Collins
School
Dictionary

HarperCollins Publishers
Westerhill Road
Bishopbriggs
Glasgow
G64 2QT
Great Britain

Second Edition 2002

Latest Reprint 2005

© HarperCollins Publishers 1999,
2002

ISBN 0-00-720213-X UK Hardback
ISBN 0-00-719639-3 UK Paperback
ISBN 0-00-713406-1 Australian
ISBN 0-00-713405-3 New Zealand
ISBN 0-00-719787-X South African

Collins® and Bank of English® are
registered trademarks of
HarperCollins Publishers Limited

www.collins.co.uk

A catalogue record for this book is
available from the British Library

Typographical design (1st edition)
by Kerry Aylin

Computing support by
Stewart C. Russell

Typeset by Wordcraft, Glasgow

Printed in Great Britain by Clays
Ltd, St Ives plc

Acknowledgements
We would like to thank those
authors and publishers who kindly
gave permission for copyright
material to be used in the Collins
Word Web. We would also like to
thank Times Newspapers Ltd for
providing valuable data.

Introduction

Being able to read, understand and write good English are vital and fundamental skills that underpin success in exams and, ultimately, success in the world beyond school. A dictionary is an essential tool for all students who want to do well in exams, because if you know how to use a dictionary effectively you can improve your performance in all subjects, not just English. This is why literacy strategies all over the world set ambitious targets for students to acquire dictionary skills at every stage of their education.

Collins New School Dictionary has been researched with teachers and students to ensure that it includes the information on language that students need to allow them to improve their performance in English and all other school subjects, and to achieve exam success. It provides:

Essential information on what words mean, how they are used, spelling, grammar and punctuation, so that students can use language well, communicate with others and express their ideas more effectively

Comprehensive coverage of core vocabulary from a wide range of curriculum subjects, such as Science, Information Technology, History, Geography and RE, to help with exam success in *all* subjects, not just English

Collins New School Dictionary is exceptionally easy to use. It is relevant to school work in all subjects, accessible and student friendly, and offers essential help on the route to success.

How To Use The Dictionary

Collins New School Dictionary is easy to use and understand. Below are some entries showing the dictionary's main features, along with an explanation of what they are.

The entry word

How to say the word

Word history 🏛 explains where the word comes from

What the word means

Other words that come from the entry word

The word's part of speech

fiend fiends
Said "feend" NOUN **1** a devil or evil spirit. **2** a very wicked or cruel person. **3** INFORMAL someone who is very keen on a particular thing E.G. *a fitness fiend.*
🏛 from Old English *feond* meaning 'enemy'

Advice on when to use the word

An example of the word being used

fish fishes fishing fished
NOUN **1** a cold-blooded creature living in water that has a spine, gills, fins, and a scaly skin. **2** Fish is the flesh of fish eaten as food. ▶ VERB **3** To fish is to try to catch fish for food or sport. **4** If you fish for information, you try to get it in an indirect way.
fishing NOUN **fisherman** NOUN
☑ The plural of the noun *fish* can be either *fish* or *fishes*, but *fish* is more common.

Other forms of the word give help with spelling

Definition number

Usage note ☑ gives more information on how the word is used

full stop full stops
NOUN the punctuation mark (.) used at the end of a sentence and after an abbreviation or initial.

What does the Full Stop do?

The **full stop** (.) marks the end of any sentence which is not a question or an exclamation:
E.G. *The train is leaving.*
A full stop is also used after an abbreviation or initial:
E.G. *etc.* ▪ *Dr. Jenkins* ▪ *J.R. Hartley*
A full stop is also used after an expression that stands by itself but is not a complete sentence:
E.G. *Good morning.*

Grammar box gives more information on the way English works

See page vi for a full list of grammar boxes in the dictionary

Similar words list ▤ shows other words with the same meaning

complain complains complaining complained
VERB **1** If you complain, you say that you are not satisfied with something. **2** If you complain of pain or illness, you say that you have it.
▤ (sense 1) find fault, grumble, moan

Ff

Spelling tips give help with finding words in the dictionary

TIP Some words which sound as if they should begin with the letter *f* actually begin with the letters *ph*, for example *pharmacy*, *pharaoh* and *phrase*. The *ph* combination, pronounced like *f*, comes in the middle of some words too, for example *amphetamine* and *emphasis*.

compare compares comparing compared
VERB 1 (EXAM TERM) When you compare things, you look at them together and see in what ways they are different or similar. 2 If you compare one thing to another, you say it is like the other thing E.G. *His voice is often compared to Michael Stipe's.*

Words used in exam questions are highlighted

comparison comparisons
NOUN (ENGLISH) When you make a comparison, you consider two things together and see in what ways they are different or similar.

Core vocabulary from all curriculum subjects, listed in the *Framework for teaching English, years 7, 8 and 9* published in the UK in 2001, is highlighted for easy learning

fabric fabrics
NOUN (D & T) 1 cloth E.G. *tough fabric for tents.* 2 The fabric of a building is its walls, roof, and other parts. 3 The fabric of a society or system is its structure, laws, and customs E.G. *the democratic fabric of American society.*

(D & T) = Design and technology

(ICT) = Information and communication technology

(PE) = Physical education

(PSHE) = Personal, social and health education

(RE) = Religious education

-ful
SUFFIX 1 '-ful' is used to form adjectives with the meaning 'full of' E.G. *careful.* 2 '-ful' is used to form nouns which mean 'the amount needed to fill' E.G. *spoonful.*
📖 from Old English

Comprehensive coverage of prefixes and suffixes help with learning new words and spelling

centi-
PREFIX 'Centi-' is used to form words that have 'hundred' as part of their meaning E.G. *centimetre.*
📖 from Latin *centum* meaning 'hundred'

Spelling notes give help with tricky words

SPELLING NOTE pAL up with the principAL and principAL staff (principal)

v

Grammar Boxes

Throughout the dictionary there are grammar boxes at the end of entries. These boxes contain rules and advice on English grammar, as well as helpful examples. In the list below, we have marked grammar boxes for *Word level* and *Sentence level* so teachers in England and Wales can see how this additional material fits in with the *Framework for teaching English, years 7, 8 and 9*.

You will find out more about grammar at the following entries:

How words are used (Word level)
a
be
not
shall
that
the
which
who
whom
whose
will

Punctuation (Sentence level)
apostrophe
bracket
colon
comma
dash
exclamation mark
full stop
hyphen
inverted comma
punctuation
question mark
semicolon

Parts of speech (Word level)
adjective
adverb
conjunction
interjection
noun
part of speech
preposition
pronoun
relative pronoun
verb

Verbs (Sentence level)
active
future
passive
past tense
present tense
tense
verb

Nouns (Word level)
noun
plural
possessive

Adjectives (Word level)
adjective
comparative
superlative

Parts of a Sentence (Sentence level)
clause
phrase
sentence

Gender (Word level)
feminine
gender
masculine
neuter

Other
Command (Sentence level)
Number (Word level)
Question (Sentence level)
Quotation (Sentence level)

BANK *of* ENGLISH

This book has been compiled by referring to the Bank of English, a unique database of the English language with examples of over 400 million words enabling Collins lexicographers to analyse how English is actually used today and how it is changing. This is the evidence on which the material in this book is based.

The Bank of English was set up as a joint initiative by HarperCollins Publishers and Birmingham University to be a resource for language research and lexicography. It contains a very wide range of material from books, newspapers, radio, TV, magazines, letters and talks reflecting the whole spectrum of English today. Its size and range make it an unequalled resource and the purpose-built software for its analysis is unique to Collins dictionaries.

This ensures that Collins Dictionaries accurately reflect English as it is used today in a way that is most helpful to the dictionary or thesaurus user as well as including the full range of rarer and historical words and meanings.

A a

a an

ADJECTIVE The indefinite article 'a', or 'an' if the next sound is a vowel, is used when you are talking about one of something E.G. *an apple… There was a car parked behind the hedge.*

The Indefinite Article

The word *a* is known as the **indefinite article**. You use it before a singular noun to refer to any example of that noun, or to avoid being specific about which example you mean:

E.G. *a school* ■ *a woman*

The word *an* is used instead of *a* when a word begins with a vowel sound:

E.G. *an elephant* ■ *an umpire*

The word *an* is also used instead of *a* when words sound as though they begin with a vowel:

E.G. *an hour* ■ *an honour*

The word *a* is used instead of *an* when words that begin with a vowel sound as though they begin with a consonant:

E.G. *a union* ■ *a European*

Also look at the grammar box at **the**.

a- an-

PREFIX **1** When 'a-' comes before an adjective it adds the meaning 'without' or 'opposite to' E.G. *amoral.* 'An-' is the form used before a vowel. **2** When 'a-' comes at the beginning of certain words it adds the meaning 'towards' or 'in the state of' E.G. *aback… asleep.*

🔠 sense 1 from Greek *a-* or *an-* meaning 'not' or 'without'

aardvark aardvarks

NOUN an ant-eating African animal with a long snout.

🔠 from obsolete Afrikaans meaning 'earth pig'

aback

ADVERB If you are taken aback, you are very surprised.

abacus abacuses

NOUN a frame with beads that slide along rods, used for counting.

🔠 from Greek *abax* meaning 'board covered with sand for doing sums on'

abalone abalones

Said "ab-a-lone-ee" NOUN a shellfish which can be eaten.

abandon abandons abandoning abandoned

VERB **1** If you abandon someone or something, you leave them or give them up for good. ▶ NOUN **2** If you do something with abandon, you do it in an uncontrolled way E.G. *He began to laugh with abandon.*

abandoned ADJECTIVE

abandonment NOUN

▣ (sense 1) desert, forsake, leave

abate abates abating abated

VERB If something abates, it becomes less E.G. *His anger abated.*

abattoir abattoirs

Said "ab-a-twahr" NOUN a place where animals are killed for meat.

abbey abbeys

NOUN a church with buildings attached to it in which monks or nuns live.

an ELegant angEL (ang**e**l) ◥ SPELLING NOTE

A B C D E F G H I J K L M N O P Q R S T U V W X Y Z

abbot abbots
NOUN the monk or priest in charge of all the monks in a monastery.

abbreviate abbreviates abbreviating abbreviated
VERB To abbreviate something is to make it shorter.

abbreviation abbreviations
NOUN a short form of a word or phrase. An example is 'W', which is short for 'West'.

abdicate abdicates abdicating abdicated
VERB If a king or queen abdicates, he or she gives up being a king or queen.
abdication NOUN

abdomen abdomens
NOUN the front part of your body below your chest, containing your stomach and intestines.
abdominal ADJECTIVE

abduct abducts abducting abducted
VERB To abduct someone is to take them away by force.
abduction NOUN

aberration aberrations
NOUN something that is not normal or usual.

abet abets abetting abetted
VERB If you abet someone, you help them to do something E.G. You've aided and abetted criminals to evade justice.

abhor abhors abhorring abhorred
VERB; FORMAL If you abhor something, you hate it.
abhorrence NOUN **abhorrent** ADJECTIVE

abide abides abiding abided
VERB 1 If you can't abide something, you dislike it very much. 2 If you

abide by a decision or law, you act in agreement with it.

ability abilities
NOUN (PSHE) the intelligence or skill needed to do something E.G. the ability to get on with others.
■ capability, proficiency, skill

abject
ADJECTIVE very bad E.G. abject failure.
abjectly ADVERB

ablaze
ADJECTIVE on fire.

able abler ablest
ADJECTIVE (PSHE) 1 If you are able to do something, you can do it. 2 Someone who is able is very clever or talented.

-able
SUFFIX 1 forming adjectives which have the meaning 'capable of' an action E.G. enjoyable… breakable. 2 forming adjectives with the meaning 'able to' or 'causing' E.G. comfortable… miserable.
▥ from the Latin suffix -ābilis meaning 'able to'
☑ When you are writing, it is easy to confuse the -able suffix with its other form, -ible. It can be helpful to know that the -able spelling is much commoner than -ible, and that you cannot make new words using -ible. Occasionally, it is correct to use either ending.

ably
Said "ay-blee" ADVERB skilfully and successfully E.G. He is ably supported by the cast.

abnormal
ADJECTIVE not normal or usual.
abnormally ADVERB

abnormality abnormalities
NOUN something that is not normal or usual.

📰 irregularity, oddity, peculiarity

aboard

PREPOSITION OR ADVERB on a ship or plane.

abode abodes

NOUN; OLD-FASHIONED Your abode is your home.

abolish abolishes abolishing abolished

VERB To abolish something is to do away with it E.G. *the campaign to abolish hunting.*

abolition NOUN

📰 do away with, eliminate, end

abominable

ADJECTIVE very unpleasant or shocking.

abominably ADVERB

Aborigine Aborigines

Said "ab-or-rij-in-ee" NOUN someone descended from the people who lived in Australia before Europeans arrived.

Aboriginal ADJECTIVE

🏛 borrowed from *aborigines*, the Latin word for the pre-Roman inhabitants of Italy

abort aborts aborting aborted

VERB 1 If a plan or activity is aborted, it is stopped before it is finished. 2 If a pregnant woman aborts, the pregnancy ends too soon and the baby dies.

abortion abortions

NOUN If a woman has an abortion, the pregnancy is ended deliberately and the baby dies.

abortive

ADJECTIVE unsuccessful E.G. *an abortive bank raid.*

abound abounds abounding abounded

VERB If things abound, there are very large numbers of them.

about

PREPOSITION OR ADVERB 1 of or concerning. 2 approximately and not exactly. ▶ ADVERB 3 in different directions E.G. *There were some bottles scattered about.* ▶ ADJECTIVE 4 present or in a place E.G. *Is Jane about?* ▶ PHRASE 5 If you are **about to** do something, you are just going to do it.

above

PREPOSITION OR ADVERB 1 directly over or higher than something E.G. *above the clouds.* 2 greater than a level or amount E.G. *The temperature didn't rise above freezing point.*

above board

ADJECTIVE completely open and legal E.G. *They assured me it was above board and properly licensed.*

🏛 an allusion to the difficulty of cheating at cards with your hands above the table

abrasion abrasions

NOUN an area where your skin has been broken.

abrasive

ADJECTIVE 1 An abrasive substance is rough and can be used to clean hard surfaces. 2 Someone who is abrasive is unpleasant and rude.

abroad

ADVERB (GEOGRAPHY) in a foreign country.

abrupt

ADJECTIVE 1 sudden and quick E.G. *His career came to an abrupt end.* 2 not friendly or polite.

abruptly ADVERB **abruptness** NOUN

abscess abscesses

Said "ab-sess" NOUN a painful swelling filled with pus.

abseiling

NOUN Abseiling is the sport of going

A Rude Idiot Thought He Might Eat Toffee In Church (<u>arithmetic</u>) 〉〉 SPELLING NOTE

A
B
C
D
E
F
G
H
I
J
K
L
M
N
O
P
Q
R
S
T
U
V
W
X
Y
Z

down a cliff or a tall building by sliding down ropes.

absent

ADJECTIVE Something that is absent is not present in a place or situation.
absence NOUN

absentee absentees

NOUN someone who is not present when they should be.

absent-minded

ADJECTIVE forgetful.

absolute

ADJECTIVE **1** total and complete E.G. *absolute honesty*. **2** having total power E.G. *the absolute ruler*.
absolutely ADVERB

absolve absolves absolving absolved

VERB To absolve someone of something is to state they are not to blame for it.

absorb absorbs absorbing absorbed

VERB (SCIENCE) If something absorbs liquid or gas, it soaks it up.
≡ soak up, take in

absorbent

ADJECTIVE Absorbent materials soak up liquid easily.

absorption

NOUN **1** the soaking up of a liquid. **2** great interest in something E.G. *my father's absorption in his business affairs*.

abstain abstains abstaining abstained

VERB **1** If you abstain from something, you do not do it or have it E.G. *The patients had to abstain from alcohol.* **2** If you abstain in a vote, you do not vote.

abstention NOUN

≡ (sense 1) forbear, keep from, refrain

abstinence

NOUN Abstinence is deliberately not doing something you enjoy.

abstract

ADJECTIVE

Said "ab-strakt" **1** An abstract idea is based on thoughts and ideas rather than physical objects or events, for example 'bravery'. **2** (ART) Abstract art is a style of art which uses shapes rather than images of people or objects. **3** Abstract nouns refer to qualities or ideas rather than to physical objects, for example 'happiness' or 'a question'. ► VERB *Said* "ab-strakt" **3** If you abstract information from a piece of writing, you summarize the main points

abstraction NOUN

📖 from Latin *abstractus* meaning 'removed'

absurd

ADJECTIVE ridiculous and stupid.

absurdly ADVERB **absurdity** NOUN

≡ ludicrous, preposterous, ridiculous

abundance

NOUN Something that exists in abundance exists in large numbers E.G. *an abundance of wildlife*.

abundant ADJECTIVE **abundantly** ADVERB

≡ plenty, profusion

abuse abuses

Said "ab-yoose" ► NOUN **1** cruel treatment of someone E.G. *child abuse*. **2** rude and unkind remarks directed towards someone. **3** the wrong use of something E.G. *an abuse of power… alcohol abuse*.

≡ (sense 1) ill-treatment, injury, maltreatment

abuse abuses abusing abused
Said "ab-**yooze**" VERB **1** If you abuse
someone, you speak insultingly to
them. **2** To abuse someone also
means to treat them cruelly. **3** If you
abuse something, you use it wrongly
or for a bad purpose.
■ (sense 2) ill-treat, maltreat

abusive
ADJECTIVE rude and unkind.
abusively ADVERB **abusiveness**
NOUN

abysmal
Said "ab-**biz**-ml" ADJECTIVE very bad
indeed E.G. *an abysmal performance*.
abysmally ADVERB

abyss abysses
NOUN a very deep hole.
🏛 from Greek *abussos* meaning
'bottomless'

acacia acacias
Said "a-**kay**-sha" NOUN a type of
thorny shrub with small yellow or
white flowers.

academic academics
ADJECTIVE **1** Academic work is work
done in a school, college, or
university. ▶ NOUN **2** someone who
teaches or does research in a college
or university.
academically ADVERB

academy academies
NOUN **1** a school or college, usually
one that specializes in one particular
subject E.G. *the Royal Academy of
Dramatic Art*. **2** an organization of
scientists, artists, writers, or
musicians.
🏛 from Greek *akadēmeia*, the name
of the grove where Plato taught

accelerate accelerates
accelerating accelerated
VERB To accelerate is to go faster.

acceleration
NOUN the rate at which the speed of
something is increasing.

accelerator accelerators
NOUN the pedal in a vehicle which
you press to make it go faster.

accent accents
NOUN **1** a way of pronouncing a
language E.G. *She had an Australian
accent*. **2** a mark placed above or
below a letter in some languages,
which affects the way the letter is
pronounced. **3** an emphasis on
something E.G. *The accent is on
action and special effects*.

accentuate accentuates
accentuating accentuated
VERB To accentuate a feature of
something is to make it more
noticeable.

accept accepts accepting
accepted
VERB **1** If you accept something, you
say yes to it or take it from someone.
2 If you accept a situation, you realize
that it cannot be changed E.G. *He
accepts criticism as part of his job*. **3** If
you accept a statement or story, you
believe it is true E.G. *The board
accepted his explanation*. **4** If a group
accepts you, they treat you as one of
the group.
acceptance NOUN **acceptable**
ADJECTIVE **acceptably** ADVERB

access accesses accessing
accessed
NOUN **1** the right or opportunity to
enter a place or to use something.
▶ VERB **2** If you access information
from a computer, you get it.

accessible
ADJECTIVE **1** easily reached or seen E.G.
The village was accessible by foot only.

a
b
c
d
e
f
g
h
i
j
k
l
m
n
o
p
q
r
s
t
u
v
w
x
y
z

2 easily understood or used E.G. *guidebooks which present information in a clear and accessible style.*

accessibility NOUN

accession

NOUN A ruler's accession is the time when he or she becomes the ruler of a country.

accessory accessories

NOUN **1** an extra part. **2** someone who helps another person commit a crime.

accident accidents

NOUN **1** an unexpected event in which people are injured or killed. **2** Something that happens by accident happens by chance.

accidental

ADJECTIVE happening by chance.

accidentally ADVERB

■ inadvert, unintentional, unplanned

acclaimed

ADJECTIVE If someone or something is acclaimed, they are praised enthusiastically.

accolade accolades

NOUN; FORMAL great praise or an award given to someone.

accommodate accommodates accommodating accommodated

VERB **1** If you accommodate someone, you provide them with a place to sleep, live, or work. **2** If a place can accommodate a number of things or people, it has enough room for them.

☑ *Accommodate* has two *c*s and two *m*s.

accommodation

NOUN a place provided for someone to sleep, live, or work in.

accompaniment accompaniments

NOUN **1** The accompaniment to a song is the music played to go with it. **2** An accompaniment to something is another thing that comes with it E.G. *Melon is a good accompaniment to cold meats.*

accompany accompanies accompanying accompanied

VERB **1** If you accompany someone, you go with them. **2** If one thing accompanies another, the two things exist at the same time E.G. *severe pain accompanied by fever.* **3** If you accompany a singer or musician, you play an instrument while they sing or play the main tune.

accomplice accomplices

NOUN a person who helps someone else to commit a crime.

accomplish accomplishes accomplishing accomplished

VERB If you accomplish something, you succeed in doing it.

☑ The *com* part of *accomplish* can sound like *kum* or *kom*.

accomplished

ADJECTIVE very talented at something E.G. *an accomplished cook.*

accomplishment accomplishments

NOUN Someone's accomplishments are the skills they have gained.

accord accords according accorded

VERB **1** If you accord someone or something a particular treatment, you treat them in that way E.G. *He was accorded a proper respect for his status.* ▶ NOUN **2** agreement. ▶ PHRASE **3** If you do something **of your own accord**, you do it willingly and not because you have been forced to do it.

accordance

PHRASE If you act **in accordance with** a rule or belief, you act in the way the rule or belief says you should.

according to

PREPOSITION **1** If something is true according to a particular person, that person says that it is true. **2** If something is done according to a principle or plan, that principle or plan is used as the basis for it.

accordion accordions

NOUN a musical instrument like an expanding box. It is played by squeezing the two sides together while pressing the keys on it.

accost accosts accosting accosted

VERB If someone accosts you, especially someone you do not know, they come up and speak to you E.G. *She says she is accosted when she goes shopping.*

account accounts accounting accounted

NOUN **1** a written or spoken report of something. **2** If you have a bank account, you can leave money in the bank and take it out when you need it. ▶ PLURAL NOUN **3** Accounts are records of money spent and received by a person or business. ▶ PHRASE **4** If you **take something into account**, you include it in your planning. **5** **On account of** means because of. ▶ VERB **6** To account for something is to explain it E.G. *This might account for her strange behaviour.* **7** If something accounts for a particular amount of something, it is that amount E.G. *The*

brain accounts for three per cent of body weight.

accountable

ADJECTIVE If you are accountable for something, you are responsible for it and have to explain your actions E.G. *The committee is accountable to Parliament.*

accountability NOUN

accountancy

NOUN the job of keeping or inspecting financial accounts.

accountant accountants

NOUN a person whose job is to keep or inspect financial accounts.

accounting

NOUN the keeping and checking of financial accounts.

accrue accrues accruing accrued

VERB If money or interest accrues, it increases gradually.

accumulate accumulates accumulating accumulated

VERB If you accumulate things or they accumulate, they collect over a period of time.

accurate

ADJECTIVE completely correct or precise.

accurately ADVERB   **accuracy** NOUN

▤ correct, exact, precise

accuse accuses accusing accused

VERB If you accuse someone of doing something wrong, you say they have done it.

accusation NOUN   **accuser** NOUN

accustom accustoms accustoming accustomed

VERB If you accustom yourself to something new or different, you get used to it.

a
b
c
d
e
f
g
h
i
j
k
l
m
n
o
p
q
r
s
t
u
v
w
x
y
z

A
B
C
D
E
F
G
H
I
J
K
L
M
N
O
P
Q
R
S
T
U
V
W
X
Y
Z

ace aces
NOUN 1 In a pack of cards, a card with a single symbol on it. ▶ ADJECTIVE 2 INFORMAL good or skilful E.G. *an ace squash player*.

acerbic
Said "as-ser-bik" ADJECTIVE; FORMAL Acerbic remarks are harsh and bitter.

ache aches aching ached
VERB 1 If you ache, you feel a continuous dull pain in a part of your body. 2 If you are aching for something, you want it very much. ▶ NOUN 3 a continuous dull pain.

achieve achieves achieving achieved
VERB (PSHE) If you achieve something, you successfully do it or cause it to happen.
■ accomplish, attain, fulfil
☑ The *i* comes before the *e* in *achieve*.

achievement achievements
NOUN (PSHE) something which you succeed in doing, especially after a lot of effort.

acid acids
NOUN (SCIENCE) 1 a chemical liquid with a pH value of less than 7 and which turns litmus paper red. Strong acids can damage skin, cloth, and metal. ▶ ADJECTIVE 2 Acid tastes are sharp or sour.
acidic ADJECTIVE **acidity** NOUN

acid rain
NOUN rain polluted by acid in the atmosphere which has come from factories.

acknowledge acknowledges acknowledging acknowledged
VERB 1 If you acknowledge a fact or situation, you agree or admit it is true. 2 If you acknowledge someone,

you show that you have seen and recognized them. 3 If you acknowledge a message, you tell the person who sent it that you have received it.

acknowledgment or **acknowledgement** NOUN
■ (sense 1) accept, admit, grant
☑ *Acknowledgment* and *acknowledgement* are both correct spellings.

acne
Said "ak-nee" NOUN lumpy spots that cover someone's face.

acorn acorns
NOUN the fruit of the oak tree, consisting of a pale oval nut in a cup-shaped base.

acoustic
Said "a-koo-stik" ADJECTIVE 1 relating to sound or hearing. 2 An acoustic guitar is not made louder with an electric amplifier.

acoustics
PLURAL NOUN The acoustics of a room are its structural features which are responsible for how clearly you can hear sounds made in it.

acquaintance acquaintances
NOUN someone you know slightly but not well

acquainted
ADJECTIVE If you are acquainted with someone, you know them slightly but not well
☑ You say that you are *acquainted with* someone.

acquire acquires acquiring acquired
VERB If you acquire something, you obtain it.

acquisition acquisitions
NOUN something you have obtained.

acquit acquits acquitting acquitted

VERB **1** If someone is acquitted of a crime, they have been tried in a court and found not guilty. **2** If you acquit yourself well on a particular occasion, you behave or perform well.

acquittal NOUN

acre acres

NOUN a unit for measuring areas of land. One acre is equal to 4840 square yards or about 4047 square metres.

📖 from Old English *æcer* meaning 'field'

acrid

ADJECTIVE sharp and bitter E.G. *the acrid smell of burning plastic*.

acrimony

Said "ak-rim-on-ee" NOUN; FORMAL bitterness and anger.

acrimonious ADJECTIVE

acrobat acrobats

NOUN an entertainer who performs gymnastic tricks.

acrobatic ADJECTIVE **acrobatics** PLURAL NOUN

📖 from Greek *akrobates* meaning 'someone who walks on tiptoe'

acronym acronyms

NOUN a word made up of the initial letters of a phrase. An example of an acronym is 'BAFTA', which stands for 'British Academy of Film and Television Arts'.

across

PREPOSITION or ADVERB **1** going from one side of something to the other. **2** on the other side of a road or river.

acrylic

Said "a-kril-lik" NOUN **1** Acrylic is a type of man-made cloth. **2** ART Acrylics,

or acrylic paints, are thick artists' paints which can be used like oil paints or thinned down with water.

act acts acting acted

VERB **1** If you act, you do something E.G. *It would be irresponsible not to act swiftly*. **2** If you act in a particular way, you behave in that way. **3** If a person or thing acts as something else, it has the function or does the job of that thing E.G. *She was able to act as an interpreter*. **4** If you act in a play or film, you play a part. ▶ NOUN **5** a single thing someone does E.G. *It was an act of disloyalty to the King*. **6** An Act of Parliament is a law passed by the government. **7** In a play, ballet, or opera, an act is one of the main parts it is divided into.

🔁 (sense 4) perform, play
🔁 (sense 5) action, deed
🔁 (sense 6) bill, decree, law

acting

NOUN the profession of performing in plays or films.

action actions

NOUN **1** something you do for a particular purpose E.G. *He had to take evasive action to avoid being hit*. **2** a physical movement. **3** In law, an action is a legal proceeding E.G. *a libel action*.

activate activates activating activated

VERB To activate something is to make it start working.

🔁 set in motion, start

active

ADJECTIVE **1** PE Active people are full of energy and are always busy. **2** If someone is active in an organization, they are involved in it and work hard for it. **3** In grammar, a

I want to see (C) your licenCe (licen*c*e) ▶ SPELLING NOTE

verb in the active voice is one where the subject does the action, rather than having it done to them.

actively ADVERB

The Active Voice

The **active** voice and the **passive** voice are two different ways of presenting information in a sentence. When a sentence is written in the **active** voice, the subject of the verb is doing the action. This is the most natural way of presenting information:

E.G. *Anna is feeding the cat.*
The cat chased a mouse.

Also look at the grammar box at **passive**.

---

activist activists
NOUN a person who tries to bring about political and social change.

activity activities
NOUN 1 Activity is a situation in which a lot of things are happening at the same time. 2 (PE) something you do for pleasure E.G. *sport and leisure activities*.

actor actors
NOUN a man or woman whose profession is acting.

actress actresses
NOUN a woman whose profession is acting.

actual
ADJECTIVE real, rather than imaginary or guessed at E.G. *That is the official figure: the actual figure is much higher.*
actually ADVERB
☑ Don't use *actual* or *actually* when they don't add anything to the meaning of a sentence. Say *it's a fact* rather than *it's an actual fact*.

acumen
NOUN the ability to make good decisions quickly E.G. *business acumen.*

acupuncture
NOUN the treatment of illness or pain by sticking small needles into specific places in a person's body.
🏛 from Latin *acus* meaning 'needle' added to 'puncture'

acute
ADJECTIVE 1 severe or intense E.G. *an acute shortage of accommodation.* 2 very intelligent E.G. *an acute mind.* 3 An acute angle is less than 90°. 4 In French and some other languages, an acute accent is a line sloping upwards from left to right placed over a vowel to indicate a change in pronunciation, as in the word *café*.

ad ads
NOUN; INFORMAL an advertisement.

AD
You use 'AD' in dates to indicate the number of years after the birth of Jesus Christ.

ad-
PREFIX 'Ad-' means 'near' or 'next to' E.G. *adjoining… adverb.*
🏛 from Latin *ad-* meaning 'towards'

adage adages
Said "**ad**-dij" NOUN a saying that expresses some general truth about life.

adamant
ADJECTIVE If you are adamant, you are determined not to change your mind.
adamantly ADVERB

Adam's apple Adam's apples
NOUN the larynx, a lump at the front of the neck which is more obvious in men than in women and young boys.

🔖 from the story that a piece of the forbidden apple got stuck in Adam's throat

adapt adapts adapting adapted
VERB 1 If you adapt to a new situation, you change so you can deal with it successfully. 2 If you adapt something, you change it so it is suitable for a new purpose or situation.
adaptable ADJECTIVE **adaptation** NOUN

adaptor adaptors; also spelt **adapter**
NOUN a type of electric plug which can be used to connect two or more plugs to one socket.

add adds adding added
VERB 1 If you add something to a number of things, you put it with the things. 2 If you add numbers together or add them up, you work out the total.

adder adders
NOUN a small poisonous snake.

addict addicts
NOUN (PSHE) someone who cannot stop taking harmful drugs.
addicted ADJECTIVE **addiction** NOUN

addictive
ADJECTIVE If a drug is addictive, the people who take it cannot stop.

addition additions
NOUN 1 something that has been added to something else. 2 (MATHS) the process of adding numbers together.
■ (sense 1) extra, supplement

additional
ADJECTIVE extra or more E.G. *They made the decision to take on additional staff.*
additionally ADVERB

additive additives
NOUN something added to something

else, usually in order to improve it.

address addresses addressing addressed
NOUN 1 the number of the house where you live, together with the name of the street and the town or village. 2 a speech given to a group of people. ▶ VERB 3 If a letter is addressed to you, it has your name and address written on it. 4 If you address a problem or task, you start to deal with it.

adept
ADJECTIVE very skilful at doing something E.G. *She is adept at motivating others.*

adequate
ADJECTIVE enough in amount or good enough for a purpose E.G. *an adequate diet.*
adequately ADVERB **adequacy** NOUN
■ enough, satisfactory, sufficient

adhere adheres adhering adhered
VERB 1 If one thing adheres to another, it sticks firmly to it. 2 If you adhere to a rule or agreement, you do what it says. 3 If you adhere to an opinion or belief, you firmly hold that opinion or belief.
adherence NOUN

adherent adherents
NOUN An adherent of a belief is someone who holds that belief.

adhesive adhesives
NOUN 1 any substance used to stick two things together, for example glue. ▶ ADJECTIVE 2 Adhesive substances are sticky and able to stick to things.

adjacent
Said "ad-**jay**-sent" ADJECTIVE; FORMAL 1 If two things are adjacent, they are next to each other E.G. *a hotel*

have a piEce of piE (pie**ce**)   **SPELLING NOTE**

A
B
C
D
E
F
G
H
I
J
K
L
M
N
O
P
Q
R
S
T
U
V
W
X
Y
Z

adjacent to the beach. **2** (MATHS)
Adjacent angles share one side and
have the same point opposite to
their bases.

adjective adjectives
NOUN a word that adds to the
description given by a noun. For
example, in 'They live in a large white
Georgian house', 'large', 'white', and
'Georgian' are all adjectives.
adjectival ADJECTIVE

What is an Adjective?

An adjective is a word that tells you
something about a noun. Adjectives are sometimes called "describing words".
Adjectives may indicate how many
of a person or thing there are:

E.G. **three** *men* ■ **some** *fish*

Adjectives may describe feelings
or qualities:

E.G. *a* **happy** *child* ■ *a* **strange** *girl*

Adjectives may describe size, age,
temperature, or measurement:

E.G. *a* **large** *envelope* ■ *an* **old**
jacket

Adjectives may indicate colour:

E.G. **red** *socks* ■ **dark** *hair*

Adjectives may indicate nationality
or origin:

E.G. *my* **Indian** *cousin* ■ *a*
northern *accent*

Adjectives may indicate the material from which something is
made:

E.G. *a* **wooden** *box* ■ **denim** *trousers*

---

adjoining
ADJECTIVE If two rooms are next to
each other and are connected, they
are adjoining.

**adjourn adjourns adjourning
adjourned**
VERB **1** If a meeting or trial is
adjourned, it stops for a time E.G. *The
case was adjourned until September*.
2 If people adjourn to another place,
they go there together after a meeting
E.G. *We adjourned to the lounge*.
adjournment NOUN

adjust adjusts adjusting adjusted
VERB **1** If you adjust something, you
change its position or alter it in some
other way. **2** If you adjust to a new
situation, you get used to it.
adjustment NOUN **adjustable**
ADJECTIVE

ad-lib ad-libs ad-libbing ad-libbed
VERB **1** If you ad-lib, you say
something that has not been
prepared beforehand E.G. *I ad-lib on
radio but use a script on TV*. ► NOUN **2** a
comment that has not been
prepared beforehand.
📖 short for Latin *ad libitum* meaning
'according to desire'.

**administer administers
administering administered**
VERB **1** To administer an organization
is to be responsible for managing it.
2 To administer the law or administer
justice is to put it into practice and
apply it. **3** If medicine is administered
to someone, it is given to them.

administration administrations
NOUN **1** Administration is the work of
organizing and supervising an
organization. **2** Administration is also
the process of administering
something E.G. *the administration of
criminal justice*. **3** The administration
is the group of people that manages
an organization or a country.
administrative ADJECTIVE

administrator NOUN

admirable
ADJECTIVE very good and deserving to
be admired.
admirably ADVERB

admiral admirals
NOUN the commander of a navy.
📖 from Arabic *amir* meaning
'commander'

admire admires admiring
admired
VERB If you admire someone or
something, you respect and approve
of them.
admiration NOUN **admirer** NOUN
admiring ADJECTIVE **admiringly**
ADVERB

admission admissions
NOUN 1 If you are allowed admission
to a place, you are allowed to go in.
2 If you make an admission of
something, you agree, often
reluctantly, it is true E.G. *It was an
admission of guilt*.

admit admits admitting admitted
VERB 1 If you admit something, you
agree, often reluctantly, it is true. 2 To
admit someone or something to a
place or organization is to allow
them to enter it. 3 If you are
admitted to hospital, you are taken
there to stay until you are better.

admittedly
ADVERB People use 'admittedly' to
show that what they are saying
contrasts with something they have
already said or are about to say, and
weakens their argument E.G. *My
studies, admittedly only from books,
taught me much.*

adolescent adolescents
NOUN a young person who is no longer
a child but who is not yet an adult.

adolescence NOUN
📖 from Latin *adolescere* meaning 'to
grow up'

adopt adopts adopting adopted
VERB 1 If you adopt a child that is not
your own, you take him or her into
your family as your son or daughter.
2 FORMAL If you adopt a particular
attitude, you start to have it.
adoption NOUN

adorable
ADJECTIVE sweet and attractive.

adore adores adoring adored
VERB If you adore someone, you feel
deep love and admiration for them.
adoration NOUN

adorn adorns adorning adorned
VERB To adorn something is to
decorate it E.G. *The cathedral is
adorned with statues*.
adornment NOUN

adrenalin or **adrenaline**
Said "a-**dren**-al-in" NOUN a substance
which is produced by your body when
you are angry, scared, or excited and
which makes your heart beat faster.

adrift
ADJECTIVE OR ADVERB If a boat is adrift or
goes adrift, it floats on the water
without being controlled.

adulation
Said "ad-yoo-**lay**-shn" NOUN great
admiration and praise for someone.
adulatory ADJECTIVE

adult adults
NOUN a mature and fully developed
person or animal.

adultery
NOUN sexual intercourse between a
married person and someone he or
she is not married to.
adulterer NOUN **adulterous**
ADJECTIVE

a
b
c
d
e
f
g
h
i
j
k
l
m
n
o
p
q
r
s
t
u
v
w
x
y
z

I went to see (C) the doctor's new practiCe (practiᴄe)   SPELLING NOTE

A
B
C
D
E
F
G
H
I
J
K
L
M
N
O
P
Q
R
S
T
U
V
W
X
Y
Z

adulthood

NOUN the time during someone's life when they are an adult.

advance advances advancing advanced

VERB **1** To advance is to move forward. **2** To advance a cause or interest is to help it to be successful. **3** If you advance someone a sum of money, you lend it to them. ▶ NOUN **4** Advance in something is progress in it E.G. *scientific advance.* **5** a sum of money lent to someone. ▶ ADJECTIVE **6** happening before an event E.G. *The event received little advance publicity.* ▶ PHRASE **7** If you do something **in advance**, you do it before something else happens E.G. *We booked up the room well in advance.* ▤ (sense 4) development, progress

advantage advantages

NOUN **1** a benefit or something that puts you in a better position. ▶ PHRASE **2** If you **take advantage of** someone, you treat them unfairly for your own benefit. **3** If you **take advantage of** something, you make use of it.

advantageous

ADJECTIVE likely to benefit you in some way E.G. *an advantageous marriage.*

advent

NOUN **1** The advent of something is its start or its coming into existence E.G. *The advent of the submarine changed naval warfare.* **2** Advent is the season just before Christmas in the Christian calendar.

adventure adventures

NOUN a series of events that are unusual and exciting.

adventurer adventurers

NOUN someone who enjoys doing dangerous and exciting things.

adventurous

ADJECTIVE willing to take risks and do new and exciting things.

adventurously ADVERB

adverb adverbs

NOUN a word that adds information about a verb or a following adjective or other adverb, for example, 'slowly', 'now', and 'here' which say how, when, or where something is done.

adverbial ADJECTIVE

What is an Adverb?

An adverb is a word that gives information about a verb. Many adverbs end with the letters -ly.

Adverbs of manner answer the question "how?":

> E.G. *She runs **quickly**.* ▪ *She sings **badly**.*

Adverbs of place answer the question "where?":

> E.G. *We travelled **northwards**.* ▪ *I live **here**.*

Adverbs of time answer the question "when?":

> E.G. *You must stop **immediately**.* *I arrived **yesterday**.*

Adverbs of degree answer the question "to what extent?":

> E.G. *I **really** hope you will stay.* ▪ *I play golf **fairly** often.*

Adverbs of frequency answer the question "how often?":

> E.G. *We **sometimes** meet for lunch.* *You **never** answer my questions.*

Sometimes adverbs can refer to the whole sentence rather than just the verb:

> E.G. ***Fortunately**, she was not badly hurt.*

---

adversary adversaries
Said "**ad**-ver-sar-ee" NOUN someone who is your enemy or who opposes what you are doing.

adverse
ADJECTIVE not helpful to you or opposite to what you want or need E.G. *adverse weather conditions*.
adversely ADVERB

adversity adversities
NOUN a time of danger or difficulty.

advert adverts
NOUN; INFORMAL an advertisement.

advertise advertises advertising advertised
VERB (ENGLISH) 1 If you advertise something, you tell people about it in a newspaper or poster, or on TV. 2 To advertise is to make an announcement in a newspaper or poster, or on TV.
advertiser NOUN **advertising** NOUN

advertisement advertisements
Said "ad-**ver**-tiss-ment" NOUN (ENGLISH) an announcement about something in a newspaper or poster, or on TV.
◼ ad, advert, commercial

advice
NOUN a suggestion from someone about what you should do.
◼ counsel, guidance, suggestion
☑ The noun *advice* is spelt with a '*c*' and the verb *advise* is spelt with an '*s*'.

advisable
ADJECTIVE sensible and likely to achieve the result you want E.G. *It is advisable to buy the visa before travelling*.
advisably ADVERB **advisability** NOUN

advise advises advising advised
VERB 1 If you advise someone to do something, you tell them you think

they should do it. 2 FORMAL If you advise someone of something, you inform them of it.
adviser NOUN **advisory** ADJECTIVE
◼ (sense 1) counsel, recommend, suggest
☑ The verb *advise* is spelt with an '*s*' and the noun *advice* is spelt with a '*c*'.

advocate advocates advocating advocated
VERB 1 If you advocate a course of action or plan, you support it publicly. ► NOUN 2 An advocate of something is someone who supports it publicly. 3 FORMAL a lawyer who represents clients in court.
advocacy NOUN

aerial aerials
Said "**air**-ee-al" ADJECTIVE 1 Aerial means happening in the air E.G. *aerial combat*. ► NOUN 2 a piece of wire for receiving television or radio signals.

aerial top dressing
NOUN In Australia and New Zealand, aerial top dressing is the spreading of fertilizer from an aeroplane onto land in remote country areas.

aero-
PREFIX 'Aero-' means involving the air, the atmosphere, or aircraft E.G. *aerobatics*.
▥ from Greek *aēr* meaning 'air'

aerobics
NOUN a type of fast physical exercise, which increases the oxygen in your blood and strengthens your heart and lungs.
aerobic ADJECTIVE

aerodynamic
ADJECTIVE having a streamlined shape that moves easily through the air.

aeroplane aeroplanes

a
b
c
d
e
f
g
h
i
j
k
l
m
n
o
p
q
r
s
t
u
v
w
x
y
z

NOUN a vehicle with wings and engines that enable it to fly.

aerosol aerosols

NOUN a small metal container in which liquid is kept under pressure so that it can be forced out as a spray

☑ *Aerosol* starts with *aer* and not with *air*.

aerospace

ADJECTIVE involved in making and designing aeroplanes and spacecraft.

aesthetic or **esthetic**

Said "eess-thet-ik" ADJECTIVE **(D&T)**; FORMAL relating to the appreciation of beauty or art.

aesthetically ADVERB **aesthetics** NOUN

afar

NOUN; LITERARY From afar means from a long way away.

affable

ADJECTIVE pleasant and easy to talk to.

affably ADVERB **affability** NOUN

affair affairs

NOUN 1 an event or series of events E.G. *The funeral was a sad affair.* 2 To have an affair is to have a secret sexual or romantic relationship, especially when one of the people is married. ▶ PLURAL NOUN 3 Your affairs are your private and personal life E.G. *Why had he meddled in her affairs?*

affect affects affecting affected

VERB 1 If something affects you, it influences you in some way. 2 FORMAL If you affect a particular way of behaving, you behave in that way E.G. *He affected an Italian accent.*

☑ Do not confuse the spelling of the verb *affect* with the noun *effect*.

Something that *affects* you has an *effect* on you.

affectation affectations

NOUN An affectation is behaviour that is not genuine but is put on to impress people.

affection affections

NOUN 1 a feeling of love and fondness for someone. ▶ PLURAL NOUN 2 Your affections are feelings of love you have for someone.

affectionate

ADJECTIVE full of fondness for someone E.G. *an affectionate embrace.*

affectionately ADVERB

affiliate affiliates affiliating affiliated

VERB If a group affiliates itself to another, larger group, it forms a close association with it E.G. *organizations affiliated to the ANC.*

affiliation NOUN

affinity affinities

NOUN a close similarity or understanding between two things or people E.G. *There are affinities between the two poets.*

affirm affirms affirming affirmed

VERB If you affirm an idea or belief, you clearly indicate your support for it E.G. *We affirm our commitment to broadcast quality programmes.*

affirmation NOUN

affirmative

ADJECTIVE An affirmative word or gesture is one that means yes.

afflict afflicts afflicting afflicted

VERB If illness or pain afflicts someone, they suffer from it E.G. *She was afflicted by depression.*

affliction NOUN

A
B
C
D
E
F
G
H
I
J
K
L
M
N
O
P
Q
R
S
T
U
V
W
X
Y
Z

affluent

ADJECTIVE having a lot of money and possessions.

affluence NOUN

afford affords affording afforded

VERB **1** If you can afford to do something, you have enough money or time to do it. **2** If you cannot afford something to happen, it would be harmful or embarrassing for you if it happened E.G. *We cannot afford to be complacent.*

affront affronts affronting affronted

VERB **1** If you are affronted by something, you are insulted and angered by it. ▶ NOUN **2** something that is an insult E.G. *Our prisons are an affront to civilized society.*

✔ Notice that *affront*, the noun, is followed by *to*.

afield

ADVERB Far afield means a long way away E.G. *competitors from as far afield as Russia and China.*

afloat

ADVERB or ADJECTIVE **1** floating on water. **2** successful and making enough money E.G. *Companies are struggling hard to stay afloat.*

afoot

ADJECTIVE or ADVERB happening or being planned, especially secretly E.G. *Plans are afoot to build a new museum.*

afraid

ADJECTIVE **1** If you are afraid, you are very frightened. **2** If you are afraid something might happen, you are worried it might happen.

▤ (sense 1) fearful, frightened, scared

afresh

ADVERB again and in a new way E.G.

The couple moved abroad to start life afresh.

Africa

NOUN Africa is the second largest continent. It is almost surrounded by sea, with the Atlantic on its west side, the Mediterranean to the north and the Indian Ocean and the Red Sea to the east.

African Africans

ADJECTIVE **1** belonging or relating to Africa. ▶ NOUN **2** someone, especially a Black person, who comes from Africa.

African-American African-Americans

NOUN an American whose ancestors came from Africa.

Afrikaans

Said "af-rik-**ahns**" NOUN a language spoken in South Africa, similar to Dutch.

Afrikaner Afrikaners

NOUN a white South African with Dutch ancestors.

aft

ADVERB or ADJECTIVE towards the back of a ship or boat.

after

PREPOSITION or ADVERB **1** later than a particular time, date, or event. **2** behind and following someone or something E.G. *They ran after her.*

▤ (sense 1) afterwards, following, later

afterlife

NOUN The afterlife is a life some people believe begins when you die.

aftermath

NOUN The aftermath of a disaster is the situation that comes after it.

afternoon afternoons

NOUN the part of the day between

a b c d e f g h i j k l m n o p q r s t u v w x y z

A
B
C
D
E
F
G
H
I
J
K
L
M
N
O
P
Q
R
S
T
U
V
W
X
Y
Z

noon and about six o'clock.

aftershave
NOUN a pleasant-smelling liquid men put on their faces after shaving.

afterthought afterthoughts
NOUN something you do or say as an addition to something else you have already done or said.

afterwards
ADVERB after an event or time.

again
ADVERB 1 happening one more time E.G. *He looked forward to becoming a father again*. 2 returning to the same state or place as before E.G. *there and back again*.
■ (sense 1) anew, once more

against
PREPOSITION 1 touching and leaning on E.G. *He leaned against the wall*. 2 in opposition to E.G. *the Test match against England*. 3 in order to prevent E.G. *precautions against fire*. 4 in comparison with E.G. *The pound is now at its lowest rate against the dollar*.

age ages ageing or aging aged
NOUN 1 The age of something or someone is the number of years they have lived or existed. 2 Age is the quality of being old E.G. *a wine capable of improving with age*. 3 a particular period in history E.G. *the Iron Age*. ► PLURAL NOUN 4 INFORMAL Ages means a very long time E.G. *He's been talking for ages*. ► VERB 5 To age is to grow old or to appear older
✓ *Ageing* and *aging* are both correct spellings.

aged
Rhymes with "raged" ADJECTIVE having a particular age E.G. *people aged 16 to 24*.

aged
Said "ay-dgid" ADJECTIVE very old E.G. *an aged invalid*.
■ elderly, old

agency agencies
NOUN an organization or business which provides certain services E.G. *a detective agency*.

agenda agendas
NOUN a list of items to be discussed at a meeting.

agent agents
NOUN 1 someone who arranges work or business for other people, especially actors or singers.
2 someone who works for their country's secret service.

aggravate aggravates aggravating aggravated
VERB 1 To aggravate a bad situation is to make it worse. 2 INFORMAL If someone or something aggravates you, they make you annoyed.
aggravating ADJECTIVE **aggravation** NOUN
☑ Some people think that using *aggravate* to mean 'annoy' is wrong.

aggregate aggregates
NOUN a total that is made up of several smaller amounts.

aggression
NOUN violent and hostile behaviour.

aggressive
ADJECTIVE full of hostility and violence.
aggressively ADVERB
aggressiveness NOUN
■ belligerent, hostile

aggressor aggressors
NOUN a person or country that starts a fight or a war.

aggrieved
ADJECTIVE upset and angry about the way you have been treated.

aghast
Said "a-gast" ADJECTIVE shocked and horrified.

agile
ADJECTIVE (PE) able to move quickly and easily E.G. *He is as agile as a cat.*
agilely ADVERB **agility** NOUN

agitate agitates agitating agitated
VERB 1 If you agitate for something, you campaign energetically to get it. 2 If something agitates you, it worries you.
agitation NOUN **agitator** NOUN

agnostic agnostics
NOUN OR ADJECTIVE Someone who believes we cannot know definitely whether God exists or not.
agnosticism NOUN
from Greek *agnōstos* meaning 'unknown'

ago
ADVERB in the past E.G. *She bought her flat three years ago.*

agog
ADJECTIVE excited and eager to know more about an event or situation E.G. *She was agog to hear his news.*

agonizing or **agonising**
ADJECTIVE extremely painful, either physically or mentally E.G. *an agonizing decision.*

agony
NOUN very great physical or mental pain.
pain, suffering, torment

agoraphobia
Said "a-gor-a-foe-bee-a" NOUN the fear of open spaces.
agoraphobic ADJECTIVE
from Greek *agora* meaning 'market place' + *phobia*

agrarian
Said "ag-rare-ee-an" ADJECTIVE; FORMAL relating to farming and agriculture E.G. *agrarian economies.*

agree agrees agreeing agreed
VERB 1 If you agree with someone, you have the same opinion as them. 2 If you agree to do something, you say you will do it. 3 If two stories or totals agree, they are the same. 4 Food that doesn't agree with you makes you ill.
(sense 1) be of the same opinion, concur
(sense 2) comply, consent

agreeable
ADJECTIVE 1 pleasant or enjoyable. 2 If you are agreeable to something, you are willing to allow it or to do it E.G. *She was agreeable to the project.*
agreeably ADVERB

agreement agreements
NOUN 1 a decision that has been reached by two or more people. 2 Two people who are in agreement have the same opinion about something.

agriculture
NOUN (HISTORY) Agriculture is farming.
agricultural ADJECTIVE

aground
ADVERB If a boat runs aground, it becomes stuck in a shallow stretch of water.

ahead
ADVERB 1 in front E.G. *He looked ahead.* 2 more advanced than someone or something else E.G. *We are five years ahead of the competition.* 3 in the future E.G. *I haven't had time to think far ahead.*

aid aids aiding aided
NOUN 1 Aid is money, equipment, or services provided for people in need E.G. *food and medical aid.* 2 something that makes a task easier

a
b
c
d
e
f
g
h
i
j
k
l
m
n
o
p
q
r
s
t
u
v
w
x
y
z

E.G. *teaching aids.* ▶ VERB **3** FORMAL If you aid a person or an organization, you help or support them.

aide aides
NOUN an assistant to an important person, especially in the government or the army E.G. *the Prime Minister's closest aides.*

AIDS
NOUN a disease which destroys the body's natural system of immunity to diseases. AIDS is an abbreviation for 'acquired immune deficiency syndrome'.

ailing
ADJECTIVE **1** sick or ill, and not getting better. **2** getting into difficulties, especially with money E.G. *an ailing company.*

ailment ailments
NOUN a minor illness.

aim aims aiming aimed
VERB **1** If you aim an object or weapon at someone or something, you point it at them. **2** If you aim to do something, you are planning or hoping to do it. ▶ NOUN **3** Your aim is what you intend to achieve. **4** If you take aim, you point an object or weapon at someone or something.
▣ (sense 1) point
▣ (sense 2) intend, mean, plan
▣ (sense 4) goal, intention, objective

aimless
ADJECTIVE having no clear purpose or plan.
aimlessly ADVERB **aimlessness** NOUN

air airs airing aired
NOUN **1** Air is the mixture of oxygen and other gases which we breathe and which forms the earth's atmosphere. **2** An air someone or something has is the impression they give E.G. *an air of defiance.* **3** 'Air' is used to refer to travel in aircraft E.G. *I have to travel by air a great deal.* ▶ VERB **4** If you air your opinions, you talk about them to other people.

airborne
ADJECTIVE in the air and flying.

air-conditioning
NOUN a system of providing cool, clean air in buildings.
air-conditioned ADJECTIVE

aircraft
NOUN any vehicle which can fly.

airfield airfields
NOUN an open area of ground with runways where small aircraft take off and land.

air force air forces
NOUN the part of a country's armed services that fights using aircraft.

air gun air guns
NOUN a gun which uses air pressure to fire pellets.

air hostess air hostesses
NOUN a woman whose job is to look after passengers on an aircraft.

airless
ADJECTIVE having no wind or fresh air.

airlift airlifts
NOUN an operation to move people or goods by air, especially in an emergency.

airline airlines
NOUN a company which provides air travel.

airmail
NOUN the system of sending letters and parcels by air.

airman airmen
NOUN a man who serves in his country's air force.

airport airports
NOUN a place where people go to catch planes.

air raid air raids
NOUN an attack by enemy aircraft, in which bombs are dropped.

airship airships
NOUN a large, light aircraft, consisting of a rigid balloon filled with gas and powered by an engine, with a passenger compartment underneath.

airstrip airstrips
NOUN a stretch of land that has been cleared for aircraft to take off and land.

airtight
ADJECTIVE not letting air in or out.

airy airier airiest
ADJECTIVE full of fresh air and light.
airily ADVERB

aisle aisles
Rhymes with "mile" NOUN a long narrow gap that people can walk along between rows of seats or shelves.

ajar
ADJECTIVE A door or window that is ajar is slightly open.

akin
ADJECTIVE; FORMAL similar E.G. *The taste is akin to veal.*

alabaster
NOUN a type of smooth stone used for making ornaments.
📖 from Latin *alabaster* meaning 'vase for perfume'

alacrity
NOUN; FORMAL eager willingness E.G. *He seized this offer with alacrity.*

alarm alarms alarming alarmed
NOUN **1** a feeling of fear and worry E.G. *The cat sprang back in alarm.* **2** an automatic device used to warn people of something E.G. *a car alarm.* ▶ VERB **3** If something alarms you, it makes you worried and anxious.
alarming ADJECTIVE

alas
ADVERB unfortunately or regrettably E.G. *But, alas, it would not be true.*

Albanian Albanians
ADJECTIVE **1** belonging or relating to Albania. ▶ NOUN **2** someone who comes from Albania. **3** Albanian is the main language spoken in Albania.

albatross albatrosses
NOUN a large white sea bird.

albeit
Said "awl-bee-it" CONJUNCTION; FORMAL although E.G. *He was making progress, albeit slowly.*

albino albinos
NOUN a person or animal with very white skin, white hair, and pink eyes.

album albums
NOUN **1** a CD, cassette, or record with a number of songs on it. **2** a book in which you keep a collection of things such as photographs or stamps.

alchemy
Said "al-kem-ee" NOUN a medieval science that attempted to change ordinary metals into gold.
alchemist NOUN

alcheringa
Said "al-cher-ring-ga" NOUN Alcheringa is the same as Dreamtime.

alcohol
NOUN Alcohol is any drink that can make people drunk; also the colourless flammable liquid found in

a b c d e f g h i j k l m n o p q r s t u v w x y z

A
B
C
D
E
F
G
H
I
J
K
L
M
N
O
P
Q
R
S
T
U
V
W
X
Y
Z

these drinks, produced by fermenting sugar.

alcoholic alcoholics
ADJECTIVE 1 An alcoholic drink contains alcohol. ▶ NOUN 2 someone who is addicted to alcohol.
alcoholism NOUN

alcopop alcopops
NOUN; INFORMAL an alcoholic drink that tastes like a soft drink.

alcove alcoves
NOUN an area of a room which is set back slightly from the main part.
🔤 from Arabic al-qubbah meaning 'arch'

ale
NOUN a type of beer.

alert alerts alerting alerted
ADJECTIVE 1 paying full attention to what is happening E.G. *The criminal was spotted by an alert member of the public.* ▶ NOUN 2 a situation in which people prepare themselves for danger E.G. *The troops were on a war alert.* ▶ VERB 3 If you alert someone to a problem or danger, you warn them of it.
alertness NOUN
▤ (sense 1) attentive, vigilant, watchful

algae
Said "al-jee" PLURAL NOUN plants that grow in water or on damp surfaces.

algebra
NOUN a branch of mathematics in which symbols and letters are used instead of numbers to express relationships between quantities.
algebraic ADJECTIVE
🔤 from Arabic al-jabr meaning 'reunion'

Algerian Algerians
ADJECTIVE 1 belonging or relating to

Algeria. ▶ NOUN 2 someone who comes from Algeria.

alias aliases
Said "ay-lee-ass" NOUN a false name E.G. *Leonard Nimoy, alias Mr Spock.*

alibi alibis
Said "al-li-bye" NOUN An alibi is evidence proving you were somewhere else when a crime was committed.

alien aliens
Said "ay-lee-an" ADJECTIVE 1 not normal to you E.G. *a totally alien culture.*
▶ NOUN 2 someone who is not a citizen of the country in which he or she lives. 3 In science fiction, an alien is a creature from outer space.

alienate alienates alienating alienated
VERB If you alienate someone, you do something that makes them stop being sympathetic to you E.G. *The Council's approach alienated many local residents.*
alienation NOUN

alight alights alighting alighted
ADJECTIVE 1 Something that is alight is burning. ▶ VERB 2 If a bird or insect alights somewhere, it lands there. 3 FORMAL When passengers alight from a vehicle, they get out of it at the end of a journey.

align aligns aligning aligned
Said "a-line" VERB 1 If you align yourself with a particular group, you support them. 2 If you align things, you place them in a straight line.
alignment NOUN

alike
ADJECTIVE 1 Things that are alike are similar in some way. ▶ ADVERB 2 If people are treated alike, they are treated in a similar way.

alimony
Said "al-li-mon-ee" NOUN money someone has to pay regularly to their wife or husband after they are divorced.

alive
ADJECTIVE **1** living. **2** lively and active.
■ (sense 1) animate, living

alkali alkalis
Said "al-kal-eye" NOUN (SCIENCE) a chemical substance that turns litmus paper blue.
alkaline ADJECTIVE **alkalinity** NOUN

all
ADJECTIVE, PRONOUN, or ADVERB **1** used when referring to the whole of something E.G. *Why did he have to say all that?… She managed to finish it all.* ► ADVERB **2** 'All' is also used when saying the two sides in a game or contest have the same score E.G. *The final score was six points all.*

Allah
PROPER NOUN the Muslim name for God.

allay allays allaying allayed
VERB To allay someone's fears or doubts is to stop them feeling afraid or doubtful.

allege alleges alleging alleged
Said "a-lej" VERB If you allege that something is true, you say it is true but do not provide any proof E.G. *It is alleged that she died as a result of neglect.*
allegation NOUN **alleged** ADJECTIVE

allegiance allegiances
Said "al-lee-jenss" NOUN loyal support for a person or organization.

allegory allegories
Said "al-li-gor-ee" NOUN a piece of writing or art in which the characters and events are symbols for something else. Allegories usually make some moral, religious, or political point. For example, George Orwell's novel 'Animal Farm' is an allegory in that the animals who revolt in the farmyard are symbols of the political leaders in the Russian Revolution.

allergy allergies
Said "al-er-jee" NOUN a sensitivity someone has to something, so that they become ill when they eat it or touch it E.G. *an allergy to cows' milk.*

alleviate alleviates alleviating alleviated
VERB To alleviate pain or a problem is to make it less severe E.G. *measures to alleviate poverty.*
alleviation NOUN

alley alleys
NOUN a narrow passage between buildings.

alliance alliances
NOUN a group of people, organizations, or countries working together for similar aims.
■ association, league, union

alligator alligators
NOUN a large animal, similar to a crocodile.
▥ from Spanish *el lagarto* meaning 'lizard'

alliteration
NOUN (ENGLISH); LITERARY the use of several words together which all begin with the same sound, for example 'around the ragged rock the ragged rascal ran'.
alliterative ADJECTIVE

allocate allocates allocating allocated
VERB If you allocate something, you decide it should be given to a person or place, or used for a

Elaine and Emily shout EE when they mEEt to grEEt each other (-ee-)   ◀ SPELLING NOTE

particular purpose E.G. *funds allocated for nursery education.*
allocation NOUN
allot allots allotting allotted
VERB If something is allotted to you, it is given to you as your share E.G. *Space was allotted for visitors' cars.*
allotment allotments
NOUN **1** a piece of land which people can rent to grow vegetables on. **2** a share of something.
allow allows allowing allowed
VERB **1** If you allow something, you say it is all right or let it happen. **2** If you allow a period of time or an amount of something, you set it aside for a particular purpose E.G. *Allow four hours for the paint to dry.*
allowable ADJECTIVE
☑ Do not confuse the spellings of the past tense form *allowed* and the adverb *aloud*, which sound the same.
allowance allowances
NOUN **1** money given regularly to someone for a particular purpose E.G. *a petrol allowance.* ▶ PHRASE **2** If you **make allowances** for something, you take it into account E.G. *The school made allowances for Muslim cultural customs.*
alloy alloys
NOUN a mixture of two or more metals.
all right or **alright**
ADJECTIVE **1** If something is all right, it is acceptable. **2** If someone is all right, they are safe and not harmed. **3** You say 'all right' to agree to something.
allude alludes alluding alluded
VERB If you allude to something, you refer to it in an indirect way.
☑ You *allude to* something. Do not confuse *allude* with *elude*.

allure
NOUN The allure of something is an exciting quality that makes it attractive E.G. *the allure of foreign travel.*
alluring ADJECTIVE
allusion allusions
NOUN an indirect reference to or comment about something E.G. *English literature is full of classical allusions.*
ally allies allying allied
NOUN **1** a person or country that helps and supports another. ▶ VERB **2** If you ally yourself with someone, you agree to help and support each other.
▦ (sense 1) friend, helper, partner
▦ (sense 2) associate, join, unite
almanac almanacs
NOUN a book published every year giving information about a particular subject.
almighty
ADJECTIVE **1** very great or serious E.G. *I've just had an almighty row with the chairman.* ▶ PROPER NOUN **2** The Almighty is another name for God.
almond almonds
NOUN a pale brown oval nut.
almost
ADVERB very nearly E.G. *Prices have almost doubled.*
▦ just about, nearly, practically
alms
PLURAL NOUN; OLD-FASHIONED Alms are gifts of money, food, or clothing to poor people.
aloft
ADVERB up in the air or in a high position E.G. *He held aloft the trophy.*
alone
ADJECTIVE or ADVERB not with other

people or things E.G. *He just wanted to be alone.*

■ by oneself, solitary, unaccompanied

along
PREPOSITION **1** moving, happening, or existing continuously from one end to the other of something, or at various points beside it E.G. *Put rivets along the top edge.* ▶ ADVERB **2** moving forward E.G. *We marched along, singing as we went.* **3** with someone E.G. *Why could she not take her along?*
▶ PHRASE **4 All along** means from the beginning of a period of time right up to now E.G. *You've known that all along.*

alongside
PREPOSITION or ADVERB **1** next to something E.G. *They had a house in the park alongside the river.*
▶ PREPOSITION **2** If you work alongside other people, you are working in the same place and cooperating with them E.G. *He was thrilled to work alongside Robert De Niro.*
✓ Do not use *of* after *alongside*.

aloof
ADJECTIVE distant from someone or something.

aloud
ADVERB When you read or speak aloud, you speak loudly enough for other people to hear you
✓ Do not confuse the spellings of *aloud* and *allowed*, the past tense form of *allow*.

alphabet alphabets
NOUN (LIBRARY) a set of letters in a fixed order that is used in writing a language.
alphabetical ADJECTIVE
alphabetically ADVERB

alpine
ADJECTIVE existing in or relating to high mountains E.G. *alpine flowers.*
▦ from *the Alps,* a mountain range in central Europe

already
ADVERB having happened before the present time or earlier than expected E.G. *She has already gone to bed.*

alright
another spelling of **all right**.
✓ Some people think that *all right* is the only correct spelling and that *alright* is wrong.

Alsatian Alsatians
Said "al-**say**-shn" NOUN a large wolflike dog.

also
ADVERB in addition to something that has just been mentioned.

altar altars
NOUN a holy table in a church or temple.

alter alters altering altered
VERB If something alters or if you alter it, it changes.
alteration NOUN
✓ Do not confuse the spellings of *alter* and *altar.*

altercation altercations
NOUN; FORMAL a noisy disagreement.

alternate alternates alternating alternated
VERB **1** If one thing alternates with another, the two things regularly occur one after the other. ▶ ADJECTIVE **2** If something happens on alternate days, it happens on the first day but not the second, and happens again on the third day but not the fourth, and so on. **3** (MATHS) Alternate angles are two angles on opposite sides of a

A
B
C
D
E
F
G
H
I
J
K
L
M
N
O
P
Q
R
S
T
U
V
W
X
Y
Z

line that crosses two other lines.
alternately ADVERB **alternation** NOUN

alternating current alternating currents
NOUN a current that regularly changes its direction, so that the electrons flow first one way and then the other.

alternative alternatives
NOUN 1 something you can do or have instead of something else E.G. *alternatives to prison such as community service.* ▶ ADJECTIVE
2 Alternative plans or actions can happen or be done instead of what is already happening or being done.
alternatively ADVERB
☑ If there are more than two choices in a situation you should say *there are three choices* rather than *there are three alternatives* because the strict meaning of *alternative* is a choice between two things.

although
CONJUNCTION in spite of the fact that E.G. *He wasn't well known in America, although he did make a film there.*

altitude altitudes
NOUN The altitude of something is its height above sea level E.G. *The mountain range reaches an altitude of 1330 metres.*

altogether
ADVERB 1 entirely E.G. *She wasn't altogether sorry to be leaving.* 2 in total; used of amounts E.G. *I get paid 1000 pounds a month altogether.*

aluminium
NOUN a silvery-white lightweight metal.

always
ADVERB all the time or for ever E.G.

She's always moaning.

am
the first person singular, present tense of **be**.

a.m.
used to specify times between 12 midnight and 12 noon, eg *I get up at 6 a.m.* It is an abbreviation for the Latin phrase 'ante meridiem', which means 'before noon'.

amalgamate amalgamates amalgamating amalgamated
VERB If two organizations amalgamate, they join together to form one new organization.
amalgamation NOUN

amandla
NOUN In South Africa, amandla is a political slogan which calls for power for Black people.

amass amasses amassing amassed
VERB If you amass something such as money or information, you collect large quantities of it E.G. *He amassed a huge fortune.*

amateur amateurs
NOUN someone who does something as a hobby rather than as a job.

amateurish
ADJECTIVE not skilfully made or done.
amateurishly ADVERB

amaze amazes amazing amazed
VERB If something amazes you, it surprises you very much.
amazement NOUN
☰ astonish, astound, stun, surprise

amazing
ADJECTIVE very surprising or remarkable.
amazingly ADVERB

ambassador ambassadors
NOUN a person sent to a foreign

country as the representative of his or her own government.

amber

NOUN **1** a hard, yellowish-brown substance used for making jewellery. ▶ NOUN or ADJECTIVE **2** orange-brown.

ambi-

PREFIX 'Ambi-' means 'both'. For example, something which is *ambiguous* can have either of two meanings.

📖 from Latin *ambo* meaning 'both'

ambidextrous

ADJECTIVE Someone who is ambidextrous is able to use both hands equally skilfully.

ambience

NOUN; FORMAL The ambience of a place is its atmosphere.

ambiguous

ADJECTIVE A word or phrase that is ambiguous has more than one meaning.

ambiguously ADVERB   **ambiguity** NOUN

ambition ambitions

NOUN **1** If you have an ambition to achieve something, you want very much to achieve it E.G. *His ambition is to be an actor.* **2** a great desire for success, power, and wealth E.G. *He's talented and full of ambition.*

ambitious

ADJECTIVE **1** Someone who is ambitious has a strong desire for success, power, and wealth. **2** An ambitious plan is a large one and requires a lot of work E.G. *an ambitious rebuilding schedule.*

ambivalent

ADJECTIVE having or showing two conflicting attitudes or emotions.

ambivalence NOUN

amble ambles ambling ambled

VERB If you amble, you walk slowly and in a relaxed manner.

ambulance ambulances

NOUN a vehicle for taking sick and injured people to hospital.

ambush ambushes ambushing ambushed

VERB **1** To ambush someone is to attack them after hiding and lying in wait for them. ▶ NOUN **2** an attack on someone after hiding and lying in wait for them.

amen

INTERJECTION Amen is said at the end of a Christian prayer. It means 'so be it'.

amenable

Said "am-**mee**-na-bl" ADJECTIVE willing to listen to suggestions, or to cooperate with someone E.G. *Both brothers were amenable to the arrangement.*

amend amends amending amended

VERB **1** To amend something that has been written or said is to alter it slightly E.G. *Our constitution had to be amended.* ▶ PLURAL NOUN **2** If you make amends for something bad you have done, you say you are sorry and try to make up for it.

amendment NOUN

amenity amenities

Said "am-**mee**-nit-ee" NOUN (GEOGRAPHY) Amenities are things that are available for the public to use, such as sports facilities or shopping centres.

America

NOUN America refers to the United States, or to the whole of North, South, and Central America.

a
b
c
d
e
f
g
h
i
j
k
l
m
n
o
p
q
r
s
t
u
v
w
x
y
z

LEt's measure the angLE (ang**le**)   SPELLING NOTE

American Americans
ADJECTIVE **1** belonging or relating to the United States, or to the whole of North, South, and Central America.
► NOUN **2** someone who comes from the United States.

amethyst amethysts
NOUN a type of purple semiprecious stone.
📖 from Greek *amethustos* meaning 'not drunk'. It was thought to prevent intoxication

amiable
ADJECTIVE pleasant and friendly E.G. *The hotel staff were very amiable.*
amiably ADVERB **amiability** NOUN

amicable
ADJECTIVE fairly friendly E.G. *an amicable divorce.*
amicably ADVERB

amid or **amidst**
PREPOSITION; FORMAL surrounded by E.G. *She enjoys cooking amid her friends.*
☑ The form *amidst* is a bit old-fashioned and *amid* is more often used.

amiss
ADJECTIVE If something is amiss, there is something wrong.

ammonia
NOUN Ammonia is a colourless, strong-smelling gas or liquid.

ammunition
NOUN anything that can be fired from a gun or other weapon, for example bullets and shells.

amnesia
NOUN loss of memory.

amnesty amnesties
NOUN an official pardon for political or other prisoners.

amoeba amoebas or amoebae
Said "am-*mee*-ba"; also spelt **ameba**
NOUN the smallest kind of living creature, consisting of one cell. Amoebas reproduce by dividing into two.

amok
Said "am-*muk*" PHRASE If a person or animal **runs amok**, they behave in a violent and uncontrolled way.
📖 a Malay word

among or **amongst**
PREPOSITION **1** surrounded by E.G. *The bike lay among piles of chains and pedals.* **2** in the company of E.G. *He was among friends.* **3** between more than two E.G. *The money will be divided among seven charities.*
☑ If there are more than two things, you should use *among*. If there are only two things you should use *between*. The form *amongst* is a bit old-fashioned and *among* is more often used.

amoral
ADJECTIVE Someone who is amoral has no moral standards by which to live
☑ Do not confuse *amoral* and *immoral*. You use *amoral* to talk about people with no moral standards, but *immoral* for people who are aware of moral standards but go against them.

amorous
ADJECTIVE passionately affectionate E.G. *an amorous relationship.*
amorously ADVERB **amorousness** NOUN

amount amounts amounting amounted (MATHS)
NOUN **1** An amount of something is how much there is of it. ► VERB **2** If something amounts to a particular total, all the parts of it add up to that total E.G. *Her vocabulary amounted*

to only 50 words.

■ (sense 1) extent, number, quantity

amp amps
NOUN An amp is the same as an ampere.

ampere amperes
Said "am-pair" NOUN a unit which is used for measuring electric current.

amphetamine amphetamines
NOUN a drug that increases people's energy and makes them excited. It can have dangerous and unpleasant side effects.

amphibian amphibians
NOUN (SCIENCE) a creature that lives partly on land and partly in water, for example a frog or a newt.

amphibious
ADJECTIVE An amphibious animal, such as a frog, lives partly on land and partly in the water.

📖 from Greek *amphibios* meaning 'having a double life'

amphitheatre amphitheatres
NOUN a large, semicircular open area with sloping sides covered with rows of seats.

ample
ADJECTIVE If there is an ample amount of something, there is more than enough of it.
amply ADVERB

amplifier amplifiers
NOUN a piece of equipment in a radio or stereo system which causes sounds or signals to become louder.

amplify amplifies amplifying amplified
VERB If you amplify a sound, you make it louder.
amplification NOUN

amplitude
NOUN In physics, the amplitude of a wave is how far its curve moves away from its normal position.

amputate amputates amputating amputated
VERB To amputate an arm or a leg is to cut it off as a surgical operation.
amputation NOUN

Amrit
NOUN 1 In the Sikh religion, Amrit is a special mixture of sugar and water used in rituals. 2 The Amrit or Amrit ceremony takes place when someone is accepted as a full member of the Sikh community, and drinks Amrit as part of the ceremony.

amuse amuses amusing amused
VERB 1 If something amuses you, you think it is funny. 2 If you amuse yourself, you find things to do which stop you from being bored.
amused ADJECTIVE **amusing** ADJECTIVE

amusement amusements
NOUN 1 Amusement is the state of thinking something is funny.
2 Amusement is also the pleasure you get from being entertained or from doing something interesting.
3 Amusements are ways of passing the time pleasantly.

an
ADJECTIVE 'An' is used instead of 'a' in front of words that begin with a vowel sound
☑ You use *an* in front of abbreviations that start with a vowel sound when they are read out loud: *an MA; an OBE*.

-an
SUFFIX '-an' comes at the end of nouns and adjectives which show where or what someone or something comes

a
b
c
d
e
f
g
h
i
j
k
l
m
n
o
p
q
r
s
t
u
v
w
x
y
z

A
B
C
D
E
F
G
H
I
J
K
L
M
N
O
P
Q
R
S
T
U
V
W
X
Y
Z

from or belongs to E.G. *American…
Victorian… Christian.*

🏛 from Latin *-ānus* meaning 'of or belonging to'

anachronism anachronisms
Said "an-**ak**-kron-izm" NOUN something that belongs or seems to belong to another time.

anachronistic ADJECTIVE

🏛 from Greek *anakhronismos* meaning 'mistake in time'

anaemia
Said "a-**nee**-mee-a" NOUN a medical condition resulting from too few red cells in a person's blood. People with anaemia look pale and feel very tired.

anaemic
ADJECTIVE

anaesthetic anaesthetics
Said "an-niss-**thet**-ik"
NOUN a substance that stops you feeling pain. A general anaesthetic stops you from feeling pain in the whole of your body by putting you to sleep, and a local anaesthetic makes just one part of your body go numb.

anaesthetist anaesthetists
NOUN a doctor who is specially trained to give anaesthetics.

anaesthetize anaesthetizes anaesthetizing anaesthetized; also spelt **anesthetize** or **anaesthetise**
VERB To anaesthetize someone is to give them an anaesthetic to make them unconscious.

anagram anagrams
NOUN a word or phrase formed by changing the order of the letters of another word or phrase. For example, 'triangle' is an anagram of 'integral'.

anal
Said "**ay**-nl" ADJECTIVE relating to the anus.

analgesic analgesics
Said "an-al-**jee**-sik" NOUN a substance that relieves pain.

analogy analogies
Said "an-**al**-o-jee" NOUN a comparison showing that two things are similar in some ways.

analogous ADJECTIVE

analyse analyses analysing analysed
VERB (EXAM TERM) To analyse something is to break it down into parts, or investigate it carefully, so that you can describe its main aspects, or find out what it consists of.

analysis analyses
NOUN the process of investigating something in order to understand it or find out what it consists of E.G. *a full analysis of the problem.*

analyst analysts
NOUN a person whose job is to analyse things to find out about them.

analytic or **analytical**
ADJECTIVE using logical reasoning E.G. *Planning in detail requires an acute analytical mind.*

analytically ADVERB

anarchy
Said "an-**nar**-kee" NOUN a situation where nobody obeys laws or rules.

🏛 from Greek *anarkhos* meaning 'without a ruler'

anatomy anatomies
NOUN 1 the study of the structure of the human body or of the bodies of animals. 2 An animal's anatomy is the structure of its body.

anatomical ADJECTIVE **anatomically** ADVERB

ANC
NOUN one of the main political parties in South Africa. ANC is an abbreviation for 'African National Congress'.

ancestor ancestors
NOUN Your ancestors are the members of your family who lived many years ago and from whom you are descended.
ancestral ADJECTIVE
■ forebear, forefather

ancestry ancestries
NOUN Your ancestry consists of the people from whom you are descended E.G. *a French citizen of Greek ancestry*.

anchor anchors anchoring anchored
NOUN 1 a heavy, hooked object at the end of a chain, dropped from a boat into the water to keep the boat in one place. ▶ VERB 2 To anchor a boat or another object is to stop it from moving by dropping an anchor or attaching it to something solid.

anchorage anchorages
NOUN a place where a boat can safely anchor.

anchovy anchovies
NOUN a type of small edible fish with a very strong salty taste.

ancient
Said "**ayn**-shent" ADJECTIVE 1 existing or happening in the distant past E.G. *ancient Greece*. 2 very old or having a very long history E.G. *an ancient monastery*.

ancillary
Said "an-**sil**-lar-ee" ADJECTIVE The ancillary workers in an institution are the people such as cooks and cleaners, whose work supports the main work of the institution.
🔲 from Latin *ancilla* meaning 'maidservant'

and
CONJUNCTION You use 'and' to link two or more words or phrases together.

androgynous
Said "an-**droj**-in-uss" ADJECTIVE; FORMAL having both male and female characteristics.

anecdote anecdotes
NOUN a short, entertaining story about a person or event.
anecdotal ADJECTIVE

anemone anemones
Said "an-**em**-on-ee" NOUN a plant with red, purple, or white flowers.

anew
ADVERB If you do something anew, you do it again E.G. *They left their life in Britain to start anew in France*.

angel angels
NOUN Angels are spiritual beings some people believe live in heaven and act as messengers for God.
angelic ADJECTIVE

anger angers angering angered
NOUN 1 the strong feeling you get when you feel someone has behaved in an unfair or cruel way. ▶ VERB 2 If something angers you, it makes you feel angry.
■ (sense 1) fury, rage, wrath
■ (sense 2) enrage, infuriate, madden

angina
Said "an-**jy**-na" NOUN a brief but very severe heart pain, caused by lack of blood supply to the heart. It is also known as 'angina pectoris'.

angle angles
NOUN 1 (MATHS) the distance between two lines at the point where they

a
b
c
d
e
f
g
h
i
j
k
l
m
n
o
p
q
r
s
t
u
v
w
x
y
z

an ELegant angEL (ang*el*) ▶ SPELLING NOTE

A

join together. Angles are measured in degrees. **2** the direction from which you look at something E.G. *He had painted the vase from all angles.* **3** An angle on something is a particular way of considering it E.G. *the same story from a German angle.*

angler anglers
NOUN someone who fishes with a fishing rod as a hobby.

angling NOUN
🔲 from Old English *angul* meaning 'fish-hook'

Anglican Anglicans
NOUN or ADJECTIVE a member of one of the churches belonging to the Anglican Communion, a group of Protestant churches which includes the Church of England.

Anglo-Saxon Anglo-Saxons
NOUN **1** The Anglo-Saxons were a race of people who settled in England from the fifth century AD and were the dominant people until the Norman invasion in 1066. They were composed of three West Germanic tribes, the Angles, Saxons, and Jutes. **2** Anglo-Saxon is another name for **Old English**.

Angolan Angolans
Said "ang-**goh**-ln" ADJECTIVE
1 belonging or relating to Angola. ▶ NOUN **2** someone who comes from Angola.

angora
ADJECTIVE **1** An angora goat or rabbit is a breed with long silky hair. ▶ NOUN **2** Angora is this hair, usually mixed with other fibres to make clothing.
🔲 from *Angora*, the former name of Ankara in Turkey

angry angrier angriest
ADJECTIVE very cross or annoyed.

angrily ADVERB
🔲 enraged, furious, infuriated, mad

anguish
NOUN extreme suffering.

anguished ADJECTIVE

angular
ADJECTIVE Angular things have straight lines and sharp points E.G. *He has an angular face and pointed chin.*

animal animals
NOUN any living being except a plant, or any mammal except a human being.
🔲 from Latin *anima* meaning 'life' or 'soul'

animate animates animating animated
VERB To animate something is to make it lively and interesting.

animated
ADJECTIVE lively and interesting E.G. *an animated conversation.*

animation
NOUN **1** a method of film-making in which a series of drawings are photographed. When the film is projected, the characters in the drawings appear to move. **2** Someone who has animation shows liveliness in the way they speak and act E.G. *The crowd showed no sign of animation.*

animator NOUN

animosity animosities
NOUN a feeling of strong dislike and anger towards someone.

ankle ankles
NOUN the joint which connects your foot to your leg.

annex annexes annexing annexed; also spelt annexe
NOUN **1** an extra building which is joined to a larger main building. **2** an

extra part added to a document.
► VERB **3** If one country annexes another, it seizes the other country and takes control of it.
annexation NOUN

annihilate annihilates annihilating annihilated
Said "an-**nye**-ill-ate" VERB If something is annihilated, it is completely destroyed.
annihilation NOUN

anniversary anniversaries
NOUN a date which is remembered because something special happened on that date in a previous year.

announce announces announcing announced
VERB If you announce something, you tell people about it publicly or officially E.G. *The team was announced on Friday morning.*
announcement NOUN
≡ broadcast, make known, proclaim

announcer announcers
NOUN someone who introduces programmes on radio and television.

annoy annoys annoying annoyed
VERB If someone or something annoys you, they irritate you and make you fairly angry.
annoyance NOUN **annoyed** ADJECTIVE
≡ bother, exasperate, irritate, vex

annual annuals
ADJECTIVE **1** happening or done once a year E.G. *their annual conference.*
2 happening or calculated over a period of one year E.G. *the United States' annual budget for national defence.* ► NOUN **3** a book or magazine published once a year. **4** a plant that grows, flowers, and dies within one year.

annually ADVERB

annuity annuities
NOUN a fixed sum of money paid to someone every year from an investment or insurance policy.

annul annuls annulling annulled
VERB If a marriage or contract is annulled, it is declared invalid, so that legally it is considered never to have existed.
annulment NOUN

anoint anoints anointing anointed
VERB To anoint someone is to put oil on them as part of a ceremony.
anointment NOUN

anomaly anomalies
Said "an-**nom**-al-ee" NOUN Something is an anomaly if it is unusual or different from normal.
anomalous ADJECTIVE

anon.
an abbreviation for **anonymous**.

anonymous
ADJECTIVE If something is anonymous, nobody knows who is responsible for it E.G. *The police received an anonymous phone call.*
anonymously ADVERB **anonymity** NOUN

anorak anoraks
NOUN a warm waterproof jacket, usually with a hood.
🔳 an Inuit word

anorexia
NOUN a psychological illness in which the person refuses to eat because they are frightened of becoming fat.
🔳 from Greek *an-* + *orexis* meaning 'no appetite'

another
ADJECTIVE or PRONOUN Another thing or person is an additional thing or person.

I always visit my FRIend on a FRIday (friend) SPELLING NOTE

a b c d e f g h i j k l m n o p q r s t u v w x y z

answer answers answering answered

VERB **1** If you answer someone, you reply to them using words or actions or in writing. ► NOUN **2** the reply you give when you answer someone. **3** a solution to a problem.

■ (sense 1) reply, respond, retort

■ (sense 2) reply, response, retort

answerable

ADJECTIVE If you are answerable to someone for something, you are responsible for it E.G. *He must be made answerable for these terrible crimes.*

answering machine answering machines

NOUN a machine which records telephone calls while you are out.

ant ants

NOUN Ants are small insects that live in large groups.

-ant

SUFFIX '-ant' is used to form adjectives E.G. *important.*

🔒

antagonism

NOUN hatred or hostility.

antagonist antagonists

NOUN an enemy or opponent.

antagonistic

ADJECTIVE Someone who is antagonistic towards you shows hate or hostility.

antagonistically ADVERB

antagonize antagonizes antagonizing antagonized; also spelt **antagonise**

VERB If someone is antagonized, they are made to feel anger and hostility.

Antarctic

NOUN The Antarctic is the region south of the Antarctic Circle.

Antarctic Circle

NOUN The Antarctic Circle is an imaginary circle around the southern part of the world.

ante-

PREFIX 'Ante-' means 'before'. For example, *antenatal* means 'before birth'.

🔒 from Latin *ante*, a preposition or adverb meaning 'before'

antecedent antecedents

Said "an-tis-**see**-dent" NOUN **1** An antecedent of a thing or event is something which happened or existed before it and is related to it in some way E.G. *the prehistoric antecedents of the horse.* **2** Your antecedents are your ancestors, the relatives from whom you are descended.

antelope antelopes

NOUN an animal which looks like a deer.

antenatal

ADJECTIVE concerned with the care of pregnant women and their unborn children E.G. *an antenatal clinic.*

antenna antennae or antennas

NOUN **1** The antennae of insects and certain other animals are the two long, thin parts attached to their heads which they use to feel with. The plural is 'antennae'. **2** In Australian, New Zealand, and American English, an antenna is a radio or television aerial. The plural is 'antennas'.

anthem anthems

NOUN a hymn written for a special occasion.

anther anthers

NOUN in a flower, the part of the stamen that makes pollen grains.

🔲 from Greek *anthos* meaning 'flower'

anthology anthologies
NOUN (LIBRARY) a collection of writings by various authors published in one book.

anthropo-
PREFIX 'Anthropo-' means involving or to do with human beings E.G. *anthropology*.
🔲 from Greek *anthrōpos* meaning 'human being'

anthropology
NOUN the study of human beings and their society and culture.
anthropological ADJECTIVE
anthropologist NOUN

anti-
PREFIX 'Anti-' means opposed to or opposite to something E.G. *antiwar marches*.
🔲 from Greek *anti-* meaning 'opposite' or 'against'

antibiotic antibiotics
NOUN a drug or chemical used in medicine to kill bacteria and cure infections.

antibody antibodies
NOUN a substance produced in the blood which can kill the harmful bacteria that cause disease.

anticipate anticipates anticipating anticipated
VERB If you anticipate an event, you are expecting it and are prepared for it E.G. *She had anticipated his visit*.
anticipation NOUN

anticlimax anticlimaxes
NOUN something that disappoints you because it is not as exciting as expected, or because it occurs after something that was very exciting.

anticlockwise
ADJECTIVE OR ADVERB moving in the opposite direction to the hands of a clock.

antics
PLURAL NOUN funny or silly ways of behaving.

antidote antidotes
NOUN a chemical substance that acts against the effect of a poison.

antihistamine antihistamines
NOUN a drug used to treat an allergy.

antipathy
NOUN a strong feeling of dislike or hostility towards something or someone.

antiperspirant antiperspirants
NOUN a substance which stops you sweating when you put it on your skin.

antipodes
Said "an-**tip**-pod-eez" PLURAL NOUN any two points on the earth's surface that are situated directly opposite each other. In Britain, Australia and New Zealand are sometimes called the Antipodes as they are opposite Britain on the globe.
antipodean ADJECTIVE
🔲 from Greek *antipous* meaning 'with the feet opposite'

antiquarian
ADJECTIVE relating to or involving old and rare objects E.G. *antiquarian books*.

antiquated
ADJECTIVE very old-fashioned E.G. *an antiquated method of teaching*.

antique antiques
Said "an-**teek**" NOUN **1** an object from the past that is collected because of its value or beauty. ▶ ADJECTIVE **2** from or concerning the past E.G. *antique furniture*.

a b c d e f g h i j k l m n o p q r s t u v w x y z

The government licenSes Schnapps (licenSes) **SPELLING NOTE**

antiquity antiquities

NOUN 1 Antiquity is the distant past, especially the time of the ancient Egyptians, Greeks, and Romans. 2 Antiquities are interesting works of art and buildings from the distant past.

anti-Semitism

NOUN hatred of Jewish people. **anti-Semitic** ADJECTIVE **anti-Semite** NOUN

antiseptic

ADJECTIVE Something that is antiseptic kills germs.

antisocial

ADJECTIVE 1 An antisocial person is unwilling to meet and be friendly with other people. 2 Antisocial behaviour is annoying or upsetting to other people E.G. Smoking in public is antisocial.

antithesis antitheses

Said "an-tith-iss-iss" NOUN; FORMAL The antithesis of something is its exact opposite E.G. Work is the antithesis of leisure.

antivenene antivenenes

NOUN a substance which reduces the effect of a venom, especially a snake venom.

antler antlers

NOUN A male deer's antlers are the branched horns on its head.

antonym antonyms

NOUN a word which means the opposite of another word. For example, 'hot' is the antonym of 'cold'.

anus anuses

NOUN the hole between the buttocks.

anvil anvils

NOUN a heavy iron block on which hot metal is beaten into shape.

anxiety anxieties

NOUN nervousness or worry.

anxious

ADJECTIVE 1 If you are anxious, you are nervous or worried. 2 If you are anxious to do something or anxious that something should happen, you very much want to do it or want it to happen E.G. She was anxious to have children.

anxiously ADVERB

any

ADJECTIVE OR PRONOUN 1 one, some, or several E.G. Do you have any paperclips I could borrow? 2 even the smallest amount or even one E.G. He was unable to tolerate any dairy products. 3 whatever or whichever, no matter what or which E.G. Any type of cooking oil will do.

anybody

PRONOUN any person.

anyhow

ADVERB 1 in any case. 2 in a careless way E.G. They were all shoved in anyhow.

anyone

PRONOUN any person.

anything

PRONOUN any object, event, situation, or action.

anyway

ADVERB in any case.

anywhere

ADVERB in, at, or to any place.

Anzac Anzacs

NOUN 1 In World War I, an Anzac was a soldier with the Australia and New Zealand Army Corps. 2 an Australian or New Zealand soldier.

aorta

Said "ay-or-ta" NOUN the main artery in the body, which carries blood away from the heart.

apart

ADVERB OR ADJECTIVE **1** When something is apart from something else, there is a space or a distance between them E.G. *The couple separated and lived apart for four years… The gliders landed about seventy metres apart.*
▶ ADVERB **2** If you take something apart, you separate it into pieces.

apartheid

Said "ap-**par**-tide" NOUN In South Africa apartheid was the government policy and laws which kept people of different races apart. It was abolished in 1994.
🏛 an Afrikaans word

apartment apartments

NOUN a set of rooms for living in, usually on one floor of a building.

apathetic

ADJECTIVE not interested in anything.
☐ indifferent, uninterested

apathy

Said "**ap**-path-ee" NOUN a state of mind in which you do not care about anything.

ape apes aping aped

NOUN **1** Apes are animals with a very short tail or no tail. They are closely related to man. Apes include chimpanzees, gorillas, and gibbons.
▶ VERB **2** If you ape someone's speech or behaviour, you imitate it.

aphid aphids

NOUN a small insect that feeds by sucking the juices from plants.

aphrodisiac aphrodisiacs

NOUN a food, drink, or drug which makes people want to have sex.

apiece

ADVERB If people have a particular number of things apiece, they have that number each.

aplomb

Said "uh-**plom**" NOUN If you do something with aplomb, you do it with great confidence.

apocalypse

Said "uh-**pok**-ka-lips" NOUN The Apocalypse is the end of the world.
apocalyptic ADJECTIVE
🏛 from Greek *apokaluptein* meaning 'to reveal'; the way the world will end is considered to be revealed in the last book of the Bible, called 'Apocalypse' or 'Revelation'

apocryphal

ADJECTIVE A story that is apocryphal is generally believed not to have really happened.

apolitical

Said "ay-poll-**it**-i-kl" ADJECTIVE not interested in politics.

apologetic

ADJECTIVE showing or saying you are sorry.
apologetically ADVERB

apologize apologizes apologizing apologized; also spelt apologise

VERB When you apologize to someone, you say you are sorry for something you have said or done.

apology apologies

NOUN something you say or write to tell someone you are sorry.

apostle apostles

NOUN The Apostles are the twelve followers who were chosen by Christ.

apostrophe apostrophes

Said "ap-**poss**-troff-ee" NOUN (ENGLISH) a punctuation mark used to show that one or more letters have been missed out of a word, for example "he's" for "he is". Apostrophes are also used with -s at the end of a noun to

a
b
c
d
e
f
g
h
i
j
k
l
m
n
o
p
q
r
s
t
u
v
w
x
y
z

show that what follows belongs to or relates to the noun, for example *my brother's books*. If the noun already has an -s at the end, for example because it is plural, you just add the apostrophe, eg *my brothers' books*, referring to more than one brother.

What does the Apostrophe do?

The **apostrophe** (') is used to show possession. It is usually added to the end of a word and followed by an *s*:

> E.G. *Matthew's book* ■ *children's programmes*

If a plural word already ends in -s, the apostrophe follows that letter:

> E.G. *my parents' generation* ■ *seven years' bad luck*

You should not use an apostrophe to form plurals or possessive pronouns:

> E.G. *a pound of tomatoes* [not *tomato's*] ■ *I happen to be a fan of hers* [not *her's*]

You can, however, add an apostrophe to form the plural of a number, letter, or symbol:

> E.G. *P's and Q's* ■ *7's* ■ *£'s*

The apostrophe is also used to show that a letter or letters have been omitted:

> E.G. *rock'n'roll* ■ *Who's next?*

---

appal appals appalling appalled
VERB If something appals you, it shocks you because it is very bad.

appalling
ADJECTIVE so bad as to be shocking E.G. *She escaped with appalling injuries.*

apparatus
NOUN (SCIENCE) The apparatus for a particular task is the equipment used for it.

apparent
ADJECTIVE 1 seeming real rather than actually being real E.G. *an apparent hit and run accident.* 2 obvious E.G. *It was apparent that he had lost interest.*
apparently ADVERB
■ (sense 1) ostensible, seeming

apparition apparitions
NOUN something you think you see but that is not really there E.G. *a ghostly apparition on the windscreen.*

appeal appeals appealing appealed
VERB 1 If you appeal for something, you make an urgent request for it E.G. *The police appealed for witnesses to come forward.* 2 If you appeal to someone in authority against a decision, you formally ask them to change it. 3 If something appeals to you, you find it attractive or interesting. ► NOUN 4 a formal or serious request E.G. *an appeal for peace.* 5 The appeal of something is the quality it has which people find attractive or appealing E.G. *the rugged appeal of the Rockies.*
appealing ADJECTIVE

appear appears appearing appeared
VERB 1 When something which you could not see appears, it moves (or you move) so that you can see it. 2 When something new appears, it begins to exist. 3 When an actor or actress appears in a film or show, they take part in it. 4 If something appears to be a certain way, it seems or looks that way E.G. *He appeared to*

be searching for something.
■ (sense 1) come into view, emerge, show up

appearance appearances
NOUN **1** The appearance of someone in a place is their arrival there, especially when it is unexpected. **2** The appearance of something new is the time when it begins to exist E.G. *the appearance of computer technology.* **3** Someone's or something's appearance is the way they look to other people E.G. *His gaunt appearance had sparked fears for his health.*

appease appeases appeasing appeased
VERB If you try to appease someone, you try to calm them down when they are angry, for example by giving them what they want.
appeasement NOUN

appendage appendages
NOUN a less important part attached to a main part.

appendicitis
Said "app-end-i-**site**-uss" NOUN a painful illness in which a person's appendix becomes infected.

appendix appendices or appendixes
NOUN **1** a small closed tube forming part of your digestive system. **2** An appendix to a book is extra information placed after the end of the main text.
✔ The plural of the part of the body is *appendixes*. The plural of the extra section in a book is *appendices*.

appetite appetites
NOUN **1** Your appetite is your desire to eat. **2** If you have an appetite for something, you have a strong desire

for it and enjoyment of it E.G. *She had lost her appetite for air travel.*

appetizing or **appetising**
ADJECTIVE Food that is appetizing looks and smells good, and makes you want to eat it.

applaud applauds applauding applauded
VERB **1** When a group of people applaud, they clap their hands in approval or praise. **2** When an action or attitude is applauded, people praise it.

applause
NOUN 〔DRAMA〕 Applause is clapping by a group of people.

apple apples
NOUN a round fruit with smooth skin and firm white flesh.

appliance appliances
NOUN any machine in your home you use to do a job like cleaning or cooking E.G. *kitchen appliances.*

applicable
ADJECTIVE Something that is applicable to a situation is relevant to it E.G. *The rules are applicable to everyone.*

applicant applicants
NOUN someone who is applying for something E.G. *We had problems recruiting applicants for the post.*

application applications
NOUN **1** a formal request for something, usually in writing. **2** The application of a rule, system, or skill is the use of it in a particular situation.

apply applies applying applied
VERB **1** If you apply for something, you formally ask for it, usually by writing a letter. **2** If you apply a rule or skill, you use it in a situation E.G. *He applied his mind to the problem.* **3** If

You must practiSe your Ss (practise)　　**SPELLING NOTE**

something applies to a person or a situation, it is relevant to that person or situation E.G. *The legislation applies only to people living in England and Wales.* **4** If you apply something to a surface, you put it on E.G. *She applied lipstick to her mouth.*

appoint appoints appointing appointed

VERB **1** If you appoint someone to a job or position, you formally choose them for it. **2** If you appoint a time or place for something to happen, you decide when or where it will happen.

appointed ADJECTIVE

appointment appointments

NOUN **1** an arrangement you have with someone to meet them. **2** The appointment of a person to do a particular job is the choosing of that person to do it. **3** a job or a position of responsibility E.G. *He applied for an appointment in Russia.*

◼ (sense 1) date, engagement, meeting

apposite

Said "**app**-o-zit" ADJECTIVE well suited for a particular purpose E.G. *He went before Cameron could think of anything apposite to say.*

appraise appraises appraising appraised

VERB If you appraise something, you think about it carefully and form an opinion about it.

appraisal NOUN

appreciable

Said "a-**pree**-shuh-bl" ADJECTIVE large enough to be noticed E.G. *an appreciable difference.*

appreciably ADVERB

appreciate appreciates appreciating appreciated

VERB **1** If you appreciate something, you like it because you recognize its good qualities E.G. *He appreciates fine wines.* **2** If you appreciate a situation or problem, you understand it and know what it involves. **3** If you appreciate something someone has done for you, you are grateful to them for it E.G. *I really appreciate you coming to visit me.* **4** If something appreciates over a period of time, its value increases E.G. *The property appreciated by 50% in two years.*

appreciation NOUN

◼ (sense 1) prize, rate highly, value

appreciative

ADJECTIVE **1** understanding and enthusiastic E.G. *They were a very appreciative audience.* **2** thankful and grateful E.G. *I am particularly appreciative of the help.*

appreciatively ADVERB

apprehend apprehends apprehending apprehended

VERB; FORMAL **1** When the police apprehend someone, they arrest them and take them into custody. **2** If you apprehend something, you understand it fully E.G. *They were unable to apprehend his hidden meaning.*

apprehensive

ADJECTIVE afraid something bad may happen E.G. *I was very apprehensive about the birth.*

apprehensively ADVERB

apprehension NOUN

apprentice apprentices

NOUN a person who works for a period of time with a skilled craftsman in order to learn a skill or trade.

apprenticeship NOUN

from Old French *aprendre*
meaning 'to learn'

approach approaches
approaching approached
VERB **1** To approach something is to
come near or nearer to it. **2** When a
future event approaches, it gradually
gets nearer E.G. *As winter
approached, tents were set up to
accommodate refugees.* **3** If you
approach someone about
something, you ask them about it.
4 If you approach a situation or
problem in a particular way, you
think about it or deal with it in that
way. ▸ NOUN **5** The approach of
something is the process of it
coming closer E.G. *the approach of
spring.* **6** An approach to a situation
or problem is a way of thinking
about it or dealing with it. **7** a road or
path that leads to a place.
approaching ADJECTIVE

appropriate appropriates
appropriating appropriated
ADJECTIVE **1** suitable or acceptable for a
particular situation E.G. *He didn't
think jeans were appropriate for a
vice-president.* ▸ VERB **2** FORMAL If you
appropriate something which does
not belong to you, you take it
without permission.
appropriately ADVERB
appropriation NOUN

approval
NOUN (PSHE) **1** Approval is agreement
given to a plan or request E.G. *The
plan will require approval from the
local authority.* **2** Approval is also
admiration E.G. *She looked at James
with approval.*
▣ (sense 1) agreement, consent,
permission

approve approves approving
approved
VERB (PSHE) **1** If you approve of
something or someone, you think
that thing or person is acceptable or
good. **2** If someone in a position of
authority approves a plan or idea,
they formally agree to it.
approved ADJECTIVE **approving**
ADJECTIVE
▣ (sense 1) commend, favour, like
▣ (sense 2) agree to, authorize, pass,
permit

approximate
ADJECTIVE almost exact E.G. *What was
the approximate distance between the
cars?*
approximately ADVERB (MATHS)
▣ close, near

apricot apricots
NOUN a small, soft, yellowish orange
fruit.
from Latin *praecox* meaning 'early
ripening'

April
NOUN the fourth month of the year.
April has 30 days.
from Latin *Aprīlis*

apron aprons
NOUN a piece of clothing worn over
the front of normal clothing to
protect it.

apse apses
NOUN a domed recess in the east wall
of a church.

apt
ADJECTIVE **1** suitable or relevant E.G. *a
very apt description.* **2** having a
particular tendency E.G. *They are apt
to jump to the wrong conclusions.*

aptitude
NOUN Someone's aptitude for
something is their ability to learn it

a
b
c
d
e
f
g
h
i
j
k
l
m
n
o
p
q
r
s
t
u
v
w
x
y
z

A

B

C

D

E

F

G

H

I

J

K

L

M

N

O

P

Q

R

S

T

U

V

W

X

Y

Z

quickly and to do it well E.G. *I have a natural aptitude for painting.*

aqua-
PREFIX 'Aqua-' means 'water'.
🏛 from Latin *aqua* meaning 'water'

aquarium aquaria or **aquariums**
NOUN a glass tank filled with water in which fish are kept.

Aquarius
NOUN Aquarius is the eleventh sign of the zodiac, represented by a person carrying water. People born between January 20th and February 18th are born under this sign.

aquatic
ADJECTIVE **1** An aquatic animal or plant lives or grows in water. **2** involving water E.G. *aquatic sports.*

aqueduct aqueducts
NOUN a long bridge with many arches carrying a water supply over a valley.

Arab Arabs
NOUN a member of a group of people who used to live in Arabia but who now live throughout the Middle East and North Africa.

Arabic
NOUN a language spoken by many people in the Middle East and North Africa.

arable
ADJECTIVE Arable land is used for growing crops.

arbiter arbiters
NOUN the person who decides about something.
📗 judge, referee, adjudicator

arbitrary
ADJECTIVE An arbitrary decision or action is one that is not based on a plan or system.
arbitrarily ADVERB

arbitrate arbitrates arbitrating arbitrated
VERB When someone arbitrates between two people or groups who are in disagreement, they consider the facts and decide who is right.
arbitration NOUN **arbitrator** NOUN

arc arcs
NOUN **1** a smoothly curving line. **2** in geometry, a section of the circumference of a circle.
☑ Do not confuse the spellings of *arc* and *ark*.

arcade arcades
NOUN a covered passage with shops or market stalls along one or both sides.

arcane
ADJECTIVE mysterious and difficult to understand.

arch arches arching arched
NOUN **1** a structure that has a curved top supported on either side by a pillar or wall. **2** the curved part of bone at the top of the foot. ► VERB **3** When something arches, it forms a curved line or shape. ► ADJECTIVE **4** most important E.G. *my arch enemy.*

arch-
PREFIX 'Arch-' means 'most important' or 'chief' E.G. *archangel.*
🏛 from Greek *arkhein* meaning 'to rule'

archaeology or **archeology**
Said "ar-kee-ol-loj-ee" NOUN the study of the past by digging up and examining the remains of buildings, tools, and other things.
archaeological ADJECTIVE
archaeologist NOUN
🏛 from Greek *arkhaios* meaning 'ancient'

archaic
Said "ar-**kay**-ik" ADJECTIVE very old or old-fashioned.

archangel archangels
Said "ark-**ain**-jel" NOUN an angel of the highest rank.

archbishop archbishops
NOUN a bishop of the highest rank in a Christian Church.

archdeacon archdeacons
NOUN an Anglican clergyman ranking just below a bishop.

archeology
another spelling of **archaeology**.

archer archers
NOUN someone who shoots with a bow and arrow.

archery
NOUN a sport in which people shoot at a target with a bow and arrow.

archipelago archipelagos
Said "ar-kip-**pel**-lag-oh" NOUN a group of small islands.
📖 from Italian *arcipelago* meaning 'chief sea'; originally referring to the Aegean Sea

architect architects
Said "ar-kit-tekt" NOUN a person who designs buildings.

architecture
NOUN the art or practice of designing buildings.
architectural ADJECTIVE

archive archives
Said "ar-kive" NOUN Archives are collections of documents and records about the history of a family or some other group of people.

arctic
NOUN 1 The Arctic is the region north of the Arctic Circle. ▶ ADJECTIVE 2 Arctic means very cold indeed E.G. *arctic conditions*.

📖 from Greek *arktos* meaning 'bear'; originally it referred to the northern constellation of the Great Bear

Arctic Circle
NOUN The Arctic Circle is an imaginary circle around the northern part of the world.

ardent
ADJECTIVE full of enthusiasm and passion.
ardently ADVERB

ardour
NOUN a strong and passionate feeling of love or enthusiasm.

arduous
Said "**ard**-yoo-uss" ADJECTIVE tiring and needing a lot of effort E.G. *the arduous task of rebuilding the country*.

are
the plural form of the present tense of **be**.

area areas
NOUN 1 a particular part of a place, country, or the world E.G. *a built-up area of the city*. 2 The area of a piece of ground or a surface is the amount of space it covers, measured in square metres or square feet.
▤ (sense 1) district, region, zone

arena arenas
NOUN 1 a place where sports and other public events take place. 2 A particular arena is the centre of attention or activity in a particular situation E.G. *the political arena*.
📖 from Latin *harena* meaning 'sand', hence the sandy centre of an amphitheatre where gladiators fought

Argentinian Argentinians
Said "ar-jen-**tin**-ee-an" ADJECTIVE
1 belonging or relating to Argentina.
▶ NOUN 2 someone who comes from Argentina.

a
b
c
d
e
f
g
h
i
j
k
l
m
n
o
p
q
r
s
t
u
v
w
x
y
z

the QUeen stood on the QUay (**quay**)   SPELLING NOTE

arguable

ADJECTIVE An arguable idea or point is not necessarily true or correct and should be questioned.

arguably ADVERB

argue argues arguing argued

VERB 1 If you argue with someone about something, you disagree with them about it, sometimes in an angry way. 2 If you argue that something is the case, you give reasons why you think it is so E.G. *She argued that her client had been wrongly accused.*

argument arguments

NOUN 1 a disagreement between two people which causes a quarrel. 2 a point or a set of reasons you use to try to convince people about something.

argumentative

ADJECTIVE An argumentative person is always disagreeing with other people.

aria arias

Said "ah-ree-a" NOUN a song sung by one of the leading singers in an opera.

📖 an Italian word meaning 'tune'

arid

ADJECTIVE Arid land is very dry because it has very little rain.

Aries

Said "air-reez" NOUN Aries is the first sign of the zodiac, represented by a ram. People born between March 21st and April 19th are born under this sign.

arise arises arising arose arisen

VERB 1 When something such as an opportunity or problem arises, it begins to exist. 2 FORMAL To arise also means to stand up from a sitting,

kneeling, or lying position.

aristocracy aristocracies

NOUN a class of people who have a high social rank and special titles.

aristocrat aristocrats

NOUN someone whose family has a high social rank, and who has a title.

aristocratic ADJECTIVE

arithmetic

NOUN the part of mathematics which is to do with the addition, subtraction, multiplication, and division of numbers.

arithmetical ADJECTIVE

arithmetically ADVERB

📖 from Greek *arithmos* meaning 'number'

ark

NOUN In the Bible, the ark was the boat built by Noah for his family and the animals during the Flood.

☑ Do not confuse the spellings of *arc* and *ark*.

arm arms arming armed

NOUN 1 Your arms are the part of your body between your shoulder and your wrist. 2 The arms of a chair are the parts on which you rest your arms. 3 An arm of an organization is a section of it E.G. *the political arm of the armed forces.* ▶ PLURAL NOUN 4 Arms are weapons used in a war. ▶ VERB 5 To arm someone is to provide them with weapons.

armada armadas

Said "ar-mah-da" NOUN a large fleet of warships.

armadillo armadillos

NOUN a mammal from South America which is covered with strong bony plates like armour.

📖 a Spanish word meaning 'little armed man'

Armageddon

NOUN In Christianity, Armageddon is the final battle between good and evil at the end of the world.

🏛 from Hebrew *har megiddon*, the mountain district of Megiddo, the site of many battles

armament armaments

NOUN Armaments are the weapons and military equipment that belong to a country.

armchair armchairs

NOUN a comfortable chair with a support on each side for your arms.

armed

ADJECTIVE A person who is armed is carrying a weapon or weapons.

armistice armistices

Said "ar-miss-tiss" NOUN an agreement in a war to stop fighting in order to discuss peace.

armour

NOUN In the past, armour was metal clothing worn for protection in battle.

armoured

ADJECTIVE covered with thick steel for protection from gunfire and other missiles E.G. *an armoured car*.

armoury armouries

NOUN a place where weapons are stored.

armpit armpits

NOUN the area under your arm where your arm joins your shoulder.

army armies

NOUN a large group of soldiers organized into divisions for fighting on land.

aroma aromas

NOUN a strong, pleasant smell.

aromatic ADJECTIVE

🏛 a Greek word meaning 'spice'

around

PREPOSITION 1 placed at various points in a place or area E.G. *There are many seats around the building.* 2 from place to place inside an area E.G. *We walked around the showroom.* 3 at approximately the time or place mentioned E.G. *The attacks began around noon.* ▶ ADVERB 4 here and there E.G. *His papers were scattered around.*

arouse arouses arousing aroused

VERB If something arouses a feeling in you, it causes you to begin to have this feeling E.G. *His death still arouses very painful feelings.*

arousal NOUN

arrange arranges arranging arranged

VERB 1 If you arrange to do something, you make plans for it. 2 If you arrange something for someone, you make it possible for them to have it or do it E.G. *The bank has arranged a loan for her.* 3 If you arrange objects, you set them out in a particular position E.G. *He started to arrange the books in piles.*

arrangement NOUN

array arrays

NOUN An array of different things is a large number of them displayed together.

arrears

PLURAL NOUN 1 Arrears are amounts of money you owe E.G. *mortgage arrears.* ▶ PHRASE 2 If you are paid **in arrears**, you are paid at the end of the period for which the payment is due.

arrest arrests arresting arrested

VERB 1 If the police arrest someone,

a b c d e f g h i j k l m n o p q r s t u v w x y z

A
B
C
D
E
F
G
H
I
J
K
L
M
N
O
P
Q
R
S
T
U
V
W
X
Y
Z

they take them into custody to decide whether to charge them with an offence. ▶ NOUN 2 An arrest is the act of taking a person into custody.

arrival arrivals
NOUN 1 the act or time of arriving E.G. *The arrival of the train was delayed.* 2 something or someone that has arrived E.G. *The tourist authority reported record arrivals over Christmas.*

arrive arrives arriving arrived
VERB 1 When you arrive at a place, you reach it at the end of your journey. 2 When a letter or a piece of news arrives, it is brought to you E.G. *A letter arrived at her lawyer's office.* 3 When you arrive at an idea or decision you reach it. 4 When a moment, event, or new thing arrives, it begins to happen E.G. *The Easter holidays arrived.*

arrogant
ADJECTIVE Someone who is arrogant behaves as if they are better than other people.
arrogantly ADVERB **arrogance** NOUN

arrow arrows
NOUN a long, thin weapon with a sharp point at one end, shot from a bow.

arsenal arsenals
NOUN a place where weapons and ammunition are stored or produced. 🏛 from Italian *arsenale* meaning 'dockyard', originally in Venice

arsenic
NOUN a very strong poison which can kill people.

arson
NOUN the crime of deliberately setting fire to something, especially a building.

art arts
NOUN 1 Art is the creation of objects such as paintings and sculptures, which are thought to be beautiful or which express a particular idea; also used to refer to the objects themselves. 2 An activity is called an art when it requires special skill or ability E.G. *the art of diplomacy.* ▶ PLURAL NOUN 3 The arts are literature, music, painting, and sculpture, considered together.

artefact artefacts
Said "ar-tif-fact" NOUN any object made by people.

artery arteries
NOUN 1 Your arteries are the tubes that carry blood from your heart to the rest of your body. 2 a main road or major section of any system of communication or transport.

artful
ADJECTIVE clever and skilful, often in a cunning way.
artfully ADVERB

arthritis
NOUN a condition in which the joints in someone's body become swollen and painful.
arthritic ADJECTIVE

artichoke artichokes
NOUN 1 A globe artichoke is a round green vegetable that has a cluster of fleshy leaves, the bottom part of which you can eat. 2 A Jerusalem artichoke is a small yellowish-white vegetable that grows underground and looks like a potato. 🏛 from Arabic *al-kharshuf*

article articles
NOUN 1 (LIBRARY) a piece of writing in a newspaper or magazine. 2 a particular item E.G. *an article of*

clothing. **3** In English grammar, 'a' and 'the' are sometimes called articles: 'a' (or 'an') is the indefinite article; 'the' is the definite article.

articulate articulates articulating articulated
ADJECTIVE **1** If you are articulate, you are able to express yourself well in words. ▶ VERB **2** When you articulate your ideas or feelings, you express in words what you think or feel E.G. *She could not articulate her grief.* **3** When you articulate a sound or word, you speak it clearly.
articulation NOUN

artificial
ADJECTIVE **1** created by people rather than occurring naturally F.G. *artificial colouring.* **2** pretending to have attitudes and feelings which other people realize are not real E.G. *an artificial smile.*
artificially ADVERB

artillery
NOUN **1** Artillery consists of large, powerful guns such as cannons. **2** The artillery is the branch of an army which uses large, powerful guns.

artist artists
NOUN **1** a person who draws or paints or produces other works of art. **2** a person who is very skilled at a particular activity.

artiste artistes
Said "ar-**teest**" NOUN a professional entertainer, for example a singer or a dancer.

artistic
ADJECTIVE **1** able to create good paintings, sculpture, or other works of art. **2** concerning or involving art or artists.
artistically ADVERB

artistry
NOUN Artistry is the creative skill of an artist, writer, actor, or musician E.G. *a supreme demonstration of his artistry as a cellist.*

arty artier artiest
ADJECTIVE; INFORMAL interested in painting, sculpture, and other works of art.

as
CONJUNCTION **1** at the same time that E.G. *She waved at fans as she arrived for the concert.* **2** in the way that E.G. *They had talked as only the best of friends can.* **3** because E.G. *As I won't be back tonight, don't bother to cook a meal.* **4** You use the structure **as ... as** when you are comparing things that are similar E.G. *It was as big as four football pitches.* ▶ PREPOSITION **5** You use 'as' when you are saying what role someone or something has E.G. *She worked as a waitress.* **6** You use **as if** or **as though** when you are giving a possible explanation for something E.G. *He looked at me as if I were mad.*

asbestos
NOUN a grey heat-resistant material used in the past to make fireproof articles.

ascend ascends ascending ascended
Said "ass-**end**" VERB; FORMAL To ascend is to move or lead upwards E.G. *We finally ascended to the brow of a steep hill.*

ascendancy
NOUN; FORMAL If one group has ascendancy over another, it has more power or influence than the other.

a b c d e f g h i j k l m n o p q r s t u v w x y z

ascendant

ADJECTIVE **1** rising or moving upwards.
▶ PHRASE **2** Someone or something **in the ascendant** is increasing in power or popularity.

ascent ascents

NOUN an upward journey, for example up a mountain.

ascertain ascertains ascertaining ascertained

Said "ass-er-**tain**"; FORMAL If you ascertain that something is the case, you find out it is the case E.G. *He had ascertained that she had given up smoking.*

ascribe ascribes ascribing ascribed

VERB **1** If you ascribe an event or state of affairs to a particular cause, you think that it is the cause of it E.G. *His stomach pains were ascribed to his intake of pork.* **2** If you ascribe a quality to someone, you think they have it.

ash ashes

NOUN **1** the grey or black powdery remains of anything that has been burnt. **2** a tree with grey bark and hard tough wood used for timber.

ashamed

ADJECTIVE **1** feeling embarrassed or guilty. **2** If you are ashamed of someone, you feel embarrassed to be connected with them.

ashen

ADJECTIVE grey or pale E.G. *Her face was ashen with fatigue.*

ashore

ADVERB on land or onto the land.

ashtray ashtrays

NOUN a small dish for ash from cigarettes and cigars.

Asia

NOUN Asia is the largest continent. It has Europe on its western side, with the Arctic to the north, the Pacific to the east, and the Indian Ocean to the south. Asia includes several island groups, including Japan, Indonesia, and the Philippines.

Asian Asians

ADJECTIVE **1** belonging or relating to Asia. ▶ NOUN **2** someone who comes from India, Pakistan, Bangladesh, or from some other part of Asia.

aside asides

ADVERB **1** If you move something aside, you move it to one side. ▶ NOUN **2** a comment made away from the main conversation or dialogue that all those talking are not meant to hear.

ask asks asking asked

VERB **1** If you ask someone a question, you put a question to them for them to answer. **2** If you ask someone to do something, you tell them you want them to do it. **3** If you ask for something, you say you would like to have it. **4** If you ask someone's permission or forgiveness, you try to obtain it. **5** If you ask someone somewhere, you invite them there E.G. *Not everybody had been asked to the wedding.*

askew

ADJECTIVE not straight.

asleep

ADJECTIVE sleeping.

asparagus

NOUN a vegetable that has long shoots which are cooked and eaten.

aspect aspects

NOUN **1** An aspect of something is one of its features E.G. *Exam results illustrate only one aspect of a school's* *success.* **2** The aspect of a building is the direction it faces E.G. *The southern aspect of the cottage faces over fields.*

asphalt
NOUN a black substance used to make road surfaces and playgrounds.

aspiration aspirations
NOUN Someone's aspirations are their desires and ambitions.

aspire aspires aspiring aspired
VERB If you aspire to something, you have an ambition to achieve it E.G. *He aspired to work in music journalism.*
aspiring ADJECTIVE

aspirin aspirins
NOUN **1** a white drug used to relieve pain, fever, and colds. **2** a tablet of this drug.

ass asses
NOUN a donkey.

assailant assailants
NOUN someone who attacks another person.

assassin assassins
NOUN someone who has murdered a political or religious leader.
📖 from Arabic *hashshashin* meaning 'people who eat hashish'; the name comes from a medieval Muslim sect who ate hashish and went about murdering Crusaders

assassinate assassinates assassinating assassinated
VERB To assassinate a political or religious leader is to murder him or her.
assassination NOUN

assault assaults assaulting assaulted
NOUN **1** a violent attack on someone.
▶ VERB **2** To assault someone is to attack them violently.

assegai assegais
Said "ass-i-guy"; also spelt **assagai**
NOUN In South African English, a sharp, light spear.

assemble assembles assembling assembled
VERB **1** To assemble is to gather together. **2** If you assemble something, you fit the parts of it together.

assembly assemblies
NOUN **1** a group of people who have gathered together for a meeting. **2** The assembly of an object is the fitting together of its parts E.G. *DIY assembly of units.*

assent assents assenting assented
Said "as-sent" NOUN **1** If you give your assent to something, you agree to it.
▶ VERB **2** If you assent to something, you agree to it.

assert asserts asserting asserted
VERB **1** If you assert a fact or belief, you state it firmly and forcefully. **2** If you assert yourself, you speak and behave in a confident and direct way, so that people pay attention to you.

assertive
ADJECTIVE If you are assertive, you speak and behave in a confident and direct way, so that people pay attention to you.
assertively ADVERB **assertiveness** NOUN

assess assesses assessing assessed
VERB (EXAM TERM) If you assess something, you consider it carefully and make a judgment about it.

'i' before 'e' except after 'c'   SPELLING NOTE

A
B
C
D
E
F
G
H
I
J
K
L
M
N
O
P
Q
R
S
T
U
V
W
X
Y
Z

assessment NOUN
▪ appraise, judge, size up

assessor assessors
NOUN someone whose job is to assess the value of something.

asset assets
NOUN **1** a person or thing considered useful E.G. *He will be a great asset to the club.* ▸ PLURAL NOUN **2** The assets of a person or company are all the things they own that could be sold to raise money.

assign assigns assigning assigned
VERB **1** To assign something to someone is to give it to them officially or to make them responsible for it. **2** If someone is assigned to do something, they are officially told to do it.
▪ (sense 1) appoint, choose, select
▪ (sense 2) allocate, allot, give

assignation assignations
Said "ass-ig-**nay**-shn" NOUN; LITERARY a secret meeting with someone, especially a lover.

assignment assignments
NOUN a job someone is given to do.

assimilate assimilates assimilating assimilated
VERB **1** If you assimilate ideas or experiences, you learn and understand them. **2** When people are assimilated into a group, they become part of it.
assimilation NOUN

assist assists assisting assisted
VERB To assist someone is to help them do something.
assistance NOUN

assistant assistants
NOUN someone whose job is to help another person in their work.

associate associates associating associated
VERB **1** If you associate one thing with another, you connect the two things in your mind. **2** If you associate with a group of people, you spend a lot of time with them. ▸ NOUN **3** Your associates are the people you work with or spend a lot of time with.
▪ (sense 1) connect, link, relate
▪ (sense 2) consort, mix, socialize

association associations
NOUN **1** an organization for people who have similar interests, jobs, or aims. **2** Your association with a person or group is the connection or involvement you have with them. **3** An association between two things is a link you make in your mind between them E.G. *The place contained associations for her.*

assonance
NOUN the use of similar vowel or consonant sounds in words near to each other or in the same word, for example 'a long storm'.

assorted
ADJECTIVE Assorted things are different in size and colour E.G. *assorted swimsuits.*

assortment assortments
NOUN a group of similar things that are different sizes and colours E.G. *an amazing assortment of old toys.*

assume assumes assuming assumed
VERB **1** If you assume that something is true, you accept it is true even though you have not thought about it E.G. *I assumed that he would turn up.* **2** To assume responsibility for something is to put yourself in charge of it.

■ (sense 1) believe, presume, suppose, take for granted

■ (sense 2) accept, shoulder, take on

assumption assumptions
NOUN **1** a belief that something is true, without thinking about it. **2** Assumption of power or responsibility is the taking of it.

assurance assurances
NOUN **1** something said which is intended to make people less worried E.G. *She was emphatic in her assurances that she wanted to stay.* **2** Assurance is a feeling of confidence E.G. *He handled the car with ease and assurance.* **3** Life assurance is a type of insurance that pays money to your dependants when you die.

assure assures assuring assured
VERB If you assure someone that something is true, you tell them it is true.

asterisk asterisks
NOUN the symbol (*) used in printing and writing.
🕮 from Greek *asterikos* meaning 'small star'

astern
ADVERB or ADJECTIVE; NAUTICAL backwards or at the back.

asteroid asteroids
NOUN one of the large number of very small planets that move around the sun between the orbits of Jupiter and Mars.

asthma
Said "**ass**-ma" NOUN a disease of the chest which causes wheezing and difficulty in breathing.
asthmatic ADJECTIVE

astonish astonishes astonishing astonished
VERB If something astonishes you, it surprises you very much.
astonished ADJECTIVE **astonishing** ADJECTIVE **astonishingly** ADVERB **astonishment** NOUN

astound astounds astounding astounded
VERB If something astounds you, it shocks and amazes you.
astounded ADJECTIVE **astounding** ADJECTIVE

astray
PHRASE **1** To **lead someone astray** is to influence them to do something wrong. **2** If something **goes astray**, it gets lost E.G. *The money had gone astray.*

astride
PREPOSITION with one leg on either side of something E.G. *He is pictured astride his new motorbike.*

astringent astringents
Said "ass-**trin**-jent" NOUN a liquid that makes skin less greasy and stops bleeding.

astro-
PREFIX 'Astro-' means involving the stars and planets. For example, *astrology* is predicting the future from the positions and movements of the stars and planets, and *astronomy* is the scientific study of the stars and planets.
🕮 from Greek *astron* meaning a 'star'

astrology
NOUN the study of the sun, moon, and stars in order to predict the future.
astrological ADJECTIVE **astrologer** NOUN

astronaut astronauts
NOUN a person who operates a

a b c d e f g h i j k l m n o p q r s t u v w x y z

an ELegant angEL (angel)   SPELLING NOTE

astronomical

ADJECTIVE 1 involved with or relating to astronomy. 2 extremely large in amount E.G. *astronomical legal costs*.
astronomically ADVERB

astronomy

NOUN the scientific study of stars and planets.
astronomer NOUN

astute

ADJECTIVE clever and quick at understanding situations and behaviour E.G. *an astute diplomat*.

asunder

ADVERB; LITERARY If something is torn asunder, it is violently torn apart.

asylum asylums

Said "ass-**eye**-lum" NOUN 1 OLD-FASHIONED a hospital for mental patients. 2 Political asylum is protection given by a government to someone who has fled from their own country for political reasons.

asymmetrical or **asymmetric**

Said "ay-sim-**met**-ri-kl" ADJECTIVE unbalanced or with one half not exactly the same as the other half.
asymmetry NOUN

at

PREPOSITION 1 used to say where someone or something is E.G. *Bert met us at the airport*. 2 used to mention the direction something is going in E.G. *He threw his plate at the wall*. 3 used to say when something happens E.G. *The game starts at 3 o'clock*. 4 used to mention the rate or price of something E.G. *The shares were priced at fifty pence*.

atheist atheists

Said "**ayth**-ee-ist" NOUN someone who believes there is no God.
atheistic ADJECTIVE **atheism** NOUN

athlete athletes

NOUN (PE) someone who is good at sport and takes part in sporting events.

athletic

ADJECTIVE (PE) 1 strong, healthy, and good at sports. 2 involving athletes or athletics E.G. *I lost two years of my athletic career because of injury*.

athletics

NOUN Sporting events such as running, jumping, and throwing are called athletics.

Atlantic

NOUN The Atlantic is the ocean separating North and South America from Europe and Africa.
from the *Atlas* mountains in North Africa; the Atlantic lies to the west of these mountains

atlas atlases

NOUN (GEOGRAPHY) a book of maps.
from the giant *Atlas* in Greek mythology, who supported the sky on his shoulders

atmosphere atmospheres

NOUN 1 the air and other gases that surround a planet; also the air in a particular place E.G. *a musty atmosphere*. 2 the general mood of a place E.G. *a relaxed atmosphere*. 3 (ENGLISH) the mood created by the writer of a novel or play.
atmospheric ADJECTIVE

atom atoms

NOUN the smallest part of an element that can take part in a chemical reaction.

spacecraft.
from Greek *astron* meaning 'star' and *nautēs* meaning 'sailor'

atomic

ADJECTIVE relating to atoms or to the power released by splitting atoms E.G. *atomic energy*.

atomic bomb atomic bombs

NOUN an extremely powerful bomb which explodes because of the energy that comes from splitting atoms.

atone atones atoning atoned

VERB; FORMAL If you atone for something wrong you have done, you say you are sorry and try to make up for it.

atrocious

ADJECTIVE extremely bad.

atrocity atrocities

NOUN an extremely cruel and shocking act.

attach attaches attaching attached

VERB If you attach something to something else, you join or fasten the two things together.

attaché attachés

Said "at-**tash**-ay" NOUN a member of staff in an embassy E.G. *the Russian Cultural Attaché*.

attached

ADJECTIVE If you are attached to someone, you are very fond of them.

attachment attachments

NOUN 1 Attachment to someone is a feeling of love and affection for them. 2 Attachment to a cause or ideal is a strong belief in it and support for it. 3 a piece of equipment attached to a tool or machine to do a particular job.

attack attacks attacking attacked

VERB 1 To attack someone is to use violence against them so as to hurt or kill them. 2 If you attack someone or their ideas, you criticize them strongly E.G. *He attacked the government's economic policies.* 3 If a disease or chemical attacks something, it damages or destroys it E.G. *fungal diseases that attack crops.* 4 In a game such as football or hockey, to attack is to get the ball into a position from which a goal can be scored. ► NOUN 5 An attack is violent physical action against someone. 6 An attack on someone or on their ideas is strong criticism of them. 7 An attack of an illness is a short time in which you suffer badly with it.

attacker NOUN

■ (sense 1) assault, set upon
■ (sense 2) censure, criticize
■ (sense 5) assault, onslaught

attain attains attaining attained

VERB; FORMAL If you attain something, you manage to achieve it E.G. *He eventually attained the rank of major.*

attainable ADJECTIVE   **attainment** NOUN

attempt attempts attempting attempted

VERB 1 If you attempt to do something, you try to do it or achieve it, but may not succeed E.G. *They attempted to escape.* ► NOUN 2 an act of trying to do something E.G. *He made no attempt to go for the ball.*

attend attends attending attended

VERB 1 If you attend an event, you are present at it. 2 To attend school, church, or hospital is to go there regularly. 3 If you attend to something, you deal with it E.G. *We have business to attend to first.*

attendance NOUN

a b c d e f g h i j k l m n o p q r s t u v w x y z

A Rude Idiot Thought He Might Eat Toffee In Church (<u>arithmetic</u>)   **SPELLING NOTE**

attendant attendants
NOUN someone whose job is to serve people in a place such as a garage or cloakroom.

attention
NOUN Attention is the thought or care you give to something E.G. *The woman needed medical attention.*

attentive
ADJECTIVE paying close attention to something E.G. *an attentive audience.*
attentively ADVERB **attentiveness** NOUN

attest attests attesting attested
VERB; FORMAL To attest something is to show or declare it is true.
attestation NOUN

attic attics
NOUN a room at the top of a house immediately below the roof.

attire
NOUN; FORMAL Attire is clothing E.G. *We will be wearing traditional wedding attire.*

attitude attitudes
NOUN Your attitude to someone or something is the way you think about them and behave towards them.

attorney attorneys
Said "at-**turn**-ee" NOUN; AMERICAN An attorney is the same as a lawyer.

attract attracts attracting attracted
VERB 1 If something attracts people, it interests them and makes them want to go to it E.G. *The trials have attracted many leading riders.* 2 If someone attracts you, you like and admire them E.G. *He was attracted to her outgoing personality.* 3 If something attracts support or publicity, it gets it.

attraction attractions
NOUN 1 Attraction is a feeling of liking someone or something very much. 2 something people visit for interest or pleasure E.G. *The temple is a major tourist attraction.* 3 a quality that attracts someone or something E.G. *the attraction of moving to seaside resorts.*

attractive
ADJECTIVE 1 interesting and possibly advantageous E.G. *an attractive proposition.* 2 pleasant to look at or be with E.G. *an attractive woman… an attractive personality.*
attractively ADVERB **attractiveness** NOUN
▤ (sense 1) appealing, tempting
▤ (sense 2) charming, lovely, pleasant

attribute attributes attributing attributed
VERB 1 If you attribute something to a person or thing, you believe it was caused or created by that person or thing E.G. *Water pollution was attributed to the use of fertilizers… a painting attributed to Raphael.* ▶ NOUN 2 a quality or feature someone or something has.
attribution NOUN **attributable** ADJECTIVE

attrition
NOUN Attrition is the constant wearing down of an enemy.

attuned
ADJECTIVE accustomed or well adjusted to something E.G. *His eyes quickly became attuned to the dark.*

aubergine aubergines
Said "**oh**-ber-jeen" NOUN a dark purple, pear-shaped vegetable. It is also called an **eggplant**.

📖 from Arabic *al-badindjan* meaning 'aubergine'

auburn
ADJECTIVE Auburn hair is reddish brown.

auction auctions auctioning auctioned
NOUN 1 a public sale in which goods are sold to the person who offers the highest price. ► VERB 2 To auction something is to sell it in an auction.

auctioneer auctioneers
NOUN the person in charge of an auction.

audacious
ADJECTIVE very daring E.G. *an audacious escape from jail.*
audaciously ADVERB **audacity** NOUN

audi-
PREFIX 'Audi-' means involving hearing or sound E.G. *audible… auditorium.*
📖 from Latin *audire* meaning 'to hear'

audible
ADJECTIVE loud enough to be heard E.G. *She spoke in a barely audible whisper.*
audibly ADVERB **audibility** NOUN

audience audiences
NOUN 1 the group of people who are watching or listening to a performance. 2 a private or formal meeting with an important person E.G. *an audience with the Queen.*

audio
ADJECTIVE used in recording and reproducing sound E.G. *audio equipment.*

audit audits auditing audited
VERB 1 To audit a set of financial accounts is to examine them officially to check they are correct. ► NOUN 2 an official examination of an organization's accounts.
auditor NOUN

audition auditions
NOUN a short performance given by an actor or musician, so that a director can decide whether they are suitable for a part in a play or film or for a place in an orchestra.

auditorium auditoriums or auditoria
NOUN the part of a theatre where the audience sits.

augment augments augmenting augmented
VERB; FORMAL To augment something is to add something to it.

August
NOUN the eighth month of the year. August has 31 days.
📖 from the name of the Roman emperor *Augustus*

aunt aunts
NOUN Your aunt is the sister of your mother or father, or the wife of your uncle.

au pair au pairs
Said "oh **pair**" NOUN a young foreign girl who lives with a family to help with the children and housework and sometimes to learn the language.
📖 a French expression meaning 'on equal terms'

aura auras
NOUN an atmosphere that surrounds a person or thing E.G. *She has a great aura of calmness.*

aural
Rhymes with "floral" ADJECTIVE relating to or done through the sense of hearing E.G. *an aural comprehension test.*

a b c d e f g h i j k l m n o p q r s t u v w x y z

auspices
*Said "**aw**-spiss-eez"* PLURAL NOUN; FORMAL
If you do something under the
auspices of a person or organization,
you do it with their support E.G.
*military intervention under the
auspices of the United Nations.*

auspicious
ADJECTIVE; FORMAL favourable and
seeming to promise success E.G. *It
was an auspicious start to the month.*

austere
ADJECTIVE plain and simple, and
without luxury E.G. *an austere grey
office block.*
austerity NOUN

Australasia
*Said "ost-ral-**lay**-sha"* NOUN
Australasia consists of Australia, New
Zealand, and neighbouring islands in
the Pacific.
Australasian ADJECTIVE

Australia
NOUN Australia is the smallest
continent and the largest island in
the world, situated between the
Indian Ocean and the Pacific.

Australian Australians
ADJECTIVE 1 belonging or relating to
Australia. ▶ NOUN 2 someone who
comes from Australia.

Austrian Austrians
ADJECTIVE 1 belonging or relating to
Austria. ▶ NOUN 2 someone who
comes from Austria.

authentic
ADJECTIVE real and genuine.
authenticity NOUN

author authors
NOUN (ENGLISH) The author of a book is
the person who wrote it.
☑ Use *author* to talk about both
men and women writers, as

authoress is now felt to be insulting.

authoritarian
ADJECTIVE believing in strict obedience
E.G. *thirty years of authoritarian
government.*
authoritarianism NOUN

authoritative
ADJECTIVE 1 having authority E.G. *his
deep, authoritative voice.* 2 accepted
as being reliable and accurate E.G.
*an authoritative biography of the
President.*
authoritatively ADVERB

authority authorities
NOUN 1 Authority is the power to
control people E.G. *the authority of
the state.* 2 (GEOGRAPHY) In Britain, an
authority is a local government
department E.G. *local health
authorities.* 3 Someone who is an
authority on something knows a lot
about it E.G. *the world's leading
authority on fashion.* ▶ PLURAL NOUN
4 The authorities are the people who
have the power to make decisions.

**authorize authorizes authorizing
authorized**; also spelt **authorise**
VERB To authorize something is to
give official permission for it to
happen.
authorization NOUN

auto-
PREFIX 'Auto-' means 'self'. For example,
an automatic machine works by
itself without needing to be
operated by hand.
📖 from Greek *autos* meaning 'self'

autobiography autobiographies
NOUN Someone's autobiography is an
account of their life which they have
written themselves.
autobiographical ADJECTIVE

autograph autographs
NOUN the signature of a famous
person.

automated
ADJECTIVE If a factory or way of making
things is automated, it works using
machinery rather than people.
automation NOUN

automatic
ADJECTIVE 1 An automatic machine is
programmed to perform tasks
without needing a person to operate
it E.G. *The plane was flying on
automatic pilot.* 2 Automatic actions
or reactions take place without
involving conscious thought. 3 A
process or punishment that is
automatic always happens as a
direct result of something E.G. *The
penalty for murder is an automatic life
sentence.*
automatically ADVERB

automobile automobiles
NOUN; AMERICAN or FORMAL a car.

autonomous
Said "aw-**ton** nom-uss" ADJECTIVE An
autonomous country governs itself
rather than being controlled by
anyone else.
autonomy NOUN

autopsy autopsies
NOUN a medical examination of a
dead body to discover the cause of
death.

autumn autumns
NOUN the season between summer
and winter.
autumnal ADJECTIVE

auxiliary auxiliaries
NOUN 1 a person employed to help
other members of staff E.G. *nursing
auxiliaries.* ► ADJECTIVE 2 Auxiliary
equipment is used when necessary

in addition to the main equipment
E.G. *Auxiliary fuel tanks were stored in
the bomb bay.*

auxiliary verb auxiliary verbs
NOUN In grammar, an auxiliary verb is
a verb which forms tenses of other
verbs or questions. For example in
'He has gone', 'has' is the auxiliary
verb and in 'Do you understand?', 'do'
is the auxiliary verb.

avail
PHRASE If something you do is **of no
avail** or **to no avail**, it is not
successful or helpful.

available
ADJECTIVE 1 Something that is available
can be obtained E.G. *Artichokes are
available in supermarkets.* 2 Someone
who is available is ready for work or
free for people to talk to E.G. *She will
no longer be available at weekends.*
availability NOUN
■ (sense 2) accessible

avalanche avalanches
Said "av-a-lahnsh" NOUN a huge mass
of snow and ice that falls down a
mountain side.

avant-garde
Said "av-vong-**gard**" ADJECTIVE
extremely modern or experimental,
especially in art, literature, or music.

avarice
NOUN; FORMAL greed for money and
possessions.
avaricious ADJECTIVE

avenge avenges avenging avenged
VERB If you avenge something
harmful someone has done to you or
your family, you punish or harm the
other person in return E.G. *He was
prepared to avenge the death of his
friend.*
avenger NOUN

a
b
c
d
e
f
g
h
i
j
k
l
m
n
o
p
q
r
s
t
u
v
w
x
y
z

avenue avenues
NOUN a street, especially one with trees along it.

average averages averaging averaged
NOUN (MATHS) **1** a result obtained by adding several amounts together and then dividing the total by the number of different amounts E.G. *Six pupils were examined in a total of 39 subjects, an average of 6.5 subjects per pupil.* ▶ ADJECTIVE **2** Average means standard or normal E.G. *the average American teenager.* ▶ VERB **3** To average a number is to produce that number as an average over a period of time E.G. *Monthly sales averaged more than 110,000.* ▶ PHRASE **4** You say **on average** when mentioning what usually happens in a situation E.G. *Men are, on average, taller than women.*
■ (sense 2) normal, ordinary, typical, usual

averse
ADJECTIVE unwilling to do something E.G. *He was averse to taking painkillers.*

aversion aversions
NOUN If you have an aversion to someone or something, you dislike them very much.

avert averts averting averted
VERB **1** If you avert an unpleasant event, you prevent it from happening. **2** If you avert your eyes from something, you turn your eyes away from it.

aviary aviaries
NOUN a large cage or group of cages in which birds are kept.

aviation
NOUN the science of flying aircraft.

aviator aviators
NOUN; OLD-FASHIONED a pilot of an aircraft.

avid
ADJECTIVE eager and enthusiastic for something.
avidly ADVERB

avocado avocados
NOUN a pear-shaped fruit, with dark green skin, soft greenish yellow flesh, and a large stone.
▦ from a South American Indian word *ahuacatl* meaning 'testicle', from its shape

avoid avoids avoiding avoided
VERB **1** If you avoid doing something, you make a deliberate effort not to do it. **2** If you avoid someone, you keep away from them.
avoidable ADJECTIVE **avoidance** NOUN
■ (sense 1) dodge, refrain from, shirk
■ (sense 2) dodge, evade, keep away from

avowed
ADJECTIVE **1** FORMAL If you are an avowed supporter or opponent of something, you have declared that you support it or oppose it. **2** An avowed belief or aim is one you hold very strongly.

avuncular
ADJECTIVE friendly and helpful in manner towards younger people, rather like an uncle.

await awaits awaiting awaited
VERB **1** If you await something, you expect it. **2** If something awaits you, it will happen to you in the future.

awake awakes awaking awoke awoken
ADJECTIVE **1** Someone who is awake is not sleeping. ▶ VERB **2** When you awake, you wake up. **3** If you are awoken by something, it wakes you up.

awaken awakens awakening awakened

VERB If something awakens an emotion or interest in you, you start to feel this emotion or interest.

award awards awarding awarded
NOUN **1** a prize or certificate for doing something well. **2** a sum of money an organization gives to students for training or study. ▶ VERB **3** If you award someone something, you give it to them formally or officially.

aware
ADJECTIVE If you are aware of something, you know about it or realize it is there.
awareness NOUN
■ conscious of, knowing about, mindful of

awash
ADJECTIVE OR ADVERB covered with water E.G. *After the downpour the road was awash*.

away
ADVERB **1** moving from a place E.G. *I saw them walk away*. **2** at a distance from a place E.G. *Our nearest vet is 12 kilometres away*. **3** in its proper place E.G. *He put his chequebook away*. **4** not at home, school, or work E.G. *She had been away from home for years*.

awe
NOUN; FORMAL a feeling of great respect mixed with amazement and sometimes slight fear.

awesome
ADJECTIVE **1** Something that is awesome is very impressive and frightening. **2** INFORMAL Awesome also means excellent or outstanding.

awful
ADJECTIVE **1** very unpleasant or very bad. **2** INFORMAL very great E.G. *It took an awful lot of courage*.

awfully ADVERB
■ (sense 1) appalling, dreadful, terrible

awkward
ADJECTIVE **1** clumsy and uncomfortable E.G. *an awkward gesture*. **2** embarrassed or nervous E.G. *He was a shy, awkward young man*. **3** difficult to deal with E.G. *My lawyer is in an awkward situation*.
📖 from Old Norse *ofugr* meaning 'turned the wrong way'

awning awnings
NOUN a large roof of canvas or plastic attached to a building or vehicle.

awry
Said "a-**rye**" ADJECTIVE wrong or not as planned E.G. *Why had their plans gone so badly awry?*

axe axes axing axed
NOUN **1** a tool with a handle and a sharp blade, used for chopping wood. ▶ VERB **2** To axe something is to end it.

axiom axioms
NOUN a statement or saying that is generally accepted to be true.

axis axes
Said "**ak**-siss"
NOUN (MATHS) **1** an imaginary line through the centre of something, around which it moves. **2** one of the two sides of a graph.

axle axles
NOUN the long bar that connects a pair of wheels on a vehicle.

ayatollah ayatollahs
NOUN an Islamic religious leader in Iran.
📖 from Arabic *ayatullah* meaning 'manifestation of God'

azure
Said "**az**-yoor" ADJECTIVE; LITERARY bright blue.

a
b
c
d
e
f
g
h
i
j
k
l
m
n
o
p
q
r
s
t
u
v
w
x
y
z

I want to see (C) your licenCe (licence)   **SPELLING NOTE**

Bb

babble babbles babbling babbled
VERB When someone babbles, they talk in a confused or excited way.

baboon baboons
NOUN an African monkey with a pointed face, large teeth, and a long tail.
📖 from Old French *baboue* meaning 'grimace'

baby babies
NOUN a child in the first year or two of its life.
babyhood NOUN **babyish** ADJECTIVE
▪ babe, infant

baby-sit baby-sits baby-sitting baby-sat
VERB To baby-sit for someone means to look after their children while that person is out.
baby-sitter NOUN **baby-sitting** NOUN

bach baches baching bached
Said "batch" NOUN 1 In New Zealand, a small holiday cottage. ▶ VERB 2 INFORMAL In Australian and New Zealand English, to bach is to live and keep a house on your own, especially when you are not used to it.

bachelor bachelors
NOUN a man who has never been married.

back backs backing backed
ADVERB 1 When people or things move back, they move in the opposite direction from the one they are facing. 2 When people or things go back to a place or situation, they return to it E.G. *She went back to sleep.* 3 If you get something back, it is returned to you. 4 If you do something back to someone, you do

to them what they have done to you E.G. *I smiled back at them.* 5 Back also means in the past E.G. *It happened back in the early eighties.* ▶ NOUN 6 the rear part of your body. 7 the part of something that is behind the front. ▶ ADJECTIVE 8 The back parts of something are the ones near the rear E.G. *an animal's back legs.* ▶ VERB 9 If a building backs onto something, its back faces in that direction. 10 When a car backs, it moves backwards. 11 To back a person or organization means to support or finance that person or organization.

back down VERB If you back down on a demand or claim, you withdraw and give up.

back out VERB If you back out of a promise or commitment, you decide not to do what you had promised to do.

back up VERB 1 If you back up a claim or story, you produce evidence to show that it is true. 2 If you back someone up, you help and support them.

backbone backbones
NOUN 1 the column of linked bones along the middle of a person's or animal's back. 2 strength of character.

backdate backdates backdating backdated
VERB If an arrangement is backdated, it is valid from a date earlier than the one on which it is completed or signed.

backdrop backdrops
NOUN the background to a situation or event E.G. *The visit occurred*

against the backdrop of the political crisis.

backer backers

NOUN The backers of a project are the people who give it financial help.

backfire backfires backfiring backfired

VERB 1 If a plan backfires, it fails.
2 When a car backfires, there is a small but noisy explosion in its exhaust pipe.

background backgrounds

NOUN 1 the circumstances which help to explain an event or caused it to happen. 2 the kind of home you come from and your education and experience E.G. *a rich background.*
3 If sounds are in the background, they are there but no one really pays any attention to them E.G. *She could hear voices in the background.*

backing

NOUN support or help E.G. *The project got government backing.*

backlash

NOUN a hostile reaction to a new development or a new policy.

backlog backlogs

NOUN a number of things which have not yet been done, but which need to be done.

backpack backpacks

NOUN a large bag that hikers or campers carry on their backs.

backside backsides

NOUN; INFORMAL the part of your body that you sit on.

backward

ADJECTIVE 1 Backward means directed behind you E.G. *without a backward glance.* 2 A backward country or society is one that does not have modern industries or technology. 3 A

backward child is one who is unable to learn as quickly as other children of the same age.

backwardness NOUN

backwards

ADVERB 1 Backwards means behind you E.G. *Lucille looked backwards.* 2 If you do something backwards, you do it the opposite of the usual way E.G. *He instructed them to count backwards.*

bacon

NOUN meat from the back or sides of a pig, which has been salted or smoked.

bacteria

PLURAL NOUN Bacteria are very tiny organisms which can cause disease.

bacterial ADJECTIVE

☑ The word *bacteria* is plural. The singular form is *bacterium.*

bad worse worst

ADJECTIVE 1 Anything harmful or upsetting can be described as bad E.G. *I have some bad news… Is the pain bad?* 2 insufficient or of poor quality E.G. *bad roads.* 3 evil or immoral in character or behaviour E.G. *a bad person.* 4 lacking skill in something E.G. *I was bad at sports.* 5 Bad language consists of swearwords. 6 If you have a bad temper, you become angry easily.

badly ADVERB **badness** NOUN

▤ (sense 3) evil, sinful, wicked, wrong

bade

a form of the past tense of **bid.**

badge badges

NOUN a piece of plastic or metal with a design or message on it that you can pin to your clothes.

have a pIEce of pIE (pie̱ce)   SPELLING NOTE

A
B
C
D
E
F
G
H
I
J
K
L
M
N
O
P
Q
R
S
T
U
V
W
X
Y
Z

badger badgers badgering badgered

NOUN 1 a wild animal that has a white head with two black stripes on it. ► VERB 2 If you badger someone, you keep asking them questions or pestering them to do something.

badminton

NOUN a game in which two or four players use rackets to hit a shuttlecock over a high net

Bafana bafana

PLURAL NOUN In South Africa, Bafana bafana is a name for the South African national soccer team.

baffle baffles baffling baffled

VERB If something baffles you, you cannot understand or explain it E.G. *The symptoms baffled the doctors.* **baffled** ADJECTIVE **baffling** ADJECTIVE

bag bags

NOUN 1 a container for carrying things in. ► PLURAL NOUN 2 INFORMAL Bags of something is a lot of it E.G. *bags of fun.*

🔲 from Old Norse *baggi* meaning 'bundle'

baggage

NOUN the suitcases and bags that you take on a journey.

baggy baggier baggiest

ADJECTIVE Baggy clothing hangs loosely.

bagpipes

PLURAL NOUN a musical instrument played by squeezing air out of a leather bag through pipes, on which a tune is played.

bail bails bailing bailed

NOUN 1 Bail is a sum of money paid to a court to allow an accused person to go free until the time of the trial E.G. *He was released on bail.* ► VERB 2 If

you bail water from a boat, you scoop it out.

bailiff bailiffs

NOUN 1 a law officer who makes sure that the decisions of a court are obeyed. 2 a person employed to look after land or property for the owner.

bait baits baiting baited

NOUN 1 a small amount of food placed on a hook or in a trap, to attract a fish or wild animal so that it gets caught. ► VERB 2 If you bait a hook or trap, you put some food on it to catch a fish or wild animal.

baize

NOUN a smooth woollen material, usually green, used for covering snooker tables.

bake bakes baking baked

VERB 1 To bake food means to cook it in an oven without using liquid or fat. 2 To bake earth or clay means to heat it until it becomes hard.

baker bakers

NOUN a person who makes and sells bread and cakes.

bakery bakeries

NOUN a building where bread and cakes are baked and sold

bakkie bakkies

Said "buck-ee" NOUN In South African English, a bakkie is a small truck.

balaclava balaclavas

NOUN a close-fitting woollen hood that covers every part of your head except your face.

balance balances balancing balanced

VERB 1 When someone or something balances, they remain steady and do not fall over. ► NOUN 2 Balance is the state of being upright and steady. 3 Balance is also a situation in which all the parts involved have a stable relationship with each other E.G. *the chemical balance of the brain.* **4** The balance in someone's bank account is the amount of money in it.

balcony balconies
NOUN **1** a platform on the outside of a building with a wall or railing round it. **2** an area of upstairs seats in a theatre or cinema.

bald balder baldest
ADJECTIVE **1** A bald person has little or no hair on their head. **2** A bald statement or question is made in the simplest way without any attempt to be polite.
baldly ADVERB   **baldness** NOUN
📖 from Middle English *ballede* meaning 'having a white patch'

bale bales baling baled
NOUN **1** a large bundle of something, such as paper or hay, tied tightly.
▶ VERB **2** If you bale water from a boat, you remove it using a container; also spelt **bail.**

balk balks balking balked; also spelt **baulk**
VERB If you balk at something, you object to it and may refuse to do it E.G. *He balked at the cost.*

ball balls
NOUN **1** a round object used in games such as cricket and soccer. **2** The ball of your foot or thumb is the rounded part where your toes join your foot or your thumb joins your hand. **3** a large formal social event at which people dance.
▣ (sense 1) globe, orb, sphere

ballad ballads
NOUN **1** a long song or poem which tells a story. **2** a slow, romantic pop song.

📖 from Old French *ballade* meaning 'song for dancing to'

ballast
NOUN any heavy material placed in a ship to make it more stable.

ballerina ballerinas
NOUN a woman ballet dancer.

ballet
Said "**bal**-lay" NOUN Ballet is a type of artistic dancing based on precise steps.

balloon balloons
NOUN **1** a small bag made of thin rubber that you blow into until it becomes larger and rounder. **2** a large, strong bag filled with gas or hot air, which travels through the air carrying passengers in a compartment underneath.
📖 from Italian *ballone* meaning 'large round object'

ballot ballots balloting balloted
NOUN **1** a secret vote in which people select a candidate in an election, or express their opinion about something. ▶ VERB **2** When a group of people are balloted, they are asked questions to find out what they think about a particular problem or question.
📖 from Italian *ballotta* meaning 'little round object'; in medieval Venice votes were cast by dropping black or white pebbles or balls into a box

ballpoint ballpoints
NOUN a pen with a small metal ball at the end which transfers the ink onto the paper.

ballroom ballrooms
NOUN a very large room used for dancing or formal balls.

balm
Said "**bahm**" NOUN; OLD-FASHIONED a

a
b
c
d
e
f
g
h
i
j
k
l
m
n
o
p
q
r
s
t
u
v
w
x
y
z

A
B
C
D
E
F
G
H
I
J
K
L
M
N
O
P
Q
R
S
T
U
V
W
X
Y
Z

sweet-smelling soothing ointment.

balmy balmier balmiest
ADJECTIVE mild and pleasant E.G. *balmy summer evenings*.

balsa
NOUN Balsa is very lightweight wood.

balustrade balustrades
NOUN a railing or wall on a balcony or staircase.

bamboo
NOUN Bamboo is a tall tropical grass with hard, hollow stems used for making furniture.

ban bans banning banned
VERB 1 If something is banned, or if you are banned from doing it or using it, you are not allowed to do it or use it. ▶ NOUN 2 If there is a ban on something, it is not allowed.
▣ (sense 1) forbid, outlaw, prohibit
▣ (sense 2) disqualification, embargo, prohibition

banal
Said "ba-**nahl**" ADJECTIVE very ordinary and not at all interesting E.G. *He made some banal remark*.
banality NOUN
🔢 Old French *banal* referred to military service which all tenants had to do; hence the word came to mean 'common to everyone' or 'ordinary'

banana bananas
NOUN a long curved fruit with a yellow skin.
🔢 from a West African language, via Portuguese

band bands
NOUN 1 a group of musicians who play jazz or pop music together, or a group who play brass instruments together. 2 a group of people who share a common purpose E.G. *a band of rebels*. 3 a narrow strip of

something used to hold things together or worn as a decoration E.G. *an elastic band… a headband*.

bandage bandages bandaging bandaged
NOUN 1 a strip of cloth wrapped round a wound to protect it. ▶ VERB 2 If you bandage a wound, you tie a bandage round it.

bandicoot bandicoots
NOUN a small Australian marsupial with a long pointed muzzle and a long tail.

bandit bandits
NOUN; OLD-FASHIONED a member of an armed gang who rob travellers.
🔢 from Italian *bandito* meaning 'man who has been banished or outlawed'

bandstand bandstands
NOUN a platform, usually with a roof, where a band can play outdoors.

bandwagon
PHRASE To **jump on the bandwagon** means to become involved in something because it is fashionable or likely to be successful.

bandy bandies bandying bandied
VERB If a name is bandied about, many people mention it.
🔢 from Old French *bander* meaning 'to hit a tennis ball back and forth'

bane
NOUN; LITERARY Someone or something that is the bane of a person or organization causes a lot of trouble for them E.G. *the bane of my life*.
🔢 from Old English *bana* meaning 'murderer'

bang bangs banging banged
VERB 1 If you bang something, you hit it or put it somewhere violently, so that it makes a loud noise E.G. *He*

banged down the receiver. **2** If you bang a part of your body against something, you accidentally bump it. ► NOUN **3** a sudden, short, loud noise. **4** a hard or painful bump against something.

Bangladeshi Bangladeshis
*Said "bang-glad-**desh**-ee"* ADJECTIVE **1** belonging or relating to Bangladesh. ► NOUN **2** someone who comes from Bangladesh.

bangle bangles
NOUN an ornamental band worn round someone's wrist or ankle.
🔲 from Hindi *bangri* meaning 'bracelet'

banish banishes banishing banished
VERB **1** To banish someone means to send them into exile. **2** To banish something means to get rid of it E.G. *It will be a long time before cancer is banished.*
banishment NOUN
🔳 (sense 1) exile, expel, outlaw

banister banisters; also spelt **bannister**
NOUN a rail supported by posts along the side of a staircase.

banjo banjos or banjoes
NOUN a musical instrument, like a small guitar with a round body.

bank banks banking banked
NOUN **1** a business that looks after people's money. **2** a bank of something is a store of it kept ready for use E.G. *a blood bank.* **3** the raised ground along the edge of a river or lake. **4** the sloping side of an area of raised ground. ► VERB **5** When you bank money, you pay it into a bank. **6** If you bank on something happening, you expect it and rely on it.

banker NOUN **banking** NOUN
bank holiday bank holidays
NOUN a public holiday, when banks are officially closed.

banknote banknotes
NOUN a piece of paper money.

bankrupt bankrupts bankrupting bankrupted
ADJECTIVE **1** People or organizations that go bankrupt do not have enough money to pay their debts. ► NOUN **2** someone who has been declared bankrupt. ► VERB **3** To bankrupt someone means to make them bankrupt E.G. *Restoring the house nearly bankrupted them.*
bankruptcy NOUN

banksia banksias
NOUN an evergreen Australian tree or shrub with yellow flowers.

banner banners
NOUN a long strip of cloth with a message or slogan on it.

bannister
another spelling of **banister**.

banquet banquets
NOUN a grand formal dinner, often followed by speeches.

banter
NOUN Banter is friendly joking and teasing.

baobab baobabs
*Said "**bay**-oh-bab"* NOUN a small fruit tree with a very thick trunk which grows in Africa and northern Australia.

baptism baptisms
NOUN (RE) a ceremony in which someone is baptized.

Baptist Baptists
NOUN or ADJECTIVE a member of a Protestant church who believe that people should be baptized when

a
b
c
d
e
f
g
h
i
j
k
l
m
n
o
p
q
r
s
t
u
v
w
x
y
z

baptize baptizes baptizing baptized; also spelt **baptise**

VERB When someone is baptized water is sprinkled on them, or they are immersed in water, as a sign that they have become a Christian.
🔲 from Greek *baptein* meaning 'to dip in water'

bar bars barring barred

NOUN 1 a counter or room where alcoholic drinks are served. 2 a long, straight piece of metal. 3 a piece of something made in a rectangular shape E.G. *a bar of soap*. 4 The bars in a piece of music are the many short parts of equal length that the piece is divided into. ▶ VERB 5 If you bar a door, you place something across it to stop it being opened. 6 If you bar someone's way, you stop them going somewhere by standing in front of them.

barb barbs

NOUN a sharp curved point on the end of an arrow or fish-hook.

barbarian barbarians

NOUN a member of a wild or uncivilised people.
🔲 from Greek *barbaros* meaning 'foreigner', originally 'person saying *bar-bar*'

barbaric

ADJECTIVE cruel or brutal E.G. *Ban the barbaric sport of fox hunting.*

barbarity NOUN

barbecue barbecues barbecuing barbecued

NOUN 1 a grill with a charcoal fire on which you cook food, usually outdoors; also an outdoor party where you eat food cooked on a barbecue. ▶ VERB 2 When food is barbecued, it is cooked over a charcoal grill.
🔲 from a Caribbean word meaning 'framework'

barbed

ADJECTIVE A barbed remark is one that seems straightforward but is really unkind or spiteful.

barbed wire

NOUN Barbed wire is strong wire with sharp points sticking out of it, used to make fences.

barber barbers

NOUN a man who cuts men's hair.

barbiturate barbiturates

NOUN a drug that people take to make them calm or to put them to sleep.

bar code bar codes

NOUN a small pattern of numbers and lines on something you buy in a shop, which can be electronically scanned at a checkout to give the price.

bard bards

NOUN; LITERARY A bard is a poet. Some people call Shakespeare the Bard.

bare bares baring bared

ADJECTIVE 1 If a part of your body is bare, it is not covered by any clothing. 2 If something is bare, it has nothing on top of it or inside it E.G. *bare floorboards… a small bare office.* 3 When trees are bare, they have no leaves on them. 4 The bare minimum or bare essentials means the very least that is needed E.G. *They were fed the bare minimum.* ▶ VERB 5 If you bare something, you uncover or show it.

▤ (sense 1) naked, nude, uncovered
▤ (sense 2) plain, stark

barefoot

ADJECTIVE or ADVERB not wearing anything on your feet.

barely

ADVERB only just E.G. *The girl was barely sixteen*.

☑ Do not use *barely* with negative words like *not*: *she was barely sixteen* rather than *she was not barely sixteen*.

bargain bargains bargaining bargained

NOUN **1** an agreement in which two people or groups discuss and agree what each will do, pay, or receive in a matter which involves them both. **2** something which is sold at a low price and which is good value. ▶ VERB **3** When people bargain with each other, they discuss and agree terms about what each will do, pay, or receive in a matter which involves both.

barge barges barging barged

NOUN **1** a boat with a flat bottom used for carrying heavy loads, especially on canals. ▶ VERB **2** INFORMAL If you barge into a place, you push into it in a rough or rude way.

baritone baritones

NOUN a man with a fairly deep singing voice.

bark barks barking barked

VERB **1** When a dog barks, it makes a short, loud noise, once or several times. ▶ NOUN **2** the short, loud noise that a dog makes. **3** the tough material that covers the outside of a tree.

barley

NOUN a cereal that is grown for food and is also used for making beer and whisky.

bar mitzvah

NOUN A Jewish boy's bar mitzvah is a ceremony that takes place on his 13th birthday, after which he is regarded as an adult.
📖 a Hebrew phrase meaning 'son of the law'

barmy barmier barmiest

ADJECTIVE; INFORMAL mad or very foolish.

barn barns

NOUN a large farm building used for storing crops or animal food.

barnacle barnacles

NOUN a small shellfish that fixes itself to rocks and to the bottom of boats.

barometer barometers

NOUN an instrument that measures air pressure and shows when the weather is changing.

baron barons

NOUN a member of the lowest rank of the nobility.
baronial ADJECTIVE

baroness baronesses

NOUN a woman who has the rank of baron, or who is the wife of a baron.

baronet baronets

NOUN a man with an honorary knighthood which has been passed to him from his father.

barracks

NOUN a building where soldiers live.
📖 from Spanish *barraca* meaning 'hut'

barracuda barracudas

NOUN a large, fierce tropical fish with sharp teeth.

barrage barrages

NOUN **1** A barrage of questions or complaints is a lot of them all coming at the same time. **2** A barrage is continuous artillery fire over a wide area, to prevent the

a
b
c
d
e
f
g
h
i
j
k
l
m
n
o
p
q
r
s
t
u
v
w
x
y
z

A

B

C

D

E

F

G

H

I

J

K

L

M

N

O

P

Q

R

S

T

U

V

W

X

Y

Z

enemy from moving.

▤ (sense 1) deluge, stream, torrent

▤ (sense 2) bombardment, fusillade, volley

barrel barrels

NOUN **1** a wooden container with rounded sides and flat ends. **2** The barrel of a gun is the long tube through which the bullet is fired.

barren

ADJECTIVE **1** Barren land has soil of such poor quality that plants cannot grow on it. **2** A barren woman or female animal is not able to have babies.

▤ (sense 1) desert, empty, unproductive

▤ (sense 2) infertile, sterile

barricade barricades barricading barricaded

NOUN **1** a temporary barrier put up to stop people getting past. ▶ VERB **2** If you barricade yourself inside a room or building, you put something heavy against the door to stop people getting in.

barrier barriers

NOUN a fence or wall that prevents people or animals getting from one area to another.

▤ barricade, fence, wall

barrister barristers

NOUN a lawyer who is qualified to represent people in the higher courts.

barrow barrows

NOUN **1** the same as a wheelbarrow. **2** a large cart from which fruit or other goods are sold in the street.

barter barters bartering bartered

VERB **1** If you barter goods, you exchange them for other goods, rather than selling them for money.

▶ NOUN **2** Barter is the activity of exchanging goods.

base bases basing based

NOUN **1** the lowest part of something, which often supports the rest. **2** A place which part of an army, navy, or air force works from. **3** In chemistry, a base is any compound that reacts with an acid to form a salt. ▶ VERB **4** To base something on something else means to use the second thing as a foundation or starting point of the first E.G. *The opera is based on a work by Pushkin.* **5** If you are based somewhere, you live there or work from there.

▤ (sense 1) bottom, foot, stand, support

baseball

NOUN Baseball is a team game played with a bat and a ball, similar to rounders.

basement basements

NOUN a floor of a building built completely or partly below the ground.

bases

NOUN **1** *Said "bay-seez"* the plural of **basis. 2** *Said "bay-siz"* the plural of **base.**

bash bashes bashing bashed

VERB; INFORMAL If you bash someone or bash into them, you hit them hard.

bashful

ADJECTIVE shy and easily embarrassed.

basic basics

ADJECTIVE **1** The basic aspects of something are the most necessary ones E.G. *the basic necessities of life.* **2** Something that is basic has only the necessary features without any extras or luxuries E.G. *The accommodation is pretty basic.*

▶ PLURAL NOUN **3** The basics of something are the things you need to know or understand E.G. *the basics of map-reading*.

basically ADVERB

■ (sense 1) essential, necessary, vital

basilica basilicas

NOUN an oblong church with a rounded end called an apse.

🏛 from Greek *basilikē* meaning 'royal hall'

basin basins

NOUN **1** a round wide container which is open at the top. **2** The basin of a river is a bowl of land from which water runs into the river.

basis bases

NOUN **1** The basis of something is the essential main principle from which it can be developed E.G. *The same colour theme is used as the basis for several patterns*. **2** The basis for a belief is the facts that support it E.G. *There is no basis for this assumption*.

■ (sense 1) base, foundation

■ (sense 2) foundation, ground, support

bask basks basking basked

VERB If you bask in the sun, you sit or lie in it, enjoying its warmth.

basket baskets

NOUN a container made of thin strips of cane woven together.

basketball

NOUN Basketball is a game in which two teams try to score goals by throwing a large ball through one of two circular nets suspended high up at each end of the court.

bass basses

Rhymes with "lace" NOUN **1** a man with a very deep singing voice. **2** a musical instrument that provides the rhythm and lowest part in the harmonies.

bass basses

Rhymes with "gas" NOUN a type of edible sea fish.

basset hound basset hounds

NOUN a smooth-haired dog with a long body and ears, and short legs.

bassoon bassoons

NOUN a large woodwind instrument.

bastard bastards

NOUN **1** OFFENSIVE People sometimes call someone a bastard when they dislike them or are very angry with them. **2** OLD-FASHIONED A bastard is someone whose parents were not married when he or she was born.

baste bastes basting basted

VERB When you baste meat that is roasting, you pour hot fat over it so that it does not become dry while cooking.

bastion bastions

NOUN; LITERARY something that protects a system or way of life E.G. *The country is the last bastion of communism*.

bat bats batting batted

NOUN **1** a specially shaped piece of wood with a handle, used for hitting the ball in a game such as cricket or table tennis. **2** a small flying animal, active at night, that looks like a mouse with wings. ▶ VERB **3** In certain sports, when someone is batting, it is their turn to try to hit the ball and score runs.

batch batches

NOUN a group of things of the same kind produced or dealt with together.

bated

PHRASE **With bated breath** means very anxiously.

a
b
c
d
e
f
g
h
i
j
k
l
m
n
o
p
q
r
s
t
u
v
w
x
y
z

Rhythmical Hounds Yap To Heavy Music (<u>rhythm</u>)   SPELLING NOTE

A
B
C
D
E
F
G
H
I
J
K
L
M
N
O
P
Q
R
S
T
U
V
W
X
Y
Z

bath baths
NOUN a long container which you fill with water and sit in to wash yourself.

bathe bathes bathing bathed
VERB 1 When you bathe, you swim or play in open water. 2 When you bathe a wound, you wash it gently. 3 LITERARY If a place is bathed in light, a lot of light reaches it E.G. *The room was bathed in spring sunshine.*
bather NOUN **bathing** NOUN

bathroom bathrooms
NOUN a room with a bath or shower, a washbasin, and often a toilet in it.

baths
NOUN The baths is a public swimming pool.

baton batons
NOUN 1 a light, thin stick that a conductor uses to direct an orchestra or choir. 2 In athletics, the baton is a short stick passed from one runner to another in a relay race.

batsman batsmen
NOUN In cricket, the batsman is the person who is batting.

battalion battalions
NOUN an army unit consisting of three or more companies.

batten battens battening battened
NOUN a strip of wood that is fixed to something to strengthen it or hold it firm.
batten down VERB If you batten something down, you make it secure by fixing battens across it.

batter batters battering battered
VERB 1 To batter someone or something means to hit them many times E.G. *The waves kept battering the life raft.* ▶ NOUN 2 Batter is a

mixture of flour, eggs, and milk, used to make pancakes, or to coat food before frying it.
battering NOUN

battery batteries
NOUN 1 a device for storing and producing electricity, for example in a torch or a car. 2 a large group of things or people. ▶ ADJECTIVE 3 A battery hen is one of a large number of hens kept in small cages for the mass production of eggs.

battle battles
NOUN 1 a fight between armed forces or a struggle between two people or groups with conflicting aims E.G. *the battle between town and country.* 2 A battle for something difficult is a determined attempt to obtain or achieve it E.G. *the battle for equality.*

battlefield battlefields
NOUN a place where a battle is or has been fought.

battlements
PLURAL NOUN The battlements of a castle consist of a wall built round the top, with gaps through which guns or arrows could be fired.

battleship battleships
NOUN a large, heavily armoured warship.

batty battier battiest
ADJECTIVE; INFORMAL crazy or eccentric.

bauble baubles
NOUN a pretty but cheap ornament or piece of jewellery.

bawdy bawdier bawdiest
ADJECTIVE a bawdy joke or song contains humorous references to sex.
📖 from Middle English *baude* meaning 'brothel keeper'

bawl bawls bawling bawled
VERB 1 INFORMAL To bawl at someone

means to shout at them loudly and
harshly. **2** When a child is bawling, it
is crying very loudly and angrily.

bay bays baying bayed
NOUN **1** a part of a coastline where the
land curves inwards. **2** a space or
area used for a particular purpose
E.G. *a loading bay.* **3** Bay is a kind of
tree similar to the laurel, with leaves
used for flavouring in cooking.
▶ PHRASE **4** If you **keep something at
bay**, you prevent it from reaching
you E.G. *Eating oranges keeps colds at
bay.* ▶ VERB **5** When a hound or wolf
bays, it makes a deep howling noise.
☰ (sense 1) cove, gulf, inlet

bayonet bayonets
NOUN a sharp blade that can be fixed
to the end of a rifle and used for
stabbing.
📖 named after *Bayonne* in France,
where it originated

bazaar bazaars
NOUN **1** an area with many small
shops and stalls, especially in Eastern
countries. **2** a sale to raise money for
charity.
📖 from Persian *bazar* meaning 'market'

BC
BC means 'before Christ' E.G. *in 49 BC.*

**be am is are; being; was were;
been**
AUXILIARY VERB **1** 'Be' is used with a present
participle to form the continuous
tense E.G. *Crimes of violence are
increasing.* **2** 'Be' is also used to say that
something will happen E.G. *We are
going to America next month.* **3** 'Be' is
used to form the passive voice E.G. *The
walls were being repaired.* ▶ VERB **4** 'Be'
is used to give more information
about the subject of a sentence E.G.
Her name is Melanie.

The Verb Be

The verb **to be** has a lot of unusual
forms, and does not follow the
usual rules.

The main form is *be*. This is used
with an auxiliary verb to make
compound tenses, and after the
preposition *to*:

> E.G. *She will **be** five years old in
> April.*

The verb forms *am*, *are*, and *is* are
used to talk about the present
time. *Am* is used for the first person
singular; *are* is used for the second
person and for all plural forms; *is* is
used for the third person singular:

> E.G. *I **am** exhausted.* ■ *You **are** very
> welcome.* ■ *Robbie **is** always
> cheerful.* ■ *They **are** a pair of
> rascals.*

The present participle is *being*. This
form is used with an auxiliary verb
to make compound tenses:

> E.G. *Matthew **was being** very
> helpful.*

The verb forms *was* and *were* talk
about past time. *Was* is used for the
first and third person singular; *were*
is used for the second person and
for all plural forms:

> E.G. *I **was** exhausted.* ■ *You **were**
> very welcome.* ■ *Robbie **was**
> always cheerful.* ■ *They **were** a
> pair of rascals.*

The past participle is *been*. This
form is used with an auxiliary verb
to make compound tenses:

> E.G. *I **shall have been** here five
> years in April.* ■ *Robbie **has
> been** polite at all times.*

A
B
C
D
E
F
G
H
I
J
K
L
M
N
O
P
Q
R
S
T
U
V
W
X
Y
Z

be-
PREFIX **1** 'Be-' is used to form verbs from nouns and adds the meaning 'treat as'. For example, to *befriend* someone is to make friends with them. **2** 'Be-' is also sometimes used to form verbs from verbs when it is used for emphasis or to mean 'covering completely'. For example, to *besmear* means to smear all over.

beach beaches
NOUN an area of sand or pebbles beside the sea.
■ seashore, seaside, shore

beacon beacons
NOUN In the past, a beacon was a light or fire on a hill, which acted as a signal or warning.

bead beads
NOUN **1** Beads are small pieces of coloured glass or wood with a hole through the middle, strung together to make necklaces. **2** Beads of liquid are drops of it.

beady
ADJECTIVE Beady eyes are small and bright like beads.

beagle beagles
NOUN a short-haired dog with long ears and short legs.

beak beaks
NOUN A bird's beak is the hard part of its mouth that sticks out.

beaker beakers
NOUN **1** a cup for drinking out of, usually made of plastic and without a handle. **2** a glass container with a lip which is used in laboratories.

beam beams beaming beamed
NOUN **1** a broad smile. **2** A beam of light is a band of light that shines from something such as a torch. **3** a long, thick bar of wood or metal,

especially one that supports a roof.
▶ VERB **4** If you beam, you smile because you are happy.

bean beans
NOUN Beans are the seeds or pods of a climbing plant, which are eaten as a vegetable; also used of some other seeds, for example the seeds from which coffee is made.

bear bears bearing bore borne
NOUN **1** a large, strong wild animal with thick fur and sharp claws. ▶ VERB **2** FORMAL To bear something means to carry it or support its weight E.G. *The ice wasn't thick enough to bear their weight.* **3** If something bears a mark or typical feature, it has it E.G. *The room bore all the signs of a violent struggle.* **4** If you bear something difficult, you accept it and are able to deal with it E.G. *He bore his last illness with courage.* **5** If you can't bear someone or something, you dislike them very much. **6** FORMAL When a plant or tree bears flowers, fruit, or leaves, it produces them.
bearable ADJECTIVE

beard beards
NOUN the hair that grows on the lower part of a man's face.
bearded ADJECTIVE

bearer bearers
NOUN The bearer of something is the person who carries or presents it E.G. *the bearer of bad news.*

bearing
NOUN **1** If something has a bearing on a situation, it is relevant to it. **2** the way in which a person moves or stands.

beast beasts
NOUN **1** OLD-FASHIONED a large wild animal. **2** INFORMAL If you call someone

a beast, you mean that they are cruel or spiteful.

beastly beastlier beastliest
ADJECTIVE; OLD-FASHIONED cruel or spiteful.

beat beats beating beat beaten
VERB 1 To beat someone or something means to hit them hard and repeatedly E.G. *He threatened to beat her.* 2 If you beat someone in a race or game, you defeat them or do better than them. 3 When a bird or insect beats its wings, it moves them up and down. 4 When your heart is beating, it is pumping blood with a regular rhythm. 5 If you beat eggs, cream, or butter, you mix them vigorously using a fork or a whisk.
▶ NOUN 6 The beat of your heart is its regular pumping action. 7 The beat of a piece of music is its main rhythm. 8 A police officer's beat is the area which he or she patrols.
■ (sense 1) batter, hit, strike
■ (sense 2) conquer, defeat, vanquish

beat up VERB To beat someone up means to hit or kick them repeatedly.
beater NOUN   **beating** NOUN

beaut beauts
NOUN; INFORMAL 1 In Australian and New Zealand English, a beaut is an outstanding person or thing.
▶ ADJECTIVE 2 In Australian and New Zealand English, beaut means good or excellent E.G. *a beaut house.*

beautiful
ADJECTIVE very attractive or pleasing E.G. *a beautiful girl… beautiful music.*
beautifully ADVERB
■ attractive, gorgeous, lovely

beauty beauties
NOUN 1 Beauty is the quality of being beautiful. 2 OLD-FASHIONED a very

attractive woman. 3 The beauty of an idea or plan is what makes it attractive or worthwhile E.G. *The beauty of the fund is its simplicity.*

beaver beavers
NOUN an animal with a big, flat tail and webbed hind feet. Beavers build dams.

because
CONJUNCTION 1 'Because' is used with a clause that gives the reason for something E.G. *I went home because I was tired.* ▶ PHRASE 2 **Because of** is used with a noun that gives the reason for something E.G. *He quit playing because of a knee injury.*

beck
PHRASE If you are at someone's **beck and call**, you are always available to do what they ask.
🔳 from Middle English *bekken* meaning 'to beckon'

beckon beckons beckoning beckoned
VERB 1 If you beckon to someone, you signal with your hand that you want them to come to you. 2 If you say that something beckons, you mean that you find it very attractive E.G. *A career in journalism beckons.*

become becomes becoming became become
VERB To become something means to start feeling or being that thing E.G. *I became very angry… He became an actor.*

bed beds
NOUN 1 a piece of furniture that you lie on when you sleep. 2 A bed in a garden is an area of ground in which plants are grown. 3 The bed of a sea or river is the ground at the bottom of it.

a b c d e f g h i j k l m n o p q r s t u v w x y z

bedclothes

PLURAL NOUN the sheets and covers that you put over you when you get into bed.

bedding

NOUN Bedding is sheets, blankets, and other covers that are used on beds.

bedlam

NOUN You can refer to a noisy and disorderly place or situation as bedlam E.G. *The delay caused bedlam at the station.*

🔲 from *Bedlam,* a shortened form of the Hospital of St. Mary of Bethlehem in London, which was an institution for the insane or mentally ill

bedpan bedpans

NOUN a container used as a toilet by people who are too ill to get out of bed.

bedraggled

ADJECTIVE A bedraggled person or animal is in a messy or untidy state.

bedridden

ADJECTIVE Someone who is bedridden is too ill or disabled to get out of bed.

bedrock

NOUN 1 Bedrock is the solid rock under the soil. 2 The bedrock of something is the foundation and principles on which it is based E.G. *His life was built on the bedrock of integrity.*

bedroom bedrooms

NOUN a room used for sleeping in.

bedspread bedspreads

NOUN a cover put over a bed, on top of the sheets and blankets.

bedstead bedsteads

NOUN the metal or wooden frame of an old-fashioned bed.

bee bees

NOUN a winged insect that makes honey and lives in large groups.

beech beeches

NOUN a tree with a smooth grey trunk and shiny leaves.

beef

NOUN Beef is the meat of a cow, bull, or ox.

🔲 from Old French *boef* meaning 'ox' or 'bull'

beefy beefier beefiest

ADJECTIVE; INFORMAL A beefy person is strong and muscular.

beehive beehives

NOUN a container in which bees live and make their honey.

beeline

PHRASE; INFORMAL If you **make a beeline** for a place, you go there as quickly and directly as possible.

been

the past participle of **be**.

beer beers

NOUN an alcoholic drink made from malt and flavoured with hops.

beet beets

NOUN a plant with an edible root and leaves, such as sugar beet or beetroot.

beetle beetles

NOUN a flying insect with hard wings which cover its body when it is not flying.

beetroot beetroots

NOUN the round, dark red root of a type of beet, eaten as a vegetable.

befall befalls befalling befell befallen

VERB; OLD-FASHIONED If something befalls you, it happens to you E.G. *A similar fate befell my cousin.*

SPELLING NOTE   'i' before 'e' except after 'c'

before

ADVERB, PREPOSITION, or CONJUNCTION

1 'Before' is used to refer to a previous time E.G. *Apply the ointment before going to bed.* ▶ ADVERB **2** If you have done something before, you have done it on a previous occasion E.G. *Never before had he seen such poverty.* ▶ PREPOSITION **3** FORMAL Before also means in front of E.G. *They stopped before a large white villa.*

🔲 (sense 1) earlier than, prior to
🔲 (sense 2) previously

beforehand

ADVERB before E.G. *It had been agreed beforehand that they would spend the night there.*

befriend befriends befriending befriended

VERB If you befriend someone, you act in a kind and helpful way and so become friends with them.

beg begs begging begged

VERB **1** When people beg, they ask for food or money, because they are very poor. **2** If you beg someone to do something, you ask them very anxiously to do it.

🔲 (sense 2) beseech, implore, plead

beggar beggars

NOUN someone who lives by asking people for money or food.

begin begins beginning began begun

VERB If you begin to do something, you start doing it. When something begins, it starts.

🔲 commence, start

beginner beginners

NOUN someone who has just started learning to do something and cannot do it very well yet.

🔲 learner, novice

beginning beginnings

NOUN The beginning of something is the first part of it or the time when it starts E.G. *They had now reached the beginning of the city.*

☑ Remember that *beginning* has one *g* and two *ns*.

begonia begonias

Said "be-**go**-nya" NOUN a plant with brightly coloured flowers.

begrudge begrudges begrudging begrudged

VERB If you begrudge someone something, you are angry or envious because they have it e.g. *No one could begrudge him the glory.*

beguiling

rhymes with "**smiling**" ADJECTIVE charming, but often in a deceptive way.

behalf

PHRASE To do something **on behalf of** someone or something means to do it for their benefit or as their representative.

behave behaves behaving behaved

VERB **1** If you behave in a particular way, you act in that way E.G. *They were behaving like animals.* **2** To behave yourself means to act correctly or properly.

behaviour

NOUN Your behaviour is the way in which you behave.

behead beheads beheading beheaded

VERB To behead someone means to cut their head off.

beheld

the past tense of **behold**.

a
b
c
d
e
f
g
h
i
j
k
l
m
n
o
p
q
r
s
t
u
v
w
x
y
z

A
B
C
D
E
F
G
H
I
J
K
L
M
N
O
P
Q
R
S
T
U
V
W
X
Y
Z

behind
PREPOSITION 1 at the back of E.G. *He was seated behind the desk.* 2 responsible for or causing E.G. *He was the driving force behind the move.* 3 supporting someone E.G. *The whole country was behind him.* ▶ ADVERB 4 If you stay behind, you remain after other people have gone. 5 If you leave something behind, you do not take it with you.

behold
INTERJECTION; LITERARY You say 'behold' when you want someone to look at something.
beholder NOUN

beige
Said "bayj" NOUN or ADJECTIVE pale creamy-brown.

being beings
1 Being is the present participle of **be**. NOUN 2 Being is the state or fact of existing E.G. *The party came into being in 1923.* 3 a living creature, either real or imaginary E.G. *alien beings from a distant galaxy.*

belated
ADJECTIVE; FORMAL A belated action happens later than it should have done E.G. *a belated birthday present.*
belatedly ADVERB

belch belches belching belched
VERB 1 If you belch, you make a sudden noise in your throat because air has risen up from your stomach. 2 If something belches smoke or fire, it sends it out in large amounts E.G. *Smoke belched from the steelworks.* ▶ NOUN 3 the noise you make when you belch.

beleaguered
ADJECTIVE 1 struggling against difficulties or criticism E.G. *the*

beleaguered meat industry. 2 besieged by an enemy E.G. *the beleaguered garrison.*

belfry belfries
NOUN the part of a church tower where the bells are.
▣ from Old French *berfrei* meaning 'tower'; because towers often contained bells this word was later changed to *belfry*

Belgian Belgians
ADJECTIVE 1 belonging or relating to Belgium. ▶ NOUN 2 someone who comes from Belgium.

belief beliefs
NOUN 1 a feeling of certainty that something exists or is true. 2 one of the principles of a religion or moral system.
▣ (sense 2) creed, doctrine, faith

believe believes believing believed
VERB 1 If you believe that something is true, you accept that it is true. 2 If you believe someone, you accept that they are telling the truth. 3 If you believe in things such as God and miracles, you accept that they exist or happen. 4 If you believe in something such as a plan or system, you are in favour of it E.G. *They really believe in education.*
believable ADJECTIVE **believer** NOUN

belittle belittles belittling belittled
VERB If you belittle someone or something, you make them seem unimportant E.G. *He belittled my opinions.*
▣ deprecate, disparage, scoff at

bell bells
NOUN 1 a cup-shaped metal object with a piece inside that swings and hits the sides, producing a ringing

sound. **2** an electrical device that
rings or buzzes in order to attract
attention.

bellbird bellbirds
NOUN an Australian or New Zealand
bird that makes a sound like a bell.

belligerent
ADJECTIVE aggressive and keen to start
a fight or an argument.
belligerence NOUN

bellow bellows bellowing bellowed
VERB **1** When an animal such as a bull
bellows, it makes a loud, deep
roaring noise. **2** If someone bellows,
they shout in a loud, deep voice.
▶ PLURAL NOUN **3** Bellows are a piece of
equipment used for blowing air into
a fire to make it burn more fiercely.

belly bellies
NOUN **1** Your belly is your stomach or
the front of your body below your
chest. **2** An animal's belly is the
underneath part of its body.

belong belongs belonging
belonged
VERB **1** If something belongs to you, it
is yours and you own it. **2** To belong
to a group means to be a member of
it. **3** If something belongs in a
particular place, that is where it
should be E.G. *It did not belong in the
music room.*

belongings
PLURAL NOUN Your belongings are the
things that you own.

beloved
Said "bil-**luv**-id" ADJECTIVE A beloved
person or thing is one that you feel
great affection for.
◩ adored, dear, loved, precious

below
PREPOSITION or ADVERB **1** If something is
below a line or the surface of

something else, it is lower down E.G.
six inches below soil level. **2** Below also
means at or to a lower point, level, or
rate E.G. *The temperature fell below
the legal minimum.*

belt belts belting belted
NOUN **1** a strip of leather or cloth that
you fasten round your waist to hold
your trousers or skirt up. **2** In a
machine, a belt is a circular strip of
rubber that drives moving parts or
carries objects along. **3** a specific
area of a country E.G. *Poland's
industrial belt.* ▶ VERB **4** INFORMAL To belt
someone means to hit them very
hard.

bemused
ADJECTIVE If you are bemused, you are
puzzled or confused.

bench benches
NOUN **1** a long seat that two or more
people can sit on. **2** a long, narrow
table for working at, for example in a
laboratory.
◩ (sense 1) form, pew, seat

bend bends bending bent
VERB **1** When you bend something,
you use force to make it curved or
angular. **2** When you bend, you move
your head and shoulders forwards
and downwards. ▶ NOUN **3** a curved
part of something.

bent ADJECTIVE
◩ (sense 1) arch, bow, curve
◩ (sense 3) arch, bow, curve

bene-
PREFIX 'Bene-' means 'good' or 'well'. For
example, something *beneficial* makes
you well or produces a good result,
and a *benevolent* person is kind and
good to others.
▥ from Latin *bene* meaning 'well'

a b c d e f g h i j k l m n o p q r s t u v w x y z

LEt's measure the angLE (an**g**le)   SPELLING NOTE

beneath

PREPOSITION, ADJECTIVE AND ADVERB **1** an old-fashioned word for **underneath**.
▶ PREPOSITION **2** If someone thinks something is beneath them, they think that it is too unimportant for them to bother with it.

benefactor benefactors

NOUN a person who helps to support a person or institution by giving money.

■ patron, sponsor, supporter

beneficial

ADJECTIVE Something that is beneficial is good for people E.G. *the beneficial effects of exercise*.

beneficially ADVERB

■ advantageous, favourable, helpful

beneficiary beneficiaries

NOUN A beneficiary of something is someone who receives money or other benefits from it.

benefit benefits benefiting benefited

NOUN **1** The benefits of something are the advantages that it brings to people E.G. *the benefits of relaxation*.
2 Benefit is money given by the government to people who are unemployed or ill. ▶ VERB **3** If you benefit from something, it helps you.

☑ *Benefit* is spelt with two *es*, not two *is*.

■ (sense 1) advantage, good, help
■ (sense 3) gain, profit

benevolent

ADJECTIVE kind and helpful.

benevolence NOUN **benevolently** ADVERB

benign

Said "be-nine" ADJECTIVE **1** Someone who is benign is kind and gentle. **2** A benign tumour is one that will not cause death or serious illness.

benignly ADVERB

bent

1 Bent is the past participle and past tense of **bend**. ▶ PHRASE **2** If you are **bent on** doing something, you are determined to do it.

bequeath bequeaths bequeathing bequeathed

VERB; FORMAL If someone bequeaths money or property to you, they give it to you in their will, so that it is yours after they have died.

bequest bequests

NOUN; FORMAL money or property that has been left to someone in a will.

berate berates berating berated

VERB; FORMAL If you berate someone, you scold them angrily E.G. *He berated them for getting caught*.

bereaved

ADJECTIVE; FORMAL You say that someone is bereaved when a close relative of theirs has recently died.

bereavement NOUN

bereft

ADJECTIVE; LITERARY If you are bereft of something, you no longer have it E.G. *The government seems bereft of ideas*.

beret berets

Said "ber-ray" NOUN a circular flat hat with no brim.

berm berms

NOUN **1** a narrow path at the edge of a slope, road, or canal. **2** In New Zealand English, a strip of grass between the road and the footpath in areas where people live.

berry berries

NOUN Berries are small, round fruits that grow on bushes or trees.

berserk

PHRASE If someone **goes berserk**, they lose control of themselves and become very violent.

📖 from Icelandic *berserkr*, a kind of Viking who wore a shirt (*serkr*) made from the skin of a bear (*björn*). They worked themselves into a frenzy before battle

berth berths

NOUN **1** a space in a harbour where a ship stays when it is being loaded or unloaded. **2** In a boat or caravan, a berth is a bed.

beseech beseeches beseeching beseeched or **besought**

VERB; LITERARY If you beseech someone to do something, you ask them very earnestly to do it E.G. *Her eyes beseeched him to show mercy.*
beseeching ADJECTIVE

beset

ADJECTIVE; FORMAL If you are beset by difficulties or doubts, you have a lot of them.

beside

PREPOSITION If one thing is beside something else, they are next to each other.

🔲 adjacent to, alongside, next to

besiege besieges besieging besieged

VERB **1** When soldiers besiege a place, they surround it and wait for the people inside to surrender. **2** If you are besieged by people, many people want something from you and continually bother you.

besought

a past tense and past participle of **beseech**.

best

1 the superlative of **good** and **well**.

▶ ADVERB **2** The thing that you like best is the thing that you prefer to everything else.

🔲 (sense 1) finest, supreme, top

best man

NOUN The best man at a wedding is the man who acts as the bridegroom's attendant.

bestow bestows bestowing bestowed

VERB; FORMAL If you bestow something on someone, you give it to them.

bet bets betting bet

VERB **1** If you bet on the result of an event, you will win money if something happens and lose money if it does not. ▶ NOUN **2** the act of betting on something, or the amount of money that you agree to risk. ▶ PHRASE; INFORMAL **3** You say **I bet** to indicate that you are sure that something is or will be so E.G. *I bet the answer is no.*
betting NOUN

betray betrays betraying betrayed

VERB **1** If you betray someone who trusts you, you do something which harms them, such as helping their enemies. **2** If you betray your feelings or thoughts, you show them without intending to.

betrayal NOUN   **betrayer** NOUN

🔲 (sense 1) be disloyal to, double-cross

🔲 (sense 2) give away, reveal

betrothal betrothals

NOUN; OLD-FASHIONED an engagement to be married.

betrothed ADJECTIVE or NOUN

better

1 the comparative of **good** and **well**.
ADVERB **2** If you like one thing better

a
b
c
d
e
f
g
h
i
j
k
l
m
n
o
p
q
r
s
t
u
v
w
x
y
z

A
B
C
D
E
F
G
H
I
J
K
L
M
N
O
P
Q
R
S
T
U
V
W
X
Y
Z

than another, you like it more than the other thing. ▶ ADJECTIVE 3 If you are better after an illness, you are no longer ill.

■ (sense 1) finer, greater, superior

between

PREPOSITION OR ADVERB 1 If something is between two other things, it is situated or happens in the space or time that separates them E.G. *flights between Europe and Asia*. 2 A relationship or difference between two people or things involves only those two.

☑ If there are two things you should use *between*. If there are more than two things you should use *among*.

beverage beverages

NOUN; FORMAL a drink.

bevy bevies

NOUN a group of people E.G. *a bevy of lawyers*.

beware

VERB If you tell someone to beware of something, you are warning them that it might be dangerous or harmful.

bewilder bewilders bewildering bewildered

VERB If something bewilders you, it is too confusing or difficult for you to understand.

bewildered ADJECTIVE **bewildering** ADJECTIVE **bewilderment** NOUN

bewitch bewitches bewitching bewitched

VERB 1 To bewitch someone means to cast a spell on them. 2 If something bewitches you, you are so delighted by it that you cannot pay attention to anything else.

bewitched ADJECTIVE **bewitching** ADJECTIVE

beyond

PREPOSITION 1 If something is beyond a certain place, it is on the other side of it E.G. *Beyond the hills was the Sahara*. 2 If something continues beyond a particular point, it continues further than that point E.G. *an education beyond the age of 16*. 3 If someone or something is beyond understanding or help, they cannot be understood or helped.

bi-

PREFIX 'Bi-' means 'two' or 'twice'. E.G. *bicycle, bigamy*.

🔠 from Latin *bis* meaning 'two'

bias

NOUN (HISTORY) Someone who shows bias favours one person or thing unfairly.

■ favouritism, partiality, prejudice

biased or **biassed**

ADJECTIVE favouring one person or thing unfairly E.G. *biased attitudes*.

■ one-sided, prejudiced

bib bibs

NOUN a piece of cloth or plastic which is worn under the chin of very young children when they are eating, to keep their clothes clean.

Bible Bibles

NOUN (RE) The Bible is the sacred book of the Christian religion.

biblical ADJECTIVE

🔠 from Greek *biblia* meaning 'the books'

bicentenary bicentenaries

NOUN The bicentenary of an event is its two-hundredth anniversary.

biceps

NOUN (PE) Your biceps are the large muscles on your upper arms.

bicker bickers bickering bickered

VERB When people bicker, they argue

or quarrel about unimportant things.

bicycle bicycles
NOUN a two-wheeled vehicle which you ride by pushing two pedals with your feet.

bid bids bidding bade bidden bid
NOUN 1 an attempt to obtain or do something E.G. *He made a bid for freedom.* 2 an offer to buy something for a certain sum of money. ▶ VERB 3 If you bid for something, you offer to pay a certain sum of money for it. 4 OLD-FASHIONED If you bid someone a greeting or a farewell, you say it to them
☑ When *bid* means 'offer to pay a certain sum of money' (sense 3), the past tense and past participle is *bid*. When *bid* means 'say a greeting or farewell' (sense 4), the past tense is *bade* and the past participle is *bidden*.

biddy-biddy biddy-biddies
NOUN a prickly low-growing plant found in New Zealand.

bide bides biding bided
PHRASE If you **bide your time**, you wait for a good opportunity before doing something.

bidet bidets
Said "bee-day" NOUN a low basin in a bathroom which is used for washing your bottom in.
🔳 a French word meaning 'small horse'

big bigger biggest
ADJECTIVE large or important.
biggish ADJECTIVE   **bigness** NOUN
🔳 enormous, huge, large

bigamy
NOUN Bigamy is the crime of marrying someone when you are already married to someone else.
bigamist NOUN

bigot bigots
NOUN someone who has strong and unreasonable opinions which they refuse to change.
bigoted ADJECTIVE   **bigotry** NOUN

bike bikes
NOUN; INFORMAL a bicycle or motorcycle.

bikini bikinis
NOUN a small two-piece swimming costume worn by women.
🔳 after *Bikini* atoll, from a comparison between the devastating effect of the atom-bomb test and the effect caused by women wearing bikinis

bilateral
ADJECTIVE A bilateral agreement is one made between two groups or countries.

bile
NOUN Bile is a bitter yellow liquid produced by the liver which helps the digestion of fat.

bilge
NOUN the lowest part of a ship, where dirty water collects.

bilingual
ADJECTIVE involving or using two languages E.G. *bilingual street signs.*

bill bills
NOUN 1 a written statement of how much is owed for goods or services. 2 a formal statement of a proposed new law that is discussed and then voted on in Parliament. 3 a notice or a poster. 4 A bird's bill is its beak.
🔳 (sense 1) charges, invoice

billabong billabongs
NOUN In Australia, a billabong is a lagoon or pool formed from part of a river.

billboard billboards
NOUN a large board on which

a
b
c
d
e
f
g
h
i
j
k
l
m
n
o
p
q
r
s
t
u
v
w
x
y
z

advertisements are displayed.

billet billets billeting billeted
VERB When soldiers are billeted in a building, arrangements are made for them to stay there.

billiards
NOUN Billiards is a game in which a long cue is used to move balls on a table.

billion billions
NOUN a thousand million. Formerly, a billion was a million million.
☑ As the meaning of *billion* has changed from one million million to one thousand million, a writer may mean either of these things when using it, depending on when the book or article was written.

billow billows billowing billowed
VERB 1 When things made of cloth billow, they swell out and flap slowly in the wind. 2 When smoke or cloud billows, it spreads upwards and outwards. ▶ NOUN 3 a large wave.

billy or **billycan billies** or **billycans**
NOUN In Australian and New Zealand English, a metal pot for boiling water over a camp fire.

bin bins
NOUN a container, especially one that you put rubbish in.

binary
Said "**by**-nar-ee" ADJECTIVE ⟨ICT⟩ The binary system expresses numbers using only two digits, 0 and 1.

bind binds binding bound
VERB 1 If you bind something, you tie rope or string round it so that it is held firmly. 2 If something binds you to a course of action, it makes you act in that way E.G. *He was bound by that decision.*

bindi-eye bindi-eyes
NOUN a small Australian plant with prickly fruits.

binding bindings
ADJECTIVE 1 If a promise or agreement is binding, it must be obeyed. ▶ NOUN 2 The binding of a book is its cover.

binge binges
NOUN; INFORMAL a wild bout of drinking or eating too much.

bingo
NOUN Bingo is a game in which players aim to match the numbers that someone calls out with the numbers on the card that they have been given.

binoculars
PLURAL NOUN Binoculars are an instrument with lenses for both eyes, which you look through in order to see objects far away.

bio-
PREFIX 'Bio-' means 'life' or 'living things'. For example, a *biography* is the story of someone's life and *biology* is the study of living things.
▥ from Greek *bios* meaning 'life'

biochemistry
NOUN Biochemistry is the study of the chemistry of living things.
biochemical ADJECTIVE **biochemist** NOUN

biodegradable
ADJECTIVE If something is biodegradable, it can be broken down into its natural elements by the action of bacteria E.G. *biodegradable cleaning products.*

biography biographies
NOUN the history of someone's life, written by someone else.
biographer NOUN **biographical** ADJECTIVE

biology

NOUN Biology is the study of living things.

biological ADJECTIVE **biologically** ADVERB **biologist** NOUN

bionic

ADJECTIVE having a part of the body that works electronically.

biopsy biopsies

NOUN an examination under a microscope of tissue from a living body to find out the cause of a disease.

birch birches

NOUN a tall deciduous tree with thin branches and thin bark.

bird birds

NOUN an animal with two legs, two wings, and feathers.

birth births

NOUN 1 The birth of a baby is when it comes out of its mother's womb at the beginning of its life. 2 The birth of something is its beginning E.G. *the birth of modern art*.

birthday birthdays

NOUN Your birthday is the anniversary of the date on which you were born.

birthmark birthmarks

NOUN a mark on someone's skin that has been there since they were born.

biscuit biscuits

NOUN a small flat cake made of baked dough.

🔲 from Old French *bes* + *cuit* meaning 'twice-cooked'

bisect bisects bisecting bisected

VERB To bisect a line or area means to divide it in half.

bisexual

ADJECTIVE sexually attracted to both men and women.

bishop bishops

NOUN 1 a high-ranking clergyman in some Christian Churches. 2 In chess, a bishop is a piece that is moved diagonally across the board.

bison

NOUN a large hairy animal related to cattle.

bistro bistros

Said "bee-stroh" NOUN a small informal restaurant.

bit bits

1 Bit is the past tense of **bite**. ▶ NOUN 2 A bit of something is a small amount of it E.G. *a bit of coal*. ▶ PHRASE; INFORMAL 3 A bit means slightly or to a small extent E.G. *That's a bit tricky*.

▤ (sense 2) fragment, part, piece

bitch bitches

NOUN 1 a female dog. 2 OFFENSIVE If someone refers to a woman as a bitch, it means that they think she behaves in a spiteful way.

bitchy ADJECTIVE

bite bites biting bit bitten

VERB 1 If you bite something, you use your teeth to cut into it or through it. 2 When an animal or insect bites you, it cuts into your skin with its teeth or mouth. ▶ NOUN 3 a small amount that you bite off something with your teeth. 4 the injury you get when an animal or insect bites you.

bitter bitterest

ADJECTIVE 1 If someone is bitter, they feel angry and resentful. 2 A bitter disappointment or experience makes people feel angry or unhappy for a long time afterwards. 3 In a bitter argument or war, people argue or fight fiercely and angrily E.G. *a bitter power struggle*. 4 A bitter wind is an extremely cold wind. 5 Something that tastes bitter has a sharp,

a
b
c
d
e
f
g
h
i
j
k
l
m
n
o
p
q
r
s
t
u
v
w
x
y
z

I always visit my FRIend on a FRIday (friend)   SPELLING NOTE

A
B
C
D
E
F
G
H
I
J
K
L
M
N
O
P
Q
R
S
T
U
V
W
X
Y
Z

unpleasant taste.

bitterly ADVERB   **bitterness** NOUN
■ (sense 1) acrimonious, resentful, sour
■ (sense 5) acid, sharp, sour

bivouac bivouacs
Said "**biv**-oo-ak" NOUN a temporary camp in the open air.

bizarre
Said "biz-**zahr**" ADJECTIVE very strange or eccentric.

blab blabs blabbing blabbed
VERB; INFORMAL When someone blabs, they give away secrets by talking carelessly.

black blacker blackest; blacks
NOUN or ADJECTIVE 1 Black is the darkest possible colour, like tar or soot.
2 Someone who is Black is a member of a dark-skinned race. ► ADJECTIVE
3 Black coffee or tea has no milk or cream added to it. 4 Black humour involves jokes about death or suffering.
blackness NOUN
■ (sense 1) dark, jet, pitch-black
☑ When you are writing about a person or people, *Black* should start with a capital letter.

blackberry blackberries
NOUN Blackberries are small black fruits that grow on prickly bushes called brambles.

blackbird blackbirds
NOUN a common European bird, the male of which has black feathers and a yellow beak.

blackboard blackboards
NOUN a dark-coloured board in a classroom, which teachers write on using chalk.

black box black boxes
NOUN an electronic device in an aircraft which collects and stores information during flights.

blackcurrant blackcurrants
NOUN Blackcurrants are very small dark purple fruits that grow in bunches on bushes.

blacken blackens blackening blackened
VERB To blacken something means to make it black E.G. *The smoke from the chimney blackened the roof.*

blackhead blackheads
NOUN a very small black spot on the skin caused by a pore being blocked with dirt.

blacklist blacklists blacklisting blacklisted
NOUN 1 a list of people or organizations who are thought to be untrustworthy or disloyal. ► VERB
2 When someone is blacklisted, they are put on a blacklist.

blackmail blackmails blackmailing blackmailed
VERB 1 If someone blackmails another person, they threaten to reveal an unpleasant secret about them unless that person gives them money or does something for them. ► NOUN
2 Blackmail is the action of blackmailing people.
blackmailer NOUN

black market
NOUN If something is bought or sold on the black market, it is bought or sold illegally.

blackout blackouts
NOUN If you have a blackout, you lose consciousness for a short time.

blacksmith blacksmiths
NOUN a person whose job is making things out of iron, such as horseshoes.

SPELLING NOTE   I want to see (C) your licenCe (licen**c**e)

bladder bladders
NOUN the part of your body where urine is held until it leaves your body.

blade blades
NOUN 1 The blade of a weapon or cutting tool is the sharp part of it. 2 The blades of a propeller are the thin, flat parts that turn round. 3 A blade of grass is a single piece of it.

blame blames blaming blamed
VERB 1 If someone blames you for something bad that has happened, they believe you caused it. ► NOUN 2 The blame for something bad that happens is the responsibility for letting it happen.
■ (sense 1) accuse, hold responsible

blameless
ADJECTIVE Someone who is blameless has not done anything wrong.

blanch blanches blanching blanched
VERB If you blanch, you suddenly become very pale.

bland blander blandest
ADJECTIVE tasteless, dull or boring E.G. a bland diet… bland pop music.
blandly ADVERB

blank blanker blankest
ADJECTIVE 1 Something that is blank has nothing on it E.G. a blank sheet of paper. 2 If you look blank, your face shows no feeling or interest. ► NOUN 3 If your mind is a blank, you cannot think of anything or remember anything.

blanket blankets
NOUN 1 a large rectangle of thick cloth that is put on a bed to keep people warm. 2 A blanket of something such as snow is a thick covering of it.

blare blares blaring blared
VERB To blare means to make a loud, unpleasant noise E.G. The radio blared pop music.

blaspheme blasphemes blaspheming blasphemed
VERB When people blaspheme, they are disrespectful about God or religion.
🏛 from Greek blapsis meaning 'evil' and phēmein meaning 'to speak'

blasphemy blasphemies
NOUN Blasphemy is speech or behaviour that shows disrespect for God or religion.
blasphemous ADJECTIVE

blast blasts blasting blasted
VERB 1 When people blast a hole in something they make a hole with an explosion. ► NOUN 2 a big explosion, especially one caused by a bomb. 3 a sudden strong rush of wind or air.

blatant
ADJECTIVE If you describe something you think is bad as blatant, you mean that rather than hide it, those responsible actually seem to be making it obvious E.G. a blatant disregard for the law.

blaze blazes blazing blazed
NOUN 1 a large, hot fire. 2 A blaze of light or colour is a great or strong amount of it E.G. a blaze of red. 3 A blaze of publicity or attention is a lot of it. ► VERB 4 If something blazes it burns or shines brightly.

blazer blazers
NOUN a kind of jacket, often in the colours of a school or sports team.

bleach bleaches bleaching bleached
VERB 1 To bleach material or hair means to make it white, usually by using a chemical. ► NOUN 2 Bleach is a

a
b
c
d
e
f
g
h
i
j
k
l
m
n
o
p
q
r
s
t
u
v
w
x
y
z

The government licenSes Schnapps (licenₛes)   SPELLING NOTE

A
B
C
D
E
F
G
H
I
J
K
L
M
N
O
P
Q
R
S
T
U
V
W
X
Y
Z

chemical that is used to make material white or to clean thoroughly and kill germs.

bleak bleaker bleakest
ADJECTIVE **1** If a situation is bleak, it is bad and seems unlikely to improve. **2** If a place is bleak, it is cold, bare, and exposed to the wind.

bleary
ADJECTIVE If your eyes are bleary, they are red and watery, usually because you are tired.

bleat bleats bleating bleated
VERB **1** When sheep or goats bleat, they make a high-pitched cry. ► NOUN **2** the high-pitched cry that a sheep or goat makes.

bleed bleeds bleeding bled
VERB When you bleed, you lose blood as a result of an injury.

bleep bleeps
NOUN a short high-pitched sound made by an electrical device such as an alarm.

blemish blemishes
NOUN a mark that spoils the appearance of something.

blend blends blending blended
VERB **1** When you blend substances, you mix them together to form a single substance. **2** When colours or sounds blend, they combine in a pleasing way. ► NOUN **3** A blend of things is a mixture of them, especially one that is pleasing. **4** a word formed by joining together the beginning and the end of two other words; for example, 'brunch' is a blend of 'breakfast' and 'lunch'.

blender blenders
NOUN a machine used for mixing liquids and foods at high speed.

bless blesses blessing blessed or blest
VERB When a priest blesses people or things, he or she asks for God's protection for them.
🔲 from Old English *blædsian* meaning 'to sprinkle with sacrificial blood'

blessed
ADJECTIVE
Said "blest" If someone is blessed with a particular quality or skill, they have it E.G. *He was blessed with a sense of humour.*
blessedly ADVERB

blessing blessings
NOUN **1** something good that you are thankful for E.G. *Good health is the greatest blessing.* ► PHRASE **2** If something is done **with someone's blessing**, they approve of it and support it.

blew
the past tense of **blow**.

blight blights blighting blighted
NOUN **1** something that damages or spoils other things E.G. *the blight of the recession.* ► VERB **2** When something is blighted, it is seriously harmed E.G. *His life had been blighted by sickness.*

blind blinds blinding blinded
ADJECTIVE **1** Someone who is blind cannot see. **2** If someone is blind to a particular fact, they do not understand it. ► VERB **3** If something blinds you, you become unable to see, either for a short time or permanently. ► NOUN **4** a roll of cloth or paper that you pull down over a window to keep out the light.
blindly ADVERB   **blindness** NOUN

blindfold blindfolds blindfolding blindfolded

NOUN **1** a strip of cloth tied over someone's eyes so that they cannot see. ▶ VERB **2** To blindfold someone means to cover their eyes with a strip of cloth.

blinding
ADJECTIVE A blinding light is so bright that it hurts your eyes E.G. *There was a blinding flash*.

blindingly
ADVERB; INFORMAL If something is blindingly obvious, it is very obvious indeed.

blink blinks blinking blinked
VERB When you blink, you close your eyes quickly for a moment.

blinkers
PLURAL NOUN Blinkers are two pieces of leather placed at the side of a horse's eyes so that it can only see straight ahead.

bliss
NOUN Bliss is a state of complete happiness.
blissful ADJECTIVE **blissfully** ADVERB

blister blisters blistering blistered
NOUN **1** a small bubble on your skin containing watery liquid, caused by a burn or rubbing. ▶ VERB **2** If someone's skin blisters, blisters appear on it as result of burning or rubbing.

blithe
ADJECTIVE casual and done without serious thought E.G. *a blithe disregard for their safety*.
blithely ADVERB

blitz blitzes blitzing blitzed
NOUN **1** a bombing attack by enemy aircraft on a city. ▶ VERB **2** When a city is blitzed, it is bombed by aircraft and is damaged or destroyed.
🔲 from German *Blitzkrieg* meaning

'lightning war'

blizzard blizzards
NOUN a heavy snowstorm with strong winds.

bloated
ADJECTIVE Something that is bloated is much larger than normal, often because there is a lot of liquid or gas inside it.

blob blobs
NOUN a small amount of a thick or sticky substance is.

bloc blocs
NOUN A group of countries or political parties with similar aims acting together is often called a bloc E.G. *the world's largest trading bloc*.

block blocks blocking blocked
NOUN **1** A block of flats or offices is a large building containing flats or offices. **2** In a town, a block is an area of land with streets on all its sides E.G. *He lives a few blocks down*. **3** A block of something is a large rectangular piece of it. ▶ VERB **4** To block a road or channel means to put something across it so that nothing can get through. **5** If something blocks your view, it is in the way and prevents you from seeing what you want to see. **6** If someone blocks something, they prevent it from happening E.G. *The council blocked his plans*.
🔲 (sense 3) bar, chunk, piece
🔲 (senses 4, 5 & 6) obstruct

blockade blockades blockading blockaded
NOUN **1** an action that prevents goods from reaching a place. ▶ VERB **2** When a place is blockaded, supplies are prevented from reaching it.

Plaice the fish has a glittering 'EYE' (I) (plaice)   SPELLING NOTE

A
B
C
D
E
F
G
H
I
J
K
L
M
N
O
P
Q
R
S
T
U
V
W
X
Y
Z

blockage blockages
NOUN When there is a blockage in a pipe or tunnel, something is clogging it. ◾ impediment, obstruction, stoppage

bloke blokes
NOUN; INFORMAL a man.

blonde blondes or **blond** blonds
ADJECTIVE 1 Blonde hair is pale yellow in colour. The spelling 'blond' is used when referring to men. ▶ NOUN 2 A blonde, or blond, is a person with light-coloured hair.

blood
NOUN 1 Blood is the red liquid that is pumped by the heart round the bodies of human beings and other mammals. ▶ PHRASE 2 If something cruel is done **in cold blood**, it is done deliberately and without showing any emotion.

bloodhound bloodhounds
NOUN a large dog with an excellent sense of smell.

bloodless
ADJECTIVE 1 If someone's face or skin is bloodless, it is very pale. 2 In a bloodless coup or revolution, nobody is killed.

blood pressure
NOUN Your blood pressure is a measure of the force with which your blood is being pumped round your body.

bloodshed
NOUN When there is bloodshed, people are killed or wounded.

bloodshot
ADJECTIVE If a person's eyes are bloodshot, the white parts have become red.

bloodstained
ADJECTIVE covered with blood.

bloodstream
NOUN the flow of blood through your body.

bloodthirsty
ADJECTIVE Someone who is bloodthirsty enjoys using or watching violence.

blood transfusion blood transfusions
NOUN a process in which blood is injected into the body of someone who has lost a lot of blood.

blood vessel blood vessels
NOUN Blood vessels are the narrow tubes in your body through which your blood flows.

bloody bloodier bloodiest
ADJECTIVE OR ADVERB 1 Bloody is a common swearword, used to express anger or annoyance. ▶ ADJECTIVE 2 A bloody event is one in which a lot of people are killed E.G. *a bloody revolution.* 3 Bloody also means covered with blood E.G. *a bloody gash on his head.*

bloom blooms blooming bloomed
NOUN 1 a flower on a plant. ▶ VERB 2 When a plant blooms, it produces flowers. 3 When something like a feeling blooms, it grows E.G. *Romance can bloom where you least expect it.*

blossom blossoms blossoming blossomed
NOUN 1 Blossom is the growth of flowers that appears on a tree before the fruit. ▶ VERB 2 When a tree blossoms, it produces blossom.

blot blots blotting blotted
NOUN 1 a drop of ink that has been spilled on a surface. 2 A blot on someone's reputation is a mistake or piece of bad behaviour that spoils

their reputation.

blot out VERB To blot something out means to be in front of it and prevent it from being seen E.G. *The smoke blotted out the sky*.

blotch blotches
NOUN a stain or a patch of a different colour.
blotchy ADJECTIVE

blouse blouses
NOUN a light shirt, worn by a girl or a woman.

blow blows blowing blew blown
VERB 1 When the wind blows, the air moves. 2 If something blows or is blown somewhere, the wind moves it there. 3 If you blow a whistle or horn, you make a sound by blowing into it. ▶ NOUN 4 If you receive a blow, someone or something hits you. 5 something that makes you very disappointed or unhappy E.G. *Marc's death was a terrible blow*.

blow up VERB 1 To blow something up means to destroy it with an explosion. 2 To blow up a balloon or a tyre means to fill it with air.

blubber
NOUN The blubber of animals such as whales and seals is the layer of fat that protects them from the cold.

bludge bludges bludging bludged
VERB INFORMAL 1 In Australian and New Zealand English, to bludge is to scrounge or cadge. 2 In Australian and New Zealand English, to bludge is also to avoid work or responsibilities.

bludgeon bludgeons bludgeoning bludgeoned
VERB To bludgeon someone means to hit them several times with a heavy object.

blue bluer bluest
ADJECTIVE or NOUN 1 Blue is the colour of the sky on a clear, sunny day. ▶ PHRASE 2 If something happens **out of the blue**, it happens suddenly and unexpectedly. ▶ ADJECTIVE 3 Blue films and jokes are about sex.
bluish or **blueish** ADJECTIVE

bluebell bluebells
NOUN a woodland plant with blue, bell-shaped flowers.

bluebottle bluebottles
NOUN 1 a large fly with a shiny dark-blue body. 2 In Australia and New Zealand, a bluebottle is also a small stinging jellyfish.

blue-collar
ADJECTIVE Blue-collar workers do physical work as opposed to office work.

blueprint blueprints
NOUN a plan of how something is expected to work E.G. *the blueprint for successful living*.

blues
NOUN The blues is a type of music which is similar to jazz, but is always slow and sad.

bluff bluffs bluffing bluffed
NOUN 1 an attempt to make someone wrongly believe that you are in a strong position. ▶ VERB 2 If you are bluffing, you are trying to make someone believe that you are in a position of strength.

blunder blunders blundering blundered
VERB 1 If you blunder, you make a silly mistake. ▶ NOUN 2 a silly mistake.

blunt blunter bluntest
ADJECTIVE 1 A blunt object has a rounded point or edge, rather than a sharp one. 2 If you are blunt, you say

a
b
c
d
e
f
g
h
i
j
k
l
m
n
o
p
q
r
s
t
u
v
w
x
y
z

A
B
C
D
E
F
G
H
I
J
K
L
M
N
O
P
Q
R
S
T
U
V
W
X
Y
Z

exactly what you think, without trying to be polite.

⊟ (sense 2) forthright, outspoken, straightforward

blur blurs blurring blurred
NOUN 1 a shape or area which you cannot see clearly because it has no distinct outline or because it is moving very fast. ► VERB 2 To blur the differences between things means to make them no longer clear E.G. *The dreams blurred confusingly with her memories.*
blurred ADJECTIVE

blurt out blurts out blurting out blurted out
VERB If you blurt something out, you say it suddenly, after trying to keep it a secret.

blush blushes blushing blushed
VERB 1 If you blush, your face becomes red, because you are embarrassed or ashamed. ► NOUN 2 the red colour on someone's face when they are embarrassed or ashamed.

bluster blusters blustering blustered
VERB 1 When someone blusters, they behave aggressively because they are angry or frightened. ► NOUN 2 Bluster is aggressive behaviour by someone who is angry or frightened.

blustery
ADJECTIVE Blustery weather is rough and windy.

boa boas
NOUN 1 A boa, or a boa constrictor, is a large snake that kills its prey by coiling round it and crushing it. 2 a woman's long thin scarf of feathers or fur.

boar boars
NOUN a male wild pig, or a male domestic pig used for breeding.

board boards boarding boarded
NOUN 1 a long, flat piece of wood. 2 the group of people who control a company or organization. 3 Board is the meals provided when you stay somewhere E.G. *The price includes full board.* ► VERB 4 If you board a ship or aircraft, you get on it or in it. ► PHRASE 5 If you are **on board** a ship or aircraft, you are on it or in it.

boarder boarders
NOUN a pupil who lives at school during term.

boarding school boarding schools
NOUN a school where the pupils live during the term.

boardroom boardrooms
NOUN a room where the board of a company meets.

boast boasts boasting boasted
VERB 1 If you boast about your possessions or achievements, you talk about them proudly. ► NOUN 2 something that you say which shows that you are proud of what you own or have done.
boastful ADJECTIVE
⊟ (sense 1) blow your own trumpet, brag, crow

boat boats
NOUN a small vehicle for travelling across water.

bob bobs bobbing bobbed
VERB 1 When something bobs, it moves up and down. ► NOUN 2 a woman's hair style in which her hair is cut level with her chin.

bobbin bobbins
NOUN a small round object on which thread or wool is wound.

bobby bobbies
NOUN; OLD-FASHIONED a policeman.

bode bodes boding boded

PHRASE; LITERARY If something **bodes ill**, or **bodes well**, it makes you think that something bad, or good, will happen.

bodice bodices

NOUN the upper part of a dress.

bodily

ADJECTIVE 1 relating to the body E.G. *bodily contact*. ▶ ADVERB 2 involving the whole of someone's body E.G. *He was carried bodily up the steps.*

body bodies

NOUN 1 Your body is either all your physical parts, or just the main part not including your head, arms, and legs. 2 a person's dead body. 3 the main part of a car or aircraft, not including the engine. 4 A body of people is also an organized group. ■ (sense 1) build, figure, form, physique

bodyguard bodyguards

NOUN a person employed to protect someone.

bodywork

NOUN the outer part of a motor vehicle

boer boers

Said "**boh**-er" NOUN In South Africa, a boer is a white farmer, especially one who is descended from the Dutch people who went to live in South Africa.

boerewors

Said "**boo**-rih-vorse" NOUN In South Africa, boerewors is a type of meat sausage.

bog bogs

NOUN an area of land which is always wet and spongy.

🔟 from Gaelic *bogach* meaning 'swamp'

boggle boggles boggling boggled

VERB If your mind boggles at something, you find it difficult to imagine or understand.

bogus

ADJECTIVE not genuine E.G. *a bogus doctor*.

bohemian

Said "boh-**hee**-mee-an" ADJECTIVE Someone who is bohemian does not behave in the same way as most other people in society, and is usually involved in the arts.

boil boils boiling boiled

VERB 1 When a hot liquid boils, bubbles appear in it and it starts to give off steam. 2 When you boil a kettle, you heat it until the water in it boils. 3 When you boil food, you cook it in boiling water. ▶ NOUN 4 a red swelling on your skin.

boiler boilers

NOUN a piece of equipment which burns fuel to provide hot water.

boiling

ADJECTIVE; INFORMAL very hot.

boisterous

ADJECTIVE Someone who is boisterous is noisy and lively. ■ loud, noisy, rowdy, unruly

bold bolder boldest

ADJECTIVE 1 confident and not shy or embarrassed E.G. *He was not bold enough to ask them*. 2 not afraid of risk or danger. 3 clear and noticeable E.G. *bold colours*.

boldly ADVERB **boldness** NOUN

bollard bollards

NOUN a short, thick post used to keep vehicles out of a road.

bolster bolsters bolstering bolstered

VERB To bolster something means to

a
b
c
d
e
f
g
h
i
j
k
l
m
n
o
p
q
r
s
t
u
v
w
x
y
z

support it or make it stronger E.G. *She relied on others to bolster her self-esteem*.

bolt bolts bolting bolted
NOUN **1** a metal bar that you slide across a door or window in order to fasten it. **2** a metal object which screws into a nut and is used to fasten things together. ▶ VERB **3** If you bolt a door or window, you fasten it using a bolt. If you bolt things together, you fasten them together using a bolt. **4** To bolt means to escape or run away. **5** To bolt food means to eat it very quickly.

bomb bombs bombing bombed
NOUN **1** a container filled with material that explodes when it hits something or is set off by a timer. ▶ VERB **2** When a place is bombed, it is attacked with bombs.
🔲 from Greek *bombos* meaning 'a booming sound'

bombard bombards bombarding bombarded
VERB **1** To bombard a place means to attack it with heavy gunfire or bombs. **2** If you are bombarded with something you are made to face a great deal of it E.G. *I was bombarded with criticism*.
bombardment NOUN

bomber bombers
NOUN an aircraft that drops bombs.

bombshell bombshells
NOUN a sudden piece of shocking or upsetting news.

bona fide
Said "boh-na **fie**-dee" ADJECTIVE genuine E.G. *We are happy to donate to bona fide charities*.
🔲 a Latin expression meaning 'in good faith'

bond bonds bonding bonded
NOUN **1** a close relationship between people. **2** LITERARY Bonds are chains or ropes used to tie a prisoner up. **3** a certificate which records that you have lent money to a business and that it will repay you the loan with interest. **4** Bonds are also feelings or obligations that force you to behave in a particular way E.G. *the social bonds of community*. ▶ VERB **5** When two things bond or are bonded, they become closely linked or attached.
▣ (sense 1) connection, link, tie

bondage
NOUN Bondage is the condition of being someone's slave.

bone bones
NOUN Bones are the hard parts that form the framework of a person's or animal's body.
boneless ADJECTIVE

bonfire bonfires
NOUN a large fire made outdoors, often to burn rubbish.
🔲 from 'bone' + 'fire'; bones were used as fuel in the Middle Ages

bonnet bonnets
NOUN **1** the metal cover over a car's engine. **2** a baby's or woman's hat tied under the chin.

bonny bonnier bonniest
ADJECTIVE; SCOTTISH AND NORTHERN ENGLISH nice to look at.

bonus bonuses
NOUN **1** an amount of money added to your usual pay. **2** Something that is a bonus is a good thing that you get in addition to something else E.G. *The view from the hotel was an added bonus*.

bony bonier boniest
ADJECTIVE Bony people or animals are

thin, with very little flesh covering their bones.

boo boos booing booed
NOUN **1** a shout of disapproval. ▶ VERB **2** When people boo, they shout 'boo' to show their disapproval.

boobook boobooks
NOUN a small brown Australian owl with a spotted back and wings.

book books booking booked
NOUN **1** a number of pages held together inside a cover. ▶ VERB **2** When you book something such as a room, you arrange to have it or use it at a particular time.

bookcase bookcases
NOUN a piece of furniture with shelves for books.

bookie bookies
NOUN; INFORMAL a bookmaker.

booking bookings
NOUN an arrangement to book something such as a hotel room.

book-keeping
NOUN Book-keeping is the keeping of a record of the money spent and received by a business.

booklet booklets
NOUN a small book with a paper cover.

bookmaker bookmakers
NOUN a person who makes a living by taking people's bets and paying them when they win.

bookmark bookmarks
NOUN a piece of card which you put between the pages of a book to mark your place.

boom booms booming boomed
NOUN **1** a rapid increase in something E.G. *the baby boom*. **2** a loud deep echoing sound. ▶ VERB **3** When something booms, it increases

rapidly E.G. *Sales are booming.* **4** To boom means to make a loud deep echoing sound.

boomerang boomerangs
NOUN a curved wooden missile that can be thrown so that it returns to the thrower, originally used as a weapon by Australian Aborigines.

boon boons
NOUN Something that is a boon makes life better or easier E.G. *Credit cards have been a boon to shoppers.*

boost boosts boosting boosted
VERB **1** To boost something means to cause it to improve or increase E.G. *The campaign had boosted sales.*
▶ NOUN **2** an improvement or increase E.G. *a boost to the economy.*
booster NOUN

boot boots booting booted
NOUN **1** Boots are strong shoes that come up over your ankle and sometimes your calf. **2** the covered space in a car, usually at the back, for carrying things in. ▶ VERB **3** INFORMAL If you boot something, you kick it.
▶ PHRASE **4** To boot means also or in addition E.G. *The story was compelling and well written to boot.*

booth booths
NOUN **1** a small partly enclosed area E.G. *a telephone booth.* **2** a stall where you can buy goods.

booty
NOUN Booty is valuable things taken from a place, especially by soldiers after a battle.

booze boozes boozing boozed
INFORMAL
NOUN **1** Booze is alcoholic drink. ▶ VERB **2** When people booze, they drink alcohol.
boozer NOUN   **boozy** ADJECTIVE

a b c d e f g h i j k l m n o p q r s t u v w x y z

A
B
C
D
E
F
G
H
I
J
K
L
M
N
O
P
Q
R
S
T
U
V
W
X
Y
Z

from Old Dutch *busen* meaning 'to drink to excess'

border borders bordering bordered

NOUN **1** the dividing line between two countries. **2** a strip or band round the edge of something E.G. *plain tiles with a bright border.* **3** a long flower bed in a garden. ▶ VERB **4** To border something means to form a boundary along the side of it E.G. *Tall poplar trees bordered the fields.*

borderline

ADJECTIVE only just acceptable as a member of a class or group E.G. *a borderline case.*

bore bores boring bored

VERB **1** If something bores you, you find it dull and not at all interesting. **2** If you bore a hole in something, you make it using a tool such as a drill. ▶ NOUN **3** someone or something that bores you.

bored

ADJECTIVE If you are bored, you are impatient because you do not find something interesting or because you have nothing to do.

boredom NOUN

✔ You can say that you are *bored with* or *bored by* someone or something, but you should not say *bored of*.

boring

ADJECTIVE dull and lacking interest.

▇ dull, tedious, uninteresting

born

VERB **1** When a baby is born, it comes out of its mother's womb at the beginning of its life. ▶ ADJECTIVE **2** You use 'born' to mean that someone has a particular quality from birth E.G. *He was a born pessimist.*

borne

the past participle of **bear**.

borough boroughs

Said "bur-uh" NOUN a town, or a district within a large town, that has its own council.

borrow borrows borrowing borrowed

VERB If you borrow something that belongs to someone else, they let you have it for a period of time.

borrower NOUN

✔ You *borrow* something *from* a person, not *off* them. Do not confuse *borrow* and *lend*. If you *borrow* something, you get it from another person for a while; if you *lend* something, someone gets it from you for a while.

Bosnian Bosnians

ADJECTIVE **1** belonging to or relating to Bosnia. ▶ NOUN **2** someone who comes from Bosnia.

bosom bosoms

NOUN **1** A woman's bosom is her breasts. ▶ ADJECTIVE **2** A bosom friend is a very close friend.

boss bosses bossing bossed

NOUN **1** Someone's boss is the person in charge of the place where they work. ▶ VERB **2** If someone bosses you around, they keep telling you what to do.

bossy bossier bossiest

ADJECTIVE A bossy person enjoys telling other people what to do.

bossiness NOUN

▇ dictatorial, domineering, overbearing

botany

NOUN Botany is the scientific study of plants.

botanic or **botanical** ADJECTIVE

botanist NOUN

botch botches botching botched
VERB; INFORMAL If you botch something, you do it badly or clumsily.
◼ bungle, mess up

both
ADJECTIVE or PRONOUN 'Both' is used when saying something about two things or people
☑ You can use *of* after *both*, but it is not essential. *Both the boys* means the same as *both of the boys*.

bother bothers bothering bothered
VERB **1** If you do not bother to do something, you do not do it because it takes too much effort or it seems unnecessary. **2** If something bothers you, you are worried or concerned about it. If you do not bother about it, you are not concerned about it E.G. *She is not bothered about money.* **3** If you bother someone, you interrupt them when they are busy. ► NOUN **4** Bother is trouble, fuss, or difficulty.

bothersome ADJECTIVE

bottle bottles bottling bottled
NOUN **1** a glass or plastic container for keeping liquids in. ► VERB **2** To bottle something means to store it in bottles.

bottleneck bottlenecks
NOUN a narrow section of road where traffic has to slow down or stop

bottle store bottle stores
NOUN In Australian, New Zealand, and South African English, a bottle store is a shop that sells sealed alcoholic drinks which can be drunk elsewhere.

bottom bottoms
NOUN **1** The bottom of something is its lowest part. **2** Your bottom is your buttocks. ► ADJECTIVE **3** The bottom thing in a series of things is the lowest one.

bottomless ADJECTIVE

bough boughs
Rhymes with "now" NOUN a large branch of a tree.

bought
the past tense and past participle of buy.
☑ Do not confuse *bought* and *brought*. *Bought* comes from *buy* and *brought* comes from *bring*.

boulder boulders
NOUN a large rounded rock.

boulevard boulevards
Said "boo-le-vard" NOUN a wide street in a city, usually with trees along each side.

bounce bounces bouncing bounced
VERB **1** When an object bounces, it springs back from something after hitting it. **2** To bounce also means to move up and down E.G. *Her long black hair bounced as she walked.* **3** If a cheque bounces, the bank refuses to accept it because there is not enough money in the account.
◼ (sense 1) rebound, recoil, ricochet

bouncy bouncier bounciest
ADJECTIVE **1** Someone who is bouncy is lively and enthusiastic. **2** Something that is bouncy is capable of bouncing or being bounced on E.G. *a bouncy ball… a bouncy castle.*

bound bounds bounding bounded
ADJECTIVE **1** If you say that something is bound to happen, you mean that it is certain to happen. **2** If a person or a vehicle is bound for a place, they are going there. **3** If someone is bound

by an agreement or regulation, they must obey it. ▶ NOUN 4 a large leap. ▶ PLURAL NOUN 5 Bounds are limits which restrict or control something E.G. *Their enthusiasm knew no bounds.* ▶ PHRASE 6 If a place is **out of bounds**, you are forbidden to go there. ▶ VERB 7 When animals or people bound, they move quickly with large leaps E.G. *He bounded up the stairway.* 8 Bound is also the past tense and past participle of **bind**.

boundary boundaries
NOUN something that indicates the farthest limit of anything E.G. *the city boundary… the boundaries of taste.*

boundless
ADJECTIVE without end or limit E.G. *her boundless energy.*

bountiful
ADJECTIVE; LITERARY freely available in large amounts E.G. *a bountiful harvest.*

bounty
NOUN 1 LITERARY Bounty is a generous supply E.G. *autumn's bounty of fruits.* 2 Someone's bounty is their generosity in giving a lot of something.

bouquet bouquets
Said "boo-kay" NOUN an attractively arranged bunch of flowers.

bourgeois
Said "boor-jhwah" ADJECTIVE typical of fairly rich middle-class people.

bourgeoisie
Said "boor-jhwah-zee" NOUN the fairly rich middle-class people in a society.

bout bouts
NOUN 1 If you have a bout of something such as an illness, you have it for a short time E.G. *a bout of flu.* 2 If you have a bout of doing

something, you do it enthusiastically for a short time. 3 a boxing or wrestling match.

boutique boutiques
Said "boo-teek" NOUN a small shop that sells fashionable clothes.

bovine
ADJECTIVE; TECHNICAL relating to cattle.

bow bows bowing bowed
Rhymes with "now" VERB 1 When you bow, you bend your body or lower your head as a sign of respect or greeting. 2 If you bow to something, you give in to it E.G. *He bowed to public pressure.* ▶ NOUN 3 the movement you make when you bow. 4 the front part of a ship.

bow bows
Rhymes with "low" NOUN 1 a knot with two loops and two loose ends. 2 a long thin piece of wood with horsehair stretched along it, which you use to play a violin. 3 a long flexible piece of wood used for shooting arrows.

bowel bowels
Rhymes with "towel" NOUN Your bowels are the tubes leading from your stomach, through which waste passes before it leaves your body. 📖 from Latin *botellus* meaning 'little sausage'

bowerbird bowerbirds
NOUN a bird found in Australia, the male of which builds a shelter during courtship.

bowl bowls bowling bowled
Rhymes with "mole" NOUN 1 a round container with a wide uncovered top, used for holding liquid or for serving food. 2 the hollow, rounded part of something E.G. *a toilet bowl.* 3 a large heavy ball used in the game

of bowls or tenpin bowling. ▶ VERB
4 In cricket, to bowl means to throw
the ball towards the batsman.
bowler NOUN

bowling
NOUN Bowling is a game in which you
roll a heavy ball down a narrow track
towards a group of wooden objects
called pins and try to knock them
down.

bowls
NOUN Bowls is a game in which the
players try to roll large wooden balls
as near as possible to a small ball.

bow tie bow ties
Rhymes with "**low**" NOUN A man's tie in
the form of a bow, often worn at
formal occasions.

box boxes boxing boxed
NOUN **1** a container with a firm base
and sides and usually a lid. **2** On a
form, a box is a rectangular space
which you have to fill in. **3** In a
theatre, a box is a small separate area
where a few people can watch the
performance together. ▶ VERB **4** To
box means to fight someone
according to the rules of boxing.

boxer boxers
NOUN **1** a person who boxes. **2** a type
of medium-sized, smooth-haired dog
with a flat face.

boxing
NOUN Boxing is a sport in which two
people fight using their fists, wearing
padded gloves.

box office box offices
NOUN the place where tickets are sold
in a theatre or cinema.

boy boys
NOUN a male child.
boyhood NOUN **boyish** ADJECTIVE
☰ lad, youngster, youth

**boycott boycotts boycotting
boycotted**
VERB **1** If you boycott an organization
or event, you refuse to have anything
to do with it. ▶ NOUN **2** the boycotting
of an organization or event E.G. *a
boycott of the elections.*
🏛 from the name of Captain C.C.
Boycott (1832–1897), an Irish land
agent, who offended the tenants, so
that they refused to pay their rents
☰ (sense 1) ban, black, embargo

boyfriend boyfriends
NOUN Someone's boyfriend is the man
or boy with whom they are having a
romantic relationship.

bra bras
NOUN a piece of underwear worn by a
woman to support her breasts

braaivleis or **braal braaivleises** or
braais
Said "**bry-**flayss" NOUN In South
African English, a braaivleis is a
picnic where meat is cooked on an
open fire.

brace braces bracing braced
VERB **1** When you brace yourself, you
stiffen your body to steady yourself
E.G. *The ship lurched and he braced
himself.* **2** If you brace yourself for
something unpleasant, you prepare
yourself to deal with it E.G. *The police
are braced for violent reprisals.* ▶ NOUN
3 an object fastened to something to
straighten or support it E.G. *a neck
brace.* ▶ PLURAL NOUN **4** Braces are a pair
of straps worn over the shoulders
and fastened to the trousers to hold
them up.

bracelet bracelets
NOUN a chain or band worn around
someone's wrist as an ornament.

a
b
c
d
e
f
g
h
i
j
k
l
m
n
o
p
q
r
s
t
u
v
w
x
y
z

Eddy Ant thinks mEAt is a grEAt trEAt to Eat (-ea-)   ◀ SPELLING NOTE

A
B
C
D
E
F
G
H
I
J
K
L
M
N
O
P
Q
R
S
T
U
V
W
X
Y
Z

bracing

ADJECTIVE Something that is bracing makes you feel fit and full of energy E.G. *the bracing sea air*.

bracken

NOUN Bracken is a plant like a large fern that grows on hills and in woods.

bracket brackets

NOUN 1 Brackets are a pair of written marks, ( ), [ ], or { }, placed round a word or sentence that is not part of the main text, or to show that the items inside the brackets belong together. 2 a range between two limits, for example of ages or prices E.G. *the four-figure price bracket*. 3 a piece of metal or wood fastened to a wall to support something such as a shelf.

What do Brackets do?

Brackets ( ) enclose material that has been added to the text, but could be omitted and still leave a meaningful sentence. In formal writing this sort of material is usually marked off with commas or dashes, and brackets are used for giving references or translations of foreign phrases:

E.G. *Buddhism is discussed in Chapter 7 (see pages 152–197).* ■ *The boat was called "La Ardilla Roja" (The Red Squirrel).*

Square brackets [ ] are used to enclose remarks and explanations which are inserted by an author to make a quotation clearer:

E.G. *The minister said, "I think that five million [pounds] should do it."*

---

brag brags bragging bragged

VERB When someone brags, they boast about their achievements E.G. *Both leaders bragged they could win by a landslide*.

Brahma

Said "brah-ma" PROPER NOUN Brahma is a Hindu god and is one of the Trimurti.

🔒 from a Sanskrit word meaning 'praise'

Brahman

Said "brah-men" NOUN In the Hindu religion Brahman is the ultimate and impersonal divine reality of the universe.

brahmin brahmins

Said "brah-min" NOUN a member of the highest or priestly caste in Hindu society.

braid braids braiding braided

NOUN 1 Braid is a strip of decorated cloth used to decorate clothes or curtains. 2 a length of hair which has been plaited and tied. ▶ VERB 3 To braid hair or thread means to plait it.

Braille

NOUN Braille is a system of printing for blind people in which letters are represented by raised dots that can be felt with the fingers.

brain brains

NOUN 1 Your brain is the mass of nerve tissue inside your head that controls your body and enables you to think and feel; also used to refer to your mind and the way that you think E.G. *I admired his legal brain*. ▶ PLURAL NOUN 2 If you say that someone has brains, you mean that they are very intelligent.

brainchild

NOUN; INFORMAL Someone's brainchild is

something that they have invented or created.

brainwash brainwashes brainwashing brainwashed
VERB If people are brainwashed into believing something, they accept it without question because they are told it repeatedly.
brainwashing NOUN

brainwave brainwaves
NOUN; INFORMAL a clever idea you think of suddenly.

brainy brainier brainiest
ADJECTIVE; INFORMAL clever.

braise braises braising braised
VERB To braise food means to fry it for a short time, then cook it slowly in a little liquid.

brake brakes braking braked
NOUN 1 a device for making a vehicle stop or slow down. ▸ VERB 2 When a driver brakes, he or she makes a vehicle stop or slow down by using its brakes
☑ Do not confuse the spellings of *brake* and *break*, or *braking* and *breaking*.

bramble brambles
NOUN a wild, thorny bush that produces blackberries.

bran
NOUN Bran is the ground husks that are left over after flour has been made from wheat grains.

branch branches branching branched
NOUN 1 The branches of a tree are the parts that grow out from its trunk.
2 A branch of an organization is one of a number of its offices or shops.
3 A branch of a subject is one of its areas of study or activity E.G. *specialists in certain branches of*

medicine. ▸ VERB 4 A road that branches off from another road splits off from it to lead in a different direction.

brand brands branding branded
NOUN 1 A brand of something is a particular kind or make of it E.G. *a popular brand of chocolate.* ▸ VERB 2 When an animal is branded, a mark is burned on its skin to show who owns it.

brandish brandishes brandishing brandished
VERB; LITERARY If you brandish something, you wave it vigorously E.G. *He brandished his sword over his head.*

brand-new
ADJECTIVE completely new.

brandy
NOUN a strong alcoholic drink, usually made from wine.
🔲 from Dutch *brandewijn* meaning 'burnt wine'

brash brasher brashest
ADJECTIVE If someone is brash, they are overconfident or rather rude.

brass
NOUN OR ADJECTIVE 1 Brass is a yellow-coloured metal made from copper and zinc. 2 In an orchestra, the brass section consists of brass wind instruments such as trumpets and trombones.

brassière brassières
NOUN; FORMAL a bra.

brat brats
NOUN; INFORMAL A badly behaved child may be referred to as a brat.

bravado
Said "bra-**vah**-doh" NOUN Bravado is a display of courage intended to impress other people.

a b c d e f g h i j k l m n o p q r s t u v w x y z

there's a rAKE in the brAKEs (br**ake**)　　**SPELLING NOTE**

brave braver bravest; braves braving braved

ADJECTIVE **1** A brave person is willing to do dangerous things and does not show any fear. ► VERB **2** If you brave an unpleasant or dangerous situation, you face up to it in order to do something E.G. *His fans braved the rain to hear him sing*.

bravely ADVERB **bravery** NOUN

■ (sense 1) courageous, daring, fearless, plucky

bravo

INTERJECTION People shout 'Bravo!' to express appreciation when something has been done well.

brawl brawls brawling brawled

NOUN **1** a rough fight. ► VERB **2** When people brawl, they take part in a rough fight.

brawn

NOUN Brawn is physical strength.

brawny ADJECTIVE

bray brays braying brayed

VERB **1** When a donkey brays, it makes a loud, harsh sound. ► NOUN **2** the sound a donkey makes.

brazen

ADJECTIVE When someone's behaviour is brazen, they do not care if other people think they are behaving wrongly.

brazenly ADVERB

brazier braziers

NOUN a metal container in which coal or charcoal is burned to keep people warm out of doors.

Brazilian Brazilians

ADJECTIVE **1** belonging or relating to Brazil. ► NOUN **2** someone who comes from Brazil.

breach breaches breaching breached

VERB **1** FORMAL If you breach an agreement or law, you break it. **2** To breach a barrier means to make a gap in it E.G. *The river breached its banks*. ► NOUN **3** A breach of an agreement or law is an action that breaks it E.G. *a breach of contract*. **4** a gap or break.

■ (sense 3) contravention, infringement, violation

bread

NOUN a food made from flour and water, usually raised with yeast, and baked.

breadth

NOUN The breadth of something is the distance between its two sides.

breadwinner breadwinners

NOUN the person who earns the money in a family.

break breaks breaking broke broken

VERB **1** When an object breaks, it is damaged and separates into pieces. **2** If you break a rule or promise you fail to keep it. **3** When a boy's voice breaks, it becomes permanently deeper. **4** When a wave breaks, it falls and becomes foam. ► NOUN **5** a short period during which you rest or do something different.

■ (sense 1) crack, fracture, separate, snap

■ (sense 2) breach, contravene, disobey, violate

break down VERB **1** When a machine or a vehicle breaks down, it stops working. **2** When a discussion or relationship breaks down, it ends because of problems or disagreements.

break up VERB If something breaks up, it ends E.G. *The marriage broke up after a year*.

breakable ADJECTIVE
☑ Do not confuse the spellings of *break* and *brake*, or *breaking* and *braking*.

breakage breakages
NOUN the act of breaking something or a thing that has been broken.

breakaway
ADJECTIVE A breakaway group is one that has separated from a larger group.

breakdown breakdowns
NOUN 1 The breakdown of something such as a system is its failure E.G. *a breakdown in communications*. 2 the same as a nervous breakdown. 3 If a driver has a breakdown, their car stops working.

breaker breakers
NOUN Breakers are big sea waves.

breakfast breakfasts
NOUN the first meal of the day.

break-in break-ins
NOUN the illegal entering of a building, especially by a burglar.

breakneck
ADJECTIVE; INFORMAL Someone or something that is travelling at breakneck speed is travelling dangerously fast.

breakthrough breakthroughs
NOUN a sudden important development E.G. *a medical breakthrough*.

breakwater breakwaters
NOUN a wall extending into the sea which protects a coast from the force of the waves.

bream breams
NOUN an edible fish.

breast breasts
NOUN A woman's breasts are the two soft, fleshy parts on her chest, which produce milk after she has had a baby.

breath breaths
NOUN 1 Your breath is the air you take into your lungs and let out again when you breathe. ► PHRASE 2 If you are **out of breath**, you are breathing with difficulty after doing something energetic. 3 If you say something **under your breath**, you say it in a very quiet voice.

breathe breathes breathing breathed
VERB When you breathe, you take air into your lungs and let it out again.

breathless
ADJECTIVE If you are breathless, you are breathing fast or with difficulty.
breathlessly ADVERB
breathlessness NOUN

breathtaking
ADJECTIVE If you say that something is breathtaking, you mean that it is very beautiful or exciting.

bred
the past tense and past participle of **breed**.

breeches
*Said "**brit-chlz**"* PLURAL NOUN Breeches are trousers reaching to just below the knee, nowadays worn especially for riding.

breed breeds breeding bred
NOUN 1 A breed of a species of domestic animal is a particular type of it. ► VERB 2 Someone who breeds animals or plants keeps them in order to produce more animals or plants with particular qualities. 3 When animals breed, they mate and produce offspring.
▤ (sense 3) multiply, procreate, reproduce

a
b
c
d
e
f
g
h
i
j
k
l
m
n
o
p
q
r
s
t
u
v
w
x
y
z

an ELegant angEL (angel)   SPELLING NOTE

breeze breezes
NOUN a gentle wind.

brevity
NOUN; FORMAL Brevity means shortness
E.G. *the brevity of his report*.

brew brews brewing brewed
VERB 1 If you brew tea or coffee, you
make it in a pot by pouring hot
water over it. 2 To brew beer means
to make it, by boiling and
fermenting malt. 3 If an unpleasant
situation is brewing, it is about to
happen E.G. *Another scandal is
brewing*.

brewer NOUN

brewery breweries
NOUN a place where beer is made, or a
company that makes it.

briar briars
NOUN a wild rose that grows on a
dense prickly bush.

bribe bribes bribing bribed
NOUN 1 a gift or money given to an
official to persuade them to make a
favourable decision. ▶ VERB 2 To bribe
someone means to give them a
bribe.

bribery NOUN

bric-a-brac
NOUN Bric-a-brac consists of small
ornaments or pieces of furniture of
no great value.
📖 from an obsolete French phrase *à
bric et à brac* meaning 'at random'

brick bricks
NOUN Bricks are rectangular blocks of
baked clay used in building.

bricklayer bricklayers
NOUN a person whose job is to build
with bricks.

bride brides
NOUN a woman who is getting
married or who has just got married.

bridal ADJECTIVE

bridegroom bridegrooms
NOUN a man who is getting married
or who has just got married.

bridesmaid bridesmaids
NOUN a woman who helps and
accompanies a bride on her
wedding day.

bridge bridges
NOUN 1 a structure built over a river,
road, or railway so that vehicles and
people can cross. 2 the platform from
which a ship is steered and
controlled. 3 the hard ridge at the
top of your nose. 4 Bridge is a card
game for four players based on
whist.

bridle bridles
NOUN a set of straps round a horse's
head and mouth, which the rider
uses to control the horse.

brief briefer briefest; briefs
briefing briefed
ADJECTIVE 1 Something that is brief
lasts only a short time. ▶ VERB
2 D & T When you brief someone
on a task, you give them all the
necessary instructions and
information about it.

briefly ADVERB
▤ (sense 1) fleeting, momentary,
quick, short

briefcase briefcases
NOUN a small flat case for carrying
papers.

briefing briefings
NOUN a meeting at which information
and instructions are given.

brier
another spelling of **briar**.

brigade brigades
NOUN an army unit consisting of three
battalions.

🔲 from Italian *brigare* meaning 'to fight'

brigadier brigadiers
Said "brig-ad-**ear**" NOUN an army officer of the rank immediately above colonel.

brigalow brigalows
NOUN a type of Australian acacia tree that grows in the bush.

bright brighter brightest
ADJECTIVE 1 strong and startling E.G. *a bright light*. 2 clever E.G. *my brightest student*. 3 cheerful E.G. *a bright smile*.
brightly ADVERB　**brightness** NOUN
▣ (sense 1) brilliant, dazzling, shining, vivid

brighten brightens brightening brightened
VERB 1 If something brightens, it becomes brighter E.G. *The weather had brightened*. 2 If someone brightens, they suddenly look happier.
brighten up VERB To brighten something up means to make it more attractive and cheerful.

brilliant
ADJECTIVE 1 A brilliant light or colour is extremely bright. 2 A brilliant person is extremely clever. 3 A brilliant career is extremely successful.
brilliantly ADVERB　**brilliance** NOUN

brim brims
NOUN 1 the wide part of a hat is the part that sticks outwards at the bottom. ▶ PHRASE 2 If a container is filled **to the brim**, it is filled right to the top.

brine
NOUN Brine is salt water.

bring brings bringing brought
VERB 1 If you bring something or someone with you when you go to a place, you take them with you E.G. *You can bring a friend to the party*. 2 To bring something to a particular state means to cause it to be like that E.G. *Bring the vegetables to the boil*.

bring about VERB To bring something about means to cause it to happen E.G. *We must try to bring about a better world*.

bring up VERB 1 To bring up children means to look after them while they grow up. 2 If you bring up a subject, you introduce it into the conversation E.G. *She brought up the subject at dinner*.

brink
NOUN If you are on the brink of something, you are just about to do it or experience it.

brisk brisker briskest
ADJECTIVE 1 A brisk action is done quickly and energetically E.G. *A brisk walk restores your energy*. 2 If someone's manner is brisk, it shows that they want to get things done quickly and efficiently.
briskly ADVERB　**briskness** NOUN

bristle bristles bristling bristled
NOUN 1 Bristles are strong animal hairs used to make brushes. ▶ VERB 2 If the hairs on an animal's body bristle, they rise up, because it is frightened.
bristly ADJECTIVE

British
ADJECTIVE belonging or relating to the United Kingdom of Great Britain and Northern Ireland.

Briton Britons
NOUN someone who comes from the United Kingdom of Great Britain and Northern Ireland.

a b c d e f g h i j k l m n o p q r s t u v w x y z

A Rude Idiot Thought He Might Eat Toffee In Church (<u>arithmetic</u>)　　**SPELLING NOTE**

A
B
C
D
E
F
G
H
I
J
K
L
M
N
O
P
Q
R
S
T
U
V
W
X
Y
Z

brittle

ADJECTIVE An object that is brittle is hard but breaks easily.

broach broaches broaching broached

VERB When you broach a subject, you introduce it into a discussion.

broad broader broadest

ADJECTIVE 1 wide E.G. *a broad smile*. 2 having many different aspects or concerning many different people E.G. *A broad range of issues was discussed*. 3 general rather than detailed E.G. *the broad concerns of the movement*. 4 If someone has a broad accent, the way that they speak makes it very clear where they come from E.G. *She spoke in a broad Irish accent*.

broadband

NOUN Broadband is a digital system used on the Internet and in other forms of telecommunication which can process and transfer information input from various sources, such as from telephones, computers or televisions.

broad bean broad beans

NOUN Broad beans are light-green beans with thick flat edible seeds.

broadcast broadcasts broadcasting broadcast

NOUN 1 a programme or announcement on radio or television. ► VERB 2 To broadcast something means to send it out by radio waves, so that it can be seen on television or heard on radio.

broadcaster NOUN **broadcasting** NOUN

broaden broadens broadening broadened

VERB 1 When something broadens, it becomes wider E.G. *His smile broadened*. 2 To broaden something means to cause it to involve more things or concern more people E.G. *We must broaden the scope of this job*.

broadly

ADVERB true to a large extent or in most cases E.G. *There are broadly two schools of thought on this*.

broad-minded

ADJECTIVE Someone who is broad-minded does not disapprove of behaviour or attitudes that many other people disapprove of.
■ liberal, open-minded, tolerant

broadsheet broadsheets

NOUN a newspaper with large pages and long news stories.

brocade

NOUN Brocade is a heavy, expensive material, often made of silk, with a raised pattern.
▥ from Spanish *brocado* meaning 'embossed fabric'

broccoli

NOUN Broccoli is a green vegetable, similar to cauliflower.

brochure brochures

Said "broh-sher" NOUN a booklet which gives information about a product or service.

brogue brogues

Said "broag" NOUN 1 a strong accent, especially an Irish one. 2 Brogues are thick leather shoes.
▥ from Irish Gaelic *bróg* meaning 'boot' or 'shoe'

broke

1 the past tense of **break**. ► ADJECTIVE 2 INFORMAL If you are broke, you have no money.

broken

the past participle of **break**.

broker brokers
NOUN a person whose job is to buy and sell shares for other people.

brolga brolgas
NOUN a large grey Australian crane with a red-and-green head.

brolly brollies
NOUN; INFORMAL an umbrella.

bronchitis
NOUN Bronchitis is an illness in which the two tubes which connect your windpipe to your lungs become infected, making you cough.

brontosaurus brontosauruses
NOUN a type of very large, plant-eating dinosaur.

bronze
NOUN Bronze is a yellowish-brown metal which is a mixture of copper and tin; also the yellowish brown colour of this metal.

brooch brooches
Rhymes with "coach" NOUN a piece of jewellery with a pin at the back for attaching to clothes.

brood broods brooding brooded
NOUN 1 a family of baby birds. ▶ VERB 2 If you brood about something, you keep thinking about it in a serious or unhappy way.

brook brooks
NOUN a stream.

broom brooms
NOUN 1 a long-handled brush. 2 Broom is a shrub with yellow flowers.

broth
NOUN Broth is soup, usually with vegetables in it.

brothel brothels
NOUN a house where men pay to have sex with prostitutes.

brother brothers

NOUN Your brother is a boy or man who has the same parents as you.
brotherly ADJECTIVE

brotherhood brotherhoods
NOUN 1 Brotherhood is the affection and loyalty that brothers or close male friends feel for each other. 2 a group of men with common interests or beliefs.

brother-in-law brothers-in-law
NOUN Someone's brother-in-law is the brother of their husband or wife, or their sister's husband.

brought
the past tense and past participle of **bring**.
☑ Do not confuse *brought* and *bought*. Brought comes from *bring* and *bought* comes from *buy*.

brow brows
NOUN 1 Your brow is your forehead. 2 Your brows are your eyebrows. 3 The brow of a hill is the top of it.

brown browner brownest
ADJECTIVE or NOUN Brown is the colour of earth or wood.

brownie brownies
NOUN a junior member of the Guides.

browse browses browsing browsed
VERB 1 If you browse through a book, you look through it in a casual way. 2 If you browse in a shop, you look at the things in it for interest rather than because you want to buy something.

browser browsers
NOUN a piece of computer software that lets you look at websites on the World Wide Web.

bruise bruises bruising bruised
NOUN 1 a purple mark that appears on your skin after something has hit it.

a
b
c
d
e
f
g
h
i
j
k
l
m
n
o
p
q
r
s
t
u
v
w
x
y
z

A
B
C
D
E
F
G
H
I
J
K
L
M
N
O
P
Q
R
S
T
U
V
W
X
Y
Z

▶ VERB **2** If something bruises you, it hits you so that a bruise appears on your skin.

brumby brumbies
NOUN In Australia and New Zealand, a wild horse.

brunette brunettes
NOUN a girl or woman with dark brown hair.

brunt
PHRASE If you **bear the brunt** of something unpleasant, you are the person who suffers most E.G. *Women bear the brunt of crime.*

brush brushes brushing brushed
NOUN **1** an object with bristles which you use for cleaning things, painting, or tidying your hair. ▶ VERB **2** If you brush something, you clean it or tidy it with a brush. **3** To brush against something means to touch it while passing it E.G. *Her lips brushed his cheek.*

brusque
Said "broosk" ADJECTIVE Someone who is brusque deals with people quickly and without considering their feelings.
brusquely ADVERB

brussels sprout brussels sprouts
NOUN Brussels sprouts are vegetables that look like tiny cabbages.

brutal
ADJECTIVE Brutal behaviour is cruel and violent E.G. *the victim of a brutal murder.*
brutally ADVERB **brutality** NOUN

brute brutes
NOUN **1** a rough and insensitive man. ▶ ADJECTIVE **2** Brute force is strength alone, without any skill E.G. *You have to use brute force to open the gates.*
brutish ADJECTIVE

bubble bubbles bubbling bubbled
NOUN **1** a ball of air in a liquid. **2** a hollow, delicate ball of soapy liquid. ▶ VERB **3** When a liquid bubbles, bubbles form in it. **4** If you are bubbling with something like excitement, you are full of it.
bubbly ADJECTIVE

buck bucks bucking bucked
NOUN **1** the male of various animals, including the deer and the rabbit. ▶ VERB **2** If a horse bucks, it jumps into the air with its feet off the ground.

bucket buckets
NOUN a deep round container with an open top and a handle.

buckle buckles buckling buckled
NOUN **1** a fastening on the end of a belt or strap. ▶ VERB **2** If you buckle a belt or strap, you fasten it. **3** If something buckles, it becomes bent because of severe heat or pressure.

bud buds budding budded
NOUN **1** a small, tight swelling on a tree or plant, which develops into a flower or a cluster of leaves. ▶ VERB **2** When a tree or plant buds, new buds appear on it.

Buddha
PROPER NOUN The Buddha is the title of Gautama Siddhartha, a religious teacher living in the 6th century BC in India and founder of Buddhism. Buddha means 'the enlightened one'

Buddhism
NOUN Buddhism is a religion, founded by the Buddha, which teaches that the way to end suffering is by overcoming your desires.
Buddhist NOUN or ADJECTIVE

budding
ADJECTIVE just beginning to develop E.G. *a budding artist.*

SPELLING NOTE ▶ there's a rAKE in the brAKEs (brake)

budge budges budging budged
VERB If something will not budge, you cannot move it.

budgerigar budgerigars
NOUN a small brightly coloured pet bird.

budget budgets budgeting budgeted
NOUN 1 a plan showing how much money will be available and how it will be spent. ► VERB 2 If you budget for something, you plan your money carefully, so that you are able to afford it.
budgetary ADJECTIVE

budgie budgies
NOUN; INFORMAL a budgerigar.

buff buffs
ADJECTIVE 1 a pale brown colour. ► NOUN 2 INFORMAL someone who knows a lot about a subject E.G. *a film buff*.

buffalo buffaloes
NOUN a wild animal like a large cow with long curved horns.

buffer buffers
NOUN 1 Buffers on a train or at the end of a railway line are metal discs on springs that reduce shock when they are hit. 2 something that prevents something else from being harmed E.G. *keep savings as a buffer against unexpected cash needs*.

buffet buffets
Said "**boof**-ay" NOUN 1 a café at a station. 2 a meal at which people serve themselves.

buffet buffets buffeting buffeted
Said "**buff**-it" VERB If the wind or sea buffets a place or person, it strikes them violently and repeatedly.

bug bugs bugging bugged
NOUN 1 an insect, especially one that causes damage. 2 a small error in a computer program which means that the program will not work properly. 3 INFORMAL a virus or minor infection E.G. *a stomach bug*. ► VERB 4 If a place is bugged, tiny microphones are hidden there to pick up what people are saying.

bugle bugles
NOUN a brass instrument that looks like a small trumpet.
bugler NOUN

build builds building built
VERB 1 To build something such as a house means to make it from its parts. 2 To build something such as an organization means to develop it gradually. ► NOUN 3 Your build is the shape and size of your body.
builder NOUN
■ (sense 1) assemble, construct, erect

building buildings
NOUN a structure with walls and a roof.

building society building societies
NOUN a business in which some people invest their money, while others borrow from it to buy a house.

bulb bulbs
NOUN 1 the glass part of an electric lamp. 2 an onion-shaped root that grows into a flower or plant.

Bulgarian Bulgarians
ADJECTIVE 1 belonging or relating to Bulgaria. ► NOUN 2 someone who comes from Bulgaria. 3 the main language spoken in Bulgaria.

bulge bulges bulging bulged
VERB 1 If something bulges, it swells out from a surface. ► NOUN 2 a lump on a normally flat surface.

bulk bulks

NOUN **1** a large mass of something E.G. *The book is more impressive for its bulk than its content.* **2** The bulk of something is most of it E.G. *the bulk of the world's great poetry.* ▶ PHRASE **3** To buy something **in bulk** means to buy it in large quantities.

bulky bulkier bulkiest

ADJECTIVE large and heavy E.G. *a bulky package.*

■ cumbersome, large, unwieldy

bull bulls

NOUN the male of some species of animals, including the cow family, elephants and whales.

bulldog bulldogs

NOUN a squat dog with a broad head and muscular body.

bulldozer bulldozers

NOUN a powerful tractor with a broad blade in front, which is used for moving earth or knocking things down.

bullet bullets

NOUN a small piece of metal fired from a gun.

bulletin bulletins

NOUN **1** a short news report on radio or television. **2** a leaflet or small newspaper regularly produced by a group or organization.

🔲 from Italian *bulletino* meaning 'small Papal edict'

bullion

NOUN Bullion is gold or silver in the form of bars.

bullock bullocks

NOUN a young castrated bull.

bullroarer bullroarers

NOUN a wooden slat attached to a string that is whirled round to make a roaring noise. Bullroarers are used especially by Australian Aborigines in religious ceremonies.

bully bullies bullying bullied

NOUN **1** someone who uses their strength or power to hurt or frighten other people. ▶ VERB **2** If someone bullies you into doing something, they make you do it by using force or threats.

🔲 a 16th century word meaning 'fine fellow' or 'hired ruffian'

bump bumps bumping bumped

VERB **1** If you bump into something, you knock into it with a jolt. ▶ NOUN **2** a soft or dull noise made by something knocking into something else. **3** a raised, uneven part of a surface.

bumpy ADJECTIVE

■ (sense 3) bulge, lump, protuberance

bumper bumpers

NOUN **1** Bumpers are bars on the front and back of a vehicle which protect it if there is a collision. ▶ ADJECTIVE **2** A bumper crop or harvest is larger than usual.

bun buns

NOUN a small, round cake.

bunch bunches bunching bunched

NOUN **1** a group of people or things. **2** A bunch of flowers is a number of them held or tied together. **3** A bunch of bananas or grapes is a group of them growing on the same stem. ▶ VERB **4** When people bunch together or bunch up, they stay very close to each other.

bundle bundles bundling bundled

NOUN **1** a number of things tied together or wrapped up in a cloth. ▶ VERB **2** If you bundle someone or something somewhere, you push them there quickly and roughly.

bung bungs bunging bunged
NOUN **1** a stopper used to close a hole in something such as a barrel. ▶ VERB **2** INFORMAL If you bung something somewhere, you put it there quickly and carelessly.

bungalow bungalows
NOUN a one-storey house.
🔲 from Hindi *bangla* meaning 'of Bengal'

bungle bungles bungling bungled
VERB To bungle something means to fail to do it properly.

bunion bunions
NOUN a painful lump on the first joint of a person's big toe.

bunk bunks
NOUN a bed fixed to a wall in a ship or caravan.

bunker bunkers
NOUN **1** On a golf course, a bunker is a large hole filled with sand. **2** A coal bunker is a storage place for coal. **3** an underground shelter with strong walls to protect it from bombing.

bunting
NOUN Bunting is strips of small coloured flags displayed on streets and buildings on special occasions.

bunyip bunyips
NOUN a legendary monster said to live in swamps and lakes in Australia.

buoy buoys
Said "boy" NOUN a floating object anchored to the bottom of the sea, marking a channel or warning of danger.

buoyant
ADJECTIVE **1** able to float. **2** lively and cheerful E.G. *She was in a buoyant mood.*

buoyancy NOUN

burble burbles burbling burbled
VERB To burble means to makes a soft bubbling sound E.G. *The water burbled over the gravel.*

burden burdens
NOUN **1** a heavy load. **2** If something is a burden to you, it causes you a lot of worry or hard work.

burdensome ADJECTIVE
▪ (sense 1) load, weight
▪ (sense 2) millstone, trouble, worry

bureau bureaux
Said "**byoo**-roh" NOUN **1** an office that provides a service E.G. *an employment bureau.* **2** a writing desk with shelves and drawers.

bureaucracy
NOUN Bureaucracy is the complex system of rules and procedures which operates in government departments.

bureaucratic ADJECTIVE

bureaucrat bureaucrats
NOUN a person who works in a government department, especially one who follows rules and procedures strictly.

burgeoning
ADJECTIVE growing or developing rapidly E.G. *a burgeoning political crisis.*

burglar burglars
NOUN a thief who breaks into a building.

burglary NOUN

burgle burgles burgling burgled
VERB If your house is burgled, someone breaks into it and steals things.

burial burials
NOUN ⟨RE⟩ a ceremony held when a dead person is buried.

a
b
c
d
e
f
g
h
i
j
k
l
m
n
o
p
q
r
s
t
u
v
w
x
y
z

burly burlier burliest
ADJECTIVE A burly man has a broad body and strong muscles.
☰ brawny, well-built

burn burns burning burned or burnt
VERB **1** If something is burning, it is on fire. **2** To burn something means to destroy it with fire. **3** If you burn yourself or are burned, you are injured by fire or by something hot. ► NOUN **4** an injury caused by fire or by something hot.
☰ (sense 1) be on fire, blaze
☰ (sense 2) incinerate, set on fire
☑ You can write either *burned* or *burnt* as the past form of *burn*.

burp burps burping burped
VERB **1** If you burp, you make a noise because air from your stomach has been forced up through your throat. ► NOUN **2** the noise that you make when you burp.

burrow burrows burrowing burrowed
NOUN **1** a tunnel or hole in the ground dug by a small animal. ► VERB **2** When an animal burrows, it digs a burrow.

bursary bursaries
NOUN a sum of money given to someone to help fund their education.

burst bursts bursting burst
VERB **1** When something bursts, it splits open because of pressure from inside it. **2** If you burst into a room, you enter it suddenly. **3** To burst means to happen or come suddenly and with force E.G. *The aircraft burst into flames.* **4** INFORMAL If you are bursting with something, you find it difficult to keep it to yourself E.G. *We were bursting with joy.* ► NOUN **5** A

burst of something is a short period of it E.G. *He had a sudden burst of energy.*
☰ (sense 5) outbreak, rush, spate

bury buries burying buried
VERB **1** When a dead person is buried, their body is put into a grave and covered with earth. **2** To bury something means to put it in a hole in the ground and cover it up. **3** If something is buried under something, it is covered by it E.G. *My bag was buried under a pile of old newspapers.*

bus buses
NOUN a large motor vehicle that carries passengers.
▦ from Latin *omnibus* meaning 'for all'; buses were originally called omnibuses

bush bushes
NOUN **1** a thick plant with many stems branching out from ground level. **2** In Australia and South Africa, an area of land in its natural state outside of city areas is called the bush. **3** In New Zealand, the bush is land covered with rain forest.

bushman bushmen
NOUN **1** In Australia and New Zealand, someone who lives or travels in the bush. **2** In New Zealand, a bushman is also someone whose job it is to clear the bush for farming.

Bushman Bushmen
NOUN A Bushman is a member of a group of people in southern Africa who live by hunting and gathering food.

bushranger bushrangers
NOUN In Australia and New Zealand in the past, an outlaw living in the bush.

bushy bushier bushiest
ADJECTIVE Bushy hair or fur grows very
thickly E.G. *bushy eyebrows*.

business businesses
NOUN **1** Business is work relating to
the buying and selling of goods and
services. **2** an organization which
produces or sells goods or provides
a service. **3** You can refer to any
event, situation, or activity as a
business E.G. *This whole business has
upset me.*
businessman NOUN
businesswoman NOUN
▣ (sense 2) company,
establishment, firm, organization

businesslike
ADJECTIVE dealing with things in an
efficient way.

busker buskers
NOUN someone who plays music or
sings for money in public places.

bust busts busting bust or
busted
NOUN **1** a statue of someone's head
and shoulders. *a bust of Beethoven.*
2 A woman's bust is her chest and
her breasts. ▶ VERB **3** INFORMAL If you
bust something, you break it.
▶ ADJECTIVE **4** INFORMAL If a business
goes bust, it becomes bankrupt and
closes down.

bustle bustles bustling bustled
VERB **1** When people bustle, they
move in a busy, hurried way. ▶ NOUN
2 Bustle is busy, noisy activity.

**busy busier busiest; busies
busying busied**
ADJECTIVE **1** If you are busy, you are in
the middle of doing something. **2** A
busy place is full of people doing
things or moving about E.G. *a busy
seaside resort.* ▶ VERB **3** If you busy

yourself with something, you occupy
yourself by doing it.
busily ADVERB
▣ (sense 1) employed, engaged,
occupied

but
CONJUNCTION **1** used to introduce an
idea that is opposite to what has
gone before E.G. *I don't miss teaching
but I miss the pupils.* **2** used when
apologizing E.G. *I'm sorry, but I can't
come tonight.* **3** except E.G. *We can't
do anything but wait.*

butcher butchers
NOUN a shopkeeper who sells meat.

butler butlers
NOUN the chief male servant in a rich
household.
▦ from Old French *bouteillier*
meaning 'a dealer in bottles'

butt butts butting butted
NOUN **1** The butt of a weapon is the
thick end of its handle. **2** If you are
the butt of teasing, you are the
target of it. ▶ VERB **3** If you butt
something, you ram it with your
head.

butt in VERB If you butt in, you join
in a private conversation or activity
without being asked to.

**butter butters buttering
buttered**
NOUN **1** Butter is a soft fatty food
made from cream, which is spread
on bread and used in cooking. ▶ VERB
2 To butter bread means to spread
butter on it.

buttercup buttercups
NOUN a wild plant with bright yellow
flowers.

butterfly butterflies
NOUN a type of insect with large
colourful wings.

A
B
C
D
E
F
G
H
I
J
K
L
M
N
O
P
Q
R
S
T
U
V
W
X
Y
Z

buttocks

PLURAL NOUN Your buttocks are the part of your body that you sit on.

button buttons buttoning buttoned

NOUN 1 Buttons are small, hard objects sewn on to clothing, and used to fasten two surfaces together. 2 a small object on a piece of equipment that you press to make it work. ► VERB 3 If you button a piece of clothing, you fasten it using its buttons.

buttonhole buttonholes

NOUN 1 a hole that you push a button through to fasten a piece of clothing. 2 a flower worn in your lapel.

buxom

ADJECTIVE A buxom woman is large, healthy, and attractive.

buy buys buying bought

VERB If you buy something, you obtain it by paying money for it. **buyer** NOUN

buzz buzzes buzzing buzzed

VERB 1 If something buzzes, it makes a humming sound, like a bee. ► NOUN 2 the sound something makes when it buzzes.

buzzard buzzards

NOUN a large brown and white bird of prey.

buzzer buzzers

NOUN a device that makes a buzzing sound, to attract attention.

by

PREPOSITION 1 used to indicate who or what has done something E.G. *The statement was issued by his solicitor.* 2 used to indicate how something is done E.G. *He frightened her by hiding behind the door.* 3 located next to E.G. *I sat by her bed.* 4 before a particular time E.G. *It should be ready by next spring.* ► PREPOSITION or ADVERB 5 going past E.G. *We drove by his house.*

by-election by-elections

NOUN an election held to choose a new member of parliament after the previous member has resigned or died.

bygone

ADJECTIVE; LITERARY happening or existing a long time ago E.G. *the ceremonies of a bygone era.*

bypass bypasses

NOUN a main road which takes traffic round a town rather than through it.

bystander bystanders

NOUN someone who is not included or involved in something but is there to see it happen.

byte bytes

NOUN (ICT) a unit of storage in a computer.

C c

TIP Some words which sound as if they might begin with *s*, actually begin with *c*, for example *centre* and *cynic*. Some words which sound as if they might begin with *sh* actually begin with *ch*, for example *chute*. Some words which sound as if they might begin with *ch* are spelt with *c* alone, for example *cello*.

cab cabs
NOUN **1** a taxi. **2** In a lorry, bus, or train, the cab is where the driver sits.
📖 from French *cabriolet* meaning 'light two-wheeled carriage'. Cabs were originally horse-drawn

cabaret cabarets
Said "kab-bar-ray" NOUN a show consisting of dancing, singing, or comedy acts.
📖 from French *cabaret* meaning 'tavern'

cabbage cabbages
NOUN a large green leafy vegetable.
📖 from Norman French *cabache* meaning 'head'

cabbage tree cabbage trees
NOUN a palm-like tree found in New Zealand with a tall bare trunk and big bunches of spiky leaves; also a similar tree found in eastern Australia.

cabin cabins
NOUN **1** a room in a ship where a passenger sleeps. **2** a small house, usually in the country and often made of wood. **3** the area where the passengers or the crew sit in a plane.

cabinet cabinets
NOUN **1** a small cupboard. **2** The cabinet in a government is a group of ministers who advise the leader and decide policies.

cable cables
NOUN **1** a strong, thick rope or chain. **2** a bundle of wires with a rubber covering, which carries electricity. **3** (ICT) a message sent abroad by using electricity.

cable car cable cars
NOUN a vehicle pulled by a moving cable, for taking people up and down mountains.

cable television
NOUN a television service people can receive from underground wires which carry the signals.

cacao
Said "ka-kah-oh" NOUN a type of small tropical evergreen tree, whose berries are used to produce chocolate and cocoa.

cache caches
Said "kash" NOUN a store of things hidden away E.G. *a cache of guns*.

cachet
Said "kash-shay" NOUN; FORMAL Cachet is the status and respect something has E.G. *the cachet of shopping at Harrods*.

cackle cackles cackling cackled
VERB **1** If you cackle, you laugh harshly.
▶ NOUN **2** a harsh laugh.

cacophony
Said "kak-koff-fon-nee" NOUN; FORMAL a loud, unpleasant noise E.G. *a*

I went to see (C) the doctor's new practiCe (practice)   **SPELLING NOTE**

A
B
C
D
E
F
G
H
I
J
K
L
M
N
O
P
Q
R
S
T
U
V
W
X
Y
Z

cacophony of barking dogs.
📖 from Greek *kakos* + *phōnē*
meaning 'bad sound'

cactus cacti or cactuses
NOUN a thick, fleshy plant that grows
in deserts and is usually covered in
spikes.

cad cads
NOUN; OLD-FASHIONED a man who treats
people unfairly.

caddie caddies; also spelt **caddy**
NOUN 1 a person who carries golf
clubs for a golf player. 2 A tea caddy
is a box for keeping tea in.

cadence cadences
NOUN The cadence of someone's voice
is the way it goes up and down as
they speak.

cadet cadets
NOUN a young person being trained
in the armed forces or police.

cadge cadges cadging cadged
VERB If you cadge something off
someone, you get it from them and
don't give them anything in return
E.G. *I cadged a lift ashore.*

caesarean caesareans
Said "siz-**air**-ee-an"; also spelt
caesarian and **cesarean**
NOUN A caesarean or caesarean
section is an operation in which a
baby is lifted out of a woman's
womb through a cut in her
abdomen.

café cafés
Said "**kaf**-fay" NOUN 1 a place where
you can buy light meals and drinks.
2 In South African English, a café is a
corner shop or grocer's shop.

cafeteria cafeterias
Said "kaf-fit-**ee**-ree-ya" NOUN a
restaurant where you serve yourself.

caffeine or **caffein**
Said "**kaf**-feen" NOUN a chemical in
coffee and tea which makes you
more active.

cage cages
NOUN a box made of wire or bars in
which birds or animals are kept.
caged ADJECTIVE

cagey cagier cagiest
Said "**kay**-jee" ADJECTIVE; INFORMAL
cautious and not open E.G. *They're
very cagey when they talk to me.*

cagoule cagoules
Said "ka-**gool**" NOUN a lightweight
waterproof jacket with a hood.

cahoots
PHRASE; INFORMAL If you are **in cahoots**
with someone, you are working
closely with them on a secret plan.

cairn cairns
NOUN a pile of stones built as a
memorial or a landmark.
📖 from Gaelic *carn* meaning 'heap of
stones' or 'hill'

cajole cajoles cajoling cajoled
VERB If you cajole someone into doing
something, you persuade them to do
it by saying nice things to them.

cake cakes caking caked
NOUN 1 a sweet food made by baking
flour, eggs, fat, and sugar. 2 a block of
a hard substance such as soap. ▶ VERB
3 If something cakes or is caked, it
forms or becomes covered with a
solid layer E.G. *caked with mud.*
📖 from Old Norse *kaka* meaning
'oatcake'

calamity calamities
NOUN an event that causes disaster or
distress.
calamitous ADJECTIVE

calcium
Said "**kal**-see-um" NOUN a soft white

substance found in bones and teeth.

calculate calculates calculating calculated

VERB 1 (MATHS) If you calculate something, you work it out, usually by doing some arithmetic. 2 If something is calculated, it is deliberately planned to have a particular effect E.G. *Everything they said to each other was calculated to wound.* **calculation** NOUN

🔲 from Latin *calculus* meaning 'stone' or 'pebble'. The Romans used pebbles to count with

calculating

ADJECTIVE carefully planning situations to get what you want E.G. *Toby was always a calculating type.*

calculator calculators

NOUN a small electronic machine used for doing mathematical calculations.

calculus

NOUN a branch of mathematics concerned with amounts that can change and rates of change.

calendar calendars

NOUN 1 a chart showing the date of each day in a particular year. 2 a system of dividing time into fixed periods of days, months, and years E.G. *the Jewish calendar.*

🔲 from Latin *kalendae* the day of the month on which interest on debts was due

calf calves

NOUN 1 a young cow, bull, elephant, whale, or seal. 2 the thick part at the back of your leg below your knee.

calibre calibres

Said "kal-lib-ber" NOUN 1 the ability or

intelligence someone has E.G. *a player of her calibre.* 2 The calibre of a gun is the width of the inside of the barrel of the gun.

🔲 from Arabic *qalib* meaning 'cobbler's last'

call calls calling called

VERB 1 If someone or something is called a particular name, that is their name E.G. *a man called Jeffrey.* 2 If you call people or situations something, you use words to describe your opinion of them E.G. *They called me crazy.* 3 If you call someone, you telephone them. 4 If you call or call out something, you say it loudly E.G. *He called out his daughter's name.* 5 If you call on someone, you pay them a short visit E.G. *Don't hesitate to call on me.*
▶ NOUN 6 If you get a call from someone, they telephone you or pay you a visit. 7 a cry or shout E.G. *a call for help.* 8 a demand for something E.G. *The call for art teachers was small.*
🔳 (sense 1) christen, label, name

call off VERB If you call something off, you cancel it.

call up VERB If someone is called up, they are ordered to join the army, navy, or air force.

call box call boxes

NOUN a telephone box.

calling

NOUN 1 a profession or career. 2 If you have a calling to a particular job, you have a strong feeling that you should do it.

callous

ADJECTIVE cruel and not concerned with other people's feelings. **callously** ADVERB **callousness** NOUN
🔳 hardhearted, heartless, unfeeling

calm calmer calmest; calms calming calmed
ADJECTIVE **1** Someone who is calm is quiet and does not show any worry or excitement. **2** If the weather or the sea is calm, it is still because there is no strong wind. ▶ NOUN **3** a state of quietness and peacefulness E.G. *He liked the calm of the evening.* ▶ VERB **4** To calm someone means to make them less upset or excited.
calmly ADVERB **calmness** NOUN
☰ (sense 1) composed, cool, self-possessed
☰ (sense 3) peacefulness, quiet
☰ (sense 4) quieten, soothe

calorie calories
NOUN a unit of measurement for the energy food gives you E.G. *All alcohol is high in calories.*

calves
the plural of **calf**.

calypso calypsos
Said "kal-**lip**-soh" NOUN a type of song from the West Indies, accompanied by a rhythmic beat, about something happening at the time.

calyx calyxes or calyces
Said "**kay**-lix" NOUN; TECHNICAL In a flower, the calyx is the ring of petal-like sepals that protects the developing bud.

camaraderie
Said "kam-mer-**rah**-der-ree" NOUN a feeling of trust and friendship between a group of people.

camber cambers
NOUN a slight downwards slope from the centre of a road to each side of it.

camel camels
NOUN a large mammal with either one or two humps on its back. Camels live in hot desert areas and are sometimes used for carrying things.
🏛 from Hebrew *gamal*

cameo cameos
NOUN **1** a small but important part in a play or film played by a well-known actor or actress. **2** a brooch with a raised stone design on a flat stone of another colour.

camera cameras
NOUN a piece of equipment used for taking photographs or for filming.
🏛 from Latin *camera* meaning 'vault'

camomile
NOUN a plant with a strong smell and daisy-like flowers which are used to make herbal tea.
🏛 from Greek *khamaimēlon* meaning 'apple on the ground'

camouflage camouflages camouflaging camouflaged
Said "**kam**-mof-flahj" NOUN **1** a way of avoiding being seen by having the same colour or appearance as the surroundings. ▶ VERB **2** To camouflage something is to hide it by giving it the same colour or appearance as its surroundings.

camp camps camping camped
NOUN **1** a place where people live in tents or stay in tents on holiday. **2** a collection of buildings for a particular group of people such as soldiers or prisoners. **3** a group of people who support a particular idea or belief E.G. *the pro-government camp.* ▶ VERB **4** If you camp, you stay in a tent.
camper NOUN **camping** NOUN

campaign campaigns campaigning campaigned
Said "kam-**pane**" NOUN **1** a set of actions aiming to achieve a

particular result E.G. *a campaign to educate people.* ▶ VERB **2** To campaign means to carry out a campaign E.G. *He has campaigned against smoking.*
campaigner NOUN

camp-drafting
NOUN In Australia, camp-drafting is a competition in which men on horseback select cattle or sheep from a herd or flock.

campus campuses
NOUN the area of land and the buildings that make up a university or college.

can could
VERB **1** If you can do something, it is possible for you to do it or you are allowed to do it E.G. *You can go to the cinema.* **2** If you can do something, you have the ability to do it E.G. *I can speak Italian.*

can cans canning canned
NOUN **1** a metal container, often a sealed one with food or drink inside. ▶ VERB **2** To can food or drink is to seal it in cans.

Canadian Canadians
ADJECTIVE **1** belonging or relating to Canada. ▶ NOUN **2** someone who comes from Canada.

canal canals
NOUN a long, narrow man-made stretch of water.

canary canaries
NOUN a small yellow bird.

can-can can-cans
NOUN a lively dance in which women kick their legs high in the air to fast music.

cancel cancels cancelling cancelled
VERB **1** If you cancel something that has been arranged, you stop it from

happening. **2** If you cancel a cheque or an agreement, you make sure that it is no longer valid.
cancellation NOUN

cancer cancers
NOUN **1** a serious disease in which abnormal cells in a part of the body increase rapidly, causing growths. **2** Cancer is also the fourth sign of the zodiac, represented by a crab. People born between June 21st and July 22nd are born under this sign.
cancerous ADJECTIVE
🔠 from Latin *cancer* meaning 'crab'

candelabra or **candelabrum** candelabras
NOUN an ornamental holder for a number of candles.

candid
ADJECTIVE honest and frank.
candidly ADVERB **candour** NOUN

candidate candidates
NOUN **1** a person who is being considered for a job. **2** a person taking an examination.
candidacy NOUN
🔠 from Latin *candidatus* meaning 'white-robed'. In Rome, a candidate wore a white toga

candied
ADJECTIVE covered or cooked in sugar E.G. *candied fruit.*

candle candles
NOUN a stick of hard wax with a wick through the middle. The lighted wick gives a flame that provides light.

candlestick candlesticks
NOUN a holder for a candle.

candy candies
NOUN; ESPECIALLY AMERICAN ENGLISH Candies are sweets.
🔠 from Arabic *qand* meaning 'cane sugar'

a
b
c
d
e
f
g
h
i
j
k
l
m
n
o
p
q
r
s
t
u
v
w
x
y
z

Psychiatrists Seldom Yell Callously Hard (**psychi**atrist)   SPELLING NOTE

cane canes caning caned
NOUN **1** Cane is the long, hollow stems of a plant such as bamboo. **2** Cane is also strips of cane used for weaving things such as baskets. **3** a long narrow stick, often one used to beat people as a punishment. ▶ VERB **4** To cane someone means to beat them with a cane as a punishment.

canine
Said "kay-nine" ADJECTIVE relating to dogs.

canister canisters
NOUN a container with a lid, used for storing foods such as sugar or tea.

cannabis
NOUN Cannabis is a drug made from the hemp plant, which some people smoke.

canned
ADJECTIVE **1** Canned food is kept in cans. **2** Canned music or laughter on a television or radio show is recorded beforehand.

cannibal cannibals
NOUN a person who eats other human beings; also used of animals that eat animals of their own type.
cannibalism NOUN

cannon cannons or cannon
NOUN a large gun, usually on wheels, used in battles to fire heavy metal balls.

cannot
VERB Cannot is the same as can not E.G. *She cannot come home yet.*

canny
ADJECTIVE clever and cautious E.G. *canny business people.*
cannily ADVERB

canoe canoes
Said "ka-**noo**" NOUN a small, narrow boat that you row using a paddle.

canoeing NOUN

canon canons
NOUN **1** a member of the clergy in a cathedral. **2** a basic rule or principle E.G. *the canons of political economy.*

canopy canopies
NOUN a cover for something, used for shelter or decoration E.G. *a frilly canopy over the bed.*
📖 from Greek *kōnōpeion* meaning 'bed with a mosquito net'

cantankerous
ADJECTIVE Cantankerous people are bad-tempered and quarrel a lot with other people.

canteen canteens
NOUN **1** the part of a workplace where the workers can go to eat. **2** A canteen of cutlery is a set of cutlery in a box.

canter canters cantering cantered
VERB When a horse canters, it moves at a speed between a gallop and a trot.

cantilever cantilevers
NOUN a long beam or bar fixed at only one end and supporting a bridge or other structure at the other end.

canton cantons
NOUN a political and administrative region of a country, especially in Switzerland.

canvas canvases
NOUN **1** Canvas is strong, heavy cloth used for making things such as sails and tents. **2** a piece of canvas on which an artist does a painting.

canvass canvasses canvassing canvassed
VERB **1** If you canvass people or a place, you go round trying to persuade people to vote for a

particular candidate or party in an election. **2** If you canvass opinion, you find out what people think about a particular subject by asking them.

canyon canyons
NOUN a narrow river valley with steep sides.

cap caps capping capped
NOUN **1** a soft, flat hat, often with a peak at the front. **2** the top of a bottle. **3** Caps are small explosives used in toy guns. ▶ VERB **4** To cap something is to cover it with something. **5** If you cap a story or a joke that someone has just told, you tell a better one.

capable
ADJECTIVE **1** able to do something E.G. *a man capable of extreme violence.* **2** skilful or talented E.G. *She was a very capable woman.*
capably ADVERB **capability** NOUN

capacity capacities
Said "kap-pas-sit-tee" NOUN **1** the maximum amount that something can hold or produce E.G. *a seating capacity of eleven thousand.* **2** A person's power or ability to do something E.G. *his capacity for consuming hamburgers.* **3** Someone's position or role E.G. *in his capacity as councillor.*

cape capes
NOUN **1** a short cloak with no sleeves. **2** a large piece of land sticking out into the sea E.G. *the Cape of Good Hope.*

caper capers
NOUN **1** Capers are the flower buds of a spiky Mediterranean shrub, which are pickled and used to flavour food. **2** a light-hearted practical joke E.G.

Jack would have nothing to do with such capers.

capillary capillaries
Said "kap-pill-lar-ree" NOUN Capillaries are very thin blood vessels.

capital capitals
NOUN **1** The capital of a country is the city where the government meets. **2** Capital is the amount of money or property owned or used by a business. **3** Capital is also a sum of money that you save or invest in order to gain interest. **4** A capital or capital letter is a larger letter used at the beginning of a sentence or a name.

capitalism
NOUN Capitalism is an economic and political system where businesses and industries are not owned and run by the government, but by individuals who can make a profit from them.
capitalist ADJECTIVE or NOUN

capitalize capitalizes capitalizing capitalized; also spelt **capitalise**
VERB If you capitalize on a situation, you use it to get an advantage.

capital punishment
NOUN Capital punishment is legally killing someone as a punishment for a crime they have committed.

capitulate capitulates capitulating capitulated
VERB To capitulate is to give in and stop fighting or resisting E.G. *The Finns capitulated in March 1940.*
capitulation NOUN

cappuccino cappuccinos
Said "kap-poot-sheen-oh" NOUN coffee made with frothy milk.

capricious
Said "kap-prish-uss" ADJECTIVE often

a
b
c
d
e
f
g
h
i
j
k
l
m
n
o
p
q
r
s
t
u
v
w
x
y
z

changing unexpectedly E.G. *the capricious English weather*.

Capricorn

NOUN Capricorn is the tenth sign of the zodiac, represented by a goat. People born between December 22nd and January 19th are born under this sign.

📖 from Latin *caper* meaning 'goat' and *cornu* meaning 'horn'

capsize capsizes capsizing capsized

VERB If a boat capsizes, it turns upside down.

capsule capsules

NOUN 1 a small container with medicine inside which you swallow. 2 the part of a spacecraft in which astronauts travel.

📖 from Latin *capsula* meaning 'little box'

captain captains captaining captained

NOUN 1 the officer in charge of a ship or aeroplane. 2 an army officer of the rank immediately above lieutenant. 3 a navy officer of the rank immediately above commander. 4 the leader of a sports team E.G. *captain of the cricket team*. ▶ VERB 5 If you captain a group of people, you are their leader.

caption captions

NOUN a title printed underneath a picture or photograph.

captivate captivates captivating captivated

VERB To captivate someone is to fascinate or attract them so that they cannot take their attention away E.G. *I was captivated by her*.

captivating ADJECTIVE

captive captives

NOUN 1 a person who has been captured and kept prisoner.
▶ ADJECTIVE 2 imprisoned or enclosed E.G. *a captive bird*.

captivity NOUN

captor captors

NOUN someone who has captured a person or animal.

capture captures capturing captured

VERB 1 To capture someone is to take them prisoner. 2 To capture a quality or mood means to succeed in representing or describing it E.G. *capturing the mood of the riots*.
▶ NOUN 3 The capture of someone or something is the capturing of them E.G. *the fifth anniversary of his capture*.

car cars

NOUN 1 a four-wheeled road vehicle with room for a small number of people. 2 a railway carriage used for a particular purpose E.G. *the buffet car*.

carafe carafes

Said "kar-**raf**" NOUN a glass bottle for serving water or wine.

📖 from Arabic *gharrafah* meaning 'vessel for liquid'

caramel caramels

NOUN 1 a chewy sweet made from sugar, butter, and milk. 2 Caramel is burnt sugar used for colouring or flavouring food.

carat carats

NOUN 1 a unit for measuring the weight of diamonds and other precious stones. 2 a unit for measuring the purity of gold.

caravan caravans

NOUN 1 a vehicle pulled by a car in

which people live or spend their holidays. **2** a group of people and animals travelling together, usually across a desert.

📖 from Persian *karwan*

carbohydrate carbohydrates

NOUN (D&T) Carbohydrate is a substance that gives you energy. It is found in foods like sugar and bread.

carbon

NOUN Carbon is a chemical element that is pure in diamonds and also found in coal. All living things contain carbon.

carbon dioxide

NOUN a colourless, odourless gas that humans and animals breathe out. Carbon dioxide is used in industry, for example in making fizzy drinks and in fire extingulshers.

carburettor carburettors

Said "kahr-bur-ret-ter" NOUN the part of the engine in a vehicle in which air and petrol are mixed together.

carcass carcasses; also spelt **carcase**

NOUN the body of a dead animal.

card cards

NOUN **1** a piece of stiff paper or plastic with information or a message on it E.G. *a birthday card*. **2** Cards can mean playing cards E.G. *a poor set of cards with which to play*. **3** When you play cards, you play any game using playing cards. **4** Card is strong, stiff paper.

📖 from Greek *khartēs* meaning 'papyrus leaf'

cardboard

NOUN Cardboard is thick, stiff paper.

cardiac

ADJECTIVE; MEDICAL relating to the heart E.G. *cardiac disease*.

cardigan cardigans

NOUN a knitted jacket that fastens up the front.

cardinal cardinals

NOUN **1** a high-ranking member of the Roman Catholic clergy who chooses and advises the Pope. ▶ ADJECTIVE **2** extremely important E.G. *a cardinal principle of law*.

📖 from Latin *cardo* meaning 'hinge'. When something is important, other things hinge on it

care cares caring cared

VERB **1** If you care about something, you are concerned about it and interested in it. **2** If you care about someone, you feel affection towards them. **3** If you care for someone, you look after them. ▶ NOUN **4** Care is concern or worry. **5** Care of someone or something is treatment for them or looking after them E.G. *the care of the elderly*. **6** If you do something with care, you do it with close attention.

career oaroers careering careered

NOUN **1** the series of jobs that someone has in life, usually in the same occupation E.G. *a career in insurance*. ▶ VERB **2** To career somewhere is to move very quickly, often out of control E.G. *His car careered off the road*.

carefree

ADJECTIVE having no worries or responsibilities.

careful

ADJECTIVE **1** acting sensibly and with care E.G. *Be careful what you say to him*. **2** complete and well done E.G. *It needs very careful planning*.

carefully ADVERB

a
b
c
d
e
f
g
h
i
j
k
l
m
n
o
p
q
r
s
t
u
v
w
x
y
z

On WEDNESday Wayne WED NESta (<u>Wednes</u>day)   SPELLING NOTE

A
B
C
D
E
F
G
H
I
J
K
L
M
N
O
P
Q
R
S
T
U
V
W
X
Y
Z

■ (sense 1) cautious, prudent

careless
ADJECTIVE **1** done badly without enough attention E.G. *careless driving*. **2** relaxed and unconcerned E.G. *careless laughter*.
carelessly ADVERB **carelessness** NOUN
■ (sense 1) slapdash, sloppy

caress caresses caressing caressed
VERB **1** If you caress someone, you stroke them gently and affectionately. ▶ NOUN **2** a gentle, affectionate stroke.
■ (sense 1) fondle, stroke

caretaker caretakers
NOUN **1** a person who looks after a large building such as a school. ▶ ADJECTIVE **2** having an important position for a short time until a new person is appointed E.G. *O'Leary was named caretaker manager*.

cargo cargoes
NOUN the goods carried on a ship or plane.

Caribbean
NOUN The Caribbean consists of the Caribbean Sea east of Central America and the islands in it.

caricature caricatures caricaturing caricatured
NOUN **1** a drawing or description of someone that exaggerates striking parts of their appearance or personality. ▶ VERB **2** To caricature someone is to give a caricature of them.

carjack carjacks carjacking carjacked
VERB If a car is carjacked, its driver is attacked and robbed, or the car is stolen.

carnage
Said "**kahr**-nij" NOUN Carnage is the violent killing of large numbers of people.

carnal
ADJECTIVE; FORMAL sexual and sensual rather than spiritual E.G. *carnal pleasure*.

carnation carnations
NOUN a plant with a long stem and white, pink, or red flowers.

carnival carnivals
NOUN a public festival with music, processions, and dancing.

carnivore carnivores
NOUN an animal that eats meat.
carnivorous ADJECTIVE

carol carols
NOUN a religious song sung at Christmas time.

carousel carousels
Said "kar-ros-**sel**" NOUN a merry-go-round.

carp carps carping carped
NOUN **1** a large edible freshwater fish. ▶ VERB **2** To carp means to complain about unimportant things.

carpel carpels
NOUN the seed-bearing female part of a flower.

carpenter carpenters
NOUN a person who makes and repairs wooden structures.
carpentry NOUN
🏛 from Latin *carpentarius* meaning 'wagon-maker'

carpet carpets carpeting carpeted
NOUN **1** a thick covering for a floor, usually made of a material like wool. ▶ VERB **2** To carpet a floor means to cover it with a carpet.

carriage carriages
NOUN **1** one of the separate sections of a passenger train. **2** an old-fashioned vehicle for carrying passengers, usually pulled by horses. **3** a machine part that moves and supports another part E.G. *a typewriter carriage.* **4** Someone's carriage is the way they hold their head and body when they move.

carriageway carriageways
NOUN one of the sides of a road which traffic travels along in one direction only.

carrier carriers
NOUN **1** a vehicle that is used for carrying things E.G. *a troop carrier.* **2** A carrier of a germ or disease is a person or animal that can pass it on to others.

carrier bag carrier bags
NOUN a bag made of plastic or paper, which is used for carrying shopping.

carrion
NOUN Carrion is the decaying flesh of dead animals.

carrot carrots
NOUN a long, thin orange root vegetable.

carry carries carrying carried
VERB **1** To carry something is to hold it and take it somewhere. **2** When a vehicle carries people, they travel in it. **3** A person or animal that carries a germ can pass it on to other people or animals E.G. *I still carry the disease.* **4** If a sound carries, it can be heard far away E.G. *Jake's voice carried over the cheering.* **5** In a meeting, if a proposal is carried, it is accepted by a majority of the people there.
■ (sense 2) bear, convey, take

carry away VERB If you are carried away, you are so excited by something that you do not behave sensibly.

carry on VERB To carry on doing something means to continue doing it.

carry out VERB To carry something out means to do it and complete it E.G. *The conversion was carried out by a local builder.*

cart carts
NOUN a vehicle with wheels, used to carry goods and often pulled by horses or cattle.

cartilage
NOUN Cartilage is a strong, flexible substance found around the joints and in the nose and ears.

carton cartons
NOUN a cardboard or plastic container.

cartoon cartoons
NOUN **1** a drawing or a series of drawings which are funny or make a point. **2** a film in which the characters and scenes are drawn.
cartoonist NOUN
▥ from Italian *cartone* meaning 'sketch on stiff paper'

cartridge cartridges
NOUN **1** a tube containing a bullet and an explosive substance, used in guns. **2** a thin plastic tube containing ink that you put in a pen. **3** (ICT) a container for ink that you insert into a printer.

cartwheel cartwheels
NOUN an acrobatic movement in which you throw yourself sideways onto one hand and move round in a circle with arms and legs stretched until you land on your feet again.

carve carves carving carved
VERB **1** To carve an object means to

a
b
c
d
e
f
g
h
i
j
k
l
m
n
o
p
q
r
s
t
u
v
w
x
y
z

cut it out of a substance such as stone or wood. **2** To carve meat means to cut slices from it.

carving carvings
NOUN a carved object.

cascade cascades cascading cascaded
NOUN **1** a waterfall or group of waterfalls. ► VERB **2** To cascade means to flow downwards quickly E.G. *Gallons of water cascaded from the attic.*

case cases
NOUN **1** a particular situation, event, or example E.G. *a clear case of mistaken identity.* **2** a container for something, or a suitcase E.G. *a camera case.* **3** Doctors sometimes refer to a patient as a case. **4** Police detectives refer to a crime they are investigating as a case. **5** In an argument, the case for an idea is the reasons used to support it. **6** In law, a case is a trial or other inquiry. **7** In grammar, the case of a noun or pronoun is the form of it which shows its relationship with other words in a sentence E.G. *the accusative case.* ► PHRASE **8** You say **in case** to explain something that you do because a particular thing might happen E.G. *I didn't want to shout in case I startled you.* **9** You say **in that case** to show that you are assuming something said before is true E.G. *In that case we won't do it.*
■ (sense 1) instance, circumstance(s), situation

casement casements
NOUN a window that opens on hinges at one side.

cash cashes cashing cashed
NOUN **1** Cash is money in notes and coins rather than cheques. ► VERB **2** If you cash a cheque, you take it to a bank and exchange it for money.
🔒 from Italian *cassa* meaning 'money-box'

cashew cashews
Said "kash-oo" NOUN a curved, edible nut.

cash flow
NOUN Cash flow is the money that a business makes and spends.

cashier cashiers
NOUN the person that customers pay in a shop or get money from in a bank.

cashmere
NOUN Cashmere is very soft, fine wool from goats.

cash register cash registers
NOUN a machine in a shop which records sales, and where the money is kept.

casing casings
NOUN a protective covering for something.

casino casinos
Said "kass-ee-noh" NOUN a place where people go to play gambling games.

cask casks
NOUN a wooden barrel.
🔒 from Spanish *casco* meaning 'helmet'

casket caskets
NOUN a small box for jewellery or other valuables.
🔒 from Old French *cassette* meaning 'little box'

casserole casseroles
NOUN a dish made by cooking a mixture of meat and vegetables slowly in an oven; also used to refer to the pot a casserole is cooked in.

🔲 from Old French *casse* meaning 'ladle' or 'dripping pan'

cassette cassettes
NOUN a small flat container with magnetic tape inside, which is used for recording and playing back sounds.

cassette recorder cassette recorders
NOUN a machine used for recording and playing cassettes.

cassock cassocks
NOUN a long robe that is worn by some members of the clergy.

cassowary cassowaries
NOUN a large bird found in Australia with black feathers and a brightly coloured neck. Cassowaries cannot fly.

cast casts casting cast
NOUN 1 all the people who act in a play or film. 2 an object made by pouring liquid into a mould and leaving it to harden E.G. *the casts of classical sculptures.* 3 a stiff plaster covering put on broken bones to keep them still so that they heal properly. ▶ VERB 4 To cast actors is to choose them for roles in a play or film. 5 When people cast their votes in an election, they vote. 6 To cast something is to throw it. 7 If you cast your eyes somewhere, you look there E.G. *I cast my eyes down briefly.* 8 To cast an object is to make it by pouring liquid into a mould and leaving it to harden E.G. *An image of him has been cast in bronze.*

cast off VERB If you cast off, you untie the rope fastening a boat to a harbour or shore.

castanets
PLURAL NOUN Castanets are a Spanish musical instrument consisting of two

small round pieces of wood that are clicked together with the fingers.
🔲 from Spanish *castañetas* meaning 'little chestnuts'

castaway castaways
NOUN a person who has been shipwrecked.

caste castes
NOUN 1 one of the four classes into which Hindu society is divided.
2 Caste is a system of social classes decided according to family, wealth, and position.
🔲 from Portuguese *casto* meaning 'pure'

caster sugar or **castor sugar**
NOUN Caster sugar is very fine white sugar used in cooking.

castigate castigates castigating castigated
VERB; FORMAL To castigate someone is to criticize them severely.

cast iron
NOUN 1 Cast iron is iron which is made into objects by casting. ▶ ADJECTIVE 2 A cast-iron excuse or guarantee is absolutely certain and firm.

castle castles
NOUN 1 (HISTORY) a large building with walls or ditches round it to protect it from attack. 2 In chess, a castle is the same as a rook.

cast-off cast-offs
NOUN a piece of outgrown or discarded clothing that has been passed on to someone else.

castor castors; also spelt **caster**
NOUN a small wheel fitted to furniture so that it can be moved easily.

castor oil
NOUN Castor oil is a thick oil that comes from the seeds of the castor oil plant. It is used as a laxative.

castrate castrates castrating castrated

VERB To castrate a male animal is to remove its testicles so that it can no longer produce sperm.

castration NOUN

casual

ADJECTIVE 1 happening by chance without planning E.G. *a casual remark*. 2 careless or without interest E.G. *a casual glance over his shoulder*. 3 Casual clothes are suitable for informal occasions. 4 Casual work is not regular or permanent.

casually ADVERB   **casualness** NOUN

■ (sense 2) careless, nonchalant, offhand

casualty casualties

NOUN a person killed or injured in an accident or war E.G. *Many of the casualties were office workers*.

casuarina casuarinas

Said "kass-you-a-**rine**-a" NOUN an Australian tree with jointed green branches.

cat cats

NOUN 1 a small furry animal with whiskers, a tail and sharp claws, often kept as a pet. 2 any of the family of mammals that includes lions and tigers.

🏛 from Latin *cattus*

catacomb catacombs

Said "**kat**-a-koom" NOUN Catacombs are underground passages where dead bodies are buried.

🏛 from Latin *catacumbas*, an underground cemetery near Rome

catalogue catalogues cataloguing catalogued

NOUN 1 a book containing pictures and descriptions of goods that you can buy in a shop or through the post. 2 (LIBRARY) a list of things such as the objects in a museum or the books in a library. ▶ VERB 3 To catalogue a collection of things means to list them in a catalogue.

catalyst catalysts

Said "**kat**-a-list" NOUN 1 something that causes a change to happen E.G. *the catalyst which provoked civil war*. 2 a substance that speeds up a chemical reaction without changing itself.

catamaran catamarans

NOUN a sailing boat with two hulls connected to each other.

🏛 from Tamil *kattumaram* meaning 'tied logs'

catapult catapults catapulting catapulted

NOUN 1 a Y-shaped object with a piece of elastic tied between the two top ends used for shooting small stones. ▶ VERB 2 To catapult something is to throw it violently through the air. 3 If someone is catapulted into a situation, they find themselves unexpectedly in that situation E.G. *Tony has been catapulted into the limelight*.

cataract cataracts

NOUN 1 an area of the lens of someone's eye that has become white instead of clear, so that they cannot see properly. 2 a large waterfall.

catarrh

Said "kat-**tahr**" NOUN Catarrh is a condition in which you get a lot of mucus in your nose and throat.

catastrophe catastrophes

Said "kat-**tass**-trif-fee" NOUN a terrible disaster.

catastrophic ADJECTIVE

catch catches catching caught
VERB 1 If you catch a ball moving in the air, you grasp hold of it when it comes near you. 2 To catch an animal means to trap it E.G. *I caught ten fish*. 3 When the police catch criminals, they find them and arrest them. 4 If you catch someone doing something they should not be doing, you discover them doing it E.G. *He caught me playing the church organ*. 5 If you catch a bus or train, you get on it and travel somewhere. 6 If you catch a cold or a disease, you become infected with it. 7 If something catches on an object, it sticks to it or gets trapped E.G. *The white fibres caught on the mesh*.
▶ NOUN 8 a hook that fastens or locks a door or window. 9 a problem or hidden complication in something.
▤ (sense 2) capture, snare, trap
▤ (sense 3) apprehend, arrest, capture
▤ (sense 6) contract, develop, go down with

catch on VERB 1 If you catch on to something, you understand it. 2 If something catches on, it becomes popular E.G. *This drink has never really caught on in New Zealand*.

catch out VERB To catch someone out is to trick them or trap them.

catch up VERB 1 To catch up with someone in front of you is to reach the place where they are by moving slightly faster than them. 2 To catch up with someone is also to reach the same level or standard as them.

catching
ADJECTIVE tending to spread very quickly E.G. *Measles is catching*.

catchy catchier catchiest
ADJECTIVE attractive and easily

remembered E.G. *a catchy little tune*.

catechism catechisms
Said "**kat**-ik-kizm" NOUN a set of questions and answers about the main beliefs of a religion.

categorical
ADJECTIVE absolutely certain and direct E.G. *a categorical denial*.
categorically ADVERB

categorize categorizes categorizing categorized; also spelt **categorise**
VERB To categorize things is to arrange them in different categories.

category categories
NOUN a set of things with a particular characteristic in common E.G. *Occupations can be divided into four categories*.

cater caters catering catored
VERB To cater for people is to provide them with what they need, especially food.

caterer caterers
NOUN a person or business that provides food for parties and groups.

caterpillar caterpillars
NOUN the larva of a butterfly or moth. It looks like a small coloured worm and feeds on plants.
▥ from Old French *catepelose* meaning 'hairy cat'

catharsis catharses
Said "**kath**-ar-siss" NOUN; FORMAL Catharsis is the release of strong emotions and feelings by expressing them through drama or literature.
▥ from Greek *kathairein* meaning 'to purge' or 'to purify'

cathedral cathedrals
NOUN (HISTORY) an important church with a bishop in charge of it.

a
b
c
d
e
f
g
h
i
j
k
l
m
n
o
p
q
r
s
t
u
v
w
x
y
z

A
B
C
D
E
F
G
H
I
J
K
L
M
N
O
P
Q
R
S
T
U
V
W
X
Y
Z

Catholic Catholics
NOUN or ADJECTIVE 1 (HISTORY) a Roman Catholic. ▶ ADJECTIVE 2 If a person has catholic interests, they have a wide range of interests.

Catholicism NOUN
📖 from Greek *katholikos* meaning 'universal'
✅ When *Catholic* begins with a capital letter, it refers to the religion. When it begins with a small letter, it means 'covering a wide range'.

cattle
PLURAL NOUN Cattle are cows and bulls kept by farmers.

catty cattier cattiest
ADJECTIVE unpleasant and spiteful.
cattiness NOUN

catwalk catwalks
NOUN a narrow pathway that people walk along, for example over a stage.

Caucasian Caucasians
Said "kaw-**kayz**-yn" NOUN a person belonging to the race of people with fair or light-brown skin.
📖 from *Caucasia*, a region in the former USSR

caught
the past tense and past participle of catch.

cauldron cauldrons
NOUN a large, round metal cooking pot, especially one that sits over a fire.

cauliflower cauliflowers
NOUN a large, round, white vegetable surrounded by green leaves.

cause causes causing caused
NOUN 1 The cause of something is the thing that makes it happen E.G. *the most common cause of back pain*.
2 an aim or principle which a group of people are working for E.G. *dedication to the cause of peace*. 3 If

you have cause for something, you have a reason for it E.G. *They gave us no cause to believe that*. ▶ VERB 4 To cause something is to make it happen E.G. *This can cause delays*.
causal ADJECTIVE

causeway causeways
NOUN a raised path or road across water or marshland.
📖 from Latin *calciatus* meaning 'paved with limestone'

caustic
ADJECTIVE 1 A caustic chemical can destroy substances E.G. *caustic liquids such as acids*. 2 bitter or sarcastic E.G. *your caustic sense of humour*.

caution cautions cautioning cautioned
NOUN 1 Caution is great care which you take to avoid danger E.G. *You will need to proceed with caution*. 2 a warning E.G. *Sutton was let off with a caution*. ▶ VERB 3 If someone cautions you, they warn you, usually not to do something again E.G. *A man has been cautioned by police*.
cautionary ADJECTIVE

cautious
ADJECTIVE acting very carefully to avoid danger E.G. *a cautious approach*.
cautiously ADVERB

cavalcade cavalcades
NOUN a procession of people on horses or in cars or carriages.

cavalier
Said "kav-val-**eer**" ADJECTIVE arrogant and behaving without sensitivity E.G. *a cavalier attitude to women*.

cavalry
NOUN The cavalry is the part of an army that uses armoured vehicles or horses.

cave caves caving caved
NOUN **1** a large hole in rock, that is underground or in the side of a cliff.
▶ VERB **2** If a roof caves in, it collapses inwards.

caveman cavemen
NOUN Cavemen were people who lived in caves in prehistoric times.

cavern caverns
NOUN a large cave.

cavernous
ADJECTIVE large, deep, and hollow E.G. *a cavernous warehouse*.

caviar or **caviare**
Said "kav-vee-ar" NOUN Caviar is the tiny salted eggs of a fish called the sturgeon.

cavity cavities
NOUN a small hole in something solid E.G. *There were dark cavities in his back teeth.*

cavort cavorts cavorting cavorted
VERB When people cavort, they jump around excitedly.

caw caws cawing cawed
VERB When a crow or rook caws, it makes a harsh sound.

cc
an abbreviation for 'cubic centimetres'.

CD
an abbreviation for 'compact disc'.

CD-ROM
(ICT) CD-ROM is a method of storing video, sound, or text on a compact disc which can be played on a computer using a laser. CD-ROM is an abbreviation for 'Compact Disc Read-Only Memory'.

cease ceases ceasing ceased
VERB **1** If something ceases, it stops happening. **2** If you cease to do something, or cease doing it, you stop doing it.

cease-fire cease-fires
NOUN an agreement between groups that are fighting each other to stop for a period and discuss peace.

ceaseless
ADJECTIVE going on without stopping E.G. *the ceaseless movement of the streets.*

ceaselessly ADVERB

cedar cedars
NOUN a large evergreen tree with wide branches and needle-shaped leaves.

cede cedes ceding ceded
Said "seed" VERB To cede something is to give it up to someone else E.G. *Haiti was ceded to France in 1697.*

ceiling ceilings
NOUN the top inside surface of a room.

celebrate celebrates celebrating celebrated
VERB **1** If you celebrate or celebrate something, you do something special and enjoyable because of it E.G. *a party to celebrate the end of the exams.* **2** (RE) When a priest celebrates Mass, he performs the ceremonies of the Mass.

celebration NOUN **celebratory** ADJECTIVE

celebrated
ADJECTIVE famous E.G. *the celebrated Italian mountaineer.*

celebrity celebrities
NOUN a famous person.

celery
NOUN Celery is a vegetable with long pale green stalks.

celestial
Said "sil-lest-yal" ADJECTIVE; FORMAL

Beautiful Elephants Are Usually Tiny (<u>beau</u>tiful)   **SPELLING NOTE**

A
B
C
D
E
F
G
H
I
J
K
L
M
N
O
P
Q
R
S
T
U
V
W
X
Y
Z

concerning the sky or heaven E.G. *The telescope is pointed at a celestial object.*

celibate
Said "**sel**-lib-bit" ADJECTIVE Someone who is celibate does not marry or have sex.
celibacy NOUN

cell cells
NOUN 1 In biology, a cell is the smallest part of an animal or plant that can exist by itself. Each cell contains a nucleus. 2 a small room where a prisoner is kept in a prison or police station. 3 a small group of people set up to work together as part of a larger organization.

cellar cellars
NOUN a room underneath a building, often used to store wine.

cello cellos
Said "**chel**-loh" NOUN a large musical stringed instrument which you play sitting down, holding the instrument upright with your knees.
cellist NOUN

Cellophane
NOUN; TRADEMARK Cellophane is thin, transparent plastic material used to wrap food or other things to protect them.

cellular
ADJECTIVE Cellular means relating to the cells of animals or plants.

celluloid
Said "**sel**-yul-loyd" NOUN Celluloid is a type of plastic which was once used to make photographic film.

Celsius
Said "**sel**-see-yuss" NOUN Celsius is a scale for measuring temperature in which water freezes at 0 degrees (0°C) and boils at 100 degrees (100°C). Celsius is the same as 'Centigrade'.

Celtic
Said "**kel**-tik" ADJECTIVE A Celtic language is one of a group of languages that includes Gaelic and Welsh.

cement cements cementing cemented
NOUN 1 Cement is a fine powder made from limestone and clay, which is mixed with sand and water to make concrete. ▶ VERB 2 To cement things is to stick them together with cement or cover them with cement.
3 Something that cements a relationship makes it stronger E.G. *to cement relations between them.*

cemetery cemeteries
NOUN an area of land where dead people are buried.

cenotaph cenotaphs
Said "**sen**-not-ahf" NOUN a monument built in memory of dead people, especially soldiers buried elsewhere.
📖 from Greek *kenos* + *taphos* meaning 'empty tomb'

censor censors censoring censored
NOUN 1 a person officially appointed to examine books or films and to ban parts that are considered unsuitable. ▶ VERB 2 If someone censors a book or film, they cut or ban parts of it that are considered unsuitable for the public.
censorship NOUN

censure censures censuring censured
Said "**sen**-sher" NOUN 1 Censure is strong disapproval of something. ▶ VERB 2 To censure someone is to criticize them severely.

SPELLING NOTE Betty Eats Cakes And Uses Seven Eggs (be<u>cause</u>)

census censuses
NOUN an official survey of the population of a country.

cent cents
NOUN a unit of currency. In the USA, a cent is worth one hundredth of a dollar; in Europe, it is worth one hundredth of a Euro.

centaur centaurs
Said "**sen**-tawr" NOUN a creature in Greek mythology with the top half of a man and the lower body and legs of a horse.

centenary centenaries
Said "sen-**teen**-er-ee" NOUN the 100th anniversary of something.

centi-
PREFIX 'Centi ' is used to form words that have 'hundred' as part of their meaning E.G. *centimetre*.
from Latin *centum* meaning 'hundred'

Centigrade
Centigrade is another name for **Celsius**.
☑ Scientists say and write *Celsius* rather than *Centigrade*.

centilitre centilitres
NOUN a unit of liquid volume equal to one hundredth of a litre.

centime centimes
Said "**sonn**-team" NOUN a unit of currency used in Switzerland and some other countries, and formerly used in France and Belgium.

centimetre centimetres
NOUN (MATHS) a unit of length equal to ten millimetres or one hundredth of a metre.

centipede centipedes
NOUN a long, thin insect-like creature with many pairs of legs.

central
ADJECTIVE 1 in or near the centre of an object or area E.G. *central ceiling lights*. 2 main or most important E.G. *the central idea of this work*.
centrally ADVERB **centrality** NOUN

Central America
NOUN Central America is another name for the Isthmus of Panama, the area of land joining North America to South America.

central heating
NOUN Central heating is a system of heating a building in which water or air is heated in a tank and travels through pipes and radiators round the building.

centralize centralizes centralizing centralized; also spelt **centralise**
VERB To centralize a system is to bring the organization of it under the control of one central group.
centralization NOUN

centre centres centring centred
NOUN 1 the middle of an object or area. 2 a building where people go for activities, meetings, or help E.G. *a health centre*. 3 Someone or something that is the centre of attention attracts a lot of attention.
▶ VERB 4 To centre something is to move it so that it is balanced or at the centre of something else. 5 If something centres on or around a particular thing, that thing is the main subject of attention E.G. *The discussion centred on his request*.
▤ (sense 1) heart, middle

centrifugal
Said "sen-**trif**-**yoo**-gl" ADJECTIVE In physics, centrifugal force is the force

a
b
c
d
e
f
g
h
i
j
k
l
m
n
o
p
q
r
s
t
u
v
w
x
y
z

A
B
C
D
E
F
G
H
I
J
K
L
M
N
O
P
Q
R
S
T
U
V
W
X
Y
Z

that makes rotating objects move outwards.

📷 from Latin *centrum* + *fugere* meaning 'to flee from the centre'

centripetal

Said "sen-**trip**-pe-tl" ADJECTIVE In physics, centripetal force is the force that makes rotating objects move inwards.

📷 from Latin *centrum* + *petere* meaning 'to seek the centre'

centurion centurions

NOUN a Roman officer in charge of a hundred soldiers.

century centuries

NOUN 1 a period of one hundred years. 2 In cricket, a century is one hundred runs scored by a batsman.

ceramic ceramics

Said "sir-**ram**-mik" NOUN 1 Ceramic is a hard material made by baking clay to a very high temperature. 2 Ceramics is the art of making objects out of clay.

cereal cereals

NOUN 1 a food made from grain, often eaten with milk for breakfast. 2 a plant that produces edible grain, such as wheat or oats.

📷 from Latin *cerealis* meaning 'concerning the growing of grain'

cerebral

Said "**ser**-reb-ral" ADJECTIVE; FORMAL relating to the brain E.G. *a cerebral haemorrhage.*

cerebral palsy

NOUN Cerebral palsy is an illness caused by damage to a baby's brain, which makes its muscles and limbs very weak.

ceremonial

ADJECTIVE relating to a E.G. *ceremonial dress.*

ceremonially ADVERB

ceremony ceremonies

NOUN 1 (RE) a set of formal actions performed at a special occasion or important public event E.G. *his recent coronation ceremony.*
2 Ceremony is very formal and polite behaviour E.G. *He hung up without ceremony.*

certain

ADJECTIVE 1 definite and with no doubt at all E.G. *He is certain to be in Italy.*
2 You use 'certain' to refer to a specific person or thing E.G. *certain aspects of the job.* 3 You use 'certain' to suggest that a quality is noticeable but not obvious E.G. *There's a certain resemblance to Joe.*

certainly

ADVERB 1 without doubt E.G. *My boss was certainly interested.* 2 of course E.G. *'Will you be there?' – 'Certainly'.*

certainty certainties

NOUN 1 Certainty is the state of being certain. 2 something that is known without doubt E.G. *There are no certainties and no guarantees.*

certificate certificates

NOUN a document stating particular facts, for example of someone's birth or death E.G. *a marriage certificate.*

certify certifies certifying certified

VERB 1 To certify something means to declare formally that it is true E.G. *certifying the cause of death.* 2 To certify someone means to declare officially that they are insane.

cervix cervixes or **cervices**

NOUN; TECHNICAL the entrance to the womb at the top of the vagina.

cervical ADJECTIVE

cessation

NOUN; FORMAL The cessation of

SPELLING NOTE you'll brEAK that Electrical Aerial, Kitty (br**eak**) something is the stopping of it E.G. *a swift cessation of hostilities.*

cf.
cf. means 'compare'. It is written after something in a text to mention something else which the the reader should compare with what has just been written.

CFC CFCs
NOUN CFCs are manufactured chemicals that are used in aerosol sprays. They damage the ozone layer. CFC is an abbreviation for 'chlorofluorocarbon'.

chaff
NOUN Chaff is the outer parts of grain separated from the seeds by beating.

chaffinch chaffinches
NOUN a small European bird with black and white wings.

chagrin
Said "shag-rin" NOUN; FORMAL Chagrin is a feeling of annoyance or disappointment.

chain chains chaining chained
NOUN 1 a number of metal rings connected together in a line E.G. *a bicycle chain.* 2 a number of things in a series or connected to each other E.G. *a chain of shops.* ▸ VERB 3 If you chain one thing to another, you fasten them together with a chain E.G. *They had chained themselves to railings.*

chain saw chain saws
NOUN a large saw with teeth fixed in a chain that is driven round by a motor.

chain-smoke chain-smokes chain-smoking chain-smoked
VERB To chain-smoke is to smoke cigarettes continually.

chair chairs chairing chaired
NOUN 1 a seat with a back and four legs for one person. 2 the person in charge of a meeting who decides when each person may speak. ▸ VERB 3 The person who chairs a meeting is in charge of it.

chair lift chair lifts
NOUN a line of chairs that hang from a moving cable and carry people up and down a mountain.

chairman chairmen
NOUN 1 the person in charge of a meeting who decides when each person may speak. 2 the head of a company or committee.

chairperson NOUN   **chairwoman**
NOUN   **chairmanship** NOUN
☑ Some people don't like to use *chairman* when talking about a woman. You can use *chair* or *chairperson* to talk about a man or a woman.

chalet chalets
Said "shall-lay" NOUN a wooden house with a sloping roof, especially in a mountain area or a holiday camp.

chalice chalices
Said "chal-liss" NOUN a gold or silver cup used in churches to hold the Communion wine.

chalk chalks chalking chalked
NOUN 1 Chalk is a soft white rock. Small sticks of chalk are used for writing or drawing on a blackboard. ▸ VERB 2 To chalk up a result is to achieve it E.G. *He chalked up his first win.*

chalky ADJECTIVE

challenge challenges challenging challenged
NOUN 1 something that is new and exciting but requires a lot of effort E.G. *It's a new challenge at the right*

a
b
c
d
e
f
g
h
i
j
k
l
m
n
o
p
q
r
s
t
u
v
w
x
y
z

time in my career. 2 a suggestion from someone to compete with them. 3 A challenge to something is a questioning of whether it is correct or true E.G. *a challenge to authority.* ▶ VERB 4 If someone challenges you, they suggest that you compete with them in some way. 5 If you challenge something, you question whether it is correct or true.

challenger NOUN **challenging** ADJECTIVE

■ (sense 5) dispute, question

chamber chambers
NOUN 1 a large room, especially one used for formal meetings E.G. *the Council Chamber.* 2 a group of people chosen to decide laws or administrative matters. 3 a hollow place or compartment inside something, especially inside an animal's body or inside a gun E.G. *the chambers of the heart.*

chambermaid chambermaids
NOUN a woman who cleans and tidies rooms in a hotel.

chameleon chameleons
Said "kam-mee-lee-on" NOUN a lizard which is able to change the colour of its skin to match the colour of its surroundings.

⬛ from Greek *khamai + leōn* meaning 'ground lion'

chamois leather chamois leathers
Said "sham-mee" NOUN a soft leather cloth used for polishing.

champagne champagnes
Said "sham-pain" NOUN Champagne is a sparkling white wine made in France.

champion champions
championing championed

NOUN 1 a person who wins a competition. 2 someone who supports or defends a cause or principle E.G. *a champion of women's causes.* ▶ VERB 3 Someone who champions a cause or principle supports or defends it.

⬛ from Latin *campus* meaning 'battlefield'

championship championships
NOUN a competition to find the champion of a sport.

chance chances chancing chanced
NOUN 1 The chance of something happening is how possible or likely it is E.G. *There's a chance of rain later.* 2 an opportunity to do something E.G. *Your chance to be a TV star!* 3 a possibility that something dangerous or unpleasant may happen E.G. *Don't take chances, he's armed.* 4 Chance is also the way things happen unexpectedly without being planned E.G. *I only found out by chance.* ▶ VERB 5 If you chance something, you try it although you are taking a risk.

■ (sense 4) accident, coincidence, luck

chancellor chancellors
NOUN 1 the head of government in some European countries. 2 In Britain, the Chancellor is the Chancellor of the Exchequer. 3 the honorary head of a university.

Chancellor of the Exchequer
NOUN In Britain, the minister responsible for finance and taxes.

chandelier chandeliers
Said "shan-del-leer" NOUN an ornamental light fitting which hangs from the ceiling.

A B C D E F G H I J K L M N O P Q R S T U V W X Y Z

change changes changing changed

NOUN **1** a difference or alteration in something E.G. *Steven soon noticed a change in Penny's attitude.* **2** a replacement of something by something else E.G. *a change of clothes.* **3** Change is money you get back when you have paid more than the actual price of something. ▶ VERB **4** When something changes or when you change it, it becomes different E.G. *It changed my life.* **5** If you change something, you exchange it for something else. **6** When you change, you put on different clothes. **7** To change money means to exchange it for smaller coins of the same total value, or to exchange it for foreign currency.

changeable

ADJECTIVE likely to change all the time. ■ erratic, Inconstant, variable

changeover changeovers

NOUN a change from one system or activity to another E.G. *the changeover between day and night.*

channel channels channelling channelled

NOUN **1** a wavelength used to receive programmes broadcast by a television or radio station; also the station itself E.G. *I was watching the other channel.* **2** a passage along which water flows or along which something is carried. **3** The Channel or the English Channel is the stretch of sea between England and France. **4** a method of achieving something E.G. *We have tried to do things through the right channels.* ▶ VERB **5** To channel something such as money or energy means to direct it in a particular way E.G. *Their efforts are being channelled into worthy causes.*

chant chants chanting chanted

NOUN **1** a group of words repeated over and over again E.G. *a rousing chant.* **2** a religious song sung on only a few notes. ▶ VERB **3** If people chant a group of words, they repeat them over and over again E.G. *Crowds chanted his name.*

Chanukah

another spelling of **Hanukkah**.

chaos

Said "kay-oss" NOUN Chaos is a state of complete disorder and confusion.
chaotic ADJECTIVE

chap chaps chapping chapped

NOUN **1** INFORMAL a man. ▶ VERB **2** If your skin chaps, it becomes dry and cracked, usually as a result of cold or wind.

chapel chapels

NOUN **1** a section of a church or cathedral with its own altar. **2** a type of small church.
🏛 from Latin *capella* meaning 'small cloak'; originally used of the place where St Martin's cloak was kept as a relic

chaperone chaperones

Said "shap-per-rone"; also spelt **chaperon**
NOUN an older woman who accompanies a young single woman on social occasions, or any person who accompanies a group of younger people.

chaplain chaplains

NOUN a member of the Christian clergy who regularly works in a hospital, school, or prison.
chaplaincy NOUN

chapter chapters

NOUN **1** one of the parts into which a

The government licenSes Schnapps (licenꟻes) ▸ SPELLING NOTE

A
B
C
D
E
F
G
H
I
J
K
L
M
N
O
P
Q
R
S
T
U
V
W
X
Y
Z

book is divided. 2 a particular period in someone's life or in history.

char chars charring charred
VERB If something chars, it gets partly burned and goes black.
charred ADJECTIVE

character characters
NOUN 1 all the qualities which combine to form the personality or atmosphere of a person or place. 2 A person or place that has character has an interesting, attractive, or admirable quality E.G. *an inn of great character and simplicity.* 3 (DRAMA) The characters in a film, play, or book are the people in it. 4 a person E.G. *an odd character.* 5 a letter, number, or other written symbol.
■ (sense 1) nature, personality, quality

characteristic characteristics
NOUN 1 (DRAMA) a quality that is typical of a particular person or thing E.G. *Silence is the characteristic of the place.* ▶ ADJECTIVE 2 Characteristic means typical of a particular person or thing E.G. *Two things are very characteristic of his driving.*
characteristically ADVERB

characterize characterizes characterizing characterized; also spelt **characterise**
VERB A quality that characterizes something is typical of it E.G. *a condition characterized by muscle stiffness.*

characterless
ADJECTIVE without atmosphere or any interesting qualities E.G. *a tiny characterless flat.*

charade charades
Said "shar-**rahd**" NOUN a ridiculous

and unnecessary activity or pretence.
🔲 from Provençal *charrado* meaning 'chat'

charcoal
NOUN (ART) Charcoal is a black form of carbon made by burning wood without air, used as a fuel and also for drawing.

charge charges charging charged
VERB 1 If someone charges you money, they ask you to pay it for something you have bought or received E.G. *The company charged 150 pounds on each loan.* 2 To charge someone means to accuse them formally of having committed a crime. 3 To charge a battery means to pass an electrical current through it to make it store electricity. 4 To charge somewhere means to rush forward, often to attack someone E.G. *The rhino charged at her.* ▶ NOUN 5 the price that you have to pay for something. 6 a formal accusation that a person is guilty of a crime and has to go to court. 7 To have charge or be in charge of someone or something means to be responsible for them and be in control of them. 8 an explosive put in a gun or other weapon. 9 An electrical charge is the amount of electricity that something carries.

charger chargers
NOUN a device for charging or recharging batteries.

chariot chariots
NOUN a two-wheeled open vehicle pulled by horses.

charisma
Said "kar-**riz**-ma" NOUN Charisma is a

special ability to attract or influence people by your personality.
charismatic ADJECTIVE

charity charities
NOUN 1 an organization that raises money to help people who are ill, poor, or disabled. 2 Charity is money or other help given to poor, disabled, or ill people E.G. *to help raise money for charity*. 3 Charity is also a kind, sympathetic attitude towards people.
charitable ADJECTIVE

charlatan charlatans
Said "shar-lat-tn" NOUN someone who pretends to have skill or knowledge that they do not really have.

charm charms charming charmed
NOUN 1 Charm is an attractive and pleasing quality that some people and things have E.G. *a man of great personal charm*. 2 a small ornament worn on a bracelet. 3 a magical spell or an object that is supposed to bring good luck. ➤ VERB 4 If you charm someone, you use your charm to please them.

charmer charmers
NOUN someone who uses their charm to influence people.

charming
ADJECTIVE very pleasant and attractive E.G. *a rather charming man*.
charmingly ADVERB

chart charts charting charted
NOUN 1 a diagram or table showing information E.G. *He noted the score on his chart*. 2 a map of the sea or stars. ➤ VERB 3 If you chart something, you observe and record it carefully.

charter charters chartering

chartered
NOUN 1 a document stating the rights or aims of a group or organization, often written by the government E.G. *the new charter for commuters*. ➤ VERB 2 To charter transport such as a plane or boat is to hire it for private use.
chartered ADJECTIVE

chase chases chasing chased
VERB 1 If you chase someone or something, you run or go after them in order to catch them or drive them away. ➤ NOUN 2 the activity of chasing or hunting someone or something E.G. *a high-speed car chase*.
■ (sense 1) hunt, pursue

chasm chasms
Said "kazm" NOUN 1 a deep crack in the earth's surface. 2 a very large difference between two ideas or groups of people E.G. *the chasm between rich and poor in America*.

chassis chassis
Said "shas-ee" NOUN the frame on which a vehicle is built.
☑ The plural of *chassis* is also *chassis*.

chaste
Said "chayst" ADJECTIVE OLD-FASHIONED not having sex with anyone outside marriage.
chastity NOUN

chastise chastises chastising chastised
VERB; FORMAL If someone chastises you, they criticize you or punish you for something that you have done.

chat chats chatting chatted
NOUN 1 a friendly talk with someone, usually about things that are not very important. ➤ VERB 2 When people chat, they talk to each other in a friendly way.

Plaice the fish has a glittering 'EYE' (I) (plaice) **SPELLING NOTE**

■ (senses 1 & 2) gossip, natter, talk

chat up VERB; INFORMAL If you chat up someone, you talk to them in a friendly way, because you are attracted to them.

chateau chateaux
Said "shat-toe" NOUN a large country house or castle in France.

chatter chatters chattering chattered
VERB 1 When people chatter, they talk very fast. 2 If your teeth are chattering, they are knocking together and making a clicking noise because you are cold. ► NOUN 3 Chatter is a lot of fast unimportant talk.

chatty chattier chattiest
ADJECTIVE talkative and friendly.

chauffeur chauffeurs
Said "show-fur" NOUN a person whose job is to drive another person's car.

chauvinist chauvinists NOUN 1 a person who thinks their country is always right. 2 A male chauvinist is a man who believes that men are superior to women.
chauvinistic ADJECTIVE **chauvinism** NOUN

cheap cheaper cheapest
ADJECTIVE 1 Something that is cheap costs very little money, and is sometimes of poor quality. 2 A cheap joke or cheap remark is unfair and unkind.
cheaply ADVERB
■ (sense 1) inexpensive, reasonable

cheat cheats cheating cheated
VERB 1 If someone cheats, they do wrong or unfair things to win or get something that they want. 2 If you are cheated of or out of something, you do not get what you are entitled

to. ► NOUN 3 a person who cheats.
■ (sense 1) con, deceive, swindle

check checks checking checked
VERB 1 To check something is to examine it in order to make sure that everything is all right. 2 To check the growth or spread of something is to make it stop E.G. *a policy to check fast population growth.* ► NOUN 3 an inspection to make sure that everything is all right. 4 Checks are different coloured squares which form a pattern. ► PHRASE 5 If you keep something **in check**, you keep it under control E.G. *She kept her emotions in check.* ► ADJECTIVE 6 Check or checked means marked with a pattern of squares E.G. *check design.*

check out VERB If you check something out, you inspect it and find out whether everything about it is right.

checkmate
NOUN In chess, checkmate is a situation where one player cannot stop their king being captured and so loses the game.
📖 from Arabic *shah mat* meaning 'the King is dead'

checkout checkouts
NOUN a counter in a supermarket where the customers pay for their goods.

checkpoint checkpoints
NOUN a place where traffic has to stop in order to be checked.

checkup checkups
NOUN an examination by a doctor to see if you are healthy.

cheek cheeks
NOUN 1 Your cheeks are the sides of your face below your eyes. 2 Cheek is speech or behaviour that is rude or

disrespectful E.G. *an expression of sheer cheek.*
■ (sense 2) impertinence, impudence, insolence

cheeky cheekier cheekiest
ADJECTIVE rather rude and disrespectful.

cheer cheers cheering cheered
VERB 1 When people cheer, they shout with approval or in order to show support for a person or team. ▶ NOUN 2 a shout of approval or support.

cheer up VERB When you cheer up, you feel more cheerful.

cheerful
ADJECTIVE 1 happy and in good spirits E.G. *I had never seen her so cheerful.* 2 bright and pleasant-looking E.G. *a cheerful and charming place.*
cheerfully ADVERB **cheerfulness** NOUN

cheerio
INTERJECTION Cheerio is a friendly way of saying goodbye.

cheery cheerier cheeriest
ADJECTIVE happy and cheerful E.G. *He gave me a cheery nod.*

cheese cheeses
NOUN a hard or creamy food made from milk.

cheesecake cheesecakes
NOUN a dessert made of biscuit covered with cream cheese.

cheetah cheetahs
NOUN a wild animal like a large cat with black spots.
▥ from Sanskrit *citra* + *kaya* meaning 'speckled body'

chef chefs
NOUN a head cook in a restaurant or hotel.

chemical chemicals
NOUN (SCIENCE) 1 Chemicals are substances manufactured by

chemistry. ▶ ADJECTIVE 2 involved in chemistry or using chemicals E.G. *chemical weapons.*
chemically ADVERB

chemist chemists
NOUN 1 a person who is qualified to make up drugs and medicines prescribed by a doctor. 2 a shop where medicines and cosmetics are sold. 3 a scientist who does research in chemistry.

chemistry
NOUN Chemistry is the scientific study of substances and the ways in which they are combined with other substances.

chemotherapy
Said "keem-oh ther-a-pee" NOUN Chemotherapy is a way of treating diseases such as cancer by using chemicals.

cheque cheques
NOUN a printed form on which you write an amount of money that you have to pay. You sign the cheque and your bank pays the money from your account.

chequered
Said "chek-kerd" ADJECTIVE 1 covered with a pattern of squares. 2 A chequered career is a varied career that has both good and bad parts.

cherish cherishes cherishing cherished
VERB 1 If you cherish something, you care deeply about it and want to keep it or look after it lovingly. 2 If you cherish a memory or hope, you have it in your mind and care deeply about it E.G. *I cherish the good memories I have of him.*

cherry cherries
NOUN 1 a small, juicy fruit with a red or

a b **c** d e f g h i j k l m n o p q r s t u v w x y z

A
B
C
D
E
F
G
H
I
J
K
L
M
N
O
P
Q
R
S
T
U
V
W
X
Y
Z

black skin and a hard stone in the centre. **2** a tree that produces cherries.

cherub cherubs or cherubim
NOUN an angel, shown in pictures as a plump, naked child with wings.
cherubic ADJECTIVE

chess
NOUN Chess is a board game for two people in which each player has 16 pieces and tries to move his or her pieces so that the other player's king cannot escape.

chessboard chessboards
NOUN A chessboard is a board divided into 64 squares of two alternating colours on which chess is played.

chest chests
NOUN **1** the front part of your body between your shoulders and your waist. **2** a large wooden box with a hinged lid.

chestnut chestnuts
NOUN **1** Chestnuts are reddish-brown nuts that grow inside a prickly green outer covering. **2** a tree that produces these nuts. ► ADJECTIVE **3** Something that is chestnut is reddish-brown.

chest of drawers chests of drawers
NOUN a piece of furniture with drawers in it, used for storing clothes.

chew chews chewing chewed
VERB When you chew something, you use your teeth to break it up in your mouth before swallowing it.
chewy ADJECTIVE

chewing gum
NOUN Chewing gum is a kind of sweet that you chew for a long time, but which you do not swallow.

chic
Said "**sheek**" ADJECTIVE elegant and fashionable E.G. *a chic restaurant*.

chick chicks
NOUN a young bird.

chicken chickens chickening chickened
NOUN **1** a bird kept on a farm for its eggs and meat; also the meat of this bird E.G. *roast chicken*. ► VERB **2** INFORMAL If you chicken out of something, you do not do it because you are afraid.

chickenpox
NOUN Chickenpox is an illness which produces a fever and blister-like spots on the skin.

chicory
NOUN Chicory is a plant with bitter leaves that are used in salads.

chide chides chiding chided
VERB; OLD-FASHIONED To chide someone is to tell them off.

chief chiefs
NOUN **1** the leader of a group or organization. ► ADJECTIVE **2** most important E.G. *the chief source of oil*.
chiefly ADVERB

chieftain chieftains
NOUN the leader of a tribe or clan.

chiffon
Said "**shif-fon**" NOUN Chiffon is a very thin lightweight cloth made of silk or nylon.

chihuahua chihuahuas
Said "**chi-wah-wah**" NOUN a breed of very small dog with short hair and pointed ears.

chilblain chilblains
NOUN a sore, itchy swelling on a finger or toe.

child children
NOUN **1** a young person who is not yet

an adult. **2** Someone's child is their son or daughter.

≡ (sense 1) baby, kid, youngster

childbirth

NOUN the act of giving birth to a child E.G. *Many women used to die in childbirth.*

childhood childhoods

NOUN Someone's childhood is the time when they are a child.

childish

ADJECTIVE immature and foolish E.G. *I don't have time for childish arguments.*

childishly ADVERB   **childishness** NOUN

≡ immature, infantile, juvenile

☑ If you call someone *childish*, you think they are immature or foolish. If you call them *childlike*, you think they are innocent like a young child.

childless

ADJECTIVE having no children.

childlike

ADJECTIVE like a child in appearance or behaviour E.G. *childlike enthusiasm.*

childminder childminders

NOUN a person who is qualified and paid to look after other people's children while they are at work.

Chilean Chileans

ADJECTIVE **1** belonging or relating to Chile. ► NOUN **2** someone who comes from Chile.

chill chills chilling chilled

VERB **1** To chill something is to make it cold E.G. *Chill the cheesecake.* **2** If something chills you, it makes you feel worried or frightened E.G. *The thought chilled her.* ► NOUN **3** a feverish cold. **4** a feeling of cold E.G. *the chill of the night air.*

chilli chillies

NOUN the red or green seed pod of a type of pepper which has a very hot, spicy taste.

chilly chillier chilliest

ADJECTIVE **1** rather cold E.G. *the chilly November breeze.* **2** unfriendly and without enthusiasm E.G. *a chilly reception.*

chilly-bin chilly-bins

NOUN; INFORMAL In New Zealand English, a container for keeping food and drink cool that can be carried.

chime chimes chiming chimed

VERB When a bell chimes, it makes a clear ringing sound.

chimney chimneys

NOUN a vertical pipe or other hollow structure above a fireplace or furnace through which smoke from a fire escapes.

🏛 from Greek *kaminos* meaning 'fireplace' or 'oven'

chimpanzee chimpanzees

NOUN a small ape with dark fur that lives in forests in Africa.

chin chins

NOUN the part of your face below your mouth

china chinas

NOUN **1** China is items like cups, saucers, and plates made from very fine clay. **2** INFORMAL In South African English, a china is a friend.

Chinese

ADJECTIVE **1** belonging or relating to China. ► NOUN **2** someone who comes from China. **3** Chinese refers to any of a group of related languages and dialects spoken by Chinese people.

chink chinks

NOUN **1** a small, narrow opening E.G. *a chink in the roof.* **2** a short, light, ringing sound, like one made by

a
b
c
d
e
f
g
h
i
j
k
l
m
n
o
p
q
r
s
t
u
v
w
x
y
z

A
B
C
D
E
F
G
H
I
J
K
L
M
N
O
P
Q
R
S
T
U
V
W
X
Y
Z

glasses touching each other.

chintz
NOUN Chintz is a type of brightly patterned cotton fabric.
📖 from Hindi *chint* meaning 'brightly coloured'

chip chips chipping chipped
NOUN 1 Chips are thin strips of fried potato. 2 In electronics, a chip is a tiny piece of silicon inside a computer which is used to form electronic circuits. 3 a small piece broken off an object, or the mark made when a piece breaks off. 4 In some gambling games, chips are counters used to represent money.
▶ VERB 5 If you chip an object, you break a small piece off it.

chipboard
NOUN Chipboard is a material made from wood scraps pressed together into hard sheets.

chipmunk chipmunks
NOUN a small rodent with a striped back.

chiropodist chiropodists
Said "kir-rop-pod-dist" NOUN a person whose job is treating people's feet.
chiropody NOUN

chirp chirps chirping chirped
VERB When a bird chirps, it makes a short, high-pitched sound.

chisel chisels chiselling chiselled
NOUN 1 a tool with a long metal blade and a sharp edge at the end which is used for cutting and shaping wood, stone, or metal. ▶ VERB 2 To chisel wood, stone, or metal is to cut or shape it using a chisel.

chivalry
Said "shiv-val-ree" NOUN Chivalry is polite and helpful behaviour, especially by men towards women.

chivalrous ADJECTIVE
📖 from Latin *caballarius* meaning 'horseman'

chive chives
NOUN Chives are grasslike hollow leaves that have a mild onion flavour.

chlorine
Said "klaw-reen" NOUN Chlorine is a poisonous greenish-yellow gas with a strong, unpleasant smell. It is used as a disinfectant for water, and to make bleach.

chloroform
Said "klor-rof-form" NOUN Chloroform is a colourless liquid with a strong, sweet smell used in cleaning products.

chlorophyll
Said "klor-rof-fil" NOUN Chlorophyll is a green substance in plants which enables them to use the energy from sunlight in order to grow.

chock-a-block or **chock-full**
ADJECTIVE completely full.

chocolate chocolates
NOUN 1 Chocolate is a sweet food made from cacao seeds. 2 a sweet made of chocolate. ▶ ADJECTIVE 3 dark brown.
📖 from Aztec *xococ + atl* meaning 'bitter water'

choice choices
NOUN 1 a range of different things that are available to choose from E.G. *a wider choice of treatments.* 2 something that you choose E.G. *You've made a good choice.* 3 Choice is the power or right to choose E.G. *I had no choice.*
▤ (sense 1) range, selection, variety

choir choirs
Said "kwire" NOUN (MUSIC) a group of singers, for example in a church.

choke chokes choking choked
VERB 1 If you choke, you stop being able to breathe properly, usually because something is blocking your windpipe E.G. *the diner who choked on a fish bone.* 2 If things choke a place, they fill it so much that it is blocked or clogged up E.G. *The canal was choked with old tyres.*

choko chokos
NOUN a fruit that is shaped like a pear and used as a vegetable in Australia and New Zealand.

cholera
Said "kol-ler-ra" NOUN Cholera is a serious disease causing severe diarrhoea and vomiting. It is caused by infected food or water.

cholesterol
Said "kol-less-ter-rol" NOUN Cholesterol is a substance found in all animal fats, tissues, and blood.

chook chooks
NOUN; INFORMAL In Australian and New Zealand English, a chicken.

choose chooses choosing chose chosen
VERB To choose something is to decide to have it or do it E.G. *He chose to live in Kenya.*
■ opt for, pick, select
☑ The present tense *chooses* and present participle *choosing* are spelt with two *o*s. The past tense *chose* and past participle *chosen* have only one *o*.

choosy choosier choosiest
ADJECTIVE fussy and difficult to satisfy E.G. *You can't be too choosy about jobs.*

chop chops chopping chopped
VERB 1 To chop something is to cut it with quick, heavy strokes using an axe or a knife. ► NOUN 2 a small piece of lamb or pork containing a bone, usually cut from the ribs.

chopper choppers
NOUN; INFORMAL a helicopter.

choppy choppier choppiest
ADJECTIVE Choppy water has a lot of waves because it is windy.

chopstick chopsticks
NOUN Chopsticks are a pair of thin sticks used by people in the Far East for eating food.

choral
ADJECTIVE relating to singing by a choir E.G. *choral music.*

chord chords
NOUN (MUSIC) a group of three or more musical notes played together.

chore chores
NOUN a boring job that has to be done E.G. *the chore of cleaning.*

choreography
Said "kor-ree-og-raf-fee" NOUN Choreography is the art of composing dance steps and movements.
choreographer NOUN

chortle chortles chortling chortled
VERB To chortle is to laugh with amusement.

chorus choruses chorusing chorused
NOUN 1 a large group of singers; also a piece of music for a large group of singers. 2 a part of a song which is repeated after each verse. 3 (ENGLISH) the chorus is a group of actors, singers or dancers that performs together, either with the main performers or between solo performances. ► VERB 4 If people chorus something, they all say or

a b c d e f g h i j k l m n o p q r s t u v w x y z

the QUeen stood on the QUay (quay)   SPELLING NOTE

sing it at the same time.

🔲 from Greek *khoros*, the group of actors who gave the commentary in Classical plays

Christ

PROPER NOUN Christ is the name for Jesus. Christians believe that Jesus is the son of God.

christen christens christening christened

VERB When a baby is christened, it is named by a member of the clergy in a religious ceremony.

Christian Christians

NOUN 1 (RE) a person who believes in Jesus Christ and his teachings.
► ADJECTIVE 2 (RE) relating to Christ and his teachings E.G. *the Christian faith*. 3 good, kind, and considerate.

Christianity NOUN

Christian name Christian names

NOUN the name given to someone when they were born or christened.

Christmas Christmases

NOUN the Christian festival celebrating the birth of Christ, falling on December 25th.

chromatic

Said "kro-**ma**-tik" ADJECTIVE (MUSIC) A chromatic scale is one which is based on an octave of 12 semitones.

chrome

Said "k**rome**" NOUN Chrome is metal plated with chromium, a hard grey metal.

chromosome chromosomes

NOUN In biology, a chromosome is a part of a cell which contains genes that determine the characteristics of an animal or plant.

chronic

Said "k**ron**-nik" ADJECTIVE lasting a very

long time or never stopping E.G. *a chronic illness*.

chronically ADVERB

chronicle chronicles chronicling chronicled

NOUN 1 a record of a series of events described in the order in which they happened. ► VERB 2 To chronicle a series of events is to record or describe them in the order in which they happened.

chronological

Said "kron-nol-**loj**-i-kl" ADJECTIVE (HISTORY) arranged in the order in which things happened E.G. *Tell me the whole story in chronological order*.

chronologically ADVERB

chronology

Said "kron-**nol**-loj-jee" NOUN (HISTORY) The chronology of events is the order in which they happened.

🔲 from Greek *khronos* meaning 'time' and *legein* meaning 'to say'

chrysalis chrysalises

Said "**kriss**-sal-liss" NOUN a butterfly or moth when it is developing from being a caterpillar to being a fully grown adult.

chrysanthemum chrysanthemums

Said "kriss-**an**-thim-mum" NOUN a plant with large, brightly coloured flowers.

chubby chubbier chubbiest

ADJECTIVE plump and round E.G. *his chubby cheeks*.

chuck chucks chucking chucked

VERB; INFORMAL To chuck something is to throw it casually.

chuckle chuckles chuckling chuckled

VERB When you chuckle, you laugh quietly.

chug chugs chugging chugged
VERB When a machine or engine
chugs, it makes a continuous dull
thudding sound.

chum chums
NOUN; INFORMAL a friend.

chunk chunks
NOUN a thick piece of something.
■ hunk, lump, piece

chunky chunkier chunkiest
ADJECTIVE Someone who is chunky is
broad and heavy but usually short.

church churches
NOUN 1 a building where Christians go
for religious services and worship.
2 In the Christian religion, a church is
one of the groups with their own
particular beliefs, customs, and
clergy E.G. *the Catholic Church.*
🔲 from Greek *kuriakon* meaning
'master's house'

Church of England
NOUN The Church of England is the
Anglican church in England, where it
is the state church, with the King or
Queen as its head.

churchyard churchyards
NOUN an area of land around a
church, often used as a graveyard.

churn churns
NOUN a container used for making
milk or cream into butter.

chute chutes
Said "shoot" NOUN a steep slope or
channel used to slide things down
E.G. *a rubbish chute.*

chutney
NOUN Chutney is a strong-tasting
thick sauce made from fruit, vinegar,
and spices.

cider
NOUN Cider is an alcoholic drink made
from apples.

cigar cigars
NOUN a roll of dried tobacco leaves
which people smoke.
🔲 from Mayan *sicar* meaning 'to
smoke'

cigarette cigarettes
NOUN a thin roll of tobacco covered in
thin paper which people smoke.

cinder cinders
NOUN Cinders are small pieces of
burnt material left after something
such as wood or coal has burned.

cinema cinemas
NOUN 1 a place where people go to
watch films. 2 Cinema is the business
of making films.

cinnamon
NOUN Cinnamon is a sweet spice
which comes from the bark of an
Asian tree.

cipher ciphers
Said "sy-fer"; also spelt **cypher**
NOUN a secret code or system of
writing used to send secret messages.

circa
Said "sir-ka" PREPOSITION; FORMAL about
or approximately; used especially
before dates E.G. *portrait of a lady,
circa 1840.*

circle circles circling circled
NOUN 1 a completely regular round
shape. Every point on its edge is the
same distance from the centre. 2 a
group of people with the same
interest or profession E.G. *a character
well known in yachting circles.* 3 an
area of seats on an upper floor of a
theatre. ▶ VERB 4 To circle is to move
round and round as though going
round the edge of a circle E.G. *A
police helicopter circled above.*

circuit circuits
Said "sir-kit" NOUN 1 any closed line or

a
b
c
d
e
f
g
h
i
j
k
l
m
n
o
p
q
r
s
t
u
v
w
x
y
z

A
B
C
D
E
F
G
H
I
J
K
L
M
N
O
P
Q
R
S
T
U
V
W
X
Y
Z

path, often circular, for example a racing track; also the distance round this path E.G. *three circuits of the 26-lap race remaining*. **2** An electrical circuit is a complete route around which an electric current can flow.

circular circulars

ADJECTIVE **1** in the shape of a circle. **2** A circular argument or theory is not valid because it uses a statement to prove a conclusion and the conclusion to prove the statement. ▶ NOUN **3** a letter or advert sent to a lot of people at the same time.

circularity NOUN

circulate circulates circulating circulated

VERB **1** (SCIENCE) When something circulates or when you circulate it, it moves easily around an area E.G. *an open position where the air can circulate freely*. **2** When you circulate something among people, you pass it round or tell it to all the people E.G. *We circulate a regular newsletter*.

circulation circulations

NOUN **1** The circulation of something is the act of circulating it or the action of it circulating E.G. *traffic circulation*. **2** The circulation of a newspaper or magazine is the number of copies that are sold of each issue. **3** (SCIENCE) Your circulation is the movement of blood through your body.

circum-

PREFIX 'Circum-' means 'around' or 'surrounding' E.G. *circumference*. 📖 from Latin *circus* meaning 'circle'

circumcise circumcises circumcising circumcised

VERB If a boy or man is circumcised, the foreskin at the end of his penis is removed. This is carried out mainly as part of a Muslim or Jewish religious ceremony.

circumcision NOUN

circumference circumferences

NOUN (MATHS) The circumference of a circle is its outer line or edge; also the length of this line.

circumstance circumstances

NOUN **1** The circumstances of a situation or event are the conditions that affect what happens E.G. *He did well in the circumstances*. **2** Someone's circumstances are their position and conditions in life E.G. *Her circumstances had changed*.

circus circuses

NOUN a show given by a travelling group of entertainers such as clowns, acrobats, and specially trained animals.

cistern cisterns

NOUN a tank in which water is stored, for example one in the roof of a house or above a toilet.

citadel citadels

NOUN a fortress in or near a city.

cite cites citing cited

VERB **1** FORMAL If you cite something, you quote it or refer to it E.G. *He cited a letter written by Newall*. **2** If someone is cited in a legal action, they are officially called to appear in court.

citizen citizens

NOUN (HISTORY) The citizens of a country or city are the people who live in it or belong to it E.G. *American citizens*.

citizenship NOUN

citrus fruit citrus fruits

NOUN Citrus fruits are juicy, sharp-tasting fruits such as oranges, lemons, and grapefruit.

city cities
NOUN a large town where many people live and work.

civic
ADJECTIVE relating to a city or citizens E.G. *the Civic Centre*.

civil
ADJECTIVE 1 relating to the citizens of a country E.G. *civil rights*. 2 relating to people or things that are not connected with the armed forces E.G. *the history of civil aviation*. 3 polite.
civilly ADVERB **civility** NOUN

civil engineering
NOUN Civil engineering is the design and construction of roads, bridges, and public buildings.

civilian civilians
NOUN a person who is not in the armed forces.

civilization civilizations; also spelt **civilisation**
NOUN (HISTORY) 1 a society which has a highly developed organization and culture E.G. *the tale of a lost civilization*. 2 Civilization is an advanced state of social organization and culture.

civilized
ADJECTIVE 1 A civilized society is one with a developed social organization and way of life. 2 A civilized person is polite and reasonable.

civil servant civil servants
NOUN a person who works in the civil service.

civil service
NOUN The civil service is the government departments responsible for the administration of a country.

civil war civil wars
NOUN a war between groups of people who live in the same country.

cl
an abbreviation for 'centilitres'.

clad
ADJECTIVE; LITERARY Someone who is clad in particular clothes is wearing them.

claim claims claiming claimed
VERB 1 If you claim that something is the case, you say that it is the case E.G. *He claims to have lived in the same house all his life*. 2 If you claim something, you ask for it because it belongs to you or you have a right to it E.G. *Cartier claimed the land for the King of France*. ► NOUN 3 a statement that something is the case, or that you have a right to something E.G. *She will make a claim for damages*.
◼ (sense 1) allege, assert, maintain

claimant claimants
NOUN someone who is making a claim, especially for money.

clairvoyant clairvoyants
ADJECTIVE 1 able to know about things that will happen in the future. ► NOUN 2 a person who is, or claims to be, clairvoyant.
▥ from French *clair* + *voyant* meaning 'clear-seeing'

clam clams
NOUN a kind of shellfish.

clamber clambers clambering clambered
VERB If you clamber somewhere, you climb there with difficulty.

clammy clammier clammiest
ADJECTIVE unpleasantly damp and sticky E.G. *clammy hands*.

clamour clamours clamouring clamoured

Eddy Ant thinks mEAt is a grEAt trEAt to EAt (-ea-)   SPELLING NOTE

A
B
C
D
E
F
G
H
I
J
K
L
M
N
O
P
Q
R
S
T
U
V
W
X
Y
Z

VERB **1** If people clamour for something, they demand it noisily or angrily E.G. *We clamoured for an explanation.* ▶ NOUN **2** Clamour is noisy or angry shouts or demands by a lot of people.

clamp clamps clamping clamped
NOUN **1** an object with movable parts that are used to hold two things firmly together. ▶ VERB **2** To clamp things together is to fasten them or hold them firmly with a clamp.

clamp down on VERB To clamp down on something is to become stricter in controlling it E.G. *The Queen has clamped down on all expenditure.*

clan clans
NOUN a group of families related to each other by being descended from the same ancestor.

clandestine
ADJECTIVE secret and hidden E.G. *a clandestine meeting with friends.*

clang clangs clanging clanged
VERB When something metal clangs or when you clang it, it makes a loud, deep sound.

clank clanks clanking clanked
VERB If something metal clanks, it makes a loud noise.

clap claps clapping clapped
VERB **1** When you clap, you hit your hands together loudly to show your appreciation. **2** If you clap someone on the back or shoulder, you hit them in a friendly way. **3** If you clap something somewhere, you put it there quickly and firmly E.G. *I clapped a hand over her mouth.* ▶ NOUN **4** a sound made by clapping your hands. **5** A clap of thunder is a sudden loud noise of thunder.

claret clarets
NOUN a type of red wine, especially one from the Bordeaux region of France.

clarify clarifies clarifying clarified
VERB (EXAM TERM) To clarify something is to make it clear and easier to understand E.G. *Discussion will clarify your thoughts.*
clarification NOUN

clarinet clarinets
NOUN a woodwind instrument with a straight tube and a single reed in its mouthpiece.

clarity
NOUN The clarity of something is its clearness.

clash clashes clashing clashed
VERB **1** If people clash with each other, they fight or argue. **2** Ideas or styles that clash are so different that they do not go together. **3** If two events clash, they happen at the same time so you cannot go to both. **4** When metal objects clash, they hit each other with a loud noise. ▶ NOUN **5** a fight or argument. **6** A clash of ideas, styles, or events is a situation in which they do not go together. **7** a loud noise made by metal objects when they hit each other.

clasp clasps clasping clasped
VERB **1** To clasp something means to hold it tightly or fasten it E.G. *He clasped his hands.* ▶ NOUN **2** a fastening such as a hook or catch.

class classes classing classed
NOUN **1** A class of people or things is a group of them of a particular type or quality E.G. *the old class of politicians.* **2** a group of pupils or students taught together, or a lesson that they

have together. **3** Someone who has class is elegant in appearance or behaviour. ▶ VERB **4** To class something means to arrange it in a particular group or to consider it as belonging to a particular group E.G. *They are officially classed as visitors.* ■ (sense 1) category, group, kind, type

classic classics
ADJECTIVE **1** typical and therefore a good model or example of something E.G. *a classic case of misuse.* **2** of very high quality E.G. *one of the classic films of all time.* **3** simple in style and form E.G. *the classic dinner suit.* ▶ NOUN **4** something of the highest quality E.G. *one of the great classics of rock music.* **5** Classics is the study of Latin and Greek, and the literature of ancient Greece and Rome.

classical
ADJECTIVE **1** traditional in style, form, and content E.G. *classical ballet.* **2** Classical music is serious music considered to be of lasting value. **3** characteristic of the style of ancient Greece and Rome E.G. *Classical friezes decorate the walls.*
classically ADVERB

classified
ADJECTIVE officially declared secret by the government E.G. *access to classified information.*

classify classifies classifying classified
VERB To classify things is to arrange them into groups with similar characteristics E.G. *We can classify the differences into three groups.*
classification NOUN (LIBRARY)

classroom classrooms
NOUN a room in a school where pupils have lessons.

classy classier classiest
ADJECTIVE; INFORMAL stylish and elegant.

clatter clatters clattering clattered
VERB **1** When things clatter, they hit each other with a loud rattling noise. ▶ NOUN **2** a loud rattling noise made by hard things hitting each other.

clause clauses
NOUN **1** a section of a legal document. **2** (ENGLISH) In grammar, a clause is a group of words with a subject and a verb, which may be a complete sentence or one of the parts of a sentence.

What is a Clause?

A **clause** is a group of words which form part of a sentence and express an Idea or describe a situation. A clause often gives information about the main idea or situation:

> E.G. *Matthew ate a cake **which was covered in chocolate**. Anna crossed the street **after looking carefully in both directions**.*

Main Clauses and Subordinate Clauses
Clauses can be either **main clauses** or **subordinate clauses**.
A **main clause** is the core of a sentence. It would make sense if it stood on its own. Every sentence contains a main clause:

> E.G. ***Matthew ate a cake*** *which was covered in chocolate.*

CONTINUED ON NEXT PAGE →

'i' before 'e' except after 'c'   **SPELLING NOTE**

a
b
c
d
e
f
g
h
i
j
k
l
m
n
o
p
q
r
s
t
u
v
w
x
y
z

*After looking carefully in both directions, **Anna crossed the road.***

A **subordinate clause** is a less important part of a sentence. It would not make sense on its own, but gives information about the main clause:

E.G. ***After looking carefully**, Anna crossed the road.*

*Anna had to cross the road, **which was often very busy**.*

Relative Clauses

Relative clauses give additional information about a person or thing mentioned in the main clause.

Relative clauses are introduced by a relative pronoun – *who, whom, whose, which* or *that*:

E.G. *Robbie has a cat **who likes fish**.*

*Anna has one sister, **whose name is Rosie**.*

claustrophobia
Said "klos-trof-**foe**-bee-ya" NOUN Claustrophobia is a fear of being in enclosed spaces.
claustrophobic ADJECTIVE

claw claws clawing clawed
NOUN **1** An animal's claws are hard, curved nails at the end of its feet. **2** The claws of a crab or lobster are the two jointed parts, used for grasping things. ▶ VERB **3** If an animal claws something, it digs its claws into it.

clay
NOUN Clay is a type of earth that is soft and sticky when wet and hard when baked dry. It is used to make pottery and bricks.

clean cleaner cleanest; cleans cleaning cleaned
ADJECTIVE **1** free from dirt or other unwanted substances or marks. **2** If humour is clean it is not rude and does not involve bad language. **3** A clean movement is skilful and accurate. **4** Clean also means free from fault or error E.G. *a clean driving licence.* ▶ VERB **5** To clean something is to remove dirt from it.
cleanly ADVERB **cleaner** NOUN

cleanliness
Said "**klen**-lin-ness" NOUN Cleanliness is the practice of keeping yourself and your surroundings clean.

cleanse cleanses cleansing cleansed
Said "klenz" VERB To cleanse something is to make it completely free from dirt.

clear clearer clearest; clears clearing cleared
ADJECTIVE **1** easy to understand, see, or hear E.G. *He made it clear he did not want to talk.* **2** easy to see through E.G. *a clear liquid.* **3** free from obstructions or unwanted things E.G. *clear of snow.* ▶ VERB **4** To clear an area is to remove unwanted things from it. **5** If you clear a fence or other obstacle, you jump over it without touching it. **6** When fog or mist clears, it disappears. **7** If someone is cleared of a crime, they are proved to be not guilty.
clearly ADVERB **clearness** NOUN
■ (sense 1) evident, obvious, plain

clear up VERB **1** If you clear up, you tidy a place and put things away. **2** When a problem or misunderstanding is cleared up, it is solved or settled.

clearance

NOUN 1 Clearance is the removal of old buildings in an area. 2 If someone is given clearance to do something, they get official permission to do it.

clearing clearings

NOUN an area of bare ground in a forest.

cleavage cleavages

NOUN the space between a woman's breasts.

cleaver cleavers

NOUN a knife with a large square blade, used especially by butchers.

cleft clefts

NOUN a narrow opening in a rock.

clementine clementines

NOUN a type of small citrus fruit that is a cross between an orange and a tangerine.

clench clenches clenching clenched

VERB 1 When you clench your fist, you curl your fingers up tightly. 2 When you clench your teeth, you squeeze them together tightly.

clergy

PLURAL NOUN The clergy are the ministers of the Christian Church.

clergyman clergymen

NOUN a male member of the clergy.

clerical

ADJECTIVE 1 relating to work done in an office E.G. *clerical jobs with the City Council*. 2 relating to the clergy.

clerk clerks

Said "klahrk" NOUN a person who keeps records or accounts in an office, bank, or law court.

clever cleverer cleverest

ADJECTIVE 1 intelligent and quick to understand things. 2 very effective or skilful E.G. *a clever plan*.

cleverly ADVERB **cleverness** NOUN

■ (sense 1) bright, intelligent, smart

clianthus

Said "klee-an-thuss" NOUN A clianthus is a plant found in Australia and New Zealand which has clusters of scarlet flowers.

cliché clichés

Said "klee-shay" NOUN (ENGLISH) an idea or phrase which is no longer effective because it has been used so much.

click clicks clicking clicked

VERB 1 When something clicks or when you click it, it makes a short snapping sound. ▶ NOUN 2 a sound of something clicking E.G. *I heard the click of a bolt*.

client clients

NOUN someone who pays a professional person or company to receive a service.

clientele

Said "klee-on-tell" PLURAL NOUN The clientele of a place are its customers.

cliff cliffs

NOUN a steep high rock face by the sea.

climate climates

NOUN 1 (GEOGRAPHY) The climate of a place is the typical weather conditions there E.G. *The climate was dry in the summer*. 2 the general attitude and opinion of people at a particular time E.G. *the American political climate*.

climatic ADJECTIVE

climax climaxes

NOUN The climax of a process, story, or piece of music is the most exciting moment in it, usually near the end.

𝄞 from Greek *klimax* meaning 'ladder'

a b c d e f g h i j k l m n o p q r s t u v w x y z

an ELegant angEL (angel)   **SPELLING NOTE**

A
B
C
D
E
F
G
H
I
J
K
L
M
N
O
P
Q
R
S
T
U
V
W
X
Y
Z

climb climbs climbing climbed
VERB 1 To climb is to move upwards.
2 If you climb somewhere, you move
there with difficulty E.G. *She climbed
out of the driving seat.* ▶ NOUN 3 a
movement upwards E.G. *this long
climb up the slope… the rapid climb in
murders*.
climber NOUN

clinch clinches clinching
clinched
VERB If you clinch an agreement or an
argument, you settle it in a definite
way E.G. *Peter clinched a deal*.

cling clings clinging clung
VERB To cling to something is to hold
onto it or stay closely attached to it
E.G. *still clinging to old-fashioned values*.

clingfilm
NOUN; TRADEMARK a clear thin plastic
used for wrapping food.

clinic clinics
NOUN a building where people go for
medical treatment.

clinical
ADJECTIVE 1 relating to the medical
treatment of patients E.G. *clinical
tests*. 2 Clinical behaviour or thought
is logical and without emotion E.G.
*the cold, clinical attitudes of his
colleagues*.
clinically ADVERB

clip clips clipping clipped
NOUN 1 a small metal or plastic object
used for holding things together. 2 a
short piece of a film shown by itself.
▶ VERB 3 If you clip things together,
you fasten them with clips. 4 If you
clip something, you cut bits from it
to shape it E.G. *clipped hedges*.

clippers
PLURAL NOUN Clippers are tools used for
cutting.

clipping clippings
NOUN an article cut from a newspaper
or magazine.

clique cliques
Rhymes with "seek" NOUN a small
group of people who stick together
and do not mix with other people.

clitoris clitorises
Said "klit-tor-riss" NOUN a small
highly sensitive piece of flesh near
the opening of a woman's vagina.

cloak cloaks cloaking cloaked
NOUN 1 a wide, loose coat without
sleeves. ▶ VERB 2 To cloak something is
to cover or hide it E.G. *a land
permanently cloaked in mist*.

cloakroom cloakrooms
NOUN a room for coats or a room with
toilets and washbasins in a public
building.

clock clocks
NOUN 1 a device that measures and
shows the time. ▶ PHRASE 2 If you work
round the clock, you work all day
and night.

clockwise
ADJECTIVE or ADVERB in the same
direction as the hands on a clock.

clockwork
NOUN 1 Toys that work by clockwork
move when they are wound up with
a key. ▶ PHRASE 2 If something
happens **like clockwork**, it happens
with no problems or delays.

clog clogs clogging clogged
VERB 1 To clog something is to block it
E.G. *pavements clogged up with
people*. ▶ NOUN 2 Clogs are heavy
wooden shoes.

cloister cloisters
NOUN a covered area in a monastery
or a cathedral for walking around a
square.

clone clones cloning cloned
NOUN **1** In biology, a clone is an animal or plant that has been produced artificially from the cells of another animal or plant and is therefore identical to it. ▶ VERB **2** To clone an animal or plant is to produce it as a clone.

close closes closing closed; closer closest
VERB **1** To close something is to shut it. **2** To close a road or entrance is to block it so that no-one can go in or out. **3** If a shop closes at a certain time, then it does not do business after that time. ▶ ADJECTIVE OR ADVERB **4** near to something E.G. *a restaurant close to their home.* ▶ ADJECTIVE **5** People who are close to each other are very friendly and know each other well. **6** You say the weather is close when it is uncomfortably warm and there is not enough air.
closely ADVERB **closeness** NOUN
closed ADJECTIVE
▪ (sense 4) near, nearby
close down VERB If a business closes down, all work stops there permanently.

closed shop closed shops
NOUN a factory or other business whose employees have to be members of a trade union.

closet closets closeting closeted
NOUN **1** a cupboard. ▶ VERB **2** If you are closeted somewhere, you shut yourself away alone or in private with another person. ▶ ADJECTIVE **3** Closet beliefs or habits are kept private and secret E.G. *a closet romantic.*

close-up close-ups
NOUN a detailed close view of something, especially a photograph taken close to the subject.

closure closures
Said "**klohz**-yur" NOUN **1** The closure of a business is the permanent shutting of it. **2** The closure of a road is the blocking of it so it cannot be used.

clot clots clotting clotted
NOUN **1** a lump, especially one that forms when blood thickens. ▶ VERB **2** When a substance such as blood clots, it thickens and forms a lump.

cloth cloths
Rhymes with "**moth**" NOUN **1** Cloth is fabric made by a process such as weaving. **2** a piece of material used for wiping or protecting things
☑ 'Cloth' and 'clothe' have different spellings and pronunciations.

clothe clothes clothing clothed
Rhymes with "**both**" PLURAL NOUN **1** Clothes are the things people wear on their bodies. ▶ VERB **2** To clothe someone is to give them clothes to wear.

clothing
NOUN Clothing is the clothes people wear.

cloud clouds clouding clouded
NOUN **1** a mass of water vapour that forms in the air and is seen as a white or grey patch in the sky. **2** A cloud of smoke or dust is a mass of it floating in the air. ▶ VERB **3** If something clouds or is clouded, it becomes cloudy or difficult to see through E.G. *The sky clouded over.* **4** Something that clouds an issue makes it more confusing.
▣ from Old English *clud* meaning 'hill'

a
b
c
d
e
f
g
h
i
j
k
l
m
n
o
p
q
r
s
t
u
v
w
x
y
z

A Rude Idiot Thought He Might Eat Toffee In Church (<u>arithmetic</u>)   SPELLING NOTE

cloudy cloudier cloudiest
ADJECTIVE 1 full of clouds E.G. *the cloudy sky.* 2 difficult to see through E.G. *a glass of cloudy liquid.*
■ (sense 1) dull, overcast

clout
NOUN; INFORMAL Someone who has clout has influence.

clove cloves
NOUN 1 Cloves are small, strong-smelling dried flower buds from a tropical tree, used as a spice in cooking. 2 A clove of garlic is one of the separate sections of the bulb.

clover
NOUN Clover is a small plant with leaves made up of three similar parts.

clown clowns clowning clowned
NOUN 1 a circus performer who wears funny clothes and make-up and does silly things to make people laugh. ► VERB 2 If you clown, you do silly things to make people laugh.

cloying
ADJECTIVE unpleasantly sickly, sweet, or sentimental E.G. *something less cloying than whipped cream.*

club clubs clubbing clubbed
NOUN 1 an organization of people with a particular interest, who meet regularly; also the place where they meet. 2 a thick, heavy stick used as a weapon. 3 a stick with a shaped head that a golf player uses to hit the ball. 4 Clubs is one of the four suits in a pack of playing cards. It is marked by a black symbol in the shape of a clover leaf. ► VERB 5 To club someone is to hit them hard with a heavy object.
■ (sense 1) association, group, society

club together VERB If people club together, they all join together to give money to buy something.

cluck clucks clucking clucked
VERB When a hen clucks, it makes a short, repeated, high-pitched sound.

clue clues
NOUN something that helps to solve a problem or mystery.

clump clumps clumping clumped
NOUN 1 a small group of things close together. ► VERB 2 If you clump about, you walk with heavy footsteps.

clumsy clumsier clumsiest
ADJECTIVE 1 moving awkwardly and carelessly. 2 said or done without thought or tact E.G. *his clumsy attempts to catch her out.*
clumsily ADVERB **clumsiness** NOUN
■ (sense 1) awkward, gauche, ungainly

cluster clusters clustering clustered
NOUN 1 A cluster of things is a group of them together E.G. *a cluster of huts at the foot of the mountains.* ► VERB 2 If people cluster together, they stay together in a close group.

clutch clutches clutching clutched
VERB 1 If you clutch something, you hold it tightly or seize it. ► PLURAL NOUN 2 If you are in someone's clutches, they have power or control over you.

clutter clutters cluttering cluttered
NOUN 1 Clutter is an untidy mess. ► VERB 2 Things that clutter a place fill it and make it untidy.

cm
an abbreviation for 'centimetres'.

co-
PREFIX Co- means together E.G. *Paula*

is now co-writing a book with Pierre.

coach coaches coaching coached

NOUN **1** a long motor vehicle used for taking passengers on long journeys. **2** a section of a train that carries passengers. **3** a four-wheeled vehicle with a roof pulled by horses, which people used to travel in. **4** a person who coaches a sport or a subject.
▶ VERB **5** If someone coaches you, they teach you and help you to get better at a sport or a subject.
≡ (sense 4) instructor, trainer
≡ (sense 5) instruct, train

coal coals

NOUN **1** Coal is a hard black rock obtained from under the earth and burned as a fuel. **2** Coals are burning pieces of coal.

coalition coalitions

NOUN a temporary alliance, especially between different political parties forming a government.

coarse coarser coarsest

ADJECTIVE **1** Something that is coarse is rough in texture, often consisting of large particles E.G. *a coarse blanket.* **2** Someone who is coarse talks or behaves in a rude or rather offensive way.

coarsely ADVERB   **coarseness** NOUN
✔ Do not confuse the spellings of *coarse* and *course.*

coast coasts coasting coasted

NOUN **1** the edge of the land where it meets the sea. ▶ VERB **2** A vehicle that is coasting is moving without engine power.

coastal ADJECTIVE

coastguard coastguards

NOUN an official who watches the sea near a coast to get help for sailors when they need it, and to prevent smuggling.

coastline coastlines

NOUN the outline of a coast, especially its appearance as seen from the sea or air.

coat coats coating coated

NOUN **1** a piece of clothing with sleeves which you wear outside over your other clothes. **2** An animal's coat is the fur or hair on its body. **3** A coat of paint or varnish is a layer of it.
▶ VERB **4** To coat something means to cover it with a thin layer of a something E.G. *walnuts coated with chocolate.*

coating NOUN

coax coaxes coaxing coaxed

VERB If you coax someone to do something, you gently persuade them to do it.
≡ cajole, persuade, talk into, wheedle

cobalt

NOUN Cobalt is a hard silvery-white metal which is used for producing a blue dye.

cobble cobbles

NOUN Cobbles or cobblestones are stones with a rounded surface that were used in the past for making roads.

cobbler cobblers

NOUN a person who makes or mends shoes.

cobra cobras

Said "koh-bra" NOUN a type of large poisonous snake from Africa and Asia.

cobweb cobwebs

NOUN the very thin net that a spider spins for catching insects.

cocaine

NOUN Cocaine is an addictive drug.

A
B
C
D
E
F
G
H
I
J
K
L
M
N
O
P
Q
R
S
T
U
V
W
X
Y
Z

🔲 from Spanish *coca* meaning 'preparation of cocoa leaves'

cock cocks

NOUN an adult male chicken; also used of any male bird.

cockatoo cockatoos

NOUN a type of parrot with a crest, found in Australia and New Guinea.

cockerel cockerels

NOUN a young cock.

Cockney Cockneys

NOUN a person born in the East End of London.

cockpit cockpits

NOUN The place in a small plane where the pilot sits.

cockroach cockroaches

NOUN a large dark-coloured insect often found in dirty rooms.

cocktail cocktails

NOUN an alcoholic drink made from several ingredients.

cocky cockier cockiest; cockies

INFORMAL

ADJECTIVE **1** cheeky or too self-confident. ▶ NOUN **2** In Australian English, a cockatoo. **3** In Australian and New Zealand English, a farmer, especially one whose farm is small.

cockiness NOUN

cocoa

NOUN Cocoa is a brown powder made from the seeds of a tropical tree and used for making chocolate; also a hot drink made from this powder.

coconut coconuts

NOUN a very large nut with white flesh, milky juice, and a hard hairy shell.

cocoon cocoons

NOUN a silky covering over the larvae of moths and some other insects.

🔲 from Provençal *coucoun* meaning 'eggshell'

cod

NOUN a large edible fish.

☑ The plural of *cod* is also *cod*.

code codes

NOUN **1** a system of replacing the letters or words in a message with other letters or words, so that nobody can understand the message unless they know the system. **2** a group of numbers and letters which is used to identify something E.G. *the telephone code for Melbourne.*

coded ADJECTIVE

coffee

NOUN Coffee is a substance made by roasting and grinding the beans of a tropical shrub; also a hot drink made from this substance.

🔲 from Arabic *qahwah* meaning 'wine' or 'coffee'

coffin coffins

NOUN a box in which a dead body is buried or cremated.

cog cogs

NOUN a wheel with teeth which turns another wheel or part of a machine.

cognac

Said "**kon**-yak" NOUN Cognac is a kind of brandy.

coherent

ADJECTIVE **1** If something such as a theory is coherent, its parts fit together well and do not contradict each other. **2** If someone is coherent, what they are saying makes sense and is not jumbled or confused.

coherence NOUN

cohesive

ADJECTIVE If something is cohesive, its parts fit together well E.G. *The team must work as a cohesive unit.*

cohesion NOUN

coil coils coiling coiled
NOUN **1** a length of rope or wire wound into a series of loops; also one of the loops. ► VERB **2** If something coils, it turns into a series of loops.

coin coins coining coined
NOUN **1** a small metal disc which is used as money. ► VERB **2** If you coin a word or a phrase, you invent it.

coinage
NOUN The coinage of a country is the coins that are used there.

coincide coincides coinciding coincided
VERB **1** If two events coincide, they happen at about the same time. **2** When two people's ideas or opinions coincide, they agree E.G. *What she said coincided exactly with his own thinking.*

coincidence coincidences
NOUN **1** what happens when two similar things occur at the same time by chance E.G. *I had moved to London, and by coincidence, Helen had too.* **2** the fact that two things are surprisingly the same.
coincidental ADJECTIVE
coincidentally ADVERB

coke
NOUN Coke is a grey fuel produced from coal.

colander colanders
Said "kol-*an-der*" NOUN a bowl-shaped container with holes in it, used for washing or draining food.

cold colder coldest; colds
ADJECTIVE **1** Something that is cold has a very low temperature. **2** If it is cold, the air temperature is very low. **3** Someone who is cold does not show much affection. ► NOUN **4** You

can refer to cold weather as the cold E.G. *She was complaining about the cold.* **5** a minor illness in which you sneeze and may have a sore throat.
coldly ADVERB **coldness** NOUN

cold-blooded
ADJECTIVE **1** Someone who is cold-blooded does not show any pity E.G. *two cold-blooded killers.* **2** A cold-blooded animal has a body temperature that changes according to the surrounding temperature.

cold war
NOUN Cold war is a state of extreme unfriendliness between countries not actually at war.

coleslaw
NOUN Coleslaw is a salad of chopped cabbage and other vegetables in mayonnaise.
📖 from Dutch *koolsla* meaning 'cabbage salad'

colic
NOUN Colic is pain in a baby's stomach.

collaborate collaborates collaborating collaborated
VERB When people collaborate, they work together to produce something E.G. *The two bands have collaborated in the past.*
collaboration NOUN **collaborator** NOUN

collage collages
Said "kol-*lahj*" NOUN ART a picture made by sticking pieces of paper or cloth onto a surface.

collapse collapses collapsing collapsed
VERB **1** If something such as a building collapses, it falls down suddenly. If a person collapses, they fall down suddenly because they are ill. **2** If

you'll brEAK that Electrical Aerial, Kitty (br**eak**) SPELLING NOTE

something such as a system or a business collapses, it suddenly stops working E.G. *50,000 small firms collapsed last year.* ▶ NOUN **3** The collapse of something is what happens when it stops working E.G. *the collapse of his marriage.*

collapsible
ADJECTIVE A collapsible object can be folded flat when it is not in use E.G. *a collapsible ironing board.*

collar collars
NOUN **1** The collar of a shirt or coat is the part round the neck which is usually folded over. **2** a leather band round the neck of a dog or cat.

collateral
NOUN Collateral is money or property which is used as a guarantee that someone will repay a loan, and which the lender can take if the loan is not repaid.

colleague colleagues
NOUN A person's colleagues are the people he or she works with.

collect collects collecting collected
VERB **1** To collect things is to gather them together for a special purpose or as a hobby E.G. *collecting money for charity.* **2** If you collect someone or something from a place, you call there and take them away E.G. *We had to collect her from school.* **3** When things collect in a place, they gather there over a period of time E.G. *Food collects in holes in the teeth.*
collector NOUN

collected
ADJECTIVE calm and self-controlled.

collection collections
NOUN **1** (ART) a group of things acquired over a period of time E.G. *a collection of paintings.* **2** the collecting of something E.G. *tax collection.* **3** the organized collecting of money, for example for charity, or the sum of money collected.
▤ (sense 1) accumulation, compilation, set

collective collectives
ADJECTIVE **1** involving every member of a group of people E.G. *The wine growers took a collective decision.*
▶ NOUN **2** a group of people who share the responsibility both for running something and for doing the work.
collectively ADVERB

collective noun collective nouns
NOUN a noun that refers to a single unit made up of a number of things, for example 'flock' and 'swarm'.

college colleges
NOUN **1** a place where students study after they have left school. **2** a name given to some secondary schools. **3** one of the institutions into which some universities are divided. **4** In New Zealand English, a college can also refer to a teacher training college.

collide collides colliding collided
VERB If a moving object collides with something, it hits it.

collie collies
NOUN a dog that is used for rounding up sheep.

colliery collieries
NOUN a coal mine.

collision collisions
NOUN A collision occurs when a moving object hits something.
▤ crash, impact, smash

colloquial
Said "kol-**loh**-kwee-al" ADJECTIVE

Colloquial words and phrases are informal and used especially in conversation.

colloquially ADVERB **colloquialism** NOUN

cologne

Said "kol-**lone**" NOUN Cologne is a kind of weak perfume.

colon colons

NOUN **1** the punctuation mark (:). **2** part of your intestine.

What does the Colon do?

The **colon** (:) and the **semicolon** (;) are often confused and used incorrectly.

The **colon** is used to introduce a list:

E.G. *I bought fruit: pears, apples, grapes and plums.*

The colon can also be used to introduce a quotation:

E.G. *He received a message which read: "You can't fool all of the people all of the time."*

Another use of the colon is to introduce an explanation of a statement:

E.G. *They did not enjoy the meal: the food was cold.*

Also look at the grammar box at **semicolon**.

---

colonel colonels

Said "kur-nl" NOUN an army officer with a fairly high rank.

colonial

ADJECTIVE **1** relating to a colony. **2** In Australia, colonial is used to relate to the period of Australian history before the Federation in 1901.

colonize colonizes colonizing colonized; also spelt **colonise**

VERB (HISTORY) When people colonize a place, they go to live there and take control of it E.G. *the Europeans who colonized North America.* When a lot of animals colonize a place, they go there and make it their home E.G. *Toads are colonizing the whole place.*

colonization NOUN **colonist** NOUN

colony colonies

NOUN (HISTORY) **1** a country controlled by a more powerful country. **2** a group of people who settle in a country controlled by their homeland.

colossal

ADJECTIVE very large indeed.

colour colours colouring coloured

NOUN **1** (ART) the appearance something has as a result of reflecting light. **2** Someone's colour is the normal colour of their skin. **3** Colour is also a quality that makes something interesting or exciting E.G. *bringing more culture and colour to the city.* ▶ VERB **4** If something colours your opinion, it affects the way you think about something.

coloured ADJECTIVE **colourful** ADJECTIVE **colourfully** ADVERB **colourless** ADJECTIVE **colouring** NOUN

☰ (sense 1) hue, shade, tint

colour blind

ADJECTIVE Someone who is colour blind cannot distinguish between colours.

colt colts

NOUN a young male horse.

column columns

NOUN **1** a tall solid upright cylinder,

a b c d e f g h i j k l m n o p q r s t u v w x y z

especially one supporting a part of a building. **2** a group of people moving in a long line.

columnist columnists
NOUN a journalist who writes a regular article in a newspaper or magazine.

com- or **con-**
PREFIX 'Com-' or 'con-' means 'together', 'with' or 'jointly' E.G. *combine… consult.*
🔲 from Latin prefix *com-* meaning 'with'

coma comas
NOUN Someone who is in a coma is in a state of deep unconsciousness.

comb combs combing combed
NOUN **1** a flat object with pointed teeth used for tidying your hair.
▶ VERB **2** When you comb your hair, you tidy it with a comb. **3** If you comb a place, you search it thoroughly to try to find someone or something.

combat combats combating combated
NOUN **1** Combat is fighting E.G. *his first experience of combat.* ▶ VERB **2** To combat something means to try to stop it happening or developing E.G. *a way to combat crime.*

combination combinations
NOUN **1** a mixture of things E.G. *a combination of charm and skill.* **2** a series of letters or numbers used to open a special lock.

combine combines combining combined
VERB **1** To combine things is to cause them to exist together E.G. *to combine a career with being a mother.* **2** To combine things also means to join them together to make a single thing E.G. *Combine all the ingredients.*

3 If something combines two qualities or features, it has them both E.G. *a film that combines great charm and scintillating performances.*

combustion
NOUN (SCIENCE) Combustion is the act of burning something or the process of burning.

come comes coming came come
VERB **1** To come to a place is to move there or arrive there. **2** To come to a place also means to reach as far as that place E.G. *The sea water came up to his waist.* **3** 'Come' is used to say that someone or something reaches a particular state E.G. *They came to power in 1997… We had come to a decision.* **4** When a particular time or event comes, it happens E.G. *The peak of his career came early in 1990.* **5** If you come from a place, you were born there or it is your home.
▶ PHRASE **6** A time or event **to come** is a future time or event E.G. *The public will thank them in years to come.*

come about VERB The way something comes about is the way it happens E.G. *The discussion came about because of the proposed changes.*

come across VERB If you come across something, you find it by chance.

come off VERB If something comes off, it succeeds E.G. *His rescue plan had come off.*

come on VERB If something is coming on, it is making progress E.G. *Let's go and see how the grapes are coming on.*

come up VERB If something comes up in a conversation or meeting, it is mentioned or discussed.

come up with VERB If you come up with a plan or idea, you suggest it.

comeback comebacks
NOUN To make a comeback means to be popular or successful again.

comedian comedians
NOUN an entertainer whose job is to make people laugh.

comedienne comediennes
Said "kom-mee-dee-**en**" NOUN a female comedian.

comedy comedies
NOUN a light-hearted play or film with a happy ending.
📖 from Greek *kōmos* meaning 'village festival' and *aeidein* meaning 'to sing'

comet comets
NOUN an object that travels around the sun leaving a bright trail behind it.

comfort comforts comforting comforted
NOUN 1 Comfort is the state of being physically relaxed E.G. *He settled back in comfort.* 2 Comfort is also a feeling of relief from worries or unhappiness E.G. *The thought is a great comfort to me.* ▶ PLURAL NOUN 3 Comforts are things which make your life easier and more pleasant E.G. *all the comforts of home.* ▶ VERB 4 To comfort someone is to make them less worried or unhappy.

comfortable
ADJECTIVE 1 If you are comfortable, you are physically relaxed. 2 Something that is comfortable makes you feel relaxed E.G. *a comfortable bed.* 3 If you feel comfortable in a particular situation, you are not afraid or embarrassed.

comfortably ADVERB

comic comics
ADJECTIVE 1 funny E.G. *a comic monologue.* ▶ NOUN 2 someone who tells jokes. 3 a magazine that contains stories told in pictures.

comical
ADJECTIVE funny E.G. *a comical sight.*

comma commas
NOUN (ENGLISH) the punctuation mark (,).

What does the Comma do?

The **comma** (,) indicates a short pause between different elements within a sentence. This happens, for example, when a sentence consists of two main clauses joined by a conjunction:

E.G. *Anna likes swimming, but Matthew prefers fishing.*

A comma may also separate an introductory phrase or a subordinate clause from the main clause in a sentence:

E.G. *After a month of sunshine, it rained on Thursday.*

However, a short introductory phrase does not need to be followed by a comma:

E.G. *After lunch the classes continued.*

When words such as *therefore, however,* and *moreover* are put into a sentence to show how a train of thought is progressing, they should be marked off by commas:

E.G. *We are confident, however, that the operation will be successful.*

CONTINUED ON NEXT PAGE →

---

a b c d e f g h i j k l m n o p q r s t u v w x y z

have a pIEce of pIE (pie̱ce)　　**SPELLING NOTE**

A
B
C
D
E
F
G
H
I
J
K
L
M
N
O
P
Q
R
S
T
U
V
W
X
Y
Z

The comma also separates items in a list or series:

E.G. *I made this soup with carrots, leeks, and potatoes.*

Commas separate the name of a person or people being addressed from the rest of the sentence:

E.G. *Thank you, ladies and gentlemen, for your attention.*

The comma also separates words in quotation marks from the rest of the sentence, if there is no question or exclamation mark at the end of the quotation:

E.G. *"This is a terrific picture," she said.*

command commands
commanding commanded
VERB **1** To command someone to do something is to order them to do it. **2** If you command something such as respect, you receive it because of your personal qualities. **3** An officer who commands part of an army or navy is in charge of it. ► NOUN **4** an order to do something. **5** Your command of something is your knowledge of it and your ability to use this knowledge E.G. *a good command of English.*

■ (sense 1) direct, order

→ *SEE BOX OPPOSITE*

commandant commandants
Said "kom-man-dant" NOUN an army officer in charge of a place or group of people.

commander commanders
NOUN an officer in charge of a military operation or organization.

commandment commandments
NOUN (RE) The commandments are

What is a Command?

Commands are used to give orders, instructions, or warnings. Commands are made by putting the verb at the start of the sentence. The verb is used in its **imperative form** which is the basic form without any endings added:

E.G. ***Come*** *over here.*

Commands do not need a subject, as people who are being told to do something already know who they are. So commands may consist of a single verb:

E.G. ***Stop!***

The negative form of a command is introduced by *do not* or *don't*:

E.G. ***Don't*** *put that on the table.*

Commands often end with an exclamation mark rather than a full stop, especially if they express urgency:

E.G. *Run for your life**!***

ten rules of behaviour that, according to the Old Testament, people should obey.

commando commandos
NOUN Commandos are soldiers who have been specially trained to carry out raids.

commemorate commemorates
commemorating commemorated
VERB **1** An object that commemorates a person or an event is intended to remind people of that person or event. **2** If you commemorate an event, you do something special to show that you remember it.
commemorative ADJECTIVE

SPELLING NOTE   Pla<u>i</u>ce the fish has a glittering 'EYE' (I) (pla<u>i</u>ce)

commemoration NOUN

commence commences
commencing commenced
VERB; FORMAL To commence is to begin.
commencement NOUN

commend commends
commending commended
VERB To commend someone or
something is to praise them E.G. *He
has been commended for his work.*
commendation NOUN
commendable ADJECTIVE

comment comments
commenting commented
VERB 1 If you comment on something,
you make a remark about it. ▶ NOUN
2 a remark about something E.G. *She
received many comments about her
appearance.*
◼ (sense 1) observe, remark

commentary commentaries
NOUN a description of an event which
is broadcast on radio or television
while the event is happening.

commentator commentators
NOUN someone who gives a radio or
television commentary.

commerce
NOUN Commerce is the buying and
selling of goods.

commercial commercials
ADJECTIVE 1 relating to commerce.
2 Commercial activities involve
producing goods on a large scale in
order to make money E.G. *the
commercial fishing world.* ▶ NOUN 3 an
advertisement on television or radio.
commercially ADVERB

commission commissions
commissioning commissioned
VERB 1 If someone commissions a
piece of work, they formally ask
someone to do it E.G. *a study*

commissioned by the government.
▶ NOUN 2 a piece of work that has
been commissioned. 3 Commission
is money paid to a salesman each
time a sale is made. 4 an official
body appointed to investigate or
control something.

commit commits committing
committed
VERB 1 To commit a crime or sin is to
do it. 2 If you commit yourself, you
state an opinion or state that you
will do something. 3 If someone is
committed to hospital or prison,
they are officially sent there.
committal NOUN
◼ (sense 1) do, perform, perpetrate

commitment commitments
NOUN 1 (RF) Commitment is a
strong belief in an idea or system.
2 something that regularly takes up
some of your time E.G. *business
commitments.*

committed
ADJECTIVE A committed person has
strong beliefs E.G. *a committed
feminist.*

committee committees
NOUN a group of people who make
decisions on behalf of a larger group.

commodity commodities
NOUN; FORMAL Commodities are things
that are sold.

common commoner
commonest; commons
ADJECTIVE 1 Something that is common
exists in large numbers or happens
often E.G. *a common complaint.* 2 If
something is common to two or
more people, they all have it or use it
E.G. *I realized we had a common
interest.* 3 'Common' is used to
indicate that something is of the

a
b
c
d
e
f
g
h
i
j
k
l
m
n
o
p
q
r
s
t
u
v
w
x
y
z

ordinary kind and not special. **4** If you describe someone as **common**, you mean they do not have good taste or good manners. ▶ NOUN **5** an area of grassy land where everyone can go. ▶ PHRASE **6** If two things or people have something **in common**, they both have it.

commonly ADVERB
▣ (sense 1) customary, frequent
▣ (sense 4) coarse, vulgar

commoner commoners
NOUN someone who is not a member of the nobility.

commonplace
ADJECTIVE Something that is commonplace happens often E.G. *Foreign holidays have become commonplace.*

common sense
NOUN Your common sense is your natural ability to behave sensibly and make good judgments.

Commonwealth
NOUN **1** The Commonwealth is an association of countries around the world that are or used to be ruled by Britain. **2** a country made up of a number of states E.G. *the Commonwealth of Australia.*

commotion
NOUN A commotion is a lot of noise and excitement.

communal
ADJECTIVE shared by a group of people E.G. *a communal canteen.*

commune communes
Said "kom-yoon" NOUN a group of people who live together and share everything.

communicate communicates communicating communicated
VERB **1** When people communicate

with each other, they exchange information, usually by talking or writing to each other. **2** If you communicate an idea or a feeling to someone, you make them aware of it.
▣ (sense 2) convey, make known

communication communications
NOUN **1** (PSHE) Communication is the process by which people or animals exchange information. ▶ PLURAL NOUN **2** Communications are the systems by which people communicate or broadcast information, especially using electricity or radio waves. ▶ NOUN **3** FORMAL a letter or telephone call.

communicative
ADJECTIVE Someone who is communicative is willing to talk to people.

communion
NOUN **1** Communion is the sharing of thoughts and feelings. **2** In Christianity, Communion is a religious service in which people share bread and wine in remembrance of the death and resurrection of Jesus Christ.

communism
NOUN Communism is the doctrine that the state should the means of production and that there should be no private property.
communist ADJECTIVE OR NOUN

community communities
NOUN all the people living in a particular area; also used to refer to particular groups within a society E.G. *the heart of the local community… the Asian community.*

commute commutes commuting commuted
VERB People who commute travel a long distance to work every day.
commuter NOUN

compact
ADJECTIVE taking up very little space E.G. *a compact microwave*.

compact disc compact discs
NOUN a music or video recording in the form of a plastic disc which is played using a laser on a special machine, and gives good quality sound or pictures. The abbreviation for compact disc is CD.

companion companions
NOUN someone you travel or spend time with.
companionship NOUN
🔲 from Latin *com-* meaning 'together' and *panis* meaning 'bread'. A companion was originally someone you shared a meal with

company companies
NOUN 1 a business that sells goods or provides a service E.G. *the record company*. 2 a group of actors, opera singers, or dancers E.G. *the Royal Shakespeare Company*. 3 If you have company, you have a friend or visitor with you E.G. *I enjoyed her company*.

comparable
Said "kom-pra-bl" ADJECTIVE If two things are comparable, they are similar in size or quality E.G. *The skill is comparable to playing the violin*.
comparably ADVERB
▣ equal, equivalent, on a par

comparative comparatives
ADJECTIVE 1 You add comparative to indicate that something is true only when compared with what is normal E.G. *eight years of comparative calm*.

▶ NOUN 2 In grammar, the comparative is the form of an adjective which indicates that the person or thing described has more of a particular quality than someone or something else. For example, 'quicker', 'better', and 'easier' are all comparatives.
comparatively ADVERB

What is a Comparative?

Many adjectives have three different forms. These are known as the **positive**, the **comparative**, and the **superlative**. The comparative and superlative are used when you make comparisons.

The **positive** form of an adjective is given as the entry in the dictionary. It is used when there is no comparison between different objects:

E.G. *Matthew is **tall**.*

The **comparative** form is usually made by adding the ending *-er* to the positive form of the adjective. It shows that something possesses a quality to a greater extent than the thing it is being compared with:

E.G. *Matthew is **taller** than Anna.*

You can also make comparisons by using the words *more* or *less* with the positive (not the comparative) form of the adjective:

E.G. *Matthew is **more energetic** than Robbie.*

Irregular Forms
When the comparative and superlative of an adjective are not formed in the regular way, the irregular forms of the adjective are

CONTINUED ON NEXT PAGE →

---

a
b
c
d
e
f
g
h
i
j
k
l
m
n
o
p
q
r
s
t
u
v
w
x
y
z

A
B
C
D
E
F
G
H
I
J
K
L
M
N
O
P
Q
R
S
T
U
V
W
X
Y
Z

shown in the dictionary after the main entry.

Many adjectives – especially ones that have more than one syllable and do not end in -y – do not have separate spelling forms for the comparative and superlative. For these adjectives comparisons must be made using *more, less, most,* and *least*:

E.G. *beautiful* ➤ *more beautiful*
➤ *most beautiful*
boring ➤ *less boring*
➤ *least boring*

Look also at the grammar box at **superlative**.

compare compares comparing compared
VERB 1 (EXAM TERM) When you compare things, you look at them together and see in what ways they are different or similar. 2 If you compare one thing to another, you say it is like the other thing E.G. *His voice is often compared to Michael Stipe's.*

comparison comparisons
NOUN (ENGLISH) When you make a comparison, you consider two things together and see in what ways they are different or similar.

compartment compartments
NOUN 1 a section of a railway carriage. 2 one of the separate parts of an object E.G. *a special compartment inside your vehicle.*

compass compasses
NOUN 1 an instrument with a magnetic needle for finding directions. ▶ PLURAL NOUN 2 Compasses are a hinged instrument for drawing circles.

☑ The proper name for the drawing instrument is *a pair of compasses.*

compassion
NOUN Compassion is pity and sympathy for someone who is suffering.
compassionate ADJECTIVE

compatible
ADJECTIVE If people or things are compatible, they can live or work together successfully.
compatibility NOUN

compatriot compatriots
NOUN Your compatriots are people from your own country.

compel compels compelling compelled
VERB To compel someone to do something is to force them to do it.

compelling
ADJECTIVE 1 If a story or event is compelling, it is extremely interesting E.G. *a compelling novel.* 2 A compelling argument or reason makes you believe that something is true or should be done E.G. *compelling new evidence.*

compensate compensates compensating compensated
VERB 1 To compensate someone is to give them money to replace something lost or damaged. 2 If one thing compensates for another, it cancels out its bad effects E.G. *The trip more than compensated for the hardship.*
compensatory ADJECTIVE
compensation NOUN
▤ (sense 1) recompense, refund
▤ (sense 2) make up for

compere comperes compering compered
Said "kom-*pare*" NOUN 1 the person

who introduces the guests or performers in a show. ► VERB 2 To compere a show is to introduce the guests or performers.

compete competes competing competed
VERB 1 When people or firms compete, each tries to prove that they or their products are the best. 2 If you compete in a contest or game, you take part in it.

competent
ADJECTIVE Someone who is competent at something can do it satisfactorily E.G. *a very competent engineer*.
competently ADVERB **competence** NOUN

competition competitions
NOUN 1 When there is competition between people or groups, they are all trying to get something that not everyone can have E.G. *There's a lot of competition for places*. 2 an event in which people take part to find who is best at something. 3 When there is competition between firms, each firm is trying to get people to buy its own goods.

competitive
ADJECTIVE 1 A competitive situation is one in which people or firms are competing with each other E.G. *a crowded and competitive market*. 2 A competitive person is eager to be more successful than others. 3 Goods sold at competitive prices are cheaper than other goods of the same kind.
competitively ADVERB

competitor competitors
NOUN a person or firm that is competing to become the most successful.

compilation compilations
NOUN A compilation is a book, record, or programme consisting of several items that were originally produced separately E.G. *this compilation of his solo work*.

compile compiles compiling compiled
VERB When someone compiles a book or report, they make it by putting together several items.

complacent
ADJECTIVE If someone is complacent, they are unconcerned about a serious situation and do nothing about it.
complacency NOUN

complain complains complaining complained
VERB 1 If you complain, you say that you are not satisfied with something. 2 If you complain of pain or illness, you say that you have it.
◼ (sense 1) find fault, grumble, moan

complaint complaints
NOUN If you make a complaint, you complain about something.

complement complements complementing complemented
VERB 1 If one thing complements another, the two things go well together E.G. *The tiled floor complements the pine furniture*. ► NOUN 2 If one thing is a complement to another, it goes well with it. 3 In grammar, a complement is a word or phrase that gives information about the subject or object of a sentence. For example, in the sentence 'Rover is a dog', 'is a dog' is a complement.
complementary ADJECTIVE

Psychiatrists Seldom Yell Callously Hard (psychiatrist)   SPELLING NOTE

A
B
C
D
E
F
G
H
I
J
K
L
M
N
O
P
Q
R
S
T
U
V
W
X
Y
Z

complete completes completing completed

ADJECTIVE **1** to the greatest degree possible E.G. *a complete mess*. **2** If something is complete, none of it is missing E.G. *a complete set of tools*. **3** When a task is complete, it is finished E.G. *The planning stage is now complete*. ▶ VERB **4** If you complete something, you finish it. **5** If you complete a form, you fill it in.

completely ADVERB **completion** NOUN

≣ (sense 1) absolute, thorough, total

≣ (sense 2) entire, full, whole

complex complexes

ADJECTIVE **1** Something that is complex has many different parts E.G. *a very complex problem*. ▶ NOUN **2** A complex is a group of buildings, roads, or other things connected with each other in some way E.G. *a hotel and restaurant complex*. **3** If someone has a complex, they have an emotional problem because of a past experience E.G. *an inferiority complex*.

complexity NOUN

≣ (sense 1) complicated, intricate, involved

complexion complexions

NOUN the quality of the skin on your face E.G. *a healthy glowing complexion*.

complicate complicates complicating complicated

VERB To complicate something is to make it more difficult to understand or deal with.

complicated

ADJECTIVE Something that is complicated has so many parts or

aspects that it is difficult to understand or deal with.

complication complications

NOUN something that makes a situation more difficult to deal with E.G. *One possible complication was that it was late in the year*.

compliment compliments complimenting complimented

NOUN **1** If you pay someone a compliment, you tell them you admire something about them. ▶ VERB **2** If you compliment someone, you pay them a compliment.

🔲 from Spanish *cumplir* meaning 'to do what is fitting'

complimentary

ADJECTIVE **1** If you are complimentary about something, you express admiration for it. **2** A complimentary seat, ticket, or publication is given to you free.

comply complies complying complied

VERB If you comply with an order or rule, you obey it.

compliance NOUN

component components

NOUN (D&T) The components of something are the parts it is made of.

compose composes composing composed

VERB **1** If something is composed of particular things or people, it is made up of them. **2** To compose a piece of music, letter, or speech means to write it. **3** If you compose yourself, you become calm after being excited or upset.

composed

ADJECTIVE calm and in control of your feelings.

composer composers
NOUN someone who writes music.

composition compositions
NOUN **1** The composition of something is the things it consists of E.G. *the composition of the ozone layer*. **2** (MUSIC) The composition of a poem or piece of music is the writing of it. **3** (MUSIC) a piece of music or writing.

compost
NOUN Compost is a mixture of decaying plants and manure added to soil to help plants grow.

composure
NOUN Someone's composure is their ability to stay calm E.G. *Jarvis was able to recover his composure.*

compound compounds compounding compounded
NOUN **1** an enclosed area of land with buildings used for a particular purpose E.G. *the prison compound*. **2** In chemistry, a compound is a substance consisting of two or more different substances or chemical elements. ▶ VERB **3** To compound something is to put together different parts to make a whole. **4** To compound a problem is to make it worse by adding to it E.G. *Water shortages were compounded by taps left running.*

comprehend comprehends comprehending comprehended
VERB; FORMAL To comprehend something is to understand or appreciate it E.G. *He did not fully comprehend what was puzzling me.*
comprehension NOUN

comprehensible
ADJECTIVE able to be understood.

comprehensive comprehensives

ADJECTIVE **1** Something that is comprehensive includes everything necessary or relevant E.G. *a comprehensive guide*. ▶ NOUN **2** a school where children of all abilities are taught together.
comprehensively ADVERB

compress compresses compressing compressed
VERB To compress something is to squeeze it or shorten it so that it takes up less space E.G. *compressed air*.
compression NOUN

comprise comprises comprising comprised
VERB; FORMAL What something comprises is what it consists of E.G. *The district then comprised 66 villages.*
✔ You do not need of after *comprise*. For example, you say *the library comprises 500,000 books.*

compromise compromises compromising compromised
NOUN **1** an agreement in which people accept less than they originally wanted E.G. *In the end they reached a compromise*. ▶ VERB **2** When people compromise, they agree to accept less than they originally wanted.
compromising ADJECTIVE

compulsion compulsions
NOUN a very strong desire to do something.

compulsive
ADJECTIVE **1** You use 'compulsive' to describe someone who cannot stop doing something E.G. *a compulsive letter writer*. **2** If you find something such as a book or television programme compulsive, you cannot stop reading or watching it.

a
b
c
d
e
f
g
h
i
j
k
l
m
n
o
p
q
r
s
t
u
v
w
x
y
z

A
B
C
D
E
F
G
H
I
J
K
L
M
N
O
P
Q
R
S
T
U
V
W
X
Y
Z

compulsory
ADJECTIVE If something is compulsory, you have to do it E.G. *School attendance is compulsory*.
■ mandatory, obligatory

computer computers
NOUN (ICT) an electronic machine that can quickly make calculations or store and find information.

computer-aided design
NOUN Computer-aided design is the use of computers and computer graphics to help design things.

computerize computerizes computerizing computerized; also spelt **computerise**
VERB When a system or process is computerized, the work is done by computers.

computing
NOUN Computing is the use of computers and the writing of programs for them.

comrade comrades
NOUN A soldier's comrades are his fellow soldiers, especially in battle.
comradeship NOUN

con cons conning conned INFORMAL
VERB 1 If someone cons you, they trick you into doing or believing something. ▶ NOUN 2 a trick in which someone deceives you into doing or believing something.

con-
PREFIX Con- is another form of **com-**.

concave
ADJECTIVE A concave surface curves inwards, rather than being level or bulging outwards.

conceal conceals concealing concealed
VERB To conceal something is to hide it E.G. *He had concealed his gun*.

concealment NOUN

concede concedes conceding conceded
Said "kon-**seed**" VERB 1 If you concede something, you admit that it is true E.G. *I conceded that he was entitled to his views*. 2 When someone concedes defeat, they accept that they have lost something such as a contest or an election.

conceit
NOUN Conceit is someone's excessive pride in their appearance or abilities.
■ pride, self-importance

conceited
ADJECTIVE Someone who is conceited is too proud of their appearance or abilities.
■ bigheaded, full of oneself, self-important

conceivable
ADJECTIVE If something is conceivable, you can believe that it could exist or be true E.G. *It's conceivable that you also met her*.
conceivably ADVERB

conceive conceives conceiving conceived
VERB 1 If you can conceive of something, you can imagine it or believe it E.G. *Could you conceive of doing such a thing yourself?* 2 If you conceive something such as a plan, you think of it and work out how it could be done. 3 When a woman conceives, she becomes pregnant.

concentrate concentrates concentrating concentrated
VERB 1 If you concentrate on something, you give it all your attention. 2 When something is concentrated in one place, it is all there rather than in several places

E.G. *They are mostly concentrated in the urban areas.*
concentration NOUN

concentrated
ADJECTIVE A concentrated liquid has been made stronger by having water removed from it E.G. *concentrated apple juice.*

concentration camp
concentration camps
NOUN a prison camp, especially one set up by the Nazis during World War Two.

concept concepts
NOUN an abstract or general idea E.G. *the concept of tolerance.*
conceptual ADJECTIVE
conceptually ADVERB

conception conceptions
NOUN 1 Your conception of something is the idea you have of it.
2 Conception is the process by which a woman becomes pregnant.

concern concerns concerning concerned
NOUN 1 Concern is a feeling of worry about something or someone E.G. *public concern about violence.* 2 If something is your concern, it is your responsibility. 3 a business E.G. *a large manufacturing concern.* ▶ VERB 4 If something concerns you or if you are concerned about it, it worries you. 5 You say that something concerns you if it affects or involves you E.G. *It concerns you and me.*
▶ PHRASE 6 If something is **of concern** to you, it is important to you.
concerned ADJECTIVE
☰ (sense 5) be relevant to, involve, regard

concerning
PREPOSITION You use 'concerning' to

show what something is about E.G. *documents concerning arm sales to Iraq.*

concert concerts
NOUN a public performance by musicians.

concerted
ADJECTIVE A concerted action is done by several people together E.G. *concerted action to cut interest rates.*

concerto concertos or **concerti**
Said "kon-cher-toe" NOUN a piece of music for a solo instrument and an orchestra.

concession concessions
NOUN If you make a concession, you agree to let someone have or do something E.G. *Her one concession was to let me come into the building.*

conch conches
NOUN a shellfish with a large, brightly coloured shell; also the shell itself.

concise
ADJECTIVE giving all the necessary information using as few words as necessary E.G. *a concise guide.*
☰ brief, short, succinct

conclude concludes concluding concluded
VERB 1 If you conclude something, you decide that it is so because of the other things that you know E.G. *An inquiry concluded that this was untrue.* 2 When you conclude something, you finish it E.G. *At that point I intend to conclude the interview.*
concluding ADJECTIVE **conclusion** NOUN

conclusive
ADJECTIVE Facts that are conclusive show that something is certainly true.
conclusively ADVERB

ABCDEFGHIJKLMNOPQRSTUVWXYZ

concoct concocts concocting concocted

VERB **1** If you concoct an excuse or explanation, you invent one. **2** If you concoct something, you make it by mixing several things together.

concoction NOUN

concourse concourses

NOUN a wide hall in a building where people walk about or gather together.

concrete

NOUN **1** Concrete is a solid building material made by mixing cement, sand, and water. ▶ ADJECTIVE **2** definite, rather than general or vague E.G. *I don't really have any concrete plans.* **3** real and physical, rather than abstract E.G. *concrete evidence.*

concubine concubines

Said "kong-kyoo-bine" NOUN; OLD-FASHIONED A man's concubine is his mistress.

concur concurs concurring concurred

VERB; FORMAL To concur is to agree E.G. *She concurred with me.*

concurrent

ADJECTIVE If things are concurrent, they happen at the same time.

concurrently ADVERB

concussed

ADJECTIVE confused or unconscious because of a blow to the head.

concussion NOUN

condemn condemns condemning condemned

VERB **1** If you condemn something, you say it is bad and unacceptable E.G. *Teachers condemned the new plans.* **2** If someone is condemned to a punishment, they are given it E.G. *She was condemned to death.* **3** If you

are condemned to something unpleasant, you must suffer it E.G. *Many women are condemned to poverty.* **4** When a building is condemned, it is going to be pulled down because it is unsafe.

condemnation NOUN

■ (sense 1) censure, criticize, disapprove

■ (sense 2) sentence

■ (sense 3) doom

condensation

NOUN (SCIENCE) Condensation is a coating of tiny drops formed on a surface by steam or vapour.

condense condenses condensing condensed

VERB **1** If you condense a piece of writing or a speech, you shorten it. **2** When a gas or vapour condenses, it changes into a liquid.

condescending

ADJECTIVE If you are condescending, you behave in a way that shows you think you are superior to other people.

■ patronizing, superior

condition conditions conditioning conditioned

NOUN **1** the state someone or something is in. ▶ PLURAL NOUN **2** The conditions in which something is done are the location and other factors likely to affect it E.G. *The very difficult conditions continued to affect our performance.* **3** a requirement that must be met for something else to be possible E.G. *He had been banned from drinking alcohol as a condition of bail.* **4** You can refer to an illness or other medical problem as a condition E.G. *a heart condition.* ▶ PHRASE **5** If you are **out of condition**, you are unfit. ▶ VERB **6** If

conditional >> confession

someone is conditioned to behave or think in a certain way, they do it as a result of their upbringing or training.

■ (sense 3) prerequisite, requirement, stipulation

conditional

ADJECTIVE If one thing is conditional on another, it can only happen if the other thing happens E.G. *You feel his love is conditional on you pleasing him.*

condolence condolences

NOUN Condolence is sympathy expressed for a bereaved person.

condom condoms

NOUN a rubber sheath worn by a man on his penis or by a woman inside her vagina as a contraceptive.

condone condones condoning condoned

VERB If you condone someone's bad behaviour, you accept it and do not try to stop it E.G. *We cannot condone violence.*

conducive

Said "kon-**joo**-siv" ADJECTIVE If something is conducive to something else, it makes it likely to happen E.G. *a situation that is conducive to relaxation.*

conduct conducts conducting conducted

VERB 1 To conduct an activity or task is to carry it out E.G. *He seemed to be conducting a conversation.* 2 FORMAL The way you conduct yourself is the way you behave. 3 When someone conducts an orchestra or choir, they stand in front of it and direct it. 4 If something conducts heat or electricity, heat or electricity can pass through it. ▶ NOUN 5 If you take part in

the conduct of an activity or task, you help to carry it out. 6 Your conduct is your behaviour.

conductor conductors

NOUN 1 (MUSIC) someone who conducts an orchestra or choir. 2 someone who moves round a bus or train selling tickets. 3 a substance that conducts heat or electricity.

cone cones

NOUN 1 a regular three-dimensional shape with a circular base and a point at the top. 2 A fir cone or pine cone is the fruit of a fir or pine tree.

confectionery

NOUN Confectionery is sweets.

confederation confederations

NOUN an organization formed for business or political purposes.

confer confers conferring conferred

VERB When people confer, they discuss something in order to make a decision.

conference conferences

NOUN a meeting at which formal discussions take place.

confess confesses confessing confessed

VERB If you confess to something, you admit it E.G. *Your son has confessed to his crimes.*

■ admit, own up

confession confessions

NOUN 1 If you make a confession, you admit you have done something wrong. 2 Confession is the act of confessing something, especially a religious act in which people confess their sins to a priest.

■ (sense 1) acknowledgment, admission

a
b
c
d
e
f
g
h
i
j
k
l
m
n
o
p
q
r
s
t
u
v
w
x
y
z

Elaine and Emily shout EE when they mEEt to grEEt each other (-ee-)   SPELLING NOTE

A
B
C
D
E
F
G
H
I
J
K
L
M
N
O
P
Q
R
S
T
U
V
W
X
Y
Z

confessional confessionals
NOUN a small room in some churches where people confess their sins to a priest.

confetti
NOUN Confetti is small pieces of coloured paper thrown over the bride and groom at a wedding.
📖 from Italian *confetto* meaning 'a sweet'

confidant confidants
Said "**kon**-fid-dant" NOUN; FORMAL a person you discuss your private problems with
☑ When the person you discuss your private problems with is a girl or a woman, the word is spelt *confidante*.

confide confides confiding confided
VERB If you confide in or to someone, you tell them a secret E.G. *Marian confided in me that she was very worried.*

confidence confidences
NOUN 1 If you have confidence in someone, you feel you can trust them. 2 Someone who has confidence is sure of their own abilities or qualities. 3 a secret you tell someone.

confident
ADJECTIVE 1 If you are confident about something, you are sure it will happen the way you want it to.
2 People who are confident are sure of their own abilities or qualities.
confidently ADVERB
▤ (sense 1) certain, positive, sure
▤ (sense 2) assured, self-assured

confidential
ADJECTIVE Confidential information is meant to be kept secret.

confidentially ADVERB
confidentiality NOUN

confine confines confining confined
VERB 1 If something is confined to one place, person, or thing, it exists only in that place or affects only that person or thing. 2 If you confine yourself to doing or saying something, it is the only thing you do or say E.G. *They confined themselves to discussing the weather.*
3 If you are confined to a place, you cannot leave it E.G. *She was confined to bed for two days.* ▶ PLURAL NOUN
4 The confines of a place are its boundaries E.G. *outside the confines of the prison.*
confinement NOUN

confined
ADJECTIVE A confined space is small and enclosed by walls.

confirm confirms confirming confirmed
VERB 1 To confirm something is to say or show that it is true E.G. *Police confirmed that they had received a call.* 2 If you confirm an arrangement or appointment, you say it is definite.
3 When someone is confirmed, they are formally accepted as a member of a Christian church.
confirmation NOUN
▤ (sense 1) prove, verify

confirmed
ADJECTIVE You use 'confirmed' to describe someone who has a belief or way of life that is unlikely to change E.G. *a confirmed bachelor.*

confiscate confiscates confiscating confiscated
VERB To confiscate something is to

take it away from someone as a punishment.

conflict conflicts conflicting conflicted

NOUN **1** Conflict is disagreement and argument E.G. *conflict between workers and management.* **2** (HISTORY) a war or battle. **3** When there is a conflict of ideas or interests, people have different ideas or interests which cannot all be satisfied. ▶ VERB **4** When ideas or interests conflict, they are different and cannot all be satisfied.

■ (sense 1) disagreement, dissension

■ (sense 2) battle, clash

■ (sense 4) be incompatible, clash, disagree

conform conforms conforming conformed

VERB **1** If you conform, you behave the way people expect you to. **2** If something conforms to a law or to someone's wishes, it is what is required or wanted.

conformist NOUN OR ADJECTIVE

confront confronts confronting confronted

VERB **1** If you are confronted with a problem or task, you have to deal with it. **2** If you confront someone, you meet them face to face like an enemy. **3** If you confront someone with evidence or a fact, you present it to them in order to accuse them of something.

confrontation confrontations

NOUN a serious dispute or fight E.G. *a confrontation between police and fans.*

confuse confuses confusing confused

VERB **1** If you confuse two things, you mix them up and think one of them is the other E.G. *You are confusing facts with opinion.* **2** To confuse someone means to make them uncertain about what is happening or what to do. **3** To confuse a situation means to make it more complicated.

confused ADJECTIVE **confusing** ADJECTIVE **confusion** NOUN

■ (sense 2) baffle, bewilder

congeal congeals congealing congealed

Said "kon-**jeel**" VERB When a liquid congeals, it becomes very thick and sticky.

congenial

Said "kon-**jeen**-yal" ADJECTIVE If something is congenial, it is pleasant and suits you E.G. *We wanted to talk in congenial surroundings.*

congenital

ADJECTIVE; MEDICAL If someone has a congenital disease or handicap, they have had it from birth but did not inherit it.

congested

ADJECTIVE **1** When a road is congested, it is so full of traffic that normal movement is impossible. **2** If your nose is congested, it is blocked and you cannot breathe properly.

congestion NOUN

conglomerate conglomerates

NOUN a large business organization consisting of several companies.

congratulate congratulates congratulating congratulated

VERB If you congratulate someone, you express pleasure at something good that has happened to them, or praise them for something they have achieved.

a
b
c
d
e
f
g
h
i
j
k
l
m
n
o
p
q
r
s
t
u
v
w
x
y
z

A
B
C
D
E
F
G
H
I
J
K
L
M
N
O
P
Q
R
S
T
U
V
W
X
Y
Z

congratulation NOUN
congratulatory ADJECTIVE
congregate congregates
congregating congregated
VERB When people congregate,
they gather together somewhere.
congregation congregations
NOUN the congregation are the
people attending a service in a
church.
congress congresses
NOUN a large meeting held to discuss
ideas or policies E.G. *a medical
congress*.
conical
ADJECTIVE shaped like a cone.
conifer conifers
NOUN any type of evergreen tree that
produces cones.
coniferous ADJECTIVE
conjecture
NOUN Conjecture is guessing about
something E.G. *There was no
evidence, only conjecture*.
conjugate conjugates
conjugating conjugated
Said "kon-joo-gate" VERB When you
conjugate a verb, you list the
different forms of it you use with the
pronouns 'I' 'you' (singular) 'he' 'she'
'it' 'you' (plural) and 'they'.
conjunction conjunctions
NOUN 1 (ENGLISH) In grammar, a
conjunction is a word that links two
other words or two clauses, for
example 'and', 'but', 'while', and 'that'.
▶ PHRASE 2 If two or more things are
done **in conjunction**, they are done
together.
→ SEE BOX OPPOSITE.
conjurer conjurers
NOUN someone who entertains
people by doing magic tricks.

What is a Conjunction?

A conjunction is a word that joins
two words or two parts of a
sentence together. Conjunctions
are sometimes called "joining
words".
Co-ordinating conjunctions join
items of equal importance:
  E.G. *I ordered fish **and** chips.*
Contrasting conjunctions are a
type of co-ordinating conjunction
which are used to join opposites or
contrasting items:
  E.G. *He was not walking **but**
  running.*
Correlative conjunctions are
pairs of conjunctions, such as *either
... or*, or *both ... and*, each of which
introduces a separate item in the
sentence:
  E.G. *She speaks **both** French **and**
  German.
  You can drink **either** tea **or**
  coffee.*
Subordinating conjunctions join
additional items to the main part
of the sentence:
  E.G. *He was happy **because** he had
  finished his work.
  I will come **if** I have time.*

---

conker conkers
NOUN Conkers are hard brown nuts
from a horse chestnut tree.
connect connects connecting
connected
VERB 1 (ICT) To connect two things is
to join them together E.G. *a modem
connecting your PC to the Internet.* **2** If
you connect something with
something else, you think of them as

being linked E.G. *High blood pressure is closely connected to heart disease.*

connection connections; also spelt **connexion**

NOUN **1** a link or relationship between things. **2** the point where two wires or pipes are joined together E.G. *a loose connection.* **3** ⟨ ICT ⟩ a link made between two telephones or computers via telephone lines or cables E.G. *a bad connection.* ▶ PLURAL NOUN **4** Someone's connections are the people they know E.G. *He had powerful connections in the army.*

connective connectives

NOUN a word or short phrase that connects clauses, phrases or words.

connoisseur connoisseurs

Said "kon-nis-**sir**" NOUN someone who knows a lot about the arts, or about food or drink E.G. *a great connoisseur of champagne.*

📖 from Old French *connoistre* meaning 'to know'

connotation connotations

NOUN The connotations of a word or name are what it makes you think of E.G. *a grey man for whom grey has no connotation of dullness.*

conquer conquers conquering conquered

VERB **1** To conquer people is to take control of their country by force. **2** If you conquer something difficult or dangerous, you succeed in controlling it E.G. *Conquer your fear!*

conqueror NOUN

conquest conquests

NOUN **1** Conquest is the conquering of a country or group of people. **2** Conquests are lands captured by conquest.

conscience consciences

Said "con-shinz" NOUN the part of your mind that tells you what is right and wrong.

☑ Do not confuse the spellings or pronunciations of *conscience* and *conscious*.

conscientious

Said "kon-shee-**en**-shus" ADJECTIVE Someone who is conscientious is very careful to do their work properly.

conscientiously ADVERB

🔲 careful, meticulous, thorough

conscious

ADJECTIVE

Said "con-shus" **1** If you are conscious of something, you are aware of it E.G. *She was not conscious of the time.* **2** A conscious action or effort is done deliberately E.G. *I made a conscious decision not to hide.* **3** Someone who is conscious is awake, rather than asleep or unconscious E.G. *Still conscious, she was taken to hospital.*

consciously ADVERB

consciousness NOUN

☑ Do not confuse the spellings or pronunciations of *conscious* and *conscience*.

consecrated

ADJECTIVE A consecrated building or place is one that has been officially declared to be holy.

consecutive

ADJECTIVE Consecutive events or periods of time happen one after the other E.G. *eight consecutive games.*

consensus

NOUN general agreement among a group of people E.G. *The consensus was that it could be done.*

☑ There are three s's in *consensus*,

a
b
c
d
e
f
g
h
i
j
k
l
m
n
o
p
q
r
s
t
u
v
w
x
y
z

do not confuse the spelling with
census. You should not say *consensus
of opinion*, as *consensus* already has
of opinion in its meaning.

**consent consents consenting
consented**
NOUN 1 permission to do something
E.G. *Thomas reluctantly gave his
consent to my writing this book.*
2 agreement between two or more
people E.G. *By common consent it
was the best game of these
championships.* ▶ VERB 3 If you
consent to something, you agree to
it or allow it.

consequence consequences
NOUN 1 The consequences of
something are its results or effects
E.G. *the dire consequences of major
war.* 2 FORMAL If something is of
consequence, it is important.

consequent
ADJECTIVE Consequent describes
something else as being the result of
something E.G. *an earthquake in
1980 and its consequent damage.*
consequently ADVERB

conservation
NOUN the preservation of the
environment.
conservationist NOUN or ADJECTIVE

conservative conservatives
NOUN 1 In Britain, a member or
supporter of the Conservative Party,
a political party that believes that
the government should interfere as
little as possible in the running of
the economy. ▶ ADJECTIVE 2 In Britain,
Conservative views and policies are
those of the Conservative Party.
3 Someone who is conservative is
not willing to accept changes or new
ideas. 4 A conservative estimate or

guess is a cautious or moderate one.
conservatively ADVERB
conservatism NOUN

conservatory conservatories
NOUN a room with glass walls and a
glass roof in which plants are kept.

**conserve conserves conserving
conserved**
VERB If you conserve a supply of
something, you make it last E.G. *the
only way to conserve energy.*

**consider considers considering
considered**
VERB 1 If you consider something to
be the case, you think or judge it to
be so E.G. *The manager does not
consider him an ideal team member.*
2 To consider something is to think
about it carefully E.G. *If an offer were
made, we would consider it.*
3 (EXAM TERM) To consider is to think
about something carefully and to
include your own opinions about it
in your answer. 4 If you consider
someone's needs or feelings, you
take account of them.
■ (sense 2) contemplate, think
about

considerable
ADJECTIVE A considerable amount of
something is a lot of it E.G. *a
considerable sum of money.*
considerably ADVERB

considerate
ADJECTIVE Someone who is considerate
pays attention to other people's
needs and feelings.

consideration considerations
NOUN 1 careful thought about
something E.G. *a decision demanding
careful consideration.* 2 If you show
consideration for someone, you take
account of their needs and feelings.

3 something that has to be taken into account E.G. *Money was also a consideration.*

■ (sense 1) deliberation, thought

considered

ADJECTIVE A considered opinion or judgment is arrived at by careful thought.

considering

CONJUNCTION or PREPOSITION You say considering to indicate that you are taking something into account E.G. *I know that must sound callous, considering that I was married to the man for seventeen years.*

consign consigns consigning consigned

VERB; FORMAL To consign something to a particular place is to send or put it there.

consignment consignments

NOUN a load of goods being delivered somewhere.

consist consists consisting consisted

VERB What something consists of is its different parts or members E.G. *The brain consists of millions of nerve cells.*

consistency consistencies

NOUN **1** the quality of being consistent. **2** The consistency of a substance is how thick or smooth it is E.G. *the consistency of single cream.*

consistent

ADJECTIVE **1** If you are consistent, you keep doing something the same way E.G. *one of our most consistent performers.* **2** If something such as a statement or argument is consistent, there are no contradictions in it.

consistently ADVERB

console consoles consoling consoled

VERB *Said "con-sole"* **1** To console someone who is unhappy is to make them more cheerful. ▶ NOUN *Said "con-sole"* **2** a panel with switches or knobs for operating a machine.

consolation NOUN

consolidate consolidates consolidating consolidated

VERB To consolidate something you have gained or achieved is to make it more secure.

consolidation NOUN

consonant consonants

NOUN (ENGLISH) a sound such as 'p' or 'm' which you make by stopping the air flowing freely through your mouth.

🔠 from Latin *consonare* meaning 'to sound at the same time'

consort consorts consorting consorted

VERB *Said "con-sort"* **1** FORMAL If you consort with someone, you spend a lot of time with them. ▶ NOUN *Said "con-sort"* **2** the wife or husband of the king or queen.

consortium consortia or consortiums

NOUN a group of businesses working together.

conspicuous

ADJECTIVE If something is conspicuous, people can see or notice it very easily.

conspicuously ADVERB

conspiracy conspiracies

NOUN When there is a conspiracy, a group of people plan something illegal, often for a political purpose.

conspirator conspirators

NOUN someone involved in a conspiracy.

a
b
c
d
e
f
g
h
i
j
k
l
m
n
o
p
q
r
s
t
u
v
w
x
y
z

A
B
C
D
E
F
G
H
I
J
K
L
M
N
O
P
Q
R
S
T
U
V
W
X
Y
Z

conspire conspires conspiring conspired

VERB 1 When people conspire, they plan together to do something illegal, often for a political purpose. 2 LITERARY When events conspire towards a particular result, they seem to work together to cause it E.G. *Circumstances conspired to doom the business.*

constable constables

NOUN a police officer of the lowest rank.

📖 from Latin *comes stabuli* meaning 'officer of the stable'

constabulary constabularies

NOUN a police force.

constant

ADJECTIVE 1 Something that is constant happens all the time or is always there E.G. *a city under constant attack.* 2 If an amount or level is constant, it stays the same. 3 People who are constant stay loyal to a person or idea.

constantly ADVERB **constancy** NOUN

■ (sense 2) fixed, steady, unchanging

constellation constellations

NOUN a group of stars.

consternation

NOUN anxiety or dismay E.G. *There was some consternation when it began raining.*

constipated

ADJECTIVE Someone who is constipated is unable to pass solid waste from their bowels.

constipation NOUN

constituency constituencies

NOUN a town or area represented by an MP.

constituent constituents

NOUN 1 An MP's constituents are the voters who live in his or her constituency. 2 The constituents of something are its parts E.G. *the major constituents of bone.*

constitute constitutes constituting constituted

VERB If a group of things constitute something, they are what it consists of E.G. *Jewellery constitutes 80 per cent of the stock.*

constitution constitutions

NOUN 1 (HISTORY) The constitution of a country is the system of laws which formally states people's rights and duties. 2 Your constitution is your health E.G. *a very strong constitution.*

constitutional ADJECTIVE

constitutionally ADVERB

constrained

ADJECTIVE If a person feels constrained to do something, they feel that they should do that.

constraint constraints

NOUN something that limits someone's freedom of action E.G. *constraints on trade union power.*

constrict constricts constricting constricted

VERB To constrict something is to squeeze it tightly.

constriction NOUN

construct constructs constructing constructed

VERB To construct something is to build or make it.

construction constructions

NOUN 1 The construction of something is the building or making of it E.G. *the construction of the harbour.* 2 something built or made E.G. *a shoddy modern construction built of concrete.*

constructive
ADJECTIVE Constructive criticisms and comments are helpful.
constructively ADVERB

consul consuls
NOUN an official who lives in a foreign city and who looks after people there who are citizens of his or her own country.
consular ADJECTIVE

consulate consulates
NOUN the place where a consul works.

consult consults consulting consulted
VERB 1 If you consult someone, you ask for their opinion or advice. 2 When people consult each other, they exchange ideas and opinions. 3 If you consult a book or map, you look at it for information.

consultancy consultancies
NOUN an organization whose members give expert advice on a subject.

consultant consultants
NOUN 1 an experienced doctor who specializes in one type of medicine. 2 someone who gives expert advice E.G. *a management consultant.*

consultation consultations
NOUN 1 a meeting held to discuss something. 2 Consultation is discussion or the seeking of advice E.G. *There has to be much better consultation with the public.*
consultative ADJECTIVE

consume consumes consuming consumed
VERB 1 FORMAL If you consume something, you eat or drink it. 2 To consume fuel or energy is to use it up.

consumer consumers
NOUN someone who buys things or uses services E.G. *two new magazines for teenage consumers.*

consumerism
NOUN Consumerism is the belief that a country will have a strong economy if its people buy a lot of goods and spend a lot of money.

consuming
ADJECTIVE A consuming passion or interest is more important to you than anything else.

consummate consummates consummating consummated
VERB *Said* "**kons**-yum-mate" 1 To consummate something is to make it complete. 2 FORMAL If two people consummate a marriage or relationship, they make it complete by having sex. ▶ ADJECTIVE 3 *Said* "kon-**sum**-mit" You use 'consummate' to describe someone who is very good at something E.G. *a consummate politician.*
consummation NOUN

consumption
NOUN The consumption of fuel or food is the using of it, or the amount used.

contact contacts contacting contacted
NOUN 1 If you are in contact with someone, you regularly talk to them or write to them. 2 When things are in contact, they are touching each other. 3 someone you know in a place or organization from whom you can get help or information. ▶ VERB 4 If you contact someone, you telephone them or write to them.
■ (sense 4) get *or* be in touch with, reach

a
b
c
d
e
f
g
h
i
j
k
l
m
n
o
p
q
r
s
t
u
v
w
x
y
z

there's a rAKE in the brAKEs (brake)　　SPELLING NOTE

A
B
C
D
E
F
G
H
I
J
K
L
M
N
O
P
Q
R
S
T
U
V
W
X
Y
Z

contact lens contact lenses
NOUN Contact lenses are small plastic
lenses that you put in your eyes
instead of wearing glasses, to help
you see better.

contagious
ADJECTIVE A contagious disease can be
caught by touching people or things
infected with it.

contain contains containing
contained
VERB 1 If a substance contains
something, that thing is a part of it
E.G. *Alcohol contains sugar.* 2 The
things a box or room contains are
the things inside it. 3 FORMAL To
contain something also means to
stop it increasing or spreading E.G.
efforts to contain the disease.
containment NOUN

container containers
NOUN 1 something such as a box or a
bottle that you keep things in. 2 a
large sealed metal box for
transporting things.
■ (sense 1) holder, receptacle

contaminate contaminates
contaminating contaminated
VERB If something is contaminated by
dirt, chemicals, or radiation, it is
made impure and harmful E.G. *foods
contaminated with lead.*
contamination NOUN

contemplate contemplates
contemplating contemplated
VERB 1 To contemplate is to think
carefully about something for a long
time. 2 If you contemplate doing
something, you consider doing it
E.G. *I never contemplated
marrying Charles.* 3 If you
contemplate something, you look
at it for a long time E.G. *He*

contemplated his drawings.
contemplation NOUN
contemplative ADJECTIVE

contemporary contemporaries
ADJECTIVE 1 produced or happening
now E.G. *contemporary literature.*
2 produced or happening at the time
you are talking about E.G.
*contemporary descriptions of Lizzie
Borden.* ▶ NOUN 3 Someone's
contemporaries are other people
living or active at the same time as
them E.G. *Shakespeare and his
contemporaries.*

contempt
NOUN If you treat someone or
something with contempt, you show
no respect for them at all.

contemptible
ADJECTIVE not worthy of any respect
E.G. *this contemptible piece of
nonsense.*

contemptuous
ADJECTIVE showing contempt.
contemptuously ADVERB

contend contends contending
contended
VERB 1 To contend with a difficulty is
to deal with it E.G. *They had to
contend with injuries.* 2 FORMAL If you
contend that something is true, you
say firmly that it is true. 3 When
people contend for something, they
compete for it.
contender NOUN

content contents contenting
contented
PLURAL NOUN *Said "con-tents"* 1 The
contents of something are the things
inside it. ▶ NOUN *Said "con-tent"*
2 (LIBRARY) The content of an article
or speech is what is expressed in it.
3 Content is the proportion of

something that a substance contains
E.G. *White bread is inferior in vitamin content.* ▶ ADJECTIVE *Said* "con-**tent**"
4 happy and satisfied with your life.
5 willing to do or have something
E.G. *He would be content to telephone her.* ▶ VERB *Said* "con-**tent**" **6** If you content yourself with doing something, you do it and do not try to do anything else E.G. *He contented himself with an early morning lecture.*

contented
ADJECTIVE happy and satisfied with your life.
contentedly ADVERB   **contentment** NOUN

contention contentions
NOUN; FORMAL Someone's contention is the idea or opinion they are expressing E.G. *It is our contention that the 1980s mark a turning point in planning.*

contest contests contesting contested
NOUN *Said* "con-**test**" **1** a competition or game E.G. *a boxing contest.* **2** a struggle for power E.G. *a presidential contest.* ▶ VERB *Said* "con-**test**" **3** If you contest a statement or decision, you object to it formally.
▤ (sense 1) competition, game, match

contestant contestants
NOUN someone taking part in a competition.
▤ competitor, player

context contexts
NOUN **1** The context of something consists of matters related to it which help to explain it E.G. *English history is treated in a European context.* **2** The context of a word or sentence consists of the words or

sentences before and after it.

continent continents
NOUN **1** a very large area of land, such as Africa or Asia. **2** The Continent is the mainland of Europe.
continental ADJECTIVE

contingency contingencies
Said "kon-**tin**-jen-see" NOUN something that might happen in the future E.G. *I need to examine all possible contingencies.*

contingent contingents
NOUN **1** a group of people representing a country or organization E.G. *a strong South African contingent.* **2** a group of police or soldiers.

continual
ADJECTIVE **1** happening all the time without stopping E.G. *continual headaches.* **2** happening again and again E.G. *the continual snide remarks.*
continually ADVERB
▤ constant, incessant

continuation continuations
NOUN **1** The continuation of something is the continuing of it E.G. *the continuation of the human race.* **2** Something that is a continuation of an event follows it and seems like a part of it E.G. *a meeting which was a continuation of a conference.*

continue continues continuing continued
VERB **1** If you continue to do something, you keep doing it. **2** If something continues, it does not stop. **3** You also say something continues when it starts again after stopping E.G. *She continued after a pause.*

a
b
c
d
e
f
g
h
i
j
k
l
m
n
o
p
q
r
s
t
u
v
w
x
y
z

I always visit my FRIend on a FRIday (<u>fri</u>end)   **SPELLING NOTE**

A
B
C
D
E
F
G
H
I
J
K
L
M
N
O
P
Q
R
S
T
U
V
W
X
Y
Z

■ (senses 2, 3 & 4) carry on, go on, proceed

continuous

ADJECTIVE **1** Continuous means happening or existing without stopping. **2** A continuous line or surface has no gaps or holes in it. **continuously** ADVERB **continuity** NOUN

contorted

ADJECTIVE twisted into an unnatural, unattractive shape.

contour contours

NOUN **1** The contours of something are its general shape. **2** (GEOGRAPHY) On a map, a contour is a line joining points of equal height.

contra-

PREFIX Contra- means against or opposite to E.G. *contraflow… contraindication.*

contraception

NOUN Contraception is methods of preventing pregnancy.

contraceptive contraceptives

NOUN a device or pill for preventing pregnancy.

contract contracts contracting contracted

NOUN *Said* "con-trakt" **1** a written legal agreement about the sale of something or work done for money. ▶ VERB *Said* "con-trakt" **2** When something contracts, it gets smaller or shorter. **3** FORMAL If you contract an illness, you get it E.G. *Her husband contracted a virus.*

contractual ADJECTIVE **contraction** NOUN

contractor contractors

NOUN a person or company who does work for other people or companies E.G. *a building contractor.*

contradict contradicts contradicting contradicted

VERB (HISTORY) If you contradict someone, you say that what they have just said is not true, and that something else is.

contradiction NOUN

contradictory ADJECTIVE

contraption contraptions

NOUN a strange-looking machine or piece of equipment.

contrary

ADJECTIVE **1** Contrary ideas or opinions are opposed to each other and cannot be held by the same person. ▶ PHRASE **2** You say **on the contrary** when you are contradicting what someone has just said.

contrast contrasts contrasting contrasted

NOUN *Said* "kon-trast" **1** a great difference between things E.G. *the real contrast between the two poems.* **2** If one thing is a contrast to another, it is very different from it E.G. *I couldn't imagine a greater contrast to Maxwell.* ▶ VERB *Said* "kon-trast" **3** (EXAM TERM) If you contrast things, you describe or emphasize the differences between them. **4** If one thing contrasts with another, it is very different from it E.G. *The interview contrasted completely with the one she gave after Tokyo.*

contravene contravenes contravening contravened

VERB; FORMAL If you contravene a law or rule, you do something that it forbids.

contribute contributes contributing contributed

VERB **1** If you contribute to something, you do things to help it succeed E.G.

The elderly have much to contribute to the community. **2** If you contribute money, you give it to help to pay for something. **3** If something contributes to an event or situation, it is one of its causes E.G. *The dry summer has contributed to perfect conditions.*
contribution NOUN **contributor** NOUN **contributory** ADJECTIVE
■ (sense 2) donate, give

contrive contrives contriving contrived
VERB; FORMAL If you contrive to do something difficult, you succeed in doing it E.G. *Anthony contrived to escape with a few companions.*

contrived
ADJECTIVE Something that is contrived is unnatural E.G. *a contrived compliment.*

control controls controlling controlled
NOUN **1** Control of a country or organization is the power to make the important decisions about how it is run. **2** (PSHE) Your control over something is your ability to make it work the way you want it to. **3** The controls on a machine are knobs or other devices used to work it. ► VERB **4** To control a country or organization means to have the power to make decisions about how it is run. **5** To control something such as a machine or system means to make it work the way you want it to. **6** (PSHE) If you control yourself, you make yourself behave calmly when you are angry or upset. ► PHRASE **7** If something is **out of control**, nobody has any power over it.
controller NOUN
■ (sense 6) hold back, restrain

controversial
ADJECTIVE Something that is controversial causes a lot of discussion and argument, because many people disapprove of it.

controversy controversies
Said "kon-**triv**-ver-see" *or* "kon-**trov**-ver-see" NOUN discussion and argument because many people disapprove of something.
🔤 from Latin *controversus* meaning 'turned in an opposite direction'
✓ Notice that there are two ways to say *controversy*. The first way is older, and the second is becoming more common.

conundrum conundrums
NOUN; FORMAL a puzzling problem.

convalesce convalesces convalescing convalesced
VERB When people convalesce, they rest and regain their health after an illness or operation.

convection
NOUN Convection is the process by which heat travels through gases and liquids.

convene convenes convening convened
VERB **1** FORMAL To convene a meeting is to arrange for it to take place. **2** When people convene, they come together for a meeting.

convenience conveniences
NOUN **1** The convenience of something is the fact that it is easy to use or that it makes something easy to do. **2** something useful.

convenient
ADJECTIVE If something is convenient, it is easy to use or it makes something easy to do.
conveniently ADVERB

a
b
c
d
e
f
g
h
i
j
k
l
m
n
o
p
q
r
s
t
u
v
w
x
y
z

The government licen**S**es Schnapps (licen**s**es)   SPELLING NOTE

■ handy, useful

convent convents
NOUN a building where nuns live, or a school run by nuns.

convention conventions
NOUN 1 an accepted way of behaving or doing something. 2 a large meeting of an organization or political group E.G. *the Democratic Convention*.

conventional
ADJECTIVE 1 You say that people are conventional when there is nothing unusual about their way of life. 2 Conventional methods are the ones that are usually used.
conventionally ADVERB

converge converges converging converged
VERB To converge is to meet or join at a particular place.

conversation conversations
NOUN If you have a conversation with someone, you spend time talking to them.
conversational ADJECTIVE
conversationalist NOUN

converse converses conversing conversed
VERB *Said "con-verse"* 1 FORMAL When people converse, they talk to each other. ▶ NOUN *Said "con-verse"* 2 The converse of something is its opposite E.G. *Don't you think that the converse might also be possible?*
conversely ADVERB

convert converts converting converted
VERB *Said "con-vert"* 1 To convert one thing into another is to change it so that it becomes the other thing. 2 If someone converts you, they persuade you to change your

religious or political beliefs. ▶ NOUN *Said "con-vert"* 3 someone who has changed their religious or political beliefs.
conversion NOUN **convertible** ADJECTIVE

convex
ADJECTIVE A convex surface bulges outwards, rather than being level or curving inwards.

convey conveys conveying conveyed
VERB 1 To convey information or ideas is to cause them to be known or understood. 2 FORMAL To convey someone or something to a place is to transport them there.

conveyor belt conveyor belts
NOUN a moving strip used in factories for moving objects along.

convict convicts convicting convicted
VERB 1 To convict someone of a crime is to find them guilty. ▶ NOUN 2 someone serving a prison sentence.

conviction convictions
NOUN 1 a strong belief or opinion. 2 The conviction of someone is what happens when they are found guilty in a court of law.

convince convinces convincing convinced
VERB To convince someone of something is to persuade them that it is true.
■ persuade, sway

convincing
ADJECTIVE 'Convincing' is used to describe things or people that can make you believe something is true E.G. *a convincing argument*.
convincingly ADVERB
■ credible, persuasive, plausible

convoluted ≫ copse

convoluted
Said "kon-vol-**yoo**-tid" ADJECTIVE
Something that is convoluted has
many twists and bends E.G. *the
convoluted patterns of these designs.*

convoy convoys
NOUN a group of vehicles or ships
travelling together.

convulsion convulsions
NOUN If someone has convulsions,
their muscles move violently and
uncontrollably.

coo coos cooing cooed
VERB When pigeons and doves coo,
they make a soft flutelike sound.

cook cooks cooking cooked
VERB 1 To cook food is to prepare it for
eating by heating it. ► NOUN
2 someone who prepares and cooks
food, often as their job.

cooker cookers
NOUN a device for cooking food.

cookery
NOUN the activity of preparing and
cooking food.

**cool cooler coolest; cools
cooling cooled**
ADJECTIVE 1 Something cool has a low
temperature but is not cold. 2 If you
are cool in a difficult situation, you
stay calm and do not get upset.
► VERB 3 When something cools or
when you cool it, it becomes less
warm.
coolly ADVERB **coolness** NOUN

**coolabah coolabahs; also spelt
coolibar**
NOUN an Australian eucalypt that
grows along rivers.

coop coops
NOUN a cage for chickens or rabbits.

**cooperate cooperates
cooperating cooperated**
Said "koh-**op**-er-ate" VERB 1 When
people cooperate, they work or act
together. 2 To cooperate also means
to do what someone asks.
cooperation NOUN

cooperative cooperatives
Said "koh-**op**-er-ut-tiv" NOUN 1 a
business or organization run by the
people who work for it, and who
share its benefits or profits. ► ADJECTIVE
2 A cooperative activity is done by
people working together. 3 Someone
who is cooperative does what you
ask them to.

**coordinates coordinating
coordinated**
Said "koh-or-din-ate" VERB 1 To
coordinate an activity is to organize
the people or things involved in it
E.G. *to coordinate the campaign.*
► PLURAL NOUN 2 (MATHS) Coordinates
are a pair of numbers or letters
which tell you how far along and up
or down a point is on a grid.
coordination NOUN **coordinator**
NOUN

cop cops
NOUN; INFORMAL a policeman.

cope copes coping coped
VERB If you cope with a problem or
task, you deal with it successfully.

copious
ADJECTIVE; FORMAL existing or produced
in large quantities E.G. *I wrote
copious notes for the solicitor.*

copper coppers
NOUN 1 Copper is a soft reddish-
brown metal. 2 Coppers are brown
metal coins of low value. 3 INFORMAL a
policeman.

copse copses
NOUN a small group of trees growing
close together.

a
b
c
d
e
f
g
h
i
j
k
l
m
n
o
p
q
r
s
t
u
v
w
x
y
z

Plaice the fish has a glittering 'EYE' (I) (plaice) SPELLING NOTE

A
B
C
D
E
F
G
H
I
J
K
L
M
N
O
P
Q
R
S
T
U
V
W
X
Y
Z

copulate copulates copulating
copulated
VERB; FORMAL To copulate is to have
sex.
copulation NOUN

copy copies copying copied
NOUN **1** something made to look like
something else. **2** A copy of a book,
newspaper, or record is one of many
identical ones produced at the same
time. ▸ VERB **3** If you copy what
someone does, you do the same
thing. **4** If you copy something, you
make a copy of it.
copier NOUN
≡ (sense 1) duplicate, replica,
reproduction
≡ (sense 4) duplicate, reproduce

copyright copyrights
NOUN (LIBRARY) If someone has the
copyright on a piece of writing or
music, it cannot be copied or
performed without their permission.

coral corals
NOUN Coral is a hard substance that
forms in the sea from the skeletons
of tiny animals called corals.

cord cords
NOUN **1** Cord is strong, thick string.
2 Electrical wire covered in rubber or
plastic is also called cord.

cordial cordials
ADJECTIVE **1** warm and friendly E.G. *the
cordial greeting.* ▸ NOUN **2** a sweet
drink made from fruit juice.

cordon cordons cordoning
cordoned
NOUN **1** a line or ring of police or
soldiers preventing people entering
or leaving a place. ▸ VERB **2** If police or
soldiers cordon off an area, they stop
people entering or leaving by forming
themselves into a line or ring.

corduroy
NOUN Corduroy is a thick cloth with
parallel raised lines on the outside.

core cores
NOUN **1** the hard central part of a fruit
such as an apple. **2** the most central
part of an object or place E.G. *the
earth's core.* **3** the most important
part of something E.G. *the core of
Asia's problems.*

cork corks
NOUN **1** Cork is the very light,
spongelike bark of a Mediterranean
tree. **2** a piece of cork pushed into
the end of a bottle to close it.

corkscrew corkscrews
NOUN a device for pulling corks out of
bottles.

cormorant cormorants
NOUN a dark-coloured bird with a
long neck.

corn corns
NOUN **1** Corn refers to crops such as
wheat and barley and to their seeds.
2 a small painful area of hard skin on
your foot.

cornea corneas
Said "kor-nee-a" NOUN the transparent
skin that covers the outside of your
eyeball.
▥ from Latin *cornea tela* meaning
'horny web'

corner corners cornering
cornered
NOUN **1** a place where two sides or
edges of something meet E.G. *a
small corner of one shelf… a street
corner.* ▸ VERB **2** To corner a person or
animal is to get them into a place
they cannot escape from.

cornet cornets
NOUN a small brass instrument used in
brass and military bands.

cornflour
NOUN Cornflour is a fine white flour made from maize and used in cooking to thicken sauces.

cornflower cornflowers
NOUN a small plant with bright flowers, usually blue.

cornice cornices
NOUN a decorative strip of plaster, wood, or stone along the top edge of a wall.

corny cornier corniest
ADJECTIVE very obvious or sentimental and not at all original E.G. *corny old love songs*.

coronary coronaries
NOUN If someone has a coronary, blood cannot reach their heart because of a blood clot.

coronation coronations
NOUN the ceremony at which a king or queen is crowned.

coroner coroners
NOUN an official who investigates the deaths of people who have died in a violent or unusual way.

coronet coronets
NOUN a small crown.

corporal corporals
NOUN an officer of low rank in the army or air force.

corporal punishment
NOUN Corporal punishment is the punishing of people by beating them.

corporate
ADJECTIVE; FORMAL belonging to or done by all members of a group together E.G. *a corporate decision*.

corporation corporations
NOUN 1 a large business. 2 a group of people responsible for running a city.

corps
Rhymes with "more" NOUN 1 a part of an army with special duties E.G. *the engineering Corps*. 2 a small group of people who do a special job E.G. *the world press corps*.
☑ The plural of *corps* is also *corps*.

corpse corpses
NOUN a dead body.

corpuscle corpuscles
Said "kor-pus-sl" NOUN a red or white blood cell.

correa correas
NOUN an Australian shrub with large green and white flowers.

correct corrects correcting corrected
ADJECTIVE 1 If something is correct, there are no mistakes in it. 2 The correct thing in a particular situation is the right one E.G. *Each has the correct number of coins*. 3 Correct behaviour is considered to be socially acceptable. ▶ VERB 4 If you correct something which is wrong, you make it right.
correctly ADVERB **correction** NOUN **corrective** ADJECTIVE or NOUN
▤ (sense 4) emend, rectify

correlate correlates correlating correlated
VERB If two things correlate or are correlated, they are closely connected or strongly influence each other E.G. *Obesity correlates with increased risk of stroke and diabetes*.
correlation NOUN

correspond corresponds corresponded
VERB 1 If one thing corresponds to another, it has a similar purpose, function, or status. 2 (MATHS) If

a b c d e f g h i j k l m n o p q r s t u v w x y z

A
B
C
D
E
F
G
H
I
J
K
L
M
N
O
P
Q
R
S
T
U
V
W
X
Y
Z

numbers or amounts correspond, they are the same. **3** When people correspond, they write to each other.

correspondence
NOUN **1** Correspondence is the writing of letters; also the letters written. **2** If there is a correspondence between two things, they are closely related or very similar.

correspondent correspondents
NOUN a newspaper, television, or radio reporter.

corresponding
ADJECTIVE **1** You use 'corresponding' to describe a change that results from a change in something else E.G. *the rise in interest rates and corresponding fall in house values*. **2** You also use 'corresponding' to describe something which has a similar purpose, status to something else E.G. *Alfard is the corresponding Western name for the star*. **3** (MATHS) 'Corresponding' is used to describe two amounts, numbers or shapes that are the same.

correspondingly ADVERB

corridor corridors
NOUN a passage in a building or train.

corroboree corroborees
NOUN an Australian Aboriginal gathering or dance that is festive or warlike.

corrode corrodes corroding corroded
VERB When metal corrodes, it is gradually destroyed by a chemical or rust.

corrosion NOUN **corrosive** ADJECTIVE

corrugated
ADJECTIVE Corrugated metal or cardboard is made in parallel folds

to make it stronger.
📖 from Latin *corrugare* meaning 'to wrinkle up'

corrupt corrupts corrupting corrupted
ADJECTIVE **1** Corrupt people act dishonestly or illegally in return for money or power E.G. *corrupt ministers*. ▶ VERB **2** To corrupt someone means to make them dishonest or immoral.

corruptible ADJECTIVE
📄 (sense 1) crooked, dishonest
📄 (sense 2) deprave

corruption
NOUN Corruption is dishonesty and illegal behaviour by people in positions of power.
📄 depravity, immorality, vice

corset corsets
NOUN Corsets are stiff underwear worn by some women round their hips and waist to make them look slimmer.

cosmetic cosmetics
NOUN **1** Cosmetics are substances such as lipstick and face powder which improve a person's appearance. ▶ ADJECTIVE **2** Cosmetic changes improve the appearance of something without changing its basic.

cosmic
ADJECTIVE belonging or relating to the universe.

cosmopolitan
ADJECTIVE A cosmopolitan place is full of people from many countries.
📖 from Greek *kosmos* meaning 'universe' and *politēs* meaning 'citizen'

cosmos
NOUN The cosmos is the universe.

cosset cossets cosseting cosseted
VERB If you cosset someone, you spoil them and protect them too much.

cost costs costing cost
NOUN 1 The cost of something is the amount of money needed to buy it, do it, or make it. 2 The cost of achieving something is the loss or injury in achieving it E.G. *the total cost in human misery.* ▶ VERB 3 You use 'cost' to talk about the amount of money you have to pay for things E.G. *The air fares were going to cost a lot.* 4 If a mistake costs you something, you lose that thing because of the mistake E.G. *a reckless gamble that could cost him his job.*

costly costlier costliest
ADJECTIVE expensive E.G. *the most costly piece of furniture.*

costume costumes
NOUN 1 (DRAMA) a set of clothes worn by an actor. 2 Costume is the clothing worn in a particular place or during a particular period E.G. *eighteenth-century costume.*

cosy cosier cosiest; cosies
ADJECTIVE 1 warm and comfortable E.G. *her cosy new flat.* 2 Cosy activities are pleasant and friendly E.G. *a cosy chat.* ▶ NOUN 3 a soft cover put over a teapot to keep the tea warm.
cosily ADVERB **cosiness** NOUN

cot cots
NOUN a small bed for a baby, with bars or panels round it to stop the baby falling out.
📖 from Hindi *khat* meaning 'bedstead'

cottage cottages
NOUN a small house in the country.

cottage cheese
NOUN Cottage cheese is a type of soft white lumpy cheese.

cotton cottons
NOUN 1 Cotton is cloth made from the soft fibres of the cotton plant. 2 Cotton is also thread used for sewing.
📖 from Arabic *qutn*

cotton wool
NOUN Cotton wool is soft fluffy cotton, often used for dressing wounds.

couch couches couching couched
NOUN 1 a long, soft piece of furniture which more than one person can sit on. ▶ VERB 2 If a statement is couched in a particular type of language, it is expressed in that language E.G. *a comment couched in impertinent terms.*

cough coughs coughing coughed
Said "koff" VERB 1 When you cough, you force air out of your throat with a sudden harsh noise. ▶ NOUN 2 an illness that makes you cough a lot; also the noise you make when you cough.

could
VERB 1 You use 'could' to say that you were able or allowed to do something E.G. *He could hear voices… She could come and go as she wanted.* 2 You also use 'could' to say that something might happen or might be the case E.G. *It could rain.* 3 You use 'could' when you are asking for something politely E.G. *Could you tell me the name of that film?*

coulomb coulombs
Said "koo-lom" NOUN a unit used to measure electric charge.

a
b
c
d
e
f
g
h
i
j
k
l
m
n
o
p
q
r
s
t
u
v
w
x
y
z

council councils

NOUN 1 a group of people elected to look after the affairs of a town, district, or county. 2 Some other groups have Council as part of their name E.G. *the World Gold Council*.

councillor councillors

NOUN an elected member of a local council.

counsel counsels counselling counselled

NOUN 1 FORMAL To give someone counsel is to give them advice. ► VERB 2 To counsel people is to give them advice about their problems.

counselling NOUN **counsellor** NOUN

count counts counting counted

VERB 1 To count is to say all the numbers in order up to a particular number. 2 If you count all the things in a group, you add them up to see how many there are. 3 What counts in a situation is whatever is most important. 4 To count as something means to be regarded as that thing E.G. *I'm not sure whether this counts as harassment.* 5 If you can count on someone or something, you can rely on them. ► NOUN 6 a number reached by counting. 7 FORMAL If something is wrong on a particular count, it is wrong in that respect. 8 a European nobleman.

countdown countdowns

NOUN the counting aloud of numbers in reverse order before something happens, especially before a spacecraft is launched.

countenance countenances

NOUN; FORMAL Someone's countenance is their face.

counter counters countering countered

NOUN 1 a long, flat surface over which goods are sold in a shop. 2 a small, flat, round object used in board games. ► VERB 3 If you counter something that is being done, you take action to make it less effective E.G. *I countered that argument with a reference to our sales report.*

counter-

PREFIX 1 'Counter-' means 'opposite' or 'contrary' E.G. *counterbalance*. 2 'Counter-' can also mean 'copy' or 'substitute' E.G. *counterfeit*. 📖 from Latin *contrā* meaning 'against' or 'opposite'

counteract counteracts counteracting counteracted

VERB To counteract something is to reduce its effect by producing an opposite effect.

counterfeit counterfeits counterfeiting counterfeited

Said "kown-ter-fit" ADJECTIVE 1 Something counterfeit is not genuine but has been made to look genuine to deceive people E.G. *counterfeit money.* ► VERB 2 To counterfeit something is to make a counterfeit version of it.

counterpart counterparts

NOUN The counterpart of a person or thing is another person or thing with a similar function in a different place E.G. *Unlike his British counterpart, the French mayor is an important personality.*

countess countesses

NOUN the wife of a count or earl, or a woman with the same rank as a count or earl.

counting

PREPOSITION You say 'counting' when including something in a calculation E.G. *nearly 4000 of us, not counting women and children.*

countless

ADJECTIVE too many to count E.G. *There had been countless demonstrations.*
■ incalculable, innumerable

country countries

NOUN (GEOGRAPHY) 1 one of the political areas the world is divided into. 2 The country is land away from towns and cities. 3 'Country' is used to refer to an area with particular features or associations E.G. *the heart of wine country.*
■ (sense 1) nation, state

countryman countrymen

NOUN Your countrymen are people from your own country.

countryside

NOUN The countryside is land away from towns and cities.

county counties

NOUN (GEOGRAPHY) a region with its own local government.
📖 from Old French *conté* meaning 'land belonging to a count'

coup coups

Rhymes with "**you**" NOUN When there is a coup, a group of people seize power in a country.
📖 from French *coup* meaning 'a blow'

couple couples coupling coupled

NOUN 1 two people who are married or having a sexual or romantic relationship. 2 A couple of things or people means two of them E.G. *a couple of weeks ago.* ► VERB 3 If one thing is coupled with another, the two things are done or dealt with together E.G. *Its stores offer high quality coupled with low prices.*

couplet couplets

NOUN two lines of poetry together, especially two that rhyme.

coupon coupons

NOUN 1 a piece of printed paper which, when you hand it in, entitles you to pay less than usual for something. 2 a form you fill in to ask for information or to enter a competition.

courage

NOUN Courage is the quality shown by people who do things knowing they are dangerous or difficult.
courageous ADJECTIVE
courageously ADVERB

courgette courgettes

Said "**koor-jet**" NOUN a type of small marrow with dark green skin. Courgettes are also called **zucchini**.
📖 from French *courgette* meaning 'little marrow'

courier couriers

Said "**koo-ree-er**" NOUN 1 someone employed by a travel company to look after people on holiday. 2 someone employed to deliver special letters quickly.

course courses

NOUN 1 a series of lessons or lectures. 2 a series of medical treatments E.G. *a course of injections.* 3 one of the parts of a meal. 4 A course or a course of action is one of the things you can do in a situation. 5 a piece of land where a sport such as golf is played. 6 the route a ship or aircraft takes. 7 If something happens in the course of a period of time, it happens during that period E.G. *Ten people died in the course of the day.*

a
b
c
d
e
f
g
h
i
j
k
l
m
n
o
p
q
r
s
t
u
v
w
x
y
z

A
B
C
D
E
F
G
H
I
J
K
L
M
N
O
P
Q
R
S
T
U
V
W
X
Y
Z

▶ PHRASE **8** If you say **of course**, you are showing that something is totally expected or that you are sure about something E.G. *Of course she wouldn't do that.*

☑ Do not confuse the spellings of *coarse* and *course*.

court courts courting courted
NOUN **1** a place where legal matters are decided by a judge and jury or a magistrate. The judge and jury or magistrate can also be referred to as the court. **2** a place where a game such as tennis or badminton is played. **3** the place where a king or queen lives and carries out ceremonial duties. ▶ VERB **4** OLD-FASHIONED If a man and a woman are courting, they are spending a lot of time together because they intend to get married.

courteous
Said "kur-tee-yuss" ADJECTIVE Courteous behaviour is polite and considerate.
🔲 from Old French *corteis* meaning 'courtly-mannered'

courtesy
NOUN Courtesy is polite, considerate behaviour.

courtier courtiers
NOUN Courtiers were noblemen and noblewomen at the court of a king or queen.

court-martial court-martials court-martialling court-martialled
NOUN **1** a military trial. ▶ VERB **2** If a member of the armed forces is court-martialled, he or she is tried by a court martial.

courtship
NOUN; FORMAL Courtship is the activity

of courting or the period of time during which a man and a woman are courting.

courtyard courtyards
NOUN a flat area of ground surrounded by buildings or walls.

cousin cousins
NOUN Your cousin is the child of your uncle or aunt.

cove coves
NOUN a small bay.

covenant covenants
Said "kuv-vi-nant" NOUN a formal written agreement or promise.

cover covers covered
VERB **1** If you cover something, you put something else over it to protect it or hide it. **2** If something covers something else, it forms a layer over it E.G. *Tears covered his face.* **3** If you cover a particular distance, you travel that distance E.G. *He covered 52 kilometres in 210 laps.* ▶ NOUN **4** something put over an object to protect it or keep it warm. **5** The cover of a book or magazine is its outside. **6** Insurance cover is a guarantee that money will be paid if something is lost or harmed. **7** In the open, cover consists of trees, rocks, or other places where you can shelter or hide.

cover up VERB If you cover up something you do not want people to know about, you hide it from them E.G. *He lied to cover up his crime.*

cover-up NOUN

coverage
NOUN The coverage of something in the news is the reporting of it.

covering coverings
NOUN a layer of something which

protects or conceals something else
E.G. *A morning blizzard left a covering of snow.*

covert
Said "kuv-vert" ADJECTIVE; FORMAL Covert activities are secret, rather than open.
covertly ADVERB

covet covets coveting coveted
Said "kuv-vit" VERB; FORMAL If you covet something, you want it very much.

cow cows
NOUN a large animal kept on farms for its milk.

coward cowards
NOUN someone who is easily frightened and who avoids dangerous or difficult situations.
cowardly ADJECTIVE **cowardice** NOUN

cowboy cowboys
NOUN a man employed to look after cattle in America.

cower cowers cowering cowered
VERB When someone cowers, they crouch or move backwards because they are afraid.
◼ cringe, shrink

cox coxes
NOUN a person who steers a boat.

coy coyer coyest
ADJECTIVE If someone is coy, they pretend to be shy and modest.
coyly ADVERB

coyote coyotes
Said "koy-ote-ee" NOUN a North American animal like a small wolf.

crab crabs
NOUN a sea creature with four pairs of legs, two pincers, and a flat, round body covered by a shell.

crack cracks cracking cracked
VERB 1 If something cracks, it becomes

damaged, with lines appearing on its surface. 2 If you crack a joke, you tell it. 3 If you crack a problem or code, you solve it. ► NOUN 4 one of the lines appearing on something when it cracks. 5 a narrow gap. ► ADJECTIVE 6 A crack soldier or sportsman is highly trained and skilful.
◼ (sense 5) break, fracture, gap

cracker crackers
NOUN 1 a thin, crisp biscuit that is often eaten with cheese. 2 a paper-covered tube that pulls apart with a bang and usually has a toy and paper hat inside.

crackle crackles crackling crackled
VERB 1 If something crackles, it makes a rapid series of short, harsh noises. ► NOUN 2 a short, harsh noise.

cradle cradles cradling cradled
NOUN 1 a box-shaped bed for a baby. ► VERB 2 If you cradle something in your arms or hands, you hold it there carefully.

craft crafts
NOUN 1 an activity such as weaving, carving, or pottery. 2 a skilful occupation E.G. *the writer's craft.* 3 a boat, plane, or spacecraft.
☑ When *craft* means 'a boat, plane, or spacecraft' (sense 3), the plural is **craft**.

craftsman craftsmen
NOUN a man who makes things skilfully with his hands.
craftsmanship NOUN
craftswoman NOUN

crafty craftier craftiest
ADJECTIVE Someone who is crafty gets what they want by tricking people in a clever way.

a b c d e f g h i j k l m n o p q r s t u v w x y z

A
B
C
D
E
F
G
H
I
J
K
L
M
N
O
P
Q
R
S
T
U
V
W
X
Y
Z

crag crags
NOUN a steep rugged rock or peak.

craggy craggier craggiest
ADJECTIVE A craggy mountain or cliff is steep and rocky.

cram crams cramming crammed
VERB If you cram people or things into a place, you put more in than there is room for.
■ pack, squeeze, stuff

cramp cramps
NOUN Cramp or cramps is a pain caused by a muscle contracting.

cramped
ADJECTIVE If a room or building is cramped, it is not big enough for the people or things in it.

cranberry cranberries
NOUN Cranberries are sour-tasting red berries, often made into a sauce.

crane cranes craning craned
NOUN 1 a machine that moves heavy things by lifting them in the air. 2 a large bird with a long neck and long legs. ▶ VERB 3 If you crane your neck, you extend your head in a particular direction to see or hear something better.

crank cranks cranking cranked
NOUN 1 INFORMAL someone with strange ideas who behaves in an odd way. 2 a device you turn to make something move E.G. *The adjustment is made by turning the crank.* ▶ VERB 3 If you crank something, you make it move by turning a handle.
cranky ADJECTIVE

cranny crannies
NOUN a very narrow opening in a wall or rock E.G. *nooks and crannies.*

crash crashes crashing crashed
NOUN 1 an accident in which a moving

vehicle hits something violently. 2 a sudden loud noise E.G. *the crash of the waves on the rocks.* 3 the sudden failure of a business or financial institution. ▶ VERB 4 When a vehicle crashes, it hits something and is badly damaged.

crash helmet crash helmets
NOUN a helmet worn by motor cyclists for protection when they are riding.

crate crates
NOUN a large box used for transporting or storing things.

crater craters
NOUN a wide hole in the ground caused by something hitting it or by an explosion.

cravat cravats
NOUN a piece of cloth a man can wear round his neck tucked into his shirt collar.
▥ from Serbo-Croat *Hrvat* meaning 'Croat'. Croat soldiers wore cravats during the Thirty Years' War

crave craves craving craved
VERB If you crave something, you want it very much E.G. *I crave her approval.*
craving NOUN

crawl crawls crawling crawled
VERB 1 When you crawl, you move forward on your hands and knees. 2 When a vehicle crawls, it moves very slowly. 3 INFORMAL If a place is crawling with people or things, it is full of them E.G. *The place is crawling with drunks.*
crawler NOUN

crayfish crayfishes or crayfish
NOUN a small shellfish like a lobster.
▥ from Old French *crevice* meaning 'crab'

crayon crayons
NOUN a coloured pencil or a stick

of coloured wax.

craze crazes
NOUN something that is very popular for a short time.

crazy crazier craziest
ADJECTIVE; INFORMAL 1 very strange or foolish E.G. *The guy is crazy… a crazy idea.* 2 If you are crazy about something, you are very keen on it E.G. *I was crazy about dancing.*
crazily ADVERB   **craziness** NOUN

creak creaks creaking creaked
VERB 1 If something creaks, it makes a harsh sound when it moves or when you stand on it. ▶ NOUN 2 a harsh squeaking noise.
creaky ADJECTIVE

cream creams
NOUN 1 Cream is a thick, yellowish-white liquid taken from the top of milk. 2 Cream is also a substance people can rub on their skin to make it soft. ▶ ADJECTIVE 3 yellowish-white.
creamy ADJECTIVE

crease creases creasing creased
NOUN 1 an irregular line that appears on cloth or paper when it is crumpled. 2 a straight line on something that has been pressed or folded neatly. ▶ VERB 3 To crease something is to make lines appear on it.
creased ADJECTIVE

create creates creating created
VERB 1 To create something is to cause it to happen or exist E.G. *This is absolutely vital but creates a problem.* 2 When someone creates a new product or process, they invent it.
creator NOUN

creation creations
NOUN 1 Creation is the creating of something or bringing it into existence. 2 A creation is something original that has been made or invented. 3 (RE) The Creation is the time when God is believed to have made the world and everything in it.

creative
ADJECTIVE 1 Creative people are able to invent and develop original ideas. 2 Creative activities involve the inventing and developing of original ideas E.G. *creative writing.*
creatively ADVERB   **creativity** NOUN

creature creatures
NOUN any living thing that moves about.

crèche crèches
Said "kresh" NOUN a place where small children are looked after while their parents are working.
from Old French *crèche* meaning 'crib' or 'manger'

credence
NOUN; FORMAL If something gives credence to a theory or story, it makes it easier to believe.

credentials
PLURAL NOUN Your credentials are your past achievements or other things in your background that make you qualified for something.

credible
ADJECTIVE If someone or something is credible, you can believe or trust them.
credibility NOUN

credit credits crediting credited
NOUN 1 If you are allowed credit, you can take something and pay for it later E.G. *to buy goods on credit.* 2 If you get the credit for something, people praise you for it. 3 If you say someone is a credit to their family or

a b **c** d e f g h i j k l m n o p q r s t u v w x y z

school, you mean that their family or school should be proud of them. ▶ PLURAL NOUN 4 The list of people who helped make a film, record, or television programme is called the credits. ▶ PHRASE 5 If someone or their bank account is **in credit**, their account has money in it. ▶ VERB 6 If you are credited with an achievement, people believe that you were responsible for it.

creditable
ADJECTIVE satisfactory or fairly good E.G. *a creditable performance*.

credit card credit cards
NOUN a plastic card that allows someone to buy goods on credit.

creditor creditors
NOUN Your creditors are the people you owe money to.

creed creeds
NOUN 1 a religion. 2 any set of beliefs E.G. *the feminist creed*.

creek creeks
NOUN a narrow inlet where the sea comes a long way into the land.
🔲 from Old Norse *kriki* meaning 'nook'

creep creeps creeping crept
VERB To creep is to move quietly and slowly.

creepy creepier creepiest
ADJECTIVE; INFORMAL strange and frightening E.G. *a creepy feeling*.

cremate cremates cremating cremated
VERB When someone is cremated, their dead body is burned during a funeral service.
cremation NOUN

crematorium crematoriums or crematoria
NOUN a building in which the bodies of dead people are burned.

crepe
Said "krayp" NOUN 1 a thin ridged material made from cotton, silk, or wool. 2 a type of rubber with a rough surface.

crescendo crescendos
Said "krish-en-doe" NOUN When there is a crescendo in a piece of music, the music gets louder.

crescent crescents
NOUN a curved shape that is wider in its middle than at the ends, which are pointed.

cress
NOUN a plant with small, strong-tasting leaves. It is used in salads.

crest crests
NOUN 1 The crest of a hill or wave is its highest part. 2 a tuft of feathers on top of a bird's head. 3 a small picture or design that is the emblem of a noble family, a town, or an organization.
crested ADJECTIVE

crevice crevices
NOUN a narrow crack or gap in rock.

crew crews
NOUN 1 The crew of a ship, aeroplane, or spacecraft are the people who operate it. 2 people with special technical skills who work together E.G. *the camera crew*.

crib cribs cribbing cribbed
VERB 1 INFORMAL If you crib, you copy what someone else has written and pretend it is your own work. ▶ NOUN 2 OLD-FASHIONED a baby's cot.

crib-wall crib-walls
NOUN In New Zealand English, a wooden wall built against a bank of earth to support it.

crick cricks
NOUN a pain in your neck or back

caused by muscles becoming stiff.

cricket crickets

NOUN **1** an outdoor game played by two teams who take turns at scoring runs by hitting a ball with a bat. **2** a small jumping insect that produces sounds by rubbing its wings together.

cricketer NOUN

crime crimes

NOUN an action for which you can be punished by law E.G. *a serious crime.*

◼ misdemeanour, offence

criminal criminals

NOUN **1** someone who has committed a crime. ▶ ADJECTIVE **2** involving or related to crime E.G. *criminal activities.*

criminally ADVERB

◼ (sense 1) crook, lawbreaker, offender

criminology

NOUN the scientific study of crime and criminals.

criminologist NOUN

crimson

NOUN or ADJECTIVE dark purplish-red.

cringe cringes cringing cringed

VERB If you cringe, you back away from someone or something because you are afraid or embarrassed.

🔟 from Old English *cringan* meaning 'to yield in battle'

crinkle crinkles crinkling crinkled

VERB **1** If something crinkles, it becomes slightly creased or folded. ▶ NOUN **2** Crinkles are small creases or folds.

cripple cripples crippling crippled

NOUN **1** someone who cannot move

their body properly because it is weak or affected by disease. ▶ VERB **2** To cripple someone is to injure them severely so that they can never move properly again.

crippled ADJECTIVE   **crippling** ADJECTIVE

crisis crises

Said "kry-*seez* in the plural" NOUN a serious or dangerous situation.

crisp crisper crispest; crisps

ADJECTIVE **1** Something that is crisp is pleasantly fresh and firm E.G. *crisp lettuce leaves.* **2** If the air or the weather is crisp, it is pleasantly fresh, cold, and dry E.G. *crisp wintry days.* ▶ NOUN **3** Crisps are thin slices of potato fried until they are hard and crunchy.

crispy crispier crispiest

ADJECTIVE Crispy food is pleasantly hard and crunchy E.G. *a crispy salad.*

criterion criteria

Said "kry-*teer*-ee-on" NOUN a standard by which you judge or decide something.

☑ *Criteria* is the plural of *criterion,* and needs to be used with a plural verb.

critic critics

NOUN **1** someone who writes reviews of books, films, plays, or musical performances. **2** A critic of a person or system is someone who criticizes them publicly E.G. *the government's critics.*

critical

ADJECTIVE **1** A critical time is one which is very important in determining what happens in the future E.G. *critical months in the history of the world.* **2** A critical situation is a very serious one E.G. *Rock music is in a*

a b c d e f g h i j k l m n o p q r s t u v w x y z

A
B
C
D
E
F
G
H
I
J
K
L
M
N
O
P
Q
R
S
T
U
V
W
X
Y
Z

critical state. **3** If an ill or injured person is critical, they are in danger of dying. **4** If you are critical of something or someone, you express severe judgments or opinions about them. **5** If you are critical, you examine and judge something carefully E.G. *a critical look at the way he led his life.*
critically ADVERB

criticism criticisms
NOUN **1** When there is criticism of someone or something, people express disapproval of them. **2** If you make a criticism, you point out a fault you think someone or something has.

criticize criticizes criticizing criticized; also spelt **criticise**
VERB If you criticize someone or something, you say what you think is wrong with them.
■ disparage, find fault with

croak croaks croaking croaked
VERB **1** When animals and birds croak, they make harsh, low sounds. ▶ NOUN **2** a harsh, low sound.
🔲 from Old Norse *kraka* meaning 'crow'

Croatian Croatians
ADJECTIVE **1** belonging to or relating to Croatia. ▶ NOUN **2** someone who comes from Croatia. **3** Croatian is the form of Serbo-Croat spoken in Croatia.

crochet
Said "kroh-shay" NOUN a way of making clothes and other things out of thread using a needle with a small hook at the end.

crockery
NOUN Crockery is plates, cups, and saucers.

crocodile crocodiles
NOUN a large scaly meat-eating reptile which lives in tropical rivers.
🔲 from Greek *krokodeilos* meaning 'lizard'

crocus crocuses
NOUN Crocuses are yellow, purple, or white flowers that grow in early spring.

croft crofts
NOUN a small piece of land, especially in Scotland, which is farmed by one family.
crofter NOUN

croissant croissants
Said "krwus-son" NOUN a light, crescent-shaped roll eaten at breakfast.
🔲 from French *croissant* meaning 'crescent'

crony cronies
NOUN; OLD-FASHIONED Your cronies are the friends you spend a lot of time with.

crook crooks
NOUN **1** INFORMAL a criminal. **2** The crook of your arm or leg is the soft inside part where you bend your elbow or knee.

crooked
Said "kroo-kid" ADJECTIVE **1** bent or twisted. **2** Someone who is crooked is dishonest.

croon croons crooning crooned
VERB To croon is to sing or hum quietly and gently E.G. *He crooned a love song.*
🔲 from Old Dutch *kronen* meaning 'to groan'

crop crops cropping cropped
NOUN **1** Crops are plants such as wheat and potatoes that are grown for food. **2** the plants collected at

King IAn went to ParlIAment in a carrIAge for his marrIAge (-ia-)

harvest time E.G. *You should have two crops in the year.* ▶ VERB 3 To crop someone's hair is to cut it very short.

croquet
Said "kroh-kay" NOUN a game in which the players use long-handled mallets to hit balls through metal arches pushed into a lawn.

cross crosses crossing crossed; crosser crossest
VERB 1 If you cross something such as a room or a road, you go to the other side of it. 2 Lines or roads that cross meet and go across each other. 3 If a thought crosses your mind, you think of it. 4 If you cross your arms, legs, or fingers, you put one on top of the other. ▶ NOUN 5 a vertical bar or line crossed by a shorter horizontal bar or line; also used to describe any object shaped like this. 6 The Cross is the cross-shaped structure on which Jesus Christ was crucified. A cross is also any symbol representing Christ's Cross. 7 a written mark shaped like an X E.G. *I drew a small bicycle and put a cross by it.* 8 Something that is a cross between two things is neither one thing nor the other, but a mixture of both. ▶ ADJECTIVE 9 Someone who is cross is rather angry. **crossly** ADVERB

crossbow crossbows
NOUN a weapon consisting of a small bow fixed at the end of a piece of wood.

cross-country
NOUN 1 Cross-country is the sport of running across open countryside, rather than on roads or on a track. ▶ ADVERB or ADJECTIVE 2 across country.

cross-eyed
ADJECTIVE A cross-eyed person has eyes that seem to look towards each other.

crossfire
NOUN gunfire crossing the same place from opposite directions.

crosshatching
NOUN (ART) Crosshatching is drawing an area of shade in a picture using two or more sets of parallel lines.

crossing crossings
NOUN 1 a place where you can cross a road safely. 2 a journey by ship to a place on the other side of the sea.

cross-legged
ADJECTIVE If you are sitting cross-legged, you are sitting on the floor with your knees pointing outwards and your feet tucked under them.

cross section cross sections
NOUN A cross section of a group of people is a representative sample of them.

crossword crosswords
NOUN a puzzle in which you work out the answers to clues and write them in the white squares of a pattern of black and white squares.

crotch crotches
NOUN the part of your body between the tops of your legs.

crotchet crotchets
NOUN (MUSIC) a musical note (♩) equal in time value to a quarter of a semibreve. In the United States and Canada, a crotchet is called a quarter note.

crouch crouches crouching crouched
VERB If you are crouching, you are leaning forward with your legs bent under you.

crow crows crowing crowed
NOUN 1 a large black bird which

an ELegant angEL (angel)   SPELLING NOTE

a b c d e f g h i j k l m n o p q r s t u v w x y z

makes a loud, harsh noise. ► VERB
2 When a cock crows, it utters a loud
squawking sound.

crowbar crowbars
NOUN a heavy iron bar used as a lever
or for forcing things open.

**crowd crowds crowding
crowded**
NOUN 1 a large group of people gathered
together. ► VERB 2 When people crowd
somewhere, they gather there close
together or in large numbers.
▣ (sense 1) mass, mob, multitude,
throng

crowded
ADJECTIVE A crowded place is full of
people.

**crown crowns crowning
crowned**
NOUN 1 a circular ornament worn on a
royal person's head. 2 The crown of
something such as your head is the
top part of it. ► VERB 3 When a king or
queen is crowned, a crown is put on
their head during their coronation
ceremony. 4 When something crowns
an event, it is the final part of it E.G.
The news crowned a dreadful week.

crucial
Said "kroo-shl" ADJECTIVE If something
is crucial, it is very important in
determining how something else
will be in the future.
▦ from Latin *crux* meaning 'a cross'
▣ critical, decisive, vital

crucifix crucifixes
NOUN a cross with a figure
representing Jesus Christ being
crucified on it.

**crucify crucifies crucifying
crucified**
VERB To crucify someone is to tie or
nail them to a large wooden cross

and leave them there to die.
crucifixion NOUN

crude cruder crudest
ADJECTIVE 1 rough and simple E.G. *a
crude weapon… a crude method of
entry*. 2 A crude person speaks or
behaves in a rude and offensive way
E.G. *You can be quite crude at times*.
crudely ADVERB **crudity** NOUN
▣ (sense 1) makeshift, primitive
▣ (sense 2) coarse, vulgar

cruel crueller cruellest
ADJECTIVE Cruel people deliberately
cause pain or distress to other
people or to animals.
cruelly ADVERB **cruelty** NOUN
▣ brutal, callous, unkind

cruise cruises cruising cruised
NOUN 1 a holiday in which you travel
on a ship and visit places. ► VERB
2 When a vehicle cruises, it moves at
a constant moderate speed.

cruiser cruisers
NOUN 1 a motor boat with a cabin you
can sleep in. 2 a large, fast warship.

crumb crumbs
NOUN Crumbs are very small pieces of
bread or cake.

**crumble crumbles crumbling
crumbled**
VERB When something crumbles, it
breaks into small pieces.

crumbly
ADJECTIVE Something crumbly easily
breaks into small pieces.

crumpet crumpets
NOUN a round, flat, breadlike cake
which you eat toasted.

**crumple crumples crumpling
crumpled**
VERB To crumple paper or cloth is to
squash it so that it is full of creases
and folds.

crunch crunches crunching crunched
VERB If you crunch something, you crush it noisily, for example between your teeth or under your feet.

crunchy crunchier crunchiest
ADJECTIVE Crunchy food is hard or crisp and makes a noise when you eat it.

crusade crusades
NOUN a long and determined attempt to achieve something E.G. *the crusade for human rights*.
crusader NOUN

crush crushes crushing crushed
VERB 1 To crush something is to destroy its shape by squeezing it. 2 To crush a substance is to turn it into liquid or powder by squeezing or grinding it. 3 To crush an army or political organization is to defeat it completely. ▶ NOUN 4 a dense crowd of people.

crust crusts
NOUN 1 the hard outside part of a loaf. 2 a hard layer on top of something E.G. *The snow had a fine crust on it*.

crusty crustier crustiest
ADJECTIVE 1 Something that is crusty has a hard outside layer. 2 Crusty people are impatient and irritable.

crutch crutches
NOUN a support like a long stick which you lean on to help you walk when you have an injured foot or leg.

crux
NOUN the most important or difficult part of a problem or argument.

cry cries crying cried
VERB 1 When you cry, tears appear in your eyes. 2 To cry something is to shout it or say it loudly E.G. *'See you soon!' they cried*. ▶ NOUN 3 If you have a cry, you cry for a period of time. 4 a

shout or other loud sound made with your voice. 5 a loud sound made by some birds E.G. *the cry of a seagull*.
■ (sense 1) sob, weep

crypt crypts
NOUN an underground room beneath a church, usually used as a burial place.
🔲 from Greek *kruptein* meaning 'to hide'

cryptic
ADJECTIVE A cryptic remark or message has a hidden meaning.

crystal crystals
NOUN 1 a piece of a mineral that has formed naturally into a regular shape. 2 Crystal is a type of transparent rock, used in jewellery. 3 Crystal is also a kind of very high quality glass.
crystalline ADJECTIVE

crystallize crystallizes crystallizing crystallized; also spelt **crystallise**
VERB 1 If a substance crystallizes, it turns into crystals. 2 If an idea crystallizes, it becomes clear in your mind.

cub cubs
NOUN 1 Some young wild animals are called cubs E.G. *a lion cub*. 2 The Cubs is an organization for young boys before they join the Scouts.

Cuban Cubans
Said "kyoo-ban" ADJECTIVE 1 belonging or relating to Cuba. ▶ NOUN 2 someone who comes from Cuba.

cube cubes cubing cubed
NOUN 1 a three-dimensional shape with six equally-sized square surfaces. 2 If you multiply a number by itself twice, you get its cube. ▶ VERB 3 To cube a number is to multiply it by itself twice.

a b c d e f g h i j k l m n o p q r s t u v w x y z

A Rude Idiot Thought He Might Eat Toffee In Church (<u>arithmetic</u>)   **SPELLING NOTE**

cubic
ADJECTIVE used in measurements of volume E.G. *cubic centimetres*.

cubicle cubicles
NOUN a small enclosed area in a place such as a sports centre, where you can dress and undress.

cuckoo cuckoos
NOUN a grey bird with a two-note call that lays its eggs in other birds' nests.

cucumber cucumbers
NOUN a long, thin, green-skinned vegetable eaten raw.

cuddle cuddles cuddling cuddled
VERB 1 If you cuddle someone, you hold them affectionately in your arms. ▶ NOUN 2 If you give someone a cuddle, you hold them affectionately in your arms.

cuddly cuddlier cuddliest
ADJECTIVE Cuddly people, animals, or toys are soft or pleasing in some way so that you want to cuddle them.

cue cues
NOUN 1 something said or done by a performer that is a signal for another performer to begin E.G. *Chris never misses a cue.* 2 a long stick used to hit the balls in snooker and billiards.

cuff cuffs
NOUN the end part of a sleeve.

cufflink cufflinks
NOUN Cufflinks are small objects for holding shirt cuffs together.

cuisine
Said "kwiz-*een*" NOUN The cuisine of a region is the style of cooking that is typical of it.
📖 from French *cuisine* meaning 'kitchen'

cul-de-sac cul-de-sacs
Said "kul-*des-sak*" NOUN a road that does not lead to any other roads

because one end is blocked off.

culinary
ADJECTIVE; FORMAL connected with the kitchen or cooking.
📖 from Latin *culina* meaning 'kitchen'

cull culls culling culled
VERB 1 If you cull things, you gather them from different places or sources E.G. *information culled from movies.* ▶ NOUN 2 When there is a cull, weaker animals are killed to reduce the numbers in a group.

culminate culminates culminating culminated
VERB To culminate in something is to finally develop into it E.G. *a campaign that culminated in a stunning success.*
culmination NOUN

culprit culprits
NOUN someone who has done something harmful or wrong.
📖 from Anglo-French *culpable* meaning 'guilty' and *prit* meaning 'ready' (i.e. ready for trial)

cult cults
NOUN 1 A cult is a religious group with special rituals, usually connected with the worship of a particular person. 2 'Cult' is used to refer to any situation in which someone or something is very popular with a large group of people E.G. *the American sports car cult.*

cultivate cultivates cultivating cultivated
VERB 1 To cultivate land is to grow crops on it. 2 If you cultivate a feeling or attitude, you try to develop it in yourself or other people.
cultivation NOUN

culture cultures
NOUN 1 Culture refers to the arts and to people's appreciation of them E.G.

He was a man of culture. **2** The culture of a particular society is its ideas, customs, and art E.G. *Japanese culture*. **3** In science, a culture is a group of bacteria or cells grown in a laboratory.
cultured ADJECTIVE **cultural** ADJECTIVE

cumulative
ADJECTIVE Something that is cumulative keeps being added to.

cunjevoi cunjevois
Said "kun-jiv-voi" NOUN a very small Australian sea creature that lives on rocks.

cunning
ADJECTIVE **1** Someone who is cunning uses clever and deceitful methods to get what they want. ▶ NOUN **2** Cunning is the ability to get what you want using clever and deceitful methods.
cunningly ADVERB
🕮 from Old Norse *kunna* meaning 'to know'
🗏 (sense 1) crafty, sly, wily

cup cups cupping cupped
NOUN **1** a small, round container with a handle, which you drink out of. **2** a large metal container with two handles, given as a prize. ▶ VERB **3** If you cup your hands, you put them together to make a shape like a cup.

cupboard cupboards
NOUN a piece of furniture with doors and shelves.

curable
ADJECTIVE If a disease or illness is curable, it can be cured.

curate curates
NOUN a clergyman who helps a vicar or a priest.

curator curators
NOUN the person in a museum or art gallery in charge of its contents.

curb curbs curbing curbed
VERB **1** To curb something is to keep it within limits E.G. *policies designed to curb inflation*. ▶ NOUN **2** If a curb is placed on something, it is kept within limits E.G. *the curb on spending*.

curdle curdles curdling curdled
VERB When milk curdles, it turns sour.

curds
PLURAL NOUN Curds are the thick white substance formed when milk turns sour.

cure cures curing cured
VERB **1** To cure an illness is to end it. **2** To cure a sick or injured person is to make them well. **3** If something cures you of a habit or attitude, it stops you having it. **4** To cure food, tobacco, or animal skin is to treat it in order to preserve it. ▶ NOUN **5** A cure for an illness is something that cures it.
🗏 (sense 2) heal, make better

curfew curfews
NOUN If there is a curfew, people must stay indoors between particular times at night.

curiosity curiosities
NOUN **1** Curiosity is the desire to know about something or about many things. **2** something unusual and interesting.

curious
ADJECTIVE **1** Someone who is curious wants to know more about something. **2** Something that is curious is unusual and hard to explain.
curiously ADVERB
🗏 (sense 1) inquiring, inquisitive, nosy

a
b
c
d
e
f
g
h
i
j
k
l
m
n
o
p
q
r
s
t
u
v
w
x
y
z

curl curls curling curled
NOUN **1** Curls are lengths of hair shaped in tight curves and circles. **2** a curved or spiral shape E.G. *the curls of morning fog.* ▶ VERB **3** If something curls, it moves in a curve or spiral.
curly ADJECTIVE

curler curlers
NOUN Curlers are plastic or metal tubes that women roll their hair round to make it curly.

curlew curlews
Said "kur-lyoo" NOUN a large brown bird with a long curved beak and a loud cry.

currant currants
NOUN **1** Currants are small dried grapes often put in cakes and puddings. **2** Currants are also blackcurrants or redcurrants.
🔳 sense 1 is from Middle English *rayson of Coraunte* meaning 'Corinth raisin'

currawong currawongs
NOUN an Australian bird like a crow.

currency currencies
NOUN **1** A country's currency is its coins and banknotes, or its system of money generally E.G. *foreign currency… a strong economy and a weak currency.* **2** If something such as an idea has currency, it is used a lot at a particular time.

current currents
NOUN **1** a strong continuous movement of the water in a river or in the sea. **2** a flowing movement in the air. **3** a flow of electricity through a wire or circuit. ▶ ADJECTIVE **4** (HISTORY) Something that is current is happening, being done, or being used now.
currently ADVERB

current affairs
PLURAL NOUN Current affairs are political and social events discussed in newspapers and on television and radio.

curriculum curriculums or curricula
Said "kur-**rik**-yoo-lum" NOUN the different courses taught at a school or university.

curriculum vitae curricula vitae
Said "vee-tie" NOUN Someone's curriculum vitae is a written account of their personal details, education, and work experience which they send when they apply for a job.

curried
ADJECTIVE Curried food has been flavoured with hot spices E.G. *curried lamb.*

curry curries currying curried
NOUN **1** Curry is an Indian dish made with hot spices. ▶ PHRASE **2** To **curry favour** with someone means to try to please them by flattering them or doing things to help them.
🔳 sense 1 is from Tamil *kari* meaning 'sauce'; sense 2 is from Old French *correer* meaning 'to make ready'

curse curses cursing cursed
VERB **1** To curse is to swear because you are angry. **2** If you curse someone or something, you say angry things about them using rude words. ▶ NOUN **3** what you say when you curse. **4** something supernatural that is supposed to cause unpleasant things to happen to someone. **5** a thing or person that causes a lot of distress E.G. *the curse of recession.*
cursed ADJECTIVE

cursor cursors
NOUN (ICT) an arrow or box on a

computer monitor which indicates where the next letter or symbol is.

cursory
ADJECTIVE When you give something a cursory glance or examination, you look at it briefly without paying attention to detail.

curt curter curtest
ADJECTIVE If someone is curt, they speak in a brief and rather rude way.
curtly ADVERB

curtail curtails curtailing curtailed
VERB; FORMAL To curtail something is to reduce or restrict it E.G. *Injury curtailed his career.*

curtain curtains
NOUN 1 a hanging piece of material which can be pulled across a window for privacy or to keep out the light. 2 (DRAMA) a large piece of material which hangs in front of the stage in a theatre until a performance begins.
📖 from Latin *cortina* meaning 'enclosed space'

curtsy curtsies curtsying curtsied; also spelt **curtsey**
VERB 1 When a woman curtsies, she lowers her body briefly, bending her knees, to show respect. ▶ NOUN 2 the movement a woman makes when she curtsies E.G. *She gave a mock curtsy.*

curve curves curving curved
NOUN 1 a smooth, gradually bending line. ▶ VERB 2 When something curves, it moves in a curve or has the shape of a curve E.G. *The track curved away below him… His mouth curved slightly.*
curved ADJECTIVE

cushion cushions cushioning cushioned
NOUN 1 a soft object put on a seat to make it more comfortable. ▶ VERB 2 To cushion something is to reduce its effect E.G. *We might have helped to cushion the shock for her.*

custard
NOUN Custard is a sweet yellow sauce made from milk and eggs or milk and a powder.

custodian custodians
NOUN the person in charge of a collection in an art gallery or a museum.

custody
NOUN 1 To have custody of a child means to have the legal right to keep it and look after it E.G. *She won custody of her younger son.* ▶ PHRASE 2 Someone who is **in custody** is being kept in prison until they can be tried in a court.
custodial ADJECTIVE

custom customs
NOUN 1 a traditional activity E.G. *an ancient Chinese custom.* 2 something usually done at a particular time or in particular circumstances by a person or by the people in a society E.G. *It was also my custom to do Christmas shows.* 3 Customs is the place at a border, airport, or harbour where you have to declare any goods you are bringing into a country. 4 FORMAL If a shop or business has your custom, you buy things or go there regularly E.G. *Banks are desperate to get your custom.*
≡ (sense 1) convention, tradition
≡ (sense 2) habit, practice

customary
ADJECTIVE usual E.G. *his customary modesty… her customary greeting.*
customarily ADVERB

a b c d e f g h i j k l m n o p q r s t u v w x y z

A
B
C
D
E
F
G
H
I
J
K
L
M
N
O
P
Q
R
S
T
U
V
W
X
Y
Z

custom-built or **custom-made**
ADJECTIVE Something that is custom-built or custom-made is made to someone's special requirements.

customer customers
NOUN 1 A shop's or firm's customers are the people who buy its goods.
2 INFORMAL You can use 'customer' to refer to someone when describing what they are like to deal with E.G. *a tough customer*.
■ (sense 1) buyer, client, consumer

cut cuts cutting cut
VERB 1 If you cut something, you use a knife, scissors, or some other sharp tool to mark it or remove parts of it.
2 If you cut yourself, you injure yourself on a sharp object. 3 If you cut the amount of something, you reduce it E.G. *Some costs could be cut*.
4 When writing is cut, parts of it are not printed or broadcast. 5 To cut from one scene or shot to another in a film is to go instantly to the other scene or shot. ▶ NOUN 6 a mark made with a knife or other sharp tool. 7 an injury caused by a sharp object. 8 a reduction E.G. *another cut in interest rates*. 9 a part in something written that is not printed or broadcast. 10 a large piece of meat ready for cooking. ▶ ADJECTIVE 11 Well cut clothes have been well designed and made E.G. *this beautifully cut coat*.

cut back VERB To cut back or cut back on spending means to reduce it.
cutback NOUN

cut down VERB If you cut down on an activity, you do it less often E.G. *cutting down on smoking*.

cut off VERB 1 To cut someone or something off means to separate them from things they are normally connected with E.G. *The President*

had cut himself off from the people.
2 If a supply of something is cut off, you no longer get it E.G. *The water had been cut off*. 3 If your telephone or telephone call is cut off, it is disconnected.

cut out VERB 1 If you cut out something you are doing, you stop doing it E.G. *Cut out drinking*. 2 If an engine cuts out, it suddenly stops working.

cute cuter cutest
ADJECTIVE pretty or attractive.

cuticle cuticles
NOUN Cuticles are the pieces of skin that cover the base of your fingernails and toenails.

cutlass cutlasses
NOUN a curved sword that was used by sailors.

cutlery
NOUN Cutlery is knives, forks, and spoons.
🏛 from Latin *culter* meaning 'knife'

cutlet cutlets
NOUN a small piece of meat which you fry or grill.

cutting cuttings
NOUN 1 something cut from a newspaper or magazine. 2 a part cut from a plant and used to grow a new plant. ▶ ADJECTIVE 3 A cutting remark is unkind and likely to hurt someone.

CV
an abbreviation for **curriculum vitae**.

cyanide
Said "**sigh-an-nide**" NOUN Cyanide is an extremely poisonous chemical.

cyber-
PREFIX Words that begin with 'cyber-' have something to do with computers in their meaning. For

example, a *cybercafé* is a place where computers are provided for customers to use.

🎏 From *cybernetic*, from Greek *kybernētēs* meaning 'a steerman'

cyberpet cyberpets

NOUN an electronic toy that imitates the activities of a pet, and needs to be fed and entertained.

cyberspace

NOUN all of the data stored in a large computer, seen as a three-dimensional model.

cycle cycles cycling cycled

VERB 1 When you cycle, you ride a bicycle. ▶ NOUN 2 a bicycle or a motorcycle. 3 a series of events which is repeated again and again in the same order E.G. *the cycle of births and deaths.* 4 (SCIENCE) a single complete series of movements or events in an electrical, electronic, mechanical, or organic process. 5 a series of songs or poems intended to be performed or read together.

🎏 from Greek *kuklos* meaning 'ring' or 'wheel'

cyclical or **cyclic**

ADJECTIVE happening over and over again in cycles E.G. *a clear cyclical pattern.*

cyclist cyclists

NOUN someone who rides a bicycle.

cyclone cyclones

NOUN a violent tropical storm.

cygnet cygnets

Said "**sig**-net" NOUN a young swan.

🎏 from Latin *cygnus* meaning 'swan'

cylinder cylinders

NOUN 1 a regular three-dimensional shape with two equally-sized flat circular ends joined by a curved surface. 2 the part in a motor engine

in which the piston moves backwards and forwards.

cylindrical ADJECTIVE

cymbal cymbals

NOUN a circular brass plate used as a percussion instrument. Cymbals are clashed together or hit with a stick.

cynic cynics

Said "**sin**-nik" NOUN a cynical person.

🎏 from Greek *kunikos* meaning 'dog-like'

cynical

ADJECTIVE believing that people always behave selfishly or dishonestly.

cynically ADVERB　**cynicism** NOUN

cypher

another spelling of **cipher**.

cypress cypresses

NOUN a type of evergreen tree with small dark green leaves and round cones.

cyst cysts

Said "**sist**" NOUN a growth containing liquid that can form under your skin or inside your body.

czar

another spelling of **tsar**.

czarina

another spelling of **tsarina**.

Czech Czechs

Said "**chek**" ADJECTIVE 1 belonging or relating to the Czech Republic. ▶ NOUN 2 someone who comes from the Czech Republic. 3 Czech is the language spoken in the Czech Republic.

Czechoslovak Czechoslovaks

Said "chek-oh-**slow**-vak" ADJECTIVE 1 belonging to or relating to the country that used to be Czechoslovakia. ▶ NOUN 2 someone who came from the country that used to be Czechoslovakia.

a
b
c
d
e
f
g
h
i
j
k
l
m
n
o
p
q
r
s
t
u
v
w
x
y
z

Dd

A
B
C
D
E
F
G
H
I
J
K
L
M
N
O
P
Q
R
S
T
U
V
W
X
Y
Z

TIP Words that sound as if they should start with *di* are often spelt with *de* instead, for example *determination* and *dessert*.

dab dabs dabbing dabbed
VERB **1** If you dab something, you touch it with quick light strokes E.G. *He dabbed some disinfectant on to the gash.* ▶ NOUN **2** a small amount of something that is put on a surface E.G. *a dab of perfume.*

dabble dabbles dabbling dabbled
VERB If you dabble in something, you work or play at it without being seriously involved in it E.G. *All his life he dabbled in poetry.*

dachshund dachshunds
Said "**daks**-hoond" NOUN a small dog with a long body and very short legs. 🔲 a German word meaning 'badger-dog'

dad or **daddy** dads or daddies
NOUN; INFORMAL Your dad or your daddy is your father.

daddy-long-legs
NOUN a harmless flying insect with very long legs.

daffodil daffodils
NOUN a plant with a yellow trumpet-shaped flower.

daft dafter daftest
ADJECTIVE stupid and not sensible. 🔲 from Old English *gedæfte* meaning 'gentle'

dagga
NOUN; INFORMAL In South African English, dagga is cannabis.

dagger daggers
NOUN a weapon like a short knife.

dahlia dahlias
Said "**dale**-ya" NOUN a type of brightly coloured garden flower.

daily
ADJECTIVE **1** occurring every day E.G. *our daily visit to the gym.* **2** of or relating to a single day or to one day at a time E.G. *the average daily wage.*

dainty daintier daintiest
ADJECTIVE very delicate and pretty.
daintily ADVERB

dairy dairies
NOUN **1** a shop or company that supplies milk and milk products. **2** In New Zealand, a small shop selling groceries, often outside of usual opening hours. ▶ ADJECTIVE **3** Dairy products are foods made from milk, such as butter, cheese, cream, and yogurt. **4** A dairy farm is one which keeps cattle to produce milk
✔ Do not confuse the order of the vowels in *dairy* and *diary*.

dais
Said "**day**-iß" NOUN a raised platform, normally at one end of a hall and used by a speaker.

daisy daisies
NOUN a small wild flower with a yellow centre and small white petals. 🔲 from Old English *dæges eage* meaning 'day's eye', because the daisy opens in the daytime and closes at night

dale dales
NOUN a valley.

dalmatian dalmatians
NOUN a large dog with short smooth white hair and black or brown spots.

dam dams
NOUN a barrier built across a river to

hold back water.

damage damages damaging damaged

VERB 1 To damage something means to harm or spoil it. ▶ NOUN 2 Damage to something is injury or harm done to it. 3 Damages is the money awarded by a court to compensate someone for loss or harm.

damaging ADJECTIVE

dame dames

NOUN the title given to a woman who has been awarded the OBE or one of the other British orders of chivalry.

damn damns damning damned

Said "*dam*" VERB 1 To damn something or someone means to curse or condemn them. ▶ INTERJECTION 2 'Damn' is a swearword.

damned ADJECTIVE

damnation

Said "dam-**nay**-shun" NOUN Damnation is eternal punishment in Hell after death.

damp damper dampest

ADJECTIVE 1 slightly wet. ▶ NOUN 2 Damp is slight wetness, especially in the air or in the walls of a building.

dampness NOUN

📖 from Old German *damp* meaning 'steam'

dampen dampens dampening dampened

VERB 1 If you dampen something, you make it slightly wet. 2 To dampen something also means to reduce its liveliness or strength E.G. *The whole episode has rather dampened my enthusiasm.*

damper

AN INFORMAL PHRASE To **put a damper on** something means to stop it being enjoyable.

damson damsons

NOUN a small blue-black plum; also the tree that the fruit grows on.

📖 from Latin *prunum Damascenum* meaning 'Damascus plum'

dance dances dancing danced

VERB 1 To dance means to move your feet and body rhythmically in time to music. ▶ NOUN 2 a series of rhythmic movements or steps in time to music. 3 a social event where people dance with each other.

dancer NOUN **dancing** NOUN

dandelion dandelions

NOUN a wild plant with yellow flowers which form a ball of fluffy seeds.

dandruff

NOUN Dandruff is small, loose scales of dead skin in someone's hair.

dandy dandies

NOUN; OLD-FASHIONED a man who always dresses in very smart clothes.

Dane Danes

NOUN someone who comes from Denmark.

danger dangers

NOUN 1 Danger is the possibility that someone may be harmed or killed. 2 something or someone that can hurt or harm you.

■ (sense 1) hazard, peril, risk

dangerous

ADJECTIVE able to or likely to cause hurt or harm.

dangerously ADVERB

■ hazardous, perilous, unsafe

dangle dangles dangling dangled

VERB When something dangles or when you dangle it, it swings or hangs loosely.

Danish

ADJECTIVE 1 belonging or relating to Denmark. ▶ NOUN 2 Danish is the main

a
b
c
d
e
f
g
h
i
j
k
l
m
n
o
p
q
r
s
t
u
v
w
x
y
z

have a plEce of plE (pie̲ce)   SPELLING NOTE

A
B
C
D
E
F
G
H
I
J
K
L
M
N
O
P
Q
R
S
T
U
V
W
X
Y
Z

language spoken in Denmark.

dank danker dankest
ADJECTIVE A dank place is unpleasantly damp and chilly.

dapper
ADJECTIVE slim and neatly dressed.
🔤 from Old Dutch *dapper* meaning 'active' or 'nimble'

dappled
ADJECTIVE marked with patches of a different or darker shade.

dare dares daring dared
VERB 1 To dare someone means to challenge them to do something in order to prove their courage. 2 To dare to do something means to have the courage to do it. ► NOUN 3 a challenge to do something dangerous.
✓ When *dare* is used in a question or with a negative, it does not add an s: *dare she come?*; *he dare not come*.

daredevil daredevils
NOUN a person who enjoys doing dangerous things.

dark darker darkest
ADJECTIVE 1 If it is dark, there is not enough light to see properly. 2 Dark colours or surfaces reflect little light and so look deep-coloured or dull. 3 'Dark' is also used to describe thoughts or ideas which are sinister or unpleasant. ► NOUN 4 The dark is the lack of light in a place.
darkly ADVERB **darkness** NOUN
▣ (sense 1) dim, murky

darken darkens darkening darkened
VERB If something darkens, or if you darken it, it becomes darker than it was.

darkroom darkrooms
NOUN a room from which daylight is shut out so that photographic film can be developed.

darling darlings
NOUN 1 Someone who is lovable or a favourite may be called a darling. ► ADJECTIVE 2 much admired or loved E.G. *his darling daughter*.

darn darns darning darned
VERB 1 To darn a hole in a garment means to mend it with crossing stitches. ► NOUN 2 a part of a garment that has been darned.

dart darts darting darted
NOUN 1 a small pointed arrow. 2 Darts is a game in which the players throw darts at a round board divided into numbered sections. ► VERB 3 To dart about means to move quickly and suddenly from one place to another.

dash dashes dashing dashed
VERB 1 To dash somewhere means to rush there. 2 If something is dashed against something else, it strikes it or is thrown violently against it. 3 If hopes or ambitions are dashed, they are ruined or frustrated. ► NOUN 4 a sudden movement or rush. 5 a small quantity of something. 6 the punctuation mark (–) which shows a change of subject, or which may be used instead of brackets.

> ### What does the Dash do?
>
> The **dash** (–) marks an abrupt change in the flow of a sentence, either showing a sudden change of subject, or marking off extra information. The dash can also show that a speech has been cut off suddenly:
>
> E.G. *I'm not sure – what was the question again?*
> *"Go ahead and –" He broke off as Robbie seized his arm.*

dashboard dashboards
NOUN the instrument panel in a motor vehicle.

dashing
ADJECTIVE A dashing man is stylish and confident E.G. *He was a dashing figure in his younger days.*

dasyure dasyures
Said "dass-ee-your" NOUN a small marsupial that lives in Australia and eats meat.

data
NOUN 1 information, usually in the form of facts or statistics. 2 (ICT) any information put into a computer and which the computer works on or processes.
🔲 from Latin *data* meaning 'things given'
✅ *Data* is really a plural word, but it is usually used as a singular.

database databases
NOUN (ICT) a collection of information stored in a computer.

date dates dating dated
NOUN 1 a particular day or year that can be named. 2 If you have a date, you have an appointment to meet someone; also used to refer to the person you are meeting. 3 a small dark-brown sticky fruit with a stone inside, which grows on palm trees. ► VERB 4 If you are dating someone, you have a romantic relationship with them. 5 If you date something, you find out the time when it began or was made. 6 If something dates from a particular time, that is when it happened or was made. ► PHRASE 7 If something is **out of date**, it is old-fashioned or no longer valid.

datum
the singular form of **data**.

daub daubs daubing daubed
VERB If you daub something such as mud or paint on a surface, you smear it there.

daughter daughters
NOUN Someone's daughter is their female child.

daughter-in-law daughters-in-law
NOUN Someone's daughter-in-law is the wife of their son.

daunt daunts daunting daunted
VERB If something daunts you, you feel worried about whether you can succeed in doing it E.G. *He was not the type of man to be daunted by adversity.*
daunting ADJECTIVE

dawn dawns dawning dawned
NOUN 1 the time in the morning when light first appears in the sky. 2 the beginning of something E.G. *the dawn of the radio age.* ► VERB 3 If day is dawning, morning light is beginning to appear. 4 If an idea or fact dawns on you, you realize it.

day days
NOUN 1 one of the seven 24-hour periods of time in a week, measured from one midnight to the next. 2 Day is the period of light between sunrise and sunset. 3 You can refer to a particular day or days meaning a particular period in history E.G. *in Gladstone's day.*

daybreak
NOUN Daybreak is the time in the morning when light first appears in the sky.

daydream daydreams daydreaming daydreamed
NOUN 1 a series of pleasant thoughts about things that you would like to

a
b
c
d
e
f
g
h
i
j
k
l
m
n
o
p
q
r
s
t
u
v
w
x
y
z

happen. ▶ VERB **2** When you daydream, you drift off into a daydream.

daylight
NOUN **1** Daylight is the period during the day when it is light. **2** Daylight is also the light from the sun.

day-to-day
ADJECTIVE happening every day as part of ordinary routine life.

day trip day trips
NOUN a journey for pleasure to a place and back again on the same day.

daze
PHRASE If you are **in a daze**, you are confused and bewildered.

dazed
ADJECTIVE If you are dazed, you are stunned and unable to think clearly.

dazzle dazzles dazzling dazzled
VERB **1** If someone or something dazzles you, you are very impressed by their brilliance. **2** If a bright light dazzles you, it blinds you for a moment.
dazzling ADJECTIVE

de-
PREFIX When de- is added to a noun or verb, it changes the meaning to its opposite E.G. *de-ice*.

deacon deacons
NOUN **1** In the Church of England or Roman Catholic Church, a deacon is a member of the clergy below the rank of priest. **2** In some other churches, a deacon is a church official appointed to help the minister.
deaconess NOUN

dead
ADJECTIVE **1** no longer living or supporting life. **2** no longer used or no longer functioning E.G. *a dead*

language. **3** If part of your body goes dead, it loses sensation and feels numb. ▶ NOUN **4** the middle part of night or winter, when it is most quiet and at its darkest or coldest.

dead end dead ends
NOUN a street that is closed off at one end.

deadline deadlines
NOUN a time or date before which something must be completed.

deadlock deadlocks
NOUN a situation in which neither side in a dispute is willing to give in.
◼ impasse, stalemate

deadly deadlier deadliest
ADJECTIVE **1** likely or able to cause death. ▶ ADVERB OR ADJECTIVE **2** 'Deadly' is used to emphasize how serious or unpleasant a situation is E.G. *He is deadly serious about his comeback.*

deadpan
ADJECTIVE OR ADVERB showing no emotion or expression.

deaf deafer deafest
ADJECTIVE **1** partially or totally unable to hear. **2** refusing to listen or pay attention to something E.G. *He was deaf to all pleas for financial help.*
deafness NOUN

deafening
ADJECTIVE If a noise is deafening, it is so loud that you cannot hear anything else.

deal deals dealing dealt
NOUN **1** an agreement or arrangement, especially in business. ▶ VERB **2** If you deal with something, you do what is necessary to sort it out E.G. *He must learn to deal with stress.* **3** If you deal in a particular type of goods, you buy and sell those goods. **4** If you deal someone

A B C D E F G H I J K L M N O P Q R S T U V W X Y Z

or something a blow, you hurt or harm them E.G. *Competition from abroad dealt a heavy blow to the industry*.

dealer dealers

NOUN a person or firm whose business involves buying or selling things.

dealings

PLURAL NOUN Your dealings with people are the relations you have with them or the business you do with them.

dean deans

NOUN 1 In a university or college, a dean is a person responsible for administration or for the welfare of students. 2 In the Church of England, a dean is a clergyman who is responsible for administration.

📖 from Latin *decanus* meaning 'someone in charge of ten people'

dear dears; dearer dearest

NOUN 1 'Dear' is used as a sign of affection E.G. *What's the matter, dear?* ➤ ADJECTIVE 2 much loved E.G. *my dear son*. 3 Something that is dear is very expensive. 4 You use 'dear' at the beginning of a letter before the name of the person you are writing to.

dearly ADVERB

❏ (sense 2) beloved, cherished
❏ (sense 3) costly, expensive

dearth

*Said "***derth***"* NOUN a shortage of something.

death deaths

NOUN Death is the end of the life of a person or animal.

debacle debacles

*Said "***day-bah-kl***"* NOUN; FORMAL a sudden disastrous failure.

debase debases debasing debased

VERB To debase something means to reduce its value or quality.

debatable

ADJECTIVE not absolutely certain E.G. *The justness of these wars is debatable*.

❏ doubtful, questionable

debate debates debating debated

NOUN 1 Debate is argument or discussion E.G. *There is much debate as to what causes depression*. 2 a formal discussion in which opposing views are expressed. ➤ VERB 3 When people debate something, they discuss it in a fairly formal manner. 4 If you are debating whether or not to do something, you are considering it E.G. *He was debating whether or not he should tell her*.

debilitating

ADJECTIVE; FORMAL If something is debilitating, it makes you very weak E.G. *a debilitating illness*

debit debits debiting debited

VERB 1 to take money from a person's bank account. ➤ NOUN 2 a record of the money that has been taken out of a person's bank account.

debrief debriefs debriefing debriefed

VERB When someone is debriefed, they are asked to give a report on a task they have just completed.

debriefing NOUN

debris

*Said "***day-bree***"* NOUN Debris is fragments or rubble left after something has been destroyed.

📖 from Old French *débriser* meaning 'to shatter'

a b c d e f g h i j k l m n o p q r s t u v w x y z

pAL up with the principAL and principAL staff (princip**al**) **SPELLING NOTE**

A
B
C
D
E
F
G
H
I
J
K
L
M
N
O
P
Q
R
S
T
U
V
W
X
Y
Z

debt debts
Said "det" NOUN **1** a sum of money that is owed to one person by another. **2** Debt is the state of owing money.

debtor debtors
NOUN a person who owes money.

debut debuts
Said "day-byoo" NOUN a performer's first public appearance.

debutante debutantes
Said "deb-yoo-tant" NOUN; OLD-FASHIONED a girl from the upper classes who has started going to social events.

dec- or **deca-**
PREFIX Words beginning with 'dec-' or 'deca-' have 'ten' in their meaning E.G. *decathlon*.
📖 from Greek *deka* meaning 'ten'

decade decades
NOUN a period of ten years.

decadence
NOUN Decadence is a decline in standards of morality and behaviour.
decadent ADJECTIVE

decaffeinated
Said "de-kaf-in-ate-ed" ADJECTIVE Decaffeinated coffee or tea has had most of the caffeine removed.

decanter decanters
NOUN a glass bottle with a stopper, from which wine and other drinks are served.

decapitate decapitates decapitating decapitated
VERB To decapitate someone means to cut off their head.

decathlon decathlons
Said "de-cath-lon" NOUN a sports contest in which athletes compete in ten different events.
📖 from Greek *deka* meaning 'ten' and *athlon* meaning 'contest'

decay decays decaying decayed
VERB **1** When things decay, they rot or go bad. ▶ NOUN **2** Decay is the process of decaying.

deceased FORMAL
ADJECTIVE **1** A deceased person is someone who has recently died. ▶ NOUN **2** The deceased is someone who has recently died.

deceit
NOUN Deceit is behaviour that is intended to mislead people into believing something that is not true.
deceitful ADJECTIVE

deceive deceives deceiving deceived
VERB If you deceive someone, you make them believe something that is not true.

decelerate decelerates decelerating decelerated
VERB If something decelerates, it slows down.
deceleration NOUN

December
NOUN December is the twelfth and last month of the year. It has 31 days.
📖 from Latin *December* meaning 'the tenth month'

decency
NOUN **1** Decency is behaviour that is respectable and follows accepted moral standards. **2** Decency is also behaviour which shows kindness and respect towards people E.G. *No one had the decency to tell me to my face*.

decent
ADJECTIVE **1** of an acceptable standard or quality E.G. *He gets a decent pension*. **2** Decent people are honest and respectable E.G. *a decent man*.
decently ADVERB

☰ (sense 2) respectable

decentralize decentralizes decentralizing decentralized; also spelt **decentralise**

VERB To decentralize an organization means to reorganize it so that power is transferred from one main administrative centre to smaller local units.

decentralization NOUN

deception deceptions

NOUN **1** something that is intended to trick or deceive someone. **2** Deception is the act of deceiving someone.

deceptive

ADJECTIVE likely to make people believe something that is not true.

deceptively ADVERB

☰ false, misleading

decibel decibels

NOUN a unit of the intensity of sound.

decide decides deciding decided

VERB If you decide to do something, you choose to do it.

☰ make up one's mind, reach *or* come to a decision

deciduous

ADJECTIVE Deciduous trees lose their leaves in the autumn every year.

decimal decimals

ADJECTIVE (MATHS) **1** The decimal system expresses numbers using all the digits from 0 to 9. ▶ NOUN **2** a fraction in which a dot called a decimal point is followed by numbers representing tenths, hundredths, and thousandths. For example, 0.5 represents $^5/_{10}$ (or $^1/_2$); 0.05 represents $^5/_{100}$ (or $^1/_{20}$).

📖 from Latin *decima* meaning 'a tenth'

decimate decimates decimating decimated

VERB To decimate a group of people or animals means to kill or destroy a large number of them.

decipher deciphers deciphering deciphered

VERB If you decipher a piece of writing or a message, you work out its meaning.

decision decisions

NOUN a choice or judgment that is made about something E.G. *The editor's decision is final.*

☰ judgment, resolution

decisive

Said "dis-**sigh**-siv" ADJECTIVE **1** having great influence on the result of something E.G. *It was the decisive moment of the race.* **2** A decisive person is able to make decisions firmly and quickly.

decisively ADVERB **decisiveness** NOUN

deck decks

NOUN **1** a floor or platform built into a ship, or one of the two floors on a bus. **2** a pack of cards.

deck chair deck chairs

NOUN a light folding chair, made from canvas and wood and used outdoors.

declaration declarations

NOUN a firm, forceful statement, often an official announcement E.G. *a declaration of war.*

☰ assertion, statement

declare declares declaring declared

VERB **1** If you declare something, you say it firmly and forcefully E.G. *He declared early he was going to be famous.* **2** To declare something means to announce it officially or formally E.G. *Catholicism was*

a
b
c
d
e
f
g
h
i
j
k
l
m
n
o
p
q
r
s
t
u
v
w
x
y
z

declared the state religion. **3** If you declare goods or earnings, you state what you have bought or earned, in order to pay tax or duty.

▣ (sense 1) announce, proclaim, state

decline declines declining declined

VERB **1** If something declines, it becomes smaller or weaker. **2** If you decline something, you politely refuse to accept it or do it. ▶ NOUN **3** a gradual weakening or decrease E.G. *a decline in the birth rate.*

decode decodes decoding decoded

VERB If you decode a coded message, you convert it into ordinary language.

decompose decomposes decomposing decomposed

VERB If something decomposes, it decays through chemical or bacterial action.

decor

Said "day-kor" NOUN The decor of a room or house is the style in which it is decorated and furnished.

decorate decorates decorating decorated

VERB **1** If you decorate something, you make it more attractive by adding some ornament or colour to it. **2** If you decorate a room or building, you paint or wallpaper it.

▣ (sense 1) adorn, ornament

decoration decorations

NOUN **1** Decorations are features added to something to make it more attractive. **2** The decoration in a building or room is the style of the furniture and wallpaper.

decorative

ADJECTIVE intended to look attractive.

decorator decorators

NOUN a person whose job is painting and putting up wallpaper in rooms and buildings.

decorum

Said "dik-**ore**-um" NOUN; FORMAL Decorum is polite and correct behaviour.

decoy decoys

NOUN a person or object that is used to lead someone or something into danger.

decrease decreases decreasing decreased

VERB **1** If something decreases or if you decrease it, it becomes less in quantity or size. ▶ NOUN **2** a lessening in the amount of something; also the amount by which something becomes less.

decreasing ADJECTIVE

decree decrees decreeing decreed

VERB **1** If someone decrees something, they state formally that it will happen. ▶ NOUN **2** an official decision or order, usually by governments or rulers.

dedicate dedicates dedicating dedicated

VERB If you dedicate yourself to something, you devote your time and energy to it.

dedication NOUN

▣ commit, devote

deduce deduces deducing deduced

VERB If you deduce something, you work it out from other facts that you know are true.

▣ conclude, reason

deduct deducts deducting deducted

VERB To deduct an amount from a

total amount means to subtract it from the total.

deduction deductions

NOUN **1** an amount which is taken away from a total. **2** a conclusion that you have reached because of other things that you know are true.

deed deeds

NOUN **1** something that is done. **2** a legal document, especially concerning the ownership of land or buildings.

deem deems deeming deemed

VERB; FORMAL If you deem something to be true, you judge or consider it to be true E.G. *His ideas were deemed unacceptable.*

deep deeper deepest

ADJECTIVE **1** situated or extending a long way down from the top surface of something, or a long way inwards E.G. *a deep hole.* **2** great or intense E.G. *deep suspicion.* **3** low in pitch E.G. *a deep voice.* **4** strong and fairly dark in colour E.G. *The wine was deep ruby in colour.*

deeply ADVERB

deepen deepens deepening deepened

VERB If something deepens or is deepened, it becomes deeper or more intense.

deer

NOUN a large, hoofed mammal that lives wild in parts of Britain.

📖 from Old English *deor* meaning 'beast'

deface defaces defacing defaced

VERB If you deface a wall or notice, you spoil it by writing or drawing on it E.G. *She spitefully defaced her sister's poster.*

default defaults defaulting defaulted

VERB **1** If someone defaults on something they have legally agreed to do, they fail to do it E.G. *He defaulted on repayment of the loan.*
▶ PHRASE **2** If something happens **by default**, it happens because something else which might have prevented it has failed to happen.

defeat defeats defeating defeated

VERB **1** If you defeat someone or something, you win a victory over them, or cause them to fail. ▶ NOUN **2** Defeat is the state of being beaten or of failing E.G. *He was gracious in defeat.* **3** an occasion on which someone is beaten or fails to achieve something E.G. *It was a crushing defeat for the government.*

defecate defecates defecating defecated

VERB To defecate means to get rid of waste matter from the bowels through the anus.

defect defects defecting defected

NOUN **1** a fault or flaw in something.
▶ VERB **2** If someone defects, they leave their own country or organization and join an opposing one.

defection NOUN

defective

ADJECTIVE imperfect or faulty E.G. *defective eyesight.*

defence defences

NOUN **1** Defence is action that is taken to protect someone or something from attack. **2** any arguments used in support of something that has been criticized or questioned. **3** the case

a b c **d** e f g h i j k l m n o p q r s t u v w x y z

A
B
C
D
E
F
G
H
I
J
K
L
M
N
O
P
Q
R
S
T
U
V
W
X
Y
Z

presented, in a court of law, by a lawyer for the person on trial; also the person on trial and his or her lawyers. **4** (HISTORY) A country's defences are its military resources, such as its armed forces and weapons.

defend defends defending defended
VERB **1** To defend someone or something means to protect them from harm or danger. **2** If you defend a person or their ideas and beliefs, you argue in support of them. **3** To defend someone in court means to represent them and argue their case for them. **4** In a game such as football or hockey, to defend means to try to prevent goals being scored by your opponents.
defender NOUN

defendant defendants
NOUN a person who has been accused of a crime in a court of law.

defensible
ADJECTIVE able to be defended against criticism or attack.

defensive
ADJECTIVE **1** intended or designed for protection E.G. *defensive weapons*. **2** Someone who is defensive feels unsure and threatened by other people's opinions and attitudes E.G. *Don't get defensive, I was only joking about your cooking.*
defensively ADVERB **defensiveness** NOUN

defer defers deferring deferred
VERB **1** If you defer something, you delay or postpone it until a future time. **2** If you defer to someone, you agree with them or do what they want because you respect them.

deference
Said "def-er-ense" NOUN Deference is polite and respectful behaviour.
deferential ADJECTIVE

defiance
NOUN Defiance is behaviour which shows that you are not willing to obey or behave in the expected way E.G. *a gesture of defiance*.
defiant ADJECTIVE **defiantly** ADVERB

deficiency deficiencies
NOUN a lack of something E.G. *vitamin deficiency*.
deficient ADJECTIVE

deficit deficits
Said "def-iss-it" NOUN the amount by which money received by an organization is less than money spent.

define defines defining defined
VERB (EXAM TERM) If you define something, you say clearly what it is or what it means E.G. *Culture can be defined in hundreds of ways*.

definite
ADJECTIVE **1** firm and unlikely to be changed E.G. *The answer is a definite 'yes'*. **2** certain or true rather than guessed or imagined E.G. *definite proof*.
definitely ADVERB

definition definitions
NOUN a statement explaining the meaning of a word or idea.

definitive
ADJECTIVE **1** final and unable to be questioned or altered E.G. *a definitive answer*. **2** most complete, o* the best of its kind E.G. *a definitive history of science fiction*.
definitively ADVERB

deflate deflates deflating deflated
VERB **1** If you deflate something such

as a tyre or balloon, you let out all the air or gas in it. **2** If you deflate someone, you make them seem less important.

deflect deflects deflecting deflected

VERB To deflect something means to turn it aside or make it change direction.

deflection NOUN

deforestation

NOUN Deforestation is the cutting down of all the trees in an area.

deformed

ADJECTIVE disfigured or abnormally shaped.

defraud defrauds defrauding defrauded

VERB If someone defrauds you, they cheat you out of something that should be yours.

defrost defrosts defrosting defrosted

VERB **1** If you defrost a freezer or refrigerator, you remove the ice from it. **2** If you defrost frozen food, you let it thaw out.

deft defter deftest

ADJECTIVE Someone who is deft is quick and skilful in their movements.

deftly ADVERB

defunct

ADJECTIVE no longer existing or functioning.

defuse defuses defusing defused

VERB **1** To defuse a dangerous or tense situation means to make it less dangerous or tense. **2** To defuse a bomb means to remove its fuse or detonator so that it cannot explode.

defy defies defying defied

VERB **1** If you defy a person or a law,

you openly refuse to obey. **2** FORMAL If you defy someone to do something that you think is impossible, you challenge them to do it.

■ (sense 1) disregard, flout, resist

degenerate degenerates degenerating degenerated

VERB **1** If something degenerates, it becomes worse E.G. *The election campaign degenerated into farce.*
► ADJECTIVE **2** having low standards of morality. ► NOUN **3** someone whose standards of morality are so low that people find their behaviour shocking or disgusting.

degeneration NOUN

degradation

NOUN Degradation is a state of poverty and misery.

degrade degrades degrading degraded

VERB If something degrades people, it humiliates them and makes them feel that they are not respected.

degrading ADJECTIVE

■ debase, demean

degree degrees

NOUN **1** an amount of a feeling or quality E.G. *a degree of pain.* **2** a unit of measurement of temperature; often written as ° after a number E.G. *20°C.* **3** (MATHS) a unit of measurement of angles in mathematics, and of latitude and longitude E.G. *The yacht was 20° off course.* **4** a course of study at a university or college; also the qualification awarded after passing the course.

dehydrated

ADJECTIVE If someone is dehydrated, they are weak or ill because they have lost too much water from their body.

deign deigns deigning deigned
*Said "**dane**"* VERB; FORMAL If you deign
to do something, you do it even
though you think you are too
important to do such a thing.

deity deities
NOUN a god or goddess.

deja vu
*Said "**day**-ja **voo**"* NOUN Deja vu is the
feeling that you have already
experienced in the past exactly the
same sequence of events as is
happening now.
📖 from French *déjà vu* meaning
literally 'already seen'

dejected
ADJECTIVE miserable and unhappy.
dejection NOUN

delay delays delaying delayed
VERB 1 If you delay doing something,
you put it off until a later time. 2 If
something delays you, it hinders you
or slows you down. ▶ NOUN 3 Delay is
time during which something is
delayed.
🔲 (sense 1) postpone, put off

delectable
ADJECTIVE very pleasing or delightful.

delegate delegates delegating
delegated
NOUN 1 a person appointed to vote or
to make decisions on behalf of a
group of people. ▶ VERB 2 If you
delegate duties, you give them to
someone who can then act on your
behalf.

delegation delegations
NOUN 1 a group of people chosen to
represent a larger group of people.
2 Delegation is the giving of duties,
responsibilities, or power to
someone who can then act on your
behalf.

delete deletes deleting deleted
VERB (ICT) To delete something
means to cross it out or remove it
E.G. *He had deleted the computer file
by mistake.*
deletion NOUN

deliberate deliberates
deliberating deliberated
ADJECTIVE 1 done on purpose or
planned in advance E.G. *It was a
deliberate insult.* 2 careful and not
hurried in speech and action E.G.
*She was very deliberate in her
movements.* ▶ VERB 3 If you deliberate
about something, you think about it
seriously and carefully.
deliberately ADVERB
🔲 (sense 1) intentional, planned

deliberation deliberations
NOUN Deliberation is careful
consideration of a subject.

delicacy delicacies
NOUN 1 Delicacy is grace and
attractiveness. 2 Something said or
done with delicacy is said or done
tactfully so that nobody is offended.
3 Delicacies are rare or expensive
foods that are considered especially
nice to eat.

delicate
ADJECTIVE 1 fine, graceful, or subtle in
character E.G. *a delicate fragrance.*
2 fragile and needing to be handled
carefully E.G. *delicate antique lace.*
3 precise or sensitive, and able to
notice very small changes E.G. *a
delicate instrument.*
delicately ADVERB

delicatessen delicatessens
NOUN a shop selling unusual or
imported foods.
📖 from German *Delikatessen*
meaning 'delicacies'

A B C D E F G H I J K L M N O P Q R S T U V W X Y Z

delicious
ADJECTIVE very pleasing, especially to taste.
deliciously ADVERB
◾ delectable, scrumptious

delight delights delighting delighted
NOUN 1 Delight is great pleasure or joy. ▶ VERB 2 If something delights you or if you are delighted by it, it gives you a lot of pleasure.
delighted ADJECTIVE

delightful
ADJECTIVE very pleasant and attractive.

delinquent delinquents
NOUN a young person who commits minor crimes.
delinquency NOUN

delirious
ADJECTIVE 1 unable to speak or act in a rational way because of illness or fever. 2 wildly excited and happy.
deliriously ADVERB

deliver delivers delivering delivered
VERB 1 If you deliver something to someone, you take it to them and give them it. 2 To deliver a lecture or speech means to give it.

delivery deliveries
NOUN 1 Delivery or a delivery is the bringing of letters or goods to a person or firm. 2 Someone's delivery is the way in which they give a speech.

dell dells
NOUN; LITERARY a small wooded valley.

delta deltas
NOUN a low, flat area at the mouth of a river where the river has split into several branches to enter the sea.

delude deludes deluding deluded
VERB To delude people means to deceive them into believing something that is not true.

deluge deluges deluging deluged
NOUN 1 a sudden, heavy downpour of rain. ▶ VERB 2 To be deluged with things means to be overwhelmed by a great number of them.

delusion delusions
NOUN a mistaken or misleading belief or idea.

de luxe
Said "de luke" ADJECTIVE rich, luxurious, or of superior quality.
▣ from French de luxe meaning literally 'of luxury'

delve delves delving delved
VERB If you delve into something, you seek out more information about it.

demand demands demanding demanded
VERB 1 If you demand something, you ask for it forcefully and urgently. 2 If a job or situation demands a particular quality, it needs it E.G. This situation demands hard work. ▶ NOUN 3 a forceful request for something. 4 If there is a demand for something, a lot of people want to buy it or have it
☑ The verb demand is either followed by of or from: at least one important decision was demanded of me; he had demanded an explanation from Daphne.

demean demeans demeaning demeaned
VERB If you demean yourself, you do something which makes people have less respect for you.
demeaning ADJECTIVE

demeanour
NOUN Your demeanour is the way you behave and the impression that this creates.

a
b
c
d
e
f
g
h
i
j
k
l
m
n
o
p
q
r
s
t
u
v
w
x
y
z

A

demented
ADJECTIVE Someone who is
demented behaves in a wild or
violent way.

dementia
Said "dee-men-sha" NOUN; MEDICAL
Dementia is a serious illness of the
mind.

demi-
PREFIX Demi- means half.

demise
Said "dee-myz" NOUN; FORMAL
Someone's demise is their death.

demo demos
NOUN; INFORMAL a demonstration.

democracy democracies
NOUN Democracy is a system of
government in which the people
choose their leaders by voting for
them in elections.

democrat democrats
NOUN a person who believes in
democracy, personal freedom, and
equality.

democratic
ADJECTIVE having representatives
elected by the people.
    democratically ADVERB
    🔟 from Greek *dēmos* meaning 'the
    people' and *kratos* meaning 'power'

demography
NOUN Demography is the study of the
changes in the size and structure of
populations.
    demographic ADJECTIVE

**demolish demolishes
demolishing demolished**
VERB To demolish a building means to
pull it down or break it up.
    demolition NOUN

demon demons
NOUN **1** an evil spirit or devil. ▶ ADJECTIVE
2 skilful, keen, and energetic E.G. *a*

demon squash player.
    demonic ADJECTIVE

**demonstrate demonstrates
demonstrating demonstrated**
VERB **1** (EXAM TERM) To demonstrate a
fact or theory means to prove or
show it to be true. **2** If you
demonstrate something to
somebody, you show and explain it
by using or doing the thing itself
E.G. *She demonstrated how to apply
the make-up.* **3** If people
demonstrate, they take part in a
march or rally to show their
opposition or support for
something.

demonstration demonstrations
NOUN **1** a talk or explanation to show
how to do or use something.
2 Demonstration is proof that
something exists or is true. **3** a public
march or rally in support of or
opposition to something.
    demonstrator NOUN

**demote demotes demoting
demoted**
VERB A person who is demoted is put
in a lower rank or position, often as a
punishment.
    demotion NOUN

demure
ADJECTIVE Someone who is demure is
quiet, shy, and behaves very
modestly.
    demurely ADVERB

den dens
NOUN **1** the home of some wild
animals such as lions or foxes. **2** a
secret place where people meet.

denial denials
NOUN **1** A denial of something is a
statement that it is untrue E.G. *He
published a firm denial of the report.*

2 The denial of a request or something to which you have a right is the refusal of it E.G. *the denial of human rights*.

denigrate denigrates denigrating denigrated
VERB; FORMAL To denigrate someone or something means to criticize them in order to damage their reputation.

denim denims
NOUN **1** Denim is strong cotton cloth, used for making clothes. ▶ PLURAL NOUN **2** Denims are jeans made from denim.
🔳 from French *serge de Nîmes*, meaning 'serge (a type of cloth) from Nîmes'

denomination denominations
NOUN **1** a particular group which has slightly different religious beliefs from other groups within the same faith. **2** a unit in a system of weights, values, or measures E.G. *a high denomination note*.

denominator denominators
NOUN (MATHS) In maths, the denominator is the bottom part of a fraction.

denote denotes denoting denoted
VERB If one thing denotes another, it is a sign of it or it represents it E.G. *Formerly, a tan denoted wealth*.

denounce denounces denouncing denounced
VERB **1** If you denounce someone or something, you express very strong disapproval of them E.G. *He publicly denounced government nuclear policy*. **2** If you denounce someone, you give information against them E.G. *He was denounced as a dangerous agitator*.

dense denser densest
ADJECTIVE **1** thickly crowded or packed together E.G. *the dense crowd*. **2** difficult to see through E.G. *dense black smoke*.
densely ADVERB

density densities
NOUN the degree to which something is filled or occupied E.G. *a very high population density*.

dent dents denting dented
VERB **1** To dent something means to damage it by hitting it and making a hollow in its surface. ▶ NOUN **2** a hollow in the surface of something.

dental
ADJECTIVE relating to the teeth.

dentist dentists
NOUN a person who is qualified to treat people's teeth.

dentistry
NOUN Dentistry is the branch of medicine concerned with disorders of the teeth.

dentures
PLURAL NOUN Dentures are false teeth.

denunciation denunciations
NOUN A denunciation of someone or something is severe public criticism of them.

deny denies denying denied
VERB **1** If you deny something that has been said, you state that it is untrue. **2** If you deny that something is the case, you refuse to believe it E.G. *He denied the existence of God*. **3** If you deny someone something, you refuse to give it to them E.G. *They were denied permission to attend*.
■ (sense 1) contradict, gainsay

deodorant deodorants
NOUN a substance or spray used to hide the smell of perspiration.

A
B
C
D
E
F
G
H
I
J
K
L
M
N
O
P
Q
R
S
T
U
V
W
X
Y
Z

depart departs departing departed

VERB When you depart, you leave.

departure NOUN

department departments

NOUN one of the sections into which an organization is divided E.G. *the marketing department*.

departmental ADJECTIVE

depend depends depending depended

VERB **1** If you depend on someone or something, you trust them and rely on them. **2** If one thing depends on another, it is influenced by it E.G. *Success depends on the quality of the workforce*.

◼ (sense 1) count on, rely on, trust

dependable

ADJECTIVE reliable and trustworthy.

dependant dependants

NOUN (PSHE) someone who relies on another person for financial support.

dependence

NOUN Dependence is a constant need that someone has for something or someone in order to survive or operate properly E.G. *He was flattered by her dependence on him*.

dependency dependencies

NOUN **1** (PSHE) Dependency is relying on someone or something to give you what you need E.G. *drug dependency*. **2** a country or area controlled by another country.

dependent

ADJECTIVE reliant on someone or something.

depict depicts depicting depicted

VERB To depict someone or something means to represent them in painting or sculpture.

deplete depletes depleting depleted

VERB To deplete something means to reduce greatly the amount of it available.

depletion NOUN

deplorable

ADJECTIVE shocking or regrettable E.G. *deplorable conditions*.

deplore deplores deploring deplored

VERB If you deplore something, you condemn it because you feel it is wrong.

deploy deploys deploying deployed

VERB To deploy troops or resources means to organize or position them so that they can be used effectively.

deployment NOUN

deport deports deporting deported

VERB If a government deports someone, it sends them out of the country because they have committed a crime or because they do not have the right to be there.

deportation NOUN

depose deposes deposing deposed

VERB If someone is deposed, they are removed from a position of power.

deposit deposits depositing deposited

VERB **1** If you deposit something, you put it down or leave it somewhere. **2** If you deposit money or valuables, you put them somewhere for safekeeping. ▶ NOUN **3** a sum of money given in part payment for goods or services.

depot depots

Said "*dep-oh*" NOUN a place where

large supplies of materials or equipment may be stored.

depraved
ADJECTIVE morally bad.

depress depresses depressing depressed
VERB 1 If something depresses you, it makes you feel sad and gloomy. 2 If wages or prices are depressed, their value falls.
depressive ADJECTIVE

depressant depressants
NOUN a drug which reduces nervous activity and so has a calming effect.

depressed
ADJECTIVE 1 unhappy and gloomy. 2 A place that is depressed has little economic activity and therefore low incomes and high unemployment E.G. *depressed industrial areas.*
■ (sense 1) dejected, despondent, low-spirited

depression depressions
NOUN 1 a state of mind in which someone feels unhappy and has no energy or enthusiasm. 2 a time of industrial and economic decline.

deprive deprives depriving deprived
VERB If you deprive someone of something, you take it away or prevent them from having it.
deprived ADJECTIVE **deprivation** NOUN

depth depths
NOUN 1 The depth of something is the measurement or distance between its top and bottom, or between its front and back. 2 The depth of something such as emotion is its intensity E.G. *the depth of her hostility.*

deputation deputations
NOUN a small group of people sent to speak or act on behalf of others.

deputy deputies
NOUN Someone's deputy is a person appointed to act in their place.

deranged
ADJECTIVE mad, or behaving in a wild and uncontrolled way.

derby derbies
Said "dar-bee" NOUN A local derby is a sporting event between two teams from the same area.

derelict
ADJECTIVE abandoned and falling into ruins.

deride derides deriding derided
VERB To deride someone or something means to mock or jeer at them with contempt.

derision
NOUN Derision is an attitude of contempt or scorn towards something or someone.

derivation derivations
NOUN The derivation of something is its origin or source.

derivative derivatives
NOUN 1 something which has developed from an earlier source.
▶ ADJECTIVE 2 not original, but based on or copied from something else E.G. *The record was not deliberately derivative.*

derive derives deriving derived
VERB 1 FORMAL If you derive something from someone or something, you get it from them E.G. *He derived so much joy from music.* 2 If something derives from something else, it develops from it.

derogatory
ADJECTIVE critical and scornful E.G. *He*

LEt's measure the angLE (angle) ◀ SPELLING NOTE

descant descants

NOUN The descant to a tune is another tune played at the same time and at a higher pitch.

descend descends descending descended

VERB 1 To descend means to move downwards. 2 If you descend on people or on a place, you arrive unexpectedly.

descendant descendants

NOUN A person's descendants are the people in later generations who are related to them.

descended

ADJECTIVE If you are descended from someone who lived in the past, your family originally derived from them.

descent descents

NOUN 1 a movement or slope from a higher to a lower position or level. 2 Your descent is your family's origins.

describe describes describing described

VERB To describe someone or something means to give an account or a picture of them in words.

description descriptions

NOUN an account or picture of something in words.

descriptive ADJECTIVE

desert deserts

Said "**dez**-ert" NOUN (GEOGRAPHY) a region of land with very little plant life, usually because of low rainfall.

desert deserts deserting deserted

Said "dez-**zert**" VERB To desert a person means to leave or abandon

them E.G. *His clients had deserted him.*

desertion NOUN

deserter deserters

NOUN someone who leaves the armed forces without permission.

deserve deserves deserving deserved

VERB If you deserve something, you are entitled to it or earn it because of your qualities, achievements, or actions E.G. *He deserved a rest.*
■ be worthy of, justify, merit

deserving

ADJECTIVE worthy of being helped, rewarded, or praised E.G. *a deserving charity.*

design designs designing designed (D&T)

VERB 1 To design something means to plan it, especially by preparing a detailed sketch or drawings from which it can be built or made. ▶ NOUN 2 a drawing or plan from which something can be built or made. 3 The design of something is its shape and style.

designer NOUN

designate designates designating designated

Said "**dez**-ig-nate" VERB 1 To designate someone or something means to formally label or name them E.G. *The room was designated a no smoking area.* 2 If you designate someone to do something, you appoint them to do it E.G. *He designated his son as his successor.*

designation designations

NOUN a name or title.

designing

ADJECTIVE crafty and cunning.

desirable

ADJECTIVE **1** worth having or doing E.G. *a desirable job*. **2** sexually attractive.
desirability NOUN

desire desires desiring desired

VERB **1** If you desire something, you want it very much. ▶ NOUN **2** a strong feeling of wanting something. **3** Desire for someone is a strong sexual attraction to them.

◼ (sense 1) long for, want, wish for
◼ (sense 2) longing, want, wish

desist desists desisting desisted

VERB; FORMAL To desist from doing something means to stop doing it.

desk desks

NOUN **1** a piece of furniture designed for working at or writing on. **2** a counter or table in a public building behind which a receptionist sits.

desktop

ADJECTIVE of a convenient size to be used on a desk or table E.G. *a desktop computer*.

desolate

ADJECTIVE **1** deserted and bleak E.G. *a desolate mountainous region*. **2** lonely, very sad, and without hope E.G. *He was desolate without her*.
desolation NOUN

despair despairs despairing despaired

NOUN **1** Despair is a total loss of hope. ▶ VERB **2** If you despair, you lose hope E.G. *He despaired of finishing it*.
despairing ADJECTIVE
◼ (sense 1) desperation, hopelessness

despatch

another spelling of **dispatch**.

desperate

ADJECTIVE **1** If you are desperate, you are so worried or frightened that you will try anything to improve your situation E.G. *a desperate attempt to save their marriage*. **2** A desperate person is violent and dangerous. **3** A desperate situation is extremely dangerous or serious.
desperately ADVERB **desperation** NOUN

despicable

ADJECTIVE deserving contempt.

despise despises despising despised

VERB If you despise someone or something, you dislike them very much.

despite

PREPOSITION In spite of E.G. *He fell asleep despite all the coffee he'd drunk*.
◼ in spite of, regardless of

despondent

ADJECTIVE dejected and unhappy.
despondency NOUN

dessert desserts

Said "diz-**ert**" NOUN a sweet food served after the main course of a meal.
🔲 from French *desservir* meaning 'to clear the table after a meal'

destination destinations

NOUN a place to which someone or something is going or is being sent.

destined

ADJECTIVE meant or intended to happen E.G. *I was destined for fame and fortune*.

destiny destinies

NOUN **1** Your destiny is all the things that happen to you in your life, especially when they are considered to be outside human control. **2** Destiny is the force which some people believe controls everyone's life.

a b c d e f g h i j k l m n o p q r s t u v w x y z

Beautiful Elephants Are Usually Tiny (<u>beauti</u>ful)   ◀ **SPELLING NOTE**

destitute

ADJECTIVE without money or possessions, and therefore in great need.

destitution NOUN

destroy destroys destroying destroyed

VERB 1 To destroy something means to damage it so much that it is completely ruined. 2 To destroy something means to put an end to it E.G. *The holiday destroyed their friendship.*

∎ (sense 1) demolish, ruin, wreck

destruction

NOUN Destruction is the act of destroying something or the state of being destroyed.

∎ devastation, ruin

destructive

ADJECTIVE causing or able to cause great harm, damage, or injury.

destructiveness NOUN

desultory

Said "dez-ul-tree" ADJECTIVE passing from one thing to another in a fitful or random way E.G. *A desultory, embarrassed chatter began again.*

detach detaches detaching detached

VERB To detach something means to remove it E.G. *The hood can be detached.*

detachable ADJECTIVE

detached

ADJECTIVE 1 separate or standing apart E.G. *a detached house.* 2 having no real interest or emotional involvement in something E.G. *He observed me with a detached curiosity.*

detachment detachments

NOUN 1 Detachment is the feeling of not being personally involved with something E.G. *A stranger can view your problems with detachment.* 2 a small group of soldiers sent to do a special job.

detail details

NOUN 1 an individual fact or feature of something E.G. *We discussed every detail of the performance.* 2 Detail is all the small features that make up the whole of something E.G. *Look at the detail.*

detailed ADJECTIVE

detain detains detaining detained

VERB 1 To detain someone means to force them to stay E.G. *She was being detained for interrogation.* 2 If you detain someone, you delay them E.G. *I mustn't detain you.*

detect detects detecting detected

VERB 1 If you detect something, you notice it E.G. *I detected a glimmer of interest in his eyes.* 2 To detect something means to find it E.G. *Cancer can be detected by X-rays.*

detectable ADJECTIVE

detection

NOUN 1 Detection is the act of noticing, discovering, or sensing something. 2 Detection is also the work of investigating crime.

detective detectives

NOUN a person, usually a police officer, whose job is to investigate crimes.

detector detectors

NOUN an instrument which is used to detect the presence of something E.G. *a metal detector.*

detention

NOUN The detention of someone is their arrest or imprisonment.

A B C D E F G H I J K L M N O P Q R S T U V W X Y Z

SPELLING NOTE Betty Eats Cakes And Uses Seven Eggs (<u>because</u>)

deter deters deterring deterred
VERB To deter someone means to discourage or prevent them from doing something by creating a feeling of fear or doubt E.G. *99 per cent of burglars are deterred by the sight of an alarm box.*

detergent detergents
NOUN a chemical substance used for washing or cleaning things.

deteriorate deteriorates deteriorating deteriorated
VERB If something deteriorates, it gets worse E.G. *My father's health has deteriorated lately.*
deterioration NOUN

determination
NOUN Determination is great firmness, after you have made up your mind to do something E.G. *They shared a determination to win the war.*

determine determines determining determined
VERB 1 If something determines a result, it causes it or controls it E.G. *The track surface determines his tactics in a race.* 2 To determine something means to decide or settle it firmly E.G. *The date has still to be determined.* 3 To determine something means to find out or calculate the facts about it E.G. *He bit the coin to determine whether it was genuine.*
▪ (sense 2) decide, settle
▪ (sense 3) ascertain, find out, verify

determined
ADJECTIVE firmly decided E.G. *She was determined not to repeat her error.*
determinedly ADVERB
▪ intent on, resolute

deterrent deterrents
NOUN something that prevents you

from doing something by making you afraid of what will happen if you do it E.G. *Capital punishment was no deterrent to domestic murders.*
deterrence NOUN

detest detests detesting detested
VERB If you detest someone or something, you strongly dislike them.

detonate detonates detonating detonated
VERB To detonate a bomb or mine means to cause it to explode.
detonator NOUN

detour detours
NOUN an alternative, less direct route.

detract detracts detracting detracted
VERB To detract from something means to make it seem less good or valuable.

detriment
NOUN Detriment is disadvantage or harm E.G. *a detriment to their health.*
detrimental ADJECTIVE

deuce deuces
Said "**joos**" NOUN In tennis, deuce is the score of forty all.

devalue devalues devaluing devalued
VERB To devalue something means to lower its status, importance, or worth.
devaluation NOUN

devastate devastates devastating devastated
VERB To devastate an area or place means to damage it severely or destroy it.
devastation NOUN

devastated
ADJECTIVE very shocked or upset E.G.

a
b
c
d
e
f
g
h
i
j
k
l
m
n
o
p
q
r
s
t
u
v
w
x
y
z

A
B
C
D
E
F
G
H
I
J
K
L
M
N
O
P
Q
R
S
T
U
V
W
X
Y
Z

The family are devastated by the news.

develop develops developing developed

VERB **1** When something develops or is developed, it grows or becomes more advanced E.G. *The sneezing developed into a full blown cold.* **2** To develop an area of land means to build on it. **3** To develop an illness or a fault means to become affected by it.

developer developers

NOUN a person or company that builds on land.

development developments

NOUN **1** Development is gradual growth or progress. **2** The development of land or water is the process of making it more useful or profitable by the expansion of industry or housing E.G. *the development of the old docks.* **3** a new stage in a series of events E.G. *developments in technology.*

developmental ADJECTIVE

deviant deviants

ADJECTIVE **1** Deviant behaviour is unacceptable or different from what people consider as normal. ▶ NOUN **2** someone whose behaviour or beliefs are different from what people consider to be acceptable.

deviate deviates deviating deviated

VERB To deviate means to differ or depart from what is usual or acceptable.

deviation NOUN

device devices

NOUN **1** a machine or tool that is used for a particular purpose E.G. *a device to warn you when the batteries need changing.* **2** a plan or scheme E.G. *a*

device to pressurise him into selling.

devil devils

NOUN **1** In Christianity and Judaism, the Devil is the spirit of evil and enemy of God. **2** an evil spirit.

📖 from Greek *diabolos* meaning 'slanderer', 'enemy', or 'devil'

devious

ADJECTIVE insincere and dishonest.

deviousness NOUN

devise devises devising devised

VERB To devise something means to work it out E.G. *Besides diets, he devised punishing exercise routines.*

devoid

ADJECTIVE lacking in a particular thing or quality E.G. *His glance was devoid of expression.*

devolution

NOUN Devolution is the transfer of power from a central government or organization to local government departments or smaller organizations.

devote devotes devoting devoted

VERB If you devote yourself to something, you give all your time, energy, or money to it E.G. *She has devoted herself to women's causes.*

devoted

ADJECTIVE very loving and loyal.

devotee devotees

NOUN a fanatical or enthusiastic follower of it.

devotion

NOUN Devotion to someone or something is great love or affection for them.

devotional ADJECTIVE

devour devours devouring devoured

VERB If you devour something, you eat

it hungrily or greedily.

devout

ADJECTIVE deeply and sincerely religious E.G. *a devout Buddhist*.

devoutly ADVERB

dew

NOUN Dew is drops of moisture that form on the ground and other cool surfaces at night.

dexterity

NOUN Dexterity is skill or agility in using your hands or mind E.G. *He had learned to use the crutches with dexterity*.

dexterous ADJECTIVE

dharma

Said "**dar-ma**" NOUN In the Buddhist religion, dharma is ideal truth as set out in the teaching of the Buddha.
📖 a Sanskrit word

diabetes

Said "**dy-a-bee-tiss**" NOUN Diabetes is a disease in which someone has too much sugar in their blood, because they do not produce enough insulin to absorb it.

diabetic NOUN or ADJECTIVE

diabolical

ADJECTIVE **1** INFORMAL dreadful and very annoying E.G. *The pain was diabolical*. **2** extremely wicked and cruel.

diagnose diagnoses diagnosing diagnosed

VERB To diagnose an illness or problem means to identify exactly what is wrong.

diagnosis diagnoses

NOUN the identification of what is wrong with someone who is ill.

diagnostic ADJECTIVE

diagonal

ADJECTIVE in a slanting direction.

diagonally ADVERB
📖 from Greek *diagōnios* meaning 'from angle to angle'

diagram diagrams

NOUN a drawing that shows or explains something.

dial dials dialling dialled

NOUN **1** the face of a clock or meter, with divisions marked on it so that a time or measurement can be recorded and read. **2** a part of a device, such as a radio, used to control or tune it. ▶ VERB **3** To dial a telephone number means to press the number keys to select the required number.

dialect dialects

NOUN a form of a language spoken in a particular geographical area.

dialogue dialogues

NOUN **1** (ENGLISH) In a novel, play, or film, dialogue is conversation. **2** Dialogue is communication or discussion between people or groups of people E.G. *The union sought dialogue with the council*.

dialysis

NOUN Dialysis is a treatment used for some kidney diseases, in which blood is filtered by a special machine to remove waste products.
📖 from Greek *dialuein* meaning 'to rip apart'

diameter diameters

NOUN (MATHS) The diameter of a circle is the length of a straight line drawn across it through its centre.

diamond diamonds

NOUN **1** a precious stone made of pure carbon. **2** a shape with four straight sides of equal length forming two opposite angles less than 90° and two opposite angles greater than

a
b
c
d
e
f
g
h
i
j
k
l
m
n
o
p
q
r
s
t
u
v
w
x
y
z

A
B
C
D
E
F
G
H
I
J
K
L
M
N
O
P
Q
R
S
T
U
V
W
X
Y
Z

90°. **3** Diamonds is one of the four suits in a pack of playing cards. It is marked by a red diamond-shaped symbol. ▶ ADJECTIVE **4** A diamond anniversary is the 60th anniversary of an event.

diaphragm diaphragms
Said "**dy**-a-fram" NOUN In mammals, the diaphragm is the muscular wall that separates the lungs from the stomach.

diarrhoea
Said "dy-a-**ree**-a" NOUN Diarrhoea is a condition in which the faeces are more liquid and frequent than usual.

diary diaries
NOUN a book which has a separate space or page for each day of the year on which to keep a record of appointments.
diarist NOUN
✔ Do not confuse the order of the vowels in *diary* and *dairy*.

dice dices dicing diced
NOUN **1** a small cube which has each side marked with dots representing the numbers one to six. ▶ VERB **2** To dice food means to cut it into small cubes.
diced ADJECTIVE

dictate dictates dictating dictated
VERB **1** If you dictate something, you say or read it aloud for someone else to write down. **2** To dictate something means to command or state what must happen E.G. *What we wear is largely dictated by our daily routine.*
dictation NOUN

dictator dictators
NOUN a ruler who has complete power in a country, especially one

who has taken power by force.
dictatorial ADJECTIVE

diction
NOUN Someone's diction is the clarity with which they speak or sing.

dictionary dictionaries
NOUN (LIBRARY) a book in which words are listed alphabetically and explained, or equivalent words are given in another language.
📖 from Latin *dictio* meaning 'phrase' or 'word'

didgeridoo didgeridoos
NOUN an Australian musical wind instrument made in the shape of a long wooden tube.

die dies dying died
VERB **1** When people, animals, or plants die, they stop living. **2** When things die or die out, they cease to exist E.G. *That custom has died out now.* **3** When something dies, dies away, or dies down, it gradually fades away E.G. *The footsteps died away.* **4** INFORMAL If you are dying to do something, you are longing to do it.
▶ NOUN **5** a dice.
■ (sense 1) expire, pass away, perish

diesel
Said "**dee**-zel" NOUN **1** a heavy fuel used in trains, buses, and lorries. **2** a vehicle with a diesel engine.

diet diets
NOUN (D&T) **1** Someone's diet is the usual food that they eat E.G. *a vegetarian diet.* **2** a special restricted selection of foods that someone eats to improve their health or regulate their weight.
dietary ADJECTIVE
📖 from Greek *diaita* meaning 'mode of living'

dietician dieticians; also spelt **dietitian**
NOUN a person trained to advise people about healthy eating.

differ differs differing differed
VERB 1 If two or more things differ, they are unlike each other. 2 If people differ, they have opposing views or disagree about something.

difference differences
NOUN 1 The difference between things is the way in which they are unlike each other. 2 The difference between two numbers is the amount by which one is less than another. 3 A difference in someone or something is a significant change in them E.G. *You wouldn't believe the difference in her.*
■ (sense 1) disparity, dissimilarity, distinction

different
ADJECTIVE 1 unlike something else. 2 unusual and out of the ordinary. 3 distinct and separate, although of the same kind E.G. *The lunch supports a different charity each year.*
differently ADVERB
■ (sense 1) dissimilar, unlike
✓ You should say that one thing is *different from* another thing. Some people think that *different to* is incorrect. *Different than* is American.

differentiate differentiates differentiating differentiated
VERB 1 To differentiate between things means to recognize or show how one is unlike the other. 2 Something that differentiates one thing from another makes it distinct and unlike the other.
differentiation NOUN

difficult
ADJECTIVE 1 not easy to do, understand, or solve E.G. *a very difficult decision to make.* 2 hard to deal with, especially because of being unreasonable or unpredictable E.G. *a difficult child.*
■ (sense 1) demanding, hard, laborious

difficulty difficulties
NOUN 1 a problem E.G. *The central difficulty is his drinking.* 2 Difficulty is the fact or quality of being difficult.

diffident
ADJECTIVE timid and lacking in self-confidence.
diffidently ADVERB **diffidence** NOUN

diffract diffracts diffracting diffracted
VERB When rays of light or sound waves diffract, they break up after hitting an obstacle.
diffraction NOUN

diffuse diffuses diffusing diffused
VERB 1 *Said* "dif-**yooz**" If something diffuses, it spreads out or scatters in all directions. ► ADJECTIVE 2 *Said* "dif-**yoos**" spread out over a wide area.
diffusion NOUN

dig digs digging dug
VERB 1 If you dig, you break up soil or sand, especially with a spade or garden fork. 2 To dig something into an object means to push, thrust, or poke it in. ► NOUN 3 a prod or jab, especially in the ribs. 4 INFORMAL A dig at someone is a spiteful or unpleasant remark intended to hurt or embarrass them. ► PLURAL NOUN 5 Digs are lodgings in someone else's house.

a
b
c
d
e
f
g
h
i
j
k
l
m
n
o
p
q
r
s
t
u
v
w
x
y
z

digest digests digesting digested

VERB (SCIENCE) **1** To digest food means to break it down in the gut so that it can be easily absorbed and used by the body. **2** If you digest information or a fact, you understand it and take it in.

digestible ADJECTIVE

digestion digestions

NOUN (SCIENCE) **1** Digestion is the process of digesting food. **2** Your digestion is your ability to digest food E.G. *Camomile tea aids poor digestion*.

digestive ADJECTIVE

digger diggers

NOUN In Australian English, digger is a friendly name to call a man.

digit digits

Said "dij-it" NOUN **1** FORMAL Your digits are your fingers or toes. **2** (MATHS) a written symbol for any of the numbers from 0 to 9.

digital

ADJECTIVE displaying information, especially time, by numbers, rather than by a pointer moving round a dial E.G. *a digital watch*.

digitally ADVERB

dignified

ADJECTIVE full of dignity.

dignitary dignitaries

NOUN a person who holds a high official position.

dignity

NOUN Dignity is behaviour which is serious, calm, and controlled E.G. *She conducted herself with dignity*.

digression digressions

NOUN A digression in speech or writing is leaving the main subject for a while.

dilapidated

ADJECTIVE falling to pieces and generally in a bad condition E.G. *a dilapidated castle*.

dilate dilates dilating dilated

VERB To dilate means to become wider and larger E.G. *The pupil of the eye dilates in the dark*.

dilated ADJECTIVE   **dilation** NOUN

dilemma dilemmas

NOUN a situation in which a choice has to be made between alternatives that are equally difficult or unpleasant.

🔲 from Greek *di-* meaning 'two' and *lemma* meaning 'assumption'

☑ A *dilemma* involves a difficult choice between two things. If there are more than two choices you should say *problem* or *difficulty*.

diligent

ADJECTIVE hard-working, and showing care and perseverance.

diligently ADVERB   **diligence** NOUN

🔲 conscientious, hard-working, industrious

dill

NOUN Dill is a herb with yellow flowers and a strong sweet smell.

dilly bag dilly bags

NOUN In Australian English, a dilly bag is a small bag used to carry food.

dilute dilutes diluting diluted

VERB To dilute a liquid means to add water or another liquid to it to make it less concentrated.

dilution NOUN

dim dimmer dimmest; dims dimming dimmed

ADJECTIVE **1** badly lit and lacking in brightness. **2** very vague and unclear in your mind E.G. *dim recollections*. **3** INFORMAL stupid or mentally dull E.G.

He is rather dim. ▶ VERB **4** If lights dim or are dimmed, they become less bright.

dimly ADVERB   **dimness** NOUN

dimension dimensions
NOUN **1** A dimension of a situation is an aspect or factor that influences the way you understand it E.G. *This process had a domestic and a foreign dimension.* **2** You can talk about the size or extent of something as its dimensions E.G. *It was an explosion of major dimensions.* **3** (ART) The dimensions of something are also its measurements, for example its length, breadth, height, or diameter.

diminish diminishes diminishing diminished
VERB If something diminishes or if you diminish it, it becomes reduced in size or importance.

diminutive
ADJECTIVE very small.

dimple dimples
NOUN a small hollow in someone's cheek or chin.

din dins
NOUN a loud and unpleasant noise.

dinar dinars
*Said "**dee**-nar"* NOUN a unit of currency in several countries in Southern Europe, North Africa and the Middle East.

dine dines dining dined
VERB; FORMAL To dine means to eat dinner in the evening E.G. *We dined together in the hotel.*

diner diners
NOUN **1** a person who is having dinner in a restaurant. **2** a small restaurant or railway restaurant car.

dinghy dinghies
*Said "**ding**-ee"* NOUN a small boat

which is rowed, sailed, or powered by outboard motor.

dingo dingoes
NOUN an Australian wild dog.

dingy dingier dingiest
*Said "**din**-jee"* ADJECTIVE dusty, dark, and rather depressing E.G. *a dingy bedsit.*

dinkum
ADJECTIVE; INFORMAL In Australian and New Zealand English, dinkum means genuine or right E.G. *a fair dinkum offer.*

dinner dinners
NOUN **1** the main meal of the day, eaten either in the evening or at lunchtime. **2** a formal social occasion in the evening, at which a meal is served.

dinosaur dinosaurs
*Said "**dy**-no-sor"* NOUN a large reptile which lived in prehistoric times. 🔲 from Greek *deinos + sauros* meaning 'fearful lizard'

dint
PHRASE **By dint of** means by means of E.G. *He succeeds by dint of hard work.*

diocese dioceses
NOUN a district controlled by a bishop.
diocesan ADJECTIVE

dip dips dipping dipped
VERB **1** If you dip something into a liquid, you lower it or plunge it quickly into the liquid. **2** If something dips, it slopes downwards or goes below a certain level E.G. *The sun dipped below the horizon.* **3** To dip also means to make a quick, slight downward movement E.G. *She dipped her fingers into the cool water.* ▶ NOUN **4** a rich creamy mixture which you scoop up with biscuits or raw vegetables and eat E.G. *an avocado dip.* **5** INFORMAL a swim.

a
b
c
d
e
f
g
h
i
j
k
l
m
n
o
p
q
r
s
t
u
v
w
x
y
z

I want to see (C) your licen**C**e (licen**c**e)   SPELLING NOTE

A
B
C
D
E
F
G
H
I
J
K
L
M
N
O
P
Q
R
S
T
U
V
W
X
Y
Z

diploma diplomas
NOUN a certificate awarded to a student who has successfully completed a course of study.
📖 from Greek *diploma* meaning 'folded paper' or 'letter of recommendation'

diplomacy
NOUN 1 Diplomacy is the managing of relationships between countries. 2 Diplomacy is also skill in dealing with people without offending or upsetting them.
diplomatic ADJECTIVE
diplomatically ADVERB

diplomat diplomats
NOUN an official who negotiates and deals with another country on behalf of his or her own country.

dire direr direst
ADJECTIVE disastrous, urgent, or terrible E.G. *people in dire need.*

direct directs directing directed
ADJECTIVE 1 moving or aimed in a straight line or by the shortest route E.G. *the direct route.*
2 straightforward, and without delay or evasion E.G. *his direct manner.*
3 without anyone or anything intervening E.G. *Schools can take direct control of their own funding.*
4 exact E.G. *the direct opposite.* ▸ VERB
5 To direct something means to guide and control it. 6 To direct people or things means to send them, tell them, or show them the way. 7 To direct a film, a play, or a television programme means to organize the way it is made and performed.
🔲 (sense 2) frank, open, straightforward

direct current
NOUN Direct current is a term used in physics to refer to an electric current that always flows in the same direction.

direction directions
NOUN 1 the general line that someone or something is moving or pointing in. 2 Direction is the controlling and guiding of something E.G. *He was chopping vegetables under the chef's direction.* ▸ PLURAL NOUN 3 Directions are instructions that tell you how to do something or how to get somewhere.

directive directives
NOUN an instruction that must be obeyed E.G. *a directive banning cigarette advertising.*

directly
ADVERB in a straight line or immediately E.G. *He looked directly at Rose.*

director directors
NOUN 1 a member of the board of a company or institution. 2 (DRAMA) the person responsible for the making and performance of a programme, play, or film.
directorial ADJECTIVE

directorate directorates
NOUN a board of directors of a company or organization.

directory directories
NOUN a book which gives lists of facts, such as names and addresses, and is usually arranged in alphabetical order.

direct speech
NOUN the reporting of what someone has said by quoting the exact words.

dirge dirges
NOUN a slow, sad piece of music,

SPELLING NOTE The government licenSes Schnapps (licen*s*es)

sometimes played or sung at funerals.

dirt
NOUN **1** Dirt is any unclean substance, such as dust, mud, or stains. **2** Dirt is also earth or soil.

🔲 from Old Norse *drit* meaning 'excrement'

▤ (sense 1) filth, grime, muck

dirty dirtier dirtiest
ADJECTIVE **1** marked or covered with dirt. **2** unfair or dishonest E.G. *a dirty fight.* **3** about sex in a way that many people find offensive E.G. *dirty jokes.*

▤ (sense 1) filthy, grubby, mucky, unclean

dis-
PREFIX Dis- is added to the beginning of a word to form a word that means the opposite E.G. *discontented.*

disability disabilities
NOUN a physical or mental condition or illness that restricts someone's way of life.

disable disables disabling disabled
VERB If something disables someone, it injures or harms them physically or mentally and severely affects their life.

disablement NOUN

disabled
ADJECTIVE lacking one or more physical powers, such as the ability to walk or to coordinate one's movements.

disadvantage disadvantages
NOUN an unfavourable or harmful circumstance.

disadvantaged ADJECTIVE

▤ drawback, handicap

disaffected
ADJECTIVE If someone is disaffected with an idea or organization, they no

longer believe in it or support it E.G. *disaffected voters.*

disagree disagrees disagreeing disagreed
VERB **1** If you disagree with someone, you have a different view or opinion from theirs. **2** If you disagree with an action or proposal, you disapprove of it and believe it is wrong E.G. *He detested her and disagreed with her policies.* **3** If food or drink disagrees with you, it makes you feel unwell.

disagreement NOUN

▤ (sense 1) differ, dispute, dissent

disagreeable
ADJECTIVE unpleasant or unhelpful and unfriendly E.G. *a disagreeable odour.*

disappear disappears disappearing disappeared
VERB **1** If something or someone disappears, they go out of sight or become lost. **2** To disappear also means to stop existing or happening E.G. *The pain has disappeared.*

disappearance NOUN

▤ fade away, vanish

disappoint disappoints disappointing disappointed
VERB If someone or something disappoints you, it fails to live up to what you expected of it.

disappointed ADJECTIVE
disappointment NOUN

disapprove disapproves disapproving disapproved
VERB To disapprove of something or someone means to believe they are wrong or bad E.G. *Everyone disapproved of their marrying so young.*

disapproval NOUN   **disapproving** ADJECTIVE

a
b
c
d
e
f
g
h
i
j
k
l
m
n
o
p
q
r
s
t
u
v
w
x
y
z

have a pIEce of pIE (p**ie**ce)   SPELLING NOTE

A
B
C
D
E
F
G
H
I
J
K
L
M
N
O
P
Q
R
S
T
U
V
W
X
Y
Z

disarm disarms disarming disarmed

VERB 1 To disarm means to get rid of weapons. 2 If someone disarms you, they overcome your anger or doubt by charming or soothing you E.G. *Mahoney was almost disarmed by the frankness.*

disarming ADJECTIVE

disarmament

NOUN Disarmament is the reducing or getting rid of military forces and weapons.

disarray

NOUN Disarray is a state of disorder and confusion E.G. *Our army was in disarray and practically weaponless.*

disassemble disassembles disassembling disassembled

VERB (D & T) To disassemble a structure or object which has been made up or built from several smaller parts is to separate its parts from one another.

disaster disasters

NOUN 1 an event or accident that causes great distress or destruction. 2 a complete failure.

disastrous ADJECTIVE **disastrously** ADVERB

■ (sense 1) calamity, catastrophe

disband disbands disbanding disbanded

VERB When a group of people disbands, it officially ceases to exist.

disc discs; also spelt **disk**

NOUN 1 a flat round object E.G. *a tax disc… a compact disc.* 2 one of the thin circular pieces of cartilage which separate the bones in your spine. 3 (ICT) a storage device used in computers.

discard discards discarding discarded

VERB To discard something means to get rid of it, because you no longer want it or find it useful.

■ dump, get rid of, throw away

discern discerns discerning discerned

Said "dis-ern" VERB; FORMAL To discern something means to notice or understand it clearly E.G. *The film had no plot that I could discern.*

discernible

ADJECTIVE able to be seen or recognized E.G. *no discernible talent.*

discerning

ADJECTIVE having good taste and judgment.

discernment NOUN

discharge discharges discharging discharged

VERB 1 If something discharges or is discharged, it is given or sent out E.G. *Oil discharged into the world's oceans.* 2 To discharge someone from hospital means to allow them to leave. 3 If someone is discharged from a job, they are dismissed from it. ▶ NOUN 4 a substance that is released from the inside of something E.G. *a thick nasal discharge.* 5 a dismissal or release from a job or an institution.

disciple disciples

Said "dis-sigh-pl" NOUN (RE) a follower of someone or something, especially one of the twelve men who were followers and helpers of Christ.

discipline disciplines disciplining disciplined

NOUN 1 (PSHE) Discipline is making people obey rules and punishing

them when they break them.
2 (PSHE) Discipline is the ability to behave and work in a controlled way. ▶ VERB (PSHE) 3 If you discipline yourself, you train yourself to behave and work in an ordered way. 4 To discipline someone means to punish them.
disciplinary ADJECTIVE   **disciplined** ADJECTIVE

disc jockey disc jockeys
NOUN someone who introduces and plays pop records on the radio or at a night club.

disclose discloses disclosing disclosed
VERB To disclose something means to make it known or allow it to be seen.
disclosure NOUN

disco discos
NOUN a party or a club where people go to dance to pop records.

discomfort discomforts
NOUN 1 Discomfort is distress or slight pain. 2 Discomfort is also a feeling of worry or embarrassment.
3 Discomforts are things that make you uncomfortable.

disconcert disconcerts disconcerting disconcerted
VERB If something disconcerts you, it makes you feel uneasy or embarrassed.
disconcerting ADJECTIVE

disconnect disconnects disconnecting disconnected
VERB 1 To disconnect something means to detach it from something else. 2 If someone disconnects your fuel supply or telephone, they cut you off.

discontent
NOUN Discontent is a feeling of

dissatisfaction with conditions or with life in general E.G. *He was aware of the discontent this policy had caused.*
discontented ADJECTIVE

discontinue discontinues discontinuing discontinued
VERB To discontinue something means to stop doing it.

discord
NOUN Discord is unpleasantness or quarrelling between people.

discount discounts discounting discounted
NOUN 1 a reduction in the price of something. ▶ VERB 2 If you discount something, you reject it or ignore it E.G. *I haven't discounted her connection with the kidnapping case.*

discourage discourages discouraging discouraged
VERB To discourage someone means to take away their enthusiasm to do something.
discouraging ADJECTIVE
discouragement NOUN
▤ demoralize, dishearten, put off

discourse discourses FORMAL
NOUN 1 a formal talk or piece of writing intended to teach or explain something. 2 Discourse is serious conversation between people on a particular subject.

discover discovers discovering discovered
VERB When you discover something, you find it or find out about it.
discovery NOUN   **discoverer** NOUN

discredit discredits discrediting discredited
VERB 1 To discredit someone means to damage their reputation. 2 To discredit an idea means to cause it

to be doubted or not believed.

discreet

ADJECTIVE If you are discreet, you avoid causing embarrassment when dealing with secret or private matters.

discreetly ADVERB

discrepancy discrepancies

NOUN a difference between two things which ought to be the same E.G. *discrepancies in his police interviews.*

discrete

ADJECTIVE; FORMAL separate and distinct E.G. *two discrete sets of nerves.*

discretion

NOUN 1 Discretion is the quality of behaving with care and tact so as to avoid embarrassment or distress to other people E.G. *You can count on my discretion.* 2 Discretion is also freedom and authority to make decisions and take action according to your own judgment E.G. *Class teachers have very limited discretion in decision-making.*

discretionary ADJECTIVE

discriminate discriminates discriminating discriminated

VERB 1 To discriminate between things means to recognize and understand the differences between them. 2 To discriminate against a person or group means to treat them unfairly, usually because of their race, colour, or sex. 3 To discriminate in favour of a person or group means to treat them more favourably than others.

discrimination NOUN

discriminatory ADJECTIVE

discus discuses

NOUN a disc-shaped object with a heavy middle, thrown by athletes.

discuss discusses discussing discussed

VERB 1 When people discuss something, they talk about it in detail. 2 (EXAM TERM) To discuss a question is to look at the points or arguments of both sides and try to reach your own opinion.

discussion discussions

NOUN (PSHE) a conversation or piece of writing in which a subject is considered in detail.

▤ conversation, discourse, talk

disdain

NOUN Disdain is a feeling of superiority over or contempt for someone or something E.G. *The candidates shared an equal disdain for the press.*

disdainful ADJECTIVE

disease diseases

NOUN (HISTORY) an unhealthy condition in people, animals, or plants.

diseased ADJECTIVE

disembark disembarks disembarking disembarked

VERB To disembark means to land or unload from a ship, aircraft, or bus.

disembodied

ADJECTIVE 1 separate from or existing without a body E.G. *a disembodied skull.* 2 seeming not to be attached or to come from anyone E.G. *disembodied voices.*

disenchanted

ADJECTIVE disappointed with something, and no longer believing that it is good or worthwhile E.G. *She is very disenchanted with the marriage.*

disenchantment NOUN

disfigure disfigures disfiguring disfigured

VERB To disfigure something means to spoil its appearance E.G. *Graffiti or posters disfigured every wall.*

disgrace disgraces disgracing disgraced

NOUN 1 Disgrace is a state in which people disapprove of someone. 2 If something is a disgrace, it is unacceptable E.G. *The overcrowded prisons were a disgrace.* 3 If someone is a disgrace to a group of people, their behaviour makes the group feel ashamed E.G. *You're a disgrace to the school.* ▶ VERB 4 If you disgrace yourself or disgrace someone else, you cause yourself or them to be strongly disapproved of by other people.

■ (sense 1) dishonour, shame
■ (sense 4) discredit, dishonour, shame

disgraceful

ADJECTIVE If something is disgraceful, people disapprove of it strongly and think that those who are responsible for it should be ashamed.

disgracefully ADVERB

■ scandalous, shameful, shocking

disgruntled

ADJECTIVE discontented or in a bad mood.

disguise disguises disguising disguised

VERB 1 To disguise something means to change its appearance so that people do not recognize it. 2 To disguise a feeling means to hide it E.G. *I tried to disguise my relief.* ▶ NOUN 3 something you wear or something you do to alter your appearance so that you cannot be

recognized by other people.

disgust disgusts disgusting disgusted

NOUN 1 Disgust is a strong feeling of dislike or disapproval. ▶ VERB 2 To disgust someone means to make them feel a strong sense of dislike or disapproval.

disgusted ADJECTIVE

■ (sense 1) loathing, repugnance, revulsion
■ (sense 2) revolt, sicken

dish dishes

NOUN 1 a shallow container for cooking or serving food. 2 food of a particular kind or food cooked in a particular way E.G. *two fish dishes to choose from.*

disheartened

ADJECTIVE If you are disheartened, you feel disappointed.

dishevelled

Said "dish-**ev**-ld" ADJECTIVE If someone looks dishevelled, their clothes or hair look untidy.

dishonest

ADJECTIVE not truthful or able to be trusted.

dishonestly ADVERB

dishonesty

NOUN Dishonesty is behaviour which is meant to deceive people, either by not telling the truth or by cheating.

disillusioned

ADJECTIVE If you are disillusioned with something, you are disappointed because it is not as good as you had expected.

disinfectant disinfectants

NOUN a chemical substance that kills germs.

disintegrate disintegrates disintegrating disintegrated

a
b
c
d
e
f
g
h
i
j
k
l
m
n
o
p
q
r
s
t
u
v
w
x
y
z

A
B
C
D
E
F
G
H
I
J
K
L
M
N
O
P
Q
R
S
T
U
V
W
X
Y
Z

VERB 1 If something disintegrates, it becomes weakened and is not effective E.G. *My confidence disintegrated.* 2 If an object disintegrates, it breaks into many pieces and so is destroyed.
disintegration NOUN

disinterest
NOUN 1 Disinterest is a lack of interest. 2 Disinterest is also a lack of personal involvement in a situation.

disinterested
ADJECTIVE If someone is disinterested, they are not going to gain or lose from the situation they are involved in, and so can act in a way that is fair to both sides E.G. *a disinterested judge.*
☑ Some people use *disinterested* to mean 'not interested', but the word they should use is *uninterested.*

disjointed
ADJECTIVE If thought or speech is disjointed, it jumps from subject to subject and so is difficult to follow.

disk
another spelling of **disc.**

dislike dislikes disliking disliked
VERB 1 If you dislike something or someone, you think they are unpleasant and do not like them.
▶ NOUN 2 Dislike is a feeling that you have when you do not like someone or something.
◪ (sense 2) aversion, distaste

dislocate dislocates dislocating dislocated
VERB To dislocate your bone or joint means to put it out of place.

dislodge dislodges dislodging dislodged
VERB To dislodge something means to move it or force it out of place.

dismal
Said "**diz**-mal" ADJECTIVE rather gloomy

and depressing E.G. *dismal weather.*
dismally ADVERB
🔲 from Latin *dies mali* meaning 'evil days'

dismantle dismantles dismantling dismantled
VERB To dismantle something means to take it apart.

dismay dismays dismaying dismayed
NOUN 1 Dismay is a feeling of fear and worry. ▶ VERB 2 If someone or something dismays you, it fills you with alarm and worry.

dismember dismembers dismembering dismembered
VERB; FORMAL To dismember a person or animal means to cut or tear their body into pieces.

dismiss dismisses dismissing dismissed
VERB 1 If you dismiss something, you decide to ignore it because it is not important enough for you to think about. 2 To dismiss an employee means to ask that person to leave their job. 3 If someone in authority dismisses you, they tell you to leave.
dismissal NOUN

dismissive
ADJECTIVE If you are dismissive of something or someone, you show that you think they are of little importance or value E.G. *a dismissive gesture.*

disobey disobeys disobeying disobeyed
VERB To disobey a person or an order means to deliberately refuse to do what you are told.

disorder disorders
NOUN 1 Disorder is a state of untidiness. 2 Disorder is also a lack of

organization E.G. *The men fled in disorder*. **3** a disease E.G. *a stomach disorder*.

■ (sense 2) chaos, confusion

disorganized or **disorganised**
ADJECTIVE If something is disorganized, it is confused and badly prepared or badly arranged.
disorganization NOUN

disown disowns disowning disowned
VERB To disown someone or something means to refuse to admit any connection with them.

disparaging
ADJECTIVE critical and scornful E.G. *disparaging remarks*.

disparate
ADJECTIVE; FORMAL Things that are disparate are utterly different from one another.
disparity NOUN

dispatch dispatches dispatching dispatched; also spelt **despatch**
VERB **1** To dispatch someone or something to a particular place means to send them there for a special reason E.G. *The president dispatched him on a fact-finding visit.*
► NOUN **2** an official written message, often sent to an army or government headquarters.

dispel dispels dispelling dispelled
VERB To dispel fears or beliefs means to drive them away or to destroy them E.G. *The myths are being dispelled.*

dispensary dispensaries
NOUN a place where medicines are prepared and given out.

dispense dispenses dispensing dispensed

VERB **1** FORMAL To dispense something means to give it out E.G. *They dispense advice.* **2** To dispense medicines means to prepare them and give them out. **3** To dispense with something means to do without it or to do away with it E.G. *We'll dispense with formalities.*

dispenser dispensers
NOUN a machine or container from which you can get things E.G. *a cash dispenser.*

disperse disperses dispersing dispersed
VERB **1** When something disperses, it scatters over a wide area. **2** When people disperse or when someone disperses them, they move apart and go in different directions.
dispersion NOUN

dispirited
ADJECTIVE depressed and having no enthusiasm for anything.

dispiriting
ADJECTIVE Something dispiriting makes you depressed E.G. *a dispiriting defeat.*

displace displaces displacing displaced
VERB **1** If one thing displaces another, it forces the thing out of its usual place and occupies that place itself. **2** If people are displaced, they are forced to leave their home or country.

displacement
NOUN Displacement is the removal of something from its usual or correct place or position.

display displays displaying displayed
VERB **1** If you display something, you show it or make it visible to people.

a b c **d** e f g h i j k l m n o p q r s t u v w x y z

Psychiatrists Seldom Yell Callously Hard (<u>psychi</u>atrist)   SPELLING NOTE

A B C D E F G H I J K L M N O P Q R S T U V W X Y Z

2 If you display something such as an emotion, you behave in a way that shows you feel it. ▶ NOUN 3 (ART) an arrangement of things designed to attract people's attention.

displease displeases displeasing displeased
VERB If someone or something displeases you, they make you annoyed, dissatisfied, or offended.
displeasure NOUN

disposable
ADJECTIVE designed to be thrown away after use E.G. *disposable nappies*.

disposal
NOUN Disposal is the act of getting rid of something that is no longer wanted or needed.

dispose disposes disposing disposed
VERB 1 To dispose of something means to get rid of it. 2 If you are not disposed to do something, you are not willing to do it.

disprove disproves disproving disproved
VERB If someone disproves an idea, belief, or theory, they show that it is not true.

dispute disputes disputing disputed
NOUN 1 an argument. ▶ VERB 2 To dispute a fact or theory means to question the truth of it.

disqualify disqualifies disqualifying disqualified
VERB If someone is disqualified from a competition or activity, they are officially stopped from taking part in it E.G. *He was disqualified from driving for 18 months*.
disqualification NOUN

disquiet
NOUN Disquiet is worry or anxiety.
disquieting ADJECTIVE

disregard disregards disregarding disregarded
VERB 1 To disregard something means to pay little or no attention to it.
▶ NOUN 2 Disregard is a lack of attention or respect for something E.G. *He exhibited a flagrant disregard of the law*.

disrepair
PHRASE If something is **in disrepair** or **in a state of disrepair**, it is broken or in poor condition.

disrespect
NOUN Disrespect is contempt or lack of respect E.G. *his disrespect for authority*.
disrespectful ADJECTIVE

disrupt disrupts disrupting disrupted
VERB To disrupt something such as an event or system means to break it up or throw it into confusion E.G. *Strikes disrupted air traffic in Italy*.
disruption NOUN **disruptive** ADJECTIVE

dissatisfied
ADJECTIVE not pleased or not contented.
dissatisfaction NOUN

dissect dissects dissecting dissected
VERB To dissect a plant or a dead body means to cut it up so that it can be scientifically examined.
dissection NOUN

dissent dissents dissenting dissented
NOUN 1 Dissent is strong difference of opinion E.G. *political dissent*. ▶ VERB 2 When people dissent, they express

a difference of opinion about something.

dissenting ADJECTIVE

dissertation dissertations
NOUN a long essay, especially for a university degree.

disservice
NOUN To do someone a disservice means to do something that harms them.

dissident dissidents
NOUN someone who disagrees with and criticizes the strict and unjust government of their country.

dissimilar
ADJECTIVE If things are dissimilar, they are unlike each other.

dissipate dissipates dissipating dissipated
VERB 1 FORMAL When something dissipates or is dissipated, it completely disappears E.G. *The cloud seemed to dissipate there.* 2 If someone dissipates time, money, or effort, they waste it.

dissipated
ADJECTIVE Someone who is dissipated shows signs of indulging too much in alcohol or other physical pleasures.

dissolve dissolves dissolving dissolved
VERB 1 (SCIENCE) If you dissolve something or if it dissolves in a liquid, it becomes mixed with and absorbed in the liquid. 2 To dissolve an organization or institution means to officially end it.

dissuade dissuades dissuading dissuaded
Said "dis-**wade**" VERB To dissuade someone from doing something or from believing something means to persuade them not to do it or not to believe it.

distance distances distancing distanced
NOUN 1 The distance between two points is how far it is between them. 2 Distance is the fact of being far away in space or time. ► VERB 3 If you distance yourself from someone or something or are distanced from them, you become less involved with them.

distant
ADJECTIVE 1 far away in space or time. 2 A distant relative is one who is not closely related to you. 3 Someone who is distant is cold and unfriendly.

distantly ADVERB
■ (sense 3) aloof, reserved, standoffish

distaste
NOUN Distaste is a dislike of something which you find offensive.

distasteful
ADJECTIVE If you find something distasteful, you think it is unpleasant or offensive.

distil distils distilling distilled
VERB (SCIENCE) When a liquid is distilled, it is heated until it evaporates and then cooled to enable purified liquid to be collected.

distillation NOUN

distillery distilleries
NOUN a place where whisky or other strong alcoholic drink is made, using a process of distillation.

distinct
ADJECTIVE 1 If one thing is distinct from another, it is recognizably different from it E.G. *A word may have two quite distinct meanings.* 2 If something is distinct, you can hear, smell, or see it clearly and plainly

a
b
c
d
e
f
g
h
i
j
k
l
m
n
o
p
q
r
s
t
u
v
w
x
y
z

Rhythmical Hounds Yap To Heavy Music (<u>rhythm</u>)   SPELLING NOTE

A
B
C
D
E
F
G
H
I
J
K
L
M
N
O
P
Q
R
S
T
U
V
W
X
Y
Z

E.G. *There was a distinct buzzing noise.*
3 If something such as a fact, idea, or intention is distinct, it is clear and definite E.G. *She had a distinct feeling someone was watching them.*
distinctly ADVERB

distinction distinctions
NOUN **1** a difference between two things E.G. *a distinction between the body and the soul.* **2** Distinction is a quality of excellence and superiority E.G. *a man of distinction.* **3** a special honour or claim E.G. *It had the distinction of being the largest square in Europe.*

distinctive
ADJECTIVE Something that is distinctive has a special quality which makes it recognizable E.G. *a distinctive voice.*
distinctively ADVERB

distinguish distinguishes distinguishing distinguished
VERB **1** To distinguish between things means to recognize the difference between them E.G. *I've learned to distinguish business and friendship.* **2** To distinguish something means to make it out by seeing, hearing, or tasting it E.G. *I heard shouting but was unable to distinguish the words.* **3** If you distinguish yourself, you do something that makes people think highly of you.
distinguishable ADJECTIVE
distinguishing ADJECTIVE

distort distorts distorting distorted
VERB **1** If you distort a statement or an argument, you represent it in an untrue or misleading way. **2** If something is distorted, it is changed so that it seems strange or unclear E.G. *His voice was distorted.* **3** If an object is distorted, it is twisted or

pulled out of shape.
distorted ADJECTIVE **distortion** NOUN

distract distracts distracting distracted
VERB If something distracts you, your attention is taken away from what you are doing.
distracted ADJECTIVE **distractedly** ADVERB **distracting** ADJECTIVE
■ divert, sidetrack

distraction distractions
NOUN **1** something that takes people's attention away from something. **2** an activity that is intended to amuse or relax someone.

distraught
ADJECTIVE so upset and worried that you cannot think clearly E.G. *He was distraught over the death of his mother.*

distress distresses distressing distressed
NOUN **1** Distress is great suffering caused by pain or sorrow. **2** Distress is also the state of needing help because of difficulties or danger.
▶ VERB **3** To distress someone means to make them feel alarmed or unhappy E.G. *Her death had profoundly distressed me.*
■ (sense 3) trouble, upset

distressing
ADJECTIVE very worrying or upsetting.

distribute distributes distributing distributed
VERB **1** To distribute something such as leaflets means to hand them out or deliver them E.G. *They publish and distribute brochures.* **2** If things are distributed, they are spread throughout an area or space E.G. *Distribute the cheese evenly on top of*

the quiche. **3** To distribute something means to divide it and share it out among a number of people.

■ (sense 3) dispense, share out

distribution distributions

NOUN **1** Distribution is the delivering of something to various people or organizations E.G. *the distribution of vicious leaflets.* **2** Distribution is the sharing out of something to various people E.G. *distribution of power.*

distributor distributors

NOUN a company that supplies goods to other businesses who then sell them to the public.

district districts

NOUN an area of a town or country E.G. *a residential district.*

district nurse district nurses

NOUN a nurse who visits and treats people in their own homes.

distrust distrusts distrusting distrusted

VERB **1** If you distrust someone, you are suspicious of them because you are not sure whether they are honest. ► NOUN **2** Distrust is suspicion.

distrustful ADJECTIVE

disturb disturbs disturbing disturbed

VERB **1** If you disturb someone, you break their peace or privacy. **2** If something disturbs you, it makes you feel upset or worried. **3** If something is disturbed, it is moved out of position or meddled with.

disturbing ADJECTIVE

■ (sense 2) trouble, upset, worry

disturbance disturbances

NOUN **1** Disturbance is the state of being disturbed. **2** a violent or unruly incident in public.

disuse

NOUN Something that has fallen into disuse is neglected or no longer used.

disused ADJECTIVE

ditch ditches

NOUN a channel at the side of a road or field, to drain away excess water.

dither dithers dithering dithered

VERB To dither means to be unsure and hesitant.

ditto

Ditto means 'the same'. In written lists, ditto is represented by a mark (,,) to avoid repetition.

🏛 from Italian *detto* meaning 'said'

ditty ditties

NOUN; OLD-FASHIONED a short simple song or poem.

diva divas

NOUN a great or leading female singer, especially in opera.

🏛 from Latin *diva* meaning 'a goddess'

dive dives diving dived

VERB **1** To dive means to jump into water with your arms held straight above your head. **2** If you go diving, you go down under the surface of the sea or a lake using special breathing equipment. **3** If an aircraft or bird dives, it flies in a steep downward path, or drops sharply.

diver NOUN   **diving** NOUN

diverge diverges diverging diverged

VERB **1** If opinions or facts diverge, they differ E.G. *Theory and practice sometimes diverged.* **2** If two things such as roads or paths which have been going in the same direction diverge, they separate and go off in different directions.

divergence NOUN   **divergent** ADJECTIVE

a
b
c
d
e
f
g
h
i
j
k
l
m
n
o
p
q
r
s
t
u
v
w
x
y
z

A
B
C
D
E
F
G
H
I
J
K
L
M
N
O
P
Q
R
S
T
U
V
W
X
Y
Z

diverse

ADJECTIVE 1 If a group of things is diverse, it is made up of different kinds of things E.G. *a diverse range of goods and services.* 2 People, ideas, or objects that are diverse are very different from each other.

diversity NOUN

diversify diversifies diversifying diversified

VERB To diversify means to increase the variety of something E.G. *Has the company diversified into new areas?*

diversification NOUN

diversion diversions

NOUN 1 a special route arranged for traffic when the usual route is closed. 2 something that takes your attention away from what you should be concentrating on E.G. *A break for tea created a welcome diversion.* 3 a pleasant or amusing activity.

divert diverts diverting diverted

VERB To divert something means to change the course or direction it is following.

diverting ADJECTIVE

divide divides dividing divided

VERB 1 When something divides or is divided, it is split up and separated into two or more parts. 2 If something divides two areas, it forms a barrier between them. 3 If people divide over something or if something divides them, it causes strong disagreement between them. 4 (MATHS) In mathematics, when you divide, you calculate how many times one number contains another. ▶ NOUN 5 a separation E.G. *the class divide.*

dividend dividends

NOUN a portion of a company's profits that is paid to shareholders.

divine divines divining divined

ADJECTIVE 1 having the qualities of a god or goddess. ▶ VERB 2 To divine something means to discover it by guessing.

divinely ADVERB

divinity divinities

NOUN 1 Divinity is the study of religion. 2 Divinity is the state of being a god. 3 a god or goddess.

division divisions

NOUN 1 Division is the separation of something into two or more distinct parts. 2 (MATHS) Division is also the process of dividing one number by another. 3 a difference of opinion that causes separation between ideas or groups of people E.G. *There were divisions in the Party on economic policy.* 4 any one of the parts into which something is split E.G. *the Research Division.*

divisional ADJECTIVE

divisive

ADJECTIVE causing hostility between people so that they split into different groups E.G. *Inflation is economically and socially divisive.*

divisor divisors

NOUN a number by which another number is divided.

divorce divorces divorcing divorced

NOUN 1 Divorce is the formal and legal ending of a marriage. ▶ VERB 2 When a married couple divorce, their marriage is legally ended.

divorced ADJECTIVE **divorcee** NOUN

divulge divulges divulging divulged

VERB To divulge information means to reveal it.

SPELLING NOTE Eddy Ant thinks mEAt is a grEAt trEAt to EAt (-ea-)

DIY

NOUN DIY is the activity of making or repairing things yourself. DIY is an abbreviation for 'do-it-yourself'.

dizzy dizzier dizziest

ADJECTIVE having or causing a whirling sensation.

dizziness NOUN

DNA

NOUN DNA is deoxyribonucleic acid, which is found in the cells of all living things. It is responsible for passing on characteristics from parents to their children.

do does doing did done; dos

VERB 1 Do is an auxiliary verb, which is used to form questions, negatives, and to give emphasis to the main verb of a sentence. 2 If someone does a task or activity, they perform it and finish it E.G. *He just didn't want to do any work.* 3 If you ask what people do, you want to know what their job is E.G. *What will you do when you leave school?* 4 If you do well at something, you are successful. If you do badly, you are unsuccessful. 5 If something will do, it is adequate but not the most suitable option E.G. *Home-made stock is best, but cubes will do.* ▶ NOUN 6 INFORMAL a party or other social event. ■ (sense 2) carry out, execute, perform

do up VERB 1 To do something up means to fasten it. 2 To do up something old means to repair and decorate it.

docile

ADJECTIVE quiet, calm, and easily controlled.

dock docks docking docked

NOUN 1 an enclosed area in a harbour where ships go to be loaded, unloaded, or repaired. 2 In a court of law, the dock is the place where the accused person stands or sits. ▶ VERB 3 When a ship docks, it is brought into dock at the end of its voyage. 4 To dock someone's wages means to deduct an amount from the sum they would normally receive. 5 To dock an animal's tail means to cut part of it off.

docker NOUN

doctor doctors doctoring doctored

NOUN 1 a person who is qualified in medicine and treats people who are ill. 2 A doctor of an academic subject is someone who has been awarded the highest academic degree E.G. *She is a doctor of philosophy.* ▶ VERB 3 To doctor something means to alter it in order to deceive people E.G. *Stamps can be doctored.*

doctorate doctorates

NOUN the highest university degree.

doctoral ADJECTIVE

doctrine doctrines

NOUN a set of beliefs or principles held by a group.

doctrinal ADJECTIVE

document documents documenting documented

NOUN 1 (HISTORY) a piece of paper which provides an official record of something. 2 (ICT) a piece of text or graphics stored in a computer as a file that can be amended or altered by document processing software. ▶ VERB 3 (HISTORY) If you document something, you make a detailed record of it.

documentation NOUN

a
b
c
d
e
f
g
h
i
j
k
l
m
n
o
p
q
r
s
t
u
v
w
x
y
z

Elaine and Emily shout EE when they mEEt to grEEt each other (-ee-)   **SPELLING NOTE**

documentary documentaries
NOUN 1 a radio or television programme, or a film, which gives information on real events. ► ADJECTIVE 2 Documentary evidence is made up of written or official records.

dodge dodges dodging dodged
VERB 1 If you dodge or dodge something, you move suddenly to avoid being seen, hit, or caught. 2 If you dodge something such as an issue or accusation, you avoid dealing with it.

dodgy
ADJECTIVE; INFORMAL dangerous, risky, or unreliable E.G. *He has a dodgy heart.*

dodo dodos
NOUN a large, flightless bird which is now extinct.

doe does
NOUN a female deer, rabbit, or hare.

does
the third person singular of the present tense of **do**.

dog dogs dogging dogged
NOUN 1 a four-legged, meat-eating animal, kept as a pet, or to guard property or go hunting. ► VERB 2 If you dog someone, you follow them very closely and never leave them.

dog collar dog collars
NOUN; INFORMAL a white collar with no front opening worn by Christian clergy.

dog-eared
ADJECTIVE A book that is dog-eared has been used so much that the corners of the pages are turned down or worn.

dogged
Said "*dog-ged*" ADJECTIVE showing determination to continue with something, even if it is very difficult

E.G. *dogged persistence.*
doggedly ADVERB

dogma dogmas
NOUN a belief or system of beliefs held by a religious or political group.

dogmatic
ADJECTIVE Someone who is dogmatic about something is convinced that they are right about it.
dogmatism NOUN

doldrums
AN INFORMAL PHRASE If you are **in the doldrums**, you are depressed or bored.

dole doles doling doled
VERB If you dole something out, you give a certain amount of it to each individual in a group.

doll dolls
NOUN a child's toy which looks like a baby or person.

dollar dollars
NOUN the main unit of currency in Australia, New Zealand, the USA, Canada, and some other countries. A dollar is worth 100 cents.

dollop dollops
NOUN an amount of food, served casually in a lump.

dolphin dolphins
NOUN a mammal which lives in the sea and looks like a large fish with a long snout.

domain domains
NOUN 1 a particular area of activity or interest E.G. *the domain of science.* 2 an area over which someone has control or influence E.G. *This reservation was the largest of the Apache domains.*

dome domes
NOUN a round roof.
domed ADJECTIVE

A B C D E F G H I J K L M N O P Q R S T U V W X Y Z

domestic
ADJECTIVE 1 happening or existing within one particular country E.G. *domestic and foreign politics*. 2 involving or concerned with the home and family E.G. *routine domestic tasks*.

domesticated
ADJECTIVE If a wild animal or plant has been domesticated, it has been controlled or cultivated.

domesticity
NOUN; FORMAL Domesticity is life at home with your family.

dominance
NOUN 1 Dominance is power or control. 2 If something has dominance over other similar things, it is more powerful or important than they are E.G. *the dominance of the United States in the film business*. **dominant** ADJECTIVE

dominate dominates dominating dominated
VERB 1 If something or someone dominates a situation or event, they are the most powerful or important thing in it and have control over it E.G. *The civil service dominated public affairs*. 2 If a person or country dominates other people or places, they have power or control over them. 3 If something dominates an area, it towers over it E.G. *The valley was dominated by high surrounding cliffs*. **dominating** ADJECTIVE **domination** NOUN

domineering
ADJECTIVE Someone who is domineering tries to control other people E.G. *a domineering mother*.

dominion
NOUN Dominion is control or authority that a person or a country has over other people.

domino dominoes
NOUN Dominoes are small rectangular blocks marked with two groups of spots on one side, used for playing the game called dominoes.

don dons donning donned
NOUN 1 a lecturer at Oxford or Cambridge university. ▶ VERB 2 LITERARY If you don clothing, you put it on.

donate donates donating donated
VERB To donate something to a charity or organization means to give it as a gift. **donation** NOUN

done
the past participle of **do**.

donkey donkeys
NOUN an animal like a horse, but smaller and with longer ears.

donor donors
NOUN 1 someone who gives some of their blood while they are alive or an organ after their death to be used to help someone who is ill E.G. *a kidney donor*. 2 someone who gives something such as money to a charity or other organization.

doodle doodles doodling doodled
NOUN 1 a drawing done when you are thinking about something else or when you are bored. ▶ VERB 2 To doodle means to draw doodles.

doom
NOUN Doom is a terrible fate or event in the future which you can do nothing to prevent.

doomed
ADJECTIVE If someone or something is doomed to an unpleasant or unhappy experience, they are certain to suffer it E.G. *doomed to failure*.

a
b
c
d
e
f
g
h
i
j
k
l
m
n
o
p
q
r
s
t
u
v
w
x
y
z

A
B
C
D
E
F
G
H
I
J
K
L
M
N
O
P
Q
R
S
T
U
V
W
X
Y
Z

doomsday

NOUN Doomsday is the end of the world.

door doors

NOUN a swinging or sliding panel for opening or closing the entrance to something; also the entrance itself.

doorway doorways

NOUN an opening in a wall for a door.

dope dopes doping doped

NOUN **1** Dope is an illegal drug. ▶ VERB **2** If someone dopes you, they put a drug into your food or drink.

🔲 from Dutch *doop* meaning 'sauce'

dormant

ADJECTIVE Something that is dormant is not active, growing, or being used E.G. *The buds will remain dormant until spring.*

dormitory dormitories

NOUN a large bedroom where several people sleep.

dormouse dormice

NOUN an animal, like a large mouse, with a furry tail.

dosage dosages

NOUN the amount of a medicine or a drug that should be taken.

dose doses

NOUN a measured amount of a medicine or drug.

dossier dossiers

Said "doss-ee-ay" NOUN a collection of papers with information on a particular subject or person.

dot dots dotting dotted

NOUN **1** a very small, round mark. ▶ VERB **2** If things dot an area, they are scattered all over it E.G. *Fishing villages dot the coastline.* ▶ PHRASE **3** If you arrive somewhere **on the dot**, you arrive there at exactly the right time.

dote dotes doting doted

VERB If you dote on someone, you love them very much.

doting ADJECTIVE

double doubles doubling doubled

ADJECTIVE **1** twice the usual size E.G. *a double whisky*. **2** consisting of two parts E.G. *a double album*. ▶ VERB **3** If something doubles, it becomes twice as large. **4** To double as something means to have a second job or use as well as the main one E.G. *Their home doubles as an office.* ▶ NOUN **5** Your double is someone who looks exactly like you. **6** Doubles is a game of tennis or badminton which two people play against two other people.

doubly ADVERB

double bass double basses

NOUN a musical instrument like a large violin, which you play standing up.

double-cross double-crosses double-crossing double-crossed

VERB If someone double-crosses you, they cheat you by pretending to do what you both planned, when in fact they do the opposite.

double-decker double-deckers

ADJECTIVE **1** having two tiers or layers. ▶ NOUN **2** a bus with two floors.

double glazing

NOUN Double glazing is a second layer of glass fitted to windows to keep the building quieter or warmer.

doubt doubts doubting doubted

NOUN **1** Doubt is a feeling of uncertainty about whether something is true or possible. ▶ VERB **2** If you doubt something, you think that it is probably not true or possible.

■ (sense 1) misgiving, qualm, uncertainty

doubtful
ADJECTIVE unlikely or uncertain.

dough
Rhymes with "go" NOUN **1** Dough is a mixture of flour and water and sometimes other ingredients, used to make bread, pastry, or biscuits. **2** INFORMAL Dough is money.

doughnut doughnuts
NOUN a ring of sweet dough cooked in hot fat.

dour
Rhymes with "poor" ADJECTIVE severe and unfriendly E.G. *a dour portrait of his personality.*

douse douses dousing doused; also spelt **dowse**
VERB If you douse a fire, you stop it burning by throwing water over it.

dove doves
NOUN a bird like a small pigeon.

dovetail dovetails dovetailing dovetailed
VERB If two things dovetail together, they fit together closely or neatly.

dowager dowagers
NOUN a woman who has inherited a title from her dead husband E.G. *the Empress Dowager.*

dowdy dowdier dowdiest
ADJECTIVE wearing dull and unfashionable clothes.

down downs downing downed
PREPOSITION or ADVERB **1** Down means towards the ground, towards a lower level, or in a lower place. **2** If you go down a road or river, you go along it. ▶ ADVERB **3** If you put something down, you place it on a surface. **4** If an amount of something goes down, it decreases. ▶ ADJECTIVE **5** If you feel down, you feel depressed. ▶ VERB **6** If you down a drink, you drink it quickly. ▶ NOUN **7** Down is the small, soft feathers on young birds.

downcast
ADJECTIVE **1** feeling sad and dejected. **2** If your eyes are downcast, they are looking towards the ground.

downfall
NOUN **1** The downfall of a successful or powerful person or institution is their failure. **2** Something that is someone's downfall is the thing that causes their failure E.G. *His pride may be his downfall.*

downgrade downgrades downgrading downgraded
VERB If you downgrade something, you give it less importance or make it less valuable.

downhill
ADVERB **1** moving down a slope. **2** becoming worse E.G. *The press has gone downhill in the last 10 years.*

downpour downpours
NOUN a heavy fall of rain.

downright
ADJECTIVE or ADVERB You use 'downright' to emphasize that something is extremely unpleasant or bad E.G. *Staff are often discourteous and sometimes downright rude.*

downstairs
ADVERB **1** going down a staircase towards the ground floor. ▶ ADJECTIVE or ADVERB **2** on a lower floor or on the ground floor.

downstream
ADJECTIVE or ADVERB Something that is downstream or moving downstream is nearer to or moving nearer to the mouth of a river from a point further up.

a
b
c
d
e
f
g
h
i
j
k
l
m
n
o
p
q
r
s
t
u
v
w
x
y
z

LEt's measure the angLE (ang*le*)   ▶ SPELLING NOTE

down-to-earth
ADJECTIVE sensible and practical E.G. *a down-to-earth approach*.

downtrodden
ADJECTIVE People who are downtrodden are treated badly by those with power and do not have the ability to fight back.

downturn downturns
NOUN a decline in the economy or in the success of a company or industry.

downwards or **downward**
ADVERB OR ADJECTIVE 1 If you move or look downwards, you move or look towards the ground or towards a lower level E.G. *His eyes travelled downwards… She slipped on the downward slope*. 2 If an amount or rate moves downwards, it decreases.

downwind
ADVERB If something moves downwind, it moves in the same direction as the wind E.G. *Sparks drifted downwind*.

dowry dowries
NOUN A woman's dowry is money or property which her father gives to the man she marries.

doze dozes dozing dozed
VERB 1 When you doze, you sleep lightly for a short period. ▶ NOUN 2 a short, light sleep.

dozen dozens
NOUN A dozen things are twelve of them.

drab drabber drabbest
ADJECTIVE dull and unattractive.
drabness NOUN
▇ dreary, dull

draft drafts drafting drafted
NOUN 1 an early rough version of it of a document or speech. ▶ VERB 2 When

you draft a document or speech, you write the first rough version of it. 3 To draft people somewhere means to move them there so that they can do a specific job E.G. *Various different presenters were drafted in*. 4 In Australian and New Zealand English, to draft cattle or sheep is to select some from a herd or flock.

drag drags dragging dragged
VERB 1 If you drag a heavy object somewhere, you pull it slowly and with difficulty. 2 If you drag someone somewhere, you make them go although they may be unwilling. 3 If things drag behind you, they trail along the ground as you move along. 4 If an event or a period of time drags, it is boring and seems to last a long time. ▶ NOUN 5 Drag is the resistance to the motion of a body passing through air or a fluid.
▇ (sense 1) draw, haul, pull

dragon dragons
NOUN In stories and legends, a dragon is a fierce animal like a large lizard with wings and claws that breathes fire.
▇ from Greek *drakōn* meaning 'serpent'

dragonfly dragonflies
NOUN a colourful insect which is often found near water.

dragoon dragoons dragooning dragooned
NOUN 1 Dragoons are soldiers. Originally, they were mounted infantry soldiers. ▶ VERB 2 If you dragoon someone into something, you force them to do it.

drain drains draining drained
VERB 1 If you drain something or if it drains, liquid gradually flows out of it

or off it. **2** If you drain a glass, you drink all its contents. **3** If something drains strength or resources, it gradually uses them up E.G. *The prolonged boardroom battle drained him of energy and money.* ▶ NOUN **4** a pipe or channel that carries water or sewage away from a place. **5** a metal grid in a road, through which rainwater flows.

drainage
NOUN **1** Drainage is the system of pipes, drains, or ditches used to drain water or other liquid away from a place. **2** Drainage is also the process of draining water away, or the way in which a place drains E.G. *To grow these well, all you need is good drainage.*

drake drakes
NOUN a male duck.

drama dramas
NOUN **1** a serious play for the theatre, television, or radio. **2** Drama is plays and the theatre in general E.G. *Japanese drama.* **3** You can refer to the exciting events or aspects of a situation as drama E.G. *the drama of real life.*

dramatic
ADJECTIVE A dramatic change or event happens suddenly and is very noticeable E.G. *a dramatic departure from tradition.*
dramatically ADVERB

dramatist dramatists
NOUN (DRAMA) a person who writes plays.

drape drapes draping draped
VERB If you drape a piece of cloth, you arrange it so that it hangs down or covers something in loose folds.

drastic
ADJECTIVE A drastic course of action is very severe and is usually taken urgently E.G. *It's time for drastic action.*
drastically ADVERB
☰ extreme, radical

draught draughts
Said "draft" NOUN **1** a current of cold air. **2** an amount of liquid that you swallow. **3** Draughts is a game for two people played on a chessboard with round pieces. ▶ ADJECTIVE **4** Draught beer is served straight from barrels rather than in bottles.

draughtsman draughtsmen
NOUN a person who prepares detailed drawings or plans.

draughty draughtier draughtiest
ADJECTIVE A place that is draughty has currents of cold air blowing through it.

draw draws drawing drew drawn
VERB **1** When you draw, you use a pen or crayon to make a picture or diagram. **2** To draw near means to move closer. To draw away or draw back means to move away. **3** If you draw something in a particular direction, you pull it there smoothly and gently E.G. *He drew his feet under the chair.* **4** If you draw a deep breath, you breathe in deeply. **5** If you draw the curtains, you pull them so that they cover or uncover the window. **6** If something such as water or energy is drawn from a source, it is taken from it. **7** If you draw a conclusion, you arrive at it from the facts you know. **8** If you draw a distinction or a comparison

a
b
c
d
e
f
g
h
i
j
k
l
m
n
o
p
q
r
s
t
u
v
w
x
y
z

Beautiful Elephants Are Usually Tiny (<u>beau</u>tiful)   SPELLING NOTE

A
B
C
D
E
F
G
H
I
J
K
L
M
N
O
P
Q
R
S
T
U
V
W
X
Y
Z

between two things, you point out that it exists. ▶ NOUN 9 the result of a game or competition in which nobody wins.

draw up VERB To draw up a plan, document, or list means to prepare it and write it out.

drawback drawbacks
NOUN a problem that makes something less acceptable or desirable E.G. *Shortcuts usually have a drawback.*

drawbridge drawbridges
NOUN a bridge that can be pulled up or lowered.

drawer drawers
NOUN a sliding box-shaped part of a piece of furniture used for storing things.

drawing drawings
NOUN 1 a picture made with a pencil, pen, or crayon. 2 Drawing is the skill or work of making drawings.

drawing room drawing rooms
NOUN; OLD-FASHIONED a room in a house where people relax or entertain guests.

drawl drawls drawling drawled
VERB If someone drawls, they speak slowly with long vowel sounds.

drawn
Drawn is the past participle of **draw**.

dread dreads dreading dreaded
VERB 1 If you dread something, you feel very worried and frightened about it E.G. *He was dreading the journey.* ▶ NOUN 2 Dread is a feeling of great fear or anxiety.
dreaded ADJECTIVE

dreadful
ADJECTIVE very bad or unpleasant.
dreadfully ADVERB
■ atrocious, awful, terrible

dream dreams dreaming dreamed or **dreamt**
NOUN 1 a series of events that you experience in your mind while asleep. 2 a situation or event which you often think about because you would very much like it to happen E.G. *his dream of winning the lottery.* ▶ VERB 3 When you dream, you see events in your mind while you are asleep. 4 When you dream about something happening, you often think about it because you would very much like it to happen. 5 If someone dreams up a plan or idea, they invent it. 6 If you say you would not dream of doing something, you are emphasizing that you would not do it E.G. *I wouldn't dream of giving the plot away.* ▶ ADJECTIVE 7 too good to be true E.G. *a dream holiday.*
dreamer NOUN

Dreamtime
NOUN In Australian Aboriginal legends, Dreamtime is the time when the world was being made and the first people were created.

dreamy dreamier dreamiest
ADJECTIVE Someone with a dreamy expression looks as if they are thinking about something very pleasant.

dreary drearier dreariest
ADJECTIVE dull or boring.

dregs
PLURAL NOUN The dregs of a liquid are the last drops left at the bottom of a container, and any sediment left with it.

drenched
ADJECTIVE soaking wet.

dress dresses dressing dressed
NOUN 1 a piece of clothing for women

or girls made up of a skirt and top attached. **2** Dress is any clothing worn by men or women. ▶ VERB **3** When you dress, you put clothes on. **4** If you dress for a special occasion, you put on formal clothes. **5** To dress a wound means to clean it up and treat it.

dresser dressers
NOUN a piece of kitchen or dining room furniture with cupboards or drawers in the lower part and open shelves in the top part.

dress rehearsal dress rehearsals
NOUN the last rehearsal of a show or play, using costumes, scenery, and lighting.

dribble dribbles dribbling dribbled
VERB **1** When liquid dribbles down a surface, it trickles down it in drops or a thin stream. **2** If a person or animal dribbles, saliva trickles from their mouth. **3** In sport, to dribble a ball means to move it along by repeatedly tapping it with your foot or a stick. ▶ NOUN **4** a small quantity of liquid flowing in a thin stream or drops.

drift drifts drifting drifted
VERB **1** When something drifts, it is carried along by the wind or by water. **2** When people drift, they move aimlessly from one place or activity to another. **3** If you drift off to sleep, you gradually fall asleep. ▶ NOUN **4** A snow drift is a pile of snow heaped up by the wind. **5** The drift of an argument or a speech is its main point.

drifter NOUN

drill drills drilling drilled

NOUN **1** a tools for making holes E.G. *an electric drill*. **2** Drill is a routine exercise or routine training E.G. *lifeboat drill*. ▶ VERB **3** To drill into something means to make a hole in it using a drill. **4** If you drill people, you teach them to do something by repetition.

drink drinks drinking drank drunk
VERB **1** When you drink, you take liquid into your mouth and swallow it. **2** To drink also means to drink alcohol E.G. *He drinks little and eats carefully*. ▶ NOUN **3** an amount of liquid suitable for drinking. **4** an alcoholic drink.

drinker NOUN
■ (sense 1) imbibe, sip, swallow
■ (sense 2) booze, tipple

drip drips dripping dripped
VERB **1** When liquid drips, it falls in small drops. **2** When an object drips, drops of liquid fall from it. ▶ NOUN **3** a drop of liquid falling from something. **4** a device for allowing liquid food to enter the bloodstream of a person who cannot eat properly because they are ill.

drive drives driving drove driven
VERB **1** To drive a vehicle means to operate it and control its movements. **2** If something or someone drives you to do something, they force you to do it E.G. *The illness of his daughter drove him to religion*. **3** If you drive a post or nail into something, you force it in by hitting it with a hammer. **4** If something drives a machine, it supplies the power that makes it work. ▶ NOUN **5** a journey in a vehicle. **6** a private road that leads from a public road to a person's house.

a
b
c
d
e
f
g
h
i
j
k
l
m
n
o
p
q
r
s
t
u
v
w
x
y
z

there's a rAKE in the brAKEs (br**a**ke)   **SPELLING NOTE**

7 Drive is energy and determination.
driver NOUN **driving** NOUN

drivel

NOUN Drivel is nonsense E.G. *He is still writing mindless drivel.*
📖 from Old English *dreflian* meaning 'to dribble'

drizzle

NOUN Drizzle is light rain.

dromedary dromedaries

NOUN a camel which has one hump.

drone drones droning droned

VERB **1** If something drones, it makes a low, continuous humming noise. **2** If someone drones on, they keep talking or reading aloud in a boring way. ▶ NOUN **3** a continuous low dull sound.

drool drools drooling drooled

VERB If someone drools, saliva dribbles from their mouth without them being able to stop it.

droop droops drooping drooped

VERB If something droops, it hangs or sags downwards with no strength or firmness.

drop drops dropping dropped

VERB **1** If you drop something, you let it fall. **2** If something drops, it falls straight down. **3** If a level or amount drops, it becomes less. **4** If your voice drops, or if you drop your voice, you speak more quietly. **5** If you drop something that you are doing or dealing with, you stop doing it or dealing with it E.G. *She dropped the subject and never mentioned it again.* **6** If you drop a hint, you give someone a hint in a casual way. **7** If you drop something or someone somewhere, you deposit or leave them there. ▶ NOUN **8** A drop of liquid is a very small quantity of it that

forms or falls in a round shape. **9** a decrease E.G. *a huge drop in income.* **10** the distance between the top and bottom of something tall, such as a cliff or building E.G. *It is a sheer drop to the foot of the cliff.*

droplet droplets

NOUN a small drop.

droppings

PLURAL NOUN Droppings are the faeces of birds and small animals.

drought droughts

Rhymes with "**shout**" NOUN a long period during which there is no rain.

drove droves droving droved

1 Drove is the past tense of **drive**.
VERB **2** To drove cattle or sheep is to drive them over a long distance.

drown drowns drowning drowned

VERB **1** When someone drowns or is drowned, they die because they have gone under water and cannot breathe. **2** If a noise drowns a sound, it is louder than the sound and makes it impossible to hear it.

drowsy drowsier drowsiest

ADJECTIVE feeling sleepy.

drudgery

NOUN Drudgery is hard boring work.

drug drugs drugging drugged

NOUN **1** a chemical given to people to treat disease. **2** Drugs are chemical substances that some people smoke, swallow, smell, or inject because of their stimulating effects. ▶ VERB **3** To drug a person or animal means to give them a drug to make them unconscious. **4** To drug food or drink means to add a drug to it in order to make someone unconscious.

drugged ADJECTIVE

druid druids
Said "*droo*-id" NOUN a priest of an ancient religion in Northern Europe.

drum drums drumming drummed
NOUN 1 a musical instrument consisting of a skin stretched tightly over a round frame. 2 an object or container shaped like a drum E.G. *an oil drum.* 3 INFORMAL In Australian English, the drum is information or advice E.G. *The manager gave me the drum.* ▶ VERB 4 If something is drumming on a surface, it is hitting it regularly, making a continuous beating sound. 5 If you drum something into someone, you keep saying it to them until they understand it or remember it.

drumstick drumsticks
NOUN 1 a stick used for beating a drum. 2 A chicken drumstick is the lower part of the leg of a chicken, which is cooked and eaten.

drunk drunks
1 Drunk is the past participle of **drink**. ▶ ADJECTIVE 2 If someone is drunk, they have drunk so much alcohol that they cannot speak clearly or behave sensibly. ▶ NOUN 3 a person who is drunk, or who often gets drunk.
drunken ADJECTIVE **drunkenly** ADVERB **drunkenness** NOUN
◼ (sense 2) inebriated, intoxicated

dry drier or **dryer driest; dries drying dried**
ADJECTIVE 1 Something that is dry contains or uses no water or liquid. 2 Dry bread or toast is eaten without a topping. 3 Dry sherry or wine does not taste sweet. 4 Dry also means plain and sometimes boring E.G. *the*

dry facts. 5 Dry humour is subtle and sarcastic. ▶ VERB 6 When you dry something, or when it dries, liquid is removed from it.
◼ (sense 1) arid, dehydrated, parched

dry up VERB 1 If something dries up, it becomes completely dry. 2 INFORMAL If you dry up, you forget what you were going to say, or find that you have nothing left to say.

dryness NOUN **drily** ADVERB

dry-clean dry-cleans dry-cleaning dry-cleaned
VERB When clothes are dry-cleaned, they are cleaned with a liquid chemical rather than with water.

dryer dryers; also spelt **drier**
NOUN a device for removing moisture from something by heating or by hot air E.G. *a hair dryer.*

dual
ADJECTIVE having two parts, functions, or aspects E.G. *a dual-purpose trimmer.*

dub dubs dubbing dubbed
VERB 1 If something is dubbed a particular name, it is given that name E.G. *Smiling has been dubbed 'nature's secret weapon'.* 2 If a film is dubbed, the voices on the soundtrack are not those of the actors, but those of other actors speaking in a different language.

dubious
Said "*dyoo*-bee-uss" ADJECTIVE 1 not entirely honest, safe, or reliable E.G. *dubious sales techniques.* 2 doubtful E.G. *I felt dubious about the entire proposition.*
dubiously ADVERB
◼ (sense 1) questionable, suspect

duchess duchesses
NOUN a woman who has the same

a b c **d** e f g h i j k l m n o p q r s t u v w x y z

A
B
C
D
E
F
G
H
I
J
K
L
M
N
O
P
Q
R
S
T
U
V
W
X
Y
Z

rank as a duke, or who is a duke's wife or widow.

duchy duchies
Said "dut-shee" NOUN the land owned and ruled by a duke or duchess.

duck ducks ducking ducked
NOUN **1** a bird that lives in water and has webbed feet and a large flat bill. ▶ VERB **2** If you duck, you move your head quickly downwards in order to avoid being hit by something. **3** If you duck a duty or responsibility, you avoid it. **4** To duck someone means to push them briefly under water.

duckling ducklings
NOUN a young duck.

duct ducts
NOUN **1** a pipe or channel through which liquid or gas is sent. **2** a bodily passage through which liquid such as tears can pass.

dud duds
NOUN something which does not function properly.

due dues
ADJECTIVE **1** expected to happen or arrive E.G. *The baby is due at Christmas.* **2** If you give something due consideration, you give it the consideration it needs. ▶ PHRASE **3 Due to** means because of E.G. *Headaches can be due to stress.* ▶ ADVERB **4** Due means exactly in a particular direction E.G. *About a mile due west lay the ocean.* ▶ PLURAL NOUN **5** Dues are sums of money that you pay regularly to an organization you belong to.

duel duels
NOUN **1** a fight arranged between two people using deadly weapons, to settle a quarrel. **2** Any contest or

conflict between two people can be referred to as a duel.

duet duets
NOUN a piece of music sung or played by two people.

dug
Dug is the past tense and past participle of **dig**.

dugong dugongs
NOUN an animal like a whale that lives in warm seas.

dugout dugouts
NOUN **1** a canoe made by hollowing out a log. **2** MILITARY a shelter dug in the ground for protection.

duke dukes
NOUN a nobleman with a rank just below that of a prince.
📖 from Latin *dux* meaning 'leader'

dull duller dullest; dulls dulling dulled
ADJECTIVE **1** not at all interesting in any way. **2** slow to learn or understand. **3** not bright, sharp, or clear. **4** A dull day or dull sky is very cloudy. **5** Dull feelings are weak and not intense E.G. *He should have been angry but felt only dull resentment.* ▶ VERB **6** If something dulls or is dulled, it becomes less bright, sharp, or clear.
dully ADVERB **dullness** NOUN
▤ (sense 4) cloudy, overcast

duly
ADVERB **1** FORMAL If something is duly done, it is done in the correct way E.G. *I wish to record my support for the duly elected council.* **2** If something duly happens, it is something that you expected to happen E.G. *Two chicks duly emerged from their eggs.*

dumb dumber dumbest
ADJECTIVE **1** unable to speak. **2** INFORMAL slow to understand or stupid.

dumbfounded
ADJECTIVE speechless with amazement
E.G. *She was too dumbfounded to
answer.*

dummy dummies
NOUN **1** a rubber teat which a baby
sucks or bites on. **2** an imitation or
model of something which is used
for display. ► ADJECTIVE **3** imitation or
substitute.

dump dumps dumping dumped
VERB **1** When unwanted waste is
dumped, it is left somewhere. **2** If you
dump something, you throw it down
or put it down somewhere in a
careless way. ► NOUN **3** a place where
rubbish is left. **4** a storage place,
especially used by the military for
storing supplies. **5** INFORMAL You refer
to a place as a dump when it is
unattractive and unpleasant to live
in.

dumpling dumplings
NOUN a small lump of dough that is
cooked and eaten with meat and
vegetables.

dunce dunces
NOUN a person who cannot learn
what someone is trying to teach
them.

dune dunes
NOUN A dune or sand dune is a hill of
sand near the sea or in the desert.

dung
NOUN Dung is the faeces from large
animals, sometimes called manure.

dungarees
PLURAL NOUN Dungarees are trousers
which have a bib covering the chest
and straps over the shoulders.

dungeon dungeons
Said "**dun**-jen" NOUN an underground
prison.

dunk dunks dunking dunked
VERB To dunk something means to dip
it briefly into a liquid E.G. *He dunked
a single tea bag into two cups.*

duo duos
NOUN **1** a pair of musical performers;
also a piece of music written for two
players. **2** Any two people doing
something together can be referred
to as a duo.

dupe dupes duping duped
VERB **1** If someone dupes you, they
trick you. ► NOUN **2** someone who has
been tricked.
📖 from Old French *de huppe*
meaning 'of the hoopoe', a bird
thought to be stupid

**duplicate duplicates duplicating
duplicated**
VERB **1** To duplicate something means
to make an exact copy of it. ► NOUN
2 something that is identical to
something else. ► ADJECTIVE **3** identical
to or an exact copy of E.G. *a
duplicate key.*
duplication NOUN

durable
ADJECTIVE strong and lasting for a long
time.
durability NOUN

duration
NOUN The duration of something is
the length of time during which it
happens or exists.

duress
Said "dyoo-**ress**" NOUN If you do
something under duress, you are
forced to do it, and you do it very
unwillingly.

during
PREPOSITION happening throughout a
particular time or at a particular
point in time E.G. *The mussels will*

a
b
c
d
e
f
g
h
i
j
k
l
m
n
o
p
q
r
s
t
u
v
w
x
y
z

open naturally during cooking.

dusk

NOUN Dusk is the time just before nightfall when it is not completely dark.

🔳 from Old English *dox* meaning 'dark' or 'swarthy'

dust dusts dusting dusted

NOUN 1 Dust is dry fine powdery material such as particles of earth, dirt, or pollen. ▸ VERB 2 When you dust furniture or other objects, you remove dust from them using a duster. 3 If you dust a surface with powder, you cover it lightly with the powder.

dustbin dustbins

NOUN a large container for rubbish.

duster dusters

NOUN a cloth used for removing dust from furniture and other objects.

dustman dustmen

NOUN someone whose job is to collect the rubbish from people's houses.

dusty dustier dustiest

ADJECTIVE covered with dust.

Dutch

ADJECTIVE 1 belonging or relating to Holland. ▸ NOUN 2 Dutch is the main language spoken in Holland.

dutiful

ADJECTIVE doing everything you are expected to do.

dutifully ADVERB

duty duties

NOUN 1 Duties are things you ought to do or feel you should do, because it is your responsibility to do them E.G. *We have a duty as adults to listen to children.* ▸ PLURAL NOUN 2 Your duties are the tasks which you do as part of your job. ▸ NOUN 3 Duty is tax paid to

the government on some goods, especially imports.

📧 (sense 1) obligation, responsibility

duty-free

ADJECTIVE Duty-free goods are sold at airports or on planes or ships at a cheaper price than usual because they are not taxed E.G. *duty-free vodka.*

duvet duvets

Said "*doo*-vay" NOUN a cotton quilt filled with feathers or other material, used on a bed in place of sheets and blankets.

dwarf dwarfs dwarfing dwarfed

VERB 1 If one thing dwarfs another, it is so much bigger that it makes it look very small. ▸ ADJECTIVE 2 smaller than average. ▸ NOUN 3 a person who is much smaller than average size.

dwell dwells dwelling dwelled or dwelt

VERB 1 LITERARY To dwell somewhere means to live there. 2 If you dwell on something or dwell upon it, you think or write about it a lot.

dwelling dwellings

NOUN; FORMAL Someone's dwelling is the house or other place where they live.

dwindle dwindles dwindling dwindled

VERB If something dwindles, it becomes smaller or weaker.

dye dyes dyeing dyed

VERB 1 To dye something means to change its colour by applying coloured liquid to it. ▸ NOUN 2 a colouring substance which is used to change the colour of something such as cloth or hair.

dyke dykes; also spelt **dike**
NOUN a thick wall that prevents water flooding onto land from a river or from the sea.

dynamic dynamics
ADJECTIVE **1** A dynamic person is full of energy, ambition, and new ideas. **2** relating to energy or forces which produce motion. ▶ PLURAL NOUN **3** In physics, dynamics is the study of the forces that change or produce the motion of bodies or particles. **4** The dynamics of a society or a situation are the forces that cause it to change. **5** (MUSIC) Dynamics is the various degrees of loudness needed in the performance of a piece of music, or the symbols used to indicate this in written music.

dynamite
NOUN Dynamite is a kind of explosive.

dynamo dynamos
NOUN a device that converts mechanical energy into electricity.

dynasty dynasties
NOUN (HISTORY) a series of rulers of a country all belonging to the same family.

dysentery
Said "diss-en-tree" NOUN an infection of the bowel which causes fever, stomach pain, and severe diarrhoea.

dyslexia
Said "dis-lek-see-a" NOUN Dyslexia is difficulty with reading caused by a slight disorder of the brain.
dyslexic ADJECTIVE AND NOUN

a
b
c
d
e
f
g
h
i
j
k
l
m
n
o
p
q
r
s
t
u
v
w
x
y
z

Plaice the fish has a glittering 'EYE' (I) (plaice)   SPELLING NOTE

Ee

TIP The words *aesthetic*, *oesophagus* and *oestrogen* sound as if they should start with letter *e*, but in British English they are spelt with *ae* and *oe*. These two combinations of letters, which both sound like *ee*, can come in the middle of words too, for example in *anaethestic* and *amoeba*.

each

ADJECTIVE OR PRONOUN **1** every one taken separately E.G. *Each time she went out, she would buy a plant.* ▶ PHRASE **2** If people do something to **each other**, each person does it to the other or others E.G. *She and Chris smiled at each other*.

☑ Wherever you use *each other* you could also use *one another*.

eager

ADJECTIVE wanting very much to do or have something.

eagerly ADVERB **eagerness** NOUN

eagle eagles

NOUN a large bird of prey.

ear ears

NOUN **1** the parts of your body on either side of your head with which you hear sounds. **2** An ear of corn or wheat is the top part of the stalk which contains seeds.

eardrum eardrums

NOUN Your eardrums are thin pieces of tightly stretched skin inside your ears which vibrate so that you can hear sounds.

earl earls

NOUN a British nobleman.

🔲 from Old English *eorl* meaning 'chieftain'

early earlier earliest

ADJECTIVE OR ADVERB **1** before the arranged or expected time E.G. *He wasn't late for our meeting, I was early.*

2 near the beginning of a day, evening, or other period of time E.G. *the early 1970s.*

🔲 (sense 1) premature, untimely

earmark earmarks earmarking earmarked

VERB If you earmark something for a special purpose, you keep it for that purpose.

🔲 from identification marks on the ears of domestic or farm animals

earn earns earning earned

VERB **1** If you earn money, you get it in return for work that you do. **2** If you earn something such as praise, you receive it because you deserve it.

earner NOUN

earnest

ADJECTIVE **1** sincere in what you say or do E.G. *I answered with an earnest smile.* ▶ PHRASE **2** If something begins **in earnest**, it happens to a greater or more serious extent than before E.G. *The battle began in earnest.*

earnestly ADVERB

earnings

PLURAL NOUN Your earnings are money that you earn.

earphones

PLURAL NOUN small speakers which you wear on your ears to listen to a radio or cassette player.

earring earrings

NOUN Earrings are pieces of jewellery that you wear on your ear lobes.

earshot

PHRASE If you are **within earshot** of something, you can hear it.

earth earths

NOUN **1** The earth is the planet on which we live. **2** Earth is the dry land on the surface of the earth, especially the soil in which things grow. **3** a hole in the ground where a fox lives. **4** The earth in a piece of electrical equipment is the wire through which electricity can pass into the ground and so make the equipment safe for use.

earthenware

NOUN pottery made of baked clay.

earthly

ADJECTIVE concerned with life on earth rather than heaven or life after death.

earthquake earthquakes

NOUN a shaking of the ground caused by movement of the earth's crust.

earthworm earthworms

NOUN a worm that lives under the ground.

earthy earthier earthiest

ADJECTIVE **1** looking or smelling like earth. **2** Someone who is earthy is open and direct, often in a crude way E.G. *earthy language*.

earwig earwigs

NOUN a small, thin, brown insect which has a pair of pincers at the end of its body.

📖 from Old English *earwicga* meaning 'ear insect'; it was believed to creep into people's ears

ease eases easing eased

NOUN **1** lack of difficulty, worry, or hardship E.G. *He had sailed through life with relative ease.* ► VERB **2** When something eases, or when you ease

it, it becomes less severe or less intense E.G. *to ease the pain.* **3** If you ease something somewhere, you move it there slowly and carefully E.G. *He eased himself into his chair.*
■ (sense 1) easiness, effortlessness
■ (sense 2) alleviate, relieve

easel easels

NOUN (ART) an upright frame which supports a picture that someone is painting.

📖 from Dutch *ezel* meaning 'ass' or 'donkey'

easily

ADVERB **1** without difficulty. **2** without a doubt E.G. *The song is easily one of their finest.*

east

NOUN **1** East is the direction in which you look to see the sun rise. **2** The east of a place is the part which is towards the east when you are in the centre E.G. *the east of Africa.* **3** The East is the countries in the south and east of Asia. ► ADJECTIVE OR ADVERB **4** East means in or towards the east E.G. *The entrance faces east.* ► ADJECTIVE **5** An east wind blows from the east.

Easter

NOUN a Christian religious festival celebrating the resurrection of Christ.

📖 from Old English *Eostre*, a pre-Christian Germanic goddess whose festival was at the spring equinox

easterly

ADJECTIVE **1** Easterly means to or towards the east. **2** An easterly wind blows from the east.

eastern

ADJECTIVE in or from the east E.G. *a remote eastern corner of the country.*

a
b
c
d
e
f
g
h
i
j
k
l
m
n
o
p
q
r
s
t
u
v
w
x
y
z

A B C D E G G H I J K L M N O P Q R S T U V W X Y Z

eastward or **eastwards**

ADVERB **1** Eastward or eastwards means towards the east E.G. *the eastward expansion of the city*.
▶ ADJECTIVE **2** The eastward part of something is the east part.

easy easier easiest

ADJECTIVE **1** able to be done without difficulty E.G. *It's easy to fall*. **2** comfortable and without any worries E.G. *an easy life*.

☑ Although *easy* is an adjective, it can be used as an adverb in fixed phrases like *take it easy*.

eat eats eating ate eaten

VERB **1** To eat means to chew and swallow food. **2** When you eat, you have a meal E.G. *We like to eat early*.

eat away VERB If something is eaten away, it is slowly destroyed E.G. *The sea had eaten away at the headland*.

eaves

PLURAL NOUN The eaves of a roof are the lower edges which jut out over the walls.

eavesdrop eavesdrops eavesdropping eavesdropped

VERB If you eavesdrop, you listen secretly to what other people are saying.

📖 from Old English *yfesdrype* meaning 'water dripping down from the eaves'; people were supposed to stand outside in the rain to hear what was being said inside the house

ebb ebbs ebbing ebbed

VERB **1** When the sea or the tide ebbs, it flows back. **2** If a person's feeling or strength ebbs, it gets weaker E.G. *The strength ebbed from his body*.

ebony

NOUN **1** a hard, dark-coloured wood,

used for making furniture. ▶ NOUN or ADJECTIVE **2** very deep black.

ebullient

ADJECTIVE; FORMAL lively and full of enthusiasm.
ebullience NOUN

EC

NOUN The EC is an old name for the European Union. EC is an abbreviation for 'European Community'.

eccentric eccentrics

Said "ik-**sen**-trik" ADJECTIVE **1** having habits or opinions which other people think are odd or peculiar.
▶ NOUN **2** someone who is eccentric.
eccentricity NOUN **eccentrically** ADVERB

🔳 (sense 1) odd, peculiar, strange
🔳 (sense 2) crank, oddball, weirdo

ecclesiastical

Said "ik-leez-ee-**ass**-ti-kl" ADJECTIVE of or relating to the Christian church.
📖 from Greek *ekklēsia* meaning 'assembly' or 'church'

echelon echelons

Said "**esh**-el-on" NOUN a level of power or responsibility in an organization.

echidna echidnas or **echidnae**

Said "ik-**kid**-na" NOUN a small, spiny mammal that lays eggs and has a long snout and claws, found in Australia.

echo echoes echoing echoed

NOUN **1** a sound which is caused by sound waves reflecting off a surface. **2** a repetition, imitation, or reminder of something E.G. *Echoes of the past are everywhere*. ▶ VERB **3** If a sound echoes, it is reflected off a surface so that you can hear it again after the original sound has stopped.

eclipse eclipses

NOUN An eclipse occurs when one

planet passes in front of another and hides it from view for a short time.

eco-

PREFIX Words beginning with 'eco-' have something to do with ecology or the environment.

📖 from Greek *oikos* meaning 'environment'

ecology

NOUN the relationship between living things and their environment; also used of the study of this relationship.
ecological ADJECTIVE **ecologically** ADVERB **ecologist** NOUN

economic

ADJECTIVE 1 (HISTORY) concerning the management of the money, industry, and trade of a country. 2 concerning making a profit E.G. *economic to produce*.

economical

ADJECTIVE 1 (HISTORY) another word for **economic**. 2 Something that is economical is cheap to use or operate. 3 Someone who is economical spends money carefully and sensibly.
economically ADVERB

economics

NOUN Economics is the study of the production and distribution of goods, services, and wealth in a society and the organization of its money, industry, and trade.

economist economists

NOUN a person who studies or writes about economics.

economy economies

NOUN 1 (HISTORY) The economy of a country is the system it uses to organize and manage its money, industry, and trade; also used of the wealth that a country gets from

business and industry. 2 Economy is the careful use of things to save money, time, or energy E.G. *Max dished up deftly, with an economy of movement*.

📖 from Greek *oikonomia* meaning 'domestic management'

ecosystem ecosystems

NOUN; TECHNICAL the relationship between plants and animals and their environment.

ecstasy ecstasies

NOUN 1 Ecstasy is a feeling of extreme happiness. 2 INFORMAL a strong illegal drug that can cause hallucinations.
ecstatic ADJECTIVE **ecstatically** ADVERB

eczema

Said "ek-sim-ma" *or* "ek soo-ma" NOUN a skin disease that causes the surface of the skin to become rough and itchy.

📖 from Greek *ekzein* meaning 'to boil over'

-ed

SUFFIX '-ed' is used to form the past tense of most English verbs E.G. *jumped… tried*.

📖 from Old English

eddy eddies

NOUN a circular movement in water or air.

edge edges edging edged

NOUN 1 The edge of something is a border or line where it ends or meets something else. 2 The edge of a blade is its thin, sharp side. 3 If you have the edge over someone, you have an advantage over them. ▶ VERB 4 If you edge something, you make a border for it E.G. *The veil was edged with matching lace*. 5 If you edge somewhere, you move there very

LEarn the principLEs (principl<u>e</u>)   SPELLING NOTE

A
B
C
D
E
F
G
H
I
J
K
L
M
N
O
P
Q
R
S
T
U
V
W
X
Y
Z

gradually E.G. *The ferry edged its way out into the river.*

■ (sense 1) border, brink, margin

edgy edgier edgiest
ADJECTIVE anxious and irritable.

edible
ADJECTIVE safe and pleasant to eat.

edifice edifices
Said "ed-if-iss" NOUN; FORMAL a large and impressive building.

edit edits editing edited
VERB 1 If you edit a piece of writing, you correct it so that it is fit for publishing. 2 To edit a film or television programme means to select different parts of it and arrange them in a particular order. 3 Someone who edits a newspaper or magazine is in charge of it.

edition editions
NOUN 1 An edition of a book or magazine is a particular version of it printed at one time. 2 An edition of a television or radio programme is a single programme that is one of a series.

editor editors
NOUN (LIBRARY) 1 a person who is responsible for the content of a newspaper or magazine. 2 a person who checks books and makes corrections to them before they are published. 3 a person who selects different parts of a television programme or a film and arranges them in a particular order.

editorship NOUN

editorial editorials
ADJECTIVE 1 involved in preparing a newspaper, book, or magazine for publication. 2 involving the contents and the opinions of a newspaper or magazine E.G. *an editorial comment.*

▶ NOUN 3 an article in a newspaper or magazine which gives the opinions of the editor or publisher on a particular topic.

editorially ADVERB

educate educates educating educated
VERB To educate someone means to teach them so that they gain knowledge about something.

educated
ADJECTIVE having a high standard of learning and culture.

education
NOUN 1 Education is the process of gaining knowledge and understanding through learning. 2 Education also refers to the system of teaching people at school or university.

educational ADJECTIVE
educationally ADVERB

eel eels
NOUN a long, thin, snakelike fish.

eerie eerier eeriest
ADJECTIVE strange and frightening E.G. *an eerie silence.*

eerily ADVERB

effect effects
NOUN 1 a direct result of someone or something on another person or thing E.G. *the effect of divorce on children.* 2 An effect that someone or something has is the overall impression or result that they have E.G. *The effect of the decor was cosy and antique.* ▶ PHRASE 3 If something **takes effect** at a particular time, it starts to happen or starts to produce results at that time E.G. *The law will take effect next year.*

☑ Remember that effect is a *noun* and *affect* is a verb.

effective

ADJECTIVE **1** working well and producing the intended results. **2** coming into operation or beginning officially E.G. *The agreement has become effective immediately.*
effectively ADVERB

effeminate

ADJECTIVE A man who is effeminate behaves, looks, or sounds like a woman.

efficient

ADJECTIVE capable of doing something well without wasting time or energy.
efficiently ADVERB   **efficiency** NOUN
■ capable, competent, proficient

effigy effigies

Said "*ef*-fij-ee" NOUN a statue or model of a person.

effluent effluents

Said "*ef*-loo-ent" NOUN Effluent is liquid waste that comes out of factories or sewage works.

effluvium effluvia

Said "*ef*-floo-vi-um" NOUN Effluvium is an unpleasant smell or gas that is given off by something, especially something that is decaying.

effort efforts

NOUN **1** (PSHE) Effort is the physical or mental energy needed to do something. **2** an attempt or struggle to do something E.G. *I went to keep-fit classes in an effort to fight the flab.*
■ (sense 1) exertion, trouble, work

effortless

ADJECTIVE done easily.
effortlessly ADVERB

eg or **e.g.**

eg means 'for example', and is abbreviated from the Latin expression 'exempli gratia'.

egalitarian

ADJECTIVE favouring equality for all people E.G. *an egalitarian country*.

egg eggs

NOUN **1** an oval or rounded object laid by female birds, reptiles, fishes, and insects. A baby creature develops inside the egg until it is ready to be born. **2** a hen's egg used as food. **3** In a female animal, an egg is a cell produced in its body which can develop into a baby if it is fertilized.

eggplant eggplants

NOUN a dark purple pear-shaped vegetable. It is also called **aubergine**.

ego egos

Said "*ee*-goh" NOUN Your ego is your opinion of what you are worth E.G. *It'll do her good and boost her ego.*
🎬 from Latin *ego* meaning 'I'

egocentric

ADJECTIVE only thinking of yourself.

egoism or **egotism**

NOUN Egoism is behaviour and attitudes which show that you believe that you are more important than other people.
egoist or **egotist** NOUN **egoistic**, **egotistic** or **egotistical** ADJECTIVE

Egyptian Egyptians

Said "ij-jip-shn" ADJECTIVE **1** belonging or relating to Egypt. ▶ NOUN **2** An Egyptian is someone who comes from Egypt.

eight eights

the number 8.
eighth

eighteen

the number 18.
eighteenth

eighty eighties

the number 80.
eightieth

a
b
c
d
e
f
g
h
i
j
k
l
m
n
o
p
q
r
s
t
u
v
w
x
y
z

the QUeen stood on the QUay (quay)   SPELLING NOTE

either

ADJECTIVE, PRONOUN, or CONJUNCTION **1** one or the other of two possible alternatives E.G. *You can spell it either way… Either of these schemes would cost billions of pounds… Either take it or leave it.* ▶ ADJECTIVE **2** both one and the other E.G. *on either side of the head.*

☑ When *either* is followed by a plural noun, the following verb can be plural too: *either of these books are useful.*

ejaculate ejaculates ejaculating ejaculated

VERB **1** When a man ejaculates, he discharges semen from his penis. **2** If you ejaculate, you suddenly say something.

ejaculation NOUN

📖 from Latin *jacere* meaning 'to throw'

eject ejects ejecting ejected

VERB If you eject something or someone, you forcefully push or send them out E.G. *He was ejected from the club.*

ejection NOUN

▤ expel, throw out

elaborate elaborates elaborating elaborated

ADJECTIVE **1** having many different parts E.G. *an elaborate system of drains.* **2** carefully planned, detailed, and exact E.G. *elaborate plans.* **3** highly decorated and complicated E.G. *elaborate designs.* ▶ VERB **4** If you elaborate on something, you add more information or detail about it.

elaborately ADVERB **elaboration** NOUN

▤ (sense 3) complicated, fancy, ornate

eland elands

NOUN a large African antelope with twisted horns.

elapse elapses elapsing elapsed

VERB When time elapses, it passes by E.G. *Eleven years elapsed before you got this job.*

elastic

ADJECTIVE **1** able to stretch easily. ▶ NOUN **2** Elastic is rubber material which stretches and returns to its original shape.

elasticity NOUN

📖 from Greek *elastikos* meaning 'pushing'

elation

NOUN Elation is a feeling of great happiness.

elated ADJECTIVE

elbow elbows elbowing elbowed

NOUN **1** Your elbow is the joint between the upper part of your arm and your forearm. ▶ VERB **2** If you elbow someone aside, you push them away with your elbow.

elder eldest; elders

ADJECTIVE **1** Your elder brother or sister is older than you. ▶ NOUN **2** a senior member of a group who has influence or authority. **3** a bush or small tree with dark purple berries.

☑ The adjectives *elder* and *eldest* can only be used when talking about the age of people within families. You can use *older* and *oldest* to talk about the age of other people or things.

elderly

ADJECTIVE **1** Elderly is a polite way to describe an old person. ▶ NOUN **2** The elderly are old people E.G. *Priority is given to services for the elderly.*

elect elects electing elected
VERB 1 If you elect someone, you choose them to fill a position, by voting E.G. *He's just been elected president.* 2 FORMAL If you elect to do something, you choose to do it E.G. *I have elected to stay.* ▶ ADJECTIVE 3 FORMAL voted into a position, but not yet carrying out the duties of the position E.G. *the vice-president elect.*

election elections
NOUN the selection of one or more people for an official position by voting.
electoral ADJECTIVE

electorate electorates
NOUN all the people who have the right to vote in an election.

electric
ADJECTIVE 1 powered or produced by electricity. 2 very tense or exciting E.G. *The atmosphere is electric.*
☑ The word *electric* is an adjective and should not be used as a noun.

electrical
ADJECTIVE using or producing electricity E.G. *electrical goods.*
electrically ADVERB

electrician electricians
NOUN a person whose job is to install and repair electrical equipment.

electricity
NOUN Electricity is a form of energy used for heating and lighting, and to provide power for machines.
🔲 from Greek *ēlektron* meaning 'amber'; in early experiments, scientists rubbed amber in order to get an electrical charge

electrified
ADJECTIVE connected to a supply of electricity.

electrifying
ADJECTIVE Something that is electrifying makes you feel very excited.

electro-
PREFIX 'Electro-' means 'electric' or involving electricity.
🔲 from Greek *ēlectron*

electrocute electrocutes electrocuting electrocuted
VERB If someone is electrocuted, they are killed by touching something that is connected to electricity.
electrocution NOUN

electrode electrodes
NOUN a small piece of metal which allows an electric current to pass between a source of power and a piece of equipment.

electron electrons
NOUN In physics, an electron is a tiny particle of matter, smaller than an atom.

electronic
ADJECTIVE (ICT) having transistors or silicon chips which control an electric current.
electronically ADVERB

electronics
NOUN Electronics is the technology of electronic devices such as televisions, and computers; also the study of how these devices work.

elegant
ADJECTIVE attractive and graceful or stylish E.G. *an elegant and beautiful city.*
elegantly ADVERB **elegance** NOUN

elegy elegies
Said "el-lij-ee" NOUN a sad poem or song about someone who has died.
🔲 from Greek *elegos* meaning 'lament sung to the flute'

element elements
NOUN 1 a part of something which

a
b
c
d
e
f
g
h
i
j
k
l
m
n
o
p
q
r
s
t
u
v
w
x
y
z

combines with others to make a whole. **2** (SCIENCE) In chemistry, an element is a substance that is made up of only one type of atom. **3** A particular element within a large group of people is a section of it which is similar E.G. *criminal elements*. **4** An element of a quality is a certain amount of it E.G. *Their attack has largely lost the element of surprise*. **5** The elements of a subject are the basic and most important points. **6** The elements are the weather conditions E.G. *Our open boat is exposed to the elements*.

elemental
ADJECTIVE; FORMAL simple and basic, but powerful E.G. *elemental emotions*.

elementary
ADJECTIVE simple, basic, and straightforward E.G. *an elementary course in woodwork*.

elephant elephants
NOUN a very large four-legged mammal with a long trunk, large ears, and ivory tusks.

elevate elevates elevating elevated
VERB **1** To elevate someone to a higher status or position means to give them greater status or importance E.G. *He was elevated to the rank of major in the army*. **2** To elevate something means to raise it up.

elevation elevations
NOUN **1** The elevation of someone or something is the raising of them to a higher level or position. **2** The elevation of a place is its height above sea level or above the ground.

eleven elevens
1 Eleven is the number 11. ▶ NOUN **2** a team of cricket or soccer players.

eleventh

elf elves
NOUN In folklore, an elf is a small mischievous fairy.

elicit elicits eliciting elicited
Said "il-**iss**-it" VERB **1** FORMAL If you elicit information, you find it out by asking careful questions. **2** If you elicit a response or reaction, you make it happen E.G. *He elicited sympathy from the audience*.

eligible
Said "el-**lij**-i-bl" ADJECTIVE suitable or having the right qualifications for something E.G. *You will be eligible for a grant in the future*.
eligibility NOUN

eliminate eliminates eliminating eliminated
VERB **1** If you eliminate something or someone, you get rid of them E.G. *They eliminated him from their inquiries*. **2** If a team or a person is eliminated from a competition, they can no longer take part.
elimination NOUN

elite elites
Said "ill-**eet**" NOUN a group of the most powerful, rich, or talented people in a society.

Elizabethan
ADJECTIVE Someone or something that is Elizabethan lived or was made during the reign of Elizabeth I.

elk elks
NOUN a large kind of deer.

ellipse ellipses
NOUN a regular oval shape, like a circle seen from an angle.

elm elms
NOUN a tall tree with broad leaves.

elocution

NOUN the art or study of speaking clearly or well in public.

elongated

ADJECTIVE long and thin.

elope elopes eloping eloped

VERB If someone elopes, they run away secretly with their lover to get married.

eloquent

ADJECTIVE able to speak or write skilfully and with ease E.G. *an eloquent politician.*

eloquently ADVERB   **eloquence** NOUN

else

ADVERB **1** other than this or more than this E.G. *Can you think of anything else?* ▶ PHRASE **2** You say **or else** to introduce a possibility or an alternative E.G. *You have to go with the flow or else be left behind in the rush.*

elsewhere

ADVERB in or to another place E.G. *He would rather be elsewhere.*

elude eludes eluding eluded

Said "ill-ood" VERB **1** If a fact or idea eludes you, you cannot understand it or remember it. **2** If you elude someone or something, you avoid them or escape from them E.G. *He eluded the authorities.*

elusive

ADJECTIVE difficult to find, achieve, describe, or remember E.G. *the elusive million dollar prize.*

elves

the plural of **elf**.

em-

PREFIX 'Em-' is another form of the prefix **en-**.

☑ em- is the form which is used before the letters *b, m* and *p*.

emaciated

*Said "im-**may**-see-ate-ed"* ADJECTIVE extremely thin and weak, because of illness or lack of food.

e-mail or **email**

NOUN the sending of messages from one computer to another.

emancipation

NOUN The emancipation of a person means the act of freeing them from harmful or unpleasant restrictions.

embargo embargoes

NOUN an order made by a government to stop trade with another country.

embark embarks embarking embarked

VERB **1** If you embark, you go onto a ship at the start of a journey. **2** If you embark on something, you start it E.G. *He embarked on a huge spending spree.*

embarrass embarrasses embarrassing embarrassed

VERB If you embarrass someone, you make them feel ashamed or awkward E.G. *I won't embarrass you by asking for details.*

embarrassed ADJECTIVE
embarrassing ADJECTIVE
embarrassment NOUN

embassy embassies

NOUN the building in which an ambassador and his or her staff work; also used of the ambassador and his or her staff.

embedded

ADJECTIVE Something that is embedded is fixed firmly and deeply E.G. *glass decorated with embedded threads.*

ember embers

NOUN Embers are glowing pieces of

a b c d e f g h i j k l m n o p q r s t u v w x y z

coal or wood from a dying fire.

embittered

ADJECTIVE If you are embittered, you are angry and resentful about things that have happened to you.

emblazoned

Said "im-**blaze**-nd" ADJECTIVE If something is emblazoned with designs, it is decorated with them E.G. *vases emblazoned with bold and colourful images.*

📖 originally a heraldic term from Old French *blason* meaning 'shield'

emblem emblems

NOUN an object or a design representing an organization or an idea E.G. *a flower emblem of Japan.*

embody embodies embodying embodied

VERB 1 To embody a quality or idea means to contain it or express it E.G. *A young dancer embodies the spirit of fun.* 2 If a number of things are embodied in one thing, they are contained in it E.G. *the principles embodied in his report.*

embodiment NOUN

embossed

ADJECTIVE decorated with designs that stand up slightly from the surface E.G. *embossed wallpaper.*

embrace embraces embracing embraced

VERB 1 If you embrace someone, you hug them to show affection or as a greeting. 2 If you embrace a belief or cause you accept it and believe in it.
► NOUN 3 a hug.

embroider embroiders embroidering embroidered

VERB If you embroider fabric, you sew a decorative design onto it.

embroidery

NOUN Embroidery is decorative designs sewn onto fabric; also the art or skill of embroidery.

embroiled

ADJECTIVE If someone is embroiled in an argument or conflict they are deeply involved in it and cannot get out of it E.G. *The two companies are now embroiled in the courts.*

embryo embryos

Said "**em**-bree-oh" NOUN an animal or human being in the very early stages of development in the womb.

embryonic ADJECTIVE

📖 from Greek *embruon* meaning 'new-born animal'

emerald emeralds

NOUN 1 a bright green precious stone.
► NOUN or ADJECTIVE 2 bright green.

emerge emerges emerging emerged

VERB 1 If someone emerges from a place, they come out of it so that they can be seen. 2 If something emerges, it becomes known or begins to be recognized as existing E.G. *It later emerged that he faced bankruptcy proceedings.*

emergence NOUN **emergent** ADJECTIVE

emergency emergencies

NOUN an unexpected and serious event which needs immediate action to deal with it.

📖 crisis, extremity

emigrant emigrants

NOUN a person who leaves their native country and goes to live permanently in another one.

emigrate emigrates emigrating emigrated

VERB If you emigrate, you leave your

native country and go to live permanently in another one.

emigration
NOUN (HISTORY) Emigration is the process of emigrating, especially by large numbers of people at various periods of history.

eminence
NOUN 1 Eminence is the quality of being well-known and respected for what you do E.G. *lawyers of eminence*. 2 'Your Eminence' is a title of respect used to address a Roman Catholic cardinal.

eminent
ADJECTIVE well-known and respected for what you do E.G. *an eminent scientist*.

eminently
ADVERB; FORMAL very E.G. *eminently reasonable*.

emir emirs
Said "em-*eer*" NOUN a Muslim ruler or nobleman.
📖 from Arabic *amir* meaning 'commander'

emission emissions
NOUN; FORMAL The emission of something such as gas or radiation is the release of it into the atmosphere.

emit emits emitting emitted
VERB To emit something means to give it out or release it E.G. *She emitted a long, low whistle*.
■ exude, give off, give out

emoticon emoticons
NOUN a symbol used in e-mail which represents a particular emotion and is made up of normal keyboard characters that are viewed sideways. For example, the symbol (:+(means 'frightened' or 'scared'.

emotion emotions
NOUN (PSHE) a strong feeling, such as love or fear.

emotional
ADJECTIVE (PSHE) 1 causing strong feelings E.G. *an emotional appeal for help*. 2 to do with feelings rather than your physical condition E.G. *emotional support*. 3 showing your feelings openly E.G. *The child is in a very emotional state*.
emotionally ADVERB

emotive
ADJECTIVE concerning emotions, or stirring up strong emotions E.G. *emotive language*.

empathize empathizes empathizing empathized; also spelt **empathise**
VERB If you empathize with someone, you understand how they are feeling.
empathy NOUN

emperor emperors
NOUN a male ruler of an empire.
📖 from Latin *imperator* meaning 'commander-in-chief'

emphasis emphases
NOUN Emphasis is special importance or extra stress given to something.

emphasize emphasizes emphasizing emphasized; also spelt **emphasise**
VERB If you emphasize something, you make it known that it is important E.G. *It was emphasized that the matter was of international concern*.

emphatic
ADJECTIVE expressed strongly and with force to show how important something is E.G. *I answered both questions with an emphatic 'Yes'*.
emphatically ADVERB

a
b
c
d
e
f
g
h
i
j
k
l
m
n
o
p
q
r
s
t
u
v
w
x
y
z

'i' before 'e' except after 'c'   SPELLING NOTE

A B C D **E** F G H I J K L M N O P Q R S T U V W X Y Z

empire empires
NOUN **1** a group of countries controlled by one country. **2** a powerful group of companies controlled by one person.
📖 from Latin *imperium* meaning 'rule'

employ employs employing employed
VERB **1** If you employ someone, you pay them to work for you. **2** If you employ something for a particular purpose, you make use of it E.G. *the techniques employed in turning grapes into wine*.
■ (sense 1) engage, hire, take on

employee employees
NOUN a person who is paid to work for another person or for an organization.

employer employers
NOUN Someone's employer is the person or organization that they work for.

employment
NOUN (GEOGRAPHY) Employment is the state of having a paid job, or the activity of recruiting people for a job.

empower empowers empowering empowered
VERB If you are empowered to do something, you have the authority or power to do it.

empress empresses
NOUN a woman who rules an empire, or the wife of an emperor.

empty emptier emptiest; empties emptying emptied
ADJECTIVE **1** having nothing or nobody inside. **2** without purpose, value, or meaning E.G. *empty promises.* ▶ VERB **3** If you empty something, or empty its contents, you remove the contents.

emptiness NOUN
☑ (sense 1) bare, blank, vacant
☐ (sense 3) clear, evacuate

emu emus
Said "ee-myoo" NOUN a large Australian bird which can run fast but cannot fly.
📖 from Portuguese *ema* meaning 'ostrich'

emulate emulates emulating emulated
VERB If you emulate someone or something, you imitate them because you admire them.

emulation NOUN

emulsion emulsions
NOUN a water-based paint.

en-
PREFIX **1** 'En-' means to surround or cover E.G. *enclose, encrusted.* **2** 'En-' means to cause to be in a certain state or condition E.G. *enamoured… endanger.*
📖 from Latin prefix *in-*

enable enables enabling enabled
VERB To enable something to happen means to make it possible.

enact enacts enacting enacted
VERB **1** If a government enacts a law or bill, it officially passes it so that it becomes law. **2** If you enact a story or play, you act it out.

enactment NOUN

enamel enamels enamelling enamelled
NOUN **1** a substance like glass, used to decorate or protect metal or china. **2** The enamel on your teeth is the hard, white substance that forms the outer part. ▶ VERB **3** If you enamel something, you decorate or cover it with enamel.

enamelled ADJECTIVE

enamoured
Said "in-**am**-erd" ADJECTIVE If you are enamoured of someone or something, you like them very much.

encapsulate encapsulates encapsulating encapsulated
VERB If something encapsulates facts or ideas, it contains or represents them in a small space.

encased
ADJECTIVE Something that is encased is surrounded or covered with a substance E.G. *encased in plaster*.

-ence
SUFFIX '-ence' is used to form nouns which mean a state, condition or quality E.G. *residence... patience*.
📖 from Latin *-ēns*

enchanted
ADJECTIVE If you are enchanted by something or someone, you are fascinated or charmed by them.

enchanting
ADJECTIVE attractive, delightful, or charming *an enchanting baby*.

encircle encircles encircling encircled
VERB To encircle something or someone means to completely surround them.

enclave enclaves
NOUN a place that is surrounded by areas that are different from it in some important way, for example because the people there are from a different culture E.G. *a Muslim enclave in Bosnia*.
📖 from Old French *enclaver* meaning 'to enclose'

enclose encloses enclosing enclosed
VERB To enclose an object or area means to surround it with

something solid.
enclosed ADJECTIVE

enclosure enclosures
NOUN an area of land surrounded by a wall or fence and used for a particular purpose.

encompass encompasses encompassing encompassed
VERB To encompass a number of things means to include all of those things E.G. *The book encompassed all aspects of maths*.

encore encores
Said "**ong**-kor" NOUN a short extra performance given by an entertainer because the audience asks for it.
📖 from French *encore* meaning 'again'

encounter encounters encountering encountered
VERB 1 If you encounter someone or something, you meet them or are faced with them E.G. *She was the most gifted child he ever encountered.*
▶ NOUN 2 a meeting, especially when it is difficult or unexpected.

encourage encourages encouraging encouraged
VERB (PSHE) 1 If you encourage someone, you give them courage and confidence to do something. 2 If someone or something encourages a particular activity, they support it E.G. *The government will encourage the creation of nursery places.*
encouraging ADJECTIVE
encouragement NOUN
▤ (sense 1) hearten, inspire

encroach encroaches encroaching encroached
VERB If something encroaches on a place or on your time or rights, it gradually takes up or takes away

a
b
c
d
e
f
g
h
i
j
k
l
m
n
o
p
q
r
s
t
u
v
w
x
y
z

an ELegant angEL (an**gel**)   SPELLING NOTE

A
B
C
D
E
F
G
H
I
J
K
L
M
N
O
P
Q
R
S
T
U
V
W
X
Y
Z

more and more of it.
encroachment NOUN
encrusted
ADJECTIVE covered with a crust or layer of something E.G. *a necklace encrusted with gold.*
encyclopedia encyclopedias
Said "en-sigh-klop-*ee*-dee-a"; also spelt **encyclopaedia**
NOUN (LIBRARY) a book or set of books giving information about many different subjects.
📖 from Greek *enkuklios paideia* meaning 'general education'
encyclopedic or **encyclopaedic**
ADJECTIVE knowing or giving information about many different things.
end ends ending ended
NOUN 1 The end of a period of time or an event is the last part. 2 The end of something is the farthest point of it E.G. *the room at the end of the passage.* 3 the purpose for which something is done E.G. *the use of taxpayers' money for overt political ends.* ▶ VERB 4 If something ends or if you end it, it comes to a finish.
endanger endangers endangering endangered
VERB To endanger something means to cause it to be in a dangerous and harmful situation E.G. *a driver who endangers the safety of others.*
📕 jeopardize, put at risk
endear endears endearing endeared
VERB If someone's behaviour endears them to you, it makes you fond of them.
endearing ADJECTIVE **endearingly** ADVERB
endeavour endeavours endeavouring endeavoured

Said "in-*dev*-er" VERB 1 FORMAL If you endeavour to do something, you try very hard to do it. ▶ NOUN 2 an effort to do or achieve something.
endless
ADJECTIVE having or seeming to have no end.
endlessly ADVERB
endorse endorses endorsing endorsed
VERB 1 If you endorse someone or something, you give approval and support to them. 2 If you endorse a document, you write your signature or a comment on it, to show that you approve of it.
endorsement NOUN
endowed
ADJECTIVE If someone is endowed with a quality or ability, they have it or are given it E.G. *He was endowed with great willpower.*
endurance
NOUN Endurance is the ability to put up with a difficult situation for a period of time.
endure endures enduring endured
VERB 1 If you endure a difficult situation, you put up with it calmly and patiently. 2 If something endures, it lasts or continues to exist E.G. *The old alliance still endures.*
enduring ADJECTIVE
enema enemas
NOUN a liquid that is put into a person's rectum in order to empty their bowels.
enemy enemies
NOUN a person or group that is hostile or opposed to another person or group.
📕 adversary, foe

energetic

ADJECTIVE having or showing energy or enthusiasm.

energetically ADVERB

■ active, lively, vigorous

energy energies

NOUN **1** the physical strength to do active things. **2** the power which drives machinery.

■ (sense 1) drive, stamina, vigour

enforce enforces enforcing enforced

VERB If you enforce a law or a rule, you make sure that it is obeyed.

enforceable ADJECTIVE

enforcement NOUN

engage engages engaging engaged

VERB **1** If you engage in an activity, you take part in it E.G. *Officials have declined to engage in a debate.* **2** To engage someone or their attention means to make or keep someone interested in something E.G. *He engaged the driver in conversation.*

engaged

ADJECTIVE **1** When two people are engaged, they have agreed to marry each other. **2** If someone or something is engaged, they are occupied or busy E.G. *Mr Anderson was otherwise engaged… The emergency number was always engaged.*

engagement engagements

NOUN **1** an appointment that you have with someone. **2** an agreement that two people have made with each other to get married.

engine engines

NOUN **1** a machine designed to convert heat or other kinds of energy into mechanical movement.

2 a railway locomotive.

🏛 from Latin *ingenium* meaning 'ingenious device'

engineer engineers engineering engineered

NOUN **1** a person trained in designing and building machinery and electrical devices, or roads and bridges. **2** a person who repairs mechanical or electrical devices.

▶ VERB **3** If you engineer an event or situation, you arrange it cleverly, usually for your own advantage.

engineering

NOUN Engineering is the profession of designing and constructing machinery and electrical devices, or roads and bridges.

English

ADJECTIVE **1** belonging or relating to England. ▶ NOUN **2** English is the main language spoken in the United Kingdom, the USA, Canada, Australia, New Zealand, and many other countries.

Englishman Englishmen

NOUN a man who comes from England.

Englishwoman NOUN

engrave engraves engraving engraved

VERB To engrave means to cut letters or designs into a hard surface with a tool.

engraving engravings

NOUN a picture or design that has been cut into a hard surface.

engraver NOUN

engrossed

ADJECTIVE If you are engrossed in something, it holds all your attention E.G. *He was engrossed in a video game.*

a
b
c
d
e
f
g
h
i
j
k
l
m
n
o
p
q
r
s
t
u
v
w
x
y
z

A Rude Idiot Thought He Might Eat Toffee In Church (<u>arithmetic</u>)   ◀ SPELLING NOTE

A
B
C
D
E
F
G
H
I
J
K
L
M
N
O
P
Q
R
S
T
U
V
W
X
Y
Z

engulf engulfs engulfing
engulfed
VERB To engulf something means to
completely cover or surround it E.G.
Black smoke engulfed him.

enhance enhances enhancing
enhanced
VERB To enhance something means to
make it more valuable or attractive
E.G. *an outfit that really enhances his
good looks.*
enhancement NOUN

enigma enigmas
NOUN anything which is puzzling or
difficult to understand.

enigmatic
ADJECTIVE mysterious, puzzling, or
difficult to understand E.G. *an
enigmatic stranger.*
enigmatically ADVERB

enjoy enjoys enjoying enjoyed
VERB 1 If you enjoy something, you
find pleasure and satisfaction in it.
2 If you enjoy something, you are
lucky to have it or experience it E.G.
The mother has enjoyed a long life.

enjoyable
ADJECTIVE giving pleasure or
satisfaction.

enjoyment
NOUN Enjoyment is the feeling of
pleasure or satisfaction you get from
something you enjoy.

enlarge enlarges enlarging
enlarged
VERB 1 When you enlarge something,
it gets bigger. 2 If you enlarge on a
subject, you give more details about
it.

enlargement enlargements
NOUN 1 An enlargement of something
is the action of making it bigger.
2 something, especially a

photograph, which has been made
bigger.

enlighten enlightens
enlightening enlightened
VERB To enlighten someone means to
give them more knowledge or
understanding of something.
enlightening ADJECTIVE
enlightenment NOUN

enlightened
ADJECTIVE well-informed and willing to
consider different opinions E.G. *an
enlightened government.*

enlist enlists enlisting enlisted
VERB 1 If someone enlists, they join
the army, navy, or air force. 2 If you
enlist someone's help, you persuade
them to help you in something you
are doing.

enliven enlivens enlivening
enlivened
VERB To enliven something means to
make it more lively or more cheerful.

en masse
Said "on mass" ADVERB If a group of
people do something en masse, they
do it together and at the same time.

enormity enormities
NOUN 1 The enormity of a problem or
difficulty is its great size and
seriousness. 2 something that is
thought to be a terrible crime or
offence.

enormous
ADJECTIVE very large in size or amount.
enormously ADVERB

enough
ADJECTIVE or ADVERB 1 as much or as
many as required E.G. *He did not
have enough money for a coffee.*
► NOUN 2 Enough is the quantity
necessary for something E.G. *There's
not enough to go round.* ► ADVERB

3 very or fairly E.G. *She could manage well enough without me.*

enquire enquires enquiring enquired; also spelt **inquire**
VERB If you enquire about something or someone, you ask about them.

enquiry enquiries; also spelt **inquiry**
NOUN **1** a question that you ask in order to find something out. **2** an investigation into something that has happened and that needs explaining.

enrage enrages enraging enraged
VERB If something enrages you, it makes you very angry.
enraged ADJECTIVE

enrich enriches enriching enriched
VERB To enrich something means to improve the quality or value of it E.G. *new woods to enrich our countryside.*
enriched ADJECTIVE **enrichment** NOUN

enrol enrols enrolling enrolled
VERB If you enrol for something such as a course or a college, you register to join or become a member of it.
enrolment NOUN

en route
Said "on root" ADVERB If something happens en route to a place, it happens on the way there.

ensconced
ADJECTIVE If you are ensconced in a particular place, you are settled there firmly and comfortably.

ensemble ensembles
Said "on-som-bl" NOUN **1** a group of things or people considered as a whole rather than separately. **2** a

small group of musicians who play or sing together.

enshrine enshrines enshrining enshrined
VERB If something such as an idea or a right is enshrined in a society, constitution, or a law, it is protected by it E.G. *Freedom of speech is enshrined in the American Constitution.*

ensign ensigns
NOUN a flag flown by a ship to show what country that ship belongs to.

ensue ensues ensuing ensued
Said "en-syoo" VERB If something ensues, it happens after another event, usually as a result of it E.G. *He entered the house and an argument ensued.*
ensuing ADJECTIVE

ensure ensures ensuring ensured
VERB To ensure that something happens means to make certain that it happens E.G. *We make every effort to ensure the information given is correct.*

entangled
ADJECTIVE If you are entangled in problems or difficulties, they are involved in them.

enter enters entering entered
VERB **1** To enter a place means to go into it. **2** If you enter an organization or institution, you join and become a member of it E.G. *He entered Parliament in 1979.* **3** If you enter a competition or examination, you take part in it. **4** If you enter something in a diary or a list, you write it down.

enterprise enterprises
NOUN **1** a business or company. **2** a

a
b
c
d
e
f
g
h
i
j
k
l
m
n
o
p
q
r
s
t
u
v
w
x
y
z

project or task, especially one that involves risk or difficulty.

📖 from French *entreprendre* meaning 'to undertake'

enterprising

ADJECTIVE ready to start new projects and tasks and full of boldness and initiative E.G. *an enterprising company*.

entertain entertains entertaining entertained

VERB 1 If you entertain people, you keep them amused or interested. 2 If you entertain guests, you receive them into your house and give them food and hospitality.

entertainer entertainers

NOUN someone whose job is to amuse and please audiences, for example a comedian or singer.

entertainment entertainments

NOUN Entertainment is anything that people watch for pleasure, such as shows and films.

enthral enthrals enthralling enthralled

Said "in-**thrawl**" VERB If you enthral someone, you hold their attention and interest completely.

enthralling ADJECTIVE

enthuse enthuses enthusing enthused

Said "inth-**yooz**" VERB If you enthuse about something, you talk about it with enthusiasm and excitement.

enthusiasm enthusiasms

NOUN Enthusiasm is interest, eagerness, or delight in something that you enjoy.

📖 from Greek *enthousiasmos* meaning 'possessed or inspired by the gods'

■ keenness, passion, zeal

enthusiastic

ADJECTIVE showing great excitement, eagerness, or approval for something E.G. *She was enthusiastic about poetry*.

enthusiastically ADVERB

entice entices enticing enticed

VERB If you entice someone to do something, you tempt them to do it E.G. *We tried to entice the mouse out of the hole*.

enticing

ADJECTIVE extremely attractive and tempting.

entire

ADJECTIVE all of something E.G. *the entire month of July*.

entirely

ADVERB wholly and completely E.G. *He and I were entirely different*.

entirety

Said "en-**tire**-it-tee" PHRASE If something happens to something **in its entirety**, it happens to all of it E.G. *This message will now be repeated in its entirety*.

entitle entitles entitling entitled

VERB If something entitles you to have or do something, it gives you the right to have or do it.

entitlement NOUN

entity entities

Said "**en**-tit-ee" NOUN any complete thing that is not divided and not part of anything else.

entourage entourages

Said "**on**-too-rahj" NOUN a group of people who follow or travel with a famous or important person.

entrails

PLURAL NOUN Entrails are the inner parts, especially the intestines, of people or animals.

entrance entrances

Said "en-truns" NOUN **1** The entrance of a building or area is its doorway or gate. **2** A person's entrance is their arrival in a place, or the way in which they arrive E.G. *Each creation is designed for you to make a dramatic entrance.* **3** (DRAMA) In the theatre, an actor makes his or her entrance when he or she comes on to the stage. **4** Entrance is the right to enter a place E.G. *He had gained entrance to the Hall by pretending to be a heating engineer.*

entrance entrances entrancing entranced

Said "en-trahnss" VERB If something entrances you, it gives you a feeling of wonder and delight.

entrancing ADJECTIVE

entrant entrants

NOUN a person who officially enters a competition or an organization.

entrenched

ADJECTIVE If a belief, custom, or power is entrenched, it is firmly established.

entrepreneur entrepreneurs

Said "on-tre-pren-**ur**" NOUN a person who sets up business deals, especially ones in which risks are involved, in order to make a profit.

entrepreneurial ADJECTIVE

entrust entrusts entrusting entrusted

VERB If you entrust something to someone, you give them the care and protection of it E.G. *Miss Fry was entrusted with the children's education.*

entry entries

NOUN **1** Entry is the act of entering a place. **2** a place through which you enter somewhere. **3** anything which is entered or recorded E.G. *Send your*

entry to the address below.

■ (sense 2) entrance, way in

envelop envelops enveloping enveloped

VERB To envelop something means to cover or surround it completely E.G. *A dense fog enveloped the area.*

envelope envelopes

NOUN a flat covering of paper with a flap that can be folded over to seal it, which is used to hold a letter.

enviable

ADJECTIVE If you describe something as enviable, you mean that you wish you had it yourself.

envious

ADJECTIVE full of envy.

enviously ADVERB

environment environments

NOUN **1** Your environment is the circumstances and conditions in which you live or work E.G. *a good environment to grow up in.* **2** The environment is the natural world around us E.G. *the waste which is dumped in the environment.*

environmental ADJECTIVE

environmentally ADVERB

☑ There is an *n* before the *m* in environment.

environmentalist environmentalists

NOUN a person who is concerned with the problems of the natural environment, such as pollution.

envisage envisages envisaging envisaged

VERB If you envisage a situation or state of affairs, you can picture it in your mind as being true or likely to happen.

envoy envoys

NOUN a messenger, sent especially

a
b
c
d
e
f
g
h
i
j
k
l
m
n
o
p
q
r
s
t
u
v
w
x
y
z

A B C E **E** F G H I J K L M N O P Q R S T U V W X Y Z

from one government to another.

envy envies envying envied

NOUN 1 Envy is a feeling of resentment you have when you wish you could have what someone else has. ▶ VERB 2 If you envy someone, you wish that you had what they have.

enzyme enzymes

NOUN a chemical substance, usually a protein, produced by cells in the body.

ephemeral

Said "if-em-er-al" ADJECTIVE lasting only a short time.

epic epics

NOUN 1 a long story of heroic events and actions. ▶ ADJECTIVE 2 very impressive or ambitious E.G. epic adventures.

epidemic epidemics

NOUN 1 an occurrence of a disease in one area, spreading quickly and affecting many people. 2 a rapid development or spread of something E.G. the country's crime epidemic.

epigram epigrams

NOUN a short saying which expresses an idea in a clever and amusing way.

epigraph

NOUN 1 a quotation at the beginning of a book. 2 an inscription on a monument or building.

epilepsy

NOUN Epilepsy is a condition of the brain which causes fits and periods of unconsciousness.

epileptic NOUN OR ADJECTIVE

episode episodes

NOUN 1 an event or period E.G. After this episode, she found it impossible to trust him. 2 one of several parts of a

novel or drama appearing for example on television E.G. I never miss an episode of Neighbours.

epistle epistles

Said "ip-piss-sl" NOUN; FORMAL a letter.

epitaph epitaphs

Said "ep-it-ahf" NOUN some words on a tomb about the person who has died.

epithet epithets

NOUN a word or short phrase used to describe some characteristic of a person.

epitome

Said "ip-pit-om-ee" NOUN; FORMAL The epitome of something is the most typical example of its sort E.G. She was the epitome of the successful woman.

☑ Do not use epitome to mean 'the peak of something'. It means 'the most typical example of something'.

epoch epochs

Said "ee-pok" NOUN a long period of time.

eponymous

Said "ip-on-im-uss" ADJECTIVE; FORMAL The eponymous hero or heroine of a play or book is the person whose name forms its title E.G. the eponymous hero of 'Eric the Viking'. 📖 from Greek eponumos meaning 'given as a name'

equal equals equalling equalled

ADJECTIVE 1 having the same size, amount, value, or standard. 2 If you are equal to a task, you have the necessary ability to deal with it. ▶ NOUN 3 Your equals are people who have the same ability, status, or rights as you. ▶ VERB 4 If one thing equals another, it is as good or remarkable as the other E.G. He

equalled the course record of 63.
equally ADVERB **equality** NOUN

equate equates equating equated
VERB If you equate a particular thing with something else, you believe that it is similar or equal E.G. *You can't equate lives with money.*

equation equations
NOUN (MATHS) a mathematical formula stating that two amounts or values are the same.

equator
Said "ik-way-tor" NOUN an imaginary line drawn round the middle of the earth, lying halfway between the North and South poles.
equatorial ADJECTIVE

equestrian
Said "ik-west ree an" ADJECTIVE relating to or involving horses.

equilateral
ADJECTIVE (MATHS) An equilateral triangle has sides that are all the same length.

equilibrium equilibria
NOUN a state of balance or stability in a situation.

equine
ADJECTIVE relating to horses.
📖 from Latin *equus* meaning 'horse'

equinox equinoxes
NOUN one of the two days in the year when the day and night are of equal length, occurring in September and March.
📖 from Latin *aequinoctium* meaning 'equal night'

equip equips equipping equipped
VERB If a person or thing is equipped with something, they have it or are provided with it E.G. *The test boat was equipped with a folding propeller.*

▣ provide, supply

equipment
NOUN Equipment is all the things that are needed or used for a particular job or activity.
▣ apparatus, gear, tools

equitable
ADJECTIVE fair and reasonable.

equity
NOUN Equity is the quality of being fair and reasonable E.G. *It is important to distribute income with some sense of equity.*

equivalent equivalents
ADJECTIVE 1 equal in use, size, value, or effect. ▶ NOUN 2 something that has the same use, value, or effect as something else E.G. *One glass of wine is the equivalent of half a pint of beer.*
equivalence NOUN
▣ (sense 2) equal, match

-er
SUFFIX 1 When '-er' is used to form some nouns it means 'for' or 'belonging to' E.G. *fastener… Highlander.* 2 '-er' is also used to form nouns which mean someone or something that does something E.G. *climber… teacher… baker.* 3 '-er' is used to make adjectives and adverbs that have the meaning 'more' E.G. *lighter… funnier.*
📖 from Old English

era eras
Said "ear-a" NOUN a period of time distinguished by a particular feature E.G. *a new era of prosperity.*
📖 from Latin *aera* meaning 'copper counters used for counting', hence for counting time

eradicate eradicates eradicating eradicated
VERB To eradicate something means

a
b
c
d
e
f
g
h
i
j
k
l
m
n
o
p
q
r
s
t
u
v
w
x
y
z

to get rid of it or destroy it completely.

eradication NOUN

erase erases erasing erased
VERB To erase something means to remove it.

erect erects erecting erected
VERB 1 To erect something means to put it up or construct it E.G. *The building was erected in 1900.*
▶ ADJECTIVE 2 in a straight and upright position E.G. *She held herself erect and looked directly at him.*
∎ (sense 2) straight, upright, vertical

erection erections
NOUN 1 the process of erecting something. 2 anything which has been erected. 3 When a man has an erection, his penis is stiff, swollen, and in an upright position.

ermine
NOUN Ermine is expensive white fur.

erode erodes eroding eroded
VERB If something erodes or is eroded, it is gradually worn or eaten away and destroyed.

erosion
NOUN (GEOGRAPHY) the gradual wearing away and destruction of something E.G. *soil erosion.*

erotic
ADJECTIVE involving or arousing sexual desire.
erotically ADVERB **eroticism** NOUN
▥ from Greek *erotikos* meaning 'of love'

err errs erring erred
VERB If you err, you make a mistake.

errand errands
NOUN a short trip you make in order to do a job for someone.

erratic
ADJECTIVE not following a regular pattern or a fixed course E.G. *Police officers noticed his erratic driving.*
erratically ADVERB

erroneous
Said "ir-**rone**-ee-uss" ADJECTIVE Ideas or methods that are erroneous are incorrect or only partly correct.
erroneously ADVERB

error errors
NOUN a mistake or something which you have done wrong.

erudite
Said "**eh**-roo-dite" ADJECTIVE having great academic knowledge.

erupt erupts erupting erupted
VERB 1 When a volcano erupts, it violently throws out a lot of hot lava and ash. 2 When a situation erupts, it starts up suddenly and violently E.G. *A family row erupted.*
eruption NOUN

escalate escalates escalating escalated
VERB If a situation escalates, it becomes greater in size, seriousness, or intensity.

escalator escalators
NOUN a mechanical moving staircase.

escapade escapades
NOUN an adventurous or daring incident that causes trouble.

escape escapes escaping escaped
VERB 1 To escape means to get free from someone or something. 2 If you escape something unpleasant or difficult, you manage to avoid it E.G. *He escaped the death penalty.* 3 If something escapes you, you cannot remember it E.G. *It was an actor whose name escapes me for the moment.* ▶ NOUN 4 an act of escaping from a particular place or situation

E.G. *his escape from North Korea.* **5** a situation or activity which distracts you from something unpleasant E.G. *Television provides an escape.*

escapee escapees
Said "is-kay-*pee*" NOUN someone who has escaped, especially an escaped prisoner.

escapism
NOUN avoiding the real and unpleasant things in life by thinking about pleasant or fantastic things E.G. *Most horror movies are simple escapism.*
escapist ADJECTIVE

eschew eschews eschewing eschewed
Said "is-*chew*" VERB; FORMAL If you eschew something, you deliberately avoid or keep away from it.

escort escorts escorting escorted
NOUN **1** a person or vehicle that travels with another in order to protect or guide them. **2** a person who accompanies another person of the opposite sex to a social event. ▶ VERB **3** If you escort someone, you go with them somewhere, especially in order to protect or guide them.

-ese
Said "-*eez*" SUFFIX '-ese' forms adjectives and nouns which show where a person or thing comes from E.G. *Japanese.*
📖 from Latin suffix *-ensis* meaning 'from'

Eskimo Eskimos
NOUN a name that was formerly used for the Inuit people and their language.

especially
ADVERB You say especially to show

that something applies more to one thing, person, or situation than to any other E.G. *Regular eye tests are important, especially for the elderly.*

espionage
Said "*ess*-pee-on-ahj" NOUN Espionage is the act of spying to get secret information, especially to find out military or political secrets.
📖 from French *espionner* meaning 'to spy'

espouse espouses espousing espoused
VERB; FORMAL If you espouse a particular policy, cause, or plan, you give your support to it E.G. *They espoused the rights of man.*

espresso
NOUN Espresso is strong coffee made by forcing steam through ground coffee.
📖 from Italian *caffè espresso* meaning 'pressed coffee'
✔ The second letter of *espresso* is s and not x.

-ess
SUFFIX '-ess' added at the end of a noun indicates a female E.G. *lioness.*
📖 from Late Latin suffix *-issa*
✔ Special words for a woman who does a particular job or activity, such as *actress, poetess* and *authoress*, are now used less often because many women prefer to be referred to simply as an *actor, poet* or *author.*

essay essays
NOUN a short piece of writing on a particular subject, for example one done as an exercise by a student.

essence essences
NOUN **1** The essence of something is its most basic and most important part, which gives it its identity E.G.

have a pIEce of pIE (pi*e*ce)   SPELLING NOTE

A
B
C
D
E
F
G
H
I
J
K
L
M
N
O
P
Q
R
S
T
U
V
W
X
Y
Z

the very essence of being a woman. **2** a concentrated liquid used for flavouring food E.G. *vanilla essence*.

essential essentials
ADJECTIVE **1** vitally important and absolutely necessary E.G. *Good ventilation is essential in the greenhouse*. **2** very basic, important, and typical E.G. *the essential aspects of international banking*. ▶ NOUN **3** something that is very important or necessary E.G. *the bare essentials of furnishing*.
essentially ADVERB

-est
SUFFIX '-est' is used to form adjectives and adverbs that have the meaning 'most' E.G. *greatest… furthest*.
📖 from Old English

establish establishes establishing established
VERB **1** To establish something means to set it up in a permanent way. **2** If you establish yourself or become established as something, you achieve a strong reputation for a particular activity E.G. *He had just established himself as a film star*. **3** If you establish a fact or establish the truth of something, you discover it and can prove it E.G. *Our first priority is to establish the cause of her death*.
established ADJECTIVE
▣ (sense 1) create, found, set up

establishment establishments
NOUN **1** The establishment of an organization or system is the act of setting it up. **2** a shop, business, or some other sort of organization or institution. **3** The Establishment is the group of people in a country who have power and influence E.G. *lawyers, businessmen and other pillars of the Establishment*.

estate estates
NOUN **1** a large area of privately owned land in the country, together with all the property on it. **2** an area of land, usually in or near a city, which has been developed for housing or industry. **3** LEGAL A person's estate consists of all the possessions they leave behind when they die.

estate agent estate agents
NOUN a person who works for a company that sells houses and land.

esteem
NOUN admiration and respect that you feel for another person.
esteemed ADJECTIVE

estimate estimates estimating estimated
VERB **1** (MATHS) If you estimate an amount or quantity, you calculate it approximately. **2** If you estimate something, you make a guess about it based on the evidence you have available E.G. *Often it's possible to estimate a person's age just by knowing their name*. ▶ NOUN **3** an approximate calculation of an amount or quantity. **4** a guess you make about something based on the evidence you have available. **5** a formal statement from a company who may do some work for you, telling you how much it is likely to cost.

estimation estimations
NOUN **1** an approximate calculation of something that can be measured. **2** the opinion or impression you form about a person or situation.

estranged
ADJECTIVE **1** If someone is estranged from their husband or wife, they no

longer live with them. **2** If someone is estranged from their family or friends, they have quarrelled with them and no longer keep in touch with them.

estrogen
NOUN a female sex hormone which regulates the reproductive cycle.

estuary estuaries
Said "**est**-yoo-ree" NOUN (GEOGRAPHY) the wide part of a river near where it joins the sea and where fresh water mixes with salt water.

etc.
a written abbreviation for **et cetera**.

et cetera
Said "it **set**-ra" 'Et cetera' is used at the end of a list to indicate that other items of the same type you have mentioned could have been mentioned if there had been time or space.

☑ As *etc.* means 'and the rest', you should not write *and etc.*

etch etches etching etched
VERB **1** If you etch a design or pattern on a surface, you cut it into the surface by using acid or a sharp tool. **2** If something is etched on your mind or memory, it has made such a strong impression on you that you feel you will never forget it.
etched ADJECTIVE

etching etchings
NOUN a picture printed from a metal plate that has had a design cut into it.

eternal
ADJECTIVE lasting forever, or seeming to last forever E.G. *eternal life.*
eternally ADVERB
■ endless, everlasting, perpetual

eternity eternities
NOUN **1** Eternity is time without end,

or a state of existing outside time, especially the state some people believe they will pass into when they die. **2** a period of time which seems to go on for ever E.G. *We arrived there after an eternity.*

ether
Said "**eeth**-er" NOUN a colourless liquid that burns easily. Used in industry as a solvent and in medicine as an anaesthetic.

ethereal
Said "ith-**ee**-ree-al" ADJECTIVE light and delicate E.G. *misty ethereal landscapes.*
ethereally ADVERB

ethical
ADJECTIVE in agreement with accepted principles of behaviour that are thought to be right E.G. *teenagers who become vegetarian for ethical reasons.*
ethically ADVERB

ethics
PLURAL NOUN Ethics are moral beliefs about right and wrong E.G. *The medical profession has a code of ethics.*

Ethiopian Ethiopians
Said "eeth-ee-**oh**-pee-an" ADJECTIVE **1** belonging to or relating to Ethiopia. ▶ NOUN **2** someone who comes from Ethiopia.

ethnic
ADJECTIVE **1** involving different racial groups of people E.G. *ethnic minorities.* **2** relating to a particular racial or cultural group, especially when very different from modern western culture E.G. *ethnic food.*
ethnically ADVERB

ethos
Said "**eeth**-oss" NOUN a set of ideas

I went to see (C) the doctor's new practiCe (practice)   SPELLING NOTE

and attitudes that is associated with a particular group of people E.G. *the ethos of journalism*.

etiquette
Said "et-ik-ket" NOUN a set of rules for behaviour in a particular social situation.

-ette
SUFFIX '-ette' is used to form nouns which have 'small' as part of their meaning E.G. *launderette… cigarette*.
📖 from French, the feminine form of the French suffix *-et*

etymology
Said "et-tim-ol-loj-ee" NOUN Etymology is the study of the origin and changes of form in words.

EU
NOUN EU is an abbreviation for 'European Union'.

eucalyptus or **eucalypt**
eucalyptuses or **eucalypts**
NOUN an evergreen tree, grown mostly in Australia; also the wood and oil from this tree.

Eucharist Eucharists
Said "yoo-kar-rist" NOUN a religious ceremony in which Christians remember and celebrate Christ's last meal with his disciples.
📖 from Greek *eucharistia* meaning 'thanksgiving'

eunuch eunuchs
Said "yoo-nuk" NOUN a man who has been castrated.

euphemism euphemisms
NOUN a polite word or expression that you can use instead of one that might offend or upset people E.G. *action movies, a euphemism for violence*.
euphemistic ADJECTIVE
euphemistically ADVERB

euphoria
NOUN a feeling of great happiness.
euphoric ADJECTIVE

euro euros
NOUN the official unit of currency in some countries of the European Union, replacing their old currencies at the beginning of January 2002.

Europe
NOUN Europe is the second smallest continent. It has Asia on its eastern side, with the Arctic to the north, the Atlantic to the west, and the Mediterranean and Africa to the south.

European Europeans
ADJECTIVE 1 belonging or relating to Europe. ► NOUN 2 someone who comes from Europe.

European Union
NOUN The group of countries who have joined together under the Treaty of Rome for economic and trade purposes are officially known as the European Union.

euthanasia
Said "yooth-a-nay-zee-a" NOUN Euthanasia is the act of painlessly killing a dying person in order to stop their suffering.
📖 from Greek *eu-* meaning 'easy' and *thanatos* meaning 'death'

evacuate evacuates evacuating evacuated
VERB If someone is evacuated, they are removed from a place of danger to a place of safety E.G. *A crowd of shoppers had to be evacuated from a store after a bomb scare*.
evacuation NOUN **evacuee** NOUN

evade evades evading evaded
VERB 1 If you evade something or someone, you keep moving in order

to keep out of their way E.G. *For two months he evaded police.* **2** If you evade a problem or question, you avoid dealing with it.

evaluate evaluates evaluating evaluated

VERB (EXAM TERM) If you evaluate something, you assess its strengths and weaknesses.

evaluation evaluations

NOUN **1** Evaluation is assessing something strengths and weaknesses. **2** (D&T) To carry out an evaluation of a design, product or system is to do an assessment to find out how well it works or will work.

evangelical

Said "ee-van-**jel**-ik-kl" ADJECTIVE Evangelical beliefs are Christian beliefs that stress the importance of the gospels and a personal belief in Christ.

evangelist evangelists

Said "iv-**van**-jel-ist" NOUN a person who travels from place to place preaching Christianity.

evangelize VERB **evangelism** NOUN 🔤 from Greek *evangelion* meaning 'good news'

evaporate evaporates evaporating evaporated (SCIENCE)

VERB **1** When a liquid evaporates, it gradually becomes less and less because it has changed from a liquid into a gas. **2** If a substance has been evaporated, all the liquid has been taken out so that it is dry or concentrated.

evaporation NOUN

evasion evasions

NOUN deliberately avoiding doing something E.G. *evasion of arrest.*

evasive

ADJECTIVE deliberately trying to avoid talking about or doing something E.G. *He was evasive about his past.*

eve eves

NOUN the evening or day before an event or occasion E.G. *on the eve of the battle.*

even evens evening evened

ADJECTIVE **1** flat and level E.G. *an even layer of chocolate.* **2** regular and without variation E.G. *an even temperature.* **3** In maths, numbers that are even can be divided exactly by two E.G. *4 is an even number.* **4** Scores that are even are exactly the same. ▶ ADVERB **5** 'Even' is used to suggest that something is unexpected or surprising E.G. *I haven't even got a bank account.* **6** 'Even' is also used to say that something is greater in degree than something else E.G. *This was an opportunity to obtain even more money.* ▶ PHRASE **7** **Even if** or **even though** is used to introduce something that is surprising in relation to the main part of the sentence E.G. *She was too kind to say anything, even though she was jealous.*

evenly ADVERB

▤ (sense 1) flat, level, straight
▤ (sense 4) equal, level

evening evenings

NOUN the part of the day between late afternoon and the time you go to bed.

event events

NOUN **1** something that happens, especially when it is unusual or important. **2** one of the competitions that are part of an organized

A
B
C
D
E
F
G
H
I
J
K
L
M
N
O
P
Q
R
S
T
U
V
W
X
Y
Z

occasion, especially in sports. ► PHRASE
3 If you say **in any event**, you mean
whatever happens E.G. *In any event
we must get on with our own lives.*
■ (sense 1) happening, incident,
occurrence

eventful
ADJECTIVE full of interesting and
important events.

eventual
ADJECTIVE happening or being
achieved in the end E.G. *He remained
confident of eventual victory.*

eventuality eventualities
NOUN a possible future event or result
E.G. *equipment to cope with most
eventualities.*

eventually
ADVERB in the end E.G. *Eventually I got
to Berlin.*

ever
ADVERB **1** at any time E.G. *Have you
ever seen anything like it?* **2** all the
time E.G. *The President will come
under ever more pressure to resign.*
3 'Ever' is used to give emphasis to
what you are saying E.G. *I'm as happy
here as ever I was in England.* ► PHRASE
4 INFORMAL **Ever so** means very E.G.
Thank you ever so much.

evergreen evergreens
NOUN a tree or bush which has green
leaves all the year round.

everlasting
ADJECTIVE never coming to an end.

every
ADJECTIVE **1** 'Every' is used to refer to all
the members of a particular group,
separately and one by one E.G. *We
eat out every night.* **2** 'Every' is used to
mean the greatest or the best
possible degree of something E.G.
He has every reason to avoid the

subject. **3** 'Every' is also used to
indicate that something happens at
regular intervals E.G. *renewable every
five years.* ► PHRASE **4 Every other**
means each alternate E.G. *I see Lisa
at least every other week.*

everybody
PRONOUN **1** all the people in a group
E.G. *He obviously thinks everybody in
the place knows him.* **2** all the people
in the world E.G. *Everybody has a
hobby.*
☑ *Everybody* and *everyone* mean the
same.

everyday
ADJECTIVE usual or ordinary E.G. *the
everyday drudgery of work.*

everyone
PRONOUN **1** all the people in a group.
2 all the people in the world
☑ *Everyone* and *everybody* mean the
same.

everything
PRONOUN **1** all or the whole of
something. **2** the most important
thing E.G. *When I was 20, friends were
everything to me.*

everywhere
ADVERB in or to all places.

evict evicts evicting evicted
VERB To evict someone means to
officially force them to leave a place
they are occupying.

eviction NOUN

evidence
NOUN **1** Evidence is anything you see,
read, or are told which gives you
reason to believe something.
2 Evidence is the information used in
court to attempt to prove or
disprove something.

evident
ADJECTIVE easily noticed or understood

E.G. *His love of nature is evident in his paintings*.

evidently ADVERB

evil evils

NOUN **1** Evil is a force or power that is believed to cause wicked or bad things to happen. **2** a very unpleasant or harmful situation or activity E.G. *the evils of war*. ▶ ADJECTIVE **3** Someone or something that is evil is morally wrong or bad E.G. *evil influences*.

evoke evokes evoking evoked

VERB To evoke an emotion, memory, or reaction means to cause it E.G. *Enthusiasm was evoked by the appearance of the Prince*.

evolution

Said "ee-vol-oo-shn" NOUN **1** Evolution is a process of gradual change taking place over many generations during which living things slowly change as they adapt to different environments. **2** Evolution is also any process of gradual change and development over a period of time E.G. *the evolution of the European Union*.

evolutionary ADJECTIVE

evolve evolves evolving evolved

VERB **1** If something evolves or if you evolve it, it develops gradually over a period of time E.G. *I was given a brief to evolve a system of training*. **2** When living things evolve, they gradually change and develop into different forms over a period of time.

ewe ewes

Said "yoo" NOUN a female sheep.

ex-

PREFIX 'Ex' means 'former' E.G. *her ex-husband*.

📖 from Greek *ek-* meaning 'out of' or 'away from'

exacerbate exacerbates exacerbating exacerbated

Said "ig-**zass**-er-bate" VERB To exacerbate something means to make it worse.

exact exacts exacting exacted

ADJECTIVE **1** correct and complete in every detail E.G. *an exact replica of the Santa Maria*. **2** accurate and precise, as opposed to approximate E.G. *Mystery surrounds the exact circumstances of his death*. ▶ VERB **3** FORMAL If somebody or something exacts something from you, they demand or obtain it from you, especially through force E.G. *The navy was on its way to exact a terrible revenge*.

exactly

ADVERB **1** with complete accuracy and precision E.G. *That's exactly what happened*. **2** You can use 'exactly' to emphasize the truth of a statement, or a similarity or close relationship between one thing and another E.G. *It's exactly the same colour*.

exaggerate exaggerates exaggerating exaggerated

VERB **1** If you exaggerate, you make the thing you are describing seem better, worse, bigger, or more important than it really is. **2** To exaggerate something means to make it more noticeable than usual E.G. *His Irish accent was exaggerated for the benefit of the joke he was telling*.

exaggeration NOUN

exalted

ADJECTIVE; FORMAL Someone who is exalted is very important.

exam exams

NOUN an official test set to find out

a
b
c
d
e
f
g
h
i
j
k
l
m
n
o
p
q
r
s
t
u
v
w
x
y
z

A
B
C
D
E
F
G
H
I
J
K
L
M
N
O
P
Q
R
S
T
U
V
W
X
Y
Z

your knowledge or skill in a subject.

examination examinations
NOUN 1 an exam. 2 If you make an examination of something, you inspect it very carefully E.G. *I carried out a careful examination of the hull.* 3 A medical examination is a check by a doctor to find out the state of your health.

examine examines examining examined
VERB 1 If you examine something, you inspect it very carefully. 2 (EXAM TERM) To examine a subject is to look closely at the issues involved and form your own opinion. 3 To examine someone means to find out their knowledge or skill in a particular subject by testing them. 4 If a doctor examines you, he or she checks your body to find out the state of your health.

examiner examiners
NOUN a person who sets or marks an exam.

example examples
NOUN 1 something which represents or is typical of a group or set E.G. *some examples of early Spanish music.* 2 If you say someone or something is an example to people, you mean that people can imitate and learn from them. ▶ PHRASE 3 You use **for example** to give an example of something you are talking about.
■ (sense 1) sample, specimen

exasperate exasperates exasperating exasperated
VERB If someone or something exasperates you, they irritate you and make you angry.
exasperating ADJECTIVE
exasperation NOUN

excavate excavates excavating excavated
VERB To excavate means to remove earth from the ground by digging.
excavation NOUN

exceed exceeds exceeding exceeded
VERB To exceed something such as a limit means to go beyond it or to become greater than it E.G. *the first aircraft to exceed the speed of sound.*

exceedingly
ADVERB extremely or very much.

excel excels excelling excelled
VERB If someone excels in something, they are very good at doing it.

Excellency Excellencies
NOUN a title used to address an official of very high rank, such as an ambassador or a governor.

excellent
ADJECTIVE very good indeed.
excellence NOUN
■ first-rate, outstanding, superb

except
PREPOSITION Except or except for means other than or apart from E.G. *All my family were musicians except my father.*

exception exceptions
NOUN somebody or something that is not included in a general statement or rule E.G. *English, like every language, has exceptions to its rules.*

exceptional
ADJECTIVE 1 unusually talented or clever. 2 unusual and likely to happen very rarely.
exceptionally ADVERB

excerpt excerpts
NOUN a short piece of writing or music which is taken from a larger piece.

excess excesses

NOUN **1** Excess is behaviour which goes beyond normally acceptable limits E.G. *a life of excess*. **2** a larger amount of something than is needed, usual, or healthy E.G. *an excess of energy*. ▶ ADJECTIVE **3** more than is needed, allowed, or healthy E.G. *excess weight*. ▶ PHRASE **4 In excess of** a particular amount means more than that amount E.G. *a fortune in excess of 150 million pounds*. **5** If you do something **to excess**, you do it too much E.G. *She drank to excess*.

excessive

ADJECTIVE too great in amount or degree E.G. *using excessive force*.
excessively ADVERB

exchange exchanges exchanging exchanged

VERB (SCIENCE) **1** To exchange things means to give or receive one thing in return for another E.G. *They exchange small presents on Christmas Eve*. ▶ NOUN **2** the act of giving or receiving something in return for something else E.G. *an exchange of letters… exchanges of gunfire*. **3** a place where people trade and do business E.G. *the stock exchange*.

exchequer

Said "iks-chek-er" NOUN The exchequer is the department in the government in Britain and other countries which is responsible for money belonging to the state.

excise

NOUN Excise is a tax put on goods produced for sale in the country that produces them.

excitable

ADJECTIVE easily excited.

excite excites exciting excited

VERB **1** If somebody or something excites you, they make you feel very happy and nervous or very interested and enthusiastic. **2** If something excites a particular feeling, it causes somebody to have that feeling E.G. *This excited my suspicion*.

excited ADJECTIVE **excitedly** ADVERB
exciting ADJECTIVE **excitement** NOUN

▣ (sense 1) arouse, thrill

exclaim exclaims exclaiming exclaimed

VERB When you exclaim, you cry out suddenly or loudly because you are excited or shocked.

exclamation exclamations

NOUN (ENGLISH) a word or phrase spoken suddenly to express a strong feeling.

exclamation mark exclamation marks

NOUN a punctuation mark (!) used in writing to express a strong feeling.

What does the Exclamation Mark do?

The **exclamation mark** (!) is used after emphatic expressions and exclamations:

  E.G. *I can't believe it!*

The exclamation mark can lose its effect if used too much. After a sentence expressing mild excitement or humour, it is better to use a full stop:

  E.G. *It is a beautiful day*.

---

exclude excludes excluding excluded

a b c d e f g h i j k l m n o p q r s t u v w x y z

VERB **1** If you exclude something, you deliberately do not include it or do not consider it. **2** If you exclude somebody from a place or an activity, you prevent them from entering the place or taking part in the activity.

exclusion NOUN

exclusive exclusives

ADJECTIVE **1** available to or for the use of a small group of rich or privileged people E.G. *an exclusive club.* **2** belonging to a particular person or group only E.G. *exclusive rights to coverage of the Olympic Games.*
▶ NOUN **3** a story or interview which appears in only one newspaper or on only one television programme.

exclusively ADVERB

excrement

Said "**eks**-krim-ment" NOUN Excrement is the solid waste matter that is passed out of a person's or animal's body through their bowels.

excrete excretes excreting excreted

VERB When you excrete waste matter from your body, you get rid of it, for example by going to the lavatory or by sweating.

excretion NOUN   **excretory** ADJECTIVE

excruciating

Said "iks-**kroo**-shee-ate-ing" ADJECTIVE unbearably painful.

excruciatingly ADVERB
📖 from Latin *excruciare* meaning 'to torture'

excursion excursions

NOUN a short journey or outing.

excuse excuses excusing excused

NOUN **1** a reason which you give to explain why something has been done, has not been done, or will not be done. ▶ VERB **2** If you excuse yourself or something that you have done, you give reasons defending your actions. **3** If you excuse somebody for something wrong they have done, you forgive them for it. **4** If you excuse somebody from a duty or responsibility, you free them from it E.G. *He was excused from standing trial because of ill health.*
▶ PHRASE **5** You say **excuse me** to try to catch somebody's attention or to apologize for an interruption or for rude behaviour.

execute executes executing executed

VERB **1** To execute somebody means to kill them as a punishment for a crime. **2** If you execute something such as a plan or an action, you carry it out or perform it E.G. *The crime had been planned and executed in Montreal.*

execution NOUN

executioner executioners

NOUN a person whose job is to execute criminals.

executive executives

NOUN **1** a person who is employed by a company at a senior level. **2** The executive of an organization is a committee which has the authority to make decisions and ensure that they are carried out. ▶ ADJECTIVE **3** concerned with making important decisions and ensuring that they are carried out E.G. *the commission's executive director.*

executor executors

Said "ig-**zek**-yoo-tor" NOUN a person you appoint to carry out the instructions in your will.

exemplary
ADJECTIVE **1** being a good example and worthy of imitation E.G. *an exemplary performance*. **2** serving as a warning E.G. *an exemplary tale*.

exemplify exemplifies exemplifying exemplified
VERB **1** To exemplify something means to be a typical example of it E.G. *This aircraft exemplifies the advantages of European technological cooperation*. **2** If you exemplify something, you give an example of it.

exempt exempts exempting exempted
ADJECTIVE **1** excused from a rule or duty E.G. *people exempt from prescription charges*. ▶ VERB **2** To exempt someone from a rule, duty, or obligation means to excuse them from it.
exemption NOUN

exercise exercises exercising exercised
NOUN **1** (PE) Exercise is any activity which you do to get fit or remain healthy. **2** Exercises are also activities which you do to practise and train for a particular skill E.G. *piano exercises… a mathematical exercise*. ▶ VERB **3** When you exercise, you do activities which help you to get fit and remain healthy. **4** If you exercise your rights or responsibilities, you use them.

exert exerts exerting exerted
VERB **1** To exert pressure means to apply it. **2** If you exert yourself, you make a physical or mental effort to do something.

exertion exertions
NOUN Exertion is vigorous physical effort or exercise.

exhale exhales exhaling exhaled
VERB When you exhale, you breathe out.

exhaust exhausts exhausting exhausted
VERB **1** To exhaust somebody means to make them very tired E.G. *Several lengths of the pool left her exhausted*. **2** If you exhaust a supply of something such as money or food, you use it up completely. **3** If you exhaust a subject, you talk about it so much that there is nothing else to say about it. ▶ NOUN **4** a pipe which carries the gas or steam out of the engine of a vehicle.
exhaustion NOUN
▣ (sense 1) fatigue, tire out, wear out

exhaustive
ADJECTIVE thorough and complete E.G. *an exhaustive series of tests*.
exhaustively ADVERB

exhibit exhibits exhibiting exhibited
VERB **1** To exhibit things means to show them in a public place for people to see. **2** If you exhibit your feelings or abilities, you display them so that other people can see them. ▶ NOUN **3** anything which is put on show for the public to see.

exhibition exhibitions
NOUN (ART) a public display of works of art, products, or skills.

exhibitor exhibitors
NOUN a person whose work is being shown in an exhibition.

exhilarating
ADJECTIVE Something that is exhilarating makes you feel very happy and excited.

a
b
c
d
e
f
g
h
i
j
k
l
m
n
o
p
q
r
s
t
u
v
w
x
y
z

A
B
C
D
E
F
G
H
I
J
K
L
M
N
O
P
Q
R
S
T
U
V
W
X
Y
Z

exile exiles exiling exiled

NOUN 1 If somebody lives in exile, they live in a foreign country because they cannot live in their own country, usually for political reasons. 2 a person who lives in exile. ▶ VERB 3 If somebody is exiled, they are sent away from their own country and not allowed to return.

exist exists existing existed

VERB If something exists, it is present in the world as a real or living thing.

existence

NOUN 1 Existence is the state of being or existing. 2 a way of living or being E.G. *an idyllic existence*.

exit exits exiting exited

NOUN 1 a way out of a place. 2 If you make an exit, you leave a place. ▶ VERB 3 To exit means to go out. 4 (DRAMA) An actor exits when he or she leaves the stage.

exodus

NOUN An exodus is the departure of a large number of people from a place.

exotic

ADJECTIVE 1 attractive or interesting through being unusual E.G. *exotic fabrics*. 2 coming from a foreign country E.G. *exotic plants*.
🔲 from Greek *exotikos* meaning 'foreign'

expand expands expanding expanded

VERB 1 If something expands or you expand it, it becomes larger in number or size. 2 If you expand on something, you give more details about it E.G. *The minister's speech expanded on the aims which he outlined last month*.

expansion NOUN

expanse expanses

NOUN a very large or widespread area E.G. *a vast expanse of pine forests*.

expansive

ADJECTIVE 1 Something that is expansive is very wide or extends over a very large area E.G. *the expansive countryside*. 2 Someone who is expansive is friendly, open, or talkative.

expatriate expatriates

Said "eks-**pat**-ree-it" NOUN someone who is living in a country which is not their own.

expect expects expecting expected

VERB 1 If you expect something to happen, you believe that it will happen E.G. *The trial is expected to end today*. 2 If you are expecting somebody or something, you believe that they are going to arrive or to happen E.G. *The Queen was expecting the chambermaid*. 3 If you expect something, you believe that it is your right to get it or have it E.G. *He seemed to expect a reply*.
🔲 (sense 1) anticipate, look forward to

expectancy

NOUN Expectancy is the feeling that something is about to happen, especially something exciting.

expectant

ADJECTIVE 1 If you are expectant, you believe that something is about to happen, especially something exciting. 2 An expectant mother or father is someone whose baby is going to be born soon.

expectantly ADVERB

expectation expectations

NOUN Expectation or an expectation

expedient expedients

Said "iks-*pee-dee-ent*" NOUN **1** an action or plan that achieves a particular purpose but that may not be morally acceptable E.G. *Many firms have improved their profitability by the simple expedient of cutting staff.* ► ADJECTIVE **2** Something that is expedient is useful or convenient in a particular situation.

expediency NOUN

expedition expeditions

NOUN **1** an organized journey made for a special purpose, such as to explore; also the party of people who make such a journey. **2** a short journey or outing E.G. *shopping expeditions.*

expeditionary ADJECTIVE

expel expels expelling expelled

VERB **1** If someone is expelled from a school or club, they are officially told to leave because they have behaved badly. **2** If a gas or liquid is expelled from a place, it is forced out of it.

expend expends expending expended

VERB To expend energy, time, or money means to use it up or spend it.

expendable

ADJECTIVE no longer useful or necessary, and therefore able to be got rid of.

expenditure

NOUN Expenditure is the total amount of money spent on something.

expense expenses

NOUN **1** Expense is the money that something costs E.G. *the expense of installing a burglar alarm.* ► PLURAL NOUN **2** Expenses are the money

somebody spends while doing something connected with their work, which is paid back to them by their employer.

■ (sense 1) cost, expenditure, outlay

expensive

ADJECTIVE costing a lot of money.

expensively ADVERB

experience experiences experiencing experienced

NOUN **1** Experience consists of all the things that you have done or that have happened to you. **2** something that you do or something that happens to you, especially something new or unusual. ► VERB **3** If you experience a situation or feeling, it happens to you or you are affected by it.

■ (sense 3) go through, undergo

experiment experiments experimenting experimented

NOUN **1** the testing of something, either to find out its effect or to prove something. ► VERB **2** If you experiment with something, you do a scientific test on it to prove or discover something.

experimentation NOUN

experimental ADJECTIVE

experimentally ADVERB

expert experts

NOUN **1** a person who is very skilled at doing something or very knowledgeable about a particular subject. ► ADJECTIVE **2** having or requiring special skill or knowledge E.G. *expert advice.*

expertly ADVERB

■ (sense 1) authority, master, specialist

expertise

Said "eks-per-*teez*" NOUN Expertise is

a
b
c
d
e
f
g
h
i
j
k
l
m
n
o
p
q
r
s
t
u
v
w
x
y
z

Elaine and Emily shout EE when they mEEt to grEEt each other (-ee-)   SPELLING NOTE

special skill or knowledge.

expire expires expiring expired

VERB When something expires, it reaches the end of the period of time for which it is valid E.G. *My contract expires in the summer.*

expiry NOUN

explain explains explaining explained

VERB If you explain something, you give details about it or reasons for it so that it can be understood.

explanation NOUN **explanatory** ADJECTIVE

■ clarify, elucidate, make clear

explicit

ADJECTIVE shown or expressed clearly and openly E.G. *an explicit death threat.*

explicitly ADVERB

explode explodes exploding exploded

VERB 1 If something such as a bomb explodes, it bursts loudly and with great force, often causing damage. 2 If somebody explodes, they express strong feelings suddenly or violently E.G. *I half expected him to explode in anger.* 3 When something increases suddenly and rapidly, it can be said to explode E.G. *Sales of men's toiletries have exploded.*

📖 from Latin *explodere* meaning 'to clap someone offstage', from *ex* meaning 'out of' + *plodere* meaning 'to clap'

exploit exploits exploiting exploited

VERB 1 If somebody exploits a person or a situation, they take advantage of them for their own ends E.G. *Critics claim he exploited black musicians.* 2 If you exploit something, you make the

best use of it, often for profit E.G. *exploiting the power of computers.*

▶ NOUN 3 something daring or interesting that somebody has done E.G. *His courage and exploits were legendary.*

exploitation NOUN

explore explores exploring explored

VERB 1 If you explore a place, you travel in it to find out what it is like. 2 If you explore an idea, you think about it carefully.

exploration NOUN **exploratory** ADJECTIVE **explorer** NOUN

explosion explosions

NOUN a sudden violent burst of energy, for example one caused by a bomb.

explosive explosives

ADJECTIVE 1 capable of exploding or likely to explode. 2 happening suddenly and making a loud noise. 3 An explosive situation is one which is likely to have serious or dangerous effects. ▶ NOUN 4 a substance or device that can explode.

exponent exponents

NOUN 1 An exponent of an idea or plan is someone who puts it forward. 2 FORMAL An exponent of a skill or activity is someone who is good at it.

export exports exporting exported

VERB 1 To export goods means to send them to another country and sell them there. ▶ NOUN 2 Exports are goods which are sent to another country and sold.

exporter NOUN

expose exposes exposing exposed

VERB 1 To expose something means to

uncover it and make it visible. **2** To expose a person to something dangerous means to put them in a situation in which it might harm them E.G. *exposed to tobacco smoke*. **3** To expose a person or situation means to reveal the truth about them.

exposition expositions
NOUN a detailed explanation of a particular subject.

exposure exposures
NOUN **1** Exposure is the exposing of something. **2** Exposure is the harmful effect on the body caused by very cold weather.

express expresses expressing expressed
VERB **1** When you express an idea or feeling, you show what you think or feel by saying or doing something. **2** If you express a quantity in a particular form, you write it down in that form E.G. *The result of the equation is usually expressed as a percentage.* ▶ ADJECTIVE **3** very fast E.G. *express delivery service.* ▶ NOUN **4** a fast train or coach which stops at only a few places.

expression expressions
NOUN **1** Your expression is the look on your face which shows what you are thinking or feeling. **2** (ENGLISH) The expression of ideas or feelings is the showing of them through words, actions, or art. **3** a word or phrase used in communicating E.G. *the expression 'nosey parker'.*

expressive
ADJECTIVE **1** showing feelings clearly. **2** full of expression.

expressway expressways
NOUN a road designed for fast-moving traffic.

expulsion expulsions
NOUN The expulsion of someone from a place or institution is the act of officially banning them from that place or institution E.G. *the high number of school expulsions.*

exquisite
ADJECTIVE extremely beautiful and pleasing.

extend extends extending extended
VERB **1** If something extends for a distance, it continues and stretches into the distance. **2** If something extends from a surface or an object, it sticks out from it. **3** If you extend something, you make it larger or longer E.G. *The table had been extended to seat fifty.*

extension extensions
NOUN **1** a room or building which is added to an existing building. **2** an extra period of time for which something continues to exist or be valid E.G. *an extension to his visa.* **3** an additional telephone connected to the same line as another telephone.

extensive
ADJECTIVE **1** covering a large area. **2** very great in effect E.G. *extensive repairs.*

extensively ADVERB

extent extents
NOUN The extent of something is its length, area, or size.

exterior exteriors
NOUN **1** The exterior of something is its outside. **2** Your exterior is your outward appearance.

exterminate exterminates exterminating exterminated
VERB When animals or people are

A
B
C
D
E
F
G
H
I
J
K
L
M
N
O
P
Q
R
S
T
U
V
W
X
Y
Z

exterminated, they are deliberately killed.

extermination NOUN

external externals
ADJECTIVE existing or happening on the outside or outer part of something.

externally ADVERB

extinct
ADJECTIVE 1 An extinct species of animal or plant is no longer in existence. 2 An extinct volcano is no longer likely to erupt.

extinction NOUN

extinguish extinguishes extinguishing extinguished
VERB To extinguish a light or fire means to put it out.

extortionate
ADJECTIVE more expensive than you consider to be fair.

extra extras
ADJECTIVE 1 more than is usual, necessary, or expected. ▶ NOUN 2 anything which is additional. 3 a person who is hired to play a very small and unimportant part in a film. ◼ (sense 1) added, additional, further

extra-
PREFIX 'Extra' means 'outside' or 'beyond' E.G. *extraordinary*. ⬚ from Latin *exterus* meaning 'outward'

extract extracts extracting extracted
VERB 1 To extract something from a place means to take it out or get it out, often by force. 2 If you extract information from someone, you get it from them with difficulty. ▶ NOUN (LIBRARY) 3 a small section taken from a book or piece of music.

extraction
NOUN 1 Your extraction is the country or people that your family originally comes from E.G. *a Malaysian citizen of Australian extraction*. 2 Extraction is the process of taking or getting something out of a place.

extraordinary
ADJECTIVE unusual or surprising.

extraordinarily ADVERB
◼ exceptional, remarkable, unusual

extravagant
ADJECTIVE 1 spending or costing more money than is reasonable or affordable. 2 going beyond reasonable limits.

extravagantly ADVERB
extravagance NOUN

extravaganza extravaganzas
NOUN a spectacular and expensive public show.

extreme extremes
ADJECTIVE 1 very great in degree or intensity E.G. *extreme caution*. 2 going beyond what is usual or reasonable E.G. *extreme weather conditions*. 3 at the furthest point or edge of something E.G. *the extreme northern corner of Spain*. ▶ NOUN 4 the highest or furthest degree of something.

extremely ADVERB

extremist extremists
NOUN a person who uses unreasonable or violent methods to bring about political change.

extremism NOUN

extremity extremities
NOUN The extremities of something are its furthest ends or edges.

extricate extricates extricating extricated
VERB To extricate someone from a

place or a situation means to free them from it.

extrovert extroverts
NOUN a person who is more interested in other people and the world around them than their own thoughts and feelings.
📖 from Latin *extra* meaning 'outwards' + *vertere* meaning 'to turn'

exuberant
ADJECTIVE full of energy and cheerfulness.
exuberantly ADVERB **exuberance** NOUN

exude exudes exuding exuded
VERB If someone exudes a quality or feeling, they seem to have it to a great degree.

eye eyes eyeing or eying eyed
NOUN 1 the organ of sight. 2 the small hole at the end of a needle through which you pass the thread. ▶ VERB 3 To eye something means to look at it carefully or suspiciously.

eyeball eyeballs
NOUN the whole of the ball-shaped part of the eye.

eyebrow eyebrows
NOUN Your eyebrows are the lines of hair which grow on the ridges of bone above your eyes.

eyelash eyelashes
NOUN Your eyelashes are hairs that grow on the edges of your eyelids.

eyelid eyelids
NOUN Your eyelids are the folds of skin which cover your eyes when they are closed.

eyesight
NOUN Your eyesight is your ability to see.

eyesore eyesores
NOUN Something that is an eyesore is extremely ugly.

eyewitness eyewitnesses
NOUN a person who has seen an event and can describe what happened.

eyrie eyries
Said "ear-ee" NOUN the nest of an eagle or other bird of prey.

a
b
c
d
e
f
g
h
i
j
k
l
m
n
o
p
q
r
s
t
u
v
w
x
y
z

Ff

A B C D E **F** G H I J K L M N O P Q R S T U V W X Y Z

> **TIP** Some words which sound as if they should begin with the letter *f* actually begin with the letters *ph*, for example *pharmacy*, *pharaoh* and *phrase*. The *ph* combination, pronounced like *f*, comes in the middle of some words too, for example *amphetamine* and *emphasis*.

fable fables
NOUN a story intended to teach a moral lesson.
📖 from Latin *fabula* meaning 'story'

fabled
ADJECTIVE well-known because many stories have been told about it E.G. *the fabled city of Troy.*

fabric fabrics
NOUN (D&T) 1 cloth E.G. *tough fabric for tents.* 2 The fabric of a building is its walls, roof, and other parts. 3 The fabric of a society or system is its structure, laws, and customs E.G. *the democratic fabric of American society.*

fabricate fabricates fabricating fabricated
VERB 1 If you fabricate a story or an explanation, you invent it in order to deceive people. 2 To fabricate something is to make or manufacture it.

fabrication NOUN

fabulous
ADJECTIVE 1 wonderful or very impressive E.G. *a fabulous picnic.* 2 not real, but happening in stories and legends E.G. *fabulous creatures.*

facade facades
Said "fas-**sahd**" NOUN 1 the front outside wall of a building. 2 a false outward appearance E.G. *the facade of honesty.*

face faces facing faced
NOUN 1 the front part of your head from your chin to your forehead. 2 the expression someone has or is making E.G. *a grim face.* 3 a surface or side of something, especially the most important side E.G. *the north face of Everest.* 4 the main aspect or general appearance of something E.G. *We have changed the face of language study.* ▶ VERB 5 To face something or someone is to be opposite them or to look at them or towards them E.G. *a room that faces on to the street.* 6 If you face something difficult or unpleasant, you have to deal with it E.G. *She faced a terrible dilemma.* ▶ PHRASE 7 **On the face of it** means judging by the appearance of something or your initial reaction to it E.G. *On the face of it the palace looks gigantic.*
▤ (sense 1) countenance, visage

faceless
ADJECTIVE without character or individuality E.G. *anonymous shops and faceless coffee-bars.*

face-lift face-lifts
NOUN 1 an operation to tighten the skin on someone's face to make them look younger. 2 If you give something a face-lift, you clean it or improve its appearance.

facet facets
Said "fas-it" NOUN 1 a single part or aspect of something E.G. *the many facets of his talent.* 2 one of the flat,

cut surfaces of a precious stone.
📷 from French *facette* meaning 'little face'

facetious
Said "fas-**see**-shuss" ADJECTIVE witty or amusing but in a rather silly or inappropriate way E.G. *He didn't appreciate my facetious suggestion.*
📷 from Latin *facetiae* meaning 'witty remarks'

facial
Said "**fay**-shal" ADJECTIVE appearing on or being part of the face E.G. *facial expressions.*

facilitate facilitates facilitating facilitated
VERB To facilitate something is to make it easier for it to happen E.G. *a process that will facilitate individual development.*

facility facilities
NOUN 1 a service or piece of equipment which makes it possible to do something E.G. *excellent shopping facilities.* 2 A facility for something is an ability to do it easily or well E.G. *a facility for novel-writing.*

fact facts
NOUN 1 a piece of knowledge or information that is true or something that has actually happened. ▶ PHRASES 2 **In fact**, **as a matter of fact**, and **in point of fact** mean 'actually' or 'really' and are used for emphasis or when making an additional comment E.G. *Very few people, in fact, have this type of skin.*
factual ADJECTIVE **factually** ADVERB

faction factions
NOUN a small group of people belonging to a larger group, but differing from the larger group in some aims or ideas E.G. *a conservative faction in the Church.*

fact of life facts of life
NOUN 1 The facts of life are details about sexual intercourse and how babies are conceived and born. 2 If you say that something is a fact of life, you mean that it is something that people expect to happen, even though they might find it shocking or unpleasant E.G. *War is a fact of life.*

factor factors
NOUN 1 something that helps to cause a result E.G. *House dust mites are a major factor in asthma.* 2 The factors of a number are the whole numbers that will divide exactly into it. For example, 2 and 5 are factors of 10. 3 If something increases by a particular factor, it is multiplied that number of times E.G. *The amount of energy used has increased by a factor of eight.*
▤ (sense 1) cause, element, part

factory factories
NOUN a building or group of buildings where goods are made in large quantities.

faculty faculties
NOUN 1 Your faculties are your physical and mental abilities E.G. *My mental faculties are as sharp as ever.* 2 In some universities, a Faculty is a group of related departments E.G. *the Science Faculty.*

fad fads
NOUN an temporary fashion or craze E.G. *the latest exercise fad.*

fade fades fading faded
VERB If something fades, the intensity of its colour, brightness, or sound is gradually reduced.

faeces or feces
Said "**fee**-seez" PLURAL NOUN the solid

a
b
c
d
e
f
g
h
i
j
k
l
m
n
o
p
q
r
s
t
u
v
w
x
y
z

A
B
C
D
E
F
G
H
I
J
K
L
M
N
O
P
Q
R
S
T
U
V
W
X
Y
Z

waste substances discharged from a person's or animal's body.

📖 from Latin *faeces* meaning 'dregs'

fag fags

NOUN INFORMAL a cigarette.

Fahrenheit

Said "**far-ren-hite**" NOUN a scale of temperature in which the freezing point of water is 32° and the boiling point is 212°.

fail fails failing failed

VERB 1 If someone fails to achieve something, they are not successful. 2 If you fail an exam, your marks are too low and you do not pass. 3 If you fail to do something that you should have done, you do not do it E.G. *They failed to phone her.* 4 If something fails, it becomes less effective or stops working properly E.G. *The power failed… His grandmother's eyesight began to fail.* ► NOUN 5 In an exam, a fail is a piece of work that is not good enough to pass. ► PHRASE 6 **Without fail** means definitely or regularly E.G. *Every Sunday her mum would ring without fail.*

🔲 (sense 1) be unsuccessful, flop

failing failings

NOUN 1 a fault in something or someone. ► PREPOSITION 2 used to introduce an alternative E.G. *Failing that, get a market stall.*

failure failures

NOUN 1 lack of success E.G. *Not all conservation programmes ended in failure.* 2 an unsuccessful person, thing, or action E.G. *The venture was a complete failure.* 3 Your failure to do something is not doing something that you were expected to do E.G. *a statement explaining his failure to turn up as a speaker.*

🔲 (sense 2) flop, loser, washout

faint fainter faintest; faints fainting fainted

ADJECTIVE 1 A sound, colour, or feeling that is faint is not very strong or intense. 2 If you feel faint, you feel weak, dizzy, and unsteady. ► VERB 3 If you faint, you lose consciousness for a short time.

faintly ADVERB

🔲 (sense 3) black out, pass out, swoon

fair fairer fairest; fairs

ADJECTIVE 1 reasonable and just E.G. *fair and prompt trials for political prisoners.* 2 quite large E.G. *a fair size envelope.* 3 moderately good or likely to be correct E.G. *He had a fair idea of what to expect.* 4 having light coloured hair or pale skin. 5 with pleasant and dry weather E.G. *Ireland's fair weather months.* ► NOUN 6 a form of entertainment that takes place outside, with stalls, sideshows, and machines to ride on. 7 an exhibition of goods produced by a particular industry E.G. *International Wine and Food Fair.*

fairly ADVERB **fairness** NOUN

🔲 (sense 1) impartial, just, unbiased

fairground fairgrounds

NOUN an outdoor area where a fair is set up.

fairway fairways

NOUN the area of trimmed grass between a tee and a green on a golf course.

fairy fairies

NOUN In stories, fairies are small, supernatural creatures with magical powers.

fairy tale fairy tales

NOUN a story of magical events.

faith faiths
NOUN 1 Faith is a feeling of confidence, trust or optimism about something. 2 `RE` someone's faith is their religion.

faithful
ADJECTIVE 1 loyal to someone or something and remaining firm in support of them. 2 accurate and truthful E.G. *a faithful copy of an original*.
faithfully ADVERB **faithfulness** NOUN
■ (sense 1) loyal, steadfast, trusty

fake fakes faking faked
NOUN 1 an imitation of something made to trick people into thinking that it is genuine. ► ADJECTIVE 2 imitation and not genuine E.G. *fake fur*. ► VERB 3 If you fake a feeling, you pretend that you are experiencing it.
■ (sense 1) copy, imitation, sham
■ (sense 2) artificial, false, phoney
■ (sense 3) feign, pretend, simulate

falcon falcons
NOUN a bird of prey that can be trained to hunt other birds or small animals.
▥ from Latin *falco* meaning 'hawk'

fall falls falling fell fallen
VERB 1 If someone or something falls or falls over, they drop towards the ground. 2 If something falls somewhere, it lands there E.G. *The spotlight fell on her*. 3 If something falls in amount or strength, it becomes less E.G. *Steel production fell about 25%*. 4 If a person or group in a position of power falls, they lose their position and someone else takes control. 5 Someone who falls in battle is killed. 6 If, for example, you fall asleep, fall ill, or fall in love, you change quite quickly to that new state. 7 If you fall for someone, you become strongly attracted to them and fall in love. 8 If you fall for a trick or lie, you are deceived by it. 9 Something that falls on a particular date occurs on that date. ► NOUN 10 If you have a fall, you accidentally fall over. 11 A fall of snow, soot, or other substance is a quantity of it that has fallen to the ground. 12 A fall in something is a reduction in its amount or strength. 13 In America, autumn is called the fall.

fall down VERB An argument or idea that falls down on a particular point is weak on that point and as a result will be unsuccessful.

fall out VERB If people fall out, they disagree and quarrel.

fall through VERB If an arrangement or plan falls through, it fails or is abandoned.

fallacy fallacies
Said "fal-lass-ee" NOUN something false that is generally believed to be true.
▥ from Latin *fallacia* meaning 'deception'

fallopian tube fallopian tubes
Said "fal-loh-pee-an" NOUN one of two tubes in a woman's body along which the eggs pass from the ovaries to the uterus.

fallout
NOUN radioactive particles that fall to the earth after a nuclear explosion.

fallow
ADJECTIVE Land that is fallow is not being used for crop growing so that it has the chance to rest and improve.

false
ADJECTIVE 1 untrue or incorrect E.G. *I*

a
b
c
d
e
f
g
h
i
j
k
l
m
n
o
p
q
r
s
t
u
v
w
x
y
z

there's a rAKE in the brAKEs (br**ake**)   SPELLING NOTE

A
B
C
D
E
F
G
H
I
J
K
L
M
N
O
P
Q
R
S
T
U
V
W
X
Y
Z

think that's a false argument. **2** not real or genuine but intended to seem real E.G. *false hair.* **3** unfaithful or deceitful.

falsely ADVERB   **falsity** NOUN

falsehood falsehoods

NOUN **1** the quality or fact of being untrue E.G. *the difference between truth and falsehood.* **2** a lie.

falsify falsifies falsifying falsified

VERB If you falsify something, you change it in order to deceive people.

falsification NOUN

falter falters faltering faltered

VERB If someone or something falters, they hesitate or become unsure or unsteady E.G. *Her voice faltered.*

fame

NOUN the state of being very well-known.

∎ prominence, renown, repute

famed

ADJECTIVE very well-known E.G. *an area famed for its beauty.*

familiar

ADJECTIVE **1** well-known or easy to recognize E.G. *familiar faces.* **2** knowing or understanding something well E.G. *Most children are familiar with stories.*

familiarity NOUN   **familiarize** VERB

∎ (sense 1) recognizable, well-known

family families

NOUN **1** a group consisting of parents and their children; also all the people who are related to each other, including aunts and uncles, cousins, and grandparents. **2** a group of related species of animals or plants.

familial ADJECTIVE

family planning

NOUN the practice of controlling the

number of children you have, usually by using contraception.

famine famines

NOUN a serious shortage of food which may cause many deaths.

famished

ADJECTIVE; INFORMAL very hungry.

famous

ADJECTIVE very well-known.

∎ prominent, renowned, well-known

famously

ADVERB; OLD-FASHIONED If people get on famously, they enjoy each other's company very much.

fan fans fanning fanned

NOUN **1** If you are a fan of someone or something, you like them very much and are very enthusiastic about them. **2** a hand-held or mechanical object which creates a draught of cool air when it moves. ▶ VERB **3** To fan someone or something is to create a draught in their direction E.G. *The gentle wind fanned her from all sides.*

∎ (sense 1) admirer, enthusiast, supporter

fan out VERB If things or people fan out, they move outwards in different directions.

fanatic fanatics

NOUN a person who is very extreme in their support for a cause or in their enthusiasm for a particular activity.

fanaticism NOUN

▦ from Latin *fanaticus* meaning 'possessed by a god'

fanatical

ADJECTIVE If you are fanatical about something, you are very extreme in your enthusiasm or support for it.

fanatically ADVERB

∎ obsessive, overenthusiastic

fancy fancies fancying fancied; fancier fanciest

VERB **1** If you fancy something, you want to have it or do it E.G. *She fancied living in Canada.* ► ADJECTIVE **2** special and elaborate E.G. *dressed up in some fancy clothes.*

fanciful ADJECTIVE

■ (sense 2) elaborate, ornate

fancy dress

NOUN clothing worn for a party at which people dress up to look like a particular character or animal.

fanfare fanfares

NOUN a short, loud, musical introduction to a special event, usually played on trumpets.

fang fangs

NOUN Fangs are long, pointed teeth.

fantail fantails

NOUN **1** a pigeon with a large tail that can be opened out like a fan. **2** In Australia and New Zealand, a fantail is also a small, insect-eating bird with a fan-shaped tail.

fantasize fantasizes fantasizing fantasized; also spelt **fantasise**

VERB If you fantasize, you imagine pleasant but unlikely events or situations.

fantastic

ADJECTIVE **1** wonderful and very pleasing E.G. *a fantastic view of the sea.* **2** extremely large in degree or amount E.G. *fantastic debts.* **3** strange and difficult to believe E.G. *fantastic animals found nowhere else on earth.*

fantastically ADVERB

■ (sense 1) marvellous, wonderful

fantasy fantasies

NOUN **1** an imagined story or situation. **2** Fantasy is the activity of imagining things or the things that you

imagine E.G. *She can't distinguish between fantasy and reality.*

3 (LIBRARY) In books and films, fantasy is the people or situations in books or films which are created in the writer's imagination and do not reflect reality.

🔲 from Greek *phantasia* meaning 'imagination'

far farther farthest; further furthest

ADVERB **1** If something is far away from other things, it is a long distance away. **2** Far also means very much or to a great extent or degree E.G. *far more important.* ► ADJECTIVE **3** Far means very distant E.G. *in the far south of Africa.* **4** Far also describes the more distant of two things rather than the nearer one E.G. *the far corner of the goal.* ► PHRASE **5** By far and **far and away** are used to say that something is the best E.G. *Walking is by far the best way to get around.* **6** So far means up to the present moment E.G. *So far, it's been good news.* **7** As far as, so far as, and in so far as mean to the degree or extent that something is true E.G. *As far as I know he is progressing well.*

■ (sense 2) considerably, much

■ (sense 3) distant, remote

☑ When you are talking about a physical distance you can use *farther* and *farthest* or *further* and *furthest*. If you are talking about extra effort or time, use *further* and *furthest*: *a further delay is likely.*

farce farces

NOUN **1** a humorous play in which ridiculous and unlikely situations occur. **2** a disorganized and ridiculous situation.

farcical ADJECTIVE

a
b
c
d
e
f
g
h
i
j
k
l
m
n
o
p
q
r
s
t
u
v
w
x
y
z

A
B
C
D
E
F
G
H
I
J
K
L
M
N
O
P
Q
R
S
T
U
V
W
X
Y
Z

fare fares faring fared
NOUN **1** the amount charged for a
journey on a bus, train, or plane.
▶ VERB **2** How someone fares in a
particular situation is how they get
on E.G. *The team have not fared well
in this tournament.*
📖 from Old English *faran* meaning
'to go'

Far East
NOUN The Far East consists of the
countries of East Asia, including
China, Japan, and Malaysia.
Far Eastern ADJECTIVE

farewell
INTERJECTION **1** Farewell means
goodbye. ▶ ADJECTIVE **2** A farewell act is
performed by or for someone who is
leaving a particular job or career E.G.
a farewell speech.

far-fetched
ADJECTIVE unlikely to be true.

farm farms farming farmed
NOUN **1** an area of land together with
buildings, used for growing crops
and raising animals. ▶ VERB
2 Someone who farms uses land to
grow crops and raise animals.
farmer NOUN **farming** NOUN
📖 from Old French *ferme* meaning
'rented land'

farmhouse farmhouses
NOUN the main house on a farm.

farmyard farmyards
NOUN an area surrounded by farm
buildings.

**fascinate fascinates fascinating
fascinated**
VERB If something fascinates you, it
interests you so much that you think
about it and nothing else.
fascinating ADJECTIVE
⬛ absorb, enthral, intrigue

fascism
Said "**fash**-izm" NOUN an extreme
right-wing political ideology or
system of government with a
powerful dictator and state control
of most activities. Nationalism is
encouraged and political opposition
is not allowed.
fascist NOUN OR ADJECTIVE

**fashion fashions fashioning
fashioned**
NOUN **1** a style of dress or way of
behaving that is popular at a
particular time. **2** The fashion in
which someone does something is
the way in which they do it. ▶ VERB **3** If
you fashion something, you make or
shape it.
⬛ (sense 1) style, trend, vogue

fashionable
ADJECTIVE Something that is
fashionable is very popular with a lot
of people at the same time.
fashionably ADVERB
⬛ in, in vogue, popular, trendy

**fast faster fastest; fasts
fasting fasted**
ADJECTIVE OR ADVERB **1** moving, doing
something, or happening quickly or
with great speed. **2** If a clock is fast, it
shows a time that is later than the
real time. ▶ ADVERB **3** Something that
is held fast is firmly fixed. ▶ PHRASE **4** If
you are **fast asleep**, you are in a
deep sleep. ▶ VERB **5** If you fast, you
eat no food at all for a period of
time, usually for religious reasons.
▶ NOUN **6** a period of time during
which someone does not eat food.
⬛ (sense 1) quick, rapid, speedy, swift

**fasten fastens fastening
fastened**
VERB **1** To fasten something is to close

it or attach it firmly to something
else. **2** If you fasten your hands or
teeth around or onto something, you
hold it tightly with them.
fastener NOUN **fastening** NOUN
■ (sense 1) fix, secure

fast food
NOUN hot food that is prepared and
served quickly after you have
ordered it.

fastidious
ADJECTIVE extremely choosy and
concerned about neatness and
cleanliness.

fast-track fast-tracks fast-
tracking fast-tracked
VERB To fast-track something is to
make it happen or put it into effect
as quickly as possible, usually giving
it priority over other things.

fat fatter fattest; fats
ADJECTIVE **1** Someone who is fat has
too much weight on their body.
2 large or great E.G. *a fat pile of
letters* ▶ NOUN **3** Fat is the greasy,
cream-coloured substance that
animals and humans have under
their skin, which is used to store
energy and to help keep them warm.
4 Fat is also the greasy solid or liquid
substance obtained from animals
and plants and used in cooking.
fatness NOUN **fatty** ADJECTIVE
■ (sense 1) overweight, plump,
podgy, tubby

fatal
ADJECTIVE **1** causing death E.G. *fatal
injuries*. **2** very important or
significant and likely to have an
undesirable effect E.G. *The mistake
was fatal to my plans.*
fatally ADVERB
■ (sense 1) deadly, lethal, mortal

fatality fatalities
NOUN a death caused by accident or
violence.

fate fates
NOUN **1** Fate is a power that is
believed to control events.
2 Someone's fate is what happens to
them E.G. *She was resigned to her fate.*
■ (sense 1) destiny, providence

fateful
ADJECTIVE having an important, often
disastrous, effect E.G. *fateful political
decisions.*

father fathers fathering
fathered
NOUN **1** A person's father is their male
parent. **2** The father of something is
the man who invented or started it
E.G. *the father of Italian painting.*
3 'Father' is used to address a priest
in some Christian churches. **4** Father
is another name for God. ▶ VERB
5 LITERARY When a man fathers a child,
he makes a woman pregnant.
fatherly ADJECTIVE **fatherhood**
NOUN

father-in-law fathers-in-law
NOUN A person's father-in-law is the
father of their husband or wife.

fathom fathoms fathoming
fathomed
NOUN **1** a unit for measuring the
depth of water. It is equal to 6 feet or
about 1.83 metres. ▶ VERB **2** If you
fathom something, you understand
it after careful thought E.G. *Daisy
tries to fathom what it means.*

fatigue fatigues fatiguing
fatigued
Said "fat-*eeg*" NOUN **1** Fatigue is
extreme tiredness. ▶ VERB **2** If you are
fatigued by something, it makes you
extremely tired.

a
b
c
d
e
f
g
h
i
j
k
l
m
n
o
p
q
r
s
t
u
v
w
x
y
z

A
B
C
D
E
F
G
H
I
J
K
L
M
N
O
P
Q
R
S
T
U
V
W
X
Y
Z

fault faults faulting faulted

NOUN 1 If something bad is your fault, you are to blame for it. 2 a weakness or imperfection in someone or something. 3 a large crack in rock caused by movement of the earth's crust. ▶ PHRASE 4 If you are **at fault**, you are mistaken or are to blame for something E.G. *If you were at fault, you accept it.* ▶ VERB 5 If you cannot fault someone, you cannot criticize them for what they are doing because they are doing it so well.
faultless ADJECTIVE **faulty** ADJECTIVE
■ (sense 2) defect, failing, flaw

favour favours favouring favoured

NOUN 1 If you regard someone or something with favour, you like or support them. 2 If you do someone a favour, you do something helpful for them. ▶ PHRASE 3 Something that is **in someone's favour** is a help or advantage to them E.G. *The arguments seemed to be in our favour.* 4 If you are **in favour of** something, you agree with it and think it should happen. ▶ VERB 5 If you favour something or someone, you prefer that person or thing.
favourable ADJECTIVE **favourably** ADVERB

favourite favourites

ADJECTIVE 1 Your favourite person or thing is the one you like best. ▶ NOUN 2 Someone's favourite is the person or thing they like best. 3 the animal or person expected to win in a race or contest.

favouritism

NOUN Favouritism is behaviour in which you are unfairly more helpful or more generous to one person than to other people.

fawn fawns fawning fawned

NOUN OR ADJECTIVE 1 pale yellowish-brown. ▶ NOUN 2 a very young deer. ▶ VERB 3 To fawn on someone is to seek their approval by flattering them.

fax faxes

NOUN an exact copy of a document sent electronically along a telephone line.

fear fears fearing feared

NOUN 1 Fear is an unpleasant feeling of danger. 2 a thought that something undesirable or unpleasant might happen E.G. *You have a fear of failure.* ▶ VERB 3 If you fear someone or something, you are frightened of them. 4 If you fear something unpleasant, you are worried that it is likely to happen E.G. *Artists feared that their pictures would be forgotten.*
fearless ADJECTIVE **fearlessly** ADVERB
■ (sense 1) dread, fright, terror

fearful

ADJECTIVE 1 afraid and full of fear. 2 extremely unpleasant or worrying E.G. *The world's in such a fearful mess.*
fearfully ADVERB

fearsome

ADJECTIVE terrible or frightening E.G. *a powerful, fearsome weapon.*

feasible

ADJECTIVE possible and likely to happen E.G. *The proposal is just not feasible.*
feasibility NOUN

feast feasts

NOUN a large and special meal for many people.

feat feats

NOUN an impressive and difficult achievement E.G. *It was an astonishing feat for Leeds to score six away from home.*

SPELLING NOTE have a pIEce of pIE (pi**e**ce)

feather feathers
NOUN one of the light fluffy things covering a bird's body.
feathery ADJECTIVE
feature features featuring featured
NOUN 1 an interesting or important part or characteristic of something. 2 Someone's features are the various parts of their face. 3 a special article or programme dealing with a particular subject. 4 the main film in a cinema programme. ▸ VERB 5 To feature something is to include it or emphasize it as an important part or subject.
featureless ADJECTIVE
February
NOUN February is the second month of the year. It has 28 days, except in a leap year, when it has 29 days.
📖 from *Februa*, a Roman festival of purification
fed
the past tense and past participle of feed.
federal
ADJECTIVE relating to a system of government in which a group of states is controlled by a central government, but each state has its own local powers E.G. *The United States of America is a federal country.*
federation federations
NOUN a group of organizations or states that have joined together for a common purpose.
fed up
ADJECTIVE; INFORMAL unhappy or bored.
fee fees
NOUN a charge or payment for a job, service, or activity.
feeble feebler feeblest
ADJECTIVE weak or lacking in power or

influence E.G. *feeble and stupid arguments.*
feed feeds feeding fed
VERB 1 To feed a person or animal is to give them food. 2 When an animal or baby feeds, it eats. 3 To feed something is to supply what is needed for it to operate or exist E.G. *The information was fed into a computer database.* ▸ NOUN 4 Feed is food for animals or babies.
feedback
NOUN 1 Feedback is comments and information about the quality or success of something. 2 Feedback is also a condition in which some of the power, sound, or information produced by electronic equipment goes back into it.
feel feels feeling felt
VERB 1 If you feel an emotion or sensation, you experience it E.G. *I felt a bit ashamed.* 2 If you feel that something is the case, you believe it to be so E.G. *She feels that she is in control of her life.* 3 If you feel something, you touch it. 4 If something feels warm or cold, for example, you experience its warmth or coldness through the sense of touch E.G. *Real marble feels cold to the touch.* 5 To feel the effect of something is to be affected by it E.G. *The shock waves of this fire will be felt by people from all over the world.* ▸ NOUN 6 The feel of something is how it feels to you when you touch it E.G. *skin with a velvety smooth feel.* ▸ PHRASE 7 If you **feel like** doing something, you want to do it.
▤ (sense 1) be aware of, experience
▤ (sense 2) believe, consider, think
feeler feelers
NOUN An insect's feelers are the two

a
b
c
d
e
f
g
h
i
j
k
l
m
n
o
p
q
r
s
t
u
v
w
x
y
z

thin antennae on its head with which it senses things around it.

feeling feelings
NOUN **1** an emotion or reaction E.G. *feelings of envy*. **2** a physical sensation E.G. *a feeling of pain*. **3** Feeling is the ability to experience the sense of touch in your body E.G. *He had no feeling in his hands*. **4** Your feelings about something are your general attitudes or thoughts about it E.G. *He has strong feelings about our national sport*.

feet
the plural of **foot**.

feign feigns feigning feigned
Rhymes with "**rain**" VERB If you feign an emotion or state, you pretend to experience it E.G. *I feigned a headache*.

feline
Said "**fee**-line" ADJECTIVE belonging or relating to the cat family.
📖 from Latin *feles* meaning 'cat'

fell fells felling felled
1 the past tense of **fall**. ▶ VERB **2** To fell a tree is to cut it down.

fellow fellows
NOUN **1** OLD-FASHIONED a man E.G. *I knew a fellow by that name*. **2** a senior member of a learned society or a university college. **3** Your fellows are the people who share work or an activity with you. ▶ ADJECTIVE **4** You use 'fellow' to describe people who have something in common with you E.G. *his fellow editors*.
📖 from Old Norse *felagi* meaning 'partner' or 'associate'

fellowship fellowships
NOUN **1** a feeling of friendliness that a group of people have when they are doing things together. **2** a group of people that join together because

they have interests in common E.G. *the Dickens Fellowship*. **3** an academic post at a university which involves research work.

felt
1 the past tense and past participle of **feel**. ▶ NOUN **2** Felt is a thick cloth made by pressing short threads together.

female females
NOUN **1** a person or animal that belongs to the sex that can have babies or young. ▶ ADJECTIVE **2** concerning or relating to females.

feminine
ADJECTIVE **1** relating to women or considered to be typical of women. **2** belonging to a particular class of nouns in some languages, such as French, German, and Latin.
femininity NOUN

What is the Feminine?

Feminine nouns denote female people and animals:

E.G. *The girl put on her coat.* ▶ *girl is feminine*

It is customary to refer to countries and vehicles as if they were feminine:

E.G. *The ship came into view, her sails swelling in the breeze.*

Common nouns may be either masculine or feminine. Other words in the sentence may tell us if they are male or female:

E.G. *The doctor parked his car.*
The doctor parked her car.

Also look at the grammar boxes at **gender**, **masculine** and **neuter**.

A B C D E F G H I J K L M N O P Q R S T U V W X Y Z

feminism

NOUN Feminism is the belief that women should have the same rights and opportunities as men.

feminist NOUN or ADJECTIVE

fen fens

NOUN The fens are an area of low, flat, very wet land in the east of England.

fence fences fencing fenced

NOUN 1 a wooden or wire barrier between two areas of land. 2 a barrier or hedge for the horses to jump over in horse racing or show jumping. ▶ VERB 3 To fence an area of land is to surround it with a fence. 4 When two people fence, they use special swords to fight each other as a sport.

fend fends fending fended

PHRASE 1 If you have to **fend for yourself**, you have to look after yourself. ▶ VERB 2 If you fend off an attack or unwelcome questions or attention, you defend and protect yourself

ferment ferments fermenting fermented

VERB When wine, beer, or fruit ferments, a chemical change takes place in it, often producing alcohol.

fermentation NOUN

fern ferns

NOUN a plant with long feathery leaves and no flowers.

ferocious

ADJECTIVE violent and fierce E.G. ferocious dogs… ferocious storms.

ferociously ADVERB   **ferocity** NOUN

📖 from Latin ferox meaning 'like a wild animal'

ferret ferrets

NOUN a small, fierce animal related to the weasel and kept for hunting rats and rabbits.

📖 from Old French furet meaning 'little thief'

ferry ferries ferrying ferried

NOUN 1 a boat that carries people and vehicles across short stretches of water. ▶ VERB 2 To ferry people or goods somewhere is to transport them there, usually on a short, regular journey.

fertile

ADJECTIVE 1 capable of producing strong, healthy plants E.G. fertile soil. 2 creative E.G. fertile minds. 3 able to have babies or young.

fertility NOUN

fertilize fertilizes fertilizing fertilized; also spelt **fertilise**

VERB 1 When an egg, plant, or female is fertilized, the process of reproduction begins by sperm joining with the egg, or by pollen coming into contact with the reproductive part of a plant. 2 To fertilize land is to put manure or chemicals onto it to feed the plants.

fertilizer fertilizers; also spelt **fertiliser**

NOUN a substance put onto soil to improve plant growth.

fervent

ADJECTIVE showing strong, sincere, and enthusiastic feeling E.G. a fervent nationalist.

fervently ADVERB

fervour

NOUN a very strong feeling for or belief in something E.G. a wave of religious fervour.

📖 from Latin fervor meaning 'heat'

fester festers festering festered

VERB If a wound festers it becomes

a
b
c
d
e
f
g
h
i
j
k
l
m
n
o
p
q
r
s
t
u
v
w
x
y
z

infected and produces pus.

🔲 from Latin *fistula* meaning 'ulcer'

festival festivals

NOUN **1** an organized series of events and performances E.G. *the Cannes Film Festival.* **2** (RE) a day or period of religious celebration.

festive

ADJECTIVE full of happiness and celebration E.G. *a festive time of singing and dancing.*

festivity festivities

NOUN celebration and happiness E.G. *the wedding festivities.*

festooned

ADJECTIVE If something is festooned with objects, the objects are hanging across it in large numbers.

fetch fetches fetching fetched

VERB **1** If you fetch something, you go to where it is and bring it back. **2** If something fetches a particular sum of money, it is sold for that amount E.G. *Portraits fetch the highest prices.*

fetching

ADJECTIVE attractive in appearance E.G. *a fetching purple frock.*

fete fetes feting feted

Rhymes with "date" NOUN **1** an outdoor event with competitions, displays, and goods for sale. ► VERB **2** Someone who is feted receives a public welcome or entertainment as an honour.

feud feuds feuding feuded

Said "fyood" NOUN **1** a long-term and very bitter quarrel, especially between families. ► VERB **2** When people feud, they take part in a feud.

feudalism

NOUN Feudalism is a social and political system that was common in the Middle Ages in Europe. Under

this system, ordinary people were given land and protection by a lord, and in return they worked and fought for him.

feudal ADJECTIVE

fever fevers

NOUN **1** Fever is a condition occurring during illness, in which the patient has a very high body temperature. **2** A fever is extreme excitement or agitation E.G. *a fever of impatience.*

feverish

ADJECTIVE **1** in a state of extreme excitement or agitation E.G. *increasingly feverish activity.* **2** suffering from a high body temperature.

feverishly ADVERB

few fewer fewest

ADJECTIVE OR NOUN **1** used to refer to a small number of things E.G. *I saw him a few moments ago… one of only a few.* ► PHRASES **2** **Quite a few** or **a good few** means quite a large number of things

☑ You use *fewer* to talk about things that can be counted: *fewer than five visits.* When you are talking about amounts that can't be counted you should use *less*.

fiancé fiancés

Said "fee-on-say" NOUN A woman's fiancé is the man to whom she is engaged.

fiancée fiancées

NOUN A man's fiancée is the woman to whom he is engaged.

fiasco fiascos

Said "fee-ass-koh" NOUN an event or attempt that fails completely, especially in a ridiculous or disorganized way E.G. *The game ended in a complete fiasco.*

fib fibs fibbing fibbed
NOUN **1** a small, unimportant lie. ▶ VERB **2** If you fib, you tell a small lie.

fibre fibres
NOUN **1** (D&T) a thin thread of a substance used to make cloth. **2** Fibre is also a part of plants that can be eaten but not digested; it helps food pass quickly through the body.
fibrous ADJECTIVE

fickle
ADJECTIVE A fickle person keeps changing their mind about who or what they like or want.
🔤 from Old English *ficol* meaning 'treacherous' or 'deceitful'

fiction fictions
NOUN **1** Fiction is stories about people and events that have been invented by the author. **2** something that is not true.
fictional ADJECTIVE   **fictitious** ADJECTIVE

fiddle fiddles fiddling fiddled
VERB **1** If you fiddle with something, you keep moving it or touching it restlessly. **2** INFORMAL If someone fiddles something such as an account, they alter it dishonestly to get money for themselves. ▶ NOUN **3** INFORMAL a dishonest action or scheme to get money. **4** a violin.
fiddler NOUN

fiddly fiddlier fiddliest
ADJECTIVE small and difficult to do or use E.G. *fiddly nuts and bolts*.

fidelity
NOUN Fidelity is remaining firm in your beliefs, friendships, or loyalty to another person.

fidget fidgets fidgeting fidgeted
VERB **1** If you fidget, you keep changing your position because of nervousness or boredom. ▶ NOUN **2** someone who fidgets.
fidgety ADJECTIVE

field fields fielding fielded
NOUN **1** an area of land where crops are grown or animals are kept. **2** (PE) an area of land where sports are played E.G. *a hockey field*. **3** A coal field, oil field, or gold field is an area where coal, oil, or gold is found. **4** a particular subject or area of interest E.G. *He was doing well in his own field of advertising.* ▶ ADJECTIVE **5** A field trip or a field study involves research or activity in the natural environment rather than theoretical or laboratory work. **6** In an athletics competition, the field events are the events such as the high jump and the javelin which do not take place on a running track. ▶ VERB **7** In cricket, when you field the ball, you stop it after the batsman has hit it. **8** To field questions is to answer or deal with them skilfully.

fielder fielders
NOUN In cricket, the fielders are the team members who stand at various parts of the pitch and try to get the batsmen out or to prevent runs from being scored.

field marshal field marshals
NOUN an army officer of the highest rank.

fieldwork
NOUN Fieldwork is the study of something in the environment where it naturally lives or occurs, rather than in a class or laboratory.

fiend fiends
Said "**feend**" NOUN **1** a devil or evil spirit. **2** a very wicked or cruel

a
b
c
d
e
f
g
h
i
j
k
l
m
n
o
p
q
r
s
t
u
v
w
x
y
z

person. **3** INFORMAL someone who is very keen on a particular thing E.G. *a fitness fiend.*

🔲 from Old English *feond* meaning 'enemy'

fierce fiercer fiercest
ADJECTIVE **1** very aggressive or angry. **2** extremely strong or intense E.G. *a sudden fierce pain… a fierce storm.*
fiercely ADVERB

🔲 (sense 1) ferocious, savage, wild

fiery fierier fieriest
ADJECTIVE **1** involving fire or seeming like fire E.G. *a huge fiery sun.* **2** showing great anger, energy, or passion E.G. *a fiery debate.*

fifteen
the number 15.
fifteenth

fifth fifths
ADJECTIVE **1** The fifth item in a series is the one counted as number five. ▶ NOUN **2** one of five equal parts.

fifty fifties
the number 50.
fiftieth

fifty-fifty
ADVERB **1** divided equally into two portions. ▶ ADJECTIVE **2** just as likely not to happen as to happen E.G. *You've got a fifty-fifty chance of being right.*

fig figs
NOUN a soft, sweet fruit full of tiny seeds. It grows in hot countries and is often eaten dried.

fight fights fighting fought
VERB **1** When people fight, they take part in a battle, a war, a boxing match, or in some other attempt to hurt or kill someone. **2** To fight for something is to try in a very determined way to achieve it E.G. *I must fight for respect.* ▶ NOUN **3** a

situation in which people hit or try to hurt each other. **4** a determined attempt to prevent or achieve something E.G. *the fight for independence.*
fighter NOUN

🔲 (sense 1) battle, come to blows, struggle

🔲 (sense 3) battle, conflict, struggle

figurative
ADJECTIVE (ENGLISH) If you use a word or expression in a figurative sense, you use it with a more abstract or imaginative meaning than its ordinary one.
figuratively ADVERB

figure figures figuring figured
NOUN **1** a written number or the amount a number stands for. **2** a geometrical shape. **3** a diagram or table in a written text. **4** the shape of a person whom you cannot see clearly E.G. *A human figure leaped at him.* **5** Your figure is the shape of your body E.G. *his slim and supple figure.* **6** a person E.G. *He was a major figure in the trial.* ▶ VERB **7** To figure in something is to appear or be included in it E.G. *the many people who have figured in his life.* **8** INFORMAL If you figure that something is the case, you guess or conclude this E.G. *We figure the fire broke out around four in the morning.*

figurehead figureheads
NOUN the leader of a movement or organization who has no real power.

figure of speech figures of speech
NOUN A figure of speech is an expression such as a simile or idiom in which the words are not used in their literal sense.

file files filing filed
NOUN **1** a box or folder in which a

group of papers or records is kept; also used of the information kept in the file. **2** In computing, a file is a stored set of related data with its own name. **3** a line of people one behind the other. **4** a long steel tool with a rough surface, used for smoothing and shaping hard materials. ► VERB **5** When someone files a document, they put it in its correct place with similar documents. **6** When a group of people file somewhere, they walk one behind the other in a line. **7** If you file something, you smooth or shape it with a file.

fill fills filling filled
VERB **1** If you fill something or if it fills up, it becomes full. **2** If something fills a need, it satisfies the need E.G. *Ella had in some small way filled the gap left by Molly's absence.* **3** To fill a job vacancy is to appoint someone to do that job. ► NOUN **4** If you have had your fill of something, you do not want any more.

fill in VERB **1** If you fill in a form, you write information in the appropriate spaces. **2** If you fill someone in, you give them information to bring them up to date.

fillet fillets filleting filleted
NOUN **1** a strip of tender, boneless beef, veal, or pork. **2** a piece of fish with the bones removed. ► VERB **3** To fillet meat or fish is to prepare it by cutting out the bones.

filling fillings
NOUN **1** the soft food mixture inside a sandwich, cake, or pie. **2** a small amount of metal or plastic put into a hole in a tooth by a dentist.

filly fillies
NOUN a female horse or pony under

the age of four.

film films filming filmed
NOUN **1** a series of moving pictures projected onto a screen and shown at the cinema or on television. **2** a thin flexible strip of plastic used in a camera to record images when exposed to light. **3** a very thin layer of powder or liquid on a surface. **4** Plastic film is a very thin sheet of plastic used for wrapping things.
► VERB **5** If you film someone, you use a video camera to record their movements on film.
📖 from Old English *filmen* meaning 'membrane'

filter filters filtering filtered
NOUN **1** a device that allows some substances, lights, or sounds to pass through it, but not others E.G. *a filter against the harmful rays of the sun.*
► VERB **2** To filter a substance is to pass it through a filter. **3** If something filters somewhere, it gets there slowly or faintly E.G. *Traffic filtered into the city*
filtration NOUN

filth
NOUN **1** Filth is disgusting dirt and muck. **2** People often use the word filth to refer to very bad language or to sexual material that is thought to be crude and offensive.
filthy ADJECTIVE
📖 from Old English *fylth* meaning 'pus' or 'corruption'
▤ (sense 1) dirt, muck, squalor

fin fins
NOUN a thin, flat structure on the body of a fish, used to help guide it through the water.

final finals
ADJECTIVE **1** last in a series or

a b c d e f g h i j k l m n o p q r s t u v w x y z

A
B
C
D
E
F
G
H
I
J
K
L
M
N
O
P
Q
R
S
T
U
V
W
X
Y
Z

happening at the end of something.
2 A decision that is final cannot be changed or questioned. ► NOUN **3** the last game or contest in a series which decides the overall winner.
► PLURAL NOUN **4** Finals are the last and most important examinations of a university or college course.
■ (sense 1) concluding, last

finale finales
Said "fin-nah-lee" NOUN the last section of a piece of music or show.

finalist finalists
NOUN a person taking part in the final of a competition.

finalize finalizes finalizing finalized; also spelt **finalise**
VERB If you finalize something, you complete all the arrangements for it.

finally
ADVERB If something finally happens, it happens after a long delay.
■ (sense 1) at last, eventually
■ (sense 2) in conclusion, lastly

finance finances financing financed
VERB **1** To finance a project or a large purchase is to provide the money for it. ► NOUN **2** Finance for something is the money or loans used to pay for it. **3** Finance is also the management of money, loans, and investments.

financial
ADJECTIVE relating to or involving money.
financially ADVERB

financier financiers
NOUN a person who deals with the finance for large businesses.

finch finches
NOUN a small bird with a short strong beak.

find finds finding found
VERB **1** If you find someone or

something, you discover them, either as a result of searching or by coming across them unexpectedly. **2** If you find that something is the case, you become aware of it or realize it E.G. *I found my fists were clenched.*
3 Something that is found in a particular place typically lives or exists there. **4** When a court or jury finds a person guilty or not guilty, they decide that the person is guilty or innocent E.G. *He was found guilty and sentenced to life imprisonment.*
► NOUN **5** If you describe something or someone as a find, you mean that you have recently discovered them and they are valuable or useful.

finder NOUN
■ (sense 1) come across, discover

find out VERB **1** If you find out something, you learn or discover something that you did not know.
2 If you find someone out, you discover that they have been doing something they should not have been doing.

findings
PLURAL NOUN Someone's findings are the conclusions they reach as a result of investigation.

fine finer finest; fines fining fined
ADJECTIVE **1** very good or very beautiful E.G. *a fine school… fine clothes.*
2 satisfactory or suitable E.G. *Pasta dishes are fine if not served with a rich sauce.* **3** very narrow or thin E.G. *fine paper.* **4** A fine net or sieve has very small holes. Fine powder or dust consists of very small particles. **5** A fine detail, adjustment, or distinction is very delicate, exact, or subtle.
6 When the weather is fine, it is not raining and is bright or sunny. ► NOUN

7 a sum of money paid as a punishment. ▸ VERB **8** Someone who is fined has to pay a sum of money as a punishment.

finery
NOUN Finery is very beautiful clothing and jewellery.

finesse
Said "fin-**ness**" NOUN If you do something with finesse, you do it with skill and subtlety.

finger fingers fingering fingered
NOUN **1** Your fingers are the four long jointed parts of your hands, sometimes including the thumbs. ▸ VERB **2** If you finger something you feel it with your fingers.

fingernail fingernails
NOUN Your fingernails are the hard coverings at the ends of your fingers.

fingerprint fingerprints
NOUN a mark made showing the pattern on the skin at the tip of a person's finger.

finish finishes finishing finished
VERB **1** When you finish something, you reach the end of it and complete it. **2** When something finishes, it ends or stops. ▸ NOUN **3** The finish of something is the end or last part of it. **4** The finish that something has is the texture or appearance of its surface E.G. *a healthy, glossy finish.*
▤ (sense 1) complete, conclude, end
▤ (sense 3) close, conclusion, end

finite
Said "**fie**-nite" ADJECTIVE having a particular size or limit which cannot be increased E.G. *There's only finite money to spend.*

Finn Finns
NOUN someone who comes from Finland.

Finnish
ADJECTIVE **1** belonging or relating to Finland. ▸ NOUN **2** Finnish is the main language spoken in Finland.

fir firs
NOUN a tall pointed evergreen tree that has thin needle-like leaves and produces cones.

fire fires firing fired
NOUN **1** Fire is the flames produced when something burns. **2** a pile or mass of burning material. **3** a piece of equipment that is used as a heater E.G. *a gas fire.* ▸ VERB **4** If you fire a weapon or fire a bullet, you operate the weapon so that the bullet or missile is released. **5** If you fire questions at someone, you ask them a lot of questions very quickly. **6** INFORMAL If an employer fires someone, he or she dismisses that person from their job. ▸ PHRASE **7** If someone **opens fire**, they start shooting.

firearm firearms
NOUN a gun.

fire brigade fire brigades
NOUN the organization which has the job of putting out fires.

fire engine fire engines
NOUN a large vehicle that carries equipment for putting out fires.

fire escape fire escapes
NOUN an emergency exit or staircase for use if there is a fire.

fire extinguisher fire extinguishers
NOUN a metal cylinder containing water or foam for spraying onto a fire.

firefighter firefighters
NOUN a person whose job is to put out fires and rescue trapped people.

a b c d e **f** g h i j k l m n o p q r s t u v w x y z

A
B
C
D
E
F
G
H
I
J
K
L
M
N
O
P
Q
R
S
T
U
V
W
X
Y
Z

firefly fireflies
NOUN an insect that glows in the dark.

fireplace fireplaces
NOUN the opening beneath a chimney where a fire can be lit.

fireproof
ADJECTIVE resistant to fire.

fire station fire stations
NOUN a building where fire engines are kept and where firefighters wait to be called out.

firework fireworks
NOUN a small container of gunpowder and other chemicals which explodes and produces coloured sparks or smoke when lit.

firing squad firing squads
NOUN a group of soldiers ordered to shoot a person condemned to death.

firm firmer firmest; firms
ADJECTIVE 1 Something that is firm does not move easily when pressed or pushed, or when weight is put on it. 2 A firm grasp or push is one with controlled force or pressure. 3 A firm decision is definite. 4 Someone who is firm behaves with authority that shows they will not change their mind. ▶ NOUN 5 a business selling or producing something.
firmly ADVERB **firmness** NOUN

first
ADJECTIVE or ADVERB 1 happening, coming, or done before everything or everyone else. ▶ ADJECTIVE 2 more important than anything else E.G. *Her cheese won first prize.* ▶ NOUN 3 something that has never happened or been before.
firstly ADVERB
■ (sense 2) chief, foremost, principal

first aid
NOUN First aid is medical treatment given to an injured person.

first class
ADJECTIVE 1 Something that is first class is of the highest quality or standard. 2 First-class accommodation on a train, aircraft, or ship is the best and most expensive type of accommodation. 3 First-class postage is quick but more expensive.

first-hand
ADJECTIVE First-hand knowledge or experience is gained directly rather than from books or other people.

First Lady First Ladies
NOUN The First Lady of a country is the wife of a president.

first-rate
ADJECTIVE excellent.

fiscal
ADJECTIVE involving government or public money, especially taxes.
🔲 from Latin *fiscus* meaning 'money-bag' or 'treasury'

fish fishes fishing fished
NOUN 1 a cold-blooded creature living in water that has a spine, gills, fins, and a scaly skin. 2 Fish is the flesh of fish eaten as food. ▶ VERB 3 To fish is to try to catch fish for food or sport. 4 If you fish for information, you try to get it in an indirect way.
fishing NOUN **fisherman** NOUN
☑ The plural of the noun *fish* can be either *fish* or *fishes*, but *fish* is more common.

fishery fisheries
NOUN an area of the sea where fish are caught commercially.

fishmonger fishmongers
NOUN a shopkeeper who sells fish; also the shop itself.

fishy fishier fishiest
ADJECTIVE 1 smelling of fish. 2 INFORMAL

suspicious or doubtful E.G. *He spotted something fishy going on*.

fission
Rhymes with "mission" NOUN 1 Fission is the splitting of something into parts. 2 Fission is also nuclear fission.

fissure fissures
NOUN a deep crack in rock.

fist fists
NOUN a hand with the fingers curled tightly towards the palm.

fit fits fitting fitted; fitter fittest
VERB 1 Something that fits is the right shape or size for a particular person or position. 2 If you fit something somewhere, you put it there carefully or securely E.G. *Very carefully he fitted the files inside the compartment*. 3 If something fits a particular situation, person, or thing, it is suitable or appropriate E.G. *a sentence that fitted the crime*. ▶ NOUN 4 The fit of something is how it fits E.G. *This bolt must be a good fit*. 5 If someone has a fit, their muscles suddenly start contracting violently and they may lose consciousness. 6 A fit of laughter, coughing, anger, or panic is a sudden uncontrolled outburst ▶ ADJECTIVE 7 good enough or suitable E.G. *Housing fit for frail elderly people*. 8 Someone who is fit is healthy and has strong muscles as a result of regular exercise.

fitness NOUN
▤ (sense 3) match, suit
▤ (sense 5) convulsion, seizure, spasm

fitful
ADJECTIVE happening at irregular intervals and not continuous E.G. *a fitful breeze*.

fitfully ADVERB

fitter fitters
NOUN a person who assembles or installs machinery.

fitting fittings
ADJECTIVE 1 right or suitable E.G. *a fitting reward for his efforts*. ▶ NOUN 2 a small part that is fixed to a piece of equipment or furniture. 3 If you have a fitting, you try on a garment that is being made to see if it fits properly.

five fives
the number 5.

fix fixes fixing fixed
VERB 1 If you fix something somewhere, you attach it or put it there securely. 2 If you fix something broken, you mend it. 3 If you fix your attention on something, you concentrate on it. 4 If you fix something, you make arrangements for it E.G. *The opening party is fixed for the 24th September*. 5 INFORMAL To fix something is to arrange the outcome unfairly or dishonestly. ▶ NOUN 6 INFORMAL something that has been unfairly or dishonestly arranged. 7 INFORMAL If you are in a fix, you are in a difficult situation. 8 an injection of a drug such as heroin.

fixed ADJECTIVE **fixedly** ADVERB
▤ (sense 2) mend, repair

fixation fixations
NOUN an extreme and obsessive interest in something.

fixture fixtures
NOUN 1 a piece of furniture or equipment that is fixed into position in a house. 2 a sports event due to take place on a particular date.

fizz fizzes fizzing fizzed
VERB Something that fizzes makes a hissing sound.

a
b
c
d
e
f
g
h
i
j
k
l
m
n
o
p
q
r
s
t
u
v
w
x
y
z

Eddy Ant thinks mEAt is a grEAt trEAt to EAt (-ea-) SPELLING NOTE

A
B
C
D
E
F
G
H
I
J
K
L
M
N
O
P
Q
R
S
T
U
V
W
X
Y
Z

fizzle fizzles fizzling fizzled
VERB Something that fizzles makes a weak hissing or spitting sound.

fizzy fizzier fizziest
ADJECTIVE Fizzy drinks have carbon dioxide in them to make them bubbly.

fjord fjords
Said "fee-ord"; also spelt **fiord**
NOUN a long narrow inlet of the sea between very high cliffs, especially in Norway.
📖 a Norwegian word

flab
NOUN Flab is large amounts of surplus fat on someone's body.

flabbergasted
ADJECTIVE extremely surprised.

flabby flabbier flabbiest
ADJECTIVE Someone who is flabby is rather fat and unfit, with loose flesh on their body.

flag flags flagging flagged
NOUN 1 a rectangular or square cloth which has a particular colour and design, and is used as the symbol of a nation or as a signal. ▶ VERB 2 If you or your spirits flag, you start to lose energy or enthusiasm.

flagrant
Said "flay-grant" ADJECTIVE very shocking and bad in an obvious way E.G. *a flagrant defiance of the rules*.

flagship flagships
NOUN 1 a ship carrying the commander of the fleet. 2 the most modern or impressive product or asset of an organization.

flail flails flailing flailed
VERB If someone's arms or legs flail about, they move in a wild, uncontrolled way.

flair
NOUN Flair is a natural ability to do

something well or stylishly.

flak
NOUN 1 Flak is anti-aircraft fire. 2 If you get flak for doing something, you get a lot of severe criticism.
📖 from the first letters of the parts of German *Fliegerabwehrkanone* meaning 'anti-aircraft gun'

flake flakes flaking flaked
NOUN 1 a small thin piece of something. ▶ VERB 2 When something such as paint flakes, small thin pieces of it come off.

flaky ADJECTIVE **flaked** ADJECTIVE

flamboyant
ADJECTIVE behaving in a very showy and confident.
flamboyance NOUN

flame flames
NOUN 1 a flickering tongue or blaze of fire. 2 A flame of passion, desire, or anger is a sudden strong feeling.
📖 from Latin *flamma* meaning 'blazing fire'

flamenco
NOUN Flamenco is a type of very lively, fast Spanish dancing, accompanied by guitar music.

flamingo flamingos or flamingoes
NOUN a long-legged wading bird with pink feathers and a long neck.

flammable
ADJECTIVE likely to catch fire and burn easily
☑ Although *flammable* and *inflammable* both mean 'likely to catch fire', *flammable* is used more often as people sometimes think that *inflammable* means 'not likely to catch fire'.

flan flans
NOUN an open sweet or savoury tart

with a pastry or cake base.

flank flanks flanking flanked
NOUN **1** the side of an animal between the ribs and the hip. ▶ VERB **2** Someone or something that is flanked by a particular thing or person has them at their side E.G. *He was flanked by four bodyguards.*

flannel flannels
NOUN **1** Flannel is a lightweight woollen fabric. **2** a small square of towelling, used for washing yourself. In Australian English it is called a **washer**.

flap flaps flapping flapped
VERB **1** Something that flaps moves up and down or from side to side with a snapping sound. ▶ NOUN **2** a loose piece of something such as paper or skin that is attached at one edge.

flare flares flaring flared
NOUN **1** a device that produces a brightly coloured flame, used especially as an emergency signal. ▶ VERB **2** If a fire flares, it suddenly burns much more vigorously. **3** If violence or a conflict flares or flares up, it suddenly starts or becomes more serious.

flash flashes flashing flashed
NOUN **1** a sudden short burst of light. ▶ VERB **2** If a light flashes, it shines for a very short period, often repeatedly. **3** Something that flashes past moves or happens so fast that you almost miss it. **4** If you flash something, you show it briefly E.G. *Michael Jackson flashed his face at the crowd.* ▶ PHRASE **5** Something that happens **in a flash** happens suddenly and lasts a very short time.

flashback flashbacks
NOUN a scene in a film, play, or book that returns to events in the past.

flashlight flashlights
NOUN a large, powerful torch.

flashy flashier flashiest
ADJECTIVE expensive and fashionable in appearance, in a vulgar way E.G. *flashy clothes.*

flask flasks
NOUN a bottle used for carrying alcoholic or hot drinks around with you.

flat flats; flats flatting flatted; flatter flattest
NOUN **1** a self-contained set of rooms, usually on one level, for living in. **2** In music, a flat is a note or key a semitone lower than that described by the same letter. It is represented by the symbol (♭). ▶ VERB **3** In Australian and New Zealand English, to flat is to live in a flat E.G. *flatting in London.* ▶ ADJECTIVE **4** Something that is flat is level and smooth. **5** A flat object is not very tall or deep E.G. *a low flat building.* **6** A flat tyre or ball has not got enough air in it. **7** A flat battery has lost its electrical charge. **8** A flat refusal or denial is complete and firm. **9** Something that is flat is without emotion or interest. **10** A flat rate or price is fixed and the same for everyone E.G. *The company charges a flat fee for its advice.* **11** A musical instrument or note that is flat is slightly too low in pitch. ▶ ADVERB **12** Something that is done in a particular time flat, takes exactly that time E.G. *They would find them in two minutes flat.*

flatly ADVERB **flatness** NOUN
■ (sense 3) even, level

flatfish
NOUN a sea fish with a wide flat body,

a
b
c
d
e
f
g
h
i
j
k
l
m
n
o
p
q
r
s
t
u
v
w
x
y
z

A
B
C
D
E
F
G
H
I
J
K
L
M
N
O
P
Q
R
S
T
U
V
W
X
Y
Z

such as a plaice or sole.

flathead flatheads
NOUN a common Australian edible fish.

flatten flattens flattening flattened
VERB If you flatten something or if it flattens, it becomes flat or flatter.

flatter flatters flattering flattered
VERB 1 If you flatter someone, you praise them in an exaggerated way, either to please them or to persuade them to do something. 2 If you are flattered by something, it makes you feel pleased and important E.G. *He was very flattered because she liked him.* 3 If you flatter yourself that something is the case, you believe, perhaps mistakenly, something good about yourself or your abilities. 4 Something that flatters you makes you appear more attractive.
flattering ADJECTIVE
■ (sense 1) butter up, praise

flattery
NOUN Flattery is flattering words or behaviour.

flatting
PHRASE In New Zealand English, to **go flatting** is to leave home and live with others in a shared house or flat.

flatulence
NOUN Flatulence is the uncomfortable state of having too much gas in your stomach or intestine.
🔲 from Latin *flatus* meaning 'gust of wind'

flaunt flaunts flaunting flaunted
VERB If you flaunt your possessions or talents, you display them too obviously or proudly
✔ Be careful not to confuse *flaunt*

with *flout*, which means 'disobey'.

flautist flautists
NOUN someone who plays the flute.

flavour flavours flavouring flavoured
NOUN 1 The flavour of food is its taste. 2 The flavour of something is its distinctive characteristic or quality.
▶ VERB 3 If you flavour food with a spice or herb, you add it to the food to give it a particular taste.
flavouring NOUN

flaw flaws
NOUN 1 a fault or mark in a piece of fabric or glass, or in a decorative pattern. 2 a weak point or undesirable quality in a theory, plan, or person's character.
flawed ADJECTIVE **flawless** ADJECTIVE
■ (sense 1) blemish, spot
■ (sense 2) fault, weakness

flax
NOUN Flax is a plant used for making rope and cloth.

flay flays flaying flayed
VERB 1 To flay a dead animal is to cut off its skin. 2 To flay someone is to criticize them severely.

flea fleas
NOUN a small wingless jumping insect which feeds on blood.

fleck flecks
NOUN a small coloured mark or particle.
flecked ADJECTIVE

fled
the past tense and past participle of **flee**.

fledgling fledglings
NOUN 1 a young bird that is learning to fly. ▶ ADJECTIVE 2 Fledgling means new, or young and inexperienced E.G. *the fledgling American President.*

flee flees fleeing fled
VERB To flee from someone or something is to run away from them.

fleece fleeces fleecing fleeced
NOUN 1 A sheep's fleece is its coat of wool. ▸ VERB 2 To fleece someone is to swindle them or charge them too much money.

fleet fleets
NOUN a group of ships or vehicles owned by the same organization or travelling together.

fleeting
ADJECTIVE lasting for a very short time.

Flemish
NOUN Flemish is a language spoken in many parts of Belgium.

flesh
NOUN 1 Flesh is the soft part of the body. 2 The flesh of a fruit or vegetable is the soft inner part that you eat.
fleshy ADJECTIVE

flew
the past tense of **fly**.

flex flexes flexing flexed
NOUN 1 a length of wire covered in plastic, which carries electricity to an appliance. ▸ VERB 2 If you flex your muscles, you bend and stretch them.

flexible
ADJECTIVE 1 able to be bent easily without breaking. 2 able to adapt to changing circumstances.
flexibility NOUN

flick flicks flicking flicked
VERB 1 If you flick something, you move it sharply with your finger. 2 If something flicks somewhere, it moves with a short sudden movement E.G. *His foot flicked forward.* ▸ NOUN 3 a sudden quick movement or sharp touch with the

finger E.G. *a sideways flick of the head.*

flicker flickers flickering flickered
VERB 1 If a light or a flame flickers, it shines and moves unsteadily. ▸ NOUN 2 a short unsteady light or movement of light E.G. *the flicker of candlelight.* 3 A flicker of a feeling is a very brief experience of it E.G. *a flicker of interest.*

flight flights
NOUN 1 a journey made by aeroplane. 2 Flight is the action of flying or the ability to fly. 3 Flight is also the act of running away. 4 A flight of stairs or steps is a set running in a single direction.

flight attendant flight attendants
NOUN a person who looks after passengers on an aircraft.

flightless
ADJECTIVE Flightless birds, such as penguins and ostriches, are birds that cannot fly.

flimsy flimsier flimsiest
ADJECTIVE 1 made of something very thin or weak and not providing much protection. 2 not very convincing E.G. *flimsy evidence.*

flinch flinches flinching flinched
VERB If you flinch, you make a sudden small movement in fear or pain.
▣ cringe, recoil, wince

fling flings flinging flung
VERB 1 If you fling something, you throw it with a lot of force. ▸ NOUN 2 a short period devoted to pleasure and free from any restrictions or rules.

flint flints
NOUN Flint is a hard greyish-black

A
B
C
D
E
F
G
H
I
J
K
L
M
N
O
P
Q
R
S
T
U
V
W
X
Y
Z

form of quartz. It produces a spark when struck with steel.

flip flips flipping flipped
VERB 1 If you flip something, you turn or move it quickly and sharply E.G. *He flipped over the first page.* 2 If you flip something, you hit it sharply with your finger or thumb.

flippant
ADJECTIVE showing an inappropriate lack of seriousness E.G. *a flippant attitude to money.*
flippancy NOUN

flipper flippers
NOUN 1 one of the broad, flat limbs of sea animals, for example seals or penguins, used for swimming.
2 Flippers are broad, flat pieces of rubber that you can attach to your feet to help you swim.

flirt flirts flirting flirted
VERB 1 If you flirt with someone, you behave as if you are sexually attracted to them but without serious intentions. 2 If you flirt with an idea, you consider it without seriously intending to do anything about it. ► NOUN 3 someone who often flirts with people.
flirtation NOUN **flirtatious** ADJECTIVE

flit flits flitting flitted
VERB To flit somewhere is to fly or move there with quick, light movements.

float floats floating floated
VERB 1 Something that floats is supported by water. 2 Something that floats through the air moves along gently, supported by the air. 3 If a company is floated, shares are sold to the public for the first time and the company gains a listing on the stock exchange. ► NOUN 4 a light

object that floats and either supports something or someone or regulates the level of liquid in a tank or cistern. 5 In Australian English, a float is also a vehicle for transporting horses.

flock flocks flocking flocked
NOUN 1 a group of birds, sheep, or goats. ► VERB 2 If people flock somewhere, they go there in large numbers.

flog flogs flogging flogged
VERB 1 INFORMAL If you flog something, you sell it. 2 To flog someone is to beat them with a whip or stick.
flogging NOUN

flood floods flooding flooded
NOUN 1 a large amount of water covering an area that is usually dry. 2 A flood of something is a large amount of it suddenly occurring E.G. *a flood of angry language.* ► VERB 3 If liquid floods an area, or if a river floods, the water or liquid overflows, covering the surrounding area. 4 If people or things flood into a place, they come there in large numbers E.G. *Refugees have flooded into Austria in the last few months.*
■ (sense 1) deluge, spate, torrent
■ (sense 2) stream, torrent

floodgates
PHRASE To **open the floodgates** is suddenly to give a lot of people the opportunity to do something they could not do before.

floodlight floodlights
NOUN a very powerful outdoor lamp used to light up public buildings and sports grounds.
floodlit ADJECTIVE

floor floors flooring floored
NOUN 1 the part of a room you walk on. 2 one of the levels in a building

E.G. *the top floor of a factory.* 3 the ground at the bottom of a valley, forest, or the sea. ► VERB 4 If a remark or question floors you, you are completely unable to deal with it or answer it.

floorboard floorboards
NOUN one of the long planks of wood from which a floor is made.

flop flops flopping flopped
VERB 1 If someone or something flops, they fall loosely and rather heavily. 2 INFORMAL Something that flops fails. ► NOUN 3 INFORMAL something that is completely unsuccessful.

floppy floppier floppiest
ADJECTIVE tending to hang downwards in a rather loose way E.G. *a floppy, outsize jacket.*
▣ droopy, limp

floppy disk floppy disks; also spelt **floppy disc**
NOUN a small flexible magnetic disk on which computer data is stored.

floral
ADJECTIVE patterned with flowers or made from flowers E.G. *floral cotton dresses.*

florid
Rhymes with "horrid" ADJECTIVE 1 highly elaborate and extravagant E.G. *florid language.* 2 having a red face.

florist florists
NOUN a person or shop selling flowers.

floss
NOUN Dental floss is soft silky threads or fibre which you use to clean between your teeth.

flotation flotations
NOUN 1 The flotation of a business is the issuing of shares in order to launch it or to raise money.

2 Flotation is the act of floating.

flotilla flotillas
Said "flot-**til**-la" NOUN a small fleet or group of small ships.
▥ from Spanish *flotilla* meaning 'little fleet'

flotsam
NOUN Flotsam is rubbish or wreckage floating at sea or washed up on the shore.

flounce flounces flouncing flounced
VERB 1 If you flounce somewhere, you walk there with exaggerated movements suggesting that you are feeling angry or impatient about something E.G. *She flounced out of the office.* ► NOUN 2 a big frill around the bottom of a dress or skirt.

flounder flounders floundering floundered
VERB 1 To flounder is to struggle to move or stay upright, for example in water or mud. 2 If you flounder in a conversation or situation, you find it difficult to decide what to say or do. ► NOUN 3 a type of edible flatfish.

flour
NOUN (D&T) Flour is a powder made from finely ground grain, usually wheat, and used for baking and cooking.
floured ADJECTIVE **floury** ADJECTIVE

flourish flourishes flourishing flourished
VERB 1 Something that flourishes develops or functions successfully or healthily. 2 If you flourish something, you wave or display it so that people notice it. ► NOUN 3 a bold sweeping or waving movement.

flout flouts flouting flouted
VERB If you flout a convention or law,

a b c d e f g h i j k l m n o p q r s t u v w x y z

A
B
C
D
E
F
G
H
I
J
K
L
M
N
O
P
Q
R
S
T
U
V
W
X
Y
Z

you deliberately disobey it

☑ Be careful not to confuse *flout* with *flaunt*, which means 'display obviously'.

flow flows flowing flowed
VERB **1** If something flows, it moves or happens in a steady continuous stream. ▶ NOUN **2** A flow of something is a steady continuous movement of it; also the rate at which it flows E.G. *a steady flow of complaints.*

flow chart flow charts
NOUN (D&T) a diagram showing the sequence of steps that lead to various results.

flower flowers flowering flowered
NOUN **1** the part of a plant containing the reproductive organs from which the fruit or seeds develop. ▶ VERB **2** When a plant flowers, it produces flowers.

flowery
ADJECTIVE Flowery language is full of elaborate expressions.

flown
the past participle of **fly**.

flu
NOUN Flu is an illness similar to a very bad cold, which causes headaches, sore throat, weakness, and aching muscles. Flu is short for 'influenza'.

fluctuate fluctuates fluctuating fluctuated
VERB Something that fluctuates is irregular and changeable E.G. *fluctuating between feeling well and not so well.*

flue flues
NOUN a pipe which takes fumes and smoke away from a stove or boiler.

fluent
ADJECTIVE **1** able to speak a foreign

language correctly and without hesitation. **2** able to express yourself clearly and without hesitation.
fluently ADVERB

fluff fluffs fluffing fluffed
NOUN **1** Fluff is soft, light, woolly threads or fibres bunched together. ▶ VERB **2** If you fluff something up or out, you brush or shake it to make it seem larger and lighter E.G. *Fluff the rice up with a fork before serving.*
fluffy ADJECTIVE

fluid fluids
NOUN **1** a liquid. ▶ ADJECTIVE **2** Fluid movement is smooth and flowing. **3** A fluid arrangement or plan is flexible and without a fixed structure.
fluidity NOUN

fluke flukes
NOUN an accidental success or piece of good luck.

flung
the past tense of **fling**.

fluorescent
Said "floo-er-ess-nt" ADJECTIVE **1** having a very bright appearance when light is shone on it, as if it is shining itself E.G. *fluorescent yellow dye.* **2** A fluorescent light is in the form of a tube and shines with a hard bright light.

fluoride
NOUN Fluoride is a mixture of chemicals that is meant to prevent tooth decay.

flurry flurries
NOUN a short rush of activity or movement.

flush flushes flushing flushed
NOUN **1** A flush is a rosy red colour E.G. *The flowers are cream with a pink flush.* **2** In cards, a flush is a hand all

of one suit. ▶ VERB **3** If you flush, your face goes red. **4** If you flush a toilet or something such as a pipe, you force water through it to clean it.

▶ ADJECTIVE **5** INFORMAL Someone who is flush has plenty of money.

6 Something that is flush with a surface is level with it or flat against it.

flustered

ADJECTIVE If you are flustered, you feel confused, nervous, and rushed.

flute flutes

NOUN a musical wind instrument consisting of a long metal tube with holes and keys. It is held sideways to the mouth and played by blowing across a hole in its side.

fluted

ADJECTIVE decorated with long grooves.

flutter flutters fluttering fluttered

VERB **1** If something flutters, it flaps or waves with small, quick movements. ▶ NOUN **2** If you are in a flutter, you are excited and nervous. **3** INFORMAL If you have a flutter, you have a small bet.

flux

NOUN Flux is a state of constant change E.G. *stability in a world of flux*.

fly flies flying flew flown

NOUN **1** an insect with two pairs of wings. **2** The front opening on a pair of trousers is the fly or the flies. **3** The fly or fly sheet of a tent is either a flap at the entrance or an outer layer providing protection from rain. ▶ VERB **4** When a bird, insect, or aircraft flies, it moves through the air. **5** If someone or something flies, they move or go very quickly. **6** If you fly at someone or let fly at them, you

attack or criticize them suddenly and aggressively.

flying ADJECTIVE or NOUN   **flyer** NOUN

fly-fishing

NOUN Fly-fishing is a method of fishing using imitation flies as bait.

flying fox flying foxes

NOUN **1** a large bat that eats fruit, found in Australia and Africa. **2** In Australia and New Zealand, a cable car used to carry people over rivers and gorges.

flying saucer flying saucers

NOUN a large disc-shaped spacecraft which some people claim to have seen.

flyover flyovers

NOUN a structure carrying one road over another at a junction or intersection.

foal foals foaling foaled

NOUN **1** a young horse. ▶ VERB **2** When a female horse foals, she gives birth.

foam foams foaming foamed

NOUN **1** Foam is a mass of tiny bubbles. **2** Foam is light spongy material used, for example, in furniture or packaging. ▶ VERB **3** When something foams, it forms a mass of small bubbles.

■ (sense 1) bubbles, froth

fob off fobs off fobbing off fobbed off

VERB; INFORMAL If you fob someone off, you provide them with something that is not very good or not adequate.

focus focuses or **focusses focusing** or **focussing focused** or **focussed; focuses** or **foci**

VERB **1** If you focus your eyes or an instrument on an object, you adjust them so that the image is clear.

a
b
c
d
e
f
g
h
i
j
k
l
m
n
o
p
q
r
s
t
u
v
w
x
y
z

focus
▸ NOUN 2 The focus of something is its centre of attention E.G. *The focus of the conversation had moved around during the meal.*

focal ADJECTIVE

☑ When you add the verb endings to *focus*, you can either add them straight to *focus* (*focuses, focusing, focused*), or you can put another *s* at the end of *focus* before adding the endings (*focusses, focussing, focussed*). Either way is correct, but the first way is much more common. The plural of the noun is either *focuses* or *foci*, but *focuses* is the commoner.

fodder
NOUN Fodder is food for farm animals or horses.

foe foes
NOUN an enemy.

foetus foetuses
Said "fee-tus"; *also spelt* **fetus**
NOUN an unborn child or animal in the womb.

foetal ADJECTIVE

fog fogs fogging fogged
NOUN 1 Fog is a thick mist of water droplets suspended in the air. ▸ VERB 2 If glass fogs up, it becomes clouded with steam or condensation.

foggy ADJECTIVE

foil foils foiling foiled
VERB 1 If you foil someone's attempt at something, you prevent them from succeeding. ▸ NOUN 2 Foil is thin, paper-like sheets of metal used to wrap food. 3 Something that is a good foil for something else contrasts with it and makes its good qualities more noticeable. 4 a thin, light sword with a button on the tip, used in fencing.

foist foists foisting foisted
VERB If you foist something on someone, you force or impose it on them.

fold folds folding folded
VERB 1 If you fold something, you bend it so that one part lies over another. 2 INFORMAL If a business folds, it fails and closes down. 3 In cooking, if you fold one ingredient into another, you mix it in gently. ▸ NOUN 4 a crease or bend in paper or cloth. 5 a small enclosed area for sheep.
▣ (sense 1) bend, crease, double over

folder folders
NOUN a thin piece of folded cardboard for keeping loose papers together.

foliage
NOUN Foliage is leaves and plants.

folk folks
NOUN 1 Folk or folks are people.
▸ ADJECTIVE 2 Folk music, dance, or art is traditional or representative of the ordinary people of an area.

folklore
NOUN Folklore is the traditional stories and beliefs of a community.

follicle follicles
NOUN a small sac or cavity in the body E.G. *hair follicles.*

follow follows following followed
VERB 1 If you follow someone, you move along behind them. If you follow a path or a sign, you move along in that direction. 2 Something that follows a particular thing happens after it. 3 Something that follows is true or logical as a result of something else being the case E.G. *Just because she is pretty, it doesn't follow that she can sing.* 4 If you follow instructions or advice, you do

what you are told. **5** If you follow an explanation or the plot of a story, you understand each stage of it.

follower followers
NOUN The followers of a person or belief are the people who support them.
■ adherent, supporter

folly follies
NOUN Folly is a foolish act or foolish behaviour.
■ foolishness, stupidity

fond fonder fondest
ADJECTIVE **1** If you are fond of someone or something, you like them. **2** A fond hope or belief is thought of with happiness but is unlikely to happen.
fondly ADVERB **fondness** NOUN
■ (sense 1) affectionate, loving

fondle fondles fondling fondled
VERB To fondle something is to stroke it affectionately.

font fonts
NOUN a large stone bowl in a church that holds the water for baptisms.

food foods
NOUN Food is any substance consumed by an animal or plant to provide energy.
■ fare, nourishment

food chain food chains
NOUN a series of living things which are linked because each one feeds on the next one in the series. For example, a plant may be eaten by a rabbit which may be eaten by a fox.

foodstuff foodstuffs
NOUN anything used for food.

food technology
NOUN Food technology is the study of foods and what they consist of, and their effect on the body.

fool fools fooling fooled
NOUN **1** someone who behaves in a silly or stupid way. **2** a dessert made from fruit, eggs, cream, and sugar whipped together. ▶ VERB **3** If you fool someone, you deceive or trick them.

foolhardy
ADJECTIVE foolish and involving too great a risk.

foolish
ADJECTIVE very silly or unwise.
foolishly ADVERB **foolishness** NOUN

foolproof
ADJECTIVE Something that is foolproof is so well designed or simple to use that it cannot fail.

foot feet
NOUN **1** the part of your body at the end of your leg. **2** the bottom, base, or lower end of something E.G. *the foot of the mountain.* **3** a unit of length equal to 12 inches or about 30.5 centimetres. **4** In poetry, a foot is the basic unit of rhythm containing two or three syllables. ▶ ADJECTIVE **5** A foot brake, pedal, or pump is operated by your foot.

footage
NOUN Footage is a length of film E.G. *library footage of prison riots.*

football footballs
NOUN **1** Football is any game in which the ball can be kicked, such as soccer, Australian Rules, rugby union, and American football. **2** a ball used in any of these games.
footballer NOUN

foothills
PLURAL NOUN Foothills are hills at the base of mountains.

foothold footholds
NOUN **1** a place where you can put your foot when climbing. **2** a position

a
b
c
d
e
f
g
h
i
j
k
l
m
n
o
p
q
r
s
t
u
v
w
x
y
z

footing

NOUN **1** Footing is a secure grip by or for your feet E.G. *He missed his footing and fell flat*. **2** a footing is the basis or nature of a relationship or situation E.G. *Steps to put the nation on a war footing*.

footman footmen

NOUN a male servant in a large house who wears uniform.

footnote footnotes

NOUN a note at the bottom of a page or an additional comment giving extra information.

footpath footpaths

NOUN a path for people to walk on.

footprint footprints

NOUN a mark left by a foot or shoe.

footstep footsteps

NOUN the sound or mark made by someone walking.

for

PREPOSITION **1** meant to be given to or used by a particular person, or done in order to help or benefit them E.G. *private beaches for their exclusive use*. **2** 'For' is used when explaining the reason, cause, or purpose of something E.G. *This is my excuse for going to Italy*. **3** You use 'for' to express a quantity, time, or distance E.G. *I'll play for ages… the only house for miles around*. **4** If you are for something, you support it or approve of it E.G. *votes for or against independence*.

forage forages foraging foraged

VERB When a person or animal forages, they search for food.

foray forays

NOUN **1** a brief attempt to do or get

something E.G. *her first foray into acting*. **2** an attack or raid by soldiers.

forbid forbids forbidding forbade forbidden

VERB If you forbid someone to do something, you order them not to do it.

forbidden ADJECTIVE

force forces forcing forced

VERB **1** To force someone to do something is to make them do it. **2** To force something is to use violence or great strength to move or open it. ▶ NOUN **3** The use of force is the use of violence or great strength. **4** The force of something is its strength or power E.G. *The force of the explosion shook buildings*. **5** a person or thing that has a lot of influence or effect E.G. *She became the dominant force in tennis*. **6** an organized group of soldiers or police. **7** In physics, force is a pushing or pulling influence that changes a body from a state of rest to one of motion, or changes its rate of motion. ▶ PHRASE **8** A law or rule that is **in force** is currently valid and must be obeyed.

▆ (sense 1) compel, drive, make

forceful

ADJECTIVE powerful and convincing E.G. *a forceful, highly political lawyer*.

forcefully ADVERB

forceps

PLURAL NOUN Forceps are a pair of long tongs or pincers used by a doctor or surgeon.

forcible

ADJECTIVE **1** involving physical force or violence. **2** convincing and making a strong impression E.G. *a forcible reminder*.

forcibly ADVERB

ford fords fording forded
NOUN 1 a shallow place in a river where it is possible to cross on foot or in a vehicle. ▶ VERB 2 To ford a river is to cross it on foot or in a vehicle.

fore
PHRASE Someone or something that comes **to the fore** becomes important or popular.

forearm forearms
NOUN the part of your arm between your elbow and your wrist.

forebear forebears
NOUN Your forebears are your ancestors.

foreboding forebodings
NOUN a strong feeling of approaching disaster.

forecast forecasts forecasting forecast or forecasted
NOUN 1 a prediction of what will happen, especially a statement about what the weather will be like. ▶ VERB 2 To forecast an event is to predict what will happen.

forecourt forecourts
NOUN an open area at the front of a petrol station or large building.

forefather forefathers
NOUN Your forefathers are your ancestors.

forefinger forefingers
NOUN the finger next to your thumb.

forefront
NOUN The forefront of something is the most important and progressive part of it.

forego foregoes foregoing forewent foregone; also spelt **forgo**
VERB If you forego something pleasant, you give it up or do not insist on having it.

foregoing
A FORMAL PHRASE You can say **the foregoing** when talking about something that has just been said E.G. *The foregoing discussion has highlighted the difficulties.*

foregone conclusion foregone conclusions
NOUN A foregone conclusion is a result or conclusion that is bound to happen.

foreground
NOUN (ART) In a picture, the foreground is the part that seems nearest to you.

forehand forehands
NOUN or ADJECTIVE a stroke in tennis, squash, or badminton made with the palm of your hand facing in the direction that you hit the ball.

forehead foreheads
NOUN the area at the front of your head, above your eyebrows and below your hairline.

foreign
ADJECTIVE 1 belonging to or involving countries other than your own E.G. *foreign coins… foreign travel.*
2 unfamiliar or uncharacteristic E.G. *Such daft enthusiasm was foreign to him.* 3 A foreign object has got into something, usually by accident, and should not be there E.G. *a foreign object in my eye.*
foreigner NOUN
▤ (sense 2) alien, unfamiliar

foreman foremen
NOUN 1 a person in charge of a group of workers, for example on a building site. 2 The foreman of a jury is the spokesman.

foremost
ADJECTIVE The foremost of a group of

a
b
c
d
e
f
g
h
i
j
k
l
m
n
o
p
q
r
s
t
u
v
w
x
y
z

things is the most important or the best.

forensic
ADJECTIVE 1 relating to or involving the scientific examination of objects involved in a crime. 2 relating to or involving the legal profession.

forerunner forerunners
NOUN The forerunner of something is the person who first introduced or achieved it, or the first example of it.

foresee foresees foreseeing foresaw foreseen
VERB If you foresee something, you predict or expect that it will happen.
foreseeable ADJECTIVE

foresight
NOUN Foresight is the ability to know what is going to happen in the future.

foreskin foreskins
NOUN A man's foreskin is the fold of skin covering the end of his penis.

forest forests
NOUN a large area of trees growing close together.

forestry
NOUN Forestry is the study and work of growing and maintaining forests.

foretaste foretastes
NOUN a slight taste or experience of something in advance.

foretell foretells foretelling foretold
VERB If you foretell something, you predict that it will happen.

forever
ADVERB permanently or continually.

forewarn forewarns forewarning forewarned
VERB If you forewarn someone, you warn them in advance about something.

foreword forewords
NOUN an introduction in a book.

forfeit forfeits forfeiting forfeited
VERB 1 If you forfeit something, you have to give it up as a penalty. ▶ NOUN 2 something that you have to give up or do as a penalty.

forge forges forging forged
NOUN 1 a place where a blacksmith works making metal goods by hand.
▶ VERB 2 To forge metal is to hammer and bend it into shape while hot.
3 To forge a relationship is to create a strong and lasting relationship.
4 Someone who forges money, documents, or paintings makes illegal copies of them. 5 To forge ahead is to progress quickly.

forgery forgeries
NOUN Forgery is the crime of forging money, documents, or paintings; also something that has been forged.
forger NOUN

forget forgets forgetting forgot forgotten
VERB 1 If you forget something, you fail to remember or think about it.
2 If you forget yourself, you behave in an unacceptable, uncontrolled way.
forgetful ADJECTIVE

forget-me-not forget-me-nots
NOUN a small plant with tiny blue flowers.

forgive forgives forgiving forgave forgiven
VERB If you forgive someone for doing something bad, you stop feeling angry and resentful towards them.
forgiveness NOUN **forgiving** ADJECTIVE
■ absolve, excuse, pardon

forgo
another spelling of **forego**.

fork forks forking forked
NOUN **1** a pronged instrument used for eating food. **2** a large garden tool with three or four prongs. **3** a Y-shaped junction or division in a road, river, or branch. ▶ VERB **4** To fork something is to move or turn it with a fork.
fork out VERB; INFORMAL If you fork out for something, you pay for it, often unwillingly.

forlorn
ADJECTIVE **1** lonely, unhappy and pitiful. **2** desperate and without any expectation of success E.G. *a forlorn fight for a draw*.
forlornly ADVERB

form forms forming formed
NOUN **1** A particular form of something is a type or kind of it E.G. *a new form of weapon*. **2** The form of something is the shape or pattern of something E.G. *a brooch in the form of a bright green lizard*. **3** a sheet of paper with questions and spaces for you to fill in the answers. **4** a class in a school. ▶ VERB **5** The things that form something are the things it consists of E.G. *events that were to form the basis of her novel*. **6** When someone forms something or when it forms, it is created, organized, or started.

formal
ADJECTIVE **1** correct, serious, and conforming to accepted conventions E.G. *a very formal letter of apology*. **2** official and publicly recognized E.G. *the first formal agreement of its kind*.
formally ADVERB

formaldehyde
Said "for-**mal**-di-hide" NOUN Formaldehyde is a poisonous, strong-smelling gas, used for preserving specimens in biology.

formality formalities
NOUN an action or process that is carried out as part of an official procedure.

format formats
NOUN the way in which something is arranged and presented.

formation formations
NOUN **1** The formation of something is the process of developing and creating it. **2** the pattern or shape of something.

formative
ADJECTIVE having an important and lasting influence on character and development E.G. *the formative days of his young manhood*.

former
ADJECTIVE **1** happening or existing before now or in the past E.G. *a former tennis champion*. ▶ NOUN **2** You use 'the former' to refer to the first of two things just mentioned E.G. *If I had to choose between happiness and money, I would have the former*.
formerly ADVERB

formidable
ADJECTIVE very difficult to deal with or overcome, and therefore rather frightening or impressive E.G. *formidable enemies*.
📖 from Latin *formido* meaning 'terror'
▤ daunting, intimidating

formula formulae or **formulas**
NOUN **1** a group of letters, numbers, and symbols which stand for a mathematical or scientific rule. **2** a list of quantities of substances that

a
b
c
d
e
f
g
h
i
j
k
l
m
n
o
p
q
r
s
t
u
v
w
x
y
z

when mixed make another substance, for example in chemistry. **3** a plan or set of rules for dealing with a particular problem E.G. *my secret formula for keeping in trim.*

formulate formulates formulating formulated
VERB If you formulate a plan or thought, you create it and express it in a clear and precise way.

fornication
NOUN; FORMAL Fornication is the sin of having sex with someone when you are not married to them.

forsake forsakes forsaking forsook forsaken
VERB To forsake someone or something is to give up or abandon them.

fort forts
NOUN **1** a strong building built for defence. ▶ PHRASE **2** If you **hold the fort** for someone, you manage their affairs while they are away.

forte fortes
Said "for-tay" **1** In music, forte is an instruction to play or sing something loudly.
NOUN **2** If something is your forte, you are particularly good at doing it.
■ (sense 2) speciality, strong point

forth
ADVERB **1** out and forward from a starting place E.G. *Christopher Columbus set forth on his epic voyage of discovery.* **2** into view E.G. *he brought forth a slim volume of his newly published verse.*

forthcoming
ADJECTIVE **1** planned to happen soon E.G. *their forthcoming holiday.* **2** given or made available E.G. *Medical aid might be forthcoming.* **3** willing to

give information E.G. *He was not too forthcoming about this.*

forthright
ADJECTIVE Someone who is forthright is direct and honest about their opinions and feelings.

fortification fortifications
NOUN Fortifications are buildings, walls, and ditches used to protect a place.

fortitude
NOUN Fortitude is calm and patient courage.

fortnight fortnights
NOUN a period of two weeks.
fortnightly ADVERB or ADJECTIVE

fortress fortresses
NOUN a castle or well-protected town built for defence.

fortuitous
Said "for-**tyoo**-it-uss" ADJECTIVE happening by chance or good luck E.G. *a fortuitous winning goal.*

fortunate
ADJECTIVE **1** Someone who is fortunate is lucky. **2** Something that is fortunate brings success or advantage.
fortunately ADVERB

fortune fortunes
NOUN **1** Fortune or good fortune is good luck. **2** A fortune is a large amount of money. ▶ PHRASE **3** If someone **tells your fortune**, they predict your future.

forty forties
the number 40.
fortieth

forum forums
NOUN **1** a place or meeting in which people can exchange ideas and discuss public issues. **2** a square in Roman towns where people met to discuss business and politics.

forward forwards forwarding forwarded

ADVERB or ADJECTIVE **1** Forward or forwards means in the front or towards the front E.G. *A photographer moved forward to capture the moment.* **2** Forward means in or towards a future time E.G. *a positive atmosphere of looking forward and making fresh starts.* **3** Forward or forwards also means developing or progressing E.G. *The new committee would push forward government plans.* ► ADVERB **4** If someone or something is put forward, they are suggested as being suitable for something. ► VERB **5** If you forward a letter that you have received, you send it on to the person to whom it is addressed at their new address. ► NOUN **6** In a game such as football or hockey, a forward is a player in an attacking position.
■ (sense 3) ahead, on

fossick fossicks fossicking fossicked

VERB **1** In Australian and New Zealand English, to fossick for gold nuggets or precious stones is to look for them in rivers or old mines. **2** In Australian and New Zealand English, to fossick for something is to search for it.

fossil fossils

NOUN the remains or impression of an animal or plant from a previous age, preserved in rock.
fossilize VERB

fossil fuel fossil fuels

NOUN Fossil fuels are fuels such as coal, oil, and natural gas, which have been formed by rotting animals and plants from millions of years ago.

foster fosters fostering fostered

VERB **1** If someone fosters a child, they are paid to look after the child for a period, but do not become its legal parent. **2** If you foster something such as an activity or an idea, you help its development and growth by encouraging people to do or think it E.G. *to foster and maintain this goodwill.*
foster child NOUN **foster home** NOUN **foster parent** NOUN

fought

the past tense and past participle of **fight**.

foul fouler foulest; fouls fouling fouled

ADJECTIVE **1** Something that is foul is very unpleasant, especially because it is dirty, wicked, or obscene. ► VERB **2** To foul something is to make it dirty, especially with faeces E.G. *Dogs must not be allowed to foul the pavement.* ► NOUN **3** In sport, a foul is an act of breaking the rules.

found founds founding founded

1 Found is the past tense and past participle of **find**. ► VERB **2** If someone founds an organization or institution, they start it and set it up.

foundation foundations

NOUN **1** The foundation of a belief or way of life is the basic ideas or attitudes on which it is built. **2** a solid layer of concrete or bricks in the ground, on which a building is built to give it a firm base. **3** an organization set up by money left in someone's will for research or charity.

founder founders foundering foundered

NOUN **1** The founder of an institution

a b c d e f g h i j k l m n o p q r s t u v w x y z

foundry foundries
or organization is the person who sets it up. ▶ VERB 2 If something founders, it fails.

NOUN a factory where metal is melted and cast.

fountain fountains
NOUN an ornamental structure consisting of a jet of water forced into the air by a pump.

fountain pen fountain pens
NOUN a pen which is supplied with ink from a container inside the pen.

four fours 1 the number 4.
PHRASE 2 If you are **on all fours**, you are on your hands and knees.

four-poster four-posters
NOUN a bed with a tall post at each corner supporting a canopy and curtains.

fourteen
the number 14.

fourteenth

fourth
The fourth item in a series is the one counted as number four.

fowl fowls
NOUN a bird such as chicken or duck that is kept or hunted for its meat or eggs.

fox foxes foxing foxed
NOUN 1 a dog-like wild animal with reddish-brown fur, a pointed face and ears, and a thick tail. ▶ VERB 2 If something foxes you, it is too confusing or puzzling for you to understand.

foxglove foxgloves
NOUN a plant with a tall spike of purple or white trumpet-shaped flowers.

foxhound foxhounds
NOUN a dog trained for hunting foxes.

foyer foyers
Said "foy-ay" NOUN a large area just inside the main doors of a cinema, hotel, or public building.

fracas
Said "frak-ah" NOUN a rough noisy quarrel or fight.

fraction fractions
NOUN 1 (MATHS) In arithmetic, a fraction is a part of a whole number. 2 a tiny proportion or amount of something E.G. *an area a fraction of the size of London.*

fractional ADJECTIVE **fractionally** ADVERB

fractious
ADJECTIVE When small children are fractious, they become upset or angry very easily, often because they are tired.

fracture fractures fracturing fractured
NOUN 1 a crack or break in something, especially a bone. ▶ VERB 2 If something fractures, it breaks.

fragile
ADJECTIVE easily broken or damaged E.G. *fragile glass… a fragile relationship.*

fragility NOUN
▤ breakable, delicate, frail

fragment fragments fragmenting fragmented
NOUN 1 a small piece or part of something. ▶ VERB 2 If something fragments, it breaks into small pieces or different parts.

fragmentation NOUN **fragmented** ADJECTIVE

fragmentary
ADJECTIVE made up of small pieces, or parts that are not connected E.G. *fragmentary notes in a journal.*

fragrance fragrances
NOUN a sweet or pleasant smell.
▤ aroma, perfume, scent

fragrant

ADJECTIVE Something that is fragrant smells sweet or pleasant.

frail frailer frailest

ADJECTIVE **1** Someone who is frail is not strong or healthy. **2** Something that is frail is easily broken or damaged. **frailty** NOUN

frame frames framing framed

NOUN **1** the structure surrounding a door, window, or picture. **2** an arrangement of connected bars over which something is built. **3** The frames of a pair of glasses are the wire or plastic parts that hold the lenses. **4** Your frame is your body E.G. *his large frame*. **5** one of the many separate photographs of which a cinema film is made up. ► VERB **6** To frame a picture is to put it into a frame E.G. *I've framed pictures I've pulled out of magazines.* **7** The language something is framed in is the language used to express it.

framework frameworks

NOUN **1** a structure acting as a support or frame. **2** a set of rules, beliefs, or ideas which you use to decide what to do.

franc francs

NOUN the main unit of currency in Switzerland, and formerly in France and Belgium. A franc is worth 100 centimes.

franchise franchises

NOUN **1** The franchise is the right to vote in an election E.G. *a franchise that gave the vote to less than 2% of the population.* **2** the right given by a company to someone to allow them to sell its goods or services.

frank franker frankest

ADJECTIVE If you are frank, you say

things in an open and honest way.
frankly ADVERB   **frankness** NOUN
▤ candid, honest, open

frantic

ADJECTIVE If you are frantic, you behave in a wild, desperate way because you are anxious or frightened.
frantically ADVERB
▥ from Greek *phrenitikis* meaning 'delirious'

fraternal

ADJECTIVE 'Fraternal' is used to describe friendly actions and feelings between groups of people E.G. *an affectional fraternal greeting.*

fraternity fraternities

NOUN **1** Fraternity is friendship between groups of people. **2** a group of people with something in common E.G. *the golfing fraternity.*

fraud frauds

NOUN **1** Fraud is the crime of getting money by deceit or trickery. **2** something that deceives people in an illegal or immoral way. **3** Someone who is not what they pretend to be.

fraudulent

ADJECTIVE dishonest or deceitful E.G. *fraudulent cheques.*

fraught

ADJECTIVE If something is fraught with problems or difficulties, it is full of them E.G. *Modern life was fraught with hazards.*

fray frays fraying frayed

VERB **1** If cloth or rope frays, its threads or strands become worn and it is likely to tear or break. ► NOUN **2** a fight or argument.

freak freaks

NOUN **1** someone whose appearance or behaviour is very unusual.
► ADJECTIVE OR NOUN **2** A freak event is

a
b
c
d
e
f
g
h
i
j
k
l
m
n
o
p
q
r
s
t
u
v
w
x
y
z

A B C D E F G H I J K L M N O P Q R S T U V W X Y Z

very unusual and unlikely to happen E.G. *a freak allergy to peanuts*.

freckle freckles
NOUN Freckles are small, light brown spots on someone's skin, especially their face.
freckled ADJECTIVE

free freer freest; frees freeing freed
ADJECTIVE 1 not controlled or limited E.G. *the free flow of aid… free trade*. 2 Someone who is free is no longer a prisoner. 3 To be free of something unpleasant is not to have it E.G. *She wanted her aunt's life to be free of worry*. 4 If someone is free, they are not busy or occupied. If a place, seat, or machine is free, it is not occupied or not being used E.G. *Are you free for dinner?* 5 If something is free, you can have it without paying for it. ► VERB 6 If you free something that is fastened or trapped, you release it E.G. *a campaign to free captive animals*. 7 When a prisoner is freed, he or she is released.
■ (sense 2) at liberty, liberated
■ (sense 5) complimentary, gratis
■ (sense 7) liberate, release

freedom
NOUN 1 If you have the freedom to do something, you have the scope or are allowed to do it E.G. *We have the freedom to decide our own futures*. 2 When prisoners gain their freedom, they escape or are released. 3 When there is freedom from something unpleasant, people are not affected by it E.G. *freedom from guilt*.
■ (sense 2) liberty, release

freehold freeholds
NOUN the right to own a house or piece of land for life without conditions.

freelance
ADJECTIVE or ADVERB A freelance journalist or photographer is not employed by one organization, but is paid for each job he or she does.

freely
ADVERB Freely means without restriction E.G. *the pleasure of being able to walk about freely*.

free-range
ADJECTIVE Free-range eggs are laid by hens that can move and feed freely on an area of open ground.

freestyle
NOUN Freestyle refers to sports competitions, especially swimming, in which competitors can use any style or method.

freeway freeways
NOUN In Australia, South Africa, and the United States, a road-designed for fast-moving traffic.

free will
PHRASE If you do something **of your own free will**, you do it by choice and not because you are forced to.

freeze freezes freezing froze frozen
VERB 1 (SCIENCE) When a liquid freezes, it becomes solid because it is very cold. 2 If you freeze, you suddenly become very still and quiet. 3 (DRAMA) To freeze the action in a film is to stop the film at a particular frame. 4 If you freeze food, you put it in a freezer to preserve it. 5 When wages or prices are frozen, they are officially prevented from rising. ► NOUN 6 an official action taken to prevent wages or prices from rising. 7 a period of freezing weather.

freezer freezers
NOUN a large refrigerator which freezes

and stores food for a long time.

freezing

ADJECTIVE extremely cold.

freight

NOUN Freight is goods moved by lorries, ships, or other transport; also the moving of these goods.

French

ADJECTIVE 1 belonging or relating to France. ▶ NOUN 2 French is the main language spoken in France, and is also spoken by many people in Belgium, Switzerland, and Canada.

French bean French beans

NOUN French beans are green pods eaten as a vegetable, which grow on a climbing plant with white or mauve flowers.

French horn French horns

NOUN a brass musical wind instrument consisting of a tube wound in a circle.

Frenchman Frenchmen

NOUN a man who comes from France. **Frenchwoman** NOUN

french window french windows

NOUN French windows are glass doors that lead into a garden or onto a balcony.

frenetic

ADJECTIVE Frenetic behaviour is wild and excited.

frenzy frenzies

NOUN If someone is in a frenzy, their behaviour is wild and uncontrolled. **frenzied** ADJECTIVE

frequency frequencies

NOUN 1 The frequency of an event is how often it happens E.G. *He was not known to call anyone with great frequency.* 2 (SCIENCE) The frequency of a sound or radio wave is the rate at which it vibrates.

frequent frequents frequenting frequented

ADJECTIVE 1 often happening E.G. *His visits were frequent… They move at frequent intervals.* ▶ VERB 2 If you frequent a place, you go there often. **frequently** ADVERB

fresco frescoes

NOUN a picture painted on a plastered wall while the plaster is still wet. 📖 from Italian *fresco* meaning 'fresh'

fresh fresher freshest

ADJECTIVE 1 A fresh thing replaces a previous one, or is added to it E.G. *footprints filled in by fresh snow… fresh evidence.* 2 Fresh food is newly made or obtained, and not tinned or frozen. 3 Fresh water is not salty, for example the water in a stream. 4 If the weather is fresh, it is fairly cold and windy. 5 If you are fresh from something, you have experienced it recently E.G. *a teacher fresh from college.* **freshly** ADVERB **freshness** NOUN

freshwater

ADJECTIVE 1 A freshwater lake or pool contains water that is not salty. 2 A freshwater creature lives in a river, lake, or pool that is not salty.

fret frets fretting fretted

VERB 1 If you fret about something, you worry about it. ▶ NOUN 2 The frets on a stringed instrument, such as a guitar, are the metal ridges across its neck. **fretful** ADJECTIVE

Freudian slip Freudian slips

NOUN something that you say or do that reveals your unconscious thoughts.

friar friars

NOUN a member of a Catholic religious order.

a
b
c
d
e
f
g
h
i
j
k
l
m
n
o
p
q
r
s
t
u
v
w
x
y
z

A B C D E F G H I J K L M N O P Q R S T U V W X Y Z

friction

NOUN 1 (SCIENCE) the force that stops things from moving freely when they rub against each other.
2 Friction between people is disagreement and quarrels.

Friday Fridays

NOUN the day between Thursday and Saturday.

📖 from Old English *Frigedæg* meaning 'Freya's day'. Freya was the Norse goddess of love

fridge fridges

NOUN the same as a **refrigerator**.

friend friends

NOUN Your friends are people you know well and like to spend time with.

■ chum, companion, mate, pal

friendly friendlier friendliest

ADJECTIVE 1 If you are friendly to someone, you behave in a kind and pleasant way to them. 2 People who are friendly with each other like each other and enjoy spending time together.

friendliness NOUN

■ (sense 1) amicable, cordial, genial

friendship friendships

NOUN 1 Your friendships are the special relationships that you have with your friends. 2 Friendship is the state of being friends with someone.

■ (sense 2) friendliness, goodwill

frieze friezes

NOUN 1 a strip of decoration or carving along the top of a wall or column. 2 (ART) a picture on a long strip of paper which is hung along a wall.

frigate frigates

NOUN a small, fast warship.

fright

NOUN Fright is a sudden feeling of fear.

frighten frightens frightening frightened

VERB If something frightens you, it makes you afraid.

frightened ADJECTIVE **frightening** ADJECTIVE

frightful

ADJECTIVE very bad or unpleasant E.G. *a frightful bully*.

frigid

ADJECTIVE Frigid behaviour is cold and unfriendly E.G. *frigid stares*.

frill frills

NOUN a strip of cloth with many folds, attached to something as a decoration.

frilly ADJECTIVE

fringe fringes

NOUN 1 the hair that hangs over a person's forehead. 2 a decoration on clothes and other objects, consisting of a row of hanging strips or threads. 3 The fringes of a place are the parts farthest from its centre E.G. *the western fringe of the Amazon basin*.

fringed ADJECTIVE

frisk frisks frisking frisked

VERB INFORMAL If someone frisks you, they search you quickly with their hands to see if you are hiding a weapon in your clothes.

frisky friskier friskiest

ADJECTIVE A frisky animal or child is energetic and wants to have fun.

fritter fritters frittering frittered

NOUN 1 Fritters consist of food dipped in batter and fried E.G. *apple fritters*.
▶ VERB 2 If you fritter away your time or money, you waste it on unimportant things.

📖 from Latin *frigere* meaning 'to fry'

frivolous

ADJECTIVE Someone who is frivolous

behaves in a silly or light-hearted way, especially when they should be serious or sensible.

frivolity NOUN
■ flippant, silly

frizzy frizzier frizziest
ADJECTIVE Frizzy hair has stiff, wiry curls.

frock frocks
NOUN; OLD-FASHIONED a dress.

frog frogs
NOUN a small amphibious creature with smooth skin, prominent eyes, and long back legs which it uses for jumping.

frolic frolics frolicking frolicked
VERB When animals or children frolic, they run around and play in a lively way.
回 from Dutch *vrolijk* meaning 'joyful'
■ frisk, play, romp

from
PREPOSITION 1 You use 'from' to say what the source, origin, or starting point of something is E.G. *a call from a public telephone… people from a city 100 miles away.* 2 If you take something from an amount, you reduce the amount by that much E.G. *A sum of money was wrongly taken from his account.* 3 You also use 'from' when stating the range of something E.G. *a score from one to five.*

frond fronds
NOUN Fronds are long feathery leaves.

front fronts fronting fronted
NOUN 1 The front of something is the part that faces forward. 2 In a war, the front is the place where two armies are fighting. 3 In meteorology, a front is the line where a mass of cold air meets a mass of warm air. 4 A front is an outward appearance, often one that is false E.G. *I put up a brave front… He's no more than a respectable front for some very dubious happenings.* ▶ PHRASE 5 In **front** means ahead or further forward. 6 If you do something in **front of** someone, you do it when they are present.

frontal ADJECTIVE

frontage frontages
NOUN The frontage of a building is the wall that faces a street.

frontier frontiers
NOUN a border between two countries.

frontispiece frontispieces
NOUN a picture opposite the title page of a book.

frost frosts
NOUN When there is a frost, the temperature outside falls below freezing.

frostbite
NOUN Frostbite is damage to your fingers, toes, or ears caused by extreme cold.

frosty frostier frostiest
ADJECTIVE 1 If it is frosty, the temperature outside is below freezing point. 2 If someone is frosty, they are unfriendly or disapproving.

froth froths frothing frothed
NOUN 1 Froth is a mass of small bubbles on the surface of a liquid. ▶ VERB 2 If a liquid froths, small bubbles appear on its surface.

frothy ADJECTIVE

frown frowns frowning frowned
VERB 1 If you frown, you move your eyebrows closer together, because you are annoyed, worried, or concentrating. ▶ NOUN 2 a cross expression on someone's face.

froze
the past tense of **freeze**.

a b c d e f g h i j k l m n o p q r s t u v w x y z

Rhythmical Hounds Yap To Heavy Music (<u>rhythm</u>) **SPELLING NOTE**

A B C D E F G H I J K L M N O P Q R S T U V W X Y Z

frozen
1 Frozen is the past participle of **freeze**. ► ADJECTIVE 2 If you say are frozen, you mean you are extremely cold.
🔲 chilled, ice-cold, icy

fructose
Said "fruck-toes" NOUN Fructose is a type of sugar found in many fruits and in honey.

frugal
ADJECTIVE 1 Someone who is frugal spends very little money. 2 A frugal meal is small and cheap.
frugality NOUN
🔲 (sense 1) economical, thrifty

fruit fruits
NOUN 1 the part of a plant that develops after the flower and contains the seeds. Many fruits are edible. ► PLURAL NOUN 2 The fruits of something is its good results E.G. *It will be a few years before the fruits of this work are apparent.*

fruitful
ADJECTIVE Something that is fruitful has good and useful results E.G. *a fruitful experience.*

fruitless
ADJECTIVE Something that is fruitless does not achieve anything E.G. *a fruitless effort.*

fruit machine fruit machines
NOUN a coin-operated gambling machine which pays out money when a particular series of symbols, usually fruit, appears on a screen.

fruit salad fruit salads
NOUN a mixture of pieces of different fruits served in a juice as a dessert.

fruity fruitier fruitiest
ADJECTIVE Something that is fruity smells or tastes of fruit.

frustrate frustrates frustrating frustrated
VERB 1 If something frustrates you, it prevents you doing what you want and makes you upset and angry E.G. *Everyone gets frustrated with their work.* 2 To frustrate something such as a plan is to prevent it E.G. *She hopes to frustrate the engagement of her son.*
frustrated ADJECTIVE **frustrating** ADJECTIVE **frustration** NOUN
🔲 (sense 2) foil, thwart

fry fries frying fried
VERB When you fry food, you cook it in a pan containing hot fat or oil.

fuchsia fuchsias
Said "fyoo-sha" NOUN a plant or small bush with pink, purple, or white flowers that hang downwards.

fudge fudges fudging fudged
NOUN 1 Fudge is a soft brown sweet made from butter, milk, and sugar.
► VERB 2 If you fudge something, you avoid making clear or definite decisions or statements about it E.G. *He was carefully fudging his message.*

fuel fuels fuelling fuelled
NOUN 1 Fuel is a substance such as coal or petrol that is burned to provide heat or power. ► VERB 2 A machine or vehicle that is fuelled by a substance works by burning the substance as a fuel E.G. *power stations fuelled by wood.*

fug
NOUN A fug is an airless, smoky atmosphere.

fugitive fugitives
Said "fyoo-jit-tiv" NOUN someone who is running away or hiding, especially from the police.

fulcrum fulcrums or fulcra

NOUN the point at which something is balancing or pivoting.

-ful

SUFFIX 1 '-ful' is used to form adjectives with the meaning 'full of' E.G. *careful*. 2 '-ful' is used to form nouns which mean 'the amount needed to fill' E.G. *spoonful*.

📖 from Old English

fulfil fulfils fulfilling fulfilled

VERB 1 If you fulfil a promise, hope, or duty, you carry it out or achieve it. 2 If something fulfils you, it gives you satisfaction.

fulfilling ADJECTIVE　**fulfilment** NOUN

full fuller fullest

ADJECTIVE 1 containing or having as much as it is possible to hold E.G. *His room is full of posters*. 2 complete or whole E.G. *They had taken a full meal… a full 20 years later*. 3 loose and made from a lot of fabric E.G. *full sleeves*. 4 rich and strong E.G. *a full, fruity wine*. ▶ ADVERB 5 completely and directly E.G. *Turn the taps full on*.
▶ PHRASE 6 Something that has been done or described **in full** has been dealt with completely.

fullness NOUN　**fully** ADVERB

■ (sense 1) filled, loaded, packed

full-blooded

ADJECTIVE having great commitment and enthusiasm E.G. *a full-blooded sprint for third place*.

full-blown

ADJECTIVE complete and fully developed E.G. *a full-blown love of music*.

full moon full moons

NOUN the moon when it appears as a complete circle.

full stop full stops

NOUN the punctuation mark (.) used at the end of a sentence and after an abbreviation or initial.

What does the Full Stop do?

The **full stop** (.) marks the end of any sentence which is not a question or an exclamation:

E.G. *The train is leaving.*

A full stop is also used after an abbreviation or initial:

E.G. *etc.* ■ *Dr. Jenkins* ■ *J.R. Hartley*

A full stop is also used after an expression that stands by itself but is not a complete sentence:

E.G. *Good morning.*

---

full-time

ADJECTIVE 1 involving work for the whole of each normal working week. ▶ NOUN 2 In games such as football, full time is the end of the match.

fully-fledged

ADJECTIVE completely developed E.G. *I was a fully-fledged and mature human being*.

fulsome

ADJECTIVE exaggerated and elaborate, and often sounding insincere E.G. *His most fulsome praise was reserved for his mother*.

fumble fumbles fumbling fumbled

VERB If you fumble, you feel or handle something clumsily.

fume fumes fuming fumed

NOUN 1 Fumes are unpleasant-smelling gases and smoke, often toxic, that are produced by burning and by some chemicals. ▶ VERB 2 If you are fuming, you are very angry.

fun

NOUN 1 Fun is pleasant, enjoyable and

a b c d e f g h i j k l m n o p q r s t u v w x y z

A
B
C
D
E
F
G
H
I
J
K
L
M
N
O
P
Q
R
S
T
U
V
W
X
Y
Z

light-hearted activity. ► PHRASE 2 If you **make fun** of someone, you tease them or make jokes about them.

function functions functioning functioned
NOUN 1 The function of something is its purpose or natural action E.G. *The function of the kidneys is to filter waste products from the blood.* 2 A person's function is the role they have in something or the job they have to do E.G. *It is one of his functions to make sure the heating system is working properly.* 3 a large formal dinner, reception, or party. ► VERB 4 When something functions, it operates or works.

functional
ADJECTIVE 1 relating to the way something works. 2 designed for practical use rather than for decoration or attractiveness E.G. *Feminine clothing has never been designed to be functional.* 3 working properly E.G. *fully functional smoke alarms.*

fund funds funding funded
NOUN 1 an amount of available money, usually for a particular purpose E.G. *a pension fund.* 2 A fund of something is a lot of it E.G. *He had a fund of hilarious tales on the subject.* ► VERB 3 Someone who funds something provides money for it E.G. *research funded by pharmaceutical companies.*
■ (sense 3) finance, subsidize

fundamental fundamentals
ADJECTIVE 1 basic and central E.G. *the fundamental right of freedom of choice… fundamental changes.* ► NOUN 2 The fundamentals of something are its most basic and important parts E.G. *teaching small*

children the fundamentals of road safety.

funeral funerals
Said "f**yoo**-ner-al" NOUN 〈 RE 〉 a ceremony or religious service for the burial or cremation of a dead person.

funereal
Said "few-**nee**-ree-al" ADJECTIVE depressing and gloomy.

funfair funfairs
NOUN a place of entertainment with things like amusement arcades and rides.

fungicide fungicides
NOUN a chemical used to kill or prevent fungus.

fungus fungi or funguses
NOUN a plant such as a mushroom or mould that does not have leaves and grows on other living things.
fungal ADJECTIVE

funk funks funking funked
VERB 1 OLD-FASHIONED If you funk something, you fail to do it because of fear. ► NOUN 2 Funk is a style of music with a strong rhythm based on jazz and blues.

funnel funnels funnelling funnelled
NOUN 1 an open cone narrowing to a tube, used to pour substances into containers. 2 a metal chimney on a ship or steam engine. ► VERB 3 If something is funnelled somewhere, it is directed through a narrow space into that place.

funny funnier funniest
ADJECTIVE 1 strange or puzzling E.G. *You get a lot of funny people coming into the libraries.* 2 causing amusement or laughter E.G. *a funny old film.*
funnily ADVERB
■ (sense 1) odd, peculiar, strange

■ (sense 2) amusing, comical, humorous

fur furs

NOUN **1** Fur is the soft thick body hair of many animals. **2** a coat made from an animal's fur.

furry ADJECTIVE

furious

ADJECTIVE **1** extremely angry. **2** involving great energy, effort, or speed E.G. *the furious speed of technological development.*

furiously ADVERB

furlong furlongs

NOUN a unit of length equal to 220 yards or about 201.2 metres. Furlong originally referred to the length of the average furrow.

furnace furnaces

NOUN a container for a very large, hot fire used, for example, in the steel industry for melting ore.

furnish furnishes furnishing furnished

VERB **1** If you furnish a room, you put furniture into it. **2** FORMAL If you furnish someone with something, you supply or provide it for them.

furnishings

PLURAL NOUN The furnishings of a room or house are the furniture and fittings in it.

furniture

NOUN Furniture is movable objects such as tables, chairs and wardrobes.

furore

Said "fyoo-**roh**-ree" NOUN an angry and excited reaction or protest.

🏛 from Italian *furore* meaning 'rage'

furrow furrows furrowing furrowed

NOUN **1** a long, shallow trench made by a plough. ► VERB **2** When someone furrows their brow, they frown.

further furthers furthering furthered

1 a comparative form of **far**.
► ADJECTIVE **2** additional or more E.G. *There was no further rain.* ► VERB **3** If you further something, you help it to progress E.G. *He wants to further his acting career.*

■ (sense 3) advance, promote

further education

NOUN Further education is education at a college after leaving school, but not at a university.

furthermore

ADVERB; FORMAL used to introduce additional information E.G. *There is no record of such a letter. Furthermore it is company policy never to send such letters.*

furthest

a superlative form of **far**.

furtive

ADJECTIVE secretive, sly, and cautious E.G. *a furtive smile.*

furtively ADVERB

fury

NOUN Fury is violent or extreme anger.

fuse fuses fusing fused

NOUN **1** a safety device in a plug or electrical appliance consisting of a piece of wire which melts to stop the electric current if a fault occurs. **2** a long cord attached to some types of simple bomb which is lit to detonate. ► VERB **3** When an electrical appliance fuses, it stops working because the fuse has melted to protect it. **4** If two things fuse, they join or become combined E.G. *Christianity slowly fused with existing beliefs.*

fuselage fuselages

Said "**fyoo**-zil-ahj" NOUN the main part of an aeroplane or rocket.

Elaine and Emily shout EE when they mEEt to grEEt each other (-ee-)   SPELLING NOTE

A
B
C
D
E
F
G
H
I
J
K
L
M
N
O
P
Q
R
S
T
U
V
W
X
Y
Z

fusion

NOUN 1 Fusion is what happens when two substances join by melting together. 2 Fusion is also nuclear fusion. ▸ ADJECTIVE 3 Fushion is used to refer to food or a style of cooking that brings together ingredients or cooking techniques from several different countries.

fuss fusses fussing fussed

NOUN 1 Fuss is unnecessarily anxious or excited behaviour. ▸ VERB 2 If someone fusses, they behave with unnecessary anxiety and concern for unimportant things.

≡ (sense 1) bother, commotion, palaver

fussy fussier fussiest

ADJECTIVE 1 likely to fuss a lot E.G. *He was unusually fussy about keeping things perfect.* 2 with too much elaborate detail or decoration E.G. *fussy chiffon evening wear.*

≡ (sense 1) finicky, particular

futile

ADJECTIVE having no chance of success E.G. *a futile attempt to calm the storm.*

futility NOUN

≡ useless, vain

future futures

NOUN 1 The future is the period of time after the present. 2 Something that has a future is likely to succeed E.G. *She sees no future in a modelling career.* ▸ ADJECTIVE 3 relating to or occurring at a time after the present E.G. *to predict future events.* 4 The future tense of a verb is the form used to express something that will happen in the future.

futuristic

ADJECTIVE very modern and strange, as if belonging to a time in the

future E.G. *futuristic cars.*

fuzz

NOUN 1 short fluffy hair. ▸ PLURAL NOUN 2 INFORMAL The fuzz are the police.

Talking about the Future

There is no simple future tense in English. To talk about an event that will happen in the future, we usually use **compound tenses**.

The auxiliary verbs *will* and *shall* are used before the basic form of the verb to show that an action will happen:

E.G. *His father **will cook** the dinner.*
*I **shall cook** the dinner.*

You can also talk about the future by putting the verbs *will have* or *shall have* before the verb, and adding the ending *-ed*. This form shows that an action will be completed in the future:

E.G. *His father **will have cooked** the dinner.*
*I **shall have cooked** the dinner.*

You can also talk about the future by using the phrase *be about to* or *be going to* in front of the dictionary form of the verb. This shows that the action will take place very soon:

E.G. *He **is about to cook** the dinner.*
*I **am going to cook** the dinner.*

You can sometimes use a form of the present tense to talk about future events, but only if the sentence contains a clear reference to the future:

E.G. *His father **is cooking** the dinner tonight.*
*The plane **leaves** at three o'clock.*

Also see the grammar box at **tense**.

G g

TIP Some words which sound as if they might begin with *g* alone, are actually spelt with the letters *gh*, for example *ghastly* and *ghost*. Some words which sound as if they might begin with the letter *n*, are spelt with *gn*, for example *gnaw*, *gnome* and *gnu*. Also take care with the spelling of words that start with *gu-* followed by the vowels *a*, *e* or *i*, because the *u* is not pronounced, for example *guarantee*, *guard*, *guerrila* and *guile*.

g
an abbreviation for 'grams'.

gabble gabbles gabbling gabbled
VERB If you gabble, you talk so fast that it is difficult for people to understand you.

gable gables
NOUN Gables are the triangular parts at the top of the outside walls at each end of a house.

gadget gadgets
NOUN a small machine or tool.
gadgetry NOUN
■ contraption, device

Gaelic
Said "gay-lik" NOUN a language spoken in some parts of Scotland and Ireland.

gaffe gaffes
Said "gaf" NOUN a social blunder or mistake.

gaffer gaffers
NOUN; INFORMAL a boss.

gag gags gagging gagged
NOUN 1 a strip of cloth that is tied round someone's mouth to stop them speaking. 2 INFORMAL a joke told by a comedian. ▶ VERB 3 To gag someone means to put a gag round their mouth. 4 If you gag, you choke and nearly vomit.

gaggle gaggles
NOUN 1 a group of geese. 2 INFORMAL a

noisy group E.G. *a gaggle of schoolboys*.
📖 from Old German *gagen* meaning 'to cry like a goose'

gaiety
Said "gay-yet-tee" NOUN liveliness and fun.

gaily
ADVERB in a happy and cheerful way.

gain gains gaining gained
VERB 1 If you gain something, you get it gradually E.G. *I spent years at night school trying to gain qualifications.* 2 If you gain from a situation, you get some advantage from it. 3 If you gain on someone, you gradually catch them up. ▶ NOUN 4 an increase E.G. *a gain in speed.* 5 an advantage that you get for yourself E.G. *People use whatever influence they have for personal gain.*

gait gaits
NOUN Someone's gait is their way of walking E.G. *an awkward gait.*

gala galas
NOUN a special public celebration or performance E.G. *the Olympics' opening gala.*

galah galahs
NOUN 1 an Australian cockatoo with a pink breast and a grey back and wings. 2 INFORMAL In Australian

A
B
C
D
E
F
G
H
I
J
K
L
M
N
O
P
Q
R
S
T
U
V
W
X
Y
Z

English, a galah is also a stupid person.

galaxy galaxies
NOUN an enormous group of stars that extends over many millions of miles.
galactic ADJECTIVE

gale gales
NOUN an extremely strong wind.

gall galls galling galled
Rhymes with "ball" NOUN 1 If someone has the gall to do something, they have enough courage or impudence to do it E.G. *He even has the gall to visit her.* ▶ VERB 2 If something galls you, it makes you extremely annoyed.

gall bladder gall bladders
NOUN an organ in your body which stores bile and which is next to your liver.

galleon galleons
NOUN a large sailing ship used in the sixteenth and seventeenth centuries.

gallery galleries
NOUN 1 (ART) a building or room where works of art are shown. 2 In a theatre or large hall, the gallery is a raised area at the back or sides E.G. *the public gallery in Parliament.*

galley galleys
NOUN 1 a kitchen in a ship or aircraft. 2 a ship, driven by oars, used in ancient and medieval times.

Gallic
Said "gal-lik" ADJECTIVE; FORMAL or LITERARY French.

gallon gallons
NOUN a unit of liquid volume equal to eight pints or about 4.55 litres.

gallop gallops galloping galloped
VERB 1 When a horse gallops, it runs very fast, so that during each stride

all four feet are off the ground at the same time. ▶ NOUN 2 a very fast run.

gallows
NOUN A gallows is a framework on which criminals used to be hanged.

gallstone gallstones
NOUN a small painful lump that can develop in your gall bladder.

galore
ADJECTIVE in very large numbers E.G. *chocolates galore.*
📖 from Irish Gaelic *go leór* meaning 'to sufficiency'

galoshes
PLURAL NOUN Galoshes are waterproof rubber shoes which you wear over your ordinary shoes to stop them getting wet.

galvanized or **galvanised**
ADJECTIVE Galvanized metal has been coated with zinc by an electrical process to protect it from rust.

gambit gambits
NOUN something which someone does to gain an advantage in a situation E.G. *Commentators are calling the plan a clever political gambit.*
📖 from Italian *gambetto* meaning 'a tripping up'

gamble gambles gambling gambled
VERB 1 When people gamble, they bet money on the result of a game or race. 2 If you gamble something, you risk losing it in the hope of gaining an advantage E.G. *The company gambled everything on the new factory.* ▶ NOUN 3 If you take a gamble, you take a risk in the hope of gaining an advantage.

gambler NOUN **gambling** NOUN
▤ (sense 1) bet, wager

game games

NOUN **1** an enjoyable activity with a set of rules which is played by individuals or teams against each other. **2** an enjoyable imaginative activity played by small children E.G. *childhood games of cowboys and Indians*. **3** You might describe something as a game when it is designed to gain advantage E.G. *the political game*. **4** Game is wild animals or birds that are hunted for sport or for food. ▶ PLURAL NOUN **5** Games are sports played at school or in a competition. ▶ ADJECTIVE **6** INFORMAL Someone who is game is willing to try something unusual or difficult.

gamely ADVERB

▣ (sense 1) amusement, pastime

gamekeeper gamekeepers

NOUN a person employed to look after game animals and birds on a country estate.

gammon

NOUN Gammon is cured meat from a pig, similar to bacon.

gamut

Said "**gam**-mut" NOUN; FORMAL The gamut of something is the whole range of things that can be included in it E.G. *the whole gamut of human emotions*.

gander ganders

NOUN a male goose.

gang gangs ganging ganged

NOUN **1** a group of people who join together for some purpose, for example to commit a crime. ▶ VERB **2** INFORMAL If people gang up on you, they join together to oppose you.

gangplank gangplanks

NOUN a plank used for boarding and leaving a ship or boat.

gangrene

Said "**gang**-green" NOUN Gangrene is decay in the tissues of part of the body, caused by inadequate blood supply.

gangrenous ADJECTIVE

▥ from Greek *gangraina* meaning 'ulcer' or 'festering sore'

gangster gangsters

NOUN a violent criminal who is a member of a gang.

gannet gannets

NOUN a large sea bird which dives to catch fish.

gaol

another spelling of **jail**.

gap gaps

NOUN **1** a space between two things or a hole in something solid. **2** A gap between things, people, or ideas is a great difference between them E.G. *the gap between fantasy and reality*.

▣ (sense 1) hole, opening, space

gape gapes gaping gaped

VERB **1** If you gape at someone or something, you stare at them with your mouth open in surprise. **2** Something that gapes is wide open E.G. *gaping holes in the wall*.

garage garages

NOUN **1** a building where a car can be kept. **2** a place where cars are repaired and where petrol is sold.

garb

NOUN; FORMAL Someone's garb is their clothes E.G. *his usual garb of a dark suit*.

garbage

NOUN **1** Garbage is rubbish, especially household rubbish. **2** If you say something is garbage, you mean it is nonsense.

a b c d e f **g** h i j k l m n o p q r s t u v w x y z

LEt's measure the angLE (ang**l**e)　　SPELLING NOTE

🔲 from Anglo-French *garbelage* meaning 'removal of discarded matter'

garbled

ADJECTIVE Garbled messages are jumbled and the details may be wrong.

garden gardens

NOUN **1** an area of land next to a house, where flowers, fruit, or vegetables are grown. ▸ PLURAL NOUN **2** Gardens are a type of park in a town or around a large house.
gardening NOUN

gardener gardeners

NOUN a person who looks after a garden as a job or as a hobby.

gargle gargles gargling gargled

VERB When you gargle, you rinse the back of your throat by putting some liquid in your mouth and making a bubbling sound without swallowing the liquid.

gargoyle gargoyles

NOUN a stone carving below the roof of an old building, in the shape of an ugly person or animal and often having a water spout at the mouth.

garish

Said "gair-rish" ADJECTIVE bright and harsh to look at E.G. *garish bright red boots*.

garland garlands

NOUN a circle of flowers and leaves which is worn around the neck or head.

garlic

NOUN Garlic is the small white bulb of an onion-like plant which has a strong taste and smell and is used in cooking.

garment garments

NOUN a piece of clothing.

garnet garnets

NOUN a type of gemstone, usually red in colour.

garnish garnishes garnishing garnished

NOUN **1** something such as a a sprig of parsley, that is used in cooking for decoration. ▸ VERB **2** To garnish food means to decorate it with a garnish.

garret garrets

NOUN an attic.

garrison garrisons

NOUN a group of soldiers stationed in a town in order to guard it; also used of the buildings in which these soldiers live.

garrotte garrottes garrotting garrotted

Said "gar-rot"; also spelt **garotte**
VERB To garrotte someone means to strangle them with a piece of wire.

garter garters

NOUN a piece of elastic worn round the top of a stocking to hold it up.

gas gases; gasses gassing gassed

NOUN **1** any airlike substance that is not liquid or solid, such as oxygen or the gas used as a fuel in heating. **2** In American English, gas is petrol. ▸ VERB **3** To gas people or animals means to kill them with poisonous gas.

☑ The plural of the noun *gas* is *gases*. The verb forms of *gas* are spelt with a double s.

gas chamber gas chambers

NOUN a room in which people or animals are killed with poisonous gas.

gash gashes gashing gashed

NOUN **1** a long, deep cut. ▸ VERB **2** If you gash something, you make a long, deep cut in it.

gas mask gas masks
NOUN a large gas mask with special filters attached which people wear over their face to protect them from poisonous gas.

gasoline
NOUN In American English, gasoline is petrol.

gasp gasps gasping gasped
VERB 1 If you gasp, you quickly draw in your breath through your mouth because you are surprised or in pain. ► NOUN 2 a sharp intake of breath through the mouth.

gastric
ADJECTIVE occurring in the stomach or involving the stomach E.G. *gastric pain.*

gate gates
NOUN 1 a barrier which can open and shut and is used to close the entrance to a garden or field. 2 The gate at a sports event is the number of people who have attended it.

gateau gateaux
Said "*gat-toe*" NOUN a rich layered cake with cream in it.

gatecrash gatecrashes gatecrashing gatecrashed
VERB If you gatecrash a party, you go to it when you have not been invited.

gateway gateways
NOUN 1 an entrance through a wall or fence where there is a gate.
2 Something that is considered to be the entrance to a larger or more important thing can be described as the gateway to the larger thing E.G. *New York is the great gateway to America.*

gather gathers gathering gathered
VERB 1 When people gather, they come together in a group. 2 If you gather a number of things, you bring them together in one place. 3 If something gathers speed or strength, it gets faster or stronger. 4 If you gather something, you learn it, often from what someone says.
■ (sense 1) assemble, congregate
■ (sense 2) amass, assemble, collect

gathering gatherings
NOUN a meeting of people who have come together for a particular purpose.

gauche
Said "*gohsh*" ADJECTIVE; FORMAL socially. awkward.
▥ from French *gauche* meaning 'left-handed'

gaudy gaudier gaudiest
Said "*gaw-dee*" ADJECTIVE very colourful in a vulgar way.
■ bright, flashy, garish

gauge gauges gauging gauged
Said "*gayj*" VERB 1 If you gauge something, you estimate it or calculate it E.G. *He gauged the wind at over 30 knots.* ► NOUN 2 a piece of equipment that measures the amount of something E.G. *a rain gauge.* 3 something that is used as a standard by which you judge a situation E.G. *They see profit as a gauge of efficiency.* 4 On railways, the gauge is the distance between the two rails on a railway line.

gaunt
ADJECTIVE A person who looks gaunt is thin and bony.

gauntlet gauntlets
NOUN 1 Gauntlets are long thick gloves worn for protection, for example by motorcyclists. ► PHRASE

a
b
c
d
e
f
g
h
i
j
k
l
m
n
o
p
q
r
s
t
u
v
w
x
y
z

A
B
C
D
E
F
G
H
I
J
K
L
M
N
O
P
Q
R
S
T
U
V
W
X
Y
Z

2 If you **throw down the gauntlet**, you challenge someone. **3** If you **run the gauntlet**, you have an unpleasant experience in which you are attacked or criticized by people.

gave
the past tense of **give**.

gay gayer gayest; gays
ADJECTIVE **1** Someone who is gay is homosexual. **2** OLD-FASHIONED Gay people or places are lively and full of fun. ▶ NOUN **3** a homosexual person
☑ The most common meaning of *gay* now is 'homosexual'. In some older books it may have its old-fashioned meaning of 'lively and full of fun'. The noun *gaiety* is related to this older meaning of *gay*. The noun that means 'the state of being homosexual' is *gayness*.

gaze gazes gazing gazed
VERB If you gaze at something, you look steadily at it for a long time.

gazelle gazelles
NOUN a small antelope found in Africa and Asia.

gazette gazettes
NOUN a newspaper or journal.

GB
an abbreviation for **Great Britain**.

GCSE GCSEs
In Britain, the GCSE is an examination taken by school students aged fifteen and sixteen. GCSE is an abbreviation for 'General Certificate of Secondary Education'.

gear gears gearing geared
NOUN **1** a piece of machinery which controls the rate at which energy is converted into movement. Gears in vehicles control the speed and power of the vehicle. **2** The gear for an activity is the clothes and equipment that you need for it. ▶ VERB **3** If someone or something is geared to a particular event or purpose, they are prepared for it.

geese
the plural of **goose**.

gel gels gelling gelled
Said "jel" NOUN **1** a smooth soft jelly-like substance E.G. *shower gel.* ▶ VERB **2** If a liquid gels, it turns into a gel. **3** If a vague thought or plan gels, it becomes more definite.

gelatine or **gelatin**
Said "jel-lat-tin" NOUN a clear tasteless substance, obtained from meat and bones, used to make liquids firm and jelly-like.

gelding geldings
Said "gel-ding" NOUN a horse which has been castrated.

gem gems
NOUN **1** a jewel or precious stone. **2** You can describe something or someone that is extremely good or beautiful as a gem E.G. *A gem of a novel.*

Gemini
Said "jem-in-nye" NOUN Gemini is the third sign of the zodiac, represented by a pair of twins. People born between May 21st and June 20th are born under this sign

gemsbok gemsbok or **gemsboks**; also spelt **gemsbuck**
NOUN In South African English, a gemsbok is an oryx, a type of large antelope with straight horns.

gen
NOUN; INFORMAL The gen on something is information about it.

gender genders
NOUN **1** (PSHE) Gender is the sex of a person or animal E.G. *the female*

gender. **2** the classification of nouns as masculine, feminine, and neuter in certain languages.

What is Gender?

When we talk about the "gender" of a noun, we mean whether it is referred to as *he*, *she*, or *it*. There are three genders: **masculine** (things referred to as *he*), **feminine** (things referred to as *she*), and **neuter** (things referred to as *it*).

Masculine nouns refer to male people and animals:

E.G. *The boy put on his coat.* ➤ *boy is **masculine***

Feminine nouns denote female people and animals:

E.G. *The girl put on her coat.* ➤ *girl is **feminine***

It is customary to refer to countries and vehicles as if they were feminine:

E.G. *The ship came into view, her sails swelling in the breeze.*

Neuter nouns refer to inanimate objects and abstract ideas:

E.G. *The kettle will switch itself off.* ➤ *kettle is **neuter***

Common nouns may be either masculine or feminine. Other words in the sentence may tell us if they are male or female:

E.G. *The doctor parked <u>his</u> car. The doctor parked <u>her</u> car.*

---

gene genes
Said "jeen" NOUN one of the parts of a living cell which controls the physical characteristics of an organism and which are passed on

from one generation to the next.

general generals
ADJECTIVE **1** relating to the whole of something or to most things in a group E.G. *your general health*. **2** true, suitable, or relevant in most situations E.G. *the general truth of science*. **3** including or involving a wide range of different things E.G. *a general hospital*. **4** having complete responsibility over a wide area of work or a large number of people E.G. *the general secretary*. ► NOUN **5** an army officer of very high rank. ► PHRASE **6** In general means usually.
generally ADVERB
▤ (sense 1) overall
▤ (sense 2) common, universal, widespread

general election general elections
NOUN an election for a new government, which all the people of a country may vote in.

generalize generalizes generalizing generalized; also spelt **generalise**
VERB To generalize means to say that something is true in most cases, ignoring minor details.
generalization NOUN

general practitioner general practitioners
NOUN a doctor who works in the community rather than in a hospital.

generate generates generating generated
VERB To generate something means to create or produce it E.G. *using wind power to generate electricity*.

generation generations
NOUN all the people of about the same age; also the period of time

a
b
c
d
e
f
g
h
i
j
k
l
m
n
o
p
q
r
s
t
u
v
w
x
y
z

between one generation and the next, usually considered to be about 25–30 years.

generator generators

NOUN a machine which produces electricity from another form of energy such as wind or water power.

generic

ADJECTIVE A generic term is a name that applies to all the members of a group of similar things.

generous

ADJECTIVE 1 (PSHE) A generous person is very willing to give money or time. 2 Something that is generous is very large E.G. *a generous waist*.

generously ADVERB **generosity** NOUN (PSHE)

■ (sense 1) lavish, liberal
■ (sense 2) abundant, ample, lavish

genesis

NOUN; FORMAL The genesis of something is its beginning.

genetics

NOUN Genetics is the science of the way that characteristics are passed on from generation to generation by means of genes.

genetic ADJECTIVE **genetically** ADVERB

genial

ADJECTIVE cheerful, friendly, and kind.

genially ADVERB

genie genies

Said "jee-nee" NOUN a magical being that obeys the wishes of the person who controls it.

📖 from Arabic *jinni* meaning 'demon'

genitals

PLURAL NOUN The genitals are the reproductive organs. The technical name is genitalia.

genital ADJECTIVE

genius geniuses

NOUN 1 a highly intelligent, creative, or talented person. 2 Genius is great intelligence, creativity, or talent E.G. *a poet of genius*.

genocide

Said "jen-nos-side" NOUN; FORMAL Genocide is the systematic murder of all members of a particular race or group.

genre genres

Said "jahn-ra" NOUN (ENGLISH) (LIBRARY) FORMAL a particular style in literature or art.

genteel

ADJECTIVE very polite and refined.

Gentile Gentiles

Said "jen-tile" NOUN a person who is not Jewish.

gentility

NOUN Gentility is excessive politeness and refinement.

gentle gentler gentlest

ADJECTIVE mild and calm; not violent or rough E.G. *a gentle man*.

gently ADVERB **gentleness** NOUN

gentleman gentlemen

NOUN a man who is polite and well-educated; also a polite way of referring to any man.

gentlemanly ADJECTIVE

gentry

PLURAL NOUN The gentry are people from the upper classes.

genuine

Said "jen-yoo-in" ADJECTIVE 1 real and not false or pretend E.G. *a genuine smile… genuine silver*. 2 A genuine person is sincere and honest.

genuinely ADVERB **genuineness** NOUN

genus genera

Said "jee-nuss" NOUN In biology, a

361

geo-

PREFIX 'Geo-' means 'earth' E.G. *geography… geologist.*
from Greek *gē* meaning 'earth'

geography

NOUN the study of the physical features of the earth, together with the climate, natural resources and population in different parts of the world.
geographic or **geographical** ADJECTIVE **geographically** ADVERB

geology

NOUN the study of the earth's structure, especially the layers of rock and soil that make up the surface of the earth.
geological ADJECTIVE **geologist** NOUN

geometric or **geometrical**

ADJECTIVE 1 consisting of regular lines and shapes, such as squares, triangles, and circles E.G. *bold geometric designs.* 2 involving geometry.

geometry

NOUN Geometry is the branch of mathematics that deals with lines, angles, curves, and spaces.

Georgian

ADJECTIVE belonging to or typical of the time from 1714 to 1830, when George I to George IV reigned in Britain.

geranium geraniums

NOUN a garden plant with red, pink, or white flowers.

gerbil gerbils

Said "**jer**-bil" NOUN a small rodent with long back legs, often kept as a pet

geriatric

Said "jer-ree-**at**-rik" ADJECTIVE 1 relating to the medical care of old people E.G. *a geriatric nurse.* 2 Someone or something that is geriatric is very old E.G. *a geriatric donkey.* ▶ NOUN 3 an old person, especially as a patient.
geriatrics NOUN

germ germs

NOUN 1 a very small organism that causes disease. 2 FORMAL The germ of an idea or plan is the beginning of it.

German Germans

ADJECTIVE 1 belonging or relating to Germany. ▶ NOUN 2 someone who comes from Germany. 3 German is the main language spoken in Germany and Austria and is also spoken by many people in Switzerland.

Germanic

ADJECTIVE 1 typical of Germany or the German people 2 The Germanic group of languages includes English, Dutch, German, Danish, Swedish, and Norwegian.

German measles

NOUN German measles is a contagious disease that gives you a sore throat and red spots.

germinate germinates germinating germinated

VERB 1 When a seed germinates, it starts to grow. 2 When an idea or plan germinates, it starts to develop.
germination NOUN

gerrymander gerrymanders gerrymandering gerrymandered

VERB To gerrymander is to change political boundaries in an area so that a particular party or politician gets a bigger share of votes in an election.

gestation

Said "jes-**tay**-shn" NOUN; TECHNICAL

I always visit my FRIend on a FRIday (<u>fri</u>end) SPELLING NOTE

Gestation is the time during which a foetus is growing inside its mother's womb.

gesticulate gesticulates gesticulating gesticulated

Said "jes-**stik**-yoo-late" VERB If you gesticulate, you move your hands and arms around while you are talking.

gesticulation NOUN

gesture gestures gesturing gestured

NOUN 1 a movement of your hands or head that conveys a message or feeling. 2 an action symbolizing something E.G. *a gesture of support.*

▶ VERB 3 If you gesture, you move your hands or head in order to communicate a message or feeling.

get gets getting got

VERB 1 Get often means the same as become E.G. *People draw the curtains once it gets dark.* 2 If you get into a particular situation, you put yourself in that situation E.G. *We are going to get into a hopeless muddle.* 3 If you get something done, you do it or you persuade someone to do it E.G. *You can get your homework done in time.* 4 If you get somewhere, you go there E.G. *I must get home.* 5 If you get something, you fetch it or are given it E.G. *I'll get us all a cup of coffee… I got your message.* 6 If you get a joke or get the point of something, you understand it. 7 If you get a train, bus, or plane, you travel on it E.G. *You can get a bus.*

 (sense 1) become, grow

 (sense 5) acquire, obtain, procure

get across VERB If you get an idea across, you make people understand it.

get at VERB 1 If someone is getting

at you, they are criticizing you in an unkind way. 2 If you ask someone what they are getting at, you are asking them to explain what they mean.

get away with VERB If you get away with something dishonest, you are not found out or punished for doing it.

get by VERB If you get by, you have just enough money to live on.

get on VERB 1 If two people get on well together, they like each other's company. 2 If you get on with a task, you do it.

get over with VERB If you want to get something unpleasant over with, you want it to be finished quickly.

get through VERB 1 If you get through to someone, you make them understand what you are saying. 2 If you get through to someone on the telephone, you succeed in talking to them.

getaway getaways

NOUN an escape made by criminals.

get-together get-togethers

NOUN; INFORMAL an informal meeting or party.

geyser geysers

Said "**gee**-zer" NOUN a spring through which hot water and steam gush up in spurts.

 from Old Norse *geysa* meaning 'to gush'

Ghanaian Ghanaians

Said "gah-**nay**-an" ADJECTIVE

1 belonging or relating to Ghana.

▶ NOUN 2 someone who comes from Ghana.

ghastly ghastlier ghastliest

ADJECTIVE extremely horrible and unpleasant E.G. *a ghastly crime… ghastly food.*

gherkin gherkins
NOUN a small pickled cucumber.

ghetto ghettoes or ghettos
NOUN a part of a city where many poor people of a particular race live. 🏛 from Italian *borghetto* meaning 'settlement outside the city walls'

ghost ghosts
NOUN the spirit of a dead person, believed to haunt people or places. ▤ phantom, spectre, spirit

ghoulish
Said "gool-ish" ADJECTIVE very interested in unpleasant things such as death and murder.

giant giants
NOUN 1 a huge person in a myth or legend. ► ADJECTIVE 2 much larger than other similar things E.G. *giant prawns… a giant wave*.

gibberish
NOUN Gibberish is speech that makes no sense at all.

gibbon gibbons
NOUN an ape with very long arms.

gibe gibes; also spelt **jibe**
NOUN an insulting remark.

giddy giddier giddiest
ADJECTIVE If you feel giddy, you feel unsteady on your feet usually because you are ill.
giddily ADVERB

gift gifts
NOUN 1 a present. 2 a natural skill or ability E.G. *a gift for comedy*.

gifted
ADJECTIVE having a special ability E.G. *gifted tennis players*.

gig gigs
NOUN a rock or jazz concert.

gigantic
ADJECTIVE extremely large.

giggle giggles giggling giggled
VERB 1 To giggle means to laugh in a nervous or embarrassed way. ► NOUN 2 a short, nervous laugh.
giggly ADJECTIVE

gilded
ADJECTIVE Something which is gilded is covered with a thin layer of gold.

gill gills
NOUN 1 *Said "gil"* The gills of a fish are the organs on its sides which it uses for breathing. 2 *Said "jil"* a unit of liquid volume equal to one quarter of a pint or about 0.142 litres.

gilt gilts
NOUN 1 a thin layer of gold. ► ADJECTIVE 2 covered with a thin layer of gold E.G. *a gilt writing-table*.

gimmick gimmicks
NOUN a device that is not really necessary but is used to attract interest E.G. *All pop stars need a good gimmick*.
gimmicky ADJECTIVE

gin
NOUN Gin is a strong, colourless alcoholic drink made from grain and juniper berries.

ginger
NOUN 1 Ginger is a plant root with a hot, spicy flavour, used in cooking. ► ADJECTIVE 2 bright orange or red E.G. *ginger hair*.

gingerbread
NOUN Gingerbread is a sweet, ginger-flavoured cake.

gingerly
ADVERB If you move gingerly, you move cautiously E.G. *They walked gingerly down the stairs*.

gingham
NOUN Gingham is checked cotton cloth.

a
b
c
d
e
f
g
h
i
j
k
l
m
n
o
p
q
r
s
t
u
v
w
x
y
z

A B C D E F G H I J K L M N O P Q R S T U V W X Y Z

🔲 from Malay *ginggang* meaning 'striped cloth'

gipsy
another spelling of **gypsy**.

giraffe giraffes
NOUN a tall, four-legged African mammal with a very long neck.
🔲 from Arabic *zarafah* meaning 'giraffe'

girder girders
NOUN a large metal beam used in the construction of a bridge or a building.

girdle girdles
NOUN a woman's corset.

girl girls
NOUN a female child.
girlish ADJECTIVE **girlhood** NOUN

girlfriend girlfriends
NOUN Someone's girlfriend is the woman or girl with whom they are having a romantic or sexual relationship.

giro giros
Said "jie-roh" NOUN 1 Giro is a system of transferring money from one account to another through a bank or post office. 2 In Britain, a cheque received regularly from the government by unemployed or sick people.

girth
NOUN The girth of something is the measurement round it.

gist
Said "jist" NOUN the general meaning or most important points in a piece of writing or speech.

give gives giving gave given
VERB 1 If you give someone something, you hand it to them or provide it for them E.G. *I gave her a tape… George gave me my job.*
2 'Give' is also used to express

physical actions and speech E.G. *He gave a fierce smile… Rosa gave a lovely performance.* 3 If you give a party or a meal, you are the host at it. 4 If something gives, it collapses under pressure. ➤ NOUN 5 If material has give, it will bend or stretch when pulled or put under pressure. ➤ PHRASE 6 You use **give or take** to indicate that an amount you are mentioning is not exact E.G. *About two years, give or take a month or so.* 7 If something **gives way** to something else, it is replaced by it. 8 If something **gives way**, it collapses.
🔲 (sense 1) grant, present, provide

give in VERB If you give in, you admit that you are defeated.

give out VERB If something gives out, it stops working E.G. *the electricity gave out.*

give up VERB 1 If you give something up, you stop doing it E.G. *I can't give up my job.* 2 If you give up, you admit that you cannot do something. 3 If you give someone up, you let the police know where they are hiding.

given
1 the past participle of **give**.
➤ ADJECTIVE 2 fixed or specified E.G. *My style can change at any given moment.*

glacé
Said "glass-say" ADJECTIVE Glacé fruits are fruits soaked and coated with sugar E.G. *glacé cherries.*

glaciation
Said "glay-see-ay-shn" NOUN In geography, glaciation is the condition of being covered with sheet ice.

glacier glaciers
Said "glass-yer" NOUN a huge frozen river of slow-moving ice.

glad gladder gladdest
ADJECTIVE happy and pleased E.G.
They'll be glad to get away from it all.
gladly ADVERB   **gladness** NOUN

glade glades
NOUN a grassy space in a forest.

gladiator gladiators
NOUN In ancient Rome, gladiators
were slaves trained to fight in arenas
to provide entertainment.
📖 from Latin *gladius* meaning
'sword'

gladiolus gladioli
NOUN a garden plant with spikes of
brightly coloured flowers on a long
stem.

glamour
NOUN The glamour of a fashionable or
attractive person or place is the
charm and excitement that they
have E.G. *the glamour of Paris.*
glamorous ADJECTIVE

glance glances glancing glanced
VERB 1 If you glance at something, you
look at it quickly. 2 If one object
glances off another, it hits it at an
angle and bounces away in another
direction. ▶ NOUN 3 a quick look.

gland glands
NOUN an organs in your body, such as
the thyroid gland and the sweat
glands, which either produce
chemical substances for your body
to use, or which help to get rid of
waste products from your body.
glandular ADJECTIVE

glare glares glaring glared
VERB 1 If you glare at someone, you
look at them angrily. ▶ NOUN 2 a hard,
angry look. 3 Glare is extremely
bright light.

glass glasses
NOUN 1 Glass is a hard, transparent
substance that is easily broken, used
to make windows and bottles. 2 a
container for drinking out of, made
from glass.

glasses
PLURAL NOUN Glasses are two lenses in
a frame, which some people wear
over their eyes to improve their
eyesight.

glassy
ADJECTIVE 1 smooth and shiny like glass
E.G. *glassy water.* 2 A glassy look
shows no feeling or expression.

glaze glazes glazing glazed
NOUN 1 A glaze on pottery or on food
is a smooth shiny surface. ▶ VERB 2 To
glaze pottery or food means to cover
it with a glaze. 3 To glaze a window
means to fit a sheet of glass into a
window frame.
glaze over VERB If your eyes glaze
over, they lose all expression, usually
because you are bored.

glazed
ADJECTIVE Someone who has a glazed
expression looks bored

gleam gleams gleaming gleamed
VERB 1 If something gleams, it shines
and reflects light. ▶ NOUN 2 a pale
shining light.

glean gleans gleaning gleaned
VERB To glean information means to
collect it from various sources.

glee
NOUN; OLD-FASHIONED Glee is joy and
delight.
gleeful ADJECTIVE   **gleefully** ADVERB

glen glens
NOUN a deep, narrow valley, especially
in Scotland or Ireland.

glide glides gliding glided
VERB 1 To glide means to move
smoothly E.G. *cygnets gliding up the*

a
b
c
d
e
f
g
h
i
j
k
l
m
n
o
p
q
r
s
t
u
v
w
x
y
z

Plaice the fish has a glittering 'EYE' (I) (plaice)   ◀ SPELLING NOTE

A
B
C
D
E
F
G
H
I
J
K
L
M
N
O
P
Q
R
S
T
U
V
W
X
Y
Z

stream. **2** When birds or aeroplanes glide, they float on air currents.

glider gliders

NOUN an aeroplane without an engine, which flies by floating on air currents.

glimmer glimmers glimmering glimmered

NOUN **1** a faint, unsteady light. **2** A glimmer of a feeling or quality is a faint sign of it E.G. *a glimmer of intelligence*.

glimpse glimpses glimpsing glimpsed

NOUN **1** a brief sight of something E.G. *They caught a glimpse of their hero*. ▶ VERB **2** If you glimpse something, you see it very briefly.

glint glints glinting glinted

VERB **1** If something glints, it reflects quick flashes of light. ▶ NOUN **2** a quick flash of light. **3** A glint in someone's eye is a brightness expressing some emotion E.G. *A glint of mischief in her blue-grey eyes.*

glisten glistens glistening glistened

Said "**gliss-ən**" VERB If something glistens, it shines or sparkles.

glitter glitters glittering glittered

VERB **1** If something glitters, it shines in a sparkling way E.G. *a glittering crown*. ▶ NOUN **2** Glitter is sparkling light.

gloat gloats gloating gloated

VERB If you gloat, you cruelly show your pleasure about your own success or someone else's failure E.G. *Their rivals were gloating over their triumph.*

global

ADJECTIVE concerning the whole world

E.G. *a global tour.*

global warming

NOUN an increase in the world's overall temperature believed to be caused by the greenhouse effect

globe globes

NOUN **1** a ball-shaped object, especially one with a map of the earth on it. **2** (GEOGRAPHY) You can refer to the world as the globe. **3** In South African, Australian, and New Zealand English, a globe is an electric light bulb.

gloom

NOUN **1** Gloom is darkness or dimness. **2** Gloom is also a feeling of unhappiness or despair.

gloomy ADJECTIVE **gloomily** ADVERB

glorify glorifies glorifying glorified

VERB If you glorify someone or something, you make them seem better than they really are E.G. *Their aggressive music glorifies violence.*

glorification NOUN

glorious

ADJECTIVE **1** beautiful and impressive to look at E.G. *glorious beaches*. **2** very pleasant and giving a feeling of happiness E.G. *glorious sunshine*. **3** involving great fame and success E.G. *a glorious career.*

gloriously ADVERB

glory glories glorying gloried

NOUN **1** Glory is fame and admiration for an achievement. **2** something considered splendid or admirable E.G. *the true glories of the Alps*. ▶ VERB **3** If you glory in something, you take great delight in it.

glory box glory boxes

NOUN; OLD-FASHIONED In Australian and New Zealand English, a chest in which a young woman stores household goods and linen for her marriage.

gloss glosses glossing glossed
NOUN **1** Gloss is a bright shine on a surface. **2** Gloss is also an attractive appearance which may hide less attractive qualities E.G. *to put a positive gloss on the events.* **3** If you gloss over a problem or fault, you try to ignore it or deal with it very quickly.

glossary glossaries
NOUN (LIBRARY) a list of explanations of specialist words, usually found at the back of a book.

glossy glossier glossiest
ADJECTIVE **1** smooth and shiny E.G. *glossy lipstick.* **2** Glossy magazines and photographs are produced on expensive, shiny paper.
■ (sense 1) lustrous, shiny

glove gloves
NOUN Gloves are coverings which you wear over your hands for warmth or protection.

glow glows glowing glowed
VERB **1** If something glows, it shines with a dull, steady light E.G. *A light glowed behind the curtains.* **2** If you are glowing, you look very happy or healthy. ▶ NOUN **3** a dull, steady light. **4** a strong feeling of pleasure or happiness.

glower glowers glowering glowered
Rhymes with "**shower**" VERB If you glower, you stare angrily.
■ glare, scowl

glowing
ADJECTIVE A glowing description praises someone or something very highly E.G. *a glowing character reference.*

glucose
NOUN Glucose is a type of sugar found in plants and that animals and people make in their bodies from food to provide energy.

glue glues gluing or **glueing glued**
NOUN **1** a substance used for sticking things together. ▶ VERB **2** If you glue one object to another, you stick them together using glue.

glum glummer glummest
ADJECTIVE miserable and depressed.
glumly ADVERB

glut gluts
NOUN a greater quantity of things than is needed.

gluten
Said "**gloo-ten**" NOUN a sticky protein found in cereal grains, such as wheat.

glutton gluttons
NOUN **1** a person who eats too much. **2** If you are a glutton for something, such as punishment or hard work, you seem very eager for it.
gluttony NOUN

gnarled
Said "**narld**" ADJECTIVE old, twisted, and rough E.G. *gnarled fingers.*

gnat gnats
Said "**nat**" NOUN a tiny flying insect that bites.

gnaw gnaws gnawing gnawed
Said "**naw**" VERB **1** To gnaw something means to bite at it repeatedly. **2** If a feeling gnaws at you, it keeps worrying you E.G. *a question gnawed at him.*

gnome gnomes
Said "**nome**" NOUN a tiny old man in fairy stories.

gnu gnus
Said "**noo**" NOUN a large African antelope.

a
b
c
d
e
f
g
h
i
j
k
l
m
n
o
p
q
r
s
t
u
v
w
x
y
z

You must practiSe your Ss (practise)　　SPELLING NOTE

go goes going went gone

VERB **1** If you go somewhere, you move or travel there. **2** You can use 'go' to mean become E.G. *She felt she was going mad.* **3** You can use 'go' to describe the state that someone or something is in E.G. *Our arrival went unnoticed.* **4** If something goes well, it is successful. If it goes badly, it is unsuccessful. **5** If you are going to do something, you will do it. **6** If a machine or clock goes, it works and is not broken. **7** You use 'go' before giving the sound something makes or before quoting a song or saying E.G. *The bell goes ding-dong.* **8** If something goes on something or to someone, it is allotted to them. **9** If one thing goes with another, they are appropriate together. **10** If one number goes into another, it can be divided into it. **11** If you go back on a promise or agreement, you do not do what you promised or agreed. **12** If someone goes for you, they attack you. **13** If you go in for something, you decide to do it as your job. **14** If you go out with someone, you have a romantic relationship with them. **15** If you go over something, you think about it or discuss it carefully. ▶ NOUN **16** an attempt at doing something. ▶ PHRASE **17** If someone is always **on the go**, they are always busy and active. **18** To go means remaining E.G. *I've got one more year of my course to go.*

go down VERB **1** If something goes down well, people like it. If it goes down badly, they do not like it. **2** If you go down with an illness, you catch it.

go off VERB **1** If you go off someone or something, you stop liking them. **2** If a bomb goes off, it explodes.

go on VERB **1** If you go on doing something, you continue to do it. **2** If you go on about something, you keep talking about it in a rather boring way. **3** Something that is going on is happening.

go through VERB **1** If you go through an unpleasant event, you experience it. **2** If a law or agreement goes through, it is approved and becomes official. **3** If you go through with something, you do it even though it is unpleasant.

goad goads goading goaded

VERB If you goad someone, you encourage them to do something by making them angry or excited E.G. *He had goaded the man into near violence.*

go-ahead

NOUN If someone gives you the go-ahead for something, they give you permission to do it.

goal goals

NOUN **1** the space, in games like football or hockey, into which the players try to put the ball in order to score a point. **2** an instance of this. **3** Your goal is something that you hope to achieve.

goalkeeper goalkeepers

NOUN the player, in games like soccer or hockey, who stands in the goal and tries to stop the other team from scoring.

goanna goannas

NOUN a large Australian lizard.

goat goats

NOUN an animal, like a sheep, with coarse hair, a beard, and horns.

go-away bird go-away birds
NOUN In South Africa, a go-away bird is a grey lourie, a type of bird which lives in open grassland.

gob gobs
NOUN INFORMAL Your gob is your mouth.

gobble gobbles gobbling gobbled
VERB 1 If you gobble food, you eat it very quickly. 2 When a turkey gobbles, it makes a loud gurgling sound.
■ devour, guzzle, wolf

gobbledygook or **gobbledegook**
NOUN Gobbledygook is language that is impossible to understand because it is so formal or complicated.

goblet goblets
NOUN a glass with a long stem.

goblin goblins
NOUN an ugly, mischievous creature in fairy stories.

god gods
PROPER NOUN 1 The name God is given to the being who is worshipped by Christians, Jews, and Muslims as the creator and ruler of the world. ▶ NOUN 2 any of the beings that are believed in many religions to have power over an aspect of life or a part of the world E.G. *Dionysus, the Greek god of wine.* 3 If someone is your god, you admire them very much. ▶ PLURAL NOUN 4 In a theatre, the gods are the highest seats farthest from the stage.

godchild godchildren
NOUN If you are someone's godchild, they agreed to be responsible for your religious upbringing when you were baptized in a Christian church.
goddaughter NOUN **godson** NOUN

goddess goddesses
NOUN a female god.

godparent godparents
NOUN A person's godparent is someone who agrees to be responsible for their religious upbringing when they are baptized in a Christian church.
godfather NOUN **godmother** NOUN

godsend godsends
NOUN something that comes unexpectedly and helps you very much.

goggles
PLURAL NOUN Goggles are special glasses that fit closely round your eyes to protect them.

going
NOUN The going is the conditions that affect your ability to do something E.G. *He found the going very slow indeed.*

gold
NOUN 1 Gold is a valuable, yellow-coloured metal. It is used for making jewellery and as an international currency. 2 'Gold' is also used to mean things that are made of gold. ▶ ADJECTIVE 3 bright yellow.

golden
ADJECTIVE 1 gold in colour E.G. *golden syrup.* 2 made of gold E.G. *a golden chain.* 3 excellent or ideal E.G. *a golden hero.*

golden rule golden rules
NOUN a very important rule to remember in order to be able to do something successfully.

golden wedding golden weddings
NOUN A married couple's golden wedding is their fiftieth wedding anniversary.

goldfish
NOUN a small orange-coloured fish,

a
b
c
d
e
f
g
h
i
j
k
l
m
n
o
p
q
r
s
t
u
v
w
x
y
z

often kept in ponds or bowls.

goldsmith goldsmiths
NOUN a person whose job is making jewellery out of gold.

golf
NOUN Golf is a game in which players use special clubs to hit a small ball into holes that are spread out over a large area of grassy land.
golfer NOUN

golf course golf courses
NOUN an area of grassy land where people play golf.

gondola gondolas
Said "**gon**-dol-la" NOUN a long narrow boat used in Venice, which is propelled with a long pole.

gone
the past participle of **go**.

gong gongs
NOUN a flat, circular piece of metal that is hit with a hammer to make a loud sound, often as a signal for something.

good better best; goods
ADJECTIVE **1** pleasant, acceptable, or satisfactory E.G. *good news… a good film.* **2** skilful or successful E.G. *good at art.* **3** kind, thoughtful, and loving E.G. *She was grateful to him for being so good to her.* **4** well-behaved E.G. *Have the children been good?* **5** used to emphasize something E.G. *a good few million pounds.* ► NOUN **6** Good is moral and spiritual justice and virtue E.G. *the forces of good and evil.* **7** Good also refers to anything that is desirable or beneficial as opposed to harmful E.G. *The break has done me good.* ► PLURAL NOUN **8** Goods are objects that people own or that are sold in shops E.G. *leather goods.* ► PHRASE **9** For good means for ever.

10 As good as means almost E.G. *The election is as good as decided.*
☑ *Good* is an adjective, and should not be used as an adverb. You should say that *a person did well* not *did good*.

goodbye
You say goodbye when you are leaving someone or ending a telephone conversation.

Good Friday
NOUN Good Friday is the Friday before Easter, when Christians remember the crucifixion of Christ.

good-natured
ADJECTIVE friendly, pleasant, and even-tempered.

goodness
NOUN **1** Goodness is the quality of being kind. ► INTERJECTION **2** People say 'Goodness!' or 'My goodness!' when they are surprised.

goodwill
NOUN Goodwill is kindness and helpfulness E.G. *Messages of goodwill were exchanged.*

goody goodies
NOUN **1** INFORMAL Goodies are enjoyable things, often food. **2** You can call a hero in a film or book a goody.

goose geese
NOUN a fairly large bird with webbed feet and a long neck.

gooseberry gooseberries
NOUN a round, green berry that grows on a bush and has a sharp taste.

gore gores goring gored
VERB **1** If an animal gores someone, it wounds them badly with its horns or tusks. ► NOUN **2** Gore is clotted blood from a wound.

gorge gorges gorging gorged
NOUN **1** a deep, narrow valley. ► VERB

2 If you gorge yourself, you eat a lot of food greedily.

gorgeous
ADJECTIVE extremely pleasant or attractive E.G. *a gorgeous man*.

gorilla gorillas
NOUN a very large, strong ape with very dark fur.
🔲 from *Gorillai*, the Greek name for an African tribe with hairy bodies

gorse
NOUN Gorse is a dark green wild shrub that has sharp prickles and small yellow flowers.

gory gorier goriest
ADJECTIVE Gory situations involve people being injured in horrible ways.

gosling goslings
Said "goz-ling" NOUN a young goose.

gospel gospels
NOUN **1** The Gospels are the four books in the New Testament which describe the life and teachings of Jesus Christ. **2** a set of ideas that someone strongly believes in E.G. *the so-called gospel of work.* ► ADJECTIVE **3** Gospel music is a style of religious music popular among Black Christians in the United States.

gossip gossips gossiping gossiped
NOUN **1** Gossip is informal conversation, often concerning people's private affairs. **2** Someone who is a gossip enjoys talking about other people's private affairs. ► VERB **3** If you gossip, you talk informally with someone, especially about other people.

got
1 Got is the past tense and past participle of **get**. **2** You can use 'have got' instead of the more formal 'have'

when talking about possessing things E.G. *The director has got a map.* **3** You can use 'have got to' instead of the more formal 'have to' when talking about something that must be done E.G. *He has got to win.*

gouge gouges gouging gouged
Said "gowj" VERB **1** If you gouge a hole in something, you make a hole in it with a pointed object. **2** If you gouge something out, you force it out of position with your fingers or a sharp tool.

goulash
Said "goo-lash" NOUN Goulash is a type of rich meat stew, originally from Hungary.

gourd gourds
Said "goord" NOUN a large fruit with a hard outside.

gourmet gourmets
Said "goor-may" NOUN a person who enjoys good food and drink and knows a lot about it.

gout
NOUN Gout is a disease which causes someone's joints to swell painfully, especially in their toes.

govern governs governing governed
VERB **1** To govern a country means to control it. **2** Something that governs a situation influences it E.G. *Our thinking is as much governed by habit as by behaviour.*

governess governesses
NOUN a woman who is employed to teach the children in a family and who lives with the family.

government governments
NOUN (HISTORY) **1** The government is the group of people who govern a country. **2** Government is the control

a
b
c
d
e
f
g
h
i
j
k
l
m
n
o
p
q
r
s
t
u
v
w
x
y
z

A
B
C
D
E
F
G
H
I
J
K
L
M
N
O
P
Q
R
S
T
U
V
W
X
Y
Z

and organization of a country.
governmental ADJECTIVE
governor governors
NOUN **1** a person who controls and
organizes a state or an institution.
2 In Australia, the Governor is the
representative of the King or Queen
in a State.
**governor-general governors-
general**
NOUN the chief representative of the
King or Queen in Australia, New
Zealand, and other Commonwealth
countries.
gown gowns
NOUN **1** a long, formal dress. **2** a long,
dark cloak worn by people such as
judges and lawyers.
GP
an abbreviation for **general
practitioner**.
grab grabs grabbing grabbed
VERB **1** If you grab something, you
take it or pick it up roughly. **2** If you
grab an opportunity, you take
advantage of it eagerly. **3** INFORMAL If
an idea grabs you, it excites you.
► NOUN **4** A grab at an object is an
attempt to grab it.
■ (senses 1 & 2) grasp, seize, snatch
grace graces gracing graced
NOUN **1** Grace is an elegant way of
moving. **2** Grace is also a pleasant,
kind way of behaving. **3** Grace is also
a short prayer of thanks said before a
meal. **4** Dukes and archbishops are
addressed as 'Your Grace' and
referred to as 'His Grace'. ► VERB
5 Something that graces a place
makes it more attractive. **6** If
someone important graces an
event, they kindly agree to be
present at it.

graceful ADJECTIVE **gracefully**
ADVERB
■ (sense 1) elegance, poise
gracious
ADJECTIVE **1** kind, polite, and pleasant.
2 'Good gracious' is an exclamation
of surprise.
graciously ADVERB
grade grades grading graded
VERB **1** To grade things means to
arrange them according to quality.
► NOUN **2** The grade of something is
its quality. **3** the mark that you get
for an exam or piece of written work.
4 Your grade in a company or
organization is your level of
importance or your rank.
gradient gradients
NOUN a slope or the steepness of a
slope.
gradual
ADJECTIVE happening or changing
slowly over a long period of time.
gradually
ADVERB happening or changing slowly
over a long period of time.
**graduate graduates graduating
graduated**
NOUN **1** a person who has completed
a first degree at a university or
college. ► VERB **2** When students
graduate, they complete a first
degree at a university or college. **3** To
graduate from one thing to another
means to progress gradually towards
the second thing.
graduation NOUN
graffiti
Said "graf-**fee**-tee" NOUN Graffiti is
slogans or drawings scribbled on
walls.
▣ from Italian *graffiare* meaning 'to
scratch a surface'

☑ Although *graffiti* is a plural in Italian, the language it comes from, in English it can be used as a singular noun or a plural noun.

graft grafts grafting grafted
NOUN **1** a piece of living tissue which is used to replace by surgery a damaged or unhealthy part of a person's body. **2** INFORMAL Graft is hard work. ► VERB **3** To graft one thing to another means to attach it.

grain grains
NOUN **1** a cereal plant, such as wheat, that is grown as a crop and used for food. **2** Grains are seeds of a cereal plant. **3** A grain of sand or salt is a tiny particle of it. **4** The grain of a piece of wood is the pattern of lines made by the fibres in it. ► PHRASE **5** If something **goes against the grain**, you find it difficult to accept because it is against your principles.
■ (sense 3) bit, granule, particle

gram grams; also spelt **gramme**
NOUN a unit of weight equal to one thousandth of a kilogram.

grammar
NOUN (ENGLISH) Grammar is the rules of a language relating to the ways you can combine words to form sentences.

grammar school grammar schools
NOUN **1** a secondary school for pupils of high academic ability. **2** In Australia, a private school, usually one controlled by a church.

grammatical
ADJECTIVE **1** relating to grammar E.G. *grammatical knowledge*. **2** following the rules of grammar correctly E.G. *grammatical sentences*.
grammatically ADVERB

gran grans
NOUN; INFORMAL Your gran is your grandmother.

granary granaries
NOUN **1** a building for storing grain.
► ADJECTIVE **2** TRADEMARK Granary bread contains whole grains of wheat.

grand grander grandest
ADJECTIVE **1** magnificent in appearance and size E.G. *a grand house*. **2** very important E.G. *the grand scheme of your life*. **3** INFORMAL very pleasant or enjoyable E.G. *It was a grand day*. **4** A grand total is the final complete amount. ► NOUN **5** INFORMAL a thousand pounds or dollars.
grandly ADVERB
■ (sense 1) impressive, magnificent, splendid

grandad grandads
NOUN; INFORMAL Your grandad is your grandfather.

grandchild grandchildren
NOUN Someone's grandchildren are the children of their son or daughter.

granddaughter granddaughters
NOUN Someone's granddaughter is the daughter of their son or daughter.

grandeur
Said "*grand*-yer" NOUN Grandeur is great beauty and magnificence.

grandfather grandfathers
NOUN Your grandfather is your father's father or your mother's father.

grandfather clock grandfather clocks
NOUN a clock in a tall wooden case that stands on the floor.

grandiose
Said "*gran-dee-ose*" ADJECTIVE intended to be very impressive, but seeming ridiculous E.G. *a grandiose gesture of love*.

a b c d e f **g** h i j k l m n o p q r s t u v w x y z

grandma grandmas
NOUN; INFORMAL Your grandma is your grandmother.

grandmother grandmothers
NOUN Your grandmother is your father's mother or your mother's mother.

grandparent grandparents
NOUN Your grandparents are your parents' parents.

grand piano grand pianos
NOUN a large flat piano with horizontal strings.

grandson grandsons
NOUN Someone's grandson is the son of their son or daughter.

grandstand grandstands
NOUN a structure with a roof and seats for spectators at a sports ground.

granite
Said "gran-nit" NOUN Granite is a very hard rock used in building.

granny grannies
NOUN; INFORMAL Your granny is your grandmother.

grant grants granting granted
NOUN 1 an amount of money that an official body gives to someone for a particular purpose E.G. a grant to carry out repairs. ▶ VERB 2 If you grant something to someone, you allow them to have it. 3 If you grant that something is true, you admit that it is true. ▶ PHRASES 4 If you **take something for granted**, you believe it without thinking about it. If you **take someone for granted**, you benefit from them without showing that you are grateful.

granule granules
NOUN a very small piece of something E.G. granules of salt.

grape grapes
NOUN a small green or purple fruit, eaten raw or used to make wine.

grapefruit grapefruits
NOUN a large, round, yellow citrus fruit.

grapevine grapevines
NOUN 1 a climbing plant which grapes grow on. 2 If you hear some news on the grapevine, it has been passed on from person to person, usually unofficially or secretly.

graph graphs
NOUN (MATHS) a diagram in which a line shows how two sets of numbers or measurements are related.

-graph
SUFFIX '-graph' means a writer or recorder of some sort or something made by writing, drawing or recording E.G. telegraph... autograph. ▣ from Greek graphein meaning 'to write'

graphic graphics
ADJECTIVE 1 A graphic description is very detailed and lifelike. 2 relating to drawing or painting. ▶ PLURAL NOUN 3 (ICT) Graphics are drawings and pictures composed of simple lines and strong colours E.G. computerized graphics.
graphically ADVERB

graphite
NOUN a black form of carbon that is used in pencil leads.

grapple grapples grappling grappled
VERB 1 If you grapple with someone, you struggle with them while fighting. 2 If you grapple with a problem, you try hard to solve it.

grasp grasps grasping grasped
VERB 1 If you grasp something, you

hold it firmly. **2** If you grasp an idea, you understand it. ► NOUN **3** A firm hold. **4** Your grasp of something is your understanding of it.

grass grasses
NOUN Grass is the common green plant that grows on lawns and in parks.
grassy ADJECTIVE

grasshopper grasshoppers
NOUN an insect with long back legs which it uses for jumping and making a high-pitched sound.

grate grates grating grated
NOUN **1** a framework of metal bars in a fireplace. ► VERB **2** To grate food means to shred it into small pieces by rubbing it against a grater. **3** When something grates on something else, it rubs against it making a harsh sound. **4** If something grates on you, it irritates you.

grateful
ADJECTIVE If you are grateful for something, you are glad you have it and want to thank the person who gave it to you.
gratefully ADVERB
▤ appreciative, thankful

grater graters
NOUN a small metal tool used for grating food.

gratify gratifies gratifying gratified
VERB **1** If you are gratified by something, you are pleased by it. **2** If you gratify a wish or feeling, you satisfy it.

grating gratings
NOUN **1** a metal frame with bars across it fastened over a hole in a wall or in the ground. ► ADJECTIVE **2** A grating

sound is harsh and unpleasant E.G. *grating melodies*.

gratis
Said "**grah-tis**" ADVERB OR ADJECTIVE free E.G. *food and drink supplied gratis*.

gratitude
NOUN Gratitude is the feeling of being grateful.
▤ appreciation, thankfulness

gratuitous
Said "**grat-yoo**-it-tuss" ADJECTIVE unnecessary E.G. *a gratuitous attack*.
gratuitously ADVERB

grave graves; graver gravest
Rhymes with "**save**" NOUN **1** a place where a corpse is buried. ► ADJECTIVE **2** FORMAL very serious E.G. *grave danger*.

grave
Said "**grahv**" ADJECTIVE In French and some other languages, a grave accent is a line sloping downwards from left to right placed over a vowel to indicate a change in pronunciation, as in the word *lèvre* (a hare).

gravel
NOUN Gravel is small stones used for making roads and paths.

gravestone gravestones
NOUN a large stone placed over someone's grave, with their name on it.

graveyard graveyards
NOUN an area of land where corpses are buried.

gravitate gravitates gravitating gravitated
VERB When people gravitate towards something, they go towards it because they are attracted by it.

gravitation
NOUN Gravitation is the force which

a
b
c
d
e
f
g
h
i
j
k
l
m
n
o
p
q
r
s
t
u
v
w
x
y
z

A
B
C
D
E
F
G
H
I
J
K
L
M
N
O
P
Q
R
S
T
U
V
W
X
Y
Z

causes objects to be attracted to each other.

gravitational ADJECTIVE

gravity

NOUN 1 Gravity is the force that makes things fall when you drop them. 2 FORMAL The gravity of a situation is its seriousness.

gravy

NOUN Gravy is a brown sauce made from meat juices.

graze grazes grazing grazed

VERB 1 When animals graze, they eat grass. 2 If something grazes a part of your body, it scrapes against it, injuring you slightly. ▶ NOUN 3 a slight injury caused by something scraping against your skin.

grease greases greasing greased

NOUN 1 Grease is an oily substance used for lubricating machines. 2 Grease is also melted animal fat, used in cooking. 3 Grease is also an oily substance produced by your skin and found in your hair. ▶ VERB 4 If you grease something, you lubricate it with grease.

greasy ADJECTIVE

great greater greatest

ADJECTIVE 1 very large E.G. *a great sea… great efforts*. 2 very important E.G. *a great artist*. 3 INFORMAL very good E.G. *Paul had a great time*.

greatly ADVERB **greatness** NOUN

Great Britain

NOUN Great Britain is the largest of the British Isles, consisting of England, Scotland, and Wales.

Great Dane Great Danes

NOUN a very large dog with short hair.

great-grandfather great-grandfathers

NOUN Your great-grandfather is your father's or mother's grandfather.

great-grandmother great-grandmothers

NOUN Your great-grandmother is your father's or mother's grandmother.

greed

NOUN Greed is a desire for more of something than you really need.

greedy greedier greediest

ADJECTIVE wanting more of something than you really need.

greedily ADVERB **greediness** NOUN
目 grasping, insatiable, voracious

Greek Greeks

ADJECTIVE 1 belonging or relating to Greece. ▶ NOUN 2 someone who comes from Greece. 3 Greek is the main language spoken in Greece.

green greener greenest; greens

ADJECTIVE or NOUN 1 Green is a colour between yellow and blue on the spectrum. ▶ NOUN 2 an area of grass in the middle of a village. 3 A putting green or bowling green is a grassy area on which putting or bowls is played. 4 an area of smooth short grass around each hole on a golf course. ▶ PLURAL NOUN 5 Greens are green vegetables. ▶ ADJECTIVE 6 'Green' is used to describe political movements which are concerned with environmental issues. 7 INFORMAL Someone who is green is young and inexperienced.

greenery

NOUN Greenery is a lot of trees, bushes, or other green plants together in one place.

greenfly

NOUN Greenfly are small green insects that damage plants.

greengrocer greengrocers
NOUN a shopkeeper who sells vegetables and fruit.

greenhouse greenhouses
NOUN a glass building in which people grow plants that need to be kept warm.

greenhouse effect
NOUN the gradual rise in temperature in the earth's atmosphere due to heat being absorbed from the sun and being trapped by gases such as carbon dioxide in the air around the earth.

green paper green papers
NOUN In Britain, Australia, and New Zealand, a report published by the government containing proposals to be discussed before decisions are made about them.

greenstone
NOUN a type of jade found in New Zealand and used for making ornaments, weapons, and tools.

greet greets greeting greeted
VERB 1 If you greet someone, you say something friendly like 'hello' to them when you meet them. 2 If you greet something in a particular way, you react to it in that way E.G. *He was greeted with deep suspicion.*
▤ (sense 1) hail, salute

greeting greetings
NOUN something friendly that you say to someone when you meet them E.G. *Her greeting was warm.*

gregarious
Said "grig-**air**-ee-uss" ADJECTIVE; FORMAL Someone who is gregarious enjoys being with other people.

grenade grenades
NOUN a small bomb, containing explosive or tear gas, which can be thrown.

▥ from Spanish *granada* meaning 'pomegranate'

grevillea grevilleas
NOUN an evergreen Australian tree or shrub.

grew
the past tense of **grow**.

grey greyer greyest; greys greying greyed
ADJECTIVE or NOUN 1 Grey is a colour between black and white. ▶ ADJECTIVE 2 dull and boring E.G. *He's a bit of a grey man.* ▶ VERB 3 If someone is greying, their hair is going grey.
greyness NOUN

greyhound greyhounds
NOUN a thin dog with long legs that can run very fast.

grid grids
NOUN 1 a pattern of lines crossing each other to form squares. 2 The grid is the network of wires and cables by which electricity is distributed throughout a country.

grief
NOUN 1 Grief is extreme sadness ▶ PHRASE 2 If someone or something **comes to grief**, they fail or are injured.
▤ (sense 1) heartache, sadness, sorrow

grievance grievances
NOUN a reason for complaining.

grieve grieves grieving grieved
VERB 1 If you grieve, you are extremely sad, especially because someone has died. 2 If something grieves you, it makes you feel very sad.
▤ (sense 1) lament, mourn

grievous
ADJECTIVE; FORMAL extremely serious E.G. *grievous damage.*
grievously ADVERB

'i' before 'e' except after 'c'   **SPELLING NOTE**

a b c d e f g h i j k l m n o p q r s t u v w x y z

grill grills grilling grilled

NOUN **1** a part on a cooker where food is cooked by strong heat from above. **2** a metal frame on which you cook food over a fire. ▶ VERB **3** If you grill food, you cook it on or under a grill. **4** INFORMAL If you grill someone, you ask them a lot of questions in a very intense way.

grille grilles

Rhymes with "pill" NOUN a metal framework over a window or piece of machinery, used for protection.

grim grimmer grimmest

ADJECTIVE **1** If a situation or piece of news is grim, it is very unpleasant and worrying E.G. *There are grim times ahead.* **2** Grim places are unattractive and depressing. **3** If someone is grim, they are very serious or stern.

grimly ADVERB

grimace grimaces grimacing grimaced

Said "grim-mace" NOUN **1** a twisted facial expression indicating disgust or pain. ▶ VERB **2** When someone grimaces, they make a grimace.

grime

NOUN Grime is thick dirt which gathers on the surface of something.

grimy ADJECTIVE

grin grins grinning grinned

VERB **1** If you grin, you smile broadly. ▶ NOUN **2** a broad smile. ▶ PHRASE **3** If you **grin and bear it**, you accept a difficult situation without complaining.

grind grinds grinding ground

VERB **1** If you grind something such as pepper, you crush it into a fine powder. **2** If you grind your teeth, you rub your upper and lower teeth

together. ▶ PHRASE **3** If something **grinds to a halt**, it stops E.G. *Progress ground to a halt.*

■ (sense 1) crush, powder, pulverize

grip grips gripping gripped

VERB **1** If you grip something, you hold it firmly. ▶ NOUN **2** a firm hold. **3** a handle on a bat or a racket. **4** Your grip on a situation is your control over it. ▶ PHRASE **5** If you **get to grips with** a situation or problem, you start to deal with it effectively.

grisly grislier grisliest

ADJECTIVE very nasty and horrible E.G. *a grisly murder scene.*

grit grits gritting gritted

NOUN **1** Grit consists of very small stones. It is put on icy roads to make them less slippery. ▶ VERB **2** When workmen grit an icy road, they put grit on it. ▶ PHRASE **3** To **grit your teeth** means to decide to carry on in a difficult situation.

gritty ADJECTIVE

grizzled

ADJECTIVE Grizzled hair is grey. A grizzled person has grey hair.

grizzly bear grizzly bears

NOUN a large, greyish-brown bear from North America.

groan groans groaning groaned

VERB **1** If you groan, you make a long, low sound of pain, unhappiness, or disapproval. ▶ NOUN **2** the sound you make when you groan.

grocer grocers

NOUN a shopkeeper who sells many kinds of food and other household goods.

grocery groceries

NOUN **1** a grocer's shop. ▶ PLURAL NOUN **2** Groceries are the goods that you buy in a grocer's shop.

grog
NOUN; INFORMAL In Australian and New Zealand English, grog is any alcoholic drink.

groin groins
NOUN the area where your legs join the main part of your body at the front.

groom grooms grooming groomed
NOUN 1 someone who looks after horses in a stable. 2 At a wedding, the groom is the bridegroom. ▶ VERB 3 To groom an animal means to clean its fur. 4 If you groom someone for a job, you prepare them for it by teaching them the skills they will need.

groove grooves
NOUN a deep line cut into a surface.
grooved ADJECTIVE

grope gropes groping groped
VERB 1 If you grope for something you cannot see, you search for it with your hands. 2 If you grope for something such as the solution to a problem, you try to think of it.

gross grosser grossest; grosses grossing grossed
ADJECTIVE 1 extremely bad E.G. *a gross betrayal.* 2 Gross speech or behaviour is very rude. 3 Gross things are ugly E.G. *gross holiday outfits.* 4 Someone's gross income is their total income before any deductions are made. 5 The gross weight of something is its total weight including the weight of its container. ▶ VERB 6 If you gross an amount of money, you earn that amount in total.
grossly ADVERB

grotesque
Said "groh-**tesk**" ADJECTIVE

1 exaggerated and absurd E.G. *It was the most grotesque thing she had ever heard.* 2 very strange and ugly E.G. *grotesque animal puppets.*
grotesquely ADVERB
▣ from Old Italian *pittura grottesca* meaning 'cave paintings'

grotto grottoes or grottos
NOUN a small cave that people visit because it is attractive.

ground grounds grounding grounded
NOUN 1 The ground is the surface of the earth. 2 a piece of land that is used for a particular purpose E.G. *the training ground.* 3 The ground covered by a book or course is the range of subjects it deals with.
▶ PLURAL NOUN 4 The grounds of a large building are the land belonging to it and surrounding it. 5 FORMAL The grounds for something are the reasons for it E.G. *genuine grounds for caution.* ▶ VERB 6 FORMAL If something is grounded in something else, it is based on it. 7 If an aircraft is grounded, it has to remain on the ground. 8 Ground is the past tense and past participle of grind.

ground floor ground floors
NOUN The ground floor of a building is the floor that is approximately level with the ground.

grounding
NOUN If you have a grounding in a skill or subject, you have had basic instruction in it.

groundless
ADJECTIVE not based on reason or evidence E.G. *groundless accusations.*

group groups grouping grouped
NOUN 1 A group of things or people is

a b c d e f g h i j k l m n o p q r s t u v w x y z

A
B
C
D
E
F
G
H
I
J
K
L
M
N
O
P
Q
R
S
T
U
V
W
X
Y
Z

a number of them that are linked together in some way. 2 a number of musicians who perform pop music together. ▶ VERB 3 When things or people are grouped together, they are linked together in some way.
◼ (sense 1) band, bunch, crowd, set

grouping groupings
NOUN a number of things or people that are linked together in some way.

grouse grouse
NOUN a fat brown or grey bird, often shot for sport.

grove groves
NOUN; LITERARY a group of trees growing close together.

grovel grovels grovelling grovelled
VERB If you grovel, you behave in an unpleasantly humble way towards someone you regard as important.

grow grows growing grew grown
VERB 1 To grow means to increase in size or amount. 2 If a tree or plant grows somewhere, it is alive there. 3 When people grow plants, they plant them and look after them. 4 If a man grows a beard or moustache, he lets it develop by not shaving. 5 If you grow to have a particular feeling, you eventually have it. 6 If one thing grows from another, it develops from it. 7 INFORMAL If something grows on you, you gradually get to like it.
◼ (sense 1) expand, get bigger, increase

grow up VERB When a child grows up, he or she becomes an adult.

growl growls growling growled
VERB 1 When an animal growls, it

makes a low rumbling sound, usually because it is angry. 2 If you growl something, you say it in a low, rough, rather angry voice. ▶ NOUN 3 the sound an animal makes when it growls.

grown-up grown-ups
NOUN 1 INFORMAL an adult. ▶ ADJECTIVE 2 Someone who is grown-up is adult, or behaves like an adult.

growth growths
NOUN 1 When there is a growth in something, it gets bigger E.G. *the growth of the fishing industry.*
2 (SCIENCE) Growth is the process by which something develops to its full size. 3 an abnormal lump that grows inside or on a person, animal, or plant.
◼ (sense 1) expansion, increase

grub grubs
NOUN 1 a wormlike insect that has just hatched from its egg. 2 INFORMAL Grub is food.

grubby grubbier grubbiest
ADJECTIVE rather dirty.

grudge grudges grudging grudged
NOUN 1 If you have a grudge against someone, you resent them because they have harmed you in the past.
▶ VERB 2 If you grudge someone something, you give it to them unwillingly, or are displeased that they have it.

grudging
ADJECTIVE done or felt unwillingly E.G. *grudging admiration.*
grudgingly ADVERB

gruel
NOUN Gruel is oatmeal boiled in water or milk.

gruelling
ADJECTIVE difficult and tiring E.G. *a gruelling race.*

gruesome
ADJECTIVE shocking and horrible E.G. *gruesome pictures*.

gruff gruffer gruffest
ADJECTIVE If someone's voice is gruff, it sounds rough and unfriendly.

grumble grumbles grumbling grumbled
VERB 1 If you grumble, you complain in a bad-tempered way. ► NOUN 2 a bad-tempered complaint.

grumpy grumpier grumpiest
ADJECTIVE bad-tempered and fed-up.
◼ ill-tempered, irritable

grunt grunts grunting grunted
VERB 1 If a person or a pig grunts, they make a short, low, gruff sound.
► NOUN 2 the sound a person or a pig makes when they grunt.

guarantee guarantees guaranteeing guaranteed
VERB 1 If something or someone guarantees something, they make certain that it will happen E.G. *Money may not guarantee success.*
► NOUN 2 If something is a guarantee of something else, it makes it certain that it will happen. 3 a written promise that if a product develops a fault it will be replaced or repaired free.
guarantor NOUN
◼ (sense 1) ensure, promise
◼ (sense 2) assurance, pledge, promise

guard guards guarding guarded
VERB 1 If you guard a person or object, you stay near to them either to protect them or to make sure they do not escape. 2 If you guard against something, you are careful to avoid it happening. ► NOUN 3 a person or group of people who guard a

person, object, or place. 4 a railway official in charge of a train. 5 Any object which covers something to prevent it causing harm can be called a guard E.G. *a fire guard.*
◼ (sense 1) defend, protect, watch over
◼ (sense 3) protector, sentry, watchman

guardian guardians
NOUN 1 someone who has been legally appointed to look after an orphaned child. 2 A guardian of something is someone who protects it E.G. *a guardian of the law.*
guardianship NOUN

guernsey guernseys
NOUN 1 In Australian and New Zealand English, a jersey. 2 a sleeveless top worn by an Australian Rules football player.

guerrilla guerrillas
Said "ger-ril-la"; also spelt **guerilla**
NOUN a member of a small unofficial army fighting an official army.
▦ from Spanish *guerrilla* meaning 'little war'

guess guesses guessing guessed
VERB 1 If you guess something, you form or express an opinion that it is the case, without having much information. ► NOUN 2 (MATHS) an attempt to give the correct answer to something without having much information, or without working it out properly.
◼ (sense 1) conjecture, suppose
◼ (sense 2) conjecture, speculation, supposition

guest guests
NOUN 1 someone who stays at your home or who attends an occasion

A Rude Idiot Thought He Might Eat Toffee In Church (<u>arithmetic</u>)   ◄ **SPELLING NOTE**

A
B
C
D
E
F
G
H
I
J
K
L
M
N
O
P
Q
R
S
T
U
V
W
X
Y
Z

because they have been invited.
2 The guests in a hotel are the people staying there.

guffaw
NOUN a loud, coarse laugh.

guidance
NOUN Guidance is help and advice.

guide guides guiding guided
NOUN **1** someone who shows you round places, or leads the way through difficult country. **2** a book which gives you information or instructions E.G. *a Sydney street guide.* **3** A Guide is a girl who is a member of an organization that encourages discipline and practical skills. ▶ VERB **4** If you guide someone in a particular direction, you lead them in that direction. **5** If you are guided by something, it influences your actions or decisions.

guidebook guidebooks
NOUN a book which gives information about a place.

guide dog guide dogs
NOUN a dog that has been trained to lead a blind person.

guideline guidelines
NOUN a piece of advice about how something should be done.

guild guilds
NOUN a society of people E.G. *the Screen Writers' Guild.*

guile
Rhymes with "mile" NOUN Guile is cunning and deceit.
guileless ADJECTIVE

guillotine guillotines
Said "gil-lot-teen" NOUN a machine used for beheading people, especially in the past in France.

guilt
NOUN **1** Guilt is an unhappy feeling of

having done something wrong.
2 Someone's guilt is the fact that they have done something wrong
E.G. *The law will decide their guilt.*

guilty guiltier guiltiest
ADJECTIVE **1** If you are guilty of doing something wrong, you did it E.G. *He was guilty of theft.* **2** If you feel guilty, you are unhappy because you have done something wrong.
guiltily ADVERB

guinea guineas
Said "gin-ee" NOUN an old British unit of money, worth 21 shillings.

guinea pig guinea pigs
NOUN **1** a small furry animal without a tail, often kept as a pet. **2** a person used to try something out on E.G. *a guinea pig for a new drug.*

guise guises
Rhymes with "prize" NOUN a misleading appearance E.G. *political statements in the guise of religious talk.*

guitar guitars
NOUN a musical instrument with six strings which are strummed or plucked.
guitarist NOUN

gulf gulfs
NOUN **1** a very large bay. **2** a wide gap or difference between two things or people.

gull gulls
NOUN a sea bird with long wings, white and grey or black feathers, and webbed feet.
🔲 from Welsh *gwylan*

gullet gullets
NOUN the tube that goes from your mouth to your stomach.

gullible
ADJECTIVE easily tricked.

SPELLING NOTE ▶ Beautiful Elephants Are Usually Tiny (<u>beautiful</u>)

gullibility NOUN
■ credulous, naive

gully gullies
NOUN a long, narrow valley.

gulp gulps gulping gulped
VERB 1 If you gulp food or drink, you swallow large quantities of it. 2 If you gulp, you swallow air, because you are nervous. ► NOUN 3 A gulp of food or drink is a large quantity of it swallowed at one time.

gum gums
NOUN 1 Gum is a soft flavoured substance that people chew but do not swallow. 2 Gum is also glue for sticking paper. 3 Your gums are the firm flesh in which your teeth are set.

gumboot gumboots
NOUN Gumboots are long waterproof boots.

gumtree gumtrees
NOUN a eucalyptus, or other tree which produces gum.

gun guns
NOUN a weapon which fires bullets or shells.

gunfire
NOUN Gunfire is the repeated firing of guns.

gunpowder
NOUN Gunpowder is an explosive powder made from a mixture of potassium nitrate and other substances.

gunshot gunshots
NOUN the sound of a gun being fired.

gunyah gunyahs
NOUN In Australia, a hut or shelter in the bush.

guppy guppies
NOUN a small, brightly coloured tropical fish.

gurdwara
NOUN a Sikh place of worship.

📖 from Sanskrit *guru* meaning 'teacher' + *dvārā* meaning 'door'

gurgle gurgles gurgling gurgled
VERB 1 To gurgle means to make a bubbling sound. ► NOUN 2 a bubbling sound.

guru gurus
Said "*goo-rooh*" NOUN a spiritual leader and teacher, especially in India.

📖 from Sanskrit *guruh* meaning 'weighty' or 'of importance'

gush gushes gushing gushed
VERB 1 When liquid gushes from something, it flows out of it in large quantities. 2 When people gush, they express admiration or pleasure in an exaggerated way.
gushing ADJECTIVE
■ (sense 1) flow, pour, spurt, stream

gust gusts
NOUN a sudden rush of wind.
gusty ADJECTIVE

gusto
NOUN Gusto is energy and enthusiasm E.G. *Her gusto for life was amazing.*

gut guts gutting gutted
PLURAL NOUN 1 Your guts are your internal organs, especially your intestines. ► VERB 2 To gut a dead fish means to remove its internal organs. 3 If a building is gutted, the inside of it is destroyed, especially by fire. ► NOUN 4 INFORMAL Guts is courage.
■ (sense 1) entrails, innards, intestines

gutter gutters
NOUN 1 the edge of a road next to the pavement, where rain collects and flows away. 2 a channel fixed to the edge of a roof, where rain collects and flows away.
guttering NOUN

A
B
C
D
E
F
G
H
I
J
K
L
M
N
O
P
Q
R
S
T
U
V
W
X
Y
Z

guttural
Said "gut-ter-al" ADJECTIVE Guttural sounds are produced at the back of a person's throat and are often considered to be unpleasant.

guy guys
NOUN 1 INFORMAL a man or boy. 2 a crude model of Guy Fawkes, that is burnt on top of a bonfire on Guy Fawkes Day (November 5).
🏛 short for *Guy* Fawkes, who plotted to blow up the British Houses of Parliament

guzzle guzzles guzzling guzzled
VERB To guzzle something means to drink or eat it quickly and greedily.

gym gyms
NOUN (PE) 1 a gymnasium. 2 Gym is gymnastics.

gymkhana gymkhanas
Said "jim-kah-na" NOUN an event in which people take part in horse-riding contests.
🏛 from Hindi *gend-khana* literally meaning 'ball house', because it is where sports were held

gymnasium gymnasiums
NOUN a room with special equipment for physical exercises.
🏛 from Greek *gumnazein* meaning 'to exercise naked'

gymnast gymnasts
NOUN someone who is trained in gymnastics.
gymnastic ADJECTIVE

gymnastics
NOUN (PE) Gymnastics is physical exercises, especially ones using equipment such as bars and ropes.

gynaecology or **gynecology**
Said "gie-nak-kol-loj-ee" NOUN Gynaecology is the branch of medical science concerned with the female reproductive system.
gynaecologist NOUN
gynaecological ADJECTIVE

gypsy gypsies; also spelt **gipsy**
NOUN a member of a race of people who travel from place to place in caravans.
🏛 from 'Egyptian', because people used to think gypsies came from Egypt

gyrate gyrates gyrating gyrated
Said "jy-rate" VERB To gyrate means to move round in a circle.

Hh

a b c d e f g h i j k l m n o p q r s t u v w x y z

TIP Some words which sound as if they might begin with letter *h*, instead begin with the letters *wh*, for example *who, whole, wholly, whom, whore,* and *whose.*

habit habits
NOUN **1** something that you do often
E.G. *He got into the habit of eating out.* **2** something that you keep doing and find it difficult to stop doing E.G. *a 20-a-day smoking habit.*
3 A monk's or nun's habit is a garment like a loose dress.
habitual ADJECTIVE **habitually** ADVERB

habitat habitats
NOUN (GEOGRAPHY) the natural home of a plant or animal.

hack hacks hacking hacked
VERB **1** If you hack at something, you cut it using rough strokes. ▶ NOUN **2** a writer or journalist who produces work fast without worrying about quality.

hacker hackers
NOUN; INFORMAL someone who uses a computer to break into the computer system of a company or government.

hackles
PLURAL NOUN **1** A dog's hackles are the hairs on the back of its neck which rise when it is angry. ▶ PHRASE **2** Something that **makes your hackles rise** makes you angry.

hackneyed
ADJECTIVE A hackneyed phrase is meaningless because it has been used too often.
■ clichéd, unoriginal

hacksaw hacksaws
NOUN a small saw with a narrow blade

set in a frame.

haddock
NOUN an edible sea fish.

haemoglobin
Said "hee-moh-gloh-bin" NOUN Haemoglobin is a substance in red blood cells which carries oxygen round the body.

haemorrhage
Said "hem-er-rij" NOUN A haemorrhage is serious bleeding especially inside a person's body.

haemorrhoids
Said "hem-er-roydz" PLURAL NOUN Haemorrhoids are painful lumps around the anus that are caused by swollen veins.

hag hags
NOUN; OFFENSIVE an ugly old woman.

haggard
ADJECTIVE A person who is haggard looks very tired and ill.

haggis
NOUN Haggis is a Scottish dish made of the internal organs of a sheep, boiled together with oatmeal and spices in a skin.

haggle haggles haggling haggled
VERB If you haggle with someone, you argue with them, usually about the cost of something.

hail hails hailing hailed
NOUN **1** Hail is frozen rain. **2** A hail of things is a lot of them falling together E.G. *a hail of bullets… a hail of protest.* ▶ VERB **3** When it is hailing,

hair hairs
NOUN Hair consists of the long, threadlike strands that grow from the skin of animals and humans.

Someone hails you, they call you to attract your attention or greet you E.G. *He hailed a taxi.*

haircut haircuts
NOUN the cutting of someone's hair; also the style in which it is cut.

hairdo hairdos
NOUN a hairstyle.

hairdresser hairdressers
NOUN someone who is trained to cut and style people's hair; also a shop where this is done.

hairdressing NOUN or ADJECTIVE

hairline hairlines
NOUN 1 the edge of the area on your forehead where your hair grows. ▶ ADJECTIVE 2 A hairline crack is so fine that you can hardly see it.

hairpin hairpins
NOUN 1 a U-shaped wire used to hold hair in position. ▶ ADJECTIVE 2 A hairpin bend is a U-shaped bend in the road.

hair-raising
ADJECTIVE very frightening or exciting.

hairstyle hairstyles
NOUN Someone's hairstyle is the way in which their hair is arranged or cut.

hairy hairier hairiest
ADJECTIVE 1 covered in a lot of hair. 2 INFORMAL difficult, exciting, and rather frightening E.G. *He had lived through many hairy adventures.*

hajj
Rhymes with "badge" NOUN The hajj is the pilgrimage to Mecca that every Muslim must make at least once in their life if they are healthy and wealthy enough to do so.

🔲 from Arabic *hajj* pilgrimage

haka haka or hakas
NOUN 1 In New Zealand, a haka is a ceremonial Maori dance made up of various postures and accompanied by a chant. 2 an imitation of this dance performed by New Zealand sports teams before matches as a challenge.

hake hakes
NOUN an edible sea fish related to the cod.

hakea hakeas
NOUN a large Australian shrub with bright flowers and hard, woody fruit.

halcyon
Said "hal-see-on" ADJECTIVE 1 LITERARY peaceful, gentle, and calm E.G. *halcyon colours of yellow and turquoise.* ▶ PHRASE 2 Halcyon days are a happy and carefree time in the past E.G. *halcyon days in the sun.*

half halves
NOUN, ADJECTIVE, or ADVERB 1 Half refers to one of two equal parts that make up a whole E.G. *the two halves of the brain… They chatted for another half hour… The bottle was only half full.* ▶ ADVERB 2 You can use 'half' to say that something is only partly true E.G. *I half expected him to explode in anger.*

half-baked
ADJECTIVE; INFORMAL Half-baked ideas or plans have not been properly thought out.

half board
NOUN Half board at a hotel includes breakfast and dinner but not lunch.

half-brother half-brothers
NOUN Your half-brother is the son of either your mother or your father but not of your other parent.

half-hearted
ADJECTIVE showing no real effort or enthusiasm.

half-pie
ADJECTIVE; INFORMAL In New Zealand English, half-pie means incomplete or not properly done E.G. *finished in a half-pie way*.

half-sister half-sisters
NOUN Your half-sister is the daughter of either your mother or your father but not of your other parent.

half-timbered
ADJECTIVE A half-timbered building has a framework of wooden beams showing in the walls.

half-time
NOUN Half-time is a short break between two parts of a game when the players have a rest.

halfway
ADVERB at the middle of the distance between two points in place or time E.G. *He stopped halfway down the ladder… halfway through the term*.

halibut halibuts
NOUN a large edible flat fish.

hall halls
NOUN 1 the room just inside the front entrance of a house which leads into other rooms. 2 a large room or building used for public events E.G. *a concert hall*.

hallmark hallmarks
NOUN 1 The hallmark of a person or group is their most typical quality E.G. *A warm, hospitable welcome is the hallmark of island people*. 2 an official mark on gold or silver indicating the quality of the metal.

hallowed
Said "hal-lode" ADJECTIVE respected as being holy E.G. *hallowed ground*.

Halloween
NOUN Halloween is October 31st, and is celebrated by children dressing up, often as ghosts and witches.
🏛 from Old English *halig* + *æfen* meaning 'holy evening', the evening before All Saints' Day

hallucinate hallucinates hallucinating hallucinated
Said "hal-loo-sin-ate" VERB If you hallucinate, you see strange things in your mind because of illness or drugs.
hallucination NOUN **hallucinatory** ADJECTIVE
🏛 from Latin *alucinari* meaning 'to wander in thought'

halo haloes or halos
NOUN a circle of light around the head of a holy figure.
🏛 from Greek *halos* meaning 'disc shape of the sun or moon'

halt halts halting halted
VERB 1 To halt when moving means to stop. 2 To halt development or action means to stop it. ► NOUN 3 a short standstill.

halter halters
NOUN a strap fastened round a horse's head so that it can be led easily.

halve halves halving halved
Said "hahv" VERB 1 If you halve something, you divide it into two equal parts. 2 To halve something also means to reduce its size or amount by half.

ham hams
NOUN 1 Ham is meat from the hind leg of a pig, salted and cured. 2 a bad actor who exaggerates emotions and gestures. 3 someone who is interested in amateur radio.

hamburger hamburgers
NOUN a flat disc of minced meat,

a
b
c
d
e
f
g
h
i
j
k
l
m
n
o
p
q
r
s
t
u
v
w
x
y
z

A
B
C
D
E
F
G
H
I
J
K
L
M
N
O
P
Q
R
S
T
U
V
W
X
Y
Z

seasoned and fried; often eaten in a bread roll.

🏛 named after its city of origin *Hamburg* in Germany

hammer hammers hammering hammered

NOUN **1** a tool consisting of a heavy piece of metal at the end of a handle, used for hitting nails into things. ▸ VERB **2** If you hammer something, you hit it repeatedly, with a hammer or with your fist. **3** If you hammer an idea into someone, you keep repeating it and telling them about it. **4** INFORMAL If you hammer someone, you criticize or attack them severely.

hammock hammocks

NOUN a piece of net or canvas hung between two supports and used as a bed.

hamper hampers hampering hampered

NOUN **1** a rectangular wicker basket with a lid, used for carrying food. ▸ VERB **2** If you hamper someone, you make it difficult for them to move or progress.

■ (sense 2) handicap, hinder, impede

hamster hamsters

NOUN a small furry rodent which is often kept as a pet.

☑ There is no *p* in *hamster*.

hamstring hamstrings

NOUN ⟨PE⟩ Your hamstring is a tendon behind your knee joining your thigh muscles to the bones of your lower leg.

hand hands handing handed

NOUN **1** Your hand is the part of your body beyond the wrist, with four fingers and a thumb. **2** Your hand is also your writing style. **3** The hand of

someone in a situation is their influence or the part they play in it E.G. *He had a hand in its design.* **4** If you give someone a hand, you help them to do something. **5** When an audience gives someone a big hand, they applaud. **6** The hands of a clock or watch are the pointers that point to the numbers. **7** In cards, your hand is the cards you are holding. ▸ VERB **8** If you hand something to someone, you give it to them.
▸ PHRASES **9** Something that is **at hand**, **to hand**, or **on hand** is available, close by, and ready for use. **10** You use **on the one hand** to introduce the first part of an argument or discussion with two different points of view. **11** You use **on the other hand** to introduce the second part of an argument or discussion with two different points of view. **12** If you do something **by hand**, you do it using your hands rather than a machine.

hand down VERB Something that is handed down is passed from one generation to another.

handbag handbags

NOUN a small bag used mainly by women to carry money and personal items.

handbook handbooks

NOUN a book giving information and instructions about something.

handcuff handcuffs

NOUN Handcuffs are two metal rings linked by a chain which are locked around a prisoner's wrists.

handful handfuls

NOUN **1** A handful of something is the amount of it you can hold in your hand E.G. *He picked up a handful of seeds.* **2** a small quantity E.G. *Only a* *handful of people knew.* **3** Someone who is a handful is difficult to control E.G. *He is a bit of a handful.*

handicap handicaps handicapping handicapped
NOUN **1** a physical or mental disability. **2** something that makes it difficult for you to achieve something. **3** In sport, a handicap is a disadvantage or advantage given to competitors according to their skill, in order to give them an equal chance of winning. ▶ VERB **4** If something handicaps someone, it makes it difficult for them to achieve something.
■ (sense 1) disability, impairment

handicraft handicrafts
NOUN Handicrafts are activities such as embroidery or pottery which involve making things with your hands; also the items produced.

handiwork
NOUN Your handiwork is something that you have done or made yourself.

handkerchief handkerchiefs
NOUN a small square of fabric used for blowing your nose.

handle handles handling handled
NOUN **1** The handle of an object is the part by which it is held or controlled. **2** a small lever used to open and close a door or window. ▶ VERB **3** If you handle an object, you hold it in your hands to examine it. **4** If you handle something, you deal with it or control it E.G. *I have learned how to handle pressure.*

handlebar handlebars
NOUN Handlebars are the bar and handles at the front of a bicycle, used for steering.

handout handouts
NOUN **1** a gift of food, clothing, or money given to a poor person. **2** a piece of paper giving information about something.

hand-picked
ADJECTIVE carefully chosen E.G. *a hand-picked team of bodyguards.*

handset handsets
NOUN The handset of a telephone is the part that you speak into and listen with.

handshake handshakes
NOUN the grasping and shaking of a person's hand by another person.

handsome
ADJECTIVE **1** very attractive in appearance. **2** large and generous E.G. *a handsome profit.*
handsomely ADVERB
■ (sense 1) attractive, good-looking

handwriting
NOUN Someone's handwriting is their style of writing as it looks on the page.

handy handier handiest
ADJECTIVE **1** conveniently near. **2** easy to handle or use. **3** skilful

hang hangs hanging hung
VERB **1** If you hang something somewhere, you attach it to a high point. If it is hanging there, it is attached by its top to something E.G. *His jacket hung from a hook behind the door.* **2** If a future event or possibility is hanging over you, it worries or frightens you E.G. *She has an eviction notice hanging over her.* **3** When you hang wallpaper, you stick it onto a wall. **4** To hang someone means to kill them by suspending them by a rope around the neck. ▶ PHRASE **5** When you **get the hang of something**, you understand it and are able to do it.

have a pIEce of pIE (piece)   SPELLING NOTE

hang about or **hang around**
VERB **1** INFORMAL To hang about or hang around means to wait somewhere. **2** To hang about or hang around with someone means to spend a lot of time with them.

hang on VERB **1** If you hang on to something, you hold it tightly or keep it. **2** INFORMAL To hang on means to wait.

hang up VERB When you hang up, you put down the receiver to end a telephone call

☑ When *hang* means 'kill someone by suspending them by a rope' (sense 4), the past tense and past participle are *hanged*: *he was hanged for murder in 1959.*

hangar hangars
NOUN a large building where aircraft are kept.

hanger hangers
NOUN a coat hanger.

hanger-on hangers-on
NOUN an unwelcome follower of an important person.

hang-glider hang-gliders
NOUN an aircraft without an engine and consisting of a large frame covered in fabric, from which the pilot hangs in a harness.

hangi hangi or hangis
Said "hung-ee" NOUN In New Zealand, a Maori oven made from a hole in the ground lined with hot stones.

hangover hangovers
NOUN a feeling of sickness and headache after drinking too much alcohol.

hang-up hang-ups
NOUN A hang-up about something is a continual feeling of embarrassment or fear about it.

hanker hankers hankering hankered
VERB If you hanker after something, you continually want it.
hankering NOUN

hanky hankies
NOUN a handkerchief.

Hanukkah or **Chanukah**
Said "hah-na-ka" NOUN Hanukkah is an eight-day Jewish festival of lights.
🏛 a Hebrew word meaning literally 'a dedication'

haphazard
Said "hap-haz-ard" ADJECTIVE not organized or planned.
haphazardly ADVERB
🏛 from Old Norse *hap* meaning 'chance' and Arabic *az-zahr* meaning 'gaming dice'

hapless
ADJECTIVE; LITERARY unlucky.

happen happens happening happened
VERB **1** When something happens, it occurs or takes place. **2** If you happen to do something, you do it by chance.
happening NOUN
▤ (sense 1) come about, occur, take place

happiness
NOUN a feeling of great contentment or pleasure.

happy happier happiest
ADJECTIVE **1** feeling, showing, or producing contentment or pleasure E.G. *a happy smile… a happy atmosphere.* **2** satisfied that something is right E.G. *I wasn't very happy about the layout.* **3** willing E.G. *I would be happy to help.* **4** fortunate or lucky E.G. *a happy coincidence.*
happily ADVERB

■ (sense 1) blissful, content, glad, joyful

happy-go-lucky

ADJECTIVE carefree and unconcerned.

harangue harangues haranguing harangued

Said "har-**rang**" NOUN **1** a long, forceful, passionate speech. ► VERB **2** To harangue someone means to talk to them at length passionately and forcefully about something.

▥ from Old Italian *aringa* meaning 'public speech'

harass harasses harassing harassed

Said "har-**rass**" VERB If someone harasses you, they trouble or annoy you continually.

harassed ADJECTIVE **harassment** NOUN

harbinger harbingers

Said "har-bin-jer" NOUN a person or thing that announces or indicates the approach of a future event E.G. *others see the shortage of cash as a harbinger of bankruptcy*.

harbour harbours harbouring harboured

NOUN **1** a protected area of deep water where boats can be moored. ► VERB **2** To harbour someone means to hide them secretly in your house. **3** If you harbour a feeling, you have it for a long time E.G. *She's still harbouring great bitterness*.

▥ from Old English *here* + *beorg* meaning 'army shelter'

hard harder hardest

ADJECTIVE or ADVERB **1** Something that is hard is firm, solid, or stiff E.G. *a hard piece of cheese… The ground was baked hard*. **2** requiring a lot of effort E.G. *hard work… They tried hard to* attract tourists. ► ADJECTIVE **3** difficult E.G. *These are hard times*. **4** Someone who is hard has no kindness or pity E.G. *Don't be hard on him*. **5** A hard colour or voice is harsh and unpleasant. **6** Hard evidence or facts can be proved to be true. **7** Hard water contains a lot of lime and does not easily produce a lather. **8** Hard drugs are very strong illegal drugs. **9** Hard drink is strong alcohol. ► ADVERB **10** An event that follows hard upon something takes place immediately afterwards.

hardness NOUN

■ (sense 1) firm, rigid, solid, stiff

hard and fast

ADJECTIVE fixed and not able to be changed E.G. *hard and fast rules*.

hardback hardbacks

NOUN a book with a stiff cover.

hard core

NOUN The hard core in an organization is the group of people who most resist change.

harden hardens hardening hardened

VERB To harden means to become hard or get harder.

hardening NOUN **hardened** ADJECTIVE

hard labour

NOUN physical work which is difficult and tiring, used in some countries as a punishment for a crime.

hardly

ADVERB **1** almost not or not quite E.G. *I could hardly believe it*. **2** certainly not E.G. *It's hardly a secret*.

☑ You should not use *hardly* with a negative word like *not* or *no: he could hardly hear her* not *he could not hardly hear her*.

a b c d e f g h i j k l m n o p q r s t u v w x y z

I went to see (C) the doctor's new practiCe (practice)   **SPELLING NOTE**

A
B
C
D
E
F
G
H
I
J
K
L
M
N
O
P
Q
R
S
T
U
V
W
X
Y
Z

hard-nosed
ADJECTIVE tough, practical, and realistic.

hard of hearing
ADJECTIVE not able to hear properly.

hardship hardships
NOUN Hardship is a time or situation of suffering and difficulty.

hard shoulder hard shoulders
NOUN the area at the edge of a motorway where a driver can stop in the event of a breakdown.

hard up
ADJECTIVE; INFORMAL having hardly any money.

hardware
NOUN 1 Hardware is tools and equipment for use in the home and garden. 2 (ICT) Hardware is also computer machinery rather than computer programs.

hard-wearing
ADJECTIVE strong, well-made, and long-lasting.

hardwood hardwoods
NOUN strong, hard wood from a tree such as an oak; also the tree itself.

hardy hardier hardiest
ADJECTIVE tough and able to endure very difficult or cold conditions E.G. a hardy race of pioneers.

hare hares haring hared
NOUN 1 an animal like a large rabbit, but with longer ears and legs. ▶ VERB 2 To hare about means to run very fast E.G. He hared off down the corridor.

harem harems
Said "har-reem" NOUN a group of wives or mistresses of one man, especially in Muslim societies; also the place where these women live.

hark harks harking harked
VERB 1 OLD-FASHIONED To hark means to

listen. 2 To hark back to something in the past means to refer back to it or recall it.

harlequin
Said "har-lik-win" ADJECTIVE having many different colours.

harm harms harming harmed
VERB 1 To harm someone or something means to injure or damage them. ▶ NOUN 2 Harm is injury or damage.
■ (sense 1) damage, hurt, injure

harmful
ADJECTIVE having a bad effect on something E.G. Whilst most stress is harmful, some is beneficial.

harmless
ADJECTIVE 1 safe to use or be near. 2 unlikely to cause problems or annoyance E.G. He's harmless really.
harmlessly ADVERB

harmonic
ADJECTIVE using musical harmony.

harmonica harmonicas
NOUN a small musical instrument which you play by blowing and sucking while moving it across your lips.

harmonious
Said "har-moh-nee-uss" ADJECTIVE 1 showing agreement, peacefulness, and friendship E.G. a harmonious relationship. 2 consisting of parts which blend well together making an attractive whole E.G. harmonious interior decor.
harmoniously ADVERB

harmony harmonies
NOUN 1 Harmony is a state of peaceful agreement and cooperation E.G. the promotion of racial harmony. 2 (MUSIC) Harmony is the structure and relationship of chords in a piece

---

SPELLING NOTE You must practiSe your Ss (practiѕe)

of music. **3** Harmony is the pleasant combination of two or more notes played at the same time.

harness harnesses harnessing harnessed

NOUN **1** a set of straps and fittings fastened round a horse so that it can pull a vehicle, or fastened round someone's body to attach something E.G. *a safety harness.* ► VERB **2** If you harness something, you bring it under control to use it E.G. *harnessing public opinion.*

harp harps harping harped

NOUN **1** a musical instrument consisting of a triangular frame with vertical strings which you pluck with your fingers. ► VERB **2** If someone harps on something, they keep talking about it, especially in a boring way.

harpoon harpoons

NOUN a barbed spear attached to a rope, thrown or fired from a gun and used for catching whales or large fish.

harpsichord harpsichords

NOUN a musical instrument like a small piano, with strings which are plucked when the keys are pressed.

harrowing

ADJECTIVE very upsetting or disturbing E.G. *a harrowing experience.*

harsh harsher harshest

ADJECTIVE severe, difficult, and unpleasant E.G. *harsh weather conditions… harsh criticism.*

harshly ADVERB   **harshness** NOUN
◼ hard, severe, tough

harvest harvests harvesting harvested

NOUN **1** the cutting and gathering of a crop; also the ripe crop when it is

gathered and the time of gathering. ► VERB **2** To harvest food means to gather it when it is ripe.

harvester NOUN
▦ from Old German *herbist* meaning 'autumn'

has-been has-beens

NOUN; INFORMAL a person who is no longer important or successful.

hash

PHRASE **1** If you **make a hash of** a job, you do it badly. ► NOUN **2** Hash is a dish made of small pieces of meat and vegetables cooked together. **3** INFORMAL Hash is also hashish.

hashish

Said "hash-eesh" NOUN Hashish is a drug made from the hemp plant. It is usually smoked, and is illegal in many countries.
▦ from Arabic *hashish* meaning 'hemp' or 'dried grass'

hassle hassles hassling hassled

NOUN **1** INFORMAL Something that is a hassle is difficult or causes trouble. ► VERB **2** If you hassle someone, you annoy them by repeatedly asking them to do something.

haste

NOUN Haste is doing something quickly, especially too quickly.

hasten hastens hastening hastened

Said "hay-sn" VERB To hasten means to move quickly or do something quickly.

hasty hastier hastiest

ADJECTIVE done or happening suddenly and quickly, often without enough care or thought.

hastily ADVERB

hat hats

NOUN a covering for the head.

a
b
c
d
e
f
g
h
i
j
k
l
m
n
o
p
q
r
s
t
u
v
w
x
y
z

A B C D E F G H I J K L M N O P Q R S T U V W X Y Z

hatch hatches hatching hatched
VERB 1 When an egg hatches, or when a bird or reptile hatches, the egg breaks open and the young bird or reptile emerges. 2 To hatch a plot means to plan it. ▶ NOUN 3 a covered opening in a floor or wall.

hatchback hatchbacks
NOUN a car with a door at the back which opens upwards.

hatchet hatchets
NOUN 1 a small axe. ▶ PHRASE 2 To **bury the hatchet** means to resolve a disagreement and become friends again.

hate hates hating hated
VERB 1 If you hate someone or something, you have a strong dislike for them. ▶ NOUN 2 Hate is a strong dislike.
▣ (sense 1) detest, loathe

hatred
Said "hay-trid" NOUN Hatred is an extremely strong feeling of dislike.

hat trick hat tricks
NOUN In sport, a hat trick is three achievements, for example when a footballer scores three goals in a match E.G. Crawford completed his hat trick in the 60th minute.

haughty haughtier haughtiest
Rhymes with "naughty" ADJECTIVE showing excessive pride E.G. He behaved in a haughty manner.
haughtily ADVERB
▣ disdainful, proud, supercilious

haul hauls hauling hauled
VERB 1 To haul something somewhere means to pull it with great effort.
▶ NOUN 2 a quantity of something obtained E.G. a good haul of fish.
▶ PHRASE 3 Something that you describe as **a long haul** takes a lot of

time and effort to achieve E.G. So women began the long haul to equality.

haulage
Said "hawl-lij" NOUN Haulage is the business or cost of transporting goods by road.

haunches
PLURAL NOUN Your haunches are your buttocks and the tops of your legs E.G. He squatted on his haunches.

haunt haunts haunting haunted
VERB 1 If a ghost haunts a place, it is seen or heard there regularly. 2 If a memory or a fear haunts you, it continually worries you. ▶ NOUN 3 A person's favourite haunt is a place they like to visit often.

haunted
ADJECTIVE 1 regularly visited by a ghost E.G. a haunted house. 2 very worried or troubled E.G. a haunted expression.

haunting
ADJECTIVE extremely beautiful or sad so that it makes a lasting impression on you E.G. haunting landscapes.

have has having had
VERB 1 Have is an auxiliary verb, used to form the past tense or to express completed actions E.G. They have never met… I have lost it. 2 If you have something, you own or possess it E.G. We have two tickets for the concert. 3 If you have something, you experience it, it happens to you, or you are affected by it E.G. I have an idea!… He had a marvellous time. 4 To have a child or baby animal means to give birth to it E.G. When is she having the baby? ▶ PHRASES 5 If you **have to** do something, you must do it. 6 If you **had better** do something, you ought to do it.

haven havens
Said "hay-ven" NOUN a safe place.

havoc
NOUN 1 Havoc is disorder and
confusion. ▶ PHRASE 2 To **play havoc**
with something means to cause
great disorder and confusion E.G.
*Food allergies often play havoc with
the immune system.*

hawk hawks hawking hawked
NOUN 1 a bird of prey which has short
rounded wings and a long tail. ▶ VERB
2 To hawk goods means to sell them
by taking them around from place to
place.

hawthorn hawthorns
NOUN a small, thorny tree producing
white blossom and red berries.

hay
NOUN Hay is grass which has been cut
and dried and is used as animal feed.

hay fever
NOUN Hay fever is an allergy to pollen
and grass, causing sneezing and
watering eyes.

haystack haystacks
NOUN a large, firmly built pile of hay,
usually covered and left out in the
open.

**hazard hazards hazarding
hazarded**
NOUN 1 (SCIENCE) a substance, object or
action which could be dangerous to
you. ▶ VERB 2 If you hazard something,
you put it at risk E.G. *hazarding the
health of his crew.* ▶ PHRASE 3 If you
hazard a guess, you make a guess.
hazardous ADJECTIVE
▥ from Arabic *az-zahr* meaning
'gaming dice'

haze
NOUN If there is a haze, you cannot
see clearly because there is moisture

or smoke in the air.

hazel hazels
NOUN 1 a small tree producing edible
nuts. ▶ ADJECTIVE 2 greenish brown in
colour.

hazy hazier haziest
ADJECTIVE dim or vague E.G. *hazy
sunshine… a hazy memory.*

he
PRONOUN 'He' is used to refer to a man,
boy, or male animal or to any person
whose sex is not mentioned.

head heads heading headed
NOUN 1 Your head is the part of your
body which has your eyes, brain, and
mouth in it. 2 Your head is also your
mind and mental abilities E.G. *He has
a head for figures.* 3 The head of
something is the top, start, or most
important end E.G. *at the head of the
table.* 4 The head of a group or
organization is the person in charge.
5 The head on beer is the layer of
froth on the top. 6 The head on a
computer or tape recorder is the
part that can read or write
information. 7 When you toss a coin,
the side called heads is the one with
the head on it. ▶ VERB 8 To head a
group or organization means to be
in charge E.G. *Bryce heads the help
organization.* 9 To head in a particular
direction means to move in that
direction E.G. *She is heading for a
breakdown.* 10 To head a ball means
to hit it with your head. ▶ PHRASE 11 If
you **lose your head**, you panic. 12 If
you say that someone is **off their
head**, you mean that they are mad
or very stupid. 13 If something is
over someone's head, it is too
difficult for them to understand. 14 If
you **can't make head nor tail of
something**, you cannot understand it.

a b c d e f g **h** i j k l m n o p q r s t u v w x y z

Psychiatrists Seldom Yell Callously Hard (<u>psychiatrist</u>)   SPELLING NOTE

A B C D E F G **H** I J K L M N O P Q R S T U V W X Y Z

head off VERB If you head off someone or something, you make them change direction or prevent something from happening E.G. *He hopes to head off a public squabble.*

headache headaches
NOUN **1** a pain in your head.
2 Something that is a headache is causing a lot of difficulty or worry E.G. *Delays in receiving money owed is a major headache for small firms.*

header headers
NOUN A header in soccer is hitting the ball with your head.

heading headings
NOUN a piece of writing that is written or printed at the top of a page.

headland headlands
NOUN a narrow piece of land jutting out into the sea.

headlight headlights
NOUN The headlights on a motor vehicle are the large powerful lights at the front.

headline headlines
NOUN **1** A newspaper headline is the title of a newspaper article printed in large, bold type. **2** The headlines are the main points of the radio or television news.

headmaster headmasters
NOUN a man who is the head teacher of a school.

headmistress headmistresses
NOUN a woman who is the head teacher of a school.

headphones
PLURAL NOUN Headphones are a pair of small speakers which you wear over your ears to listen to a radio without other people hearing.

headquarters
NOUN The headquarters of an

organization is the main place or from which it is run.

headroom
NOUN Headroom is the amount of space below a roof or surface under which an object must pass or fit.

headstone headstones
NOUN a large stone standing at one end of a grave and showing the name of the person buried there.

headstrong
ADJECTIVE determined to do something in your own way and ignoring other people's advice.

head teacher head teachers
NOUN the teacher who is in charge of a school.

headway
PHRASE If you are **making headway**, you are making progress.

headwind headwinds
NOUN a wind blowing in the opposite direction to the way you are travelling.

heady
ADJECTIVE extremely exciting E.G. *the heady days of the civil rights era.*

heal heals healing healed
VERB If something heals or if you heal it, it becomes healthy or normal again E.G. *He had a nasty wound which had not healed properly.*
healer NOUN

health
NOUN Health is the normally good condition of someone's body and the extent to which it is free from illness E.G. *Vitamins are essential for health.*
📖 from Old English *hælth* a toast drunk to a person's wellbeing
■ fitness, wellbeing

health food health foods
NOUN food which is free from added

chemicals and is considered to be good for your health.

healthy healthier healthiest
ADJECTIVE **1** Someone who is healthy is fit and strong and does not have any diseases. **2** Something that is healthy is good for you E.G. *a healthy diet*. **3** An organization or system that is healthy is successful E.G. *a healthy economy*.
healthily ADVERB
■ (sense 1) fit, well

heap heaps heaping heaped
NOUN **1** a pile of things. **2** INFORMAL Heaps of something means plenty of it E.G. *His performance earned him heaps of praise*. ▶ VERB **3** If you heap things, you pile them up. **4** To heap something such as praise on someone means to give them a lot of it.
■ (sense 1) mass, mound, pile

hear hears hearing heard
VERB **1** When you hear sounds, you are aware of them because they reach your ears. **2** When you hear from someone, they write to you or phone you. **3** When a judge hears a case, he or she listens to it in court in order to make a decision on it. ▶ PHRASE **4** If you say that you **won't hear of** something, you mean you refuse to allow it.
hear out VERB If you hear someone out, you listen to all they have to say without interrupting.

hearing hearings
NOUN **1** Hearing is the sense which makes it possible for you to be aware of sounds E.G. *My hearing is poor*. **2** a court trial or official meeting to hear facts about an incident. **3** If someone gives you a hearing, they let you give your point

of view and listen to you.

hearsay
NOUN Hearsay is information that you have heard from other people rather than something that you know personally to be true.

hearse hearses
Rhymes with "verse" NOUN a large car that carries the coffin at a funeral.

heart hearts
NOUN **1** the organ in your chest that pumps the blood around your body. **2** Your heart is also thought of as the centre of your emotions. **3** Heart is courage, determination, or enthusiasm E.G. *They were losing heart*. **4** The heart of something is the most central and important part of it. **5** a shape similar to a heart, used especially as a symbol of love. **6** Hearts is one of the four suits in a pack of playing cards. It is marked by a red heart-shaped symbol.

heartache heartaches
NOUN Heartache is very great sadness and emotional suffering.

heart attack heart attacks
NOUN a serious medical condition in which the heart suddenly beats irregularly or stops completely.

heartbreak heartbreaks
NOUN Heartbreak is great sadness and emotional suffering.
heartbreaking ADJECTIVE

heartbroken
ADJECTIVE very sad and emotionally upset E.G. *She was heartbroken at his death*.

heartburn
NOUN Heartburn is a painful burning sensation in your chest, caused by indigestion.

a b c d e f g h i j k l m n o p q r s t u v w x y z

Rhythmical Hounds Yap To Heavy Music (<u>rhythm</u>)   **SPELLING NOTE**

A
B
C
D
E
F
G
H
I
J
K
L
M
N
O
P
Q
R
S
T
U
V
W
X
Y
Z

heartening
ADJECTIVE encouraging or uplifting E.G. *heartening news*.

heart failure
NOUN Heart failure is a serious condition in which someone's heart does not work as well as it should, sometimes stopping completely.

heartfelt
ADJECTIVE sincerely and deeply felt E.G. *Our heartfelt sympathy goes out to you.*

hearth hearths
Said "harth" NOUN the floor of a fireplace.

heartless
ADJECTIVE cruel and unkind.

heart-rending
ADJECTIVE causing great sadness and pity E.G. *a heart-rending story*.

heart-throb heart-throbs
NOUN someone who is attractive to a lot of people.

heart-to-heart heart-to-hearts
NOUN a discussion in which two people talk about their deepest feelings.

hearty heartier heartiest
ADJECTIVE 1 cheerful and enthusiastic E.G. *hearty congratulations*. 2 strongly felt E.G. *a hearty dislike for her teacher*. 3 A hearty meal is large and satisfying.
heartily ADVERB

heat heats heating heated
NOUN 1 Heat is warmth or the quality of being hot; also the temperature of something that is warm or hot. 2 Heat is strength of feeling, especially of anger or excitement. 3 a contest or race in a competition held to decide who will play in the final. ▶ VERB 4 To heat something means to raise its temperature. ▶ PHRASE 5 When

a female animal is **on heat**, she is ready for mating.
heater NOUN

heath heaths
NOUN an area of open land covered with rough grass or heather.

heathen heathens
NOUN; OLD-FASHIONED someone who does not believe in one of the established religions.

heather
NOUN a plant with small purple or white flowers that grows wild on hills and moorland.

heating
NOUN Heating is the equipment used to heat a building; also the process and cost of running the equipment to provide heat.

heatwave heatwaves
NOUN a period of time during which the weather is much hotter than usual.

heave heaves heaving heaved
VERB 1 To heave something means to move or throw it with a lot of effort. 2 If your stomach heaves, you vomit or suddenly feel sick. 3 If you heave a sigh, you sigh loudly. ▶ NOUN 4 If you give something a heave, you move or throw it with a lot of effort.

heaven heavens
NOUN 1 a place of happiness where God is believed to live and where good people are believed to go when they die. 2 If you describe a situation or place as heaven, you mean that it is wonderful E.G. *The cake was pure heaven.* ▶ PHRASE 3 You say **'Good heavens'** to express surprise.

heavenly
ADJECTIVE 1 relating to heaven E.G. *a*

heavenly choir. **2** INFORMAL wonderful
E.G. *his heavenly blue eyes.*

heavy heavier heaviest; heavies
ADJECTIVE **1** great in weight or force
E.G. *How heavy are you?… a heavy
blow.* **2** great in degree or amount
E.G. *heavy casualties.* **3** solid and thick
in appearance E.G. *heavy shoes.*
4 using a lot of something quickly
E.G. *The van is heavy on petrol.*
5 serious and difficult to deal with or
understand E.G. *It all got a bit heavy
when the police arrived… a heavy
speech.* **6** Food that is heavy is solid
and difficult to digest E.G. *a heavy
meal.* **7** When it is heavy, the weather
is hot, humid, and still. **8** Someone
with a heavy heart is very sad. ► NOUN
9 INFORMAL a large, strong man
employed to protect someone or
something.
heavily ADVERB **heaviness** NOUN

heavy-duty
ADJECTIVE Heavy-duty equipment is
strong and hard-wearing.

heavy-handed
ADJECTIVE showing a lack of care or
thought and using too much
authority E.G. *heavy-handed police
tactics.*

heavyweight heavyweights
NOUN **1** a boxer in the heaviest weight
group. **2** an important person with a
lot of influence.

Hebrew Hebrews
Said "hee-broo" NOUN **1** Hebrew is an
ancient language now spoken in
Israel, where it is the official
language. **2** In the past, the Hebrews
were Hebrew-speaking Jews who
lived in Israel. ► ADJECTIVE **3** relating to
the Hebrews and their customs.
📖 from Hebrew *ibhri* meaning 'one

from beyond (the river)'

heckle heckles heckling heckled
VERB If members of an audience
heckle a speaker, they interrupt and
shout rude remarks.
heckler NOUN

hectare hectares
NOUN a unit for measuring areas of
land, equal to 10,000 square metres
or about 2.471 acres.

hectic
ADJECTIVE involving a lot of rushed
activity E.G. *a hectic schedule.*

hedge hedges hedging hedged
NOUN **1** a row of bushes forming a
barrier or boundary. ► VERB **2** If you
hedge against something
unpleasant happening, you protect
yourself. **3** If you hedge, you avoid
answering a question or dealing
with a problem. ► PHRASE **4** If you
hedge your bets, you support two
or more people or courses of action
to avoid the risk of losing a lot.

hedgehog hedgehogs
NOUN a small, brown animal with
sharp spikes covering its back.

hedonism
Said "hee-dn-izm" NOUN Hedonism is
the belief that gaining pleasure is
the most important thing in life.
hedonistic ADJECTIVE

heed heeds heeding heeded
VERB **1** If you heed someone's advice,
you pay attention to it. ► NOUN **2** If
you take or pay heed to something,
you give it careful attention.
■ (sense 1) listen to, mind, pay
attention to

heel heels heeling heeled
NOUN **1** the back part of your foot.
2 The heel of a shoe or sock is the
part that fits over your heel. ► VERB

3 To heel a pair of shoes means to put a new piece on the heel. ► PHRASE **4** A person or place that looks **down at heel** looks untidy and in poor condition.

heeler heelers
NOUN In Australia, a dog that herds cattle by biting at their heels.

hefty heftier heftiest
ADJECTIVE of great size, force, or weight E.G. *a hefty fine… hefty volumes.*

height heights
NOUN **1** The height of an object is its measurement from the bottom to the top. **2** a high position or place E.G. *Their nesting rarely takes place at any great height.* **3** The height of something is its peak, or the time when it is most successful or intense E.G. *the height of the tourist season… at the height of his career.*

heighten heightens heightening heightened
VERB If something heightens a feeling or experience, it increases its intensity.

heinous
Said "hay-nuss or hee-nuss" ADJECTIVE evil and terrible E.G. *heinous crimes.*

heir heirs
Said "air" NOUN A person's heir is the person who is entitled to inherit their property or title.

heiress heiresses
Said "air-iss" NOUN a female with the right to inherit property or a title.

heirloom heirlooms
Said "air-loom" NOUN something belonging to a family that has been passed from one generation to another.

helicopter helicopters
NOUN an aircraft with rotating blades above it which enable it to take off vertically, hover, and fly.
📖 from Greek *heliko* + *pteron* meaning 'spiral wing'

helium
Said "hee-lee-um" NOUN Helium is a gas that is lighter than air and that is used to fill balloons.

hell
NOUN **1** Hell is the place where souls of evil people are believed to go to be punished after death. **2** INFORMAL If you say that something is hell, you mean it is very unpleasant. ► INTERJECTION **3** 'Hell' is also a swearword.

hell-bent
ADJECTIVE determined to do something whatever the consequences.

hellish
ADJECTIVE; INFORMAL very unpleasant.

hello
INTERJECTION You say 'Hello' as a greeting or when you answer the phone.

helm helms
NOUN **1** The helm on a boat is the position from which it is steered and the wheel or tiller. ► PHRASE **2** **At the helm** means in a position of leadership or control.

helmet helmets
NOUN a hard hat worn to protect the head.

help helps helping helped
VERB **1** To help someone means to make something easier or better for them. ► NOUN **2** If you need or give help, you need or give assistance. **3** someone or something that helps you E.G. *He really is a good help.* ► PHRASE **4** If you **help yourself** to something, you take it. **5** If you **can't**

help something, you cannot control it or change it E.G. *I can't help feeling sorry for him.*
helper NOUN

helpful
ADJECTIVE **1** If someone is helpful, they help you by doing something for you. **2** Something that is helpful makes a situation more pleasant or easier to tolerate.
helpfully ADVERB
■ (sense 1) cooperative, supportive
■ (sense 2) beneficial, useful

helping helpings
NOUN an amount of food that you get in a single serving.

helpless
ADJECTIVE **1** unable to cope on your own E.G. *a helpless child.* **2** weak or powerless E.G. *helpless despair.*
helplessly ADVERB　**helplessness** NOUN

hem hems hemming hemmed
NOUN **1** The hem of a garment is an edge which has been turned over and sewn in place. ▶ VERB **2** To hem something means to make a hem on it.
hem in VERB If someone is hemmed in, they are surrounded and prevented from moving.

hemisphere hemispheres
Said "hem-iss-feer" NOUN one half of the earth, the brain, or a sphere.

hemp
NOUN Hemp is a tall plant, some varieties of which are used to make rope, and others to produce the drug cannabis.

hen hens
NOUN a female chicken; also any female bird.

hence
ADVERB **1** FORMAL for this reason E.G. *It*
sells more papers, hence more money is made.* **2** from now or from the time mentioned E.G. *The convention is due to start two weeks hence.*

henceforth
ADVERB; FORMAL from this time onward E.G. *His life henceforth was to revolve around her.*

henchman henchmen
NOUN The henchmen of a powerful person are the people employed to do violent or dishonest work for that person.

hepatitis
NOUN Hepatitis is a serious infectious disease causing inflammation of the liver.

her
PRONOUN or ADJECTIVE 'Her' is used to refer to a woman, girl or female animal that has already been mentioned, or to show that something belongs to a particular female.

herald heralds heralding heralded
NOUN **1** In the past, a herald was a messenger. ▶ VERB **2** Something that heralds a future event is a sign of that event.

herb herbs
NOUN a plant whose leaves are used in medicine or to flavour food.
herbal ADJECTIVE　**herbalist** NOUN

herbivore herbivores
NOUN an animal that eats only plants.

herd herds herding herded
NOUN **1** a large group of animals. ▶ VERB **2** To herd animals or people means to make them move together as a group.

here
ADVERB **1** at, to, or in the place where

you are, or the place mentioned or indicated. ▸ PHRASE 2 **Here and there** means in various unspecified places E.G. *dense forests broken here and there by small towns.*

hereafter
ADVERB; FORMAL after this time or point E.G. *the South China Morning Post (referred to hereafter as SCMP).*

hereby
ADVERB; FORMAL used in documents and statements to indicate that a declaration is official E.G. *All leave is hereby cancelled.*

hereditary
ADJECTIVE passed on to a child from a parent E.G. *a hereditary disease.*

heredity
NOUN Heredity is the process by which characteristics are passed from parents to their children through the genes.

herein
ADVERB; FORMAL in this place or document.

heresy heresies
Said "herr-ess-ee" NOUN Heresy is belief or behaviour considered to be wrong because it disagrees with what is generally accepted, especially with regard to religion.
heretic NOUN **heretical** ADJECTIVE

herewith
ADVERB; FORMAL with this letter or document E.G. *I herewith return your cheque.*

heritage
NOUN the possessions or traditions that have been passed from one generation to another.

hermit hermits
NOUN a person who lives alone with a simple way of life, especially for religious reasons.
🔲 from Greek *erēmitēs* meaning 'living in the desert'

hernia hernias
Said "her-nee-a" NOUN a medical condition in which part of the intestine sticks through a weak point in the surrounding tissue.

hero heroes
NOUN 1 the main male character in a book, film, or play. 2 a person who has done something brave or good.

heroic
ADJECTIVE brave, courageous, and determined.
heroically ADVERB

heroin
Said "herr-oh-in" NOUN Heroin is a powerful drug formerly used as an anaesthetic and now taken illegally by some people for pleasure.

heroine heroines
Said "herr-oh-in" NOUN 1 the main female character in a book, film, or play. 2 a woman who has done something brave or good.

heroism
Said "herr-oh-i-zm" NOUN Heroism is great courage and bravery.

heron herons
NOUN a wading bird with very long legs and a long beak and neck.

herpes
Said "her-peez" NOUN Herpes is a virus which causes painful red spots on the skin.

herring herrings
NOUN a silvery fish that lives in large shoals in northern seas.

hers
PRONOUN 'Hers' refers to something that belongs to or relates to a woman, girl, or female animal.

herself

PRONOUN 1 'Herself' is used when the same woman, girl, or female animal does an action and is affected by it E.G. *She pulled herself out of the water.* 2 'Herself' is used to emphasize 'she'.

hertz

NOUN A hertz is a unit of frequency equal to one cycle per second.

hesitant

ADJECTIVE If you are hesitant, you do not do something immediately because you are uncertain or worried.
hesitantly ADVERB
▣ irresolute, uncertain, unsure

hesitate hesitates hesitating hesitated

VERB To hesitate means to pause or show uncertainty.
hesitation NOUN

hessian

NOUN Hessian is a thick, rough fabric used for making sacks.

heterosexual heterosexuals

Said "het-roh-**seks**-yool" ADJECTIVE 1 involving a sexual relationship between a man and a woman E.G. *heterosexual couples.* ▶ NOUN 2 a person who is sexually attracted to people of the opposite sex.

hewn

ADJECTIVE carved from a substance E.G. *a cave, hewn out of the hillside.*

hexagon hexagons

NOUN a shape with six straight sides.
hexagonal ADJECTIVE

heyday

Said "**hay**-day" NOUN The heyday of a person or thing is the period when they are most successful or popular E.G. *Hollywood in its heyday.*

hi

INTERJECTION 'Hi!' is an informal greeting.

hiatus hiatuses

Said "high-**ay**-tuss" NOUN; FORMAL a pause or gap.

hibernate hibernates hibernating hibernated

VERB Animals that hibernate spend the winter in a state like deep sleep.
hibernation NOUN
▦ from Latin *hibernare* meaning 'to spend the winter'

hibiscus hibiscuses

Said "hie-**bis**-kuss" NOUN a type of tropical shrub with brightly coloured flowers.

hiccup hiccups hiccupping hiccupped

Said "**hik**-kup"
NOUN 1 Hiccups are short, uncontrolled choking sounds in your throat that you sometimes get if you have been eating or drinking too quickly. 2 INFORMAL a minor problem. ▶ VERB 3 When you hiccup, you make these little choking sounds.

hide hides hiding hid hidden

VERB 1 To hide something means to put it where it cannot be seen, or to prevent it from being discovered E.G. *He was unable to hide his disappointment.* ▶ NOUN 2 the skin of a large animal.
▣ (sense 1) conceal, disguise

hideous

Said "**hid**-ee-uss" ADJECTIVE extremely ugly or unpleasant.
hideously ADVERB

hideout hideouts

NOUN a hiding place.

hierarchy hierarchies

Said "**high**-er-ar-kee" NOUN a system in

hierarchical ADJECTIVE

hi-fi hi-fis

NOUN a set of stereo equipment on which you can play compact discs and tapes.

high higher highest; highs

ADJECTIVE OR ADVERB **1** tall or a long way above the ground. **2** great in degree, quantity, or intensity E.G. *high interest rates… There is a high risk of heart disease.* **3** towards the top of a scale of importance or quality E.G. *high fashion.* **4** close to the top of a range of sound or notes E.G. *the human voice reaches a very high pitch.* ▶ ADJECTIVE **5** INFORMAL Someone who is high on a drug is affected by having taken it. ▶ NOUN **6** a high point or level E.G. *Morale reached a new high.* **7** INFORMAL Someone who is on a high is in a very excited and optimistic mood.
■ (sense 1) lofty, tall, towering

highbrow

ADJECTIVE concerned with serious, intellectual subjects.

higher education

NOUN Higher education is education at universities and colleges.

high jump

NOUN The high jump is an athletics event involving jumping over a high bar.

highlands

PLURAL NOUN Highlands are mountainous or hilly areas of land.

highlight highlights highlighting highlighted

VERB **1** If you highlight a point or problem, you emphasize and draw attention to it. ▶ NOUN **2** The highlight of something is the most interesting

part of it E.G. *His show was the highlight of the Festival.* **3** ⟨ART⟩ a lighter area of a painting, showing where light shines on things.
4 Highlights are also light-coloured streaks in someone's hair.

highly

ADVERB **1** extremely E.G. *It is highly unlikely I'll be able to replace it.*
2 towards the top of a scale of importance, admiration, or respect E.G. *She thought highly of him… highly qualified personnel.*

high-minded

ADJECTIVE Someone who is high-minded has strong moral principles.

Highness

'Highness' is used in titles and forms of address for members of the royal family other than a king or queen E.G. *Her Royal Highness, Princess Alexandra.*

high-pitched

ADJECTIVE A high-pitched sound is high and often rather shrill.

high-rise

ADJECTIVE High-rise buildings are very tall.

high school high schools

NOUN a secondary school.

high technology

NOUN High technology is the development and use of advanced electronics and computers.

high tide

NOUN On a coast, high tide is the time, usually twice a day, when the sea is at its highest level.

highway highways

NOUN a road along which vehicles have the right to pass.

highwayman highwaymen

NOUN In the past, highwaymen were

A B C D E F G **H** I J K L M N O P Q R S T U V W X Y Z

robbers on horseback who used to rob travellers.

hijack hijacks hijacking hijacked
VERB If someone hijacks a plane or vehicle, they illegally take control of it during a journey.
hijacking NOUN

hike hikes hiking hiked
NOUN 1 a long country walk. ▶ VERB 2 To hike means to walk long distances in the country.
hiker NOUN

hilarious
ADJECTIVE very funny.
hilariously ADVERB
▤ funny, humorous, uproarious

hilarity
NOUN Hilarity is great amusement and laughter E.G. *His antics caused great hilarity*.

hill hills
NOUN a rounded area of land higher than the land surrounding it.
hilly ADJECTIVE

hillbilly hillbillies
NOUN someone who lives in the country away from other people, especially in remote areas in the southern United States.

hilt hilts
NOUN The hilt of a sword or knife is its handle.

him
PRONOUN You use 'him' to refer to a man, boy, or male animal that has already been mentioned, or to any person whose sex is not known.

himself
PRONOUN 1 'Himself' is used when the same man, boy, or male animal does an action and is affected by it E.G. *He discharged himself from hospital*.
2 'Himself' is used to emphasize 'he'.

hind hinds
Rhymes with "blind" ADJECTIVE 1 used to refer to the back part of an animal E.G. *the hind legs*. ▶ NOUN 2 a female deer.

hinder hinders hindering hindered
Said "hin-der" VERB If you hinder someone or something, you get in their way and make something difficult for them.

Hindi
Said "hin-dee" NOUN Hindi is a language spoken in northern India.
▥ from Old Persian *Hindu* meaning 'the river Indus'

hindrance hindrances
NOUN 1 Someone or something that is a hindrance causes difficulties or is an obstruction. 2 Hindrance is the act of hindering someone or something.

hindsight
NOUN Hindsight is the ability to understand an event after it has actually taken place E.G. *With hindsight, I realized how odd he is*

Hindu Hindus
Said "hin-doo" NOUN ⟨ RE ⟩ a person who believes in Hinduism, an Indian religion which has many gods and believes that people have another life on earth after death.
Hinduism NOUN

hinge hinges hinging hinged
NOUN 1 the movable joint which attaches a door or window to its frame. ▶ VERB 2 Something that hinges on a situation or event depends entirely on that situation or event E.G. *Victory or defeat hinged on her final putt*.

hint hints hinting hinted
NOUN 1 a suggestion, clue, or helpful

a
b
c
d
e
f
g
h
i
j
k
l
m
n
o
p
q
r
s
t
u
v
w
x
y
z

LEt's measure the angLE (angLe)   ▶ SPELLING NOTE

A
B
C
D
E
F
H
I
J
K
L
M
N
O
P
Q
R
S
T
U
V
W
X
Y
Z

piece of advice. ▶ VERB **2** If you hint at something, you suggest it indirectly.
■ (sense 1) clue, indication, suggestion
■ (sense 2) imply, insinuate, suggest

hinterland hinterlands
NOUN The hinterland of a coastline or a port is the area of land behind it or around it.

hip hips
NOUN Your hips are the two parts at the sides of your body between your waist and your upper legs.

hippo hippos
NOUN; INFORMAL a hippopotamus.

hippopotamus hippopotamuses or **hippopotami**
NOUN a large African animal with thick wrinkled skin and short legs, that lives near rivers.
▦ from Greek *hippo* + *potamos* meaning 'river horse'

hippy hippies; also spelt **hippie**
NOUN In the 1960s and 1970s hippies were people who rejected conventional society and tried to live a life based on peace and love.

hire hires hiring hired
VERB **1** If you hire something, you pay money to be able to use it for a period of time. **2** If you hire someone, you pay them to do a job for you.
▶ PHRASE **3** Something that is **for hire** is available for people to hire.

hirsute
Said "hir-syoot" ADJECTIVE; FORMAL hairy.

his
ADJECTIVE or PRONOUN 'His' refers to something that belongs or relates to a man, boy, or male animal that has already been mentioned, or to any person whose sex is not known.

hiss hisses hissing hissed
VERB **1** To hiss means to make a long 's' sound, especially to show disapproval or aggression. ▶ NOUN **2** a long 's' sound.

histogram histograms
NOUN a graph consisting of rectangles of varying sizes, that shows the frequency of values of a quantity.

historian historians
NOUN a person who studies and writes about history.

historic
ADJECTIVE important in the past or likely to be seen as important in the future.

historical
ADJECTIVE **1** occurring in the past, or relating to the study of the past E.G. *historical events*. **2** describing or representing the past E.G. *historical novels*.
historically ADVERB

history histories
NOUN History is the study of the past. A history is a record of the past E.G. *The village is steeped in history… my family history*.

histrionic histrionics
Said "hiss-tree-on-ik" ADJECTIVE
1 Histrionic behaviour is very dramatic and full of exaggerated emotion E.G. *The setting was unbelievably histrionic*. **2** FORMAL relating to drama and acting E.G. *a young man of marked histrionic ability*. ▶ PLURAL NOUN **3** Histrionics are histrionic behaviour.

hit hits hitting hit
VERB **1** To hit someone or something means to strike them forcefully, usually causing hurt or damage. **2** To hit a ball or other object means to

make it move by hitting it with something. **3** If something hits you, it affects you badly and suddenly E.G. *The recession has hit the tourist industry hard.* **4** If something hits a particular point or place, it reaches it E.G. *The book hit Britain just at the right time.* **5** If you hit on an idea or solution, you suddenly think of it. ▶ NOUN **6** a person or thing that is popular and successful. **7** the action of hitting something E.G. *Give it a good hard hit with the hammer.* ▶ PHRASE **8** INFORMAL If you **hit it off** with someone, you become friendly with them the first time you meet them.

hit and miss
ADJECTIVE happening in an unpredictable way or without being properly organized.

hit-and-run
ADJECTIVE A hit-and-run car accident is one in which the person who has caused the damage drives away without stopping.

hitch hitches hitching hitched
NOUN **1** a slight problem or difficulty E.G. *The whole process was completed without a hitch.* ▶ VERB **2** INFORMAL If you hitch, you travel by getting lifts from passing vehicles E.G. *America is no longer a safe place to hitch round.*

hitchhiking
NOUN Hitchhiking is travelling by getting free lifts from passing vehicles.

hi tech
ADJECTIVE designed using the most modern methods and equipment, especially electronic equipment.

hither OLD-FASHIONED
ADVERB **1** used to refer to movement

towards the place where you are. ▶ PHRASE **2** Something that moves **hither and thither** moves in all directions.

hitherto
ADVERB; FORMAL until now E.G. *What he was aiming at had not hitherto been attempted.*

HIV
NOUN HIV is a virus that reduces people's resistance to illness and can cause AIDS. HIV is an abbreviation for 'human immunodeficiency virus'.

hive hives hiving hived
NOUN **1** a beehive. **2** A place that is a hive of activity is very busy with a lot of people working hard. ▶ VERB **3** If part of something such as a business is hived off, it is transferred to new ownership E.G. *The company is poised to hive off its music interests.*

hoard hoards hoarding hoarded
VERB **1** To hoard things means to save them even though they may no longer be useful. ▶ NOUN **2** a store of things that has been saved or hidden.
◼ (sense 1) save, stockpile, store
◼ (sense 2) cache, stash, store
☑ Do not confuse *hoard* with *horde*.

hoarding hoardings
NOUN a large advertising board by the side of the road.

hoarse hoarser hoarsest
ADJECTIVE A hoarse voice sounds rough and unclear.
hoarsely ADVERB

hoax hoaxes hoaxing hoaxed
NOUN **1** a trick or an attempt to deceive someone. ▶ VERB **2** To hoax someone means to trick or deceive them.

hob hobs
NOUN a surface on top of a cooker

a b c d e f g h i j k l m n o p q r s t u v w x y z

which can be heated in order to cook things.

hobble hobbles hobbling hobbled
VERB **1** If you hobble, you walk awkwardly because of pain or injury. **2** If you hobble an animal, you tie its legs together to restrict its movement.

hobby hobbies
NOUN something that you do for enjoyment in your spare time.

hock hocks
NOUN The hock of a horse or other animal is the angled joint in its back leg.

hockey
NOUN Hockey is a game in which two teams use long sticks with curved ends to try to hit a small ball into the other team's goal.

hoe hoes hoeing hoed
NOUN **1** a long-handled gardening tool with a small square blade, used to remove weeds and break up the soil. ▶ VERB **2** To hoe the ground means to use a hoe on it.

hog hogs hogging hogged
NOUN **1** a castrated male pig. ▶ VERB **2** INFORMAL If you hog something, you take more than your share of it, or keep it for too long. ▶ PHRASE **3** INFORMAL If you **go the whole hog**, you do something completely or thoroughly in a bold or extravagant way.

hoist hoists hoisting hoisted
VERB **1** To hoist something means to lift it, especially using a crane or other machinery. ▶ NOUN **2** a machine for lifting heavy things.

hokey-pokey
NOUN In New Zealand, hokey-pokey is a kind of brittle toffee.

hold holds holding held
VERB **1** To hold something means to carry or keep it in place, usually with your hand or arms. **2** Someone who holds power, office, or an opinion has it or possesses it. **3** If you hold something such as a meeting or an election, you arrange it and cause it to happen. **4** If something holds, it is still available or valid E.G. *The offer still holds.* **5** If you hold someone responsible for something, you consider them responsible for it. **6** If something holds a certain amount, it can contain that amount E.G. *The theatre holds 150 people.* **7** If you hold something such as theatre tickets, a telephone call, or the price of something, you keep or reserve it for a period of time E.G. *The line is engaged – will you hold?* **8** To hold something down means to keep it or to keep it under control E.G. *How could I have children and hold down a job like this?* **9** If you hold on to something, you continue it or keep it even though it might be difficult E.G. *They are keen to hold on to their culture.* **10** To hold something back means to prevent it, keep it under control, or not reveal it E.G. *She failed to hold back the tears.* ▶ NOUN **11** If someone or something has a hold over you, they have power, control, or influence over you E.G. *The party has a considerable hold over its own leader.* **12** a way of holding something or the act of holding it E.G. *He grabbed the rope and got a hold on it.* **13** the place where cargo or luggage is stored in a ship or a plane.
holder NOUN

A B C D E F G H I J K L M N O P Q R S T U V W X Y Z

holdall holdalls
NOUN a large, soft bag for carrying clothing.

hole holes holing holed
NOUN 1 an opening or hollow in something. 2 INFORMAL If you are in a hole, you are in a difficult situation. 3 INFORMAL A hole in a theory or argument is a weakness or error in it. 4 In golf, a hole is one of the small holes into which you have to hit the ball. ► VERB 5 When you hole the ball in golf, you hit the ball into one of the holes.
▤ (sense 1) aperture, gap, opening

Holi
NOUN Holi is a Hindu festival celebrated in spring.
▦ from *Holika*, a legendary female demon

holiday holidays holidaying holidayed
NOUN 1 a period of time spent away from home for enjoyment. 2 a time when you are not working or not at school. ► VERB 3 When you holiday somewhere, you take a holiday there E.G. *She is currently holidaying in Italy.*
▦ from Old English *haligdæg* meaning 'holy day'

holidaymaker holidaymakers
NOUN a person who is away from home on holiday.

holiness
NOUN 1 Holiness is the state or quality of being holy. 2 'Your Holiness' and 'His Holiness' are titles used to address or refer to the Pope or to leaders of some other religions.

hollow hollows hollowing hollowed
ADJECTIVE 1 Something that is hollow has space inside it rather than being solid. 2 An opinion or situation that is hollow has no real value or worth E.G. *a hollow gesture.* 3 A hollow sound is dull and has a slight echo E.G. *the hollow sound of his footsteps on the stairs.* ► NOUN 4 a hole in something or a part of a surface that is lower than the rest E.G. *It is a pleasant village in a lush hollow.* ► VERB 5 To hollow means to make a hollow E.G. *They hollowed out crude dwellings from the soft rock.*

holly
NOUN Holly is an evergreen tree or shrub with spiky leaves. It often has red berries in winter.

holocaust holocausts
Said "hol-o-kawst" NOUN 1 a large-scale destruction or loss of life, especially the result of war or fire. 2 The Holocaust was the mass murder of the Jews in Europe by the Nazis during World War II.
▦ from Greek *holos* + *kaustos* meaning 'completely burnt'

holster holsters
NOUN a holder for a hand gun, worn at the side of the body or under the arm.

holy holier holiest
ADJECTIVE 1 relating to God or to a particular religion E.G. *the holy city.* 2 Someone who is holy is religious and leads a pure and good life.
▤ (sense 1) hallowed, sacred
▤ (sense 2) devout, pious

homage
Said "hom-ij" NOUN Homage is an act of respect and admiration E.G. *The thronging crowds paid homage to their assassinated president.*

home homes
NOUN 1 Your home is the building or

a
b
c
d
e
f
g
h
i
j
k
l
m
n
o
p
q
r
s
t
u
v
w
x
y
z

A B C D E F G **H** I J K L M N O P Q R S T U V W X Y Z

place in which you live or feel you belong. **2** a building in which elderly or ill people live and are looked after E.G. *He has been confined to a nursing home since his stroke.* ▶ ADJECTIVE **3** connected with or involving your home or country E.G. *He gave them his home phone number… The government is expanding the home market.*

🔲 (sense 1) abode, dwelling, residence

homeland homelands
NOUN Your homeland is your native country.

homeless
ADJECTIVE **1** having no home. ▶ PLURAL NOUN **2** The homeless are people who have no home.
homelessness NOUN

homely
ADJECTIVE simple, ordinary and comfortable E.G. *The room was small and homely.*

homeopathy
Said "home-ee-op-path-ee" NOUN Homeopathy is a way of treating illness by giving the patient tiny amounts of a substance that would normally cause illness in a healthy person.
homeopathic ADJECTIVE

homeowner homeowners
NOUN a person who owns the home in which he or she lives.

homesick
ADJECTIVE unhappy because of being away from home and missing family and friends.

homespun
ADJECTIVE not sophisticated or complicated E.G. *The book is simple homespun philosophy.*

homestead homesteads
NOUN a house and its land and other buildings, especially a farm.

home truth home truths
NOUN Home truths are unpleasant facts about yourself that you are told by someone else.

homeward or **homewards**
ADJECTIVE or ADVERB towards home E.G. *the homeward journey.*

homework
NOUN **1** Homework is school work given to pupils to be done in the evening at home. **2** Homework is also research and preparation E.G. *You certainly need to do your homework before buying a horse.*

homicide homicides
NOUN Homicide is the crime of murder.
homicidal ADJECTIVE

homing
ADJECTIVE A homing device is able to guide itself to a target. An animal with a homing instinct is able to guide itself home.

homophone homophones
NOUN Homophones are words with different meanings which are pronounced in the same way but are spelt differently. For example, 'write' and 'right' are homophones.

homo sapiens
Said "hoh-moh sap-ee-enz" NOUN; FORMAL Homo sapiens is the scientific name for human beings.
🔲 from Latin *homo* meaning 'man' and *sapiens* meaning 'wise'

homosexual homosexuals
NOUN **1** a person who is sexually attracted to someone of the same sex. ▶ ADJECTIVE **2** sexually attracted to people of the same sex.
homosexuality NOUN

hone hones honing honed
VERB **1** If you hone a tool, you sharpen it. **2** If you hone a quality or ability, you develop and improve it E.G. *He had a sharply honed sense of justice.*

honest
ADJECTIVE truthful and trustworthy.
honestly ADVERB
■ honourable, trustworthy, truthful

honesty
NOUN Honesty is the quality of being truthful and trustworthy.
■ honour, integrity, truthfulness

honey
NOUN **1** Honey is a sweet, edible, sticky substance produced by bees. **2** Honey means 'sweetheart' or 'darling' E.G. *What is it, honey?*

honeycomb honeycombs
NOUN a wax structure consisting of rows of six-sided cells made by bees for storage of honey and the eggs.

honeyeater honeyeaters
NOUN a small Australian bird that feeds on nectar from flowers.

honeymoon honeymoons
NOUN a holiday taken by a couple who have just got married.

honeysuckle
NOUN Honeysuckle is a climbing plant with fragrant pink or cream flowers.

hongi
Said "hong-ee" NOUN In New Zealand, hongi is a Maori greeting in which people touch noses.

honk honks honking honked
NOUN **1** a short, loud sound like that made by a car horn or a goose. ► VERB **2** When something honks, it makes a short, loud sound.

honorary
ADJECTIVE An honorary title or job is given as a mark of respect, and does not involve the usual qualifications or work E.G. *She was awarded an honorary degree.*

honour honours honouring honoured
NOUN **1** Your honour is your good reputation and the respect that other people have for you E.G. *This is a war fought by men totally without honour.* **2** an award or privilege given as a mark of respect. **3** Honours is a class of university degree which is higher than a pass or ordinary degree. ► PHRASE **4** If something is done **in honour of** someone, it is done out of respect for them E.G. *Egypt celebrated frequent minor festivals in honour of the dead.* ► VERB **5** If you honour someone, you give them special praise or attention, or an award. **6** If you honour an agreement or promise, you do what was agreed or promised E.G. *There is enough cash to honour the existing pledges.*

honourable
ADJECTIVE worthy of respect or admiration E.G. *He should do the honourable thing and resign.*

hood hoods
NOUN **1** a loose covering for the head, usually part of a coat or jacket. **2** a cover on a piece of equipment or vehicle, usually curved and movable E.G. *The mechanic had the hood up to work on the engine.*
hooded ADJECTIVE

-hood
SUFFIX '-hood' is added at the end of words to form nouns that indicate a state or condition E.G. *childhood… priesthood.*
▥ from the Old English suffix *-hād*

A
B
C
D
E
F
G
H
I
J
K
L
M
N
O
P
Q
R
S
T
U
V
W
X
Y
Z

hoof hooves or **hoofs**
NOUN The hard bony part of certain animals' feet.

hook hooks hooking hooked
NOUN 1 a curved piece of metal or plastic that is used for catching, holding, or hanging things E.G. *picture hooks.* 2 a curving movement, for example of the fist in boxing, or of a golf ball. ▶ VERB 3 If you hook one thing onto another, you attach it there using a hook. ▶ PHRASE 4 If you are **let off the hook**, something happens so that you avoid punishment or a difficult situation.

hooked
ADJECTIVE addicted to something; also obsessed by something E.G. *hooked on alcohol… I'm hooked on exercise.*

hooligan hooligans
NOUN a destructive and violent young person.

hooliganism NOUN
■ delinquent, ruffian, yob

hoop hoops
NOUN a large ring, often used as a toy.

hooray
INTERJECTION another spelling of **hurray**.

hoot hoots hooting hooted
VERB 1 To hoot means to make a long 'oo' sound like an owl E.G. *hooting with laughter.* 2 If a car horn hoots, it makes a loud honking noise. ▶ NOUN 3 a sound like that made by an owl or a car horn.

hoover hoovers hoovering hoovered
NOUN 1 TRADEMARK a vacuum cleaner.
▶ VERB 2 When you hoover, you use a vacuum cleaner to clean the floor.

hooves
a plural of **hoof**.

hop hops hopping hopped
VERB 1 If you hop, you jump on one foot. 2 When animals or birds hop, they jump with two feet together. 3 INFORMAL If you hop into or out of something, you move there quickly and easily E.G. *You only have to hop on the ferry to get there.* ▶ NOUN 4 a jump on one leg. 5 Hops are flowers of the hop plant, which are dried and used for making beer.

hope hopes hoping hoped
VERB 1 If you hope that something will happen or hope that it is true, you want it to happen or be true. ▶ NOUN 2 Hope is a wish or feeling of desire and expectation E.G. *There was little hope of recovery.*

hopeful ADJECTIVE   **hopefully** ADVERB
☑ Some people do not like the use of *hopeful* to mean 'it is hoped', for example *hopefully, we can get a good result on Saturday.* Although it is very common in speech, it should be avoided in written work.

hopeless
ADJECTIVE 1 having no hope E.G. *She shook her head in hopeless bewilderment.* 2 certain to fail or be unsuccessful. 3 unable to do something well E.G. *I'm hopeless at remembering birthdays.*

hopelessly ADVERB   **hopelessness** NOUN

hopper hoppers
NOUN a large, funnel-shaped container for storing things such as grain or sand.

horde hordes
Rhymes with "bored" NOUN a large group or number of people or animals E.G. *hordes of tourists.*
☑ Do not confuse *horde* with *hoard.*

horizon horizons
Said "hor-**eye**-zn" NOUN **1** the distant line where the sky seems to touch the land or sea. **2** Your horizons are the limits of what you want to do or are interested in E.G. *Travel broadens your horizons.* ▶ PHRASE **3** If something is **on the horizon**, it is almost certainly going to happen or be done in the future E.G. *Political change was on the horizon.*

horizontal
Said "hor-riz-**zon**-tl" ADJECTIVE (MATHS)
flat and parallel with the horizon or with a line considered as a base E.G. *a patchwork of vertical and horizontal black lines.*
horizontally ADVERB

hormone hormones
NOUN a chemical made by one part of your body that stimulates or has a specific effect on another part of your body.
hormonal ADJECTIVE

horn horns
NOUN **1** one of the hard, pointed growths on the heads of animals such as goats. **2** a musical instrument made of brass, consisting of a pipe or that is narrow at one end and wide at the other. **3** On vehicles, a horn is a warning device which makes a loud noise.

hornet hornets
NOUN a type of very large wasp.

horoscope horoscopes
Said "hor-ros-kope" NOUN a prediction about what is going to happen to someone, based on the position of the stars when they were born.
🔾 from Greek *hora* + *skopos* meaning 'hour observer'

horrendous
ADJECTIVE very unpleasant and shocking E.G. *horrendous injuries.*

horrible
ADJECTIVE **1** disagreeable and unpleasant E.G. *A horrible nausea rose within him.* **2** causing shock, fear, or disgust E.G. *horrible crimes.*
horribly ADVERB
▤ (sense 1) disagreeable, nasty, unpleasant
▤ (sense 2) dreadful, ghastly, shocking

horrid
ADJECTIVE very unpleasant indeed E.G. *We were all so horrid to him.*

horrific
ADJECTIVE so bad or unpleasant that people are horrified E.G. *a horrific attack.*

horrify horrifies horrifying horrified
VERB If something horrifies you, it makes you feel dismay or disgust E.G. *a crime trend that will horrify parents.*
horrifying ADJECTIVE

horror horrors
NOUN **1** a strong feeling of alarm, dismay, and disgust E.G. *He gazed in horror at the knife.* **2** If you have a horror of something, you fear it very much E.G. *He had a horror of fire.*

horse horses
NOUN **1** a large animal with a mane and long tail, on which people can ride. **2** a piece of gymnastics equipment with four legs, used for jumping over.

horseback
NOUN and ADJECTIVE You refer to someone who is riding a horse as someone **on horseback**, or a horseback rider.

a
b
c
d
e
f
g
h
i
j
k
l
m
n
o
p
q
r
s
t
u
v
w
x
y
z

The government licenSes Schnapps (licenₔes)   SPELLING NOTE

A
B
C
D
E
F
G
H
I
J
K
L
M
N
O
P
Q
R
S
T
U
V
W
X
Y
Z

horsepower

NOUN Horsepower is a unit used for measuring how powerful an engine is, equal to about 746 watts.

horseradish

NOUN Horseradish is the white root of a plant made into a hot-tasting sauce, often served cold with beef.

horseshoe horseshoes

NOUN a U-shaped piece of metal, nailed to the hard surface of a horse's hoof to protect it; also anything of this shape, often regarded as a good luck symbol.

horsey or **horsy**

ADJECTIVE 1 very keen on horses and riding. 2 having a face similar to that of a horse.

horticulture

NOUN Horticulture is the study and practice of growing flowers, fruit, and vegetables.

horticultural ADJECTIVE

hose hoses hosing hosed

NOUN 1 a long flexible tube through which liquid or gas can be passed E.G. *He left the garden hose on.* ▶ VERB 2 If you hose something, you wash or water it using a hose E.G. *The street cleaners need to hose the square down.*

hosiery

Said "hoze-yer-ee" NOUN Hosiery consists of tights, socks, and similar items, especially in shops.

hospice hospices

Said "hoss-piss" NOUN a hospital which provides care for people who are dying.

hospitable

ADJECTIVE friendly, generous, and welcoming to guests or strangers.

hospitality NOUN

hospital hospitals

NOUN a place where sick and injured people are treated and cared for.

host hosts hosting hosted

NOUN 1 The host of an event is the person that welcomes guests and provides food or accommodation for them E.G. *He is a most generous host who takes his guests to the best restaurants in town.* 2 a plant or animal with smaller plants or animals living on or in it. 3 A host of things is a large number of them E.G. *a host of close friends.* 4 In the Christian church, the Host is the consecrated bread used in Mass or Holy Communion. ▶ VERB 5 To host an event means to organize it or act as host at it.

hostage hostages

NOUN a person who is illegally held prisoner and threatened with injury or death unless certain demands are met by other people.

hostel hostels

NOUN a large building in which people can stay or live E.G. *a hostel for battered women.*

hostess hostesses

NOUN a woman who welcomes guests or visitors and provides food or accommodation for them.

hostile

ADJECTIVE 1 unfriendly, aggressive, and unpleasant E.G. *a hostile audience.* 2 relating to or involving the enemies of a country E.G. *hostile territory.*

hostility NOUN

hot hotter hottest

ADJECTIVE 1 having a high temperature E.G. *a hot climate.* 2 very spicy and causing a burning sensation in your mouth E.G. *a hot curry.* **3** new, recent, and exciting E.G. *hot news from tinseltown.* **4** dangerous or difficult to deal with E.G. *Animal testing is a hot issue.*

hotly ADVERB

hotbed hotbeds
NOUN A hotbed of some type of activity is a place that seems to encourage it E.G. *The city was a hotbed of rumour.*

hot dog hot dogs
NOUN a sausage served in a roll split lengthways.

hotel hotels
NOUN a building where people stay, paying for their room and meals.

hothouse hothouses
NOUN **1** a large heated greenhouse. **2** a place or situation of intense intellectual or emotional activity E.G. *a hothouse of radical socialist ideas.*

hot seat
NOUN; INFORMAL Someone who is in the hot seat has to make difficult decisions for which they will be held responsible.

hound hounds hounding hounded
NOUN **1** a dog, especially one used for hunting or racing. ▶ VERB **2** If someone hounds you, they constantly pursue or trouble you.

hour hours
NOUN **1** a unit of time equal to 60 minutes, of which there are 24 in a day. **2** The hour for something is the time when it happens E.G. *The hour for launching approached.* **3** The hour is also the time of day E.G. *What are you doing up at this hour?* **4** an important or difficult time E.G. *The hour has come... He is the hero of the hour.* ▶ PLURAL NOUN **5** The hours that

you keep are the times that you usually go to bed and get up.

hourly ADJECTIVE or ADVERB

house houses housing housed
NOUN *Said "hows"* **1** a building where a person or family lives. **2** a building used for a particular purpose E.G. *an auction house... the opera house.* **3** In a theatre or cinema, the house is the part where the audience sits; also the audience itself E.G. *The show had a packed house calling for more.* ▶ VERB *Said "howz"* **4** To house something means to keep it or contain it E.G. *The west wing housed a store of valuable antiques.*

houseboat houseboats
NOUN a small boat which people live on that is tied up at a particular place on a river or canal.

household households
NOUN **1** all the people who live as a group in a house or flat. ▶ PHRASE **2** Someone who is **a household name** is very well-known.
householder NOUN

housekeeper housekeepers
NOUN a person who is employed to do the cooking and cleaning in a house.

House of Commons
NOUN The House of Commons is the more powerful of the two parts of the British Parliament. Its members are elected by the public.

House of Lords
NOUN The House of Lords is the less powerful of the two parts of the British Parliament. Its members are unelected and come from noble families or are appointed by the Queen as an honour for a life of public service.

a b c d e f g h i j k l m n o p q r s t u v w x y z

Plaice the fish has a glittering 'EYE' (I) (pla*i*ce)   SPELLING NOTE

A B C D E F G H I J K L M N O P Q R S T U V W X Y Z

House of Representatives

NOUN **1** In Australia, the House of Representatives is the larger of the two parts of the Federal Parliament. **2** In New Zealand, the House of Representatives is the Parliament.

housewife housewives

NOUN a married woman who does the chores in her home, and does not have a paid job.

housing

NOUN Housing is the buildings in which people live E.G. *the serious housing shortage.*

hovel hovels

NOUN a small hut or house that is dirty or badly in need of repair.

hover hovers hovering hovered

VERB **1** When a bird, insect, or aircraft hovers, it stays in the same position in the air. **2** If someone is hovering they are hesitating because they cannot decide what to do E.G. *He was hovering nervously around the sick animal.*

hovercraft hovercraft or hovercrafts

NOUN a vehicle which can travel over water or land supported by a cushion of air.

how

ADVERB **1** 'How' is used to ask about, explain, or refer to the way in which something is done, known, or experienced E.G. *How did this happen?… He knew how quickly rumours could spread.* **2** 'How' is used to ask about or refer to a measurement or quantity E.G. *How much is it for the weekend?… I wonder how old he is.* **3** 'How' is used to emphasize the following word or statement E.G. *How odd!*

however

ADVERB **1** You use 'however' when you are adding a comment that seems to contradict or contrast with what has just been said E.G. *For all his compassion, he is, however, surprisingly restrained.* **2** You use 'however' to say that something makes no difference to a situation E.G. *However hard she tried, nothing seemed to work.*

howl howls howling howled

VERB **1** To howl means to make a long, loud wailing noise such as that made by a dog when it is upset E.G. *A distant coyote howled at the moon… The wind howled through the trees.* ► NOUN **2** a long, loud wailing noise.

HQ

an abbreviation for **headquarters**.

hub hubs

NOUN **1** the centre part of a wheel. **2** the most important or active part of a place or organization E.G. *The kitchen is the hub of most households.*

hubbub

NOUN Hubbub is great noise or confusion E.G. *the general hubbub of conversation.*

huddle huddles huddling huddled

VERB **1** If you huddle up or are huddled, you are curled up with your arms and legs close to your body. **2** When people or animals huddle together, they sit or stand close to each other, often for warmth. ► NOUN **3** A huddle of people or things is a small group of them.

hue hues

NOUN **1** LITERARY a colour or a particular shade of a colour. ► PHRASE **2** If people raise a **hue and cry**, they are very angry about something and protest.

huff

PHRASE If you are **in a huff**, you are sulking or offended about something.

huffy ADJECTIVE

hug hugs hugging hugged

VERB 1 If you hug someone, you put your arms round them and hold them close to you. 2 To hug the ground or a stretch of water or land means to keep very close to it E.G. *The road hugs the coast for hundreds of miles.* ▸ NOUN 3 If you give someone a hug, you hold them close to you. ▨ from Old Norse *hugga* meaning 'to comfort' or 'console'

huge huger hugest

ADJECTIVE extremely large in amount, size, or degree E.G. *a huge success… a huge crowd.*

hugely ADVERB

■ enormous, gigantic, vast

hui hui or **huis**

Said "hoo-ee" NOUN 1 In New Zealand, a meeting of Maori people. 2 INFORMAL In New Zealand English, a party.

hulk hulks

NOUN 1 a large, heavy person or thing. 2 the body of a ship that has been wrecked or abandoned.

hulking ADJECTIVE

hull hulls

NOUN The hull of a ship is the main part of its body that sits in the water.

hum hums humming hummed

VERB 1 To hum means to make a continuous low noise E.G. *The generator hummed faintly.* 2 If you hum, you sing with your lips closed. ▸ NOUN 3 a continuous low noise E.G. *the hum of the fridge.*

human humans

ADJECTIVE 1 relating to, concerning, or typical of people E.G. *Intolerance appears deeply ingrained in human nature.* ▸ NOUN 2 a person.

humanly ADVERB

human being human beings

NOUN a person.

humane

ADJECTIVE showing kindness and sympathy towards others E.G. *Medicine is regarded as the most humane of professions.*

humanely ADVERB

humanism

NOUN Humanism is the belief in mankind's ability to achieve happiness and fulfilment without the need for religion.

humanitarian humanitarians

NOUN 1 a person who works for the welfare of mankind. ▸ ADJECTIVE 2 concerned with the welfare of mankind E.G. *humanitarian aid.*

humanitarianism NOUN

humanity

NOUN 1 Humanity is people in general E.G. *I have faith in humanity.* 2 Humanity is also the condition of being human E.G. *He denies his humanity.* 3 Someone who has humanity is kind and sympathetic.

human rights

PLURAL NOUN Human rights are the rights of individuals to freedom and justice.

humble humbler humblest; humbles humbling humbled

ADJECTIVE 1 A humble person is modest and thinks that he or she has very little value. 2 Something that is humble is small or not very important E.G. *Just a splash of wine will transform a humble casserole.* ▸ VERB 3 To humble someone means

a
b
c
d
e
f
g
h
i
j
k
l
m
n
o
p
q
r
s
t
u
v
w
x
y
z

You must practiSe your Ss (practi_se_)   SPELLING NOTE

humbly ADVERB   **humbled** ADJECTIVE
◼ (sense 1) modest, unassuming

humbug humbugs
NOUN 1 a hard black and white striped sweet that tastes of peppermint.
2 Humbug is speech or writing that is obviously dishonest or untrue E.G. *hypocritical humbug*.

humdrum
ADJECTIVE ordinary, dull, and boring E.G. *humdrum domestic tasks*.

humid
ADJECTIVE If it is humid, the air feels damp, heavy, and warm.

humidity
NOUN Humidity is the amount of moisture in the air, or the state of being humid.

humiliate humiliates humiliating humiliated
VERB To humiliate someone means to make them feel ashamed or appear stupid to other people.
humiliation NOUN
◼ embarrass, mortify, shame

humility
NOUN Humility is the quality of being modest and humble.

hummingbird hummingbirds
NOUN a small bird with powerful wings that make a humming noise as they beat.

humour humours humouring humoured
NOUN 1 Humour is the quality of being funny E.G. *They discussed it with tact and humour.* 2 Humour is also the ability to be amused by certain things E.G. *Helen's got a peculiar sense of humour.* 3 Someone's humour is the mood they are in E.G. *He hasn't been in a good humour*

lately. ▶ VERB 4 If you humour someone, you are especially kind to them and do whatever they want.
humorous ADJECTIVE
◼ (sense 1) comedy, funniness, wit

hump humps humping humped
NOUN 1 a small, rounded lump or mound E.G. *a camel's hump.* ▶ VERB 2 INFORMAL If you hump something heavy, you carry or move it with difficulty.

hunch hunches hunching hunched
NOUN 1 a feeling or suspicion about something, not based on facts or evidence. ▶ VERB 2 If you hunch your shoulders, you raise your shoulders and lean forwards.

hunchback hunchbacks
NOUN; OLD-FASHIONED someone who has a large hump on their back.

hundred hundreds
the number 100.
hundredth

Hungarian Hungarians
Said "hung-*gair-ee-an*" ADJECTIVE
1 belonging or relating to Hungary.
▶ NOUN 2 someone who comes from Hungary. 3 Hungarian is the main language spoken in Hungary.

hunger hungers hungering hungered
NOUN 1 Hunger is the need to eat or the desire to eat. 2 A hunger for something is a strong need or desire for it E.G. *a hunger for winning.* ▶ VERB 3 If you hunger for something, you want it very much.

hunger strike hunger strikes
NOUN a refusal to eat anything at all, especially by prisoners, as a form of protest.

hungry hungrier hungriest
ADJECTIVE needing or wanting to eat
E.G. *People are going hungry.*
hungrily ADVERB

hunk hunks
NOUN A hunk of something is a large
piece of it.

hunt hunts hunting hunted
VERB 1 To hunt means to chase wild
animals to kill them for food or for
sport. 2 If you hunt for something,
you search for it. ▶ NOUN 3 the act of
hunting E.G. *Police launched a hunt
for an abandoned car.*
hunter NOUN **hunting** ADJECTIVE or
NOUN

huntaway huntaways
NOUN In Australia and New Zealand, a
dog trained to drive sheep forward.

hurdle hurdles
NOUN 1 one of the frames or barriers
that you jump over in an athletics
race called hurdles E.G. *She won the
four hundred metre hurdles.* 2 a
problem or difficulty E.G. *Several
hurdles exist for anyone seeking to do
postgraduate study.*

hurl hurls hurling hurled
VERB 1 To hurl something means to
throw it with great force. 2 If you hurl
insults at someone, you insult them
aggressively and repeatedly.

hurray or **hurrah** or **hooray**
INTERJECTION an exclamation of
excitement or approval.

hurricane hurricanes
NOUN a violent wind or storm.

hurry hurries hurrying hurried
VERB 1 To hurry means to move or do
something as quickly as possible
E.G. *She hurried through the empty
streets.* 2 To hurry something means
to make it happen more quickly E.G.

You can't hurry nature. ▶ NOUN 3 Hurry
is the speed with which you do
something quickly E.G. *He was in a
hurry to leave.*
hurried ADJECTIVE **hurriedly** ADVERB
◼ (sense 1) dash, fly, rush
◼ (sense 3) haste, rush

hurt hurts hurting hurt
VERB 1 To hurt someone means to
cause them physical pain. 2 If a part
of your body hurts, you feel pain
there. 3 If you hurt yourself, you
injure yourself. 4 To hurt someone
also means to make them unhappy
by being unkind or thoughtless
towards them E.G. *I didn't want to
hurt his feelings.* ▶ ADJECTIVE 5 If
someone feels hurt, they feel
unhappy because of someone's
unkindness towards them E.G. *He felt
hurt by all the lies.*
hurtful ADJECTIVE

hurtle hurtles hurtling hurtled
VERB To hurtle means to move or
travel very fast indeed, especially in
an uncontrolled way.

husband husbands
NOUN A woman's husband is the man
she is married to.

husbandry
NOUN 1 Husbandry is the art or skill of
farming. 2 Husbandry is also the art
or skill of managing something
carefully and economically.

hush hushes hushing hushed
VERB 1 If you tell someone to hush,
you are telling them to be quiet. 2 To
hush something up means to keep it
secret, especially something
dishonest involving important
people E.G. *The government has
hushed up a series of scandals.* ▶ NOUN
3 If there is a hush, it is quiet and still

a
b
c
d
e
f
g
h
i
j
k
l
m
n
o
p
q
r
s
t
u
v
w
x
y
z

LEarn the principLEs (princip<u>le</u>s)   **SPELLING NOTE**

A

E.G. *A graveyard hush fell over the group.*

hushed ADJECTIVE

B

C

husk husks

NOUN Husks are the dry outer coverings of grain or seed.

D

E

F

husky huskier huskiest; huskies

ADJECTIVE 1 A husky voice is rough or hoarse. ▶ NOUN 2 a large, strong dog with a thick coat, often used to pull sledges across snow.

G

H

hustle hustles hustling hustled

VERB To hustle someone means to make them move by pushing and jostling them E.G. *The guards hustled him out of the car.*

I

J

hut huts

NOUN a small, simple building, with one or two rooms.

K

L

hutch hutches

NOUN a wooden box with wire mesh at one side, in which small pets can be kept.

M

N

hyacinth hyacinths

Said "high-as-sinth" NOUN a spring flower with many small, bell-shaped flowers.

O

P

hybrid hybrids

NOUN 1 a plant or animal that has been bred from two different types of plant or animal. 2 anything that is a mixture of two other things.

Q

R

S

hydra hydras or hydrae

NOUN a microscopic freshwater creature that has a slender tubular body and tentacles round the mouth.

T

U

V

hydrangea hydrangeas

Said "high-**drain**-ja" NOUN a garden shrub with large clusters of pink or blue flowers.

W

X

hydraulic

Said "high-**drol**-lik" ADJECTIVE operated

Y

Z

by water or other fluid which is under pressure.

hydro-

PREFIX 'Hydro-' means 'water'. For example, *hydroelectricity* is electricity made using water power.

▦ from Greek *hudōr* meaning 'water'

hydrogen

NOUN Hydrogen is the lightest gas and the simplest chemical element.

hyena hyenas

Said "high-**ee**-na"; also spelt **hyaena**

NOUN a wild doglike animal of Africa and Asia that hunts in packs.

hygiene

Said "**high**-jeen" NOUN (D&T) Hygiene is the practice of keeping yourself and your surroundings clean, especially to stop the spread of disease.

hygienic ADJECTIVE

hymn hymns

NOUN (RE) a Christian song in praise of God.

hyper-

PREFIX 'Hyper-' means 'very much' or 'excessively' E.G. *hyperactive*.

▦ from Greek *huper* meaning 'over'

hyperactive

ADJECTIVE A hyperactive person is unable to relax and is always in a state of restless activity.

hyperbole

Said "high-**per**-bol-lee" NOUN Hyperbole is a style of speech or writing which uses exaggeration.

hypertension

NOUN Hypertension is a medical condition in which a person has high blood pressure.

hyphen hyphens

NOUN a punctuation mark used to join together words or parts of words, as for example in the word 'left-handed'.

hyphenate VERB **hyphenation** NOUN

What does the Hyphen do?

The **hyphen** (-) separates the different parts of certain words. A hyphen is often used when there would otherwise be an awkward combination of letters, or confusion with another word:

E.G. *Anna was re-elected president. She adopted a no-nonsense approach.*

In printed texts, the hyphen also divides a word that will not fit at the end of a line and has to be continued on the next line.

---

hypnosis
Said "hip-**noh**-siss" NOUN Hypnosis is an artificially produced state of relaxation in which the mind is very receptive to suggestion.
🔲 from Greek *hupnos* meaning 'sleep'

hypnotize hypnotizes hypnotizing hypnotized; also spelt **hypnotise**
VERB To hypnotize someone means to put them into a state in which they seem to be asleep but can respond to questions and suggestions.
hypnotic ADJECTIVE **hypnotism** NOUN **hypnotist** NOUN

hypochondriac hypochondriacs
Said "high-pok-**kon**-dree-ak" NOUN a person who continually worries about their health, being convinced that they are ill when there is actually nothing wrong with them.

hypocrisy hypocrisies
NOUN Hypocrisy is pretending to have beliefs or qualities that you do not really have, so that you seem a better person than you are.
hypocritical ADJECTIVE **hypocrite** NOUN

hypodermic hypodermics
NOUN a medical instrument with a hollow needle, used for giving people injections, or taking blood samples.

hypothermia
NOUN Hypothermia is a condition in which a person is very ill because their body temperature has been unusually low for a long time.

hypothesis hypotheses
NOUN an explanation or theory which has not yet been proved to be correct.

hypothetical
ADJECTIVE based on assumption rather than on fact or reality.

hysterectomy hysterectomies
Said "his-ter-**rek**-tom-ee" NOUN an operation to remove a woman's womb.

hysteria
Said "hiss-**teer**-ee-a" NOUN Hysteria is a state of uncontrolled excitement or panic.

hysterical
ADJECTIVE 1 Someone who is hysterical is in a state of uncontrolled excitement or panic. 2 INFORMAL Something that is hysterical is extremely funny.
hysterically ADVERB **hysterics** NOUN
▬ (sense 1) frantic, frenzied

a b c d e f g **h** i j k l m n o p q r s t u v w x y z

I i

I
PRONOUN A speaker or writer uses 'I' to refer to himself or herself E.G. *I like the colour.*

ibis ibises
Said "eye-biss" NOUN a large wading bird with a long, thin, curved bill that lives in warm countries.

-ible
SUFFIX another form of the suffix **-able**.

-ic or -ical
SUFFIX '-ic' and '-ical' form adjectives from nouns. For example, *ironic* or *ironical* formed from *irony.*

ice ices icing iced
NOUN 1 water that has frozen solid. 2 an ice cream. ▶ VERB 3 If you ice cakes, you cover them with icing. 4 If something ices over or ices up, it becomes covered with a layer of ice. ▶ PHRASE 5 If you do something to **break the ice**, you make people feel relaxed and comfortable.

Ice Age Ice Ages
NOUN a period of time lasting thousands of years when a lot of the earth's surface was covered with ice.

iceberg icebergs
NOUN a large mass of ice floating in the sea.
🔟 from Dutch *ijsberg* meaning 'ice mountain'

icecap icecaps
NOUN a layer of ice and snow that permanently covers the North or South Pole.

ice cream ice creams
NOUN a very cold sweet food made from frozen cream.

ice cube ice cubes
NOUN Ice cubes are small cubes of ice put in drinks to make them cold.

ice hockey
NOUN a type of hockey played on ice, with two teams of six players.

Icelandic
NOUN the main language spoken in Iceland.

ice-skate ice-skates ice-skating ice-skated
NOUN 1 a boot with a metal blade on the bottom, which you wear when skating on ice. ▶ VERB 2 If you ice-skate, you move about on ice wearing ice-skates.

icicle icicles
Said "eye-sik-kl" NOUN a piece of ice shaped like a pointed stick that hangs down from a surface.

icing
NOUN a mixture of powdered sugar and water or egg whites, used to decorate cakes.

icon icons
Said "eye-kon" NOUN 1 (ICT) a picture on a computer screen representing a program that can be activated by moving the cursor over it. 2 in the Orthodox Churches, a holy picture of Christ, the Virgin Mary, or a saint.
🔟 from Greek *eikōn* meaning 'likeness' or 'image'

icy icier iciest
ADJECTIVE 1 Something which is icy is very cold E.G. *an icy wind.* 2 An icy road has ice on it.
icily ADVERB

id
NOUN In psychology, your id is your

A B C D E F G H I J K L M N O P Q R S T U V W X Y Z

basic instincts and unconscious thoughts.

idea ideas
NOUN **1** a plan, suggestion, or thought that you have after thinking about a problem. **2** an opinion or belief E.G. *old-fashioned ideas about women.*
3 An idea of something is what you know about it E.G. *They had no idea of their position.*
■ (sense 1) impression, thought
■ (sense 2) belief, notion, opinion

ideal ideals
NOUN **1** a principle or idea that you try to achieve because it seems perfect to you. **2** Your ideal of something is the person or thing that seems the best example of it. ▶ ADJECTIVE **3** The ideal person or thing is the best possible person or thing for the situation.

idealism
Said "eye-**dee**-il-izm" NOUN behaviour that is based on a person's ideals.
idealist NOUN **idealistic** ADJECTIVE

idealize idealizes idealizing idealized; also spelt **idealise**
VERB If you idealize someone or something, you regard them as being perfect.
idealization NOUN

ideally
ADVERB **1** If you say that ideally something should happen, you mean that you would like it to happen but you know that it is not possible. **2** Ideally means perfectly E.G. *The hotel is ideally placed for business travellers.*

identical
ADJECTIVE exactly the same E.G. *identical twins.*
identically ADVERB

identification
NOUN **1** The identification of someone or something is the act of identifying them. **2** Identification is a document such as a driver's licence or passport, which proves who you are.

identify identifies identifying identified
VERB **1** To identify someone or something is to recognize them or name them. **2** If you identify with someone, you understand their feelings and ideas.
identifiable ADJECTIVE

identity identities
NOUN the characteristics that make you who you are.

ideology ideologies
NOUN a set of political beliefs.
ideological ADJECTIVE **ideologically** ADVERB

idiom idioms
NOUN a group of words whose meaning together is different from all the words taken individually. For example, 'It is raining cats and dogs' is an idiom.
📖 from Greek *idiōma* meaning 'special phraseology'

idiosyncrasy idiosyncrasies
Said "id-ee-oh-**sing**-krass-ee" NOUN Someone's idiosyncrasies are their own habits and likes or dislikes.
idiosyncratic ADJECTIVE

idiot idiots
NOUN someone who is stupid or foolish.
📖 from Greek *idiōtēs* meaning 'ignorant person'
■ fool, halfwit, moron

idiotic
ADJECTIVE extremely foolish or silly.
■ foolish, senseless, stupid

a
b
c
d
e
f
g
h
i
j
k
l
m
n
o
p
q
r
s
t
u
v
w
x
y
z

there's SAND in my SANDwich (<u>sand</u>wich)   SPELLING NOTE

idle idles idling idled
ADJECTIVE If you are idle, you are doing nothing.
idleness NOUN **idly** ADVERB
📖 from Saxon *idal* meaning 'worthless' or 'empty'

idol idols
Said "eye-doll" NOUN **1** a famous person who is loved and admired by fans. **2** a picture or statue which is worshipped as if it were a god.
📖 from Greek *eidōlon* meaning 'image' or 'phantom'

idyll idylls
Said "id-ill" NOUN a situation which is peaceful and beautiful.
idyllic ADJECTIVE

i.e.
i.e. means 'that is', and is used before giving more information. It is an abbreviation for the Latin expression 'id est'.

if
CONJUNCTION **1** on the condition that E.G. *I shall stay if I can. I asked her if she wanted to go.* **2** whether E.G. *I asked her if she wanted to go.*

igloo igloos
NOUN a dome-shaped house built out of blocks of snow by the Inuit, or Eskimo, people.
📖 from *igdlu*, an Inuit word meaning 'house'

igneous
Said "ig-nee-uss" ADJECTIVE; TECHNICAL Igneous rocks are formed by hot liquid rock cooling and going hard.
📖 from Latin *igneus* meaning 'fiery'

ignite ignites igniting ignited
VERB If you ignite something or if it ignites, it starts burning.
📖 from Latin *ignis* meaning 'fire'

ignition ignitions
NOUN In a car, the ignition is the part of the engine where the fuel is ignited.

ignominious
ADJECTIVE shameful or considered wrong E.G. *It was an ignominious end to a brilliant career.*
ignominiously ADVERB **ignominy** NOUN

ignoramus ignoramuses
Said "ig-nor-ray-muss" NOUN an ignorant person.
📖 from the character *Ignoramus*, an uneducated lawyer in a 17th-century play by Ruggle. In Latin *ignoramus* means 'we do not know'

ignorant
ADJECTIVE **1** If you are ignorant of something, you do not know about it E.G. *He was completely ignorant of the rules.* **2** Someone who is ignorant does not know about things in general E.G. *I thought of asking, but didn't want to seem ignorant.*
ignorantly ADVERB **ignorance** NOUN
🔳 (sense 1) unaware, unconscious, uninformed

ignore ignores ignoring ignored
VERB If you ignore someone or something, you deliberately do not take any notice of them.

iguana iguanas
Said "ig-wah-na" NOUN a large, tropical lizard.

il-
PREFIX 'Il-' means 'not' or 'the opposite of', and is the form of 'in-' that is used before the letter E.G. *illegible.*

ill ills
ADJECTIVE **1** unhealthy or sick. **2** harmful or unpleasant E.G. *ill effects.* ▶ PLURAL NOUN **3** Ills are difficulties or problems.
📖 from Norse *illr* meaning 'bad'
🔳 (sense 1) sick, unhealthy, unwell

ill at ease
PHRASE If you feel **ill at ease**, you feel unable to relax.

illegal
ADJECTIVE forbidden by the law.
illegally ADVERB **illegality** NOUN
■ criminal, illicit, unlawful

illegible
Said "il-lej-i-bl" ADJECTIVE Writing which is illegible is unclear and very difficult to read.

illegitimate
Said "il-lij-it-tim-it" ADJECTIVE A person who is illegitimate was born to parents who were not married at the time.
illegitimacy NOUN

ill-fated
ADJECTIVE doomed to end unhappily E.G. his ill-fated attempt on the world record.

illicit
Said "il-liss-it" ADJECTIVE not allowed by law or not approved of by society E.G. illicit drugs.

illiterate
ADJECTIVE unable to read or write.
illiteracy NOUN

illness illnesses
NOUN 1 Illness is the experience of being ill. 2 a particular disease E.G. the treatment of common illnesses.
■ (sense 2) ailment, disease, malady, sickness

illogical
ADJECTIVE An illogical feeling or action is not reasonable or sensible.
illogically ADVERB

ill-treat ill-treats ill-treating ill-treated
VERB If you ill-treat someone or something you hurt or damage them or treat them cruelly.
ill-treatment NOUN

illuminate illuminates illuminating illuminated
VERB To illuminate something is to shine light on it to make it easier to see.

illumination illuminations
NOUN 1 Illumination is lighting. 2 Illuminations are the coloured lights put up to decorate a town, especially at Christmas.

illusion illusions
NOUN 1 a false belief which you think is true E.G. Their hopes proved to be an illusion. 2 (ART) a false appearance of reality which deceives the eye E.G. Painters create the illusion of space.

illusory
Said "ill-yoo-ser-ee" ADJECTIVE seeming to be true, but actually false E.G. an illusory truce.

illustrate illustrates illustrating illustrated
VERB 1 (EXAM TERM) If you illustrate a point, you explain it or make it clearer, often by using examples. 2 If you illustrate a book, you put pictures in it.
illustrator NOUN **illustrative** ADJECTIVE

illustration illustrations
NOUN 1 an example or a story which is used to make a point clear. 2 a picture in a book.

illustrious
ADJECTIVE An illustrious person is famous and respected.

ill will
NOUN Ill will is a feeling of hostility.

im-
PREFIX 'Im-' means 'not' or 'the opposite of', and is the form of 'in-' which is used before the letters b, m and p E.G. imbalance… impatient… immature.

a b c d e f g h i j k l m n o p q r s t u v w x y z

A
B
C
D
E
F
G
H
I
J
K
L
M
N
O
P
Q
R
S
T
U
V
W
X
Y
Z

image images
NOUN 1 a mental picture of someone or something. 2 the appearance which a person, group, or organization presents to the public.

imagery
NOUN (ENGLISH) The imagery of a poem or book is the descriptive language used in it.

imaginary
ADJECTIVE Something that is imaginary exists only in your mind, not in real life.

imagination imaginations
NOUN the ability to form new and exciting ideas.

imaginative
ADJECTIVE Someone who is imaginative can easily form new or exciting ideas in their mind.
imaginatively ADVERB

imagine imagines imagining imagined
VERB 1 If you imagine something, you form an idea of it in your mind, or you think you have seen or heard it but you have not really. 2 If you imagine that something is the case, you believe it is the case E.G. *I imagine that's what you aim to do.*
imaginable ADJECTIVE
■ (sense 1) conceive, envisage, picture, visualize
■ (sense 2) believe, suppose, think

imam
Said "ih-**mam**" NOUN a person who leads a group in prayer in a mosque.

imbalance imbalances
NOUN If there is an imbalance between things, they are unequal E.G. *the imbalance between rich and poor.*

imbecile imbeciles
Said "im-bis-**seel**" NOUN a stupid person.
🔲 from Latin *imbecillus* meaning 'physically or mentally feeble'

imitate imitates imitating imitated
VERB To imitate someone or something is to copy them.
imitator NOUN **imitative** ADJECTIVE
■ copy, mimic

imitation imitations
NOUN a copy of something else.

immaculate
Said "im-**mak**-yoo-lit" ADJECTIVE 1 completely clean and tidy E.G. *The flat was immaculate.* 2 without any mistakes at all E.G. *his usual immaculate guitar accompaniment.*
immaculately ADVERB

immaterial
ADJECTIVE Something that is immaterial is not important.

immature
ADJECTIVE 1 Something that is immature has not finished growing or developing. 2 A person who is immature does not behave in a sensible adult way.
immaturity NOUN

immediate
ADJECTIVE 1 Something that is immediate happens or is done without delay. 2 Your immediate relatives and friends are the ones most closely connected or related to you.

immediately
ADVERB 1 If something happens immediately it happens right away. 2 Immediately means very near in time or position E.G. *immediately behind the house.*

immemorial

ADJECTIVE If something has been happening from time immemorial, it has been happening longer than anyone can remember.

immense

ADJECTIVE very large or huge.

immensely ADVERB   **immensity** NOUN

immerse immerses immersing immersed

VERB 1 If you are immersed in an activity you are completely involved in it. 2 If you immerse something in a liquid, you put it into the liquid so that it is completely covered.

immersion NOUN

immigrant immigrants

NOUN (HISTORY) someone who has come to live permanently in a new country.

immigrate VERB   **Immigration** NOUN

imminent

ADJECTIVE If something is imminent, it is going to happen very soon.

imminently ADVERB   **imminence** NOUN

■ coming, impending, near

immobile

ADJECTIVE not moving.

immobility NOUN

immoral

ADJECTIVE (RE) If you describe someone or their behaviour as immoral, you mean that they do not fit in with most people's idea of what is right and proper.

immorality NOUN

✔ Do not confuse *immoral* and *amoral*. You use *immoral* to talk about people who are aware of moral standards, but go against

them. *Amoral* applies to people with no moral standards.

immortal

ADJECTIVE 1 Something that is immortal is famous and will be remembered for a long time E.G. *Emily Bronte's immortal love story*. 2 In stories, someone who is immortal will never die.

immortality

NOUN (RE) Immortality is never dying. In many religions, people believe that the soul or some other essential part of a person lives forever or continues to exist in some form.

immovable or **immoveable**

ADJECTIVE Something that is immovable is fixed and cannot be moved.

immovably ADVERB

immune

Said "im-*yoon*" ADJECTIVE 1 If you are immune to a particular disease, you cannot catch it. 2 If someone or something is immune to something, they are able to avoid it or are not bound by it E.G. *The captain was immune to prosecution*.

immunity NOUN

immune system

NOUN Your body's immune system consists of your white blood cells, which fight disease by producing antibodies or germs to kill germs which come into your body.

imp imps

NOUN a small mischievous creature in fairy stories.

impish ADJECTIVE

impact impacts

NOUN 1 The impact that someone or something has is the impression that

a b c d e f g h i j k l m n o p q r s t u v w x y z

A
B
C
D
E
F
G
H
I
J
K
L
M
N
O
P
Q
R
S
T
U
V
W
X
Y
Z

they make or the effect that they have. **2** Impact is the action of one object hitting another, usually with a lot of force E.G. *The aircraft crashed into a ditch, exploding on impact.*

impair impairs impairing impaired
VERB To impair something is to damage it so that it stops working properly E.G. *Travel had made him weary and impaired his judgement.*

impale impales impaling impaled
VERB If you impale something, you pierce it with a sharp object.

impart imparts imparting imparted
VERB; FORMAL To impart information to someone is to pass it on to them.

impartial
ADJECTIVE Someone who is impartial has a view of something which is fair or not biased.
impartially ADVERB **impartiality** NOUN
■ fair, neutral, objective

impasse
Said "am-pass" NOUN a difficult situation in which it is impossible to find a solution.
🔲 from French *impasse* meaning 'dead end'

impassioned
ADJECTIVE full of emotion E.G. *an impassioned plea.*

impassive
ADJECTIVE showing no emotion.
impassively ADVERB

impasto
NOUN (ART) a technique of painting with thick paint so that brush strokes or palette knife marks can be seen.
🔲 an Italian word, from *pasta* meaning 'paste'

impatient
ADJECTIVE **1** Someone who is impatient becomes annoyed easily or is quick to lose their temper when things go wrong. **2** If you are impatient to do something, you are eager and do not want to wait E.G. *He was impatient to get back.*
impatiently ADVERB **impatience** NOUN

impeccable
Said "im-pek-i-bl" ADJECTIVE excellent, without any faults.
impeccably ADVERB

impede impedes impeding impeded
VERB If you impede someone, you make their progress difficult.

impediment impediments
NOUN something that makes it difficult to move, develop, or do something properly E.G. *a speech impediment.*

impelled
ADJECTIVE If you feel impelled to do something, you feel strongly that you must do it.

impending
ADJECTIVE; FORMAL You use 'impending' to describe something that is going to happen very soon E.G. *a sense of impending doom.*

impenetrable
ADJECTIVE impossible to get through.

imperative
ADJECTIVE **1** Something that is imperative is extremely urgent or important. ▶ NOUN **2** In grammar, an imperative is the form of a verb that is used for giving orders.

imperfect
ADJECTIVE **1** Something that is imperfect has faults or problems.

▶ NOUN **2** In grammar, the imperfect is a tense used to describe continuous or repeated actions which happened in the past.

imperfectly ADVERB **imperfection** NOUN

■ (sense 1) faulty, flawed

imperial

ADJECTIVE **1** (HISTORY) Imperial means relating to an empire or an emperor or empress E.G. *the Imperial Palace.* **2** The imperial system of measurement is the measuring system which uses inches, feet, and yards, ounces and pounds, and pints and gallons.

imperialism

NOUN (HISTORY) a system of rule in which a rich and powerful nation controls other nations.

imperialist ADJECTIVE OR NOUN

imperious

ADJECTIVE proud and domineering E.G. *an imperious manner.*

imperiously ADVERB

impersonal

ADJECTIVE Something that is impersonal makes you feel that individuals and their feelings do not matter E.G. *impersonal cold rooms.*

impersonally ADVERB

■ detached, dispassionate, inhuman

impersonate impersonates impersonating impersonated

VERB If you impersonate someone, you pretend to be that person.

impersonation NOUN

impersonator NOUN

impertinent

ADJECTIVE disrespectful and rude E.G. *impertinent questions.*

impertinently ADVERB

impertinence NOUN

impetuous

ADJECTIVE If you are impetuous, you act quickly without thinking E.G. *an impetuous gamble.*

impetuously ADVERB **impetuosity** NOUN

impetus

NOUN **1** An impetus is the stimulating effect that something has on a situation, which causes it to develop more quickly. **2** In physics, impetus is the force that starts an object moving and resists changes in speed or direction.

impinge impinges impinging impinged

VERB If something impinges on your life, it has an effect on you and influences you E.G. *My private life doesn't impinge on my professional life.*

implacable

Said "im-plak-a-bl" ADJECTIVE Someone who is implacable is being harsh and refuses to change their mind.

implacably ADVERB

implant implants implanting implanted

VERB **1** To implant something into a person's body is to put it there, usually by means of an operation. ▶ NOUN **2** something that has been implanted into someone's body.

implausible

ADJECTIVE very unlikely E.G. *implausible stories.*

implausibly ADVERB

implement implements implementing implemented

VERB **1** If you implement something such as a plan, you carry it out E.G. *The government has failed to implement promised reforms.* ▶ NOUN

a
b
c
d
e
f
g
h
i
j
k
l
m
n
o
p
q
r
s
t
u
v
w
x
y
z

A
B
C
D
E
F
G
H
I
J
K
L
M
N
O
P
Q
R
S
T
U
V
W
X
Y
Z

2 An implement is a tool.
implementation NOUN

implicate implicates implicating
implicated
VERB If you are implicated in a crime,
you are shown to be involved in it.

implication implications
NOUN something that is suggested or
implied but not stated directly.

implicit
Said "im-**pliss**-it" ADJECTIVE **1** expressed
in an indirect way E.G. *implicit
criticism*. **2** If you have an implicit
belief in something, you have no
doubts about it E.G. *He had implicit
faith in the noble intentions of the
Emperor*.
implicitly ADVERB

implore implores imploring
implored
VERB If you implore someone to do
something, you beg them to do it.

imply implies implying implied
VERB If you imply that something is
the case, you suggest it in an indirect
way.

import imports importing
imported
VERB **1** If you import something from
another country, you bring it into
your country or have it sent there.
▸ NOUN **2** a product that is made in
another country and sent to your
own country for use there.
importation NOUN **importer** NOUN

important
ADJECTIVE **1** Something that is
important is very valuable, necessary,
or significant. **2** An important person
has great influence or power.
importantly ADVERB **importance**
NOUN
■ (sense 1) momentous, significant

impose imposes imposing
imposed
VERB **1** If you impose something on
people, you force it on them E.G. *The
allies had imposed a ban on all flights
over Iraq*. **2** If someone imposes on
you, they unreasonably expect you
to do something for them.
imposition NOUN

imposing
ADJECTIVE having an impressive
appearance or manner E.G. *an
imposing building*.

impossible
ADJECTIVE Something that is
impossible cannot happen, be done,
or be believed.
impossibly ADVERB **impossibility**
NOUN

imposter imposters; also spelt
impostor
NOUN a person who pretends to be
someone else in order to get things
they want.

impotent
ADJECTIVE **1** Someone who is impotent
has no power to influence people or
events. **2** A man who is impotent is
unable to have or maintain an
erection during sexual intercourse.
impotently ADVERB **impotence**
NOUN

impound impounds impounding
impounded
VERB If something you own is
impounded, the police or other
officials take it.

impoverished
ADJECTIVE Someone who is
impoverished is poor.

impractical
ADJECTIVE not practical, sensible, or
realistic.

impregnable
ADJECTIVE A building or other structure that is impregnable is so strong that it cannot be broken into or captured.

impregnated
ADJECTIVE If something is impregnated with a substance, it has absorbed the substance so that it spreads right through it E.G. *sponges impregnated with detergent and water*.

impresario impresarios
Said "im-pris-**sar**-ee-oh" NOUN a person who manages theatrical or musical events or companies.

impress impresses impressing impressed
VERB 1 If you impress someone, you make them admire or respect you. 2 If you impress something on someone, you make them understand the importance of it.

impression impressions
NOUN 1 An impression of someone or something is the way they look or seem to you. 2 If you **make an impression**, you have a strong effect on people you meet.

impressionable
ADJECTIVE easy to influence E.G. *impressionable teenagers*.

impressionism
NOUN a style of painting which is concerned with the impressions created by light and shapes, rather than with exact details.
impressionist NOUN

impressive
ADJECTIVE If something is impressive, it impresses you E.G. *an impressive display of old-fashioned American cars*.

imprint imprints imprinting imprinted
NOUN 1 If something leaves an imprint

on your mind, it has a strong and lasting effect. 2 the mark left by the pressure of one object on another.
▶ VERB 3 If something is imprinted on your memory, it is firmly fixed there.

imprison imprisons imprisoning imprisoned
VERB If you are imprisoned, you are locked up, usually in a prison.
imprisonment NOUN

improbable
ADJECTIVE not probable or likely to happen.
improbably ADVERB
■ doubtful, unlikely

impromptu
Said "im-**prompt**-yoo" ADJECTIVE An impromptu action is one done without planning or organization.
▥ from Latin *in promptu* meaning 'in readiness'
■ improvised, off the cuff, unprepared

improper
ADJECTIVE 1 rude or shocking E.G. *improper behaviour*. 2 illegal or dishonest E.G. *improper dealings*. 3 not suitable or correct E.G. *an improper diet*.
improperly ADVERB

improve improves improving improved
VERB If something improves or if you improve it, it gets better or becomes more valuable.
improvement NOUN
■ better, enhance

improvise improvises improvising improvised
VERB 1 If you improvise something, you make or do something without planning in advance, and with whatever materials are available.

A Rude Idiot Thought He Might Eat Toffee In Church (<u>arithmetic</u>)   SPELLING NOTE

A
B
C
D
E
F
G
H
I
J
K
L
M
N
O
P
Q
R
S
T
U
V
W
X
Y
Z

2 (DRAMA) When musicians or actors improvise, they make up the music or words as they go along.

improvised ADJECTIVE

improvisation NOUN

impudent

ADJECTIVE If someone is impudent, something they say or do is cheeky and lacking in respect.

impudently ADVERB   **impudence** NOUN

impulse impulses

NOUN a strong urge to do something E.G. *She felt a sudden impulse to confide in her.*

impulsive

ADJECTIVE If you are impulsive, you do things suddenly, without thinking about them carefully.

impulsively ADVERB

impure

ADJECTIVE Something which is impure contains small amounts of other things, such as dirt.

impurity impurities

NOUN **1** Impurity is the quality of being impure E.G. *the impurity of the water.* **2** If something contains impurities, it contains small amounts of dirt or other substances that should not be there.

in

PREPOSITION or ADVERB 'In' is used to indicate position, direction, time, and manner E.G. *boarding schools in England… in the past few years.*

in-

PREFIX **1** 'In-' is added to the beginning of some words to form a word with the opposite meaning E.G. *insincere.* **2** 'In-' also means in, into, or in the course of E.G. *infiltrate.*

📖 from a Latin prefix

inability

NOUN a lack of ability to do something.

inaccessible

ADJECTIVE impossible or very difficult to reach.

inaccurate

ADJECTIVE not accurate or correct.

inadequate

ADJECTIVE **1** If something is inadequate, there is not enough of it, or it is not good enough in quality for a particular purpose. **2** If someone feels inadequate, they feel they do not possess the skills necessary to do a particular job or to cope with life in general.

inadequately ADVERB   **inadequacy** NOUN

📘 (sense 1) insufficient, meagre

inadvertent

ADJECTIVE not intentional E.G. *the murder had been inadvertent.*

inadvertently ADVERB

inane

ADJECTIVE silly or stupid.

inanely ADVERB   **inanity** NOUN

inanimate

ADJECTIVE An inanimate object is not alive.

inappropriate

ADJECTIVE not suitable for a particular purpose or occasion E.G. *It was quite inappropriate to ask such questions.*

inappropriately ADVERB

📘 out of place, unfitting, unsuitable

inarticulate

ADJECTIVE If you are inarticulate, you are unable to express yourself well or easily in speech.

inasmuch

CONJUNCTION 'Inasmuch as' means to the extent that E.G. *She's giving herself a hard time inasmuch as she feels guilty.*

inaudible
ADJECTIVE not loud enough to be heard.
inaudibly ADVERB

inaugurate inaugurates inaugurating inaugurated
Said "in-**awg**-yoo-rate" VERB **1** To inaugurate a new scheme is to start it. **2** To inaugurate a new leader is to officially establish them in their new position in a special ceremony E.G. *Albania's Orthodox Church inaugurated its first archbishop in 25 years.*
inauguration NOUN **inaugural** ADJECTIVE

inborn
ADJECTIVE An inborn quality is one that you were born with.

incandescent
ADJECTIVE Something which is incandescent gives out light when it is heated.
incandescence NOUN
📖 from Latin *candescere* meaning 'to glow white'

incapable
ADJECTIVE **1** Someone who is incapable of doing something is not able to do it E.G. *He is incapable of changing a fuse.* **2** An incapable person is weak and helpless.

incarcerate incarcerates incarcerating incarcerated
Said "in-**kar**-ser-rate" VERB To incarcerate someone is to lock them up.
incarceration NOUN

Incarnation
NOUN The Incarnation is the Christian belief that God took human form in Jesus Christ.

incendiary
Said "in-**send**-yer-ee" ADJECTIVE An incendiary weapon is one which sets fire to things E.G. *incendiary bombs.*

incense
NOUN Incense is a spicy substance which is burned to create a sweet smell, especially during religious services.

incensed
ADJECTIVE If you are incensed by something, it makes you extremely angry.

incentive incentives
NOUN something that encourages you to do something.
📖 from Latin *incentivus* meaning 'the beginning of a song'

inception
NOUN; FORMAL The inception of a project is the start of it.

incessant
ADJECTIVE continuing without stopping E.G. *her incessant talking.*
incessantly ADVERB

Incest
NOUN Incest is the crime of two people who are closely related having sex with each other.
incestuous ADJECTIVE

inch inches inching inched
NOUN **1** a unit of length equal to about 2.54 centimetres. ▶ VERB **2** To inch forward is to move forward slowly.
📖 from Latin *uncia* meaning 'twelfth part'; there are twelve inches to the foot

incident incidents
NOUN an event E.G. *a shooting incident.*

incidental
ADJECTIVE occurring as a minor part of

a b c d e f g h i j k l m n o p q r s t u v w x y z

A
B
C
D
E
F
G
H
I
J
K
L
M
N
O
P
Q
R
S
T
U
V
W
X
Y
Z

something E.G. *vivid incidental detail.*
incidentally ADVERB
incinerate **incinerates**
incinerating **incinerated**
VERB If you incinerate something, you
burn it.
incineration NOUN
incinerator **incinerators**
NOUN a furnace for burning rubbish.
incipient
ADJECTIVE beginning to happen or
appear E.G. *incipient panic.*
incision **incisions**
NOUN a sharp cut, usually made by a
surgeon operating on a patient.
incisive
ADJECTIVE Incisive language is clear
and forceful.
incite **incites** **inciting** **incited**
VERB If you incite someone to do
something, you encourage them to
do it by making them angry or excited.
incitement NOUN
◼ encourage, provoke, spur
inclination **inclinations**
NOUN If you have an inclination to do
something, you want to do it.
incline **inclines** **inclining** **inclined**
VERB 1 If you are inclined to behave in
a certain way, you often behave that
way or you want to behave that way.
▶ NOUN 2 a slope.
include **includes** **including**
included
VERB If one thing includes another, it
has the second thing as one of its
parts.
including PREPOSITION
◼ contain, incorporate
inclusion
NOUN The inclusion of one thing in
another is the act of making it part
of the other thing.

inclusive
ADJECTIVE A price that is inclusive
includes all the goods and services
that are being offered, with no extra
charge for any of them.
incognito
Said "in-kog-**nee**-*toe*" ADVERB If you are
travelling incognito, you are
travelling in disguise.
📖 from Latin *in-* + *cognitus* meaning
'not known'
incoherent
ADJECTIVE If someone is incoherent,
they are talking in an unclear or
rambling way.
incoherently ADVERB **incoherence**
NOUN
income **incomes**
NOUN the money a person earns.
income tax
NOUN Income tax is a part of
someone's salary which they have to
pay regularly to the government.
incoming
ADJECTIVE coming in E.G. *incoming
trains… an incoming phone call.*
incomparable
ADJECTIVE Something that is
incomparable is so good that it
cannot be compared with anything
else.
incomparably ADVERB
◼ matchless, unequalled,
unparalleled
incompatible
ADJECTIVE Two things or people are
incompatible if they are unable to
live or exist together because they
are completely different.
incompatibility NOUN
incompetent
ADJECTIVE Someone who is
incompetent does not have the

ability to do something properly.
incompetently ADVERB
incompetence NOUN

incomplete
ADJECTIVE not complete or finished.
incompletely ADVERB

incomprehensible
ADJECTIVE not able to be understood.

inconceivable
ADJECTIVE impossible to believe.

inconclusive
ADJECTIVE not leading to a decision or to a definite result.

incongruous
ADJECTIVE Something that is incongruous seems strange because it does not fit in to a place or situation.
incongruously ADVERB

inconsequential
ADJECTIVE Something that is inconsequential is not very important.

inconsistent
ADJECTIVE Someone or something which is inconsistent is unpredictable and behaves differently in similar situations.
inconsistently ADVERB
inconsistency NOUN

inconspicuous
ADJECTIVE not easily seen or obvious.
inconspicuously ADVERB

incontinent
ADJECTIVE Someone who is incontinent is unable to control their bladder or bowels.

inconvenience inconveniences inconveniencing inconvenienced
NOUN **1** If something causes inconvenience, it causes difficulty or problems. ▶ VERB **2** To inconvenience someone is to cause them trouble,

difficulty or problems.
inconvenient ADJECTIVE
inconveniently ADVERB

incorporate incorporates incorporating incorporated
VERB If something is incorporated into another thing, it becomes part of that thing.
incorporation NOUN

incorrect
ADJECTIVE wrong or untrue.
incorrectly ADVERB

increase increases increasing increased
VERB **1** If something increases, it becomes larger in amount. ▶ NOUN **2** a rise in the number, level, or amount of something.
increasingly ADVERB

incredible
ADJECTIVE totally amazing or impossible to believe.
incredibly ADVERB
≡ amazing, unbelievable

incredulous
ADJECTIVE If you are incredulous, you are unable to believe something because it is very surprising or shocking.
incredulously ADVERB   **incredulity** NOUN

increment increments
NOUN the amount by which something increases, or a regular increase in someone's salary.
incremental ADJECTIVE

incriminate incriminates incriminating incriminated
VERB If something incriminates you, it suggests that you are involved in a crime.

incubate incubates incubating incubated
Said "in-kyoo-bate" VERB When eggs

you'll brEAK that Electrical Aerial, Kitty (br<u>eak</u>)   **SPELLING NOTE**

A
B
C
D
E
F
G
H
I
J
K
L
M
N
O
P
Q
R
S
T
U
V
W
X
Y
Z

incubate, they are kept warm until they are ready to hatch.

incubation NOUN

incubator incubators

NOUN a piece of hospital equipment in which sick or weak newborn babies are kept warm.

incumbent incumbents FORMAL

ADJECTIVE 1 If it is incumbent on you to do something, it is your duty to do it. ► NOUN 2 the person in a particular official po klklksition.

incur incurs incurring incurred

VERB If you incur something unpleasant, you cause it to happen.

incurable

ADJECTIVE 1 An incurable disease is one which cannot be cured. 2 An incurable habit is one which cannot be changed E.G. *an incurable romantic*.

incurably ADVERB

indebted

ADJECTIVE If you are indebted to someone, you are grateful to them.

indecent

ADJECTIVE Something that is indecent is shocking or rude, usually because it concerns nakedness or sex.

indecently ADVERB   **indecency** NOUN

indeed

ADVERB You use 'indeed' to strengthen a point that you are making E.G. *The desserts are very good indeed*. from Middle English *in dede* meaning 'in fact'

indefatigable

Said "in-dif-**fat**-ig-a-bl" ADJECTIVE

People who never get tired of doing something are indefatigable.

indefinite

ADJECTIVE 1 If something is indefinite, no time to finish has been decided

E.G. *an indefinite strike*. 2 Indefinite also means vague or not exact E.G. *Indefinite words and pictures*.

indefinitely ADVERB

indefinite article indefinite articles

NOUN the grammatical term for 'a' and 'an'.

indelible

ADJECTIVE unable to be removed E.G. *indelible ink*.

indelibly ADVERB

indemnity

NOUN; FORMAL Indemnity is protection against damage or loss.

indentation indentations

NOUN a dent or a groove in a surface or on the edge of something.

independence

NOUN 1 Independence is not relying on anyone else. 2 (HISTORY) A nation or state gains its independence when it stops being ruled or governed by another country and has its own government and laws.

independent

ADJECTIVE 1 Something that is independent happens or exists separately from other people or things E.G. *Results are assessed by an independent panel*. 2 Someone who is independent does not need other people's help E.G. *a fiercely independent woman*. 3 An independent nation is one that is not ruled or governed by another country.

independently ADVERB

≡ (sense 1 and 3) autonomous, self-governing

indeterminate

ADJECTIVE not certain or definite E.G. *some indeterminate point in the future*.

index indexes

NOUN **1** an alphabetical list at the back of a book, referring to items in the book. **2** (LIBRARY) an alphabetical list of all the books in a library, arranged by title, author or subject.

index finger index fingers

NOUN your first finger, next to your thumb.

Indian Indians

ADJECTIVE **1** belonging or relating to India. ▶ NOUN **2** someone who comes from India. **3** someone descended from the people who lived in North, South, or Central America before Europeans arrived.

indicate indicates indicating indicated

VERB **1** If something indicates something, it shows that it Is true E.G. *a gesture which clearly indicates his relief.* **2** If you Indicate something to someone, you point to it. **3** If you indicate a fact, you mention it. **4** If the driver of a vehicle indicates, they give a signal to show which way they are going to turn.

■ (sense 1) denote, show, signify

indication indications

NOUN a sign of what someone feels or what is likely to happen.

indicative

ADJECTIVE **1** If something is indicative of something else, it is a sign of that thing E.G. *Clean, pink tongues are indicative of a good, healthy digestion.* ▶ NOUN **2** If a verb is used in the indicative, it is in the form used for making statements.

indicator indicators

NOUN **1** something which tells you what something is like or what is happening. **2** A car's indicators are the lights at the front and back which are used to show when it is turning left or right. **3** a substance used in chemistry that shows if another substance is an acid or alkali by changing colour when it comes into contact with it.

indict indicts indicting indicted

Said "in-**dite**" VERB; FORMAL To indict someone is to charge them officially with a crime.

indictment NOUN   **indictable** ADJECTIVE

indifferent

ADJECTIVE **1** If you are indifferent to something, you have no interest in it. **2** If something is indifferent, it is of a poor quality or low standard E.G. *a pair of rather indifferent paintings.*

indifferently ADVERB   **indifference** NOUN

indigenous

Said "in-**dij**-in-uss" ADJECTIVE If something is indigenous to a country, it comes from that country E.G. *a plant indigenous to Asia.*

indigestion

NOUN Indigestion is a pain you get when you find it difficult to digest food.

indignant

ADJECTIVE If you are indignant, you feel angry about something that you think is unfair.

indignantly ADVERB

indignation

NOUN Indignation is anger about something that you think is unfair.

indignity indignities

NOUN something that makes you feel embarrassed or humiliated E.G. *the indignity of having to flee angry protesters.*

a
b
c
d
e
f
g
h
i
j
k
l
m
n
o
p
q
r
s
t
u
v
w
x
y
z

indigo

NOUN or ADJECTIVE dark violet-blue.

indirect

ADJECTIVE Something that is indirect is not done or caused directly by a particular person or thing, but by someone or something else.

indirectly ADVERB

▪ circuitous, roundabout

indiscriminate

ADJECTIVE not involving careful thought or choice E.G. *an indiscriminate bombing campaign.*

indiscriminately ADVERB

indispensable

ADJECTIVE If something is indispensable, you cannot do without it E.G. *A good pair of walking shoes is indispensable.*

indistinct

ADJECTIVE not clear E.G. *indistinct voices.*

indistinctly ADVERB

individual individuals

ADJECTIVE 1 relating to one particular person or thing E.G. *Each family needs individual attention.*
2 Someone who is individual behaves quite differently from the way other people behave. ▶ NOUN 3 a person, different from any other person E.G. *wealthy individuals.*

individually ADVERB

individualist individualists

NOUN someone who likes to do things in their own way.

individualistic ADJECTIVE

individuality

NOUN If something has individuality, it is different from all other things, and therefore is very interesting and noticeable.

indomitable

ADJECTIVE; FORMAL impossible to overcome E.G. *an indomitable spirit.*

Indonesian Indonesians

Said "in-don-**nee**-zee-an" ADJECTIVE
1 belonging or relating to Indonesia.
▶ NOUN 2 someone who comes from Indonesia. 3 Indonesian is the official language of Indonesia.

indoor

ADJECTIVE situated or happening inside a building.

indoors

ADVERB If something happens indoors, it takes place inside a building.

induce induces inducing induced

VERB 1 To induce a state is to cause it E.G. *His manner was rough and suspicious but he did not induce fear.*
2 If you induce someone to do something, you persuade them to do it.

inducement inducements

NOUN something offered to encourage someone to do something.

indulge indulges indulging indulged

VERB 1 If you indulge in something, you allow yourself to do something that you enjoy. 2 If you indulge someone, you let them have or do what they want, often in a way that is not good for them.

indulgence indulgences

NOUN 1 something you allow yourself to have because it gives you pleasure. 2 Indulgence is the act of indulging yourself or another person.

indulgent

ADJECTIVE If you are indulgent, you treat someone with special kindness

E.G. *a rich, indulgent father.*

indulgently ADJECTIVE

industrial
ADJECTIVE relating to industry.

industrial action
NOUN Industrial action is action such as striking taken by workers in protest over pay or working conditions.

industrialist industrialists
NOUN a person who owns or controls a lot of factories.

Industrial Revolution
NOUN The Industrial Revolution took place in Britain in the late eighteenth and early nineteenth century, when machines began to be used more in factories and more goods were produced as a result.

industrious
ADJECTIVE An industrious person works very hard.

industry industries
NOUN 1 Industry is the work and processes involved in manufacturing things in factories. 2 all the people and processes involved in manufacturing a particular thing.

inedible
ADJECTIVE too nasty or poisonous to eat.

inefficient
ADJECTIVE badly organized, wasteful, and slow E.G. *a corrupt and inefficient administration.*

inefficiently ADVERB **inefficiency** NOUN

inept
ADJECTIVE without skill E.G. *an inept lawyer.*

ineptitude NOUN

inequality inequalities
NOUN a difference in size, status,

wealth, or position, between different things, groups, or people.

inert
ADJECTIVE Something that is inert does not move and appears lifeless E.G. *an inert body lying on the floor.*

inertia
Said "in-ner-sha" NOUN If you have a feeling of inertia, you feel very lazy and unwilling to do anything.

inevitable
ADJECTIVE certain to happen.

inevitably ADVERB **inevitability** NOUN

inexhaustible
ADJECTIVE Something that is inexhaustible will never be used up E.G. *an inexhaustible supply of ideas.*

inexorable
ADJECTIVE; FORMAL Something that is inexorable cannot be prevented from continuing E.G. *the inexorable increase in the number of cars.*

inexorably ADVERB

inexpensive
ADJECTIVE not costing much.

inexperienced
ADJECTIVE lacking experience of a situation or activity E.G. *inexperienced drivers.*

inexperience NOUN
■ new, raw, unpractised

inexplicable
ADJECTIVE If something is inexplicable, you cannot explain it E.G. *For some inexplicable reason I still felt uneasy.*

inexplicably ADVERB

inextricably
ADVERB If two or more things are inextricably linked, they cannot be separated.

infallible
ADJECTIVE never wrong E.G. *No*

a
b
c
d
e
f
g
h
i
j
k
l
m
n
o
p
q
r
s
t
u
v
w
x
y
z

A B C D E F G H I J K L M N O P Q R S T U V W X Y Z

machine is infallible.
infallibility NOUN

infamous
Said "in-fe-muss" ADJECTIVE well-known because of something bad or evil E.G. *a book about the country's most infamous murder cases.*

infant infants
NOUN 1 a baby or very young child.
▶ ADJECTIVE 2 designed for young children E.G. *an infant school.*
infancy NOUN **infantile** ADJECTIVE
📖 from Latin *infans* meaning 'unable to speak'

infantry
NOUN In an army, the infantry are soldiers who fight on foot rather than in tanks or on horses.

infatuated
ADJECTIVE If you are infatuated with someone, you have such strong feelings of love or passion that you cannot think sensibly about them.
infatuation NOUN

infect infects infecting infected
VERB To infect someone or something is to cause disease in them.

infection infections
NOUN 1 a disease caused by germs E.G. *a chest infection.* 2 Infection is the state of being infected E.G. *a very small risk of infection.*

infectious
ADJECTIVE spreading from one person to another E.G. *an infectious disease.*
🔁 catching, contagious

infer infers inferring inferred
VERB If you infer something, you work out that it is true on the basis of information that you already have.
inference NOUN
☑ Do not use *infer* to mean the same as *imply*.

inferior inferiors
ADJECTIVE 1 having a lower position or worth less than something else E.G. *inferior quality cassette tapes.* ▶ NOUN 2 Your inferiors are people in a lower position than you.
inferiority NOUN

infernal
ADJECTIVE very unpleasant E.G. *an infernal bore.*
📖 from Latin *infernus* meaning 'hell'

inferno infernos
NOUN a very large dangerous fire.

infertile
ADJECTIVE 1 Infertile soil is of poor quality and plants cannot grow well in it. 2 Someone who is infertile cannot have children.

infested
ADJECTIVE Something that is infested has a large number of animals or insects living on it and causing damage E.G. *The flats are damp and infested with rats.*
infestation NOUN

infidelity infidelities
NOUN Infidelity is being unfaithful to your husband, wife, or lover.

infighting
NOUN Infighting is quarrelling or rivalry between members of the same organization.

infiltrate infiltrates infiltrating infiltrated
VERB If people infiltrate an organization, they gradually enter it in secret to spy on its activities.
infiltration NOUN

infinite
ADJECTIVE without any limit or end E.G. *an infinite number of possibilities.*
infinitely ADVERB
🔁 limitless, never-ending

SPELLING NOTE Plaice the fish has a glittering 'EYE' (I) (plaice)

infinitive infinitives

NOUN In grammar, the infinitive is the base form of the verb. It often has 'to' in front of it, for example 'to go' or 'to see'.

infinity

NOUN 1 Infinity is a number that is larger than any other number and can never be given an exact value. 2 Infinity is also a point that can never be reached, further away than any other point E.G. *skies stretching on into infinity*.

infirmary infirmaries

NOUN a hospital.

inflamed

ADJECTIVE If part of your body is inflamed, it is red and swollen, usually because of infection.

inflammable

ADJECTIVE An inflammable material burns easily

☑ Although *inflammable* and *flammable* both mean 'likely to catch fire', *flammable* is used more often as people sometimes think that *inflammable* means 'not likely to catch fire'.

inflammation

NOUN Inflammation is painful redness or swelling of part of the body.

inflammatory

ADJECTIVE Inflammatory actions are likely to make people very angry.

inflate inflates inflating inflated

VERB When you inflate something, you fill it with air or gas to make it swell.

inflatable ADJECTIVE

inflation

NOUN Inflation is an increase in the price of goods and services in a country.

inflationary ADJECTIVE

inflection inflections; also spelt **inflexion**

NOUN a change in the form of a word that shows its grammatical function, for example a change that makes a noun plural.

inflexible

ADJECTIVE fixed and unable to be altered E.G. *an inflexible routine*.

inflict inflicts inflicting inflicted

VERB If you inflict something unpleasant on someone, you make them suffer it.

influence influences influencing influenced

NOUN 1 Influence is power that a person has over other people. 2 An influence is also the effect that someone or something has E.G. *under the influence of alcohol*. ► VERB 3 To influence someone or something means to have an effect on them.

📖 from Latin *influentia* meaning 'power flowing from the stars'

🔲 (sense 1) hold, power, pull

influential

ADJECTIVE Someone who is influential has a lot of influence over people.

influenza

NOUN; FORMAL Influenza is flu.

influx

NOUN a steady arrival of of people or things E.G. *a large influx of tourists*.

inform informs informing informed

VERB 1 If you inform someone of something, you tell them about it. 2 If you inform on a person, you tell the police about a crime they have committed.

informant NOUN

🔲 (sense 1) notify, tell

a b c d e f g h i j k l m n o p q r s t u v w x y z

A
B
C
D
E
F
G
H
I
J
K
L
M
N
O
P
Q
R
S
T
U
V
W
X
Y
Z

◼ (sense 2) betray, grass, shop

informal
ADJECTIVE relaxed and casual E.G. *an informal meeting*.
informally ADVERB **informality** NOUN

information
NOUN If you have information on or about something, you know something about it.
◼ data, facts

informative
ADJECTIVE Something that is informative gives you useful information.

informer informers
NOUN someone who tells the police that another person has committed a crime.

infrastructure infrastructures
NOUN (GEOGRAPHY) The infrastructure of a country consists of things like factories, schools, and roads, which show how much money the country has and how strong its economy is.

infringe infringes infringing infringed
VERB 1 If you infringe a law, you break it. 2 To infringe people's rights is to not allow them the rights to which they are entitled.
infringement NOUN

infuriate infuriates infuriating infuriated
VERB If someone infuriates you, they make you very angry.
infuriating ADJECTIVE

infuse infuses infusing infused
VERB 1 If you infuse someone with a feeling such as enthusiasm or joy, you fill them with it. 2 If you infuse a substance such as a herb or medicine, you pour hot water onto it

and leave it for the water to absorb the flavour.
infusion NOUN

ingenious
Said "in-**jeen**-yuss" ADJECTIVE very clever and using new ideas E.G. *his ingenious invention*.
ingeniously ADVERB

ingenuity
Said "in-jen-**yoo**-it-ee" NOUN Ingenuity is cleverness and skill at inventing things or working out plans.

ingot ingots
NOUN a brick-shaped lump of metal, especially gold.

ingrained
ADJECTIVE If habits and beliefs are ingrained, they are difficult to change or destroy.

ingredient ingredients
NOUN (D & T) Ingredients are the things that something is made from, especially in cookery.

inhabit inhabits inhabiting inhabited
VERB If you inhabit a place, you live there.

inhabitant inhabitants
NOUN The inhabitants of a place are the people who live there.
◼ citizen, dweller, resident

inhale inhales inhaling inhaled
VERB When you inhale, you breathe in.
inhalation NOUN

inherent
ADJECTIVE Inherent qualities or characteristics in something are a natural part of it E.G. *her inherent common sense*.
inherently ADVERB

inherit inherits inheriting inherited
VERB 1 If you inherit money or

property, you receive it from someone who has died. **2** If you inherit a quality or characteristic from a parent or ancestor, it is passed on to you at birth.
inheritance NOUN **inheritor** NOUN

inhibit inhibits inhibiting inhibited
VERB If you inhibit someone from doing something, you prevent them from doing it.

inhibited
ADJECTIVE People who are inhibited find it difficult to relax and to show their emotions.

inhibition inhibitions
NOUN Inhibitions are feelings of fear or embarrassment that make it difficult for someone to relax and to show their emotions.

inhospitable
ADJECTIVE **1** An inhospitable place is unpleasant or difficult to live in. **2** If someone is inhospitable, they do not make people who visit them feel welcome.

inhuman
ADJECTIVE not human or not behaving like a human E.G. *the inhuman killing of their enemies.*

inhumane
ADJECTIVE extremely cruel.
inhumanity NOUN

inimitable
ADJECTIVE If you have an inimitable characteristic, no-one else can imitate it E.G. *her inimitable sense of style.*

initial initials
Said "in-**nish**-l" ADJECTIVE **1** first, or at the beginning E.G. *Shock and dismay were my initial reactions.* ▶ NOUN **2** the first letter of a name.

initially ADVERB

initiate initiates initiating initiated
Said "in-**nish**-ee-ate" VERB **1** If you initiate something, you make it start or happen. **2** If you initiate someone into a group or club, you allow them to become a member of it, usually by means of a special ceremony.
initiation NOUN

initiative initiatives
Said "in-**nish**-at-ive" NOUN **1** an attempt to get something done. **2** If you have initiative, you decide what to do and then do it, without needing the advice of other people.

inject injects injecting injected
VERB **1** If a doctor or nurse injects you with a substance, they use a needle and syringe to put the substance into your body. **2** If you inject something new into a situation, you add it.
injection NOUN

injunction injunctions
NOUN an order issued by a court of law to stop someone doing something.

injure injures injuring injured
VERB To injure someone is to damage part of their body.

injury injuries
NOUN ⟨PE⟩ hurt or damage, especially to part of a person's body or to their feelings E.G. *He suffered acute injury to his pride… The knee injury forced him to retire from the professional game.*

injustice injustices
NOUN **1** Injustice is lack of justice and fairness. **2** If you do someone an injustice, you judge them too harshly.

a
b
c
d
e
f
g
h
i
j
k
l
m
n
o
p
q
r
s
t
u
v
w
x
y
z

ink
NOUN Ink is the coloured liquid used for writing or printing.

inkling inklings
NOUN a vague idea about something.

inlaid
ADJECTIVE decorated with small pieces of wood, metal, or stone E.G. *decorative plates inlaid with brass.*
inlay NOUN

inland
ADVERB OR ADJECTIVE towards or near the middle of a country, away from the sea.

in-law in-laws
NOUN Your in-laws are members of your husband's or wife's family.

inlet inlets
NOUN a narrow bay.

inmate inmates
NOUN someone who lives in a prison or psychiatric hospital.

inn inns
NOUN a small old country pub or hotel.

innards
PLURAL NOUN The innards of something are its inside parts.

innate
ADJECTIVE An innate quality is one that you were born with E.G. *an innate sense of fairness.*
innately ADVERB

inner
ADJECTIVE contained inside a place or object E.G. *an inner room.*

innermost
ADJECTIVE deepest and most secret E.G. *our innermost feelings.*

innings
NOUN In cricket, an innings is a period when a particular team is batting.

innocent
ADJECTIVE 1 not guilty of a crime.

2 without experience of evil or unpleasant things E.G. *an innocent child.*
innocently ADVERB **innocence** NOUN

innocuous
Said "in-**nok**-yoo-uss" ADJECTIVE not harmful.

innovation innovations
NOUN (D & T) a completely new idea, product, or system of doing things.

innuendo innuendos or innuendoes
Said "in-yoo-**en**-doe" NOUN an indirect reference to something rude or unpleasant.
🔲 from Latin *innuendo* meaning 'by hinting', from *innuere* meaning 'to convey by a nod'

innumerable
ADJECTIVE too many to be counted E.G. *innumerable cups of tea.*

input inputs
NOUN 1 Input consists of all the money, information, and other resources that are put into a job, project, or company to make it work.
2 (ICT) In computing, input is information which is fed into a computer.

inquest inquests
NOUN an official inquiry to find out what caused a person's death.

inquire inquires inquiring inquired; also spelt **enquire**
VERB If you inquire about something, you ask for information about it.
inquiring ADJECTIVE **inquiry** NOUN

inquisition inquisitions
NOUN an official investigation, especially one which is very thorough and uses harsh methods of questioning.

inquisitive
ADJECTIVE Someone who is inquisitive is keen to find out about things.
inquisitively ADVERB

inroads
PLURAL NOUN If something makes inroads on or into something, it starts affecting it.

insane
ADJECTIVE Someone who is insane is mad.
insanely ADVERB **insanity** NOUN

insatiable
Said "in-**saysh**-a-bl" ADJECTIVE A desire or urge that is insatiable is very great E.G. *an insatiable curiosity*.
insatiably ADVERB

inscribe inscribes inscribing inscribed
VERB If you inscribe words on an object, you write or carve them on it.

inscription inscriptions
NOUN the words that are written or carved on something.

inscrutable
Said "in-**skroot**-a-bl" ADJECTIVE Someone who is inscrutable does not show what they are really thinking.

insect insects
NOUN (SCIENCE) a small creature with six legs, and usually wings.

insecticide insecticides
NOUN a poisonous chemical used to kill insects.

insecure
ADJECTIVE 1 If you are insecure, you feel unsure of yourself and doubt whether other people like you.
2 Something that is insecure is not safe or well protected E.G. *People still feel their jobs are insecure*.
insecurity NOUN

insensitive
ADJECTIVE If you are insensitive, you do not notice when you are upsetting people.
insensitivity NOUN

insert inserts inserting inserted
VERB If you insert an object into something, you put it inside.
insertion NOUN

inshore
ADJECTIVE at sea but close to the shore E.G. *inshore boats*.

inside insides
ADVERB, PREPOSITION, or ADJECTIVE 1 Inside refers to the part of something which is surrounded by the main part and is often hidden E.G. *Tom had to stay inside and work… inside the house… an inside pocket*. ▶ PLURAL NOUN 2 Your insides are the parts inside your body. ▶ PHRASE 3 **Inside out** means with the inside part facing outwards
☑ Do not use *of* after *inside*. You should write *she was waiting inside the school* and not *inside of the school*.

insider insiders
NOUN a person who is involved in a situation and so knows more about it than other people.

insidious
ADJECTIVE Something that is insidious is unpleasant and develops slowly without being noticed E.G. *the insidious progress of the disease*.
insidiously ADVERB

insight insights
NOUN If you gain insight into a problem, you gradually get a deep and accurate understanding of it.

insignia
Said "in-**sig**-nee-a" NOUN the badge or a sign of a particular organization.

Psychiatrists Seldom Yell Callously Hard (<u>psychi</u>atrist)　　SPELLING NOTE

insignificant

ADJECTIVE small and unimportant.
insignificance NOUN

insincere

ADJECTIVE Someone who is insincere pretends to have feelings which they do not really have.

insinuate insinuates insinuating insinuated

VERB If you insinuate something unpleasant, you hint about it.
insinuation NOUN

insipid

ADJECTIVE 1 An insipid person or activity is dull and boring. 2 Food that is insipid has very little taste.
 (sense 1) bland, colourless, uninteresting

insist insists insisting insisted

VERB If you insist on something, you demand it forcefully.
insistent ADJECTIVE **insistence** NOUN

insolent

ADJECTIVE very rude and disrespectful.
insolently ADVERB **insolence** NOUN

insoluble

Said "in-soll-yoo-bl" ADJECTIVE
1 impossible to solve E.G. *an insoluble problem.* 2 unable to dissolve E.G. *substances which are insoluble in water.*

insolvent

ADJECTIVE unable to pay your debts.
insolvency NOUN

insomnia

NOUN Insomnia is difficulty in sleeping.
insomniac NOUN

inspect inspects inspecting inspected

VERB To inspect something is to examine it carefully to check that

everything is all right.
inspection NOUN

inspector inspectors

NOUN 1 someone who inspects things. 2 a police officer just above a sergeant in rank.

inspire inspires inspiring inspired

VERB 1 (DRAMA) If something inspires you, it gives you new ideas and enthusiasm to do something. 2 To inspire an emotion in someone is to make them feel this emotion.
inspired ADJECTIVE **inspiring** ADJECTIVE **inspiration** NOUN

instability

NOUN Instability is a lack of stability in a place E.G. *political instability.*

install installs installing installed

VERB 1 If you install a piece of equipment in a place, you put it there so it is ready to be used. 2 To install someone in an important job is to officially give them that position. 3 If you install yourself in a place, you settle there and make yourself comfortable.
installation NOUN

instalment instalments

NOUN 1 If you pay for something in instalments, you pay small amounts of money regularly over a period of time. 2 one of the parts of a story or television series.

instance instances

NOUN 1 a particular example or occurrence of an event, situation, or person E.G. *a serious instance of corruption.* ▶ PHRASE 2 You use **for instance** to give an example of something you are talking about.

instant instants

NOUN **1** a moment or short period of time E.G. *In an instant they were gone.* ▶ ADJECTIVE **2** immediate and without delay E.G. *The record was an instant success.*

instantly ADVERB

instantaneous

ADJECTIVE happening immediately and without delay E.G. *The applause was instantaneous.*

instantaneously ADVERB

instead

ADVERB in place of something E.G. *Take the stairs instead of the lift.*

instigate instigates instigating instigated

VERB Someone who instigates a situation makes it happen.

instigation NOUN   **instigator** NOUN

instil instils instilling instilled

VERB If you instil an idea or feeling into someone, you make them feel or think it.

instinct instincts

NOUN a natural tendency to do something E.G. *My first instinct was to protect myself.*

instinctive ADJECTIVE   **instinctively** ADVERB

institute institutes instituting instituted

NOUN **1** an organization for teaching or research. ▶ VERB **2** FORMAL If you institute a rule or system, you introduce it.

institution institutions

NOUN **1** a custom or system regarded as an important tradition within a society E.G. *The family is an institution to be cherished.* **2** a large, important organization, for example a university or bank.

institutional ADJECTIVE

instruct instructs instructing instructed

VERB **1** If you instruct someone to do something, you tell them to do it. **2** If someone instructs you in a subject or skill, they teach you about it.

instructor NOUN   **instructive** ADJECTIVE   **instruction** NOUN

instrument instruments

NOUN **1** a tool or device used for a particular job E.G. *a special instrument which cut through the metal.* **2** (MUSIC) A musical instrument is an object, such as a piano or flute, played to make music.

instrumental

ADJECTIVE **1** If you are instrumental in doing something, you help to make it happen. **2** (MUSIC) Instrumental music is performed using only musical instruments, and not voices.

insufficient

ADJECTIVE not enough for a particular purpose.

insufficiently ADVERB

insular

Said "inss-yoo-lar" ADJECTIVE Someone who is insular is unwilling to meet new people or to consider new ideas.

insularity NOUN

insulate insulates insulating insulated

VERB If you insulate something, you cover it with a layer to keep it warm or to stop electricity passing through it.

insulation NOUN   **insulator** NOUN

insulin

Said "inss-yoo-lin" NOUN Insulin is a substance which controls the level of sugar in the blood. People who have

a b c d e f g h i j k l m n o p q r s t u v w x y z

A
B
C
D
E
F
G
H
I
J
K
L
M
N
O
P
Q
R
S
T
U
V
W
X
Y
Z

diabetes do not produce insulin naturally and have to take regular doses of it.

insult insults insulting insulted
VERB 1 If you insult someone, you offend them by being rude to them. ➤ NOUN 2 a rude remark which offends you.
insulting ADJECTIVE
■ (sense 1) abuse, affront, offend
■ (sense 2) abuse, affront, offence

insure insures insuring insured
VERB 1 If you insure something or yourself, you pay money regularly to a company so that if there is an accident or damage, the company will pay for medical treatment or repairs. 2 If you do something to insure against something unpleasant happening, you do it to prevent the unpleasant thing from happening or to protect yourself if it does happen.
insurance NOUN

insurrection insurrections
NOUN a violent action taken against the rulers of a country.

intact
ADJECTIVE complete, and not changed or damaged in any way E.G. *The rear of the aircraft remained intact when it crashed.*

intake intakes
NOUN A person's intake of food, drink, or air is the amount they take in.

integral
ADJECTIVE If something is an integral part of a whole thing, it is an essential part.

integrate integrates integrating integrated
VERB 1 If a person integrates into a group, they become part of it. 2 To

integrate things is to combine them so that they become closely linked or form one thing E.G. *his plan to integrate the coal and steel industries.*
integration NOUN

integrity
NOUN 1 Integrity is the quality of being honest and following your principles. 2 The integrity of a group of people is their being united as one whole.

intellect intellects
NOUN Intellect is the ability to understand ideas and information.

intellectual intellectuals
ADJECTIVE 1 involving thought, ideas, and understanding E.G. *an intellectual exercise.* ➤ NOUN
2 someone who enjoys thinking about complicated ideas.
intellectually ADVERB

intelligence
NOUN A person's intelligence is their ability to understand and learn things quickly and well.
intelligent ADJECTIVE **intelligently** ADVERB
■ brains, intellect, understanding

intelligentsia
Said "in-tell-lee-jent-sya" NOUN The intelligentsia are intellectual people, considered as a group.

intelligible
ADJECTIVE able to be understood E.G. *very few intelligible remarks.*

intend intends intending intended
VERB 1 If you intend to do something, you have decided or planned to do it E.G. *She intended to move back to Cape Town.* 2 If something is

intended for a particular use, you have planned that it should have this use E.G. *The booklet is intended to be kept handy.*

intense

ADJECTIVE **1** very great in strength or amount E.G. *intense heat.* **2** If a person is intense, they take things very seriously and have very strong feelings.

intensely ADVERB   **intensity** NOUN

intensify intensifies intensifying intensified

VERB To intensify something is to make it greater or stronger.

intensive

ADJECTIVE involving a lot of energy or effort over a very short time E.G. *an intensive training course.*

intent intents

NOUN **1** FORMAL A person's intent is their purpose or intention. ▶ ADJECTIVE **2** If you are intent on doing something, you are determined to do it.

intently ADVERB

intention intentions

NOUN If you have an intention to do something, you have a plan of what you are going to do.

intentional

ADJECTIVE If something is intentional, it is done on purpose.

intentionally ADVERB

inter-

PREFIX 'Inter-' means 'between' E.G. *inter-school competitions.*
📖 a Latin word

interact interacts interacting interacted

VERB The way two people or things interact is the way they work together, communicate, or react with each other.

interaction NOUN

interactive

ADJECTIVE ICT Interactive television, computers and games react to decisions taken by the viewer, user or player.

intercept intercepts intercepting intercepted

Said "in-ter-**sept**" VERB If you intercept someone or something that is going from one place to another, you stop them.

interchange interchanges

NOUN An interchange is the act or process of exchanging things or ideas.

interchangeable ADJECTIVE

intercom intercoms

NOUN a device consisting of a microphone and a loudspeaker, which you use to speak to people in another room.

intercourse

NOUN Intercourse or sexual intercourse is the act of having sex.

interest interests interesting interested

NOUN **1** If you have an interest in something or if something is of interest, you want to learn or hear more about it. **2** Your interests are your hobbies. **3** If you have an interest in something being done, you want it to be done because it will benefit you. **4** Interest is an extra payment made to the lender by someone who has borrowed a sum of money, or by a bank or company to someone who has invested money in them. Interest is worked out as a percentage of the sum of

a
b
c
d
e
f
g
h
i
j
k
l
m
n
o
p
q
r
s
t
u
v
w
x
y
z

A
B
C
D
E
F
G
H
I
J
K
L
M
N
O
P
Q
R
S
T
U
V
W
X
Y
Z

money borrowed or invested. ► VERB
5 Something that interests you attracts your attention so that you want to learn or hear more about it.
interesting ADJECTIVE **interestingly** ADVERB **interested** ADJECTIVE

interface interfaces
NOUN 1 The interface between two subjects or systems is the area in which they affect each other or are linked. 2 ICT The user interface of a computer program is how it is presented on the computer screen and how easy it is to operate.

interfere interferes interfering interfered
VERB 1 If you interfere in a situation, you try to influence it, although it does not really concern you.
2 Something that interferes with a situation has a damaging effect on it.
interference NOUN **interfering** ADJECTIVE
🏛 from Old French *s'entreferir* meaning 'to collide'
🟰 (sense 1) butt in, intrude, meddle

interim
ADJECTIVE intended for use only until something permanent is arranged
E.G. *an interim government.*
☑ from Latin *interim* meaning 'meanwhile'

interior interiors
NOUN 1 the inside part of something.
► ADJECTIVE 2 Interior means inside
E.G. *They painted the interior walls white.*

interjection interjections
NOUN a word or phrase spoken suddenly to express surprise, pain, or anger.

What is an Interjection?

An interjection is a word that expresses a strong emotion, such as anger, surprise, or excitement. Interjections often stand alone rather than as part of a sentence. Some interjections express greetings:
E.G. *Hello.* ■ *Congratulations!*
Some interjections express agreement or disagreement:
E.G. *Indeed.* ■ *No.*
Some interjections express pain, anger, or annoyance:
E.G. *Ouch!* ■ *Blast!*
Some interjections express approval, pleasure, or excitement:
E.G. *Bravo!* ■ *Hooray!*
Some interjections express surprise or relief:
E.G. *Wow!* ■ *Phew!*
Sometimes an interjection is more like a noise than a word:
E.G. *Sh!* ■ *Psst!*
A group of words can be used together as an interjection:
E.G. *Happy birthday!* ■ *Hey presto!*
When an interjection does occur within a sentence, it is usually separated by commas or dashes:
E.G. *I turned the key and, **bingo**, the engine started.*

interlude interludes
Rhymes with "rude" NOUN a short break from an activity.

intermediary intermediaries
Said "in-ter-**meed**-yer-ee" NOUN someone who tries to get two groups of people to come to an agreement.

intermediate
ADJECTIVE An intermediate level occurs in the middle, between two other stages E.G. *intermediate students*.

interminable
ADJECTIVE If something is interminable, it goes on for a very long time E.G. *an interminable wait for the bus*.
interminably ADVERB

intermission intermissions
NOUN an interval between two parts of a film or play.

intermittent
ADJECTIVE happening only occasionally.
intermittently ADVERB

internal
ADJECTIVE happening inside a person, place, or object.
internally ADVERB

international internationals
ADJECTIVE (GEOGRAPHY) 1 involving different countries. ► NOUN 2 a sports match between two countries.
internationally ADVERB

Internet
NOUN (ICT) The Internet is a worldwide communication system which people use through computers.

interplay
NOUN The interplay between two things is the way they react with one another.

interpret interprets interpreting interpreted
VERB 1 If you interpret what someone says or does, you decide what it means. 2 If you interpret a foreign language that someone is speaking, you translate it.
interpretation NOUN **interpreter** NOUN

interrogate interrogates interrogating interrogated
VERB If you interrogate someone, you question them thoroughly to get information from them.
interrogation NOUN **interrogator** NOUN
≡ cross-examine, question

interrupt interrupts interrupting interrupted
VERB 1 If you interrupt someone, you start talking while they are talking. 2 If you interrupt a process or activity, you stop it continuing for a time.
interruption NOUN

intersect intersects intersecting intersected
VERB When two roads intersect, they cross each other.
intersection NOUN

interspersed
ADJECTIVE If something is interspersed with things, these things occur at various points in it.

interval intervals
NOUN 1 the period of time between two moments or dates. 2 a short break during a play or concert.
(MUSIC)
≡ (sense 2) break, interlude, intermission

intervene intervenes intervening intervened
VERB If you intervene in a situation, you step in to prevent conflict between people.
intervention NOUN
≡ mediate, step in

intervening
ADJECTIVE An intervening period of time is one which separates two events.

a
b
c
d
e
f
g
h
i
j
k
l
m
n
o
p
q
r
s
t
u
v
w
x
y
z

Elaine and Emily shout EE when they mEEt to grEEt each other (-ee-)   **SPELLING NOTE**

A
B
C
D
E
F
G
H
I
J
K
L
M
N
O
P
Q
R
S
T
U
V
W
X
Y
Z

interview interviews
NOUN **1** a meeting at which someone asks you questions about yourself to see if you are suitable for a particular job. **2** a conversation in which a journalist asks a famous person questions. ▶ VERB **3** If you interview someone, you ask them questions about themselves.

intestine intestines
NOUN Your intestines are a long tube which carries food from your stomach through to your bowels, and in which the food is digested.
intestinal ADJECTIVE

intimate intimates intimating intimated
ADJECTIVE **1** If two people are intimate, there is a close relationship between them. **2** An intimate matter is very private and personal. **3** An intimate knowledge of something is very deep and detailed. ▶ VERB **4** If you intimate something, you hint at it E.G. *He did intimate that he is considering legal action.*
intimately ADVERB **intimacy** NOUN
intimation NOUN

intimidate intimidates intimidating intimidated
VERB If you intimidate someone, you frighten them in a threatening way.
intimidated ADJECTIVE **intimidating** ADJECTIVE **intimidation** NOUN

into
PREPOSITION **1** If something goes into something else, it goes inside it. **2** If you bump or crash into something, you hit it. **3** INFORMAL If you are into something, you like it very much E.G. *Nowadays I'm really into healthy food.*

intolerable
ADJECTIVE If something is intolerable, it

is so bad that it is difficult to put up with it.
intolerably ADVERB

intonation
NOUN Your intonation is the way that your voice rises and falls as you speak.

intoxicated
ADJECTIVE If someone is intoxicated, they are drunk.
intoxicating ADJECTIVE **intoxication** NOUN

intra-
PREFIX 'Intra-' means 'within' or 'inside' E.G. *intra-European conflicts.*
📖 from Latin *intra* meaning 'within'

intractable
ADJECTIVE; FORMAL stubborn and difficult to deal with or control.

intransitive
ADJECTIVE An intransitive verb is one that does not have a direct object. For example, 'sings' is intransitive in 'She sings', but not in 'She sings a song'.

intravenous
Said "in-trav-**vee**-nuss" ADJECTIVE Intravenous foods or drugs are given to sick people through their veins.
intravenously ADVERB

intrepid
ADJECTIVE not worried by danger E.G. *an intrepid explorer.*
intrepidly ADVERB

intricate
ADJECTIVE Something that is intricate has many fine details E.G. *walls and ceilings covered with intricate patterns.*
intricately ADVERB **intricacy** NOUN

intrigue intrigues intriguing intrigued
NOUN **1** Intrigue is the making of

secret plans, often with the intention of harming other people E.G. *political intrigue.* ▶ VERB **2** If something intrigues you, you are fascinated by it and curious about it.
intriguing ADJECTIVE

intrinsic
ADJECTIVE; FORMAL The intrinsic qualities of something are its basic qualities.
intrinsically ADVERB

introduce introduces introducing introduced
VERB **1** If you introduce one person to another, you tell them each other's name so that they can get to know each other. **2** When someone introduces a radio or television show, they say a few words at the beginning to tell you about it. **3** If you introduce someone to something, they learn about it for the first time.
introductory ADJECTIVE

introduction introductions
NOUN **1** The introduction of someone or something is the act of presenting them for the first time. **2** a piece of writing at the beginning of a book, which usually tells you what the book is about.
■ (sense 2) foreword, opening, preface

introvert introverts
NOUN someone who spends more time thinking about their private feelings than about the world around them, and who often finds it difficult to talk to others.
introverted ADJECTIVE

intrude intrudes intruding intruded
VERB To intrude on someone or something is to disturb them E.G. *I*

don't want to intrude on your parents.
intruder NOUN   **intrusion** NOUN
intrusive ADJECTIVE
■ butt in, trespass

intuition intuitions
Said "int-yoo-**ish**-n" NOUN Your intuition is a feeling you have about something that you cannot explain E.G. *My intuition is right about him.*
intuitive ADJECTIVE   **intuitively** ADVERB

Inuit Inuits; also spelt **Innuit**
NOUN a member of a group of people who live in Northern Canada, Greenland, Alaska, and Eastern Siberia, formerly known as Eskimos.

inundated
ADJECTIVE If you are inundated by letters or requests, you receive so many that you cannot deal with them all.

invade invades invading invaded
VERB **1** If an army invades a country, it enters it by force. **2** If someone invades your privacy, they disturb you when you want to be alone.
invader NOUN

invalid invalids
Said "**in**-va-lid" NOUN someone who is so ill that they need to be looked after by someone else.
🔲 from Latin *invalidus* meaning 'infirm'

invalid
Said "in-**val**-id" ADJECTIVE **1** If an argument or result is invalid, it is not acceptable because it is based on a mistake. **2** If a law, marriage, or election is invalid, it is illegal because it has not been carried out properly.
invalidate VERB
🔲 from Latin *invalidus* meaning 'without legal force'

invalidity
Said "in-va-**lid**-dit-ee" NOUN Invalidity

a
b
c
d
e
f
g
h
i
j
k
l
m
n
o
p
q
r
s
t
u
v
w
x
y
z

is the condition of being very ill for a very long time.

invaluable

ADJECTIVE extremely useful E.G. *This book contains invaluable tips*.

invariably

ADVERB If something invariably happens, it almost always happens.

invasion invasions

NOUN 1 (HISTORY) The invasion of a country or territory is the act of entering it by force. 2 an unwanted disturbance or intrusion E.G. *an invasion of her privacy*.

invective

NOUN; FORMAL Invective is abusive language used by someone who is angry.

invent invents inventing invented

VERB 1 If you invent a device or process, you are the first person to think of it or to use it. 2 If you invent a story or an excuse, you make it up.

inventor NOUN **invention** NOUN **inventive** ADJECTIVE **inventiveness** NOUN

■ (sense 1) conceive, create, devise

inventory inventories

NOUN a written list of all the objects in a place.

inverse

ADJECTIVE; FORMAL If there is an inverse relationship between two things, one decreases as the other increases.

invertebrate invertebrates

NOUN; TECHNICAL a creature which does not have a spine

inverted

ADJECTIVE upside down or back to front.

inverted comma inverted commas

NOUN Inverted commas are the punctuation marks " " or ' ', used to show where speech begins and ends.

What do Inverted Commas do?

Inverted commas or **quotation marks** (" " or ' ') mark the beginning and end of a speaker's exact words or thoughts:

E.G. *"I would like some more," said Matthew*.

Inverted commas are not used when a speaker's words are reported indirectly rather than in their exact form:

E.G. *Matthew said that he would like some more*.

Inverted commas can also be used to indicate the title of a book, piece of music, etc:

E.G. *The class had been reading "The Little Prince"*.

Inverted commas are also used to draw attention to the fact that a word or phrase is being used in an unusual way, or that a word itself is the subject of discussion:

E.G. *Braille allows a blind person to "see" with the fingers. What rhymes with "orange"?*

---

invest invests investing invested

VERB 1 If you invest money, you pay it into a bank or buy shares so that you will receive a profit. 2 If you invest in something useful, you buy it because it will help you do something better. 3 If you invest money, time, or energy in something, you try to make it a success.

investor NOUN **investment** NOUN

investigate investigates investigating investigated

VERB To investigate something is to try to find out all the facts about it.
investigator NOUN **investigation** NOUN

■ examine, look into, study

inveterate

ADJECTIVE having lasted for a long time and not likely to stop E.G. *an inveterate gambler*.

invincible

ADJECTIVE unable to be defeated.
invincibility NOUN

invisible

ADJECTIVE If something is invisible, you cannot see it, because it is hidden, very small, or imaginary.
invisibly ADVERB **invisibility** NOUN

invite invites inviting invited

VERB 1 If you invite someone to an event, you ask them to come to it. 2 If you invite someone to do something, you ask them to do it E.G. *Andrew has been invited to speak at the conference.*
inviting ADJECTIVE **invitation** NOUN

invoice invoices

NOUN a bill for services or goods.

invoke invokes invoking invoked

VERB 1 FORMAL If you invoke a law, you use it to justify what you are doing. 2 If you invoke certain feelings, you cause someone to have these feelings.

📖 from Latin *invocare* meaning 'to call upon'

involuntary

ADJECTIVE sudden and uncontrollable.
involuntarily ADVERB

involve involves involving involved

VERB (PSHE) If a situation involves someone or something, it includes them as a necessary part.
involvement NOUN

inward or **inwards**

ADJECTIVE 1 Your inward thoughts and feelings are private. ▶ ADJECTIVE or ADVERB 2 If something moves inward or inwards, it moves towards the inside or centre of something.
inwardly ADVERB

iodine

Said "eye-oh-deen" NOUN Iodine is a bluish-black substance used in medicine and photography.

ion ions

Said "eye-on" NOUN Ions are electrically charged atoms.

iota

NOUN an extremely small amount E.G. *He did not have an iota of proof.*

IQ IQs

NOUN Your IQ is your level of intelligence shown by the results of a special test. IQ is an abbreviation for 'intelligence quotient'.

Ir-

PREFIX 'Ir-' means 'not' or 'the opposite of', and is the form of 'in-' which is used before the letter E.G. *irrational*.

Iranian Iranians

Said "ir-rain-ee-an" ADJECTIVE 1 belonging or relating to Iran. ▶ NOUN 2 someone who comes from Iran. 3 Iranian is the main language spoken in Iran. It is also known as Farsi.

Iraqi Iraqis

Said "ir-ah-kee" ADJECTIVE 1 belonging or relating to Iraq. ▶ NOUN 2 someone who comes from Iraq.

irate

Said "eye-rate" ADJECTIVE very angry.

a b c d e f g h i j k l m n o p q r s t u v w x y z

LEt's measure the angLE (ang**le**)   SPELLING NOTE

iris irises

Said "eye-riss" NOUN 1 the round, coloured part of your eye. 2 a tall plant with long leaves and large blue, yellow, or white flowers.

🔺 from Greek *iris* meaning 'rainbow' or 'coloured circle'

Irish

ADJECTIVE 1 belonging or relating to the Irish Republic, or to the whole of Ireland. ▶ NOUN 2 Irish or Irish Gaelic is a language spoken in some parts of Ireland.

Irishman Irishmen

NOUN a man who comes from Ireland. **Irishwoman** NOUN

irk irks irking irked

VERB If something irks you, it annoys you. **irksome** ADJECTIVE

iron irons ironing ironed

NOUN 1 Iron is a hard dark metal used to make steel, and things like gates and fences. Small amounts of iron are found in blood. 2 a device which heats up and which you rub over clothes to remove creases. ▶ VERB 3 If you iron clothes, you use a hot iron to remove creases from them.

ironing NOUN

iron out VERB If you iron out difficulties, you solve them.

Iron Age

NOUN The Iron Age was a time about three thousand years ago when people first started to make tools out of iron.

ironbark ironbarks

NOUN an Australian eucalypt with a hard, rough bark.

irony

Said "eye-ron-ee" NOUN 1 Irony is a form of humour in which you say the opposite of what you really mean

E.G. *This group could be described, without irony, as the fortunate ones.* 2 There is irony in a situation when there is an unexpected or unusual connection between things or events E.G. *It's a sad irony of life: once you are lost, a map is useless.*

ironic or **ironical** ADJECTIVE **ironically** ADVERB

irrational

ADJECTIVE Irrational feelings are not based on logical reasons E.G. *irrational fears.*

irrationally ADVERB **irrationality** NOUN

irregular

ADJECTIVE 1 Something that is irregular is not smooth or straight, or does not form a regular pattern E.G. *irregular walls.* 2 (MATHS) Irregular things are uneven or unequal, or are not symmetrical.

irregularly ADVERB **irregularity** NOUN

🔲 haphazard, random, variable

irrelevant

ADJECTIVE (LIBRARY) not directly connected with a subject E.G. *He either ignored questions or gave irrelevant answers.*

irrelevance NOUN

irrepressible

ADJECTIVE Someone who is irrepressible is lively and cheerful.

irresistible

ADJECTIVE 1 unable to be controlled E.G. *an irresistible urge to yawn.* 2 extremely attractive E.G. *Women always found him irresistible.*

irresistibly ADVERB

irrespective

ADJECTIVE If you say something will be

done irrespective of certain things, you mean it will be done without taking those things into account.

irresponsible

ADJECTIVE An irresponsible person does things without considering the consequences E.G. *an irresponsible driver*.

irresponsibly ADVERB
irresponsibility NOUN

■ careless, reckless, thoughtless

irrigate irrigates irrigating irrigated

VERB To irrigate land is to supply it with water brought through pipes or ditches.

irrigated ADJECTIVE   **irrigation** NOUN

irritate irritates irritating irritated

VERB 1 If something irritates you, it annoys you. 2 If something irritates part of your body, it makes it tender, sore, or itchy.

irritable ADJECTIVE   **irritant** NOUN
irritation NOUN

■ (sense 1) annoy, get on one's nerves

is

the third person, present tense of *be*.

-ish

SUFFIX '-ish' forms adjectives that mean 'fairly' or 'rather' E.G. *smallish, greenish*.

📖 from an Old English suffix

Islam

Said "iz-lahm" NOUN ⟨ RE ⟩ Islam is the Muslim religion, which teaches that there is only one God, Allah, and Mohammed is his prophet. The holy book of Islam is the Koran.

Islamic ADJECTIVE

📖 from Arabic *islam* meaning 'surrender to God'

island islands

Said "eye-land" NOUN a piece of land surrounded on all sides by water.

islander NOUN

isle isles

Rhymes with "mile" NOUN; LITERARY an island.

-ism

SUFFIX 1 '-ism' forms nouns that refer to an action or condition E.G. *criticism, heroism*. 2 '-ism' forms nouns that refer to a political or economic system or a system of beliefs E.G. *Marxism, Sikhism*. 3 '-ism' forms nouns that refer to a type of prejudice E.G. *racism, sexism*.

📖 from the Greek suffix *-ismos*

isolate isolates Isolating isolated

VERB 1 If something isolates you or if you isolate yourself, you are set apart from other people. 2 If you isolate something, you separate it from everything else.

isolated ADJECTIVE   **isolation** NOUN

isosceles

Said "eye-**soss**-il-eez" ADJECTIVE ⟨ MATHS ⟩ An isosceles triangle has two sides of the same length.

📖 from Greek *iso-* meaning 'equal' and *skelos* meaning 'leg'

Israeli Israelis

Said "iz-rail-ee" ADJECTIVE ⟨ RE ⟩ 1 belonging or relating to Israel. ▶ NOUN 2 someone who comes from Israel.

issue issues issuing issued

Said "ish-yoo" NOUN 1 an important subject that people are talking about. 2 a particular edition of a newspaper or magazine. ▶ VERB 3 If you issue a statement or a warning, you say it formally and publicly. 4 If

a
b
c
d
e
f
g
h
i
j
k
l
m
n
o
p
q
r
s
t
u
v
w
x
y
z

someone issues something, they officially give it E.G. *Staff were issued with plastic cards*.

🔲 (sense 4) distribute, give out

-ist

SUFFIX 1 '-ist' forms nouns and adjectives which refer to someone who is involved in a certain activity, or who believes in a certain system or religion E.G. *chemist... motorist... Buddhist*. 2 '-ist' forms nouns and adjectives which refer to someone who has a certain prejudice E.G. *racist*.

🔲 from the Greek suffix *istēs*

isthmus isthmuses

NOUN a narrow strip of land connecting two larger areas.

it

PRONOUN 1 'It' is used to refer to something that has already been mentioned, or to a situation or fact E.G. *It was a difficult decision*. 2 'It' is used to refer to people or animals whose sex is not known E.G. *If a baby is thirsty, it feeds more often*. 3 You use 'it' to make statements about the weather, time, or date E.G. *It's noon*.

Italian Italians

ADJECTIVE 1 belonging or relating to Italy. ▸ NOUN 2 someone who comes from Italy. 3 Italian is the main language spoken in Italy.

italics

PLURAL NOUN Italics are letters printed in a special sloping way, and are often used to emphasize something. All the examples in this dictionary are in italics.

italic ADJECTIVE

itch itches itching itched

VERB 1 When your skin itches, it has an unpleasant feeling and you want to scratch it. 2 If you are itching to do something, you are impatient to do it. ▸ NOUN 3 an unpleasant feeling on your skin that you want to scratch.

itchy ADJECTIVE

🔲 from Old English *giccean* meaning 'to itch'

item items

NOUN 1 one of a collection or list of objects. 2 a newspaper or magazine article.

🔲 (sense 2) article, feature, piece

itinerary itineraries

NOUN a plan of a journey, showing a route to follow and places to visit.

-itis

SUFFIX '-itis' is added to the name of a part of the body to refer to disease or inflammation in that part E.G. *appendicitis... tonsillitis*.

🔲 from Greek, the feminine form of *-itēs* meaning 'belonging to'

its

ADJECTIVE OR PRONOUN 'Its' refers to something belonging to or relating to things, children, or animals that have already been mentioned E.G. *The lion lifted its head*.

✔ Many people are confused about the difference between *its* and *it's*. *Its*, without the apostrophe, is the possessive form of *it*: *the cat has hurt its paw*. *It's*, with the apostrophe, is a short form of *it is* or *it has*: *it's green... it's been snowing again*.

itself

PRONOUN 1 'Itself' is used when the same thing, child, or animal does an action and is affected by it E.G. *Paris prides itself on its luxurious hotels*. 2 'Itself' is used to emphasize 'it'.

-ity

SUFFIX '-ity' forms nouns that refer to a

state or condition E.G. *continuity… technicality.*

🔲 from the Latin suffix *-itas*

-ive

SUFFIX '-ive' forms adjectives and some nouns E.G. *massive… detective.*

🔲 from Latin suffix *-īvus*

ivory

NOUN **1** the valuable creamy-white bone which forms the tusk of an elephant. It is used to make ornaments. ▶ NOUN OR ADJECTIVE **2** creamy-white.

ivy

NOUN an evergreen plant which creeps along the ground and up walls.

iwi iwi or **iwis**

NOUN In New Zealand, a Maori tribe.

-ize or **-ise**

SUFFIX '-ize' and '-ise' forms verbs. Most verbs can be spelt with either ending, though there are some that can only be spelt with '-ise', for example *advertise, improvise* and *revise*.

🔲 from the Greek suffix *-izein*

a
b
c
d
e
f
g
h
i
j
k
l
m
n
o
p
q
r
s
t
u
v
w
x
y
z

J j

TIP Many words which sound as if they ought to begin with letter *j* are spelt instead with letter *g*, for example *gender, geranium, giraffe* and *gym*.

jab jabs jabbing jabbed
VERB **1** To jab something means to poke at it roughly. ► NOUN **2** a sharp or sudden poke. **3** INFORMAL an injection.

jabiru jabirus
NOUN a white-and-green Australian stork with red legs.

jack jacks jacking jacked
NOUN **1** a piece of equipment for lifting heavy objects, especially for lifting a car when changing a wheel. **2** In a pack of cards, a jack is a card whose value is between a ten and a queen. ► VERB **3** To jack up an object means to raise it, especially by using a jack.

jackal jackals
NOUN a wild animal related to the dog.

jackaroo jackaroos; also spelt **jackeroo**
NOUN In Australia, a young person learning the work of a sheep or cattle station.

jackdaw jackdaws
NOUN a bird like a small crow with black and grey feathers.

jacket jackets
NOUN **1** a short coat reaching to the waist or hips. **2** an outer covering for something E.G. *a book jacket*. **3** The jacket of a baked potato is its skin.

jackpot jackpots
NOUN In a gambling game, the jackpot is the top prize.

jack up jacks up jacking up jacked up
VERB; INFORMAL In New Zealand English,

to jack up is to organize or prepare something.

jade
NOUN Jade is a hard green stone used for making jewellery and ornaments.

jagged
ADJECTIVE sharp and spiky.
◼ serrated, spiked, uneven

jaguar jaguars
NOUN a large member of the cat family with spots on its back.

jail jails jailing jailed; also spelt **gaol**
NOUN **1** a building where people convicted of a crime are locked up.
► VERB **2** To jail someone means to lock them up in a jail.
◼ (sense 1) nick, penitentiary, prison

jailer jailers; also spelt **gaoler**
NOUN a person who is in charge of the prisoners in a jail.

jam jams jamming jammed
NOUN **1** a food, made by boiling fruit and sugar together until it sets. **2** a situation in which it is impossible to move E.G. *a traffic jam*. ► AN INFORMAL PHRASE **3** If someone is **in a jam**, they are in a difficult situation. ► VERB **4** If people or things are jammed into a place, they are squeezed together so closely that they can hardly move. **5** To jam something somewhere means to push it there roughly E.G. *He jammed his foot on the brake*. **6** If something is jammed, it is stuck or unable to work properly. **7** To jam a radio signal means to interfere with it and prevent it from

being received clearly.

■ (sense 3) fix, predicament, tight spot

Jamaican Jamaicans
Said "jam-**may**-kn" ADJECTIVE
1 belonging or relating to Jamaica.
► NOUN 2 someone who comes from Jamaica.

jamboree jamborees
NOUN a gathering of large numbers of people enjoying themselves.

Jandal Jandals
NOUN; TRADEMARK In New Zealand, a sandal with a strap between the big toe and other toes and over the foot.

jangle jangles jangling jangled
VERB 1 If something jangles, it makes a harsh metallic ringing noise. ► NOUN 2 the sound made by metal objects striking against each other.

janitor janitors
NOUN the caretaker of a building.

January
NOUN January is the first month of the year. It has 31 days.
⊞ from Latin *Januarius* meaning 'the month of Janus', named after a Roman god

Japanese
ADJECTIVE 1 belonging or relating to Japan. ► NOUN 2 someone who comes from Japan. 3 Japanese is the main language spoken in Japan.

jar jars jarring jarred
NOUN 1 a glass container with a wide top used for storing food. ► VERB 2 If something jars on you, you find it unpleasant or annoying.

jargon
NOUN Jargon consists of words that are used in special or technical ways by particular groups of people, often

making the language difficult to understand.

jarrah jarrahs
NOUN an Australian eucalypt tree that produces wood used for timber.

jasmine
NOUN Jasmine is a climbing plant with small sweet-scented white flowers.

jaundice
NOUN Jaundice is an illness affecting the liver, in which the skin and the whites of the eyes become yellow.

jaundiced
ADJECTIVE pessimistic and lacking enthusiasm E.G. *He takes a rather jaundiced view of politicians.*

jaunt jaunts
NOUN a journey or trip you go on for pleasure.

jaunty jauntier jauntiest
ADJECTIVE expressing cheerfulness and self-confidence E.G. *a jaunty tune.*
jauntily ADVERB

javelin javelins
NOUN a long spear that is thrown in sports competitions.

jaw jaws
NOUN 1 A person's or animal's jaw is the bone in which the teeth are set.
2 A person's or animal's mouth and teeth are their jaws.

jay jays
NOUN a kind of noisy chattering bird.

jazz jazzes jazzing jazzed
NOUN 1 Jazz is a style of popular music with a forceful rhythm. ► VERB
2 INFORMAL To jazz something up means to make it more colourful or exciting.

jazzy jazzier jazziest
ADJECTIVE; INFORMAL bright and showy.

jealous
ADJECTIVE 1 If you are jealous, you feel

a b c d e f g h i j k l m n o p q r s t u v w x y z

I always visit my FRIend on a FRIday (**fri**end)   SPELLING NOTE

A
B
C
D
E
F
G
H
I
J
K
L
M
N
O
P
Q
R
S
T
U
V
W
X
Y
Z

bitterness towards someone who has something that you would like to have. **2** If you are jealous of something you have, you feel you must try to keep it from other people.
jealously ADVERB **jealousy** NOUN
■ (sense 1) covetous, envious
■ (sense 2) possessive

jeans
PLURAL NOUN Jeans are casual denim trousers.

jeep jeeps
NOUN; TRADEMARK a small road vehicle with four-wheel drive.

jeer jeers jeering jeered
VERB **1** If you jeer at someone, you insult them in a loud, unpleasant way. ▶ NOUN **2** Jeers are rude and insulting remarks.
jeering ADJECTIVE

Jehovah
Said "ji-**hove**-ah" PROPER NOUN Jehovah is the name of God in the Old Testament.
▥ from adding vowels to the Hebrew *JHVH*, the sacred name of God

jelly jellies
NOUN **1** a clear, sweet food eaten as a dessert. **2** a type of clear, set jam.

jellyfish jellyfishes
NOUN a sea animal with a clear soft body and tentacles which may sting.

jeopardize jeopardizes jeopardizing jeopardized
Said "**jep**-par-dyz"; also spelt **jeopardise**
VERB To jeopardize something means to do something which puts it at risk
E.G. *Elaine jeopardized her health.*

jeopardy
NOUN If someone or something is in jeopardy, they are at risk of failing or

of being destroyed.

jerk jerks jerking jerked
VERB **1** To jerk something means to give it a sudden, sharp pull. **2** If something jerks, it moves suddenly and sharply. ▶ NOUN **3** a sudden sharp movement. **4** INFORMAL If you call someone a jerk, you mean they are stupid.
jerky ADJECTIVE **jerkily** ADVERB

jerkin jerkins
NOUN a short sleeveless jacket.

jersey jerseys
NOUN **1** a knitted garment for the upper half of the body. **2** Jersey is a type of knitted woollen or cotton fabric used to make clothing.

jest jests jesting jested
NOUN **1** a joke. ▶ VERB **2** To jest means to speak jokingly.

jester jesters
NOUN In the past, a jester was a man who was kept to amuse the king or queen.

jet jets jetting jetted
NOUN **1** a plane which is able to fly very fast. **2** a stream of liquid, gas, or flame forced out under pressure. **3** Jet is a hard black stone, usually highly polished and used in jewellery and ornaments. ▶ VERB **4** To jet somewhere means to fly there in a plane, especially a jet.

jet boat jet boats
NOUN In New Zealand, a motor boat that is powered by a jet of water at the rear.

jet lag
NOUN Jet lag is a feeling of tiredness or confusion that people have after a long flight across different time zones.

jettison jettisons jettisoning jettisoned
VERB If you jettison something, you

throw it away because you no longer want it.

jetty jetties
NOUN a wide stone wall or wooden platform at the edge of the sea or a river, where boats can be moored.

Jew Jews
Said "joo" (RE) NOUN a person who practises the religion of Judaism, or who is of Hebrew descent.
Jewish ADJECTIVE
🔳 from *Judah*, the name of a Jewish patriarch

jewel jewels
NOUN a precious stone used to decorate valuable ornaments or jewellery.
jewelled ADJECTIVE

jeweller jewellers
NOUN a person who makes jewellery or who sells and repairs jewellery and watches.

jewellery
NOUN Jewellery consists of ornaments that people wear, such as rings or necklaces, made of valuable metals and sometimes decorated with precious stones.

jib jibs
NOUN a small sail towards the front of a sailing boat.

jibe
another spelling of **gibe**.

jig jigs jigging jigged
NOUN 1 a type of lively folk dance. ▸ VERB 2 If you jig, you dance around in a lively bouncy manner.

jiggle jiggles jiggling jiggled
VERB If you jiggle something, you move it around with quick jerky movements.

jigsaw jigsaws
NOUN a puzzle consisting of a picture

on cardboard that has been cut up into small pieces, which have to be put together again.

jilt jilts jilting jilted
VERB If you jilt someone, you suddenly break off your relationship with them.
jilted ADJECTIVE

jingle jingles jingling jingled
NOUN 1 a short, catchy phrase or rhyme set to music and used to advertise something on radio or television. 2 the sound of something jingling. ▸ VERB 3 When something jingles, it makes a tinkling sound like small bells.

jinks
PLURAL NOUN High jinks is boisterous and mischievous behaviour.

jinx jinxes
NOUN someone or something that is thought to bring bad luck E.G. *He was beginning to think he was a jinx.*

jinxed
ADJECTIVE If something is jinxed it is considered to be unlucky E.G. *I think this house is jinxed.*

jitters
PLURAL NOUN; INFORMAL If you have got the jitters, you are feeling very nervous.
jittery ADJECTIVE

job jobs
NOUN 1 the work that someone does to earn money. 2 a duty or responsibility E.G. *It is a captain's job to lead from the front.* ▸ PHRASE 3 If something is **just the job**, it is exactly right or exactly what you wanted.
▤ (sense 1) employment, occupation, work

job centre job centres
NOUN a government office where

a
b
c
d
e
f
g
h
i
j
k
l
m
n
o
p
q
r
s
t
u
v
w
x
y
z

people can find out about job vacancies.

jobless

ADJECTIVE without any work.

jockey jockeys jockeying jockeyed

NOUN **1** someone who rides a horse in a race. ▶ VERB **2** To jockey for a position means to manoeuvre in order to gain an advantage over other people.

jocular

ADJECTIVE A jocular comment is intended to make people laugh.

jodhpurs

Said "jod-purz" PLURAL NOUN Jodhpurs are close-fitting trousers worn when riding a horse.

from *Jodhpur*, the name of a town in N. India

joey joeys

NOUN; INFORMAL In Australian English, a young kangaroo or other young animal.

jog jogs jogging jogged

VERB **1** To jog means to run slowly and rhythmically, often as a form of exercise. **2** If you jog something, you knock it slightly so that it shakes or moves. **3** If someone or something jogs your memory, they remind you of something. ▶ NOUN **4** a slow run.

jogger NOUN **jogging** NOUN

join joins joining joined

VERB **1** When two things join, or when one thing joins another, they come together. **2** If you join a club or organization, you become a member of it or start taking part in it. **3** To join two things means to fasten them. ▶ NOUN **4** a place where two things are fastened together.

■ (senses 1 & 3) connect, link, unite

■ (sense 2) enlist, enrol, sign up

join up VERB If someone joins up, they become a member of the armed forces.

joiner joiners

NOUN a person who makes wooden window frames, doors, and furniture.

joinery

NOUN Joinery is the work done by a joiner.

joint joints jointing jointed

ADJECTIVE **1** shared by or belonging to two or more people E.G. *a joint building society account*. ▶ NOUN **2** a part of the body where two bones meet and are joined together so that they can move, for example a knee or hip. **3** a place where two things are fixed together. **4** a large piece of meat suitable for roasting. **5** INFORMAL any place of entertainment, such as a nightclub or pub. ▶ VERB **6** To joint meat means to cut it into large pieces according to where the bones are.

jointly ADVERB **jointed** ADJECTIVE

joist joists

NOUN a large beam used to support floors or ceilings.

joke jokes joking joked

NOUN **1** something that you say or do to make people laugh, such as a funny story. **2** anything that you think is ridiculous and not worthy of respect E.G. *The decision was a joke*. ▶ VERB **3** If you are joking, you are teasing someone.

jokingly ADVERB

■ (sense 1) gag, jest

■ (sense 3) jest, kid

joker jokers

NOUN In a pack of cards, a joker is an extra card that does not belong to

A B C D E F G H I J K L M N O P Q R S T U V W X Y Z

any of the four suits, but is used in some games.

jolly jollier jolliest
ADJECTIVE **1** happy, cheerful, and pleasant. ► ADVERB **2** INFORMAL Jolly also means very E.G. *jolly good fun.*

jolt jolts jolting jolted
VERB **1** To jolt means to move or shake roughly and violently. **2** If you are jolted by something, it gives you an unpleasant surprise. ► NOUN **3** a sudden jerky movement. **4** an unpleasant shock or surprise.

jostle jostles jostling jostled
VERB To jostle means to push roughly against people in a crowd.

jot jots jotting jotted
VERB **1** If you jot something down, you write it quickly in the form of a short informal note. ► NOUN **2** a very small amount.
jotting NOUN

jotter jotters
NOUN a pad or notebook.

joule joules
Rhymes with "school" NOUN a unit of energy or work.

journal journals
NOUN **1** a magazine that deals with a particular subject, trade, or profession. **2** a diary which someone keeps regularly.

journalism
NOUN Journalism is the work of collecting, writing, and publishing news in newspapers, magazines, and on television and radio.
journalist NOUN **journalistic** ADJECTIVE

journey journeys journeying journeyed
NOUN **1** the act of travelling from one place to another. ► VERB **2** FORMAL To journey somewhere means to travel there E.G. *He intended to journey up the Amazon.*

joust jousts
NOUN In medieval times, a joust was a competition between knights fighting on horseback, using lances.

jovial
ADJECTIVE cheerful and friendly.
jovially ADVERB **joviality** NOUN

joy joys
NOUN **1** Joy is a feeling of great happiness. **2** INFORMAL Joy also means success or luck E.G. *Any joy with your insurance claim?* **3** something that makes you happy or gives you pleasure.

joyful
ADJECTIVE **1** causing pleasure and happiness. **2** Someone who is joyful is extremely happy.
joyfully ADVERB

joyous
ADJECTIVE; FORMAL joyful.
joyously ADVERB

joyride joyrides
NOUN a drive in a stolen car for pleasure.
joyriding NOUN **joyrider** NOUN

joystick joysticks
NOUN a lever in an aircraft which the pilot uses to control height and direction.

jube jubes
NOUN; INFORMAL In Australian and New Zealand English, a fruit-flavoured jelly sweet.

jubilant
ADJECTIVE feeling or expressing great happiness or triumph.
jubilantly ADVERB

jubilation
NOUN Jubilation is a feeling of great happiness and triumph.

Plaice the fish has a glittering 'EYE' (I) (plaice)　　SPELLING NOTE

A B C D E F G H I J K L M N O P Q R S T U V W X Y Z

jubilee jubilees
NOUN a special anniversary of an event such as a coronation E.G. *Queen Elizabeth's Silver Jubilee in 1977.*
📖 from Hebrew *yobhel* meaning 'ram's horn'; rams' horns were blown during festivals and celebrations

Judaism
Said "joo-day-i-zm" NOUN ⟨ RE ⟩
Judaism is the religion of the Jewish people. It is based on a belief in one God, and draws its laws and authority from the Old Testament.
Judaic ADJECTIVE

judder judders juddering juddered
VERB To judder means to shake and vibrate noisily and violently.

judder bar judder bars
NOUN In New Zealand English, a bump built across a road to stop drivers from going too fast. In Britain it is called a sleeping policeman.

judge judges judging judged
NOUN 1 the person in a law court who decides how the law should be applied to people who appear in the court. 2 someone who decides the winner in a contest or competition.
▶ VERB 3 If you judge someone or something, you form an opinion about them based on the evidence that you have. 4 To judge a contest or competition means to decide on the winner.

judgment or **judgement** NOUN
🟰 (sense 2) adjudicator, referee, umpire
🟰 (sense 4) adjudicate, referee, umpire
✔ *Judgment* and *judgement* are both correct spellings.

judicial
ADJECTIVE relating to judgment or to justice E.G. *a judicial review.*

judiciary
NOUN The judiciary is the branch of government concerned with justice and the legal system.

judicious
ADJECTIVE sensible and showing good judgment.
judiciously ADVERB

judo
NOUN Judo is a sport in which two people try to force each other to the ground using special throwing techniques.

jug jugs
NOUN a container with a lip or spout used for holding or serving liquids.

juggernaut juggernauts
NOUN a large heavy lorry.
📖 from Hindi *Jagannath*, the name of a huge idol of the god Krishna, which every year is wheeled through the streets of Puri in India

juggle juggles juggling juggled
VERB To juggle means to throw objects into the air, catching them in sequence, and tossing them up again so there are several in the air at one time.
juggler NOUN

jugular jugulars
NOUN The jugular or jugular vein is one of the veins in the neck which carry blood from the head back to the heart.

juice juices
NOUN 1 Juice is the liquid that can be squeezed or extracted from fruit or other food. 2 Juices in the body are fluids E.G. *gastric juices.*

juicy juicier juiciest
ADJECTIVE **1** Juicy food has a lot of juice in it. **2** Something that is juicy is interesting, exciting, or scandalous E.G. *a juicy bit of gossip*.

jukebox jukeboxes
NOUN a large record player found in cafés and pubs which automatically plays a selected record when coins are inserted.

July
NOUN July is the seventh month of the year. It has 31 days.
📖 from Latin *Julius*, the month of July, named after Julius Caesar by the Romans

jumble jumbles jumbling jumbled
NOUN **1** an untidy muddle of things. **2** Jumble consists of articles for a jumble sale. ▸ VERB **3** To jumble things means to mix them up untidily.

jumble sale jumble sales
NOUN an event at which cheap second-hand clothes and other articles are sold to raise money, usually for a charity.

jumbo jumbos
NOUN **1** A jumbo or jumbo jet is a large jet aeroplane that can carry several hundred passengers.
▸ ADJECTIVE **2** very large E.G. *jumbo packs of elastic bands*.
📖 from *Jumbo*, the name of a famous 19th-century elephant

jumbuck jumbucks
NOUN; OLD-FASHIONED In Australian English, a sheep.

jump jumps jumping jumped
VERB **1** To jump means to spring off the ground using your leg muscles. **2** To jump something means to spring off the ground and move over or across it. **3** If you jump at

something such as an opportunity, you accept it eagerly. **4** If you jump on someone, you criticize them suddenly and forcefully. **5** If someone jumps, they make a sudden sharp movement of surprise. **6** If an amount or level jumps, it suddenly increases. ▸ NOUN **7** a spring into the air, sometimes over an object.
■ (senses 1 & 7) bound, leap, spring

jumper jumpers
NOUN a knitted garment for the top half of the body.

jumpy jumpier jumpiest
ADJECTIVE nervous and worried.

junction junctions
NOUN a place where roads or railway lines meet or cross.

June
NOUN June is the sixth month of the year. It has 30 days.
📖 from Latin *Junius*, the month of June, probably from the name of an important Roman family

jungle jungles
NOUN **1** a dense tropical forest. **2** a tangled mass of plants or other objects.

junior juniors
ADJECTIVE **1** Someone who is junior to other people has a lower position in an organization. **2** Junior also means younger. **3** relating to childhood E.G. *a junior school*. ▸ NOUN **4** someone who holds an unimportant position in an organization.

juniper junipers
NOUN an evergreen shrub with purple berries used in cooking and medicine.

junk junks
NOUN **1** Junk is old or second-hand articles which are sold cheaply or thrown away. **2** If you think something

a
b
c
d
e
f
g
h
i
j
k
l
m
n
o
p
q
r
s
t
u
v
w
x
y
z

is junk, you think it is worthless rubbish. **3** a Chinese sailing boat with a flat bottom and square sails.

junk food
NOUN Junk food is food low in nutritional value which is eaten as well as or instead of proper meals.

junkie junkies
NOUN; INFORMAL a drug addict.

Jupiter
NOUN Jupiter is the largest planet in the solar system and the fifth from the sun.

jurisdiction
NOUN **1** FORMAL Jurisdiction is the power or right of the courts to apply laws and make legal judgments E.G. *The Court held that it did not have the jurisdiction to examine the merits of the case.* **2** Jurisdiction is power or authority E.G. *The airport was under French jurisdiction.*

juror jurors
NOUN a member of a jury.

jury juries
NOUN a group of people in a court of law who have been selected to listen to the facts of a case on trial, and to decide whether the accused person is guilty or not.

just
ADJECTIVE **1** fair and impartial E.G. *She arrived at a just decision.* **2** morally right or proper E.G. *a just reward.* ► ADVERB **3** If something has just happened, it happened a very short time ago. **4** If you just do something, you do it by a very small amount E.G. *They only just won.* **5** simply or only E.G. *It was just an excuse not to mow the lawn.* **6** exactly E.G. *It's just what she wanted.* ► PHRASE **7** In South

African English, **just now** means in a little while.

justly ADVERB

justice justices
NOUN **1** Justice is fairness and reasonableness. **2** The system of justice in a country is the way in which laws are maintained by the courts. **3** a judge or magistrate.

justify justifies justifying justified
VERB **1** If you justify an action or idea, you prove or explain why it is reasonable or necessary. **2** ICT To justify text that you have typed or keyed into a computer is to adjust the spaces between the words so each full line in a paragraph fills the space between the left and right hand margins of the page.

justification NOUN **justifiable** ADJECTIVE

jut juts jutting jutted
VERB If something juts out, it sticks out beyond or above a surface or edge.
■ project, protrude, stick out

jute
NOUN Jute is a strong fibre made from the bark of an Asian plant, used to make rope and sacking.

juvenile juveniles
ADJECTIVE **1** suitable for young people. **2** childish and rather silly E.G. *a juvenile game.* ► NOUN **3** a young person not old enough to be considered an adult.

juxtapose juxtaposes juxtaposing juxtaposed
VERB If you juxtapose things or ideas, you put them close together, often to emphasize the difference between them.

juxtaposition NOUN

K k

> **TIP** Some words that begin with a *k-* sound are spelt with the letters *ch-*, for example *chlorophyll*, *chlorine*, and *choir*. Some words that begin with a *k-* sound are spelt with letter *q*, for example *quite* and *quiet*.

kaffir kaffirs or **kaffir**
NOUN; VERY OFFENSIVE In South African English, a kaffir is a Black person.

kaleidoscope kaleidoscopes
Said "kal-**eye**-*dos-skope*" NOUN A toy consisting of a tube with a hole at one end. When you look through the hole and twist the other end of the tube, you can see a changing pattern of colours.
▦ from Greek *kalos* meaning 'beautiful', *eidos* meaning 'shape', and *skopein* meaning 'to look at'

kamikaze
NOUN In the Second World War, a kamikaze was a Japanese pilot who flew an aircraft loaded with explosives directly into an enemy target knowing he would be killed doing so.
▦ from Japanese *kami* meaning 'divine' + *kaze* meaning 'wind'

kangaroo kangaroos
NOUN a large Australian animal with very strong back legs which it uses for jumping.

karate
Said "kar-**rat**-*ee*" NOUN Karate is a sport in which people fight each other using only their hands, elbows, feet, and legs.
▦ from Japanese *kara* + *te* meaning 'empty hand'

karma
NOUN In Buddhism and Hinduism, karma is actions you take which affect you in your present and future lives

Karoo Karoos; also spelt **Karroo**
NOUN In South Africa, the Karoos are areas of very dry land.

karri karris
NOUN an Australian eucalypt that produces a dark red wood used for building.

katipo katipo or **katipos**
NOUN a small, poisonous spider with a red or orange stripe on its back, found in New Zealand.

kauri kauri or **kauris**
NOUN a large tree found in New Zealand which produces wood used for building and making furniture.

kayak kayaks
Said "ky-ak" NOUN a covered canoe with a small opening for the person sitting in it, originally used by the Inuit people.

kea kea or **keas**
Said "kay-ah" NOUN **1** a large, greenish parrot found in New Zealand. **2** In New Zealand, Keas are the youngest members of the Scouts.

kebab kebabs
NOUN pieces of meat or vegetable stuck on a stick and grilled.

keel keels keeling keeled
NOUN **1** the specially shaped bottom of a ship which supports the sides and sits in the water. ▶ VERB **2** If someone or something keels over, they fall down sideways.

keen keener keenest
ADJECTIVE 1 Someone who is keen shows great eagerness and enthusiasm. 2 If you are keen on someone or something, you are attracted to or fond of them. 3 Keen senses let you see, hear, smell, and taste things very clearly or strongly.
keenly ADVERB **keenness** NOUN
■ (sense 1) avid, eager, enthusiastic

keep keeps keeping kept
VERB 1 To keep someone or something in a particular condition means to make them stay in that condition E.G. *We'll walk to keep warm.* 2 If you keep something, you have it and look after it. 3 If you keep doing something, you do it repeatedly or continuously E.G. *I kept phoning the hospital.* 4 If you keep a promise, you do what you promised to do. 5 If you keep a secret, you do not tell anyone else. 6 If you keep a diary, you write something in it every day. 7 If you keep someone from going somewhere, you delay them so that they are late. 8 To keep someone means to provide them with money, food, and clothing.
► NOUN 9 Your keep is the cost of the food you eat, your housing, and your clothing E.G. *He does not contribute towards his keep.* 10 the main tower inside the walls of a castle.
■ (sense 2) hold, maintain, preserve
keep up VERB If you keep up with other people, you move or work at the same speed as they do.

keeper keepers
NOUN 1 a person whose job is to look after the animals in a zoo. 2 a goalkeeper in soccer or hockey.

keeping
NOUN 1 If something is in your keeping, it has been given to you to look after for a while. ► PHRASE 2 If one thing is **in keeping with** another, the two things are suitable or appropriate together.

keepsake keepsakes
NOUN something that someone gives you to remind you of a particular person or event.
■ memento, souvenir

keg kegs
NOUN a small barrel.

kelpie kelpies; also spelt **kelpy**
NOUN a smooth-haired Australian sheepdog with upright ears.

kennel kennels
NOUN 1 a shelter for a dog. 2 A kennels is a place where dogs can be kept for a time, or where they are bred.

Kenyan Kenyans
Said "keen-yan" ADJECTIVE 1 belonging or relating to Kenya. ► NOUN 2 someone who comes from Kenya.

kerb kerbs
NOUN the raised edge at the point where a pavement joins onto a road.

kernel kernels
NOUN the part of a nut that is inside the shell.

kerosene
NOUN Kerosene is the same as paraffin.

kestrel kestrels
NOUN a type of small falcon.

ketchup
NOUN Ketchup is a cold sauce, usually made from tomatoes.

kettle kettles
NOUN a metal container with a spout, in which you boil water.

key keys keying keyed
NOUN 1 a shaped piece of metal that fits into a hole so that you can

unlock a door, wind something that is clockwork, or start a car. **2** The keys on a typewriter, piano, or cash register are the buttons that you press to use it. **3** an explanation of the symbols used in a map or diagram. **4** In music, a key is a scale of notes. ▶ VERB **5** If you key in information on a computer keyboard, you type it.

keyboard keyboards
NOUN (ICT) a row of levers or buttons on a piano, typewriter, or computer.

kg
an abbreviation for 'kilograms'.

khaki
Said "kah-kee" NOUN **1** Khaki is a strong yellowish-brown material, used especially for military uniforms. ▶ NOUN or ADJECTIVE **2** yellowish-brown.
🔲 from Urdu *kaki* meaning 'dusty'

khanda khandas
Said "kun-dah" NOUN a sword used by Sikhs in the Amrit ceremony.

kia ora
Said "ki-or-ah" In New Zealand, 'kia ora' is a Maori greeting.

kibbutz kibbutzim
Said "kib-boots" NOUN a place of work in Israel, for example a farm or factory, where the workers live together and share all the duties and income.

kick kicks kicking kicked
VERB **1** If you kick something, you hit it with your foot. ▶ NOUN **2** If you give something a kick, you hit it with your foot. **3** INFORMAL If you get a kick out of doing something, you enjoy doing it very much.

kick off VERB When players kick off, they start a soccer or rugby match.
kick-off NOUN

kid kids kidding kidded
NOUN **1** INFORMAL a child. **2** a young goat. ▶ VERB **3** If you kid people, you tease them by deceiving them in fun.

kidnap kidnaps kidnapping kidnapped
VERB To kidnap someone is to take them away by force and demand a ransom in exchange for returning them.
kidnapper NOUN **kidnapping** NOUN
☰ abduct, seize

kidney kidneys
NOUN Your kidneys are two organs in your body that remove waste products from your blood.

kill kills killing killed
VERB **1** To kill a person, animal, or plant is to make them die. **2** If something is killing you, it is causing you severe pain or discomfort E.G. *My arms are killing me.* ▶ NOUN **3** The kill is the moment when a hunter kills an animal.
killer NOUN
☰ (sense 1) murder, slay

kiln kilns
NOUN (ART) an oven for baking china or pottery until it becomes hard and dry.

kilo kilos
NOUN a kilogram.

kilogram kilograms
NOUN (MATHS) a unit of weight equal to 1000 grams.

kilohertz
NOUN a unit of measurement of radio waves equal to one thousand hertz.

kilometre kilometres
NOUN (MATHS) a unit of distance equal to one thousand metres.

kilowatt kilowatts
NOUN a unit of power equal to one thousand watts.

a b c d e f g h i j k l m n o p q r s t u v w x y z

A
B
C
D
E
F
G
H
I
J
K
L
M
N
O
P
Q
R
S
T
U
V
W
X
Y
Z

kilt kilts
NOUN a tartan skirt worn by men as part of Scottish Highland dress.

kimono kimonos
NOUN a long, loose garment with wide sleeves and a sash, worn in Japan.

kin
PLURAL NOUN Your kin are your relatives.
☰ family, kindred, relatives

kind kinds; kinder kindest
NOUN **1** A particular kind of thing is something of the same type or sort as other things E.G. *that kind of film*.
▶ ADJECTIVE **2** Someone who is kind is considerate and generous towards other people.
kindly ADVERB **kindness** NOUN
☰ (sense 1) class, sort, type
☰ (sense 2) considerate, generous
☑ When you use *kind* in its singular form, the adjective before it should also be singular: *that kind of dog*. When you use the plural form *kinds*, the adjective before it should be plural: *those kinds of dog... those kinds of dogs*.

kindergarten kindergartens
NOUN a school for children who are too young to go to primary school.
▥ from German *Kinder* + *Garten* meaning 'children's garden'

kindle kindles kindling kindled
VERB **1** If you kindle a fire, you light it. **2** If something kindles a feeling in you, it causes you to have that feeling.

kindling
NOUN Kindling is bits of dry wood or paper that you use to start a fire.

kindred
ADJECTIVE If you say that someone is a kindred spirit, you mean that they have the same interests or opinions as you.

kinetic energy
NOUN Kinetic energy is the energy that is produced when something moves.

king kings
NOUN **1** a man who is the head of state in a country, and who inherited his position from his parents. **2** a chess piece which can only move one square at a time. **3** In a pack of cards, a king is a card with a picture of a king on it.

kingdom kingdoms
NOUN **1** a country that is governed by a king or queen. **2** The divisions of the natural world are called kingdoms E.G. *the animal kingdom*.

kingfisher kingfishers
NOUN a brightly coloured bird that lives near water and feeds on fish.

king-size or **king-sized**
ADJECTIVE larger than the normal size E.G. *a king-size bed*.

kink kinks
NOUN a dent or curve in something which is normally straight.

kinky
ADJECTIVE; INFORMAL having peculiar sexual tastes.

kinship
NOUN Kinship is a family relationship to other people.

kiosk kiosks
Said "kee-osk" NOUN a covered stall on a street where you can buy newspapers, sweets, or cigarettes.
▥ from Turkish *kösk* meaning 'pavilion'

kip kips kipping kipped INFORMAL
NOUN **1** a period of sleep. ▶ VERB **2** When you kip, you sleep.

kipper kippers
NOUN a smoked herring.

kirk kirks

NOUN In Scotland, a kirk is a church.

kiss kisses kissing kissed

VERB 1 When you kiss someone, you touch them with your lips as a sign of love or affection. ► NOUN 2 When you give someone a kiss, you kiss them.

kiss of life

NOUN The kiss of life is a method of reviving someone by blowing air into their lungs.

kit kits

NOUN 1 a collection of things that you use for a sport or other activity. 2 a set of parts that you put together to make something.

kitchen kitchens

NOUN a room used for cooking and preparing food.

kite kites

NOUN 1 a frame covered with paper or cloth which is attached to a piece of string, and which you fly in the air. 2 a shape with four sides, with two pairs of the same length, and none of the sides parallel to each other. 3 a large bird of prey with a long tail and long wings.

kitset kitsets

NOUN In New Zealand English, a set of parts which you have to put together yourself to make an item such as a house or a piece of furniture.

kitten kittens

NOUN a young cat.

kitty kitties

NOUN a fund of money that has been given by a group of people who will use it to pay for or do things together.

kiwi kiwi or kiwis

Said "kee-wee" NOUN 1 a type of bird found in New Zealand. Kiwis cannot fly. 2 someone who comes from New Zealand. The plural of this sense is 'kiwis'.

kiwi fruit kiwi fruits

NOUN a fruit with a brown hairy skin and green flesh.

kloof kloofs

NOUN In South Africa, a kloof is a narrow valley.

km

an abbreviation for 'kilometres'.

knack

NOUN an ability to do something difficult whilst making it look easy E.G. *the knack of making friends*.

knead kneads kneading kneaded

VERB If you knead dough, you press it and squeeze it with your hands before baking it.

knee knees

NOUN the joint in your leg between your ankle and your hip.

kneecap kneecaps

NOUN Your kneecaps are the bones at the front of your knees.

kneel kneels kneeling knelt

VERB When you kneel, you bend your legs and lower your body until your knees are touching the ground.

knell knells

NOUN; LITERARY the sound of a bell rung to announce a death or at a funeral.

knickers

PLURAL NOUN Knickers are underpants worn by women and girls.

knick-knacks

PLURAL NOUN Knick-knacks are small ornaments.

knife knives; knifes knifing knifed

NOUN 1 (D&T) a sharp metal tool

a b c d e f g h i j **k** l m n o p q r s t u v w x y z

A B C D E F G H I J **K** L M N O P Q R S T U V W X Y Z

that you use to cut things. ▶ VERB 2 To knife someone is to stab them with a knife.

knight knights knighting knighted

NOUN 1 a man who has been given the title 'Sir' by the King or Queen. 2 In medieval Europe, a knight was a man who served a monarch or lord as a mounted soldier. 3 a chess piece that is usually in the shape of a horse's head. ▶ VERB 4 To knight a man is to give him the title 'Sir'.

knighthood NOUN

knit knits knitting knitted

VERB 1 If you knit a piece of clothing, you make it by working lengths of wool together, either using needles held in the hand, or with a machine. 2 If you knit your brows, you frown.

knitting NOUN

knob knobs

NOUN 1 a round handle. 2 a round switch on a machine E.G. *the knobs of a radio*.

knobkerrie knobkerries

NOUN In South Africa, a knobkerrie is a club or stick with a rounded end.

knock knocks knocking knocked

VERB 1 If you knock on something, you strike it with your hand or fist. 2 If you knock a part of your body against something, you bump into it quite forcefully. 3 INFORMAL To knock someone is to criticize them. ▶ NOUN 4 a firm blow on something solid E.G. *There was a knock at the door*.

knock out VERB To knock someone out is to hit them so hard that they become unconscious.

knocker knockers

NOUN a metal lever attached to a

door, which you use to knock on the door.

knockout knockouts

NOUN 1 a punch in boxing which knocks a boxer unconscious. 2 a competition in which competitors are eliminated in each round until only the winner is left.

knoll knolls

Rhymes with "**roll**" NOUN; LITERARY a gently sloping hill with a rounded top.

knot knots knotting knotted

NOUN 1 a fastening made by looping a piece of string around itself and pulling the ends tight. 2 a small lump visible on the surface of a piece of wood. 3 A knot of people is a small group of them. 4 TECHNICAL a unit of speed used for ships and aircraft. ▶ VERB 5 If you knot a piece of string, you tie a knot in it.

know knows knowing knew known

VERB 1 If you know a fact, you have it in your mind and you do not need to learn it. 2 People you know are not strangers because you have met them and spoken to them. ▶ AN INFORMAL PHRASE 3 If you are **in the know**, you are one of a small number of people who share a secret.

know-how

NOUN Know-how is the ability to do something that is quite difficult or technical.

knowing

ADJECTIVE A knowing look is one that shows that you know or understand something that other people do not.

knowingly ADVERB

SPELLING NOTE   On WEDNESday Wayne WED NESta (<u>Wednes</u>day)

knowledge
NOUN Knowledge is all the information and facts that you know.

knowledgeable
ADJECTIVE Someone who is knowledgeable knows a lot about a subject E.G. *She was very knowledgeable about Irish mythology.*

knuckle knuckles
NOUN Your knuckles are the joints at the end of your fingers where they join your hand.

koala koalas
NOUN an Australian animal with grey fur and small tufted ears. Koalas live in trees and eat eucalyptus leaves.

kohanga reo or **kohanga kohanga reo**
NOUN In New Zealand, an infant class where children are taught in Maori.
🔲 a Maori term meaning 'language nest'

koppie koppies
Said "**kop**-i"; also spelt **kopje**
NOUN In South Africa, a koppie is a small hill with no other hills around it.

Koran or **Qur'an**
Said "kaw-**rahn**" NOUN The Koran is the holy book of Islam.
🔲 from Arabic *kara'a* meaning 'to read'

Korean Koreans
Said "kor-**ree**-an" ADJECTIVE 1 relating or belonging to Korea. ▶ NOUN
2 someone who comes from Korea. 3 Korean is the main language spoken in Korea.

kosher
Said "**koh**-sher" ADJECTIVE Kosher food has been specially prepared to be eaten according to Jewish law.

🔲 from Hebrew *kasher* meaning 'right' or 'proper'

kowhai kowhai or **kowhais**
Said "**ko**-wigh" a small New Zealand tree with clusters of yellow flowers.

kraal kraals
NOUN In South Africa, a kraal is a village in which a tribe lives and which is often surrounded by a fence.

kudu kudus; also spelt **koodoo**
NOUN a large African antelope with curled horns.

kumara or **kumera kumara** or **kumaras**
Said "koo-**mih**-rah" NOUN In New Zealand English, a kumara is a sweet potato, a vegetable with yellow or orange flesh.

kumquat kumquats
NOUN a very small round or oval citrus fruit.

kung fu
Said "kung **foo**" NOUN Kung fu is a Chinese style of fighting which involves using your hands and feet.

kura kaupapa Maori kura kaupapa Maori
Said "**koo**-ra **kow**-puh-puh" NOUN In New Zealand, a primary school where teaching is based on Maori language and culture.

Kurd Kurds
NOUN The Kurds are a group of people who live mainly in eastern Turkey, northern Iraq, and western Iran.

Kurdish
ADJECTIVE 1 belonging or relating to the Kurds E.G. *Kurdish culture*. ▶ NOUN 2 Kurdish is the language spoken by the Kurds.

a
b
c
d
e
f
g
h
i
j
k
l
m
n
o
p
q
r
s
t
u
v
w
x
y
z

Eddy Ant thinks mEAt is a grEAt trEAt to EAt (-ea-)   SPELLING NOTE

LI

l
an abbreviation for 'litres'.

lab labs
NOUN; INFORMAL a laboratory.

label labels labelling labelled
NOUN **1** a piece of paper or plastic attached to something as an identification. ▶ VERB **2** If you label something, you put a label on it.

laboratory laboratories
NOUN (SCIENCE) a place where scientific experiments are carried out.

laborious
ADJECTIVE needing a lot of effort or time.
laboriously ADVERB

Labor Party
NOUN In Australia, the Labor Party is one of the major political parties.

labour labours labouring laboured
NOUN **1** Labour is hard work. **2** The workforce of a country or industry is sometimes called its labour E.G. *unskilled labour.* **3** In Britain, the Labour Party is a political party that believes that the government should provide free health care and education for everyone. **4** New Zealand, the Labour Party is one of the main political parties. **5** Labour is also the last stage of pregnancy when a woman gives birth to a baby. ▶ VERB **6** OLD-FASHIONED To labour means to work hard.
labourer NOUN
■ (sense 1) toil, work
■ (sense 6) slave, toil, work

labrador labradors
NOUN a large dog with short black or golden hair.

labyrinth labyrinths
Said "**lab-er-inth**" NOUN a complicated series of paths or passages.

lace laces lacing laced
NOUN **1** Lace is a very fine decorated cloth made with a lot of holes in it. **2** Laces are cords with which you fasten your shoes. ▶ VERB **3** When you lace up your shoes, you tie a bow in the laces. **4** To lace someone's food or drink means to put a small amount of alcohol, a drug, or poison in it E.G. *black coffee laced with vodka.*
lacy ADJECTIVE

lack lacks lacking lacked
NOUN **1** If there is a lack of something, it is not present when or where it is needed. ▶ VERB **2** If something is lacking, it is not present when or where it is needed. **3** If someone or something is lacking something, they do not have it or do not have enough of it E.G. *Francis was lacking in stamina.*
■ (sense 1) absence, scarcity, shortage

lacklustre
Said "**lak-luss-ter**" ADJECTIVE not interesting or exciting.

laconic
Said "**lak-kon-ik**" ADJECTIVE using very few words.
🔲 from Greek *Lakonikas* meaning 'Spartan'. The Spartans were famous for using few words

lacquer lacquers
Said "**lak-er**" NOUN Lacquer is thin, clear paint that you put on wood to protect it and make it shiny.

lacrosse
NOUN Lacrosse is an outdoor ball game in which two teams try to score goals using long sticks with

nets on the end of them.
🔲 from Canadian French *la crosse*
meaning 'the hooked stick'

lad lads
NOUN a boy or young man.

ladder ladders laddering
laddered
NOUN 1 a wooden or metal frame
used for climbing which consists of
horizontal steps fixed to two vertical
poles. 2 If your stockings or tights
have a ladder in them, they have a
vertical, ladder-like tear in them.
▶ VERB 3 If you ladder your stockings
or tights, you get a ladder in them.

laden
Said "lay-den" ADJECTIVE To be laden
with something means to be
carrying a lot of it E.G. *bushes laden
with ripe fruit.*

ladle ladles ladling ladled
NOUN 1 a long-handled spoon with a
deep, round bowl, which you use to
serve soup. ▶ VERB 2 If you ladle out
food, you serve it with a ladle.

lady ladies
NOUN 1 a woman, especially one who
is considered to be well mannered.
2 Lady is a title used in front of the
name of a woman from the nobility,
such as a lord's wife.

ladybird ladybirds
NOUN a small flying beetle with a round
red body patterned with black spots.

lady-in-waiting ladies-in-waiting
NOUN a woman who acts as
companion to a queen or princess.

ladylike
ADJECTIVE behaving in a polite and
socially correct way.

Ladyship Ladyships
NOUN You address a woman who has
the title 'Lady' as 'Your Ladyship'.

lag lags lagging lagged
VERB 1 To lag behind is to make slower
progress than other people. 2 To lag
pipes is to wrap cloth round them to
stop the water inside freezing in cold
weather.

lager lagers
NOUN Lager is light-coloured beer.
🔲 from German *Lagerbier* meaning
'beer for storing'

lagoon lagoons
NOUN an area of water separated from
the sea by reefs or sand.

laid
the past tense and past participle of
lay.

lain
the past participle of some
meanings of **lie**.

lair lairs
NOUN a place where a wild animal
lives.

laird lairds
Rhymes with "**dared**" NOUN a
landowner in Scotland.

lake lakes
NOUN an area of fresh water
surrounded by land.

lama lamas
NOUN a Buddhist priest or monk.

lamb lambs
NOUN 1 a young sheep. 2 Lamb is the
meat from a lamb.

lame
ADJECTIVE 1 Someone who is lame has
an injured leg and cannot walk
easily. 2 A lame excuse is not very
convincing.
lamely ADVERB **lameness** NOUN
▤ (sense 2) feeble, flimsy, weak

lament laments lamenting
lamented
VERB 1 To lament something means to

a
b
c
d
e
f
g
h
i
j
k
l
m
n
o
p
q
r
s
t
u
v
w
x
y
z

express sorrow or regret about it. ► NOUN **2** an expression of sorrow or regret. **3** a song or poem expressing grief at someone's death.

lamentable
ADJECTIVE disappointing and regrettable.

laminated
ADJECTIVE consisting of several thin sheets or layers stuck together E.G. *laminated glass*.

lamp lamps
NOUN a device that produces light.

lamppost lampposts
NOUN a tall column in a street, with a lamp at the top.

lampshade lampshades
NOUN a decorative covering over an electric light bulb which prevents the bulb giving out too harsh a light.

lance lances lancing lanced
VERB **1** To lance a boil or abscess means to stick a sharp instrument into it in order to release the fluid. ► NOUN **2** a long spear that used to be used by soldiers on horseback.

land lands landing landed
NOUN **1** Land is an area of ground. **2** Land is also the part of the earth that is not covered by water. **3** a country E.G. *our native land*. ► VERB **4** When a plane lands, it arrives back on the ground after a flight. **5** If you land something you have been trying to get, you succeed in getting it E.G. *She eventually landed a job with a local radio station*. **6** To land a fish means to catch it while fishing. **7** If you land someone with something unpleasant, you cause them to have to deal with it.

landing landings
NOUN **1** a flat area in a building at the

top of a flight of stairs. **2** The landing of an aeroplane is its arrival back on the ground after a flight E.G. *a smooth landing*.

landlady landladies
NOUN a woman who owns a house or small hotel and who lets rooms to people.

landlord landlords
NOUN a man who owns a house or small hotel and who lets rooms to people.

landmark landmarks
NOUN **1** a noticeable feature in a landscape, which you can use to check your position. **2** an important stage in the development of something E.G. *The play is a landmark in Japanese theatre*.

landowner landowners
NOUN someone who owns land, especially a large area of the countryside.

landscape landscapes
NOUN **1** (GEOGRAPHY) The landscape is the view over an area of open land. **2** (ART) a painting of the countryside.

landslide landslides
NOUN **1** a large amount of loose earth and rocks falling down a mountain side. **2** a victory in an election won by a large number of votes.

lane lanes
NOUN **1** a narrow road, especially in the country. **2** one of the strips on a road marked with lines to guide drivers.

language languages
NOUN **1** the system of words that the people of a country use to communicate with each other. **2** Your language is the style in which you

express yourself E.G. *His language is often obscure.* **3** Language is the study of the words and grammar of a particular language.

■ (sense 2) expression, speech

languid
Said "lang-gwid" ADJECTIVE slow and lacking energy.
languidly ADVERB

languish languishes languishing languished
VERB If you languish, you endure an unpleasant situation for a long time E.G. *Many languished in poverty.*

lanky lankier lankiest
ADJECTIVE Someone who is lanky is tall and thin and moves rather awkwardly.

lantana lantanas
NOUN In Australia, a shrub with yellow or orange flowers which is regarded as a pest in some areas.

lantern lanterns
NOUN a lamp in a metal frame with glass sides.

lap laps lapping lapped
NOUN **1** Your lap is the flat area formed by your thighs when you are sitting down. **2** one circuit of a running track or racecourse. ▶ VERB **3** When an animal laps up liquid, it drinks using its tongue to get the liquid into its mouth. **4** If you lap someone in a race, you overtake them when they are still on the previous lap. **5** When water laps against something, it gently moves against it in little waves.

lapel lapels
Said "lap-el" NOUN a flap which is joined on to the collar of a jacket or coat.

lapse lapses lapsing lapsed
NOUN **1** a moment of bad behaviour

by someone who usually behaves well. **2** a slight mistake. **3** a period of time between two events. ▶ VERB **4** If you lapse into a different way of behaving, you start behaving that way E.G. *The offenders lapsed into a sullen silence.* **5** If a legal document or contract lapses, it is not renewed on the date when it expires.

lard
NOUN Lard is fat from a pig, used in cooking.

larder larders
NOUN a room in which you store food, often next to a kitchen.

large larger largest
ADJECTIVE **1** Someone or something that is large is much bigger than average. ▶ PHRASE **2** If a prisoner is **at large**, he or she has escaped from prison.

largely
ADVERB to a great extent E.G. *The public are largely unaware of this.*

lark larks
NOUN **1** a small brown bird with a distinctive song. **2** If you do something for a lark, you do it in a high-spirited or mischievous way for fun.

larrikin larrikins
NOUN; INFORMAL In Australian and New Zealand English, a young person who behaves in a wild or irresponsible way.

larva larvae
NOUN an insect, which looks like a short, fat worm, at the stage before it becomes an adult.

laryngitis
Said "lar-in-jie-tiss" NOUN Laryngitis is an infection of the throat which causes you to lose your voice.

a
b
c
d
e
f
g
h
i
j
k
l
m
n
o
p
q
r
s
t
u
v
w
x
y
z

an ELegant angEL (ang**e**l)   SPELLING NOTE

A

larynx larynxes or **larynges**
NOUN the part of your throat containing the vocal cords, through which air passes between your nose and lungs.

lasagne
Said "laz-**zan**-ya" NOUN Lasagne is an Italian dish made with wide flat sheets of pasta, meat, and cheese sauce.

📖 from Latin *lasanum* meaning 'cooking pot'

laser lasers
NOUN a machine that produces a powerful concentrated beam of light which is used to cut very hard materials and in some kinds of surgery.

📖 from the first letters of 'Light Amplification by Stimulated Emission of Radiation'

lash lashes lashing lashed
NOUN 1 Your lashes are the hairs growing on the edge of your eyelids. 2 a strip of leather at the end of a whip. 3 Lashes are blows struck with a whip.

lash out VERB To lash out at someone means to criticize them severely.

lass lasses
NOUN a girl or young woman.

lasso lassoes or **lassos lassoing lassoed**
Said "las-**soo**" NOUN 1 a length of rope with a noose at one end, used by cowboys to catch cattle and horses. ▶ VERB 2 To lasso an animal means to catch it by throwing the noose of a lasso around its neck.

last lasts lasting lasted
ADJECTIVE 1 The last thing or event is the most recent one E.G. *last year.*

2 The last thing that remains is the only one left after all the others have gone E.G. *The last family left in 1950.* ▶ ADVERB 3 If you last did something on a particular occasion, you have not done it since then E.G. *They last met in Rome.* 4 The thing that happens last in a sequence of events is the final one E.G. *He added the milk last.* ▶ VERB 5 If something lasts, it continues to exist or happen E.G. *Her speech lasted fifty minutes.* 6 To last also means to remain in good condition E.G. *The mixture will last for up to 2 weeks in the fridge.* ▶ PHRASE 7 **At last** means after a long time.
lastly ADVERB

last-ditch
ADJECTIVE A last-ditch attempt to do something is a final attempt to succeed when everything else has failed.

latch latches latching latched
NOUN 1 a simple door fastening consisting of a metal bar which falls into a hook. 2 a type of door lock which locks automatically when you close the door and which has to be opened with a key. ▶ VERB 3 INFORMAL If you latch onto someone or something, you become attached to them.

late later latest
ADJECTIVE or ADVERB 1 Something that happens late happens towards the end of a period of time E.G. *the late evening… late in the morning.* 2 If you arrive late, or do something late, you arrive or do it after the time you were expected to. ▶ ADJECTIVE 3 A late event happens after the time when it usually takes place E.G. *a late breakfast.* 4 FORMAL Late means dead E.G. *my late grandmother.*

◼ (sense 2) belated, overdue, tardy

lately
ADVERB Events that happened lately happened recently.

latent
ADJECTIVE A latent quality is hidden at the moment, but may emerge in the future E.G. *a latent talent for art*.

lateral
ADJECTIVE relating to the sides of something, or moving in a sideways direction.

lathe lathes
NOUN a machine which holds and turns a piece of wood or metal against a tool to cut and shape it.

lather lathers
NOUN Lather is the foam that you get when you rub soap in water.

Latin Latins
NOUN 1 Latin is the language of ancient Rome. ▶ NOUN OR ADJECTIVE 2 Latins are people who speak languages closely related to Latin, such as French, Italian, Spanish, and Portuguese.

Latin America
NOUN Latin America consists of the countries in North, South, and Central America where Spanish or Portuguese is the main language.
Latin American ADJECTIVE

latitude latitudes
NOUN (GEOGRAPHY) The latitude of a place is its distance north or south of the equator measured in degrees.

latrine latrines
Said "lat-*reen*" NOUN a hole or trench in the ground used as a toilet at a camp.

latter
ADJECTIVE OR NOUN 1 You use 'latter' to refer to the second of two things

that are mentioned E.G. *They were eating sandwiches and cakes (the latter bought from Mrs Paul's bakery).*
▶ ADJECTIVE 2 'Latter' also describes the second or end part of something E.G. *The latter part of his career.*
☑ You use *latter* to talk about the second of two items. To talk about the last of three or more items you should use *last-named*.

latterly
ADVERB; FORMAL Latterly means recently E.G. *It's only latterly that this has become an issue.*

lattice lattices
NOUN a structure made of strips which cross over each other diagonally leaving holes in between.

laudable
ADJECTIVE; FORMAL deserving praise E.G. *It is a laudable enough aim.*

laugh laughs laughing laughed
VERB 1 When you laugh, you make a noise which shows that you are amused or happy. ▶ NOUN 2 the noise you make when you laugh.
laughter NOUN

laughable
ADJECTIVE quite absurd.

laughing stock
NOUN someone who has been made to seem ridiculous.

launch launches launching launched
VERB 1 To launch a ship means to send it into the water for the first time.
2 To launch a rocket means to send it into space. 3 When a company launches a new product, they have an advertising campaign to promote it as they start to sell it. ▶ NOUN 4 a motorboat.

a
b
c
d
e
f
g
h
i
j
k
l
m
n
o
p
q
r
s
t
u
v
w
x
y
z

A Rude Idiot Thought He Might Eat Toffee In Church (<u>arithmetic</u>)   SPELLING NOTE

A B C D E F G H I J K L M N O P Q R S T U V W X Y Z

launch pad launch pads
NOUN A launch pad, or a launching pad, is the place from which space rockets take off.

launder launders laundering laundered
VERB; OLD-FASHIONED To launder clothes, sheets, or towels means to wash and iron them.

laundry laundries
NOUN 1 a business that washes and irons clothes and sheets. 2 Laundry is also the dirty clothes and sheets that are being washed, or are about to be washed.

laurel laurels
NOUN an evergreen tree with shiny leaves.

lava
NOUN Lava is the very hot liquid rock that comes shooting out of an erupting volcano, and becomes solid as it cools.

lavatory lavatories
NOUN a toilet.

lavender
NOUN 1 Lavender is a small bush with bluish-pink flowers that have a strong, pleasant scent. ▶ ADJECTIVE 2 bluish-pink.

lavish lavishes lavishing lavished
ADJECTIVE 1 If you are lavish, you are very generous with your time, money, or gifts. 2 A lavish amount is a large amount. ▶ VERB 3 If you lavish money or affection on someone, you give them a lot of it.
lavishly ADVERB

law laws
NOUN 1 The law is the system of rules developed by the government of a country, which regulate what people may and may not do and deals with

people who break these rules. 2 The law is also the profession of people such as lawyers, whose job involves the application of the laws of a country. 3 one of the rules established by a government or a religion, which tells people what they may or may not do. 4 a scientific fact which allows you to explain how things work in the physical world.
lawful ADJECTIVE **lawfully** ADVERB

law-abiding
ADJECTIVE obeying the law and not causing any trouble.

lawless
ADJECTIVE having no regard for the law.

lawn lawns
NOUN an area of cultivated grass.

lawnmower lawnmowers
NOUN a machine for cutting grass.

lawsuit lawsuits
NOUN a civil court case between two people, as opposed to the police prosecuting someone for a criminal offence.

lawyer lawyers
NOUN a person who is qualified in law, and whose job is to advise people about the law and represent them in court.

lax
ADJECTIVE careless and not keeping up the usual standards E.G. *a lax accounting system*.

laxative laxatives
NOUN something that you eat or drink to stop you being constipated.

lay lays laying laid
VERB 1 When you lay something somewhere, you put it down so that it lies there. 2 If you lay the table, you put cutlery on the table ready for a meal. 3 When a bird lays an egg, it

produces the egg out of its body. **4** If you lay a trap for someone, you create a situation in which you will be able to catch them out. **5** If you lay emphasis on something, you refer to it in a way that shows you think it is very important. **6** If you lay odds on something, you bet that it will happen. ▶ ADJECTIVE **7** You use 'lay' to describe people who are involved with a Christian church but are not members of the clergy E.G. *a lay preacher.* **8** Lay is the past tense of some senses of **lie**.

lay off VERB **1** When workers are laid off, their employers tell them not to come to work for a while because there is a shortage of work. **2** INFORMAL If you tell someone to lay off, you want them to stop doing something annoying.

lay on VERB If you lay on a meal or entertainment, you provide it

☑ People often get confused about *lay* and *lie*. The verb *lay* takes an object: *lay the table please… the Queen laid a wreath.* The verb *lie* does not take an object: *the book was lying on the table… I'm going to lie down.*

lay-by lay-bys
NOUN **1** an area by the side of a main road where motorists can stop for a short while. **2** In Australia and New Zealand, lay-by is a system where you pay a deposit on an item in a shop so that it will be kept for you until you pay the rest of the price.

layer layers
NOUN a single thickness of something E.G. *layers of clothing.*

layman laymen
NOUN **1** someone who does not have specialized knowledge of a subject E.G. *a layman's guide to computers.*

2 someone who belongs to the church but is not a member of the clergy.

layout layouts
NOUN The layout of something is the pattern in which it is arranged.

laze lazes lazing lazed
VERB If you laze, you relax and do no work E.G. *We spent a few days lazing around by the pool.*

lazy lazier laziest
ADJECTIVE idle and unwilling to work.
lazily ADVERB **laziness** NOUN
🔲 idle, indolent, slothful

lb
an abbreviation for 'pounds' E.G. *3lb of sugar.*

lbw
In cricket lbw is an abbreviation for 'leg before wicket', which is a way of dismissing a batsman when his legs prevent the ball from hitting the wicket.

leach leaches leaching leached
VERB When minerals are leached from rocks, they are dissolved by water which filters through the rock.

lead leads leading led
Rhymes with "feed" VERB **1** If you lead someone somewhere, you go in front of them in order to show them the way. **2** If one thing leads to another, it causes the second thing to happen. **3** a person who leads a group of people is in charge of them. ▶ NOUN **4** a length of leather or chain attached to a dog's collar, so that the dog can be kept under control. **5** If the police have a lead, they have a clue which might help them to solve a crime.

leading ADJECTIVE
🔲 (sense 1) conduct, escort, guide

a b c d e f g h i j k l m n o p q r s t u v w x y z

A B C D E F G H I J K L M N O P Q R S T U V W X Y Z

lead
Rhymes with "fed" NOUN Lead is a soft, grey, heavy metal.

leaden
Said "led-en" ADJECTIVE 1 dark grey E.G. *a leaden sky.* 2 heavy and slow-moving.

leader leaders
NOUN 1 someone who is in charge of a country, an organization, or a group of people. 2 the person who is winning in a competition or race. 3 a newspaper article that expresses the newspaper's opinions.

leadership
NOUN 1 the group of people in charge of an organization. 2 Leadership is the ability to be a good leader.

leaf leaves; leafs leafing leafed
NOUN 1 the flat green growth on the end of a twig or branch of a tree or other plant. ► VERB 2 If you leaf through a book, magazine, or newspaper, you turn the pages over quickly.
leafy ADJECTIVE

leaflet leaflets
NOUN a piece of paper with information or advertising printed on it.

league leagues
Said "leeg" NOUN 1 ⬭ PE ⬭ a group of countries, clubs, or people who have joined together for a particular purpose or because they share a common interest E.G. *the League of Red Cross Societies… the Australian Football League.* 2 a unit of distance used in former times, equal to about 3 miles.

leak leaks leaking leaked
VERB 1 If a pipe or container leaks, it has a hole which lets gas or liquid escape. 2 If liquid or gas leaks, it

escapes from a pipe or container. 3 If someone in an organization leaks information, they give the information to someone who is not supposed to have it E.G. *The letter was leaked to the press.* ► NOUN 4 If a pipe or container has a leak, it has a hole which lets gas or liquid escape. 5 If there is a leak in an organization, someone inside the organization is giving information to people who are not supposed to have it.
leaky ADJECTIVE

leakage leakages
NOUN an escape of gas or liquid from a pipe or container.

lean leans leaning leant or leaned; leaner leanest
VERB 1 When you lean in a particular direction, you bend your body in that direction. 2 When you lean on something, you rest your body against it for support. 3 If you lean on someone, you depend on them. 4 If you lean towards particular ideas, you approve of them and follow them E.G. *parents who lean towards strictness.* ► ADJECTIVE 5 having little or no fat E.G. *lean cuts of meat.* 6 A lean period is a time when food or money is in short supply.

leap leaps leaping leapt or leaped
VERB 1 If you leap somewhere, you jump over a long distance or high in the air. ► NOUN 2 a jump over a long distance or high in the air.

leap year leap years
NOUN a year, occurring every four years, in which there are 366 days.

learn learns learning learnt or learned
VERB 1 When you learn something,

you gain knowledge or a skill through studying or training. **2** If you learn of something, you find out about it E.G. *She had first learnt of the bomb attack that morning.*

learner NOUN

■ (sense 2) discover, find out, hear

learned

Said "ler-nid" ADJECTIVE A learned person has a lot of knowledge gained from years of study.

learning

NOUN Learning is knowledge that has been acquired through serious study.

lease leases leasing leased

NOUN **1** an agreement which allows someone to use a house or flat in return for rent. ► VERB **2** To lease property to someone means to allow them to use it in return for rent.

leash leashes

NOUN a length of leather or chain attached to a dog's collar so that the dog can be controlled.

least

NOUN **1** The least is the smallest possible amount of something. ► ADJECTIVE OR ADVERB **2** Least is a superlative form of **little.** ► PHRASE **3** You use **at least** to show that you are referring to the minimum amount of something, and that you think the true amount is greater E.G. *At least 200 hundred people were injured.*

leather

NOUN Leather is the tanned skin of some animals, used to make shoes and clothes.

leathery ADJECTIVE

leave leaves leaving left

VERB **1** When you leave a place, you go away from it. **2** If you leave someone somewhere, they stay behind after you go away. **3** If you leave a job or organization, you stop being part of it E.G. *He left his job shortly after Christmas.* **4** If someone leaves money or possessions to someone, they arrange for them to be given to them after their death. **5** In subtraction, when you take one number from another, it leaves a third number. ► NOUN **6** a period of holiday or absence from a job.

■ (sense 1) depart, exit, go

Lebanese

ADJECTIVE **1** belonging or relating to Lebanon. ► NOUN **2** someone who comes from Lebanon.

lecherous

ADJECTIVE constantly thinking about sex.

lectern lecterns

NOUN a sloping desk which people use to rest books or notes on.

lecture lectures lecturing lectured

NOUN **1** a formal talk intended to teach people about a particular subject. **2** a talk intended to tell someone off. ► VERB **3** Someone who lectures teaches in a college or university.

lecturer lecturers

NOUN a teacher in a college or university.

led

the past tense and past participle of **lead**.

ledge ledges

NOUN a narrow shelf on the side of a cliff or rock face, or on the outside of a building, directly under a window.

a b c d e f g h i j k l m n o p q r s t u v w x y z

A
B
C
D
E
F
G
H
I
J
K
L
M
N
O
P
Q
R
S
T
U
V
W
X
Y
Z

ledger ledgers

NOUN a book in which accounts are kept.

lee

NOUN 1 the sheltered side of a place E.G. *the lee of the mountain*. ▶ ADJECTIVE 2 the side of a ship away from the wind.

leech leeches

NOUN a small worm that lives in water and feeds by sucking the blood from other animals.

leek leeks

NOUN a long vegetable of the onion family, which is white at one end and has green leaves at the other.

leer leers leering leered

VERB 1 To leer at someone means to smile at them in an unpleasant or sexually suggestive way. ▶ NOUN 2 an unpleasant or sexually suggestive smile.

leeway

NOUN If something gives you some leeway, it allows you more flexibility in your plans, for example by giving you time to finish an activity.

left

NOUN 1 The left is one of two sides of something. For example, on a page, English writing begins on the left. 2 People and political groups who hold socialist or communist views are referred to as the Left. 3 Left is the past tense and past participle of **leave**. ▶ ADJECTIVE OR ADVERB 4 Left means on or towards the left side of something E.G. *Turn left down Govan Road*.

left-handed

ADJECTIVE OR ADVERB Someone who is left-handed does things such as writing with their left hand.

leftist leftists

NOUN OR ADJECTIVE someone who holds left-wing political views.

leftovers

PLURAL NOUN the bits of food which have not been eaten at the end of the meal.

left-wing

ADJECTIVE believing more strongly in socialism, or less strongly in capitalism or conservatism, than other members of the same party or group.

left-winger NOUN

leg legs

NOUN 1 Your legs are the two limbs which stretch from your hips to your feet. 2 The legs of a pair of trousers are the parts that cover your legs. 3 The legs of an object such as a table are the parts which rest on the floor and support the object's weight. 4 A leg of a journey is one part of it. 5 one of two matches played between two sports teams E.G. *He will miss the second leg of their UEFA Cup tie.*

legacy legacies

NOUN 1 property or money that someone gets in the will of a person who has died. 2 something that exists as a result of a previous event or time E.G. *the legacy of a Catholic upbringing.*

■ (sense 1) bequest, inheritance

legal

ADJECTIVE 1 relating to the law E.G. *the Dutch legal system*. 2 allowed by the law E.G. *The strike was perfectly legal.*

legally ADVERB

legal aid

NOUN Legal aid is a system which provides the services of a lawyer free, or very cheaply, to people who cannot afford the full fees.

legality

NOUN The legality of an action means whether or not it is allowed by the law E.G. *They challenged the legality of the scheme.*

legalize legalizes legalizing legalized; also spelt **legalise**

VERB To legalize something that is illegal means to change the law so that it becomes legal.

legalization NOUN

legend legends

NOUN 1 an old story which was once believed to be true, but which is probably untrue. 2 If you refer to someone or something as a legend, you mean they are very famous E.G. *His career has become a legend.*

legendary ADJECTIVE

leggings

PLURAL NOUN 1 Leggings are very close-fitting trousers made of stretch material, worn mainly by young women. 2 Leggings are also a waterproof covering worn over ordinary trousers to protect them.

legible

ADJECTIVE Writing that is legible is clear enough to be read.

legion legions

NOUN 1 In ancient Rome, a legion was a military unit of between 3000 and 6000 soldiers. 2 a large military force E.G. *the French Foreign Legion.* 3 Legions of people are large numbers of them.

legislate legislates legislating legislated

VERB; FORMAL When a government legislates, it creates new laws.

legislation

NOUN Legislation is a law or set of laws created by a government.

legislative

ADJECTIVE relating to the making of new laws E.G. *a legislative council.*

legislator legislators

NOUN; FORMAL a person involved in making or passing laws.

legislature

NOUN; FORMAL the parliament in a country, which is responsible for making new laws.

legitimate

Said "lij-it-tim-it" ADJECTIVE Something that is legitimate is reasonable or acceptable according to existing laws or standards E.G. *a legitimate charge for parking the car.*

legitimacy NOUN **legitimately** ADVERB

leisure

Rhymes with "measure" NOUN 1 Leisure is time during which you do not have to work, and can do what you enjoy doing. ▶ PHRASES 2 If you do something **at leisure**, or **at your leisure**, you do it at a convenient time.

leisurely

ADJECTIVE or ADVERB A leisurely action is done in an unhurried and calm way.

lekker

ADJECTIVE; SLANG 1 In South African English, lekker means pleasant. 2 In South African English, lekker can also mean tasty.

lemming lemmings

NOUN a small rodent which lives in cold, northern countries. Lemmings were believed in the past to jump off cliffs to their death in large numbers.

I want to see (C) your licenCe (licence)   **SPELLING NOTE**

a
b
c
d
e
f
g
h
i
j
k
l
m
n
o
p
q
r
s
t
u
v
w
x
y
z

lemon lemons

NOUN 1 a yellow citrus fruit with a sour taste. ▶ ADJECTIVE 2 pale yellow.

lemonade

NOUN a sweet, fizzy drink made from lemons, water, and sugar.

lend lends lending lent

VERB 1 If you lend someone something, you give it to them for a period of time and then they give it back to you. 2 If a bank lends money, it gives the money to someone and the money has to be repaid in the future, usually with interest. ▶ PHRASE 3 If you **lend someone a hand**, you help them.

lender NOUN

length lengths

NOUN 1 The length of something is the horizontal distance from one end to the other. 2 The length of an event or activity is the amount of time it lasts for. 3 The length of something is also the fact that it is long rather than short E.G. *Despite its length, it is a rewarding read.* 4 a long piece of something.

lengthen lengthens lengthening lengthened

VERB To lengthen something means to make it longer.

◼ elongate, extend, prolong

lengthways or **lengthwise**

ADVERB If you measure something lengthways, you measure the horizontal distance from one end to the other.

lengthy lengthier lengthiest

ADJECTIVE Something that is lengthy lasts for a long time.

lenient

ADJECTIVE If someone in authority is lenient, they are less severe than expected.

leniently ADVERB **leniency** NOUN

lens lenses

NOUN 1 a curved piece of glass designed to focus light in a certain way, for example in a camera, telescope, or pair of glasses. 2 The lens in your eye is the part behind the iris, which focuses light.

lent

1 the past tense and past participle of **lend**. ▶ NOUN 2 Lent is the period of forty days leading up to Easter, during which Christians give up something they enjoy.

lentil lentils

NOUN Lentils are small dried red or brown seeds which are cooked and eaten in soups and curries.

Leo

NOUN Leo is the fifth sign of the zodiac, represented by a lion. People born between July 23rd and August 22nd are born under this sign.

leopard leopards

NOUN a wild Asian or African big cat, with yellow fur and black or brown spots.

leotard leotards

Said "lee-eh-tard" NOUN a tight-fitting costume covering the body and legs, which is worn for dancing or exercise.

leper lepers

NOUN someone who has leprosy.

🏛 from Greek *lepros* meaning 'scaly'

leprosy

NOUN Leprosy is an infectious disease which attacks the skin and nerves, and which can lead to fingers or toes dropping off.

lesbian lesbians
NOUN a homosexual woman.
lesbianism NOUN

lesion lesions
Said "lee-shen" NOUN a wound or injury.

less
ADJECTIVE or ADVERB 1 Less means a smaller amount, or not as much in quality E.G. *They left less than three weeks ago… She had become less frightened of him now.* 2 Less is a comparative form of **little**.
▶ PREPOSITION 3 You use 'less' to show that you are subtracting one number from another E.G. *Eight less two leaves six.*
✓ You use *less* to talk about things that can't be counted: *less time.* When you are talking about amounts that can be counted you should use *fewer*.

-less
SUFFIX '-less' means without E.G. *hopeless… fearless.*
⬛ from an Old English suffix

lessen lessens lessening lessened
VERB If something lessens, it is reduced in amount, size, or quality.
▤ decrease, diminish, reduce

lesser
ADJECTIVE smaller in importance or amount than something else.

lesson lessons
NOUN 1 a fixed period of time during which a class of pupils is taught by a teacher. 2 an experience that makes you understand something important which you had not realized before.

lest
CONJUNCTION; OLD-FASHIONED as a precaution in case something

unpleasant or unwanted happens E.G. *I was afraid to open the door lest he should follow me.*

let lets letting let
VERB 1 If you let someone do something, you allow them to do it. 2 If someone lets a house or flat that they own, they rent it out. 3 You can say 'let's' or 'let us' when you want to suggest doing something with someone else E.G. *Let's go.* 4 If you let yourself in for something, you agree to do it although you do not really want to.

let off VERB 1 If someone in authority lets you off, they do not punish you for something you have done wrong. 2 If you let off a firework or explosive, you light it or detonate it.

lethal
Said "lee-thal" ADJECTIVE able to kill someone E.G. *a lethal weapon.*

lethargic
Said "lith-**ar**-jik" ADJECTIVE If you feel lethargic, you have no energy or enthusiasm.

lethargy
Said "**leth**-ar-jee" NOUN Lethargy is a lack of energy and enthusiasm.

letter letters
NOUN 1 Letters are written symbols which go together to make words. 2 a piece of writing addressed to someone, and usually sent through the post.

letter box letter boxes
NOUN 1 an oblong gap in the front door of a house or flat, through which letters are delivered. 2 a large metal container in the street, where you post letters.

a
b
c
d
e
f
g
h
i
j
k
l
m
n
o
p
q
r
s
t
u
v
w
x
y
z

have a pIEce of pIE (pie̱ce)   ◀ SPELLING NOTE

A
B
C
D
E
F
G
H
I
J
K
L
M
N
O
P
Q
R
S
T
U
V
W
X
Y
Z

lettering

NOUN Lettering is writing, especially when you are describing the type of letters used E.G. *bold lettering*.

lettuce lettuces

NOUN a vegetable with large green leaves eaten raw in salad.

leukaemia or **leukemia**

Said "loo-**kee**-mee-a" NOUN Leukaemia is a serious illness which affects the blood.

level levels levelling levelled

ADJECTIVE 1 A surface that is level is smooth, flat, and parallel to the ground. ▶ VERB 2 To level a piece of land means to make it flat. 3 If you level a criticism at someone, you say or write something critical about them. ▶ ADVERB 4 If you draw level with someone, you get closer to them so that you are moving next to them. ▶ NOUN 5 a point on a scale which measures the amount, importance, or difficulty of something. 6 The level of a liquid is the height it comes up to in a container.

■ (sense 5) grade, position, stage

level off or **level out**

VERB If something levels off or levels out, it stops increasing or decreasing E.G. *Profits are beginning to level off.*

level crossing level crossings

NOUN a place where road traffic is allowed to drive across a railway track.

level-headed

ADJECTIVE Someone who is level-headed is sensible and calm in emergencies.

lever levers

NOUN 1 a handle on a machine that you pull in order to make the machine work. 2 a long bar that you wedge underneath a heavy object and press down on to make the object move.

leverage

NOUN Leverage is knowledge or influence that you can use to make someone do something.

leveret leverets

NOUN a young hare.

levy levies levying levied

Said "**lev**-ee" NOUN 1 FORMAL an amount of money that you pay in tax. ▶ VERB 2 When a government levies a tax, it makes people pay the tax and organizes the collection of the money.

lewd

Rhymes with "**rude**" ADJECTIVE sexually coarse and crude.

lexicography

NOUN the profession of writing dictionaries.

lexicographer NOUN

🔳 from Greek *lexis* meaning 'word' and *graphein* meaning 'to write'

liability liabilities

NOUN 1 Someone's liability is their responsibility for something they have done wrong. 2 In business, a company's liabilities are its debts. 3 INFORMAL If you describe someone as a liability, you mean that they cause a lot of problems or embarrassment.

liable

ADJECTIVE 1 If you say that something is liable to happen, you mean that you think it will probably happen. 2 If you are liable for something you have done, you are legally responsible for it.

☑ It used to be wrong to use *liable* to mean 'probable or likely', but that use is now considered correct.

liaise liaises liaising liaised
Said "lee-*aze*" VERB To liaise with someone or an organization means to cooperate with them and keep them informed.

liaison liaisons
Said "lee-*aze*-on" NOUN Liaison is communication between two organizations or two sections of an organization.

liar liars
NOUN a person who tells lies.

libel libels libelling libelled
Said "*lie*-bel" NOUN 1 Libel is something written about someone which is not true, and for which the writer can be made to pay damages in court. ▶ VERB 2 To libel someone means to write or say something untrue about them.
libellous ADJECTIVE

liberal liberals
NOUN 1 someone who believes in political progress, social welfare, and individual freedom. ▶ ADJECTIVE 2 Someone who is liberal is tolerant of a wide range of behaviour, standards, or opinions. 3 To be liberal with something means to be generous with it. 4 A liberal quantity of something is a large amount of it.
liberally ADVERB **liberalism** NOUN
📖 from Latin *liberalis* meaning 'of freedom'

Liberal Democrat Liberal Democrats
NOUN In Britain, a member or supporter of the Liberal Democrats, a political party that believes that individuals should have more rights and freedom.

liberate liberates liberating liberated
VERB To liberate people means to free them from prison or from an unpleasant situation.
liberation NOUN **liberator** NOUN

liberty
NOUN Liberty is the freedom to choose how you want to live, without government restrictions.

libido libidos
Said "lib *bee* doe" NOUN Someone's libido is their sexual drive.
📖 from Latin *libido* meaning 'desire'

Libra
NOUN Libra is the seventh sign of the zodiac, represented by a pair of scales. People born between September 23rd and October 22nd are born under this sign.

librarian librarians
NOUN (LIBRARY) a person who works in, or is in charge of, a library.

library libraries
NOUN 1 a building in which books are kept for people to come and read or borrow. 2 a collection of books, records, or videos.

Libyan Libyans
ADJECTIVE 1 belonging or relating to Libya. ▶ NOUN 2 someone who comes from Libya.

lice
the plural of **louse**.

licence licences
NOUN 1 an official document which entitles you to carry out a particular activity, for example to drive a car. 2 Licence is the freedom to do what you want, especially when other people consider that it is being used irresponsibly.
☑ The noun *licence* ends in *ce*.

a
b
c
d
e
f
g
h
i
j
k
l
m
n
o
p
q
r
s
t
u
v
w
x
y
z

A
B
C
D
E
F
G
H
I
J
K
L
M
N
O
P
Q
R
S
T
U
V
W
X
Y
Z

license licenses licensing licensed

VERB To license an activity means to give official permission for it to be carried out

☑ The verb *license* ends in *se*.

lichen lichens

Said "lie-ken" NOUN Lichen is a green, moss-like growth on rocks or tree trunks.

lick licks licking licked

VERB 1 If you lick something, you move your tongue over it. ▶ NOUN 2 the action of licking.

lid lids

NOUN the top of a container, which you open in order to reach what is inside.

lie lies lying lay lain

VERB 1 To lie somewhere means to rest there horizontally. 2 If you say where something lies, you are describing where it is E.G. *The farm lies between two valleys.*

☑ The past tense of this verb *lie* is *lay*. Do not confuse it with the verb *lay* meaning 'put'.

lie lies lying lied

VERB 1 To lie means to say something that is not true. ▶ NOUN 2 something you say which is not true.

lieu

Said "lyoo" PHRASE If one thing happens **in lieu** of another, it happens instead of it.

lieutenant lieutenants

Said "lef-ten-ent" NOUN a junior officer in the army or navy.

🔤 from Old French *lieutenant* meaning literally 'holding a place'

life lives

NOUN 1 Life is the quality of being able to grow and develop, which is present in people, plants, and animals. 2 Your life is your existence from the time you are born until the time you die. 3 The life of a machine is the period of time for which it is likely to work. 4 If you refer to the life in a place, you are talking about the amount of activity there E.G. *The town was full of life.* 5 If criminals are sentenced to life, they are sent to prison for the rest of their lives, or until they are granted parole.

life assurance

NOUN Life assurance is an insurance which provides a sum of money in the event of the policy holder's death.

lifeblood

NOUN The lifeblood of something is the most essential part of it.

lifeboat lifeboats

NOUN 1 a boat kept on shore, which is sent out to rescue people who are in danger at sea. 2 a small boat kept on a ship, which is used if the ship starts to sink.

life expectancy life expectancies

NOUN Your life expectancy is the number of years you can expect to live.

lifeguard lifeguards

NOUN a person whose job is to rescue people who are in difficulty in the sea or in a swimming pool.

life jacket life jackets

NOUN a sleeveless inflatable jacket that keeps you afloat in water.

lifeless

ADJECTIVE 1 Someone who is lifeless is dead. 2 If you describe a place or person as lifeless, you mean that they are dull.

SPELLING NOTE ▶ You must practiSe your Ss (practi*se*)

lifelike
ADJECTIVE A picture or sculpture that is lifelike looks very real or alive.

lifeline lifelines
NOUN 1 something which helps you to survive or helps an activity to continue. 2 a rope thrown to someone who is in danger of drowning.

lifelong
ADJECTIVE existing throughout someone's life E.G. *He had a lifelong interest in music.*

lifesaver lifesavers
NOUN In Australia and New Zealand, a person whose job is to rescue people who are in difficulty in the sea.

life span life spans
NOUN 1 Someone's life span is the length of time during which they are alive. 2 The life span of a product or organization is the length of time it exists or is useful.

lifetime lifetimes
NOUN Your lifetime is the period of time during which you are alive.

lift lifts lifting lifted
VERB 1 To lift something means to move it to a higher position. 2 When fog or mist lifts, it clears away. 3 To lift a ban on something means to remove it. 4 INFORMAL To lift things means to steal them. ► NOUN 5 a machine like a large box which carries passengers from one floor to another in a building. 6 If you give someone a lift, you drive them somewhere in a car or on a motorcycle.
▣ (sense 1) elevate, raise

ligament ligaments
NOUN a piece of tough tissue in your body which connects your bones.

light lights lighting lighted or lit; lighter lightest
NOUN 1 Light is brightness from the sun, fire, or lamps, that enables you to see things. 2 a lamp or other device that gives out brightness. 3 If you give someone a light, you give them a match or lighter to light their cigarette. ► ADJECTIVE 4 A place that is light is bright because of the sun or the use of lamps. 5 A light colour is pale. 6 A light object does not weigh much. 7 A light task is fairly easy. 8 Light books or music are entertaining and are not intended to be serious. ► VERB 9 To light a place means to cause it to be filled with light. 10 To light a fire means to make it start burning. 11 To light upon something means to find it by accident.
lightly ADVERB   **lightness** NOUN

lighten lightens lightening lightened
VERB 1 When something lightens, it becomes less dark. 2 To lighten a load means to make it less heavy.

lighter lighters
NOUN a device for lighting a cigarette or cigar.

light-headed
ADJECTIVE If you feel light-headed, you feel slightly dizzy or drunk.

light-hearted
ADJECTIVE Someone who is light-hearted is cheerful and has no worries.
▣ blithe, carefree, happy-go-lucky

lighthouse lighthouses
NOUN a tower by the sea, which sends out a powerful light to guide ships and warn them of danger.

a
b
c
d
e
f
g
h
i
j
k
l
m
n
o
p
q
r
s
t
u
v
w
x
y
z

lighting
NOUN **1** The lighting in a room or building is the way that it is lit. **2** (DRAMA) Lighting in the theatre or for a film is the special lights that are directed on the performers or scene.

lightning
NOUN Lightning is the bright flashes of light in the sky which are produced by natural electricity during a thunder storm.

lightweight lightweights
NOUN **1** a boxer in one of the lighter weight groups. ► ADJECTIVE **2** Something that is lightweight does not weigh very much E.G. *a lightweight jacket.*

light year light years
NOUN a unit of distance equal to the distance that light travels in a year.

likable or **likeable**
ADJECTIVE Someone who is likable is very pleasant and friendly.

like likes liking liked
PREPOSITION **1** If one thing is like another, it is similar to it. ► NOUN **2** 'The like' means other similar things of the sort just mentioned E.G. *nappies, prams, cots, and the like.* ► PHRASE **3** If you **feel like** something, you want to do it or have it E.G. *I feel like a walk.* ► VERB **4** If you like something or someone, you find them pleasant.

-like
SUFFIX '-like' means resembling or similar to E.G. *a balloonlike object.*

likelihood
NOUN If you say that there is a likelihood that something will happen, you mean that you think it will probably happen.

likely likelier likeliest
ADJECTIVE Something that is likely will probably happen or is probably true.

liken likens likening likened
VERB If you liken one thing to another, you say that they are similar.

likeness likenesses
NOUN If two things have a likeness to each other, they are similar in appearance.

likewise
ADVERB Likewise means similarly E.G. *She sat down and he did likewise.*

liking
NOUN If you have a liking for someone or something, you like them.

lilac
NOUN **1** a shrub with large clusters of pink, white, or mauve flowers. ► ADJECTIVE **2** pale mauve.

lilt lilts
NOUN A lilt in someone's voice is a pleasant rising and falling sound in it.
lilting ADJECTIVE

lily lilies
NOUN a plant with trumpet-shaped flowers of various colours.

limb limbs
NOUN **1** Your limbs are your arms and legs. **2** The limbs of a tree are its branches. ► PHRASE **3** If you have gone **out on a limb**, you have said or done something risky.

limber up limbers up limbering up limbered up
VERB If you limber up, you stretch your muscles before doing a sport.

limbo
NOUN **1** If you are in limbo, you are in an uncertain situation over which you feel you have no control. **2** The limbo is a West Indian dance in

which the dancer has to pass under a low bar while leaning backwards. 📖 sense 1 is from Latin *in limbo* meaning 'on the border (of Hell)'

lime limes
NOUN **1** a small, green citrus fruit, rather like a lemon. **2** A lime tree is a large tree with pale green leaves. **3** Lime is a chemical substance that is used in cement and as a fertilizer.

limelight
NOUN If someone is in the limelight, they are getting a lot of attention.

limerick limericks
NOUN an amusing nonsense poem of five lines.

limestone
NOUN Limestone is a white rock which is used for building and making cement.

limit limits limiting limited
NOUN **1** a boundary or an extreme beyond which something cannot go E.G. *the speed limit.* ▶ VERB **2** To limit something means to prevent it from becoming bigger, spreading, or making progress E.G. *He did all he could to limit the damage.*

limitation limitations
NOUN **1** The limitation of something is the reducing or controlling of it. **2** If you talk about the limitations of a person or thing, you are talking about the limits of their abilities.

limited
ADJECTIVE Something that is limited is rather small in amount or extent E.G. *a limited number of bedrooms.*

limousine limousines
Said "lim-o-zeen" NOUN a large, luxurious car, usually driven by a chauffeur.

limp limps limping limped; limper limpest
VERB **1** If you limp, you walk unevenly because you have hurt your leg or foot. ▶ NOUN **2** an uneven way of walking. ▶ ADJECTIVE **3** Something that is limp is soft and floppy, and not stiff or firm E.G. *a limp lettuce.*

limpet limpets
NOUN a shellfish with a pointed shell, that attaches itself very firmly to rocks.

line lines lining lined
NOUN **1** a long, thin mark. **2** a number of people or things positioned one behind the other. **3** a route along which someone or something moves E.G. *a railway line.* **4** In a piece of writing, a line is a number of words together E.G. *I often used to change my lines as an actor.* **5** Someone's line of work is the kind of work they do. **6** The line someone takes is the attitude they have towards something E.G. *He took a hard line with terrorism.* **7** In a shop or business, a line is a type of product E.G. *That line has been discontinued.* ▶ VERB **8** To line something means to cover its inside surface or edge with something E.G. *Cottages lined the edge of the harbour.*

line up VERB **1** When people line up, they stand in a line. **2** When you line something up, you arrange it for a special occasion E.G. *A tour is being lined up for July.*

lineage lineages
Said "lin-ee-ij" NOUN Someone's lineage is all the people from whom they are directly descended.

linear
Said "lin-ee-ar" ADJECTIVE arranged in a

a b c d e f g h i j k l m n o p q r s t u v w x y z

line or in a strict sequence, or happening at a constant rate.

line dancing

NOUN a type of dancing performed by rows of people to country music.

linen

NOUN ⟨D&T⟩ **1** Linen is a type of cloth made from a plant called flax. **2** Linen is also household goods made of cloth, such as sheets and tablecloths.

liner liners

NOUN a large passenger ship that makes long journeys.

linesman linesmen

NOUN an official at a sports match who watches the lines of the field or court and indicates when the ball goes outside them.

-ling

SUFFIX '-ling' means 'small' E.G. *duckling*.

🔲 from an Old English suffix

linger lingers lingering lingered

VERB To linger means to remain for a long time E.G. *Economic problems lingered in the background*.

lingerie

Said "lan-jer-ee" NOUN Lingerie is women's nightclothes and underclothes.

lingo lingoes

NOUN; INFORMAL a foreign language.

linguist linguists

NOUN someone who studies foreign languages or the way in which language works.

lining linings

NOUN any material used to line the inside of something.

link links linking linked

NOUN **1** a relationship or connection between two things E.G. *the link*

between sunbathing and skin cancer. **2** a physical connection between two things or places E.G. *a high-speed rail link between the cities*. **3** one of the rings in a chain. ▶ VERB **4** To link people, places, or things means to join them together.

linkage NOUN

lino

NOUN Lino is the same as linoleum.

linoleum

NOUN a floor covering with a shiny surface.

lint

NOUN soft cloth made from linen, used to dress wounds.

lion lions

NOUN a large member of the cat family which comes from Africa. Lions have light brown fur, and the male has a long mane. A female lion is called a lioness.

lip lips

NOUN **1** Your lips are the edges of your mouth. **2** The lip of a jug is the slightly pointed part through which liquids are poured out.

lip-read lip-reads lip-reading lip-read

VERB To lip-read means to watch someone's lips when they are talking in order to understand what they are saying. Deaf people often lip-read.

lipstick lipsticks

NOUN a coloured substance which women wear on their lips.

liqueur liqueurs

Said "lik-yoor" NOUN a strong sweet alcoholic drink, usually drunk after a meal.

liquid liquids ⟨SCIENCE⟩

NOUN **1** any substance which is not a solid or a gas, and which can be

A B C D E F G H I J K L M N O P Q R S T U V W X Y Z

poured. ► ADJECTIVE **2** Something that is liquid is in the form of a liquid E.G. *liquid nitrogen*. **3** In commerce and finance a person's or company's liquid assets are the things that can be sold quickly to raise cash.

liquidate liquidates liquidating liquidated

VERB **1** To liquidate a company means to close it down and to use its assets to pay off its debts. **2** INFORMAL To liquidate a person means to murder them.

liquidation NOUN　**liquidator** NOUN

liquor

NOUN Liquor is any strong alcoholic drink.

liquorice

Said "lik-ker-iss" NOUN Liquorice is a root used to flavour sweets; also the sweets themselves.

lira lire

NOUN a unit of currency formerly used in Italy.

lisp lisps lisping lisped

NOUN **1** Someone who has a lisp pronounces the sounds 's' and 'z' like 'th'. ► VERB **2** To lisp means to speak with a lisp.

list lists listing listed

NOUN **1** a set of words or items written one below the other. ► VERB **2** If you list a number of things, you make a list of them.

listen listens listening listened

VERB If you listen to something, you hear it and pay attention to it.

listener NOUN

listless

ADJECTIVE lacking energy and enthusiasm.

listlessly ADVERB

🔲 from Old English *list* meaning 'desire'

lit

a past tense and past participle of **light**.

litany litanies

NOUN **1** a part of a church service in which the priest says or chants prayers and the people give responses. **2** something, especially a list of things, that is repeated often or in a boring or insincere way E.G. *a tedious litany of complaints*.

literacy

NOUN Literacy is the ability to read and write.

literate ADJECTIVE

literal

ADJECTIVE **1** The literal meaning of a word is its most basic meaning. **2** A literal translation from a foreign language is one that has been translated exactly word for word.

literally ADVERB

✅ Be careful where you use *literally*. It can emphasize something without changing the meaning: *the house was literally only five minutes walk away*. However, it can make nonsense of some things: *he literally swept me off my feet*. This sentence is ridiculous unless *he* actually took a broom and swept the speaker over.

literary

ADJECTIVE connected with literature E.G. *literary critics*.

literature

NOUN **1** Literature consists of novels, plays, and poetry. **2** The literature on a subject is everything that has been written about it.

lithe

ADJECTIVE supple and graceful.

litmus

NOUN In chemistry, litmus is a

Rhythmical Hounds Yap To Heavy Music (**rhythm**) SPELLING NOTE

A
B
C
D
E
F
G
H
I
J
K
L
M
N
O
P
Q
R
S
T
U
V
W
X
Y
Z

substance that turns red under acid and blue under alkali conditions.

litmus test litmus tests
NOUN something which is regarded as a simple and accurate test of a particular thing, such as a person's attitude to an issue E.G. *The conflict was seen as a litmus test of Britain's will to remain a major power.*

litre litres
NOUN (MATHS) a unit of liquid volume equal to about 1.76 pints.

litter litters littering littered
NOUN 1 Litter is rubbish in the street and other public places. 2 Cat litter is a gravelly substance you put in a container where you want your cat to urinate and defecate. 3 a number of baby animals born at the same time to the same mother. ► VERB 4 If things litter a place, they are scattered all over it.

little less lesser least
ADJECTIVE 1 small in size or amount. ► NOUN or ADVERB 2 A little is a small amount or degree E.G. *Would you like a little fruit juice?* 3 Little also means not much E.G. *He has little to say.*

live lives living lived
VERB 1 If you live in a place, that is where your home is. 2 To live means to be alive. 3 If something lives up to your expectations, it is as good as you thought it would be. ► ADJECTIVE or ADVERB 4 Live television or radio is broadcast while the event is taking place E.G. *a live football match… The concert will go out live.* ► ADJECTIVE 5 Live animals or plants are alive, rather than dead or artificial E.G. *a live spider.* 6 Something is live if it is directly connected to an electricity supply E.G. *Careful – those wires are*

live. 7 Live bullets or ammunition have not yet been exploded.

live down VERB If you cannot live down a mistake or failure, you cannot make people forget it.

livelihood livelihoods
NOUN Someone's livelihood is their job or the source of their income.

lively
ADJECTIVE full of life and enthusiasm E.G. *lively conversation.*
liveliness NOUN
▤ brisk, energetic, vigorous

liven livens livening livened
VERB To liven things up means to make them more lively or interesting.

liver livers
NOUN 1 Your liver is a large organ in your body which cleans your blood and helps digestion. 2 Liver is also the liver of some animals, which may be cooked and eaten.
▥ from Greek *liparos* meaning 'fat'

livestock
NOUN Livestock is farm animals.

livid
ADJECTIVE 1 extremely angry. 2 dark purple or bluish E.G. *livid bruises.*

living
ADJECTIVE 1 If someone is living, they are alive E.G. *her only living relative.* ► NOUN 2 The work you do for a living is the work you do in order to earn money to live.

living room living rooms
NOUN the room where people relax and entertain in their homes.

lizard lizards
NOUN a long, thin, dry-skinned reptile found in hot, dry countries.

llama llamas
NOUN a South American animal

related to the camel.

load loads loading loaded
NOUN 1 something being carried.
2 INFORMAL Loads means a lot E.G.
loads of work. ▶ VERB 3 To load a
vehicle or animal means to put a
large number of things into it or
onto it.

loaf loaves; loafs loafing loafed
NOUN 1 a large piece of bread baked
in a shape that can be cut into slices.
▶ VERB 2 To loaf around means to be
lazy and not do any work.

loan loans loaning loaned
NOUN 1 a sum of money that you
borrow. 2 the act of borrowing or
lending something E.G. *I am grateful
to Jane for the loan of her book*. ▶ VERB
3 If you loan something to someone,
you lend it to them.

loath
Rhymes with "both" ADJECTIVE If you
are loath to do something, you are
very unwilling to do it
☑ Do not confuse *loath* with *loathe*.

loathe loathes loathing loathed
VERB To loathe someone or
something means to feel strong
dislike for them.
loathing NOUN **loathsome** ADJECTIVE
☑ Do not confuse *loathe* with *loath*.

lob lobs lobbing lobbed
VERB 1 If you lob something, you
throw it high in the air. ▶ NOUN 2 In
tennis, a lob is a stroke in which the
player hits the ball high in the air.

lobby lobbies lobbying lobbied
NOUN 1 The lobby in a building is the
main entrance area with corridors
and doors leading off it. 2 a group of
people trying to persuade an
organization that something should
be done E.G. *the environmental*

lobby. ▶ VERB 3 To lobby an MP or an
organization means to try to
persuade them to do something, for
example by writing them lots of
letters.

lobe lobes
NOUN 1 The lobe of your ear is the
rounded soft part at the bottom.
2 any rounded part of something
E.G. *the frontal lobe of the brain*.

lobster lobsters
NOUN an edible shellfish with two
front claws and eight legs.

local locals
ADJECTIVE 1 Local means in, near, or
belonging to the area in which you
live E.G. *the local newspaper*. 2 A local
anaesthetic numbs only one part of
your body and does not send you to
sleep. ▶ NOUN 3 The locals are the
people who live in a particular area.
4 INFORMAL Someone's local is the pub
nearest their home.

locally ADVERB
■ (sense 1) provincial, regional

locality localities
NOUN an area of a country or city E.G.
a large map of the locality.

localized or **localised**
ADJECTIVE existing or happening in
only one place E.G. *localized pain*.

locate locates locating located
VERB 1 To locate someone or
something means to find out where
they are. 2 If something is located in
a place, it is in that place

location locations
NOUN 1 (GEOGRAPHY) a place, or the
position of something. 2 In South
Africa, a location was a small town
where only Black people or Coloured
people were allowed to live. ▶ PHRASE
3 If a film is made **on location**, it is

a
b
c
d
e
f
g
h
i
j
k
l
m
n
o
p
q
r
s
t
u
v
w
x
y
z

A
B
C
D
E
F
G
H
I
J
K
L
M
N
O
P
Q
R
S
T
U
V
W
X
Y
Z

made away from a studio.
■ (sense 1) place, position

loch lochs
NOUN In Scottish English, a loch is a lake.

lock locks locking locked
VERB 1 If you lock something, you close it and fasten it with a key. 2 If something locks into place, it moves into place and becomes firmly fixed there. ▶ NOUN 3 a device on something which fastens it and prevents it from being opened except with a key. 4 A lock on a canal is a place where the water level can be raised or lowered to allow boats to go between two parts of the canal which have different water levels. 5 A lock of hair is a small bunch of hair.

locker lockers
NOUN a small cupboard for your personal belongings, for example in a changing room.

locket lockets
NOUN a piece of jewellery consisting of a small case which you can keep a photograph in, and which you wear on a chain round your neck.

locksmith locksmiths
NOUN a person who makes or mends locks.

locomotive locomotives
NOUN a railway engine.

locust locusts
NOUN an insect like a large grasshopper, which travels in huge swarms and eats crops.

lodge lodges lodging lodged
NOUN 1 a small house in the grounds of a large country house, or a small house used for holidays. ▶ VERB 2 If you lodge in someone else's house, you live there and pay them rent. 3 If something lodges somewhere, it

gets stuck there E.G. *The bullet lodged in his pelvis.* 4 If you lodge a complaint, you formally make it.

lodger lodgers
NOUN a person who lives in someone's house and pays rent.

lodgings
PLURAL NOUN If you live in lodgings, you live in someone else's house and pay them rent.

loft lofts
NOUN the space immediately under the roof of a house, often used for storing things.

lofty loftier loftiest
ADJECTIVE 1 very high E.G. *a lofty hall.* 2 very noble and important E.G. *lofty ideals.* 3 proud and superior E.G. *her lofty manner.*

log logs logging logged
NOUN 1 a thick branch or piece of tree trunk which has fallen or been cut down. 2 the captain's official record of everything that happens on board a ship. ▶ VERB 3 If you log something, you officially make a record of it, for example in a ship's log. 4 To log into a computer system means to gain access to it, usually by giving your name and password. To log out means to finish using the system.

logic
NOUN Logic is a way of reasoning involving a series of statements, each of which must be true if the statement before it is true.

logical
ADJECTIVE 1 A logical argument uses logic. 2 A logical course of action or decision is sensible or reasonable in the circumstances E.G. *the logical conclusion.*
logically ADVERB

logistics
NOUN; FORMAL The logistics of a complicated undertaking is the skilful organization of it.

logo logos
Said "**loh**-goh" NOUN The logo of an organization is a special design that is put on all its products.
▣ from Greek *logos* meaning 'word'

-logy
SUFFIX '-logy' is used to form words that refer to the study of something E.G. *biology… geology.*
▣ from Greek *logos* meaning 'reason', 'speech', or 'discourse'

loin loins
NOUN 1 OLD-FASHIONED Your loins are the front part of your body between your waist and your thighs, especially your sexual parts. 2 Loin is a piece of meat from the back or sides of an animal E.G. *loin of pork.*

loiter loiters loitering loitered
VERB To loiter means to stand about idly with no real purpose.

loll lolls lolling lolled
VERB 1 If you loll somewhere, you sit or lie there in an idle, relaxed way. 2 If your head or tongue lolls, it hangs loosely.

lollipop lollipops
NOUN a hard sweet on the end of a stick.

lolly lollies
NOUN 1 a lollipop. 2 a piece of flavoured ice or ice cream on a stick. 3 In Australian and New Zealand English, a sweet.

lolly scramble lolly scrambles
NOUN In New Zealand, a lolly scramble is a lot of sweets thrown on the ground for children to pick up.

lone
ADJECTIVE A lone person or thing is the only one in a particular place E.G. *a lone climber.*
▤ single, solitary

lonely lonelier loneliest
ADJECTIVE 1 If you are lonely, you are unhappy because you are alone. 2 A lonely place is an isolated one which very few people visit E.G. *a lonely hillside.*
loneliness NOUN

loner loners
NOUN a person who likes to be alone.

lonesome
ADJECTIVE lonely and sad.

long longer longest; longs longing longed
ADJECTIVE or ADVERB 1 continuing for a great amount of time E.G. *There had been no rain for a long time… The equipment will not last much longer.*
▶ ADJECTIVE 2 great in length or distance E.G. *a long dress… a long road.* ▶ PHRASE 3 If something **no longer** happens, it does not happen any more. 4 **Before long** means soon. 5 If one thing is true **as long as** another thing is true, it is true only if the other thing is true. ▶ VERB 6 If you long for something, you want it very much.
longing NOUN

longevity
Said "lon-**jev**-it-ee" NOUN; FORMAL Longevity is long life.

longhand
NOUN If you write something in longhand, you do it in your own handwriting rather than using shorthand or a typewriter.

longitude longitudes
NOUN (GEOGRAPHY) The longitude of a

a
b
c
d
e
f
g
h
i
j
k
l
m
n
o
p
q
r
s
t
u
v
w
x
y
z

A
B
C
D
E
F
G
H
I
J
K
L
M
N
O
P
Q
R
S
T
U
V
W
X
Y
Z

place is its distance east or west of a line passing through Greenwich, measured in degrees.

long jump
NOUN The long jump is an athletics event in which you jump as far as possible after taking a long run.

long-range
ADJECTIVE 1 able to be used over a great distance E.G. *long-range artillery*. 2 extending a long way into the future E.G. *a long-range weather forecast*.

long-sighted
ADJECTIVE If you are long-sighted, you have difficulty seeing things that are close.

long-standing
ADJECTIVE having existed for a long time E.G. *a long-standing tradition*.

long-suffering
ADJECTIVE very patient E.G. *her long-suffering husband*.

long-term
ADJECTIVE extending a long way into the future E.G. *a long-term investment*.

long-winded
ADJECTIVE long and boring E.G. *a long-winded letter*.

loo loos
NOUN; INFORMAL a toilet.

look looks looking looked
VERB 1 If you look at something, you turn your eyes towards it so that you can see it. 2 If you look for someone or something, you try to find them. 3 If you look at a subject or situation, you study it or judge it. 4 If you look down on someone, you think that they are inferior to you. 5 If you are looking forward to something, you want it to happen because you think

you will enjoy it. 6 If you look up to someone, you admire and respect them. 7 If you describe the way that something looks, you are describing its appearance. ► NOUN 8 If you have a look at something, you look at it. 9 The look on your face is the expression on it. 10 If you talk about someone's looks, you are talking about how attractive they are.
► INTERJECTION 11 You say 'look out' to warn someone of danger.
■ (sense 1) gaze, glance, see, watch
■ (sense 8) glance, glimpse, peek
■ (sense 9) appearance, expression

look after VERB If you look after someone or something, you take care of them.

look up VERB 1 To look up information means to find it out in a book. 2 If you look someone up, you go to see them after not having seen them for a long time. 3 If a situation is looking up, it is improving.

lookalike lookalikes
NOUN a person who looks very like someone else E.G. *an Elvis lookalike*.

lookout lookouts
NOUN 1 someone who is watching for danger, or a place where they watch for danger. ► PHRASE 2 If you are **on the lookout** for something, you are watching for it or waiting expectantly for it.

loom looms looming loomed
NOUN 1 a machine for weaving cloth.
► VERB 2 If something looms in front of you, it suddenly appears as a tall, unclear, and sometimes frightening shape. 3 If a situation or event is looming, it is likely to happen soon and is rather worrying.

loony loonies INFORMAL
ADJECTIVE 1 People or behaviour can be

described as loony if they are mad or eccentric. ▶ NOUN **2** a mad or eccentric person.

loop loops looping looped
NOUN **1** a curved or circular shape in something long such as a piece of string. ▶ VERB **2** If you loop rope or string around an object, you place it in a loop around the object.

loophole loopholes
NOUN a small mistake or omission in the law which allows you to do something that the law really intends that you should not do.

loose looser loosest
ADJECTIVE **1** If something is loose, it is not firmly held, fixed, or attached. **2** Loose clothes are rather large and do not fit closely. ▶ ADVERB **3** To set animals loose means to set them free after they have been tied up or kept in a cage.
loosely ADVERB
☑ The adjective and adverb *loose* is spelt with two *o*s. Do not confuse it with the verb *lose*.

loosen loosens loosening loosened
VERB To loosen something means to make it looser.

loot loots looting looted
VERB **1** To loot shops and houses means to steal goods from them during a battle or riot. ▶ NOUN **2** Loot is stolen money or goods.
🔲 from Hindi *lut*
🔳 (sense 1) pillage, plunder, ransack
🔳 (sense 2) booty, plunder, spoils

lop lops lopping lopped
VERB If you lop something off, you cut it off with one quick stroke.

lopsided
ADJECTIVE Something that is lopsided

is uneven because its two sides are different sizes or shapes.

lord lords
NOUN **1** a nobleman. **2** Lord is a title used in front of the names of some noblemen, and of bishops, archbishops, judges, and some high-ranking officials E.G. *the Lord Mayor of London*. **3** In Christianity, Lord is a name given to God and Jesus Christ.

Lordship Lordships
NOUN You address a lord, judge, or bishop as Your Lordship.

lore
NOUN The lore of a place, people, or subject is all the traditional knowledge and stories about it.

lorikeet lorikeets
NOUN a type of small parrot found in Australia.

lorry lorries
NOUN a large vehicle for transporting goods by road.

lory lories
Said "law-ree" NOUN a small, brightly coloured parrot found in Australia.

lose loses losing lost
VERB **1** If you lose something, you cannot find it, or you no longer have it because it has been taken away from you E.G. *I lost my airline ticket*. **2** If you lose a relative or friend, they die E.G. *She lost her brother in the war*. **3** If you lose a fight or an argument, you are beaten. **4** If a business loses money, it is spending more money than it is earning.
loser NOUN
☑ The verb *lose* is spelt with one *o*. Do not confuse it with the adjective and adverb *loose*.

loss losses
NOUN **1** The loss of something is the

a b c d e f g h i j k l m n o p q r s t u v w x y z

A
B
C
D
E
F
G
H
I
J
K
L
M
N
O
P
Q
R
S
T
U
V
W
X
Y
Z

losing of it. ► PHRASE **2** If you are **at a loss**, you do not know what to do.

lost

ADJECTIVE **1** If you are lost, you do not know where you are. **2** If something is lost, you cannot find it. ► **3** Lost is the past tense and past participle of **lose**.

lot lots

NOUN **1** A lot of something, or lots of something, is a large amount of it. **2** A lot means very much or very often E.G. *I love him a lot.* **3** an amount of something or a number of things E.G. *He bet all his wages and lost the lot.* **4** In an auction, a lot is one of the things being sold.

■ (sense 1) abundance, load(s), plenty

lotion lotions

NOUN a liquid that you put on your skin to protect or soften it E.G. *suntan lotion.*

lottery lotteries

NOUN a method of raising money by selling tickets by which a winner is selected at random.

lotus lotuses

NOUN a large water lily, found in Africa and Asia.

loud louder loudest

ADJECTIVE or ADVERB **1** A loud noise has a high volume of sound E.G. *a loud explosion.* **2** If you describe clothing as loud, you mean that it is too bright E.G. *a loud tie.*

loudly ADVERB

loudspeaker loudspeakers

NOUN a piece of equipment that makes your voice louder when you speak into a microphone connected to it.

lounge lounges lounging lounged

NOUN **1** a room in a house or hotel with comfortable chairs where people can relax. **2** The lounge or lounge bar in a pub or hotel is a more expensive and comfortably furnished bar. ► VERB **3** If you lounge around, you lean against something or sit or lie around in a lazy and comfortable way.

lourie louries

Rhymes with "Maori" NOUN one of two types of bird found in South Africa. The grey lourie lives in open grassland and the other more brightly coloured species lives in forests and wooded areas.

louse lice

NOUN Lice are small insects that live on people's bodies E.G. *head lice.*

lousy lousier lousiest

ADJECTIVE INFORMAL **1** of bad quality or very unpleasant E.G. *The weather is lousy.* **2** ill or unhappy.

lout louts

NOUN a young man who behaves in an aggressive and rude way.

lovable or **loveable**

ADJECTIVE having very attractive qualities and therefore easy to love E.G. *a lovable black mongrel.*

love loves loving loved

VERB **1** If you love someone, you have strong emotional feelings of affection for them. **2** If you love something, you like it very much E.G. *We both love fishing.* **3** If you would love to do something, you want very much to do it E.G. *I would love to live there.* ► NOUN **4** Love is a strong emotional feeling of affection for someone or something. **5** In tennis, love is a score of zero. ► PHRASE **6** If

you are **in love** with someone, you feel strongly attracted to them romantically or sexually. **7** When two people **make love**, they have sex.
loving ADJECTIVE   **lovingly** ADVERB
■ (sense 1) adore, dote on

love affair love affairs
NOUN a romantic and often sexual relationship between two people who are not married to each other.

love life love lives
NOUN a person's romantic and sexual relationships.

lovely lovelier loveliest
ADJECTIVE very beautiful, attractive, and pleasant.
loveliness NOUN

lover lovers
NOUN **1** A person's lover is someone that they have a sexual relationship with but are not married to.
2 Someone who is a lover of something, for example art or music, is very fond of it.

low lower lowest
ADJECTIVE or ADVERB **1** Something that is low is close to the ground, or measures a short distance from the ground to the top E.G. *a low stool.*
2 'Low' is used to describe people who are considered not respectable E.G. *mixing with low company.* ► NOUN **3** a level or amount that is less than before E.G. *Sales hit a new low.*

lowboy lowboys
NOUN In Australian and New Zealand English, a small wardrobe or chest of drawers.

lower lowers lowering lowered
VERB To lower something means to move it downwards or to make it less in value or amount.

lowlands
PLURAL NOUN Lowlands are an area of flat, low land.
lowland ADJECTIVE

lowly lowlier lowliest
ADJECTIVE low in importance, rank or status.

low tide
NOUN On a coast, low tide is the time, usually twice a day, when the sea is at its lowest level.

loyal
ADJECTIVE firm in your friendship or support for someone or something.
loyally ADVERB   **loyalty** NOUN

loyalist loyalists
NOUN a person who remains firm in their support for a government or ruler.

lozenge lozenges
NOUN **1** a type of sweet with medicine in it, which you suck to relieve a sore throat or cough. **2** a diamond shape.

LP LPs
NOUN a long-playing record. LP is short for 'long playing record'.

LSD
NOUN LSD is a very powerful drug which causes hallucinations. LSD is an abbreviation for 'lysergic acid diethylamide'.

Ltd
an abbreviation for 'limited'; used after the names of limited companies.

lubra lubras
NOUN an Australian Aboriginal woman.

lubricate lubricates lubricating lubricated
VERB To lubricate something such as a machine means to put oil or an oily substance onto it, so that it moves

lubrication NOUN **lubricant** NOUN

lucid

ADJECTIVE 1 Lucid writing or speech is clear and easy to understand. 2 Someone who is lucid after having been ill or delirious is able to think clearly again.

luck

NOUN Luck is anything that seems to happen by chance and not through your own efforts.

■ chance, fortune

luckless

ADJECTIVE unsuccessful or unfortunate E.G. *We reduced our luckless opponents to shattered wrecks.*

lucky luckier luckiest

ADJECTIVE 1 Someone who is lucky has a lot of good luck. 2 Something that is lucky happens by chance and has good effects or consequences.

luckily ADVERB

lucrative

ADJECTIVE Something that is lucrative earns you a lot of money E.G. *a lucrative sponsorship deal.*

ludicrous

ADJECTIVE completely foolish, unsuitable, or ridiculous.

lug lugs lugging lugged

VERB If you lug a heavy object around, you carry it with difficulty.

luggage

NOUN Your luggage is the bags and suitcases that you take with you when you travel.

lukewarm

ADJECTIVE 1 slightly warm E.G. *a mug of lukewarm tea.* 2 not very enthusiastic or interested E.G. *The report was given a polite but lukewarm response.*

lull lulls lulling lulled

NOUN 1 a pause in something, or a short time when it is quiet and nothing much happens E.G. *There was a temporary lull in the fighting.*
► VERB 2 If you are lulled into feeling safe, someone or something casues you to feel safe at a time when you are not safe E.G. *We had been lulled into a false sense of security.*

lullaby lullabies

NOUN a song used for sending a baby or child to sleep.

lumber lumbers lumbering lumbered

NOUN 1 Lumber is wood that has been roughly cut up. 2 Lumber is also old unwanted furniture and other items.
► VERB 3 If you lumber around, you move heavily and clumsily. 4 INFORMAL If you are lumbered with something, you are given it to deal with even though you do not want it E.G. *Women are still lumbered with the housework.*

luminary luminaries

NOUN; LITERARY a person who is famous or an expert in a particular subject.

luminous

ADJECTIVE Something that is luminous glows in the dark, usually because it has been treated with a special substance E.G. *The luminous dial on her clock.*

luminosity NOUN

lump lumps lumping lumped

NOUN 1 A lump of something is a solid piece of it, of any shape or size E.G. *a big lump of dough.* 2 a bump on the surface of something. ► VERB 3 If you lump people or things together, you combine them into one group or consider them as being similar in some way.

lumpy ADJECTIVE

lump sum lump sums
NOUN a large sum of money given or received all at once.

lunacy
NOUN 1 Lunacy is extremely foolish or eccentric behaviour. 2 OLD-FASHIONED Lunacy is also severe mental illness.

lunar
ADJECTIVE relating to the moon.
📖 from Latin *luna* meaning 'moon'

lunatic lunatics
NOUN 1 If you call someone a lunatic, you mean that they are very foolish E.G. *He drives like a lunatic!*
2 someone who is insane. ▶ ADJECTIVE
3 Lunatic behaviour is very stupid, foolish, or dangerous.

lunch lunches lunching lunched
NOUN 1 a meal eaten in the middle of the day. ▶ VERB 2 When you lunch, you eat lunch.

luncheon luncheons
Said "lun-shen" NOUN; FORMAL
Luncheon is lunch.

lung lungs
NOUN Your lungs are the two organs inside your ribcage with which you breathe.

lunge lunges lunging lunged
NOUN 1 a sudden forward movement E.G. *He made a lunge for her.* ▶ VERB
2 To lunge means to make a sudden movement in a particular direction.

lurch lurches lurching lurched
VERB 1 To lurch means to make a sudden, jerky movement. ▶ NOUN 2 a sudden, jerky movement.

lure lures luring lured
VERB 1 To lure someone means to attract them into going somewhere

or doing something. ▶ NOUN
2 something that you find very attractive.

lurid
Said "loo-rid" ADJECTIVE 1 involving a lot of sensational detail E.G. *lurid stories in the press.* 2 very brightly coloured or patterned.

lurk lurks lurking lurked
VERB To lurk somewhere means to remain there hidden from the person you are waiting for.

luscious
ADJECTIVE very tasty E.G. *luscious fruit.*

lush lusher lushest
ADJECTIVE In a lush field or garden, the grass or plants are healthy and growing thickly.

lust lusts lusting lusted
NOUN 1 Lust is a very strong feeling of sexual desire for someone. 2 A lust for something is a strong desire to have it E.G. *a lust for money.* ▶ VERB
3 To lust for or after someone means to desire them sexually. 4 If you lust for or after something, you have a very strong desire to possess it E.G. *She lusted after fame.*

lustre
Said "lus-ter" NOUN Lustre is soft shining light reflected from the surface of something E.G. *the lustre of silk.*

lute lutes
NOUN an old-fashioned stringed musical instrument which is plucked like a guitar.

luxuriant
ADJECTIVE Luxuriant plants, trees, and gardens are large, healthy and growing strongly.

luxurious
ADJECTIVE very expensive and full of luxury.

a
b
c
d
e
f
g
h
i
j
k
l
m
n
o
p
q
r
s
t
u
v
w
x
y
z

Beautiful Elephants Are Usually Tiny (<u>beautiful</u>)   SPELLING NOTE

A
B
C
D
E
F
G
H
I
J
K
L
M
N
O
P
Q
R
S
T
U
V
W
X
Y
Z

luxuriously ADVERB
■ opulent, splendid, sumptuous
luxury luxuries
NOUN **1** Luxury is great comfort in expensive and beautiful surroundings E.G. *a life of luxury*. **2** something that you enjoy very much but do not have very often, usually because it is expensive.
■ (sense 1) extravagance, indulgence, treat

-ly
SUFFIX **1** '-ly' forms adjectives that describe a quality E.G. *friendly*. **2** '-ly' forms adjectives that refer to how often something happens or is done E.G. *yearly*. **3** '-ly' forms adverbs that refer to how or in what way something is done E.G. *quickly… nicely*.

lying
NOUN **1** Lying is telling lies. **2** Lying is

also the present participle of **lie**.
lynch lynches lynching lynched
VERB If a crowd lynches someone, it kills them in a violent way without first holding a legal trial.

lynx lynxes
NOUN a wildcat with a short tail and tufted ears.

lyre lyres
NOUN a stringed instrument rather like a small harp, which was used in ancient Greece.

lyric lyrics
NOUN **1** (MUSIC) The lyrics of a song are the words. ▶ ADJECTIVE **2** Lyric poetry is written in a simple and direct style, and is usually about love.

lyrical
ADJECTIVE poetic and romantic.

Mm

m
an abbreviation for 'metres' or 'miles'.

macabre
Said "mak-**kahb**-ra" ADJECTIVE A macabre event is strange and horrible E.G. *a macabre horror story*.

macadamia macadamias
Said "ma-ka-**dame**-ee-a" NOUN an Australian tree, also grown in New Zealand, that produces edible nuts.

macaroni
NOUN Macaroni is short hollow tubes of pasta.
🏛 an Italian word; from Greek *makaria* meaning 'food made from barley'

macaroon macaroons
NOUN a sweet biscuit flavoured with almonds or coconut.

mace maces
NOUN an ornamental pole carried by an official during ceremonies as a symbol of authority.

machete machetes
Said "mash-**ett**-ee" NOUN a large, heavy knife with a big blade.

machine machines machining machined
NOUN 1 (D&T) a piece of equipment which uses electricity or power from an engine to make it work. ▶ VERB 2 If you machine something, you make it or work on it using a machine.

machine-gun machine-guns
NOUN a gun that works automatically, firing bullets one after the other.

machinery
NOUN Machinery is machines in general.

machismo
Said "mak-**kiz**-moe" NOUN Machismo is exaggerated aggressive male behaviour.

macho
Said "**mat**-shoh" ADJECTIVE A man who is described as macho behaves in an aggressively masculine way.
🏛 from Spanish *macho* meaning 'male'

mackerel mackerels
NOUN a sea fish with blue and silver stripes.

mackintosh mackintoshes
NOUN a raincoat made from specially treated waterproof cloth.

mad madder maddest
ADJECTIVE 1 Someone who is mad has a mental illness which often causes them to behave in strange ways. 2 If you describe someone as mad, you mean that they are very foolish E.G. *He said we were mad to share a flat.* 3 INFORMAL Someone who is mad is angry. 4 If you are mad about someone or something, you like them very much E.G. *Alan was mad about golf.*
madness NOUN **madman** NOUN
▣ (sense 1) crazy, deranged, insane
▣ (sense 2) daft, foolish

madam
'Madam' is a very formal way of addressing a woman.

maddening
ADJECTIVE irritating or frustrating E.G. *She had many maddening habits.*

madly
ADVERB If you do something madly, you do it in a fast, excited way.

madrigal madrigals
NOUN a song sung by several people without instruments.

Mafia
NOUN The Mafia is a large crime

A
B
C
D
E
F
G
H
I
J
K
L
M
N
O
P
Q
R
S
T
U
V
W
X
Y
Z

organization operating in Sicily, Italy, and the USA.

magazine magazines
NOUN 1 (LIBRARY) a weekly or monthly publication with articles and photographs. **2** a compartment in a gun for cartridges.
📖 from Arabic *makhzan* meaning 'storehouse'

magenta
Said "maj-**jen**-ta" NOUN or ADJECTIVE dark reddish-purple.

maggot maggots
NOUN a creature that looks like a small worm and lives on decaying things. Maggots turn into flies.

magic
NOUN 1 In fairy stories, magic is a special power that can make impossible things happen. **2** Magic is the art of performing tricks to entertain people.
magical ADJECTIVE   **magically** ADVERB

magician magicians
NOUN 1 a person who performs tricks as entertainment. **2** In fairy stories, a magician is a man with magical powers.

magistrate magistrates
NOUN an official who acts as a judge in a law court that deals with less serious crimes.

magnanimous
ADJECTIVE generous and forgiving.

magnate magnates
NOUN someone who is very rich and powerful in business.

magnet magnets
NOUN a piece of iron which attracts iron or steel towards it, and which points towards north if allowed to swing freely.
magnetic ADJECTIVE   **magnetism** NOUN

magnificent
ADJECTIVE extremely beautiful or impressive.
magnificently ADVERB
magnificence NOUN

magnify magnifies magnifying magnified
VERB When a microscope or lens magnifies something, it makes it appear bigger than it actually is.
magnification NOUN

magnifying glass magnifying glasses
NOUN a lens which makes things appear bigger than they really are.

magnitude
NOUN The magnitude of something is its great size or importance.

magnolia magnolias
NOUN a tree which has large white or pink flowers in spring.

magpie magpies
NOUN a large black and white bird with a long tail.

mahogany
NOUN Mahogany is a hard reddish brown wood used for making furniture.

maid maids
NOUN a female servant.

maiden maidens
NOUN 1 LITERARY a young woman.
▶ ADJECTIVE **2** first E.G. *a maiden voyage*.

maiden name maiden names
NOUN the surname a woman had before she married.

mail mails mailing mailed
NOUN 1 Your mail is the letters and parcels delivered to you by the post office. ▶ VERB **2** If you mail a letter, you send it by post.

mail order

NOUN Mail order is a system of buying goods by post.

maim maims maiming maimed

VERB To maim someone is to injure them very badly for life.

main mains

ADJECTIVE 1 most important E.G. *the main event.* ▶ NOUN 2 The mains are large pipes or wires that carry gas, water or electricity.

mainly ADVERB

■ (sense 1) chief, major, principal

mainframe mainframes

NOUN a large computer which can be used by many people at the same time.

mainland

NOUN The mainland is the main part of a country in contrast to islands around its coast.

mainstay

NOUN The mainstay of something is the most important part of it.

mainstream

NOUN The mainstream is the most ordinary and conventional group of people or ideas in a society.

maintain maintains maintaining maintained

VERB 1 If you maintain something, you keep it going or keep it at a particular rate or level E.G. *I wanted to maintain our friendship.* 2 If you maintain someone, you provide them regularly with money for what they need. 3 To maintain a machine or a building is to keep it in good condition. 4 If you maintain that something is true, you believe it is true and say so.

maintenance

NOUN 1 Maintenance is the process of keeping something in good condition. 2 Maintenance is also money that a person sends regularly to someone to provide for the things they need.

maize

NOUN Maize is a tall plant which produces sweet corn.

majesty majesties 1 You say 'His Majesty' when you are talking about a king, and 'Her Majesty' when you are talking about a queen.

NOUN 2 Majesty is great dignity and impressiveness.

majestic ADJECTIVE **majestically** ADVERB

major majors

ADJECTIVE 1 more important or more significant than other things E.G. *There were over fifty major injuries.* 2 (MUSIC) A major key is one of the keys in which most European music is written. ▶ NOUN 3 an army officer of the rank immediately above captain.

majority majorities

NOUN 1 The majority of people or things in a group is more than half of the group. 2 In an election, the majority is the difference between the number of votes gained by the winner and the number gained by the runner-up

✔ You should use *majority* only to talk about things that can be counted: *the majority of car owners.* To talk about an amount that cannot be counted you should use *most*: *most of the harvest was saved.*

make makes making made

VERB 1 To make something is to produce or construct it, or to cause it

a
b
c
d
e
f
g
h
i
j
k
l
m
n
o
p
q
r
s
t
u
v
w
x
y
z

A B C D E F G H I J K L **M** N O P Q R S T U V W X Y Z

to happen. **2** To make something is to do it E.G. *He was about to make a speech.* **3** To make something is to prepare it E.G. *I'll make some salad dressing.* **4** If someone makes you do something, they force you to do it E.G. *Mum made me clean the bathroom.* ▸ NOUN **5** The make of a product is the name of the company that manufactured it E.G. *'What make of car do you drive?' – 'Toyota'.*

■ (sense 1) create, fashion, form, produce

■ (sense 5) brand, kind, type

make up VERB **1** If a number of things make up something, they form that thing. **2** If you make up a story, you invent it. **3** If you make yourself up, you put make-up on. **4** If two people make it up, they become friends again after a quarrel.

make-up

NOUN **1** Make-up is coloured creams and powders which women put on their faces to make themselves look more attractive. **2** Someone's make-up is their character or personality.

making

NOUN **1** The making of something is the act or process of creating or producing it. ▸ PHRASE **2** When you describe someone as something **in the making**, you mean that they are gradually becoming that thing E.G. *a captain in the making.*

maladjusted

ADJECTIVE A maladjusted person has psychological or behaviour problems.

malaise

Said "mal-**laze**" NOUN; FORMAL Malaise is a feeling of dissatisfaction or unhappiness.

malaria

Said "mal-**lay**-ree-a" NOUN Malaria is a tropical disease caught from mosquitoes which causes fever and shivering.

Malaysian Malaysians

ADJECTIVE **1** belonging or relating to Malaysia. ▸ NOUN **2** someone who comes from Malaysia.

male males

NOUN **1** a person or animal belonging to the sex that cannot give birth or lay eggs. ▸ ADJECTIVE **2** concerning or affecting men rather than women.

male chauvinist male chauvinists

NOUN a man who thinks that men are better than women.

malevolent

Said "mal-**lev**-oh-lent" ADJECTIVE; FORMAL wanting or intending to cause harm. **malevolence** NOUN

■ malicious, spiteful, vindictive

malfunction malfunctions malfunctioning malfunctioned

VERB **1** If a machine malfunctions, it fails to work properly. ▸ NOUN **2** the failure of a machine to work properly.

malice

NOUN Malice is a desire to cause harm to people.

malicious

ADJECTIVE Malicious talk or behaviour is intended to harm someone.

malign maligns maligning maligned

VERB; FORMAL To malign someone is to say unpleasant and untrue things about them.

malignant

ADJECTIVE **1** harmful and cruel. **2** A malignant disease or tumour could cause death if it is allowed to continue.

mallard mallards

NOUN a kind of wild duck. The male has a green head.

mallee mallees

NOUN a eucalypt that grows close to the ground in dry areas of Australia.

mallet mallets

NOUN a wooden hammer with a square head.

malnutrition

NOUN Malnutrition is not eating enough healthy food.

malodorous

ADJECTIVE If you describe something as malodorous, you means it smells bad.

malpractice

NOUN If someone such as a doctor or lawyer breaks the rules of their profession, their behaviour is called malpractice.

malt

NOUN Malt is roasted grain, usually barley, that is used in making beer and whisky.

mammal mammals

NOUN (SCIENCE) Animals that give birth to live babies and feed their young with milk from the mother's body are called mammals. Human beings, dogs, and whales are all mammals.

mammoth mammoths

ADJECTIVE 1 very large indeed E.G. *a mammoth outdoor concert.* ▶ NOUN 2 a huge animal that looked like a hairy elephant with long tusks. Mammoths became extinct a long time ago.

man men; mans manning manned

NOUN 1 an adult male human being. ▶ PLURAL NOUN 2 Human beings in

general are sometimes referred to as men E.G. *All men are equal.* ▶ VERB 3 To man something is to be in charge of it or operate it E.G. *Two officers were manning the radar screens.*

▤ (sense 1) bloke, chap, guy
▤ (sense 2) humanity, mankind

mana

NOUN Mana is authority and influence such as that held by a New Zealand Maori chief.

manacle manacles

NOUN Manacles are metal rings or clamps attached to a prisoner's wrists or ankles.

manage manages managing managed

VERB 1 If you manage to do something, you succeed in doing it E.G. *We managed to find somewhere to sit.* 2 If you manage an organization or business, you are responsible for controlling it.

▤ (sense 1) accomplish, succeed

manageable

ADJECTIVE able to be dealt with.

management

NOUN 1 The management of a business is the controlling and organizing of it. 2 The people who control an organization are called the management.

▤ (sense 1) administration, control, running

manager managers

NOUN a person responsible for running a business or organization E.G. *a bank manager.*

☑ In business, the word *manager* can apply to either a man or a woman.

manageress manageresses

NOUN a woman responsible for

running a business or organization.

managing director managing
directors

NOUN a company director who is
responsible for the way the company
is managed.

mandarin mandarins

NOUN a type of small orange which is
easy to peel.

mandate mandates

NOUN FORMAL A government's mandate
is the authority it has to carry out
particular policies as a result of
winning an election.

mandatory

ADJECTIVE If something is mandatory,
there is a law or rule stating that it
must be done E.G. *a mandatory life
sentence for murder.*

mandir mandirs

Said "mun-dir" NOUN a Hindu temple.
🏛 a Hindi word

mandolin mandolins

NOUN a musical instrument like a
small guitar with a deep, rounded
body.

mane manes

NOUN the long hair growing from the
neck of a lion or horse.

manger mangers

NOUN a feeding box in a barn or
stable.

mangle mangles mangling
mangled

VERB 1 If something is mangled, it is
crushed and twisted. ▶ NOUN 2 an old-
fashioned piece of equipment
consisting of two large rollers
which squeeze water out of wet
clothes.

mango mangoes or mangos

NOUN a sweet yellowish fruit which
grows in tropical countries.

manhole manholes

NOUN a covered hole in the ground
leading to a drain or sewer.

manhood

NOUN Manhood is the state of being a
man rather than a boy.

mania manias

NOUN 1 a strong liking for something
E.G. *my wife's mania for plant
collecting.* 2 a mental illness.
🏛 from Greek *mania* meaning
'madness'

maniac maniacs

NOUN a mad person who is violent
and dangerous.

manic

ADJECTIVE energetic and excited E.G. *a
manic attack.*

manicure manicures

NOUN a special treatment for the
hands and nails.
manicurist NOUN

manifest manifests manifesting
manifested FORMAL

ADJECTIVE 1 obvious or easily seen E.G.
his manifest enthusiasm. ▶ VERB 2 To
manifest something is to make
people aware of it E.G. *Fear can
manifest itself in many ways.*

manifestation manifestations

NOUN; FORMAL A manifestation of
something is a sign that it is
happening or exists E.G. *The illness
may be a manifestation of stress.*

manifesto manifestoes or
manifestos

NOUN a published statement of the
aims and policies of a political party.

manipulate manipulates
manipulating manipulated

VERB 1 To manipulate people or
events is to control or influence
them to produce a particular result.

2 If you manipulate a piece of equipment, you control it in a skilful way.

manipulation NOUN **manipulator** NOUN **manipulative** ADJECTIVE

mankind

NOUN 'Mankind' is used to refer to all human beings E.G. *a threat to mankind*.

manly manlier manliest

ADJECTIVE having qualities that are typically masculine E.G. *He laughed a deep, manly laugh*.

manna

NOUN If something appears like manna from heaven, it appears suddenly as if by a miracle and helps you in a difficult situation.

manner manners

NOUN **1** The manner in which you do something is the way you do it. **2** Your manner is the way in which you behave and talk E.G. *his kind manner*. ▶ PLURAL NOUN **3** If you have good manners, you behave very politely.

mannerism mannerisms

NOUN a gesture or a way of speaking which is characteristic of a person.

manoeuvre manoeuvres manoeuvring manoeuvred

Said "man-noo-ver" VERB **1** If you manoeuvre something into a place, you skilfully move it there E.G. *It took expertise to manoeuvre the boat so close to the shore*. ▶ NOUN **2** a clever move you make in order to change a situation to your advantage.

manor manors

NOUN a large country house with land.

manpower

NOUN Workers can be referred to as manpower.

mansion mansions

NOUN a very large house.

manslaughter

NOUN; LEGAL Manslaughter is the accidental killing of a person.

mantelpiece mantelpieces

NOUN a shelf over a fireplace.

mantle mantles

NOUN LITERARY To take on the mantle of something is to take on responsibility for it E.G. *He has taken over the mantle of England's greatest living poet*.

mantra mantras

NOUN a word or short piece of sacred text or prayer continually repeated to help concentration.

manual manuals

ADJECTIVE **1** Manual work involves physical strength rather than mental skill. **2** operated by hand rather than by electricity or by motor E.G. *a manual typewriter*. ▶ NOUN **3** an instruction book which tells you how to use a machine.

manually ADVERB

manufacture manufactures manufacturing manufactured

(D&T) VERB **1** To manufacture goods is to make them in a factory. ▶ NOUN **2** The manufacture of goods is the making of them in a factory E.G. *the manufacture of nuclear weapons*.

manufacturer NOUN

manure

NOUN Manure is animal faeces used to fertilize the soil.

manuscript manuscripts

NOUN a handwritten or typed document, especially a version of a book before it is printed.

a
b
c
d
e
f
g
h
i
j
k
l
m
n
o
p
q
r
s
t
u
v
w
x
y
z

Manx

ADJECTIVE belonging or relating to the Isle of Man.

many

ADJECTIVE 1 If there are many people or things, there are a large number of them. 2 You also use 'many' to ask how great a quantity is or to give information about it E.G. *How many tickets do you require?* ▶ PRONOUN 3 a large number of people or things E.G. *Many are too weak to walk.*

Maori Maoris

NOUN 1 someone descended from the people who lived in New Zealand before Europeans arrived. 2 Maori is a language spoken by Maoris.

map maps mapping mapped

NOUN 1 a detailed drawing of an area as it would appear if you saw it from above. ▶ VERB 2 If you map out a plan, you work out in detail what you will do.

maple maples

NOUN a tree that has large leaves with five points.

mar mars marring marred

VERB To mar something is to spoil it E.G. *The game was marred by violence.*

marae marae or **maraes**

NOUN *Said* "ma-**rye**" In New Zealand, a Maori meeting house; also the enclosed space in front of it.

marathon marathons

NOUN 1 a race in which people run 26 miles along roads. ▶ ADJECTIVE 2 A marathon task is a large one that takes a long time.

marble marbles

NOUN 1 Marble is a very hard, cold stone which is often polished to show the coloured patterns in it. 2 Marbles is a children's game played with small coloured glass balls. These balls are also called marbles.

march marches marching marched

NOUN 1 March is the third month of the year. It has 31 days. 2 an organized protest in which a large group of people walk somewhere together. ▶ VERB 3 When soldiers march, they walk with quick regular steps in time with each other. 4 To march somewhere is to walk quickly in a determined way E.G. *He marched out of the room.*

▣ sense 1 is from Latin *Martius* (month) of Mars, the Roman god of war

mare mares

NOUN an adult female horse.

margarine

Said "mar-jar-**reen**" **margarines**
NOUN Margarine is a substance that is similar to butter but is made from vegetable oil and animal fats.

margin margins

NOUN 1 If you win a contest by a large or small margin, you win it by a large or small amount. 2 an extra amount that allows you more freedom in doing something E.G. *a small margin of error.* 3 the blank space at each side on a written or printed page.

marginal

ADJECTIVE 1 small and not very important E.G. *a marginal increase.* 2 A marginal seat or constituency is a political constituency where the previous election was won by a very small majority.

marginally ADVERB

marigold marigolds

NOUN a type of yellow or orange garden flower.

marijuana
Said "mar-rih-**hwan**-a" NOUN Marijuana is an illegal drug which is smoked in cigarettes.

marina marinas
NOUN a harbour for pleasure boats and yachts.

marinate marinates marinating marinated; also spelt **marinade**
VERB To marinate food is to soak it in a mixture of oil and vinegar to flavour it before cooking.

marine marines
NOUN 1 a soldier who serves with the navy. ▶ ADJECTIVE 2 relating to or involving the sea E.G. *marine life*.

marital
ADJECTIVE relating to or involving marriage E.G. *marital problems*.

maritime
ADJECTIVE relating to the sea and ships E.G. *maritime trade*.

marjoram
NOUN Marjoram is a herb with small, rounded leaves and tiny, pink flowers.

mark marks marking marked
NOUN 1 a small stain or damaged area on a surface E.G. *I can't get this mark off the curtain.* 2 a written or printed symbol E.G. *He made a few marks with his pen.* 3 a letter or number showing how well you have done in homework or in an exam. 4 a unit of currency formerly used in Germany. ▶ VERB 5 If something marks a surface, it damages it in some way. 6 If you mark something, you write a symbol on it or identify it in some other way. 7 When a teacher marks your work, he or she decides how good it is and gives it a mark. 8 To mark something is to be a sign of it E.G. *The accident marked a tragic end to the day.* 9 In soccer or hockey, if you mark your opposing player, you stay close to them, trying to prevent them from getting the ball.

marked
ADJECTIVE very obvious E.G. *a marked improvement.*
markedly ADVERB

market markets marketing marketed
NOUN 1 a place where goods or animals are bought and sold. 2 a place with many small stalls selling different goods. 3 The market for a product is the number of people who want to buy it E.G. *the market for cars.* ▶ VERB 4 To market a product is to sell it in an organized way.
▤ (sense 1) bazaar, fair, mart

marketing
NOUN Marketing is the part of a business concerned with the way a product is sold.

market research
NOUN Market research is research into what people want and buy.

marksman marksmen
NOUN someone who can shoot very accurately.

marlin marlins
NOUN a large fish found in tropical seas which has a very long upper jaw.

marmalade
NOUN Marmalade is a jam made from citrus fruit, usually eaten at breakfast.
▥ from Latin *marmelo* meaning 'quince'

maroon
NOUN OR ADJECTIVE dark reddish-purple.

marooned
ADJECTIVE If you are marooned in a place, you are stranded there and cannot leave it.

a b c d e f g h i j k l **m** n o p q r s t u v w x y z

A B C D E F G H I J K L **M** N O P Q R S T U V W X Y Z

marquee marquees
Said "mar-**kee**" NOUN a very large tent used at a fair or other outdoor entertainment.

marquis marquises
Said "mar-**kwiss**"; also spelt
marquess
NOUN a male member of the nobility of the rank between duke and earl.

marriage marriages
NOUN **1** the relationship between a husband and wife. **2** (RE) Marriage is the act of marrying someone.
■ (sense 1) matrimony, wedlock

marrow marrows
NOUN a long, thick green vegetable with cream-coloured flesh.

marry marries marrying married
VERB **1** When a man and a woman marry, they become each other's husband and wife during a special ceremony. **2** When a clergyman or registrar marries a couple, he or she is in charge of their marriage ceremony.
married ADJECTIVE

Mars
NOUN Mars is the planet in the solar system which is fourth from the sun.

marsh marshes
NOUN an area of land which is permanently wet.

marshal marshals marshalling marshalled
VERB **1** If you marshal things or people, you gather them together and organize them E.G. *Shipping was being marshalled into convoys.* ▶ NOUN **2** an official who helps to organize a public event.

marshmallow marshmallows
NOUN a soft, spongy, pink or white

sweet made using gelatine.

marsupial marsupials
Said "mar-**syoo**-pee-al" NOUN an animal that carries its young in a pouch. Koala bears and kangaroos are marsupials.
▣ from Greek *marsupion* meaning 'purse'

martial
Said "mar-shal" ADJECTIVE relating to or involving war or soldiers E.G. *martial music.*

martial arts
PLURAL NOUN The martial arts are the techniques of self-defence that come from the Far East, for example karate or judo.

Martian Martians
Said "mar-shan" NOUN an imaginary creature from the planet Mars.

martyr martyrs martyring martyred
NOUN **1** someone who suffers or is killed rather than change their beliefs. ▶ VERB **2** If someone is martyred, they are killed because of their beliefs.
martyrdom NOUN

marvel marvels marvelling marvelled
VERB **1** If you marvel at something, it fills you with surprise or admiration E.G. *Modern designers can only marvel at his genius.* ▶ NOUN **2** something that makes you feel great surprise or admiration E.G. *a marvel of high technology.*

marvellous
ADJECTIVE wonderful or excellent.
marvellously ADVERB

Marxism
NOUN Marxism is a political philosophy based on the writings of

Karl Marx. It states that society will develop towards communism through the struggle between different social classes.

Marxist ADJECTIVE or NOUN

marzipan
NOUN Marzipan is a paste made of almonds, sugar, and egg. It is put on top of cakes or used to make small sweets.

mascara
NOUN Mascara is a substance that can be used to colour eyelashes and make them look longer.

mascot mascots
NOUN a person, animal, or toy which is thought to bring good luck E.G. *Celtic's mascot, Hoopy the Huddle Hound.*

masculine
ADJECTIVE 1 typical of men, rather than women E.G. *the masculine world of motorsport.* 2 belonging to a particular class of nouns in some languages, such as French, German, and Latin

masculinity NOUN

What is Masculine?

Masculine nouns refer to male people and animals:

E.G. *The boy put on his coat.* ▶ *boy is masculine*

Common nouns may be either masculine or feminine. Other words in the sentence may tell us if they are male or female:

E.G. *The doctor parked his car.*
The doctor parked her car.

Also look at the grammar boxes at **gender**, **feminine** and **neuter**.

---

mash mashes mashing mashed
VERB If you mash vegetables, you crush them after they have been cooked.

mask masks masking masked
NOUN 1 something you wear over your face for protection or disguise E.G. *a surgical mask.* ▶ VERB 2 If you mask something, you cover it so that it is protected or cannot be seen.

masochist masochists
Said "mass-so-kist" NOUN someone who gets pleasure from their own suffering.
masochism NOUN
🏛 named after the Austrian novelist Leopold von Sacher Masoch (1836–1895), who wrote about masochism

mason masons
NOUN a person who is skilled at making things with stone.

masonry
NOUN Masonry is pieces of stone which form part of a wall or building.

masquerade masquerades masquerading masqueraded
Said "mass-ker-raid" VERB If you masquerade as something, you pretend to be it E.G. *He masqueraded as a doctor.*

mass masses massing massed
NOUN 1 a large amount of something. 2 The masses are the ordinary people in society considered as a group E.G. *opera for the masses.* 3 In physics, the mass of an object is the amount of physical matter that it has. 4 In the Roman Catholic Church, Mass is a religious service in which people share bread and wine in remembrance of the death and resurrection of Jesus Christ.

a
b
c
d
e
f
g
h
i
j
k
l
m
n
o
p
q
r
s
t
u
v
w
x
y
z

ADJECTIVE 5 involving a large number of people E.G. *mass unemployment*.
▶ **VERB 6** When people mass, they gather together in a large group.

massacre massacres massacring massacred
Said "**mass**-ik-ker" NOUN **1** the killing of a very large number of people in a violent and cruel way. ▶ VERB **2** To massacre people is to kill large numbers of them in a violent and cruel way.

massage massages massaging massaged
VERB **1** To massage someone is to rub their body in order to help them relax or to relieve pain. ▶ NOUN **2** A massage is treatment which involves rubbing the body.

massive
ADJECTIVE extremely large E.G. *a massive iceberg*.
massively ADVERB

mass-produce mass-produces mass-producing mass-produced
VERB To mass-produce something is to make it in large quantities E.G. *They began mass-producing cameras after the war*.

mast masts
NOUN the tall upright pole that supports the sails of a boat.

master masters mastering mastered
NOUN **1** a man who has authority over others, such as the employer of servants, or the owner of slaves or animals. **2** If you are master of a situation, you have control over it E.G. *He was master of his own destiny*. **3** a male teacher at some schools.
▶ VERB **4** If you master a difficult situation, you succeed in controlling

it. **5** If you master something, you learn how to do it properly E.G. *She found it easy to master the typewriter*.

masterful
ADJECTIVE showing control and authority.

masterly
ADJECTIVE extremely clever or well done E.G. *a masterly exhibition of batting*.

mastermind masterminds masterminding masterminded
VERB **1** If you mastermind a complicated activity, you plan and organize it. ▶ NOUN **2** The mastermind behind something is the person responsible for planning it.

masterpiece masterpieces
NOUN an extremely good painting or other work of art.

masturbate masturbates masturbating masturbated
VERB If someone masturbates, they stroke or rub their own genitals in order to get sexual pleasure.
masturbation NOUN

mat mats
NOUN **1** a small round or square piece of cloth, card, or plastic that is placed on a table to protect it from plates or glasses. **2** a small piece of carpet or other thick material that is placed on the floor.

matador matadors
NOUN a man who fights and tries to kill bulls as part of a public entertainment, especially in Spain. 🎏 from Spanish *matar* meaning 'to kill'

match matches matching matched
NOUN **1** an organized game of football, cricket, or some other sport.

2 a small, thin stick of wood that produces a flame when you strike it against a rough surface. ▶ VERB **3** If one thing matches another, the two things look the same or have similar qualities.

mate mates mating mated
NOUN **1** INFORMAL Your mates are your friends. **2** The first mate on a ship is the officer who is next in importance to the captain. **3** An animal's mate is its sexual partner. ▶ VERB **4** When a male and female animal mate, they come together sexually in order to breed.

material materials
NOUN **1** Material is cloth. **2** a substance from which something is made E.G. *the materials to make red dye.* **3** The equipment for a particular activity can be referred to as materials E.G. *building materials.* **4** Material for a book, play, or film is the information or ideas on which it is based. ▶ ADJECTIVE **5** involving possessions and money E.G. *concerned with material comforts.*
materially ADVERB

materialism
NOUN Materialism is thinking that money and possessions are the most important things in life.
materialistic ADJECTIVE

materialize materializes
materializing materialized; also spelt **materialise**
VERB If something materializes, it actually happens or appears E.G. *Fortunately, the attack did not materialize.*

maternal
ADJECTIVE relating to or involving a mother E.G. *her maternal instincts.*

maternity
ADJECTIVE relating to or involving pregnant women and birth E.G. *a maternity hospital.*

mathematics
NOUN Mathematics is the study of numbers, quantities, and shapes.
mathematical ADJECTIVE
mathematically ADVERB
mathematician NOUN

maths
NOUN Maths is mathematics.

Matilda
NOUN; OLD-FASHIONED In Australia, Matilda is the pack of belongings carried by a swagman in the bush. The word is now used only in the phrase 'waltzing Matilda', meaning to travel in the bush with few possessions.

matinee matinees
Said "mat-in-nay"; also spelt **matinée**
NOUN an afternoon performance of a play or film.

matrimony
NOUN; FORMAL Matrimony is marriage.
matrimonial ADJECTIVE

matrix matrices
Said "may-trix" NOUN **1** FORMAL the framework in which something grows and develops. **2** In maths, a matrix is a set of numbers or elements set out in rows and columns.

matron matrons
NOUN In a hospital, a senior nurse in charge of all the nursing staff used to be known as matron.

matt
ADJECTIVE A matt surface is dull rather than shiny E.G. *matt black plastic.*

a
b
c
d
e
f
g
h
i
j
k
l
m
n
o
p
q
r
s
t
u
v
w
x
y
z

matted

ADJECTIVE Hair that is matted is tangled with the strands sticking together.

matter matters mattering mattered

NOUN 1 something that you have to deal with. 2 Matter is any substance E.G. *The atom is the smallest divisible particle of matter.* 3 Books and magazines are reading matter. ▶ VERB 4 If something matters to you, it is important. ▶ PHRASE 5 If you ask **What's the matter?**, you are asking what is wrong.

■ (sense 1) affair, business, situation, subject

matter-of-fact

ADJECTIVE showing no emotion.

matting

NOUN Matting is thick woven material such as rope or straw, used as a floor covering.

mattress mattresses

NOUN a large thick pad filled with springs or feathers that is put on a bed to make it comfortable.

mature matures maturing matured

VERB 1 When a child or young animal matures, it becomes an adult. 2 When something matures, it reaches complete development. ▶ ADJECTIVE 3 Mature means fully developed and emotionally balanced.

maturely ADVERB **maturity** NOUN

maudlin

ADJECTIVE Someone who is maudlin is sad and sentimental when they are drunk.

maul mauls mauling mauled

VERB If someone is mauled by an animal, they are savagely attacked

and badly injured by it.

mausoleum mausoleums

Said "maw-sal-**lee**-um" NOUN a building which contains the grave of a famous person.

mauve

Rhymes with "**grove**" NOUN OR ADJECTIVE pale purple.

maxim maxims

NOUN a short saying which gives a rule for good or sensible behaviour E.G. *Instant action: that's my maxim.*

maximize maximizes maximizing maximized; also spelt **maximise**

VERB To maximize something is to make it as great or effective as possible E.G. *Their objective is to maximize profits.*

maximum

ADJECTIVE 1 The maximum amount is the most that is possible E.G. *the maximum recommended intake.* ▶ NOUN 2 The maximum is the most that is possible E.G. *a maximum of fifty men.*

may

VERB 1 If something may happen, it is possible that it will happen E.G. *It may happen quite soon.* 2 If someone may do something, they are allowed to do it E.G. *Please may I be excused?* 3 You can use 'may' when saying that, although something is true, something else is also true E.G. *This may be true, but it is only part of the story.* 4 FORMAL You also use 'may' to express a wish that something will happen E.G. *May you live to be a hundred.* ▶ NOUN 5 May is the fifth month of the year. It has 31 days.

▥ sense 5 is probably from *Maia*, a Roman goddess

☑ It used to be that you used *may*

instead of *can* when asking for or giving someone permission to do something: *you may leave the table.* Nowadays *may* is usually only used in polite questions: *may I open the window?*

maybe

ADVERB You use 'maybe' when you are stating a possibility that you are not certain about E.G. *Maybe I should lie about my age.*

mayhem

NOUN You can refer to a confused and chaotic situation as mayhem E.G. *There was complete mayhem in the classroom.*

mayonnaise

Said "may-on-**nayz**" NOUN Mayonnaise is a thick salad dressing made with egg yolks and oil.

mayor mayors

NOUN a person who has been elected to lead and represent the people of a town.

maze mazes

NOUN a system of complicated passages which it is difficult to find your way through E.G. *a maze of dark tunnels.*

MBE MBEs

NOUN a British honour granted by the King or Queen. MBE is an abbreviation for 'Member of the Order of the British Empire' E.G. *Ally McCoist, MBE.*

MD

an abbreviation for 'Doctor of Medicine' or 'Managing Director'.

me

PRONOUN A speaker or writer uses 'me' to refer to himself or herself.

meadow meadows

NOUN a field of grass.

meagre

Said "**mee**-ger" ADJECTIVE very small and poor E.G. *his meagre pension.*

meal meals

NOUN an occasion when people eat, or the food they eat at that time

mealie mealies; also spelt **mielie**

NOUN In South African English, mealie is maize or an ear of maize.

mean means meaning meant; meaner meanest

VERB 1 If you ask what something means, you want it explained to you. 2 If you mean what you say, you are serious E.G. *The boss means what he says.* 3 If something means a lot to you, it is important to you. 4 If one thing means another, it shows that the second thing is true or will happen E.G. *Major roadworks will mean long delays.* 5 If you mean to do something, you intend to do it E.G. *I meant to phone you, but didn't have time.* 6 If something is meant to be true, it is supposed to be true E.G. *I found a road that wasn't meant to be there.* ▸ ADJECTIVE 7 Someone who is mean is unwilling to spend much money. 8 Someone who is mean is unkind or cruel E.G. *He apologized for being so mean to her.* ▸ NOUN 9 A means of doing something is a method or object which makes it possible E.G. *The tests were marked by means of a computer.* ▸ PLURAL NOUN 10 Someone's means are their money and income E.G. *He's obviously a man of means.* ▸ NOUN 11 In mathematics, the mean is the average of a set of numbers.

meanness NOUN

▤ (sense 5) aim, intend, plan
▤ (sense 7) miserly, parsimonious, stingy, tight-fisted

a
b
c
d
e
f
g
h
i
j
k
l
m
n
o
p
q
r
s
t
u
v
w
x
y
z

meander meanders meandering meandered

Said "mee-an-der" VERB If a road or river meanders, it has a lot of bends in it.

meaning meanings

NOUN 1 The meaning of a word, expression, or gesture is what it refers to or expresses. 2 The meaning of what someone says, or of a book or a film, is the thoughts or ideas that it is intended to express. 3 If something has meaning, it seems to be worthwhile and to have real purpose.

meaningful ADJECTIVE **meaningfully** ADVERB **meaningless** ADJECTIVE

■ (sense 1) gist, sense, significance

means test means tests

NOUN a check of a person's money and income to see whether they need money or benefits from the government or other organization.

meantime

PHRASE **In the meantime** means in the period of time between two events E.G. I'll call the nurse; in the meantime, you must rest.

meanwhile

ADVERB 1 Meanwhile means while something else is happening. ▶ NOUN 2 Meanwhile also means the time between two events.

measles

NOUN Measles is an infectious illness in which you have red spots on your skin.

measly

ADJECTIVE; INFORMAL very small or inadequate E.G. a measly ten cents.

measure measures measuring measured

VERB 1 (MATHS) When you measure something, you find out how big it is by using a ruler or tape measure. 2 (MATHS) If something measures a particular distance, its length or depth is that distance E.G. slivers of glass measuring a few millimetres across. ▶ NOUN 3 A measure of something is a certain amount of it E.G. There has been a measure of agreement. 4 (MATHS) a unit in which size, speed, or depth is expressed. 5 Measures are actions carried out to achieve a particular result E.G. Tough measures are needed to maintain order.

measurement NOUN

measured

ADJECTIVE careful and deliberate E.G. walking at the same measured pace.

measurement measurements

NOUN 1 the result that you obtain when you measure something. 2 Measurement is the activity of measuring something. 3 Your measurements are the sizes of your chest, waist, and hips that you use to buy the correct size of clothes.

meat meats

NOUN Meat is the flesh of animals that is cooked and eaten.

meaty ADJECTIVE

Mecca

NOUN 1 Mecca is the holiest city of Islam, to which many Muslims make pilgrimages. 2 If a place is a mecca for people of a particular kind, many of them go there because it is of special interest to them E.G. The island is a mecca for bird lovers.

☑ Most Muslims dislike this form and use the Arabic Makkah.

mechanic mechanics

NOUN 1 a person who repairs and

maintains engines and machines.
► PLURAL NOUN 2 The mechanics of something are the way in which it works or is done E.G. *the mechanics of accounting.* ► NOUN 3 Mechanics is also the scientific study of movement and the forces that affect objects.

mechanical
ADJECTIVE 1 A mechanical device has moving parts and is used to do a physical task. 2 A mechanical action is done automatically without thinking about it E.G. *He gave a mechanical smile.*
mechanically ADVERB

mechanism mechanisms
NOUN 1 a part of a machine that does a particular task E.G. *a locking mechanism.* 2 part of your behaviour that is automatic E.G. *the body's defence mechanisms.*

medal medals
NOUN a small disc of metal given as an award for bravery or as a prize for sport.

medallion medallions
NOUN a round piece of metal worn as an ornament on a chain round the neck.

medallist medallists
NOUN a person who has won a medal in sport E.G. *a gold medallist at the Olympics.*

meddle meddles meddling meddled
VERB To meddle is to interfere and try to change things without being asked.

media
PLURAL NOUN You can refer to the television, radio, and newspapers as the media.

☑ Although *media* is a plural noun, it is becoming more common for it

to be used as a singular: *the media is obsessed with violence.*

mediaeval
another spelling of **medieval**.

median medians
Said "mee-dee-an" ADJECTIVE 1 The median value of a set is the middle value when the set is arranged in order. ► NOUN 2 In geometry, a straight line drawn from one of the angles of a triangle to the middle point of the opposite side.

mediate mediates mediating mediated
VERB If you mediate between two groups, you try to settle a dispute between them.
mediation NOUN   **mediator** NOUN

medical medicals
ADJECTIVE 1 relating to the prevention and treatment of illness and injuries.
► NOUN 2 a thorough examination of your body by a doctor.
medically ADVERB

medication medications
NOUN Medication is a substance that is used to treat illness.

medicinal
ADJECTIVE relating to the treatment of illness E.G. *a valuable medicinal herb.*

medicine medicines
NOUN (PE) 1 Medicine is the treatment of illness and injuries by doctors and nurses. 2 a substance that you drink or swallow to help cure an illness.

medieval or **mediaeval**
Said "med-dee-ee-vul" ADJECTIVE relating to the period between about 1100 AD and 1500 AD, especially in Europe.
🏛 from Latin *medium aevum* meaning 'the middle age'

a
b
c
d
e
f
g
h
i
j
k
l
m
n
o
p
q
r
s
t
u
v
w
x
y
z

A
B
C
D
E
F
G
H
I
J
K
L
M
N
O
P
Q
R
S
T
U
V
W
X
Y
Z

mediocre
Said "meed-dee-oh-ker" ADJECTIVE of rather poor quality E.G. *a mediocre string of performances.*
mediocrity NOUN

meditate meditates meditating meditated
VERB 1 If you meditate on something, you think about it very deeply. 2 If you meditate, you remain in a calm, silent state for a period of time, often as part of a religious training.
meditation NOUN

Mediterranean
NOUN 1 The Mediterranean is the large sea between southern Europe and northern Africa. ► ADJECTIVE 2 relating to or typical of the Mediterranean or the European countries adjoining it.

medium mediums or media
ADJECTIVE 1 If something is of medium size or degree, it is neither large nor small E.G. *a medium sized hotel.*
► NOUN 2 a means that you use to communicate something E.G. *the medium of television.* 3 a person who claims to be able to speak to the dead and to receive messages from them.

medley medleys
NOUN 1 a mixture of different things creating an interesting effect. 2 a number of different songs or tunes sung or played one after the other.

meek meeker meekest
ADJECTIVE A meek person is timid and does what other people say.
meekly ADVERB
■ submissive, timid

meet meets meeting met
VERB 1 If you meet someone, you happen to be in the same place as them. 2 If you meet a visitor you go

to be with them when they arrive. 3 When a group of people meet, they gather together for a purpose. 4 If something meets a need, it can fulfil it E.G. *services intended to meet the needs of the elderly.* 5 If something meets with a particular reaction, it gets that reaction from people E.G. *I was met with silence.*

meeting meetings
NOUN 1 an event in which people discuss proposals and make decisions together. 2 what happens when you meet someone.

megabyte megabytes
NOUN (ICT) a unit of storage in a computer, equal to 1 048 576 bytes.

melaleuca melaleucas
Said "mel-a-loo-ka" NOUN an Australian tree or shrub that has black branches and a white trunk.

melancholy
ADJECTIVE or NOUN If you feel melancholy, you feel sad.

mêlée mêlées
Said "mel-lay" NOUN a situation where there are a lot of people rushing around.

mellow mellower mellowest; mellows mellowing mellowed
ADJECTIVE 1 Mellow light is soft and golden. 2 A mellow sound is smooth and pleasant to listen to E.G. *his mellow clarinet.* ► VERB 3 If someone mellows, they become more pleasant or relaxed E.G. *He certainly hasn't mellowed with age.*

melodic
ADJECTIVE relating to melody.

melodious
ADJECTIVE pleasant to listen to E.G. *soft melodious music.*

melodrama melodramas
NOUN a story or play in which people's emotions are exaggerated.

melodramatic
ADJECTIVE behaving in an exaggerated, emotional way.
■ histrionic, overdramatic, theatrical

melody melodies
NOUN (MUSIC) a tune.

melon melons
NOUN a large, juicy fruit with a green or yellow skin and many seeds inside.

melt melts melting melted
VERB 1 When something melts or when you melt it, it changes from a solid to a liquid because it has been heated. 2 If something melts, it disappears E.G. *The crowd melted away… Her inhibitions melted.*

member members
NOUN 1 A member of a group is one of the people or things belonging to the group E.G. *members of the family.* 2 A member of an organization is a person who has joined the organization. ▶ ADJECTIVE 3 A country belonging to an international organization is called a member country or a member state.

Member of Parliament
Members of Parliament
NOUN a person who has been elected to represent people in a country's parliament.

membership
NOUN 1 Membership of an organization is the state of being a member of it. 2 The people who belong to an organization are its membership.

membrane membranes
NOUN a very thin piece of skin or tissue which connects or covers plant or animal organs or cells E.G. *the nasal membrane.*

memento mementos
NOUN an object which you keep because it reminds you of a person or a special occasion E.G. *a lasting memento of their romance.*

memo memos
NOUN a note from one person to another within the same organization. Memo is short for 'memorandum'.

memoirs
Said "mem-wahrz" PLURAL NOUN If someone writes their memoirs, they write a book about their life and experiences.

memorable
ADJECTIVE If something is memorable, it is likely to be remembered because it is special or unusual E.G. *a memorable victory.*
memorably ADVERB

memorandum memorandums or memoranda
NOUN a memo.

memorial memorials
NOUN 1 a structure built to remind people of a famous person or event E.G. *a war memorial.* ▶ ADJECTIVE 2 A memorial event or prize is in honour of someone who has died, so that they will be remembered.

memory memories
NOUN 1 Your memory is your ability to remember things. 2 something you remember about the past E.G. *memories of their school days.* 3 (ICT) the part in which information is stored in a computer.
■ (sense 1) recall, recollection, remembrance

a
b
c
d
e
f
g
h
i
j
k
l
m
n
o
p
q
r
s
t
u
v
w
x
y
z

'i' before 'e' except after 'c'   SPELLING NOTE

men

the plural of **man**.

menace menaces menacing menaced

NOUN **1** someone or something that is likely to cause serious harm E.G. *the menace of drugs in sport.* **2** Menace is the quality of being threatening E.G. *an atmosphere of menace.* ▶ VERB **3** If someone or something menaces you, they threaten to harm you.

menacingly ADVERB

menagerie menageries

Said "men-**naj**-er-ree" NOUN a collection of different wild animals. 🏛 from French *menagerie* meaning 'household management', which used to include the care of domestic animals

mend mends mending mended

VERB If you mend something that is broken, you repair it.

menial

ADJECTIVE Menial work is boring and tiring and the people who do it have low status.

meningitis

NOUN Meningitis is a serious infectious illness which affects your brain and spinal cord.

menopause

NOUN The menopause is the time during which a woman gradually stops menstruating. This usually happens when she is about fifty.

menorah menorahs

Said "mi-**naw**-rah" NOUN a candelabra that usually has seven parts and is used in Jewish temples.

menstruate menstruates menstruating menstruated

VERB When a woman menstruates, blood comes from her womb. This normally happens once a month.

menstruation NOUN **menstrual** ADJECTIVE

-ment

SUFFIX '-ment' forms nouns which refer to a state or a feeling E.G. *contentment… resentment.*
🏛 from Latin suffix *-mentum*

mental

ADJECTIVE **1** relating to the process of thinking or intelligence E.G. *mental arithmetic.* **2** relating to the health of the mind E.G. *mental health.*

mentally ADVERB

mentality mentalities

NOUN an attitude or way of thinking E.G. *the traditional military mentality.*

mention mentions mentioning mentioned

VERB **1** If you mention something, you talk about it briefly. ▶ NOUN **2** a brief comment about someone or something E.G. *He made no mention of his criminal past.*

🔲 (sense 1) bring up, refer to, touch upon

mentor mentors

NOUN Someone's mentor is a person who teaches them and gives them advice.

menu menus

NOUN **1** a list of the foods you can eat in a restaurant. **2** a list of different options shown on a computer screen which the user must choose from.

mercenary mercenaries

NOUN **1** a soldier who is paid to fight for a foreign country. ▶ ADJECTIVE **2** Someone who is mercenary is mainly interested in getting money.

merchandise

NOUN; FORMAL Merchandise is goods

that are sold E.G. *He had left me with more merchandise than I could sell.*

merchant merchants
NOUN a trader who imports and exports goods E.G. *a coal merchant.*

merchant navy
NOUN The merchant navy is the boats and sailors involved in carrying goods for trade.

merciful
ADJECTIVE 1 considered to be fortunate as a relief from suffering E.G. *Death came as a merciful release.* 2 showing kindness and forgiveness.
mercifully ADVERB
◼ (sense 2) compassionate, humane, kind

merciless
ADJECTIVE showing no kindness or forgiveness.
mercilessly ADVERB
◼ cruel, heartless, ruthless

mercury
NOUN 1 Mercury is a silver-coloured metallic element that is liquid at room temperature. It is used in thermometers. 2 Mercury is also the planet in the solar system which is nearest to the sun.

mercy mercies
NOUN If you show mercy, you show kindness and forgiveness and do not punish someone as severely as you could.
◼ compassion, kindness, pity

mere merest
ADJECTIVE used to emphasize how unimportant or small something is E.G. *It's a mere 7-minute journey by boat.*
merely ADVERB

merge merges merging merged
VERB When two things merge, they

combine together to make one thing E.G. *The firms merged in 1983.*
merger NOUN

meringue meringues
Said "mer-**rang**" NOUN a type of crisp, sweet cake made with egg whites and sugar.

merino merinos
Said "mer-**ree**-no" NOUN a breed of sheep, common in Australia and New Zealand, with long, fine wool.

merit merits meriting merited
NOUN 1 If something has merit, it is good or worthwhile. 2 The merits of something are its advantages or good qualities. ▶ VERB 3 If something merits a particular treatment, it deserves that treatment E.G. *He merits a place in the team.*

mermaid mermaids
NOUN In stories, a mermaid is a woman with a fish's tail instead of legs, who lives in the sea.

merry merrier merriest
ADJECTIVE happy and cheerful E.G. *He was, for all his shyness, a merry man.*
merrily ADVERB

merry-go-round merry-go-rounds
NOUN a large rotating platform with models of animals or vehicles on it, on which children ride at a fair.

mesh
NOUN Mesh is threads of wire or plastic twisted together like a net E.G. *a fence made of wire mesh.*

mess messes messing messed
NOUN 1 something untidy. 2 a situation which is full of problems and trouble. 3 a room or building in which members of the armed forces eat E.G. *the officers' mess.* ▶ VERB 4 If you mess about or mess around, you

a
b
c
d
e
f
g
h
i
j
k
l
m
n
o
p
q
r
s
t
u
v
w
x
y
z

an ELegant angEL (ang**e**l)　　**SPELLING NOTE**

A
B
C
D
E
F
G
H
I
J
K
L
M
N
O
P
Q
R
S
T
U
V
W
X
Y
Z

do things without any particular purpose. **5** If you mess something up, you spoil it or do it wrong.
messy ADJECTIVE

message messages
NOUN **1** a piece of information or a request that you send someone or leave for them. **2** an idea that someone tries to communicate to people, for example in a play or a speech E.G. *the story's anti-drugs message.*

messaging
NOUN Messaging or text messaging is the sending and receiving of short pieces of information between mobile phones, using both letters and numbers to produce shortened forms of words.

messenger messengers
NOUN someone who takes a message to someone for someone else.
▤ courier, emissary, envoy

Messiah
Said "miss-**eye**-ah" PROPER NOUN **1** For Jews, the Messiah is the king of the Jews who will be sent by God. **2** For Christians, the Messiah is Jesus Christ.
🏛 from Hebrew *mashiach* meaning 'anointed'

Messrs
Said "**mes**-serz" Messrs is the plural of **Mr.** It is often used in the names of businesses E.G. *Messrs Brown and Humberley, Solicitors.*

met
the past tense and past participle of **meet.**

metabolism metabolisms
NOUN Your metabolism is the chemical processes in your body that use food for growth and energy.
metabolic ADJECTIVE

metal metals
NOUN Metal is a chemical element such as iron, steel, copper, or lead. Metals are good conductors of heat and electricity.
metallic ADJECTIVE

metamorphic
ADJECTIVE Metamorphic rock is rock that has been altered from its original state by heat or pressure.

metamorphosis metamorphoses
Said "met-am-**mor**-fiss-iss" NOUN; FORMAL When a metamorphosis occurs, a person or thing changes into something completely different E.G. *the metamorphosis of a larva into an insect.*

metaphor metaphors
NOUN (ENGLISH) an imaginative way of describing something as another thing, and so suggesting that it has the typical qualities of that other thing. For example, if you wanted to say that someone is shy, you might say they are a mouse.
metaphorical ADJECTIVE
metaphorically ADVERB

meteor meteors
NOUN a piece of rock or metal that burns very brightly when it enters the earth's atmosphere from space.

meteoric
ADJECTIVE A meteoric rise to power or success happens very quickly.

meteorite meteorites
NOUN a piece of rock from space that has landed on earth.

meteorological
ADJECTIVE relating to or involving the weather or weather forecasting.
meteorology NOUN

meter meters

NOUN a device that measures and records something E.G. *a gas meter*.

methane

Said "**mee**-thane" NOUN Methane is a colourless gas with no smell that is found in coal gas and produced by decaying vegetable matter. It burns easily and can be used as a fuel.

method methods

NOUN 1 a particular way of doing something E.G. *the traditional method of making wine*. 2 (SCIENCE) a way that an experiment or test is carried out E.G. *Describe the method as well as the result obtained*.

methodical

ADJECTIVE Someone who is methodical does things carefully and in an organized way.

methodically ADVERB

Methodist Methodists

NOUN or ADJECTIVE someone who belongs to the Methodist Church, a Protestant church whose members worship God in a way begun by John Wesley and his followers.

meticulous

ADJECTIVE A meticulous person does things very carefully and with great attention to detail.

meticulously ADVERB

metre metres

NOUN 1 (MATHS) a unit of length equal to 100 centimetres. 2 In poetry, metre is the rhythmic arrangement of words and syllables.

metric

ADJECTIVE relating to the system of measurement that uses metres, grams, and litres.

metropolis metropolises

NOUN a very large city.

📖 from Greek *mētēr* + *polis* meaning 'mother city'

metropolitan

ADJECTIVE relating or belonging to a large, busy city E.G. *metropolitan districts*.

mettle

NOUN If you are on your mettle, you are ready to do something as well as you can because you know you are being tested or challenged.

mew mews mewing mewed

VERB 1 When a cat mews, it makes a short high-pitched noise. ▶ NOUN 2 the short high-pitched sound that a cat makes. 3 A mews is a quiet yard or street surrounded by houses.

Mexican Mexicans

ADJECTIVE 1 belonging or relating to Mexico. ▶ NOUN 2 someone who comes from Mexico.

mg

an abbreviation for 'milligrams'.

miasma miasmas or **miasmata**

NOUN an unhealthy or unpleasant atmosphere, especially one caused by decaying things.

mice

the plural of **mouse**.

micro-

PREFIX 'Micro-' means very small.
📖 from Greek *micros* meaning 'small'

microchip microchips

NOUN a small piece of silicon on which electronic circuits for a computer are printed.

microphone microphones

NOUN a device that is used to make sounds louder or to record them on a tape recorder.

microprocessor microprocessors

NOUN a microchip which can be

a b c d e f g h i j k l **m** n o p q r s t u v w x y z

programmed to do a large number of tasks or calculations.

microscope microscopes
NOUN a piece of equipment which magnifies very small objects so that you can study them.

microscopic
ADJECTIVE very small indeed E.G. *microscopic parasites*.

microwave microwaves
NOUN A microwave or microwave oven is a type of oven which cooks food very quickly by radiation.

mid-
PREFIX 'Mid-' is used to form words that refer to the middle part of a place or period of time E.G. *mid-Atlantic… the mid-70s*.
🔲 from Old English

midday
NOUN Midday is twelve o'clock in the middle of the day.

middle middles
NOUN 1 The middle of something is the part furthest from the edges, ends, or outside surface. ▶ ADJECTIVE 2 The middle one in a series or a row is the one that has an equal number of people or things each side of it E.G. *the middle house*.

middle age
NOUN Middle age is the period of your life when you are between about 40 and 60 years old.
middle-aged ADJECTIVE

Middle Ages
PLURAL NOUN In European history, the Middle Ages were the period between about 1100 AD and 1500 AD.

middle class middle classes
NOUN The middle classes are the people in a society who are not working class or upper class, for example managers and lawyers.

Middle East
NOUN The Middle East consists of Iran and the countries in Asia to the west and south-west of Iran.

Middle English
NOUN Middle English was the English language from about 1100 AD until about 1450 AD.

middle-of-the-road
ADJECTIVE Middle-of-the-road opinions are moderate.

middle school middle schools
NOUN In England and Wales, a middle school is for children aged between about 8 and 12.

middling
ADJECTIVE of average quality or ability.

midge midges
NOUN a small flying insect which can bite people.

midget midgets
NOUN a very short person.

midnight
NOUN Midnight is twelve o'clock at night.

midriff midriffs
NOUN the middle of your body between your waist and your chest.

midst
NOUN If you are in the midst of a crowd or an event, you are in the middle of it.

midsummer
ADJECTIVE relating to the period in the middle of summer E.G. *a lovely midsummer morning in July*.

midway
ADVERB in the middle of a distance or period of time E.G. *They scored midway through the second half*.

midwife midwives
NOUN a nurse who is trained to help

A B C D E F G H I J K L M N O P Q R S T U V W X Y Z

women at the birth of a baby.

midwifery NOUN

might

VERB **1** If you say something might happen, you mean that it is possible that it will happen E.G. *I might stay a while.* **2** If you say that someone might do something, you are suggesting that they do it E.G. *You might like to go and see it.* **3** Might is also the past tense of **may**. ▶ NOUN **4** LITERARY Might is strength or power E.G. *the full might of the Navy.*
☑ You can use *might* or *may* to make a very polite request: *might I ask a favour?… may I ask a favour?*

mightily

ADVERB; LITERARY to a great degree or extent E.G. *I was mightily relieved by the decision.*

mighty mightier mightiest

ADJECTIVE; LITERARY very powerful or strong E.G. *a mighty army on the march.*

migraine migraines

*Said "**mee**-grane or **my**-grane"* NOUN a severe headache that makes you feel very ill.
🔟 from Latin *hemicrania* meaning 'pain in half the head'

migrate migrates migrating migrated

VERB **1** If people migrate, they move from one place to another, especially to find work. **2** When birds or animals migrate, they move at a particular season to a different place, usually to breed or to find new feeding grounds E.G. *the birds migrate each year to Mexico.*

migration NOUN   **migratory** ADJECTIVE   **migrant** NOUN or ADJECTIVE

mike mikes

NOUN; INFORMAL a microphone.

mild milder mildest

ADJECTIVE **1** Something that is mild is not strong and does not have any powerful or damaging effects E.G. *a mild shampoo.* **2** Someone who is mild is gentle and kind. **3** Mild weather is warmer than usual E.G. *The region has mild winters and hot summers.* **4** Mild emotions or attitudes are not very great or extreme E.G. *mild surprise.*

mildly ADVERB

mildew

NOUN Mildew is a soft white fungus that grows on things when they are warm and damp.

mile miles

NOUN a unit of distance equal to 1760 yards or about 1.6 kilometres.
🔟 from Latin *milia passuum* meaning 'a thousand paces'

mileage mileages

NOUN **1** Your mileage is the distance that you have travelled, measured in miles. **2** The amount of mileage that you get out of something is how useful it is to you.

militant militants

ADJECTIVE **1** A militant person is very active in trying to bring about extreme political or social change E.G. *a militant socialist.* ▶ NOUN **2** a person who tries to bring about extreme political or social change.

militancy NOUN

military

ADJECTIVE **1** related to or involving the armed forces of a country E.G. *military bases.* ▶ NOUN **2** The military are the armed forces of a country.

militarily ADVERB

a
b
c
d
e
f
g
h
i
j
k
l
m
n
o
p
q
r
s
t
u
v
w
x
y
z

A
B
C
D
E
F
G
H
I
J
K
L
M
N
O
P
Q
R
S
T
U
V
W
X
Y
Z

militia militias
Said "mil-lish-a" NOUN an organization that operates like an army but whose members are not professional soldiers.

milk milks milking milked
NOUN **1** Milk is the white liquid produced by female cows, goats, and some other animals to feed their young. People drink milk and use it to make butter, cheese, and yogurt. **2** Milk is also the white liquid that a baby drinks from its mother's breasts. ▶ VERB **3** When someone milks a cow or a goat, they get milk from it by pulling its udders. **4** If you milk a situation, you get as much personal gain from it as possible E.G. *They milked money from a hospital charity*.

milk tooth milk teeth
NOUN Your milk teeth are your first teeth which fall out and are replaced by the permanent set.

milky milkier milkiest
ADJECTIVE **1** pale creamy white E.G. *milky white skin*. **2** containing a lot of milk E.G. *a large mug of milky coffee*.

Milky Way
NOUN The Milky Way is a strip of stars clustered closely together, appearing as a pale band in the sky.

mill mills
NOUN **1** a building where grain is crushed to make flour. **2** a factory for making materials such as steel, wool, or cotton. **3** a small device for grinding coffee or spices into powder E.G. *a pepper mill*.

millennium millennia or **millenniums**
NOUN; FORMAL a period of 1000 years.

millennium bug
NOUN a computer software problem

caused by the change of date at the start of the year 2000.

miller millers
NOUN the person who operates a flour mill.

milligram milligrams
NOUN a unit of weight equal to one thousandth of a gram.

millilitre millilitres
NOUN a unit of liquid volume equal to one thousandth of a litre.

millimetre millimetres
NOUN a unit of length equal to a tenth of a centimetre or one thousandth of a metre.

million millions
the number 1,000,000.

millionth

millionaire millionaires
NOUN a very rich person who has property worth millions of pounds or dollars.

millstone millstones
PHRASE If something is **a millstone round your neck**, it is an unpleasant problem or responsibility you cannot escape from.

mime mimes miming mimed
NOUN **1** Mime is the use of movements and gestures to express something or to tell a story without using speech. ▶ VERB **2** If you mime something, you describe or express it using mime.

mimic mimics mimicking mimicked
VERB **1** If you mimic someone's actions or voice, you imitate them in an amusing way. ▶ NOUN **2** a person who can imitate other people.

mimicry NOUN

minaret minarets
NOUN a tall, thin tower on a mosque.

mince minces mincing minced

NOUN **1** Mince is meat which has been chopped into very small pieces in a special machine. ▶ VERB **2** If you mince meat, you chop it into very small pieces. **3** To mince about is to walk with small quick steps in an affected, effeminate way.

mind minds minding minded

NOUN **1** Your mind is your ability to think, together with all the thoughts you have and your memory. ▶ PHRASE **2** If you **change your mind**, you change a decision that you have made or an opinion that you have. ▶ VERB **3** If you do not mind something, you are not annoyed by it or bothered about it. **4** If you say that you wouldn't mind something, you mean that you would quite like it E.G. *I wouldn't mind a drink.* **5** If you mind a child or mind something for someone, you look after it for a while E.G. *My mother is minding the office.*

mindful

ADJECTIVE; FORMAL If you are mindful of something, you think about it carefully before taking action E.G. *mindful of their needs.*

mindless

ADJECTIVE **1** Mindless actions are regarded as stupid and destructive E.G. *mindless violence.* **2** A mindless job or activity is simple and repetitive.

mine mines mining mined

PRONOUN **1** 'Mine' refers to something belonging or relating to the person who is speaking or writing E.G. *a friend of mine.* ▶ NOUN **2** a series of holes or tunnels in the ground from which diamonds, coal, or other

minerals are dug out E.G. *a diamond mine.* **3** a bomb hidden in the ground or underwater, which explodes when people or things touch it. ▶ VERB **4** To mine diamonds, coal, or other minerals is to obtain these substances from underneath the ground.

miner NOUN   **mining** NOUN

minefield minefields

NOUN an area of land or water where mines have been hidden.

mineral minerals

NOUN （D & T） a substance such as tin, salt, or coal that is formed naturally in rocks and in the earth E.G. *rich mineral deposits.*

mineral water

NOUN Mineral water is water which comes from a natural spring.

minestrone

Said "min-nes-**strone**-ee" NOUN Minestrone is soup containing small pieces of vegetable and pasta. 🎴 from Italian *minestrare* meaning 'to serve'

minesweeper minesweepers

NOUN a ship for clearing away underwater mines.

mingle mingles mingling mingled

VERB If things mingle, they become mixed together E.G. *His cries mingled with theirs.*

mini-

PREFIX 'Mini-' is used to form nouns referring to something smaller or less important than similar things E.G. *a TV mini-series.*

miniature miniatures

Said "min-nit-cher" ADJECTIVE **1** a tiny copy of something much larger. ▶ NOUN **2** a very small detailed painting, often of a person.

a b c d e f g h i j k l m n o p q r s t u v w x y z

A
B
C
D
E
F
G
H
I
J
K
L
M
N
O
P
Q
R
S
T
U
V
W
X
Y
Z

minibus minibuses
NOUN a van with seats in the back which is used as a small bus.

minim minims
NOUN (MUSIC) a musical note (♩) that has a time value equal to half a semibreve. In the United States and Canada, a minim is called a half note.

minimal
ADJECTIVE very small in quality, quantity, or degree E.G. *He has minimal experience.*
minimally ADVERB

minimize minimizes minimizing minimized; also spelt **minimise**
VERB If you minimize something, you reduce it to the smallest amount possible E.G. *His route was changed to minimize jet lag.*

minimum
ADJECTIVE 1 The minimum amount is the smallest amount that is possible E.G. *a minimum wage.* ▸ NOUN 2 The minimum is the smallest amount that is possible E.G. *a minimum of three weeks.*

minister ministers
NOUN 1 A minister is a person who is in charge of a particular government department E.G. *Portugal's deputy foreign minister.* 2 A minister in a Protestant church is a member of the clergy.

ministerial
ADJECTIVE relating to a government minister or ministry E.G. *ministerial duties.*

ministry ministries
NOUN 1 a government department that deals with a particular area of work E.G. *the Ministry of Defence.* 2 Members of the clergy can be referred to as the ministry E.G. *Her son is in the ministry.*

mink minks
NOUN Mink is an expensive fur used to make coats or hats.

minnow minnows
NOUN a very small freshwater fish.

minor minors
ADJECTIVE 1 not as important or serious as other things E.G. *a minor injury.* 2 (MUSIC) A minor key is one of the keys in which most European music is written. ▸ NOUN 3 FORMAL a young person under the age of 18 E.G. *laws concerning the employment of minors.*

minority minorities
NOUN 1 The minority of people or things in a group is a number of them forming less than half of the whole E.G. *Only a minority of people want this.* 2 A minority is a group of people of a particular race or religion living in a place where most people are of a different race or religion E.G. *ethnic minorities.*

minstrel minstrels
NOUN a singer and entertainer in medieval times.

mint mints minting minted
NOUN 1 Mint is a herb used for flavouring in cooking. 2 a peppermint-flavoured sweet. 3 The mint is the place where the official coins of a country are made. ▸ VERB 4 When coins or medals are minted, they are made. ▸ ADJECTIVE 5 If something is in mint condition, it is in very good condition, like new.

minus (MATHS) 1 You use 'minus' to show that one number is being subtracted from another E.G. *Ten minus six equals four.*
ADJECTIVE 2 'Minus' is used when

SPELLING NOTE I always visit my FRIend on a FRIday (fri**end**) talking about temperatures below 0°C or 0°F.

minuscule
Said "**min**-nus-kyool" ADJECTIVE very small indeed.

minute minutes minuting minuted
Said "**min**-nit" NOUN **1** a unit of time equal to sixty seconds. **2** The minutes of a meeting are the written records of what was said and decided. ▶ VERB **3** To minute a meeting is to write the official notes of it.

minute
Said "my-**nyoot**" ADJECTIVE extremely small E.G. *a minute amount of pesticide.*
minutely ADVERB

minutiae
Said "my-**nyoo**-shee-aye" PLURAL NOUN; FORMAL Minutiae are small, unimportant details.

miracle miracles
NOUN **1** (RE) a wonderful and surprising event, believed to have been caused by God. **2** any very surprising and fortunate event E.G. *My father got a job. It was a miracle.*
miraculous ADJECTIVE
miraculously ADVERB

mirage mirages
Said "mir-**ahj**" NOUN an image which you can see in the distance in very hot weather, but which does not actually exist.

mire
NOUN; LITERARY Mire is swampy ground or mud.

mirror mirrors mirroring mirrored
NOUN **1** a piece of glass which reflects light and in which you can see your reflection. ▶ VERB **2** To mirror

something is to have similar features to it E.G. *His own shock was mirrored on her face.*

mirth
NOUN; LITERARY Mirth is great amusement and laughter.

mis-
PREFIX 'Mis-' means 'wrong' or 'false' E.G. *misbehaviour… misconception.* 🔲 from Old English

misbehave misbehaves misbehaving misbehaved
VERB If a child misbehaves, he or she is naughty or behaves badly.
misbehaviour NOUN

miscarriage miscarriages
NOUN **1** If a woman has a miscarriage she gives birth to a baby before it is properly formed and it dies. **2** A miscarriage of justice is a wrong decision made by a court, which causes an innocent person to be punished.

miscellaneous
ADJECTIVE A miscellaneous group is made up of people or things that are different from each other.

mischief
NOUN Mischief is eagerness to have fun by teasing people or playing tricks.
mischievous ADJECTIVE

misconception misconceptions
NOUN a wrong idea about something E.G. *Another misconception is that cancer is infectious.*

misconduct
NOUN Misconduct is bad or unacceptable behaviour by a professional person E.G. *The Football Association found him guilty of misconduct.*

misdemeanour misdemeanours
Said "miss-dem-**mee**-ner" NOUN; FORMAL

a
b
c
d
e
f
g
h
i
j
k
l
m
n
o
p
q
r
s
t
u
v
w
x
y
z

I want to see (C) your licenCe (licen*c*e)   ◀ SPELLING NOTE

A B C D E F G H I J K L M N O P Q R S T U V W X Y Z

an act that is shocking or unacceptable.

miser misers
NOUN a person who enjoys saving money but hates spending it.
miserly ADJECTIVE

miserable
ADJECTIVE 1 If you are miserable, you are very unhappy. 2 If a place or a situation is miserable, it makes you feel depressed E.G. *a miserable little flat.*
miserably ADVERB
■ (sense 1) dejected, unhappy, wretched
■ (sense 2) gloomy, wretched

misery miseries
NOUN Misery is great unhappiness.

misfire misfires misfiring misfired
VERB If a plan misfires, it goes wrong.

misfit misfits
NOUN a person who is not accepted by other people because of being rather strange or eccentric.

misfortune misfortunes
NOUN an unpleasant occurrence that is regarded as bad luck E.G. *I had the misfortune to fall off my bike.*

misgiving misgivings
NOUN If you have misgivings, you are worried or unhappy about something E.G. *I had misgivings about his methods.*

misguided
ADJECTIVE A misguided opinion or action is wrong because it is based on a misunderstanding or bad information.

misinform misinforms misinforming misinformed
VERB If you are misinformed, you are

given wrong or inaccurate information.
misinformation NOUN

misinterpret misinterprets misinterpreting misinterpreted
VERB To misinterpret something is to understand it wrongly E.G. *You completely misinterpreted what I wrote.*

misjudge misjudges misjudging misjudged
VERB If you misjudge someone or something, you form an incorrect idea or opinion about them.

mislay mislays mislaying mislaid
VERB If you mislay something, you lose it because you have forgotten where you put it.

mislead misleads misleading misled
VERB To mislead someone is to make them believe something which is not true.

misplaced
ADJECTIVE A misplaced feeling is inappropriate or directed at the wrong thing or person E.G. *misplaced loyalty.*

misprint misprints
NOUN a mistake such as a spelling mistake in something that has been printed.

misrepresent misrepresents misrepresenting misrepresented
VERB To misrepresent someone is to give an inaccurate or misleading account of what they have said or done.
misrepresentation NOUN

miss misses missing missed
VERB 1 If you miss something, you do not notice it E.G. *You can't miss it. It's*

on the second floor. **2** If you miss someone or something, you feel sad that they are no longer with you E.G. *The boys miss their father.* **3** If you miss a chance or opportunity, you fail to take advantage of it. **4** If you miss a bus, plane, or train, you arrive too late to catch it. **5** If you miss something, you fail to hit it when you aim at it E.G. *His shot missed the target and went wide.* ▶ NOUN **6** an act of missing something that you were aiming at. **7** 'Miss' is used before the name of a woman or girl who is not married as a form of address E.G. *Did you know Miss Smith?*

missile missiles
NOUN a weapon that moves long distances through the air and explodes when it reaches its target; also used of any object thrown as a weapon.

mission missions
NOUN **1** an important task that you have to do. **2** a group of people who have been sent to a foreign country to carry out an official task E.G. *He became head of the Israeli mission.* **3** a journey made by a military aeroplane or space rocket to carry out a task. **4** If you have a mission, there is something that you believe it is your duty to try to achieve. **5** the workplace of a group of Christians who are working for the Church.

missionary missionaries
NOUN a Christian who has been sent to a foreign country to work for the Church.

missive missives
NOUN; OLD-FASHIONED a letter or message.

mist mists misting misted
NOUN **1** Mist consists of a large number of tiny drops of water in the

air, which make it hard to see clearly. ▶ VERB **2** If your eyes mist, you cannot see very far because there are tears in your eyes. **3** If glass mists over or mists up, it becomes covered with condensation so that you cannot see through it.

mistake mistakes mistaking mistook mistaken
NOUN **1** an action or opinion that is wrong or is not what you intended. ▶ VERB **2** If you mistake someone or something for another person or thing, you wrongly think that they are the other person or thing E.G. *I mistook him for the owner of the house.*
■ (sense 1) blunder, error, miscalculation, slip

mistaken
ADJECTIVE **1** If you are mistaken about something, you are wrong about it. **2** If you have a mistaken belief or opinion, you believe something which is not true.
mistakenly ADVERB

mister
A man is sometimes addressed in a very informal way as 'mister' E.G. *Where do you live, mister?*

mistletoe
Said "mis-sel-toe" NOUN Mistletoe is a plant which grows on trees and has white berries on it. It is used as a Christmas decoration.

mistook
the past tense of **mistake**.

mistreat mistreats mistreating mistreated
VERB To mistreat a person or animal is to treat them badly and make them suffer.

mistress mistresses
NOUN **1** A married man's mistress is a

a
b
c
d
e
f
g
h
i
j
k
l
m
n
o
p
q
r
s
t
u
v
w
x
y
z

mistrust >> **ml**

woman who is not his wife and who he is having a sexual relationship with. **2** A school mistress is a female teacher. **3** A servant's mistress is the woman who is the servant's employer.

mistrust mistrusts mistrusting mistrusted
VERB **1** If you mistrust someone, you do not feel that you can trust them. ▶ NOUN **2** Mistrust is a feeling that you cannot trust someone.

misty mistier mistiest
ADJECTIVE full of or covered with mist.

misunderstand misunderstands misunderstanding misunderstood
VERB If you misunderstand someone, you do not properly understand what they say or do E.G. *He misunderstood the problem.*

misunderstanding misunderstandings
NOUN If two people have a misunderstanding, they have a slight quarrel or disagreement.

misuse misuses misusing misused
Said "mis-**yooz**" NOUN The misuse of something is the incorrect or dishonest use of it E.G. *the misuse of public money. Said* "mis-**yooss**" VERB To misuse something is to use it incorrectly or dishonestly.

mite mites
NOUN a very tiny creature that lives in the fur of animals.

mitigating
ADJECTIVE; FORMAL Mitigating circumstances make a crime easier to understand, and perhaps justify it.

mitten mittens
NOUN Mittens are gloves which have

one section that covers your thumb and another section for the rest of your fingers together.

mix mixes mixing mixed
VERB If you mix things, you combine them or shake or stir them together.
☰ blend, combine, merge, mingle

mix up VERB If you mix up two things or people, you confuse them E.G. *People often mix us up and greet us by each other's names.*

mixed
ADJECTIVE **1** consisting of several things of the same general kind E.G. *a mixed salad*. **2** involving people from two or more different races E.G. *mixed marriages*. **3** Mixed education or accommodation is for both males and females E.G. *a mixed comprehensive*.

mixed up
ADJECTIVE **1** If you are mixed up, you are confused E.G. *I'm mixed up about which country I want to play for.* **2** If you are mixed up in a crime or a scandal, you are involved in it.

mixer mixers
NOUN a machine used for mixing things together E.G. *a cement mixer*.

mixture mixtures
NOUN several different things mixed together. a substance that consists of other substances which have been stirred or shaken together E.G. *Spoon the mixture into serving glasses.*
☰ blend, medley, mix

mix-up mix-ups
NOUN a mistake in something that was planned E.G. *a mix-up with the bookings.*

ml
an abbreviation for 'millilitres'.

mm
an abbreviation for 'millimetres'.

moa moa or moas
NOUN a large, flightless bird that lived in New Zealand and which became extinct in the late 18th century.

moan moans moaning moaned
VERB 1 If you moan, you make a low, miserable sound because you are in pain or suffering. 2 INFORMAL If you moan about something, you complain about it. ▶ NOUN 3 a low cry of pain or misery.

moat moats
NOUN a wide, water-filled ditch around a building such as a castle.

mob mobs mobbing mobbed
NOUN 1 a large, disorganized crowd of people E.G. *A violent mob attacked the team bus.* ▶ VERB 2 If a lot of people mob someone, they crowd around the person in a disorderly way E.G. *The band was mobbed by over a thousand fans.*
🔲 from Latin *mobile vulgus* meaning 'the fickle public'

mobile mobiles
ADJECTIVE 1 able to move or be moved freely and easily E.G. *a mobile phone.* 2 (PE) If you are mobile, you are able to travel or move about from one place to another E.G. *a mobile workforce.* ▶ NOUN 3 a decoration consisting of several small objects which hang from threads and move around when a breeze blows. 4 a mobile phone.
mobility NOUN

moccasin moccasins
NOUN Moccasins are flat, soft leather shoes with a raised seam above the toe.
🔲 from *mocussin*, a North American

Indian word meaning 'shoe'

mock mocks mocking mocked
VERB 1 If you mock someone, you say something scornful or imitate their foolish behaviour. ▶ ADJECTIVE 2 not genuine E.G. *mock surprise… a mock Tudor house.* 3 A mock examination is one that you do as a practice before the real examination.
🔲 (sense 1) laugh at, make fun of, ridicule

mockery
NOUN Mockery is the expression of scorn or ridicule of someone.
🔲 derision, ridicule

mode modes
NOUN 1 A mode of life or behaviour is a particular way of living or behaving. 2 In mathematics, the mode is the biggest in a set of groups.

model models modelling modelled
NOUN OR ADJECTIVE 1 a copy of a something that shows what it looks like or how it works E.G. *a model aircraft.* ▶ NOUN 2 Something that is described as, for example, a model of clarity or a model of perfection, is extremely clear or absolutely perfect. 3 a type or version of a machine E.G. *Which model of washing machine did you choose?* 4 a person who poses for a painter or a photographer. 5 a person who wears the clothes that are being displayed at a fashion show. ▶ ADJECTIVE 6 Someone who is described as, for example, a model wife or a model student is an excellent wife or student. ▶ VERB 7 If you model yourself on someone, you copy their behaviour because you admire them. 8 To model clothes is to display them by wearing them.

a
b
c
d
e
f
g
h
i
j
k
l
m
n
o
p
q
r
s
t
u
v
w
x
y
z

A
B
C
D
E
F
G
H
I
J
K
L
M
N
O
P
Q
R
S
T
U
V
W
X
Y
Z

9 To model shapes or figures is to make them out of clay or wood.
■ (sense 2) example, ideal, pattern

modem modems
Said "moe-dem" NOUN (ICT) a piece of equipment that links a computer to the telephone system so that data can be transferred from one machine to another via the telephone line.

moderate moderates moderating moderated
ADJECTIVE **1** Moderate views are not extreme, and usually favour gradual changes rather than major ones. **2** A moderate amount of something is neither large nor small. ▶ NOUN **3** a person whose political views are not extreme. ▶ VERB **4** If you moderate something or if it moderates, it becomes less extreme or violent E.G. *The weather moderated.*
moderately ADVERB

moderation
NOUN Moderation is control of your behaviour that stops you acting in an extreme way E.G. *a man of fairness and moderation.*

modern
ADJECTIVE **1** relating to the present time E.G. *modern society.* **2** new and involving the latest ideas and equipment E.G. *modern technology.*
modernity NOUN
■ (sense 1) contemporary, current, present-day

modernize modernizes modernizing modernized; also spelt **modernise**
VERB To modernize something is to introduce new methods or equipment to it.

modest
ADJECTIVE **1** quite small in size or amount. **2** Someone who is modest does not boast about their abilities or possessions. **3** shy and easily embarrassed.
modestly ADVERB **modesty** NOUN

modification modifications
NOUN a small change made to improve something E.G. *Modifications to the undercarriage were made.*

modify modifies modifying modified
VERB If you modify something, you change it slightly in order to improve it.

module modules
NOUN **1** one of the parts which when put together form a whole unit or object E.G. *The college provides modules for trainees.* **2** (ICT) a part of a machine or system that does a particular task. **3** a part of a spacecraft which can do certain things away from the main body E.G. *the lunar module.*
modular ADJECTIVE

mohair
NOUN Mohair is very soft, fluffy wool obtained from angora goats.

moist moister moistest
ADJECTIVE slightly wet.

moisten moistens moistening moistened
VERB If you moisten something, you make it slightly wet.

moisture
NOUN Moisture is tiny drops of water in the air or on the ground.

molar molars
NOUN Your molars are the large teeth at the back of your mouth.

SPELLING NOTE You must practiSe your Ss (practi*se*)

mole moles

NOUN **1** a dark, slightly raised spot on your skin. **2** a small animal with black fur. Moles live in tunnels underground. **3** INFORMAL a member of an organization who is working as a spy for a rival organization.

molecule molecules

NOUN the smallest amount of a substance that can exist.

molecular ADJECTIVE

molest molests molesting molested

VERB To molest a child is to touch the child in a sexual way. This is illegal.

molester NOUN

mollify mollifies mollifying mollified

VERB To mollify someone is to do something to make them less upset or angry.

mollusc molluscs

NOUN an animal with a soft body and no backbone. Snails, slugs, clams, and mussels are all molluscs.

molten

ADJECTIVE Molten rock or metal has been heated to a very high temperature and has become a thick liquid.

moment moments

NOUN **1** a very short period of time E.G. *He paused for a moment.* **2** The moment at which something happens is the point in time at which it happens E.G. *At that moment, the doorbell rang.* ▶ PHRASE **3** If something is happening **at the moment**, it is happening now.

▤ (sense 1) instant, second

momentary

ADJECTIVE Something that is momentary lasts for only a few seconds E.G. *a momentary lapse of concentration.*

momentarily ADVERB

☑ Some Americans say *momentarily* when they mean 'very soon', rather than 'for a moment'.

momentous

ADJECTIVE; FORMAL very important, often because of its future effect E.G. *a momentous occasion.*

momentum

NOUN **1** Momentum is the ability that something has to keep developing E.G. *The campaign is gaining momentum.* **2** Momentum is also the ability that an object has to continue moving as a result of the speed it already has.

monarch monarchs

Said "**mon-nark**" NOUN a queen, king, or other royal person who reigns over a country.

monarchy monarchies

NOUN a system in which a queen or king reigns in a country.

monastery monasteries

NOUN a building in which monks live.

monastic ADJECTIVE

Monday Mondays

NOUN Monday is the day between Sunday and Tuesday.

▦ from Old English *monandæg* meaning 'moon's day'

money

NOUN Money is the coins or banknotes that you use to buy something.

mongrel mongrels

NOUN a dog with parents of different breeds.

monitor monitors monitoring monitored

VERB **1** If you monitor something, you

a
b
c
d
e
f
g
h
i
j
k
l
m
n
o
p
q
r
s
t
u
v
w
x
y
z

A B C D E F G H I J K L **M** N O P Q R S T U V W X Y Z

regularly check its condition and progress E.G. *Her health will be monitored daily.* ▶ NOUN **2** a machine used to check or record things. **3** (ICT) the visual display unit of a computer. **4** a school pupil chosen to do special duties by the teacher.

monk monks
NOUN a member of a male religious community.

monkey monkeys
NOUN an animal which has a long tail and climbs trees. Monkeys live in hot countries.

mono-
PREFIX 'Mono-' is used at the beginning of nouns and adjectives that have 'one' as part of their meaning E.G. *monopoly… monogamy.*
🏛 from Greek *monos* meaning 'single'

monocle monocles
NOUN a glass lens worn in front of one eye only and held in place by the curve of the eye socket.

monogamy
NOUN; FORMAL Monogamy is the custom of being married to only one person at a time.
monogamous ADJECTIVE

monologue monologues
Said "mon-nol-og" NOUN a long speech by one person during a play or a conversation.

monopoly monopolies
NOUN control of most of an industry by one or a few large firms.

monotone monotones
NOUN a tone which does not vary E.G. *He droned on in a boring monotone.*

monotonous
ADJECTIVE having a regular pattern which is very dull and boring E.G. *monotonous work.*

monotony NOUN

monotreme monotremes
NOUN an Australian mammal that has a single opening in its body.

monounsaturated
ADJECTIVE Monounsaturated oils are made mainly from vegetable fats and are considered to be healthier than saturated oils.
monounsaturate NOUN

monsoon monsoons
NOUN the season of very heavy rain in South-east Asia.

monster monsters
NOUN **1** a large, imaginary creature that looks very frightening. **2** a cruel or frightening person. ▶ ADJECTIVE **3** extremely large E.G. *a monster truck.*
🏛 from Latin *monstrum* meaning 'omen' or 'warning'

monstrosity monstrosities
NOUN something that is large and extremely ugly E.G. *a concrete monstrosity in the middle of the city.*

monstrous
ADJECTIVE extremely shocking or unfair E.G. *a monstrous crime.*
monstrously ADVERB

montage montages
Said "mon-tahj" NOUN a picture or film consisting of a combination of several different items arranged to produce an unusual effect.

month months
NOUN one of the twelve periods that a year is divided into.

monthly monthlies
ADJECTIVE Monthly describes something that happens or appears once a month E.G. *monthly staff meetings.*

monument monuments
NOUN a large stone structure built to remind people of a famous person or event E.G. *a monument to the dead*.

monumental
ADJECTIVE **1** A monumental building or sculpture is very large and important. **2** very large or extreme E.G. *We face a monumental task.*

moo moos mooing mooed
VERB When a cow moos, it makes a long, deep sound.

mood moods
NOUN the way you are feeling at a particular time E.G. *She was in a really cheerful mood.*
■ humour, state of mind, temper

moody moodier moodiest
ADJECTIVE **1** Someone who is moody is depressed or unhappy E.G. *Tony, despite his charm, could sulk and be moody.* **2** Someone who is moody often changes their mood for no apparent reason.
■ (sense 1) morose, sulky, sullen
■ (sense 2) mercurial, temperamental

moon moons
NOUN The moon is an object moving round the earth which you see as a shining circle or crescent in the sky at night. Some other planets have moons.

moonlight moonlights moonlighting moonlighted
NOUN **1** Moonlight is the light that comes from the moon at night. ▶ VERB **2** INFORMAL If someone is moonlighting, they have a second job that they have not informed the tax office about.

moonlit ADJECTIVE

moor moors mooring moored
NOUN **1** a high area of open land.
▶ VERB **2** If a boat is moored, it is attached to the land with a rope.

mooring moorings
NOUN a place where a boat can be tied.

moose
NOUN a large North American deer with flat antlers.

moot moots mooting mooted
VERB; FORMAL When something is mooted, it is suggested for discussion E.G. *The project was first mooted in 1988.*

mop mops mopping mopped
NOUN **1** a tool for washing floors, consisting of a sponge or string head attached to a long handle. **2** a large amount of loose or untidy hair. ▶ VERB **3** To mop a floor is to clean it with a mop. **4** To mop a surface is to wipe it with a dry cloth to remove liquid.

mope mopes moping moped
VERB If you mope, you feel miserable and not interested in anything.

moped mopeds
Said "moe-ped" NOUN a type of small motorcycle.

mopoke mopokes
NOUN a small, spotted owl found in Australia and New Zealand. In New Zealand it is called a **morepork**.

moral morals
PLURAL NOUN **1** (RE) Morals are values based on beliefs about the correct and acceptable way to behave.
▶ ADJECTIVE **2** concerned with whether behaviour is right or acceptable E.G. *moral values.*

morality NOUN **morally** ADVERB

morale
Said "mor-rahl" NOUN Morale is the

a b c d e f g h i j k l **m** n o p q r s t u v w x y z

A
B
C
D
E
F
G
H
I
J
K
L
M
N
O
P
Q
R
S
T
U
V
W
X
Y
Z

amount of confidence and optimism that you have E.G. *The morale of the troops was high.*

morbid

ADJECTIVE having a great interest in unpleasant things, especially death.

more

ADJECTIVE or PRONOUN 1 More means a greater number or extent than something else E.G. *He's got more chips than me… I've got more than you.* 2 used to refer to an additional thing or amount of something E.G. *He found some more clues.* ▶ ADVERB 3 to a greater degree or extent E.G. *more amused than concerned.* 4 You can use 'more' in front of adjectives and adverbs to form comparatives E.G. *You look more beautiful than ever.*

moreover

ADVERB used to introduce a piece of information that supports or expands the previous statement E.G. *They have accused the government of corruption. Moreover, they have named names.*

morepork moreporks

NOUN In New Zealand English, the same as a mopoke.

morgue morgues

Said "morg" NOUN a building where dead bodies are kept before being buried or cremated.

moribund

ADJECTIVE no longer having a useful function and about to come to an end E.G. *a moribund industry.*

morning mornings

NOUN 1 the early part of the day until lunchtime. 2 the part of the day between midnight and noon E.G. *He was born at three in the morning.*

Moroccan Moroccans

Said "mor-rok-an" ADJECTIVE 1 belonging or relating to Morocco. ▶ NOUN 2 someone who comes from Morocco.

moron morons

NOUN; INFORMAL a very stupid person.

moronic ADJECTIVE

morose

ADJECTIVE miserable and bad-tempered.

morphine

NOUN Morphine is a drug which is used to relieve pain.

Morse or **Morse code**

NOUN Morse or Morse code is a code used for sending messages in which each letter is represented by a series of dots and dashes.

morsel morsels

NOUN a small piece of food.

mortal mortals

ADJECTIVE 1 unable to live forever E.G. *Remember that you are mortal.* 2 A mortal wound is one that causes death. ▶ NOUN 3 an ordinary person.

mortality

NOUN 1 Mortality is the fact that all people must die. 2 Mortality also refers to the number of people who die at any particular time E.G. *a low infant mortality rate.*

mortar mortars

NOUN 1 a short cannon which fires missiles high into the air for a short distance. 2 Mortar is a mixture of sand, water, and cement used to hold bricks firmly together.

mortgage mortgages mortgaging mortgaged

Said "mor-gij" NOUN 1 a loan which you get from a bank or a building society in order to buy a house.

SPELLING NOTE   the QUeen stood on the QUay (quay)

► VERB **2** If you **mortgage** your house, you use it as a guarantee to a company in order to borrow money from them. They can take the house from you if you do not pay back the money you have borrowed.

mortifying
ADJECTIVE embarrassing or humiliating E.G. *There were some mortifying setbacks.*

mortuary mortuaries
NOUN a special room in a hospital where dead bodies are kept before being buried or cremated.

mosaic mosaics
*Said "moe-**zay**-yik"* NOUN a design made of small coloured stones or pieces of coloured glass set into concrete or plaster.

Moslem
another spelling of **Muslim**.

mosque mosques
Said "mosk" NOUN a building where Muslims go to worship.
📖 from Arabic *masjid* meaning 'temple'

mosquito mosquitoes or mosquitos
*Said "moss-**skee**-toe"* NOUN Mosquitoes are small insects which bite people in order to suck their blood.
📖 from Spanish *mosquito* meaning 'little fly'

moss mosses
NOUN Moss is a soft, low-growing, green plant which grows on damp soil or stone.
mossy ADJECTIVE

most
ADJECTIVE or PRONOUN **1** Most of a group of things or people means nearly all of them E.G. *Most people don't share your views.* **2** The most means a larger amount than anyone or anything else E.G. *She has the most talent.* ► ADVERB **3** You can use 'most' in front of adjectives or adverbs to form superlatives E.G. *the most beautiful women in the world.*

mostly
ADVERB 'Mostly' is used to show that a statement is generally true E.G. *Her friends are mostly men.*

MOT MOTs
NOUN In Britain, an annual test for road vehicles to check that they are safe to drive.

motel motels
NOUN a hotel providing overnight accommodation for people in the middle of a car journey.

moth moths
NOUN an insect like a butterfly which usually flies at night.

mother mothers mothering mothered
NOUN **1** Your mother is the woman who gave birth to you. **2** Your mother could also be the woman who has looked after you and brought you up. ► VERB **3** To mother someone is to look after them and bring them up.

motherhood
NOUN Motherhood is the state of being a mother.

mother-in-law mothers-in-law
NOUN Someone's mother-in-law is the mother of their husband or wife.

motif motifs
*Said "moe-**teef**"* NOUN a design which is used as a decoration.

motion motions motioning motioned
NOUN **1** Motion is the process of continually moving or changing

a
b
c
d
e
f
g
h
i
j
k
l
m
n
o
p
q
r
s
t
u
v
w
x
y
z

position E.G. *the motion of the ship.*
2 an action or gesture E.G. *Apply with a brush using circular motions.* **3** a proposal which people discuss and vote on at a meeting. ▶ VERB **4** If you motion to someone, you make a movement with your hand in order to show them what they should do E.G. *I motioned him to proceed.*

motionless
ADJECTIVE not moving at all E.G. *He sat motionless.*

motivate motivates motivating motivated
VERB **1** If you are motivated by something, it makes you behave in a particular way E.G. *He is motivated by duty rather than ambition.* **2** If you motivate someone, you make them feel determined to do something. **motivated** ADJECTIVE **motivation** NOUN

■ (sense 1) drive, inspire, prompt

motive motives
NOUN (HISTORY) a reason or purpose for doing something E.G. *There was no motive for the attack.*

motley
ADJECTIVE A motley collection is made up of people or things of very different types.

motor motors
NOUN **1** a part of a vehicle or a machine that uses electricity or fuel to produce movement so that the machine can work. ▶ ADJECTIVE **2** concerned with or relating to vehicles with a petrol or diesel engine E.G. *the motor industry.*

motorboat motorboats
NOUN a boat with an engine.

motorcycle motorcycles
NOUN a two-wheeled vehicle with an

engine which is ridden like a bicycle.
motorcyclist NOUN

motoring
ADJECTIVE relating to cars and driving E.G. *a motoring correspondent.*

motorist motorists
NOUN a person who drives a car.

motorway motorways
NOUN a wide road built for fast travel over long distances.

mottled
ADJECTIVE covered with patches of different colours E.G. *mottled leaves.*

motto mottoes or mottos
NOUN a short sentence or phrase that is a rule for good or sensible behaviour.

mould moulds moulding moulded
VERB **1** To mould someone or something is to influence and change them so they develop in a particular way E.G. *Early experiences mould our behaviour for life.* **2** To mould a substance is to make it into a particular shape E.G. *Mould the mixture into flat round cakes.* ▶ NOUN **3** a container used to make something into a particular shape E.G. *a jelly mould.* **4** Mould is a soft grey or green substance that can form on old food or damp walls.
mouldy ADJECTIVE

moult moults moulting moulted
VERB When an animal or bird moults, it loses its hair or feathers so new ones can grow.

mound mounds
NOUN **1** a small man-made hill. **2** a large, untidy pile E.G. *a mound of blankets.*

mount mounts mounting mounted
VERB **1** To mount a campaign or event

is to organize it and carry it out. **2** If something is mounting, it is increasing E.G. *Economic problems are mounting.* **3** FORMAL To mount something is to go to the top of it E.G. *He mounted the steps.* **4** If you mount a horse, you climb on its back. **5** If you mount an object in a particular place, you fix it there to display it. ▶ NOUN **6** 'Mount' is also used as part of the name of a mountain E.G. *Mount Everest.*

mountain mountains
NOUN **1** a very high piece of land with steep sides. **2** a large amount of something E.G. *mountains of paperwork.*

mountaineer mountaineers
NOUN a person who climbs mountains.

mountainous
ADJECTIVE A mountainous area has a lot of mountains.

mourn mourns mourning mourned
VERB **1** If you mourn for someone who has died, you are very sad and think about them a lot. **2** If you mourn something, you are sad because you no longer have it E.G. *He mourned the end of his marriage.*

mourner mourners
NOUN a person who attends a funeral.

mournful
ADJECTIVE very sad.

mourning
NOUN If someone is in mourning, they wear special black clothes or behave in a quiet and restrained way because a member of their family has died.

mouse mice
NOUN **1** a small rodent with a long tail. **2** a small device moved by hand to control the position of the cursor on a computer screen.

mousse mousses
Said "**moos**" NOUN Mousse is a light, fluffy food made from whipped eggs and cream.

moustache moustaches
Said "mus-**stahsh**" NOUN A man's moustache is hair growing on his upper lip.
📖 from Greek *mustax* meaning 'upper lip'

mouth mouths mouthing mouthed
NOUN **1** your lips, or the space behind them where your tongue and teeth are. **2** The mouth of a cave or a hole is the entrance to it. **3** The mouth of a river is the place where it flows into the sea. ▶ VERB **4** If you mouth something, you form words with your lips without making any sound E.G. *He mouthed 'Thank you' to the jurors.*

mouthful NOUN

mouthpiece mouthpieces
NOUN **1** the part you speak into on a telephone. **2** the part of a musical instrument you put to your mouth. **3** The mouthpiece of an organization is the person who publicly states its opinions and policies.

movable
ADJECTIVE Something that is movable can be moved from one place to another.

move moves moving moved
VERB **1** To move means to go to a different place or position. To move something means to change its place or position. **2** If you move, or move house, you go to live in a different house. **3** If something

a
b
c
d
e
f
g
h
i
j
k
l
m
n
o
p
q
r
s
t
u
v
w
x
y
z

moves you, it causes you to feel a deep emotion E.G. *Her story moved us to tears.* ▶ NOUN 4 a change from one place or position to another E.G. *We were watching his every move.* 5 an act of moving house. 6 the act of putting a piece or counter in a game in a different position E.G. *It's your move next.*

■ (sense 1) budge, go, shift, stir

movement movements

NOUN 1 (DRAMA) Movement involves changing position or going from one place to another. ▶ PLURAL NOUN 2 FORMAL Your movements are everything you do during a period of time E.G. *They asked him for an account of his movements during the previous morning.* ▶ NOUN 3 a group of people who share the same beliefs or aims E.G. *the peace movement.* 4 one of the major sections of a piece of classical music.

moving

ADJECTIVE Something that is moving makes you feel deep sadness or emotion.

movingly ADVERB

mow mows mowing mowed mown

VERB 1 To mow grass is to cut it with a lawnmower. 2 To mow down a large number of people is to kill them all violently.

mower mowers

NOUN a machine for cutting grass.

MP MPs

NOUN a person who has been elected to represent people in a country's parliament. MP is an abbreviation for 'Member of Parliament'.

mpg

an abbreviation for 'miles per gallon'.

mph

an abbreviation for 'miles per hour'.

Mr

Said "miss-ter" 'Mr' is used before a man's name when you are speaking or referring to him.

Mrs

Said "miss-iz" 'Mrs' is used before the name of a married woman when you are speaking or referring to her.

Ms

Said "miz" 'Ms' is used before a woman's name when you are speaking or referring to her. Ms does not specify whether a woman is married or not.

much

ADVERB 1 You use 'much' to emphasize that something is true to a great extent E.G. *I feel much better now.* 2 If something does not happen much, it does not happen very often.

▶ ADJECTIVE or PRONOUN 3 You use 'much' to ask questions or give information about the size or amount of something E.G. *How much money do you need?*

muck mucks mucking mucked

NOUN 1 INFORMAL Muck is dirt or some other unpleasant substance. 2 Muck is also manure. ▶ VERB 3 INFORMAL If you muck about, you behave stupidly and waste time.

mucky ADJECTIVE

mucus

Said "myoo-kuss" NOUN Mucus is a liquid produced in parts of your body, for example in your nose.

mud

NOUN Mud is wet, sticky earth.

muddle muddles muddling muddled

NOUN 1 A muddle is a state of disorder

or untidiness E.G. *Our finances are in a muddle.* ▶ VERB **2** If you muddle things, you mix them up.
 📰 (sense 2) jumble, mix up

muddy muddier muddiest
ADJECTIVE **1** covered in mud. **2** A muddy colour is dull and not clear E.G. *a mottled, muddy brown.*

muesli
Said "myooz-lee" NOUN Muesli is a mixture of chopped nuts, cereal flakes, and dried fruit that you can eat for breakfast with milk.

muffin muffins
NOUN a small, round cake which you eat hot.

muffled
ADJECTIVE A muffled sound is quiet or difficult to hear E.G. *a muffled explosion.*

mug mugs mugging mugged
NOUN **1** a large, deep cup. **2** INFORMAL someone who is stupid and easily deceived. ▶ VERB **3** INFORMAL If someone mugs you, they attack you in order to steal your money.
mugging NOUN **mugger** NOUN

muggy muggier muggiest
ADJECTIVE Muggy weather is unpleasantly warm and damp.

mule mules
NOUN the offspring of a female horse and a male donkey.

mulga
NOUN **1** Mulga are acacia shrubs that are found in the desert regions of Australia. **2** INFORMAL In Australian English, mulga is also the bush or outback.

mull mulls mulling mulled
VERB If you mull something over, you think about it for a long time before making a decision.

mullet mullets
NOUN a common edible fish found in Australian and New Zealand waters.

mulloway mulloways
NOUN a large edible fish found in Australian waters.

multi-
PREFIX 'Multi-' is used to form words that refer to something that has many parts or aspects E.G. *a multistorey car park.*
 🏛 from Latin *multus* meaning 'much' or 'many'

multimedia
NOUN **1** ICT in computing, you use multimedia to refer to products which use sound, pictures, film and ordinary text to convey information. **2** In the classroom, all the things like TV, computers, and books which are used as teaching aids are called multimedia.

multinational multinationals
NOUN a very large company with branches in many countries.

multiple multiples
ADJECTIVE **1** having or involving many different functions or things E.G. *He died from multiple injuries in the crash.* ▶ NOUN **2** The multiples of a number are other numbers that it will divide into exactly. For example, 6, 9, and 12 are multiples of 3.

multiple sclerosis
Said "skler-roe-siss" NOUN Multiple sclerosis is a serious disease which attacks the nervous system, affecting your ability to move.

multiplication
NOUN **1** MATHS Multiplication is the process of multiplying one number by another. **2** The multiplication of things is a large increase in their

a
b
c
d
e
f
g
h
i
j
k
l
m
n
o
p
q
r
s
t
u
v
w
x
y
z

A
B
C
D
E
F
G
H
I
J
K
L
M
N
O
P
Q
R
S
T
U
V
W
X
Y
Z

number E.G. *the multiplication of universities*.

multiplicity

NOUN If there is a multiplicity of things, there is a large number or variety of them.

multiply multiplies multiplying multiplied

VERB 1 When something multiplies, it increases greatly in number E.G. *The trip wore on and the hazards multiplied*. 2 (MATHS) When you multiply one number by another, you calculate the total you would get if you added the first number to itself a particular number of times. For example, two multiplied by three is equal to two plus two plus two, which equals six.

multitude multitudes

NOUN; FORMAL a very large number of people or things.

mum mums

NOUN; INFORMAL Your mum is your mother.

mumble mumbles mumbling mumbled

VERB If you mumble, you speak very quietly and indistinctly.

mummy mummies

NOUN 1 AN INFORMAL USE, USED ESPECIALLY BY CHILDREN Your mummy is your mother. 2 a dead body which was preserved long ago by being rubbed with special oils and wrapped in cloth.

mumps

NOUN Mumps is a disease that causes painful swelling in the neck glands.

munch munches munching munched

VERB If you munch something, you chew it steadily and thoroughly.

mundane

ADJECTIVE very ordinary and not interesting or unusual E.G. *a mundane job*.

municipal

Said "myoo-**nis**-si-pl" ADJECTIVE belonging to a city or town which has its own local government E.G. *a municipal golf course*.

📖 from Latin *municipium* meaning 'free town'

munitions

PLURAL NOUN Munitions are bombs, guns, and other military supplies.

mural murals

NOUN a picture painted on a wall.

murder murders murdering murdered

NOUN 1 Murder is the deliberate killing of a person. ► VERB 2 To murder someone is to kill them deliberately.
murderer NOUN
☰ (sense 1) homicide, killing

murderous

ADJECTIVE 1 likely to murder someone E.G. *murderous gangsters*. 2 A murderous attack or other action results in the death of many people E.G. *murderous acts of terrorism*.

murky murkier murkiest

ADJECTIVE dark or dirty and unpleasant E.G. *He rushed through the murky streets*.

murmur murmurs murmuring murmured

VERB 1 If you murmur, you say something very softly. ► NOUN 2 something that someone says which can hardly be heard.

muscle muscles muscling muscled

NOUN 1 (PE) Your muscles are pieces of flesh which you can expand or contract in order to move parts of your body. ▶ VERB **2** INFORMAL If you muscle in on something, you force your way into a situation in which you are not welcome.

🔲 from Latin *musculus* meaning 'little mouse', because muscles were thought to look like mice

muscular
Said "**musk**-yool-lar" ADJECTIVE
1 involving or affecting your muscles E.G. *muscular strength*. **2** Someone who is muscular has strong, firm muscles.

muse muses musing mused
VERB LITERARY To muse is to think about something for a long time.

museum museums
NOUN a building where many interesting or valuable objects are kept and displayed.

mush
NOUN A mush is a thick, soft paste.

mushroom mushrooms mushrooming mushroomed
NOUN **1** a fungus with a short stem and a round top. Some types of mushroom are edible. ▶ VERB **2** If something mushrooms, it appears and grows very quickly E.G. *The mill towns mushroomed into cities*.

mushy mushier mushiest
ADJECTIVE **1** Mushy fruits or vegetables are too soft E.G. *mushy tomatoes*. **2** INFORMAL Mushy stories are too sentimental.

music
NOUN **1** Music is a pattern of sounds performed by people singing or playing instruments. **2** Music is also the written symbols that represent musical sounds E.G. *I taught myself to read music*.

musical musicals
ADJECTIVE **1** relating to playing or studying music E.G. *a musical instrument*. ▶ NOUN **2** a play or film that uses songs and dance to tell the story.
musically ADVERB

musician musicians
NOUN (MUSIC) a person who plays a musical instrument as their job or hobby.

musk
NOUN Musk is a substance with a strong, sweet smell. It is used to make perfume.
musky ADJECTIVE

musket muskets
NOUN an old-fashioned gun with a long barrel.

Muslim Muslims; also spelt **Moslem**
NOUN (RE) **1** a person who believes in Islam and lives according to its rules. ▶ ADJECTIVE **2** relating to Islam.

muslin
NOUN Muslin is a very thin cotton material.

mussel mussels
NOUN Mussels are a kind of shellfish with black shells.

must
VERB **1** If something must happen, it is very important or necessary that it happens E.G. *You must be over 18*. **2** If you tell someone they must do something, you are suggesting that they do it E.G. *You must try this pudding: it's delicious*. ▶ NOUN **3** something that is absolutely necessary E.G. *The museum is a must for all visitors*.

mustard
NOUN Mustard is a spicy-tasting

a
b
c
d
e
f
g
h
i
j
k
l
m
n
o
p
q
r
s
t
u
v
w
x
y
z

yellow or brown paste made from seeds.

muster musters mustering mustered

VERB If you muster something such as energy or support, you gather it together E.G. *as much calm as he could muster.*

musty mustier mustiest

ADJECTIVE smelling stale and damp E.G. *musty old books.*

mutate mutates mutating mutated

VERB; TECHNICAL If something mutates, its structure or appearance alters in some way E.G. *Viruses react to change and can mutate fast.*
mutation NOUN **mutant** NOUN or ADJECTIVE

mute

ADJECTIVE; FORMAL not giving out sound or speech E.G. *mute amazement.*

muted

ADJECTIVE 1 Muted colours or sounds are soft and gentle. 2 A muted reaction is not very strong

muti

Said "**moo**-ti" NOUN; INFORMAL In South African English, muti is medicine.

mutilate mutilates mutilating mutilated

VERB 1 If someone is mutilated, their body is badly injured E.G. *His leg was badly mutilated.* 2 If you mutilate something, you deliberately damage or spoil it E.G. *Almost every book had been mutilated.*
mutilation NOUN

mutiny mutinies

NOUN A mutiny is a rebellion against someone in authority.

mutter mutters muttering muttered

VERB To mutter is to speak in a very low and perhaps cross voice E.G. *Rory muttered something under his breath.*

mutton

NOUN Mutton is the meat of an adult sheep.

muttonbird muttonbirds

NOUN a seabird in the Pacific Ocean that is often hunted for its flesh, which is said to taste like mutton.

mutual

ADJECTIVE used to describe something that two or more people do to each other or share E.G. *They had a mutual interest in rugby.*

☑ It used to be that *mutual* could only be used of something that was shared between two people or groups. Nowadays you can use it to mean 'shared between two or more people or groups'.

mutually

ADVERB Mutually describes a situation in which two or more people feel the same way about each other E.G. *a mutually supportive relationship.*

muzzle muzzles muzzling muzzled

NOUN 1 the nose and mouth of an animal. 2 a cover or a strap for a dog's nose and mouth to prevent it from biting. 3 the open end of a gun through which the bullets come out.
► VERB 4 To muzzle a dog is to put a muzzle on it.

my

ADJECTIVE 'My' refers to something belonging or relating to the person speaking or writing E.G. *I held my breath.*

mynah bird mynah birds
NOUN a tropical bird which can mimic speech and sounds.

myriad myriads
Said "mir-ree-ad" NOUN OR ADJECTIVE; LITERARY a very large number of people or things.

myrrh
Rhymes with "purr" NOUN Myrrh is a fragrant substance used in perfume and incense.

myself
PRONOUN 1 'Myself' is used when the person speaking or writing does an action and is affected by it E.G. *I was ashamed of myself.* 2 'Myself' is also used to emphasize 'I' E.G. *I find it a bit odd myself.*

mysterious
ADJECTIVE 1 strange and not well understood. 2 secretive about something E.G. *Stop being so mysterious.*
mysteriously ADVERB
■ (sense 2) enigmatic, secretive

mystery mysteries
NOUN something that is not understood or known about.

mystic mystics
NOUN 1 a religious person who spends long hours meditating. ▶ ADJECTIVE 2 Mystic means the same as mystical.

mystical
ADJECTIVE involving spiritual powers and influences E.G. *a mystical experience.*
mysticism NOUN

mystify mystifies mystifying mystified
VERB If something mystifies you, you find it impossible to understand.

mystique
Said "mis-steek" NOUN Mystique is an atmosphere of mystery and importance associated with a particular person or thing.

myth myths
NOUN 1 an untrue belief or explanation. 2 (ENGLISH) a story which was made up long ago to explain natural events and religious beliefs E.G. *Viking myths.*

mythical
ADJECTIVE imaginary, untrue, or existing only in myths E.G. *a mythical beast.*

mythology
NOUN Mythology refers to stories that have been made up in the past to explain natural events or justify religious beliefs.
mythological ADJECTIVE

a
b
c
d
e
f
g
h
i
j
k
l
m
n
o
p
q
r
s
t
u
v
w
x
y
z

Nn

TIP Some words which sound as if they should begin with letter *n*, are spelt with *gn*, for example *gnaw*, *gnome* and *gnu*. Other words that sound as if they ought to begin with letter *n* are actually spelt with *kn*, for example *knee*, *knight*, *knock* and *knot*. Other words that sound as if they ought to begin with letter *n* are actually spelt with *pn*, for example *pneumatic* and *pneumonia*.

naartjie naartjies
Said "**nar**-chi" NOUN In South African English, a tangerine.

nag nags nagging nagged
VERB 1 If you nag someone, you keep complaining to them about something. 2 If something nags at you, it keeps worrying you.

nail nails nailing nailed
NOUN 1 a small piece of metal with a sharp point at one end, which you hammer into objects to hold them together. 2 Your nails are the thin hard areas covering the ends of your fingers and toes. ▶ VERB 3 If you nail something somewhere, you fit it there using a nail.

naive or **naïve**
Said "ny-**eev**" ADJECTIVE foolishly believing that things are easier or less complicated than they really are.
naively ADVERB **naivety** NOUN

naked
ADJECTIVE 1 not wearing any clothes or not covered by anything. 2 shown openly E.G. *naked aggression*.
nakedness NOUN

name names naming named
NOUN 1 a word that you use to identify a person, place, or thing. 2 Someone's name is also their reputation E.G. *My only wish now is to clear my name*. ▶ VERB 3 If you name

someone or something, you give them a name or you say their name. 4 If you name a price or a date, you say what you want it to be.

nameless
ADJECTIVE You describe someone or something as nameless when you do not know their name, or when a name has not yet been given to them.

namely
ADVERB that is; used to introduce more detailed information about what you have just said E.G. *The state stripped them of their rights, namely the right to own land*.

namesake namesakes
NOUN Your namesake is someone with the same name as you E.G. *Audrey Hepburn and her namesake Katharine*.

nanny nannies
NOUN a woman whose job is looking after young children.

nap naps napping napped
NOUN 1 a short sleep. ▶ VERB 2 When you nap, you have a short sleep.

nape napes
NOUN The nape of your neck is the back of it.

napkin napkins
NOUN a small piece of cloth or paper used to wipe your hands and mouth after eating.

nappy nappies
NOUN a piece of towelling or paper worn round a baby's bottom.

narcotic narcotics
NOUN a drug which makes you sleepy and unable to feel pain.
🔲 from Greek *narkoun* meaning 'to make numb'

narrate narrates narrating narrated
VERB If you narrate a story, you tell it.
narration NOUN

narrative narratives
Said "nar-rat-tiv" NOUN (ENGLISH) a story or an account of events.

narrator narrators
NOUN 1 a person who is reading or telling a story out loud. 2 (ENGLISH) a character in a novel who tells the story.

narrow narrower narrowest; narrows narrowing narrowed
ADJECTIVE 1 having a small distance from one side to the other E.G. *a narrow stream*. 2 concerned only with a few aspects of something and ignoring the important points E.G. *people with a narrow point of view*. 3 A narrow escape or victory is one that you only just achieve. ▶ VERB 4 To narrow means to become less wide E.G. *The road narrowed*.
narrowly ADVERB

narrow-minded
ADJECTIVE unwilling to consider new ideas or opinions.
🟰 bigoted, intolerant

nasal
Said "nay-zal" ADJECTIVE 1 relating to the nose E.G. *the nasal passages*. 2 Nasal sounds are made by breathing out through your nose as you speak.

nasty nastier nastiest
ADJECTIVE very unpleasant E.G. *a nasty shock*.
nastily ADVERB **nastiness** NOUN

nation nations
NOUN (GEOGRAPHY) a large group of people sharing the same history and language and usually inhabiting a particular country.

national nationals (GEOGRAPHY)
ADJECTIVE 1 relating to the whole of a country E.G. *a national newspaper*. 2 typical of a particular country E.G. *women in Polish national dress*. ▶ NOUN 3 A national of a country is a citizen of that country E.G. *Turkish nationals*.
nationally ADVERB

national anthem national anthems
NOUN A country's national anthem is its official song.

nationalism
NOUN 1 Nationalism is a desire for the independence of a country; also a political movement aiming to achieve such independence. 2 Nationalism is also love of your own country.
nationalist NOUN **nationalistic** ADJECTIVE

nationality nationalities
NOUN Nationality is the fact of belonging to a particular country.

nationalize nationalizes nationalizing nationalized; also spelt **nationalise**
VERB To nationalize an industry means to bring it under the control and ownership of the state.
nationalization NOUN

National Party
NOUN In Australia and New Zealand,

a
b
c
d
e
f
g
h
i
j
k
l
m
n
o
p
q
r
s
t
u
v
w
x
y
z

the National Party is a major political party.

national service

NOUN National service is a compulsory period of service in the armed forces.

nationwide

ADJECTIVE or ADVERB happening all over a country E.G. *a nationwide search*.

native natives

ADJECTIVE 1 Your native country is the country where you were born. 2 Your native language is the language that you first learned to speak. 3 Animals or plants that are native to a place live or grow there naturally and have not been brought there by people.
► NOUN 4 A native of a place is someone who was born there.

Nativity

NOUN In Christianity, the Nativity is the birth of Christ or the festival celebrating this.

natter natters nattering nattered

VERB; INFORMAL If you natter, you talk about unimportant things.

natural naturals

ADJECTIVE 1 normal and to be expected E.G. *It was only natural that he was tempted*. 2 not trying to pretend or hide anything E.G. *Caitlin's natural manner reassured her.* (D&T) existing or happening in nature E.G. *natural disasters*. 4 A natural ability is one you were born with. 5 Your natural mother or father is your real mother or father and not someone who has adopted you. ► NOUN 6 someone who is born with a particular ability E.G. *She's a natural at bridge*. 7 In music, a natural is a note that is not a sharp or a flat. It is

represented by the symbol (♮).

naturally ADVERB

≣ (sense 4) inborn, inherent, innate

nature natures

NOUN 1 Nature is animals, plants, and all the other things in the world not made by people. 2 The nature of a person or thing is their basic character E.G. *She liked his warm, generous nature*.

🏛 from Latin *natura* meaning 'birth'

naughty naughtier naughtiest

ADJECTIVE 1 behaving badly. 2 rude or indecent E.G. *naughty films*.

naughtiness NOUN

nausea

Said "naw-zee-ah" NOUN Nausea is a feeling in your stomach that you are going to be sick.

nauseous ADJECTIVE

nautical

Said "naw-tik-kl" ADJECTIVE relating to ships or navigation.

naval

ADJECTIVE relating to or having a navy E.G. *naval officers… naval bases*.

navel navels

NOUN the small hollow on the front of your body just below your waist.

navigate navigates navigating navigated

VERB 1 When someone navigates, they work out the direction in which a ship, plane, or car should go, using maps and sometimes instruments. 2 To navigate a stretch of water means to travel safely across it E.G. *It was the first time I had navigated the ocean*.

navigation NOUN **navigator** NOUN

navy navies

NOUN 1 the part of a country's armed

forces that fights at sea. ▶ ADJECTIVE **2** dark blue.

Nazi Nazis
Said "**naht**-*see*" NOUN The Nazis were members of the National Socialist German Workers' Party, which was led by Adolf Hitler.

NB
You write NB to draw attention to what you are going to write next. NB is an abbreviation for the Latin 'nota bene', which means 'note well'.

near nearer nearest; nears nearing neared
PREPOSITION OR ADVERB **1** not far from. ▶ ADJECTIVE **2** You can also use 'near' to mean almost E.G. *a night of near disaster.* ▶ VERB **3** When you are nearing something, you are approaching it and will soon reach it E.G. *The dog began to bark as he neared the porch.*

nearby
ADJECTIVE OR ADVERB only a short distance away.

nearly
ADVERB not completely but almost.

neat neater neatest
ADJECTIVE **1** tidy and smart. **2** A neat alcoholic drink does not have anything added to it E.G. *a small glass of neat vodka.*
neatly ADVERB **neatness** NOUN

necessarily
ADVERB Something that is not necessarily the case is not always or inevitably the case.

necessary
ADJECTIVE **1** Something that is necessary is needed or must be done. **2** FORMAL Necessary also means certain or inevitable E.G. *a necessary consequence of war.*

▣ (sense 1) essential, needed, requisite

necessity necessities
NOUN **1** Necessity is the need to do something E.G. *There is no necessity for any of this.* **2** Necessities are things needed in order to live.

neck necks
NOUN **1** the part of your body which joins your head to the rest of your body. **2** the long narrow part at the top of a bottle.

necklace necklaces
NOUN **1** a piece of jewellery which a woman wears around her neck. **2** In South Africa, a name for a tyre filled with petrol which is placed round a person's neck and set on fire in order to kill that person.

nectar
NOUN Nectar is a sweet liquid produced by flowers and attractive to insects.

nectarine nectarines
NOUN a kind of peach with a smooth skin.

née
Rhymes with "**day**" 'Née' is used to indicate what a woman's surname was before she got married E.G. *Sara Black, née Wells.*

need needs needing needed
VERB **1** If you need something, you believe that you must have it or do it. ▶ NOUN **2** Your needs are the things that you need to have. **3** a strong feeling that you must have or do something E.G. *I just felt the need to write about it.*

▣ (sense 2) necessity, requirement

needle needles needling needled
NOUN **1** a small thin piece of metal with a pointed end and a hole at the other, which is used for sewing.

a
b
c
d
e
f
g
h
i
j
k
l
m
n
o
p
q
r
s
t
u
v
w
x
y
z

there's a rAKE in the brAKEs (br**ake**)   **SPELLING NOTE**

A
B
C
D
E
F
G
H
I
J
K
L
M
N
O
P
Q
R
S
T
U
V
W
X
Y
Z

2 Needles are also long thin pieces of steel or plastic, used for knitting. **3** the small pointed part in a record player that touches the record and picks up the sound signals. **4** the part of a syringe which a doctor or nurse sticks into your body. **5** the thin piece of metal or plastic on a dial which moves to show a measurement.
6 The needles of a pine tree are its leaves. ▸ VERB **7** INFORMAL If someone needles you, they annoy or provoke you.

needless
ADJECTIVE unnecessary.
needlessly ADVERB

needy needier neediest
ADJECTIVE very poor.

negative negatives
ADJECTIVE **1** A negative answer means 'no'. **2** Someone who is negative sees only problems and disadvantages E.G. *Why are you so negative about everything?* **3** If a medical or scientific test is negative, it shows that something has not happened or is not present E.G. *The pregnancy test came back negative.* **4** (MATHS) A negative number is less than zero.
▸ NOUN **5** the image that is first produced when you take a photograph.
negatively ADVERB

neglect neglects neglecting neglected
VERB **1** If you neglect something, you do not look after it properly. **2** FORMAL If you neglect to do something, you fail to do it E.G. *He had neglected to give her his address.* ▸ NOUN **3** Neglect is failure to look after something or someone properly E.G. *Most of her plants died from neglect.*
neglectful ADJECTIVE

negligent
ADJECTIVE not taking enough care E.G. *her negligent driving.*
negligence NOUN

negligible
ADJECTIVE very small and unimportant E.G. *a negligible amount of fat.*

negotiable
ADJECTIVE able to be changed or agreed by discussion E.G. *All contributions are negotiable.*

negotiate negotiates negotiating negotiated
VERB **1** When people negotiate, they have formal discussions in order to reach an agreement about something. **2** If you negotiate an obstacle, you manage to get over it or round it.
negotiation NOUN **negotiator** NOUN

Negro Negroes
NOUN; OLD-FASHIONED a person with black skin who comes from Africa or whose ancestors came from Africa.

neigh neighs neighing neighed
Rhymes with "day" VERB **1** When a horse neighs, it makes a loud high-pitched sound. ▸ NOUN **2** a loud sound made by a horse.

neighbour neighbours
NOUN **1** Your neighbour is someone who lives next door to you or near you. **2** Your neighbour is also someone standing or sitting next to you E.G. *I got chatting with my neighbour in the studio.*

neighbourhood neighbourhoods
NOUN a district where people live E.G. *a safe neighbourhood.*

neighbouring
ADJECTIVE situated nearby E.G. *schools in neighbouring areas.*

SPELLING NOTE   you'll brEAK that Electrical Aerial, Kitty (br<u>ea</u>k)

neither

ADJECTIVE OR PRONOUN used to indicate that a negative statement refers to two or more things or people E.G. *It's neither a play nor a musical… Neither of them spoke.*

☑ When *neither* is followed by a plural noun, the verb can be plural too: *neither of these books are useful.* When you have two singular subjects the verb should be singular too: *neither Jack nor John has done the work.*

neo-

PREFIX new or modern E.G. *neo-fascism.*
🔲 from Greek *neos* meaning 'new'

nephew nephews

NOUN Someone's nephew is the son of their sister or brother.

Neptune

NOUN Neptune is the planet in the solar system which is eighth from the sun.
🔲 from *Neptune*, the Roman god of the sea

nerve nerves

NOUN **1** a long thin fibre that sends messages between your brain and other parts of your body. **2** If you talk about someone's nerves, you are referring to how able they are to remain calm in a difficult situation E.G. *It needs confidence and strong nerves.* **3** Nerve is courage E.G. *O'Meara held his nerve to sink the putt.* **4** INFORMAL Nerve is boldness or rudeness E.G. *He had the nerve to swear at me.* ▶ AN INFORMAL PHRASE **5** If someone **gets on your nerves**, they irritate you.

nerve-racking

ADJECTIVE making you feel very worried and tense E.G. *a nerve-racking experience.*

nervous

ADJECTIVE **1** worried and frightened. **2** A nervous illness affects your emotions and mental health.
nervously ADVERB **nervousness** NOUN
📧 (sense 1) apprehensive, edgy, jumpy

nervous breakdown nervous breakdowns

NOUN an illness in which someone suffers from deep depression and needs psychiatric treatment.

nervous system nervous systems

NOUN Your nervous system is the nerves in your body together with your brain and spinal cord.

-ness

SUFFIX ' ness' forms nouns from adjectives E.G. *tenderness… happiness.*
🔲 from an Old English suffix

nest nests nesting nested

NOUN **1** a place that a bird makes to lay its eggs in; also a place that some insects and other animals make to rear their young in. ▶ VERB **2** When birds nest, they build a nest and lay eggs in it.

nestle nestles nestling nestled

*Said "**ness-sl**"* VERB If you nestle somewhere, you settle there comfortably, often pressing up against someone else E.G. *A new puppy nestled in her lap.*

nestling nestlings

NOUN a young bird that has not yet learned to fly and so has not left the nest.

net nets

NOUN **1** a piece of material made of

I always visit my FRIend on a FRIday (friend)   SPELLING NOTE

A
B
C
D
E
F
G
H
I
J
K
L
M
N
O
P
Q
R
S
T
U
V
W
X
Y
Z

threads woven together with small spaces in between. **2** The net is the same as the **Internet**. ▶ ADJECTIVE **3** A net result or amount is final, after everything has been considered E.G. *a net profit of 171 million*. **4** The net weight of something is its weight without its wrapping.

netball
NOUN Netball is a game played by two teams of seven players in which each team tries to score goals by throwing a ball through a net at the top of a pole.

netting
NOUN Netting is material made of threads or metal wires woven together with small spaces in between.

nettle nettles
NOUN a wild plant covered with little hairs that sting.

network networks
NOUN **1** a large number of lines or roads which cross each other at many points E.G. *a small network of side roads*. **2** A network of people or organizations is a large number of them that work together as a system E.G. *the public telephone network*. **3** A television network is a group of broadcasting stations that all transmit the same programmes at the same time. **4** (ICT) a group of computers connected to each other.

neuron neurons
NOUN a cell that is part of the nervous system and conducts messages to and from the brain.

neurone neurones
NOUN the same as a **neuron**.

neurosis neuroses
Said "nyoor-**roh**-siss" NOUN Neurosis is

mental illness which causes people to have strong and unreasonable fears and worries.

neurotic
Said "nyoor-**rot**-ik" ADJECTIVE having strong and unreasonable fears and worries E.G. *He was almost neurotic about being followed*.

neuter neuters neutering neutered
Said "**nyoo**-ter" VERB **1** When an animal is neutered, its reproductive organs are removed. ▶ ADJECTIVE **2** In some languages, a neuter noun or pronoun is one which is not masculine or feminine.

What is Neuter?

Neuter nouns refer to inanimate objects and abstract ideas:
E.G. *The kettle will switch itself off.*
▶ *kettle is **neuter***
Also look at the grammar boxes at **gender**, **masculine** and **feminine**.

neutral neutrals
ADJECTIVE **1** People who are neutral do not support either side in a disagreement or war. **2** The neutral wire in an electric plug is the one that is not earth or live. **3** A neutral colour is not definite or striking, for example pale grey. **4** In chemistry, a neutral substance is neither acid nor alkaline. ▶ NOUN **5** a person or country that does not support either side in a disagreement or war. **6** Neutral is the position between the gears of a vehicle in which the gears are not connected to the engine and so the vehicle cannot move.
neutrality NOUN

neutron neutrons
NOUN an atomic particle that has no electrical charge.

never
ADVERB at no time in the past, present, or future
✅ Do not use *never* to mean 'not' in writing. You should say *I didn't see her* not *I never saw her*.

nevertheless
ADVERB in spite of what has just been said E.G. *They dress rather plainly but nevertheless look quite smart.*

new newer newest
ADJECTIVE 1 recently made or created E.G. *a new house… a new plan.* 2 only recently discovered E.G. *a new virus.* 3 not used or owned before E.G. *We've got a new car.* 4 different or unfamiliar E.G. *a name which was new to me.*
▤ (sense 1) latest, modern, recent

newborn
ADJECTIVE born recently.

newcomer newcomers
NOUN someone who has recently arrived in a place.

newly
ADVERB recently E.G. *the newly born baby.*

new moon new moons
NOUN The moon is a new moon when it is a thin crescent shape at the start of its four-week cycle.

news
NOUN News is information about things that have happened.

newsagent newsagents
NOUN a person or shop that sells newspapers and magazines.

newspaper newspapers
NOUN a publication, on large sheets of paper, that is produced regularly and contains news and articles.

newt newts
NOUN a small amphibious creature with a moist skin, short legs, and a long tail.
▥ from a mistaken division of Middle English *an ewt*

New Testament
NOUN The New Testament is the second part of the Bible, which deals with the life of Jesus Christ and with the early Church.

New Year
NOUN New Year is the time when people celebrate the start of a year.

New Zealander New Zealanders
NOUN someone who comes from New Zealand.

next
ADJECTIVE or ADVERB 1 coming immediately after something else E.G. *They lived in the next street.*
► PHRASE 2 If one thing is **next to** another, it is at the side of it.
▤ (sense 1) following, subsequent

next door
ADJECTIVE or ADVERB in the house next to yours.

NHS
In Britain, an abbreviation for 'National Health Service'.

nib nibs
NOUN the pointed end of a pen.

nibble nibbles nibbling nibbled
VERB 1 When you nibble something, you take small bites of it. ► NOUN 2 a small bite of something.

nice nicer nicest
ADJECTIVE pleasant or attractive.

nicely ADVERB

nicety niceties
Said "nigh-se-tee" NOUN a small detail E.G. *the social niceties.*

a
b
c
d
e
f
g
h
i
j
k
l
m
n
o
p
q
r
s
t
u
v
w
x
y
z

The government licenSes Schnapps (licenses)   SPELLING NOTE

A B C D E F G H I J K L M **N** O P Q R S T U V W X Y Z

niche niches
Said "neesh" NOUN **1** a hollow area in a wall. **2** If you say that you have found your niche, you mean that you have found a job or way of life that is exactly right for you.

nick nicks nicking nicked
VERB **1** If you nick something, you make a small cut in its surface E.G. *He nicked his chin*. **2** INFORMAL To nick something also means to steal it.
▶ NOUN **3** a small cut in the surface of something.

nickel
NOUN Nickel is a silver-coloured metal that is used in making steel.

nickname nicknames nicknaming nicknamed
NOUN **1** an informal name given to someone. ▶ VERB **2** If you nickname someone, you give them a nickname.
📖 from Middle English *an ekename* meaning 'an additional name'

nicotine
NOUN Nicotine is an addictive substance found in tobacco.

niece nieces
NOUN Someone's niece is the daughter of their sister or brother.

nifty
ADJECTIVE neat and pleasing or cleverly done.

Nigerian Nigerians
Said "nie-jeer-ee-an" ADJECTIVE **1** belonging or relating to Nigeria.
▶ NOUN **2** someone from Nigeria.

niggle niggles niggling niggled
VERB **1** If something niggles you, it worries you slightly. ▶ NOUN **2** a small worry that you keep thinking about.

night nights
NOUN Night is the time between sunset and sunrise when it is dark.

nightclub nightclubs
NOUN a place where people go late in the evening to drink and dance.

nightdress nightdresses
NOUN a loose dress that a woman or girl wears to sleep in.

nightfall
NOUN Nightfall is the time of day when it starts to get dark.

nightie nighties
NOUN; INFORMAL a nightdress.

nightingale nightingales
NOUN a small brown European bird, the male of which sings very beautifully, especially at night.

nightly
ADJECTIVE or ADVERB happening every night E.G. *the nightly news programme*.

nightmare nightmares
NOUN a very frightening dream; also used of any very unpleasant or frightening situation E.G. *The meal itself was a nightmare*.
nightmarish ADJECTIVE
📖 from *night* + Middle English *mare* meaning 'evil spirit'

nil
NOUN Nil means zero or nothing. It is used especially in sports scores.

nimble nimbler nimblest
ADJECTIVE **1** able to move quickly and easily. **2** able to think quickly and cleverly.
nimbly ADVERB

nine
the number 9.
ninth

nineteen
the number 19.
nineteenth

ninety nineties
the number 90.
ninetieth

nip nips nipping nipped
VERB 1 INFORMAL If you nip somewhere, you go there quickly. 2 To nip someone or something means to pinch or them slightly. ▶ NOUN 3 a light pinch.

nipple nipples
NOUN Your nipples are the two small pieces of projecting flesh on your chest. Babies suck milk through the nipples on their mothers' breasts.

nirvana
Said "neer-**vah**-na" NOUN Nirvana is the ultimate state of spiritual enlightenment which can be achieved in the Hindu and Buddhist religions.

nit nits
NOUN Nits are the eggs of a kind of louse that sometimes lives in people's hair.

nitrogen
NOUN Nitrogen is a chemical element usually found as a gas. It forms about 78% of the earth's atmosphere.

no
INTERJECTION 1 used to say that something is not true or to refuse something. ▶ ADJECTIVE 2 none at all or not at all E.G. *She gave no reason… You're no friend of mine.* ▶ ADVERB 3 used with a comparative to mean 'not' E.G. *no later than 24th July.*

no.
a written abbreviation for **number.**

nobility
NOUN 1 Nobility is the quality of being noble E.G. *the unmistakable nobility of his character.* 2 The nobility of a society are all the people who have titles and high social rank.

noble nobler noblest; nobles
ADJECTIVE 1 honest and brave, and deserving admiration. 2 very impressive E.G. *broad cheekbones which gave them a noble appearance.* ▶ NOUN 3 a member of the nobility.
nobly ADVERB

nobleman noblemen
NOUN a man who is a member of the nobility.
noblewoman NOUN

nobody nobodies
PRONOUN 1 not a single person. ▶ NOUN 2 Someone who is a nobody is not at all important
☑ *Nobody* and *no-one* mean the same.

nocturnal
ADJECTIVE 1 happening at night E.G. *a nocturnal journey through New York.* 2 active at night E.G. *a nocturnal animal.*

nod nods nodding nodded
VERB 1 When you nod, you move your head up and down, usually to show agreement. ▶ NOUN 2 a movement of your head up and down.
nod off VERB If you nod off, you fall asleep.

noise noises
NOUN a sound, especially one that is loud or unpleasant.
☰ din, racket, sound

noisy noisier noisiest
ADJECTIVE making a lot of noise or full of noise E.G. *a noisy crowd.*
noisily ADVERB **noisiness** NOUN

nomad nomads
NOUN a person who belongs to a tribe which travels from place to place rather than living in just one place.
nomadic ADJECTIVE

nominal
ADJECTIVE 1 Something that is nominal is supposed to have a particular

a
b
c
d
e
f
g
h
i
j
k
l
m
n
o
p
q
r
s
t
u
v
w
x
y
z

identity or status, but in reality does not have it E.G. *the nominal leader of his party.* **2** A nominal amount of money is very small compared to the value of something E.G. *I am prepared to sell my shares at a nominal price.*
nominally ADVERB

nominate nominates nominating nominated
VERB If you nominate someone for a job or position, you formally suggest that they have it.
nomination NOUN
■ name, propose, suggest

non-
PREFIX not E.G. *non-smoking.*
🏛 from Latin

nonchalant
Said "**non-shal-nt**" ADJECTIVE seeming calm and not worried.
nonchalance NOUN **nonchalantly** ADVERB

noncommissioned officer noncommissioned officers
NOUN an officer such as a sergeant or corporal who has been promoted from the lower ranks.

nondescript
ADJECTIVE Someone or something nondescript has no special or interesting qualities or details E.G. *a nondescript coat.*

none
PRONOUN not a single thing or person, or not even a small amount of something.

nonfiction
NOUN (LIBRARY) Nonfiction is writing that gives facts and information rather than telling a story.

nonplussed
ADJECTIVE confused and unsure about how to react.

nonsense
NOUN Nonsense is foolish and meaningless words or behaviour.
nonsensical ADJECTIVE

nonstop
ADJECTIVE or ADVERB continuing without any pauses or breaks E.G. *nonstop excitement.*

noodle noodles
NOUN Noodles are a kind of pasta shaped into long, thin pieces.

nook nooks
NOUN; LITERARY a small sheltered place.

noon
NOUN Noon is midday.

no-one or **no one**
PRONOUN not a single person
☑ *No-one* and *nobody* mean the same.

noose nooses
NOUN a loop at the end of a piece of rope, with a knot that tightens when the rope is pulled.

nor
CONJUNCTION used after 'neither' or after a negative statement, to add something else that the negative statement applies to E.G. *They had neither the time nor the money for the sport.*

norm
NOUN If something is the norm, it is the usual and expected thing E.G. *cultures where large families are the norm.*
■ from Latin *norma* meaning 'carpenter's rule'

normal
ADJECTIVE usual and ordinary E.G. *I try to lead a normal life.*
normality NOUN
■ conventional, ordinary, usual

normally
ADVERB **1** usually E.G. *I don't normally*

like dancing. **2** in a way that is normal E.G. *The foetus is developing normally.*

north

NOUN **1** The north is the direction to your left when you are looking towards the place where the sun rises. **2** The north of a place or country is the part which is towards the north when you are in the centre. ► ADVERB or ADJECTIVE **3** North means towards the north E.G. *The helicopter took off and headed north.* ► ADJECTIVE **4** A north wind blows from the north.

North America

NOUN North America is the third largest continent, consisting of Canada, the United States, and Mexico.

North American ADJECTIVE

north-east

NOUN, ADVERB, or ADJECTIVE North-east is halfway between north and east.

north-easterly

ADJECTIVE **1** North-easterly means to or towards the north-east. **2** A north-easterly wind blows from the north-east.

north-eastern

ADJECTIVE in or from the north-east.

northerly

ADJECTIVE **1** Northerly means to or towards the north E.G. *travelling in a northerly direction.* **2** A northerly wind blows from the north.

northern

ADJECTIVE in or from the north E.G. *the mountains of northern Italy.*

North Pole

NOUN The North Pole is the most northerly point of the earth's surface.

northward or northwards

ADVERB **1** Northward or northwards means towards the north E.G. *We continued northwards.* ► ADJECTIVE **2** The northward part of something is the north part.

north-west

NOUN, ADVERB, or ADJECTIVE North-west is halfway between north and west.

north-westerly

ADJECTIVE **1** North-westerly means to or towards the north-west. **2** A north-westerly wind blows from the north-west.

north-western

ADJECTIVE in or from the north-west.

Norwegian Norwegians

Said "nor-**wee**-jn" ADJECTIVE **1** belonging or relating to Norway. ► NOUN **2** someone who comes from Norway. **3** Norwegian is the main language spoken in Norway.

nose noses

NOUN **1** the part of your face above your mouth which you use for smelling and breathing. **2** the front part of a car or plane.

nostalgia

Said "nos-**tal**-ja" NOUN Nostalgia is a feeling of affection for the past, and sadness that things have changed.

nostalgic ADJECTIVE

nostril nostrils

NOUN Your nostrils are the two openings in your nose which you breathe through.

nosy nosier nosiest; also spelt nosey

ADJECTIVE trying to find out about things that do not concern you.

not

ADVERB used to make a sentence negative, to refuse something, or to deny something.

a
b
c
d
e
f
g
h
i
j
k
l
m
n
o
p
q
r
s
t
u
v
w
x
y
z

You must practiSe your Ss (practi**se**)   SPELLING NOTE

A
B
C
D
E
F
G
H
I
J
K
L
M
N
O
P
Q
R
S
T
U
V
W
X
Y
Z

What does 'not' do?

You can turn most sentences into negatives if you want to express the opposite meaning.

You can usually make a sentence into a negative by adding the word *not*:

E.G. *Robbie was **not** feeling tired.*

If a sentence already contains an auxiliary verb, such as *have*, *will*, *be*, or *must*, the word *not* should go after this verb:

E.G. *She has **not** gone to the shops.*

If the sentence does not already contain an auxiliary verb, a form of the verb *do* is added, and the word *not* is placed after this:

E.G. *We **do not** expect to win.*

In spoken and informal English, the ending -*n't* may be added to an auxiliary verb in place of *not*:

E.G. *She **hasn't** gone to the shops.*

notable

ADJECTIVE important or interesting E.G. *The production is notable for some outstanding performances.*
notably ADVERB

notch notches

NOUN a small V-shaped cut in a surface.

■ from a mistaken division of Middle English *an otch*

note notes noting noted

NOUN **1** a short letter. **2** a written piece of information that helps you to remember something E.G. *You should make a note of that.* **3** In music, a note is a musical sound of a particular pitch, or a written symbol that represents it. **4** a banknote. **5** an atmosphere, feeling, or quality E.G. *There was a note of regret in his voice… I'm determined to close on an optimistic note.* ▶ VERB **6** If you note a fact, you become aware of it or you mention it E.G. *I noted that the rain had stopped.* ▶ PHRASE **7** If you **take note** of something, you pay attention to it E.G. *The world hardly took note of this crisis.*

note down VERB If you note something down, you write it down so that you will remember it.

notebook notebooks

NOUN a small book for writing notes in.

noted

ADJECTIVE well-known and admired E.G. *a noted Hebrew scholar.*

nothing

PRONOUN not anything E.G. *There was nothing to do.*

■ nil, nought, zero

✔ *Nothing* is usually followed by a singular verb: *nothing was in the bag.* If the expression *nothing but* is followed by a plural noun, the verb should be plural too: *a large room where nothing but souvenirs were sold.*

notice notices noticing noticed

VERB **1** If you notice something, you become aware of it. ▶ NOUN **2** Notice is attention or awareness E.G. *I'm glad he brought it to my notice.* **3** a written announcement. **4** Notice is also advance warning about something E.G. *We were lucky to get you at such short notice.* ▶ PHRASE **5** If you **hand in your notice**, you tell your employer that you intend to leave your job after a fixed period of time.

■ (sense 1) detect, observe, perceive

noticeable
ADJECTIVE obvious and easy to see E.G. *a noticeable improvement*.
noticeably ADVERB

noticeboard noticeboards
NOUN a board for notices.

notify notifies notifying notified
VERB To notify someone of something means to officially inform them of it E.G. *You must notify us of any change of address*.
notification NOUN

notion notions
NOUN an idea or belief.

notorious
ADJECTIVE well known for something bad E.G. *The area has become notorious for violence against tourists*.
notoriously ADVERB **notoriety** NOUN

notwithstanding
PREPOSITION; FORMAL in spite of E.G. *Notwithstanding his age, Sikorski had an important job*.

nougat
Said "noo-gah" NOUN Nougat is a kind of chewy sweet containing nuts and sometimes fruit.
📖 from Provençal *noga* meaning 'nut'

nought
the number 0.

noun nouns
NOUN a word which refers to a person, thing, or idea. Examples of nouns are 'president', 'table', 'sun', and 'beauty'. → *SEE BOX OPPOSITE*

nourish nourishes nourishing nourished
Said "nur-rish" VERB To nourish people or animals means to provide them with food.

What is a Noun?

A noun is a word that labels a person, a thing or an idea. In any sentence, the nouns will tell you which people or things are involved. They are sometimes called "naming words".

Common nouns are words which indicate every example of a certain type of thing. They begin with small letters:

  E.G. *girl* ■ *city* ■ *picture*

Proper nouns are words which give the name of a particular person, place, or object. They begin with capital letters:

  E.G. *Anna Jamieson* ■ *Los Angeles*
       The Mona Lisa

Some common nouns are **concrete nouns**. These are words that indicate things that you *can* touch :

  E.G. *cat* ■ *pen* ■ *apple*

Other common nouns are **abstract nouns**. These are words that indicate things that you *cannot* touch :

  E.G. *beauty* ■ *ambition* ■ *popularity*

Some common nouns are **collective nouns**. These are words that indicate a group or collection of things:

  E.G. *pack* ■ *bunch* ■ *flock*

---

nourishing
ADJECTIVE Food that is nourishing makes you strong and healthy.

nourishment
NOUN Nourishment is food that your body needs in order to remain healthy E.G. *poor nourishment*.

a b c d e f g h i j k l m n o p q r s t u v w x y z

A
B
C
D
E
F
G
H
I
J
K
L
M
N
O
P
Q
R
S
T
U
V
W
X
Y
Z

novel novels

NOUN 1 (LIBRARY) a book that tells an invented story. ▶ ADJECTIVE 2 new and interesting E.G. *a very novel experience*.

novelist novelists

NOUN a person who writes novels.

novelty novelties

NOUN 1 Novelty is the quality of being new and interesting E.G. *The novelty had worn off*. 2 something new and interesting E.G. *Steam power was still a bit of a novelty*. 3 a small, unusual object sold as a gift or souvenir.

November

NOUN November is the eleventh month of the year. It has 30 days.
📖 from Latin *November* meaning 'the ninth month'

novice novices

NOUN 1 someone who is not yet experienced at something. 2 someone who is preparing to become a monk or nun.

now

ADVERB 1 at the present time or moment. ▶ CONJUNCTION 2 as a result or consequence of a particular fact E.G. *Things have got better now there is a new board*. ▶ PHRASE 3 **Just now** means very recently E.G. *I drove Brenda back to the camp just now*. 4 If something happens **now and then**, it happens sometimes but not regularly.

nowadays

ADVERB at the present time E.G. *Nowadays most fathers choose to be present at the birth*.

nowhere

ADVERB not anywhere.

noxious

Said "**nok**-shus" ADJECTIVE harmful or

poisonous E.G. *a noxious gas*.

nozzle nozzles

NOUN a spout fitted onto the end of a pipe or hose to control the flow of a liquid.

nuance nuances

Said "**nyoo**-ahnss" NOUN a small difference in sound, colour, or meaning E.G. *the nuances of his music*.

nubile

Said "**nyoo**-bile" ADJECTIVE A woman who is nubile is young and sexually attractive.
📖 from Latin *nubere* meaning 'to take a husband'

nuclear

ADJECTIVE 1 relating to the energy produced when the nuclei of atoms are split E.G. *nuclear power… the nuclear industry*. 2 relating to weapons that explode using the energy released by atoms E.G. *nuclear war*. 3 relating to the structure and behaviour of the nuclei of atoms E.G. *nuclear physics*.

nuclear reactor nuclear reactors

NOUN A nuclear reactor is a device which is used to obtain nuclear energy.

nucleus nuclei

Said "**nyoo**-klee-uss" NOUN 1 the central part of an atom or cell. 2 The nucleus of something is the basic central part of it to which other things are added E.G. *They have retained the nucleus of the team that won the World Cup*.
📖 from Latin *nucleus* meaning 'kernel'

nude nudes

ADJECTIVE 1 naked. ▶ NOUN 2 a picture or

statue of a naked person.
nudity NOUN

nudge nudges nudging nudged
VERB **1** If you nudge someone, you push them gently, usually with your elbow. ▶ NOUN **2** a gentle push.

nudist nudists
NOUN a person who believes in wearing no clothes.

nugget nuggets
NOUN a small rough lump of something, especially gold.

nuisance nuisances
NOUN someone or something that is annoying or inconvenient.
■ bother, inconvenience, problem

null
PHRASE **Null and void** means not legally valid E.G. *Other documents were declared to be null and void.*

nulla-nulla nulla-nullas
NOUN a thick heavy stick used as a weapon by Australian Aborigines.

numb numbs numbing numbed
ADJECTIVE **1** unable to feel anything E.G. *My legs felt numb… numb with grief.* ▶ VERB **2** If something numbs you, it makes you unable to feel anything E.G. *The cold numbed my fingers.*

numbat numbats
NOUN a small Australian marsupial with a long snout and tongue and strong claws which it uses for hunting and eating insects.

number numbers numbering numbered
NOUN **1** a word or a symbol used for counting or calculating. **2** Someone's number is the series of numbers that you dial when you telephone them. **3** A number of things is a quantity of them E.G. *Adrian has introduced me*

to a large number of people. **4** a song or piece of music. ▶ VERB **5** If things number a particular amount, there are that many of them E.G. *At that time London's population numbered about 460,000.* **6** If you number something, you give it a number E.G. *The picture is signed and numbered by the artist.* **7** To be numbered among a particular group means to belong to it E.G. *Only the best are numbered among their champions.*
■ (sense 1) digit, figure, numeral

What do Numbers do?

Numbers tell you how many of a thing there are.
Cardinal numbers tell you the total number of a thing:
  E.G. ***Three*** figures huddled in the doorway.
Ordinal numbers tell you the order of something. They often end with the letters -th:
  E.G. Her ***sixth*** novel was the most successful yet.

---

numeral numerals
NOUN a symbol that represents a number E.G. *a wristwatch with Roman numerals.*

numerical
ADJECTIVE expressed in numbers or relating to numbers E.G. *a numerical value.*

numerous
ADJECTIVE existing or happening in large numbers.

nun nuns
NOUN a woman who has taken religious vows and lives in a convent.

a b c d e f g h i j k l m n o p q r s t u v w x y z

nurse nurses nursing nursed
NOUN **1** a person whose job is to look after people who are ill. ▶ VERB **2** If you nurse someone, you look after them when they are ill. **3** If you nurse a feeling, you feel it strongly for a long time E.G. *He nursed a grudge against the USA*.

nursery nurseries
NOUN **1** a place where young children are looked after while their parents are working. **2** a room in which young children sleep and play. **3** a place where plants are grown and sold.

nursery school nursery schools
NOUN a school for children from three to five years old.

nursing home nursing homes
NOUN a privately run hospital, especially for old people.

nurture nurtures nurturing nurtured
VERB; FORMAL If you nurture a young child or a plant, you look after it carefully.

nut nuts
NOUN **1** a fruit with a hard shell and an edible centre that grows on certain trees. **2** a piece of metal with a hole in the middle which a bolt screws into.

nutmeg
NOUN Nutmeg is a spice used for flavouring in cooking.

nutrient nutrients
NOUN (SCIENCE) Nutrients are substances that help plants or animals to grow E.G. *the nutrients in the soil*.

nutrition
NOUN (D & T) Nutrition is the food that you eat, considered from the point of view of how it helps you to grow and remain healthy E.G. *The effects of poor nutrition are evident*.
nutritional ADJECTIVE **nutritionist** NOUN

nutritious
ADJECTIVE containing substances that help you to grow and remain healthy.

nutty nuttier nuttiest
ADJECTIVE **1** INFORMAL mad or very foolish. **2** tasting of nuts.

nylon nylons
NOUN **1** Nylon is a type of strong artificial material E.G. *nylon stockings*. **2** Nylons are stockings or tights.

Oo

oaf oafs
NOUN a clumsy and stupid person.
📖 from Old Norse *alfr* meaning 'elf'

oak oaks
NOUN a large tree which produces acorns. It has a hard wood which is often used to make furniture.

OAP OAPs
NOUN In Britain, a man over the age of 65 or a woman over the age of 60 who receives a pension. OAP is an abbreviation for 'old age pensioner'.

oar oars
NOUN a wooden pole with a wide, flat end, used for rowing a boat.

oasis oases
Said "oh-ay-siss" NOUN a small area in a desert where water and plants are found.

oat oats
NOUN Oats are a type of grain.

oath oaths
NOUN a formal promise, especially a promise to tell the truth in a court of law.
🟦 pledge, promise, vow

oatmeal
NOUN Oatmeal is a rough flour made from oats.

OBE OBEs
NOUN a British honour awarded by the King or Queen. OBE is an abbreviation for 'Officer of the Order of the British Empire'.

obedient
ADJECTIVE If you are obedient, you do what you are told to do.
obediently ADVERB **obedience** NOUN

obelisk obelisks
NOUN a stone pillar built in honour of a person or an event.

obese
Said "oh-bees" ADJECTIVE extremely fat.
obesity NOUN
📖 from Latin *ob-* meaning 'much' and *edere* meaning 'to eat'

obey obeys obeying obeyed
VERB If you obey a person or an order, you do what you are told to do.

obituary obituaries
NOUN a piece of writing about the life and achievements of someone who has just died.

object objects objecting objected
NOUN 1 anything solid that you can touch or see, and that is not alive. 2 an aim or purpose. 3 The object of your feelings or actions is the person that they are directed towards. 4 In grammar, the object of a verb or preposition is the word or phrase which follows it and describes the person or thing affected. ▶ VERB 5 If you object to something, you dislike it or disapprove of it.
🟦 (sense 5) oppose, protest, take exception

objection objections
NOUN If you have an objection to something, you dislike it or disapprove of it.

objectionable
ADJECTIVE unpleasant and offensive.

objective objectives
NOUN 1 an aim E.G. *The protection of the countryside is their main objective.*
▶ ADJECTIVE 2 If you are objective, you are not influenced by personal feelings or prejudices E.G. *an objective approach.*
objectively ADVERB **objectivity** NOUN

a b c d e f g h i j k l m n o p q r s t u v w x y z

A
B
C
D
E
F
G
H
I
J
K
L
M
N
O
P
Q
R
S
T
U
V
W
X
Y
Z

obligation obligations
NOUN something that you must do because it is your duty.

obligatory
Said "ob-lig-a-tree" ADJECTIVE required by a rule or law E.G. *Religious education was made obligatory*.

oblige obliges obliging obliged
VERB 1 If you are obliged to do something, you have to do it. 2 If you oblige someone, you help them.
obliging ADJECTIVE

oblique
Said "o-bleek" ADJECTIVE 1 An oblique remark is not direct, and is therefore difficult to understand. 2 An oblique line slopes at an angle.

obliterate obliterates obliterating obliterated
VERB To obliterate something is to destroy it completely.
obliteration NOUN

oblivion
NOUN Oblivion is unconsciousness or complete lack of awareness of your surroundings.
oblivious ADJECTIVE **obliviously** ADVERB

oblong oblongs
NOUN 1 a four-sided shape with two parallel short sides, two parallel long sides, and four right angles.
▶ ADJECTIVE 2 shaped like an oblong.

obnoxious
Said "ob-nok-shuss" ADJECTIVE extremely unpleasant.

oboe oboes
NOUN a woodwind musical instrument with a double reed.
oboist NOUN
🎵 from French *haut bois* meaning literally 'high wood', a reference to the instrument's pitch

obscene
ADJECTIVE indecent and likely to upset people E.G. *obscene pictures*.
obscenely ADVERB **obscenity** NOUN
■ filthy, indecent, pornographic

obscure obscures obscuring obscured
ADJECTIVE 1 Something that is obscure is known by only a few people E.G. *an obscure Mongolian dialect*.
2 Something obscure is difficult to see or to understand E.G. *The news was shrouded in obscure language*.
▶ VERB 3 To obscure something is to make it difficult to see or understand E.G. *His view was obscured by trees*.
obscurity NOUN
■ (sense 2) cryptic, unclear, vague

observance
NOUN The observance of a law or custom is the practice of obeying or following it.

observant
ADJECTIVE Someone who is observant notices things that are not easy to see.

observation observations
NOUN 1 Observation is the act of watching something carefully E.G. *Success hinges on close observation*.
2 something that you have seen or noticed. 3 a remark. 4 Observation is the ability to notice things that are not easy to see.

observatory observatories
NOUN a room or building containing telescopes and other equipment for studying the sun, moon, and stars.

observe observes observing observed
VERB 1 To observe something is to watch it carefully. 2 To observe something is to notice it. 3 If you

observe that something is the case, you make a comment about it. **4** To observe a law or custom is to obey or follow it.
observer NOUN   **observable** ADJECTIVE

obsession obsessions
NOUN If someone has an obsession about something, they cannot stop thinking about that thing.
obsessional ADJECTIVE   **obsessed** ADJECTIVE   **obsessive** ADJECTIVE

obsolete
ADJECTIVE out of date and no longer used.
◼ outmoded, passé

obstacle obstacles
NOUN something which is in your way and makes it difficult to do something.
◼ difficulty, stumbling block

obstetrics
NOUN Obstetrics is the branch of medicine concerned with pregnancy and childbirth.
obstetrician NOUN

obstinate
ADJECTIVE Someone who is obstinate is stubborn and unwilling to change their mind.
obstinately ADVERB   **obstinacy** NOUN

obstruct obstructs obstructing obstructed
VERB If something obstructs a road or path, it blocks it.
obstruction NOUN   **obstructive** ADJECTIVE

obtain obtains obtaining obtained
VERB If you obtain something, you get it.
obtainable ADJECTIVE

obtrusive
ADJECTIVE noticeable in an unpleasant way E.G. *a remarkably obtrusive cigar*.

obtuse
ADJECTIVE **1** Someone who is obtuse is stupid or slow to understand things. **2** An obtuse angle is an angle between 90° and 180°.

obvious
ADJECTIVE easy to see or understand.
obviously ADVERB
◼ clear, evident, plain

occasion occasions occasioning occasioned
NOUN **1** a time when something happens. **2** an important event. **3** An occasion for doing something is an opportunity for doing it. ▶ VERB
4 FORMAL To occasion something is to cause it E.G. *damage occasioned by fire*.

occasional
ADJECTIVE happening sometimes but not often E.G. *an occasional outing*.
occasionally ADVERB

occult
NOUN The occult is the knowledge and study of supernatural and magical forces or powers.

occupancy
NOUN The occupancy of a building is the act of living or working in it.

occupant occupants
NOUN The occupants of a building are the people who live or work in it.

occupation occupations
NOUN **1** a job or profession. **2** a hobby or something you do for pleasure. **3** The occupation of a country is the act of invading it and taking control of it.
occupational ADJECTIVE

a
b
c
d
e
f
g
h
i
j
k
l
m
n
o
p
q
r
s
t
u
v
w
x
y
z

Eddy Ant thinks mEAt is a grEAt trEAt to EAt (-ea-)   **SPELLING NOTE**

A
B
C
D
E
F
G
H
I
J
K
L
M
N
O
P
Q
R
S
T
U
V
W
X
Y
Z

occupy occupies occupying occupied

VERB 1 The people who occupy a building are the people who live or work there. 2 When people occupy a place, they move into it and take control of it E.G. *Demonstrators occupied the building.* 3 To occupy a position in a system or plan is to have that position E.G. *His phone-in show occupies a daytime slot.* 4 If something occupies you, you spend your time doing it E.G. *That problem occupies me night and day.*

occupier NOUN

occur occurs occurring occurred

VERB 1 If something occurs, it happens or exists E.G. *The second attack occurred at a swimming pool.* 2 If something occurs to you, you suddenly think of it

☑ If an event has been planned, you should not say that it *occurred* or *happened: the wedding took place on Saturday.* Only something unexpected *occurs* or *happens: an accident has occurred; the burglary happened last night.*

occurrence occurrences

NOUN 1 an event. 2 The occurrence of something is the fact that it happens or exists E.G. *the occurrence of diseases.*

ocean oceans

NOUN 1 LITERARY the sea. 2 The five oceans are the five very large areas of sea E.G. *the Atlantic Ocean.*

oceanic ADJECTIVE

o'clock

ADVERB You use 'o'clock' after the number of the hour to say what the time is.

octagon octagons

NOUN a shape with eight straight sides.

octagonal ADJECTIVE

octave octaves

NOUN (MUSIC) the difference in pitch between the first note and the eighth note of a musical scale.

October

NOUN October is the tenth month of the year. It has 31 days.
📖 from Latin *october* meaning 'the eighth month'

octopus octopuses

NOUN a sea creature with eight long tentacles which it uses to catch food.
📖 from Greek *okto* + *pous* meaning 'eight feet'

odd odder oddest; odds

ADJECTIVE 1 Something odd is strange or unusual. 2 Odd things do not match each other E.G. *odd socks.* 3 Odd numbers are numbers that cannot be divided exactly by two.
► ADVERB 4 You use 'odd' after a number to say that it is approximate E.G. *I've written twenty odd plays.*
► PLURAL NOUN 5 In gambling, the probability of something happening is called the odds E.G. *The odds are against the record being beaten.*

oddly ADVERB **oddness** NOUN

oddity oddities

NOUN something very strange.

oddments

PLURAL NOUN Oddments are things that are left over after other things have been used.

odds and ends

PLURAL NOUN You can refer to a collection of small unimportant things as odds and ends.

ode odes
NOUN a poem written in praise of someone or something.

odious
ADJECTIVE extremely unpleasant.

odour odours
NOUN; FORMAL a strong smell.
odorous ADJECTIVE

odyssey odysseys
Said "*od*-i-*see*" NOUN a long and eventful journey.

oesophagus oesophaguses
Said "*ee*-*sof*-fag-uss" NOUN the tube that carries food from your throat to your stomach.

oestrogen
another spelling of **estrogen**.

of
PREPOSITION 1 consisting of or containing E.G. *a collection of short stories… a cup of tea.* 2 used when naming something or describing a characteristic of something E.G. *the city of Canberra… a woman of great power and influence.* 3 belonging to or connected with E.G. *a friend of Rachel… the cover of the book.*
☑ Where *of* means 'belonging to', it can be replaced by an apostrophe: *the cover of the book* is the same as *the book's cover.*

off
PREPOSITION or ADVERB 1 indicating movement away from or out of a place E.G. *They had just stepped off the plane… She got up and marched off.* 2 indicating separation or distance from a place E.G. *some islands off the coast of Australia… The whole crescent has been fenced off.* 3 not working E.G. *It was Frank's night off.* ► ADVERB or ADJECTIVE 4 not switched on E.G. *He turned the radio*

off, the off switch. ► ADJECTIVE 5 cancelled or postponed E.G. *The concert was off.* 6 Food that is off has gone sour or bad. ► PREPOSITION 7 not liking or not using something E.G. *He went right off alcohol.*
☑ Do not use *of* after *off*. You should say *he stepped off the bus* not *he stepped off of the bus.* It is very informal to use *off* where you mean 'from': *they bought milk off a farmer* instead of *they bought milk from a farmer.* Always use *from* in written work.

offal
NOUN Offal is liver, kidneys, and other parts of animals, which can be eaten.

offence offences
NOUN 1 a crime E.G. *a drink-driving offence.* ► PHRASES 2 If something **gives offence**, it upsets people. If you **take offence**, you are upset by someone or something.

offend offends offending offended
VERB 1 If you offend someone, you upset them. 2 FORMAL To offend or to offend a law is to commit a crime.
offender NOUN

offensive offensives
ADJECTIVE 1 Something offensive is rude and upsetting E.G. *offensive behaviour.* 2 Offensive actions or weapons are used in attacking someone. ► NOUN 3 an attack E.G. *a full-scale offensive against the rebels.*
offensively ADVERB

offer offers offering offered
VERB 1 If you offer something to someone, you ask them if they would like it. ► NOUN 2 something that someone says they will give you or do for you if you want them to E.G.

a
b
c
d
e
f
g
h
i
j
k
l
m
n
o
p
q
r
s
t
u
v
w
x
y
z

He refused the offer of a drink. **3** a specially low price for a product in a shop E.G. *You will need a voucher to qualify for the special offer.*

offering offerings
NOUN something that is offered or given to someone.

offhand
ADJECTIVE **1** If someone is offhand, they are unfriendly and slightly rude. ► ADVERB **2** If you know something offhand, you know it without having to think very hard E.G. *I couldn't tell you offhand how long he's been here.*

office offices
NOUN **1** a room where people work at desks. **2** a government department E.G. *the Office of Fair Trading.* **3** a place where people can go for information, tickets, or other services. **4** Someone who holds office has an important job or position in government or in an organization.

officer officers
NOUN a person with a position of authority in the armed forces, the police, or a government organization.

official officials
ADJECTIVE **1** approved by the government or by someone in authority E.G. *the official figures.* **2** done or used by someone in authority as part of their job E.G. *official notepaper.* ► NOUN **3** a person who holds a position of authority in an organization.
officially ADVERB

officialdom
NOUN You can refer to officials in government or other organizations as officialdom, especially when you find them difficult to deal with.

officiate officiates officiating officiated
VERB To officiate at a ceremony is to be in charge and perform the official part of the ceremony.

offing
PHRASE If something is **in the offing**, it is likely to happen soon E.G. *A change is in the offing.*

off-licence off-licences
NOUN a shop which sells alcoholic drinks.

offset offsets offsetting offset
VERB If one thing is offset by another thing, its effect is reduced or cancelled out by that thing E.G. *This tedium can be offset by watching the television.*

offshoot offshoots
NOUN something that has developed from another thing E.G. *The technology we use is an offshoot of the motor industry.*

offshore
ADJECTIVE OR ADVERB in or from the part of the sea near the shore E.G. *an offshore wind... a wreck fifteen kilometres offshore.*

offside
ADJECTIVE **1** If a soccer, rugby, or hockey player is offside, they have broken the rules by moving too far forward. ► NOUN **2** the side of a vehicle that is furthest from the pavement.

offspring
NOUN A person's or animal's offspring are their children.

often
ADVERB happening many times or a lot of the time.

ogle ogles ogling ogled
Said "oh-gl" VERB To ogle someone is to stare at them in a way that

ogre ogres
Said "oh-gur" NOUN a cruel, frightening giant in a fairy story.

ohm ohms
Rhymes with "home" NOUN In physics, an ohm is a unit used to measure electrical resistance.

oil oils oiling oiled
NOUN 1 Oil is a thick, sticky liquid used as a fuel and for lubrication. 2 Oil is also a thick, greasy liquid made from plants or animals E.G. *cooking oil… bath oil.* ▶ VERB 3 If you oil something, you put oil in it or on it.

oil painting oil paintings
NOUN a picture that has been painted with thick paints made from coloured powder and a kind of oil.

oilskin oilskins
NOUN a piece of clothing made from a thick, waterproof material, worn especially by fishermen.

oily
ADJECTIVE Something that is oily is covered with or contains oil E.G. *an oily rag… oily skin.*

ointment ointments
NOUN a smooth, thick substance that you put on sore skin to heal it

okay or **OK**
ADJECTIVE or ADVERB; INFORMAL Okay means all right E.G. *Tell me if this sounds okay.*
■ acceptable, all right, satisfactory

old older oldest
ADJECTIVE 1 having lived or existed for a long time E.G. *an old lady… old clothes.* 2 'Old' is used to give the age of someone or something E.G. *This photo is five years old.* 3 'Old' also means former E.G. *my old art teacher.*

olden
PHRASE **In the olden days** means long ago.

Old English
NOUN Old English was the English language from the fifth century AD until about 1100. Old English is also known as Anglo-Saxon.

old-fashioned
ADJECTIVE 1 Something which is old-fashioned is no longer fashionable E.G. *old-fashioned shoes.* 2 Someone who is old-fashioned believes in the values and standards of the past.
■ (sense 1) dated, outmoded, passé

Old Norse
NOUN Old Norse was a language spoken in Scandinavia and Iceland from about 700 AD to about 1350 AD. Many English words are derived from Old Norse.

Old Testament
NOUN The Old Testament is the first part of the Christian Bible. It is also the holy book of the Jewish religion and contains writings which relate to the history of the Jews.

oleander oleanders
NOUN an evergreen shrub with fragrant white, pink, or purple flowers.

olive olives
NOUN 1 a small green or black fruit containing a stone. Olives are usually pickled and eaten as a snack or crushed to produce oil. ▶ ADJECTIVE or NOUN 2 dark yellowish-green.

-ology
SUFFIX -ology is used to form words that refer to the study of something E.G. *biology… geology.*
🔳 from Greek *logos* meaning 'reason', 'speech', or 'discourse'

a
b
c
d
e
f
g
h
i
j
k
l
m
n
o
p
q
r
s
t
u
v
w
x
y
z

an ELegant angEL (angel)   SPELLING NOTE

A
B
C
D
E
F
G
H
I
J
K
L
M
N
O
P
Q
R
S
T
U
V
W
X
Y
Z

Olympic Games
Said "ol-lim-pik" PLURAL NOUN The Olympic Games are a set of sporting contests held in a different city every four years.

ombudsman ombudsmen
NOUN The ombudsman is a person who investigates complaints against the government or a public organization.

omelette omelettes
Said "om-lit" NOUN a dish made by beating eggs together and cooking them in a flat pan.

omen omens
NOUN something that is thought to be a sign of what will happen in the future E.G. *John saw this success as a good omen for his trip.*
▤ portent, sign

ominous
ADJECTIVE suggesting that something unpleasant is going to happen E.G. *an ominous sign.*
ominously ADVERB
▤ sinister, threatening

omission omissions
NOUN 1 something that has not been included or done E.G. *There are some striking omissions in the survey.* 2 Omission is the act of not including or not doing something E.G. *controversy over the omission of female novelists.*

omit omits omitting omitted
VERB 1 If you omit something, you do not include it. 2 FORMAL If you omit to do something, you do not do it.

omnibus omnibuses
NOUN 1 a book containing a collection of stories or articles by the same author or about the same subject.
▸ ADJECTIVE 2 An omnibus edition of a

radio or television show contains two or more programmes that were originally broadcast separately.

omnipotent
Said "om-nip-a-tent" ADJECTIVE having very great or unlimited power E.G. *omnipotent emperors.*
omnipotence NOUN

omnivore
NOUN An omnivore is an animal that eats all kinds of food, including meat and plants.
omnivorous ADJECTIVE

on
PREPOSITION 1 touching or attached to something E.G. *The woman was sitting on the sofa.* 2 If you are on a bus, plane, or train, you are inside it. 3 If something happens on a particular day, that is when it happens E.G. *It is his birthday on Monday.* 4 If something is done on an instrument or machine, it is done using that instrument or machine E.G. *He preferred to play on his computer.* 5 A book or talk on a particular subject is about that subject. ▸ ADVERB 6 If you have a piece of clothing on, you are wearing it. ▸ ADJECTIVE 7 A machine or switch that is on is working. 8 If an event is on, it is happening or taking place E.G. *The race is definitely on.*

once
ADVERB 1 If something happens once, it happens one time only. 2 If something was once true, it was true in the past, but is no longer true. ▸ CONJUNCTION 3 If something happens once another thing has happened, it happens immediately afterwards E.G. *Once you get used to working for yourself, it's tough working for anybody else.* ▸ PHRASES 4 If you do

something **at once**, you do it immediately. If several things happen **at once**, they all happen at the same time.

one ones 1 One is the number 1. ADJECTIVE **2** If you refer to the one person or thing of a particular kind, you mean the only person or thing of that kind E.G. *My one aim is to look after the horses well.* **3** One also means 'a'; used when emphasizing something E.G. *They got one almighty shock.* ▶ PRONOUN **4** One refers to a particular thing or person E.G. *Alf Brown's business was a good one.* **5** One also means people in general E.G. *One likes to have the opportunity to chat.*

one-off one-offs
NOUN something that happens or is made only once.

onerous
Said "ohn-er-uss" ADJECTIVE; FORMAL difficult or unpleasant E.G. *an onerous task.*

oneself
PRONOUN 'Oneself' is used when you are talking about people in general E.G. *One could hardly hear oneself talk.*

one-sided
ADJECTIVE **1** If an activity or relationship is one-sided, one of the people has a lot more success or involvement than the other E.G. *a one-sided contest.* **2** A one-sided argument or report considers the facts or a situation from only one point of view.

one-way
ADJECTIVE **1** One-way streets are streets along which vehicles can drive in only one direction. **2** A one-way

ticket is one that you can use to travel to a place, but not to travel back again.

ongoing
ADJECTIVE continuing to happen E.G. *an ongoing process of learning.*

onion onions
NOUN a small, round vegetable with a brown skin like paper and a very strong taste.

onlooker onlookers
NOUN someone who is watching an event.

only
ADVERB **1** You use 'only' to indicate the one thing or person involved E.G. *Only Keith knows whether he will continue.* **2** You use 'only' to emphasize that something is unimportant or small E.G. *He's only a little boy.* **3** You can use 'only' to introduce something which happens immediately after something else E.G. *She had thought of one plan, only to discard it for another.* ▶ ADJECTIVE **4** If you talk about the only thing or person, you mean that there are no others E.G. *their only hit single.* **5** If you are an only child, you have no brothers or sisters. ▶ CONJUNCTION **6** 'Only' also means but or except E.G. *He was like you, only blond.* ▶ PHRASE **7 Only too** means extremely E.G. *I would be only too happy to swap places.*

onomatopoeia
Said "on-o-mat-o-**pee**-a" NOUN (ENGLISH) the use of words which sound like the thing that they represent. 'Hiss' and 'buzz' are examples of onomatopoeia.
📖 from Greek *onoma* meaning 'name' and *poiein* meaning 'to make'

a
b
c
d
e
f
g
h
i
j
k
l
m
n
o
p
q
r
s
t
u
v
w
x
y
z

A
B
C
D
E
F
G
H
I
J
K
L
M
N
O
P
Q
R
S
T
U
V
W
X
Y
Z

onset
NOUN The onset of something unpleasant is the beginning of it E.G. *the onset of war*.

onslaught onslaughts
Said "on-slawt" NOUN a violent attack.

onto or **on to**
PREPOSITION If you put something onto an object, you put it on it.

onus
Rhymes with "bonus" NOUN; FORMAL If the onus is on you to do something, it is your duty to do it.

onwards or **onward**
ADVERB 1 continuing to happen from a particular time E.G. *He could not speak a word from that moment onwards.* 2 travelling forwards E.G. *Duncliffe escorted the pair onwards to his own room.*

onyx
Said "on-iks" NOUN Onyx is a semiprecious stone used for making ornaments and jewellery.

ooze oozes oozing oozed
VERB When a thick liquid oozes, it flows slowly E.G. *The cold mud oozed over her new footwear.*

opal opals
NOUN a pale or whitish semiprecious stone used for making jewellery.

opaque
Said "oh-pake" ADJECTIVE If something is opaque, you cannot see through it E.G. *opaque glass windows.*

open opens opening opened
VERB 1 When you open something, or when it opens, you move it so that it is no longer closed E.G. *She opened the door.* 2 When a shop or office opens, people are able to go in. 3 To open something also means to start it E.G. *He tried to open a bank*

account. ► ADJECTIVE 4 Something that is open is not closed or fastened E.G. *an open box of chocolates.* 5 If you have an open mind, you are willing to consider new ideas or suggestions. 6 Someone who is open is honest and frank. 7 When a shop or office is open, people are able to go in. 8 An open area of sea or land is a large, empty area E.G. *open country.* 9 If something is open to you, it is possible for you to do it E.G. *There is no other course open to us but to fight it out.* 10 If a situation is still open, it is still being considered E.G. *Even if the case remains open, the full facts may never be revealed.* ► PHRASE 11 **In the open** means outside. 12 **In the open** also means not secret.

openly ADVERB

opening openings
ADJECTIVE 1 Opening means coming first E.G. *the opening day of the season.* ► NOUN 2 The opening of a book or film is the first part of it. 3 a hole or gap. 4 an opportunity E.G. *The two men circled around, looking for an opening to attack.*

▣ (sense 3) aperture, gap, hole

open-minded
ADJECTIVE willing to consider new ideas and suggestions.

open-plan
ADJECTIVE An open-plan office or building has very few dividing walls inside.

opera operas
NOUN a play in which the words are sung rather than spoken.

operatic ADJECTIVE
🏛 from Latin *opera* meaning 'works'

operate operates operating operated
VERB 1 To operate is to work E.G. *We*

are shocked at the way that businesses operate. **2** When you operate a machine, you make it work. **3** When surgeons operate, they cut open a patient's body to remove or repair a damaged part.

operation operations
NOUN **1** a complex, planned event E.G. *a full-scale military operation.* **2** a form of medical treatment in which a surgeon cuts open a patient's body to remove or repair a damaged part.
▶ PHRASE **3** If something is **in operation**, it is working or being used E.G. *The system is in operation from April to the end of September.*

operational
ADJECTIVE working or able to be used E.G. *an operational aircraft.*

operative
ADJECTIVE Something that is operative is working or having an effect.

operator operators
NOUN **1** someone who works at a telephone exchange or on a switchboard. **2** someone who operates a machine E.G. *a computer operator.* **3** someone who runs a business E.G. *a tour operator.*

opinion opinions
NOUN a belief or view.
▤ belief, judgment, view

opinionated
ADJECTIVE Someone who is opinionated has strong views and refuses to accept that they might be wrong.

opium
NOUN Opium is a drug made from the seeds of a poppy. It is used in medicine to relieve pain.
▥ from Latin *opium* meaning 'poppy juice'

opponent opponents
NOUN someone who is against you in an argument or a contest.

opportune
ADJECTIVE; FORMAL happening at a convenient time E.G. *The king's death was opportune for the prince.*

opportunism
NOUN Opportunism is taking advantage of any opportunity to gain money or power for yourself.
opportunist NOUN

opportunity opportunities
NOUN a chance to do something.

oppose opposes opposing opposed
VERB If you oppose something, you disagree with it and try to prevent it.

opposed
ADJECTIVE **1** If you are opposed to something, you disagree with it E.G. *He was totally opposed to bullying in schools.* **2** Opposed also means opposite or very different E.G. *two opposed schools of thought.* ▶ PHRASE **3** If you refer to one thing **as opposed to** another, you are emphasizing that it is the first thing rather than the second which concerns you E.G. *Real spectators, as opposed to invited guests, were hard to spot.*

opposite opposites
PREPOSITION or ADVERB **1** If one thing is opposite another, it is facing it E.G. *the shop opposite the station... the house opposite.* ▶ ADJECTIVE **2** The opposite part of something is the part farthest away from you E.G. *the opposite side of town.* **3** If things are opposite, they are completely different E.G. *I take the opposite view to you.* ▶ NOUN **4** If two things are

a
b
c
d
e
f
g
h
i
j
k
l
m
n
o
p
q
r
s
t
u
v
w
x
y
z

A
B
C
D
E
F
G
H
I
J
K
L
M
N
O
P
Q
R
S
T
U
V
W
X
Y
Z

completely different, they are opposites.

■ (sense 4) antithesis, contrary, reverse

opposition

NOUN 1 If there is opposition to something, people disagree with it and try to prevent it. 2 The political parties who are not in power are referred to as the Opposition. 3 In a game or sports event, the opposition is the person or team that you are competing against.

oppressed

ADJECTIVE People who are oppressed are treated cruelly or unfairly.

oppress VERB **oppression** NOUN
oppressor NOUN

oppressive

ADJECTIVE 1 If the weather is oppressive, it is hot and humid. 2 An oppressive situation makes you feel depressed or concerned E.G. *The silence became oppressive.* 3 An oppressive system treats people cruelly or unfairly E.G. *Married women were subject to oppressive laws.*

oppressively ADVERB

opt opts opting opted

VERB If you opt for something, you choose it. If you opt out of something, you choose not to be involved in it.

optical

ADJECTIVE 1 concerned with vision, light, or images E.G. *an optical scanner.* 2 relating to the appearance of things E.G. *an optical illusion.*

optic ADJECTIVE

optician opticians

NOUN someone who tests people's

eyes, and makes and sells glasses and contact lenses.

optimism

NOUN Optimism is a feeling of hopefulness about the future.

optimist NOUN **optimistic** ADJECTIVE
optimistically ADVERB

optimum

ADJECTIVE the best that is possible E.G. *Six is the optimum number of participants for a good meeting.*

option options

NOUN a choice between two or more things.

optional ADJECTIVE

opulent

Said "op-yool-nt" ADJECTIVE grand and expensive-looking E.G. *an opulent seafront estate.*

opus opera

NOUN an artistic work, especially a piece of music.

or

CONJUNCTION 1 used to link two different things E.G. *I didn't know whether to laugh or cry.* 2 used to introduce a warning E.G. *Do what I say or else I will fire.*

-or

SUFFIX '-or' is used to form nouns from verbs E.G. *actor… conductor.*
🏛from Latin

oracle oracles

NOUN 1 In ancient Greece, an oracle was a place where a priest or priestess made predictions about the future. 2 a prophecy made by a priest or other person with great authority or wisdom.

oral orals

ADJECTIVE 1 spoken rather than written E.G. *oral history.* 2 Oral describes things that are used in your mouth or done with your mouth E.G. *an oral vaccine.* ▶ NOUN 3 an examination that is spoken rather than written.

orally ADVERB

■ (sense 1) spoken, verbal

orange oranges

NOUN 1 a round citrus fruit that is juicy and sweet and has a thick reddish-yellow skin. ▶ ADJECTIVE OR NOUN 2 reddish-yellow.

🔟 from Sanskrit *naranga* meaning 'orange'

orang-utan orang-utans; also spelt **orang-utang**

NOUN a large ape with reddish-brown hair.

orator orators

NOUN someone who is good at making speeches.

oratory

NOUN Oratory is the art and skill of making formal public speeches.

orbit orbits orbiting orbited

NOUN 1 the curved path followed by an object going round a planet or the sun. ▶ VERB 2 If something orbits a planet or the sun, it goes round and round it.

orchard orchards

NOUN a piece of land where fruit trees are grown.

orchestra orchestras

Said "or-kess-tra" NOUN (MUSIC) a large group of musicians who play musical instruments together.

orchestral ADJECTIVE

🔟 from Greek *orkhestra* meaning 'the area in a theatre reserved for musicians'

orchestrate orchestrates orchestrating orchestrated

VERB 1 To orchestrate something is to organize it very carefully in order to

produce a particular result. 2 To orchestrate a piece of music is to rewrite it so that it can be played by an orchestra.

orchestration NOUN

orchid orchids

Said "or-kid" NOUN Orchids are plants with beautiful and unusual flowers.

ordain ordains ordaining ordained

VERB When someone is ordained, they are made a member of the clergy.

ordeal ordeals

NOUN a difficult and extremely unpleasant experience E.G. *the ordeal of being arrested and charged with attempted murder.*

■ hardship, torture, tribulation

order orders ordering ordered

NOUN 1 a command given by someone in authority. 2 If things are arranged or done in a particular order, they are arranged or done in that sequence E.G. *in alphabetical order.* 3 Order is a situation in which everything is in the correct place and done at the correct time. 4 something that you ask to be brought to you or sent to you. ▶ VERB 5 To order someone to do something is to tell them firmly to do it. 6 When you order something, you ask for it to be brought or sent to you. ▶ PHRASE 7 If you do something **in order to** achieve a particular thing, you do it because you want to achieve that thing.

orderly

ADJECTIVE Something that is orderly is well organized or arranged.

■ methodical, well-organized

ordinarily

ADVERB If something ordinarily happens, it usually happens.

A
B
C
D
E
F
G
H
I
J
K
L
M
N
O
P
Q
R
S
T
U
V
W
X
Y
Z

ordinary

ADJECTIVE Ordinary means not special or different in any way.

■ conventional, normal, usual

ordination

NOUN When someone's ordination takes place, they are made a member of the clergy.

ordnance

NOUN Weapons and other military supplies are referred to as ordnance.

ore ores

NOUN Ore is rock or earth from which metal can be obtained.

oregano

*Said "or-rig-**garh**-no"* NOUN Oregano is a herb used for flavouring in cooking.

organ organs

NOUN 1 Your organs are parts of your body that have a particular function, for example your heart or lungs. 2 a large musical instrument with pipes of different lengths through which air is forced. It has various keyboards which are played like a piano.

organic

ADJECTIVE 1 Something that is organic is produced by or found in plants or animals E.G. *decaying organic matter.* 2 Organic food is produced without the use of artificial fertilizers or pesticides.

organically ADVERB

organism organisms

NOUN (SCIENCE) any living animal or plant.

organist organists

NOUN someone who plays the organ.

organization organizations; also spelt **organisation**

NOUN 1 any group or business. 2 The organization of something is the act of planning and arranging it.

organizational ADJECTIVE

■ (sense 1) body, company, group

organize organizes organizing organized; also spelt **organise**

VERB 1 If you organize an event, you plan and arrange it. 2 If you organize things, you arrange them in a sensible order.

organized ADJECTIVE **organizer** NOUN

orgasm orgasms

NOUN the moment of greatest pleasure and excitement during sexual activity.

orgy orgies

Said "or-jee" NOUN 1 a wild, uncontrolled party involving a lot of drinking and sexual activity. 2 You can refer to a period of intense activity as an orgy of that activity E.G. *an orgy of violence.*

▥ from Greek *orgia* meaning 'nocturnal festival'

orient

NOUN LITERARY The Orient is eastern and south-eastern Asia.

oriental

ADJECTIVE relating to eastern or south-eastern Asia.

orientated

ADJECTIVE If someone is interested in a particular thing, you can say that they are orientated towards it E.G. *These men are very career-orientated.*

orientation

NOUN You can refer to an organization's activities and aims as its orientation E.G. *Poland's political and military orientation.*

oriented

ADJECTIVE Oriented means the same as orientated.

orienteering

NOUN Orienteering is a sport in which people run from one place to another in the countryside, using a map and compass to guide them.

origin origins

NOUN 1 You can refer to the beginning or cause of something as its origin or origins. 2 You can refer to someone's family background as their origin or origins E.G. *She was of Swedish origin.*
■ (sense 1) root, source

original originals

ADJECTIVE 1 Original describes things that existed at the beginning, rather than being added later, or things that were the first of their kind to exist E.G. *the original owner of the cottage.* 2 Original means imaginative and clever E.G. *a stunningly original idea.* ▶ NOUN 3 A work of art or a document that is the one that was first produced, and not a copy.

originally ADVERB   **originality** NOUN

originate originates originating originated

VERB When something originates, or you originate it, it begins to happen or exist.

originator NOUN

ornament ornaments

NOUN a small, attractive object that you display in your home or that you wear in order to look attractive.

ornamental

ADJECTIVE designed to be attractive rather than useful E.G. *an ornamental lake.*

ornamentation

NOUN Ornamentation is decoration on a building, a piece of furniture, or a work of art.

ornate

ADJECTIVE Something that is ornate has a lot of decoration on it.

ornithology

NOUN Ornithology is the study of birds.

ornithologist NOUN
🏛 from Greek *ornis* meaning 'bird' and *-logia* meaning 'study of'

orphan orphans orphaning orphaned

NOUN 1 a child whose parents are dead. ▶ VERB 2 If a child is orphaned, its parents die.

orphanage orphanages

NOUN a place where orphans are looked after.

orthodox

ADJECTIVE 1 Orthodox beliefs or methods are the ones that most people have or use and that are considered standard. 2 People who are orthodox believe in the older, more traditional ideas of their religion or political party. 3 The Orthodox church is the part of the Christian church which separated from the western European church in the 11th century and is the main church in Greece and Russia.

orthodoxy NOUN

osmosis

Said "oz-**moh**-siss" NOUN TECHNICAL Osmosis is the process by which a liquid moves through a semipermeable membrane from a weaker solution to a more concentrated one.

osprey ospreys

Said "**oss**-pree" NOUN a large bird of prey which catches fish with its feet.

ostensibly

ADVERB If something is done

a b c d e f g h i j k l m n o p q r s t u v w x y z

ostensibly for a reason, that seems to be the reason for it E.G. *Byrnes submitted his resignation, ostensibly on medical grounds.*

ostentatious

ADJECTIVE **1** Something that is ostentatious is intended to impress people, for example by looking expensive E.G. *ostentatious sculptures.* **2** People who are ostentatious try to impress other people with their wealth or importance.
ostentatiously ADVERB
ostentation NOUN

ostinato

NOUN AND ADJECTIVE (MUSIC) a musical phrase that is continuously repeated throughout a piece.

ostrich ostriches

NOUN The ostrich is the largest bird in the world. Ostriches cannot fly.

other others

ADJECTIVE or PRONOUN **1** Other people or things are different people or things E.G. *All the other children had gone home… One of the cabinets came from the palace; the other is a copy.*
▶ PHRASES **2 The other day** or **the other week** means recently E.G. *She had bought four pairs of shoes the other day.*

otherwise

ADVERB **1** You use 'otherwise' to say a different situation would exist if a particular fact or occurrence was not the case E.G. *You had to learn to swim pretty quickly, otherwise you sank.* **2** 'Otherwise' means apart from the thing mentioned E.G. *She had written to her daughter, but otherwise refused to take sides.* **3** 'Otherwise' also means in a different way E.G. *The majority voted otherwise.*

otter otters

NOUN a small, furry animal with a long tail. Otters swim well and eat fish.

ouch

INTERJECTION You say ouch when you suddenly feel pain.

ought

Said "awt" VERB If you say that someone ought to do something, you mean that they should do it E.G. *He ought to see a doctor.*
☑ Do not use *did* and *had* with *ought*: *He ought not to come* is correct: *he didn't ought to come* is not correct.

ounce ounces

NOUN a unit of weight equal to one sixteenth of a pound or about 28.35 grams.

our

ADJECTIVE 'Our' refers to something belonging or relating to the speaker or writer and one or more other people E.G. *We recently sold our house.*
☑ Some people pronounce *our* and *are* in the same way, so do not confuse the spellings of these words.

ours

PRONOUN 'Ours' refers to something belonging or relating to the speaker or writer and one or more other people E.G. *a friend of ours from Korea.*

ourselves

PRONOUN **1** 'Ourselves' is used when the same speaker or writer and one or more other people do an action and are affected by it E.G. *We haven't damaged ourselves too badly.* **2** 'Ourselves' is used to emphasize 'we'.

oust ousts ousting ousted

VERB If you oust someone, you force

them out of a job or a place E.G. *Cole was ousted from the board.*

out

ADVERB **1** towards the outside of a place E.G. *Two dogs rushed out of the house.* **2** not at home E.G. *She was out when I rang last night.* **3** in the open air E.G. *They are playing out in bright sunshine.* **4** no longer shining or burning E.G. *The lights went out.*
▶ ADJECTIVE **5** on strike E.G. *1000 construction workers are out in sympathy.* **6** unacceptable or unfashionable E.G. *Miniskirts are out.* **7** incorrect E.G. *Logan's timing was out in the first two rounds.*

out-

SUFFIX **1** 'Out-' means 'exceeding' or 'going beyond'. E.G. *outdo… outclass.* **2** 'Out-' also means on the outside or away from the centre E.G. *outback… outpost.*

out-and-out

ADJECTIVE entire or complete E.G. *an out-and-out lie.*

outback

NOUN In Australia, the outback is the remote parts where very few people live.

outboard motor outboard motors

NOUN a motor that can be fixed to the back of a small boat.

outbreak outbreaks

NOUN If there is an outbreak of something unpleasant, such as war, it suddenly occurs.

outburst outbursts

NOUN **1** a sudden, strong expression of an emotion, especially anger E.G. *John broke into an angry outburst about how unfairly the work was divided.* **2** a sudden occurrence of

violent activity E.G. *an outburst of gunfire.*

outcast outcasts

NOUN someone who is rejected by other people.

outclassed

ADJECTIVE If you are outclassed, you are much worse than your opponent at a particular activity.

outcome outcomes

NOUN a result E.G. *the outcome of the election.*

outcrop outcrops

NOUN a large piece of rock that sticks out of the ground.

outcry outcries

NOUN If there is an outcry about something, a lot of people are angry about it E.G. *a public outcry over alleged fraud.*

outdated

ADJECTIVE no longer in fashion.

outdo outdoes outdoing outdid outdone

VERB If you outdo someone, you do a particular thing better than they do.

outdoor

ADJECTIVE happening or used outside E.G. *outdoor activities.*

outdoors

ADVERB outside E.G. *It was too chilly to sit outdoors.*

outer

ADJECTIVE The outer parts of something are the parts furthest from the centre E.G. *the outer door of the office.*

outer space

NOUN Outer space is everything beyond the Earth's atmosphere.

outfit outfits

NOUN **1** a set of clothes. **2** INFORMAL an organization.

a
b
c
d
e
f
g
h
i
j
k
l
m
n
o
p
q
r
s
t
u
v
w
x
y
z

A
B
C
D
E
F
G
H
I
J
K
L
M
N
O
P
Q
R
S
T
U
V
W
X
Y
Z

outgoing outgoings
ADJECTIVE **1** Outgoing describes someone who is leaving a job or place E.G. *the outgoing President*. **2** Someone who is outgoing is friendly and not shy. ▶ PLURAL NOUN **3** Your outgoings are the amount of money that you spend.

outgrow outgrows outgrowing outgrew outgrown
VERB **1** If you outgrow a piece of clothing, you grow too big for it. **2** If you outgrow a way of behaving, you stop it because you have grown older and more mature.

outhouse outhouses
NOUN a small building in the grounds of a house to which it belongs.

outing outings
NOUN a trip made for pleasure.

outlandish
ADJECTIVE very unusual or odd E.G. *outlandish clothes*.

outlaw outlaws outlawing outlawed
VERB **1** If something is outlawed, it is made illegal. ▶ NOUN **2** In the past, an outlaw was a criminal.

outlay outlays
NOUN an amount of money spent on something E.G. *a cash outlay of 300 dollars*.

outlet outlets
NOUN **1** An outlet for your feelings or ideas is a way of expressing them. **2** a hole or pipe through which water or air can flow away. **3** a shop which sells goods made by a particular manufacturer.

outline outlines outlining outlined
VERB **1** If you outline a plan or idea, you explain it in a general way. **2** You

say that something is outlined when you can see its shape because there is a light behind it. ▶ NOUN **3** a general explanation or description of something. **4** The outline of something is its shape.

outlive outlives outliving outlived
VERB To outlive someone is to live longer than they do.

outlook
NOUN **1** Your outlook is your general attitude towards life. **2** The outlook of a situation is the way it is likely to develop E.G. *The Japanese economy's outlook is uncertain*.

outlying
ADJECTIVE Outlying places are far from cities.

outmoded
ADJECTIVE old-fashioned and no longer useful E.G. *an outmoded form of transport*.

outnumber outnumbers outnumbering outnumbered
VERB If there are more of one group than of another, the first group outnumbers the second.

out of
PREPOSITION **1** If you do something out of a particular feeling, you are motivated by that feeling E.G. *Out of curiosity she went along*. **2** 'Out of' also means from E.G. *old instruments made out of wood*. **3** If you are out of something, you no longer have any of it E.G. *I do hope we're not out of fuel again*. **4** If you are out of the rain, sun, or wind, you are sheltered from it. **5** You also use 'out of' to indicate proportion. For example, one out of five means one in every five.

out of date
ADJECTIVE old-fashioned and no longer useful.

SPELLING NOTE   Plaice the fish has a glittering 'EYE' (I) (plaice)

out of doors
ADVERB outside E.G. *Sometimes we eat out of doors.*

outpatient outpatients
NOUN Outpatients are people who receive treatment in hospital without staying overnight.

outpost outposts
NOUN a small collection of buildings a long way from a main centre E.G. *a remote mountain outpost.*

output outputs
NOUN 1 Output is the amount of something produced by a person or organization. 2 (ICT) The output of a computer is the information that it produces.

outrage outrages outraging outraged
VERB 1 If something outrages you, it angers and shocks you E.G. *I was outraged at what had happened to her.* ► NOUN 2 Outrage is a feeling of anger and shock. 3 something very shocking or violent.
outrageous ADJECTIVE
outrageously ADVERB

outright
ADJECTIVE 1 absolute E.G. *an outright rejection.* ► ADVERB 2 in an open and direct way E.G. *Have you asked him outright?* 3 completely and totally E.G. *I own the company outright.*

outset
NOUN The outset of something is the beginning of it E.G. *the outset of his journey.*

outshine outshines outshining outshone
VERB If you outshine someone, you perform better than they do.

outside
NOUN 1 The outside of something is the part which surrounds or encloses the rest of it. ► ADVERB, ADJECTIVE, or PREPOSITION 2 Outside means not inside E.G. *houses just outside the airport… He stood outside and shouted… an outside toilet.* 3 Outside also means not included in something E.G. *outside office hours.*

☑ Do not use *of* after *outside.* You should write *she was waiting outside the school* and not *outside of the school.*

outsider outsiders
NOUN 1 someone who does not belong to a particular group. 2 a competitor considered unlikely to win in a race.

outsize or **outsized**
ADJECTIVE much larger than usual E.G. *outsize feet.*

outskirts
PLURAL NOUN The outskirts of a city or town are the parts around the edge of it.

outspoken
ADJECTIVE Outspoken people give their opinions openly, even if they shock other people.

outstanding
ADJECTIVE 1 extremely good E.G. *The collection contains hundreds of outstanding works of art.* 2 Money that is outstanding is still owed E.G. *an outstanding mortgage of 46,000 pounds.*

outstretched
ADJECTIVE If your arms are outstretched, they are stretched out as far as possible.

outstrip outstrips outstripping outstripped
VERB If one thing outstrips another thing, it becomes bigger or more

a b c d e f g h i j k l m n o p q r s t u v w x y z

I went to see (C) the doctor's new practiCe (practice)   SPELLING NOTE

A B C D E F G H I J K L M N O P Q R S T U V W X Y Z

successful or moves faster than the other thing.

outward

ADJECTIVE OR ADVERB **1** Outward means away from a place or towards the outside E.G. *the outward journey.*

▶ ADJECTIVE **2** The outward features of someone are the ones they appear to have, rather than the ones they actually have E.G. *He never showed any outward signs of emotion.*

outwardly ADVERB

outwards

ADVERB away from a place or towards the outside E.G. *The door opened outwards.*

outweigh outweighs outweighing outweighed

VERB If you say that the advantages of something outweigh its disadvantages, you mean that the advantages are more important than the disadvantages.

outwit outwits outwitting outwitted

VERB If you outwit someone, you use your intelligence to defeat them.

oval ovals

NOUN **1** a round shape, similar to a circle but wider in one direction than the other. ▶ ADJECTIVE **2** shaped like an oval E.G. *an oval table.*

ovary ovaries

Said "oh-var-ree" NOUN A woman's ovaries are the two organs in her body that produce eggs.

ovation ovations

NOUN a long burst of applause.

oven ovens

NOUN the part of a cooker that you use for baking or roasting food.

over overs

PREPOSITION **1** Over something means

directly above it or covering it E.G. *the picture over the fireplace… He put his hands over his eyes.* **2** A view over an area is a view across that area E.G. *The pool and terrace look out over the sea.* **3** If something is over a road or river it is on the opposite side of the road or river. **4** Something that is over a particular amount is more than that amount. **5** 'Over' indicates a topic which is causing concern E.G. *An American was arguing over the bill.* **6** If something happens over a period of time, it happens during that period E.G. *I went to New Zealand over Christmas.* ▶ ADVERB OR PREPOSITION **7** If you lean over, you bend your body in a particular direction E.G. *He bent over and rummaged in a drawer… She was hunched over her typewriter.* ▶ ADVERB **8** 'Over' is used to indicate a position E.G. *over by the window… Come over here.* **9** If something rolls or turns over, it is moved so that its other side is facing upwards E.G. *He flipped over the envelope.* ▶ ADJECTIVE **10** Something that is over is completely finished.

▶ PHRASE **11 All over** a place means everywhere in that place E.G. *studios all over America.* ▶ NOUN **12** In cricket, an over is a set of six balls bowled by a bowler from the same end of the pitch.

over-

PREFIX 'Over' means to too great an extent or too much E.G. *overprotective… overindulge… overact.*

📖 from Old English *ofer*

overall overalls

ADJECTIVE OR ADVERB **1** Overall means taking into account all the parts or aspects of something E.G. *The overall* *quality of pupils' work had shown a marked improvement… Overall, things are not really too bad.* ► PLURAL NOUN **2** Overalls are a piece of clothing that looks like trousers and a jacket combined. You wear overalls to protect your other clothes when you are working. ► NOUN **3** An overall is a piece of clothing like a coat that you wear to protect your other clothes when you are working.

overawed
ADJECTIVE If you are overawed by something, you are very impressed by it and a little afraid of it.

overbearing
ADJECTIVE trying to dominate other people E.G. *Mozart had a difficult relationship with his overbearing father.*

overboard
ADVERB If you fall overboard, you fall over the side of a ship into the water.

overcast
ADJECTIVE If it is overcast, the sky is covered by cloud.

overcoat overcoats
NOUN a thick, warm coat.

overcome overcomes overcoming overcame overcome
VERB **1** If you overcome a problem or a feeling, you manage to deal with it or control it. ► ADJECTIVE **2** If you are overcome by a feeling, you feel it very strongly.

overcrowded
ADJECTIVE If a place is overcrowded, there are too many things or people in it.

overdo overdoes overdoing overdid overdone
VERB If you overdo something, you do it too much or in an exaggerated

way E.G. *It is important never to overdo new exercises.*

overdose overdoses
NOUN a larger dose of a drug than is safe.

overdraft overdrafts
NOUN an agreement with a bank that allows someone to spend more money than they have in their account.

overdrawn
ADJECTIVE If someone is overdrawn, they have taken more money from their bank account than the account has in it.

overdrive
NOUN Overdrive is an extra, higher gear in a vehicle, which is used at high speeds to reduce engine wear and save petrol.

overdue
ADJECTIVE If someone or something is overdue, they are late E.G. *The payments are overdue.*

overestimate overestimates overestimating overestimated
VERB If you overestimate something, you think that it is bigger, more important, or better than it really is E.G. *We had overestimated his popularity.*

overflow overflows overflowing overflowed overflown
VERB If a liquid overflows, it spills over the edges of its container. If a river overflows, it flows over its banks.

overgrown
ADJECTIVE A place that is overgrown is covered with weeds because it has not been looked after E.G. *an overgrown path.*

overhang overhangs overhanging overhung
VERB If one thing overhangs another,

a
b
c
d
e
f
g
h
i
j
k
l
m
n
o
p
q
r
s
t
u
v
w
x
y
z

A
B
C
D
E
F
G
H
I
J
K
L
M
N
O
P
Q
R
S
T
U
V
W
X
Y
Z

it sticks out sideways above it E.G. *old trees whose branches overhang a footpath.*

overhaul overhauls overhauling overhauled
VERB 1 If you overhaul something, you examine it thoroughly and repair any faults. ▶ NOUN 2 If you give something an overhaul, you examine it and repair or improve it.

overhead overheads
ADVERB OR ADJECTIVE 1 Overhead means above you E.G. *seagulls flying overhead.* ▶ PLURAL NOUN 2 The overheads of a business are the costs of running it.

overhear overhears overhearing overheard
VERB If you overhear someone's conversation, you hear what they are saying to someone else.

overjoyed
ADJECTIVE extremely pleased E.G. *Colm was overjoyed to see me.*
◼ delighted, over the moon

overlaid
ADJECTIVE If something is overlaid by something else, it is covered by it.

overland
ADJECTIVE OR ADVERB travelling across land rather than going by sea or air E.G. *an overland trek to India… Wray was returning to England overland.*

overlander overlanders
NOUN In Australian history, an overlander was a man who drove cattle or sheep long distances through the outback.

overlap overlaps overlapping overlapped
VERB If one thing overlaps another, one part of it covers part of the other thing.

overleaf
ADVERB on the next page E.G. *Write to us at the address shown overleaf.*

overload overloads overloading overloaded
VERB If you overload someone or something, you give them too much to do or to carry.

overlook overlooks overlooking overlooked
VERB 1 If a building or window overlooks a place, it has a view over that place. 2 If you overlook something, you ignore it or do not notice it.

overly
ADVERB excessively E.G. *I'm not overly fond of jazz.*

overnight
ADJECTIVE OR ADVERB 1 during the night E.G. *Further rain was forecast overnight.* 2 sudden or suddenly E.G. *an overnight success… Good players don't become bad ones overnight.*
▶ ADJECTIVE 3 for use when you go away for one or two nights E.G. *an overnight bag.*

overpower overpowers overpowering overpowered
VERB 1 If you overpower someone, you seize them despite their struggles, because you are stronger than them. 2 If a feeling overpowers you, it affects you very strongly.
overpowering ADJECTIVE

overrate overrates overrating overrated
VERB If you overrate something, you think that it is better or more important than it really is.
overrated ADJECTIVE

overreact overreacts
overreacting overreacted
VERB If you overreact, you react in an
extreme way.

overriding
ADJECTIVE more important than
anything else E.G. *an overriding duty*.

overrule overrules overruling
overruled
VERB To overrule a person or their
decisions is to decide that their
decisions are incorrect.
■ countermand, override, reverse

overrun overruns overrunning
overran overrun
VERB 1 If an army overruns a country, it
occupies it very quickly. 2 If animals
or plants overrun a place, they
spread quickly over it. 3 If an event
overruns, it continues for longer than
it was meant to.

overseas
ADJECTIVE or ADVERB 1 abroad E.G. *an
overseas tour… travelling overseas.*
▸ ADJECTIVE 2 from abroad E.G.
overseas students.

oversee oversees overseeing
oversaw overseen
VERB To oversee a job is to make sure
it is done properly.
overseer NOUN

overshadow overshadows
overshadowing overshadowed
VERB If something is overshadowed, it
is made unimportant by something
else that is better or more important.

oversight oversights
NOUN something which you forget to
do or fail to notice.

overspill
NOUN or ADJECTIVE Overspill refers to the
moving of people from overcrowded
cities to houses in smaller towns E.G.

an East End overspill… overspill estates.

overstate overstates
overstating overstated
VERB If you overstate something, you
exaggerate its importance.

overstep oversteps
overstepping overstepped
PHRASE If you **overstep the mark**, you
behave in an unacceptable way.

overt
ADJECTIVE open and obvious E.G. *overt
signs of stress.*
overtly ADVERB

overtake overtakes overtaking
overtook overtaken
VERB If you overtake someone, you
pass them because you are moving
faster than them.

overthrow overthrows
overthrowing overthrew
overthrown
VERB If a government is overthrown, it
is removed from power by force.

overtime
NOUN 1 Overtime is time that
someone works in addition to their
normal working hours. ▸ ADVERB 2 If
someone works overtime, they do
work in addition to their normal
working hours.

overtones
PLURAL NOUN If something has
overtones of an emotion or attitude,
it suggests it without showing it
openly E.G. *the political overtones of
the trial.*

overture overtures
NOUN 1 a piece of music that is the
introduction to an opera or play. 2 If
you make overtures to someone, you
approach them because you want to
start a friendly or business
relationship with them.

a
b
c
d
e
f
g
h
i
j
k
l
m
n
o
p
q
r
s
t
u
v
w
x
y
z

Psychiatrists Seldom Yell Callously Hard (psychiatrist)   SPELLING NOTE

A
B
C
D
E
F
G
H
I
J
K
L
M
N
O
P
Q
R
S
T
U
V
W
X
Y
Z

overturn overturns overturning overturned
VERB 1 To overturn something is to turn it upside down or onto its side. 2 If someone overturns a legal decision, they change it by using their higher authority.

overview overviews
NOUN a general understanding or description of a situation.

overweight
ADJECTIVE too fat, and therefore unhealthy E.G. *overweight businessmen*.

overwhelm overwhelms overwhelming overwhelmed
VERB 1 If you are overwhelmed by something, it affects you very strongly E.G. *The priest appeared overwhelmed by the news.* 2 If one group of people overwhelm another, they gain complete control or victory over them.
overwhelming ADJECTIVE
overwhelmingly ADVERB

overwork overworks overworking overworked
VERB If you overwork, you work too hard.

overwrought
Said "oh-ver-**rawt**" ADJECTIVE extremely upset E.G. *He didn't get angry or overwrought.*

ovulate ovulates ovulating ovulated
Said "**ov**-yool-late" VERB When a woman or female animal ovulates, she produces ova or eggs from her ovary.

ovum ova
Said "**oh**-vum" NOUN a reproductive cell of a woman or female animal. The ovum is fertilized by a male

sperm to produce young.
📖 a Latin word meaning 'egg'

owe owes owing owed
VERB 1 If you owe someone money, they have lent it to you and you have not yet paid it back. 2 If you owe a quality or skill to someone, they are responsible for giving it to you E.G. *He owes his success to his mother.* 3 If you say that you owe someone gratitude or loyalty, you mean that they deserve it from you.

owl owls
NOUN Owls are birds of prey that hunt at night. They have large eyes and short, hooked beaks.

own owns owning owned
ADJECTIVE 1 If something is your own, it belongs to you or is associated with you E.G. *She stayed in her own house.*
▶ VERB 2 If you own something, it belongs to you. ▶ PHRASE 3 **On your own** means alone.

owner owners
NOUN The owner of something is the person it belongs to.

ownership
NOUN If you have ownership of something, you own it E.G. *He shared the ownership of a sailing dinghy.*

ox oxen
NOUN Oxen are cattle which are used for carrying or pulling things.

oxide oxides
NOUN a compound of oxygen and another chemical element.

oxidize oxidizes oxidizing oxidized; also spelt **oxidise**
VERB When a substance oxidizes, it changes chemically by reacting with oxygen.
oxidation NOUN

oxygen

NOUN (SCIENCE) a colourless gas in the air. It makes up about 21% of the Earth's atmosphere. All animals and plants need oxygen to live, and things cannot burn without it.

oxymoron oxymora or oxymorons

NOUN two words that contradict each other placed beside each other, for example 'deafening silence'.

oyster oysters

NOUN Oysters are large, flat shellfish. Some oysters can be eaten, and others produce pearls.

🏛 from Greek *ostrakon* meaning 'shell'

oz

an abbreviation for 'ounces'.

ozone

NOUN Ozone is a form of oxygen that is poisonous and has a strong smell. There is a layer of ozone high above the Earth's surface.

ozone layer

NOUN The ozone layer is that part of the Earth's atmosphere that protects living things from the harmful radiation of the sun.

a
b
c
d
e
f
g
h
i
j
k
l
m
n
o
p
q
r
s
t
u
v
w
x
y
z

Pp

p
1 p is an abbreviation for 'pence'. 2 p is also a written abbreviation for 'page'. The plural is pp.

pa pa or pas
NOUN In New Zealand, a Maori village or settlement.

pace paces pacing paced
NOUN 1 The pace of something is the speed at which it moves or happens. 2 a step; also used as a measurement of distance. ▶ VERB 3 If you pace up and down, you continually walk around because you are anxious or impatient.

pacemaker pacemakers
NOUN a small electronic device put into someone's heart to control their heartbeat.

Pacific
Said "pas-**sif**-ik" NOUN The Pacific is the ocean separating North and South America from Asia and Australia.

pacifist pacifists
NOUN someone who is opposed to all violence and war.
pacifism NOUN

pacify pacifies pacifying pacified
VERB If you pacify someone who is angry, you calm them.
■ appease, calm, placate

pack packs packing packed
VERB 1 If you pack, you put things neatly into a suitcase, bag, or box. 2 If people pack into a place, it becomes crowded with them. ▶ NOUN 3 a bag or rucksack carried on your back. 4 a packet or collection of something E.G. *a pack of cigarettes*. 5 A pack of playing cards is a complete set. 6 A pack of dogs or wolves is a group of them.

pack up VERB If you pack up your belongings, you put them in a bag because you are leaving.

package packages
NOUN 1 a small parcel. 2 a set of proposals or offers presented as a whole E.G. *a package of beauty treatments*.
packaged ADJECTIVE

packaging
NOUN Packaging is the container or wrapping in which an item is sold or sent.

packed
ADJECTIVE very full E.G. *The church was packed with people*.

packet packets
NOUN a thin cardboard box or paper container in which something is sold.

pact pacts
NOUN a formal agreement or treaty.

pad pads padding padded
NOUN 1 a thick, soft piece of material. 2 a number of pieces of paper fixed together at one end. 3 The pads of an animal such as a cat or dog are the soft, fleshy parts on the bottom of its paws. 4 a flat surface from which helicopters take off or rockets are launched. ▶ VERB 5 If you pad something, you put a pad inside it or over it to protect it or change its shape. 6 If you pad around, you walk softly.
padding NOUN

paddle paddles paddling paddled
NOUN 1 a short pole with a broad blade at one or both ends, used to

move a small boat or a canoe. ▸ VERB
2 If someone paddles a boat, they
move it using a paddle. **3** If you
paddle, you walk in shallow water.

paddock paddocks
NOUN a small field where horses are
kept.

paddy paddies
NOUN A paddy or paddy field is an
area in which rice is grown.

padlock padlocks padlocking
padlocked
NOUN **1** a lock made up of a metal
case with a U-shaped bar attached
to it, which can be put through a
metal loop and then closed. It is
unlocked by turning a key in the lock
on the case. ▸ VERB **2** If you padlock
something, you lock it with a
padlock.

padre padres
Said "**pah**-dray" NOUN a priest,
especially a chaplain to the armed
forces.
🔲 from Italian or Spanish *padre*
meaning 'father'

paediatrician paediatricians
Said "pee-dee-ya-**trish**-n"; also spelt
pediatrician
NOUN a doctor who specializes in
treating children.
🔲 from Greek *pais* meaning 'child'
and *iatros* meaning 'physician'

paediatrics
Said "pee-dee-ya-**triks**"; also spelt
pediatrics
NOUN Paediatrics is the area of
medicine which deals with children's
diseases.
paediatric ADJECTIVE

pagan pagans
Said "**pay**-gan" ADJECTIVE **1** involving
beliefs and worship outside the main

religions of the world E.G. *pagan
myths and cults*. ▸ NOUN **2** someone
who believes in a pagan religion.
paganism NOUN

page pages paging paged
NOUN **1** one side of one of the pieces
of paper in a book or magazine; also
the sheet of paper itself. **2** In
medieval times, a page was a young
boy servant who was learning to be
a knight. ▸ VERB **3** To page someone is
to send a signal or message to a
small electronic device which they
are carrying.

pageant pageants
Said "**paj**-jent" NOUN a grand, colourful
show or parade.

pagoda pagodas
NOUN a tall, elaborately decorated
Buddhist or Hindu temple.

pail pails
NOUN a bucket.

pain pains paining pained
NOUN **1** Pain is an unpleasant feeling
of physical hurt or deep
unhappiness. ▸ VERB **2** If something
pains you, it makes you very
unhappy.
painless ADJECTIVE **painlessly**
ADVERB
🔳 (sense 1) ache, hurt, pang, twinge

painful
ADJECTIVE causing emotional or
physical pain.
painfully ADVERB

painkiller painkillers
NOUN a drug that reduces or stops
pain.

painstaking
ADJECTIVE very careful and thorough
E.G. *years of painstaking research*.

paint paints painting painted
NOUN **1** Paint is a coloured liquid used

a
b
c
d
e
f
g
h
i
j
k
l
m
n
o
p
q
r
s
t
u
v
w
x
y
z

A B C D E F G H I J K L M N O P Q R S T U V W X Y Z

to decorate buildings, or to make a picture. ► VERB **2** If you paint something or paint a picture of it, you make a picture of it using paint. **3** When you paint something such as a wall, you cover it with paint.
painter NOUN **painting** NOUN

pair pairs pairing paired
NOUN **1** two things of the same type or that do the same thing E.G. *a pair of earrings*. **2** You use 'pair' when referring to certain objects which have two main matching parts E.G. *a pair of scissors*. ► VERB **3** When people pair off, they become grouped in pairs. **4** If you pair up with someone, you agree to do something together
☑ The verb following *pair* can be singular or plural. If *pair* refers to a unit, the verb is singular: *a pair of good shoes is essential*. If *pair* refers to two individual things, the verb is plural: *the pair are said to dislike each other*.

pakeha pakeha or **pakehas**
Said "**pa**-ki-ha" NOUN In New Zealand English, someone who is of European rather than Maori descent.

Pakistani Pakistanis
Said "pah-kiss-**tah**-nee" ADJECTIVE **1** belonging or relating to Pakistan. ► NOUN **2** someone who comes from Pakistan.

pal pals
NOUN; INFORMAL a friend.

palace palaces
NOUN a large, grand house, especially the official home of a king or queen.

palagi palagi or **palagis**
Said "pa-**lang**-ee" NOUN a Samoan name for a New Zealander of European descent.

palatable
ADJECTIVE Palatable food tastes pleasant.

palate palates
Said "**pall**-lat" NOUN **1** the top of the inside of your mouth. **2** Someone's palate is their ability to judge good food and wine E.G. *dishes to tempt every palate*.

pale paler palest
ADJECTIVE rather white and without much colour or brightness.

Palestinian Palestinians
NOUN an Arab from the region formerly called Palestine situated between the River Jordan and the Mediterranean.

palette palettes
NOUN (ART) a flat piece of wood on which an artist mixes colours.

pall palls palling palled
Rhymes with "fall" VERB **1** If something palls, it becomes less interesting or less enjoyable E.G. *This record palls after ten minutes*. ► NOUN **2** a thick cloud of smoke. **3** a cloth covering a coffin.

palm palms
NOUN **1** A palm or palm tree is a tropical tree with no branches and a crown of long leaves. **2** the flat surface of your hand which your fingers bend towards.

Palm Sunday
NOUN Palm Sunday is the Sunday before Easter.

palpable
ADJECTIVE obvious and easily sensed E.G. *Happiness was palpable in the air*.
palpably ADVERB
▥ from Latin *palpabilis* meaning 'able to be touched'

paltry
Said "**pawl**-tree" ADJECTIVE A paltry sum
of money is a very small amount.
■ insignificant, trifling, trivial

pamper pampers pampering pampered
VERB If you pamper someone, you give
them too much kindness and comfort.

pamphlet pamphlets
NOUN (ENGLISH) a very thin book in
paper covers giving information
about something.

pan pans panning panned
NOUN 1 a round metal container with
a long handle, used for cooking
things in on top of a cooker. ▶ VERB
2 When a film camera pans, it moves
in a wide sweep. 3 INFORMAL To pan
something is to criticize it strongly.

panacea panaceas
Said "pan-nass-**see**-ah" NOUN
something that is supposed to cure
everything.

panache
Said "pan-**nash**" NOUN Something that
is done with panache is done
confidently and stylishly.

pancake pancakes
NOUN a thin, flat piece of fried batter
which can be served with savoury or
sweet fillings.

pancreas pancreases
Said "**pang**-kree-ass" NOUN an organ
in the body situated behind the
stomach. It helps the body to digest
food.

panda pandas
NOUN A panda or giant panda is a
large animal rather like a bear that
lives in China. It has black fur with
large patches of white.

panda car panda cars
NOUN In Britain, a police patrol car.

pandemonium
Said "pan-dim-**moan**-ee-um" NOUN
Pandemonium is a state of noisy
confusion E.G. *scenes of
pandemonium*.
▥ from *Pandemonium*, the capital of
Hell in Milton's 'Paradise Lost'

pander panders pandering pandered
VERB If you pander to someone, you
do everything they want.

pane panes
NOUN a sheet of glass in a window or
door.

panel panels
NOUN 1 a small group of people who
are chosen to do something E.G. *a
panel of judges*. 2 a flat piece of wood
that is part of a larger object E.G.
door panels. 3 A control panel is a
surface containing switches and
instruments to operate a machine.
panelled ADJECTIVE

panelling
NOUN Panelling is rectangular pieces
of wood covering an inside wall.

pang pangs
NOUN a sudden strong feeling of
sadness or pain.

panic panics panicking panicked
NOUN 1 Panic is a sudden
overwhelming feeling of fear or
anxiety. ▶ VERB 2 If you panic, you
become so afraid or anxious that you
cannot act sensibly.

panorama panoramas
NOUN an extensive view over a wide
area of land E.G. *a fine panorama
over the hills*.
panoramic ADJECTIVE

pansy pansies
NOUN a small garden flower with large
round petals.

a
b
c
d
e
f
g
h
i
j
k
l
m
n
o
p
q
r
s
t
u
v
w
x
y
z

Elaine and Emily shout EE when they mEEt to grEEt each other (-ee-)   SPELLING NOTE

A

pant pants panting panted
VERB If you pant, you breathe quickly
and loudly through your mouth.

B

C

panther panthers
NOUN a large wild animal belonging
to the cat family, especially the black
leopard.

D

E

pantomime pantomimes
NOUN a musical play, usually based on
a fairy story and performed at
Christmas.

F

G

pantry pantries
NOUN a small room where food is kept.
📖 from Old French *paneterie*
meaning 'bread store'

H

I

J

pants
PLURAL NOUN 1 Pants are a piece of
underwear with holes for your legs
and elastic around the waist or hips.
2 Pants are also trousers.

K

L

papaya papayas
NOUN a fruit with sweet yellow flesh
that grows in the West Indies and
tropical Australia.

M

N

paper papers papering papered
NOUN 1 Paper is a material made from
wood pulp and used for writing on
or wrapping things. 2 a newspaper.
► PLURAL NOUN 3 Papers are official
documents, for example a passport
for identification. ► NOUN 4 part of a
written examination. ► VERB 5 If you
paper a wall, you put wallpaper on it.
📖 from *papyrus,* the plant from
which paper was made in ancient
Egypt, Greece, and Rome

O

P

Q

R

S

T

U

paperback paperbacks
NOUN a book with a thin cardboard
cover.

V

W

paperwork
NOUN Paperwork is the part of a job
that involves dealing with letters and
records.

X

Y

Z

papier-mâché
Said "pap-yay **mash**-shay" NOUN
Papier-mâché is a hard substance
made from mashed wet paper mixed
with glue and moulded when moist
to make things such as bowls and
ornaments.
📖 from French *papier-mâché*
meaning literally 'chewed paper'

paprika
NOUN Paprika is a red powder made
from a kind of pepper.
📖 a Hungarian word

par
PHRASE 1 Something that is **on a par**
with something else is similar in
quality or amount E.G. *This match
was on a par with the German Cup
Final.* 2 Something that is **below par**
or **under par** is below its normal
standard. ► NOUN 3 In golf, par is the
number of strokes which it is
thought a good player should take
for a hole or all the holes on a
particular golf course.

parable parables
NOUN ⟨RE⟩ a short story which
makes a moral or religious point.

parachute parachutes
Said "**par**-rash-oot" NOUN a circular
piece of fabric attached by lines to a
person or package so that they can
fall safely to the ground from an
aircraft.

parade parades parading
paraded
NOUN 1 a line of people or vehicles
standing or moving together as a
display. ► VERB 2 When people parade,
they walk together in a group as a
display.

Paradise
NOUN According to some religions,

Paradise is a wonderful place where good people go when they die.
🔲 from Greek *paradeisos* meaning 'garden'

paradox paradoxes
NOUN something that contains two ideas that seem to contradict each other E.G. *the paradox of having to drink in order to stay sober.*
paradoxical ADJECTIVE

paraffin
NOUN Paraffin is a strong-smelling liquid which is used as a fuel.

paragon paragons
NOUN someone whose behaviour is perfect in some way E.G. *a paragon of elegance.*

paragraph paragraphs
NOUN (ENGLISH) a section of a piece of writing. Paragraphs begin on a new line.

parallel parallels
NOUN 1 Something that is a parallel to something else has similar qualities or features to it. ▶ ADJECTIVE 2 (MATHS) If two lines are parallel, they are the same distance apart along the whole of their length.

parallelogram parallelograms
NOUN (MATHS) a four-sided shape in which each side is parallel to the opposite side.

paralyse paralyses paralysing paralysed
VERB If something paralyses you, it causes loss of feeling and movement in your body.
🟩 freeze, immobilize, numb

paralysis
Said "par-**ral**-liss-iss" NOUN Paralysis is loss of the power to move.

paramedic paramedics
Said "par-ram-**med**-dik" NOUN a person

who does some types of medical work, for example for the ambulance service.

parameter parameters
Said "par-**ram**-met-ter" NOUN a limit which affects the way something is done E.G. *the general parameters set by the president.*

paramilitary
ADJECTIVE A paramilitary organization has a military structure but is not the official army of a country.

paramount
ADJECTIVE more important than anything else E.G. *Safety is paramount.*

paranoia
Said "par-ran-**noy**-ah" NOUN Paranoia is a mental illness in which someone believes that other people are trying to harm them.

paranoid
Said "**par**-ran-noyd" ADJECTIVE Someone who is paranoid believes wrongly that other people are trying to harm them.

parapet parapets
NOUN a low wall along the edge of a bridge or roof.
🔲 from Italian *parapetto* meaning 'chest-high wall'

paraphernalia
Said "par-raf-fan-**ale**-yah" NOUN Someone's paraphernalia is all their belongings or equipment.
🔲 from Latin *parapherna* meaning 'personal property of a married woman'

paraphrase paraphrases paraphrasing paraphrased
NOUN 1 A paraphrase of a piece of writing or speech is the same thing said in a different way E.G. *a*

King IAn went to ParlIAment in a carrIAge for his marrIAge (-ia-) ◀ **SPELLING NOTE**

A B C D E F G H I J K L M N O **P** Q R S T U V W X Y Z

paraphrase of the popular song. ▶ VERB **2** If you paraphrase what someone has said, you express it in a different way.

parasite parasites
NOUN a small animal or plant that lives on or inside a larger animal or plant.
parasitic ADJECTIVE
🔲 from Greek *parasitos* meaning 'someone who eats at someone else's table'

parasol parasols
NOUN an object like an umbrella that provides shelter from the sun.

paratroops or **paratroopers**
PLURAL NOUN Paratroops are soldiers trained to be dropped by parachute.

parcel parcels parcelling parcelled
NOUN **1** something wrapped up in paper. ▶ VERB **2** If you parcel something up, you make it into a parcel.

parched
ADJECTIVE **1** If the ground is parched, it is very dry and in need of water. **2** If you are parched, you are very thirsty.

parchment
NOUN Parchment is thick yellowish paper of very good quality.

pardon pardons pardoning pardoned **1** You say **pardon** or **beg your pardon** to express surprise or apology, or when you have not heard what someone has said.
VERB **2** If you pardon someone, you forgive them for doing something wrong.

pare pares paring pared
VERB When you pare fruit or vegetables, you cut off the skin.

parent parents
NOUN Your parents are your father and mother.
parental ADJECTIVE

parentage
NOUN A person's parentage is their parents and ancestors.

parish parishes
NOUN an area with its own church and clergyman, and often its own elected council.

parishioner parishioners
NOUN A clergyman's parishioners are the people who live in his parish and attend his church.

parity
NOUN; FORMAL If there is parity between things, they are equal E.G. *By 1943 the USA had achieved a rough parity of power with the British.*

park parks parking parked
NOUN **1** a public area with grass and trees. **2** a private area of grass and trees around a large country house. ▶ VERB **3** When someone parks a vehicle, they drive it into a position where it can be left.
parked ADJECTIVE **parking** NOUN

parliament parliaments
NOUN (HISTORY) the group of elected representatives who make the laws of a country.
parliamentary ADJECTIVE

parlour parlours
NOUN; OLD-FASHIONED a sitting room.
🔲 from Old French *parleur* meaning 'room for talking to visitors (in a convent)'

parochial
Said "par-**roe**-key-yal" ADJECTIVE concerned only with local matters E.G. *narrow parochial interests.*

parody parodies parodying parodied

NOUN **1** an amusing imitation of the style of an author or of a familiar situation. ▶ VERB **2** If you parody something, you make a parody of it.

■ (sense 1) send-up, spoof, takeoff

parole

NOUN When prisoners are given parole, they are released early on condition that they behave well.

📖 from French *parole d'honneur* meaning 'word of honour'

parrot parrots

NOUN a brightly coloured tropical bird with a curved beak.

parry parries parrying parried

VERB **1** If you parry a question, you cleverly avoid answering it E.G. *My searching questions are simply parried with evasions.* **2** If you parry a blow, you push aside your attacker's arm to defend yourself.

parsley

NOUN Parsley is a herb with curly leaves used for flavouring in cooking.

parsnip parsnips

NOUN a long, pointed, cream-coloured root vegetable.

parson parsons

NOUN a vicar or other clergyman.

part parts parting parted

NOUN **1** one of the pieces or aspects of something. **2** one of the roles in a play or film, played by an actor or actress. **3** Someone's part in something is their involvement in it E.G. *He was jailed for eleven years for his part in the plot.* ▶ PHRASE **4** If you **take part** in an activity, you do it together with other people. ▶ VERB **5** If things that are next to each other part, they move away from each

other. **6** If two people part, they leave each other.

■ (sense 1) bit, component, constituent, piece

partake partakes partaking partook partaken

VERB; FORMAL If you partake of food, you eat it E.G. *She partook of the refreshments offered.*

partial

ADJECTIVE **1** not complete or whole E.G. *a partial explanation… partial success.* **2** liking something very much E.G. *I'm very partial to marigolds.* **3** supporting one side in a dispute, rather than being fair and without bias.

partially ADVERB

participate participates participating participated

VERB If you participate in an activity, you take part in it.

participant NOUN **participation** NOUN

■ be involved in, join in, take part

participle participles

NOUN In grammar, a participle is a form of a verb used with an auxiliary verb in compound tenses and often as an adjective. English has two participles: the past participle, which describes a completed action, and the present participle, which describes a continuing action. For example in 'He has gone', 'gone' is a past participle and in 'She was winning', 'winning' is a present participle.

particle particles

NOUN **1** (SCIENCE) a basic unit of matter, such as an atom, molecule or electron. **2** a very small piece of something.

a b c d e f g h i j k l m n o p q r s t u v w x y z

A B C D E F G H I J K L M N O P Q R S T U V W X Y Z

particular particulars

ADJECTIVE **1** relating or belonging to only one thing or person E.G. *That particular place is dangerous.*
2 especially great or intense E.G. *Pay particular attention to the forehead.*
3 Someone who is particular has high standards and is not easily satisfied. ▶ PLURAL NOUN **4** Particulars are facts or details.

particularly ADVERB

parting partings

NOUN an occasion when one person leaves another.

partisan partisans

ADJECTIVE **1** favouring or supporting one person or group E.G. *a partisan crowd.* ▶ NOUN **2** a member of an unofficial armed force fighting to free their country from enemy occupation E.G. *Norwegian partisans.*

partition partitions partitioning partitioned

NOUN **1** a screen separating one part of a room or vehicle from another.
2 Partition is the division of a country into independent areas. ▶ VERB **3** To partition something is to divide it into separate parts.

partly

ADVERB to some extent but not completely.

partner partners partnering partnered

NOUN **1** Someone's partner is the person they are married to or are living with. **2** Your partner is the person you are doing something with, for example in a dance or a game. **3** Business partners are joint owners of their business. ▶ VERB **4** If you partner someone, you are their

partner for a game or social occasion.

partnership NOUN

part of speech parts of speech

NOUN a particular grammatical class of word, such as 'noun' or 'adjective'.

What is a Part of Speech?

Every word in the dictionary can be classified into a group. These groups are known as **parts of speech**. If we know which group a word belongs to, we can understand what sort of idea the word represents, and how it can be combined with other words to produce meaningful statements. You can check the part of speech of any word by looking it up in the dictionary. The part of speech is given after the main entry word. The most common parts of speech in this dictionary are noun, verb, adjective, adverb, pronoun, pre-position, interjection and con-junction. There are grammar boxes for all of these.

---

partook

the past tense of **partake**.

partridge partridges

NOUN a brown game bird with a round body and a short tail.

part-time

ADJECTIVE involving work for only a part of the working day or week.

party parties

NOUN **1** a social event held for people to enjoy themselves. **2** an organization whose members share the same political beliefs and campaign for election to government. **3** a group who are doing something together. **4** FORMAL one of the people involved in a legal agreement or dispute.

pass passes passing passed

VERB **1** To pass something is to move past it. **2** To pass in a particular direction is to move in that direction E.G. *We passed through the gate.* **3** If you pass something to someone, you hand it to them or transfer it to them. **4** If you pass a period of time doing something, you spend it that way E.G. *He hoped to pass the long night in meditation.* **5** When a period of time passes, it happens and finishes. **6** If you pass a test, you are considered to be of an acceptable standard. **7** When a new law or proposal is passed, it is formally approved. **8** When a judge passes sentence on someone, the judge states what the punishment will be. **9** If you pass the ball in a ball game, you throw, kick, or hit it to another player in your team. ► NOUN **10** the transfer of the ball in a ball game to another player in the same team. **11** an official document that allows you to go somewhere. **12** a narrow route between mountains.

■ (sense 1) go past, overtake

■ (sense 5) elapse, go by, lapse

pass away or **pass on**

VERB Someone who has passed away has died.

pass out VERB If someone passes out, they faint.

passable

ADJECTIVE of an acceptable standard E.G. *a passable imitation of his dad.*

passage passages

NOUN **1** a long, narrow corridor or space that connects two places. **2** a section of a book or piece of music.

passé

Said "pas-say" ADJECTIVE no longer fashionable.

passenger passengers

NOUN a person travelling in a vehicle, aircraft, or ship.

passer-by passers-by

NOUN someone who is walking past someone or something.

passing

ADJECTIVE lasting only for a short time E.G. *a passing phase.*

■ brief, fleeting, momentary

passion passions

NOUN Passion is a very strong feeling, especially of sexual attraction.

■ emotion, fervour, intensity

passionate

ADJECTIVE expressing very strong feelings about something.

passionately ADVERB

■ emotional, fervent, intense

passive

ADJECTIVE **1** remaining calm and showing no feeling when provoked. ► NOUN **2** In grammar, the passive or passive voice is the form of the verb in which the person or thing to which an action is being done is the grammatical subject of the sentence, and is given more emphasis as a result. For example, the passive of *The committee rejected your application* is *Your application was rejected by the committee.*

passively ADVERB **passivity** NOUN

■ (sense 1) inactive, submissive

The Passive Voice

The **passive** voice and the **active** voice are two different ways of presenting information in a sentence. The **passive** always uses a form of the auxiliary verb *to be* with the past participle of the verb.

CONTINUED ON NEXT PAGE →

a b c d e f g h i j k l m n o p q r s t u v w x y z

Beautiful Elephants Are Usually Tiny (beautiful)   SPELLING NOTE

A
B
C
D
E
F
G
H
I
J
K
L
M
N
O
P
Q
R
S
T
U
V
W
X
Y
Z

When a sentence is in the passive voice, the subject of the verb is affected by the action, rather than doing it:

E.G. *The cat **is being fed** by Anna.*
*The mouse **was chased** by a cat.*

It usually sounds more natural to use the active rather than the passive. However, it is sometimes better to use the passive if you want to avoid giving blame or if the name of the subject is not known:

E.G. *The book has been mislaid.*
We are being followed.

Also look at the grammar box at **active**.

Passover
NOUN The Passover is an eight day Jewish festival held in spring.

passport passports
NOUN an official identification document which you need to show when you travel abroad.

password passwords
NOUN 1 a secret word known to only a few people. It allows people on the same side to recognize a friend.
2 (ICT) a word you need to know to get into some computers or computer files.

past
NOUN 1 The past is the period of time before the present. ▶ ADJECTIVE 2 Past things are things that happened or existed before the present E.G. *the past 30 years.* ▶ PREPOSITION OR ADVERB
3 You use 'past' when you are telling the time E.G. *It was ten past eleven.*
4 If you go past something, you

move towards it and continue until you are on the other side E.G. *They drove rapidly past their cottage.*
▶ PREPOSITION 5 Something that is past a place is situated on the other side of it E.G. *It's just past the church there.*

Talking about the Past

You can talk about events that have already happened by using **simple past tenses** or **compound tenses**.

The **simple past tense** is formed without any auxiliary verbs. It is usually formed by taking the dictionary form of the verb and adding the ending -*ed*. (If the verb already ends in -*e*, then you only need to add -*d*.)

E.G. *I **cooked** the dinner.*
*She **liked** fish.*

You can also use **compound tenses** to talk about actions that have happened.

One compound past tense is formed by using *was* or *were* in front of the main verb, and adding the ending -*ing*. This shows that an action happening in the past was continuous:

E.G. *I **was cooking** the dinner.*
*We **were dining**.*

Notice that if the verb ends in *e*, the *e* is dropped.

Another compound past tense is formed by using a form of the verb *to have* in front of the main verb, and adding the ending -*ed*. This shows that an action has been completed:

E.G. *I **have cooked** the dinner.*
*We **have dined**.*

CONTINUED ON NEXT PAGE →

SPELLING NOTE   Betty Eats Cakes And Uses Seven Eggs (<u>because</u>)

Notice that if the verb already ends in e you don't need to add one. Another compound past tense is formed by using *had* in front of the main verb, and adding the ending -*ed*. This form shows that an action in the past had been completed before something else took place:

E.G. *I **had cooked** the dinner.
We **had dined**.*

Another compound past tense is formed by using *did* in front of the basic form of the verb. This can add emphasis:

E.G. *We **did enjoy** that!*

pasta
NOUN Pasta is a dried mixture of flour, eggs, and water, formed into different shapes.

paste pastes pasting pasted
NOUN 1 Paste is a soft, rather sticky mixture that can be easily spread E.G. *tomato paste.* ▶ VERB 2 If you paste something onto a surface, you stick it with glue.

pastel
ADJECTIVE Pastel colours are pale and soft. (ART)

pasteurized
Said "past-yoor-ized"; also spelt **pasteurised**
ADJECTIVE Pasteurized milk has been treated with a special heating process to kill bacteria.

pastime pastimes
NOUN a hobby or something you do just for pleasure.
■ activity, hobby, recreation

pastor pastors
NOUN a clergyman in charge of a congregation.

pastoral
ADJECTIVE 1 characteristic of peaceful country life and landscape E.G. *pastoral scenes.* 2 relating to the duties of the clergy in caring for the needs of their parishioners E.G. *a pastoral visit.*

past participle past participles
NOUN In grammar, the past participle of a verb is the form, usually ending in 'ed' or 'en', that is used to make some past tenses and the passive. For example 'killed' in 'She has killed the goldfish' and 'broken' in 'My leg was broken' are past participles.

pastry pastries
NOUN 1 Pastry is a mixture of flour, fat, and water, rolled flat and used for making pies. 2 a small cake.

past tense
NOUN In grammar, the past tense is the tense of a verb that you use mainly to refer to things that happened or existed before the time of writing or speaking.

pasture pastures
NOUN Pasture is an area of grass on which farm animals graze.

pasty pasties
ADJECTIVE 1
Rhymes with "hasty" Someone who is pasty looks pale and unhealthy.
▶ NOUN 2
Said "pass-tee" a small pie containing meat and vegetables.

pat pats patting patted
VERB 1 If you pat something, you tap it lightly with your hand held flat.
▶ NOUN 2 a small lump of butter.

patch patches patching patched
NOUN 1 a piece of material used to cover a hole in something. 2 an area of a surface that is different in

a
b
c
d
e
f
g
h
i
j
k
l
m
n
o
p
q
r
s
t
u
v
w
x
y
z

there's a rAKE in the brAKEs (br**a**ke) ◀ **SPELLING NOTE**

appearance from the rest E.G. *a bald patch.* ▸ VERB 3 If you patch something, you mend it by fixing a patch over the hole.

patch up VERB If you patch something up, you mend it hurriedly or temporarily.

patchwork
ADJECTIVE 1 A patchwork quilt is made from many small pieces of material sewn together. ▸ NOUN 2 Something that is a patchwork is made up of many parts.

patchy patchier patchiest
ADJECTIVE Something that is patchy is unevenly spread or incomplete in parts E.G. *patchy fog on the hills.*

pâté
Said "pa-tay" NOUN Pâté is a mixture of meat, fish, or vegetables blended into a paste and spread on bread or toast.

patent patents patenting patented
NOUN 1 an official right given to an inventor to be the only person or company allowed to make or sell a new product. ▸ VERB 2 If you patent something, you obtain a patent for it. ▸ ADJECTIVE 3 obvious E.G. *This was patent nonsense.*
patently ADVERB

paternal
ADJECTIVE relating to a father E.G. *paternal pride.*

paternity
NOUN Paternity is the state or fact of being a father.

path paths
NOUN 1 a strip of ground for people to walk on. 2 Your path is the area ahead of you and the direction in which you are moving.

pathetic
ADJECTIVE 1 If something is pathetic, it makes you feel pity. 2 Pathetic also means very poor or unsuccessful E.G. *a pathetic attempt.*
pathetically ADVERB
■ (sense 1) heart-rending, moving, sad

pathological
ADJECTIVE extreme and uncontrollable E.G. *a pathological fear of snakes.*
pathologically ADVERB

pathology
NOUN Pathology is the study of diseases and the way they develop.
pathologist NOUN

pathos
Said "pay-thoss" NOUN Pathos is a quality in literature or art that causes great sadness or pity.

pathway pathways
NOUN a path.

patience
NOUN Patience is the ability to stay calm in a difficult or irritating situation.
■ forbearance, tolerance

patient patients
ADJECTIVE 1 If you are patient, you stay calm in a difficult or irritating situation. ▸ NOUN 2 a person receiving medical treatment from a doctor or in a hospital.
patiently ADVERB

patio patios
NOUN a paved area close to a house.

patriarch patriarchs
Said "pay-tree-ark" NOUN the male head of a family or tribe.
patriarchal ADJECTIVE

patrician
ADJECTIVE; FORMAL belonging to a family of high rank.

patriot patriots

NOUN someone who loves their country and feels very loyal towards it.

patriotic ADJECTIVE   **patriotism** NOUN

patrol patrols patrolling patrolled

VERB 1 When soldiers, police, or guards patrol an area, they walk or drive around to make sure there is no trouble. ► NOUN 2 a group of people patrolling an area.

🔲 from French *patouiller* meaning 'to flounder in mud'

patron patrons

NOUN 1 a person who supports or gives money to artists, writers, or musicians. 2 The patrons of a hotel, pub, or shop are the people who use it.

patronage NOUN

patronize patronizes patronizing patronized; also spelt **patronise**

VERB 1 If someone patronizes you, they treat you kindly, but in a way that suggests that you are less intelligent than them or inferior to them. 2 If you patronize a hotel, pub, or shop, you are a customer there.

patronizing ADJECTIVE

patron saint patron saints

NOUN The patron saint of a group of people or place is a saint who is believed to look after them.

patter patters pattering pattered

VERB 1 If something patters on a surface, it makes quick, light, tapping sounds. ► NOUN 2 a series of light tapping sounds E.G. *a patter of light rain*.

pattern patterns

NOUN 1 a decorative design of repeated shapes. 2 The pattern of something is the way it is usually done or happens E.G. *a perfectly normal pattern of behaviour*. 3 a diagram or shape used as a guide for making something, for example clothes.

patterned ADJECTIVE

paunch paunches

NOUN If a man has a paunch, he has a fat stomach.

pauper paupers

NOUN; OLD-FASHIONED a very poor person.

pause pauses pausing paused

VERB 1 If you pause, you stop what you are doing for a short time. ► NOUN 2 a short period when you stop what you are doing. 3 a short period of silence.

pave paves paving paved

VERB When an area of ground is paved, it is covered with flat blocks of stone or concrete.

pavement pavements

NOUN a path with a hard surface at the side of a road.

pavilion pavilions

NOUN a building at a sports ground where players can wash and change.

paw paws pawing pawed

NOUN 1 The paws of an animal such as a cat or bear are its feet with claws and soft pads. ► VERB 2 If an animal paws something, it hits it or scrapes at it with its paws.

pawn pawns pawning pawned

VERB 1 If you pawn something, you leave it with a pawnbroker in exchange for money. ► NOUN 2 the smallest and least valuable playing piece in chess.

a
b
c
d
e
f
g
h
i
j
k
l
m
n
o
p
q
r
s
t
u
v
w
x
y
z

I always visit my FRIend on a FRIday (<u>fri</u>end)   SPELLING NOTE

A
B
C
D
E
F
G
H
I
J
K
L
M
N
O
P
Q
R
S
T
U
V
W
X
Y
Z

pawnbroker pawnbrokers
NOUN a dealer who lends money in return for personal property left with him or her, which may be sold if the loan is not repaid on time.

pawpaw pawpaws
NOUN the same as a **papaya**.

pay pays paying paid
VERB 1 When you pay money to someone, you give it to them because you are buying something or owe it to them. 2 If it pays to do something, it is to your advantage to do it E.G. *They say it pays to advertise.* 3 If you pay for something that you have done, you suffer as a result. 4 If you pay attention to something, you give it your attention. 5 If you pay a visit to someone, you visit them.
▶ NOUN 6 Someone's pay is their salary or wages.
■ (sense 1) give, reimburse, settle

payable
ADJECTIVE 1 An amount of money that is payable has to be paid or can be paid E.G. *All fees are payable in advance.* 2 If a cheque is made payable to you, you are the person who should receive the money.

payment payments
NOUN 1 Payment is the act of paying money. 2 a sum of money paid.

payroll payrolls
NOUN Someone who is on an organization's payroll is employed and paid by them.

PC PCs
NOUN 1 In Britain, a police constable. 2 a personal computer.

PE
NOUN PE is a lesson in which gymnastics or sports are taught. PE is

an abbreviation for 'physical education'.

pea peas
NOUN Peas are small round green seeds that grow in pods and are eaten as a vegetable.

peace
NOUN 1 Peace is a state of calm and quiet when there is no disturbance of any kind. 2 When a country is at peace, it is not at war.
peaceable ADJECTIVE
■ (sense 1) stillness, tranquillity

peaceful
ADJECTIVE quiet and calm.
peacefully ADVERB
■ serene, tranquil

peach peaches
NOUN 1 a soft, round fruit with yellow flesh and a yellow and red skin.
▶ ADJECTIVE 2 pale pink with a hint of orange.

peacock peacocks
NOUN a large bird with green and blue feathers. The male has a long tail which it can spread out in a fan.

peak peaks peaking peaked
NOUN 1 The peak of an activity or process is the point at which it is strongest or most successful. 2 the pointed top of a mountain. ▶ VERB 3 When something peaks, it reaches its highest value or its greatest level of success.
peaked ADJECTIVE
■ (sense 1) climax, culmination, high point

peal peals pealing pealed
NOUN 1 A peal of bells is the musical sound made by bells ringing one after another. ▶ VERB 2 When bells peal, they ring one after the other.

peanut peanuts
NOUN Peanuts are small oval nuts that grow under the ground.

pear pears
NOUN a fruit which is narrow at the top and wide and rounded at the bottom.

pearl pearls
NOUN a hard, round, creamy-white object used in jewellery. Pearls grow inside the shell of an oyster.

peasant peasants
NOUN a person who works on the land, especially in a poor country.

peat
NOUN Peat is dark-brown decaying plant material found in cool, wet regions. Dried peat can be used as fuel.

pebble pebbles
NOUN a smooth, round stone.

peck pecks pecking pecked
VERB 1 If a bird pecks something, it bites at it quickly with its beak. 2 If you peck someone on the cheek, you give them a quick kiss. ▶ NOUN 3 a quick bite by a bird. 4 a quick kiss on the cheek.

peculiar
ADJECTIVE 1 strange and perhaps unpleasant. 2 relating or belonging only to a particular person or thing E.G. *a gesture peculiar to her.*
peculiarly ADVERB **peculiarity** NOUN

pedal pedals pedalling pedalled
NOUN 1 a control lever on a machine or vehicle that you press with your foot. ▶ VERB 2 When you pedal a bicycle, you push the pedals round with your feet to move along.

pedantic
ADJECTIVE If a person is pedantic, they are too concerned with unimportant details and traditional rules.

peddle peddles peddling peddled
VERB Someone who peddles something sells it.

pedestal pedestals
NOUN a base on which a statue stands.

pedestrian pedestrians
NOUN 1 someone who is walking. ▶ ADJECTIVE 2 Pedestrian means ordinary and rather dull E.G. *a pedestrian performance.*

pedestrian crossing pedestrian crossings
NOUN a specially marked place where you can cross the road safely.

pediatrician
another spelling of **paediatrician**.

pediatrics
another spelling of **paediatrics**.

pedigree pedigrees
ADJECTIVE 1 A pedigree animal is descended from a single breed and its ancestors are known and recorded. ▶ NOUN 2 Someone's pedigree is their background or ancestry.

peek peeks peeking peeked
VERB 1 If you peek at something, you have a quick look at it E.G. *I peeked round the corner.* ▶ NOUN 2 a quick look at something.

peel peels peeling peeled
NOUN 1 The peel of a fruit is the skin when it has been removed. ▶ VERB 2 When you peel fruit or vegetables, you remove the skin. 3 If a surface is peeling, it is coming off in thin layers.
peelings PLURAL NOUN

peep peeps peeping peeped
VERB 1 If you peep at something, you have a quick look at it. 2 If something peeps out from behind something

a
b
c
d
e
f
g
h
i
j
k
l
m
n
o
p
q
r
s
t
u
v
w
x
y
z

A
B
C
D
E
F
G
H
I
J
K
L
M
N
O
P
Q
R
S
T
U
V
W
X
Y
Z

else, a small part of it becomes visible E.G. *a handkerchief peeping out of his breast pocket.* ▶ NOUN 3 a quick look at something.

peer peers peering peered
VERB 1 If you peer at something, you look at it very hard. ▶ NOUN 2 a member of the nobility. 3 Your peers are the people who are of the same age and social status as yourself.

peerage peerages
NOUN 1 The peers in a country are called the peerage. 2 A peerage is also the rank of being a peer.

peer group peer groups
NOUN Your peer group is the people who are of the same age and social status as yourself.

peerless
ADJECTIVE so magnificent or perfect that nothing can equal it E.G. *peerless wines.*

peewee peewees
NOUN a small black-and-white Australian bird with long, thin legs.

peg pegs pegging pegged
NOUN 1 a plastic or wooden clip used for hanging wet clothes on a line. 2 a hook on a wall where you can hang things. ▶ VERB 3 If you peg clothes on a line, you fix them there with pegs. 4 If a price is pegged at a certain level, it is fixed at that level.

peggy square peggy squares
NOUN In New Zealand, a small square of knitted wool which is sewn together with others to make a rug.

pejorative
Said "pej-**jor**-ra-tiv" ADJECTIVE A pejorative word expresses criticism.

pekinese pekineses
Said "pee-kin-**eez**"; also spelt
pekingese

NOUN a small long-haired dog with a flat nose.

pelican pelicans
NOUN a large water bird with a pouch beneath its beak in which it stores fish.

pellet pellets
NOUN a small ball of paper, lead, or other material.

pelt pelts pelting pelted
VERB 1 If you pelt someone with things, you throw the things with force at them. 2 If you pelt along, you run very fast. ▶ NOUN 3 the skin and fur of an animal.

pelvis pelvises
NOUN the wide, curved group of bones at hip-level at the base of your spine.
pelvic ADJECTIVE

pen pens penning penned
NOUN 1 a long, thin instrument used for writing with ink. 2 a small fenced area in which farm animals are kept for a short time. ▶ VERB 3 LITERARY If someone pens a letter or article, they write it. 4 If you are penned in or penned up, you have to remain in an uncomfortably small area.
📖 from Latin *penna* meaning 'feather'; pens used to be made from feathers

penal
ADJECTIVE relating to the punishment of criminals.

penalize penalizes penalizing penalized; also spelt **penalise**
VERB If you are penalized, you are made to suffer some disadvantage as a punishment for something.

penalty penalties
NOUN 1 a punishment or disadvantage that someone is made to suffer. 2 In soccer, a penalty is a free kick at goal

that is given to the attacking team if the defending team have committed a foul near their goal.

penance

NOUN If you do penance, you do something unpleasant to show that you are sorry for something wrong that you have done.

pence

a plural form of **penny**.

penchant

Said "pon-shon" NOUN; FORMAL If you have a penchant for something, you have a particular liking for it E.G. *a penchant for crime*.

pencil pencils

NOUN a long thin stick of wood with graphite in the centre, used for drawing or writing.

pendant pendants

NOUN a piece of jewellery attached to a chain and worn round the neck.

pending FORMAL

ADJECTIVE 1 Something that is pending is waiting to be dealt with or will happen soon. ▶ PREPOSITION
2 Something that is done pending a future event is done until the event happens E.G. *The army should stay in the west pending a future war.*

pendulum pendulums

NOUN a rod with a weight at one end in a clock which swings regularly from side to side to control the clock.

penetrate penetrates penetrating penetrated

VERB To penetrate an area that is difficult to get into is to succeed in getting into it.

penetration NOUN

penetrating

ADJECTIVE 1 loud and high-pitched E.G. *a penetrating voice.* 2 having or

showing deep understanding E.G. *penetrating questions.*

pen friend pen friends

NOUN someone living in a different place or country whom you write to regularly, although you may never have met each other.

penguin penguins

NOUN a black and white bird with webbed feet and small wings like flippers.

penicillin

NOUN Penicillin is a powerful antibiotic obtained from fungus and used to treat infections.

peninsula peninsulas

NOUN an area of land almost surrounded by water.

penis penises

NOUN A man's penis is the part of his body that he uses when urinating and having sexual intercourse.

penitent

ADJECTIVE Someone who is penitent is deeply sorry for having done something wrong.

penitence NOUN

penknife penknives

NOUN a small knife with a blade that folds back into the handle.

pennant pennants

NOUN a triangular flag, especially one used by ships as a signal.

penniless

ADJECTIVE Someone who is penniless has no money.

penny pennies or pence

NOUN a unit of currency in Britain and some other countries. In Britain a penny is worth one-hundredth of a pound.

pension pensions

Said "pen-shn" NOUN a regular sum of

Plaice the fish has a glittering 'EYE' (I) (plaice)   **SPELLING NOTE**

money paid to an old or retired person.

pensioner pensioners
NOUN an old retired person who gets a pension paid by the state.

pensive
ADJECTIVE deep in thought.
▤ dreamy, meditative, thoughtful

pentagon pentagons
NOUN a shape with five straight sides.

pentathlon pentathlons
Said "pen-**tath**-lon" NOUN a sports contest in which athletes compete in five different events.

penthouse penthouses
NOUN a luxurious flat at the top of a building.

pent-up
ADJECTIVE Pent-up emotions have been held back for a long time without release.
▤ bottled up, suppressed

penultimate
ADJECTIVE The penultimate thing in a series is the one before the last.

peony peonies
Said "**pee**-yon-ee" NOUN a garden plant with large pink, white, or red flowers.

people peoples peopling peopled
PLURAL NOUN 1 People are men, women, and children. ▶ NOUN 2 all the men, women, and children of a particular country or race. ▶ VERB 3 If an area is peopled by a particular group, that group of people live there.
▤ (sense 1) humanity, mankind, persons
▤ (sense 2) nation, population, race

pepper peppers
NOUN 1 Pepper is a hot-tasting powdered spice used for flavouring in cooking. 2 a hollow green, red, or

yellow vegetable, with sweet-flavoured flesh.

peppermint peppermints
NOUN Peppermint is a plant with a strong taste. It is used for making sweets and in medicine.

per
PREPOSITION 'Per' is used to mean 'each' when expressing rates and ratios E.G. *The class meets two evenings per week.*

perceive perceives perceiving perceived
VERB If you perceive something that is not obvious, you see it or realize it.
▤ notice, see, spot

per cent
PHRASE You use **per cent** to talk about amounts as a proportion of a hundred. An amount that is 10 per cent (10%) of a larger amount is equal to 10 hundredths of the larger amount E.G. *86 per cent of Americans believe Presley is alive.*
▥ from Latin *per* meaning 'each' and *centum* meaning 'hundred'

percentage percentages
NOUN (MATHS) a fraction expressed as a number of hundredths E.G. *the high percentage of failed marriages.*

perceptible
ADJECTIVE Something that is perceptible can be seen E.G. *a barely perceptible nod.*

perception perceptions
NOUN 1 Perception is the recognition of things using the senses, especially the sense of sight. 2 Someone who has perception realizes or notices things that are not obvious. 3 Your perception of something or someone is your understanding of them.

perceptive
ADJECTIVE Someone who is perceptive realizes or notices things that are not obvious.
perceptively ADVERB
■ astute, observant, sharp

perch perches perching perched
VERB 1 If you perch on something, you sit on the edge of it. 2 When a bird perches on something, it stands on it. ▶ NOUN 3 a short rod for a bird to stand on. 4 an edible freshwater fish.

percolator percolators
NOUN a special pot for making and serving coffee.

percussion
NOUN or ADJECTIVE (MUSIC) Percussion instruments are musical instruments that you hit to produce sounds.
percussionist NOUN

perennial
ADJECTIVE continually occurring or never ending E.G. *The damp cellar was a perennial problem.*

perfect perfects perfecting perfected
ADJECTIVE 1 of the highest standard and without fault E.G. *His English was perfect.* 2 complete or absolute E.G. *They have a perfect right to say so.* 3 In English grammar, the perfect tense of a verb is formed with the present tense of 'have' and the past participle of the main verb E.G. *I have lost my home.* ▶ VERB 4 If you perfect something, you make it as good as it can possibly be.
perfectly ADVERB **perfection** NOUN
■ (sense 1) faultless, flawless
■ (sense 4) improve, refine

perfectionist perfectionists
NOUN someone who always tries to do everything perfectly.

perforated
ADJECTIVE Something that is perforated has had small holes made in it.
perforation NOUN

perform performs performing performed
VERB 1 To perform a task or action is to do it. 2 (DRAMA) To perform is to act, dance, or play music in front of an audience.
performer NOUN

performance performances
NOUN 1 (DRAMA) an entertainment provided for an audience. 2 The performance of a task or action is the doing of it. 3 Someone's or something's performance is how successful they are E.G. *the poor performance of the American economy.*

perfume perfumes
NOUN 1 Perfume is a pleasant-smelling liquid which women put on their bodies. 2 The perfume of something is its pleasant smell.
perfumed ADJECTIVE

perfunctory
ADJECTIVE done quickly without interest or care E.G. *a perfunctory kiss.*

perhaps
ADVERB You use 'perhaps' when you are not sure whether something is true or possible.

peril perils
NOUN; FORMAL Peril is great danger.
perilous ADJECTIVE **perilously** ADVERB

perimeter perimeters
NOUN (MATHS) The perimeter of an area or figure is the whole of its outer edge.

period periods
NOUN 1 a particular length of time.

a
b
c
d
e
f
g
h
i
j
k
l
m
n
o
p
q
r
s
t
u
v
w
x
y
z

You must practiSe your Ss (practiSe)   **SPELLING NOTE**

2 one of the parts the day is divided into at school. **3** A woman's period is the monthly bleeding from her womb. ▶ ADJECTIVE **4** relating to a historical period of time E.G. *period furniture*.

periodic ADJECTIVE **periodically** ADVERB

periodical periodicals
NOUN a magazine.

peripheral
Said "per-**rif**-fer-ral" ADJECTIVE **1** of little importance in comparison with other things E.G. *a peripheral activity*. **2** on or relating to the edge of an area.

periphery peripheries
NOUN The periphery of an area is its outside edge.

perish perishes perishing perished
VERB **1** FORMAL If someone or something perishes, they are killed or destroyed. **2** If fruit or fabric perishes, it rots.

perishable ADJECTIVE

perjury
NOUN; A FORMAL or LEGAL WORD If someone commits perjury, they tell a lie in court while under oath.

perjure VERB

perk perks perking perked
NOUN **1** an extra, such as a company car, offered by an employer in addition to a salary. Perk is an abbreviation of 'perquisite'. ▶ VERB **2** INFORMAL When someone perks up, they become more cheerful.

perky ADJECTIVE

perm perms perming permed
NOUN **1** If you have a perm, your hair is curled and treated with chemicals to keep the curls for several months.

▶ VERB **2** To perm someone's hair means to put a perm in it.

permanent
ADJECTIVE lasting for ever, or present all the time.

permanently ADVERB **permanence** NOUN

permeable
Said "**per**-mee-a-bl" ADJECTIVE; FORMAL If something is permeable, liquids are able to pass through it E.G. *permeable rock*.

permeate permeates permeating permeated
VERB To permeate something is to spread through it and affect every part of it E.G. *The feeling of failure permeates everything I do*.

permissible
ADJECTIVE allowed by the rules.
▣ allowable, permitted

permission
NOUN If you have permission to do something, you are allowed to do it.
▣ authorization, go-ahead

permissive
ADJECTIVE A permissive society allows things which some people disapprove of, especially freedom in sexual behaviour.

permissiveness NOUN

permit permits permitting permitted
VERB **1** To permit something is to allow it or make it possible. ▶ NOUN **2** an official document which says that you are allowed to do something.
▣ (sense 1) allow, give permission, let

permutation permutations
NOUN one possible arrangement of a number of things.

pernicious
ADJECTIVE; FORMAL very harmful E.G. *the pernicious influence of television.*

peroxide
NOUN Peroxide is a chemical used for bleaching hair or as an antiseptic.

perpendicular
ADJECTIVE (MATHS) upright, or at right angles to a horizontal line.
📖 from Latin *perpendiculum* meaning 'plumb line'

perpetrate perpetrates perpetrating perpetrated
VERB; FORMAL To perpetrate a crime is to commit it.
perpetrator NOUN

perpetual
ADJECTIVE never ending E.G. *a perpetual toothache.*
perpetually ADVERB **perpetuity** NOUN

perpetuate perpetuates perpetuating perpetuated
VERB To perpetuate a situation or belief is to cause it to continue E.G. *The television series will perpetuate the myths.*

perplexed
ADJECTIVE If you are perplexed, you are puzzled and do not know what to do.

persecute persecutes persecuting persecuted
VERB To persecute someone is to treat them cruelly and unfairly over a long period of time.
persecution NOUN **persecutor** NOUN
🔳 pick on, victimize

persevere perseveres persevering persevered
VERB If you persevere, you keep trying to do something and do not give up.

perseverance NOUN
🔳 carry on, continue, keep going

Persian
Said "per-shn" ADJECTIVE or NOUN an old word for **Iranian**, used especially when referring to the older forms of the language.

persimmon persimmons
NOUN a sweet, red, tropical fruit.

persist persists persisting persisted
VERB 1 If something undesirable persists, it continues to exist. 2 If you persist in doing something, you continue in spite of opposition or difficulty.
persistence NOUN **persistent** ADJECTIVE

person people or persons
NOUN 1 a man, woman, or child. 2 In grammar, the first person is the speaker (I), the second person is the person being spoken to (you), and the third person is anyone else being referred to (he, she, they).
🔳 (sense 1) human being, individual
☑ The usual plural of *person* is *people. Persons* is much less common, and is used only in formal or official English.

personal
ADJECTIVE 1 Personal means belonging or relating to a particular person rather than to people in general E.G. *my personal feeling.* 2 (PE) Personal matters relate to your feelings, relationships, and health which you may not wish to discuss with other people.
personally ADVERB
🔳 (sense 1) individual, own, private

personality personalities
NOUN 1 Your personality is your

a
b
c
d
e
f
g
h
i
j
k
l
m
n
o
p
q
r
s
t
u
v
w
x
y
z

A
B
C
D
E
F
G
H
I
J
K
L
M
N
O
P
Q
R
S
T
U
V
W
X
Y
Z

character and nature. **2** a famous person in entertainment or sport.

personification

NOUN **1** (ENGLISH) Personification is a form of imagery in which something inanimate is described as if it has human qualities E.G. *The trees sighed and whispered as the impatient breeze stirred their branches.* **2** Someone who is the personification of some quality is a living example of that quality E.G. *He was the personification of evil.*

personify personifies personifying personified

VERB Someone who personifies a particular quality seems to be a living example of it. If you personify a thing or concept, you write or speak of it as if it has human abilities or qualities, for example 'The sun is trying to come out'.

personnel

Said "per-son-**nell**" NOUN The personnel of an organization are the people who work for it.

perspective perspectives

NOUN **1** A particular perspective is one way of thinking about something.
2 (ART) Perspective is a method atrists use to make some people and things seem further away than others.

perspiration

NOUN Perspiration is the moisture that appears on your skin when you are hot or frightened.

perspire perspires perspiring perspired

VERB If someone perspires, they sweat.

persuade persuades persuading persuaded

VERB If someone persuades you to do

something or persuades you that something is true, they make you do it or belleve it by giving you very good reasons.

persuasion NOUN **persuasive** ADJECTIVE

■ convince, talk into

pertaining

ADJECTIVE; FORMAL If information or questions are pertaining to a place or thing, they are about that place or thing E.G. *issues pertaining to women.*

pertinent

ADJECTIVE especially relevant to the subject being discussed E.G. *He asks pertinent questions.*

perturbed

ADJECTIVE Someone who is perturbed is worried.

Peruvian Peruvians

Said "per-**roo**-vee-an" ADJECTIVE
1 belonging or relating to Peru.
▶ NOUN **2** someone who comes from Peru.

pervade pervades pervading pervaded

VERB Something that pervades a place is present and noticeable throughout it E.G. *a fear that pervades the community.*

pervasive ADJECTIVE

perverse

ADJECTIVE Someone who is perverse deliberately does things that are unreasonable or harmful.

perversely ADVERB **perversity** NOUN

pervert perverts perverting perverted

VERB **1** FORMAL To pervert something is to interfere with it so that it is no longer what it should be E.G. *a conspiracy to pervert the course of* justice. ► NOUN 2 a person whose sexual behaviour is disgusting or harmful.

perversion NOUN

🔲 from Latin *pervertere* meaning 'to turn the wrong way'

perverted

ADJECTIVE 1 Someone who is perverted has disgusting or unacceptable behaviour or ideas, especially sexual behaviour or ideas. 2 Something that is perverted is completely wrong E.G. *a perverted sense of value.*

peseta pesetas

Said "pes-say-ta" NOUN a unit of currency formerly used in Spain.

peso pesos

Said "pay-soh" NOUN the main unit of currency in several South American countries.

pessimism

NOUN Pessimism is the tendency to believe that bad things will happen.

pessimist NOUN **pessimistic** ADJECTIVE

pest pests

NOUN 1 an insect or small animal which damages plants or food supplies. 2 someone who keeps bothering or annoying you.

pester pesters pestering pestered

VERB If you pester someone, you keep bothering them or asking them to do something.

📰 annoy, badger, hassle

pesticide pesticides

NOUN Pesticides are chemicals sprayed onto plants to kill insects and grubs.

pet pets petting petted

NOUN 1 a tame animal kept at home. ► ADJECTIVE 2 Someone's pet theory or

pet project is something that they particularly support or feel strongly about. ► VERB 3 If you pet a person or animal, you stroke them affectionately.

petal petals

NOUN The petals of a flower are the coloured outer parts.

peter out peters out petering out petered out

VERB If something peters out, it gradually comes to an end.

petite

Said "pet-teet" ADJECTIVE A woman who is petite is small and slim.

petition petitions petitioning petitioned

NOUN 1 a document demanding official action which is signed by a lot of people. 2 an formal request to a court for legal action to be taken. ► VERB 3 If you petition someone in authority, you make a formal request to them E.G. *I petitioned the Chinese government for permission to visit its country.*

petrified

ADJECTIVE If you are petrified, you are very frightened.

petrol

NOUN Petrol is a liquid obtained from petroleum and used as a fuel for motor vehicles.

petroleum

NOUN Petroleum is thick, dark oil found under the earth or under the sea bed.

🔲 from Latin *petra* meaning 'rock' and *oleum* meaning 'oil'

petticoat petticoats

NOUN a piece of women's underwear like a very thin skirt.

petty pettier pettiest

ADJECTIVE 1 Petty things are small and

a b c d e f g h i j k l m n o **p** q r s t u v w x y z

unimportant. **2** Petty behaviour consists of doing small things which are selfish and unkind.

petulant
ADJECTIVE showing unreasonable and childish impatience or anger.
petulantly ADVERB **petulance** NOUN

petunia petunias
Said "pit-**yoon**-nee-ah" NOUN a garden plant with large trumpet-shaped flowers.

pew pews
NOUN a long wooden seat with a back, which people sit on in church.

pewter
NOUN Pewter is a silvery-grey metal made from a mixture of tin and lead.

pH
NOUN The pH of a solution or of the soil is a measurement of how acid or alkaline it is. Acid solutions have a pH of less than 7 and alkaline solutions have a pH greater than 7. pH is an abbreviation for 'potential hydrogen'.

phalanger phalangers
Said "fal-**lan**-jer" NOUN an Australian marsupial with thick fur and a long tail. In Australia and New Zealand, it is also called a possum.

phallus phalluses
NOUN a penis or a symbolic model of a penis.
phallic ADJECTIVE

phantom phantoms
NOUN **1** a ghost. ▶ ADJECTIVE **2** imagined or unreal E.G. a phantom pregnancy.

pharaoh pharaohs
Said "**fair**-oh" NOUN The pharaohs were kings of ancient Egypt.

pharmaceutical
Said "far-mass-**yoo**-tik-kl" ADJECTIVE connected with the industrial production of medicines.

pharmacist pharmacists
NOUN a person who is qualified to prepare and sell medicines.

pharmacy pharmacies
NOUN a shop where medicines are sold.

phase phases phasing phased
NOUN **1** a particular stage in the development of something. ▶ VERB **2** To phase something is to cause it to happen gradually in stages.

PhD PhDs
NOUN a degree awarded to someone who has done advanced research in a subject. PhD is an abbreviation for 'Doctor of Philosophy'.

pheasant pheasants
NOUN a large, long-tailed game bird.

phenomenal
Said "fin-**nom**-in-nal" ADJECTIVE extraordinarily great or good.
phenomenally ADVERB

phenomenon phenomena
NOUN something that happens or exists, especially something remarkable or something being considered in a scientific way E.G. a well-known geographical phenomenon.
☑ The word phenomenon is singular. The plural form is phenomena.

philanthropist philanthropists
Said "fil-**lan**-throp-pist" NOUN someone who freely gives help or money to people in need.
philanthropic ADJECTIVE
philanthropy NOUN

philistine philistines
NOUN If you call someone a philistine, you mean that they do not like art, literature, or music.

philosophical or **philosophic**
ADJECTIVE Someone who is philosophical does not get upset when disappointing things happen.

philosophy philosophies
NOUN **1** Philosophy is the study or creation of ideas about existence, knowledge or beliefs. **2** a set of beliefs that a person has.
philosopher NOUN
📖 from Greek *philosophos* meaning 'lover of wisdom'

phlegm
Said "flem" NOUN Phlegm is a thick mucus which you get in your throat when you have a cold.

phobia phobias
NOUN an great fear or hatred of something E.G. *The man had a phobia about flying.*
phobic ADJECTIVE

-phobia
SUFFIX '-phobia' means 'fear of' E.G. *claustrophobia.*
📖 from Greek *phobos* meaning 'fear'

phoenix phoenixes
Said "fee-niks" NOUN an imaginary bird which, according to myth, burns itself to ashes every five hundred years and rises from the fire again.

phone phones phoning phoned
NOUN **1** a piece of electronic equipment which allows you to speak to someone in another place by keying in or dialling their number. ▶ VERB **2** If you phone someone, you key in or dial their number and speak to them using a phone.

-phone
SUFFIX '-phone' means 'giving off sound' E.G. *telephone… gramophone.*
📖 from Greek *phōnē* meaning 'voice' or 'sound'

phoney phonier phoniest; also spelt **phony**
ADJECTIVE; INFORMAL false and intended to deceive.

photo photos
NOUN; INFORMAL a photograph.

photo-
PREFIX 'Photo-' means 'light' or 'using light' E.G. *photography.*

photocopier photocopiers
NOUN a machine which makes instant copies of documents by photographing them.

photocopy photocopies photocopying photocopied
(LIBRARY)
NOUN **1** a copy of a document produced by a photocopier. ▶ VERB **2** If you photocopy a document, you make a copy of it using a photocopier.

photogenic
ADJECTIVE Someone who is photogenic always looks nice in photographs.

photograph photographs photographing photographed
NOUN **1** a picture made using a camera. ▶ VERB **2** When you photograph someone, you take a picture of them by using a camera.
photographer NOUN
photography NOUN

photographic
ADJECTIVE connected with photography.

photosynthesis
NOUN Photosynthesis is the process by which the action of sunlight on the chlorophyll in plants produces the substances that keep the plants alive.

phrasal verb phrasal verbs
NOUN a verb such as 'take over' or 'break in', which is made up of a verb and an adverb or preposition.

phrase phrases phrasing phrased
NOUN **1** a group of words considered

a b c d e f g h i j k l m n o p q r s t u v w x y z

there's SAND in my SANDwich (<u>sand</u>wich)   SPELLING NOTE

as a unit. ▶ VERB **2** If you phrase something in a particular way, you choose those words to express it E.G. *I should have phrased that better.*

What is a Phrase?

A **phrase** is a group of words which combine together but is not usually capable of standing on its own to describe an idea or situation. It requires additional words to form a meaningful sentence:

E.G. *She drank **a cup of tea**.
I **was reading** a book.*

Some phrases act as nouns:

E.G. ***A stack of newspapers** lay on the floor.
My sister's friend lives in Canada.*

Some phrases act as verbs. Verb phrases often contain an auxiliary verb. They may also contain adverbs:

E.G. *She **was always complaining** about the buses.
He **used to play** the piano.*

Some phrases act as adjectives. When words combine to act as an adjective, they are usually hyphenated if they occur before the noun:

E.G. *The food here is **of the highest quality**.
He asked for an **up-to-the-minute** report.*

Some phrases act as adverbs. Adverb phrases often begin with a preposition:

E.G. *She disappeared **in the blink of an eye**.
They played **with great gusto**.*

CONTINUED →

Some phrases are acceptable as substitutes for sentences. Although they do not contain a subject and a verb, they can be understood on their own:

E.G. *Happy Birthday!* ■ *Good morning.* ■ *All right?*

---

physical
ADJECTIVE **1** concerning the body rather than the mind. **2** (GEOGRAPHY) relating to things that can be touched or seen, especially with regard to their size or shape E.G. *the physical characteristics of their machinery… the physical world.*
physically ADVERB

physical education
NOUN Physical education consists of the sport that you do at school.

physician physicians
NOUN a doctor.

physics
NOUN Physics is the scientific study of matter, energy, gravity, electricity, heat, and sound.
physicist NOUN

physio-
PREFIX 'Physio-' means to do with the body or natural functions E.G. *physiotherapy.*
📖 from Greek *physio*, from *phuein* meaning 'to make grow'

physiology
NOUN Physiology is the scientific study of the way the bodies of living things work.

physiotherapy
NOUN Physiotherapy is medical treatment which involves exercise and massage.
physiotherapist NOUN

SPELLING NOTE On WEDNESday Wayne WED NESta (<u>Wednes</u>day)

physique >> picture

physique physiques
Said "fiz-**zeek**" NOUN A person's physique is the shape and size of their body.

pi
Rhymes with "fly" NOUN Pi is a number, approximately 3.142 and symbolized by the Greek letter π. Pi is the ratio of the circumference of a circle to its diameter.

piano pianos
NOUN a large musical instrument with a row of black and white keys. When the keys are pressed, little hammers hit wires to produce the different notes.

pianist NOUN
🎹 originally called 'pianoforte', from Italian *gravecembalo col piano e forte* meaning 'harpsichord with soft and loud (sounds)'

piccolo piccolos
NOUN a high-pitched wind instrument like a small flute.
🎹 from Italian *piccolo* meaning 'small'

pick picks picking picked
VERB 1 To pick something is to choose it. 2 If you pick a flower or fruit, or pick something from a place, you remove it with your fingers. 3 If someone picks a lock, they open it with a piece of wire instead of a key.
► NOUN 4 a pickaxe.

pick on VERB If you pick on someone, you criticize them unfairly or treat them unkindly.

pick up VERB If you pick someone or something up, you collect them from the place where they are waiting.

pickaxe pickaxes
NOUN a tool consisting of a curved

pointed iron bar attached in the middle to a long handle.

picket pickets picketing picketed
VERB 1 When a group of people picket a place of work, they stand outside to persuade other workers to join a strike. ► NOUN 2 someone who is picketing a place.

pickings
PLURAL NOUN Pickings are goods or money that can be obtained very easily E.G. *rich pickings*.

pickle pickles pickling pickled
NOUN 1 Pickle or pickles consists of vegetables or fruit preserved in vinegar or salt water. ► VERB 2 To pickle food is to preserve it in vinegar or salt water.

pickpocket pickpockets
NOUN a thief who steals from people's pockets or handbags.

picnic picnics picnicking picnicked
NOUN 1 a meal eaten out of doors.
► VERB 2 People who are picnicking are having a picnic.

pictorial
ADJECTIVE relating to or using pictures E.G. *a pictorial record of the railway*.

picture pictures picturing pictured
NOUN 1 a drawing, painting, or photograph of someone or something. 2 If you have a picture of something in your mind, you have an idea or impression of it. ► PLURAL NOUN 3 If you go to the pictures, you go to see a film at the cinema. ► VERB 4 If someone is pictured in a newspaper or magazine, a photograph of them is printed in it. 5 If you picture something, you think of it and

a
b
c
d
e
f
g
h
i
j
k
l
m
n
o
p
q
r
s
t
u
v
w
x
y
z

Eddy Ant thinks mEAt is a grEAt trEAt to EAt (-ea-)　　SPELLING NOTE

imagine it clearly E.G. *That is how I always picture him.*

picturesque
Said "pik-chur-**esk**" ADJECTIVE A place that is picturesque is very attractive and unspoiled.

pie pies
NOUN a dish of meat, vegetables, or fruit covered with pastry.

piece pieces piecing pieced
NOUN 1 a portion or part of something. 2 something that has been written or created, such as a work of art or a musical composition. 3 a coin E.G. *a 50 pence piece.* ▶ VERB 4 If you piece together a number of things, you gradually put them together to make something complete.

piecemeal
ADVERB or ADJECTIVE done gradually and at irregular intervals E.G. *a piecemeal approach to career management.*

pier piers
NOUN a large structure which sticks out into the sea at a seaside town, and which people can walk along.

pierce pierces piercing pierced
VERB If a sharp object pierces something, it goes through it, making a hole.
■ penetrate, puncture

piercing
ADJECTIVE 1 A piercing sound is high-pitched and unpleasant. 2 Someone with piercing eyes seems to look at you very intensely.
■ (sense 1) penetrating, shrill

piety
Said "**pie**-it-tee" NOUN Piety is strong and devout religious belief or behaviour.

pig pigs
NOUN a farm animal kept for its meat. It has pinkish skin, short legs, and a snout.

pigeon pigeons
NOUN a largish bird with grey feathers, often seen in towns.

pigeonhole pigeonholes
NOUN one of the sections in a frame on a wall where letters can be left.

piggyback piggybacks
NOUN If you give someone a piggyback, you carry them on your back, supporting them under their knees.

piglet piglets
NOUN a young pig.

pigment pigments
NOUN a substance that gives something a particular colour.
pigmentation NOUN

pigsty pigsties
NOUN a hut with a small enclosed area where pigs are kept.

pigtail pigtails
NOUN a length of plaited hair.

pike pikes
NOUN 1 a large freshwater fish of northern countries with strong teeth. 2 a medieval weapon consisting of a pointed metal blade attached to a long pole.

pilchard pilchards
NOUN a small sea fish.

pile piles piling piled
NOUN 1 a quantity of things lying one on top of another. 2 the soft surface of a carpet consisting of many threads standing on end. ▶ PLURAL NOUN 3 Piles are painful swellings that appear in the veins inside or just outside a person's anus. ▶ VERB 4 If you pile things somewhere, you

put them one on top of the other.

pile-up pile-ups
NOUN; INFORMAL a road accident involving several vehicles.

pilfer pilfers pilfering pilfered
VERB Someone who pilfers steals small things over a period of time.
🔲 from Old French *pelfre* meaning 'booty'

pilgrim pilgrims
NOUN (RE) a person who travels to a holy place for religious reasons.
pilgrimage NOUN

pill pills
NOUN 1 a small, hard tablet of medicine that you swallow. 2 The pill is a type of drug that women can take regularly to prevent pregnancy.
🔲 from Latin *pilula* meaning 'little ball'

pillage pillages pillaging pillaged
VERB If a group of people pillage a place, they steal from it using violence.

pillar pillars
NOUN 1 a tall, narrow, solid structure, usually supporting part of a building. 2 Someone who is described as a pillar of a particular group is an active and important member of it
E.G. *a pillar of the Church*.

pillar box pillar boxes
NOUN a red cylinder or box in which you post letters.

pillory pillories pillorying pilloried
VERB If someone is pilloried, they are criticized severely by a lot of people.

pillow pillows
NOUN a rectangular cushion which you rest your head on when you are in bed.

pillowcase pillowcases
NOUN a cover for a pillow which can be removed and washed.

pilot pilots piloting piloted
NOUN 1 a person who is trained to fly an aircraft. 2 a person who goes on board ships to guide them through local waters to a port. ► VERB 3 To pilot something is to control its movement or to guide it. ► ADJECTIVE 4 a small test of a scheme or product, done to see if it would be successful.

pimp pimps
NOUN a man who finds clients for prostitutes and takes a large part of their earnings.

pimple pimples
NOUN a small spot on the skin.
pimply ADJECTIVE

pin pins pinning pinned
NOUN 1 a thin, pointed piece of metal used to fasten together things such as pieces of fabric or paper. ► VERB 2 If you pin something somewhere, you fasten it there with a pin or a drawing pin. 3 If someone pins you in a particular position, they hold you there so that you cannot move. 4 If you try to pin something down, you try to get or give a clear and exact description of it or statement about it.

pinafore pinafores
NOUN a dress with no sleeves, worn over a blouse.

pincers
PLURAL NOUN 1 Pincers are a tool used for gripping and pulling things. They consist of two pieces of metal hinged in the middle. 2 The pincers of a crab or lobster are its front claws.

a
b
c
d
e
f
g
h
i
j
k
l
m
n
o
p
q
r
s
t
u
v
w
x
y
z

'i' before 'e' except after 'c'   **SPELLING NOTE**

A B C D E F G H I J K L M N O P Q R S T U V W X Y Z

pinch pinches pinching pinched
VERB 1 If you pinch something, you squeeze it between your thumb and first finger. 2 INFORMAL If someone pinches something, they steal it. ▶ NOUN 3 A pinch of something is the amount that you can hold between your thumb and first finger E.G. *a pinch of salt.*

pinched
ADJECTIVE If someone's face is pinched, it looks thin and pale.

pine pines pining pined
NOUN 1 A pine or pine tree is an evergreen tree with very thin leaves. ▶ VERB 2 If you pine for something, you are sad because you cannot have it.

pineapple pineapples
NOUN a large, oval fruit with sweet, yellow flesh and a thick, lumpy brown skin.

ping-pong
NOUN the same as **table tennis**.

pink pinker pinkest
ADJECTIVE pale reddish-white.

pinnacle pinnacles
NOUN 1 a tall pointed piece of stone or rock. 2 The pinnacle of something is its best or highest level E.G. *the pinnacle of his career.*

pinpoint pinpoints pinpointing pinpointed
VERB If you pinpoint something, you explain or discover exactly what or where it is.

pinstripe
ADJECTIVE Pinstripe cloth has very narrow vertical stripes.

pint pints
NOUN a unit of liquid volume equal to one eighth of a gallon or about 0.568 litres.

pioneer pioneers pioneering pioneered
Said "pie-on-ear" NOUN 1 Someone who is a pioneer in a particular activity is one of the first people to develop it. ▶ VERB 2 Someone who pioneers a new process or invention is the first person to develop it.

pious
Said "pie-uss" ADJECTIVE very religious and moral.

pip pips
NOUN Pips are the hard seeds in a fruit.

pipe pipes piping piped
NOUN 1 a long, hollow tube through which liquid or gas can flow. 2 an object used for smoking tobacco. It consists of a small hollow bowl attached to a tube. ▶ VERB 3 To pipe a liquid or gas somewhere is to transfer it through a pipe.

pipeline pipelines
NOUN a large underground pipe that carries oil or gas over a long distance.

piper pipers
NOUN a person who plays the bagpipes.

piping
NOUN Piping consists of pipes and tubes.

piranha piranhas
Said "pir-rah-nah" NOUN a small, fierce fish with sharp teeth.
📖 a Portuguese word

pirate pirates
NOUN Pirates were sailors who attacked and robbed other ships.

pirouette pirouettes
Said "pir-roo-et" NOUN In ballet, a pirouette is a fast spinning step done on the toes.

Pisces
Said "pie-*seez*" NOUN Pisces is the twelfth sign of the zodiac, represented by two fish. People born between February 19th and March 20th are born under this sign.
🔲 the plural of Latin *piscis* meaning 'a fish'

pistil pistils
NOUN in a flower, the pistil is the female reproductive part made up of the carpel or two or more carpels fused together.

pistol pistols
NOUN a small gun held in the hand.

piston pistons
NOUN a cylinder or disc that slides up and down inside a tube. Pistons make parts of engines move.

pit pits
NOUN **1** a large hole In the ground. **2** a small hollow in the surface of something. **3** a coal mine.

pitch pitches pitching pitched
NOUN **1** (PE) an area of ground marked out for playing a game such as football. **2** (MUSIC) The pitch of a sound is how high or low it is. **3** a black substance used in road tar and also for making boats and roofs waterproof. ▶ VERB **4** If you pitch something somewhere, you throw it with a lot of force. **5** If you pitch something at a particular level of difficulty, you set it at that level E.G. *Any film must be pitched at a level to suit its intended audience.* **6** When you pitch a tent, you fix it in an upright position.

pitcher pitchers
NOUN a large jug.

pitfall pitfalls
NOUN The pitfalls of a situation are its difficulties or dangers.

pith
NOUN the white substance between the outer skin and the flesh of an orange or lemon.

pitiful
ADJECTIVE Someone or something that is pitiful is in such a sad or weak situation that you feel pity for them.

pittance
NOUN a very small amount of money.

pitted
ADJECTIVE covered in small hollows E.G. *Nails often become pitted.*

pity pities pitying pitied
VERB **1** If you pity someone, you feel very sorry for them. ▶ NOUN **2** Pity is a feeling of being sorry for someone. **3** If you say that it is a pity about something, you are expressing your disappointment about it.

pivot pivots pivoting pivoted
VERB **1** If something pivots, it balances or turns on a central point E.G. *The keel pivots on a large stainless steel pin.* ▶ NOUN **2** the central point on which something balances or turns.
pivotal ADJECTIVE

pixie pixies
NOUN an imaginary little creature in fairy stories.

pizza pizzas
Said "peet-*sah*" NOUN a flat piece of dough covered with cheese, tomato, and other savoury food.

placard placards
NOUN a large notice carried at a demonstration or displayed in a public place.

placate placates placating placated
VERB If you placate someone, you stop them feeling angry by doing something to please them.

a
b
c
d
e
f
g
h
i
j
k
l
m
n
o
p
q
r
s
t
u
v
w
x
y
z

an ELegant angEL (angel)   SPELLING NOTE

A
B
C
D
E
F
G
H
I
J
K
L
M
N
O
P
Q
R
S
T
U
V
W
X
Y
Z

place places placing placed
NOUN **1** any point, building, or area.
2 the position where something
belongs E.G. *She set the holder in its
place on the table.* **3** a space at a table
set with cutlery where one person
can eat. **4** If you have a place in a
group or at a college, you are a
member or are accepted as a
student. **5** a particular point or stage
in a sequence of things E.G. *second
place in the race.* ▶ PHRASE **6** When
something **takes place**, it happens.
▶ VERB **7** If you place something
somewhere, you put it there. **8** If you
place an order, you order something.
≡ (sense 1) location, site, spot

placebo placebos
Said "plas-**see**-boh" NOUN a substance
given to a patient in place of a drug
and from which, though it has no
active ingredients, the patient
may imagine they get some
benefit.

placenta placentas
Said "plas-**sen**-tah" NOUN The
placenta is the mass of veins and
tissues in the womb of a pregnant
woman or animal. It gives the foetus
food and oxygen.

placid
ADJECTIVE calm and not easily excited
or upset.
placidly ADVERB
≡ even-tempered, unexcitable

plagiarism
Said "**play**-jer-rizm" NOUN Plagiarism is
copying someone else's work or
ideas and pretending that it is your
own.
plagiarist NOUN **plagiarize** VERB
▣ from Latin *plagiarus* meaning
'plunderer'

plague plagues plaguing plagued
Said "**playg**" NOUN **1** Plague is a very
infectious disease that kills large
numbers of people. **2** A plague of
unpleasant things is a large number
of them occurring at the same time
E.G. *a plague of rats.* ▶ VERB **3** If
problems plague you, they keep
causing you trouble.

plaice
NOUN an edible European flat fish.

plaid plaids
Said "**plad**" NOUN Plaid is woven
material with a tartan design.

plain plainer plainest; plains
ADJECTIVE **1** very simple in style with no
pattern or decoration E.G. *plain
walls.* **2** obvious and easy to
recognize or understand E.G. *plain
language.* **3** A person who is plain is
not at all beautiful or attractive.
▶ ADVERB **4** You can use 'plain' before a
noun or adjective to emphasize it
E.G. *You were just plain stupid.* ▶ NOUN
5 a large, flat area of land with very
few trees.
plainly ADVERB
≡ (sense 1) bare, simple, unadorned

plaintiff plaintiffs
NOUN a person who has brought a
court case against another person.

plait plaits plaiting plaited
VERB **1** If you plait three lengths of hair
or rope together, you twist them
over each other in turn to make one
thick length. ▶ NOUN **2** a length of hair
that has been plaited.

plan plans planning planned
NOUN **1** a method of achieving
something that has been worked
out beforehand. **2** a detailed diagram
or drawing of something that is to
be made. ▶ VERB **3** If you plan

something, you decide in detail what it is to be and how to do it. **4** If you are planning to do something, you intend to do it E.G. *They plan to marry in the summer.*

■ (sense 1) scheme, strategy

■ (sense 3) devise, scheme, think out

■ (sense 4) intend, mean, propose

plane planes planing planed

NOUN **1** a vehicle with wings and engines that enable it to fly. **2** a flat surface. **3** You can refer to a particular level of something as a particular plane E.G. *to take the rock and roll concert to a higher plane.* **4** a tool with a flat bottom with a sharp blade in it. You move it over a piece of wood to remove thin pieces from the surface. ▶ VERB **5** If you plane a piece of wood, you smooth its surface with a plane.

planet planets

NOUN a round object in space which moves around the sun or a star and is lit by light from it.

planetary ADJECTIVE

plank planks

NOUN a long rectangular piece of wood.

plankton

NOUN Plankton is a layer of tiny plants and animals that live just below the surface of a sea or lake.

plant plants planting planted

NOUN **1** a living thing that grows in the earth and has stems, leaves, and roots. **2** a factory or power station E.G. *a giant bottling plant.* ▶ VERB **3** When you plant a seed or plant, you put it into the ground. **4** If you plant something somewhere, you put it there firmly or secretly.

plantation plantations

NOUN **1** a large area of land where crops such as tea, cotton, or sugar are grown. **2** a large number of trees planted together.

plaque plaques

Rhymes with "black" NOUN **1** a flat piece of metal which is fixed to a wall and has an inscription in memory of a famous person or event. **2** Plaque is a substance which forms around your teeth and consists of bacteria, saliva, and food.

plasma

Said "plaz-mah" NOUN Plasma is the clear fluid part of blood.

plaster plasters plastering plastered

NOUN **1** Plaster is a paste made of sand, lime, and water, which is used to form a smooth surface for inside walls and ceilings. **2** a strip of sticky material with a small pad, used for covering cuts on your body. ▶ VERB **3** To plaster a wall is to cover it with a layer of plaster. ▶ PHRASE **4** If your arm or leg is **in plaster**, it has a plaster cast on it to protect a broken bone.

plasterer NOUN

plastered

ADJECTIVE **1** If something is plastered to a surface, it is stuck there. **2** If something is plastered with things, they are all over its surface.

plastic plastics

NOUN **1** Plastic is a substance made by a chemical process that can be moulded when soft to make a wide range of objects. ▶ ADJECTIVE **2** made of plastic.

plastic surgery

NOUN Plastic surgery is surgery to replace or repair damaged skin or to

a
b
c
d
e
f
g
h
i
j
k
l
m
n
o
p
q
r
s
t
u
v
w
x
y
z

A
B
C
D
E
F
G
H
I
J
K
L
M
N
O
P
Q
R
S
T
U
V
W
X
Y
Z

improve a person's appearance by changing the shape of their features.

plate plates
NOUN 1 a flat dish used to hold food. 2 a flat piece of metal or other hard material used for various purposes in machinery or building E.G. *heavy steel plates used in shipbuilding.*

plateau plateaus or **plateaux**
Rhymes with "snow" NOUN a large area of high and fairly flat land.

plated
ADJECTIVE Metal that is plated is covered with a thin layer of silver or gold.

platform platforms
NOUN 1 a raised structure on which someone or something can stand. 2 the raised area in a railway station where passengers get on and off trains.

platinum
NOUN Platinum is a valuable silver-coloured metal.

platitude platitudes
NOUN a statement made as if it were significant but which has become meaningless or boring because it has been used so many times before.

platonic
ADJECTIVE A platonic relationship is simply one of friendship and does not involve sexual attraction.
🎞 from the name of the Greek philospher Plato

platoon platoons
NOUN a small group of soldiers, commanded by a lieutenant.

platter platters
NOUN a large serving plate.

platypus platypuses
NOUN A platypus or duck-billed platypus is an Australian mammal

which lives in rivers. It has brown fur, webbed feet, and a snout like a duck.
🎞 from Greek *platus* meaning 'flat' and *pous* meaning 'foot'

plaudits
PLURAL NOUN; FORMAL Plaudits are expressions of admiration.

plausible
ADJECTIVE An explanation that is plausible seems likely to be true.
plausibility NOUN

play plays playing played
VERB 1 When children play, they take part in games or use toys. 2 When you play a sport or match, you take part in it. 3 If an actor plays a character in a play or film, he or she performs that role. 4 If you play a musical instrument, you produce music from it. 5 If you play a record or tape, you listen to it. ▶ NOUN 6 a piece of drama performed in the theatre or on television.
player NOUN

playboy playboys
NOUN a rich man who spends his time enjoying himself.

playful
ADJECTIVE 1 friendly and light-hearted E.G. *a playful kiss on the tip of his nose.* 2 lively E.G. *a playful puppy.*
playfully ADVERB

playground playgrounds
NOUN a special area for children to play in.

playgroup playgroups
NOUN an informal kind of school for very young children where they learn by playing.

playing card playing cards
NOUN Playing cards are cards printed with numbers or pictures which are used to play various games.

SPELLING NOTE ⟩ Beautiful Elephants Are Usually Tiny (<u>beauti</u>ful)

playing field playing fields
NOUN an area of grass where people
play sports.

playwright playwrights
NOUN (DRAMA) (ENGLISH) a person who
writes plays.

plaza plazas
Said "plah-za" NOUN an open square
in a city.

plea pleas
NOUN 1 an emotional request E.G. *a
plea for help.* 2 In a court of law,
someone's plea is their statement
that they are guilty or not guilty.

plead pleads pleading pleaded
VERB 1 If you plead with someone, you
ask them in an intense emotional
way to do something. 2 When a
person pleads guilty or not guilty,
they state in court that they are
guilty or not guilty of a crime.

pleasant
ADJECTIVE enjoyable, likable, or
attractive.
pleasantly ADVERB
◼ agreeable, nice, pleasing

please pleases pleasing pleased
1 You say please when you are
asking someone politely to do
something.
VERB 2 If something pleases you, it
makes you feel happy and satisfied.
pleased ADJECTIVE
◼ (sense 2) delight, gladden, satisfy

pleasing
ADJECTIVE attractive, satisfying, or
enjoyable E.G. *a pleasing appearance.*

pleasure pleasures
NOUN 1 Pleasure is a feeling of
happiness, satisfaction, or
enjoyment. 2 an activity that you
enjoy.
pleasurable ADJECTIVE

pleat pleats
NOUN a permanent fold in fabric
made by folding one part over
another.

plebiscite plebiscites
Said "pleb-iss-ite" NOUN; FORMAL a vote
on a matter of national importance
in which all the voters in a country
can take part.
▥ from Latin *plebiscitum* meaning
'decree of the people'

pledge pledges pledging pledged
NOUN 1 a solemn promise. ▶ VERB 2 If
you pledge something, you promise
that you will do it or give it.

plentiful
ADJECTIVE existing in large numbers or
amounts and readily available E.G.
Fruit and vegetables were plentiful.
plentifully ADVERB

plenty
NOUN If there is plenty of something,
there is a lot of it.

plethora
Said "pleth-thor-ah" NOUN A plethora
of something is an amount that is
greater than you need.

pleurisy
Said "ploor-ris-see" NOUN Pleurisy is a
serious illness in which a person's
lungs become inflamed and
breathing is difficult.

pliable
ADJECTIVE 1 If something is pliable, you
can bend it without breaking it.
2 Someone who is pliable can be
easily influenced or controlled.
◼ (sense 1) bendy, flexible,
supple

pliers
PLURAL NOUN Pliers are a small tool with
metal jaws for holding small objects
and bending wire.

a
b
c
d
e
f
g
h
i
j
k
l
m
n
o
p
q
r
s
t
u
v
w
x
y
z

plight

NOUN Someone's plight is the very difficult or dangerous situation that they are in E.G. *the plight of the refugees.*

plinth plinths

NOUN a block of stone on which a statue or pillar stands.

plod plods plodding plodded

VERB If you plod somewhere, you walk there slowly and heavily.

plonk plonks plonking plonked

VERB If you plonk something down, you put it down heavily and carelessly.

plop plops plopping plopped

NOUN 1 a gentle sound made by something light dropping into a liquid. ➤ VERB 2 If something plops into a liquid, it drops into it with a gentle sound.

plot plots plotting plotted

NOUN 1 a secret plan made by a group of people. 2 The plot of a novel or play is the story. 3 a small piece of land. ➤ VERB 4 If people plot to do something, they plan it secretly E.G. *His family is plotting to disinherit him.* 5 If someone plots the course of a plane or ship on a map, or plots a graph, they mark the points in the correct places.

☰ (sense 1) conspiracy, scheme

☰ (sense 4) conspire, plan, scheme

plough ploughs ploughing ploughed

Rhymes with "cow" NOUN 1 a large farming tool that is pulled across a field to turn the soil over before planting seeds. ➤ VERB 2 When someone ploughs land, they use a plough to turn over the soil.

ploy ploys

NOUN a clever plan or way of behaving in order to get something that you want.

pluck plucks plucking plucked

VERB 1 To pluck a fruit or flower is to remove it with a sharp pull. 2 To pluck a chicken or other dead bird means to pull its feathers out before cooking it. 3 When you pluck a stringed instrument, you pull the strings and let them go. ➤ NOUN 4 Pluck is courage.

plucky ADJECTIVE

plug plugs plugging plugged

NOUN 1 a plastic object with metal prongs that can be pushed into a socket to connect an appliance to the electricity supply. 2 a disc of rubber or metal with which you block up the hole in a sink or bath. ➤ VERB 3 If you plug a hole, you block it with something.

plum plums

NOUN a small fruit with a smooth red or yellow skin and a large stone in the middle.

plumage

*Said "**ploom**-mage"* NOUN A bird's plumage is its feathers.

plumber plumbers

NOUN a person who connects and repairs water pipes.

🔲 from Old French *plommier* meaning 'worker in lead'

plumbing

NOUN The plumbing in a building is the system of water pipes, sinks, and toilets.

plume plumes

NOUN a large, brightly coloured feather.

plummet plummets plummeting plummeted

VERB If something plummets, it falls very quickly E.G. *Sales have plummeted.*

plump plumper plumpest

ADJECTIVE rather fat E.G. *a small plump baby.*

☐ chubby, podgy, tubby

plunder plunders plundering plundered

VERB If someone plunders a place, they steal things from it.

plunge plunges plunging plunged

VERB 1 If something plunges, it falls suddenly. 2 If you plunge an object into something, you push it in quickly. 3 If you plunge into an activity or state, you suddenly become involved in it or affected by it E.G. *The United States had just plunged into the war.* ► NOUN 4 a sudden fall.

☐ (sense 1) dive, drop, fall, plummet

Plunket Society

NOUN In New Zealand, the Plunket Society was an organization for the care of mothers and babies. It is now called the Royal New Zealand Society for the Health of Women and Children.

plural plurals

NOUN (ENGLISH) the form of a word that is used to refer to two or more people or things, for example the plural of 'chair' is 'chairs', and the plural of 'mouse' is 'mice'.

→ SEE BOX ON NEXT PAGE

pluralism

NOUN Pluralism is the belief that it is possible for different social and religious groups to live together peacefully while keeping their own beliefs and traditions.

pluralist ADJECTIVE or NOUN

plural noun plural nouns

NOUN In this dictionary, 'plural noun' is the name given to a noun that is normally used only in the plural, for example 'scissors' or 'police'.
See box on p 636

plus 1 You use 'plus' to show that one number is being added to another E.G. *Two plus two equals four.*
ADJECTIVE 2 slightly more than the number mentioned E.G. *a career of 25 years plus.* ► PREPOSITION 3 You can use 'plus' when you mention an additional item E.G. *He wrote a history of Scotland plus a history of British literature.*

☑ Although you can use *plus* to mean 'additionally' in spoken language, you should avoid it in written work: *plus, you could win a holiday in Florida.*

plush

ADJECTIVE very expensive and smart E.G. *a plush hotel.*

Pluto

NOUN Pluto is the smallest planet in the solar system and the furthest from the sun.

ply plies plying plied

VERB 1 If you ply someone with things or questions, you keep giving them things or asking them questions. 2 To ply a trade is to do a particular job as your work. ► NOUN 3 Ply is the thickness of wool or thread, measured by the number of strands it is made from.

plywood

NOUN Plywood is wooden board made from several thin sheets of wood glued together under pressure.

a
b
c
d
e
f
g
h
i
j
k
l
m
n
o
p
q
r
s
t
u
v
w
x
y
z

A
B
C
D
E
F
G
H
I
J
K
L
M
N
O
P
Q
R
S
T
U
V
W
X
Y
Z

What is a Plural?

Most nouns can exist in either the singular or plural.

The **singular** form of the noun is used to mean only one instance of a thing. This is the main form given in the dictionary:

E.G. *one book* ■ *a raven*

The **plural** form of the noun is used to mean more than one instance of a thing. The plural form is given in the dictionary in smaller type after the main form:

E.G. *two books* ■ *some ravens*

The plural form of the noun is usually formed by adding the letter -s to the singular:

E.G. *book* ➤ *books* ■ *raven* ➤ *ravens*

Words that end in -s, -z, -x, -ch, or -sh in the singular are made plural by adding the letters -es:

E.G. *cross* ➤ *crosses* ■ *box* ➤ *boxes*

Words that end in a consonant + -y in the singular are made plural by removing the -y and adding -ies:

E.G. *pony* ➤ *ponies* ■ *party* ➤ *parties*

Words that end in -ife in the singular are made plural by removing the -fe and adding -ves:

E.G. *knife* ➤ *knives* ■ *life* ➤ *lives*

Some words that end in -f in the singular are made plural by removing the -f and adding -ves. Other words that end in -f in the singular are made plural by simply adding -s:

E.G. *hoof* ➤ *hooves* ■ *roof* ➤ *roofs*

BE CAREFUL not to use an apostrophe (') when you add an -s to make a plural.

Irregular Plurals

Some words that have come to English from a foreign language have plurals that do not end in -s.

Some words that came into English from French have plurals ending in -x:

E.G. *bureau* ➤ *bureaux* ■ *gateau* ➤ *gateaux*

Some words that came into English from Italian have plurals ending in -i:

E.G. *paparazzo* ➤ *paparazzi* *graffito* ➤ *graffiti*

Some words that came into English from Hebrew have plurals ending in -im:

E.G. *cherub* ➤ *cherubim* ■ *kibbutz* ➤ *kibbutzim*

Some words that came into English from Latin have plurals ending in -i, -a, or -ae:

E.G. *cactus* ➤ *cacti* ■ *medium* ➤ *media* ■ *formula* ➤ *formulae*

Some words that came into English from Ancient Greek have plurals ending in -a:

E.G. *phenomenon* ➤ *phenomena* *criterion* ➤ *criteria*

The plural forms of a few words are not formed according to any regular rule. However, there are very few words like this. Here are some of the most common ones: *child, children; deer, deer; fish, fish* or *fishes; foot, feet; man, men; mouse, mice; ox, oxen; sheep, sheep; woman, women.*

I always visit my FRIend on a FRIday (<u>friend</u>)

p.m.
used to specify times between 12 noon and 12 midnight, eg *He went to bed at 9 p.m.* It is an abbreviation for the Latin phrase 'post meridiem', which means 'after noon'.

pneumatic
Said "new-**mat**-ik" ADJECTIVE operated by or filled with compressed air E.G. *a pneumatic drill.*
📖 from Latin *pneumaticus* meaning 'of air or wind'

pneumonia
Said "new-**moan**-ee-ah" NOUN Pneumonia is a serious disease which affects a person's lungs and makes breathing difficult.

poach poaches poaching poached
VERB 1 If someone poaches animals from someone else's land, they illegally catch the animals for food. 2 When you poach food, you cook it gently in hot liquid.
poacher NOUN

pocket pockets
NOUN 1 a small pouch that forms part of a piece of clothing. 2 A pocket of something is a small area of it E.G. *There are still pockets of resistance.*

pocket money
NOUN Pocket money is an amount of money given regularly to children by their parents.

pod pods
NOUN a long narrow seed container that grows on plants such as peas or beans.

poddy poddies
NOUN In Australian English, a calf or lamb that is being fed by hand.

podium podiums
NOUN a small platform, often one on which someone stands to make a speech.

poem poems
NOUN a piece of writing in which the words are arranged in short rhythmic lines, often with a rhyme.

poet poets
NOUN a person who writes poems.

poetic
ADJECTIVE 1 very beautiful and expressive E.G. *a pure and poetic love.* 2 relating to poetry.
poetically ADVERB

poetry
NOUN Poetry is poems, considered as a form of literature.

poignant
Said "**poyn**-yant" ADJECTIVE Something that is poignant has a strong emotional effect on you, often making you feel sad E.G. *a moving and poignant moment.*
poignancy NOUN

point points pointing pointed
NOUN 1 an opinion or fact expressed by someone E.G. *You've made a good point.* 2 a quality E.G. *Tact was never her strong point.* 3 the purpose or meaning something has E.G. *He completely missed the point in most of his argument.* 4 a position or time E.G. *At some point during the party, a fight erupted.* 5 a single mark in a competition. 6 the thin, sharp end of something such as a needle or knife. 7 The points of a compass are the 32 directions indicated on it. 8 The decimal point in a number is the dot separating the whole number from the fraction. 9 On a railway track, the points are the levers and rails which enable a train to move from one track to another. ▶ VERB 10 If you point

I want to see (C) your licenCe (licen*c*e)   SPELLING NOTE

at something, you stick out your finger to show where it is. **11** If something points in a particular direction, it faces that way.

point-blank

ADJECTIVE **1** Something that is shot at point-blank range is shot with a gun held very close to it. ► ADVERB **2** If you say something point-blank, you say it directly without explanation or apology.

pointed

ADJECTIVE **1** A pointed object has a thin, sharp end. **2** Pointed comments express criticism.

pointedly ADVERB

pointer pointers

NOUN a piece of information which helps you to understand something E.G. *Here are a few pointers to help you make a choice.*

pointless

ADJECTIVE Something that is pointless has no purpose.

pointlessly ADVERB

point of view points of view

NOUN Your point of view is your opinion about something or your attitude towards it.

poise

NOUN Someone who has poise is calm and dignified.

poised

ADJECTIVE If you are poised to do something, you are ready to do it at any moment.

poison poisons poisoning poisoned

NOUN **1** Poison is a substance that can kill people or animals if they swallow it or absorb it. ► VERB **2** To poison someone is to try to kill them with poison.

poisonous ADJECTIVE

poke pokes poking poked

VERB **1** If you poke someone or something, you push at them quickly with your finger or a sharp object. **2** Something that pokes out of another thing appears from underneath or behind it E.G. *roots poking out of the earth.*

■ (sense 1) dig, jab, prod

poker pokers

NOUN **1** Poker is a card game in which the players make bets on the cards dealt to them. **2** a long metal rod used for moving coals or logs in a fire.

polar

ADJECTIVE relating to the area around the North and South Poles.

polar bear polar bears

NOUN a large white bear which lives in the area around the North Pole.

pole poles

NOUN **1** a long rounded piece of wood or metal. **2** The earth's poles are the two opposite ends of its axis E.G. *the North Pole.*

Pole Poles

NOUN someone who comes from Poland.

pole vault

NOUN The pole vault is an athletics event in which contestants jump over a high bar using a long flexible pole to lift themselves into the air.

police polices policing policed

PLURAL NOUN **1** The police are the people who are officially responsible for making sure that people obey the law. ► VERB **2** To police an area is to keep law and order there by means of the police or an armed force.

policeman policemen
NOUN a man who is a member of a police force.
policewoman NOUN

policy policies
NOUN 1 a set of plans, especially in politics or business E.G. *the new economic policy.* 2 An insurance policy is a document which shows an agreement made with an insurance company.

polio
NOUN Polio is an infectious disease that is caused by a virus and often results in paralysis. Polio is short for 'poliomyelitis'.

polish polishes polishing polished
VERB 1 If you polish something, you put polish on it or rub it with a cloth to make it shine. ► NOUN 2 Polish is a substance that you put on an object to clean it and make it shine E.G. *shoe polish.*
polished ADJECTIVE

Polish
Said "pole-ish" ADJECTIVE 1 belonging or relating to Poland. ► NOUN 2 Polish is the main language spoken in Poland.

polite
ADJECTIVE Someone who is polite has good manners and behaves considerately towards other people.
politely ADVERB **politeness** NOUN
▣ civil, courteous, well-mannered

politician politicians
NOUN a person involved in the government of a country.

politics
NOUN (HISTORY) Politics is the activity and planning concerned with achieving power and control in a country or organization.
political ADJECTIVE **politically** ADVERB

polka polkas
NOUN a fast dance in which couples dance together in circles around the room.

poll polls polling polled
NOUN 1 a survey in which people are asked their opinions about something. ► PLURAL NOUN 2 A political election can be referred to as the polls. ► VERB 3 If you are polled on something, you are asked your opinion about it as part of a survey.

pollen
NOUN Pollen is a fine yellow powder produced by flowers in order to fertilize other flowers of the same species.

pollinate pollinates pollinating pollinated
VERB To pollinate a plant is to fertilize it with pollen.
pollination NOUN

pollutant pollutants
NOUN a substance that causes pollution.

pollute pollutes polluting polluted
VERB To pollute water or air is to make it dirty and dangerous to use or live in.
polluted ADJECTIVE
▣ contaminate, foul, poison

pollution
NOUN (GEOGRAPHY) Pollution of the environment happens when dirty or dangerous substances get into the air, water or soil.

polo
NOUN Polo is a game played between two teams of players on horseback. The players use wooden hammers with long handles to hit a ball.

a
b
c
d
e
f
g
h
i
j
k
l
m
n
o
p
q
r
s
t
u
v
w
x
y
z

A
B
C
D
E
F
G
H
I
J
K
L
M
N
O
P
Q
R
S
T
U
V
W
X
Y
Z

polo-necked
ADJECTIVE A polo-necked jumper has a deep fold of material at the neck.

polyester
NOUN (D&T) a man-made fibre, used especially to make clothes.

polygamy
Said "pol-**lig**-gam-ee" NOUN Polygamy is having more than one wife at the same time.
polygamous ADJECTIVE

polygon polygons
NOUN any two-dimensional shape whose sides are all straight.

polystyrene
NOUN Polystyrene is a very light plastic, used especially as insulating material or to make containers.

polythene
NOUN Polythene is a type of plastic that is used to make thin sheets or bags.

polyunsaturated
ADJECTIVE Polyunsaturated oils and margarines are made mainly from vegetable fats and are considered to be healthier than saturated oils.
polyunsaturate NOUN

pomegranate pomegranates
NOUN a round fruit with a thick reddish skin. It contains a lot of small seeds.
📖 from Latin *pomum granatum* meaning 'apple full of seeds'

pomp
NOUN Pomp is the use of ceremony, fine clothes, and decorations on special occasions E.G. *Sir Patrick was buried with much pomp.*

pompous
ADJECTIVE behaving in a way that is too serious and self-important.
pomposity NOUN

pond ponds
NOUN a small, usually man-made area of water.

ponder ponders pondering pondered
VERB If you ponder, you think about something deeply E.G. *He was pondering the problem when Phillipson drove up.*
■ consider, mull over, think

ponderous
ADJECTIVE dull, slow, and serious E.G. *the ponderous commentary.*

pong pongs
NOUN; INFORMAL an unpleasant smell.

pontiff pontiffs
NOUN; FORMAL The pontiff is the Pope.

pony ponies
NOUN a small horse.

ponytail ponytails
NOUN a hairstyle in which long hair is tied at the back of the head and hangs down like a tail.

pony trekking
NOUN Pony trekking is a leisure activity in which people ride across country on ponies.

poodle poodles
NOUN a type of dog with curly hair.

pool pools pooling pooled
NOUN 1 a small area of still water.
2 Pool is a game in which players try to hit coloured balls into pockets around the table using long sticks called cues. 3 A pool of people, money, or things is a group or collection used or shared by several people. ► PLURAL NOUN 4 The pools are a competition in which people try to guess the results of football matches. ► VERB 5 If people pool their resources, they gather together the things they have so that they can be

shared or used by all of them.

poor poorer poorest
ADJECTIVE **1** Poor people have very little money and few possessions. **2** Poor places are inhabited by people with little money and show signs of neglect. **3** You use 'poor' to show sympathy E.G. *Poor you!* **4** 'Poor' also means of a low quality or standard E.G. *a poor performance.*
■ (sense 1) impoverished, penniless, poverty-stricken

poorly
ADJECTIVE **1** feeling unwell or ill.
► ADVERB **2** badly E.G. *a poorly planned operation.*

pop pops popping popped
NOUN **1** Pop is modern music played and enjoyed especially by young people. **2** You can refer to fizzy, nonalcoholic drinks as pop. **3** A short, sharp sound. ► VERB **4** If something pops, it makes a sudden sharp sound. **5** If you pop something somewhere, you put it there quickly E.G. *I'd just popped the pie in the oven.* **6** If you pop somewhere, you go there quickly E.G. *His mother popped out to buy him an ice cream.*

popcorn
NOUN Popcorn is a snack consisting of grains of maize heated until they puff up and burst.

Pope Popes
NOUN The Pope is the head of the Roman Catholic Church.
🏛 from Latin *Papa* meaning 'bishop' or 'father'

poplar poplars
NOUN a type of tall thin tree.

poppy poppies
NOUN a plant with a large red flower on a hairy stem.

populace
NOUN; FORMAL The populace of a country is its people.

popular
ADJECTIVE **1** liked or approved of by a lot of people. **2** involving or intended for ordinary people E.G. *the popular press.*
popularly ADVERB **popularity** NOUN
popularize VERB
■ (sense 1) fashionable, well-liked

populate populates populating populated
VERB The people or animals that populate an area live there.

population populations
NOUN The population of a place is the people who live there, or the number of people living there.

porcelain
NOUN Porcelain is a delicate, hard material used to make crockery and ornaments.

porch porches
NOUN a covered area at the entrance to a building.

porcupine porcupines
NOUN a large rodent with long spines covering its body.
🏛 from Old French *porc d'espins* meaning 'pig with spines'

pore pores poring pored
NOUN **1** The pores in your skin or on the surface of a plant are very small holes which allow moisture to pass through. ► VERB **2** If you pore over a piece of writing or a diagram, you study it carefully.

pork
NOUN Pork is meat from a pig which has not been salted or smoked.

pornography
NOUN Pornography refers to magazines and films that are

a
b
c
d
e
f
g
h
i
j
k
l
m
n
o
p
q
r
s
t
u
v
w
x
y
z

A
B
C
D
E
F
G
H
I
J
K
L
M
N
O
P
Q
R
S
T
U
V
W
X
Y
Z

designed to cause sexual excitement by showing naked people and sexual acts.

pornographic ADJECTIVE

📖 from Greek *pornos* meaning 'prostitute' and *graphein* meaning 'to write'

porpoise porpoises

Said "**por**-pus" NOUN a sea mammal related to the dolphin.

📖 from Latin *porcus* meaning 'pig' and *piscis* meaning 'fish'

porridge

NOUN Porridge is a thick, sticky food made from oats cooked in water or milk.

port ports

NOUN 1 a town or area which has a harbour or docks. 2 Port is a kind of strong, sweet red wine. ▶ ADJECTIVE 3 The port side of a ship is the left side when you are facing the front.

-port

SUFFIX '-port' comes at the end of words that have something to do with 'carrying' in their meaning E.G. *transport*.

📖 from Latin *portāre* meaning 'to carry'

portable

ADJECTIVE designed to be easily carried E.G. *a portable television*.

porter porters

NOUN 1 a person whose job is to be in charge of the entrance of a building, greeting and directing visitors. 2 A porter in a railway station or hospital is a person whose job is to carry or move things.

portfolio portfolios

NOUN 1 a thin, flat case for carrying papers. 2 (D&T) A portfolio is also a group of selected duties, investments, or items of artwork.

📖 from Italian *portafoglio* meaning

'carrier for papers'

porthole portholes

NOUN a small window in the side of a ship or aircraft.

portion portions

NOUN a part or amount of something E.G. *a portion of fresh fruit*.

🔲 bit, part, piece

portrait portraits

NOUN (ART) a picture or photograph of someone.

portray portrays portraying portrayed

VERB When an actor, artist, or writer portrays someone or something, they represent or describe them.

portrayal NOUN

Portuguese

Said "por-tyoo-**geez**" ADJECTIVE

1 belonging or relating to Portugal.

▶ NOUN 2 someone who comes from Portugal. 3 Portuguese is the main language spoken in Portugal and Brazil.

pose poses posing posed

VERB 1 If something poses a problem, it is the cause of the problem. 2 If you pose a question, you ask it. 3 If you pose as someone else, you pretend to be that person in order to deceive people. ▶ NOUN 4 a way of standing, sitting, or lying E.G. *Mr Clark assumes a pose for the photographer*.

🔲 (sense 4) attitude, posture

poser posers

NOUN 1 someone who behaves or dresses in an exaggerated way in order to impress people. 2 a difficult problem.

posh posher poshest

ADJECTIVE 1 INFORMAL smart, fashionable, and expensive E.G. *a posh restaurant*.

2 upper class E.G. *the man with the posh voice.*

position positions positioning positioned

NOUN **1** (DRAMA) The position of someone or something is the place where they are or ought to be E.G. *Would the cast take their positions, please.* **2** When someone or something is in a particular position, they are sitting or lying in that way E.G. *I raised myself to a sitting position.* **3** a job or post in an organization. **4** The position that you are in at a particular time is the situation that you are in E.G. *This puts the president in a difficult position.* ▶ VERB **5** To position something somewhere is to put it there E.G. *Llewelyn positioned a cushion behind Joanna's back.*

positive

ADJECTIVE **1** completely sure about something E.G. *I was positive he'd known about that money.* **2** confident and hopeful E.G. *I felt very positive about everything.* **3** showing approval or encouragement E.G. *I anticipate a positive response.* **4** providing definite proof of the truth or identity of something E.G. *positive evidence.* **5** (MATHS) A positive number is greater than zero.

positively ADVERB

■ (sense 4) absolute, certain, definite

possess possesses possessing possessed

VERB **1** If you possess something, you own it or have it. **2** If a feeling or belief possesses you, it strongly influences you E.G. *Absolute terror possessed her.*

possessor NOUN

possession possessions

NOUN **1** If something is in your possession or if you are in possession of it, you have it. **2** Your possessions are the things that you own or that you have with you.

■ (sense 2) belongings, property

possessive

ADJECTIVE **1** A person who is possessive about someone or something wants to keep them to themselves. ▶ NOUN **2** In grammar, the possessive is the form of a noun or pronoun used to show possession E.G. *my car… That's hers.*

What is the Possessive?

The possessive case is formed by adding an apostrophe (') and the letter *s* to the dictionary form of the word.

The **possessive** is used when a noun indicates a person or thing that owns another person or thing:

E.G. *The **cat's** fur was wet.*
*The **doctor's** cat was called Joey.*

If the noun is plural and already ends in *-s*, the possessive is formed by simply adding an apostrophe:

E.G. *The vet often trims **cats'** claws.*
***Doctors'** surgeries make me nervous.*

The possessive can also be shown by using the word of in front of the noun. This is usually used when you are talking about something that is not alive or cannot be touched:

E.G. *We climbed to the top **of the hill**.*
*He is a master **of disguise**.*

When a possessive is not followed by another noun, it refers to the place where that person lives or works:

E.G. *I am going to stay at my **aunt's**.*
*I bought a loaf at the **baker's**.*

---

a
b
c
d
e
f
g
h
i
j
k
l
m
n
o
p
q
r
s
t
u
v
w
x
y
z

A
B
C
D
E
F
G
H
I
J
K
L
M
N
O
P
Q
R
S
T
U
V
W
X
Y
Z

possibility possibilities
NOUN something that might be true or might happen E.G. *the possibility of a ban.*
■ chance, likelihood, probability

possible
ADJECTIVE **1** likely to happen or able to be done. **2** likely or capable of being true or correct.
possibly ADVERB
■ (sense 1) feasible, practicable

possum possums
NOUN In Australian and New Zealand English, a possum is a phalanger, a marsupial with thick fur and a long tail.

post posts posting posted
NOUN **1** The post is the system by which letters and parcels are collected and delivered. **2** a job or official position in an organization. **3** a strong upright pole fixed into the ground E.G. *They are tied to a post.*
▶ VERB **4** If you post a letter, you send it to someone by putting it into a postbox. **5** If you are posted somewhere, you are sent by your employers to work there.
postal ADJECTIVE

post-
PREFIX after a particular time or event E.G. *his postwar career.*
🔟 from Latin *post* meaning 'after'

postage
NOUN Postage is the money that you pay to send letters and parcels by post.

postal order postal orders
NOUN a piece of paper representing a sum of money which you can buy at a post office.

postbox postboxes
NOUN a metal box with a hole in it

which you put letters into for collection by the postman.

postcard postcards
NOUN a card, often with a picture on one side, which you write on and send without an envelope.

postcode postcodes
NOUN a short sequence of letters and numbers at the end of an address which helps the post office to sort the mail.

poster posters
NOUN a large notice or picture that is stuck on a wall as an advertisement or for decoration.

posterior posteriors
NOUN; A HUMOROUS USE A person's posterior is their bottom.

posterity
NOUN; FORMAL You can refer to the future and the people who will be alive then as posterity E.G. *to record the voyage for posterity.*
🔟 from Latin *posteritas* meaning 'future generations'

posthumous
Said "**poss**-tyum-uss" ADJECTIVE happening or awarded after a person's death E.G. *a posthumous medal.*
posthumously ADVERB

postman postmen
NOUN someone who collects and delivers letters and parcels sent by post.

postmortem postmortems
NOUN a medical examination of a dead body to find out how the person died.

post office post offices
NOUN **1** The Post Office is the national organization responsible for postal services. **2** a building where you can

buy stamps and post letters.

postpone postpones postponing postponed
VERB If you postpone an event, you arrange for it to take place at a later time than was originally planned.
postponement NOUN
■ put off, shelve

posture postures
NOUN Your posture is the position or manner in which you hold your body.

posy posies
NOUN a small bunch of flowers.

pot pots
NOUN a deep round container; also used to refer to its contents.

potassium nitrate
NOUN a white chemical compound used to make gunpowder, fireworks and fertilizers. Potassium nitrate is also called saltpetre.

potato potatoes
NOUN a white vegetable that has a brown or red skin and grows underground.

potent
ADJECTIVE effective or powerful E.G. *a potent cocktail*.
potency NOUN

potential
ADJECTIVE 1 capable of becoming the thing mentioned E.G. *potential customers… potential sources of finance*. ► NOUN 2 Your potential is your ability to achieve success in the future.
potentially ADVERB

potential energy
NOUN Potential energy is the energy stored in something.

pothole potholes
NOUN 1 a hole in the surface of a road

caused by bad weather or traffic.
2 an underground cavern.

potion potions
NOUN a drink containing medicine, poison, or supposed magical powers.
🔲 from Latin *potio* meaning 'a drink'

potted
ADJECTIVE Potted meat or fish is cooked and put into a small sealed container to preserve it.

potter potters pottering pottered
NOUN 1 a person who makes pottery.
► VERB 2 If you potter about, you pass the time doing pleasant, unimportant things.

pottery
NOUN 1 Pottery is pots, dishes, and other items made from clay and fired in a kiln. 2 Pottery is also the craft of making pottery.

potty potties; pottier pottiest
NOUN 1 a bowl which a small child can sit on and use instead of a toilet.
► ADJECTIVE 2 INFORMAL crazy or foolish.

pouch pouches
NOUN 1 a small, soft container with a fold-over top E.G. *a tobacco pouch*.
2 Animals like kangaroos have a pouch, which is a pocket of skin in which they carry their young.

poultry
NOUN Chickens, turkeys, and other birds kept for their meat or eggs are referred to as poultry.

pounce pounces pouncing pounced
VERB If an animal or person pounces on something, they leap and grab it.

pound pounds pounding pounded
NOUN 1 The pound is the main unit of currency in Britain and in some other

a
b
c
d
e
f
g
h
i
j
k
l
m
n
o
p
q
r
s
t
u
v
w
x
y
z

A
B
C
D
E
F
G
H
I
J
K
L
M
N
O
P
Q
R
S
T
U
V
W
X
Y
Z

countries. **2** a unit of weight equal to 16 ounces or about 0.454 kilograms. ▶ VERB **3** If you pound something, you hit it repeatedly with your fist E.G. *Someone was pounding on the door*. **4** If you pound a substance, you crush it into a powder or paste E.G. *Wooden mallets were used to pound the meat*. **5** If your heart is pounding, it is beating very strongly and quickly. **6** If you pound somewhere, you run there with heavy noisy steps.

pour pours pouring poured
VERB **1** If you pour a liquid out of a container, you make it flow out by tipping the container. **2** If something pours somewhere, it flows there quickly and in large quantities E.G. *Sweat poured down his face*. **3** When it is raining heavily, you can say that it is pouring.

pout pouts pouting pouted
VERB If you pout, you stick out your lips or bottom lip.

poverty
NOUN (GEOGRAPHY) the state of being very poor.
◼ destitution, pennilessness, want

powder powders powdering powdered
NOUN **1** Powder consists of many tiny particles of a solid substance. ▶ VERB **2** If you powder a surface, you cover it with powder.
powdery ADJECTIVE

power powers powering powered
NOUN **1** Someone who has power has a lot of control over people and activities. **2** Someone who has the power to do something has the ability to do it E.G. *the power of*

speech. **3** The power of something is the physical strength that it has to move things. **4** Power is energy obtained, for example, by burning fuel or using the wind or waves. **5** In physics, power is the energy transferred from one thing to another in one second. It is measured in watts. ▶ VERB **6** Something that powers a machine provides the energy for it to work.
powerful ADJECTIVE **powerfully** ADVERB
◼ (sense 3) force, strength

powerless
ADJECTIVE unable to control or influence events E.G. *I was powerless to save her*.
◼ helpless, impotent, incapable

power station power stations
NOUN a place where electricity is generated.

practicable
ADJECTIVE If a task or plan is practicable, it can be carried out successfully E.G. *a practicable option*.

practical practicals
ADJECTIVE **1** The practical aspects of something are those that involve experience and real situations rather than ideas or theories E.G. *the practical difficulties of teaching science*. **2** sensible and likely to be effective E.G. *practical low-heeled shoes*. **3** Someone who is practical is able to deal effectively and sensibly with problems. ▶ NOUN **4** an examination in which you make or perform something rather than simply write.
practicality NOUN
◼ (sense 2) functional, utilitarian

practically
ADVERB **1** almost but not completely or

exactly E.G. *The house was practically a wreck.* **2** in a practical way E.G. *practically minded.*

practice practices
NOUN **1** You can refer to something that people do regularly as a practice E.G. *the practice of kissing hands.* **2** Practice is regular training or exercise E.G. *I need more practice.* **3** A doctor's or lawyer's practice is his or her business.

☑ The noun *practice* ends in *ice*.

practise practises practising practised
VERB **1** If you practise something, you do it regularly in order to improve. **2** People who practise a religion, custom, or craft regularly take part in the activities associated with it E.G. *a practising Buddhist.* **3** Someone who practises medicine or law works as a doctor or lawyer

☑ The verb *practise* ends in *ise*.

practised
ADJECTIVE Someone who is practised at doing something is very skilful at it E.G. *a practised performer.*

practitioner practitioners
NOUN You can refer to someone who works in a particular profession as a practitioner E.G. *a medical practitioner.*

pragmatic
ADJECTIVE A pragmatic way of considering or doing something is a practical rather than theoretical way E.G. *He is pragmatic about the risks involved.*

pragmatically ADVERB
pragmatism NOUN

prairie prairies
NOUN a large area of flat, grassy land in North America.

praise praises praising praised
VERB **1** If you praise someone or something, you express strong approval of their qualities or achievements. ▶ NOUN **2** Praise is what is said or written in approval of someone's qualities or achievements.

■ (sense 1) acclaim, approve, compliment

■ (sense 2) acclaim, approval, commendation

pram prams
NOUN a baby's cot on wheels.

prance prances prancing pranced
VERB Someone who is prancing around is walking with exaggerated movements.

prank pranks
NOUN a childish trick.

prattle prattles prattling prattled
VERB If someone prattles on, they talk a lot without saying anything important.

prawn prawns
NOUN a small, pink, edible shellfish with a long tail.

pray prays praying prayed
VERB (RE) When someone prays, they speak to God to give thanks or to ask for help.

prayer prayers
NOUN (RE) **1** Prayer is the activity of praying. **2** the words said when someone prays.

pre-
PREFIX 'Pre-' means before a particular time or event E.G. *pre-war.*

🏛 from Latin *prae* meaning 'before'

preach preaches preaching preached
VERB When someone preaches, they

a
b
c
d
e
f
g
h
i
j
k
l
m
n
o
p
q
r
s
t
u
v
w
x
y
z

give a short talk on a religious or moral subject as part of a church service.

preacher NOUN

precarious

ADJECTIVE 1 If your situation is precarious, you may fail in what you are doing at any time. 2 Something that is precarious is likely to fall because it is not well balanced or secured.

precariously ADVERB

■ (sense 2) insecure, shaky, unsafe

precaution precautions

NOUN an action that is intended to prevent something from happening E.G. *It's still worth taking precautions against accidents.*

precautionary ADJECTIVE

precede precedes preceding preceded

VERB 1 Something that precedes another thing happens or occurs before it. 2 If you precede someone somewhere, you go in front of them.

preceding ADJECTIVE

precedence

Said "press-id-ens" NOUN If something takes precedence over other things, it is the most important thing and should be dealt with first.

precedent precedents

NOUN An action or decision that is regarded as a precedent is used as a guide in taking similar action or decisions later.

precinct precincts

NOUN 1 A shopping precinct is a pedestrian shopping area. ▶ PLURAL NOUN 2 The precincts of a place are its buildings and land.

precious

ADJECTIVE Something that is precious is

valuable or very important and should be looked after or used carefully.

precipice precipices

Said "press-sip-piss" NOUN a very steep rock face.

precipitate precipitates precipitating precipitated

VERB FORMAL If something precipitates an event or situation, it causes it to happen suddenly.

precipitation

NOUN; FORMAL Precipitation is rain, snow, or hail; used especially when stating the amount that falls during a particular period.

precise

ADJECTIVE exact and accurate in every detail E.G. *precise measurements*.

precisely ADVERB **precision** NOUN

preclude precludes precluding precluded

VERB; FORMAL If something precludes an event or situation, it prevents it from happening E.G. *The meal precluded serious conversation.*

precocious

ADJECTIVE Precocious children behave in a way that seems too advanced for their age.

preconceived

ADJECTIVE Preconceived ideas about something have been formed without any real experience or information.

preconception NOUN

precondition preconditions

NOUN If something is a precondition for another thing, it must happen before the second thing can take place.

precursor precursors

NOUN A precursor of something that

exists now is a similar thing that existed at an earlier time E.G. *real tennis, an ancient precursor of the modern game.*

predator predators
Said "pred-dat-tor" NOUN (SCIENCE) an animal that kills and eats other animals.
predatory ADJECTIVE

predecessor predecessors
NOUN Someone's predecessor is a person who used to do their job before.

predetermined
ADJECTIVE decided in advance or controlled by previous events rather than left to chance.

predicament predicaments
NOUN a difficult situation.
■ dilemma, fix, jam

predict predicts predicting predicted
VERB If someone predicts an event, they say that it will happen in the future.
prediction NOUN
■ forecast, foretell, prophesy

predominant
ADJECTIVE more important or more noticeable than anything else in a particular set of people or things E.G. *Yellow is the predominant colour in the house.*
predominantly ADVERB
■ chief, main, prevailing

predominate predominates predominating predominated
VERB If one type of person or thing predominates, it is the most common, frequent, or noticeable E.G. *Fresh flowers predominate in the bouquet.*
predominance NOUN

pre-eminent
ADJECTIVE recognized as being the most important in a particular group E.G. *the pre-eminent experts in the area.*
pre-eminence NOUN

pre-empt pre-empts pre-empting pre-empted
VERB; FORMAL If you pre-empt something, you prevent it by doing something else which makes it pointless or impossible E.G. *a wish to pre-empt any further publicity.*

preen preens preening preened
VERB When a bird preens its feathers, it cleans them using its beak.

preface prefaces
Said "pref-fiss" NOUN an introduction at the beginning of a book explaining what the book is about or why it was written.

prefect prefects
NOUN a pupil who has special duties at a school.
📖 from Latin *praefectus* meaning 'someone put in charge'

prefer prefers preferring preferred
VERB If you prefer one thing to another, you like it better than the other thing.
preferable ADJECTIVE **preferably** ADVERB

preference preferences
Said "pref-fer-enss" NOUN 1 If you have a preference for something, you like it more than other things E.G. *a preference for white.* 2 When making a choice, if you give preference to one type of person or thing, you try to choose that type.

preferential
ADJECTIVE A person who gets

a b c d e f g h i j k l m n o p q r s t u v w x y z

A B C D E F G H I J K L M N O P Q R S T U V W X Y Z

preferential treatment is treated better than others.

prefix prefixes

NOUN (ENGLISH) a letter or group of letters added to the beginning of a word to make a new word, for example 'semi-','pre-', and 'un-'.

pregnant

ADJECTIVE A woman who is pregnant has a baby developing in her womb.

pregnancy NOUN

prehistoric

ADJECTIVE existing at a time in the past before anything was written down.

prejudice prejudices

NOUN (RE) Prejudice is an unreasonable and unfair dislike of, or preference for, a particular type of person or thing.

prejudiced ADJECTIVE **prejudicial** ADJECTIVE

preliminary

ADJECTIVE Preliminary activities take place before something starts, in preparation for it E.G. *the preliminary rounds of the competition.*

■ first, initial, preparatory

prelude preludes

NOUN Something that is an introduction to a more important event can be described as a prelude to that event.

premature

ADJECTIVE happening too early, or earlier than expected E.G. *premature baldness.*

prematurely ADVERB

premeditated

ADJECTIVE planned in advance E.G. *a premeditated attack.*

premier premiers

NOUN 1 The leader of a government is sometimes referred to as the

premier. 2 In Australia, the leader of a State government. ► ADJECTIVE 3 considered to be the best or most important E.G. *Wellington's premier jewellers.*

premiere premieres

Said "prem-mee-er" NOUN the first public performance of a new play or film.

premise premises

Said "prem-iss" PLURAL NOUN 1 The premises of an organization are all the buildings it occupies on one site. ► NOUN 2 a statement which you suppose is true and use as the basis for an idea or argument.

premium premiums

NOUN an extra sum of money that has to be paid E.G. *Paying a premium for space is worthwhile.*

premonition premonitions

Said "prem-on-ish-on" NOUN a feeling that something unpleasant is going to happen.

■ (sense 1) feeling, foreboding, presentiment

preoccupation preoccupations

NOUN If you have a preoccupation with something, it is very important to you and you keep thinking about it.

preoccupied

ADJECTIVE Someone who is preoccupied is deep in thought or totally involved with something.

preparatory

ADJECTIVE Preparatory activities are done before doing something else in order to prepare for it.

prepare prepares preparing prepared

VERB If you prepare something, you make it ready for a particular

purpose or event E.G. *He was preparing the meal.*
preparation NOUN

prepared
ADJECTIVE If you are prepared to do something, you are willing to do it.

preposition prepositions
NOUN (ENGLISH) a word such as 'by', 'for', 'into', or 'with', which usually has a noun as its object.

What is a Preposition?

A preposition is a word that is used before a noun or pronoun to relate it to other words.
Prepositions may tell you the **place** of something in relation to another thing:

E.G. *She saw the cat **in** the garden.*
*The cat was sheltering **under** a bench.*

Prepositions may also indicate **movement**:

E.G. *The train came **into** the station.*
*We pushed **through** the crowd.*

Prepositions may indicate **time**:

E.G. *They will arrive **on** Friday.*
*They will stay **for** two days.*

---

preposterous
ADJECTIVE extremely unreasonable and ridiculous E.G. *a preposterous statement.*

prerequisite prerequisites
Said "pree-**rek**-wiz-zit" NOUN; FORMAL
Something that is a prerequisite for another thing must happen or exist before the other thing is possible E.G. *Self-esteem is a prerequisite for a happy life.*

prerogative prerogatives
Said "prir-**rog**-at-tiv" NOUN; FORMAL
Something that is the prerogative of a person is their special privilege or right.

prescribe prescribes prescribing prescribed
VERB When a doctor prescribes treatment, he or she states what treatment a patient should have.

prescription prescriptions
NOUN a piece of paper on which the doctor has written the name of a medicine needed by a patient.

presence
NOUN 1 Someone's presence in a place is the fact of their being there E.G. *His presence made me happy.* 2 If you are in someone's presence, you are in the same place as they are.
3 Someone who has presence has an impressive appearance or manner.

present presents presenting presented
ADJECTIVE
Said "**prez**-ent" 1 If someone is present somewhere, they are there E.G. *He had been present at the birth of his son.* 2 A present situation is one that exists now rather than in the past or the future. ▶ NOUN
Said "**prez**-ent" 3 The present is the period of time that is taking place now. 4 something that you give to someone for them to keep. ▶ VERB
Said "pri-**zent**" 5 If you present someone with something, you give it to them E.G. *She presented a bravery award to the girl.* 6 Something that presents a difficulty or a challenge causes it or provides it. 7 The person who presents a radio or television

a
b
c
d
e
f
g
h
i
j
k
l
m
n
o
p
q
r
s
t
u
v
w
x
y
z

A
B
C
D
E
F
G
H
I
J
K
L
M
N
O
P
Q
R
S
T
U
V
W
X
Y
Z

show introduces each part or each guest.

presenter NOUN
▤ (sense 2) contemporary, current, existing

presentable
ADJECTIVE neat or attractive and suitable for people to see.

presentation presentations
NOUN 1 the act of presenting or a way of presenting something. 2 The presentation of a piece of work is the way it looks or the impression it gives. 3 (D&T) To give a presentation is to give a talk or demonstration to an audience of something you have been studying or working on.

present-day
ADJECTIVE existing or happening now E.G. *present-day farming practices*.

presently
ADVERB 1 If something will happen presently, it will happen soon E.G. *I'll finish the job presently*. 2 Something that is presently happening is happening now E.G. *Some progress is presently being made*.

present participle present participles
NOUN In grammar, the present participle of an English verb is the form that ends in '-ing'. It is used to form some tenses, and can be used to form adjectives and nouns from a verb.

present tense
NOUN In grammar, the present tense is the tense of a verb that you use mainly to talk about things that happen or exist at the time of writing or speaking.

Talking about the Present

You can talk about events that are happening now by using **simple tenses** or **compound tenses**.

The **simple present tense** is formed by using the verb on its own, without any auxiliary verbs. For the first and second person, and for all plural forms, the simple present tense of the verb is the same as the main form given in the dictionary:

E.G. *I **cook** the dinner*.

For the third person singular, however, you need to add an -s to the dictionary form to make the simple present tense:

E.G. *He **cooks** the dinner*.

You can also talk about an event that is happening in the present by using **compound tenses**. Compound tenses are formed by adding an auxiliary verb to a form of the main verb.

The most common compound present tense is formed by putting a form of the verb *to be* in front of the main verb, and adding the ending -ing. This shows that the action is going on at the present time and is continuous:

E.G. *I **am listening** to the radio*.

You can also talk about the present using a form of the verb *to do* in front of the basic form of the verb. This can add emphasis:

E.G. *I **do like** fish*.

preservative preservatives
NOUN a substance or chemical that stops things decaying.

SPELLING NOTE   'i' before 'e' except after 'c'

preserve preserves preserving preserved

VERB 1 If you preserve something, you take action so that it remains as it is. 2 If you preserve food, you treat it to prevent it from decaying. ▶ NOUN 3 Preserves are foods such as jam or chutney that have been made with a lot of sugar or vinegar.

preservation NOUN

preside presides presiding presided

VERB A person who presides over a formal event is in charge of it.

president presidents

NOUN 1 In a country which has no king or queen, the president is the elected leader E.G. *the President of the United States of America.* 2 The president of an organization is the person who has the highest position.

presidency NOUN **presidential** ADJECTIVE

press presses pressing pressed

VERB 1 If you press something, you push it or hold it firmly against something else E.G. *Lisa pressed his hand… Press the blue button.* 2 If you press clothes, you iron them. 3 If you press for something, you try hard to persuade someone to agree to it E.G. *She was pressing for improvements to the education system.* 4 If you press charges, you make an accusation against someone which has to be decided in a court of law. ▶ NOUN 5 Newspapers and the journalists who work for them are called the press.

press conference press conferences

NOUN When someone gives a press conference, they have a meeting to answer questions put by reporters.

pressing

ADJECTIVE Something that is pressing needs to be dealt with immediately E.G. *pressing needs.*

pressure pressures pressuring pressured

NOUN 1 (SCIENCE) Pressure is the force that is produced by pushing on something. 2 (PSHE) If you are under pressure, you have too much to do and not enough time, or someone is trying hard to persuade you to do something. ▶ VERB 3 If you pressure someone, you try hard to persuade them to do something.

pressurize pressurizes pressurizing pressurized; also spelt **pressurise**

VERB If you pressurize someone, you try hard to persuade them to do something.

prestige

Said "press-**teezh**" NOUN If you have prestige, people admire you because of your position.

prestigious ADJECTIVE

▤ honour, standing, status

presumably

ADVERB If you say that something is presumably the case, you mean you assume that it is E.G. *Your audience, presumably, are younger.*

presume presumes presuming presumed

Said "priz-**yoom**" VERB If you presume something, you think that it is the case although you have no proof.

presumption NOUN

▤ assume, believe, suppose

presumptuous

ADJECTIVE Someone who behaves in a presumptuous way does things that they have no right to do.

a
b
c
d
e
f
g
h
i
j
k
l
m
n
o
p
q
r
s
t
u
v
w
x
y
z

King IAn went to ParllAment in a carrIAge for his marrIAge (-ia-)   SPELLING NOTE

A
B
C
D
E
F
G
H
I
J
K
L
M
N
O
P
Q
R
S
T
U
V
W
X
Y
Z

pretence pretences
NOUN a way of behaving that is false and intended to deceive people.

pretend pretends pretending pretended
VERB If you pretend that something is the case, you try to make people believe that it is, although in fact it is not E.G. *Latimer pretended not to notice.*
■ affect, feign, sham

pretender pretenders
NOUN A pretender to a throne or title is someone who claims it but whose claim is being questioned.

pretension pretensions
NOUN Someone with pretensions claims that they are more important than they really are.

pretentious
ADJECTIVE Someone or something that is pretentious is trying to seem important when in fact they are not.

pretext pretexts
NOUN a false reason given to hide the real reason for doing something.

pretty prettier prettiest
ADJECTIVE 1 attractive in a delicate way.
► ADVERB 2 INFORMAL quite or rather E.G. *He spoke pretty good English.*
prettily ADVERB **prettiness** NOUN

prevail prevails prevailing prevailed
VERB 1 If a custom or belief prevails in a particular place, it is normal or most common there E.G. *This attitude has prevailed in Britain for many years.* 2 If someone or something prevails, they succeed in their aims E.G. *In recent years better sense has prevailed.*
prevailing ADJECTIVE

prevalent
ADJECTIVE very common or widespread E.G. *the hooliganism so prevalent today.*
prevalence NOUN

prevent prevents preventing prevented
VERB If you prevent something, you stop it from happening or being done.
preventable ADJECTIVE **prevention** NOUN
■ avert, forestall, stop

preventive or **preventative**
ADJECTIVE intended to help prevent things such as disease or crime E.G. *preventive health care.*

preview previews
NOUN 1 an opportunity to see something, such as a film or exhibition, before it is shown to the public. 2 (ICT) a part of a computer program which allows you to look at what you have keyed or added to a document or spreadsheet as it will appear when it is printed.

previous
ADJECTIVE happening or existing before something else in time or position E.G. *previous reports… the previous year.*
previously ADVERB
■ earlier, former, preceding

prey preys preying preyed
Rhymes with "say" NOUN 1 The creatures that an animal hunts and eats are called its prey. ► VERB 2 An animal that preys on a particular kind of animal lives by hunting and eating it.

price prices pricing priced
NOUN 1 The price of something is the amount of money you have to pay to

buy it. ► VERB **2** To price something at a particular amount is to fix its price at that amount.

■ (sense 1) charge, cost, expense

priceless

ADJECTIVE Something that is priceless is so valuable that it is difficult to work out how much it is worth.

pricey pricier priciest

ADJECTIVE; INFORMAL expensive.

prick pricks pricking pricked

VERB **1** If you prick something, you stick a sharp pointed object into it. ► NOUN **2** a small, sharp pain caused when something pricks you.

prickle prickles prickling prickled

NOUN **1** Prickles are small sharp points or thorns on plants. ► VERB **2** If your skin prickles, it feels as if a lot of sharp points are being stuck into it.

prickly ADJECTIVE

pride prides priding prided

NOUN **1** Pride is a feeling of satisfaction you have when you have done something well. **2** Pride is also a feeling of being better than other people. ► VERB **3** If you pride yourself on a quality or skill, you are proud of it E.G. *She prides herself on punctuality.*

■ (sense 1) gratification, pleasure, satisfaction

priest priests

NOUN (RE) **1** a member of the clergy in some Christian Churches. **2** In many non-Christian religions, a priest is a man who has special duties in the place where people worship.

priestly ADJECTIVE

priestess priestesses

NOUN a female priest in a non-Christian religion.

priesthood

NOUN The priesthood is the position of being a priest.

prim primmer primmest

ADJECTIVE Someone who is prim always behaves very correctly and is easily shocked by anything rude.

■ priggish, prudish, strait-laced

primaeval

another spelling of **primeval**.

primarily

ADVERB You use 'primarily' to indicate the main or most important feature of something E.G. *I still rated people primarily on their looks.*

primary

ADJECTIVE 'Primary' is used to describe something that is extremely important for someone or something E.G. *the primary aim of his research.*

primary colour primary colours

NOUN In art, the primary colours are red, yellow, and blue, from which other colours can be obtained by mixing.

primary school primary schools

NOUN a school for children aged up to 11.

primate primates

NOUN **1** an archbishop. **2** a member of the group of animals which includes humans, monkeys, and apes.

prime primes priming primed

ADJECTIVE **1** main or most important E.G. *a prime cause of brain damage.* **2** of the best quality E.G. *in prime condition.* ► NOUN **3** Someone's prime is the stage when they are at their strongest, most active, or most successful. ► VERB **4** If you prime someone, you give them information about something in advance to

a
b
c
d
e
f
g
h
i
j
k
l
m
n
o
p
q
r
s
t
u
v
w
x
y
z

LEt's measure the angLE (ang*le*)   **SPELLING NOTE**

prepare them E.G. *We are primed for every lesson*.

■ (sense 3) height, heyday, peak

prime minister prime ministers

NOUN The prime minister is the leader of the government.

primeval or **primaeval**

Said "pry-**mee**-vl" ADJECTIVE belonging to a very early period in the history of the world.

primitive

ADJECTIVE 1 connected with a society that lives very simply without industries or a writing system E.G. *the primitive peoples of the world*. 2 very simple, basic, or old-fashioned E.G. *a very small primitive cottage*.

primrose primroses

NOUN a small plant that has pale yellow flowers in spring.

🔲 from Latin *prima rosa* meaning 'first rose'

prince princes

NOUN a male member of a royal family, especially the son of a king or queen.

princely ADJECTIVE

🔲 from Latin *princeps* meaning 'chief' or 'ruler'

princess princesses

NOUN a female member of a royal family, usually the daughter of a king or queen, or the wife of a prince.

principal principals

ADJECTIVE 1 main or most important E.G. *the principal source of food*.

▶ NOUN 2 the person in charge of a school or college.

principally ADVERB

☑ Do not confuse *principal* with *principle*: *my principal objection*.

principality principalities

NOUN a country ruled by a prince.

principle principles

NOUN 1 a belief you have about the way you should behave E.G. *a woman of principle*. 2 a general rule or scientific law which explains how something happens or works E.G. *the principle of evolution in nature*.

■ (sense 1) precept, standard, rule

☑ Do not confuse *principle* with *principal*: *a man with no principles*.

print prints printing printed

VERB 1 To print a newspaper or book is to reproduce it in large quantities using a mechanical or electronic copying process. 2 If you print when you are writing, you do not join the letters together. ▶ NOUN 3 The letters and numbers on the pages of a book or newspaper are referred to as the print. 4 a photograph, or a printed copy of a painting. 5 Footprints and fingerprints can be referred to as prints.

printer NOUN

print-out print-outs

NOUN a printed copy of information from a computer.

prior priors

ADJECTIVE 1 planned or done at an earlier time E.G. *I have a prior engagement*. ▶ PHRASE 2 Something that happens **prior to** a particular time or event happens before it.

▶ NOUN 3 a monk in charge of a small group of monks in a priory.

prioress NOUN

priority priorities

NOUN something that needs to be dealt with first E.G. *The priority is building homes*.

prioritize prioritizes prioritizing prioritized or **prioritise**

VERB To prioritize things is to decide

which is the most important and deal with it first.

priory priories

NOUN a place where a small group of monks live under the charge of a prior.

prise prises prising prised

VERB If you prise something open or away from a surface, you force it open or away E.G. *She prised his fingers loose.*

prism prisms

NOUN **1** an object made of clear glass with many flat sides. It separates light passing through it into the colours of the rainbow. **2** In maths, a prism is any polyhedron with two identical parallel ends and sides which are parallelograms.

prison prisons

NOUN a building where criminals are kept in captivity.

prisoner prisoners

NOUN someone who is kept in prison or held in captivity against their will.

pristine

Said "priss-teen" ADJECTIVE; FORMAL very clean or new and in perfect condition.

private privates

ADJECTIVE **1** for the use of one person rather than people in general E.G. *a private bathroom.* **2** taking place between a small number of people and kept secret from others E.G. *a private conversation.* **3** owned or run by individuals or companies rather than by the state E.G. *a private company.* ▶ NOUN **4** a soldier of the lowest rank.

privacy NOUN   **privately** ADVERB

private school private schools

NOUN a school that does not receive money from the government, and parents pay for their children to attend.

privatize privatizes privatizing privatized; also spelt **privatise**

VERB If the government privatizes a state-owned industry or organization, it allows it to be bought and owned by a private individual or group.

privilege privileges

NOUN a special right or advantage given to a person or group E.G. *the privileges of monarchy.*

privileged ADJECTIVE

privy

ADJECTIVE FORMAL If you are privy to something secret, you have been told about it.

prize prizes prizing prized

NOUN **1** a reward given to the winner of a competition or game. ▶ ADJECTIVE **2** of the highest quality or standard E.G. *his prize dahlia.* ▶ VERB **3** Something that is prized is wanted and admired for its value or quality.

■ (sense 1) award, reward, trophy

pro pros

NOUN **1** INFORMAL a professional. ▶ PHRASE **2** The **pros and cons** of a situation are its advantages and disadvantages.

▦ sense 2 is from Latin *pro* meaning 'for' and *contra* meaning 'against'

pro-

PREFIX 'Pro-' means supporting or in favour of E.G. *pro-democracy protests.*

probability probabilities

NOUN **1** The probability of something happening is how likely it is to happen E.G. *the probability of success.* **2** If something is a

a
b
c
d
e
f
g
h
i
j
k
l
m
n
o
p
q
r
s
t
u
v
w
x
y
z

probability, it is likely to happen E.G.
The probability is that you will be feeling better.

■ (sense 1) chance(s), likelihood, odds

probable
ADJECTIVE Something that is probable is likely to be true or correct, or likely to happen E.G. *the most probable outcome.*

probably
ADVERB Something that is probably the case is likely but not certain.

probation
NOUN Probation is a period of time during which a person convicted of a crime is supervised by a probation officer instead of being sent to prison.

probationary ADJECTIVE

probe probes probing probed
VERB 1 If you probe, you ask a lot of questions to discover the facts about something. ▶ NOUN 2 a long thin instrument used by doctors and dentists when examining a patient.

problem problems
NOUN 1 an unsatisfactory situation that causes difficulties. 2 a puzzle or question that you solve using logical thought or mathematics.

problematic ADJECTIVE

■ (sense 1) difficulty, predicament

procedure procedures
NOUN a way of doing something, especially the correct or usual way E.G. *It's standard procedure.*

procedural ADJECTIVE

proceed proceeds proceeding proceeded
VERB 1 If you proceed to do something, you start doing it, or continue doing it E.G. *She proceeded*

to tell them. 2 FORMAL If you proceed in a particular direction, you move in that direction E.G. *I he taxi proceeded along a lonely road.* ▶ PLURAL NOUN
3 The proceeds from a fund-raising event are the money obtained from it.

proceedings
PLURAL NOUN 1 You can refer to an organized and related series of events as the proceedings E.G. *She was determined to see the proceedings from start to finish.* 2 Legal proceedings are legal action taken against someone.

process processes processing processed
NOUN 1 a series of actions intended to achieve a particular result or change.
▶ PHRASE 2 If you are **in the process** of doing something, you have started doing it but have not yet finished.
▶ VERB 3 When something such as food or information is processed, it is treated or dealt with.

procession processions
NOUN a group of people or vehicles moving in a line, often as part of a ceremony.

processor processors
NOUN (ICT) In computing, a processor is the central chip in a computer which controls its operations.

proclaim proclaims proclaiming proclaimed
VERB If someone proclaims something, they announce it or make it known E.G. *You have proclaimed your innocence.*

proclamation NOUN

procure procures procuring procured
VERB; FORMAL If you procure something,

you obtain it.

prod prods prodding prodded
VERB If you prod something, you give it a push with your finger or with something pointed.

prodigy prodigies
Said "prod-dij-ee" NOUN someone who shows an extraordinary natural ability at an early age.

produce produces producing produced
VERB 1 To produce something is to make it or cause it E.G. *a white wine produced mainly from black grapes.* 2 If you produce something from somewhere, you bring it out so it can be seen. ▶ NOUN 3 Produce is food that is grown to be sold E.G. *fresh produce.*

producer producers
NOUN The producer of a record, film, or show is the person in charge of making it or putting it on.

product products
NOUN 1 something that is made to be sold E.G. *high-quality products.* 2 In maths, the product of two or more numbers or quantities is the result of multiplying them together.

production productions
NOUN (D&T) 1 Production is the process of manufacturing or growing something in large quantities E.G. *modern methods of production.* 2 Production is also the amount of goods manufactured or food grown by a country or company E.G. *Production has fallen by 13.2%.* 3 A production of a play, opera, or other show is a series of performances of it.

productive
ADJECTIVE 1 To be productive means to

produce a large number of things E.G. *Farms were more productive in these areas.* 2 If something such as a meeting is productive, good or useful things happen as a result of it. ■ (sense 2) beneficial, useful, worthwhile

productivity
NOUN Productivity is the rate at which things are produced or dealt with.

profane
ADJECTIVE FORMAL showing disrespect for a religion or religious things E.G. *profane language.*

profess professes professing professed
VERB 1 FORMAL If you profess to do or have something, you claim to do or have it. 2 If you profess a feeling or opinion, you express it E.G. *He professes a lasting affection for Trinidad.*

profession professions
NOUN 1 a type of job that requires advanced education or training. 2 You can use 'profession' to refer to all the people who have a particular profession E.G. *the medical profession.*

professional professionals
ADJECTIVE 1 Professional means relating to the work of someone who is qualified in a particular profession E.G. *I think you need professional advice.* 2 Professional also describes activities when they are done to earn money rather than as a hobby E.G. *professional football.* 3 A professional piece of work is of a very high standard. ▶ NOUN 4 a person who has been trained in a profession. 5 someone who plays a sport to earn money rather than as a hobby.

a
b
c
d
e
f
g
h
i
j
k
l
m
n
o
p
q
r
s
t
u
v
w
x
y
z

A
B
C
D
E
F
G
H
I
J
K
L
M
N
O
P
Q
R
S
T
U
V
W
X
Y
Z

professor professors
NOUN the senior teacher in a department of a British university.
professorial ADJECTIVE

proficient
ADJECTIVE If you are proficient at something, you can do it well.
proficiency NOUN

profile profiles
NOUN 1 Your profile is the outline of your face seen from the side. 2 A profile of someone is a short description of their life and character.
📖 from Italian *profilare* meaning 'to sketch lightly'

profit profits profiting profited
NOUN 1 When someone sells something, the profit is the amount they gain by selling it for more than it cost them to buy or make. ▶ VERB 2 If you profit from something, you gain or benefit from it.
profitable ADJECTIVE
🔲 (sense 1) gain, proceeds, return

profound
ADJECTIVE 1 great in degree or intensity E.G. *a profound need to please.* 2 showing great and deep intellectual understanding E.G. *a profound question.*
profoundly ADVERB **profundity** NOUN

profuse
Said "prof-**yooss**" ADJECTIVE very large in quantity or number E.G. *There were profuse apologies for his absence.*
profusely ADVERB

program programs programming programmed
(ICT) NOUN 1 a set of instructions

that a computer follows to perform a particular task. ▶ VERB 2 When someone programs a computer, they write a program and put it into the computer.
programmer NOUN

programme programmes
NOUN 1 a planned series of events E.G. *a programme of official engagements.* 2 a particular piece presented as a unit on television or radio, such as a play, show, or discussion. 3 a booklet giving information about a play, concert, or show that you are attending.
🔲 (sense 1) agenda, plan, schedule

progress progresses progressing progressed
NOUN 1 Progress is the process of gradually improving or getting near to achieving something E.G. *Gerry is now making some real progress towards fitness.* 2 The progress of something is the way in which it develops or continues E.G. *news on the progress of the war.* ▶ PHRASE 3 Something that is **in progress** is happening E.G. *A cricket match was in progress.* ▶ VERB 4 If you progress, you become more advanced or skilful. 5 To progress is to continue E.G. *As the evening progressed, sadness turned to rage.*
progression NOUN
🔲 (sense 1) advance, headway
🔲 (sense 2) course, movement

progressive
ADJECTIVE 1 having modern ideas about how things should be done. 2 happening gradually E.G. *a progressive illness.*

prohibit prohibits prohibiting prohibited
VERB If someone prohibits something,

they forbid it or make it illegal.
prohibition NOUN

☑ You *prohibit* a person *from* doing something.

prohibitive
ADJECTIVE If the cost of something is prohibitive, it is so high that people cannot afford it.

project projects projecting projected
NOUN 1 a carefully planned attempt to achieve something or to study something over a period of time. ▶ VERB 2 Something that is projected is planned or expected to happen in the future E.G. *The population aged 65 or over is projected to increase.* 3 To project an image onto a screen is to make it appear there using equipment such as a projector. 4 Something that projects sticks out beyond a surface or edge.
projection NOUN

projector projectors
NOUN a piece of equipment which produces a large image on a screen by shining light through a photographic slide or film strip.

proletariat
NOUN; FORMAL Working-class people are sometimes referred to as the proletariat.
proletarian ADJECTIVE

proliferate proliferates proliferating proliferated
VERB If things proliferate, they quickly increase in number.
proliferation NOUN
📖 from Latin *prolifer* meaning 'having children'

prolific
ADJECTIVE producing a lot of something E.G. *this prolific artist.*

prologue prologues
NOUN a speech or section that introduces a play or book.

prolong prolongs prolonging prolonged
VERB If you prolong something, you make it last longer.
prolonged ADJECTIVE

prom proms
NOUN; INFORMAL a concert at which some of the audience stand.

promenade promenades
Said "prom-min-**ahd**" NOUN a road or path next to the sea at a seaside resort.
📖 a French word, from *se promener* meaning 'to go for a walk'

prominent
ADJECTIVE 1 Prominent people are important. 2 Something that is prominent is very noticeable E.G. *a prominent nose.*
prominence NOUN **prominently** ADVERB

promiscuous
Said "prom-**misk**-yoo-uss" ADJECTIVE Someone who is promiscuous has sex with many different people.
promiscuity NOUN

promise promises promising promised
VERB 1 If you promise to do something, you say that you will definitely do it. 2 Something that promises to have a particular quality shows signs that it will have that quality E.G. *This promised to be a very long night.* ▶ NOUN 3 a statement made by someone that they will definitely do something E.G. *He made a promise to me.* 4 Someone or something that shows promise seems likely to be very successful.
promising ADJECTIVE

a
b
c
d
e
f
g
h
i
j
k
l
m
n
o
p
q
r
s
t
u
v
w
x
y
z

A B C D E F G H I J K L M N O **P** Q R S T U V W X Y Z

■ (sense 1) guarantee, pledge, vow
■ (sense 3) guarantee, oath, vow

promontory promontories
Said "prom-mon-tree" NOUN an area of high land sticking out into the sea.

promote promotes promoting promoted
VERB 1 If someone promotes something, they try to make it happen or become more popular E.G. *to promote their latest film.* 2 If someone is promoted, they are given a more important job at work.
promoter NOUN **promotion** NOUN

prompt prompts prompting prompted
VERB 1 If something prompts someone to do something, it makes them decide to do it E.G. *Curiosity prompted him to push at the door.* 2 If you prompt someone when they stop speaking, you tell them what to say next or encourage them to continue. ► ADVERB 3 exactly at the time mentioned E.G. *Wednesday morning at 10.40 prompt.* ► ADJECTIVE 4 A prompt action is done without any delay E.G. *a prompt reply.*
promptly ADVERB

prone
ADJECTIVE 1 If you are prone to something, you have a tendency to be affected by it or to do it E.G. *She is prone to depression.* 2 If you are prone, you are lying flat and face downwards E.G. *lying prone on the grass.*
■ (sense 1) inclined, liable, subject

prong prongs
NOUN The prongs of a fork are the long, narrow, pointed parts.

pronoun pronouns
NOUN In grammar, a pronoun is a word that is used to replace a noun. 'He', 'she', and 'them' are all pronouns.

What is a Pronoun?

A **pronoun** is a word that is used in place of a noun. Pronouns may be used instead of naming a person or thing.

Personal pronouns replace the subject or object of a sentence:
E.G. ***She** caught a fish.*
*The nurse reassured **him**.*

Reflexive pronouns replace the object when it is the same person or thing as the subject:
E.G. *Matthew saw **himself** in the mirror.*

Demonstrative pronouns replace the subject or object when you want to show where something is:
E.G. ***That** is a nice jacket.*
*Have you seen **this**?*

Possessive pronouns replace the subject or object when you want to show who owns it:
E.G. *The blue car is **mine**.*
***Hers** is a strange story.*

Relative pronouns replace a noun to link two different parts of the sentence:
E.G. *Do you know the man **who** lives next door?*
*I watched a programme **that** I had recorded yesterday.*

Interrogative pronouns ask questions:
E.G. ***What** are you doing?*

Indefinite pronouns replace a

CONTINUED ON NEXT PAGE →

SPELLING NOTE   I want to see (C) your licenCe (licen**c**e) subject or object to talk about a broad or vague range of people or things:

E.G. ***Everybody*** *knew the exercise was a waste of time.*
Some *say he cheats at cards.*

Also look at the grammar box at **relative pronoun**.

pronounce pronounces pronouncing pronounced
VERB When you pronounce a word, you say it.
☑ There is an *o* before the *u* in *pronounce*. Compare this spelling with *pronunciation*.

pronounced
ADJECTIVE very noticeable E.G. *He talks with a pronounced lowland accent.*

pronouncement pronouncements
NOUN a formal statement.

pronunciation pronunciations
Said "pron-nun-see-**ay**-shn" NOUN the way a word is usually said
☑ There is no *o* before the *u* in *pronunciation*. Compare this spelling with *pronounce*.

proof
NOUN If you have proof of something, you have evidence which shows that it is true or exists.
▤ confirmation, evidence, verification

prop props propping propped
VERB 1 If you prop an object somewhere, you support it or rest it against something E.G. *The barman propped himself against the counter.*
▶ NOUN 2 a stick or other object used to support something. 3 The props in a play are all the objects and furniture used by the actors.

propaganda
NOUN (HISTORY) Propaganda is exaggerated or false information that is published or broadcast in order to influence people.

propagate propagates propagating propagated
VERB 1 If people propagate an idea, they spread it to try to influence many other people. 2 If you propagate plants, you grow more of them from an original one.
propagation NOUN

propel propels propelling propelled
VERB To propel something is to cause it to move in a particular direction.

propeller propellers
NOUN a device on a boat or aircraft with rotating blades which make the boat or aircraft move.

propensity propensities
NOUN; FORMAL a tendency to behave in a particular way.

proper
ADJECTIVE 1 real and satisfactory E.G. *He was no nearer having a proper job.* 2 correct or suitable E.G. *Put things in their proper place.*
properly ADVERB

proper noun proper nouns
NOUN the name of a person, place, or institution.

property properties
NOUN 1 A person's property is the things that belong to them. 2 a building and the land belonging to it. 3 a characteristic or quality E.G. *Mint has powerful healing properties.*

prophecy prophecies
NOUN a statement about what

a
b
c
d
e
f
g
h
i
j
k
l
m
n
o
p
q
r
s
t
u
v
w
x
y
z

someone believes will happen in the future

☑ The noun *prophecy* ends in *cy*.

prophesy prophesies prophesying prophesied

VERB If someone prophesies something, they say it will happen

☑ The verb *prophesy* ends in *sy*.

prophet prophets

NOUN (RE) a person who predicts what will happen in the future.

prophetic

ADJECTIVE correctly predicting what will happen E.G. *It was a prophetic warning*.

proportion proportions

NOUN 1 A proportion of an amount or group is a part of it E.G. *a tiny proportion of the population*. 2 The proportion of one amount to another is its size in comparison with the other amount E.G. *the highest proportion of single women to men*.

▶ PLURAL NOUN 3 You can refer to the size of something as its proportions E.G. *a red umbrella of vast proportions*.

proportional or **proportionate**

ADJECTIVE If one thing is proportional to another, it remains the same size in comparison with the other E.G. *proportional increases in profit*.

proportionally or **proportionately**

ADVERB

proportional representation

NOUN Proportional representation is a system of voting in elections in which the number of representatives of each party is in proportion to the number of people who voted for it.

proposal proposals

NOUN a plan that has been suggested E.G. *business proposals*.

propose proposes proposing proposed

VERB 1 If you propose a plan or idea, you suggest it. 2 If you propose to do something, you intend to do it E.G. *And how do you propose to do that?* 3 When someone proposes a toast to a particular person, they ask people to drink a toast to that person. 4 If someone proposes to another person, they ask that person to marry them.

proposition propositions

NOUN 1 a statement expressing a theory or opinion. 2 an offer or suggestion E.G. *I made her a proposition*.

proprietor proprietors

NOUN The proprietor of a business is the owner.

propriety

NOUN; FORMAL Propriety is what is socially or morally acceptable E.G. *a model of propriety*.

propulsion

NOUN Propulsion is the power that moves something.

prose

NOUN Prose is ordinary written language in contrast to poetry.

📖 from Latin *prosa oratorio* meaning 'straightforward speech'

prosecute prosecutes prosecuting prosecuted

VERB If someone is prosecuted, they are charged with a crime and have to stand trial.

prosecutor NOUN

prosecution

NOUN The lawyers who try to prove that a person on trial is guilty are called the prosecution.

prospect prospects prospecting prospected

NOUN **1** If there is a prospect of something happening, there is a possibility that it will happen E.G. *There was little prospect of going home.* **2** Someone's prospects are their chances of being successful in the future. ▶ VERB **3** If someone prospects for gold or oil, they look for it.

prospector NOUN

prospective

ADJECTIVE 'Prospective' is used to say that someone wants to be or is likely to be something. For example, the prospective owner of something is the person who wants to own it.

prospectus prospectuses

NOUN a booklet giving details about a college or a company.

prosper prospers prospering prospered

VERB When people or businesses prosper, they are successful and make a lot of money.

prosperous ADJECTIVE   **prosperity** NOUN

prostitute prostitutes

NOUN a person, usually a woman, who has sex with men in exchange for money.

prostitution NOUN

prostrate

ADJECTIVE lying face downwards on the ground.

protagonist protagonists

NOUN FORMAL **1** Someone who is a protagonist of an idea or movement is a leading supporter of it. **2** a main character in a play or story.

▥ from Greek *prōtagonistēs* meaning 'main actor in a play'

protea proteas

NOUN an evergreen African shrub with colourful flowers.

protect protects protecting protected

VERB To protect someone or something is to prevent them from being harmed or damaged.

protection NOUN   **protective** ADJECTIVE

protégé protégés

Said "proh-tij-ay" NOUN Someone who is the protégé of an older, more experienced person is helped and guided by that person.

protein proteins

NOUN ⟨D&T⟩ Protein is a substance that is found in meat, eggs, and milk and that is needed by bodies for growth.

protest protests protesting protested

VERB **1** If you protest about something, you say or demonstrate publicly that you disagree with it E.G. *They protested against the killing of a teenager.* ▶ NOUN **2** a demonstration or statement showing that you disagree with something.

Protestant Protestants

NOUN OR ADJECTIVE ⟨HISTORY⟩ a member of one of the Christian Churches which separated from the Catholic Church in the sixteenth century.

protestation protestations

NOUN a strong declaration that something is true or not true E.G. *his protestations of love.*

protocol

NOUN Protocol is the system of rules about the correct way to behave in formal situations.

a
b
c
d
e
f
g
h
i
j
k
l
m
n
o
p
q
r
s
t
u
v
w
x
y
z

Plaice the fish has a glittering 'EYE' (I) (pla<u>i</u>ce)   **SPELLING NOTE**

proton protons
NOUN a particle which forms part of the nucleus of an atom and has a positive electrical charge.

prototype prototypes
NOUN a first model of something that is made so that the design can be tested and improved.

protracted
ADJECTIVE lasting longer than usual E.G. *a protracted dispute*.

protractor protractors
NOUN a flat, semicircular piece of plastic used for measuring angles.

protrude protrudes protruding protruded
VERB; FORMAL If something is protruding from a surface or edge, it is sticking out.
protrusion NOUN

proud prouder proudest
ADJECTIVE 1 feeling pleasure and satisfaction at something you own or have achieved E.G. *I was proud of our players today*. 2 having great dignity and self-respect E.G. *too proud to ask for money*.
proudly ADVERB

prove proves proving proved or proven
VERB 1 To prove that something is true is to provide evidence that it is definitely true E.G. *A letter from Kathleen proved that he lived there*. 2 If something proves to be the case, it becomes clear that it is so E.G. *His first impressions of her proved wrong*.
■ (sense 1) confirm, show, verify

proverb proverbs
NOUN a short sentence which gives advice or makes a comment about life.
proverbial ADJECTIVE

provide provides providing provided
VERB 1 If you provide something for someone, you give it to them or make it available for them. 2 If you provide for someone, you give them the things they need.
■ (sense 1) furnish, supply

provided or providing
CONJUNCTION If you say that something will happen provided something else happens, you mean that the first thing will happen only if the second thing does
☑ *Provided* is followed by *that*, but *providing* is not: *I'll come, providing he doesn't… You can go, provided that you phone as soon as you get there*.

providence
NOUN Providence is God or a force which is believed to arrange the things that happen to us.

province provinces
NOUN 1 one of the areas into which some large countries are divided, each province having its own administration. 2 You can refer to the parts of a country which are not near the capital as the provinces.
🏛 from Latin *provincia* meaning 'a conquered territory'

provincial
ADJECTIVE 1 connected with the parts of a country outside the capital E.G. *a provincial theatre*. 2 narrow-minded and lacking sophistication.

provision provisions
NOUN (GEOGRAPHY) 1 The provision of something is the act of making it available to people E.G. *the provision of health care*. ▶ PLURAL NOUN
2 Provisions are supplies of food.

provisional
ADJECTIVE A provisional arrangement has not yet been made definite and so might be changed.

proviso provisos
Said "prov-**eye**-zoh" NOUN a condition in an agreement.

provocation provocations
NOUN an act done deliberately to annoy someone.

provocative
ADJECTIVE 1 intended to annoy people or make them react E.G. *a provocative speech*. 2 intended to make someone feel sexual desire E.G. *provocative poses*.

provoke provokes provoking provoked
VERB 1 If you provoke someone, you deliberately try to make them angry. 2 If something provokes an unpleasant reaction, it causes it E.G. *illness provoked by tension or worry*.

prow prows
NOUN the front part of a boat.

prowess
NOUN Prowess is outstanding ability E.G. *his prowess at tennis*.

prowl prowls prowling prowled
VERB If a person or animal prowls around, they move around quietly and secretly, as if hunting.

proximity
NOUN; FORMAL Proximity is nearness to someone or something.

proxy
PHRASE If you do something **by proxy**, someone else does it on your behalf E.G. *voting by proxy*.

prude prudes
NOUN someone who is too easily shocked by sex or nudity.
prudish ADJECTIVE

🔲 from Old French *prode femme* meaning 'respectable woman'

prudent
ADJECTIVE behaving in a sensible and cautious way E.G. *It is prudent to plan ahead*.
prudence NOUN **prudently** ADVERB

prune prunes pruning pruned
NOUN 1 a dried plum. ▶ VERB 2 When someone prunes a tree or shrub, they cut back some of the branches.

pry pries prying pried
VERB If someone is prying, they are trying to find out about something secret or private.

PS
PS is written before an additional message at the end of a letter. PS is an abbreviation for 'postscript'.

psalm psalms
Said "**sahm**" NOUN one of the 150 songs, poems, and prayers which together form the Book of Psalms in the Bible.

pseudo-
Said "**syoo**-doh" PREFIX 'Pseudo-' is used to form adjectives and nouns indicating that something is not what it is claimed to be E.G. *pseudo-scientific theories*.
🔲 from Greek *pseudēs* meaning 'false'

pseudonym pseudonyms
Said "**syoo**-doe-nim" NOUN a name an author uses rather than their real name.

psyche psyches
Said "**sigh**-kee" NOUN your mind and your deepest feelings.

psychiatry
NOUN Psychiatry is the branch of

A
B
C
D
E
F
G
H
I
J
K
L
M
N
O
P
Q
R
S
T
U
V
W
X
Y
Z

medicine concerned with mental illness.

psychiatrist NOUN **psychiatric** ADJECTIVE

psychic
ADJECTIVE having unusual mental powers such as the ability to read people's minds or predict the future.

psychoanalysis
NOUN Psychoanalysis is the examination and treatment of someone who is mentally ill by encouraging them to talk about their feelings and past events in order to discover the cause of the illness.

psychoanalyst NOUN
psychoanalyse VERB

psychology
NOUN Psychology is the scientific study of the mind and of the reasons for people's behaviour.

psychological ADJECTIVE
psychologist NOUN

psychopath psychopaths
NOUN a mentally ill person who behaves violently without feeling guilt.

psychopathic ADJECTIVE

psychosis psychoses
Said "sigh-**koe**-siss" NOUN a severe mental illness.

psychotic ADJECTIVE

pterodactyl pterodactyls
Said "ter-rod-**dak**-til" NOUN
Pterodactyls were flying reptiles in prehistoric times.
📖 from Greek *pteron* meaning 'wing' and *daktulos* meaning 'finger'

PTO
PTO is an abbreviation for 'please turn over'. It is written at the bottom

of a page to indicate that the writing continues on the other side.

pub pubs
NOUN a building where people go to buy and drink alcoholic or soft drinks and talk with their friends.

puberty
Said "**pyoo**-ber-tee" NOUN Puberty is the stage when a person's body changes from that of a child into that of an adult.

pubic
Said "**pyoo**-bik" ADJECTIVE relating to the area around and above a person's genitals.

public
NOUN 1 You can refer to people in general as the public. ▶ ADJECTIVE
2 relating to people in general E.G. *There was some public support for the idea*. 3 provided for everyone to use, or open to anyone E.G. *public transport*.

publicly ADVERB

publican publicans
NOUN a person who owns or manages a pub.

publication publications
NOUN 1 The publication of a book is the act of printing it and making it available. 2 a book or magazine E.G. *medical publications*.

publicity
NOUN Publicity is information or advertisements about an item or event.

publicize publicizes publicizing publicized; also spelt **publicise**
VERB When someone publicizes a fact or event, they advertise it and make it widely known.

public school public schools
NOUN In Britain, a public school is a

school that is privately run and that charges fees for the pupils to attend.

public servant public servants

NOUN In Australia and New Zealand, someone who works in the public service.

public service

NOUN In Australia and New Zealand, the public service is the government departments responsible for the administration of the country.

publish publishes publishing published

VERB When a company publishes a book, newspaper, or magazine, they print copies of it and distribute it.

publishing NOUN

publisher publishers

NOUN (LIBRARY) The publisher of a book, newspaper or magazine is the person or company that prints copies of it and distributes it.

pudding puddings

NOUN 1 a sweet cake mixture cooked with fruit or other flavouring and served hot. 2 You can refer to the sweet course of a meal as the pudding.

puddle puddles

NOUN a small shallow pool of liquid.

puerile

Said "pyoo-rile" ADJECTIVE Puerile behaviour is silly and childish.

🏛 from Latin _puerilis_, from _puer_ meaning 'boy'

puff puffs puffing puffed

VERB 1 To puff a cigarette or pipe is to smoke it. 2 If you are puffing, you are breathing loudly and quickly with your mouth open. 3 If something puffs out or puffs up, it swells and

becomes larger and rounder. ➤ NOUN 4 a small amount of air or smoke that is released.

puffin puffins

NOUN a black and white sea bird with a large brightly coloured beak.

pug pugs

NOUN a small, short-haired dog with a flat nose.

puja

Said "poo-jah" NOUN Puja is a variety of practices which make up Hindu worship.

puke pukes puking puked

VERB; INFORMAL If someone pukes, they vomit.

pull pulls pulling pulled

VERB 1 When you pull something, you hold it and move it towards you. 2 When something is pulled by a vehicle or animal, it is attached to it and moves along behind it E.G. _Four oxen can pull a single plough_. 3 When you pull a curtain or blind, you move it so that it covers or uncovers the window. 4 If you pull a muscle, you injure it by stretching it too far or too quickly. 5 When a vehicle pulls away, pulls out, or pulls in, it moves in that direction. ➤ NOUN 6 The pull of something is its attraction or influence E.G. _the pull of the past_.

pull down VERB When a building is pulled down, it is deliberately destroyed.

pull out VERB If you pull out of something, you leave it or decide not to continue with it E.G. _The German government has pulled out of the project_.

pull through VERB When someone pulls through, they recover from a serious illness.

a b c d e f g h i j k l m n o **p** q r s t u v w x y z

A
B
C
D
E
F
G
H
I
J
K
L
M
N
O
P
Q
R
S
T
U
V
W
X
Y
Z

pulley pulleys
NOUN a device for lifting heavy weights. The weight is attached to a rope which passes over a wheel or series of wheels.

pullover pullovers
NOUN a woollen piece of clothing that covers the top part of your body.

pulmonary
ADJECTIVE; FORMAL relating to the lungs or to the veins and arteries carrying blood between the lungs and the heart.

pulp
NOUN If something is turned into a pulp, it is crushed until it is soft and moist.

pulpit pulpits
Said "pool-pit". NOUN the small raised platform in a church where a member of the clergy stands to preach.

pulse pulses pulsing pulsed
NOUN 1 Your pulse is the regular beating of blood through your body, the rate of which you can feel at your wrists and elsewhere. 2 The seeds of beans, peas, and lentils are called pulses when they are used for food. ▶ VERB 3 If something is pulsing, it is moving or vibrating with rhythmic, regular movements E.G. *She could feel the blood pulsing in her eardrums.*

puma pumas
Said "pyoo-mah" NOUN a wild animal belonging to the cat family.

pumice
Said "pum-miss" NOUN Pumice stone is very light-weight grey stone that can be used to soften areas of hard skin.

pummel pummels pummelling pummelled
VERB If you pummel something, you beat it with your fists.

pump pumps pumping pumped
NOUN 1 a machine that is used to force a liquid or gas to move in a particular direction. 2 Pumps are light shoes with flat soles which people wear for sport or leisure.
▶ VERB 3 To pump a liquid or gas somewhere is to force it to flow in that direction, using a pump. 4 If you pump money into something, you put a lot of money into it.

pumpkin pumpkins
NOUN a very large, round, orange vegetable.

pun puns
NOUN a clever and amusing use of words so that what you say has two different meanings, such as *my dog's a champion boxer.*

punch punches punching punched
VERB 1 If you punch someone, you hit them hard with your fist. ▶ NOUN 2 a hard blow with the fist. 3 a tool used for making holes. 4 Punch is a drink made from a mixture of wine, spirits, and fruit.

punctual
ADJECTIVE arriving at the correct time.
punctually ADVERB **punctuality** NOUN
▤ on time, prompt

punctuate punctuates punctuating punctuated
VERB 1 Something that is punctuated by a particular thing is interrupted by it at intervals E.G. *a grey day punctuated by bouts of rain.* 2 When you punctuate a piece of writing, you put punctuation into it.

punctuation

NOUN The marks in writing such as full stops, question marks, and commas are called punctuation or punctuation marks.

What does Punctuation do?

Punctuation marks are essential parts of written language. They help the reader to understand what is being read.
Look at the grammar boxes at **apostrophe**, **bracket**, **colon**, **comma**, **dash**, **exclamation mark**, **full stop**, **hyphen**, **inverted comma**, **question mark**, and **semicolon**.

puncture punctures puncturing punctured

NOUN 1 If a tyre has a puncture, a small hole has been made in it and it has become flat. ▶ VERB 2 To puncture something is to make a small hole in it.

pungent

ADJECTIVE having a strong, unpleasant smell or taste.

pungency NOUN

punish punishes punishing punished

VERB To punish someone who has done something wrong is to make them suffer because of it.

◼ chastise, discipline, penalize

punishment punishments

NOUN something unpleasant done to someone because they have done something wrong.

punitive

Said "**pyoo**-nit-tiv" ADJECTIVE harsh and intended to punish people E.G. *punitive military action*.

Punjabi Punjabis

Said "pun-**jah**-bee" ADJECTIVE
1 belonging or relating to the Punjab, a state in north-western India. ▶ NOUN 2 someone who comes from the Punjab. 3 Punjabi is a language spoken in the Punjab.

punk

NOUN Punk or punk rock is an aggressive style of rock music.

punt punts

NOUN a long, flat-bottomed boat. You move it along by pushing a pole against the river bottom.

puny punier puniest

ADJECTIVE very small and weak.

pup pups

NOUN a young dog. Some other young animals such as seals are also called pups.

pupil pupils

NOUN 1 The pupils at a school are the children who go there. 2 Your pupils are the small, round, black holes in the centre of your eyes.

puppet puppets

NOUN a doll or toy animal that is moved by pulling strings or by putting your hand inside its body.

puppy puppies

NOUN a young dog.

purchase purchases purchasing purchased

VERB 1 When you purchase something, you buy it. ▶ NOUN 2 something you have bought.

purchaser NOUN

pure purer purest

ADJECTIVE 1 Something that is pure is not mixed with anything else E.G. *pure wool… pure white*. 2 Pure also means clean and free from harmful substances E.G. *The water is pure*

a
b
c
d
e
f
g
h
i
j
k
l
m
n
o
p
q
r
s
t
u
v
w
x
y
z

A B C D E F G H I J K L M N O P Q R S T U V W X Y Z

enough to drink. **3** People who are pure have not done anything considered to be sinful. **4** Pure also means complete and total E.G. *a matter of pure luck.*

purity NOUN
■ (sense 2) clean, uncontaminated
■ (sense 3) chaste, innocent, virtuous

purée purées
Said "pyoo-ray" NOUN a food which has been mashed or blended to a thick, smooth consistency.

purely
ADVERB involving only one feature and not including anything else E.G. *purely professional.*

Purgatory
NOUN Roman Catholics believe that Purgatory is a place where spirits of the dead are sent to suffer for their sins before going to Heaven.

purge purges purging purged
VERB To purge something is to remove undesirable things from it E.G. *to purge the country of criminals.*

purify purifies purifying purified
VERB To purify something is to remove all dirty or harmful substances from it.

purification NOUN

purist purists
NOUN someone who believes that something should be done in a particular, correct way E.G. *a football purist.*

puritan puritans
NOUN someone who believes in strict moral principles and avoids physical pleasures.

puritanical ADJECTIVE

purple
NOUN or ADJECTIVE reddish-blue.

purport purports purporting purported
Said "pur-port" VERB; FORMAL Something that purports to be or have a particular thing is claimed to be or have it E.G. *a country which purports to disapprove of smokers.*

purpose purposes
NOUN **1** The purpose of something is the reason for it E.G. *the purpose of the meeting.* **2** If you have a particular purpose, this is what you want to achieve E.G. *To make music is my purpose in life.* ▶ PHRASE **3** If you do something **on purpose**, you do it deliberately.

purposely ADVERB **purposeful** ADJECTIVE

purr purrs purring purred
VERB When a cat purrs, it makes a low vibrating sound because it is contented.

purse purses pursing pursed
NOUN **1** a small leather or fabric container for carrying money. ▶ VERB **2** If you purse your lips, you move them into a tight, rounded shape.

purser pursers
NOUN the officer responsible for the paperwork and the welfare of passengers on a ship.

pursue pursues pursuing pursued
VERB **1** If you pursue an activity or plan, you do it or make efforts to achieve it E.G. *I decided to pursue a career in photography.* **2** If you pursue someone, you follow them to try to catch them.

pursuer NOUN **pursuit** NOUN

purveyor purveyors
NOUN; FORMAL A purveyor of goods or

services is a person who sells them or provides them.

pus

NOUN Pus is a thick yellowish liquid that forms in an infected wound.

push pushes pushing pushed

VERB **1** When you push something, you press it using force in order to move it. **2** If you push someone into doing something, you force or persuade them to do it E.G. *His mother pushed him into auditioning for a part.* **3** INFORMAL Someone who pushes drugs sells them illegally.

◼ (sense 1) shove, thrust

push off VERB; INFORMAL If you tell someone to push off, you are telling them rudely to go away.

pushchair pushchairs

NOUN a small folding chair on wheels in which a baby or toddler can be wheeled around.

pusher pushers

NOUN; INFORMAL someone who sells illegal drugs.

pushing

PREPOSITION Someone who is pushing a particular age is nearly that age E.G. *pushing sixty.*

pushover

NOUN INFORMAL **1** something that is easy. **2** someone who is easily persuaded or defeated.

pushy pushier pushiest

ADJECTIVE; INFORMAL behaving in a forceful and determined way.

pussy pussies

NOUN; INFORMAL a cat.

put puts putting put

VERB **1** When you put something somewhere, you move it into that place or position. **2** If you put an idea or remark in a particular way, you

express it that way E.G. *I think you've put that very well.* **3** To put someone or something in a particular state or situation means to cause them to be in it E.G. *It puts us both in an awkward position.* **4** You can use 'put' to express an estimate of the size or importance of something E.G. *Her wealth is now put at 290 million.*

◼ (sense 1) place, position, set

put down VERB **1** To put someone down is to criticize them and make them appear foolish. **2** If an animal is put down, it is killed because it is very ill or dangerous.

put off VERB **1** If you put something off, you delay doing it. **2** To put someone off is to discourage them.

put out VERB **1** If you put a fire out or put the light out, you make it stop burning or shining. **2** If you are put out, you are annoyed or upset.

put up VERB **1** If you put up resistance to something, you argue or fight against it E.G. *She put up a tremendous struggle.* **2** If you put up with something, you tolerate it even though you disagree with it or dislike it.

putt putts

NOUN In golf, a putt is a gentle stroke made when the ball is near the hole.

putting

NOUN Putting is a game played on a small grass course with no obstacles. You hit a ball gently with a club so that it rolls towards one of a series of holes around the course.

putty

NOUN Putty is a paste used to fix panes of glass into frames.

puzzle puzzles puzzling puzzled

VERB **1** If something puzzles you, it confuses you and you do not

a
b
c
d
e
f
g
h
i
j
k
l
m
n
o
p
q
r
s
t
u
v
w
x
y
z

there's SAND in my SANDwich (<u>sand</u>wich)   SPELLING NOTE

A
B
C
D
E
F
G
H
I
J
K
L
M
N
O
P
Q
R
S
T
U
V
W
X
Y
Z

understand it E.G. *There was something about her that puzzled me.*
▶ NOUN **2** A puzzle is a game or question that requires a lot of thought to complete or solve.
puzzled ADJECTIVE **puzzlement** NOUN
■ (sense 1) baffle, mystify, perplex

PVC
NOUN PVC is a plastic used for making clothing, pipes, and many other things. PVC is an abbreviation for 'polyvinyl chloride'.

pygmy pygmies
Said "pig-mee"; also spelt **pigmy**
NOUN a very small person, especially one who belongs to a racial group in which all the people are small.
🔲 from Greek *pugmaios* meaning 'undersized'

pyjamas
PLURAL NOUN Pyjamas are loose trousers and a jacket or top that you

wear in bed.
🔲 from Persian *pay jama* meaning 'leg clothing'

pylon pylons
NOUN a very tall metal structure which carries overhead electricity cables.

pyramid pyramids
NOUN **1** a three-dimensional shape with a flat base and flat triangular sides sloping upwards to a point.
2 The Pyramids are ancient stone structures built over the tombs of Egyptian kings and queens.

pyre pyres
NOUN a high pile of wood on which a dead body or religious offering is burned.

python pythons
NOUN a large snake that kills animals by squeezing them with its body.
🔲 from Greek *Puthon*, a huge mythical serpent

Q q

quack quacks quacking quacked
VERB When a duck quacks, it makes a
loud harsh sound.

quad quads
Said "kwod" NOUN Quad is the same as
quadruplet.

quadrangle quadrangles
Said "kwod-rang-gl" NOUN a courtyard
with buildings all round it.

quadri-
PREFIX 'Quadri-' means 'four'.
🔤 a Latin word

quadriceps
NOUN (PE) a large muscle in four
parts at the front of your thigh.

quadrilateral quadrilaterals
Said "kwod-rll-lat-ral" NOUN (MATHS) a
shape with four straight sides.

quadruped quadrupeds
Said "kwod-roo-ped" NOUN any animal
with four legs.

quadruple quadruples
quadrupling quadrupled
Said "kwod-roo-pl" VERB When an
amount or number quadruples, it
becomes four times as large as it
was.

quadruplet quadruplets
Said "kwod-roo-plet" NOUN
Quadruplets are four children born
at the same time to the same
mother.

quagmire quagmires
Said "kwag-mire" NOUN a soft, wet area
of land which you sink into if you
walk on it.

quail quails quailing quailed
NOUN 1 a type of small game bird with
a round body and short tail. ▶ VERB 2 If
you quail, you feel or look afraid.

quaint quainter quaintest
ADJECTIVE attractively old-fashioned or
unusual E.G. *quaint customs.*
quaintly ADVERB

quake quakes quaking quaked
VERB If you quake, you shake and
tremble because you are very
frightened.

Quaker Quakers
NOUN a member of a Christian group,
the Society of Friends.

qualification qualifications
NOUN 1 Your qualifications are your
skills and achievements, especially as
officially recognized at the end of a
course of training or study.
2 something you add to a statement
to make it less strong E.G. *It is a good
novel and yet cannot be
recommended without qualification.*

qualify qualifies qualifying
qualified
VERB 1 (PE) When you qualify, you
pass the examinations or tests that
you need to pass to do a particular
job or to take part in a sporting
event. 2 If you qualify a statement,
you add a detail or explanation to
make it less strong E.G. *I would
qualify that by putting it into context.*
3 If you qualify for something, you
become entitled to have it E.G. *You
qualify for a discount.*
qualified ADJECTIVE

quality qualities
NOUN 1 The quality of something is
how good it is E.G. *The quality of food
is very poor.* 2 a characteristic E.G.
These qualities are essential for success.

qualm qualms
Said "kwahm" NOUN If you have

a
b
c
d
e
f
g
h
i
j
k
l
m
n
o
p
q
r
s
t
u
v
w
x
y
z

Eddy Ant thinks mEAt is a grEAt trEAt to EAt (-ea-) **SPELLING NOTE**

qualms about what you are doing, you worry that it might not be right.

quandary quandaries
Said "kwon-dree" NOUN If you are in a quandary, you cannot decide what to do.

quango quangos
NOUN a body responsible for a particular area of public administration, which is financed by the government but is outside direct government control. Quango is short for quasi-autonomous non-governmental organization.

quantity quantities
NOUN 1 an amount you can measure or count E.G. *a small quantity of alcohol*. 2 Quantity is the amount of something that there is E.G. *emphasis on quantity rather than quality*.

quarantine
Said "kwor-an-teen" NOUN If an animal is in quarantine, it is kept away from other animals for a time because it might have an infectious disease.
📖 from Italian *quarantina* meaning 'forty days'

quarrel quarrels quarrelling quarrelled
NOUN 1 an angry argument. ▶ VERB 2 If people quarrel, they have an angry argument.
☰ (sense 1) argument, disagreement, fight
☰ (sense 2) argue, disagree, fall out

quarry quarries quarrying quarried
Said "kwor-ree" NOUN 1 a place where stone is removed from the ground by digging or blasting. 2 A person's or animal's quarry is the animal that they are hunting. ▶ VERB 3 To quarry stone means to remove it from a quarry by digging or blasting.

📖 sense 2 is from Middle English *quirre* meaning 'entrails given to the hounds to eat'

quart quarts
Said "kwort" NOUN a unit of liquid volume equal to two pints or about 1.136 litres.

quarter quarters
NOUN 1 one of four equal parts. 2 an American coin worth 25 cents. 3 You can refer to a particular area in a city as a quarter E.G. *the French quarter*. 4 You can use 'quarter' to refer vaguely to a particular person or group of people E.G. *You are very popular in certain quarters*. ▶ PLURAL NOUN 5 A soldier's or a servant's quarters are the rooms that they live in.

quarterly quarterlies
ADJECTIVE OR ADVERB 1 Quarterly means happening regularly every three months E.G. *my quarterly report*.
▶ NOUN 2 a magazine or journal published every three months.

quartet quartets
Said "kwor-tet" NOUN a group of four musicians who sing or play together; also a piece of music written for four instruments or singers.

quartz
NOUN Quartz is a kind of hard, shiny crystal used in making very accurate watches and clocks.

quash quashes quashing quashed
Said "kwosh" VERB To quash a decision or judgment means to reject it officially E.G. *The judges quashed their convictions*.

quasi-
Said "kway-sie" PREFIX Quasi- means resembling something but not

actually being that thing E.G. *a quasi-religious order.*

📖 a Latin word meaning 'as if'

quaver quavers quavering quavered

Said "kway-ver" VERB 1 If your voice quavers, it sounds unsteady, usually because you are nervous. NOUN 2 (MUSIC) a musical note (♪) that has a time value of an eighth of a semibreve. In the United States and Canada, a quaver is known as an eighth note.

quay quays

Said "kee" NOUN a place where boats are tied up and loaded or unloaded.

queasy queasier queasiest

Said "kwee-zee" ADJECTIVE feeling slightly sick.

queen queens

NOUN 1 a female monarch or a woman married to a king. 2 a female bee or ant which can lay eggs. 3 In chess, the queen is the most powerful piece, which can move in any direction. 4 In a pack of cards, a queen is a card with a picture of a queen on it.

queen mother queen mothers

NOUN the widow of a king and the mother of the reigning monarch.

queer queerer queerest

ADJECTIVE Queer means very strange.

quell quells quelling quelled

VERB 1 To quell a rebellion or riot means to put an end to it by using force. 2 If you quell a feeling such as fear or grief, you stop yourself from feeling it E.G. *trying to quell the loneliness.*

quench quenches quenching quenched

VERB If you quench your thirst, you have a drink so that you are no longer thirsty.

query queries querying queried

Said "qweer-ree" NOUN 1 a question.
▶ VERB 2 If you query something, you ask about it because you think it might not be right E.G. *No-one queried my decision.*

quest quests

NOUN a long search for something.

question questions questioning questioned

NOUN 1 a sentence which asks for information. 2 If there is some question about something, there is doubt about it. 3 a problem that needs to be discussed E.G. *Can we get back to the question of the car?*
▶ VERB 4 If you question someone, you ask them questions. 5 If you question something, you express doubts about it E.G. *He never stopped questioning his own beliefs.* ▶ PHRASE 6 If something is **out of the question**, it is impossible.

🔲 (sense 1) inquiry, query
🔲 (sense 5) challenge, dispute

What is a Question?

Questions are used to ask for information.
A question has a question mark at the end of the sentence:
  E.G. *What is your name?*
Questions are often introduced by a questioning word such as *what, who, where, when, why,* or *how*:
  E.G. ***Where** do you live?*
If a sentence does not already contain an auxiliary verb, a form of the auxiliary verb *do* may be placed at the start to turn it into a question:
  E.G. ***Does** Anna have a sister?*

CONTINUED ON NEXT PAGE →

---

a b c d e f g h i j k l m n o p **q** r s t u v w x y z

the QUeen stood on the QUay (**qu**ay)   **SPELLING NOTE**

A B C D E F G H I J K L M N O P Q R S T U V W X Y Z

If there is already an auxiliary verb in the sentence, you can turn it into a question by reversing the word order so the auxiliary verb comes before the subject instead of after it:

E.G. **Are** you going to the swimming baths?
Must they keep doing that?

A question can also be made by adding a phrase, such as *isn't it?* or *don't you?*, on to the end of a statement:

E.G. It is hot today, **isn't it?**
You like chocolate, **don't you?**

questionable

ADJECTIVE possibly not true or not honest.

question mark question marks

NOUN the punctuation mark (?) which is used at the end of a question.

What does the Question Mark do?

The **question mark** (?) marks the end of a question:

E.G. *When is the train leaving?*

After an indirect question or a polite request, a full stop is used rather than a question mark:

E.G. *Anna asked when the train was leaving.*
Will you please send me an application form.

questionnaire questionnaires

NOUN (MATHS) a list of questions which asks for information for a survey.

queue queues queuing or queueing queued

Said "kyoo" NOUN 1 a line of people or vehicles waiting for something. ▶ VERB 2 When people queue, they stand in a line waiting for something.

quibble quibbles quibbling quibbled

VERB 1 If you quibble, you argue about something unimportant. ▶ NOUN 2 a minor objection.

quiche quiches

Said "keesh" NOUN a tart with a savoury filling.

📖 a French word, originally from German *Kuchen* meaning 'cake'

quick quicker quickest

ADJECTIVE 1 moving with great speed. 2 lasting only a short time E.G. *a quick chat.* 3 happening without any delay E.G. *a quick response.* 4 intelligent and able to understand things easily.

quickly ADVERB

quicksand quicksands

NOUN an area of deep wet sand that you sink into if you walk on it.

quid

NOUN; INFORMAL In British English, a pound in money.

quiet quieter quietest

ADJECTIVE 1 Someone or something that is quiet makes very little noise or no noise at all. 2 Quiet also means peaceful E.G. *a quiet evening at home.* 3 A quiet event happens with very little fuss or publicity E.G. *a quiet wedding.* ▶ NOUN 4 Quiet is silence.

quietly ADVERB

☑ Do not confuse the spellings of *quiet* and the adverb *quite*.

quieten quietens quietening quietened

VERB To quieten someone means to make them become quiet.

quill quills

NOUN 1 a pen made from a feather. 2 A bird's quills are the large feathers on its wings and tail. 3 A porcupine's quills are its spines.

quilt quilts

NOUN A quilt for a bed is a cover, especially a cover that is padded.

quilted

ADJECTIVE Quilted clothes or coverings are made of thick layers of material sewn together.

quin quins

NOUN Quin is the same as **quintuplet**.

quince quinces

NOUN an acid-tasting fruit used for making jam and marmalade.

quintessential

ADJECTIVE; FORMAL A person or thing that is quintessential seems to represent the basic nature of something in a pure, concentrated form E.G. *It was the quintessential Hollywood party.*

quintet quintets

Said "kwin-**tet**" NOUN a group of five musicians who sing or play together; also a piece of music written for five instruments or singers.

quintuplet quintuplets

Said "kwin-**tyoo**-plit" NOUN Quintuplets are five children born at the same time to the same mother.

quip quips quipping quipped

NOUN 1 an amusing or clever remark. ▶ VERB 2 To quip means to make an amusing or clever remark.

quirk quirks

NOUN 1 an odd habit or characteristic

E.G. *an interesting quirk of human nature.* 2 an unexpected event or development E.G. *a quirk of fate.*

quirky ADJECTIVE

quit quits quitting quit

VERB If you quit something, you leave it or stop doing it E.G. *Leigh quit his job as a salesman.*

quite

ADVERB 1 fairly but not very E.G. *quite old.* 2 completely E.G. *Jane lay quite still.* ▶ PHRASE 3 You use **quite a** to emphasize that something is large or impressive E.G. *It was quite a party.*

☑ You should be careful about using *quite*. It can mean 'completely': *quite amazing.* It can also mean 'fairly but not very': *quite friendly.* Do not confuse the spellings of *quite* and the adjective *quiet*.

quiver quivers quivering quivered

VERB 1 If something quivers, it trembles. ▶ NOUN 2 a trembling movement E.G. *a quiver of panic.*

quiz quizzes quizzing quizzed

NOUN 1 a game in which the competitors are asked questions to test their knowledge. ▶ VERB 2 If you quiz someone, you question them closely about something.

quizzical

Said "**kwiz**-ik-kl" ADJECTIVE amused and questioning E.G. *a quizzical smile.*

quota quotas

NOUN a number or quantity of something which is officially allowed E.G. *a quota of three foreign players allowed in each team.*

quotation quotations

NOUN an extract from a book or speech which is quoted.

→ SEE BOX ON NEXT PAGE

a
b
c
d
e
f
g
h
i
j
k
l
m
n
o
p
q
r
s
t
u
v
w
x
y
z

an ELegant angEL (ang**e**l)   SPELLING NOTE

A
B
C
D
E
F
G
H
I
J
K
L
M
N
O
P
Q
R
S
T
U
V
W
X
Y
Z

What is a Quotation?

There are two ways of writing what people say. You can write down the exact words that are spoken. This is called **direct speech**. The second way is to write down the meaning of what they say without using the exact words. This is called **indirect speech** or **reported speech**.

When you use direct speech, the exact words spoken go into quotation marks:

E.G. *Robbie said,* **"Thank you very much for the prize."**

The sentence will contain a main verb which indicates speaking, such as *say, tell, ask,* or *answer.* The words contained in quotation marks begin with a capital letter. If there is no other punctuation, they are separated from the rest of the sentence by a comma:

E.G. *"This is the best picture," said the judge.*

When you use indirect or reported speech, there is a subordinate clause which reports the meaning of what was said.

E.G. *The judge said* **that Robbie's picture was the best**.

When the reported words are a statement, the clause that reports them is usually introduced by *that*. The main clause usually contains a verb such as *say, tell, explain,* or *reply*:

E.G. *The judge said* **that Robbie should win first prize.**

Sometimes the word *that* can be left out.

E.G. *The judge said Robbie should win first prize.*

quote quotes quoting quoted
VERB **1** If you quote something that someone has written or said, you repeat their exact words. **2** If you quote a fact, you state it because it supports what you are saying. ▶ NOUN **3** an extract from a book or speech. **4** an estimate of how much a piece of work will cost.

Qur'an
another spelling of **Koran**.

Rr

a
b
c
d
e
f
g
h
i
j
k
l
m
n
o
p
q
r
s
t
u
v
w
x
y
z

TIP Some words which sound as if they should begin with letter *r* are spelt with *wr*, for example *wrangle, wretch, write* and *wrong*. Other words which sound as if they ought to begin with letter *r* alone are actually spelt with *rh*, for example *rhapsody, rheumatism, rhino* and *rhododendron*.

RAAF
In Australia, an abbreviation for 'Royal Australian Air Force'.

rabbi rabbis
Said "rab-by" NOUN a Jewish religious leader.
📖 from Hebrew *rabh* + *-i* meaning 'my master'

rabbit rabbits
NOUN a small animal with long ears.

rabble
NOUN a noisy, disorderly crowd.

rabid
ADJECTIVE 1 used to describe someone with strong views that you do not approve of E.G. *a rabid Nazi.* 2 A rabid dog or other animal has rabies.

rabies
Said "ray-beez" NOUN an infectious disease which causes people and animals, especially dogs, to go mad and die.

raccoon raccoons; also spelt **racoon**
NOUN a small North American animal with a long striped tail.

race races racing raced
NOUN 1 a competition to see who is fastest, for example in running or driving. 2 one of the major groups that human beings can be divided into according to their physical features. ► VERB 3 If you race someone, you compete with them in a race. 4 If you race something or if it races, it goes at its greatest rate E.G. *Her heart raced uncontrollably.* 5 If you race somewhere, you go there as quickly as possible E.G. *The hares raced away out of sight.*
racing NOUN

racecourse racecourses
NOUN a grass track, sometimes with jumps, along which horses race.

racehorse racehorses
NOUN a horse trained to run in races.

racial
ADJECTIVE relating to the different races that people belong to E.G. *racial harmony.*
racially ADVERB

racism or **racialism**
NOUN (PSHE) Racism or racialism is the treatment of some people as inferior because of their race.
racist NOUN or ADJECTIVE

rack racks racking racked
NOUN 1 a piece of equipment for holding things or hanging things on. ► VERB 2 If you are racked by something, you suffer because of it E.G. *She was racked by guilt.* ► AN INFORMAL PHRASE 3 If you **rack your brains**, you try hard to think of or remember something.

racket rackets
NOUN 1 If someone is making a racket, they are making a lot of noise. 2 an illegal way of making money E.G. *a*

drugs racket. **3** Racket is another spelling of **racquet**.

racquet racquets; also spelt **racket**
NOUN a bat with strings across it used in tennis and similar games.
🔲 from Arabic *rahat* meaning 'palm of the hand'

radar
NOUN Radar is equipment used to track ships or aircraft that are out of sight by using radio signals that are reflected back from the object and shown on a screen.
🔲 from *RA(dio) D(etecting) A(nd) R(anging)*

radiant
ADJECTIVE **1** Someone who is radiant is so happy that it shows in their face. **2** glowing brightly.
radiance NOUN

radiate radiates radiating radiated
VERB **1** If things radiate from a place, they form a pattern like lines spreading out from the centre of a circle. **2** If you radiate a quality or emotion, it shows clearly in your face and behaviour E.G. *He radiated health*.

radiation
NOUN the stream of particles given out by a radioactive substance.

radiator radiators
NOUN **1** a hollow metal device for heating a room, usually connected to a central heating system. **2** the part of a car that is filled with water to cool the engine.

radical radicals
NOUN **1** Radicals are people who think there should be great changes in society, and try to make them

happen. ► ADJECTIVE **2** very significant, important, or basic E.G. *a radical change in the law*.
radically ADVERB **radicalism** NOUN

radii
the plural of **radius**.

radio radios radioing radioed
NOUN **1** Radio is a system of sending sound over a distance by transmitting electrical signals. **2** Radio is also the broadcasting of programmes to the public by radio. **3** a piece of equipment for listening to radio programmes. ► VERB **4** To radio someone means to send them a message by radio E.G. *The pilot radioed that a fire had started*.

radioactive
ADJECTIVE giving off powerful and harmful rays.
radioactivity NOUN

radiotherapy
NOUN the treatment of diseases such as cancer using radiation.
radiotherapist NOUN

radish radishes
NOUN a small salad vegetable with a red skin and white flesh and a hot taste.

radium
NOUN a radioactive element which is used in the treatment of cancer.

radius radii
NOUN (MATHS) The radius of a circle is the length of a straight line drawn from its centre to its circumference.

RAF
In Britain, an abbreviation for 'Royal Air Force'.

raffia
NOUN a material made from palm leaves and used for making mats and baskets.

A B C D E F G H I J K L M N O P Q R S T U V W X Y Z

raffle raffles
NOUN a competition in which people buy numbered tickets and win a prize if they have the ticket that is chosen.

raft rafts
NOUN a floating platform made from long pieces of wood tied together.

rafter rafters
NOUN Rafters are the sloping pieces of wood that support a roof.

rag rags
NOUN 1 a piece of old cloth used to clean or wipe things. 2 If someone is dressed in rags, they are wearing old torn clothes.

rage rages raging raged
NOUN 1 Rage is great anger. ▶ VERB 2 To rage about something means to speak angrily about it. 3 If something such as a storm or battle is raging, it is continuing with great force or violence E.G. *The fire still raged out of control.*
■ (sense 1) anger, fury, wrath

ragged
ADJECTIVE Ragged clothes are old and torn.

raid raids raiding raided
VERB 1 To raid a place means to enter it by force to attack it or steal something. ▶ NOUN 2 the raiding of a building or a place E.G. *an armed raid on a bank.*

rail rails
NOUN 1 a fixed horizontal bar used as a support or for hanging things on. 2 Rails are the steel bars which trains run along. 3 Rail is the railway considered as a means of transport E.G. *I plan to go by rail.*

railing railings
NOUN Railings are a fence made from metal bars.

railway railways
NOUN a route along which trains travel on steel rails.

rain rains raining rained
NOUN 1 water falling from the clouds in small drops. ▶ VERB 2 When it is raining, rain is falling.
rainy ADJECTIVE

rainbird rainbirds
NOUN a bird whose call is believed to be a sign that it will rain.

rainbow rainbows
NOUN an arch of different colours that sometimes appears in the sky after it has been raining.

raincoat raincoats
NOUN a waterproof coat.

rainfall
NOUN the amount of rain that falls in a place during a particular period.

rainforest rainforests
NOUN a dense forest of tall trees in a tropical area where there is a lot of rain.

rainwater
NOUN rain that has been stored.

raise raises raising raised
VERB 1 If you raise something, you make it higher E.G. *She went to the window and raised the blinds… a drive to raise standards of literacy.* 2 If you raise your voice, you speak more loudly. 3 To raise money for a cause means to get people to donate money towards it. 4 To raise a child means to look after it until it is grown up. 5 If you raise a subject, you mention it.

raisin raisins
NOUN Raisins are dried grapes.

rake rakes raking raked
NOUN a garden tool with a row of

a
b
c
d
e
f
g
h
i
j
k
l
m
n
o
p
q
r
s
t
u
v
w
x
y
z

A
B
C
D
E
F
G
H
I
J
K
L
M
N
O
P
Q
R
S
T
U
V
W
X
Y
Z

metal teeth and a long handle.

rake up VERB If you rake up something embarrassing from the past, you remind someone about it.

rally rallies rallying rallied
NOUN 1 a large public meeting held to show support for something. 2 a competition in which vehicles are raced over public roads. 3 In tennis or squash, a rally is a continuous series of shots exchanged by the players. ▶ VERB 4 When people rally to something, they gather together to continue a struggle or to support something.

ram rams ramming rammed
VERB 1 If one vehicle rams another, it crashes into it. 2 To ram something somewhere means to push it there firmly E.G. *He rammed his key into the lock.* ▶ NOUN 3 an adult male sheep.

RAM
NOUN In computing, RAM is a storage space which can be filled with data but which loses its contents when the machine is switched off. RAM stands for 'random access memory'.

Ramadan
NOUN the ninth month of the Muslim year, during which Muslims eat and drink nothing during daylight.
📖 from Arabic *Ramadan* meaning literally 'the hot month'

ramble rambles rambling rambled
NOUN 1 a long walk in the countryside. ▶ VERB 2 To ramble means to go for a ramble. 3 To ramble also means to talk in a confused way E.G. *He then started rambling and repeating himself.*

rambler NOUN

ramification ramifications
NOUN The ramifications of a decision or plan are all its consequences and effects.

ramp ramps
NOUN a sloping surface connecting two different levels.

rampage rampages rampaging rampaged
VERB 1 To rampage means to rush about wildly causing damage.
▶ PHRASE 2 To **go on the rampage** means to rush about in a wild or violent way.
▤ (sense 1) go berserk, run amok

rampant
ADJECTIVE If something such as crime or disease is rampant, it is growing or spreading uncontrollably.

rampart ramparts
NOUN Ramparts are earth banks, often with a wall on top, built to protect a castle or city.

ramshackle
ADJECTIVE A ramshackle building is in very poor condition.

ranch ranches
NOUN a large farm where cattle or horses are reared, especially in the USA.
📖 from Mexican Spanish *rancho* meaning 'small farm'

rancid
Said "ran-sid" ADJECTIVE Rancid food has gone bad.
📖 from Latin *rancere* meaning 'to stink'

rancour
Said "rang-kur" NOUN; FORMAL Rancour is bitter hatred.

rancorous ADJECTIVE

rand
NOUN The rand is the main unit of currency in South Africa.

random

ADJECTIVE **1** A random choice or arrangement is not based on any definite plan. ▶ PHRASE **2** If you do something **at random**, you do it without any definite plan E.G. *He chose his victims at random.*
randomly ADVERB
■ (sense 1) chance, haphazard, incidental

range ranges ranging ranged

NOUN **1** The range of something is the maximum distance over which it can reach things or detect things E.G. *This mortar has a range of 15,000 metres.* **2** a number of different things of the same kind E.G. *A wide range of colours are available.* **3** a set of values on a scale E.G. *The average age range is between 35 and 55.* **4** A range of mountains is a line of them. **5** A rifle range or firing range is a place where people practise shooting at targets. ▶ VERB **6** When a set of things ranges between two points, they vary within these points on a scale E.G. *prices ranging between 370 and 1200 pounds.*
■ (sense 2) series, variety

ranger rangers

NOUN someone whose job is to look after a forest or park.

rank ranks ranking ranked

NOUN **1** Someone's rank is their official level in a job or profession. **2** The ranks are the ordinary members of the armed forces, rather than the officers. **3** The ranks of a group are its members E.G. *We welcomed five new members to our ranks.* **4** a row of people or things. ▶ VERB **5** To rank as something means to have that status or position on a scale E.G. *His dismissal ranks as the worst*

humiliation he has ever known.
▶ ADJECTIVE **6** complete and absolute E.G. *rank stupidity.* **7** having a strong, unpleasant smell E.G. *the rank smell of unwashed clothes.*

ransack ransacks ransacking ransacked

VERB To ransack a place means to disturb everything and leave it in a mess, in order to search for or steal something.
🔳 from Old Norse *rann* meaning 'house' and *saka* meaning 'to search'

ransom ransoms

NOUN money that is demanded to free someone who has been kidnapped.

rant rants ranting ranted

VERB To rant means to talk loudly in an excited or angry way.

rap raps rapping rapped

VERB **1** If you rap something, you hit it with a series of quick blows. ▶ NOUN **2** a quick knock or blow on something E.G. *A rap on the door signalled his arrival.* **3** Rap is a style of poetry spoken to music with a strong rhythmic beat.

rape rapes raping raped

VERB **1** If a man rapes a woman, he violently forces her to have sex with him against her will. ▶ NOUN **2** Rape is the act or crime of raping a woman E.G. *victims of rape.* **3** Rape is a plant with yellow flowers that is grown as a crop for oil and fodder.
rapist NOUN

rapid rapids

ADJECTIVE **1** happening or moving very quickly E.G. *rapid industrial expansion… He took a few rapid steps.*
▶ PLURAL NOUN **2** An area of a river where the water moves extremely

a
b
c
d
e
f
g
h
i
j
k
l
m
n
o
p
q
r
s
t
u
v
w
x
y
z

A
B
C
D
E
F
G
H
I
J
K
L
M
N
O
P
Q
R
S
T
U
V
W
X
Y
Z

fast over rocks is referred to as rapids.
rapidly ADVERB **rapidity** NOUN

rapier rapiers
NOUN a long thin sword with a sharp point.

rapport
Said "rap-*por*" NOUN; FORMAL If there is a rapport between two people, they find it easy to understand each other's feelings and attitudes.

rapt
ADJECTIVE If you are rapt, you are so interested in something that you are not aware of other things E.G. *sitting with rapt attention in front of the screen.*

rapture
NOUN Rapture is a feeling of extreme delight.
rapturous ADJECTIVE **rapturously** ADVERB

rare rarer rarest
ADJECTIVE 1 Something that is rare is not common or does not happen often E.G. *a rare flower… Such major disruptions are rare.* 2 Rare meat has been lightly cooked.
rarely ADVERB

rarefied
Said "rare-*if-eyed*" ADJECTIVE seeming to have little connection with ordinary life E.G. *He grew up in a rarefied literary atmosphere.*

raring
ADJECTIVE If you are raring to do something, you are very eager to do it.

rarity rarities
NOUN 1 something that is interesting or valuable because it is unusual. 2 The rarity of something is the fact that it is not common.

rascal rascals
NOUN If you refer to someone as a

rascal, you mean that they do bad or mischievous things.

rash rashes
ADJECTIVE 1 If you are rash, you do something hasty and foolish. ▶ NOUN 2 an area of red spots that appear on your skin when you are ill or have an allergy. 3 A rash of events is a lot of them happening in a short time E.G. *a rash of strikes.*
rashly ADVERB
■ (sense 1) foolhardy, reckless

rasher rashers
NOUN a thin slice of bacon.

rasp rasps rasping rasped
VERB 1 To rasp means to make a harsh unpleasant sound. ▶ NOUN 2 a coarse file with rows of raised teeth, used for smoothing wood or metal.

raspberry raspberries
NOUN a small soft red fruit that grows on a bush.

rat rats
NOUN a long-tailed animal which looks like a large mouse.

rate rates rating rated
NOUN 1 The rate of something is the speed or frequency with which it happens E.G. *New diet books appear at the rate of nearly one a week.* 2 The rate of interest is its level E.G. *a further cut in interest rates.* 3 Rates are a local tax paid by people who own buildings. ▶ PHRASE 4 If you say **at this rate** something will happen, you mean it will happen if things continue in the same way E.G. *At this rate we'll be lucky to get home before six.* 5 You say **at any rate** when you want to add to or amend what you have just said E.G. *He is the least appealing character, to me at any rate.*
▶ VERB 6 The way you rate someone or

something is your opinion of them
E.G. *He was rated as one of England's
top young players.*

rather

ADVERB **1** Rather means to a certain
extent E.G. *We got along rather
well… The reality is rather more
complex.* ▶ PHRASE **2** If you **would
rather** do a particular thing, you
would prefer to do it. **3** If you do one
thing **rather than** another, you
choose to do the first thing instead
of the second.

▤ (sense 1) quite, relatively,
somewhat

▤ (sense 2) preferably, sooner

ratify ratifies ratifying ratified

VERB; FORMAL To ratify a written
agreement means to approve it
formally, usually by signing
it.

ratification NOUN

rating ratings

NOUN **1** a score based on the quality
or status of something. **2** The ratings
are statistics showing how popular
each television programme is.

ratio ratios

NOUN a relationship which shows how
many times one thing is bigger than
another E.G. *The adult to child ratio is
1 to 6.*

ration rations rationing rationed

NOUN **1** Your ration of something is
the amount you are allowed to have.
2 Rations are the food given each
day to a soldier or member of an
expedition. ▶ VERB **3** When something
is rationed, you are only allowed a
limited amount of it, because there is
a shortage.

rational

ADJECTIVE When people are rational,

their judgments are based on reason
rather than emotion.

rationally ADVERB   **rationality** NOUN

rationale

Said "rash-on-nahl" NOUN The
rationale for a course of action or for
a belief is the set of reasons on
which it is based.

rattle rattles rattling rattled

VERB **1** When something rattles, it
makes short, regular knocking
sounds. **2** If something rattles you, it
upsets you E.G. *He was obviously
rattled by events.* ▶ NOUN **3** the noise
something makes when it rattles. **4** a
baby's toy which makes a noise
when it is shaken.

rattlesnake rattlesnakes

NOUN a poisonous American snake.

raucous

Said "raw-kuss" ADJECTIVE A raucous
voice is loud and rough.

**ravage ravages ravaging
ravaged** FORMAL

VERB **1** To ravage something means to
seriously harm or damage it E.G. *a
country ravaged by floods.* ▶ NOUN
2 The ravages of something are its
damaging effects E.G. *the ravages of
two world wars.*

rave raves raving raved

VERB **1** If someone raves, they talk in
an angry, uncontrolled way E.G. *He
started raving about being treated
badly.* **2** INFORMAL If you rave about
something, you talk about it very
enthusiastically. ▶ ADJECTIVE **3** INFORMAL
If something gets a rave review, it is
praised enthusiastically. ▶ NOUN
4 INFORMAL a large party with
electronic dance music.

raven ravens

NOUN **1** a large black bird with a deep,

a
b
c
d
e
f
g
h
i
j
k
l
m
n
o
p
q
r
s
t
u
v
w
x
y
z

I want to see (C) your licenCe (licence)   SPELLING NOTE

A
B
C
D
E
F
G
H
I
J
K
L
M
N
O
P
Q
R
S
T
U
V
W
X
Y
Z

harsh call. ▶ ADJECTIVE 2 Raven hair is black and shiny.

ravenous

ADJECTIVE very hungry.

ravine ravines

NOUN a deep, narrow valley with steep sides.

raving ravings

ADJECTIVE 1 If someone is raving, they are mad E.G. *a raving lunatic.* ▶ NOUN 2 Someone's ravings are crazy things they write or say.

ravioli

Said "rav-ee-**oh**-lee" NOUN Ravioli consists of small squares of pasta filled with meat and served with a sauce.

ravishing

ADJECTIVE Someone or something that is ravishing is very beautiful E.G. *a ravishing landscape.*

raw

ADJECTIVE 1 Raw food has not been cooked. 2 A raw substance is in its natural state E.G. *raw sugar.* 3 If part of your body is raw, the skin has come off or been rubbed away. 4 Someone who is raw is too young or too new in a job or situation to know how to behave.

raw material raw materials

NOUN Raw materials are the natural substances used to make something.

ray rays

NOUN 1 a beam of light or radiation. 2 A ray of hope is a small amount that makes an unpleasant situation seem slightly better. 3 a large sea fish with eyes on the top of its body, and a long tail.

raze razes razing razed

VERB To raze a building, town, or forest means to completely destroy it E.G. *The town was razed to the ground during the occupation.*

razor razors

NOUN a tool that people use for shaving.

razor blade razor blades

NOUN a small, sharp, flat piece of metal fitted into a razor for shaving.

re-

PREFIX 1 'Re-' is used to form nouns and verbs that refer to the repetition of an action or process E.G. *reread… remarry.* 2 'Re-' is also used to form verbs that refer to going back to a previous condition E.G. *refresh… renew.* 🏛 from a Latin prefix

reach reaches reaching reached

VERB 1 When you reach a place, you arrive there. 2 When you reach for something, you stretch out your arm to it. 3 If something reaches a place or point, it extends as far as that place or point E.G. *She has a cloak that reaches to the ground.* 4 If something or someone reaches a stage or level, they get to it E.G. *Unemployment has reached record levels.* 5 To reach an agreement or decision means to succeed in achieving it. ▶ PHRASE 6 If a place is **within reach**, you can get there E.G. *a cycle route well within reach of most people.* 7 If something is **out of reach**, you cannot get it to it by stretching out your arm E.G. *Store out of reach of children.*

react reacts reacting reacted

VERB 1 When you react to something, you behave in a particular way because of it E.G. *He reacted badly to the news.* 2 If one substance reacts with another, a chemical change takes place when they are put together.

reaction reactions

NOUN 1 Your reaction to something is what you feel, say, or do because of it

E.G. *Reaction to the visit is mixed.*
2 Your reactions are your ability to move quickly in response to something that happens E.G. *Squash requires fast reactions.* **3** If there is a reaction against something, it becomes unpopular E.G. *a reaction against Christianity.* **4** In a chemical reaction, a chemical change takes place when two substances are put together.

reactionary reactionaries
ADJECTIVE **1** Someone who is reactionary tries to prevent political or social change. ► NOUN
2 Reactionaries are reactionary people.

reactor reactors
NOUN a device which is used to produce nuclear energy.

read reads reading read
VERB **1** When you read, you look at something written and follow it or say it aloud. **2** If you can read someone's moods or mind, you can judge what they are feeling or thinking. **3** When you read a meter or gauge, you look at it and record the figure on it. **4** If you read a subject at university, you study it.

reader readers
NOUN **1** The readers of a newspaper or magazine are the people who read it regularly. **2** At a university, a reader is a senior lecturer just below the rank of professor.

readership
NOUN The readership of a newspaper or magazine consists of the people who read it regularly.

readily
ADVERB **1** willingly and eagerly E.G. *She readily agreed to see Alex.* **2** easily done or quickly obtainable E.G. *Help is readily available.*

reading readings
NOUN **1** Reading is the activity of reading books. **2** The reading on a meter or gauge is the figure or measurement it shows.

readjust readjusts readjusting readjusted
Said "ree-aj-**just**" VERB **1** If you readjust, you adapt to a new situation. **2** If you readjust something, you alter it to a different position.

ready
ADJECTIVE **1** having reached the required stage, or prepared for action or use E.G. *In a few days time the plums will be ready to eat.*
2 willing or eager to do something E.G. *She says she's not ready for marriage.* **3** If you are ready for something, you need it E.G. *I'm ready for bed.* **4** easily produced or obtained E.G. *ready cash.*
readiness NOUN

ready-made
ADJECTIVE already made and therefore able to be used immediately.

reaffirm reaffirms reaffirming reaffirmed
VERB To reaffirm something means to state it again E.G. *He reaffirmed his support for the campaign.*

real
ADJECTIVE **1** actually existing and not imagined or invented. **2** genuine and not imitation E.G. *Who's to know if they're real guns?* **3** true or actual and not mistaken E.G. *This was the real reason for her call.*
■ (sense 1) authentic, genuine, true

real estate
NOUN Real estate is property in the form of land and buildings rather than personal possessions.

a
b
c
d
e
f
g
h
i
j
k
l
m
n
o
p
q
r
s
t
u
v
w
x
y
z

A
B
C
D
E
F
G
H
I
J
K
L
M
N
O
P
Q
R
S
T
U
V
W
X
Y
Z

realism

NOUN Realism is the recognition of the true nature of a situation E.G. *a triumph of muddled thought over realism and common sense.*

realist NOUN

realistic

ADJECTIVE 1 recognizing and accepting the true nature of a situation. 2 representing things in a way that is true to real life E.G. *His novels are more realistic than his short stories.*

realistically ADVERB

reality

NOUN (PSHE) 1 Reality is the real nature of things, rather than the way someone imagines it E.G. *Fiction and reality were increasingly blurred.* 2 If something has become reality, it actually exists or is actually happening. ▤ (sense 1) fact, truth

realize realizes realizing realized; also spelt **realise**

VERB 1 If you realize something, you become aware of it. 2 FORMAL If your hopes or fears are realized, what you hoped for or feared actually happens E.G. *Our worst fears were realized.* 3 To realize a sum of money means to receive it as a result of selling goods or shares.

realization NOUN

really

ADVERB 1 used to add emphasis to what is being said E.G. *I'm not really surprised.* 2 used to indicate that you are talking about the true facts about something E.G. *What was really going on?*

☑ If you want to emphasize an adjective you should always use *really* rather than *real*: *really interesting.*

realm realms

Said "relm" NOUN FORMAL 1 You can

refer to any area of thought or activity as a realm E.G. *the realm of politics.* 2 a country with a king or queen E.G. *defence of the realm.*

reap reaps reaping reaped

VERB 1 To reap a crop such as corn means to cut and gather it. 2 When people reap benefits or rewards, they get them as a result of hard work or careful planning.

reaper NOUN

reappear reappears reappearing reappeared

VERB When people or things reappear, you can see them again, because they have come back E.G. *The stolen ring reappeared three years later in a pawn shop.*

reappearance NOUN

reappraisal reappraisals

NOUN; FORMAL If there is a reappraisal, people think about something and decide whether they want to change it E.G. *a reappraisal of the government's economic policies.*

rear rears rearing reared

NOUN 1 The rear of something is the part at the back. ► VERB 2 To rear children or young animals means to bring them up until they are able to look after themselves. 3 When a horse rears, it raises the front part of its body, so that its front legs are in the air.

rear admiral rear admirals

NOUN A senior officer in the navy.

rearrange rearranges rearranging rearranged

VERB To rearrange something means to organize or arrange it in a different way.

reason reasons reasoning reasoned

NOUN 1 The reason for something is

the fact or situation which explains why it happens or which causes it to happen. **2** If you have reason to believe or feel something, there are definite reasons why you believe it or feel it E.G. *He had every reason to be upset*. **3** Reason is the ability to think and make judgments. ▶ VERB **4** If you reason that something is true, you decide it is true after considering all the facts. **5** If you reason with someone, you persuade them to accept sensible arguments.
▤ (sense 1) cause, motive
▤ (sense 3) rationality, sense(s), understanding

reasonable
ADJECTIVE **1** Reasonable behaviour is fair and sensible. **2** If an explanation is reasonable, there are good reasons for thinking it is correct. **3** A reasonable amount is a fairly large amount. **4** A reasonable price is fair and not too high.
reasonably ADVERB

reasoning
NOUN Reasoning is the process by which you reach a conclusion after considering all the facts.

reassess reassesses reassessing reassessed
VERB If you reassess something, you consider whether it still has the same value or importance.
reassessment NOUN

reassure reassures reassuring reassured
VERB If you reassure someone, you say or do things that make them less worried.
reassurance NOUN

rebate rebates
NOUN money paid back to someone

who has paid too much tax or rent.

rebel rebels rebelling rebelled
NOUN **1** (HISTORY) Rebels are people who are fighting their own country's army to change the political system. **2** Someone who is a rebel rejects society's values and behaves differently from other people. ▶ VERB **3** To rebel means to fight against authority and reject accepted values.

rebellion rebellions
NOUN (HISTORY) A rebellion is organized and often violent opposition to authority.
▤ mutiny, revolution, uprising

rebellious
ADJECTIVE unwilling to obey and likely to rebel against authority.

rebuff rebuffs rebuffing rebuffed
VERB **1** If you rebuff someone, you reject what they offer E.G. *She rebuffed their offers of help*. ▶ NOUN **2** a rejection of an offer.

rebuild rebuilds rebuilding rebuilt
VERB When a town or building is rebuilt, it is built again after being damaged or destroyed.

rebuke rebukes rebuking rebuked
Said "rib-**yook**" VERB To rebuke someone means to speak severely to them about something they have done.

recall recalls recalling recalled
VERB **1** To recall something means to remember it. **2** If you are recalled to a place, you are ordered to return there. **3** If a company recalls products, it asks people to return them because they are faulty.

recap recaps recapping recapped
VERB To recap means to repeat and

a
b
c
d
e
f
g
h
i
j
k
l
m
n
o
p
q
r
s
t
u
v
w
x
y
z

A
B
C
D
E
F
G
H
I
J
K
L
M
N
O
P
Q
R
S
T
U
V
W
X
Y
Z

summarize the main points of an explanation or discussion.

recapture recaptures recapturing recaptured

VERB **1** When you recapture a pleasant feeling, you experience it again E.G. *She may never recapture that past assurance.* **2** When soldiers recapture a place, they capture it from the people who took it from them. **3** When animals or prisoners are recaptured, they are caught after they have escaped.

recede recedes receding receded

VERB **1** When something recedes, it moves away into the distance. **2** If a man's hair is receding, he is starting to go bald at the front.

receipt receipts

*Said "ris-**seet**"* NOUN **1** a piece of paper confirming that money or goods have been received. **2** In a shop or theatre, the money received is often called the receipts E.G. *Box-office receipts were down last month.* **3** FORMAL The receipt of something is the receiving of it E.G. *You have to sign here and acknowledge receipt.*

receive receives receiving received

VERB **1** When you receive something, someone gives it to you, or you get it after it has been sent to you. **2** To receive something also means to have it happen to you E.G. *injuries she received in a car crash.* **3** When you receive visitors or guests, you welcome them. **4** If something is received in a particular way, that is how people react to it E.G. *The decision has been received with great disappointment.*

receiver receivers

NOUN the part of a telephone you hold near to your ear and mouth.

recent

ADJECTIVE Something recent happened a short time ago.

recently ADVERB

reception receptions

NOUN **1** In a hotel or office, reception is the place near the entrance where appointments or enquiries are dealt with. **2** a formal party. **3** The reception someone or something gets is the way people react to them E.G. *Her tour met with a rapturous reception.* **4** If your radio or television gets good reception, the sound or picture is clear.

receptionist receptionists

NOUN The receptionist in a hotel or office deals with people when they arrive, answers the telephone, and arranges appointments.

receptive

ADJECTIVE Someone who is receptive to ideas or suggestions is willing to consider them.

recess recesses

NOUN **1** a period when no work is done by a committee or parliament E.G. *the Christmas recess.* **2** a place where part of a wall has been built further back than the rest.

recession recessions

NOUN a period when a country's economy is less successful and more people become unemployed.

recharge recharges recharging recharged

VERB To recharge a battery means to charge it with electricity again after it has been used.

recipe recipes
Said "res-sip-ee" NOUN 1 (D&T) a list
of ingredients and instructions for
cooking something. **2** If something is
a recipe for disaster or for success, it
is likely to result in disaster or
success.

recipient recipients
NOUN The recipient of something is
the person receiving it.

reciprocal
ADJECTIVE A reciprocal agreement
involves two people, groups, or
countries helping each other in a
similar way E.G. *a reciprocal
agreement on trade.*

reciprocate reciprocates
reciprocating reciprocated
VERB If you reciprocate someone's
feelings or behaviour, you feel or
behave in the same way towards
them.

recital recitals
NOUN a performance of music or
poetry, usually by one person.

recite recites reciting recited
VERB If you recite a poem or
something you have learnt, you say it
aloud.
recitation NOUN

reckless
ADJECTIVE showing a complete lack of
care about danger or damage E.G. *a
reckless tackle.*
recklessly ADVERB   **recklessness**
NOUN

reckon reckons reckoning
reckoned
VERB **1** INFORMAL If you reckon that
something is true, you think it is true
E.G. *I reckoned he was still fond of her.*
2 INFORMAL If someone reckons to do
something, they claim or expect to

do it E.G. *Officers on the case are
reckoning to charge someone shortly.*
3 To reckon an amount means to
calculate it. **4** If you reckon on
something, you rely on it happening
when making your plans E.G. *He
reckons on being world champion.* **5** If
you had not reckoned with
something, you had not expected it
and therefore were unprepared
when it happened E.G. *Giles had not
reckoned with the strength of Sally's
feelings.*

reckoning reckonings
NOUN a calculation E.G. *There were a
thousand or so, by my reckoning.*

reclaim reclaims reclaiming
reclaimed
VERB **1** When you reclaim something,
you collect it after leaving it
somewhere or losing it. **2** To reclaim
land means to make it suitable for
use, for example by draining it.
reclamation NOUN

recline reclines reclining
reclined
VERB To recline means to lie or lean
back at an angle E.G. *a photo of him
reclining on his bed.*

recluse recluses
NOUN Someone who is a recluse lives
alone and avoids other people.
reclusive ADJECTIVE

recognize recognizes
recognizing recognized; also spelt
recognise
VERB **1** If you recognize someone or
something, you realize that you
know who or what they are E.G. *The
receptionist recognized me at once.*
2 To recognize something
also means to accept and
acknowledge it E.G. *The RAF*

pAL up with the principAL and principAL staff (princip*al*)   SPELLING NOTE

recognized him as an outstanding pilot.

recognition NOUN **recognizable** ADJECTIVE **recognizably** ADVERB
■ (sense 1) identify, know, place

recommend recommends recommending recommended
VERB If you recommend something to someone, you praise it and suggest they try it.
recommendation NOUN

reconcile reconciles reconciling reconciled
VERB 1 To reconcile two things that seem to oppose one another, means to make them work or exist together successfully E.G. *The designs reconciled style with comfort.* 2 When people are reconciled, they become friendly again after a quarrel. 3 If you reconcile yourself to an unpleasant situation, you accept it.
reconciliation NOUN

reconnaissance
Said "rik-**kon**-iss-sanss" NOUN
Reconnaissance is the gathering of military information by soldiers, planes, or satellites.

reconsider reconsiders reconsidering reconsidered
VERB To reconsider something means to think about it again to decide whether to change it.
reconsideration NOUN

reconstruct reconstructs reconstructing reconstructed
VERB 1 To reconstruct something that has been damaged means to build it again. 2 To reconstruct a past event means to get a complete description of it from small pieces of information.
reconstruction NOUN

record records recording recorded
NOUN 1 If you keep a record of something, you keep a written account or store information in a computer E.G. *medical records.* 2 a round, flat piece of plastic on which music has been recorded. 3 an achievement which is the best of its type. 4 Your record is what is known about your achievements or past activities E.G. *He had a distinguished war record.* ▸ VERB 5 If you record information, you write it down or put it into a computer. 6 To record sound means to put it on tape, record, or compact disc. ▸ ADJECTIVE 7 higher, lower, better, or worse than ever before E.G. *Profits were at a record level.*
■ (sense 1) document, file, register
■ (sense 5) note, register, write down

recorder recorders
NOUN a small woodwind instrument.

recording recordings
NOUN A recording of something is a record, tape, or video of it.

recount recounts recounting recounted
VERB 1 If you recount a story, you tell it. ▸ NOUN 2 a second count of votes in an election when the result is very close.

recoup recoups recouping recouped
Said "rik-**koop**" VERB If you recoup money that you have spent or lost, you get it back.

recourse
NOUN; FORMAL If you have recourse to something, you use it to help you E.G. *The members settled their differences without recourse to war.*

recover recovers recovering recovered
VERB 1 To recover from an illness or unhappy experience means to get well again or get over it. 2 If you recover a lost object or your ability to do something, you get it back.
recovery NOUN
■ (sense 1) convalesce, get better, recuperate
■ (sense 2) regain, retrieve

recreate recreates recreating recreated
VERB To recreate something means to succeed in making it happen or exist again E.G. *a museum that faithfully recreates an old farmhouse.*

recreation recreations
Said "rek-kree-**ay**-shn" NOUN Recreation is all the things that you do for enjoyment in your spare time.
recreational ADJECTIVE

recrimination recriminations
NOUN Recriminations are accusations made by people about each other.

recruit recruits recruiting recruited
VERB 1 To recruit people means to get them to join a group or help with something. ▶ NOUN 2 someone who has joined the army or some other organization.
recruitment NOUN

rectangle rectangles
NOUN a four-sided shape with four right angles.
rectangular ADJECTIVE

rectify rectifies rectifying rectified
VERB; FORMAL If you rectify something that is wrong, you put it right.

rector rectors
NOUN a Church of England priest in charge of a parish.

rectory rectories
NOUN a house where a rector lives.

rectum rectums
NOUN; MEDICAL the bottom end of the tube down which waste food passes out of your body.
rectal ADJECTIVE

recuperate recuperates recuperating recuperated
VERB When you recuperate, you gradually recover after being ill or injured.
recuperation NOUN

recur recurs recurring recurred
VERB If something recurs, it happens or occurs again E.G. *His hamstring injury recurred after the first game.*
recurrence NOUN **recurrent** ADJECTIVE

recurring
ADJECTIVE 1 happening or occurring many times E.G. *a recurring dream.* 2 (MATHS) In maths, a recurring digit is one that is repeated over and over again after the decimal point in a decimal fraction.

recycle recycles recycling recycled
VERB To recycle used products means to process them so that they can be used again E.G. *recycled glass.*

red redder reddest; reds
NOUN or ADJECTIVE 1 Red is the colour of blood or of a ripe tomato. ▶ ADJECTIVE 2 Red hair is between orange and brown in colour.

redback redbacks
NOUN a small Australian spider with a poisonous bite.

redcurrant redcurrants
NOUN Redcurrants are very small,

a
b
c
d
e
f
g
h
i
j
k
l
m
n
o
p
q
r
s
t
u
v
w
x
y
z

Psychiatrists Seldom Yell Callously Hard (<u>psych</u>iatrist)   **SPELLING NOTE**

A
B
C
D
E
F
G
H
I
J
K
L
M
N
O
P
Q
R
S
T
U
V
W
X
Y
Z

bright red fruits that grow in bunches on a bush.

redeem redeems redeeming redeemed

VERB 1 If a feature redeems an unpleasant thing or situation, it makes it seem less bad. 2 If you redeem yourself, you do something that gives people a good opinion of you again. 3 If you redeem something, you get it back by paying for it. 4 In Christianity, to redeem someone means to free them from sin by giving them faith in Jesus Christ.

redemption

NOUN Redemption is the state of being redeemed.

red-handed

PHRASE To **catch someone red-handed** means to catch them doing something wrong.

red-hot

ADJECTIVE Red-hot metal has been heated to such a high temperature that it has turned red.

redress redresses redressing redressed FORMAL

VERB 1 To redress a wrong means to put it right. ▶ NOUN 2 If you get redress for harm done to you, you are compensated for it.

red tape

NOUN Red tape is official rules and procedures that seem unnecessary and cause delay.

reduce reduces reducing reduced

VERB 1 To reduce something means to make it smaller in size or amount. 2 You can use 'reduce' to say that someone or something is changed to a weaker or inferior state E.G. *She reduced them to tears… The village*

was reduced to rubble.

■ (sense 1) cut, decrease, lessen

reduction reductions

NOUN When there is a reduction in something, it is made smaller.

redundancy redundancies

NOUN 1 Redundancy is the state of being redundant. 2 The number of redundancies is the number of people made redundant.

redundant

ADJECTIVE 1 When people are made redundant, they lose their jobs because there is no more work for them or no money to pay them. 2 When something becomes redundant, it is no longer needed.

reed reeds

NOUN 1 Reeds are hollow stemmed plants that grow in shallow water or wet ground. 2 a thin piece of cane or metal inside some wind instruments which vibrates when air is blown over it.

reef reefs

NOUN a long line of rocks or coral close to the surface of the sea.

reek reeks reeking reeked

VERB 1 To reek of something means to smell strongly and unpleasantly of it. ▶ NOUN 2 If there is a reek of something, there is a strong unpleasant smell of it.

reel reels reeling reeled

NOUN 1 a cylindrical object around which you wrap something; often part of a device which you turn as a control. 2 a fast Scottish dance. ▶ VERB 3 When someone reels, they move unsteadily as if they are going to fall. 4 If your mind is reeling, you are confused because you have too much to think about.

reel off VERB If you reel off information, you repeat it from memory quickly and easily.

re-elect re-elects re-electing re-elected
VERB When someone is re-elected, they win an election again and are able to stay in power.

refer refers referring referred
VERB 1 If you refer to something, you mention it. 2 If you refer to a book or record, you look at it to find something out. 3 When a problem or issue is referred to someone, they are formally asked to deal with it E.G. *The case was referred to the European Court.*
▦ from Latin *referre* meaning 'to carry back'
☑ The word *refer* contains the sense 'back' in its meaning. Therefore, you should not use *back* after *refer*: this *refers* to what has already been said not *refers back.*

referee referees
NOUN 1 the official who controls a football game or a boxing or wrestling match. 2 someone who gives a reference to a person who is applying for a job.

reference references
NOUN 1 A reference to something or someone is a mention of them. 2 Reference is the act of referring to something or someone for information or advice E.G. *He makes that decision without reference to her.* 3 a number or name that tells you where to find information or identifies a document. 4 If someone gives you a reference when you apply for a job, they write a letter about your abilities.

referendum referendums or referenda
NOUN a vote in which all the people in a country are officially asked whether they agree with a policy or proposal.

refine refines refining refined
VERB To refine a raw material such as oil or sugar means to process it to remove impurities.

refined
ADJECTIVE very polite and well-mannered.

refinement refinements
NOUN 1 Refinements are minor improvements. 2 Refinement is politeness and good manners.

refinery refineries
NOUN a factory where substances such as oil or sugar are refined.

reflect reflects reflecting reflected
VERB 1 If something reflects an attitude or situation, it shows what it is like E.G. *His off-duty hobbies reflected his maritime interests.* 2 If something reflects light or heat, the light or heat bounces off it. 3 When something is reflected in a mirror or water, you can see its image in it. 4 (MATHS) If something reflects, its direction is reversed. 5 When you reflect, you think about something.

reflective ADJECTIVE **reflectively** ADVERB

reflection reflections
NOUN 1 If something is a reflection of something else, it shows what it is like E.G. *This is a terrible reflection of the times.* 2 an image in a mirror or water. 3 Reflection is the process by which light and heat are bounced off a surface. 4 (MATHS) In maths, reflection is also the turning back of something on itself E.G. *reflection of*

a
b
c
d
e
f
g
h
i
j
k
l
m
n
o
p
q
r
s
t
u
v
w
x
y
z

A
B
C
D
E
F
G
H
I
J
K
L
M
N
O
P
Q
R
S
T
U
V
W
X
Y
Z

an axis. **5** Reflection is also thought
E.G. *After days of reflection she
decided to leave.*

reflex reflexes
NOUN **1** A reflex or reflex action is a
sudden uncontrollable movement
that you make as a result of pressure
or a blow. **2** If you have good
reflexes, you respond very quickly
when something unexpected
happens. ▶ ADJECTIVE **3** A reflex angle is
between 180° and 360°.

reflexive reflexives
ADJECTIVE or NOUN In grammar, a
reflexive verb or pronoun is one that
refers back to the subject of the
sentence E.G. *She washed herself.*

reform reforms reforming
reformed
NOUN **1** Reforms are major changes to
laws or institutions E.G. *a programme
of economic reform.* ▶ VERB **2** When
laws or institutions are reformed,
major changes are made to them.
3 When people reform, they stop
committing crimes or doing other
unacceptable things.
reformer NOUN

Reformation
NOUN The Reformation was a religious
and political movement in Europe in
the 16th century that began as an
attempt to reform the Roman
Catholic Church, but ended in the
establishment of the Protestant
Churches.

refraction
NOUN Refraction is the bending of a
ray of light, for example when it
enters water or glass.

refrain refrains refraining
refrained
VERB **1** FORMAL If you refrain from doing

something, you do not do it E.G.
*Please refrain from smoking in the
hall.* ▶ NOUN **2** The refrain of a song is
a short, simple part, repeated many
times.

refresh refreshes refreshing
refreshed
VERB **1** If something refreshes you
when you are hot or tired, it makes
you feel cooler or more energetic
E.G. *A glass of fruit juice will refresh
you.* ▶ PHRASE **2** To **refresh someone's
memory** means to remind them of
something they had forgotten.

refreshing
ADJECTIVE You say that something is
refreshing when it is pleasantly
different from what you are used to
E.G. *She is a refreshing contrast to her
father.*

refreshment refreshments
NOUN Refreshments are drinks and
small amounts of food provided at
an event.

refrigerator refrigerators
NOUN an electrically cooled container
in which you store food to keep it fresh.

refuel refuels refuelling
refuelled
VERB When an aircraft or vehicle is
refuelled, it is filled with more fuel.

refuge refuges
NOUN **1** a place where you go for
safety. **2** If you take refuge, you go
somewhere for safety or behave in a
way that will protect you E.G. *They
took refuge in a bomb shelter…
Father Rowan took refuge in silence.*
■ (sense 1) haven, sanctuary, shelter

refugee refugees
NOUN Refugees are people who have
been forced to leave their country
and live elsewhere.

refund refunds refunding refunded

NOUN **1** money returned to you because you have paid too much for something or because you have returned goods. ▶ VERB **2** To refund someone's money means to return it to them after they have paid for something with it.

refurbish refurbishes refurbishing refurbished

VERB; FORMAL To refurbish a building means to decorate it and repair damage.
refurbishment NOUN

refusal refusals

NOUN A refusal is when someone says firmly that they will not do, allow, or accept something.

refuse refuses refusing refused

Said "rif-yooz" VERB **1** If you refuse to do something, you say or decide firmly that you will not do it. **2** If someone refuses something, they do not allow it or do not accept it E.G. The United States has refused him a visa… He offered me a second drink which I refused.

refuse

Said "ref-yoos" NOUN Refuse is rubbish or waste.

refute refutes refuting refuted

VERB; FORMAL To refute a theory or argument means to prove that it is wrong.

☑ Refute does not mean the same as deny. If you refute something, you provide evidence to show that it is not true. If you deny something, you say that it is not true.

regain regains regaining regained

VERB To regain something means to get it back.

regal

ADJECTIVE very grand and suitable for a king or queen E.G. regal splendour.
regally ADVERB

regard regards regarding regarded

VERB **1** To regard someone or something in a particular way means to think of them in that way or have that opinion of them E.G. We all regard him as a friend… Many disapprove of the tax, regarding it as unfair. **2** LITERARY To regard someone in a particular way also means to look at them in that way E.G. She regarded him curiously for a moment. ▶ NOUN **3** If you have a high regard for someone, you have a very good opinion of them. ▶ PHRASES **4** **Regarding**, **as regards**, **with regard to**, and **in regard to** are all used to indicate what you are talking or writing about E.G. There was always some question regarding education… As regards the war, he believed in victory at any price. **5** 'Regards' is used in various expressions to express friendly feelings E.G. Give my regards to your husband.

regardless

PREPOSITION or ADVERB done or happening in spite of something else E.G. He led from the front, regardless of the danger.

regatta regattas

NOUN a race meeting for sailing or rowing boats.

regency regencies

NOUN a period when a country is ruled by a regent.

regenerate regenerates regenerating regenerated

VERB; FORMAL To regenerate something

a
b
c
d
e
f
g
h
i
j
k
l
m
n
o
p
q
r
s
t
u
v
w
x
y
z

A
B
C
D
E
F
G
H
I
J
K
L
M
N
O
P
Q
R
S
T
U
V
W
X
Y
Z

means to develop and improve it after it has been declining E.G. *a scheme to regenerate the docks area of the city.*

regeneration NOUN

regent regents
NOUN someone who rules in place of a king or queen who is ill or too young to rule.

reggae
NOUN Reggae is a type of music, originally from the West Indies, with a strong beat.

regime regimes
Said "ray-**jeem**" NOUN a system of government, and the people who are ruling a country E.G. *a communist regime.*

regiment regiments
NOUN a large group of soldiers commanded by a colonel.

regimental ADJECTIVE

regimented
ADJECTIVE very strictly controlled E.G. *the regimented life of the orphanage.*

regimentation NOUN

region regions
NOUN 1 (GEOGRAPHY) a large area of land. 2 You can refer to any area or part as a region E.G. *the pelvic region.*
▶ PHRASE 3 **In the region of** means approximately E.G. *The scheme will cost in the region of six million.*

regional ADJECTIVE **regionally** ADVERB
■ (sense 1) area, district, territory

register registers registering registered
NOUN 1 an official list or record of things E.G. *the electoral register.* 2 TECHNICAL a style of speaking or writing used in particular circumstances or social occasions.
▶ VERB 3 When something is

registered, it is recorded on an official list E.G. *The car was registered in my name.* 4 If an instrument registers a measurement, it shows it. 5 If your face registers a feeling, it expresses it.

registration NOUN

registrar registrars
NOUN 1 a person who keeps official records of births, marriages, and deaths. 2 At a college or university, the registrar is a senior administrative official. 3 a senior hospital doctor.

registration number registration numbers
NOUN the sequence of letters and numbers on the front and back of a motor vehicle that identify it.

registry registries
NOUN a place where official records are kept.

registry office registry offices
NOUN a place where births, marriages, and deaths are recorded, and where people can marry without a religious ceremony.

regret regrets regretting regretted
VERB 1 If you regret something, you are sorry that it happened. 2 You can say that you regret something as a way of apologizing E.G. *We regret any inconvenience to passengers.*
▶ NOUN 3 If you have regrets, you are sad or sorry about something.

regretful ADJECTIVE **regretfully** ADVERB
■ (sense 1) repent, rue

regrettable
ADJECTIVE unfortunate and undesirable E.G. *a regrettable accident.*

regrettably ADVERB

regular regulars

ADJECTIVE **1** even and equally spaced E.G. *soft music with a regular beat*. **2** (MATHS) A regular shape has equal angles and equal sides E.G. *a regular polygon*. **3** Regular events or activities happen often and according to a pattern, for example each day or each week E.G. *The trains to London are fairly regular*. **4** If you are a regular customer or visitor somewhere, you go there often. **5** usual or normal E.G. *I was filling in for the regular bartender*. **6** having a well balanced appearance E.G. *a regular geometrical shape*. ▶ NOUN **7** People who go to a place often are known as its regulars.

regularly ADVERB **regularity** NOUN
◼ (sense 1) even, steady, uniform

regulate regulates regulating regulated

VERB To regulate something means to control the way it operates E.G. *Sweating helps to regulate the body's temperature*. **regulator** NOUN

regulation regulations

NOUN **1** Regulations are official rules. **2** Regulation is the control of something E.G. *regulation of the betting industry*.

regurgitate regurgitates regurgitating regurgitated

Said "rig-gur-jit-tate" VERB To regurgitate food means to bring it back from the stomach before it is digested.

rehabilitate rehabilitates rehabilitating rehabilitated

VERB To rehabilitate someone who has been ill or in prison means to help them lead a normal life. **rehabilitation** NOUN

rehearsal rehearsals

NOUN (DRAMA) a practice of a performance in preparation for the actual event.

rehearse rehearses rehearsing rehearsed

VERB (DRAMA) To rehearse a performance means to practise it in preparation for the actual event.

reign reigns reigning reigned

Said "rain" VERB **1** When a king or queen reigns, he or she rules a country. **2** You can say that something reigns when it is a noticeable feature of a situation or period of time E.G. *Panic reigned after his assassination*. ▶ NOUN **3** (HISTORY) The reign of a king or queen is the period during which he or she reigns.

rein reins

NOUN **1** Reins are the thin leather straps which you hold when you are riding a horse. ▶ PHRASE **2** To **keep a tight rein on** someone or something means to control them firmly.

reincarnation

NOUN People who believe in reincarnation believe that when you die, you are born again as another creature.

reindeer

NOUN Reindeer are deer with large antlers, that live in northern regions.

reinforce reinforces reinforcing reinforced

VERB **1** To reinforce something means to strengthen it E.G. *a reinforced steel barrier*. **2** If something reinforces an idea or claim, it provides evidence to support it.

a
b
c
d
e
f
g
h
i
j
k
l
m
n
o
p
q
r
s
t
u
v
w
x
y
z

A
B
C
D
E
F
G
H
I
J
K
L
M
N
O
P
Q
R
S
T
U
V
W
X
Y
Z

reinforcement reinforcements
NOUN **1** Reinforcements are additional
soldiers sent to join an army in
battle. **2** Reinforcement is the
reinforcing of something.

reinstate reinstates reinstating
reinstated
VERB **1** To reinstate someone means to
give them back a position they have
lost. **2** To reinstate something means
to bring it back E.G. *Parliament voted
against reinstating capital
punishment.*
reinstatement NOUN

reiterate reiterates reiterating
reiterated
Said "ree-**it**-er-ate" VERB; FORMAL If you
reiterate something, you say it again.
reiteration NOUN

reject rejects rejecting rejected
VERB **1** If you reject a proposal or
request, you do not accept it or
agree to it. **2** If you reject a belief,
political system, or way of life, you
decide that it is not for you. ▶ NOUN
3 a product that cannot be used,
because there is something wrong
with it.
rejection NOUN
■ (sense 1) decline, refuse, turn
down

rejoice rejoices rejoicing
rejoiced
VERB To rejoice means to be very
pleased about something E.G. *The
whole country rejoiced after his
downfall.*

rejoin rejoins rejoining rejoined
VERB If you rejoin someone, you go
back to them soon after leaving
them E.G. *She rejoined her friends in
the bar.*

rejuvenate rejuvenates
rejuvenating rejuvenated
Said "ree-joo-vin-ate" VERB To
rejuvenate someone means to make
them feel young again.
rejuvenation NOUN

relapse relapses
NOUN If a sick person has a relapse,
their health suddenly gets worse
after improving.

relate relates relating related
VERB **1** If something relates to
something else, it is connected or
concerned with it E.G. *The statistics
relate only to western Germany.* **2** If
you can relate to someone, you can
understand their thoughts and
feelings. **3** To relate a story means to
tell it.

relation relations
NOUN **1** If there is a relation between
two things, they are similar or
connected in some way E.G. *This
theory bears no relation to reality.*
2 Your relations are the members of
your family. **3** Relations between
people are their feelings and
behaviour towards each other E.G.
*Relations between husband and wife
had not improved.*

relationship relationships
NOUN (PSHE) **1** The relationship
between two people or groups is the
way they feel and behave towards
each other. **2** a close friendship,
especially one involving romantic or
sexual feelings. **3** The relationship
between two things is the way in
which they are connected E.G. *the
relationship between slavery and the
sugar trade.*

relative relatives
ADJECTIVE **1** compared to other things

or people of the same kind E.G. *The fighting resumed after a period of relative calm… He is a relative novice.* **2** You use 'relative' when comparing the size or quality of two things E.G. *the relative strengths of the British and German forces.* ► NOUN **3** Your relatives are the members of your family.

relative pronoun relative pronouns

NOUN a pronoun that replaces a noun that links two parts of a sentence.

What is a Relative Pronoun?

Relative pronouns are used to replace a noun which links two different parts of a sentence. The relative pronouns are *who, whom, whose, which,* and *that.*

Relative pronouns always refer back to a word in the earlier part of the sentence. The word they refer to is called the **antecedent**. (In the examples that follow, the antecedents are underlined.)

> E.G. *I have <u>a friend</u> **who** lives in Rome.*
> *We could go to <u>a place</u> **that** I know.*

The forms *who, whom,* and *whose* are used when the antecedent is a person. *Who* indicates the subject of the verb, while *whom* indicates the object of the verb:

> E.G. *It was <u>the same person</u> **who** saw me yesterday.*
> *It was <u>the person</u> **whom** I saw yesterday.*

The distinction between *who* and *whom* is often ignored in everyday English, and *who* is often used as the object:

> E.G. *It was <u>the person</u> **who** I saw yesterday.*

Whom is used immediately after a preposition. However, if the preposition is separated from the relative pronoun, *who* is usually used:

> E.G. *He is <u>a man</u> **in whom** I have great confidence.*
> *He is <u>a man</u> **who** I have great confidence **in**.*

Whose is the possessive form of the relative pronoun. It can refer to things as well as people:

> E.G. *Anna has <u>a sister</u> **whose** name is Rosie.*
> *I found <u>a book</u> **whose** pages were torn.*

Which is only used when the antecedent is not a person:

> E.G. *We took <u>the road</u> **which** leads to the sea.*

That refers to things or people. It is never used immediately after a preposition, but it can be used if the preposition is separated from the relative pronoun:

> E.G. *It was <u>a film</u> **that** I had little interest **in**.*

---

relax relaxes relaxing relaxed

VERB **1** If you relax, you become calm and your muscles lose their tension. **2** If you relax your hold, you hold something less tightly. **3** To relax something also means to make it less strict or controlled E.G. *The rules governing student conduct were relaxed.*

relaxation NOUN

▤ (sense 1) rest, take it easy, unwind
▤ (sense 2) lessen, loosen, slacken

CONTINUED →

a b c d e f g h i j k l m n o p q r s t u v w x y z

A
B
C
D
E
F
G
H
I
J
K
L
M
N
O
P
Q
R
S
T
U
V
W
X
Y
Z

relay relays relaying relayed

NOUN 1 (PE) A relay race or relay is a race between teams, with each team member running one part of the race. ▶ VERB 2 To relay a television or radio signal means to send it on. 3 If you relay information, you tell it to someone else.

release releases releasing released

VERB 1 To release someone or something means to set them free or remove restraints from them. 2 To release something also means to issue it or make it available E.G. *He is releasing an album of love songs.* ▶ NOUN 3 When the release of someone or something takes place, they are set free. 4 A press release or publicity release is an official written statement given to reporters. 5 A new release is a new record or video that has just become available.

relegate relegates relegating relegated

VERB To relegate something or someone means to give them a less important position or status. **relegation** NOUN

relent relents relenting relented

VERB If someone relents, they agree to something they had previously not allowed.

relentless

ADJECTIVE never stopping and never becoming less intense E.G. *the relentless rise of business closures.* **relentlessly** ADVERB

relevant

ADJECTIVE (LIBRARY) If something is relevant, it is connected with and is appropriate to what is being discussed E.G. *We have passed all relevant information on to the police.*

relevance NOUN

■ appropriate, pertinent, significant

reliable

ADJECTIVE 1 Reliable people and things can be trusted to do what you want. 2 If information is reliable, you can assume that it is correct.

reliably ADVERB **reliability** NOUN

reliant

ADJECTIVE If you are reliant on someone or something, you depend on them E.G. *They are not wholly reliant on charity.*

reliance NOUN

relic relics

NOUN 1 Relics are objects or customs that have survived from an earlier time. 2 an object regarded as holy because it is thought to be connected with a saint.

relief

NOUN 1 If you feel relief, you are glad and thankful because a bad situation is over or has been avoided. 2 Relief is also money, food, or clothing provided for poor or hungry people.

relief map relief maps

NOUN a map showing the shape of mountains and hills by shading.

relieve relieves relieving relieved

VERB 1 If something relieves an unpleasant feeling, it makes it less unpleasant E.G. *Drugs can relieve much of the pain.* 2 FORMAL If you relieve someone, you do their job or duty for a period. 3 If someone is relieved of their duties, they are dismissed from their job. 4 If you relieve yourself, you urinate.

religion religions

NOUN (RE) 1 Religion is the belief in a god or gods and all the activities connected with such beliefs. **2** a system of religious belief.

religious

ADJECTIVE **1** (HISTORY) connected with religion E.G. *religious worship*.
2 (RE) Someone who is religious has a strong belief in a god or gods.
■ (sense 2) devout, pious

religiously

ADVERB If you do something religiously, you do it regularly as a duty E.G. *He stuck religiously to the rules.*

relinquish relinquishes relinquishing relinquished

Said "ril-**ling**-kwish" VERB; FORMAL If you relinquish something, you give it up.

relish relishes relishing relished

VERB **1** If you relish something, you enjoy it E.G. *He relished the idea of getting some cash.* ▶ NOUN **2** Relish is enjoyment E.G. *He told me with relish of the wonderful times he had.* **3** Relish is also a savoury sauce or pickle.

relive relives reliving relived

VERB If you relive a past experience, you remember it and imagine it happening again.

relocate relocates relocating relocated

VERB If people or businesses are relocated, they are moved to a different place.

relocation NOUN

reluctant

ADJECTIVE If you are reluctant to do something, you are unwilling to do it.

reluctance NOUN

reluctantly

ADVERB If you do something reluctantly, you do it although you do not want to.

rely relies relying relied

VERB **1** If you rely on someone or something, you need them and depend on them E.G. *She has to rely on hardship payments.* **2** If you can rely on someone to do something, you can trust them to do it E.G. *They can always be relied on to turn up.*

remain remains remaining remained

VERB **1** If you remain in a particular place or state, you stay there or stay the same and do not change E.G. *The three men remained silent.*
2 Something that remains still exists or is left over E.G. *Huge amounts of weapons remain to be collected.*
▶ PLURAL NOUN **3** The remains of something are the parts that are left after most of it has been destroyed E.G. *the remains of an ancient mosque.* **4** You can refer to a dead body as remains E.G. *More human remains have been unearthed today.*
■ (sense 3) debris, remnants

remainder

NOUN The remainder of something is the part that is left E.G. *He gulped down the remainder of his coffee.*

remand remands remanding remanded

VERB **1** If a judge remands someone who is accused of a crime, the trial is postponed and the person is ordered to come back at a later date.
▶ PHRASE **2** If someone is on **remand**, they are in prison waiting for their trial to begin.

remark remarks remarking remarked

VERB **1** If you remark on something, you mention it or comment on it E.G. *She had remarked on the boy's*

LEt's measure the ang**LE** (ang**le**) SPELLING NOTE

A
B
C
D
E
F
G
H
I
J
K
L
M
N
O
P
Q
R
S
T
U
V
W
X
Y
Z

improvement. ▶ NOUN 2 something you say, often in a casual way.

remarkable
ADJECTIVE impressive and unexpected
E.G. *It was a remarkable achievement.*

remarkably ADVERB
■ extraordinary, outstanding, wonderful

remarry remarries remarrying remarried
VERB If someone remarries, they get married again.

remedial
ADJECTIVE 1 Remedial activities are to help someone improve their health after they have been ill. 2 Remedial exercises are designed to improve someone's ability in something E.G. *the remedial reading class.*

remedy remedies remedying remedied
NOUN 1 a way of dealing with a problem E.G. *a remedy for colic.* ▶ VERB 2 If you remedy something that is wrong, you correct it E.G. *We have to remedy the situation immediately.*

remember remembers remembering remembered
VERB 1 If you can remember someone or something from the past, you can bring them into your mind or think about them. 2 If you remember to do something, you do it when you intended to E.G. *Ben had remembered to book reservations.*
■ (sense 1) recall, recollect

remembrance
NOUN If you do something in remembrance of a dead person, you are showing that they are remembered with respect and affection.

remind reminds reminding reminded
VERB 1 If someone reminds you of a fact, they say something to make you think about it E.G. *Remind me to buy a bottle of wine, will you?* 2 If someone reminds you of another person, they look similar and make you think of them.

reminder reminders
NOUN 1 If one thing is a reminder of another, the first thing makes you think of the second E.G. *a reminder of better times.* 2 a note sent to tell someone they have forgotten to do something.

reminiscent
ADJECTIVE Something that is reminiscent of something else reminds you of it.

remission
NOUN When prisoners get remission for good behaviour, their sentences are reduced.

remit remits
NOUN; FORMAL The remit of a person or committee is the subject or task they are responsible for E.G. *Their remit is to research into a wide range of health problems.*

remittance remittances
NOUN; FORMAL payment for something sent through the post.

remnant remnants
NOUN a small part of something left after the rest has been used or destroyed.

remorse
NOUN; FORMAL Remorse is a strong feeling of guilt.

remorseful ADJECTIVE
■ contrition, regret, repentance

remote remoter remotest
ADJECTIVE **1** Remote areas are far away from places where most people live. **2** far away in time E.G. *the remote past.* **3** If you say a person is remote, you mean they do not want to be friendly E.G. *She is severe, solemn, and remote.* **4** If there is only a remote possibility of something happening, it is unlikely to happen.
remoteness NOUN

remote control
NOUN Remote control is a system of controlling a machine or vehicle from a distance using radio or electronic signals.

remotely
ADVERB used to emphasize a negative statement E.G. *He isn't remotely keen.*

removal
NOUN **1** The removal of something is the act of taking it away. **2** A removal company transports furniture from one building to another.

remove removes removing removed
VERB **1** If you remove something from a place, you take it off or away. **2** If you are removed from a position of authority, you are not allowed to continue your job. **3** If you remove an undesirable feeling or attitude, you get rid of it E.G. *Most of her fears had been removed.*
removable ADJECTIVE
■ (sense 1) extract, take away, withdraw

Renaissance
Said "ren-**nay**-*sonss*" NOUN The Renaissance was a period from the 14th to 16th centuries in Europe when there was a great revival in the arts and learning.

▥ a French word, meaning literally 'rebirth'

renal
ADJECTIVE; TECHNICAL concerning the kidneys E.G. *renal failure.*

rename renames renaming renamed
VERB If you rename something, you give it a new name.

render renders rendering rendered
VERB You can use 'render' to say that something is changed into a different state E.G. *The bomb was quickly rendered harmless.*

rendezvous
Said "**ron**-day-voo" NOUN **1** a meeting E.G. *Baxter arranged a six o'clock rendezvous.* **2** a place where you have arranged to meet someone E.G. *The pub became a popular rendezvous.*

rendition renditions
NOUN; FORMAL a performance of a play, poem, or piece of music.

renew renews renewing renewed
VERB **1** To renew an activity or relationship means to begin it again. **2** To renew a licence or contract means to extend the period of time for which it is valid.
renewal NOUN

renounce renounces renouncing renounced
VERB; FORMAL If you renounce something, you reject it or give it up.
renunciation NOUN

renovate renovates renovating renovated
VERB If you renovate an old building or machine, you repair it and restore it to good condition.
renovation NOUN

a
b
c
d
e
f
g
h
i
j
k
l
m
n
o
p
q
r
s
t
u
v
w
x
y
z

A
B
C
D
E
F
G
H
I
J
K
L
M
N
O
P
Q
R
S
T
U
V
W
X
Y
Z

renowned
ADJECTIVE well-known for something good E.G. *He is not renowned for his patience.*
renown NOUN

rent rents renting rented
VERB 1 If you rent something, you pay the owner a regular sum of money in return for being able to use it. ► NOUN 2 Rent is the amount of money you pay regularly to rent land or accommodation.

rental
ADJECTIVE 1 concerned with the renting out of goods and services E.G. *Scotland's largest video rental company.* ► NOUN 2 the amount of money you pay when you rent something.

reorganize reorganizes reorganizing reorganized; also spelt **reorganise**
VERB To reorganize something means to organize it in a new way in order to make it more efficient or acceptable.
reorganization NOUN

rep reps
NOUN; INFORMAL a travelling salesman or saleswoman. Rep is an abbreviation for representative.

repair repairs repairing repaired
NOUN 1 something you do to mend something that is damaged or broken. ► VERB 2 If you repair something, you mend it.

repay repays repaying repaid
VERB 1 To repay money means to give it back to the person who lent it. 2 If you repay a favour, you do something to help the person who helped you.
repayment NOUN

repeal repeals repealing repealed
VERB If the government repeals a law, it cancels it so that it is no longer valid.

repeat repeats repeating repeated
VERB 1 If you repeat something, you say, write, or do it again. 2 If you repeat what someone has said, you tell someone else about it E.G. *I trust you not to repeat that to anyone.*
► NOUN 3 something which is done or happens again E.G. *the number of repeats shown on TV.*
repeated ADJECTIVE **repeatedly** ADVERB

repel repels repelling repelled
VERB 1 If something repels you, you find it horrible and disgusting. 2 When soldiers repel an attacking force, they successfully defend themselves against it. 3 When a magnetic pole repels an opposite pole, it forces the opposite pole away.
■ (sense 1) disgust, revolt, sicken

repellent repellents
ADJECTIVE 1 FORMAL horrible and disgusting E.G. *I found him repellent.*
► NOUN 2 Repellents are chemicals used to keep insects or other creatures away.

repent repents repenting repented
VERB; FORMAL If you repent, you are sorry for something bad you have done.
repentance NOUN **repentant** ADJECTIVE

repercussion repercussions
NOUN The repercussions of an event are the effects it has at a later time.

repertoire repertoires
Said "rep-et-twar" NOUN A performer's repertoire is all the pieces of music or dramatic parts he or she has learned and can perform

repertory repertories
NOUN 1 Repertory is the practice of performing a small number of plays in a theatre for a short time, using the same actors in each play. 2 In Australian, New Zealand and South African English, repertory is the same as **repertoire**.

repetition repetitions
NOUN If there is a repetition of something, it happens again E.G. *We don't want a repetition of last week's fiasco.*

repetitive
ADJECTIVE A repetitive activity involves a lot of repetition and is boring E.G. *dull and repetitive work.*

replace replaces replacing replaced
VERB 1 When one thing replaces another, the first thing takes the place of the second. 2 If you replace something that is damaged or lost, you get a new one. 3 If you replace something, you put it back where it was before E.G. *She replaced the receiver.*
■ (sense 1) supersede, supplant

replacement replacements
NOUN 1 The replacement for someone or something is the person or thing that takes their place. 2 The replacement of a person or thing happens when they are replaced by another person or thing.

replay replays replaying replayed
VERB 1 If a match is replayed, the teams play it again. 2 If you replay a tape or film, you play it again E.G. *Replay the first few seconds of the tape please.* ▶ NOUN 3 a match that is played for a second time.

replenish replenishes replenishing replenished
VERB; FORMAL If you replenish something, you make it full or complete again.

replica replicas
NOUN an accurate copy of something E.G. *a replica of Columbus's ship.*
replicate VERB

reply replies replying replied
VERB 1 If you reply to something, you say or write an answer. ▶ NOUN 2 what you say or write when you answer someone.

report reports reporting reported
VERB 1 If you report that something has happened, you tell someone about it or give an official account of it E.G. *He reported the theft to the police.* 2 To report someone to an authority means to make an official complaint about them. 3 If you report to a person or place, you go there and say you have arrived.
▶ NOUN 4 an account of an event or situation.
■ (sense 4) account, description

reported speech
NOUN a report of what someone said that gives the content of the speech without repeating the exact words.

reporter reporters
NOUN someone who writes news articles or broadcasts news reports.

repossess repossesses repossessing repossessed
VERB If a shop or company

there's a rAKE in the brAKEs (bra̲ke)   **SPELLING NOTE**

repossesses goods that have not been paid for, they take them back.

represent represents representing represented
VERB (PSHE) 1 If you represent someone, you act on their behalf E.G. *lawyers representing relatives of the victims.* 2 If a sign or symbol represents something, it stands for it. 3 To represent something in a particular way means to describe it in that way E.G. *The popular press tends to represent him as a hero.*

representation representations
NOUN 1 Representation is the state of being represented by someone E.G. *Was there any student representation?* 2 You can describe a picture or statue of someone as a representation of them.

representative representatives
NOUN 1 (PSHE) a person chosen to act on behalf of another person or a group. ▸ ADJECTIVE 2 A representative selection is typical of the group it belongs to E.G. *The photos chosen are not representative of his work.*

repress represses repressing repressed
VERB 1 If you repress a feeling, you succeed in not showing or feeling it E.G. *I couldn't repress my anger any longer.* 2 To repress people means to restrict their freedom and control them by force.
repression NOUN

repressive
ADJECTIVE Repressive governments use force and unjust laws to restrict and control people.

reprieve reprieves reprieving reprieved
Said "rip-**preev**" VERB 1 If someone who has been sentenced to death is reprieved, their sentence is changed and they are not killed. ▸ NOUN 2 a delay before something unpleasant happens E.G. *The zoo won a reprieve from closure.*

reprimand reprimands reprimanding reprimanded
VERB 1 If you reprimand someone, you officially tell them that they should not have done something. ▸ NOUN 2 something said or written by a person in authority when they are reprimanding someone.

reprisal reprisals
NOUN Reprisals are violent actions taken by one group of people against another group that has harmed them.

reproach reproaches reproaching reproached FORMAL
NOUN 1 If you express reproach, you show that you feel sad and angry about what someone has done E.G. *a long letter of reproach.* ▸ VERB 2 If you reproach someone, you tell them, rather sadly, that they have done something wrong.
reproachful ADJECTIVE

reproduce reproduces reproducing reproduced
VERB (SCIENCE) 1 To reproduce something means to make a copy of it. 2 When living things reproduce, they produce more of their own kind E.G. *Bacteria reproduce by splitting into two.*

reproduction reproductions
NOUN 1 a modern copy of a painting or piece of furniture. 2 Reproduction is the process by which a living thing produces more of its kind E.G. *the study of animal reproduction.*

reproductive
ADJECTIVE relating to the reproduction of living things E.G. *the female reproductive system*.

reptile reptiles
NOUN a cold-blooded animal, such as a snake or a lizard, which has scaly skin and lays eggs.
reptilian ADJECTIVE
📖 from Latin *reptilis* meaning 'creeping'

republic republics
NOUN a country which has a president rather than a king or queen.
republican NOUN or ADJECTIVE
republicanism NOUN
📖 from Latin *res publica* meaning literally 'public thing'

repulse repulses repulsing repulsed
VERB 1 If you repulse someone who is being friendly, you put them off by behaving coldly towards them E.G. *He repulses friendly advances*. 2 To repulse an attacking force means to fight it and cause it to retreat. 3 If something repulses you, you find it horrible and disgusting and you want to avoid it.

repulsion
NOUN 1 Repulsion is a strong feeling of disgust. 2 Repulsion is a force separating two objects, such as the force between two like electric charges.

repulsive
ADJECTIVE horrible and disgusting.

reputable
ADJECTIVE known to be good and reliable E.G. *a well-established and reputable firm*.

reputation reputations
NOUN The reputation of something or someone is the opinion that people have of them E.G. *The college had a good reputation*.
■ name, renown, standing

reputed
ADJECTIVE If something is reputed to be true, some people say that it is true E.G. *the reputed tomb of Christ*.
reputedly ADVERB

request requests requesting requested
VERB 1 If you request something, you ask for it politely or formally. ▶ NOUN 2 If you make a request for something, you request it.

requiem requiems
Said "rek-wee-em" NOUN 1 A requiem or requiem mass is a mass celebrated for someone who has recently died. 2 a piece of music for singers and an orchestra, originally written for a requiem mass E.G. *Mozart's Requiem*.
📖 from Latin *requies* meaning 'rest'

require requires requiring required
VERB 1 If you require something, you need it. 2 If you are required to do something, you have to do it because someone says you must E.G. *The rules require employers to provide safety training*.

requirement requirements
NOUN something that you must have or must do E.G. *A good degree is a requirement for entry*.

requisite requisites FORMAL
ADJECTIVE 1 necessary for a particular purpose E.G. *She filled in the requisite paperwork*. ▶ NOUN 2 something that is necessary for a particular purpose.

rescue rescues rescuing rescued
VERB 1 If you rescue someone, you

a b c d e f g h i j k l m n o p q **r** s t u v w x y z

save them from a dangerous or unpleasant situation. ▶ NOUN 2 Rescue is help which saves someone from a dangerous or unpleasant situation.
rescuer NOUN

research researches researching researched
NOUN 1 Research is work that involves studying something and trying to find out facts about it. ▶ VERB 2 If you research something, you try to discover facts about it.
researcher NOUN

resemblance
NOUN If there is a resemblance between two things, they are similar to each other E.G. *There was a remarkable resemblance between them*.
■ likeness, similarity

resemble resembles resembling resembled
VERB To resemble something means to be similar to it.

resent resents resenting resented
VERB If you resent something, you feel bitter and angry about it.
resentment NOUN

resentful
ADJECTIVE bitter and angry E.G. *He felt very resentful about losing his job*.
resentfully ADVERB

reservation reservations
NOUN 1 If you have reservations about something, you are not sure that it is right. 2 If you make a reservation, you book a place in advance. 3 an area of land set aside for American Indian peoples E.G. *a Cherokee reservation*.

reserve reserves reserving reserved
VERB 1 If something is reserved for a particular person or purpose, it is kept specially for them. ▶ NOUN 2 a supply of something for future use. 3 In sport, a reserve is someone who is available to play in case one of the team is unable to play. 4 A nature reserve is an area of land where animals, birds, or plants are officially protected. 5 If someone shows reserve, they keep their feelings hidden.
reserved ADJECTIVE
■ (sense 1) put by, save, set aside

reservoir reservoirs
Said "**rez**-ev-wahr" NOUN a lake used for storing water before it is supplied to people.

reshuffle reshuffles
NOUN a reorganization of people or things.

reside resides residing resided
Said "riz-**zide**" VERB; FORMAL If a quality resides in something, the quality is in that thing.

residence residence
NOUN; FORMAL a house.

resident residents
NOUN 1 A resident of a house or area is someone who lives there.
▶ ADJECTIVE 2 If someone is resident in a house or area, they live there.

residential
ADJECTIVE 1 A residential area contains mainly houses rather than offices or factories. 2 providing accommodation E.G. *residential care for the elderly*.

residue residues
NOUN a small amount of something that remains after most of it has gone E.G. *an increase in toxic residues found in drinking water*.
residual ADJECTIVE

A B C D E F G H I J K L M N O P Q R S T U V W X Y Z

resign resigns resigning resigned

VERB 1 If you resign from a job, you formally announce that you are leaving it. 2 If you resign yourself to an unpleasant situation, you realize that you have to accept it.

resigned ADJECTIVE

resignation resignations

NOUN 1 Someone's resignation is a formal statement of their intention to leave a job. 2 Resignation is the reluctant acceptance of an unpleasant situation or fact.

resilient

ADJECTIVE able to recover quickly from unpleasant or damaging events.

resilience NOUN

resin resins

NOUN 1 Resin is a sticky substance produced by some trees. 2 Resin is also a substance produced chemically and used to make plastics.

resist resists resisting resisted

VERB 1 If you resist something, you refuse to accept it and try to prevent it E.G. *The pay squeeze will be fiercely resisted by the unions.* 2 If you resist someone, you fight back against them.

■ (sense 1) fight, oppose

resistance resistances

NOUN 1 Resistance to something such as change is a refusal to accept it. 2 Resistance to an attack consists of fighting back E.G. *The demonstrators offered no resistance.* 3 Your body's resistance to germs or disease is its power to not be harmed by them. 4 Resistance is also the power of a substance to resist the flow of an electrical current through it.

resistant

ADJECTIVE 1 opposed to something and wanting to prevent it E.G. *People were very resistant to change.* 2 If something is resistant to a particular thing, it is not harmed or affected by it E.G. *Certain insects are resistant to this spray.*

resolute

Said "rez-ol-loot" ADJECTIVE; FORMAL Someone who is resolute is determined not to change their mind.

resolutely ADVERB

resolution resolutions

NOUN 1 Resolution is determination. 2 If you make a resolution, you promise yourself to do something. 3 a formal decision taken at a meeting. 4 (ENGLISH) FORMAL The resolution of a problem is the solving of it.

resolve resolves resolving resolved

VERB 1 If you resolve to do something, you firmly decide to do it. 2 If you resolve a problem, you find a solution to it. ► NOUN 3 Resolve is absolute determination.

resonance resonances

NOUN 1 Resonance is sound produced by an object vibrating as a result of another sound nearby. 2 Resonance is also a deep, clear, and echoing quality of sound.

resonate resonates resonating resonated

VERB If something resonates, it vibrates and produces a deep, strong sound.

resort resorts resorting resorted

VERB 1 If you resort to a course of

a b c d e f g h i j k l m n o p q **r** s t u v w x y z

The government licenSes Schnapps (licenses)   **SPELLING NOTE**

A
B
C
D
E
F
G
H
I
J
K
L
M
N
O
P
Q
R
S
T
U
V
W
X
Y
Z

action, you do it because you have no alternative. ► NOUN **2** a place where people spend their holidays. ► PHRASE **3** If you do something **as a last resort**, you do it because you can find no other way of solving a problem.

resounding
ADJECTIVE **1** loud and echoing E.G. *a resounding round of applause.* **2** A resounding success is a great success.

resource resources
NOUN The resources of a country, organization, or person are the materials, money, or skills they have.

resourceful
ADJECTIVE A resourceful person is good at finding ways of dealing with problems.
resourcefulness NOUN

respect respects respecting respected
VERB **1** If you respect someone, you have a good opinion of their character or ideas. **2** If you respect someone's rights or wishes, you do not do things that they would not like, or would consider wrong E.G. *It is about time they started respecting the law.* ► NOUN **3** If you have respect for someone, you respect them. ► PHRASE **4** You can say **in this respect** to refer to a particular feature E.G. *At least in this respect we are equals.*

respectable
ADJECTIVE **1** considered to be acceptable and morally correct E.G. *respectable families.* **2** adequate or reasonable E.G. *a respectable rate of economic growth.*
respectability NOUN **respectably** ADVERB

respectful
ADJECTIVE showing respect for someone E.G. *Our children are always respectful to their elders.*
respectfully ADVERB

respective
ADJECTIVE belonging or relating individually to the people or things just mentioned E.G. *They went into their respective rooms to pack.*

respectively
ADVERB in the same order as the items just mentioned E.G. *They finished first and second respectively.*

respiration
NOUN (SCIENCE) TECHNICAL Your respiration is your breathing.

respiratory
ADJECTIVE; TECHNICAL relating to breathing E.G. *respiratory diseases.*

respire respires respiring respired
VERB (SCIENCE) To respire is to breathe.

respite
NOUN; FORMAL a short rest from something unpleasant.

respond responds responding responded
VERB When you respond to something, you react to it by doing or saying something.

respondent respondents
NOUN **1** a person who answers a questionnaire or a request for information. **2** In a court case, the respondent is the defendant.

response responses
NOUN Your response to an event is your reaction or reply to it E.G. *There has been no response to his remarks yet.*

responsibility responsibilities
NOUN **1** If you have responsibility for

something, it is your duty to deal with it or look after it E.G. *The garden was to have been his responsibility*. **2** If you accept responsibility for something that has happened, you agree that you caused it or were to blame E.G. *We must all accept responsibility for our own mistakes.*

responsible

ADJECTIVE **1** If you are responsible for something, it is your duty to deal with it and you are to blame if it goes wrong. **2** If you are responsible to someone, that person is your boss and tells you what you have to do. **3** A responsible person behaves properly and sensibly without needing to be supervised. **4** A responsible job involves making careful judgments about important matters.

responsibly ADVERB

■ (sense 1) accountable, answerable, liable

responsive

ADJECTIVE **1** quick to show interest and pleasure. **2** taking notice of events and reacting in an appropriate way E.G. *The course is responsive to students' needs.*

rest rests resting rested

NOUN **1** The rest of something is all the remaining parts of it. **2** If you have a rest, you sit or lie quietly and relax.
▶ VERB **3** If you rest, you relax and do not do anything active for a while.

restaurant restaurants

*Said "***rest-ront***"* NOUN a place where you can buy and eat a meal.
🔠 a French word; from *restaurer* meaning 'to restore'

restaurateur restaurateurs

*Said "***rest-er-a-tur***"* NOUN someone who owns or manages a restaurant.

restful

ADJECTIVE Something that is restful helps you feel calm and relaxed.

restless

ADJECTIVE finding it hard to remain still or relaxed because of boredom or impatience.

restlessness NOUN **restlessly** ADVERB

restore restores restoring restored

VERB **1** To restore something means to cause it to exist again or to return to its previous state E.G. *He was anxious to restore his reputation.* **2** To restore an old building or work of art means to clean and repair it.

restoration NOUN

■ (sense 2) refurbish, renovate

restrain restrains restraining restrained

VERB To restrain someone or something means to hold them back or prevent them from doing what they want to.

restrained

ADJECTIVE behaving in a controlled way.

restraint restraints

NOUN **1** Restraints are rules or conditions that limit something E.G. *wage restraints.* **2** Restraint is calm, controlled behaviour.

restrict restricts restricting restricted

VERB **1** If you restrict something, you prevent it becoming too large or varied. **2** To restrict people or animals means to limit their movement or actions.

restrictive ADJECTIVE

restriction restrictions

NOUN a rule or situation that limits

a
b
c
d
e
f
g
h
i
j
k
l
m
n
o
p
q
r
s
t
u
v
w
x
y
z

Plaice the fish has a glittering 'EYE' (I) (pla*i*ce) **SPELLING NOTE**

A
B
C
D
E
F
G
H
I
J
K
L
M
N
O
P
Q
R
S
T
U
V
W
X
Y
Z

what you can do E.G. *financial restrictions*.

result results resulting resulted

NOUN 1 The result of an action or situation is the situation that is caused by it E.G. *As a result of the incident he got a two-year suspension*. 2 The result is also the final marks, figures, or situation at the end of an exam, calculation, or contest E.G. *election results… The result was calculated to three decimal places*.
▶ VERB 3 If something results in a particular event, it causes that event to happen. 4 If something results from a particular event, it is caused by that event E.G. *The fire had resulted from carelessness*.
resultant ADJECTIVE
■ (sense 1) consequence, outcome, upshot

resume resumes resuming resumed
Said "riz-**yoom**" VERB If you resume an activity or position, you return to it after a break.
resumption NOUN

resurgence
NOUN If there is a resurgence of an attitude or activity, it reappears and grows stronger.
resurgent ADJECTIVE

resurrect resurrects resurrecting resurrected
VERB If you resurrect something, you make it exist again after it has disappeared or ended.
resurrection NOUN

Resurrection
NOUN In Christian belief, the Resurrection is the coming back to life of Jesus Christ three days after he had been killed.

resuscitate resuscitates resuscitating resuscitated
Said "ris-**suss**-it-tate" VERB If you resuscitate someone, you make them conscious again after an accident.
resuscitation NOUN

retail
NOUN The retail price is the price at which something is sold in the shops.
retailer NOUN

retain retains retaining retained
VERB To retain something means to keep it.
retention NOUN

retaliate retaliates retaliating retaliated
VERB If you retaliate, you do something to harm or upset someone because they have already acted in a similar way against you.
retaliation NOUN

retarded
ADJECTIVE If someone is retarded, their mental development is much less advanced than average.

rethink rethinks rethinking rethought
VERB If you rethink something, you think about how it should be changed E.G. *We have to rethink our strategy*.

reticent
ADJECTIVE Someone who is reticent is unwilling to tell people about things.
reticence NOUN

retina retinas
NOUN the light-sensitive part at the back of your eyeball, which receives an image and sends it to your brain.

retinue retinues
NOUN a group of helpers or friends travelling with an important person.

retire retires retiring retired
VERB 1 When older people retire, they give up work. 2 FORMAL If you retire, you leave to go into another room, or to bed E.G. *She retired early with a good book.*
retired ADJECTIVE   **retirement** NOUN

retort retorts retorting retorted
VERB 1 To retort means to reply angrily. ▶ NOUN 2 a short, angry reply.

retract retracts retracting retracted
VERB 1 If you retract something you have said, you say that you did not mean it. 2 When something is retracted, it moves inwards or backwards E.G. *The undercarriage was retracted shortly after takeoff.*
retraction NOUN   **retractable** ADJECTIVE

retreat retreats retreating retreated
VERB 1 To retreat means to move backwards away from something or someone. 2 If you retreat from something difficult or unpleasant, you avoid doing it. ▶ NOUN 3 If an army moves away from the enemy, this is referred to as a retreat. 4 a quiet place that you can go to rest or do things in private.

retribution
NOUN; FORMAL Retribution is punishment E.G. *the threat of retribution.*

retrieve retrieves retrieving retrieved
VERB If you retrieve something, you get it back.
retrieval NOUN

retriever retrievers
NOUN a large dog often used by hunters to bring back birds and animals which have been shot.

retro-
PREFIX 'Retro-' means 'back' or 'backwards' E.G. *retrospective.*
📖 from Latin *retro* meaning 'behind' or 'backwards'

retrospect
NOUN When you consider something in retrospect, you think about it afterwards and often have a different opinion from the one you had at the time E.G. *In retrospect, I probably shouldn't have resigned.*

retrospective
ADJECTIVE 1 concerning things that happened in the past. 2 taking effect from a date in the past.
retrospectively ADVERB

return returns returning returned
VERB 1 When you return to a place, you go back after you have been away. 2 If you return something to someone, you give it back to them. 3 When you return a ball during a game, you hit it back to your opponent. 4 When a judge or jury returns a verdict, they announce it. ▶ NOUN 5 Your return is your arrival back at a place. 6 The return on an investment is the profit or interest you get from it. 7 a ticket for the journey to a place and back again. ▶ PHRASE 8 If you do something in return for a favour, you do it to repay the favour.

reunion reunions
NOUN a party or meeting for people who have not seen each other for a long time.

reunite reunites reuniting reunited
VERB If people are reunited, they meet

a
b
c
d
e
f
g
h
i
j
k
l
m
n
o
p
q
r
s
t
u
v
w
x
y
z

again after they have been
separated for some time.

rev revs revving revved INFORMAL
VERB 1 When you rev the engine of a
vehicle, you press the accelerator to
increase the engine speed. ► NOUN
2 The speed of an engine is
measured in revolutions per minute,
referred to as revs E.G. *I noticed that
the engine revs had dropped.*

Rev or **Revd**
abbreviations for **Reverend**.

revamp revamps revamping
revamped
VERB To revamp something means to
improve or repair it.

reveal reveals revealing
revealed
VERB 1 To reveal something means to
tell people about it E.G. *They were
not ready to reveal any of the details.*
2 If you reveal something that has
been hidden, you uncover it.

revel revels revelling revelled
VERB If you revel in a situation, you
enjoy it very much.
revelry NOUN

revelation revelations
NOUN 1 a surprising or interesting fact
made known to people. 2 If an
experience is a revelation, it makes
you realize or learn something.

revenge revenges revenging
revenged
NOUN 1 Revenge involves hurting
someone who has hurt you. ► VERB 2 If
you revenge yourself on someone
who has hurt you, you hurt them in
return.
■ (sense 1) retaliation, vengeance
■ (sense 2) avenge, retaliate

revenue revenues
NOUN Revenue is money that a

government, company, or
organization receives E.G.
government tax revenues.

revered
ADJECTIVE If someone is revered, he or
she is respected and admired E.G. *He
is still revered as the father of the nation.*

reverence
NOUN Reverence is a feeling of great
respect.

Reverend
Reverend is a title used before the
name of a member of the clergy E.G.
the Reverend George Young.

reversal reversals
NOUN If there is a reversal of a process
or policy, it is changed to the
opposite process or policy.

reverse reverses reversing
reversed
VERB 1 When someone reverses a
process, they change it to the
opposite process E.G. *They won't
reverse the decision to increase prices.*
2 If you reverse the order of things,
you arrange them in the opposite
order. 3 When you reverse a car, you
drive it backwards. ► NOUN 4 The
reverse is the opposite of what has
just been said or done. ► ADJECTIVE
5 Reverse means opposite to what is
usual or to what has just been
described.

reversible
ADJECTIVE Reversible clothing can be
worn with either side on the outside.

revert reverts reverting
reverted
VERB; FORMAL To revert to a former state
or type of behaviour means to go
back to it.

review reviews reviewing
reviewed

NOUN **1** an article or an item on television or radio, giving an opinion of a new book or play. **2** When there is a review of a situation or system, it is examined to decide whether changes are needed. ▶ VERB **3** To review a play or book means to write an account expressing an opinion of it. **4** To review something means to examine it to decide whether changes are needed.
reviewer NOUN
■ (sense 2) examination, survey
■ (sense 4) reassess, reconsider, revise

revise revises revising revised
VERB **1** If you revise something, you alter or correct it. **2** When you revise for an examination, you go over your work to learn things thoroughly.
revision NOUN

revive revives reviving revived
VERB **1** When a feeling or practice is revived, it becomes active or popular again. **2** When you revive someone who has fainted, they become conscious again.
revival NOUN

revolt revolts revolting revolted
NOUN (HISTORY) **1** a violent attempt by a group of people to change their country's political system. ▶ VERB **2** When people revolt, they fight against the authority that governs them. **3** If something revolts you, it is so horrible that you feel disgust.

revolting
ADJECTIVE horrible and disgusting E.G. *The smell in the cell was revolting.*

revolution revolutions
NOUN **1** (HISTORY) a violent attempt by a large group of people to change the political system of their country. **2** an important change in an area of

human activity E.G. *the Industrial Revolution.* **3** one complete turn in a circle.

revolutionary revolutionaries
ADJECTIVE **1** involving great changes E.G. *a revolutionary new cooling system.* ▶ NOUN **2** a person who takes part in a revolution.

revolve revolves revolving revolved
VERB **1** If something revolves round something else, it centres on that as the most important thing E.G. *My job revolves around the telephone.* **2** When something revolves, it turns in a circle around a central point E.G. *The moon revolves round the earth.*

revolver revolvers
NOUN a small gun held in the hand.

revulsion
NOUN Revulsion is a strong feeling of disgust or disapproval.

reward rewards rewarding rewarded
NOUN (PSHE) **1** something you are given because you have done something good. ▶ VERB **2** If you reward someone, you give them a reward.

rewarding
ADJECTIVE Something that is rewarding gives you a lot of satisfaction.

rewind rewinds rewinding rewound
VERB If you rewind a tape on a tape recorder or video, you make the tape go backwards.

rhapsody rhapsodies
Said "rap-sod-ee" NOUN a short piece of music which is very passionate and flowing.

rhetoric
NOUN Rhetoric is speech or writing that is intended to impress people.

a
b
c
d
e
f
g
h
i
j
k
l
m
n
o
p
q
r
s
t
u
v
w
x
y
z

LEarn the principLEs (princip**le**)   SPELLING NOTE

A
B
C
D
E
F
G
H
I
J
K
L
M
N
O
P
Q
R
S
T
U
V
W
X
Y
Z

rhetorical

ADJECTIVE **1** A rhetorical question is one which is asked in order to make a statement rather than to get an answer. **2** Rhetorical language is intended to be grand and impressive.

rheumatism

Said "room-at-izm" NOUN Rheumatism is an illness that makes your joints and muscles stiff and painful.
rheumatic ADJECTIVE

rhino rhinos

NOUN; INFORMAL a rhinoceros.

rhinoceros rhinoceroses

NOUN a large African or Asian animal with one or two horns on its nose. 🔲 from Greek *rhin* meaning 'of the nose' and *keras* meaning 'horn'

rhododendron rhododendrons

NOUN an evergreen bush with large coloured flowers.

rhombus rhombuses or **rhombi**

NOUN (MATHS) a shape with four equal sides and no right angles.

rhubarb

NOUN Rhubarb is a plant with long red stems which can be cooked with sugar and eaten.

rhyme rhymes rhyming rhymed

(ENGLISH) VERB **1** If two words rhyme, they have a similar sound E.G. *Sally rhymes with valley*. ▶ NOUN **2** a word that rhymes with another. **3** a short poem with rhyming lines.

rhythm rhythms

NOUN **1** (MUSIC) Rhythm is a regular movement or beat. **2** a regular pattern of changes, for example, in the seasons.
rhythmic ADJECTIVE **rhythmically** ADVERB

rib ribs

NOUN Your ribs are the curved bones that go from your backbone to your chest.
ribbed ADJECTIVE

ribbon ribbons

NOUN a long, narrow piece of cloth used for decoration.

ribcage ribcages

NOUN Your ribcage is the framework of bones made up of your ribs which protects your internal organs like your heart and lungs.

rice

NOUN Rice is a tall grass that produces edible grains. Rice is grown in warm countries on wet ground.

rich richer richest; riches

ADJECTIVE **1** Someone who is rich has a lot of money and possessions. **2** Something that is rich in something contains a large amount of it E.G. *Liver is particularly rich in vitamin A*. **3** Rich food contains a large amount of fat, oil, or sugar. **4** Rich colours, smells, and sounds are strong and pleasant. ▶ PLURAL NOUN **5** Riches are valuable possessions or large amounts of money E.G. *the oil riches of the Middle East*.
richness NOUN

richly

ADVERB **1** If someone is richly rewarded, they are rewarded well with something valuable. **2** If you feel strongly that someone deserves something, you can say it is richly deserved.

rick ricks

NOUN a large pile of hay or straw.

rickets

NOUN Rickets is a disease that causes soft bones in children if they do not get enough vitamin D.

rickety

ADJECTIVE likely to collapse or break
E.G. *a rickety wooden jetty*.

rickshaw rickshaws

NOUN a hand-pulled cart used in Asia
for carrying passengers.

ricochet ricochets ricocheting or
ricochetting ricocheted or
ricochetted

Said "rik-*osh*-ay" VERB When a bullet
ricochets, it hits a surface and
bounces away from it.

rid rids ridding rid

PHRASE 1 When you **get rid** of
something you do not want, you
remove or destroy it. ► VERB 2 FORMAL
To rid a place of something
unpleasant means to succeed in
removing it.

riddle riddles

NOUN 1 a puzzle which seems to be
nonsense, but which has an
entertaining solution. 2 Something
that is a riddle puzzles and confuses
you.

■ (sense 2) enigma, mystery

riddled

ADJECTIVE full of something
undesirable E.G. *The report was
riddled with errors*.

🔟 from Old English *hriddel* meaning
'sieve'

ride rides riding rode ridden

VERB 1 When you ride a horse or a
bike, you sit on it and control it as it
moves along. 2 When you ride in a
car, you travel in it. ► NOUN 3 a journey
on a horse or bike or in a vehicle.

rider riders

NOUN 1 a person riding on a horse or
bicycle. 2 an additional statement
which changes or puts a condition

on what has already been said.

ridge ridges

NOUN 1 a long, narrow piece of high
land. 2 a raised line on a flat surface.

**ridicule ridicules ridiculing
ridiculed**

VERB 1 To ridicule someone means to
make fun of them in an unkind way.
► NOUN 2 Ridicule is unkind laughter
and mockery.

ridiculous

ADJECTIVE very foolish.

ridiculously ADVERB

rife

ADJECTIVE; FORMAL very common E.G.
Unemployment was rife.

rifle rifles rifling rifled

NOUN 1 a gun with a long barrel. ► VERB
2 When someone rifles something,
they make a quick search through it
to steal things.

rift rifts

NOUN 1 a serious quarrel between
friends that damages their
friendship. 2 a split in something
solid, especially in the ground.

rig rigs rigging rigged

VERB 1 If someone rigs an election or
contest, they dishonestly arrange for
a particular person to succeed.
► NOUN 2 a large structure used for
extracting oil or gas from the ground
or sea bed.

rig up VERB If you rig up a device or
structure, you make it quickly and fix
it in place E.G. *They had even rigged
up a makeshift aerial*.

right rights righting righted

ADJECTIVE or ADVERB 1 correct and in
accordance with the facts E.G. *That
clock never tells the right time… That's
absolutely right*. 2 'Right' means on or
towards the right side of something.

a
b
c
d
e
f
g
h
i
j
k
l
m
n
o
p
q
r
s
t
u
v
w
x
y
z

A
B
C
D
E
F
G
H
I
J
K
L
M
N
O
P
Q
R
S
T
U
V
W
X
Y
Z

▶ ADJECTIVE **3** The right choice or decision is the best or most suitable one. **4** The right people or places are those that have influence or are socially admired E.G. *He was always to be seen in the right places.* **5** The right side of something is the side intended to be seen and to face outwards. ▶ NOUN **6** 'Right' is used to refer to principles of morally correct behaviour E.G. *At least he knew right from wrong.* **7** If you have a right to do something, you are morally or legally entitled to do it. **8** The right is one of the two sides of something. For example, when you look at the word 'to', the 'o' is to the right of the 't'. **9** The Right refers to people who support the political ideas of capitalism and conservatism rather than socialism. ▶ ADVERB **10** 'Right' is used to emphasize a precise place E.G. *I'm right here.* **11** 'Right' means immediately E.G. *I had to decide right then.* ▶ VERB **12** If you right something, you correct it or put it back in an upright position.

rightly ADVERB

◧ (sense 3) appropriate, proper, suitable

◧ (sense 7) prerogative, privilege

right angle right angles
NOUN an angle of 90°.

righteous
ADJECTIVE Righteous people behave in a way that is morally good and religious.

rightful
ADJECTIVE Someone's rightful possession is one which they have a moral or legal right to.

rightfully ADVERB

right-handed
ADJECTIVE or ADVERB Someone who is

right-handed does things such as writing and painting with their right hand.

right-wing
ADJECTIVE believing more strongly in capitalism or conservatism, or less strongly in socialism, than other members of the same party or group.

right-winger NOUN

rigid
ADJECTIVE **1** Rigid laws or systems cannot be changed and are considered severe. **2** A rigid object is stiff and does not bend easily.

rigidly ADVERB **rigidity** NOUN

◧ (sense 1) inflexible, strict

rigorous
ADJECTIVE very careful and thorough.

rigorously ADVERB

rigour rigours
NOUN; FORMAL The rigours of a situation are the things which make it hard or unpleasant E.G. *the rigours of childbirth.*

rim rims
NOUN the outside or top edge of an object such as a wheel or a cup.

rimu rimu or rimus
Said "ree-moo" NOUN a New Zealand tree with narrow, pointed leaves, which produces wood used for furniture.

rind rinds
NOUN Rind is the thick outer skin of fruit, cheese, or bacon.

ring rings ringing rang rung
VERB **1** If you ring someone, you phone them. **2** When a bell rings, it makes a clear, loud sound. **3** To ring something means to draw a circle around it. **4** If something is ringed with something else, it has that thing

all the way around it E.G. *The courthouse was ringed with police.*
▶ NOUN 5 the sound made by a bell. 6 a small circle of metal worn on your finger. 7 an object or group of things in the shape of a circle. 8 At a boxing match or circus, the ring is the place where the fight or performance takes place. 9 an organized group of people who are involved in an illegal activity E.G. *an international spy ring.*

☑ The past tense of *ring* is *rang*, and the past participle is *rung*. Do not confuse these words: *she rang the bell… I had rung the police.*

ringbark ringbarks ringbarking ringbarked
VERB If you ringbark a tree, you kill it by cutting away a strip of bark from around its trunk.

ringer ringers
NOUN 1 a person or thing that is almost identical to another. 2 In Australian English, someone who works on a sheep farm. 3 In Australian and New Zealand English, the fastest shearer in a woolshed.

ring-in ring-ins
NOUN INFORMAL 1 In Australian English, a person or thing that is not normally a member of a particular group. 2 In Australian and New Zealand English, someone who is brought in at the last minute as a replacement for someone else.

ringleader ringleaders
NOUN the leader of a group of people who get involved in mischief or crime.

rink rinks
NOUN a large indoor area for ice-skating or roller-skating.

rinse rinses rinsing rinsed
VERB 1 When you rinse something, you wash it in clean water. ▶ NOUN 2 a liquid you can put on your hair to give it a different colour.

riot riots rioting rioted
NOUN 1 When there is a riot, a crowd of people behave noisily and violently. ▶ VERB 2 To riot means to behave noisily and violently. ▶ PHRASE 3 To **run riot** means to behave in a wild and uncontrolled way.

rip rips ripping ripped
VERB 1 When you rip something, you tear it violently. 2 If you rip something away, you remove it quickly and violently. ▶ NOUN 3 a long split in cloth or paper.

rip off VERB; INFORMAL If someone rips you off, they cheat you by charging you too much money.

RIP
RIP is an abbreviation often written on gravestones, meaning 'rest in peace'.

ripe riper ripest
ADJECTIVE 1 When fruit or grain is ripe, it is fully developed and ready to be eaten. 2 If a situation is ripe for something to happen, it is ready for it.

ripeness NOUN

ripen ripens ripening ripened
VERB When crops ripen, they become ripe.

ripper rippers
NOUN; INFORMAL In Australia and New Zealand English, an excellent person or thing.

ripple ripples rippling rippled
NOUN 1 Ripples are little waves on the surface of calm water. 2 If there is a ripple of laughter or applause,

a
b
c
d
e
f
g
h
i
j
k
l
m
n
o
p
q
r
s
t
u
v
w
x
y
z

A
B
C
D
E
F
G
H
I
J
K
L
M
N
O
P
Q
R
S
T
U
V
W
X
Y
Z

people laugh or applaud gently for a short time. ▶ VERB **3** When the surface of water ripples, little waves appear on it.

rise rises rising rose risen

VERB **1** If something rises, it moves upwards. **2** FORMAL When you rise, you stand up. **3** To rise also means to get out of bed. **4** When the sun rises, it first appears. **5** The place where a river rises is where it begins. **6** If land rises, it slopes upwards. **7** If a sound or wind rises, it becomes higher or stronger. **8** If an amount rises, it increases. **9** If you rise to a challenge or a remark, you respond to it rather than ignoring it E.G. *He rose to the challenge with enthusiasm*. **10** When people rise up, they start fighting against people in authority. ▶ NOUN **11** an increase. **12** Someone's rise is the process by which they become more powerful or successful E.G. *his rise to fame*.

▣ (sense 1) ascend, climb, go up

riser risers

NOUN An early riser is someone who likes to get up early in the morning.

risk risks risking risked

NOUN **1** a chance that something unpleasant or dangerous might happen. ▶ VERB **2** If you risk something unpleasant, you do something knowing that the unpleasant thing might happen as a result E.G. *If he doesn't play, he risks losing his place in the team*. **3** If you risk someone's life, you put them in a dangerous situation in which they might be killed.

risky ADJECTIVE

▦ from Italian *rischiare* meaning 'to be in danger'

rite rites

NOUN a religious ceremony.

ritual rituals

NOUN **1** a series of actions carried out according to the custom of a particular society or group E.G. *This is the most ancient of the Buddhist rituals*. ▶ ADJECTIVE **2** Ritual activities happen as part of a tradition or ritual E.G. *fasting and ritual dancing*.

ritualistic ADJECTIVE

rival rivals rivalling rivalled

NOUN **1** Your rival is the person you are competing with. ▶ VERB **2** If something rivals something else, it is of the same high standard or quality E.G. *As a holiday destination, South Africa rivals Kenya for weather*.

▣ (sense 1) adversary, opponent

rivalry rivalries

NOUN Rivalry is active competition between people.

river rivers

NOUN a natural feature consisting of water flowing for a long distance between two banks.

rivet rivets

NOUN a short, round pin with a flat head which is used to fasten sheets of metal together.

riveting

ADJECTIVE If you find something riveting, you find it fascinating and it holds your attention E.G. *I find tennis riveting*.

road roads

NOUN a long piece of hard ground specially surfaced so that people and vehicles can travel along it easily.

road rage

NOUN Road rage is aggressive behaviour by a driver as a reaction to the behaviour of another driver.

road train road trains
NOUN In Australia, a line of linked trailers pulled by a truck, used for transporting cattle or sheep.

roadworks
PLURAL NOUN Roadworks are repairs being done on a road.

roam roams roaming roamed
VERB If you roam around, you wander around without any particular purpose E.G. *Hens were roaming around the yard.*

roar roars roaring roared
VERB 1 If something roars, it makes a very loud noise. 2 To roar with laughter or anger means to laugh or shout very noisily. 3 When a lion roars, it makes a loud, angry sound. ▶ NOUN 4 a very loud noise.

roast roasts roasting roasted
VERB 1 When you roast meat or other food, you cook it using dry heat in an oven or over a fire. ▶ ADJECTIVE 2 Roast meat has been roasted. ▶ NOUN 3 a piece of meat that has been roasted.

rob robs robbing robbed
VERB 1 If someone robs you, they steal your possessions. 2 If you rob someone of something they need or deserve, you deprive them of it E.G. *He robbed me of my childhood.*

robber robbers
NOUN Robbers are people who steal money or property using force or threats E.G. *bank robbers.*
robbery NOUN

robe robes
NOUN a long, loose piece of clothing which covers the body E.G. *He knelt in his white robes before the altar.*

robin robins
NOUN a small bird with a red breast.

robot robots
NOUN a machine which is programmed to move and perform tasks automatically.
📷 from Czech *robota* meaning 'work'

robust
ADJECTIVE very strong and healthy.
robustly ADVERB

rock rocks rocking rocked
NOUN 1 Rock is the hard mineral substance that forms the surface of the earth. 2 a large piece of rock E.G. *She picked up a rock and threw it into the lake.* 3 Rock or rock music is music with simple tunes and a very strong beat. 4 Rock is also a sweet shaped into long, hard sticks, sold in holiday resorts. ▶ VERB 5 When something rocks or when you rock it, it moves regularly backwards and forwards or from side to side E.G. *She rocked the baby.* 6 If something rocks people, it shocks and upsets them E.G. *Palermo was rocked by a crime wave.* 7 If someone's marriage or relationship is **on the rocks**, it is unsuccessful and about to end.

rock and roll
NOUN Rock and roll is a style of music with a strong beat that was especially popular in the 1950s.

rocket rockets rocketing rocketed
NOUN 1 a space vehicle, usually shaped like a long pointed tube. 2 an explosive missile E.G. *They fired rockets into a number of government buildings.* 3 a firework that explodes when it is high in the air. ▶ VERB 4 If prices rocket, they increase very quickly.

rocking chair rocking chairs
NOUN a chair on two curved pieces of

rock melon rock melons

NOUN In Australian, New Zealand, and American English a rock melon is a cantaloupe, a melon with orange flesh and a hard, lumpy skin.

rocky

ADJECTIVE covered with rocks.

rod rods

NOUN a long, thin pole or bar, usually made of wood or metal E.G. *a fishing rod*.

rodent rodents

NOUN a small mammal with sharp front teeth which it uses for gnawing.

🏛 from Latin *rodere* meaning 'to gnaw'

rodeo rodeos

NOUN a public entertainment in which cowboys show different skills.

roe

NOUN Roe is the eggs of a fish.

rogue rogues

NOUN 1 You can refer to a man who behaves dishonestly as a rogue. ► ADJECTIVE 2 a vicious animal that lives apart from its herd or pack.

role roles; also spelt rôle

NOUN 1 Someone's role is their position and function in a situation or society. 2 (DRAMA) An actor's role is the character that he or she plays E.G. *her first leading role*.

roll rolls rolling rolled

VERB 1 When something rolls or when you roll it, it moves along a surface, turning over and over. 2 When vehicles roll along, they move E.G. *Tanks rolled into the village.* 3 If you roll your eyes, you make them turn up or go from side to side. 4 If you

roll something flexible into a cylinder or ball, you wrap it several times around itself E.G. *He rolled up the bag with the money in it.* ► NOUN 5 A roll of paper or cloth is a long piece of it that has been rolled into a tube E.G. *a roll of film.* 6 a small, rounded, individually baked piece of bread. 7 an official list of people's names E.G. *the electoral roll.* 8 A roll on a drum is a long, rumbling sound made on it.

roll-call roll-calls

NOUN If you take a roll-call, you call a register of names to see who is present.

roller rollers

NOUN 1 a cylinder that turns round in a machine or piece of equipment. 2 Rollers are tubes which you can wind your hair around to make it curly.

Rollerblade Rollerblades

NOUN; TRADEMARK Rollerblades are roller-skates which have the wheels set in one straight line on the bottom of the boot.

roller-coaster roller-coasters

NOUN a pleasure ride at a fair, consisting of a small railway that goes up and down very steep slopes.

roller-skate roller-skates roller-skating roller-skated

NOUN 1 Roller-skates are shoes with four small wheels underneath. ► VERB 2 If you roller-skate, you move along wearing roller-skates.

rolling pin rolling pins

NOUN a wooden cylinder used for rolling pastry dough to make it flat.

ROM

NOUN In computing, ROM is a storage device that holds data permanently and cannot be altered by the programmer. ROM stands for 'read only memory'.

Roman Catholic Roman Catholics
ADJECTIVE **1** relating or belonging to the branch of the Christian church that accepts the Pope in Rome as its leader. ► NOUN **2** someone who belongs to the Roman Catholic church.
Roman Catholicism NOUN

romance romances
NOUN **1** a relationship between two people who are in love with each other. **2** Romance is the pleasure and excitement of doing something new and unusual E.G. *the romance of foreign travel.* **3** (LIBRARY) a novel about a love affair.

Romanian Romanians
Said "roe-may-nee-an"; *also spelt* **Rumanian**
ADJECTIVE **1** belonging or relating to Romania. ► NOUN **2** someone who comes from Romania. **3** Romanian is the main language spoken in Romania.

romantic romantics
ADJECTIVE or NOUN **1** A romantic person has ideas that are not realistic, for example about love or about ways of changing society E.G. *a romantic idealist.* ► ADJECTIVE **2** connected with sexual love E.G. *a romantic relationship.* **3** Something that is romantic is beautiful in a way that strongly affects your feelings E.G. *It is one of the most romantic ruins in Scotland.* **4** Romantic describes a style of music, literature, and art popular in Europe in the late 18th and early 19th centuries, which emphasized feeling and imagination

rather than order and form.
romantically ADVERB **romanticism** NOUN

rondavel rondavels
NOUN In South Africa, a rondavel is a small circular building with a conical roof.

roo roos
NOUN; INFORMAL In Australian English, a kangaroo.

roof roofs
NOUN **1** The roof of a building or car is the covering on top of it. **2** The roof of your mouth or of a cave is the highest part.

roofing
NOUN Roofing is material used for covering roofs.

rooftop rooftops
NOUN the outside part of the roof of a building.

rook rooks
NOUN **1** a large black bird. **2** a chess piece which can move any number of squares in a straight but not diagonal line.

room rooms
NOUN **1** a separate section in a building, divided from other rooms by walls. **2** If there is plenty of room, there is a lot of space E.G. *There wasn't enough room for his gear.*

roost roosts roosting roosted
NOUN **1** a place where birds rest or build their nests. ► VERB **2** When birds roost, they settle somewhere for the night.

root roots rooting rooted
NOUN **1** The roots of a plant are the parts that grow under the ground. **2** The root of a hair is the part beneath the skin. **3** You can refer to the place or culture that you grew

a b c d e f g h i j k l m n o p q r s t u v w x y z

'i' before 'e' except after 'c'   SPELLING NOTE

up in as your roots. **4** The root of something is its original cause or basis E.G. *We got to the root of the problem.* ➤ VERB **5** To root through things means to search through them, pushing them aside E.G. *She rooted through his bag.*

root out VERB If you root something or someone out, you find them and force them out E.G. *a major drive to root out corruption.*

rooted
ADJECTIVE developed from or strongly influenced by something E.G. *songs rooted in traditional African music.*

rope ropes roping roped
NOUN **1** a thick, strong length of twisted cord. ➤ VERB **2** If you rope one thing to another, you tie them together with rope.

rosary rosaries
NOUN a string of beads that Catholics use for counting prayers.

rose roses
NOUN **1** a large garden flower which has a pleasant smell and grows on a bush with thorns. ➤ NOUN or ADJECTIVE **2** reddish-pink.

rosella rosellas
NOUN a brightly coloured Australian parrot.

rosemary
NOUN Rosemary is a herb with fragrant spiky leaves, used for flavouring in cooking.

rosette rosettes
NOUN a large badge of coloured ribbons gathered into a circle, which is worn as a prize in a competition or to support a political party.

Rosh Hashanah or **Rosh Hashana**
NOUN the festival celebrating the Jewish New Year.
🔲 a Hebrew phrase meaning 'head of the year'

roster rosters
NOUN a list of people who take it in turn to do a particular job E.G. *He put himself first on the new roster for domestic chores.*

rostrum rostrums or **rostra**
NOUN a raised platform on which someone stands to speak to an audience or conduct an orchestra.
🔲 from Latin *rostrum* meaning 'ship's prow'; Roman orators' platforms were decorated with the prows of captured ships

rosy rosier rosiest
ADJECTIVE **1** reddish-pink. **2** If a situation seems rosy, it is likely to be good or successful. **3** If a person looks rosy, they have pink cheeks and look healthy.

rot rots rotting rotted
VERB **1** When food or wood rots, it decays and can no longer be used. **2** When something rots another substance, it causes it to decay E.G. *Sugary drinks rot your teeth.* ➤ NOUN **3** Rot is the condition that affects things when they rot E.G. *The timber frame was not protected against rot.*
▤ (sense 1) decay, decompose

rota rotas
NOUN a list of people who take turns to do a particular job.

rotate rotates rotating rotated
VERB (MATHS) When something rotates, it turns with a circular movement E.G. *He rotated the camera 180°.*
rotation NOUN

rotor rotors
NOUN **1** The rotor is the part of a machine that turns. **2** The rotors or

rotor blades of a helicopter are the four long flat pieces of metal on top of it which rotate and lift it off the ground.

rotten

ADJECTIVE **1** decayed and no longer of use E.G. *The front bay window is rotten.* **2** INFORMAL of very poor quality E.G. *I think it's a rotten idea.* **3** INFORMAL very unfair, unkind, or unpleasant E.G. *That's a rotten thing to say!*

rouble roubles

Said "roo-bl" NOUN the main unit of currency in Russia.

🔳 In Russian *rubl* means literally 'silver bar'

rough rougher roughest; roughs

Said "ruff" ADJECTIVE **1** uneven and not smooth. **2** not using enough care or gentleness E.G. *Don't be so rough or you'll break it.* **3** difficult or unpleasant E.G. *Teachers have been given a rough time.* **4** approximately correct E.G. *At a rough guess it is five times more profitable.* **5** If the sea is rough, there are large waves because of bad weather. **6** A rough town or area has a lot of crime or violence. ► NOUN OR ADJECTIVE **7** A rough or a rough sketch is a drawing or description that shows the main features but does not show the details. **8** On a golf course, the rough is the part of the course next to a fairway where the grass has not been cut.

roughly ADVERB   **roughness** NOUN

roulette

Said "roo-let" NOUN Roulette is a gambling game in which a ball is dropped onto a revolving wheel with numbered holes in it.

round rounder roundest; rounds rounding rounded

ADJECTIVE **1** Something round is shaped like a ball or a circle. **2** complete or whole E.G. *round numbers.* ► PREPOSITION OR ADVERB **3** If something is round something else, it surrounds it. **4** The distance round something is the length of its circumference or boundary E.G. *I'm about two inches larger round the waist.* **5** You can refer to an area near a place as the area round it E.G. *There's nothing to do round here.* ► PREPOSITION **6** If something moves round you, it keeps moving in a circle with you in the centre. **7** When someone goes to the other side of something, they have gone round it. ► ADVERB OR PREPOSITION **8** If you go round a place, you go to different parts of it to look at it E.G. *We went round the museum.* ► ADVERB **9** If you turn or look round, you turn so you are facing in a different direction. **10** When someone comes round, they visit you E.G. *He came round with a bottle of wine.* ► NOUN **11** one of a series of events E.G. *After round three, two Americans shared the lead.* **12** If you buy a round of drinks, you buy a drink for each member of the group you are with.

🔲 (sense 1) globular, spherical

round up VERB If you round up people or animals, you gather them together.

roundabout roundabouts

NOUN **1** a meeting point of several roads with a circle in the centre which vehicles have to travel around. **2** a circular platform which rotates and which children can ride on in a

a
b
c
d
e
f
g
h
i
j
k
l
m
n
o
p
q
r
s
t
u
v
w
x
y
z

A
B
C
D
E
F
G
H
I
J
K
L
M
N
O
P
Q
R
S
T
U
V
W
X
Y
Z

playground. **3** the same as a merry-go-round.

rounded

ADJECTIVE curved in shape, without any points or sharp edges.

rounders

NOUN a game played by two teams, in which a player scores points by hitting a ball and running around four sides of a square pitch.

round-the-clock

ADJECTIVE happening continuously.

rouse rouses rousing roused

VERB **1** If someone rouses you, they wake you up. **2** If you rouse yourself to do something, you make yourself get up and do it. **3** If something rouses you, it makes you feel very emotional and excited.

rouseabout rouseabouts

NOUN In Australian and New Zealand English, an unskilled worker who does odd jobs, especially on a farm.

rout routs routing routed

Rhymes with "out" VERB To rout your opponents means to defeat them completely and easily.

route routes

Said "root" NOUN a way from one place to another.

routine routines

ADJECTIVE **1** Routine activities are done regularly. ▶ NOUN **2** the usual way or order in which you do things. **3** a boring repetition of tasks.

routinely ADVERB

roving

ADJECTIVE **1** wandering or roaming E.G. *roving gangs of youths.* **2** not restricted to any particular location or area E.G. *a roving reporter.*

row rows rowing rowed

Rhymes with "snow" NOUN **1** A row of

people or things is several of them arranged in a line. ▶ VERB **2** When you row a boat, you use oars to make it move through the water.

row rows rowing rowed

Rhymes with "now" NOUN **1** a serious argument. **2** If someone is making a row, they are making too much noise. ▶ VERB **3** If people are rowing, they are quarrelling noisily.

rowdy rowdier rowdiest

ADJECTIVE rough and noisy.

royal royals

ADJECTIVE **1** belonging to or involving a queen, a king, or a member of their family. **2** 'Royal' is used in the names of organizations appointed or supported by a member of a royal family. ▶ NOUN **3** INFORMAL Members of the royal family are sometimes referred to as the royals.

◼ (sense 1) imperial, regal

royalist royalists

NOUN someone who supports their country's royal family.

royalty royalties

NOUN **1** The members of a royal family are sometimes referred to as royalty. **2** Royalties are payments made to authors and musicians from the sales of their books or records.

rub rubs rubbing rubbed

VERB If you rub something, you move your hand or a cloth backwards and forwards over it.

rub out VERB To rub out something written means to remove it by rubbing it with a rubber or a cloth.

rubber rubbers

NOUN **1** Rubber is a strong, elastic substance used for making tyres, boots, and other products. **2** a small piece of rubber used to rub out pencil mistakes.

rubbish
NOUN **1** Rubbish is unwanted things or waste material. **2** You can refer to nonsense or something of very poor quality as rubbish.
■ (sense 1) garbage, refuse, trash, waste
■ (sense 2) garbage, nonsense, twaddle

rubble
NOUN Bits of old brick and stone are referred to as rubble.

rubric rubrics
Said "roo-brik" NOUN; FORMAL a set of instructions at the beginning of an official document.

ruby rubies
NOUN a type of red Jewel.

rucksack rucksacks
NOUN a bag with shoulder straps for carrying things on your back.

rudder rudders
NOUN a piece of wood or metal at the back of a boat or plane which is moved to make the boat or plane turn.

rude ruder rudest
ADJECTIVE **1** not polite. **2** embarrassing or offensive because of reference to sex or other bodily functions E.G. *rude jokes.* **3** unexpected and unpleasant E.G. *a rude awakening.*
rudely ADVERB **rudeness** NOUN
■ (sense 1) discourteous, ill-mannered, impolite, uncivil

rudimentary
ADJECTIVE; FORMAL very basic or not developed E.G. *He had only a rudimentary knowledge of French.*

rudiments
PLURAL NOUN When you learn the rudiments of something, you learn only the simplest and most basic things about it.
📖 from Latin *rudimentum* meaning 'beginning'

ruff ruffs
NOUN **1** a stiff circular collar with many pleats in it, worn especially in the 16th century. **2** a thick band of fur or feathers around the neck of a bird or animal.

ruffle ruffles ruffling ruffled
VERB **1** If you ruffle someone's hair, you move your hand quickly backwards and forwards over their head. **2** If something ruffles you, it makes you annoyed or upset. ▶ NOUN **3** Ruffles are small folds made in a piece of material for decoration.

rug rugs
NOUN **1** a small, thick carpet. **2** a blanket which you can use to cover your knees or for sitting on outdoors.

rugby
NOUN Rugby is a game played by two teams, who try to kick and throw an oval ball to their opponents' end of the pitch. Rugby League is played with 13 players in each side, Rugby Union is played with 15 players in each side.

rugged
ADJECTIVE **1** rocky and wild E.G. *the rugged west coast of Ireland.* **2** having strong features E.G. *his rugged good looks.*

rugger
NOUN Rugger is the same as rugby.

ruin ruins ruining ruined
VERB **1** If you ruin something, you destroy or spoil it completely. **2** If someone is ruined, they have lost all

A
B
C
D
E
F
G
H
I
J
K
L
M
N
O
P
Q
R
S
T
U
V
W
X
Y
Z

their money. ▶ NOUN **3** Ruin is the state of being destroyed or completely spoilt. **4** A ruin or the ruins of something refers to the parts that are left after it has been severely damaged E.G. *the ruins of a thirteenth-century monastery*.

rule rules ruling ruled
NOUN **1** Rules are statements which tell you what you are allowed to do. ▶ VERB **2** To rule a country or group of people means to have power over it and be in charge of its affairs. **3** FORMAL When someone in authority rules on a particular matter, they give an official decision about it. ▶ PHRASE **4 As a rule**, means usually or generally E.G. *As a rule, I eat my meals in front of the TV*.
■ (sense 1) law, regulation

rule out VERB **1** If you rule out an idea or course of action, you reject it. **2** If one thing rules out another, it prevents it from happening or being possible E.G. *The accident ruled out a future for him in football*.

ruler rulers
NOUN **1** a person who rules a country. **2** a long, flat piece of wood or plastic with straight edges marked in centimetres or inches, used for measuring or drawing straight lines.

rum
NOUN Rum is a strong alcoholic drink made from sugar cane juice.

Rumanian
Said "roo-**may**-nee-an" another spelling of **Romanian**.

rumble rumbles rumbling rumbled
VERB **1** If something rumbles, it makes a continuous low noise E.G. *Another train rumbled past the house*. ▶ NOUN

2 a continuous low noise E.G. *the distant rumble of traffic*.

rummage rummages rummaging rummaged
VERB If you rummage somewhere, you search for something, moving things about carelessly.

rumour rumours rumoured
NOUN **1** a story that people are talking about, which may or may not be true. ▶ VERB **2** If something is rumoured, people are suggesting that it is has happened.
▥ from Latin *rumor* meaning 'common talk'
■ (sense 1) gossip, hearsay, story

rump rumps
NOUN **1** An animal's rump is its rear end. **2** Rump or rump steak is meat cut from the rear end of a cow.

run runs running ran
VERB **1** When you run, you move quickly, leaving the ground during each stride. **2** If you run away from a place, you leave it suddenly and secretly. **3** If you say that a road or river runs in a particular direction, you are describing its course. **4** If you run your hand or an object over something, you move it over it. **5** If someone runs in an election, they stand as a candidate E.G. *He announced he would run for President*. **6** If you run a business or an activity, you are in charge of it. **7** If you run an experiment, a computer program, or tape, you start it and let it continue E.G. *He ran a series of computer checks*. **8** To run a car means to have it and use it. **9** If you run someone somewhere in a car, you drive them there E.G. *Could you run me up to town?* **10** If you run water, you turn on a tap to make it flow E.G. *We*

heard him running the kitchen tap.
11 If your nose is running, it is producing a lot of mucus. **12** If the dye in something runs, the colour comes out when it is washed. **13** If a feeling runs through your body, it affects you quickly and strongly. **14** If an amount is running at a particular level, it is at that level E.G. *Inflation is currently running at 2.6%.* **15** If someone or something is running late, they have taken more time than was planned. **16** If an event or contract runs for a particular time, it lasts for that time. ▶ NOUN **17** If you go for a run, you run for pleasure or exercise. **18** a journey somewhere E.G. *It was quite a run to the village.* **19** If a play or show has a run of a particular length of time, it is on for that time. **20** A run of success or failure is a series of successes or failures. **21** In cricket or baseball, a player scores one run by running between marked places on the pitch after hitting the ball.

▤ (sense 1) dash, race, sprint
▤ (sense 2) bolt, flee

run out VERB If you run out of something, you have no more left.
run over VERB If someone is run over, they are hit by a moving vehicle.

runaway runaways
NOUN a person who has escaped from a place or left it secretly and hurriedly.

rundown
ADJECTIVE **1** tired and not well. **2** neglected and in poor condition. ▶ NOUN **3** INFORMAL If you give someone the rundown on a situation, you tell them the basic, important facts about it.

rung rungs
NOUN The rungs on a ladder are the bars that form the steps.

runner runners
NOUN **1** a person who runs, especially as a sport. **2** a person who takes messages or runs errands. **3** A runner on a plant such as a strawberry is a long shoot from which a new plant develops. **4** The runners on drawers and ice skates are the thin strips on which they move.

runner bean runner beans
NOUN Runner beans are long green pods eaten as a vegetable, which grow on a climbing plant.

runner-up runners-up
NOUN a person or team that comes second in a race or competition.

running
ADJECTIVE **1** continuing without stopping over a period of time E.G. *a running commentary.* **2** Running water is flowing rather than standing still.

runny runnier runniest
ADJECTIVE **1** more liquid than usual E.G. *Warm the honey until it becomes runny.* **2** If someone's nose or eyes are runny, liquid is coming out of them.

runt runts
NOUN The runt of a litter of animals is the smallest and weakest.

runway runways
NOUN a long strip of ground used by aeroplanes for taking off or landing.

rupee rupees
Said "roo-**pee**" NOUN the main unit of currency in India, Pakistan, and some other countries.

rupture ruptures rupturing ruptured
NOUN **1** a severe injury in which part

a
b
c
d
e
f
g
h
i
j
k
l
m
n
o
p
q
r
s
t
u
v
w
x
y
z

of your body tears or bursts open.
► VERB **2** To rupture part of the body means to cause it to tear or burst E.G. *a ruptured spleen*.

rural
ADJECTIVE (GEOGRAPHY) relating to or involving the countryside.

ruse ruses
NOUN; FORMAL an action which is intended to trick someone.

rush rushes rushing rushed
VERB **1** To rush means to move fast or do something quickly. **2** If you rush someone into doing something, you make them do it without allowing them enough time to think. ► NOUN **3** If you are in a rush, you are busy and do not have enough time to do things. **4** If there is a rush for something, there is a sudden increase in demand for it E.G. *There was a rush for tickets*. **5** Rushes are plants with long, thin stems that grow near water.

rush hour rush hours
NOUN The rush hour is one of the busy parts of the day when most people are travelling to or from work.

rusk rusks
NOUN a hard, dry biscuit given to babies.

Russian Russians
ADJECTIVE **1** belonging or relating to Russia. ► NOUN **2** someone who comes from Russia. **3** Russian is the main language spoken in Russia.

rust rusts rusting rusted
NOUN **1** Rust is a reddish-brown substance that forms on iron or steel which has been in contact with water and which is decaying gradually. ► NOUN or ADJECTIVE **2** reddish-brown. ► VERB **3** When a metal object rusts, it becomes covered in rust.

rustic
ADJECTIVE simple in a way considered to be typical of the countryside E.G. *a rustic old log cabin*.

rustle rustles rustling rustled
VERB When something rustles, it makes soft sounds as it moves.
rustling ADJECTIVE or NOUN

rusty rustier rustiest
ADJECTIVE **1** affected by rust E.G. *a rusty iron gate*. **2** If someone's knowledge is rusty, it is not as good as it used to be because they have not used it for a long time E.G. *My German is a bit rusty these days*.

rut ruts
NOUN **1** a deep, narrow groove in the ground made by the wheels of a vehicle. ► PHRASE **2** If someone is **in a rut**, they have become fixed in their way of doing things.

ruthless
ADJECTIVE very harsh or cruel E.G. *a ruthless drug dealer*.
ruthlessness NOUN **ruthlessly** ADVERB

rye
NOUN a type of grass that produces light brown grain.

A B C D E F G H I J K L M N O P Q R S T U V W X Y Z

Ss

TIP Some words which sound as if they begin with s actually begin with c, for example *city*. Some words which sound as if they begin with sh actually begin with ch, for example *chivalry*. Other words which sound as if they begin with s actually begin with the letters ps, for example *psychiatry* and *psychology*.

Sabbath
NOUN The Sabbath is the day of the week when members of some religious groups, especially Jews and Christians, do not work.
📖 from Hebrew *shabbath* meaning 'to rest'

sable sables
NOUN a very expensive fur used for making coats and hats; also the wild animal from which this fur is obtained.

sabotage sabotages sabotaging sabotaged
Said "**sab**-ot-ahj" NOUN **1** the deliberate damaging of things such as machinery and railway lines. ▶ VERB **2** If something is sabotaged, it is deliberately damaged.

saboteur NOUN
📖 from French *saboter* meaning 'to spoil through clumsiness'

sabre sabres
NOUN **1** a heavy curved sword. **2** a light sword used in fencing.

saccharine or **saccharin**
Said "**sak**-er-rine" NOUN a chemical used instead of sugar to sweeten things.

sachet sachets
Said "**sash**-ay" NOUN a small closed packet, containing a small amount of something such as sugar or shampoo.

sack sacks sacking sacked
NOUN **1** a large bag made of rough material used for carrying or storing goods. ▶ VERB **2** INFORMAL If someone is sacked, they are dismissed from their job by their employer. ▶ PHRASE **3** INFORMAL If someone **gets the sack**, they are sacked by their employer.
📕 (sense 2) dismiss, fire

sacrament sacraments
NOUN an important Christian ceremony such as communion, baptism, or marriage.

sacred
Said "**say**-krid" ADJECTIVE holy, or connected with religion or religious ceremonies E.G. *sacred ground*.

sacrifice sacrifices sacrificing sacrificed
Said "**sak**-riff-ice" VERB **1** If you sacrifice something valuable or important, you give it up. **2** To sacrifice an animal means to kill it as an offering to a god. ▶ NOUN **3** the killing of an animal as an offering to a god or gods.

sacrificial ADJECTIVE
📕 (sense 1) forfeit, give up

sacrilege
Said "**sak**-ril-ij" NOUN Sacrilege is behaviour that shows great disrespect for something holy.

sacrilegious ADJECTIVE

you'll brEAK that Electrical Aerial, Kitty (**break**) **SPELLING NOTE**

A B C D E F G H I J K L M N O P Q R S T U V W X Y Z

sacrosanct
Said "**sak**-roe-sangkt" ADJECTIVE
regarded as too important to be
criticized or changed E.G. *Freedom of
the press is sacrosanct.*

sad sadder saddest
ADJECTIVE 1 If you are sad, you feel
unhappy. 2 Something sad makes
you feel unhappy E.G. *a sad story.*
sadly ADVERB **sadness** NOUN
■ (sense 1) low, melancholy,
unhappy

**sadden saddens saddening
saddened**
VERB If something saddens you, it
makes you feel sad.

saddle saddles saddling saddled
NOUN 1 a leather seat that you sit on
when you are riding a horse. 2 The
saddle on a bicycle is the seat. ▶ VERB
3 If you saddle a horse, you put a
saddle on it.

sadism
Said "**say**-diz-m" NOUN Sadism is the
obtaining of pleasure, especially
sexual pleasure, from making people
suffer pain or humiliation.
sadist NOUN **sadistic** ADJECTIVE
🏛 from the Marquis de Sade
(1740–1814), who got his pleasure in
this way

safari safaris
NOUN an expedition for hunting or
observing wild animals.
🏛 from Swahili *safari* meaning
'journey'

safari park safari parks
NOUN a large park where wild animals
such as lions and elephants roam
freely.

safe safer safest; safes
ADJECTIVE 1 Something that is safe
does not cause harm or danger. 2 If

you are safe, you are not in any
danger. 3 If it is safe to say
something, you can say it with little
risk of being wrong. ▶ NOUN 4 a strong
metal box with special locks, in
which you can keep valuable things.
safely ADVERB **safety** NOUN
■ (sense 2) out of danger, secure

**safeguard safeguards
safeguarding safeguarded**
VERB 1 To safeguard something means
to protect it. ▶ NOUN 2 a rule or law
designed to protect something or
someone.

safekeeping
NOUN If something is given to you for
safekeeping, it is given to you to look
after.

sag sags sagging sagged
VERB When something sags, it hangs
down loosely or sinks downwards in
the middle.
sagging ADJECTIVE

saga sagas
Said "**sah**-ga" NOUN a very long story,
usually with many different
adventures E.G. *a saga of rivalry,
honour and love.*
🏛 from Old Norse *saga* meaning
'story'

sage sages
NOUN 1 LITERARY a very wise person.
2 Sage is also a herb used for
flavouring in cooking.
🏛 sense 1 is from Latin *sapere*
meaning 'to be wise'; sense 2 is from
Latin *salvus* meaning 'healthy',
because of the supposed medicinal
properties of the plant

Sagittarius
Said "saj-it-**tair**-ee-uss" NOUN
Sagittarius is the ninth sign of the
zodiac, represented by a creature

half-horse, half-man holding a bow and arrow. People born between November 22nd and December 21st are born under this sign.

📖 from Latin *sagittarius* meaning 'archer'

sail sails sailing sailed
NOUN 1 Sails are large pieces of material attached to a ship's mast. The wind blows against the sail and moves the ship. ▶ VERB 2 When a ship sails, it moves across water. 3 If you sail somewhere, you go there by ship.

sailor sailors
NOUN a member of a ship's crew.

saint saints
NOUN a person who after death is formally recognized by a Christian Church as deserving special honour because of having lived a very holy life.

📖 from Latin *sanctus* meaning 'holy'

saintly
ADJECTIVE behaving in a very good or holy way.

sake sakes
PHRASE 1 If you do something **for someone's sake**, you do it to help or please them. 2 You use **for the sake of** to say why you are doing something E.G. *a one-off expedition for interest's sake*.

salad salads
NOUN a mixture of raw vegetables.

📖 from Old Provençal *salar* meaning 'to season with salt'

salami
Said "sal-**lah**-mee" NOUN Salami is a kind of spicy sausage.

salary salaries
NOUN a regular monthly payment to an employee.

📖 from Latin *salarium* meaning 'money given to soldiers to buy salt'

sale sales
NOUN 1 The sale of goods is the selling of them. 2 an occasion when a shop sells things at reduced prices.
▶ PLURAL NOUN 3 The sales of a product are the numbers that are sold.

salesman salesmen
NOUN someone who sells products for a company.

saleswoman NOUN

salient
Said "**say**-lee-ent" ADJECTIVE; FORMAL The salient points or facts are the important ones.

saliva
Said "sal-**live**-a" NOUN Saliva is the watery liquid in your mouth that helps you chew and digest food.

sallow
ADJECTIVE Sallow skin is pale and unhealthy.

salmon salmons or **salmon**
Said "**sam**-on" NOUN a large edible silver-coloured fish with pink flesh.

salmonella
Said "sal-mon-**nell**-a" NOUN Salmonella is a kind of bacteria which can cause severe food poisoning.

salon salons
NOUN a place where hairdressers work.

saloon saloons
NOUN 1 a car with a fixed roof and a separate boot. 2 In America, a place where alcoholic drinks are sold and drunk.

salt salts
NOUN 1 Salt is a white substance found naturally in sea water. It is used to flavour and preserve food. 2 a chemical compound formed from an acid base.

I want to see (C) your licen**C**e (licen**c**e)   **SPELLING NOTE**

A
B
C
D
E
F
G
H
I
J
K
L
M
N
O
P
Q
R
S
T
U
V
W
X
Y
Z

salty saltier saltiest

ADJECTIVE containing salt or tasting of salt.

salute salutes saluting saluted

NOUN **1** a formal sign of respect. Soldiers give a salute by raising their right hand to their forehead. ▶ VERB **2** If you salute someone, you give them a salute.

salvage salvages salvaging salvaged

VERB **1** If you salvage things, you save them, for example from a wrecked ship or a destroyed building. ▶ NOUN **2** You refer to things saved from a wrecked ship or destroyed building as salvage.

salvation

NOUN **1** When someone's salvation takes place, they are saved from harm or evil. **2** To be someone's salvation means to save them from harm or evil. ·

salvo salvos or salvoes

NOUN The firing of several guns or missiles at the same time.

same

ADJECTIVE or PRONOUN **1** If two things are the same, they look like one another. **2** Same means just one thing and not two different ones E.G. *They were born in the same town.*

Samoan Samoans

ADJECTIVE **1** belonging or relating to Samoa. ▶ NOUN **2** someone who comes from Samoa.

sample samples sampling sampled

NOUN **1** A sample of something is a small amount of it that you can try or test E.G. *a sample of new wine.* ▶ VERB **2** If you sample something, you try it E.G. *I sampled his cooking.*

samurai

*Said "***sam***-oor-eye"* NOUN A samurai was a member of an ancient Japanese warrior class.

sanctimonious

*Said "sank-tim-***moan***-ee-uss"* ADJECTIVE pretending to be very religious and virtuous.

sanction sanctions sanctioning sanctioned

VERB (PSHE) **1** To sanction something means to officially approve of it or allow it. ▶ NOUN **2** Sanction is official approval of something. **3** a severe punishment or penalty intended to make people obey the law.
4 Sanctions are sometimes taken by countries against a country that has broken international law.

sanctity

NOUN If you talk about the sanctity of something, you are saying that it should be respected because it is very important E.G. *the sanctity of marriage.*

sanctuary sanctuaries

NOUN **1** a place where you are safe from harm or danger. **2** a place where wildlife is protected E.G. *a bird sanctuary.*

sand sands sanding sanded

NOUN **1** Sand consists of tiny pieces of stone. Beaches are made of sand. ▶ VERB **2** If you sand something, you rub sandpaper over it to make it smooth.

sandal sandals

NOUN Sandals are light shoes with straps, worn in warm weather.

sandpaper

NOUN Sandpaper is strong paper with a coating of sand on it, used for rubbing surfaces to make them smooth.

SPELLING NOTE The government licenSes Schnapps (licenSes)

sandshoe sandshoes
NOUN In British, Australian, and New
Zealand English, a light canvas shoe
with a rubber sole.

sandstone
NOUN Sandstone is a type of rock
formed from sand, often used for
building.

sandwich sandwiches
sandwiching sandwiched
NOUN 1 two slices of bread with a
filling between them. ➤ VERB 2 If one
thing is sandwiched between two
others, it is in a narrow space
between them E.G. *a small shop
sandwiched between a bar and an
office.*
🔲 sense 1 is named after the 4th Earl
of Sandwich (1718–1792), for whom
they were invented so that he
could eat and gamble at the same
time

sandy sandier sandiest
ADJECTIVE 1 A sandy area is covered
with sand. 2 Sandy hair is light
orange-brown.

sane saner sanest
ADJECTIVE 1 If someone is sane, they
have a normal and healthy mind. 2 A
sane action is sensible and
reasonable.

sanguine
Said "**sang**-gwin" ADJECTIVE; FORMAL
cheerful and confident.

sanitary
ADJECTIVE Sanitary means concerned
with keeping things clean and
hygienic E.G. *improving the sanitary
conditions.*

sanitary towel sanitary towels
NOUN Sanitary towels are pads of
thick, soft material which women
wear during their periods.

sanitation
NOUN Sanitation is the process of
keeping places clean and hygienic,
especially by providing a sewage
system and clean water supply.

sanity
NOUN Your sanity is your ability to
think and act normally and
reasonably.

sap saps sapping sapped
VERB 1 If something saps your
strength or confidence, it gradually
weakens and destroys it. ➤ NOUN 2 Sap
is the watery liquid in plants.

sapling saplings
NOUN a young tree.

sapphire sapphires
NOUN a blue precious stone.

sarcastic
ADJECTIVE saying or doing the opposite
of what you really mean in order to
mock or insult someone E.G. *a
sarcastic remark.*

sarcasm NOUN **sarcastically**
ADVERB
🔲 from Greek *sarkazein* meaning 'to
tear the flesh'

sarcophagus sarcophagi or
sarcophaguses
Said "sar-**kof**-fag-uss" NOUN a stone
coffin used in ancient times.

sardine sardines
NOUN a small edible sea fish.

sardonic
ADJECTIVE mocking or scornful E.G. *a
sardonic grin.*

sardonically ADVERB

sari saris
Said "**sah**-ree" NOUN a piece of
clothing worn especially by Indian
women, consisting of a long piece of
material folded around the body.
🔲 a Hindi word

a
b
c
d
e
f
g
h
i
j
k
l
m
n
o
p
q
r
s
t
u
v
w
x
y
z

there's SAND in my SANDwich (**sand**wich)   **SPELLING NOTE**

sarmie sarmies
NOUN; SLANG In South African English, a sarmie is a sandwich.

sartorial
ADJECTIVE; FORMAL relating to clothes E.G. *sartorial elegance*.

sash sashes
NOUN a long piece of cloth worn round the waist or over one shoulder.
from Arabic *shash* meaning 'muslin'

Satan
NOUN Satan is the Devil.
from Hebrew *satan* meaning 'to plot against'

satanic
Said "sa-**tan**-ik" ADJECTIVE caused by or influenced by Satan E.G. *satanic forces*.

satchel satchels
NOUN a leather or cloth bag with a long strap.

satellite satellites
NOUN 1 a spacecraft sent into orbit round the earth to collect information or as part of a communications system. 2 a natural object in space that moves round a planet or star.

satin satins
NOUN Satin is a kind of smooth, shiny silk.

satire satires
NOUN Satire is the use of mocking or ironical humour, especially in literature, to show how foolish or wicked some people are.
satirical ADJECTIVE

satisfaction
NOUN Satisfaction is the feeling of pleasure you get when you do something you wanted or needed to do.

satisfactory
ADJECTIVE acceptable or adequate E.G. *a satisfactory explanation*.
satisfactorily ADVERB

satisfy satisfies satisfying satisfied
VERB 1 To satisfy someone means to give them enough of something to make them pleased or contented. 2 To satisfy someone that something is the case means to convince them of it. 3 To satisfy the requirements for something means to fulfil them.
satisfied ADJECTIVE
■ (sense 1) content, indulge, please

satisfying
ADJECTIVE Something that is satisfying gives you a feeling of pleasure and fulfilment.

satsuma satsumas
Said "sat-**soo**-ma" NOUN a fruit like a small orange.

saturated
ADJECTIVE 1 very wet. 2 If a place is saturated with things, it is completely full of them.
saturation NOUN

Saturday Saturdays
NOUN the day between Friday and Sunday.
from Latin *Saturni dies* meaning 'day of Saturn'

Saturn
NOUN Saturn is the planet in the solar system which is sixth from the sun.

sauce sauces
NOUN a liquid eaten with food to give it more flavour.
✓ Do not confuse the spellings of *sauce* and *source*, which can sound very similar.

saucepan saucepans
NOUN a deep metal cooking pot with a handle and a lid.

saucer saucers
NOUN a small curved plate for a cup.

saucy saucier sauciest
ADJECTIVE cheeky in an amusing way.

Saudi Saudis
Rhymes with "cloudy" ADJECTIVE
1 belonging or relating to Saudi Arabia. ▶ NOUN 2 someone who comes from Saudi Arabia.

sauna saunas
Said "saw-na" NOUN If you have a sauna, you go into a very hot room in order to sweat, then have a cold bath or shower.
📖 a Finnish word

saunter saunters sauntering sauntered
VERB To saunter somewhere means to walk there slowly and casually.

sausage sausages
NOUN a mixture of minced meat and herbs formed into a tubular shape and served cooked.

sauté sautés sautéing or sautéeing sautéed
Said "soh-tay" VERB To sauté food means to fry it quickly in a small amount of oil or butter.

savage savages savaging savaged
ADJECTIVE 1 cruel and violent E.G. *savage fighting.* ▶ NOUN 2 If you call someone a savage, you mean that they are violent and uncivilized.
▶ VERB 3 If an animal savages you, it attacks you and bites you.

savagely ADVERB
■ (sense 1) brutal, cruel, vicious

savagery
NOUN Savagery is cruel and violent behaviour.

save saves saving saved
VERB 1 If you save someone, you rescue them or help to keep them safe E.G. *He saved my life.* 2 If you save something, you keep it so that you can use it later E.G. *He'd saved up enough money for the deposit.* 3 To save time, money, or effort means to prevent it from being wasted E.G. *You could have saved us the trouble.*
▶ PREPOSITION 4 FORMAL Save means except E.G. *I was alone in the house save for a very old woman.*

saving savings
NOUN 1 a reduction in the amount of time or money used. ▶ PLURAL NOUN 2 Your savings are the money you have saved.

saviour saviours
NOUN 1 If someone saves you from danger, you can refer to them as your saviour. ▶ PROPER NOUN 2 In Christianity, the Saviour is Jesus Christ.

savour savours savouring savoured
VERB If you savour something, you take your time with it and enjoy it fully E.G. *These spirits should be sipped and savoured like fine whiskies.*

savoury
ADJECTIVE 1 Savoury is salty or spicy. 2 Something that is not very savoury is not very pleasant or respectable E.G. *the less savoury places.*

saw saws sawing sawed sawn
1 Saw is the past tense of **see**. NOUN 2 a tool, with a blade with sharp teeth along one edge, for cutting wood. ▶ VERB 3 If you saw something, you cut it with a saw.

a
b
c
d
e
f
g
h
i
j
k
l
m
n
o
p
q
r
s
t
u
v
w
x
y
z

I went to see (C) the doctor's new practiCe (practice)   SPELLING NOTE

sawdust

NOUN Sawdust is the fine powder produced when you saw wood.

saxophone saxophones

NOUN a curved metal wind instrument often played in jazz bands.

🏛 named after Adolphe Sax (1814–1894), who invented the instrument

say says saying said

VERB 1 When you say something, you speak words. 2 'Say' is used to give an example E.G. *a maximum fee of, say, a million.* ▶ NOUN 3 If you have a say in something, you can give your opinion and influence decisions.

≡ (sense 1) remark, speak, utter

saying sayings

NOUN a well-known sentence or phrase that tells you something about human life.

≡ adage, proverb

scab scabs

NOUN a hard, dry covering that forms over a wound.

scabby ADJECTIVE

scaffolding

NOUN Scaffolding is a framework of poles and boards that is used by workmen to stand on while they are working on the outside structure of a building.

scald scalds scalding scalded

Said "skawld" VERB 1 If you scald yourself, you burn yourself with very hot liquid or steam. ▶ NOUN 2 a burn caused by scalding.

scale scales scaling scaled

NOUN 1 The scale of something is its size or extent E.G. *the sheer scale of the disaster.* 2 a set of levels or numbers used for measuring things. 3 The scale of a map, plan, or model is the relationship between the size of something in the map, plan, or model and its size in the real world E.G. *a scale of 1:10,000.* 4 (MUSIC) an upward or downward sequence of musical notes. 5 The scales of a fish or reptile are the small pieces of hard skin covering its body. ▶ PLURAL NOUN 6 Scales are a piece of equipment used for weighing things. ▶ VERB 7 If you scale something high, you climb it.

scalene

ADJECTIVE A scalene triangle has sides which are all of different lengths.

scallop scallops

NOUN Scallops are edible shellfish with two flat fan-shaped shells.

scalp scalps scalping scalped

NOUN 1 Your scalp is the skin under the hair on your head. 2 the piece of skin and hair removed when someone is scalped. ▶ VERB 3 To scalp someone means to remove the skin and hair from their head in one piece.

scalpel scalpels

NOUN a knife with a thin, sharp blade, used by surgeons.

scaly

ADJECTIVE covered with scales.

scamper scampers scampering scampered

VERB To scamper means to move quickly and lightly.

scampi

PLURAL NOUN Scampi are large prawns often eaten fried in breadcrumbs.

scan scans scanning scanned

VERB 1 If you scan something, you look at all of it carefully E.G. *I scanned the horizon to the north-east.* 2 If a machine scans something, it examines it by means of a beam of light or X-rays. ▶ NOUN **3** an examination or search by a scanner E.G. *a brain scan*.

scandal scandals
NOUN a situation or event that people think is shocking and immoral.
scandalous ADJECTIVE

Scandinavia
Said "skan-din-**nay**-vee-a" NOUN Scandinavia is the name given to a group of countries in Northern Europe, including Norway, Sweden, Denmark, and sometimes Finland and Iceland.
Scandinavian NOUN or ADJECTIVE

scanner scanners
NOUN **1** a machine which is used to examine, identify, or record things by means of a beam of light or X-rays. **2** (ICT) a machine which converts text or images into a form that can be stored on a computer.

scant scanter scantest
ADJECTIVE If something receives scant attention, it does not receive enough attention.

scapegoat scapegoats
NOUN If someone is made a scapegoat, they are blamed for something, although it may not be their fault.

scar scars scarring scarred
NOUN **1** a mark left on your skin after a wound has healed. **2** a permanent effect on someone's mind that results from a very unpleasant experience E.G. *the scars of war*. ▶ VERB **3** If an injury scars you, it leaves a permanent mark on your skin. **4** If an unpleasant experience scars you, it has a permanent effect on you.

scarce scarcer scarcest
ADJECTIVE If something is scarce, there is not very much of it.
scarcity NOUN

scarcely
ADVERB Scarcely means hardly E.G. *I can scarcely hear her*.
☑ As *scarcely* already has a negative sense, it is followed by *ever* or *any*, and not by *never* or *no*.

scare scares scaring scared
VERB **1** If something scares you, it frightens you. ▶ NOUN **2** If something gives you a scare, it scares you. **3** If there is a scare about something, a lot of people are worried about it E.G. *an AIDS scare*.
scared ADJECTIVE
▦ (sense 1) alarm, frighten, startle

scarecrow scarecrows
NOUN an object shaped like a person put in a field to scare birds away.

scarf scarfs or **scarves**
NOUN a piece of cloth worn round your neck or head to keep you warm.

scarlet
NOUN or ADJECTIVE bright red.

scary scarier scariest
ADJECTIVE; INFORMAL frightening.

scathing
Said "**skayth**-ing" ADJECTIVE harsh and scornful E.G. *They were scathing about his job*.

scatter scatters scattering scattered
VERB **1** To scatter things means to throw or drop them all over an area. **2** If people scatter, they suddenly move away in different directions.
▦ (sense 1) sprinkle, strew, throw about

a
b
c
d
e
f
g
h
i
j
k
l
m
n
o
p
q
r
s
t
u
v
w
x
y
z

A
B
C
D
E
F
G
H
I
J
K
L
M
N
O
P
Q
R
S
T
U
V
W
X
Y
Z

scattering
NOUN A scattering of things is a small number of them spread over a large area E.G. *the scattering of islands*.

scavenge scavenges scavenging scavenged
VERB If you scavenge for things, you search for them among waste and rubbish.
scavenger NOUN

scenario scenarios
Said "sin-**nar**-ee-oh" NOUN 1 (DRAMA) The scenario of a film or play is a summary of its plot. 2 the way a situation could possibly develop in the future E.G. *the worst possible scenario*.

scene scenes
NOUN 1 (ENGLISH) (DRAMA) part of a play or film in which a series of events happen in one place. 2 Pictures and views are sometimes called scenes E.G. *a village scene*. 3 The scene of an event is the place where it happened. 4 an area of activity E.G. *the music scene*.

scenery
NOUN 1 In the countryside, you can refer to everything you see as the scenery. 2 In a theatre, the scenery is the painted cloth on the stage which represents the place where the action is happening.

scenic
ADJECTIVE A scenic place or route has nice views.

scent scents scenting scented
NOUN 1 a smell, especially a pleasant one. 2 Scent is perfume. ▶ VERB 3 When an animal scents something, it becomes aware of it by smelling it.

sceptic sceptics
Said "**skep**-tik" NOUN someone who

has doubts about things that other people believe.
sceptical ADJECTIVE **scepticism** NOUN

sceptre sceptres
Said "**sep**-ter" NOUN an ornamental rod carried by a king or queen as a symbol of power.

schedule schedules scheduling scheduled
Said "**shed**-yool" NOUN 1 a plan that gives a list of events or tasks, together with the times at which each thing should be done. ▶ VERB 2 If something is scheduled to happen, it has been planned and arranged E.G. *Their journey was scheduled for the beginning of May*.

schema schemata
Said "**skee**-ma" NOUN 1 TECHNICAL an outline of a plan or theory. 2 a mental model which the mind uses to understand new experiences or to view the world.

scheme schemes scheming schemed
NOUN 1 a plan or arrangement E.G. *a five-year development scheme*. ▶ VERB 2 When people scheme, they make secret plans.

schism schisms
Said "**skizm**" NOUN a split or division within a group or organization.

schizophrenia
Said "skit-soe-**free**-nee-a" NOUN Schizophrenia is a serious mental illness which prevents someone relating their thoughts and feelings to what is happening around them.
schizophrenic NOUN OR ADJECTIVE
🔲 from Greek *skhizein* meaning 'to split' and *phren* meaning 'mind'

scholar scholars
NOUN 1 a person who studies an

academic subject and knows a lot about it. **2** In South African English, a scholar is a school pupil.

scholarly
ADJECTIVE having or showing a lot of knowledge.

scholarship scholarships
NOUN **1** If you get a scholarship to a school or university, your studies are paid for by the school or university or by some other organization. **2** Scholarship is academic study and knowledge.

school schools schooling schooled
NOUN **1** a place where children are educated. **2** University departments and colleges are sometimes called schools E.G. *My oldest son is in medical school.* **3** You can refer to a large group of dolphins or fish as a school. ▶ VERB **4** When someone is schooled in something, they are taught it E.G. *They were schooled in the modern techniques.*

schoolchild schoolchildren
NOUN Schoolchildren are children who go to school.

schoolboy NOUN **schoolgirl** NOUN

schooling
NOUN Your schooling is the education you get at school.

schooner schooners
NOUN a sailing ship.

science sciences
NOUN **1** Science is the study of the nature and behaviour of natural things and the knowledge obtained about them. **2** a branch of science, for example physics or biology.

science fiction
NOUN Stories about events happening in the future or in other parts of the

universe are called science fiction.

scientific
ADJECTIVE **1** relating to science or to a particular science E.G. *scientific knowledge.* **2** done in a systematic way, using experiments or tests E.G. *this scientific method.*

scientifically ADVERB

scientist scientists
NOUN an expert in one of the sciences who does work connected with it.

scintillating
Said "sin-til-late-ing" ADJECTIVE lively and witty E.G. *scintillating conversation.*

scissors
PLURAL NOUN Scissors are a cutting tool with two sharp blades.

scoff scoffs scoffing scoffed
VERB **1** If you scoff, you speak in a scornful, mocking way about something. **2** INFORMAL If you scoff food, you eat it quickly and greedily.

scold scolds scolding scolded
VERB If you scold someone, you tell them off.
■ rebuke, reprimand, tell off

scone scones
Said "skon or skone" NOUN Scones are small cakes made from flour and fat and usually eaten with butter.

scoop scoops scooping scooped
VERB **1** If you scoop something up, you pick it up using a spoon or the palm of your hand. ▶ NOUN **2** an object like a large spoon which is used for picking up food such as ice cream.

scooter scooters
NOUN **1** a small, light motorcycle. **2** a simple cycle which a child rides by standing on it and pushing the ground with one foot.

scope
NOUN **1** If there is scope for doing

a
b
c
d
e
f
g
h
i
j
k
l
m
n
o
p
q
r
s
t
u
v
w
x
y
z

something, the opportunity to do it exists. **2** The scope of something is the whole subject area which it deals with or includes.

-scope

SUFFIX '-scope' is used to form nouns which refer to an instrument used for observing or detecting E.G. *microscope… telescope.*

📖 from Greek *skopein* meaning 'to look at'

scorch scorches scorching scorched ▸ VERB To scorch something means to burn it slightly.

scorching

ADJECTIVE extremely hot E.G. *another scorching summer.*

score scores scoring scored

VERB **1** If you score in a game, you get a goal, run, or point. **2** To score in a game also means to record the score obtained by the players. **3** If you score a success or victory, you achieve it. **4** To score a surface means to cut a line into it. ▸ NOUN **5** The score in a game is the number of goals, runs, or points obtained by the two teams. **6** Scores of things means very many of them E.G. *Ros entertained scores of celebrities.* **7** OLD-FASHIONED A score is twenty. **8** (MUSIC) The score of a piece of music is the written version of it.

scorer NOUN

scorn scorns scorning scorned

NOUN **1** Scorn is great contempt E.G. *a look of scorn.* ▸ VERB **2** FORMAL If you scorn something, you refuse to accept it.

scornful

ADJECTIVE showing contempt E.G. *his scornful comment.*

scornfully ADVERB

▣ contemptuous, disdainful, sneering

Scorpio

NOUN Scorpio is the eighth sign of the zodiac, represented by a scorpion. People born between October 23rd and November 21st are born under this sign.

📖 from Latin *scorpio* meaning 'scorpion'

scorpion scorpions

NOUN an animal that looks like a small lobster, with a long tail with a poisonous sting on the end.

Scot Scots

NOUN **1** a person who comes from Scotland. ▸ ADJECTIVE **2** Scots means the same as **Scottish**.

scotch scotches

NOUN Scotch is whisky made in Scotland.

Scotsman Scotsmen

NOUN a man who comes from Scotland.

Scotswoman NOUN

Scottish

ADJECTIVE belonging or relating to Scotland.

scoundrel scoundrels

NOUN; OLD-FASHIONED a man who cheats and deceives people.

scour scours scouring scoured

VERB **1** If you scour a place, you look all over it in order to find something E.G. *The police scoured the area.* **2** If you scour something such as a pan, you clean it by rubbing it with something rough.

scourge scourges

*Rhymes with "**urge**"* NOUN something that causes a lot of suffering E.G. *hay fever, that scourge of summer.*

scout scouts scouting scouted

NOUN **1** a boy who is a member of the Scout Association, an organization for boys which aims to develop character and responsibility. **2** someone who is sent to an area to find out the position of an enemy army. ▶ VERB **3** If you scout around for something, you look around for it.

scowl scowls scowling scowled

VERB **1** If you scowl, you frown because you are angry E.G. *They were scowling at me.* ▶ NOUN **2** an angry expression.

scrabble scrabbles scrabbling scrabbled

VERB If you scrabble at something, you scrape at it with your hands or feet.

📖 from Old Dutch *schrabbelen* meaning 'to scrape repeatedly'

scramble scrambles scrambling scrambled

VERB **1** If you scramble over something, you climb over it using your hands to help you. ▶ NOUN **2** a motorcycle race over rough ground.

scrap scraps scrapping scrapped

NOUN **1** A scrap of something is a very small piece of it E.G. *a scrap of cloth.* ▶ PLURAL NOUN **2** Scraps are pieces of leftover food. ▶ ADJECTIVE or NOUN **3** Scrap metal or scrap is metal from old machinery or cars that can be re-used. ▶ VERB **4** If you scrap something, you get rid of it E.G. *They considered scrapping passport controls.*

scrapbook scrapbooks

NOUN a book in which you stick things such as pictures or newspaper articles.

scrape scrapes scraping scraped

VERB **1** If you scrape something off a surface, you remove it by pulling a rough or sharp object over it E.G. *to scrape the fallen snow off the track.* **2** If something scrapes, it makes a harsh noise by rubbing against something E.G. *his shoes scraping across the stone ground.*

scratch scratches scratching scratched

VERB **1** To scratch something means to make a small cut on it accidentally E.G. *They were always getting scratched by cats.* **2** If you scratch, you rub your skin with your nails because it is itching. ▶ NOUN **3** a small cut.

scratchcard scratchcards

NOUN a ticket in a competition with a surface that you scratch off to show whether or not you have won a prize.

scrawl scrawls scrawling scrawled

VERB **1** If you scrawl something, you write it in a careless and untidy way. ▶ NOUN **2** You can refer to careless and untidy writing as a scrawl.

scrawny scrawnier scrawniest

ADJECTIVE thin and bony E.G. *a small scrawny man.*

scream screams screaming screamed

VERB **1** If you scream, you shout or cry in a loud, high-pitched voice. ▶ NOUN **2** a loud, high-pitched cry.

🔊 cry, shriek, yell

screech screeches screeching screeched

VERB **1** To screech means to make an unpleasant high-pitched noise E.G.

a
b
c
d
e
f
g
h
i
j
k
l
m
n
o
p
q
r
s
t
u
v
w
x
y
z

Rhythmical Hounds Yap To Heavy Music (<u>rhythm</u>)   SPELLING NOTE

The car wheels screeched. ▶ NOUN **2** an unpleasant high-pitched noise.

screen screens screening screened

NOUN **1** a flat vertical surface on which a picture is shown E.G. *a television screen*. **2** a vertical panel used to separate different parts of a room or to protect something. ▶ VERB **3** To screen a film or television programme means to show it. **4** If you screen someone, you put something in front of them to protect them.

screenplay screenplays

NOUN The screenplay of a film is the script.

screw screws screwing screwed

NOUN **1** a small, sharp piece of metal used for fixing things together or for fixing something to a wall. ▶ VERB **2** If you screw things together, you fix them together using screws. **3** If you screw something onto something else, you fix it there by twisting it round and round E.G. *He screwed the top on the ink bottle.*

screw up VERB If you screw something up, you twist it or squeeze it so that it no longer has its proper shape E.G. *Amy screwed up her face.*

screwdriver screwdrivers

NOUN a tool for turning screws.

scribble scribbles scribbling scribbled

VERB **1** If you scribble something, you write it quickly and roughly. **2** To scribble also means to make meaningless marks E.G. *When Caroline was five she scribbled on a wall.* ▶ NOUN **3** You can refer to

something written or drawn quickly and roughly as a scribble.

scrimp scrimps scrimping scrimped

VERB If you scrimp, you live cheaply and spend as little money as you can.

script scripts

NOUN (DRAMA) the written version of a play or film.

scripture scriptures

NOUN Scripture refers to sacred writings, especially the Bible.

scriptural ADJECTIVE

scroll scrolls

NOUN a long roll of paper or parchment with writing on it.

scrounge scrounges scrounging scrounged

VERB; INFORMAL If you scrounge something, you get it by asking for it rather than by earning or buying it.

scrounger NOUN

▣ cadge, sponge

scrub scrubs scrubbing scrubbed

VERB **1** If you scrub something, you clean it with a stiff brush and water. ▶ NOUN **2** If you give something a scrub, you scrub it. **3** Scrub consists of low trees and bushes.

scruff

NOUN The scruff of your neck is the back of your neck or collar.

scruffy scruffier scruffiest

ADJECTIVE dirty and untidy E.G. *four scruffy youths.*

▣ tatty, unkempt

scrum scrums

NOUN When rugby players form a scrum, they form a group and push against each other with their heads down in an attempt to get the ball.

scrunchie scrunchies
NOUN a loop of elastic loosely covered with material which is used to hold hair in a ponytail.

scruple scruples
Said "skroo-pl" NOUN Scruples are moral principles that make you unwilling to do something that seems wrong E.G. *The West must drop its scruples and fight back.*

scrupulous
ADJECTIVE 1 always doing what is honest or morally right. 2 paying very careful attention to detail E.G. *a long and scrupulous search.*
scrupulously ADVERB

scrutiny
NOUN If something is under scrutiny, it is being observed very carefully.

scuba diving
NOUN Scuba diving is the sport of swimming underwater with tanks of compressed air on your back.

scuff scuffs scuffing scuffed
VERB 1 If you scuff your feet, you drag them along the ground when you are walking. 2 If you scuff your shoes, you mark them by scraping or rubbing them.

scuffle scuffles scuffling scuffled
NOUN 1 a short, rough fight. ► VERB 2 When people scuffle, they fight roughly.

scullery sculleries
NOUN a small room next to a kitchen where washing and cleaning are done.

sculpt sculpts sculpting sculpted
VERB When something is sculpted, it is carved or shaped in stone, wood, or clay.

sculptor sculptors
NOUN someone who makes sculptures.

sculpture sculptures
NOUN 1 a work of art produced by carving or shaping stone or clay. 2 Sculpture is the art of making sculptures.

scum
NOUN Scum is a layer of a dirty substance on the surface of a liquid.

scurrilous
Said "skur-ril-luss" ADJECTIVE abusive and damaging to someone's good name E.G. *scurrilous stories.*

scurry scurries scurrying scurried
VERB To scurry means to run quickly with short steps.

scurvy
NOUN Scurvy is a disease caused by a lack of vitamin C.

scuttle scuttles scuttling scuttled
VERB 1 To scuttle means to run quickly. 2 To scuttle a ship means to sink it deliberately by making holes in the bottom. ► NOUN 3 a container for coal.

scythe scythes
NOUN a tool with a long handle and a curved blade used for cutting grass or grain.

sea seas
NOUN 1 The sea is the salty water that covers much of the earth's surface. 2 A sea of people or things is a very large number of them E.G. *a sea of red flags.*

seagull seagulls
NOUN Seagulls are common white, grey, and black birds that live near the sea.

seahorse seahorses
NOUN a small fish which swims

On WEDNESday Wayne WED NESta (<u>Wednes</u>day)   SPELLING NOTE

A
B
C
D
E
F
G
H
I
J
K
L
M
N
O
P
Q
R
S
T
U
V
W
X
Y
Z

upright, with a head that resembles a horse's head.

seal seals sealing sealed

NOUN **1** an official mark on a document which shows that it is genuine. **2** a piece of wax fixed over the opening of a container. **3** a large mammal with flippers, that lives partly on land and partly in the sea. ▶ VERB **4** If you seal an envelope, you stick down the flap. **5** If you seal an opening, you cover it securely so that air, gas, or liquid cannot get through.

sea lion sea lions

NOUN a type of large seal.

seam seams

NOUN **1** a line of stitches joining two pieces of cloth. **2** A seam of coal is a long, narrow layer of it beneath the ground.

seaman seamen

NOUN a sailor.

seance seances

Said "say-ahnss"; also spelt **séance**
NOUN a meeting in which people try to communicate with the spirits of dead people.

search searches searching searched

VERB **1** If you search for something, you look for it in several places. **2** If a person is searched their body and clothing is examined to see if they are hiding anything. ▶ NOUN **3** an attempt to find something.

■ (sense 1) hunt, look, scour
■ (sense 3) look, hunt, quest

searching

ADJECTIVE intended to discover the truth about something E.G. *searching questions.*

searchlight searchlights

NOUN a powerful light whose beam can be turned in different directions.

searing

ADJECTIVE A searing pain is very sharp.

seashore

NOUN The seashore is the land along the edge of the sea.

seasick

ADJECTIVE feeling sick because of the movement of a boat.

seasickness NOUN

seaside

NOUN The seaside is an area next to the sea.

season seasons seasoning seasoned

NOUN **1** The seasons are the periods into which a year is divided and which have their own typical weather conditions. The seasons are spring, summer, autumn, and winter. **2** a period of the year when something usually happens E.G. *the football season… the hunting season.* ▶ VERB **3** If you season food, you add salt, pepper, or spices to it.

seasonal

ADJECTIVE happening during one season or one time of the year E.G. *seasonal work.*

seasoned

ADJECTIVE very experienced E.G. *a seasoned professional.*

seasoning

NOUN Seasoning is flavouring such as salt and pepper.

season ticket season tickets

NOUN a train or bus ticket that you can use as many times as you like within a certain period.

seat seats seating seated

NOUN **1** something you can sit on.

2 The seat of a piece of clothing is the part that covers your bottom. **3** If someone wins a seat in parliament, they are elected. ▶ VERB **4** If you seat yourself somewhere, you sit down. **5** If a place seats a particular number of people, it has enough seats for that number E.G. *The theatre seats 570 people.*

seat belt seat belts
NOUN a strap that you fasten across your body for safety when travelling in a car or an aircraft.

seating
NOUN The seating in a place is the number or arrangement of seats there.

seaweed
NOUN Plants that grow in the sea are called seaweed.

secateurs
Said "sek-at-**turz**" PLURAL NOUN Secateurs are small shears for pruning garden plants.

secluded
ADJECTIVE quiet and hidden from view E.G. *a secluded beach.*
seclusion NOUN

second seconds seconding seconded
ADJECTIVE **1** The second item in a series is the one counted as number two. ▶ NOUN **2** one of the sixty parts that a minute is divided into. ▶ PLURAL NOUN **3** Seconds are goods that are sold cheaply because they are slightly faulty. ▶ VERB **4** If you second a proposal, you formally agree with it so that it can be discussed or voted on. **5** If you are seconded somewhere, you are sent there temporarily to work.
secondly ADVERB

☑ Senses 1–4 are pronounced "*seck-ond*", but sense 5 is pronounced "sick-**kond**".

secondary
ADJECTIVE **1** Something that is secondary is less important than something else. **2** Secondary education is education for pupils between the ages of eleven and eighteen.

secondary school secondary schools
NOUN a school for pupils between the ages of eleven and eighteen.

second-class
ADJECTIVE **1** Second-class things are regarded as less important than other things of the same kind E.G. *He has been treated as a second-class citizen.* ▶ ADJECTIVE or ADVERB **2** Second-class services are cheaper and therefore slower or less comfortable than first-class ones.

second cousin second cousins
NOUN Your second cousins are the children of your parents' cousins.

second-hand
ADJECTIVE or ADVERB **1** Something that is second-hand has already been owned by someone else E.G. *a second-hand car.* **2** If you hear a story second-hand, you hear it indirectly, rather than from the people involved.

second-rate
ADJECTIVE of poor quality E.G. *a second-rate movie.*

secret secrets
ADJECTIVE **1** Something that is secret is told to only a small number of people and hidden from everyone else E.G. *a secret meeting.* ▶ NOUN **2** a fact told to only a small number of

Elaine and Emily shout EE when they mEEt to grEEt each other (-ee-)   **SPELLING NOTE**

people and hidden from everyone else.

secretly ADVERB **secrecy** NOUN
■ (sense 1) confidential, concealed, hidden

secret agent secret agents
NOUN a spy.

secretary secretaries
NOUN **1** a person employed by an organization to keep records, write letters, and do office work. **2** Ministers in charge of some government departments are also called secretaries E.G. *the Health Secretary*.
secretarial ADJECTIVE

secrete secretes secreting secreted
Said "sik-**kreet**" VERB **1** When part of a plant or animal secretes a liquid, it produces it. **2** FORMAL If you secrete something somewhere, you hide it.
secretion NOUN

secretive
ADJECTIVE Secretive people tend to hide their feelings and intentions.
■ reticent, tight-lipped

secret service
NOUN A country's secret service is the government department in charge of espionage.

sect sects
NOUN a religious or political group which has broken away from a larger group.

sectarian
Said "sek-**tair**-ee-an" ADJECTIVE strongly supporting a particular sect E.G. *sectarian violence*.

section sections
NOUN (LIBRARY) A section of something is one of the parts it is divided into E.G. *this section of the motorway*.

■ part, portion, segment

sector sectors
NOUN **1** A sector of something, especially a country's economy, is one part of it E.G. *the private sector*. **2** A sector of a circle is one of the two parts formed when you draw two straight lines from the centre to the circumference.

secular
ADJECTIVE having no connection with religion E.G. *secular education*.

secure secures securing secured
VERB **1** FORMAL If you secure something, you manage to get it E.G. *They secured the rights to her story*. **2** If you secure a place, you make it safe from harm or attack. **3** To secure something also means to fasten it firmly E.G. *One end was secured to the pier*. ▶ ADJECTIVE **4** If a place is secure, it is tightly locked or well protected. **5** If an object is secure, it is firmly fixed in place. **6** If you feel secure, you feel safe and confident.
securely ADVERB

security
NOUN or ADJECTIVE **1** Security means all the precautions taken to protect a place E.G. *Security forces arrested one member*. ▶ NOUN **2** A feeling of security is a feeling of being safe.

sedate sedates sedating sedated
Said "sid-**date**" ADJECTIVE **1** quiet and dignified. ▶ VERB **2** To sedate someone means to give them a drug to calm them down or make them sleep.
sedately ADVERB

sedative sedatives
Said "**sed**-at-tiv" NOUN **1** a drug that calms you down or makes you sleep.

▶ ADJECTIVE **2** having a calming or soothing effect E.G. *antihistamines which have a sedative effect.*
sedation NOUN

sedentary
Said "**sed**-en-tree" ADJECTIVE A sedentary occupation is one in which you spend most of your time sitting down.

sediment
NOUN **1** Sediment is solid material that settles at the bottom of a liquid E.G. *a bottle of beer with sediment in it is usually a guarantee of quality.*
2 Sediment is also small particles of rock that have been worn down and deposited together by water, ice, and wind.

sedimentary
ADJECTIVE Sedimentary rocks are formed from fragments of shells or rocks that have become compressed. Sandstone and limestone are sedimentary rocks.

seduce seduces seducing seduced
VERB **1** To seduce someone means to persuade them to have sex. **2** If you are seduced into doing something, you are persuaded to do it because it seems very attractive.

seductive
ADJECTIVE **1** A seductive person is sexually attractive. **2** Something seductive is very attractive and tempting.
seductively ADVERB

see sees seeing saw seen
VERB **1** If you see something, you are looking at it or you notice it. **2** If you see someone, you visit them or meet them E.G. *I went to see my dentist.* **3** If you see someone to a place, you

accompany them there. **4** To see something also means to realize or understand it E.G. *I see what you mean.* **5** If you say you will see what is happening, you mean you will find out. **6** If you say you will see if you can do something, you mean you will try to do it. **7** If you see that something is done, you make sure that it is done. **8** If you see to something, you deal with it. **9** 'See' is used to say that an event takes place during a particular period of time E.G. *The next couple of years saw two momentous developments.* ▶ PHRASES **10** INFORMAL **Seeing that** or **seeing as** means because E.G. *I took John for lunch, seeing as it was his birthday.* ▶ NOUN **11** A bishop's see is his diocese.
◼ (sense 1) notice, perceive, spot

seed seeds
NOUN **1** The seeds of a plant are the small, hard parts from which new plants can grow. **2** The seeds of a feeling or process are its beginning or origins E.G. *the seeds of mistrust.*

seedling seedlings
NOUN a young plant grown from a seed.

seedy seedier seediest
ADJECTIVE untidy and shabby E.G. *a seedy hotel.*

seek seeks seeking sought
VERB FORMAL **1** To seek something means to try to find it, obtain it, or achieve it E.G. *The police were still seeking information.* **2** If you seek to do something, you try to do it E.G. *De Gaulle sought to reunite the country.*

seem seems seeming seemed
VERB If something seems to be the

a
b
c
d
e
f
g
h
i
j
k
l
m
n
o
p
q
r
s
t
u
v
w
x
y
z

case, it appears to be the case or you think it is the case E.G. *He seemed such a quiet chap.*

seeming

ADJECTIVE appearing to be real or genuine E.G. *this seeming disregard for human life.*

seemingly ADVERB

seep seeps seeping seeped

VERB If a liquid or gas seeps through something, it flows through very slowly.

seesaw seesaws

NOUN a long plank, supported in the middle, on which two children sit, one on each end, and move up and down in turn.

seething

ADJECTIVE If you are seething about something, you are very angry but it does not show.

segment segments

NOUN 1 A segment of something is one part of it. 2 The segments of an orange or grapefruit are the sections which you can divide it into. 3 A segment of a circle is one of the two parts formed when you draw a straight line across it.

segregate segregates segregating segregated

VERB To segregate two groups of people means to keep them apart from each other.

segregated ADJECTIVE **segregation** NOUN

seize seizes seizing seized

VERB 1 If you seize something, you grab it firmly E.G. *He seized the phone.* 2 To seize a place or to seize control of it means to take control of it quickly and suddenly. 3 If you seize an opportunity, you take advantage

of it. 4 If you seize on something, you immediately show great interest in it E.G. *MPs have seized on a new report.*

seizure seizures

Said "seez-yer" NOUN 1 a sudden violent attack of an illness, especially a heart attack or a fit. 2 If there is a seizure of power, a group of people suddenly take control using force.

seldom

ADVERB not very often E.G. *They seldom speak to each other.*

select selects selecting selected

VERB 1 If you select something, you choose it. ▶ ADJECTIVE 2 of good quality E.G. *a select gentlemen's club.*

selector NOUN

selection selections

NOUN 1 Selection is the choosing of people or things E.G. *the selection of parliamentary candidates.* 2 A selection of people or things is a set of them chosen from a larger group. 3 The selection of goods in a shop is the range of goods available E.G. *a good selection of wines.*

selective

ADJECTIVE choosing things carefully E.G. *I am selective about what I eat.*

selectively ADVERB

self selves

NOUN Your self is your basic personality or nature E.G. *Hershey is her normal dependable self.*

self-

PREFIX 1 done to yourself or by yourself E.G. *self-help... self-control.* 2 doing something automatically E.G. *a self-loading rifle.*

self-assured

ADJECTIVE behaving in a way that shows confidence in yourself.

self-centred

ADJECTIVE thinking only about yourself and not about other people.

self-confessed

ADJECTIVE admitting to having bad habits or unpopular opinions E.G. *a self-confessed liar.*

self-confident

ADJECTIVE confident of your own abilities or worth.

self-confidence NOUN

self-conscious

ADJECTIVE nervous and easily embarrassed, and worried about what other people think of you.

self-consciously ADVERB

self-control

NOUN Self-control Is the ability to restrain yourself and not show your feelings.

self-defence

NOUN Self-defence is the use of special physical techniques to protect yourself when someone attacks you.

self-employed

ADJECTIVE working for yourself and organizing your own finances, rather than working for an employer.

self-esteem

NOUN Your self-esteem is your good opinion of yourself.

self-evident

ADJECTIVE Self-evident facts are completely obvious and need no proof or explanation.

self-indulgent

ADJECTIVE allowing yourself to do or have things you enjoy, especially as a treat.

self-interest

NOUN If you do something out of self-interest, you do it for your own

benefit rather than to help other people.

selfish

ADJECTIVE caring only about yourself, and not about other people.

selfishly ADVERB **selfishness** NOUN

selfless

ADJECTIVE putting other people's interests before your own.

self-made

ADJECTIVE rich and successful through your own efforts E.G. *a self-made man.*

self-raising

ADJECTIVE Self-raising flour contains baking powder to make it rise.

self-respect

NOUN Self-respect is a feeling of confidence and pride in your own abilities and worth.

self-righteous

ADJECTIVE convinced that you are better or more virtuous than other people.

self-righteousness NOUN

▣ holier-than-thou, sanctimonious

self-service

ADJECTIVE A self-service shop or restaurant is one where you serve yourself.

self-sufficient

ADJECTIVE 1 producing or making everything you need, and so not needing to buy things. 2 able to live in a way in which you do not need other people.

sell sells selling sold

VERB 1 If you sell something, you let someone have it in return for money. 2 If a shop sells something, it has it available for people to buy E.G. *a tobacconist that sells stamps.* 3 If something sells, people buy it E.G. *This book will sell.*

a
b
c
d
e
f
g
h
i
j
k
l
m
n
o
p
q
r
s
t
u
v
w
x
y
z

LEt's measure the angLE (ang**le**)   SPELLING NOTE

A
B
C
D
E
F
G
H
I
J
K
L
M
N
O
P
Q
R
S
T
U
V
W
X
Y
Z

■ (sense 2) deal in, retail, stock

sell out VERB If a shop has sold out of something, it has sold it all.

seller NOUN

Sellotape

NOUN; TRADEMARK Sellotape is a transparent sticky tape.

semblance

NOUN If there is a semblance of something, it seems to exist, although it might not really exist E.G. *an effort to restore a semblance of normality*.

semen

Said "see-men" NOUN Semen is the liquid containing sperm produced by a man's or male animal's sex organs.

semi-

PREFIX 'Semi-' means half or partly E.G. *semiskilled workers*.

■ from Latin *semi-* meaning 'half' or 'partly'

semibreve semibreves

NOUN (MUSIC) a musical note (o) which can be divided by any power of 2 to give all other notes. In the United States and Canada, a semibreve is known as a whole note.

semicircle semicircles

NOUN a half of a circle, or something with this shape.

semicircular ADJECTIVE

semicolon semicolons

NOUN the punctuation mark (;), used to separate different parts of a sentence or to indicate a pause. → *SEE BOX OPPOSITE*

semidetached

ADJECTIVE A semidetached house is joined to another house on one side.

semifinal semifinals

NOUN The semifinals are the two

matches in a competition played to decide who plays in the final.

semifinalist NOUN

What does the Semicolon do?

The **semicolon** (;) and the **colon** (:) are often confused and used incorrectly.

The **semicolon** is stronger than a comma, but weaker than a full stop. It can be used to mark the break between two main clauses, especially where there is balance or contrast between them:

E.G. *I'm not that interested in jazz; I prefer classical music.*

The semicolon can also be used instead of a comma to separate clauses or items in a long list:

E.G. *They did not enjoy the meal: the food was cold; the service was poor; and the music was too loud.*

Also look at the grammar box at **colon**.

---

seminar seminars

NOUN a meeting of a small number of university students or teachers to discuss a particular topic.

semipermeable

ADJECTIVE A semipermeable material is one that certain substances with small enough molecules can pass through but which others with larger molecules can not.

semiprecious

ADJECTIVE Semiprecious stones are stones such as opals or turquoises that are used in jewellery. They are less valuable than precious stones.

semitone semitones

NOUN (MUSIC) an interval representing the difference in pitch between a note and its sharpened or flattened equivalent. Two semitones are equal to one tone.

Senate Senates

NOUN The Senate is the smaller, more important of the two councils in the government of some countries, for example Australia, Canada, and the USA.

senator senators

NOUN a member of a Senate.

send sends sending sent

VERB **1** If you send something to someone, you arrange for it to be delivered to them. **2** To send a radio signal or message means to transmit it. **3** If you send someone somewhere, you tell them to go there or arrange for them to go. **4** If you send for someone, you send a message asking them to come and see you. **5** If you send off for something, you write and ask for it to be sent to you. **6** To send people or things in a particular direction means to make them move in that direction E.G. *It should have sent him tumbling from the saddle.*

■ (sense 1) direct, dispatch, forward

senile

ADJECTIVE If old people become senile, they become confused and cannot look after themselves.

senility NOUN

senior seniors

ADJECTIVE **1** The senior people in an organization or profession have the highest and most important jobs. ► NOUN **2** Someone who is your senior is older than you.

seniority NOUN

senior citizen senior citizens

NOUN an elderly person, especially one receiving an old-age pension.

sensation sensations

NOUN **1** a feeling, especially a physical feeling. **2** If something is a sensation, it causes great excitement and interest.

sensational

ADJECTIVE **1** causing great excitement and interest. **2** INFORMAL extremely good E.G. *a sensational party.*

sensationally ADVERB

sense senses sensing sensed

NOUN **1** Your senses are the physical abilities of sight, hearing, smell, touch, and taste. **2** a feeling E.G. *a sense of guilt.* **3** A sense of a word is one of its meanings. **4** Sense is the ability to think and behave sensibly. ► VERB **5** If you sense something, you become aware of it. ► PHRASE **6** If something **makes sense**, you can understand it or it seems sensible E.G. *It makes sense to find out as much as you can.*

senseless

ADJECTIVE **1** A senseless action has no meaning or purpose E.G. *senseless destruction.* **2** If someone is senseless, they are unconscious.

sensibility sensibilities

NOUN Your sensibility is your ability to experience deep feelings E.G. *a man of sensibility rather than reason.*

sensible

ADJECTIVE showing good sense and judgment.

sensibly ADVERB

■ prudent, rational, wise

sensitive

ADJECTIVE **1** If you are sensitive to other

a
b
c
d
e
f
g
h
i
j
k
l
m
n
o
p
q
r
s
t
u
v
w
x
y
z

A
B
C
D
E
F
G
H
I
J
K
L
M
N
O
P
Q
R
S
T
U
V
W
X
Y
Z

people's feelings, you understand them. **2** If you are sensitive about something, you are worried or easily upset about it E.G. *He was sensitive about his height.* **3** A sensitive subject or issue needs to be dealt with carefully because it can make people angry or upset. **4** Something that is sensitive to a particular thing is easily affected or harmed by it.
sensitively ADVERB **sensitivity** NOUN

sensor sensors
NOUN (ICT) an instrument which reacts to physical conditions such as light or heat.

sensual
Said "senss-yool" ADJECTIVE **1** showing or suggesting a liking for sexual pleasures E.G. *He was a very sensual person.* **2** giving pleasure to your physical senses rather than to your mind E.G. *the sensual rhythm of his voice.*
sensuality NOUN

sensuous
ADJECTIVE giving pleasure through the senses.
sensuously ADVERB

sentence sentences sentencing sentenced
NOUN **1** a group of words which make a statement, question, or command. When written down a sentence begins with a capital letter and ends with a full stop. **2** In a law court, a sentence is a punishment given to someone who has been found guilty. ▶ VERB **3** When a guilty person is sentenced, they are told officially what their punishment will be.
→ *SEE BOX OPPOSITE.*

sentiment sentiments
NOUN **1** a feeling, attitude, or opinion E.G. *I doubt my parents share my sentiments.* **2** Sentiment consists of feelings such as tenderness or sadness E.G. *There's no room for sentiment in business.*

sentimental
ADJECTIVE **1** feeling or expressing tenderness or sadness to an exaggerated extent E.G. *sentimental love stories.* **2** relating to a person's emotions E.G. *things of sentimental value.*
sentimentality NOUN
■ (sense 1) emotional, romantic, slushy

sentinel sentinels
NOUN; OLD-FASHIONED a sentry.

sentry sentries
NOUN a soldier who keeps watch and guards a camp or building.

separate separates separating separated
ADJECTIVE **1** If something is separate from something else, the two things are not connected. ▶ VERB **2** To separate people or things means to cause them to be apart from each other. **3** If people or things separate, they move away from each other. **4** If a married couple separate, they decide to live apart.
separately ADVERB **separation** NOUN
■ (sense 2) divide, split, part
■ (sense 3) diverge, part, part company

sepia
Said "see-pee-a" ADJECTIVE or NOUN deep brown, like the colour of old photographs.
📖 from Latin *sepia* meaning 'cuttlefish', because the brown dye is obtained from the ink of this fish

What is a Sentence?

The different types of word can go together to make sentences. A sentence is a group of words which expresses an idea or describes a situation.

Sentences begin with a **capital letter**:

E.G. *The child was sleeping.*

Sentences usually end with a **full stop**:

E.G. *Anna lives in Lisbon.*

If a sentence is a question, it ends with a **question mark** instead of a full stop:

E.G. *Where is my purse?*

If a sentence is an exclamation of surprise, anger, or excitement, it ends with an **exclamation mark** instead of a full stop:

E.G. *You must be joking!*

Sentences have a **subject**, which indicates a person or thing. The rest of the sentence usually says something about the subject. The subject is usually the first word or group of words in a sentence:

E.G. ***Anna*** *laughed.*
Robbie *likes bananas.*

Most sentences have a **verb**. The verb says what the subject of the sentence is doing or what is happening to the subject. The verb usually follows immediately after the subject:

E.G. *Matthew **smiled**.*

Simple, Compound and Complex Sentences

Simple sentences consist of only one main clause, and no subordinate clause:

E.G. *Anna fed the cat.*

The **subject** of a simple sentence is the person or thing that the sentence is about. It usually comes at the start of the sentence. The subject may be a noun, a pronoun, or a noun phrase:

E.G. ***We*** *often go to the cinema.*

The remaining part of the sentence is called the **predicate**. The predicate says something about the subject:

E.G. *Anna **likes to go swimming**.*
*She **is a strong swimmer**.*
*A ginger cat **was sitting on the stair**.*

Compound sentences consist of two or more main clauses joined together by a conjunction. Both clauses are equally important:

E.G. *Anna likes to go swimming, but Matthew likes to go fishing.*

Complex sentences consist of a main clause with one or more subordinate clauses joined to it. Numerous subordinate clauses can be added to a main clause:

E.G. ***After looking at all the pictures***, *the judges gave the first prize*, ***which was a silver trophy***, *to Robbie*, ***because his work was the best***.

a
b
c
d
e
f
g
h
i
j
k
l
m
n
o
p
q
r
s
t
u
v
w
x
y
z

September
NOUN September is the ninth month of the year. It has 30 days.
📖 from Latin *September* meaning

'the seventh month'
septic
ADJECTIVE If a wound becomes septic, it becomes infected with poison.

there's a rAKE in the brAKEs (br**ake**)   **SPELLING NOTE**

A
B
C
D
E
F
G
H
I
J
K
L
M
N
O
P
Q
R
S
T
U
V
W
X
Y
Z

sepulchre sepulchres
Said "**sep**-pul-ka" NOUN; LITERARY a large tomb.

sequel sequels
NOUN 1 A sequel to a book or film is another book or film which continues the story. 2 The sequel to an event is a result or consequence of it E.G. *There's a sequel to my egg story.*

sequence sequences
NOUN 1 A sequence of events is a number of them coming one after the other E.G. *the whole sequence of events that had brought me to this place.* 2 The sequence in which things are arranged is the order in which they are arranged E.G. *Do things in the right sequence.*

sequin sequins
NOUN Sequins are small, shiny, coloured discs sewn on clothes to decorate them.

Serbian Serbians
ADJECTIVE 1 belonging to or relating to Serbia. ▶ NOUN 2 someone who comes from Serbia. 3 Serbian is the form of Serbo-Croat spoken in Serbia.

Serbo-Croat
Said "ser-boh-**kroh**-at" NOUN Serbo-Croat is the main language spoken in Serbia and Croatia.

serenade serenades serenading serenaded
VERB 1 If you serenade someone you love, you sing or play music to them outside their window. ▶ NOUN 2 a song sung outside a woman's window by a man who loves her.

serene
ADJECTIVE peaceful and calm E.G. *She had a serene air.*
serenely ADVERB **serenity** NOUN

serf serfs
NOUN Serfs were servants in medieval Europe who had to work on their master's land and could not leave without his permission.

sergeant sergeants
NOUN 1 a noncommissioned officer of middle rank in the army or air force. 2 a police officer just above a constable in rank.

sergeant major sergeant majors
NOUN a noncommissioned army officer of the highest rank.

serial serials
NOUN a story which is broadcast or published in a number of parts over a period of time E.G. *a television serial.*

serial number serial numbers
NOUN An object's serial number is a number you can see on it which identifies it and distinguishes it from other objects of the same kind.

series
NOUN 1 (LIBRARY) A series of things is a number of them coming one after the other E.G. *a series of loud explosions.* 2 A radio or television series is a set of programmes with the same title.
■ (sense 1) sequence, set, succession

serious
ADJECTIVE 1 A serious problem or situation is very bad and worrying. 2 Serious matters are important and should be thought about carefully. 3 If you are serious about something, you are sincere about it E.G. *You are really serious about having a baby.* 4 People who are serious are

thoughtful, quiet, and do not laugh much.

seriousness NOUN
■ (sense 1) grave, severe
■ (sense 4) grave, solemn

seriously
ADVERB **1** You say seriously to emphasize that you mean what you say E.G. *Seriously, though, something must be done.* ▶ PHRASE **2** If you **take something seriously**, you regard it as important.

sermon sermons
NOUN a talk on a religious or moral subject given as part of a church service.

serpent serpents
NOUN; LITERARY a snake.

serrated
ADJECTIVE having a row of V-shaped points along the edge, like a saw E.G. *green serrated leaves.*

servant servants
NOUN someone who is employed to work in another person's house.

serve serves serving served
VERB **1** If you serve a country, an organization, or a person, you do useful work for them. **2** To serve as something means to act or be used as that thing E.G. *the room that served as their office.* **3** If something serves people in a particular place, it provides them with something they need E.G. *a recycling plant which serves the whole of the county.* **4** If you serve food or drink to people, you give it to them. **5** To serve customers in a shop means to help them and provide them with what they want. **6** To serve a prison sentence or an apprenticeship means to spend time doing it. **7** When you serve in tennis

or badminton, you throw the ball or shuttlecock into the air and hit it over the net to start playing. ▶ NOUN **8** the act of serving in tennis or badminton.

server servers
NOUN ICT a computer or computer program which supplies information or resources to a number of computers on a network.

service services servicing serviced
NOUN **1** a system organized to provide something for the public E.G. *the bus service.* **2** Some government organizations are called services E.G. *the diplomatic service.* **3** The services are the army, the navy, and the air force. **4** If you give your services to a person or organization, you work for them or help them in some way E.G. *services to the community.* **5** In a shop or restaurant, service is the process of being served. **6** a religious ceremony. **7** When it is your service in a game of tennis or badminton, it is your turn to serve. ▶ PLURAL NOUN **8** Motorway services consist of a garage, restaurant, shop, and toilets. ▶ VERB **9** When a machine or vehicle is serviced, it is examined and adjusted so that it will continue working efficiently.

serviceman servicemen
NOUN a man in the army, navy, or air force.
servicewoman NOUN

service station service stations
NOUN a garage that sells petrol, oil, spare parts, and snacks.

servile
ADJECTIVE too eager to obey people.
servility NOUN
■ obsequious, subservient

a
b
c
d
e
f
g
h
i
j
k
l
m
n
o
p
q
r
s
t
u
v
w
x
y
z

I always visit my FRIend on a FRIday (<u>fri</u>end)   SPELLING NOTE

A
B
C
D
E
F
G
H
I
J
K
L
M
N
O
P
Q
R
S
T
U
V
W
X
Y
Z

serving servings
NOUN **1** a helping of food. ▶ ADJECTIVE
2 A serving spoon or dish is used for serving food.

session sessions
NOUN **1** a meeting of an official group
E.G. *the emergency session of the Indiana Supreme Court.* **2** a period during which meetings are held regularly E.G. *the end of the parliamentary session.* **3** The period during which an activity takes place can also be called a session E.G. *a drinking session.*

set sets setting set
NOUN **1** Several things make a set when they belong together or form a group E.G. *a set of weights.* **2** In maths, a set is a collection of numbers or other things which are treated as a group. **3** A television set is a television. **4** The set for a play or film is the scenery or furniture on the stage or in the studio. **5** In tennis, a set is a group of six or more games. There are usually several sets in a match. ▶ VERB **6** If something is set somewhere, that is where it is E.G. *The house was set back from the beach.* **7** When the sun sets, it goes below the horizon. **8** When you set the table, you prepare it for a meal by putting plates and cutlery on it. **9** When you set a clock or a control, you adjust it to a particular point or position. **10** If you set someone a piece of work or a target, you give it to them to do or to achieve. **11** When something such as jelly or cement sets, it becomes firm or hard. ▶ ADJECTIVE **12** Something that is set is fixed and not varying E.G. *a set charge.* **13** If you are set to do something, you are ready or likely to

do it. **14** If you are set on doing something, you are determined to do it. **15** If a play or story is set at a particular time or in a particular place, the events in it take place at that time or in that place.
■ (sense 12) fixed, hard and fast, inflexible

set about VERB If you set about doing something, you start doing it.

set back VERB If something sets back a project or scheme, it delays it.

set off VERB **1** When you set off, you start a journey. **2** To set something off means to cause it to start.

set out VERB **1** When you set out, you start a journey. **2** If you set out to do something, you start trying to do it.

set up VERB If you set something up, you make all the necessary preparations for it E.G. *We have done all we can about setting up a system of communication.*

setback setbacks
NOUN something that delays or hinders you.

settee settees
NOUN a long comfortable seat for two or three people to sit on.

setter setters
NOUN a long-haired breed of dog originally used in hunting.

setting settings
NOUN **1** The setting of something is its surroundings or circumstances E.G. *The Irish setting made the story realistic.* **2** The settings on a machine are the different positions to which the controls can be adjusted.

settle settles settling settled
VERB **1** To settle an argument means to put an end to it E.G. *The dispute*

was settled. **2** If something is settled, it has all been decided and arranged. **3** If you settle on something or settle for it, you choose it E.G. *We settled for orange juice and coffee.* **4** When you settle a bill, you pay it. **5** If you settle in a place, you make it your permanent home. **6** If you settle yourself somewhere, you sit down and make yourself comfortable. **7** If something settles, it sinks slowly down and comes to rest E.G. *A black dust settled on the walls.*

settle down VERB **1** When someone settles down, they start living a quiet life in one place, especially when they get married. **2** To settle down means to become quiet or calm.

settlement settlements
NOUN **1** an official agreement between people who have been involved in a conflict E.G. *the last chance for a peaceful settlement.* **2** (GEOGRAPHY) a place where people have settled and built homes.

settler settlers
NOUN someone who settles in a new country E.G. *the first settlers in Cuba.*

seven
the number 7.

seventeen
the number 17.

seventeenth

seventh sevenths
1 The seventh item in a series is the one counted as number seven. NOUN **2** one of seven equal parts.

seventy seventies
the number 70.

seventieth

sever severs severing severed
VERB **1** To sever something means to

cut it off or cut right through it. **2** If you sever a connection with someone or something, you end it completely E.G. *She severed her ties with England.*

several
ADJECTIVE or PRONOUN Several people or things means a small number of them.

severe
ADJECTIVE **1** extremely bad or unpleasant E.G. *severe stomach pains.* **2** stern and harsh E.G. *Perhaps I was too severe with that young man.*
severely ADVERB **severity** NOUN

sew sews sewing sewed sewn
Said "so" VERB (D & T) When you sew things together, you join them using a needle and thread.
sewing NOUN

sewage
NOUN Sewage is dirty water and waste which is carried away in sewers.

sewer sewers
NOUN an underground channel that carries sewage to a place where it is treated to make it harmless.

sewerage
NOUN Sewerage is the system by which sewage is carried away and treated.

sex sexes
NOUN **1** The sexes are the two groups, male and female, into which people and animals are divided. **2** The sex of a person or animal is their characteristic of being either male or female. **3** Sex is the physical activity by which people and animals produce young.

sexism
NOUN (PSHE) Sexism is discrimination against the members of one sex, usually women.
sexist ADJECTIVE or NOUN

The government licenSes Schnapps (licenses) ◤ **SPELLING NOTE**

sextet sextets

NOUN a group of six musicians who sing or play together; also a piece of music written for six instruments or singers.

sextuplet sextuplets

NOUN Sextuplets are six children born at the same time to the same mother.

sexual

ADJECTIVE **1** connected with the act of sex or with people's desire for sex E.G. *sexual attraction*. **2** relating to the difference between males and females E.G. *sexual equality*. **3** relating to the biological process by which people and animals produce young E.G. *sexual reproduction*. **sexually** ADVERB

sexual intercourse

NOUN Sexual intercourse is the physical act of sex between two people.

sexuality

Said "seks-yoo-**a**l-it-ee" NOUN A person's sexuality is their ability to experience sexual feelings.

sexy sexier sexiest

ADJECTIVE sexually attractive or exciting E.G. *these sexy blue eyes*.

shabby shabbier shabbiest

ADJECTIVE **1** old and worn in appearance E.G. *a shabby overcoat*. **2** dressed in old, worn-out clothes E.G. *a shabby figure crouching in a doorway*. **3** behaving in a mean or unfair way E.G. *shabby treatment*. **shabbily** ADVERB

■ (sense 1) tatty, threadbare, worn

shack shacks

NOUN a small hut.

shackle shackles shackling shackled

NOUN **1** In the past, shackles were two metal rings joined by a chain fastened around a prisoner's wrists or ankles. ▶ VERB **2** To shackle someone means to put shackles on them. **3** LITERARY If you are shackled by something, it restricts or hampers you.

shade shades shading shaded

NOUN **1** Shade is an area of darkness and coolness which the sun does not reach E.G. *The table was in the shade*. **2** a lampshade. **3** The shades of a colour are its different forms. For example, olive green is a shade of green. ▶ VERB **4** If a place is shaded by trees or buildings, they prevent the sun from shining on it. **5** If you shade your eyes, you put your hand in front of them to protect them from a bright light.

shadow shadows shadowing shadowed

NOUN **1** the dark shape made when an object prevents light from reaching a surface. **2** Shadow is darkness caused by light not reaching a place. ▶ VERB **3** To shadow someone means to follow them and watch them closely.

shadow cabinet

NOUN The shadow cabinet consists of the leaders of the main opposition party, each of whom is concerned with a particular policy.

shadowy

ADJECTIVE **1** A shadowy place is dark and full of shadows. **2** A shadowy figure or shape is difficult to see because it is dark or misty.

shady shadier shadiest

ADJECTIVE A shady place is sheltered from sunlight by trees or buildings.

shaft shafts

NOUN **1** a vertical passage, for example one for a lift or one in a mine. **2** A shaft of light is a beam of light. **3** A shaft in a machine is a rod which revolves and transfers movement in the machine E.G. *the drive shaft*.

shaggy shaggier shaggiest

ADJECTIVE Shaggy hair or fur is long and untidy.

shake shakes shaking shook shaken

VERB **1** To shake something means to move it quickly from side to side or up and down. **2** If something shakes, it moves from side to side or up and down with small, quick movements. **3** If your voice shakes, it trembles because you are nervous or angry. **4** If something shakes you, it shocks and upsets you. **5** When you shake your head, you move it from side to side in order to say 'no'. ▶ NOUN **6** If you give something a shake, you shake it. ▶ PHRASE **7** When you **shake hands** with someone, you grasp their hand as a way of greeting them.

■ (sense 2) quiver, tremble, vibrate

shaky shakier shakiest

ADJECTIVE rather weak and unsteady E.G. *Confidence in the economy is still shaky.*

shakily ADVERB

shall

VERB **1** If I say I shall do something, I mean that I intend to do it. **2** If I say something shall happen, I am emphasizing that it will definitely happen, or I am ordering it to happen E.G. *There shall be work and security!* **3** 'Shall' is also used in questions when you are asking what

to do, or making a suggestion E.G. *Shall we sit down… Shall I go and check for you?*

The verbs Shall and Will

The verbs *shall* and *will* have only one form. They do not have a present form ending in *-s*, and they do not have a present participle, a past tense, or a past participle. These verbs are used as auxiliary verbs to form the future tense:

E.G. *We **shall** arrive on Thursday.*
*She **will** give a talk about Chinese history.*

People used to use *shall* to indicate the first person, and *will* to indicate the second person and the third person. However, this distinction is often ignored now:

E.G. *I **shall** see you on Sunday.*
*I **will** see you on Sunday.*

Shall is always used in questions involving *I* and *we*. *Will* is avoided in these cases:

E.G. ***Shall** I put the cat out?*
***Shall** we dance?*

Will is always used when making polite requests, giving orders, and indicating persistence. *Shall* is avoided in these cases:

E.G. ***Will** you please help me?*
***Will** you be quiet!*
*She **will** keep going on about Al Pacino.*

---

shallow shallower shallowest; shallows

ADJECTIVE **1** Shallow means not deep. **2** Shallow also means not involving serious thought or sincere feelings E.G. *a well-meaning but shallow man.*

a
b
c
d
e
f
g
h
i
j
k
l
m
n
o
p
q
r
s
t
u
v
w
x
y
z

Plaice the fish has a glittering 'EYE' (I) (pla**i**ce)   **SPELLING NOTE**

A
B
C
D
E
F
G
H
I
J
K
L
M
N
O
P
Q
R
S
T
U
V
W
X
Y
Z

➤ PLURAL NOUN **3** The shallows are the shallow part of a river or lake.

sham shams

NOUN **1** Something that is a sham is not real or genuine. ➤ ADJECTIVE **2** not real or genuine E.G. *a sham display of affection*.

shambles

NOUN If an event is a shambles, it is confused and badly organized

shame shames shaming shamed

NOUN **1** Shame is the feeling of guilt or embarrassment you get when you know you have done something wrong or foolish. **2** To bring shame on someone means to make people lose respect for them E.G. *the scenes that brought shame to English soccer*. **3** If you say something is a shame, you mean you are sorry about it E.G. *It's a shame you can't come round.* ➤ INTERJECTION **4** INFORMAL In South African English, you say 'Shame!' to show sympathy. ➤ VERB **5** If something shames you, it makes you feel ashamed. **6** If you shame someone into doing something, you force them to do it by making them feel ashamed not to E.G. *Two children shamed their parents into giving up cigarettes.*

shameful

ADJECTIVE If someone's behaviour is shameful, they ought to be ashamed of it.

shamefully ADVERB

shameless

ADJECTIVE behaving in an indecent or unacceptable way, but showing no shame E.G. *shameless dishonesty*.

shamelessly ADVERB

◼ barefaced, brazen, flagrant

shampoo shampoos shampooing shampooed

NOUN **1** Shampoo is a soapy liquid used for washing your hair. ➤ VERB **2** When you shampoo your hair, you wash it with shampoo.

▦ from Hindi *champna* meaning 'to knead'

shamrock shamrocks

NOUN a plant with three round leaves on each stem which is the national emblem of Ireland.

▦ from Irish Gaelic *seamrog* meaning 'little clover'

shanghai shanghais shanghaiing shanghaied INFORMAL

VERB **1** If someone is shanghaied, they are kidnapped and forced to work on a ship. **2** If you shanghai someone, you trick or force them into doing something. ➤ NOUN **3** In Australian and New Zealand English, a catapult.

shanty shanties

NOUN **1** a small, rough hut. **2** A sea shanty is a song sailors used to sing.

shape shapes shaping shaped

NOUN **1** The shape of something is the form or pattern of its outline, for example whether it is round or square. **2** something with a definite form, for example a circle or triangle **3** The shape of something such as an organization is its structure and size. ➤ VERB **4** If you shape an object, you form it into a particular shape E.G. *Shape the dough into an oblong.* **5** To shape something means to cause it to develop in a particular way E.G. *events that shaped the lives of some of the leading characters.*

◼ (sense 1) figure, form, outline

shapeless

ADJECTIVE not having a definite shape.

shapely shapelier shapeliest
ADJECTIVE A shapely woman has an attractive figure.

shard shards
NOUN a small fragment of pottery, glass, or metal.

share shares sharing shared
VERB (DRAMA) 1 If two people share something, they both use it, do it, or have it E.G. *We shared a bottle of champagne.* 2 If you share an idea or a piece of news with someone, you tell it to them. ▶ NOUN 3 A share of something is a portion of it. 4 The shares of a company are the equal parts into which its ownership is divided. People can buy shares as an investment.

■ (sense 3) lot, part, portion

share out VERB If you share something out, you give it out equally among a group of people.

shareholder shareholders
NOUN a person who owns shares in a company.

share-milker share-milkers
NOUN In New Zealand, someone who works on a dairy farm and shares the profit from the sale of its produce.

shark sharks
NOUN 1 Sharks are large, powerful fish with sharp teeth. 2 a person who cheats people out of money.

sharp sharper sharpest; sharps
ADJECTIVE 1 A sharp object has a fine edge or point that is good for cutting or piercing things. 2 A sharp outline or distinction is easy to see. 3 A sharp person is quick to notice or understand things. 4 A sharp change is sudden and significant E.G. *a sharp rise in prices.* 5 If you say something in a sharp way, you say it firmly and

rather angrily. 6 A sharp sound is short, sudden, and quite loud. 7 A sharp pain is sudden and painful. 8 A sharp taste is slightly sour. 9 A musical instrument or note that is sharp is slightly too high in pitch. ▶ ADVERB 10 If something happens at a certain time sharp, it happens at that time precisely E.G. *You'll begin at eight o'clock sharp.* ▶ NOUN 11 In music, a sharp is a note or key a semitone higher than that described by the same letter. It is represented by the symbol (♯).

sharply ADVERB   **sharpness** NOUN
■ (sense 3) astute, perceptive, quick-witted

sharpen sharpens sharpening sharpened
VERB 1 To sharpen an object means to make its edge or point sharper. 2 If your senses or abilities sharpen, you become quicker at noticing or understanding things.

sharpener NOUN

shatter shatters shattering shattered
VERB 1 If something shatters, it breaks into a lot of small pieces. 2 If something shatters your hopes or beliefs, it destroys them completely. 3 If you are shattered by an event or piece of news, you are shocked and upset by it.

shattered
ADJECTIVE; INFORMAL completely exhausted E.G. *He must be absolutely shattered after all his efforts.*

shattering
ADJECTIVE making you feel shocked and upset E.G. *a shattering event.*

shave shaves shaving shaved
VERB 1 When a man shaves, he

a
b
c
d
e
f
g
h
i
j
k
l
m
n
o
p
q
r
s
t
u
v
w
x
y
z

A B C D E F G H I J K L M N O P Q R S T U V W X Y Z

removes hair from his face with a razor. **2** If you shave off part of a piece of wood, you cut thin pieces from it. ▶ NOUN **3** When a man has a shave, he shaves.

shaven

ADJECTIVE If part of someone's body is shaven, it has been shaved E.G. *a shaven head*.

shaver shavers

NOUN an electric razor.

shavings

PLURAL NOUN Shavings are small, very thin pieces of wood which have been cut from a larger piece.

shawl shawls

NOUN a large piece of woollen cloth worn round a woman's head or shoulders or used to wrap a baby in.

she

PRONOUN 'She' is used to refer to a woman or girl whose identity is clear. 'She' is also used to refer to a country, a ship, or a car.

sheaf sheaves

NOUN **1** A sheaf of papers is a bundle of them. **2** A sheaf of corn is a bundle of ripe corn tied together.

shear shears shearing sheared shorn

VERB **1** To shear a sheep means to cut the wool off it. ▶ PLURAL NOUN **2** Shears are a tool like a large pair of scissors, used especially for cutting hedges.

shearer shearers

NOUN someone whose job is to shear sheep.

sheath sheaths

NOUN **1** a covering for the blade of a knife. **2** a condom.

shed sheds shedding shed

NOUN **1** a small building used for storing things. ▶ VERB **2** When an

animal sheds hair or skin, some of its hair or skin drops off. When a tree sheds its leaves, its leaves fall off. **3** FORMAL To shed something also means to get rid of it E.G. *The firm is to shed 700 jobs.* **4** If a lorry sheds its load, the load falls off the lorry onto the road. **5** If you shed tears, you cry.

sheen

NOUN a gentle brightness on the surface of something.

sheep

NOUN A sheep is a farm animal with a thick woolly coat. Sheep are kept for meat and wool

☑ The plural of *sheep* is *sheep*.

sheep-dip sheep-dips

NOUN a liquid disinfectant used to keep sheep clean and free of pests.

sheepdog sheepdogs

NOUN a breed of dog often used for controlling sheep.

sheepish

ADJECTIVE If you look sheepish, you look embarrassed because you feel shy or foolish.

sheepishly ADVERB

sheepskin

NOUN Sheepskin is the skin and wool of a sheep, used for making rugs and coats.

sheer sheerer sheerest

ADJECTIVE **1** Sheer means complete and total E.G. *sheer exhaustion*. **2** A sheer cliff or drop is vertical. **3** Sheer fabrics are very light and delicate.

sheet sheets

NOUN **1** a large rectangular piece of cloth used to cover a bed. **2** A sheet of paper is a rectangular piece of it. **3** A sheet of glass or metal is a large, flat piece of it.

sheik sheiks

Said "shake"; also spelt **sheikh**

NOUN an Arab chief or ruler.

📖 from Arabic *shaykh* meaning 'old man'

shelf shelves

NOUN a flat piece of wood, metal, or glass fixed to a wall and used for putting things on.

shell shells shelling shelled

NOUN 1 The shell of an egg or nut is its hard covering. 2 The shell of a tortoise, snail, or crab is the hard protective covering on its back. 3 The shell of a building or other structure is its frame E.G. *The room was just an empty shell.* 4 a container filled with explosives that can be fired from a gun. ▶ VERB 5 If you shell peas or nuts, you remove their natural covering. 6 To shell a place means to fire large explosive shells at it.

shellfish shellfish or **shellfishes**

NOUN a small sea creature with a shell.

shelter shelters sheltering sheltered

NOUN 1 a small building made to protect people from bad weather or danger. 2 If a place provides shelter, it provides protection from bad weather or danger. ▶ VERB 3 If you shelter in a place, you stay there and are safe. 4 If you shelter someone, you provide them with a place to stay when they are in danger.

sheltered

ADJECTIVE 1 A sheltered place is protected from wind and rain. 2 If you lead a sheltered life, you do not experience unpleasant or upsetting things. 3 Sheltered accommodation is accommodation designed for old or handicapped people.

shelve shelves shelving shelved

VERB If you shelve a plan, you decide to postpone it for a while.

shepherd shepherds shepherding shepherded

NOUN 1 a person who looks after sheep. ▶ VERB 2 If you shepherd someone somewhere, you accompany them there.

sheriff sheriffs

NOUN 1 In America, a sheriff is a person elected to enforce the law in a county. 2 In Australia, an administrative officer of the Supreme Court who carries out writs and judgments.

📖 from Old English *scir* meaning 'shire' and *gerefa* meaning 'reeve', an official

sherry sherries

NOUN Sherry is a kind of strong wine.

📖 from the Spanish town *Jerez* where it was first made

shield shields shielding shielded

NOUN 1 a large piece of a strong material like metal or plastic which soldiers or policeman carry to protect themselves. 2 If something is a shield against something, it gives protection from it. ▶ VERB 3 To shield someone means to protect them from something.

shift shifts shifting shifted

VERB 1 If you shift something, you move it. If something shifts, it moves E.G. *to shift the rubble.* 2 If an opinion or situation shifts, it changes slightly. ▶ NOUN 3 A shift in an opinion or situation is a slight change. 4 a set period during which people work in a factory E.G. *the night shift.*

shilling shillings

NOUN a former British, Australian, and

a
b
c
d
e
f
g
h
i
j
k
l
m
n
o
p
q
r
s
t
u
v
w
x
y
z

New Zealand coin worth one-twentieth of a pound.

shimmer shimmers shimmering shimmered

VERB 1 If something shimmers, it shines with a faint, flickering light. ▸ NOUN 2 a faint, flickering light.

shin shins shinning shinned

NOUN 1 Your shin is the front part of your leg between your knee and your ankle. ▸ VERB 2 If you shin up a tree or pole, you climb it quickly by gripping it with your hands and legs.

shine shines shining shone

VERB 1 When something shines, it gives out or reflects a bright light E.G. *The stars shone brilliantly.* 2 If you shine a torch or lamp somewhere, you point it there.

shingle shingles

NOUN 1 Shingle consists of small pebbles on the seashore. 2 Shingles are small wooden roof tiles.
3 Shingles is a disease that causes a painful red rash, especially around the waist.

shining

ADJECTIVE 1 Shining things are very bright, usually because they are reflecting light E.G. *shining stainless steel tables.* 2 A shining example of something is a very good or typical example of that thing E.G. *a shining example of courage.*

⬛ (sense 1) bright, gleaming

shiny shinier shiniest

ADJECTIVE Shiny things are bright and look as if they have been polished E.G. *a shiny brass plate.*

ship ships shipping shipped

NOUN 1 a large boat which carries passengers or cargo. ▸ VERB 2 If people or things are shipped somewhere, they are transported there.

-ship

SUFFIX '-ship' is used to form nouns that refer to a condition or position E.G. *fellowship.*
🏛 from Old English

shipment shipments

NOUN 1 a quantity of goods that are transported somewhere E.G. *a shipment of olive oil.* 2 The shipment of goods is the transporting of them.

shipping

NOUN 1 Shipping is the transport of cargo on ships. 2 You can also refer to ships generally as shipping E.G. *Attention all shipping!*

shipwreck shipwrecks

NOUN When there is a shipwreck, a ship is destroyed in an accident at sea E.G. *He was drowned in a shipwreck.*

shipyard shipyards

NOUN a place where ships are built and repaired.

shiralee shiralees

NOUN; OLD-FASHIONED In Australian English, the bundle of possessions carried by a swagman.

shire shires

NOUN 1 OLD-FASHIONED In Britain, a county. 2 In Australia, a rural district with its own local council.

shirk shirks shirking shirked

VERB To shirk a task means to avoid doing it.

shirt shirts

NOUN a piece of clothing worn on the upper part of the body, having a collar, sleeves, and buttons down the front

shiver shivers shivering shivered

VERB 1 When you shiver, you tremble

slightly because you are cold or scared. ▶ NOUN 2 a slight trembling caused by cold or fear.

shoal shoals
NOUN A shoal of fish is a large group of them swimming together.

shock shocks shocking shocked
NOUN 1 If you have a shock, you have a sudden upsetting experience. 2 Shock is a person's emotional and physical condition when something very unpleasant or upsetting has happened to them. 3 In medicine, shock is a serious physical condition in which the blood cannot circulate properly because of an injury. 4 a slight movement in something when it is hit by something else E.G. *The straps help to absorb shocks.* 5 A shock of hair is a thick mass of it.
▶ VERB 6 If something shocks you, it upsets you because it is unpleasant and unexpected E.G. *I was shocked by his appearance.* 7 You can say that something shocks you when it offends you because it is rude or immoral.

shocked ADJECTIVE
■ (sense 6) appal, horrify
■ (sense 7) disgust, scandalize

shock absorber shock absorbers
NOUN Shock absorbers are devices fitted near the wheels of a vehicle. They help to prevent the vehicle from bouncing up and down.

shocking
ADJECTIVE 1 INFORMAL very bad E.G. *It's been a shocking year.* 2 rude or immoral E.G. *a shocking video.*

shoddy shoddier shoddiest
ADJECTIVE badly made or done E.G. *a shoddy piece of work.*

shoe shoes shoeing shod
NOUN 1 Shoes are strong coverings for your feet. They cover most of your foot, but not your ankle. ▶ VERB 2 To shoe a horse means to fix horseshoes onto its hooves.

shoestring
NOUN If you do something on a shoestring, you do it using very little money.

shoot shoots shooting shot
VERB 1 To shoot a person or animal means to kill or injure them by firing a gun at them. 2 To shoot an arrow means to fire it from a bow. 3 If something shoots in a particular direction, it moves there quickly and suddenly E.G. *They shot back into Green Street.* 4 When a film is shot, it is filmed E.G. *The whole film was shot in California.* 5 In games such as football or hockey, to shoot means to kick or hit the ball towards the goal.
▶ NOUN 6 an occasion when people hunt animals or birds with guns. 7 a plant that is beginning to grow, or a new part growing from a plant.

shooting shootings
NOUN an incident in which someone is shot.

shooting star shooting stars
NOUN a meteor.

shop shops shopping shopped
NOUN 1 a place where things are sold. 2 a place where a particular type of work is done E.G. *a bicycle repair shop.* ▶ VERB 3 When you shop, you go to the shops to buy things.
shopper NOUN

shopkeeper shopkeepers
NOUN someone who owns or manages a small shop.

a
b
c
d
e
f
g
h
i
j
k
l
m
n
o
p
q
r
s
t
u
v
w
x
y
z

the QUeen stood on the QUay (quay)   SPELLING NOTE

A
B
C
D
E
F
G
H
I
J
K
L
M
N
O
P
Q
R
S
T
U
V
W
X
Y
Z

shoplifting

NOUN Shoplifting is stealing goods from shops.

shoplifter NOUN

shopping

NOUN Your shopping is the goods you have bought from the shops.

shop steward shop stewards

NOUN a trade union member elected to represent the workers in a factory or office.

shore shores shoring shored

NOUN 1 The shore of a sea, lake, or wide river is the land along the edge of it. ▶ VERB 2 If you shore something up, you reinforce it or strengthen it E.G. *a short-term solution to shore up the worst defence in the League.*

shoreline shorelines

NOUN the edge of a sea, lake, or wide river.

shorn

1 Shorn is the past participle of **shear.** ▶ ADJECTIVE 2 Grass or hair that is shorn is cut very short.

short shorter shortest; shorts

ADJECTIVE 1 not lasting very long. 2 small in length, distance, or height E.G. *a short climb… the short road.* 3 If you are short with someone, you speak to them crossly. 4 If you have a short temper, you get angry very quickly. 5 If you are short of something, you do not have enough of it. 6 If a name is short for another name, it is a short version of it. ▶ PLURAL NOUN 7 Shorts are trousers with short legs. ▶ ADVERB 8 If you stop short of a place, you do not quite reach it. ▶ PHRASE 9 **Short of** is used to say that a level or amount has not quite been reached E.G. *a hundred votes short of a majority.* ■ (sense 3) abrupt, curt, sharp

shortage shortages

NOUN If there is a shortage of something, there is not enough of it.

shortbread

NOUN Shortbread is a crumbly biscuit made from flour and butter.
🔲 from an old-fashioned use of *short* meaning 'crumbly'

short circuit short circuits

NOUN a fault in an electrical system when two points accidentally become connected and the electricity travels directly between them rather than through the complete circuit.

shortcoming shortcomings

NOUN Shortcomings are faults or weaknesses.

shortcut shortcuts

NOUN 1 a quicker way of getting somewhere than the usual route. 2 a quicker way of doing something E.G. *Stencils have been used as a shortcut to hand painting.*

shorten shortens shortening shortened

VERB If you shorten something or if it shortens, it becomes shorter E.G. *This might help to shorten the conversation.*

shortfall shortfalls

NOUN If there is a shortfall in something, there is less than you need.

shorthand

NOUN Shorthand is a way of writing in which signs represent words or syllables. It is used to write down quickly what someone is saying.

short-list short-lists short-listing short-listed

NOUN 1 a list of people selected from a larger group, from which one person is finally selected for a job or prize. ▶ VERB **2** If someone is short-listed for a job or prize, they are put on a short-list.

shortly

ADVERB **1** Shortly means soon E.G. *I'll be back shortly.* **2** If you speak to someone shortly, you speak to them in a cross and impatient way.

short-sighted

ADJECTIVE **1** If you are short-sighted, you cannot see things clearly when they are far away. **2** A short-sighted decision does not take account of the way things may develop in the future.

short-term

ADJECTIVE happening or having an effect within a short time or for a short time.

shot shots

1 Shot is the past tense and past participle of **shoot**. NOUN **2** the act of firing a gun. **3** Someone who is a good shot can shoot accurately. **4** In football, golf, and tennis, a shot is the act of kicking or hitting the ball. **5** a photograph or short film sequence E.G. *I'd like to get some shots of the river.* **6** INFORMAL If you have a shot at something, you try to do it.

shotgun shotguns

NOUN a gun that fires a lot of small pellets all at once.

shot put

NOUN In athletics, the shot put is an event in which the contestants throw a heavy metal ball called a shot as far as possible.

shot putter NOUN

should

VERB **1** You use 'should' to say that something ought to happen E.G.

Ward should have done better. **2** You also use 'should' to say that you expect something to happen E.G. *He should have heard by now.* **3** FORMAL You can use 'should' to announce that you are about to do or say something E.G. *I should like to express my thanks to the Professor.* **4** 'Should' is used in conditional sentences E.G. *If they should discover the fact, what use would the knowledge be to them?* **5** 'Should' is sometimes used in 'that' clauses E.G. *It is inevitable that you should go.* **6** If you say that you should think something, you mean that it is probably true E.G. *I should think that's unlikely.*

shoulder shoulders shouldering shouldered

NOUN **1** Your shoulders are the parts of your body between your neck and the tops of your arms. ▶ VERB **2** If you shoulder something heavy, you put it across one of your shoulders to carry it. **3** If you shoulder the responsibility or blame for something, you accept it.

shoulder blade shoulder blades

NOUN Your shoulder blades are the two large, flat bones in the upper part of your back, below your shoulders.

shout shouts shouting shouted

NOUN **1** a loud call or cry. ▶ VERB **2** If you shout something, you say it very loudly E.G. *He shouted something to his brother.*

⬛ call, cry, yell

shove shoves shoving shoved

VERB **1** If you shove someone or something, you push them roughly E.G. *He shoved his wallet into a back pocket.* ▶ NOUN **2** a rough push.

shove off VERB; INFORMAL If you tell

a b c d e f g h i j k l m n o p q r **s** t u v w x y z

someone to shove off, you are telling them angrily and rudely to go away.

shovel shovels shovelling shovelled

NOUN 1 a tool like a spade, used for moving earth or snow. ▶ VERB 2 If you shovel earth or snow, you move it with a shovel.

show shows showing showed shown

VERB 1 To show that something exists or is true means to prove it E.G. *The survey showed that 29 per cent would now approve the treaty.* 2 If a picture shows something, it represents it E.G. *The painting shows supporters and crowd scenes.* 3 If you show someone something, you let them see it E.G. *Show me your passport.* 4 If you show someone to a room or seat, you lead them there. 5 If you show someone how to do something, you demonstrate it to them. 6 If something shows, it is visible. 7 If something shows a quality or characteristic, you can see that it has it E.G. *Her sketches and watercolours showed promise.* 8 If you show your feelings, you let people see them E.G. *She was flustered, but too proud to show it.* 9 If you show affection or mercy, you behave in an affectionate or merciful way E.G. *the first person who showed me some affection.* 10 To show a film or television programme means to let the public see it. ▶ NOUN 11 a form of light entertainment at the theatre or on television. 12 an exhibition E.G. *the Napier Antiques Show.* 13 A show of a feeling or attitude is behaviour in which you show it E.G. *a show of optimism.* ▶ PHRASE 14 If something is **on show**, it is being exhibited for the public to see.

■ (sense 1) demonstrate, prove
■ (sense 7) display, indicate, reveal
■ (sense 12) display, exhibition

show off VERB INFORMAL If someone is showing off, they are trying to impress people.

show up VERB 1 INFORMAL If you show up, you arrive at a place where you are expected. 2 If something shows up, it can be seen clearly E.G. *Her bones were too soft to show up on an X-ray.*

show business

NOUN Show business is entertainment in the theatre, films, and television.

showdown showdowns

NOUN; INFORMAL a major argument or conflict intended to end a dispute.

shower showers showering showered

NOUN 1 a device which sprays you with water so that you can wash yourself. 2 If you have a shower, you wash yourself by standing under a shower. 3 a short period of rain. 4 You can refer to a lot of things falling at once as a shower E.G. *a shower of confetti.* ▶ VERB 5 If you shower, you have a shower. 6 If you are showered with a lot of things, they fall on you.

showing showings

NOUN A showing of a film or television programme is a presentation of it so that the public can see it.

showjumping

NOUN Showjumping is a horse-riding competition in which the horses jump over a series of high fences.

show-off show-offs

NOUN; INFORMAL someone who tries to impress people with their knowledge or skills.

showroom showrooms

NOUN a shop where goods such as cars or electrical appliances are displayed.

showy showier showiest

ADJECTIVE large or bright and intended to impress people E.G. *a showy house.*

≡ flamboyant, flashy, ostentatious

shrapnel

NOUN Shrapnel consists of small pieces of metal scattered from an exploding shell.

🏛 named after General Henry *Shrapnel* (1761–1842), who invented it

shred shreds shredding shredded

VERB 1 If you shred something, you cut or tear it into very small pieces. ▶ NOUN 2 A shred of paper or material is a small, narrow piece of it. 3 If there is not a shred of something, there is absolutely none of it E.G. *He was left without a shred of self-esteem.*

shrew shrews

Said "shroo" NOUN a small mouse-like animal with a long pointed nose.

shrewd shrewder shrewdest

ADJECTIVE Someone who is shrewd is intelligent and makes good judgments.

shrewdly ADVERB **shrewdness** NOUN

≡ astute, clever, sharp

shriek shrieks shrieking shrieked

NOUN 1 a high-pitched scream. ▶ VERB 2 If you shriek, you make a high-pitched scream.

shrift

NOUN If you give someone or something short shrift, you pay very little attention to them.

🏛 from Old English *scrift* meaning 'confession'; 'short shrift' referred to the short time allowed to prisoners before they were put to death to make their confession

shrill shriller shrillest

ADJECTIVE A shrill sound is unpleasantly high-pitched and piercing.

shrilly ADVERB

shrimp shrimps

NOUN a small edible shellfish with a long tail and many legs.

shrine shrines

NOUN (RE) a place of worship associated with a sacred person or object.

shrink shrinks shrinking shrank shrunk

VERB 1 If something shrinks, it becomes smaller. 2 If you shrink from something, you move away from it because you are afraid of it.

shrinkage NOUN

shrivel shrivels shrivelling shrivelled

VERB When something shrivels, it becomes dried and withered.

shroud shrouds shrouding shrouded

NOUN 1 a cloth in which a dead body is wrapped before it is buried. ▶ VERB 2 If something is shrouded in darkness or fog, it is hidden by it.

shrub shrubs

NOUN a low, bushy plant.

shrug shrugs shrugging shrugged

VERB 1 If you shrug your shoulders, you raise them slightly as a sign of indifference. ▶ NOUN 2 If you give a shrug of your shoulders, you shrug them.

a
b
c
d
e
f
g
h
i
j
k
l
m
n
o
p
q
r
s
t
u
v
w
x
y
z

A B C D E F G H I J K L M N O P Q R S T U V W X Y Z

shrunken

ADJECTIVE; FORMAL Someone or something that is shrunken has become smaller than it used to be E.G. *a shrunken old man.*

shudder shudders shuddering shuddered

VERB 1 If you shudder, you tremble with fear or horror. 2 If a machine or vehicle shudders, it shakes violently.
▶ NOUN 3 a shiver of fear or horror.

shuffle shuffles shuffling shuffled

VERB 1 If you shuffle, you walk without lifting your feet properly off the ground. 2 If you shuffle about, you move about and fidget because you feel uncomfortable or embarrassed. 3 If you shuffle a pack of cards, you mix them up before you begin a game. ▶ NOUN 4 the way someone walks when they shuffle.

shun shuns shunning shunned

VERB If you shun someone or something, you deliberately avoid them.

shunt shunts shunting shunted

VERB; INFORMAL If you shunt people or things to a place, you move them there E.G. *You are shunted from room to room.*

shut shuts shutting shut

VERB 1 If you shut something, you close it. 2 When a shop or pub shuts, it is closed and you can no longer go into it. ▶ ADJECTIVE 3 If something is shut, it is closed.

shut up VERB; INFORMAL If you shut up, you stop talking.

shutter shutters

NOUN Shutters are hinged wooden or metal covers fitted on the outside or inside of a window.

shuttle shuttles

ADJECTIVE 1 A shuttle service is an air, bus, or train service which makes frequent journeys between two places. ▶ NOUN 2 a plane used in a shuttle service.

shuttlecock shuttlecocks

NOUN the feathered object used as a ball in the game of badminton.

shy shyer shyest; shies shying shied

ADJECTIVE 1 A shy person is nervous and uncomfortable in the company of other people. ▶ VERB 2 When a horse shies, it moves away suddenly because something has frightened it. 3 If you shy away from doing something, you avoid doing it because you are afraid or nervous.

shyly ADVERB **shyness** NOUN

■ (sense 1) bashful, self-conscious, timid

sibling siblings

NOUN; FORMAL Your siblings are your brothers and sisters.

sick sicker sickest

ADJECTIVE 1 If you are sick, you are ill. 2 If you feel sick, you feel as if you are going to vomit. If you are sick, you vomit. 3 INFORMAL If you are sick of doing something, you feel you have been doing it too long. 4 INFORMAL A sick joke or story deals with death or suffering in an unpleasantly frivolous way. ▶ PHRASE 5 If something **makes you sick**, it makes you angry.

sickness NOUN

■ (sense 2) nauseous, queasy

sicken sickens sickening sickened

VERB If something sickens you, it makes you feel disgusted.

sickening ADJECTIVE

sickle sickles
NOUN a tool with a short handle and a curved blade used for cutting grass or grain.

sickly sicklier sickliest
ADJECTIVE **1** A sickly person or animal is weak and unhealthy. **2** Sickly also means very unpleasant to smell or taste.

side sides siding sided
NOUN **1** Side refers to a position to the left or right of something E.G. *the two armchairs on either side of the fireplace.* **2** The sides of a boundary or barrier are the two areas it separates E.G. *this side of the border.* **3** Your sides are the parts of your body from your armpits down to your hips. **4** The sides of something are its outside surfaces, especially the surfaces which are not its front or back. **5** The sides of a hill or valley are the parts that slope. **6** The two sides in a war, argument, or relationship are the two people or groups involved. **7** A particular side of something is one aspect of it E.G. *the sensitive, caring side of human nature.* ► ADJECTIVE **8** situated on a side of a building or vehicle E.G. *the side door.* **9** A side road is a small road leading off a larger one. **10** A side issue is an issue that is less important than the main one. ► VERB **11** If you side with someone in an argument, you support them.

sideboard sideboards
NOUN **1** a long, low cupboard for plates and glasses. ► PLURAL NOUN **2** A man's sideboards are his sideburns.

sideburns
PLURAL NOUN A man's sideburns are areas of hair growing on his cheeks in front of his ears.
🖼 from a 19th century US army general called *Burnside* who wore his whiskers like this

side effect side effects
NOUN The side effects of a drug are the effects it has in addition to its main effects.

sidekick sidekicks
NOUN; INFORMAL Someone's sidekick is their close friend who spends a lot of time with them.

sideline sidelines
NOUN an extra job in addition to your main job.

sideshow sideshows
NOUN Sideshows are stalls at a fairground.

sidestep sidesteps sidestepping sidestepped
VERB If you sidestep a difficult problem or question, you avoid dealing with it.

sidewalk sidewalks
NOUN In American English, a sidewalk is a pavement.

sideways
ADVERB from or towards the side of something or someone.

siding sidings
NOUN a short railway track beside the main tracks, where engines and carriages are left when not in use.

sidle sidles sidling sidled
VERB If you sidle somewhere, you walk there cautiously and slowly, as if you do not want to be noticed.

siege sieges
Said "seej" NOUN (HISTORY) a military operation in which an army surrounds a place and prevents food or help from reaching the people inside.

a
b
c
d
e
f
g
h
i
j
k
l
m
n
o
p
q
r
s
t
u
v
w
x
y
z

'i' before 'e' except after 'c'   SPELLING NOTE

A
B
C
D
E
F
G
H
I
J
K
L
M
N
O
P
Q
R
S
T
U
V
W
X
Y
Z

sieve sieves sieving sieved
Said "siv" NOUN **1** a kitchen tool made of mesh, used for sifting or straining things. ▶ VERB **2** If you sieve a powder or liquid, you pass it through a sieve.

sift sifts sifting sifted
VERB **1** If you sift a powdery substance, you pass it through a sieve to remove lumps. **2** If you sift through something such as evidence, you examine it all thoroughly.

sigh sighs sighing sighed
VERB **1** When you sigh, you let out a deep breath. ▶ NOUN **2** the breath you let out when you sigh.

sight sights sighting sighted
NOUN **1** Sight is the ability to see E.G. *His sight was so poor that he could not follow the cricket.* **2** something you see E.G. *It was a ghastly sight.* ▶ PLURAL NOUN **3** Sights are interesting places which tourists visit. ▶ VERB **4** If you sight someone or something, you see them briefly or suddenly E.G. *He had been sighted in Cairo.* ▶ PHRASES **5** If something is **in sight**, you can see it. If it is **out of sight**, you cannot see it. ☑ Do not confuse the spellings of *sight* and *site*.

sighted
ADJECTIVE Someone who is sighted can see.

sighting sightings
NOUN A sighting of something rare or unexpected is an occasion when it is seen.

sightseeing
NOUN Sightseeing is visiting the interesting places that tourists usually visit.
sightseer NOUN

sign signs signing signed
NOUN **1** a mark or symbol that always has a particular meaning, for example in mathematics or music. **2** a gesture with a particular meaning. **3** A sign can also consist of words, a picture, or a symbol giving information or a warning. **4** ⟨RE⟩ A sign is an event or happening that some people believe God has sent as a warning or instruction to an individual or to people in general. **5** If there are signs of something, there is evidence that it exists or is happening E.G. *We are now seeing the first signs of recovery.* ▶ VERB **6** If you sign a document, you write your name on it E.G. *He hurriedly signed the death certificate.* **7** If you sign, you communicate by using sign language. ▤ (sense 2) gesture, signal

sign on VERB **1** If you sign on for a job or course, you officially agree to do it by signing a contract. **2** When people sign on, they officially state that they are unemployed and claim benefit from the state.

sign up VERB If you sign up for a job or course, you officially agree to do it by signing a contract.

signal signals signalling signalled
NOUN **1** a gesture, sound, or action intended to give a message to someone. **2** A railway signal is a piece of equipment beside the track which tells train drivers whether to stop or not. ▶ VERB **3** If you signal to someone, you make a gesture or sound to give them a message.

signature signatures
NOUN If you write your signature, you write your name the way you usually write it.

significant
ADJECTIVE **1** A significant amount is a

large amount. **2** Something that is
significant is important E.G. *a
significant victory*.

significance NOUN **significantly**
ADVERB

**signify signifies signifying
signified**
VERB A gesture that signifies
something has a particular meaning
E.G. *They signified a desire to leave*.

sign language
NOUN Sign language is a way of
communicating using your hands,
used especially by deaf people.

signpost signposts
NOUN a road sign with information on
it such as the name of a town and
how far away it is.

Sikh Sikhs
Said "**seek**" NOUN RE a person who
believes in Sikhism, an Indian
religion which separated from
Hinduism in the sixteenth century
and which teaches that there is only
one God.

Sikhism NOUN
📖 from Hindi *sikh* meaning 'disciple'

**silence silences silencing
silenced**
NOUN **1** Silence is quietness.
2 Someone's silence about
something is their failure or refusal
to talk about it. ▶ VERB **3** To silence
someone or something means to
stop them talking or making a noise.

silent
ADJECTIVE **1** If you are silent, you are not
saying anything. **2** If you are silent
about something, you do not tell
people about it. **3** When something
is silent, it makes no noise. **4** A silent
film has only pictures and no sound.

silently ADVERB

■ (sense 1) dumb, mute, speechless

silhouette silhouettes
Said "**sil-loo-ett**" NOUN the outline of a
dark shape against a light
background.

silhouetted ADJECTIVE

silicon
NOUN Silicon is an element found in
sand, clay, and stone. It is used to
make parts of computers.

silk silks
NOUN Silk is a fine, soft cloth made
from a substance produced by
silkworms.

📖 from Chinese *ssu* meaning 'silk'

silkworm silkworms
NOUN Silkworms are the larvae of a
particular kind of moth.

silky silkier silkiest
ADJECTIVE smooth and soft.

sill sills
NOUN a ledge at the bottom of a
window.

silly sillier silliest
ADJECTIVE foolish or childish.

■ daft, foolish, stupid

silt
NOUN Silt is fine sand or soil which is
carried along by a river.

silver
NOUN **1** Silver is a valuable greyish-
white metallic element used for
making jewellery and ornaments.
2 Silver is also coins made from silver
or from silver-coloured metal.
▶ ADJECTIVE OR NOUN **3** greyish-white.

silver beet silver beets
NOUN a type of beet grown in
Australia and New Zealand.

silver fern
NOUN a tall fern that is found in New
Zealand. It is the symbol of New
Zealand national sports teams.

a
b
c
d
e
f
g
h
i
j
k
l
m
n
o
p
q
r
s
t
u
v
w
x
y
z

A
B
C
D
E
F
G
H
I
J
K
L
M
N
O
P
Q
R
S
T
U
V
W
X
Y
Z

silverfish silverfishes or silverfish

NOUN a small silver insect with no wings that eats paper and clothing.

silver jubilee silver jubilees

NOUN the 25th anniversary of an important event.

silver medal silver medals

NOUN a medal made from silver awarded to the competitor who comes second in a competition.

silver wedding silver weddings

NOUN A couple's silver wedding is the 25th anniversary of their wedding.

silvery

ADJECTIVE having the appearance or colour of silver E.G. *the silvery moon*.

similar

ADJECTIVE 1 If one thing is similar to another, or if two things are similar, they are like each other. 2 In maths, two triangles are similar if the angles in one correspond exactly to the angles in the other.

similarly ADVERB

✓ Be careful when deciding whether to use *similar* or *same*. *Similar* means 'alike but not identical', and *same* means 'identical'. Do not put *as* after *similar*: her dress was similar to mine.

similarity similarities

NOUN If there is a similarity between things, they are similar in some way.

■ likeness, resemblance

simile similes

Said "**sim**-ill-*ee*" NOUN (ENGLISH) an expression in which a person or thing is described as being similar to someone or something else. Examples of similes are *She runs like a deer* and *He's as white as a sheet*.

simmer simmers simmering simmered

VERB When food simmers, it cooks gently at just below boiling point.

simple simpler simplest

ADJECTIVE 1 Something that is simple is uncomplicated and easy to understand or do. 2 Simple also means plain and not elaborate in style E.G. *a simple coat*. 3 A simple way of life is uncomplicated. 4 Someone who is simple is mentally retarded. 5 You use 'simple' to emphasize that what you are talking about is the only important thing E.G. *simple stubbornness*.

simplicity NOUN

simple-minded

ADJECTIVE not very intelligent or sophisticated E.G. *simple-minded pleasures*.

simplify simplifies simplifying simplified

VERB To simplify something means to make it easier to do or understand.

simplification NOUN

simplistic

ADJECTIVE too simple or naive E.G. *a rather simplistic approach to the subject*.

simply

ADVERB 1 Simply means merely E.G. *It was simply a question of making the decision*. 2 You use 'simply' to emphasize what you are saying E.G. *It is simply not true*. 3 If you say or write something simply, you do it in a way that makes it easy to understand.

simulate simulates simulating simulated

VERB To simulate something means to

imitate it E.G. *The wood has been painted to simulate stone.*

simulation NOUN

simultaneous

ADJECTIVE Things that are simultaneous happen at the same time.

simultaneously ADVERB

sin sins sinning sinned

NOUN **1** Sin is wicked and immoral behaviour. ▶ VERB **2** To sin means to do something wicked and immoral.

■ (sense 1) evil, iniquity, wrongdoing

■ (sense 2) lapse, transgress

since

PREPOSITION, CONJUNCTION, or ADVERB **1** Since means from a particular time until now E.G. *I've been waiting patiently since half past three.* ▶ ADVERB **2** Since also means at some time after a particular time in the past E.G. *They split up and he has since remarried.* ▶ CONJUNCTION **3** Since also means because E.G. *I'm forever on a diet, since I put on weight easily.*

☑ Do not put *ago* before *since*, as it is not needed: *it is ten years since she wrote her book* not *ten years ago since.*

sincere

ADJECTIVE If you are sincere, you say things that you really mean E.G. *a sincere expression of friendliness.*

sincerity NOUN

■ genuine, honest

sincerely

ADVERB **1** If you say or feel something sincerely, you mean it or feel it genuinely. ▶ PHRASE **2** You write **Yours sincerely** before your signature at the end of a letter in which you have named the person you are writing to in the greeting at the beginning of the letter. For example, if you began your letter 'Dear Mr Brown' you would use 'Yours sincerely'.

sinew sinews

Said "sin-yoo" NOUN a tough cord in your body that connects a muscle to a bone.

sinful

ADJECTIVE wicked and immoral.

sing sings singing sang sung

VERB **1** When you sing, you make musical sounds with your voice, usually producing words that fit a tune. **2** When birds or insects sing, they make pleasant sounds.

singer NOUN

☑ The past tense of *sing* is *sang*, and the past participle is *sung*. Do not confuse these words: *the team sang the national anthem; we have sung together many times.*

singe singes singeing singed

VERB **1** To singe something means to burn it slightly so that it goes brown but does not catch fire. ▶ NOUN **2** a slight burn.

single singles singling singled

ADJECTIVE **1** Single means only one and not more E.G. *A single shot was fired.* **2** People who are single are not married. **3** A single bed or bedroom is for one person. **4** A single ticket is a one-way ticket. ▶ NOUN **5** a recording of one or two short pieces of music on a small record, CD, or cassette. **6** Singles is a game of tennis, badminton, or squash between just two players.

single out VERB If you single someone out from a group, you give them special treatment E.G. *He'd been singled out for some special award.*

a
b
c
d
e
f
g
h
i
j
k
l
m
n
o
p
q
r
s
t
u
v
w
x
y
z

single-handed

ADVERB If you do something single-handed, you do it on your own, without any help.

single-minded

ADJECTIVE A single-minded person has only one aim and is determined to achieve it.

singly

ADVERB If people do something singly, they do it on their own or one by one.

singular

NOUN 1 In grammar, the singular is the form of a word that refers to just one person or thing. ► ADJECTIVE 2 FORMAL unusual and remarkable E.G. *her singular beauty.*

singularity NOUN **singularly** ADVERB

sinister

ADJECTIVE seeming harmful or evil E.G. *something cold and sinister about him.*
from Latin *sinister* meaning 'left-hand side', because the left side was considered unlucky

sink sinks sinking sank sunk

NOUN 1 a basin with taps supplying water, usually in a kitchen or bathroom. ► VERB 2 If something sinks, it moves downwards, especially through water E.G. *An Indian cargo ship sank in icy seas.* 3 To sink a ship means to cause it to sink by attacking it. 4 If an amount or value sinks, it decreases. 5 If you sink into an unpleasant state, you gradually pass into it E.G. *He sank into black despair.* 6 To sink something sharp into an object means to make it go deeply into it E.G. *The tiger sank its teeth into his leg.*

sink in VERB When a fact sinks in, you fully understand it or realize it E.G. *The truth was at last sinking in.*

sinner sinners

NOUN someone who has committed a sin.

sinus sinuses

NOUN Your sinuses are the air passages in the bones of your skull, just behind your nose.

sip sips sipping sipped

VERB 1 If you sip a drink, you drink it by taking a small amount at a time. ► NOUN 2 a small amount of drink that you take into your mouth.

siphon siphons siphoning siphoned

Said "sigh-fn"; also spelt **syphon**

VERB If you siphon off a liquid, you draw it out of a container through a tube and transfer it to another place.

sir

NOUN 1 Sir is a polite, formal way of addressing a man. 2 Sir is also the title used in front of the name of a knight or baronet.

siren sirens

NOUN a warning device, for example on a police car, which makes a loud, wailing noise.
the Sirens in Greek mythology were sea nymphs who had beautiful voices and sang in order to lure sailors to their deaths on the rocks where the nymphs lived

sirloin

NOUN Sirloin is a prime cut of beef from the lower part of a cow's back.
from Old French *sur* meaning 'above' and *longe* meaning 'loin'

sis or **sies**

Said "siss" INTERJECTION; INFORMAL In South African English, you say 'Sis!' to show disgust.

sister sisters

NOUN 1 Your sister is a girl or woman

who has the same parents as you. **2** a member of a female religious order. **3** In a hospital, a sister is a senior nurse who supervises a ward. ▶ ADJECTIVE **4** Sister means closely related to something or very similar to it E.G. *Citroen and its sister company Peugeot*.

sisterhood
NOUN Sisterhood is a strong feeling of companionship between women.

sister-in-law sisters-in-law
NOUN Your sister-in-law is the wife of your brother, the sister of your husband or wife, or the woman married to your wife's or husband's brother.

sit sits sitting sat
VERB **1** If you are sitting, your weight is supported by your buttocks rather than your feet. **2** When you sit or sit down somewhere, you lower your body until you are sitting. **3** If you sit an examination, you take it. **4** FORMAL When a parliament, law court, or other official body sits, it meets and officially carries out its work.

sitcom sitcoms
NOUN; INFORMAL a television comedy series which shows characters in amusing situations that are similar to everyday life.
🔲 shortened from *situation comedy*

site sites siting sited
NOUN **1** a piece of ground where a particular thing happens or is situated E.G. *a building site*. ▶ VERB **2** If something is sited in a place, it is built or positioned there.
✅ Do not confuse the spellings of *site* and *sight*.

sitting sittings
NOUN **1** one of the times when a meal is served. **2** one of the occasions

when a parliament or law court meets and carries out its work.

sitting room sitting rooms
NOUN a room in a house where people sit and relax.

situated
ADJECTIVE If something is situated somewhere, that is where it is E.G. *a town situated 45 minutes from Geneva*.

situation situations
NOUN **1** what is happening in a particular place at a particular time E.G. *the political situation*.
2 (GEOGRAPHY) The situation of a building or town is its surroundings E.G. *a beautiful situation*.
≡ (sense 1) circumstances, condition, state of affairs

Siva
PROPER NOUN Siva is a Hindu god and is one of the Trimurti.
🔲 from a Sanskrit word meaning 'auspicious'

six
Six is the number 6.

sixteen
the number 16.

sixteenth

sixth sixths
1 The sixth item in a series is the one counted as number six.
NOUN **2** one of six equal parts.

sixth sense
NOUN You say that someone has a sixth sense when they know something instinctively, without having any evidence of it.

sixty sixties
the number 60.

sixtieth

sizable or sizeable
ADJECTIVE fairly large E.G. *a sizable amount of money*.

a b c d e f g h i j k l m n o p q r **s** t u v w x y z

A
B
C
D
E
F
G
H
I
J
K
L
M
N
O
P
Q
R
S
T
U
V
W
X
Y
Z

size sizes

NOUN 1 The size of something is how big or small it is E.G. *the size of the audience.* 2 The size of something is also the fact that it is very large E.G. *the sheer size of Australia.* 3 one of the standard graded measurements of clothes and shoes.

☰ (sense 1) dimensions, magnitude, proportions

sizzle sizzles sizzling sizzled

VERB If something sizzles, it makes a hissing sound like the sound of frying food

sjambok sjamboks

Said "sham-bok" NOUN In South African English, a sjambok is a long whip made from animal hide.

skate skates skating skated

NOUN 1 Skates are ice skates or roller skates. 2 a flat edible sea fish. ➤ VERB 3 If you skate, you move about on ice wearing ice skates. 4 If you skate round a difficult subject, you avoid discussing it.

skateboard skateboards

NOUN a narrow board on wheels which you stand on and ride for fun.

skeleton skeletons

NOUN Your skeleton is the framework of bones in your body.

sketch sketches sketching sketched

NOUN 1 (ART) a quick, rough drawing. 2 A sketch of a situation or incident is a brief description of it. 3 a short, humorous piece of acting, usually forming part of a comedy show. ➤ VERB 4 If you sketch something, you draw it quickly and roughly.

sketchy sketchier sketchiest

ADJECTIVE giving only a rough description or account E.G. *Details*

surrounding his death are sketchy.

skew or **skewed**

Said "skyoo" ADJECTIVE in a slanting position, rather than straight or upright.

skewer skewers skewering skewered

NOUN 1 a long metal pin used to hold pieces of food together during cooking. ➤ VERB 2 If you skewer something, you push a skewer through it.

ski skis skiing skied

NOUN 1 Skis are long pieces of wood, metal, or plastic that you fasten to special boots so you can move easily on snow. ➤ VERB 2 When you ski, you move on snow wearing skis, especially as a sport.

⊞ from Old Norse *skith* meaning 'snowshoes'

skid skids skidding skidded

VERB If a vehicle skids, it slides in an uncontrolled way, for example because the road is wet or icy.

skilful

ADJECTIVE If you are skilful at something, you can do it very well. **skilfully** ADVERB

☰ able, expert, proficient

skill skills

NOUN 1 Skill is the knowledge and ability that enables you to do something well. 2 a type of work or technique which requires special training and knowledge.

☰ (sense 1) ability, expertise, proficiency

skilled

ADJECTIVE 1 A skilled person has the knowledge and ability to do something well. 2 Skilled work is work which can only be done by people who have had special training.

skim skims skimming skimmed
VERB **1** If you skim something from the surface of a liquid, you remove it. **2** If something skims a surface, it moves along just above it E.G. *seagulls skimming the waves.*

skimmed milk
NOUN Skimmed milk has had the cream removed.

skin skins skinning skinned
NOUN **1** Your skin is the natural covering of your body. An animal skin is the skin and fur of a dead animal. **2** The skin of a fruit or vegetable is its outer covering. **3** a solid layer which forms on the surface of a liquid. ► VERB **4** If you skin a dead animal, you remove its skin. **5** If you skin a part of your body, you accidentally graze it.

skinny skinnier skinniest
ADJECTIVE extremely thin.

skip skips skipping skipped
VERB **1** If you skip along, you move along jumping from one foot to the other. **2** If you skip something, you miss it out or avoid doing it E.G. *It is all too easy to skip meals.* ► NOUN **3** Skips are the movements you make when you skip. **4** a large metal container for holding rubbish and rubble.

skipper skippers
NOUN; INFORMAL The skipper of a ship or boat is its captain.
🔲 from Old Dutch *schipper* meaning 'shipper'

skirmish skirmishes
NOUN a short, rough fight.

skirt skirts skirting skirted
NOUN **1** A woman's skirt is a piece of clothing which fastens at her waist and hangs down over her legs. ► VERB **2** Something that skirts an area is situated around the edge of it. **3** If you skirt something, you go around the edge of it E.G. *We skirted the town.* **4** If you skirt a problem, you avoid dealing with it E.G. *He was skirting the real question.*
🔲 from Old Norse *skyrta* meaning 'shirt'

skirting skirtings
NOUN A skirting or skirting board is a narrow strip of wood running along the bottom of a wall in a room.

skite skites skiting skited
INFORMAL
VERB **1** In Australian and New Zealand English, to skite is to talk in a boastful way about something that you own or that you have done. ► NOUN **2** In Australian and New Zealand English, someone who boasts.

skittle skittles
NOUN Skittles is a game in which players roll a ball and try to knock down wooden objects called skittles.

skull skulls
NOUN Your skull is the bony part of your head which surrounds your brain.

skunk skunks
NOUN a small black and white animal from North America which gives off an unpleasant smell when it is frightened.
🔲 a North American Indian word

sky skies
NOUN The sky is the space around the earth which you can see when you look upwards.
🔲 from Old Norse *sky* meaning 'cloud'

a
b
c
d
e
f
g
h
i
j
k
l
m
n
o
p
q
r
s
t
u
v
w
x
y
z

skylight skylights
NOUN a window in a roof or ceiling.

skyline skylines
NOUN The skyline is the line where the sky meets buildings or the ground E.G. *the New York City skyline.*

skyscraper skyscrapers
NOUN a very tall building.

slab slabs
NOUN a thick, flat piece of something.

slack slacker slackest; slacks
ADJECTIVE **1** Something that is slack is loose and not firmly stretched or positioned. **2** A slack period is one in which there is not much work to do. ▶ NOUN **3** The slack in a rope is the part that hangs loose. ▶ PLURAL NOUN **4** Slacks are casual trousers.
slackness NOUN

slacken slackens slackening slackened
VERB **1** If something slackens, it becomes slower or less intense E.G. *The rain had slackened to a drizzle.* **2** To slacken also means to become looser E.G. *Her grip slackened on Arnold's arm.*

slag slags slagging slagged
NOUN **1** Slag is the waste material left when ore has been melted down to remove the metal E.G. *a slag heap.* ▶ VERB **2** INFORMAL To slag someone off means to criticize them in an unpleasant way, usually behind their back.

slalom slaloms
Said "slah-lom" NOUN a skiing competition in which the competitors have to twist and turn quickly to avoid obstacles.
🔲 from Norwegian *slad + lom* meaning 'sloping path'

slam slams slamming slammed
VERB **1** If you slam a door or if it slams, it shuts noisily and with great force. **2** If you slam something down, you throw it down violently E.G. *She slammed the phone down.*

slander slanders slandering slandered
NOUN **1** Slander is something untrue and malicious said about someone. ▶ VERB **2** To slander someone means to say untrue and malicious things about them.
slanderous ADJECTIVE
▤ (sense 1) defamation, smear

slang
NOUN Slang consists of very informal words and expressions.

slant slants slanting slanted
VERB **1** If something slants, it slopes E.G. *The back can be adjusted to slant into the most comfortable position.* **2** If news or information is slanted, it is presented in a biased way. ▶ NOUN **3** a slope. **4** A slant on a subject is one way of looking at it, especially a biased one.

slap slaps slapping slapped
VERB **1** If you slap someone, you hit them with the palm of your hand. **2** If you slap something onto a surface, you put it there quickly and noisily. ▶ NOUN **3** If you give someone a slap, you slap them.
🔲 from German *Schlappe* an imitation of the sound

slash slashes slashing slashed
VERB **1** If you slash something, you make a long, deep cut in it. **2** INFORMAL To slash money means to reduce it greatly E.G. *Car makers could be forced to slash prices.* ▶ NOUN **3** a diagonal line that separates letters, words, or numbers, for example in the number 340/21/K.

slat slats
NOUN Slats are the narrow pieces of wood or metal plastic in things such as Venetian blinds.
slatted ADJECTIVE

slate slates slating slated
NOUN **1** Slate is a dark grey rock that splits easily into thin layers. **2** Slates are small, flat pieces of slate used for covering roofs. ▶ VERB **3** INFORMAL If critics slate a play, film, or book, they criticize it severely.

slaughter slaughters slaughtering slaughtered
VERB **1** To slaughter a large number of people means to kill them unjustly or cruelly. **2** To slaughter farm animals means to kill them for meat. ▶ NOUN **3** Slaughter is the killing of many people.
■ (sense 3) carnage, massacre, murder

slave slaves slaving slaved
NOUN **1** someone who is owned by another person and must work for them. ▶ VERB **2** If you slave for someone, you work very hard for them.
slavery NOUN
▥ from Latin *Sclavus* meaning 'a Slav', because the Slavonic races were frequently conquered and made into slaves

slay slays slaying slew slain
VERB; LITERARY To slay someone means to kill them.

sleazy sleazier sleaziest
ADJECTIVE A sleazy place looks dirty, run-down, and not respectable.

sled sleds
NOUN a sledge.

sledge sledges
NOUN a vehicle on runners used for travelling over snow.

sledgehammer sledgehammers
NOUN a large, heavy hammer.

sleek sleeker sleekest
ADJECTIVE **1** Sleek hair is smooth and shiny. **2** Someone who is sleek looks rich and dresses elegantly.

sleep sleeps sleeping slept
NOUN **1** Sleep is the natural state of rest in which your eyes are closed and you are unconscious. **2** If you have a sleep, you sleep for a while E.G. *He'll be ready for a sleep soon.*
▶ VERB **3** When you sleep, you rest in a state of sleep. ▶ PHRASE **4** If a sick or injured animal **is put to sleep**, it is painlessly killed.
■ (sense 2) doze, nap, slumber

sleeper sleepers
NOUN **1** You use 'sleeper' to say how deeply someone sleeps E.G. *I'm a very heavy sleeper.* **2** a bed on a train, or a train which has beds on it. **3** Railway sleepers are the large beams that support the rails of a railway track.

sleeping bag sleeping bags
NOUN a large, warm bag for sleeping in, especially when you are camping.

sleeping pill sleeping pills
NOUN A sleeping pill or a sleeping tablet is a pill which you take to help you sleep.

sleepout sleepouts
NOUN **1** In Australia, an area of veranda or porch which has been closed off to be used as a bedroom. **2** In New Zealand, a small building outside a house, used for sleeping.

sleepwalk sleepwalks sleepwalking sleepwalked
VERB If you sleepwalk, you walk around while you are asleep.

a
b
c
d
e
f
g
h
i
j
k
l
m
n
o
p
q
r
s
t
u
v
w
x
y
z

I want to see (C) your licenCe (licen<u>c</u>e)   SPELLING NOTE

A
B
C
D
E
F
G
H
I
J
K
L
M
N
O
P
Q
R
S
T
U
V
W
X
Y
Z

sleepy sleepier sleepiest
ADJECTIVE **1** tired and ready to go to sleep. **2** A sleepy town or village is very quiet.
sleepily ADVERB **sleepiness** NOUN

sleet
NOUN Sleet is a mixture of rain and snow.

sleeve sleeves
NOUN The sleeves of a piece of clothing are the parts that cover your arms.
sleeveless ADJECTIVE

sleigh sleighs
Said "slay" NOUN a sledge.

slender
ADJECTIVE **1** attractively thin and graceful. **2** small in amount or degree E.G. *the first slender hopes of peace.*
■ (sense 1) slim, willowy

sleuth sleuths
Said "slooth" NOUN; OLD-FASHIONED a detective.
▥ a shortened form of *sleuthhound*, a tracker dog, from Old Norse *sloth* meaning 'track'

slew slews slewing slewed
1 Slew is the past tense of **slay**.
▶ VERB **2** If a vehicle slews, it slides or skids E.G. *The bike slewed into the crowd.*

slice slices slicing sliced
NOUN **1** A slice of cake, bread, or other food is a piece of it cut from a larger piece. **2** a kitchen tool with a broad, flat blade E.G. *a fish slice.* **3** In sport, a slice is a stroke in which the player makes the ball go to one side, rather than straight ahead. ▶ VERB **4** If you slice food, you cut it into thin pieces. **5** To slice through something means to cut or move through it quickly, like a knife E.G. *The ship sliced through the water.*

slick slicker slickest; slicks
ADJECTIVE **1** A slick action is done quickly and smoothly E.G. *slick passing and strong running.* **2** A slick person speaks easily and persuasively but is not sincere E.G. *a slick TV presenter.* ▶ NOUN **3** An oil slick is a layer of oil floating on the surface of the sea or a lake.

slide slides sliding slid
VERB **1** When something slides, it moves smoothly over or against something else. ▶ NOUN **2** a small piece of photographic film which can be projected onto a screen so that you can see the picture. **3** a small piece of glass on which you put something that you want to examine through a microscope. **4** In a playground, a slide is a structure with a steep, slippery slope for children to slide down.

slight slighter slightest; slights slighting slighted
ADJECTIVE **1** Slight means small in amount or degree E.G. *a slight dent.* **2** A slight person has a slim body.
▶ PHRASE **3** **Not in the slightest** means not at all E.G. *This doesn't surprise me in the slightest.* ▶ VERB **4** If you slight someone, you insult them by behaving rudely towards them.
▶ NOUN **5** A slight is rude or insulting behaviour.
slightly ADVERB

slim slimmer slimmest; slims slimming slimmed
ADJECTIVE **1** A slim person is attractively thin. **2** A slim object is thinner than usual E.G. *a slim book.* **3** If there is only a slim chance that something will happen, it is unlikely to happen. ▶ VERB **4** If you are

slimming, you are trying to lose weight.

slimmer NOUN

slime

NOUN Slime is an unpleasant, thick, slippery substance.

📖 from Old English *slim* meaning 'soft sticky mud'

slimy slimier slimiest

ADJECTIVE **1** covered in slime. **2** Slimy people are friendly and pleasant in an insincere way E.G. *a slimy business partner*.

sling slings slinging slung

VERB **1** INFORMAL If you sling something somewhere, you throw it there. **2** If you sling a rope between two points, you attach it so that it hangs loosely between them. ► NOUN **3** a piece of cloth tied round a person's neck to support a broken or injured arm. **4** a device made of ropes or cloth used for carrying things.

slip slips slipping slipped

VERB **1** If you slip, you accidentally slide and lose your balance. **2** If something slips, it slides out of place accidentally E.G. *One of the knives slipped from her grasp.* **3** If you slip somewhere, you go there quickly and quietly E.G. *She slipped out of the house.* **4** If you slip something somewhere, you put it there quickly and quietly. **5** If something slips to a lower level or standard, it falls to that level or standard E.G. *The shares slipped to an all-time low.* ► NOUN **6** a small mistake. **7** A slip of paper is a small piece of paper. **8** a piece of clothing worn under a dress or skirt.

slipped disc slipped discs

NOUN a painful condition in which one of the discs in your spine has

moved out of its proper position.

slipper slippers

NOUN Slippers are loose, soft shoes that you wear indoors.

slippery

ADJECTIVE **1** smooth, wet, or greasy, and difficult to hold or walk on. **2** You describe a person as slippery when they cannot be trusted.

slippery dip slippery dips

NOUN; INFORMAL In Australian English, a children's slide at a playground or funfair.

slip rail slip rails

NOUN In Australian and New Zealand English, a rail in a fence that can be slipped out of place to make an opening.

slipstream slipstreams

NOUN The slipstream of a car or plane is the flow of air directly behind it.

slit slits slitting slit

VERB **1** If you slit something, you make a long, narrow cut in it. ► NOUN **2** a long, narrow cut or opening.

slither slithers slithering slithered

VERB To slither somewhere means to move there by sliding along the ground in an uneven way E.G. *The snake slithered into the water.*

sliver slivers

NOUN a small, thin piece of something.

slob slobs

NOUN; INFORMAL a lazy, untidy person.

slog slogs slogging slogged

VERB; INFORMAL If you slog at something, you work hard and steadily at it E.G. *They are still slogging away at algebra.*

slogan slogans

NOUN a short, easily-remembered

have a pIEce of pIE (pi<u>e</u>ce) ◄ **SPELLING NOTE**

phrase used in advertising or by a political party.

🔲 from Gaelic *sluagh-ghairm* meaning 'war cry'

▣ catch-phrase, motto

slop slops slopping slopped

VERB **1** If a liquid slops, it spills over the edge of a container in a messy way. ▶ PLURAL NOUN **2** You can refer to dirty water or liquid waste as slops.

slope slopes sloping sloped

NOUN **1** a flat surface that is at an angle, so that one end is higher than the other. **2** The slope of something is the angle at which it slopes. ▶ VERB **3** If a surface slopes, it is at an angle. **4** If something slopes, it leans to one side rather than being upright E.G. *sloping handwriting*.

▣ (sense 1) incline, slant, tilt

▣ (sense 2) gradient, inclination

sloppy sloppier sloppiest

ADJECTIVE INFORMAL **1** very messy or careless E.G. *two sloppy performances*. **2** foolishly sentimental E.G. *some sloppy love story*.

sloppily ADVERB **sloppiness** NOUN

slot slots slotting slotted

NOUN **1** a narrow opening in a machine or container, for example for putting coins in. ▶ VERB **2** When you slot something into something else, you put it into a space where it fits.

sloth sloths

Rhymes with "growth" NOUN **1** FORMAL Sloth is laziness. **2** a South and Central American animal that moves very slowly and hangs upside down from the branches of trees.

slouch slouches slouching slouched

VERB If you slouch, you stand or sit

with your shoulders and head drooping forwards.

slouch hat slouch hats

NOUN a hat with a wide, flexible brim, especially an Australian army hat with the left side of the brim turned up.

Slovak Slovaks

ADJECTIVE **1** belonging to or relating to Slovakia. ▶ NOUN **2** someone who comes from Slovakia. **3** Slovak is the language spoken in Slovakia.

slow slower slowest; slows slowing slowed

ADJECTIVE **1** moving, happening, or doing something with very little speed E.G. *His progress was slow*. **2** Someone who is slow is not very clever. **3** If a clock or watch is slow, it shows a time earlier than the correct one. ▶ VERB **4** If something slows, slows down, or slows up, it moves or happens more slowly.

slowly ADVERB **slowness** NOUN

slow motion

NOUN Slow motion is movement which is much slower than normal, especially in a film E.G. *It all seemed to happen in slow motion*.

sludge

NOUN Sludge is thick mud or sewage.

slug slugs

NOUN **1** a small, slow-moving creative with a slimy body, like a snail without a shell. **2** INFORMAL A slug of a strong alcoholic drink is a mouthful of it.

sluggish

ADJECTIVE moving slowly and without energy E.G. *the sluggish waters*.

sluice sluices sluicing sluiced

Said "sloose" NOUN **1** a channel which carries water, with an opening called a sluicegate which can be opened or

closed to control the flow of water.
► VERB **2** If you sluice something, you wash it by pouring water over it E.G. *He had sluiced his hands under a tap.*
📖 from Latin *exclusa aqua* meaning 'water shut out'

slum slums
NOUN a poor, run-down area of a city.

slumber slumbers slumbering slumbered LITERARY
NOUN **1** Slumber is sleep. ► VERB **2** When you slumber, you sleep.

slump slumps slumping slumped
VERB **1** If an amount or a value slumps, it falls suddenly by a large amount. **2** If you slump somewhere, you fall or sit down heavily E.G. *He slumped against the side of the car.* ► NOUN **3** a sudden, severe drop in an amount or value E.G. *the slump in house prices.* **4** a time when there is economic decline and high unemployment.

slur slurs slurring slurred
NOUN **1** an insulting remark. ► VERB **2** When people slur their speech, they do not say their words clearly, often because they are drunk or ill.

slurp slurps slurping slurped
VERB If you slurp a drink, you drink it noisily.
📖 from Old Dutch *slorpen* meaning 'to sip'

slush
NOUN **1** Slush is wet melting snow. **2** INFORMAL You can refer to sentimental love stories as slush.
slushy ADJECTIVE

slut sluts
NOUN; OFFENSIVE a dirty, untidy woman, or one considered to be immoral.

sly slyer or slier slyest or sliest
ADJECTIVE **1** A sly expression or remark shows that you know something other people do not know E.G. *a sly smile.* **2** A sly person is cunning and good at deceiving people.
slyly ADVERB
■ (sense 2) crafty, cunning, devious

smack smacks smacking smacked
VERB **1** If you smack someone, you hit them with your open hand. **2** If something smacks of something else, it reminds you of it E.G. *His tale smacks of fantasy.* ► NOUN **3** If you give someone a smack, you smack them. **4** a loud, sharp noise E.G. *He landed with a smack on the tank.*

small smaller smallest; smalls
ADJECTIVE **1** Small means not large in size, number, or amount. **2** Small means not important or significant E.G. *small changes.* ► NOUN **3** The small of your back is the narrow part where your back curves slightly inwards.
■ (sense 1) little, tiny
■ (sense 2) insignificant, minor, trivial

smallpox
NOUN Smallpox is a serious contagious disease that causes a fever and a rash.

small talk
NOUN Small talk is conversation about unimportant things.

smart smarter smartest; smarts smarting smarted
ADJECTIVE **1** A smart person is clean and neatly dressed. **2** Smart means clever E.G. *a smart idea.* **3** A smart movement is quick and sharp. ► VERB **4** If a wound smarts, it stings. **5** If you are smarting from criticism or unkindness, you are feeling upset by it.
smartly ADVERB

a
b
c
d
e
f
g
h
i
j
k
l
m
n
o
p
q
r
s
t
u
v
w
x
y
z

A
B
C
D
E
F
G
H
I
J
K
L
M
N
O
P
Q
R
S
T
U
V
W
X
Y
Z

smarten smartens smartening smartened
VERB If you smarten something up, you make it look neater and tidier.

smash smashes smashing smashed
VERB 1 If you smash something, you break it into a lot of pieces by hitting it or dropping it. 2 To smash through something such as a wall means to go through it by breaking it. 3 To smash against something means to hit it with great force E.G. *An immense wave smashed against the hull.* ▶ NOUN 4 INFORMAL If a play or film is a smash or a smash hit, it is very successful. 5 a car crash. 6 In tennis, a smash is a stroke in which the player hits the ball downwards very hard.

smashing
ADJECTIVE; INFORMAL If you describe something as smashing, you mean you like it very much.

smattering
NOUN A smattering of knowledge or information is a very small amount of it E.G. *a smattering of Russian.*

smear smears smearing smeared
NOUN 1 a dirty, greasy mark on a surface E.G. *a smear of pink lipstick.* 2 an untrue and malicious rumour. ▶ VERB 3 If something smears a surface, it makes dirty, greasy marks on it E.G. *The blade was chipped and smeared.* 4 If you smear a surface with a greasy or sticky substance, you spread a layer of the substance over the surface.

smell smells smelling smelled or smelt
NOUN 1 The smell of something is a quality it has which you perceive

through your nose E.G. *a smell of damp wood.* 2 Your sense of smell is your ability to smell things. ▶ VERB 3 If something smells or if you can smell it, it has a quality you can perceive through your nose E.G. *He smelled of tobacco and garlic.* 4 If you can smell something such as danger or trouble, you feel it is present or likely to happen.
▤ (sense 1) odour, scent

smelly smellier smelliest
ADJECTIVE having a strong, unpleasant smell.

smelt smelts smelting smelted
VERB To smelt a metal ore means to heat it until it melts, so that the metal can be extracted.

smile smiles smiling smiled
VERB 1 When you smile, the corners of your mouth move outwards and slightly upwards because you are pleased or amused. ▶ NOUN 2 the expression you have when you smile.

smirk smirks smirking smirked
VERB 1 When you smirk, you smile in a sneering or sarcastic way E.G. *The boy smirked and turned the volume up.* ▶ NOUN 2 a sneering or sarcastic smile.

smith smiths
NOUN someone who makes things out of iron, gold, or another metal.

smitten
ADJECTIVE If you are smitten with someone or something, you are very impressed with or enthusiastic about them E.G. *They were totally smitten with each other.*

smock smocks
NOUN a loose garment like a long blouse.

smog

NOUN Smog is a mixture of smoke and fog which occurs in some industrial cities.

smoke smokes smoking smoked

NOUN **1** Smoke is a mixture of gas and small particles sent into the air when something burns. ▶ VERB **2** If something is smoking, smoke is coming from it. **3** When someone smokes a cigarette or pipe, they suck smoke from it into their mouth and blow it out again. **4** To smoke fish or meat means to hang it over burning wood so that the smoke preserves it and gives it a pleasant flavour E.G. *smoked bacon*.

smoker NOUN   **smoking** NOUN

smoky smokier smokiest

ADJECTIVE A smoky place is full of smoke.

smooth smoother smoothest; smooths smoothing smoothed

ADJECTIVE **1** A smooth surface has no roughness and no holes in it. **2** A smooth liquid or mixture has no lumps in it. **3** A smooth movement or process happens evenly and steadily E.G. *smooth acceleration*. **4** Smooth also means successful and without problems E.G. *staff responsible for the smooth running of the hall*. ▶ VERB **5** If you smooth something, you move your hands over it to make it smooth and flat.

smoothly ADVERB   **smoothness** NOUN

smoothie smoothies

NOUN a thick type of drink made in an electric blender from milk, fruit and crushed ice.

smother smothers smothering smothered

VERB **1** If you smother a fire, you cover it with something to put it out. **2** To smother a person means to cover their face with something so that they cannot breathe. **3** To smother someone also means to give them too much love and protection E.G. *She loved her own children, almost smothering them with love.* **4** If you smother an emotion, you control it so that people do not notice it E.G. *They tried to smother their glee.*

smothered

ADJECTIVE completely covered with something E.G. *a spectacular trellis smothered in climbing roses.*

smoulder smoulders smouldering smouldered

VERB **1** When something smoulders, it burns slowly, producing smoke but no flames. **2** If a feeling is smouldering inside you, you feel it very strongly but do not show it E.G. *smouldering with resentment.*

smudge smudges smudging smudged

NOUN **1** a dirty or blurred mark or a smear on something. ▶ VERB **2** If you smudge something, you make it dirty or messy by touching it or marking it.

smug smugger smuggest

ADJECTIVE Someone who is smug is very pleased with how good or clever they are.

smugly ADVERB   **smugness** NOUN

smuggle smuggles smuggling smuggled

VERB To smuggle things or people into or out of a place means to take them there illegally or secretly.

smuggler smugglers

NOUN someone who smuggles goods illegally into a country.

a b c d e f g h i j k l m n o p q r **s** t u v w x y z

A
B
C
D
E
F
G
H
I
J
K
L
M
N
O
P
Q
R
S
T
U
V
W
X
Y
Z

snack snacks
NOUN a light, quick meal.

snag snags snagging snagged
NOUN **1** a small problem or disadvantage E.G. *There is one snag: it is not true.* ► VERB **2** If you snag your clothing, you damage it by catching it on something sharp. ► NOUN; INFORMAL **3** In Australian and New Zealand English, a sausage.

snail snails
NOUN a small, slow-moving creature with a long, shiny body and a shell on its back.

snail mail
NOUN; INFORMAL the conventional postal system, as opposed to email.

snake snakes snaking snaked
NOUN **1** a long, thin, scaly reptile with no legs. ► VERB **2** Something that snakes moves in long winding curves E.G. *The queue snaked out of the shop.*

snap snaps snapping snapped
VERB **1** If something snaps or if you snap it, it breaks with a sharp cracking noise. **2** If you snap something into a particular position, you move it there quickly with a sharp sound. **3** If an animal snaps at you, it shuts its jaws together quickly as if to bite you. **4** If someone snaps at you, they speak in a sharp, unfriendly way. **5** If you snap someone, you take a quick photograph of them. ► NOUN **6** the sound of something snapping. **7** INFORMAL a photograph taken quickly and casually. ► ADJECTIVE **8** A snap decision or action is taken suddenly without careful thought.

snapper snappers
NOUN a fish with edible pink flesh,

found in waters around Australia and New Zealand.

snapshot snapshots
NOUN a photograph taken quickly and casually.

snare snares snaring snared
NOUN **1** a trap for catching birds or small animals. ► VERB **2** To snare an animal or bird means to catch it using a snare.

snarl snarls snarling snarled
VERB **1** When an animal snarls, it bares its teeth and makes a fierce growling noise. **2** If you snarl, you say something in a fierce, angry way. ► NOUN **3** the noise an animal makes when it snarls.

snatch snatches snatching snatched
VERB **1** If you snatch something, you reach out for it quickly and take it. **2** If you snatch an amount of time or an opportunity, you quickly make use of it. ► NOUN **3** If you make a snatch at something, you reach out for it quickly to try to take it. **4** A snatch of conversation or song is a very small piece of it.

sneak sneaks sneaking sneaked
VERB **1** If you sneak somewhere, you go there quickly trying not to be seen or heard. **2** If you sneak something somewhere, you take it there secretly. ► NOUN **3** INFORMAL someone who tells people in authority that someone else has done something wrong.

sneaker sneakers
NOUN Sneakers are casual shoes with rubber soles.

sneaking
ADJECTIVE If you have a sneaking feeling about something or

someone, you have this feeling rather reluctantly E.G. *I had a sneaking suspicion that she was enjoying herself.*

sneaky sneakier sneakiest
ADJECTIVE; INFORMAL Someone who is sneaky does things secretly rather than openly.

sneer sneers sneering sneered
VERB 1 If you sneer at someone or something, you show by your expression and your comments that you think they are stupid or inferior. ▶ NOUN 2 the expression on someone's face when they sneer.

sneeze sneezes sneezing sneezed
VERB 1 When you sneeze, you suddenly take in breath and blow it down your nose noisily, because there is a tickle in your nose. ▶ NOUN 2 an act of sneezing.

snide
ADJECTIVE A snide comment or remark criticizes someone in a nasty and unfair way.

sniff sniffs sniffing sniffed
VERB 1 When you sniff, you breathe in air through your nose hard enough to make a sound. 2 If you sniff something, you smell it by sniffing. 3 You can say that a person sniffs at something when they do not think very much of it E.G. *Bessie sniffed at his household arrangements.* ▶ NOUN 4 the noise you make when you sniff. 5 A sniff of something is a smell of it E.G. *a sniff at the flowers.*

snigger sniggers sniggering sniggered
VERB 1 If you snigger, you laugh in a quiet, sly way E.G. *They were sniggering at her accent.* ▶ NOUN 2 a

quiet, disrespectful laugh.

snip snips snipping snipped
VERB 1 If you snip something, you cut it with scissors or shears in a single quick action. ▶ NOUN 2 a small cut made by scissors or shears.

snippet snippets
NOUN A snippet of something such as information or news is a small piece of it.

snob snobs
NOUN 1 someone who admires upper-class people and looks down on lower-class people. 2 someone who believes that they are better than other people.
snobbery NOUN **snobbish** ADJECTIVE

snooker
NOUN Snooker is a game played on a large table covered with smooth green cloth. Players score points by hitting different coloured balls into side pockets using a long stick called a cue.

snoop snoops snooping snooped
VERB; INFORMAL Someone who is snooping is secretly looking round a place to find out things.
📖 from Dutch *snoepen* meaning 'to eat furtively'

snooze snoozes snoozing snoozed INFORMAL
VERB 1 If you snooze, you sleep lightly for a short time, especially during the day. ▶ NOUN 2 a short, light sleep.

snore snores snoring snored
VERB 1 When a sleeping person snores, they make a loud noise each time they breathe. ▶ NOUN 2 the noise someone makes when they snore.

snorkel snorkels
NOUN a tube you can breathe through when you are swimming just under

a b c d e f g h i j k l m n o p q r **s** t u v w x y z

A
B
C
D
E
F
G
H
I
J
K
L
M
N
O
P
Q
R
S
T
U
V
W
X
Y
Z

the surface of the sea.

snorkelling NOUN
🔲 from German *Schnorchel*, originally an air pipe for a submarine

snort snorts snorting snorted
VERB 1 When people or animals snort, they force breath out through their nose in a noisy way E.G. *Sarah snorted with laughter.* ▶ NOUN 2 the noise you make when you snort.

snout snouts
NOUN An animal's snout is its nose.

snow snows snowing snowed
NOUN 1 Snow consists of flakes of ice crystals which fall from the sky in cold weather. ▶ VERB 2 When it snows, snow falls from the sky.

snowball snowballs snowballing snowballed
NOUN 1 a ball of snow for throwing. ▶ VERB 2 When something such as a project snowballs, it grows rapidly.

snowdrift snowdrifts
NOUN a deep pile of snow formed by the wind.

snowdrop snowdrops
NOUN a small white flower which appears in early spring.

snowman snowmen
NOUN a large mound of snow moulded into the shape of a person.

snub snubs snubbing snubbed
VERB 1 To snub someone means to behave rudely towards them, especially by making an insulting remark or ignoring them. ▶ NOUN 2 an insulting remark or a piece of rude behaviour. ▶ ADJECTIVE 3 A snub nose is short and turned-up.
▤ (sense 2) affront, insult, slap in the face

snuff
NOUN Snuff is powdered tobacco

which people take by sniffing it up their noses.

snug
ADJECTIVE A snug place is warm and comfortable. If you are snug, you are warm and comfortable.

snugly ADVERB

snuggle snuggles snuggling snuggled
VERB If you snuggle somewhere, you cuddle up more closely to something or someone.

so
ADVERB 1 'So' is used to refer back to what has just been mentioned E.G. *Had he locked the car? If so, where were the keys?* 2 'So' is used to mean also E.G. *He laughed, and so did Jarvis.* 3 'So' can be used to mean 'therefore' E.G. *It's a bit expensive, so I don't think I will get one.* 4 'So' is used when you are talking about the degree or extent of something E.G. *Why are you so cruel?* 5 'So' is used before words like 'much' and 'many' to say that there is a definite limit to something E.G. *There are only so many questions that can be asked about the record.* ▶ CONJUNCTION 6 'So that' and 'so as' are used to introduce the reason for doing something E.G. *to die so that you might live.*

soak soaks soaking soaked
VERB 1 To soak something or leave it to soak means to put it in a liquid and leave it there. 2 When a liquid soaks something, it makes it very wet. 3 When something soaks up a liquid, the liquid is drawn up into it.
▤ (sense 2) saturate, wet

soaked
ADJECTIVE extremely wet.

soaking

ADJECTIVE If something is soaking, it is very wet.

soap soaps

NOUN Soap is a substance made of natural oils and fats and used for washing yourself.

soapy ADJECTIVE

soap opera soap operas

NOUN a popular television drama serial about people's daily lives.

soar soars soaring soared

VERB 1 If an amount soars, it quickly increases by a great deal E.G. *Property prices soared.* 2 If something soars into the air, it quickly goes up into the air.

soaring ADJECTIVE

sob sobs sobbing sobbed

VERB 1 When someone sobs, they cry in a noisy way, breathing in short breaths. ▶ NOUN 2 the noise made when you cry.

sober soberer soberest; sobers sobering sobered

ADJECTIVE 1 If someone is sober, they are not drunk. 2 Sober also means serious and thoughtful. 3 Sober colours are plain and rather dull. ▶ VERB 4 To sober up means to become sober after being drunk.

soberly ADVERB

sobering

ADJECTIVE Something which is sobering makes you serious and thoughtful E.G. *the sobering lesson of the last year.*

so-called

ADJECTIVE You use 'so-called' to say that the name by which something is called is incorrect or misleading E.G. *so-called environmentally-friendly products.*

soccer

NOUN Soccer is a game played by two teams of eleven players kicking a ball in an attempt to score goals.

🏛 formed from *Association Football*

sociable

ADJECTIVE Sociable people are friendly and enjoy talking to other people.

sociability NOUN

🔲 friendly, gregarious, outgoing

social

ADJECTIVE 1 to do with society or life within a society E.G. *women from similar social backgrounds.* 2 to do with leisure activities that involve meeting other people.

socially ADVERB

socialism

NOUN Socialism is the political belief that the state should own industries on behalf of the people and that everyone should be equal.

socialist ADJECTIVE OR NOUN

socialize socializes socializing socialized; also spelt **socialise**

VERB When people socialize, they meet other people socially, for example at parties.

social security

NOUN Social security is a system by which the government pays money regularly to people who have no other income or only a very small income.

social work

NOUN Social work involves giving help and advice to people with serious financial or family problems.

social worker NOUN

society societies

NOUN 1 Society is the people in a particular country or region E.G. *a major problem in society.* 2 an

a
b
c
d
e
f
g
h
i
j
k
l
m
n
o
p
q
r
s
t
u
v
w
x
y
z

A
B
C
D
E
F
G
H
I
J
K
L
M
N
O
P
Q
R
S
T
U
V
W
X
Y
Z

organization for people who have the same interest or aim E.G. *the school debating society*. **3** Society is also rich, upper-class, fashionable people.

■ (sense 1) civilization, culture

sociology

NOUN Sociology is the study of human societies and the relationships between groups in these societies.

sociological ADJECTIVE **sociologist** NOUN

sock socks

NOUN Socks are pieces of clothing covering your foot and ankle.

🔲 from Old English *socc* meaning 'light shoe'

socket sockets

NOUN **1** a place on a wall or on a piece of electrical equipment into which you can put a plug or bulb. **2** Any hollow part or opening into which another part fits can be called a socket E.G. *eye sockets*.

sod

NOUN; LITERARY The sod is the surface of the ground, together with the grass and roots growing in it.

soda sodas

NOUN **1** Soda is the same as **soda water**. **2** Soda is also sodium in the form of crystals or a powder, and is used for baking or cleaning.

soda water soda waters

NOUN Soda water is fizzy water used for mixing with alcoholic drinks or fruit juice.

sodden

ADJECTIVE soaking wet.

sodium

NOUN Sodium is a silvery-white chemical element which combines

with other chemicals. Salt is a sodium compound.

sofa sofas

NOUN a long comfortable seat with a back and arms for two or three people.

🔲 from Arabic *suffah* meaning 'an upholstered raised platform'

soft softer softest

ADJECTIVE **1** Something soft is not hard, stiff, or firm. **2** Soft also means very gentle E.G. *a soft breeze*. **3** A soft sound or voice is quiet and not harsh. **4** A soft colour or light is not bright.

softly ADVERB

soft drink soft drinks

NOUN any cold, nonalcoholic drink.

soften softens softening softened

VERB **1** If something is softened or softens, it becomes less hard, stiff, or firm. **2** If you soften, you become more sympathetic and less critical E.G. *Phillida softened as she spoke.*

software

NOUN (ICT) Computer programs are known as software.

soggy soggier soggiest

ADJECTIVE unpleasantly wet or full of water.

🔲 from American dialect *sog* meaning 'marsh'

soil soils soiling soiled

NOUN **1** Soil is the top layer on the surface of the earth in which plants grow. ▶ VERB **2** If you soil something, you make it dirty.

soiled ADJECTIVE

■ (sense 1) earth, ground

solace

NOUN; LITERARY Solace is something

that makes you feel less sad E.G. *I found solace in writing*.

solar

ADJECTIVE **1** relating or belonging to the sun. **2** using the sun's light and heat as a source of energy E.G. *a solar-powered calculator*.

solar system

NOUN The solar system is the sun and all the planets, comets, and asteroids that orbit round it.

solder solders soldering soldered

VERB **1** To solder two pieces of metal together means to join them with molten metal. ► NOUN **2** Solder is the soft metal used for soldering.

soldier soldiers

NOUN a person in an army.

sole soles soling soled

ADJECTIVE **1** The sole thing or person of a particular type is the only one of that type. ► NOUN **2** The sole of your foot or shoe is the underneath part. **3** a flat sea-water fish which you can eat. ► VERB **4** When a shoe is soled, a sole is fitted to it.

solely

ADVERB If something involves solely one thing, it involves that thing and nothing else.

solemn

ADJECTIVE Solemn means serious rather than cheerful or humorous.

solemnly ADVERB **solemnity** NOUN

solicitor solicitors

NOUN a lawyer who gives legal advice and prepares legal documents and cases.

solid solids

ADJECTIVE **1** A solid substance or object is hard or firm, and not in the form of a liquid or gas. **2** You say that

something is solid when it is not hollow E.G. *solid steel*. **3** You say that a structure is solid when it is strong and not likely to fall down E.G. *solid fences*. **4** You use 'solid' to say that something happens for a period of time without interruption E.G. *I cried for two solid days*. ► NOUN **5** a solid substance or object.

solidly ADVERB

solidarity

NOUN If a group of people show solidarity, they show unity and support for each other.

soliloquy soliloquies

Said "sol-lill-ok-wee" NOUN (ENGLISH) a speech in a play made by a character who is alone on the stage.

🔤 from Latin *solus* meaning 'alone' and *loqui* meaning 'to speak'

solitary

ADJECTIVE **1** A solitary activity is one that you do on your own. **2** A solitary person or animal spends a lot of time alone. **3** If there is a solitary person or object somewhere, there is only one.

solitary confinement

NOUN A prisoner in solitary confinement is being kept alone in a prison cell.

solitude

NOUN Solitude is the state of being alone.

■ isolation, seclusion

solo solos

NOUN **1** a piece of music played or sung by one person alone. ► ADJECTIVE **2** A solo performance or activity is done by one person alone E.G. *my first solo flight*. ► ADVERB **3** Solo means alone E.G. *to sail solo around the world*.

a b c d e f g h i j k l m n o p q r s t u v w x y z

A
B
C
D
E
F
G
H
I
J
K
L
M
N
O
P
Q
R
S
T
U
V
W
X
Y
Z

soloist soloists
NOUN a person who performs a solo.

solstice solstices
NOUN one of the two times in the year when the sun is at its furthest point south or north of the equator.
📖 from Latin *sol* meaning 'sun' and *sistere* meaning 'to stand still'

soluble
ADJECTIVE A soluble substance is able to dissolve in liquid.

solution solutions
NOUN 1 a way of dealing with a problem or difficult situation E.G. *a quick solution to our problem.* 2 The solution to a riddle or a puzzle is the answer. 3 (SCIENCE) a liquid in which a solid substance has been dissolved.

solve solves solving solved
VERB If you solve a problem or a question, you find a solution or answer to it.
■ answer, resolve, work out

solvent
ADJECTIVE 1 If a person or company is solvent, they have enough money to pay all their debts. ► NOUN 2 a liquid that can dissolve other substances.
solvency NOUN

Somali Somalis
ADJECTIVE 1 belonging or relating to Somalia. ► NOUN 2 The Somalis are a group of people who live in Somalia. 3 Somali is the language spoken by Somalis.

sombre
ADJECTIVE 1 Sombre colours are dark and dull. 2 A sombre person is serious, sad, or gloomy.

some 1 You use 'some' to refer to a quantity or number when you are not stating the quantity or number exactly E.G. *There's some money on*

the table. 2 You use 'some' to emphasize that a quantity or number is fairly large E.G. *She had been there for some days.*
ADVERB 3 You use 'some' in front of a number to show that it is not exact E.G. *a fishing village some seven miles north.*

somebody
PRONOUN Somebody means someone
✔ *Somebody* and *someone* mean the same.

some day
ADVERB Some day means at a date in the future that is unknown or that has not yet been decided.

somehow
ADVERB 1 You use 'somehow' to say that you do not know how something was done or will be done E.G. *You'll find a way of doing it somehow.* 2 You use 'somehow' to say that you do not know the reason for something E.G. *Somehow it didn't feel quite right.*

someone
PRONOUN You use 'someone' to refer to a person without saying exactly who you mean
✔ *Someone* and *somebody* mean the same.

somersault somersaults
NOUN a forwards or backwards roll in which the head is placed on the ground and the body is brought over it.
📖 from Old Provençal *sobre* meaning 'over' and *saut* meaning 'jump'

something
PRONOUN You use 'something' to refer to anything that is not a person without saying exactly what you mean.

sometime

ADVERB **1** at a time in the future or the past that is unknown or that has not yet been fixed E.G. *He has to find out sometime.* ► ADJECTIVE **2** FORMAL 'Sometime' is used to say that a person had a particular job or role in the past E.G. *a sometime actress, dancer and singer.*

sometimes

ADVERB occasionally, rather than always or never.

somewhat

ADVERB to some extent or degree E.G. *The future seemed somewhat bleak.*

somewhere

ADVERB **1** 'Somewhere' is used to refer to a place without stating exactly where it is E.G. *There has to be a file somewhere.* **2** 'Somewhere' is used when giving an approximate amount, number, or time E.G. *somewhere between the winter of 1989 and the summer of 1991.*

son sons

NOUN Someone's son is their male child.

sonar

NOUN Sonar is equipment on a ship which calculates the depth of the sea or the position of an underwater object using sound waves. 🏛 from *So(und) Na(vigation) R(anging)*

sonata sonatas

NOUN a piece of classical music, usually in three or more movements, for piano or for another instrument with or without piano.

song songs

NOUN a piece of music with words that are sung to the music.

songbird songbirds

NOUN a bird that produces musical sounds like singing.

son-in-law sons-in-law

NOUN Someone's son-in-law is the husband of their daughter.

sonnet sonnets

NOUN a poem with 14 lines, in which lines rhyme according to fixed patterns. 🏛 from Old Provençal *sonet* meaning 'little poem'

soon sooner soonest

ADVERB If something is going to happen soon, it will happen in a very short time.

soot

NOUN Soot is black powder which rises in the smoke from a fire. **sooty** ADJECTIVE

soothe soothes soothing soothed

VERB **1** If you soothe someone who is angry or upset, you make them calmer. **2** Something that soothes pain makes the pain less severe. **soothing** ADJECTIVE

sophisticated

ADJECTIVE **1** Sophisticated people have refined or cultured tastes or habits. **2** A sophisticated machine or device is made using advanced and complicated methods. **sophistication** NOUN

■ (sense 1) cultured, urbane

soppy soppier soppiest

ADJECTIVE; INFORMAL silly or foolishly sentimental.

soprano sopranos

NOUN a woman, girl, or boy with a singing voice in the highest range of musical notes.

sorcerer sorcerers

Said "sor-ser-er" NOUN a person who

a
b
c
d
e
f
g
h
i
j
k
l
m
n
o
p
q
r
s
t
u
v
w
x
y
z

A
B
C
D
E
F
G
H
I
J
K
L
M
N
O
P
Q
R
S
T
U
V
W
X
Y
Z

performs magic by using the power of evil spirits.

sorceress sorceresses
NOUN a female sorcerer.

sorcery
NOUN Sorcery is magic that uses the power of evil spirits.

sordid
ADJECTIVE **1** dishonest or immoral E.G. *a rather sordid business.* **2** dirty, unpleasant, or depressing E.G. *the sordid guest house.*
■ (sense 2) seedy, sleazy, squalid

sore sorer sorest; sores
ADJECTIVE **1** If part of your body is sore, it causes you pain and discomfort. **2** LITERARY 'Sore' is used to emphasize something E.G. *The President is in sore need of friends.* ▶ NOUN **3** a painful place where your skin has become infected.
sorely ADVERB **soreness** NOUN
■ (sense 1) painful, sensitive, tender

sorghum
Said "*saw*-gum" NOUN a type of tropical grass that is grown for hay, grain, and syrup.

sorrow sorrows
NOUN **1** Sorrow is deep sadness or regret. **2** Sorrows are things that cause sorrow E.G. *the sorrows of this world.*

sorry sorrier sorriest
ADJECTIVE **1** If you are sorry about something, you feel sadness, regret, or sympathy because of it E.G. *I was so sorry to hear about your husband.* **2** 'Sorry' is used to describe people and things that are in a bad physical or mental state E.G. *She was in a pretty sorry state when we found her.*
■ (sense 1) apologetic, contrite, regretful

sort sorts sorting sorted
NOUN **1** The different sorts of something are the different types of it. ▶ VERB **2** To sort things means to arrange them into different groups or sorts.
■ (sense 1) kind, type, variety

sort out VERB If you sort out a problem or misunderstanding, you deal with it and find a solution to it.
☑ When you use *sort* in its singular form, the adjective before it should also be singular: *that sort of car.* When you use the plural form *sorts,* the adjective before it should be plural: *those sorts of shop; those sorts of shops.*

SOS
NOUN An SOS is a signal that you are in danger and need help.

so-so
ADJECTIVE neither good nor bad E.G. *The food is so-so.*

soufflé soufflés
Said "*soo*-flay"; also spelt **souffle**
NOUN a light, fluffy food made from beaten egg whites and other ingredients that is baked in the oven.

sought
the past tense and past participle of **seek**.

soul souls
NOUN **1** A person's soul is the spiritual part of them that is supposed to continue after their body is dead. **2** People also use 'soul' to refer to a person's mind, character, thoughts, and feelings. **3** 'Soul' can be used to mean person E.G. *There was not a soul there.* **4** Soul is a type of pop music.

sound sounds sounding sounded; sounder soundest
NOUN **1** Sound is everything that can

be heard. **2** A particular sound is something that you hear. **3** The sound of someone or something is the impression you have of them E.G. *I like the sound of your father's grandfather.* ▶ VERB **4** If something sounds or if you sound it, it makes a noise. **5** To sound something deep, such as a well or the sea, means to measure how deep it is using a weighted line or sonar. ▶ ADJECTIVE **6** in good condition E.G. *a guarantee that a house is sound.* **7** reliable and sensible E.G. *The logic behind the argument seems sound.*

soundly ADVERB

sound bite sound bites
NOUN a short and memorable sentence or phrase extracted from a longer speech for use on radio or television.

sound effect sound effects
NOUN Sound effects are sounds created artificially to make a play more realistic, especially a radio play.

soundproof
ADJECTIVE If a room is soundproof, sound cannot get into it or out of it.

soundtrack soundtracks
NOUN The soundtrack of a film is the part you hear.

soup soups
NOUN Soup is liquid food made by boiling meat, fish, or vegetables in water.

sour sours souring soured
ADJECTIVE **1** If something is sour, it has a sharp, acid taste. **2** Sour milk has an unpleasant taste because it is no longer fresh. **3** A sour person is bad-tempered and unfriendly. ▶ VERB **4** If a friendship, situation, or attitude sours or if something sours it, it becomes

less friendly, enjoyable, or hopeful.

source sources
NOUN **1** The source of something is the person, place, or thing that it comes from E.G. *the source of his confidence.* **2** (HISTORY) **3** The source of a river or stream is the place where it begins.

☑ Do not confuse the spellings of *source* and *sauce*, which can sound very similar.

sour grapes
PLURAL NOUN You describe someone's behaviour as sour grapes when they say something is worthless but secretly want it and cannot have it.

south
NOUN **1** The south is the direction to your right when you are looking towards the place where the sun rises. **2** The south of a place or country is the part which is towards the south when you are in the centre. ▶ ADVERB or ADJECTIVE **3** South means towards the south E.G. *The taxi headed south… the south end of the site.* ▶ ADJECTIVE **4** A south wind blows from the south.

South America
NOUN South America is the fourth largest continent. It has the Pacific Ocean on its west side, the Atlantic on the east, and the Antarctic to the south. South America is joined to North America by the Isthmus of Panama.
South American ADJECTIVE

south-east
NOUN, ADVERB, or ADJECTIVE South-east is halfway between south and east.

south-easterly
ADJECTIVE **1** South-easterly means to or towards the south-east. **2** A south-

a
b
c
d
e
f
g
h
i
j
k
l
m
n
o
p
q
r
s
t
u
v
w
x
y
z

easterly wind blows from the south-east.

south-eastern

ADJECTIVE in or from the south-east.

southerly

ADJECTIVE 1 Southerly means to or towards the south. 2 A southerly wind blows from the south.

southern

ADJECTIVE in or from the south.

Southern Cross

NOUN The Southern Cross is a small group of stars which can be seen from the southern part of the earth, and which is represented on the national flags of Australia and New Zealand.

South Pole

NOUN The South Pole is the place on the surface of the earth that is farthest towards the south.

southward or **southwards**

ADVERB 1 Southward or southwards means towards the south E.G. *the dusty road which led southwards*. ▸ ADJECTIVE 2 The southward part of something is the south part.

south-west

NOUN, ADVERB, or ADJECTIVE South-west is halfway between south and west.

south-westerly

ADJECTIVE 1 South-westerly means to or towards the south-west. 2 A south-westerly wind blows from the south-west.

south-western

ADJECTIVE in or from the south-west.

souvenir souvenirs

NOUN something you keep to remind you of a holiday, place, or event.
🔲 from French *se souvenir* meaning 'to remember'

sovereign sovereigns

Said "**sov**-rin" NOUN 1 a king, queen, or royal ruler of a country. 2 In the past, a sovereign was a British gold coin worth one pound. ▸ ADJECTIVE 3 A sovereign state or country is independent and not under the authority of any other country.

sovereignty

Said "**sov**-rin-tee" NOUN Sovereignty is the political power that a country has to govern itself.

Soviet Soviets

Said "**soe**-vee-et" ADJECTIVE 1 belonging or relating to the country that used to be the Soviet Union. ▸ NOUN 2 The people and the government of the country that used to be the Soviet Union were sometimes referred to as the Soviets.

sow sows sowing sowed sown

Said "**soh**" VERB 1 To sow seeds or sow an area of land with seeds means to plant them in the ground. 2 To sow undesirable feelings or attitudes means to cause them E.G. *You have sown discontent*.

sow sows

Rhymes with "**now**" NOUN an adult female pig.

soya

NOUN Soya flour, margarine, oil, and milk are made from soya beans.
🔲 from Chinese *chiang yu* meaning 'paste sauce'

soya bean soya beans

NOUN Soya beans are a type of edible Asian bean.

spa spas

NOUN a place where water containing minerals bubbles out of the ground, at which people drink or bathe in the water to improve their health.

🏛 from the Belgian town *Spa* where there are mineral springs

space spaces spacing spaced
NOUN **1** Space is the area that is empty or available in a place, building, or container. **2** Space is the area beyond the earth's atmosphere surrounding the stars and planets. **3** a gap between two things E.G. *the space between the tables.* **4** Space can also refer to a period of time E.G. *two incidents in the space of a week.* ▶ VERB **5** If you space a series of things, you arrange them with gaps between them.

spacecraft
NOUN a rocket or other vehicle that can travel in space.

spaceman spacemen
NOUN someone who travels in space.

spaceship spaceships
NOUN a spacecraft that carries people through space.

space shuttle space shuttles
NOUN a spacecraft designed to be used many times for travelling out into space and back again.

spacious
ADJECTIVE having or providing a lot of space E.G. *the spacious living room.*
▪ capacious, commodious, roomy

spade spades
NOUN **1** a tool with a flat metal blade and a long handle used for digging. **2** Spades is one of the four suits in a pack of playing cards. It is marked by a black symbol in the shape of a heart-shaped leaf with a stem.

spaghetti
Said "spag-get-ee" NOUN Spaghetti consists of long, thin pieces of pasta.

span spans spanning spanned
NOUN **1** the period of time during which something exists or functions E.G. *looking back today over a span of forty years.* **2** The span of something is the total length of it from one end to the other. ▶ VERB **3** If something spans a particular length of time, it lasts throughout that time E.G. *a career that spanned 50 years.* **4** A bridge that spans something stretches right across it.

spangle spangles spangling spangled
VERB **1** If something is spangled, it is covered with small, sparkling objects. ▶ NOUN **2** Spangles are small sparkling pieces of metal or plastic used to decorate clothing or hair.

Spaniard Spaniards
Said "span-yard" NOUN someone who comes from Spain.

spaniel spaniels
NOUN a dog with long drooping ears and a silky coat.
🏛 from Old French *espaigneul* meaning 'Spanish dog'

Spanish
ADJECTIVE **1** belonging or relating to Spain. ▶ NOUN **2** Spanish is the main language spoken in Spain, and is also spoken by many people in Central and South America.

spank spanks spanking spanked
VERB If a child is spanked, it is punished by being slapped, usually on its leg or bottom.

spanner spanners
NOUN a tool with a specially shaped end that fits round a nut to turn it.

spar spars sparring sparred
VERB **1** When boxers spar, they hit each other with light punches for practice. **2** To spar with someone also means to argue with them, but not

a b c d e f g h i j k l m n o p q r s t u v w x y z

LEt's measure the angLE (angle)   **SPELLING NOTE**

A
B
C
D
E
F
G
H
I
J
K
L
M
N
O
P
Q
R
S
T
U
V
W
X
Y
Z

in an unpleasant or serious way.
▶ NOUN **3** a strong pole that a sail is attached to on a yacht or ship.

spare spares sparing spared
ADJECTIVE **1** extra to what is needed E.G. *What does she do in her spare time?* ▶ NOUN **2** a thing that is extra to what is needed. ▶ VERB **3** If you spare something for a particular purpose, you make it available E.G. *Few troops could be spared to go abroad.* **4** If someone is spared an unpleasant experience, they are prevented from suffering it E.G. *The capital was spared the misery of an all-out train strike.*

sparing
ADJECTIVE If you are sparing with something, you use it in very small quantities.
sparingly ADVERB

spark sparks sparking sparked
NOUN **1** a tiny, bright piece of burning material thrown up by a fire. **2** a small flash of light caused by electricity. **3** A spark of feeling is a small amount of it E.G. *that tiny spark of excitement.* ▶ VERB **4** If something sparks, it throws out sparks. **5** If one thing sparks another thing off, it causes the second thing to start happening E.G. *The tragedy sparked off a wave of sympathy among staff.*

sparkle sparkles sparkling sparkled
VERB **1** If something sparkles, it shines with a lot of small, bright points of light. ▶ NOUN **2** Sparkles are small, bright points of light.
sparkling ADJECTIVE
■ (sense 1) gleam, glitter, twinkle
sparrow sparrows
NOUN a common, small bird with

brown and grey feathers.

sparse sparser sparsest
ADJECTIVE small in number or amount and spread out over an area E.G. *the sparse audience.*
sparsely ADVERB

spartan
ADJECTIVE A spartan way of life is very simple with no luxuries E.G. *spartan accommodation.*
🔟 from *Sparta*, a city in Ancient Greece, whose inhabitants were famous for their discipline, military skill, and stern and plain way of life

spasm spasms
NOUN **1** a sudden tightening of the muscles. **2** a sudden, short burst of something E.G. *a spasm of fear.*

spasmodic
ADJECTIVE happening suddenly for short periods of time at irregular intervals E.G. *spasmodic movements.*

spastic spastics
ADJECTIVE **1** A spastic person is born with a disability which makes it difficult for them to control their muscles. ▶ NOUN **2** a spastic person.
🔟 from Greek *spasmos* meaning 'cramp' or 'convulsion'

spate
NOUN A spate of things is a large number of them that happen or appear in a rush E.G. *a recent spate of first novels from older writers.*

spatial
Said "**spay**-shl" ADJECTIVE to do with size, area, or position.

spatter spatters spattering spattered
VERB **1** If something spatters a surface, it covers the surface with drops of liquid. ▶ NOUN **2** A spatter of something is a small amount of it in

drops or tiny pieces.

spawn spawns spawning spawned

NOUN **1** Spawn is a jelly-like substance containing the eggs of fish or amphibians. ▶ VERB **2** When fish or amphibians spawn, they lay their eggs. **3** If something spawns something else, it causes it E.G. *The depressed economy spawned the riots.*

speak speaks speaking spoke spoken

VERB **1** When you speak, you use your voice to say words. **2** If you speak a foreign language, you know it and can use it.

■ (sense 1) say, talk, utter

speak out VERB To speak out about something means to publicly state an opinion about it.

speaker speakers

NOUN **1** a person who is speaking, especially someone making a speech. **2** A speaker on a radio or hi-fi is a loudspeaker.

spear spears spearing speared

NOUN **1** a weapon consisting of a long pole with a sharp point. ▶ VERB **2** To spear something means to push or throw a spear or other pointed object into it.

spearhead spearheads spearheading spearheaded

VERB If someone spearheads a campaign, they lead it.

spec specs INFORMAL

PLURAL NOUN **1** Someone's specs are their glasses. ▶ PHRASE **2** If you do something **on spec**, you do it hoping for a result but without any certainty E.G. *He turned up at the same event on spec.*

special

ADJECTIVE (RE) **1** Something special is more important or better than other things of its kind. **2** Special describes someone who is officially appointed, or something that is needed for a particular purpose E.G. *Karen actually had to get special permission to go there.* **3** Special also describes something that belongs or relates to only one particular person, group, or place E.G. *the special needs of the chronically sick.*

specialist specialists

NOUN **1** someone who has a particular skill or who knows a lot about a particular subject E.G. *a skin specialist.* ▶ ADJECTIVE **2** having a skill or knowing a lot about a particular subject E.G. *a specialist teacher.*

specialism NOUN

speciality specialities

NOUN A person's speciality is something they are especially good at or know a lot about E.G. *Roses are her speciality.*

specialize specializes specializing specialized; also spelt **specialise**

VERB If you specialize in something, you make it your speciality E.G. *a shop specializing in ceramics.*

specialization NOUN

specialized or **specialised**

ADJECTIVE developed for a particular purpose or trained in a particular area of knowledge E.G. *a specialized sales team.*

specially

ADVERB If something has been done specially for a particular person or purpose, it has been done only for that person or purpose.

species

Said "spee-sheez" NOUN a class of

a
b
c
d
e
f
g
h
i
j
k
l
m
n
o
p
q
r
s
t
u
v
w
x
y
z

plants or animals whose members have the same characteristics and are able to breed with each other.

specific
ADJECTIVE **1** particular E.G. *specific areas of difficulty*. **2** precise and exact E.G. *She will ask for specific answers.*
specifically ADVERB

specification specifications
NOUN (D & T) a detailed description of what is needed for something, such as the necessary features in the design of something E.G. *I like to build it to my own specifications.*

specify specifies specifying specified
VERB To specify something means to state or describe it precisely E.G. *In his will he specified that these documents were never to be removed.*

specimen specimens
NOUN A specimen of something is an example or small amount of it which gives an idea of what the whole is like E.G. *a specimen of your writing.*

speck specks
NOUN a very small stain or amount of something.

speckled
ADJECTIVE Something that is speckled is covered in very small marks or spots.

spectacle spectacles
PLURAL NOUN **1** Someone's spectacles are their glasses. ▶ NOUN **2** a strange or interesting sight or scene E.G. *an astonishing spectacle.* **3** a grand and impressive event or performance.

spectacular spectaculars
ADJECTIVE **1** Something spectacular is very impressive or dramatic. ▶ NOUN **2** a grand and impressive show or performance.

■ (sense 1) impressive, sensational, stunning

spectator spectators
NOUN a person who is watching something.
■ observer, onlooker, watcher

spectra
the plural of **spectrum**.

spectre spectres
NOUN **1** a frightening idea or image E.G. *the spectre of war.* **2** a ghost.

spectrum spectra or spectrums
NOUN **1** (ART) The spectrum is the range of different colours produced when light passes through a prism or a drop of water. A rainbow shows the colours in a spectrum. **2** A spectrum of opinions or emotions is a range of them.

speculate speculates speculating speculated
VERB If you speculate about something, you think about it and form opinions about it.
speculation NOUN

speculative
ADJECTIVE **1** A speculative piece of information is based on guesses and opinions rather than known facts. **2** Someone with a speculative expression seems to be trying to guess something E.G. *His mother regarded him with a speculative eye.*

speech speeches
NOUN **1** Speech is the ability to speak or the act of speaking. **2** a formal talk given to an audience. **3** In a play, a speech is a group of lines spoken by one of the characters.
■ (sense 2) address, talk

speechless
ADJECTIVE Someone who is speechless is unable to speak for a short time

because something has shocked them.

speed speeds speeding sped or speeded

NOUN **1** The speed of something is the rate at which it moves or happens. **2** Speed is very fast movement or travel. ▶ VERB **3** If you speed somewhere, you move or travel there quickly. **4** Someone who is speeding is driving a vehicle faster than the legal speed limit.

■ (sense 2) rapidity, swiftness, velocity

speedboat speedboats

NOUN a small, fast motorboat.

speed limit speed limits

NOUN The speed limit is the maximum speed at which vehicles are legally allowed to drive on a particular road.

speedway

NOUN Speedway is the sport of racing lightweight motorcycles on special tracks.

speedy speedier speediest

ADJECTIVE done very quickly.

speedily ADVERB

spell spells spelling spelt or spelled

VERB **1** When you spell a word, you name or write its letters in order. **2** When letters spell a word, they form that word when put together in a particular order. **3** If something spells a particular result, it suggests that this will be the result E.G. *This haphazard method could spell disaster for you.* ▶ NOUN **4** A spell of something is a short period of it E.G. *a spell of rough weather.* **5** a word or sequence of words used to perform magic.

spell out VERB If you spell

something out, you explain it in detail E.G. *I don't have to spell it out, do I?*

spellbound

ADJECTIVE so fascinated by something that you cannot think about anything else E.G. *She had sat spellbound through the film.*

spelling spellings

NOUN The spelling of a word is the correct order of letters in it.

spend spends spending spent

VERB **1** When you spend money, you buy things with it. **2** To spend time or energy means to use it.

spent

ADJECTIVE **1** Spent describes things which have been used and therefore cannot be used again E.G. *spent matches.* **2** If you are spent, you are exhausted and have no energy left.

sperm sperms

NOUN a cell produced in the sex organ of a male animal which can enter a female animal's egg and fertilize it.

spew spews spewing spewed

VERB **1** When things spew from something or when it spews them out, they come out of it in large quantities. **2** INFORMAL To spew up means to vomit.

sphere spheres

NOUN **1** a perfectly round object, such as a ball. **2** An area of activity or interest can be referred to as a sphere of activity or interest.

spherical ADJECTIVE

sphinx sphinxes

Said "**sfingks**" NOUN In mythology, the sphinx was a monster with a person's head and a lion's body.

spice spices spicing spiced

NOUN **1** Spice is powder or seeds from

a
b
c
d
e
f
g
h
i
j
k
l
m
n
o
p
q
r
s
t
u
v
w
x
y
z

a plant added to food to give it flavour. **2** Spice is something which makes life more exciting E.G. *Variety is the spice of life.* ► VERB **3** To spice food means to add spice to it. **4** If you spice something up, you make it more exciting or lively.

spicy spicier spiciest
ADJECTIVE strongly flavoured with spices.

spider spiders
NOUN a small insect-like creature with eight legs that spins webs to catch insects for food.
📖 from Old English *spinnan* meaning 'to spin'

spike spikes
NOUN **1** a long pointed piece of metal. **2** The spikes on a sports shoe are the pointed pieces of metal attached to the sole. **3** Some other long pointed objects are called spikes E.G. *beautiful pink flower spikes.*

spiky spikier spikiest
ADJECTIVE Something spiky has sharp points.

spill spills spilling spilled or **spilt**
VERB **1** If you spill something or if it spills, it accidentally falls or runs out of a container. **2** If people or things spill out of a place, they come out of it in large numbers.

spillage spillages
NOUN the spilling of something, or something that has been spilt E.G. *the oil spillage in the Shetlands.*

spin spins spinning spun
VERB **1** If something spins, it turns quickly around a central point. **2** When spiders spin a web, they give out a sticky substance and make it into a web. **3** When people spin, they make thread by twisting together

pieces of fibre using a machine. **4** If your head is spinning, you feel dizzy or confused. ► NOUN **5** a rapid turn around a central point E.G. *a golf club which puts more spin on the ball.*

spinach
Said "spin-ij" NOUN Spinach is a vegetable with large green leaves.

spinal
ADJECTIVE to do with the spine.

spine spines
NOUN **1** Your spine is your backbone. **2** Spines are long, sharp points on an animal's body or on a plant.

spinifex
NOUN Spinifex is a coarse, spiny Australian grass.

spinning wheel spinning wheels
NOUN a wooden machine for spinning flax or wool.

spin-off spin-offs
NOUN something useful that unexpectedly results from an activity.

spinster spinsters
NOUN a woman who has never married.
📖 originally a person whose occupation was spinning; later, the official label of an unmarried woman

spiny
ADJECTIVE covered with spines.

spiral spirals spiralling spiralled
NOUN **1** a continuous curve which winds round and round, with each curve above or outside the previous one. ► ADJECTIVE **2** in the shape of a spiral E.G. *a spiral staircase.* ► VERB **3** If something spirals, it moves up or down in a spiral curve E.G. *The aircraft spiralled down.* **4** If an amount or level spirals, it rises or falls quickly at an increasing rate E.G.

Prices have spiralled recently.

spire spires

NOUN The spire of a church is the tall cone-shaped structure on top.

spirit spirits spiriting spirited

NOUN 1 Your spirit is the part of you that is not physical and that is connected with your deepest thoughts and feelings. 2 (RE) The spirit of a dead person is a nonphysical part that is believed to remain alive after death. 3 a supernatural being, such as a ghost. 4 Spirit is liveliness, energy, and self-confidence E.G. *a band full of spirit.* 5 Spirit can refer to an attitude E.G. *his old fighting spirit.* ▶ PLURAL NOUN 6 Spirits can describe how happy or unhappy someone is E.G. *in good spirits.* 7 Spirits are strong alcoholic drinks such as whisky and gin. ▶ VERB 8 If you spirit someone or something into or out of a place, you get them in or out quickly and secretly.

spirited

ADJECTIVE showing energy and courage.

spirit level spirit levels

NOUN a device for finding out if a surface is level, consisting of a bubble of air sealed in a tube of liquid in a wooden or metal frame.

spiritual spirituals

ADJECTIVE (RE) 1 to do with people's thoughts and beliefs, rather than their bodies and physical surroundings. 2 to do with people's religious beliefs E.G. *spiritual guidance.* ▶ NOUN 3 a religious song originally sung by Black slaves in America.

spiritually ADVERB **spirituality** NOUN

spit spits spitting spat

NOUN 1 Spit is saliva. 2 a long stick made of metal or wood which is pushed through a piece of meat so that it can be hung over a fire and cooked. 3 a long, flat, narrow piece of land sticking out into the sea. ▶ VERB 4 If you spit, you force saliva or some other substance out of your mouth. 5 When it is spitting, it is raining very lightly.

spite spites spiting spited

PHRASE 1 **In spite of** is used to introduce a statement which makes the rest of what you are saying seem surprising E.G. *In spite of all the gossip, Virginia stayed behind.* ▶ VERB 2 If you do something to spite someone, you do it deliberately to hurt or annoy them. ▶ NOUN 3 If you do something out of spite, you do it to spite someone.

spiteful

ADJECTIVE A spiteful person does or says nasty things to people deliberately to hurt them.
▤ malicious, nasty, vindictive

spitting image

NOUN If someone is the spitting image of someone else, they look just like them.

splash splashes splashing splashed

VERB 1 If you splash around in water, your movements disturb the water in a noisy way. 2 If liquid splashes something, it scatters over it in a lot of small drops. ▶ NOUN 3 A splash is the sound made when something hits or falls into water. 4 A splash of liquid is a small quantity of it that has been spilt on something.

a
b
c
d
e
f
g
h
i
j
k
l
m
n
o
p
q
r
s
t
u
v
w
x
y
z

I always visit my FRIend on a FRIday (<u>fri</u>end) ◀ SPELLING NOTE

splatter splatters splattering splattered

VERB When something is splattered with a substance, the substance is splashed all over it E.G. *fur coats splattered with paint*.

spleen spleens

NOUN Your spleen is an organ near your stomach which controls the quality of your blood.

splendid

ADJECTIVE 1 very good indeed E.G. *a splendid career*. 2 beautiful and impressive E.G. *a splendid old mansion*.

splendidly ADVERB

■ (sense 2) grand, magnificent

splendour splendours

NOUN 1 If something has splendour, it is beautiful and impressive. ▶ PLURAL NOUN 2 The splendours of something are its beautiful and impressive features.

splint splints

NOUN a long piece of wood or metal fastened to a broken limb to hold it in place.

splinter splinters splintering splintered

NOUN 1 a thin, sharp piece of wood or glass which has broken off a larger piece. ▶ VERB 2 If something splinters, it breaks into thin, sharp pieces.

split splits splitting split

VERB 1 If something splits or if you split it, it divides into two or more parts. 2 If something such as wood or fabric splits, a long crack or tear appears in it. 3 If people split something, they share it between them. ▶ NOUN 4 A split in a piece of wood or fabric is a crack or tear. 5 A split between two things is a division

or difference between them E.G. *the split between rugby league and rugby union*.

■ (sense 1) break, divide, separate
■ (sense 5) division, schism

split up VERB If two people split up, they end their relationship or marriage.

split second

NOUN an extremely short period of time.

splitting

ADJECTIVE A splitting headache is very painful.

splutter splutters spluttering spluttered

VERB 1 If someone splutters, they speak in a confused way because they are embarrassed. 2 If something splutters, it makes a series of short, sharp sounds.

spoil spoils spoiling spoiled or **spoilt**

VERB 1 If you spoil something, you prevent it from being successful or satisfactory. 2 To spoil children means to give them everything they want, with harmful effects on their character. 3 To spoil someone also means to give them something nice as a treat. ▶ PLURAL NOUN 4 Spoils are valuable things obtained during war or as a result of violence E.G. *the spoils of war*.

■ (sense 1) mess up, ruin, wreck
■ (sense 2) overindulge, pamper

spoilsport spoilsports

NOUN someone who spoils people's fun.

spoke spokes

NOUN The spokes of a wheel are the bars which connect the hub to the rim.

spokesperson spokespersons
NOUN someone who speaks on behalf
of another person or a group.
spokesman NOUN **spokeswoman**
NOUN

sponge sponges sponging
sponged
NOUN 1 a sea creature with a body
made up of many cells. 2 part of the
very light skeleton of a sponge, used
for bathing and cleaning. 3 A sponge
or sponge cake is a very light cake.
▶ VERB 4 If you sponge something,
you clean it by wiping it with a wet
sponge.

sponsor sponsors sponsoring
sponsored
VERB 1 To sponsor something, such as
an event or someone's training,
means to support it financially E.G.
*The visit was sponsored by the London
Natural History Society.* 2 If you
sponsor someone who is doing
something for charity, you agree to
give them a sum of money for the
charity if they manage to do it. 3 If
you sponsor a proposal or
suggestion, you officially put it
forward and support it E.G. *the MP
who sponsored the Bill.* ▶ NOUN 4 a
person or organization sponsoring
something or someone.
sponsorship NOUN

spontaneous
ADJECTIVE 1 Spontaneous acts are not
planned or arranged, but are done
because you feel like it. 2 A
spontaneous event happens
because of processes within
something rather than being caused
by things outside it E.G. *spontaneous
bleeding.*
spontaneously ADVERB
spontaneity NOUN

spoof spoofs
NOUN something such as an article or
television programme that seems to
be about a serious matter but is
actually a joke.

spooky spookier spookiest
ADJECTIVE eerie and frightening.

spool spools
NOUN a cylindrical object onto which
thread, tape, or film can be wound.

spoon spoons
NOUN an object shaped like a small
shallow bowl with a long handle,
used for eating, stirring, and serving
food.

spoonful spoonfuls or spoonsful
NOUN the amount held by a spoon.

sporadic
ADJECTIVE happening at irregular
intervals E.G. *a few sporadic attempts
at keeping a diary.*
sporadically ADVERB

spore spores
NOUN; TECHNICAL Spores are cells
produced by bacteria and
nonflowering plants such as fungi
which develop into new bacteria or
plants.

sporran sporrans
NOUN a large purse made of leather or
fur, worn by a Scotsman over his kilt.
📖 from Scottish Gaelic *sporan*
meaning 'purse'

sport sports sporting sported
NOUN 1 Sports are games and other
enjoyable activities which need
physical effort and skill. 2 You say
that someone is a sport when they
accept defeat or teasing cheerfully
E.G. *Be a sport, Minister!* ▶ VERB 3 If you
sport something noticeable or
unusual, you wear it E.G. *A German
boy sported a ponytail.*

A
B
C
D
E
F
G
H
I
J
K
L
M
N
O
P
Q
R
S
T
U
V
W
X
Y
Z

sporting

ADJECTIVE **1** relating to sport.
2 behaving in a fair and decent way.

sports car sports cars

NOUN a low, fast car, usually with room for only two people.

sportsman sportsmen

NOUN a man who takes part in sports and is good at them.

sportswoman sportswomen

NOUN a woman who takes part in sports and is good at them.

sporty sportier sportiest

ADJECTIVE **1** A sporty car is fast and flashy. **2** A sporty person is good at sports.

spot spots spotting spotted

NOUN **1** Spots are small, round, coloured areas on a surface. **2** Spots on a person's skin are small lumps, usually caused by an infection or allergy. **3** A spot of something is a small amount of it E.G. *spots of rain.* **4** A place can be called a spot E.G. *the most beautiful spot in the garden.* ▶ VERB **5** If you spot something, you notice it. ▶ PHRASE **6** If you do something **on the spot**, you do it immediately.

spot check spot checks

NOUN a random examination made without warning on one of a group of things or people E.G. *spot checks by road safety officers.*

spotless

ADJECTIVE perfectly clean.

spotlessly ADVERB

■ clean, immaculate, impeccable

spotlight spotlights spotlighting spotlit or **spotlighted**

NOUN **1** (DRAMA) a powerful light which can be directed to light up a small area. ▶ VERB **2** If something spotlights

a situation or problem, it draws the public's attention to it E.G. *a national campaign to spotlight the problem.*

spot-on

ADJECTIVE; INFORMAL exactly correct or accurate.

spotted

ADJECTIVE Something spotted has a pattern of spots on it.

spotter spotters

NOUN a person whose hobby is looking out for things of a particular kind E.G. *a train spotter.*

spotty spottier spottiest

ADJECTIVE Someone who is spotty has spots or pimples on their skin, especially on their face.

spouse spouses

NOUN Someone's spouse is the person they are married to.

spout spouts spouting spouted

VERB **1** When liquid or flame spouts out of something, it shoots out in a long stream. **2** When someone spouts what they have learned, they say it in a boring way. ▶ NOUN **3** a tube with a lip-like end for pouring liquid E.G. *a teapot with a long spout.*

sprain sprains spraining sprained

VERB **1** If you sprain a joint, you accidentally damage it by twisting it violently. ▶ NOUN **2** the injury caused by spraining a joint.

sprawl sprawls sprawling sprawled

VERB **1** If you sprawl somewhere, you sit or lie there with your legs and arms spread out. **2** A place that sprawls is spread out over a large area E.G. *a Monday market which sprawls all over town.* ▶ NOUN
3 anything that spreads in an untidy

and uncontrolled way E.G. *a sprawl of skyscrapers*.

sprawling ADJECTIVE

spray sprays spraying sprayed

NOUN **1** Spray consists of many drops of liquid splashed or forced into the air E.G. *The salt spray stung her face.* **2** Spray is also a liquid kept under pressure in a can or other container E.G. *hair spray.* **3** a piece of equipment for spraying liquid E.G. *a garden spray.* **4** A spray of flowers or leaves consists of several of them on one stem. ► VERB **5** To spray a liquid over something means to cover it with drops of the liquid.

spread spreads spreading spread

VERB **1** If you spread something out, you open it out or arrange it so that it can be seen or used easily E.G. *He spread the map out on his knees.* **2** If you spread a substance on a surface, you put a thin layer on the surface. **3** If something spreads, it gradually reaches or affects more people E.G. *The news spread quickly.* **4** If something spreads over a period of time, it happens regularly or continuously over that time E.G. *His four international appearances were spread over eight years.* **5** If something such as work is spread, it is distributed evenly. ► NOUN **6** The spread of something is the extent to which it gradually reaches or affects more people E.G. *the spread of Buddhism.* **7** A spread of ideas, interests, or other things is a wide variety of them. **8** soft food put on bread E.G. *cheese spread.*

spread-eagled

ADJECTIVE Someone who is spread-eagled is lying with their arms

and legs spread out.

spreadsheet spreadsheets

NOUN (ICT) a computer program that is used for entering and arranging figures, used mainly for financial planning.

spree sprees

NOUN a period of time spent doing something enjoyable E.G. *a shopping spree.*

sprig sprigs

NOUN **1** a small twig with leaves on it. **2** In Australian and New Zealand English, sprigs are studs on the sole of a football boot.

sprightly sprightlier sprightliest

ADJECTIVE lively and active.

spring springs springing sprang sprung

NOUN **1** Spring is the season between winter and summer. **2** a coil of wire which returns to its natural shape after being pressed or pulled. **3** a place where water comes up through the ground. **4** an act of springing E.G. *With a spring he had opened the door.* ► VERB **5** To spring means to jump upwards or forwards E.G. *Martha sprang to her feet.* **6** If something springs in a particular direction, it moves suddenly and quickly E.G. *The door sprang open.* **7** If one thing springs from another, it is the result of it E.G. *The failures sprang from three facts.*

springboard springboards

NOUN **1** a flexible board on which a diver or gymnast jumps to gain height. **2** If something is a springboard for an activity or enterprise, it makes it possible for it to begin.

springbok springboks

NOUN **1** a small South African antelope

which moves in leaps. **2** a Springbok is a person who has represented South Africa in a sports team.

spring-clean spring-cleans spring-cleaning spring-cleaned
VERB To spring-clean a house means to clean it thoroughly throughout.

spring onion spring onions
NOUN a small onion with long green shoots, often eaten raw in salads.

sprinkle sprinkles sprinkling sprinkled
VERB If you sprinkle a liquid or powder over something, you scatter it over it.

sprinkling sprinklings
NOUN A sprinkling of something is a small quantity of it E.G. *a light sprinkling of snow*.

sprint sprints sprinting sprinted
NOUN **1** a short, fast race. ► VERB **2** To sprint means to run fast over a short distance.

sprinter sprinters
NOUN an athlete who runs fast over short distances.

sprite sprites
NOUN a type of fairy.

sprout sprouts sprouting sprouted
VERB **1** When something sprouts, it grows. **2** If things sprout up, they appear rapidly E.G. *Their houses sprouted up in that region.* ► NOUN **3** Sprouts are the same as **brussels sprouts**.

spruce spruces; sprucer sprucest; spruces sprucing spruced
NOUN **1** an evergreen tree with needle-like leaves. ► ADJECTIVE **2** Someone who is spruce is very neat and smart. ► VERB **3** To spruce

something up means to make it neat and smart.

spunk spunks
NOUN INFORMAL **1** OLD-FASHIONED Spunk is courage. **2** In Australian and New Zealand English, someone who is good-looking.

spur spurs spurring spurred
VERB **1** If something spurs you to do something or spurs you on, it encourages you to do it. ► NOUN **2** Something that acts as a spur encourages a person to do something. **3** Spurs are sharp metal points attached to the heels of a rider's boots and used to urge a horse on. ► PHRASE **4** If you do something **on the spur of the moment**, you do it suddenly, without planning it.

spurious
Said "spyoor-ee-uss" ADJECTIVE not genuine or real.

spurn spurns spurning spurned
VERB If you spurn something, you refuse to accept it E.G. *You spurned his last offer.*

spurt spurts spurting spurted
VERB **1** When a liquid or flame spurts out of something, it comes out quickly in a thick, powerful stream. ► NOUN **2** A spurt of liquid or flame is a thick powerful stream of it E.G. *a small spurt of blood.* **3** A spurt of activity or effort is a sudden, brief period of it.

spy spies spying spied
NOUN **1** a person sent to find out secret information about a country or organization. ► VERB **2** Someone who spies tries to find out secret information about another country or organization. **3** If you spy on

someone, you watch them secretly.
4 If you spy something, you notice it.

squabble squabbles squabbling squabbled

VERB **1** When people squabble, they quarrel about something trivial.
▶ NOUN **2** a quarrel.

squad squads

NOUN (PE) a small group chosen to do a particular activity E.G. *the fraud squad… the England football squad.*
📖 from Old Spanish *escuadra* meaning 'square', because of the square formation used by soldiers

squadron squadrons

NOUN a section of one of the armed forces, especially the air force.
📖 from Italian *squadrone* meaning 'soldiers drawn up in a square formation'

squalid

ADJECTIVE **1** dirty, untidy, and in bad condition. **2** Squalid activities are unpleasant and often dishonest.

squall squalls

NOUN a brief, violent storm.

squalor

NOUN Squalor consists of bad or dirty conditions or surroundings.

squander squanders squandering squandered

VERB To squander money or resources means to waste them E.G. *They have squandered huge amounts of money.*

square squares squaring squared

NOUN **1** (MATHS) a shape with four equal sides and four right angles. **2** In a town or city, a square is a flat, open place, bordered by buildings or streets. **3** The square of a number is the number multiplied by itself. For example, the square of 3, written 3^2,

is 3×3. ▶ ADJECTIVE **4** shaped like a square E.G. *her delicate square face.*
5 'Square' is used before units of length when talking about the area of something E.G. $24m^2$. **6** 'Square' is used after units of length when you are giving the length of each side of something square E.G. *a towel measuring a foot square.* ▶ VERB **7** If you square a number, you multiply it by itself.

squarely

ADVERB **1** Squarely means directly rather than indirectly or at an angle E.G. *I looked squarely in the mirror.* **2** If you approach a subject squarely, you consider it fully, without trying to avoid unpleasant aspects of it.

square root square roots

NOUN A square root of a number is a number that makes the first number when it is multiplied by itself. For example, the square roots of 25 are 5 and –5.

squash squashes squashing squashed

VERB **1** If you squash something, you press it, so that it becomes flat or loses its shape. ▶ NOUN **2** If there is a squash in a place, there are a lot of people squashed in it. **3** Squash is a game in which two players hit a small rubber ball against the walls of a court using rackets. **4** Squash is a drink made from fruit juice, sugar, and water.

squat squats squatting squatted; squatter squattest

VERB **1** If you squat down, you crouch, balancing on your feet with your legs bent. **2** A person who squats in an unused building lives there as a squatter. ▶ NOUN **3** a building used by squatters. ▶ ADJECTIVE **4** short and thick.

a b c d e f g h i j k l m n o p q r s t u v w x y z

You must practiSe your Ss (practiSe)　　SPELLING NOTE

squatter squatters

NOUN **1** a person who lives in an unused building without permission and without paying rent. **2** In Australian English, someone who owns a large amount of land for sheep or cattle farming. **3** In Australia and New Zealand in the past, someone who rented land from the King or Queen.

squawk squawks squawking squawked

VERB **1** When a bird squawks, it makes a loud, harsh noise. ► NOUN **2** a loud, harsh noise made by a bird.

squeak squeaks squeaking squeaked

VERB **1** If something squeaks, it makes a short high-pitched sound. ► NOUN **2** a short, high-pitched sound.

squeaky ADJECTIVE

squeal squeals squealing squealed

VERB **1** When things or people squeal, they make long, high-pitched sounds. ► NOUN **2** a long, high-pitched sound.

squeamish

ADJECTIVE easily upset by unpleasant sights or situations.

squeeze squeezes squeezing squeezed

VERB **1** When you squeeze something, you press it firmly from two sides. **2** If you squeeze something into a small amount of time or space, you manage to fit it in. ► NOUN **3** If you give something a squeeze, you squeeze it E.G. *She gave my hand a quick squeeze.* **4** If getting into something is a squeeze, it is just possible to fit into it E.G. *It would take four comfortably, but six*

would be a squeeze.

squelch squelches squelching squelched

VERB **1** To squelch means to make a wet, sucking sound. ► NOUN **2** a wet, sucking sound.

squid squids

NOUN a sea creature with a long soft body and many tentacles.

squiggle squiggles

NOUN a wriggly line.

squint squints squinting squinted

VERB **1** If you squint at something, you look at it with your eyes screwed up. ► NOUN **2** If someone has a squint, their eyes look in different directions from each other.

squire squires

NOUN In a village, the squire was a gentleman who owned a large house with a lot of land.

squirm squirms squirming squirmed

VERB If you squirm, you wriggle and twist your body about, usually because you are nervous or embarrassed.

squirrel squirrels

NOUN a small furry animal with a long bushy tail.

📖 from Greek *skia* meaning 'shadow' and *oura* meaning 'tail'

squirt squirts squirting squirted

VERB **1** If a liquid squirts, it comes out of a narrow opening in a thin, fast stream. ► NOUN **2** a thin, fast stream of liquid.

Sri Lankan Sri Lankans

Said "sree-**lang**-kan" ADJECTIVE

1 belonging to or relating to Sri Lanka. ► NOUN **2** someone who comes from Sri Lanka.

stab stabs stabbing stabbed
VERB 1 To stab someone means to wound them by pushing a knife into their body. 2 To stab at something means to push at it sharply with your finger or with something long and narrow. ► PHRASE 3 INFORMAL If you **have a stab** at something, you try to do it. ► NOUN 4 You can refer to a sudden unpleasant feeling as a stab of something E.G. *He felt a stab of guilt.*

stable stables
ADJECTIVE 1 not likely to change or come to an end suddenly E.G. *I am in a stable relationship.* 2 firmly fixed or balanced and not likely to move, wobble, or fall. ► NOUN 3 a building in which horses are kept.
stability NOUN   **stabilize** VERB

staccato
Said "stak-kah-toe" ADJECTIVE consisting of a series of short, sharp, separate sounds.

stack stacks stacking stacked
NOUN 1 A stack of things is a pile of them, one on top of the other. ► PLURAL NOUN 2 INFORMAL If someone has stacks of something, they have a lot of it. ► VERB 3 If you stack things, you arrange them one on top of the other in a pile.

stadium stadiums
NOUN a sports ground with rows of seats around it.
🏛 from Greek *stadion* meaning 'racecourse'

staff staffs staffing staffed
NOUN 1 The staff of an organization are the people who work for it. ► VERB 2 To staff an organization means to find and employ people to work in it. 3 If an organization is staffed by

particular people, they are the people who work for it.

stag stags
NOUN an adult male deer.

stage stages staging staged
NOUN 1 a part of a process that lasts for a period of time. 2 (DRAMA) In a theatre, the stage is a raised platform where the actors or entertainers perform. 3 (DRAMA) You can refer to the profession of acting as the stage. ► VERB 4 If someone stages a play or event, they organize it and present it or take part in it.
■ (sense 1) period, phase, point

stagecoach stagecoaches
NOUN a large carriage pulled by horses which used to carry passengers and mail.

stagger staggers staggering staggered
VERB 1 If you stagger, you walk unsteadily because you are ill or drunk. 2 If something staggers you, it amazes you. 3 If events are staggered, they are arranged so that they do not all happen at the same time.
staggering ADJECTIVE
■ (sense 1) lurch, reel, totter

stagnant
ADJECTIVE Stagnant water is not flowing and is unhealthy and dirty.

stag night stag nights
NOUN a party for a man who is about to get married, which only men go to.

staid
ADJECTIVE serious and dull.

stain stains staining stained
NOUN 1 a mark on something that is difficult to remove. ► VERB 2 If a substance stains something, the

a b c d e f g h i j k l m n o p q r s t u v w x y z

LEarn the principLEs (principle)   SPELLING NOTE

A
B
C
D
E
F
G
H
I
J
K
L
M
N
O
P
Q
R
S
T
U
V
W
X
Y
Z

thing becomes marked or coloured by it.

stained glass
NOUN Stained glass is coloured pieces of glass held together with strips of lead.

stainless steel
NOUN Stainless steel is a metal made from steel and chromium which does not rust.

stair stairs
NOUN Stairs are a set of steps inside a building going from one floor to another.

staircase staircases
NOUN a set of stairs.

stairway stairways
NOUN a set of stairs.

stake stakes staking staked
PHRASE 1 If something is **at stake**, it might be lost or damaged if something else is not successful E.G. *The whole future of the company was at stake.* ► PLURAL NOUN 2 The stakes involved in something are the things that can be lost or gained. ► VERB 3 If you say you would stake your money, life, or reputation on the success or truth of something, you mean you would risk it E.G. *He is prepared to stake his own career on this.* ► NOUN 4 If you have a stake in something such as a business, you own part of it and its success is important to you. 5 a pointed wooden post that can be hammered into the ground and used as a support.

stale staler stalest
ADJECTIVE 1 Stale food or air is no longer fresh. 2 If you feel stale, you have no new ideas and are bored.
■ (sense 1) fusty, musty, old

stalemate
NOUN 1 Stalemate is a situation in which neither side in an argument or contest can win. 2 In chess, stalemate is a situation in which a player cannot make any move permitted by the rules, so that the game ends and no-one wins.

stalk stalks stalking stalked
Said "**stawk**" NOUN 1 The stalk of a flower or leaf is its stem. ► VERB 2 To stalk a person or animal means to follow them quietly in order to catch, kill, or observe them. 3 If someone stalks into a room, they walk in a stiff, proud, or angry way.

stall stalls stalling stalled
NOUN 1 a large table containing goods for sale or information. ► PLURAL NOUN 2 In a theatre, the stalls are the seats at the lowest level, in front of the stage. ► VERB 3 When a vehicle stalls, the engine suddenly stops. 4 If you stall when someone asks you to do something, you try to avoid doing it until a later time.

stallion stallions
NOUN an adult male horse that can be used for breeding.

stamina
NOUN Stamina is the physical or mental energy needed to do something for a very long time.

stammer stammers stammering stammered
VERB 1 When someone stammers, they speak with difficulty, repeating words and sounds and hesitating awkwardly. ► NOUN 2 Someone who has a stammer tends to stammer when they speak.

stamp stamps stamping stamped

NOUN **1** a small piece of gummed paper which you stick on a letter or parcel before posting it. **2** a small block with a pattern cut into it, which you press onto an inky pad and make a mark with it on paper; also the mark made by the stamp. **3** If something bears the stamp of a particular quality or person, it shows clear signs of that quality or of the person's style or characteristics. ▶ VERB **4** If you stamp a piece of paper, you make a mark on it using a stamp. **5** If you stamp, you lift your foot and put it down hard on the ground.

stamp out VERB To stamp something out means to put an end to it E.G. *the battle to stamp out bullying in schools*.

stampede stampedes stampeding stampeded

VERB **1** When a group of animals stampede, they run in a wild, uncontrolled way. ▶ NOUN **2** a group of animals stampeding.
📖 from Spanish *estampida* meaning 'crash' or 'din'

stance stances

NOUN Your stance on a particular matter is your attitude and way of dealing with it E.G. *He takes no particular stance on animal rights*.

stand stands standing stood

VERB **1** If you are standing, you are upright, your legs are straight, and your weight is supported by your feet. When you stand up, you get into a standing position. **2** If something stands somewhere, that is where it is E.G. *The house stands alone on the top of a small hill*. **3** If you

stand something somewhere, you put it there in an upright position E.G. *Stand the containers on bricks*. **4** If a decision or offer stands, it is still valid E.G. *My offer still stands*. **5** You can use 'stand' when describing the state or condition of something E.G. *Youth unemployment stands at 35%*. **6** If a letter stands for a particular word, it is an abbreviation for that word. **7** If you say you will not stand for something, you mean you will not tolerate it. **8** If something can stand a situation or test, it is good enough or strong enough not to be damaged by it. **9** If you cannot stand something, you cannot bear it E.G. *I can't stand that woman*. **10** If you stand in an election, you are one of the candidates. ▶ PHRASE **11** When someone **stands trial**, they are tried in a court of law. ▶ NOUN **12** a stall or very small shop outdoors or in a large public building. **13** a large structure at a sports ground, where the spectators sit to watch what is happening. **14** a piece of furniture designed to hold something E.G. *an umbrella stand*.

stand by VERB **1** If you stand by to provide help or take action, you are ready to do it if necessary. **2** If you stand by while something happens, you do nothing to stop it.

stand down VERB If someone stands down, they resign from their job or position.

stand in VERB If you stand in for someone, you take their place while they are ill or away.

stand out VERB If something stands out, it can be easily noticed or is more important than other similar things.

the QUeen stood on the QUay (quay)   SPELLING NOTE

A
B
C
D
E
F
G
H
I
J
K
L
M
N
O
P
Q
R
S
T
U
V
W
X
Y
Z

stand up VERB 1 If something stands up to rough treatment, it is not damaged or harmed. 2 If you stand up to someone who is criticizing or attacking you, you defend yourself.

standard standards
NOUN 1 a level of quality or achievement that is considered acceptable E.G. *The work is not up to standard.* ► PLURAL NOUN 2 Standards are moral principles of behaviour. ► ADJECTIVE 3 usual, normal, and correct E.G. *The practice became standard procedure for most motor companies.*

standard English
NOUN Standard English is the form of English taught in schools, used in text books and broadsheet newspapers, and spoken and written by most educated people.

standardize standardizes standardizing standardized; also spelt **standardise**
VERB To standardize things means to change them so that they all have a similar set of features E.G. *We have decided to standardize our equipment.*

stand-by stand-bys
NOUN 1 something available for use when you need it E.G. *a useful stand-by.* ► ADJECTIVE 2 A stand-by ticket is a cheap ticket that you buy just before a theatre performance or a flight if there are any seats left.

stand-in stand-ins
NOUN someone who takes a person's place while the person is ill or away E.G. *stand-in teachers.*

standing
ADJECTIVE 1 permanently in existence or used regularly E.G. *a standing joke.* ► NOUN 2 A person's standing is their status and reputation. 3 'Standing' is used to say how long something has existed E.G. *a friend of 20 years' standing.*

standpoint standpoints
NOUN If you consider something from a particular standpoint, you consider it from that point of view E.G. *from a military standpoint.*

standstill
NOUN If something comes to a standstill, it stops completely.

stanza stanzas
NOUN a verse of a poem.
🔳 from Italian *stanza* meaning 'stopping place'

staple staples stapling stapled
NOUN 1 Staples are small pieces of wire that hold sheets of paper firmly together. ► VERB 2 If you staple sheets of paper, you fasten them together with staples. ► ADJECTIVE 3 A staple food forms a regular and basic part of someone's everyday diet.

star stars starring starred
NOUN 1 a large ball of burning gas in space that appears as a point of light in the sky at night. 2 a shape with four, five, or more points sticking out in a regular pattern. 3 Famous actors, sports players, and musicians are referred to as stars. ► PLURAL NOUN 4 The horoscope in a newspaper or magazine can be referred to as the stars E.G. *I'm a Virgo, but don't read my stars every day.* ► VERB 5 If an actor or actress stars in a film or if the film stars that person, he or she has one of the most important parts in it.

starboard
ADJECTIVE OR NOUN The starboard side of a ship is the right-hand side when you are facing the front.

🔲 from Old English *steorbord* meaning 'steering side', because boats were formerly steered with a paddle over the right-hand side

starch starches starching starched

NOUN **1** Starch is a substance used for stiffening fabric such as cotton and linen. **2** Starch is a carbohydrate found in foods such as bread and potatoes. ▶ VERB **3** To starch fabric means to stiffen it with starch.

stare stares staring stared

VERB **1** If you stare at something, you look at it for a long time. ▶ NOUN **2** a long fixed look at something.

🔳 (sense 1) gawp, gaze, goggle

starfish starfishes or starfish

NOUN a flat, star-shaped sea creature with five limbs.

stark starker starkest

ADJECTIVE **1** harsh, unpleasant and plain E.G. *the stark choice.* ▶ PHRASE **2** If someone is **stark-naked**, they have no clothes on at all.

starling starlings

NOUN a common European bird with shiny dark feathers.

start starts starting started

VERB **1** To start means to begin. To start doing something means to begin doing it E.G. *School starts next week... Suzy started crying.* **2** If you start a machine or car, you operate the controls to make it work. **3** If you start, your body suddenly jerks because of surprise or fear. ▶ NOUN **4** The start of something is the point or time at which it begins. **5** If you do something with a start, you do it with a sudden jerky movement because of surprise or fear E.G. *I awoke with a start.*

starter starters

NOUN a small quantity of food served as the first part of a meal.

startle startles startling startled

VERB If something sudden and unexpected startles you, it surprises you and makes you slightly frightened.

startled ADJECTIVE   **startling** ADJECTIVE

starve starves starving starved

VERB **1** If people are starving, they are suffering from a serious lack of food and are likely to die. **2** To starve a person or animal means to prevent them from having any food. **3** INFORMAL If you say you are starving, you mean you are very hungry. **4** If someone or something is starved of something they need, they are suffering because they are not getting enough of it E.G. *The hospital was starved of cash.*

starvation NOUN

stash stashes stashing stashed

VERB; INFORMAL If you stash something away in a secret place, you store it there to keep it safe.

state states stating stated

NOUN **1** The state of something is its condition, what it is like, or its circumstances. **2** Countries are sometimes referred to as states E.G. *the state of Denmark.* **3** Some countries are divided into regions called states which make some of their own laws E.G. *the State of Vermont.* **4** You can refer to the government or administration of a country as the state. ▶ PHRASE **5** If you are **in a state**, you are nervous or upset and unable to control your

a
b
c
d
e
f
g
h
i
j
k
l
m
n
o
p
q
r
s
t
u
v
w
x
y
z

emotions. ➤ ADJECTIVE 6 A state ceremony involves the ruler or leader of a country. ➤ VERB 7 If you state something, you say it or write it, especially in a formal way.

state house state houses
NOUN In New Zealand, a house built and owned by the government and rented out.

stately home stately homes
NOUN In Britain, a very large old house which belongs to an upper-class family.

statement statements
NOUN 1 something you say or write when you give facts or information in a formal way. 2 a document provided by a bank showing all the money paid into and out of an account during a period of time.

state school state schools
NOUN a school maintained and financed by the government in which education is free.

statesman statesmen
NOUN an important and experienced politician.

static
ADJECTIVE 1 never moving or changing E.G. *The temperature remains fairly static.* ➤ NOUN 2 Static is an electrical charge caused by friction. It builds up in metal objects.

station stations stationing stationed
NOUN 1 a building and platforms where trains stop for passengers. 2 A bus or coach station is a place where some buses start their journeys. 3 A radio station is the frequency on which a particular company broadcasts. 4 In Australian and New Zealand English, a large sheep or

cattle farm. 5 OLD-FASHIONED A person's station is their position or rank in society. ➤ VERB 6 Someone who is stationed somewhere is sent there to work or do a particular job E.G. *Her husband was stationed in Vienna.*

stationary
ADJECTIVE not moving E.G. *a stationary car.*
■ fixed, motionless

stationery
NOUN Stationery is paper, pens, and other writing equipment.

statistic statistics
NOUN 1 Statistics are facts obtained by analysing numerical information. 2 Statistics is the branch of mathematics that deals with the analysis of numerical information.
statistical ADJECTIVE

statistician statisticians
Said "stat-iss-**tish**-an" NOUN a person who studies or works with statistics.

statue statues
NOUN a sculpture of a person.

stature
NOUN 1 Someone's stature is their height and size. 2 Someone's stature is also their importance and reputation E.G. *the desire to gain international stature.*

status statuses
Said "**stay**-tuss" NOUN 1 A person's status is their position and importance in society. 2 Status is also the official classification given to someone or something E.G. *I am not sure what your legal status is.*
■ (sense 1) position, prestige, standing

status quo
Said "**stay**-tuss kwoh" NOUN The status quo is the situation that exists

at a particular time E.G. *They want to keep the status quo.*

📖 a Latin expression, meaning literally 'the state in which'

statute statutes
NOUN a law.

statutory ADJECTIVE

staunch stauncher staunchest
ADJECTIVE A staunch supporter is a strong and loyal supporter.

stave staves staving staved
NOUN 1 In music, a stave is the five lines that music is written on. ▶ VERB 2 If you stave something off, you try to delay or prevent it

stay stays staying stayed
VERB 1 If you stay in a place, you do not move away from it E.G. *She stayed in bed until noon.* 2 If you stay at a hotel or a friend's house, you spend some time there as a guest or visitor. 3 If you stay in a particular state, you continue to be in it E.G. *I stayed awake the first night.* 4 In Scottish and South African English, to stay in a place can also mean to live there. ▶ NOUN 5 a short time spent somewhere E.G. *a very pleasant stay in Cornwall.*

📘 (sense 1) linger, remain

stead
NOUN; FORMAL Something that will stand someone in good stead will be useful to them in the future.

steady steadier steadiest; steadies steadying steadied
ADJECTIVE 1 continuing or developing gradually without major interruptions or changes E.G. *a steady rise in profits.* 2 firm and not shaking or wobbling E.G. *O'Brien held out a steady hand.* 3 A steady look or voice is calm and controlled.

4 Someone who is steady is sensible and reliable. ▶ VERB 5 When you steady something, you hold on to prevent it from shaking or wobbling. 6 When you steady yourself, you control and calm yourself.

steadily ADVERB

📘 (sense 2) firm, secure, stable

steak steaks
NOUN 1 Steak is good-quality beef without much fat. 2 A fish steak is a large piece of fish.

📖 from Old Norse *steik* meaning 'roast'

steal steals stealing stole stolen
VERB 1 To steal something means to take it without permission and without intending to return it. 2 To steal somewhere means to move there quietly and secretively.

📘 (sense 1) nick, purloin, take

stealth
Rhymes with "health" NOUN If you do something with stealth, you do it quietly and secretively.

stealthy ADJECTIVE   **stealthily** ADVERB

steam steams steaming steamed
NOUN 1 Steam is the hot vapour formed when water boils. ▶ ADJECTIVE 2 Steam engines are operated using steam as a means of power. ▶ VERB 3 If something steams, it gives off steam. 4 To steam food means to cook it in steam.

steamy ADJECTIVE

steam-engine steam-engines
NOUN any engine that uses the energy of steam to produce mechanical work.

steamer steamers
NOUN 1 a ship powered by steam. 2 a

a
b
c
d
e
f
g
h
i
j
k
l
m
n
o
p
q
r
s
t
u
v
w
x
y
z

A
B
C
D
E
F
G
H
I
J
K
L
M
N
O
P
Q
R
S
T
U
V
W
X
Y
Z

container with small holes in the bottom in which you steam food.

steed steeds

NOUN; LITERARY a horse.

steel steels steeling steeled

NOUN 1 Steel is a very strong metal containing mainly iron with a small amount of carbon. ▶ VERB 2 To steel yourself means to prepare to deal with something unpleasant.

steel band steel bands

NOUN a group of people who play music on special metal drums.

steep steeper steepest; steeps steeping steeped

ADJECTIVE 1 A steep slope rises sharply and is difficult to go up. 2 A steep increase is large and sudden. ▶ VERB 3 To steep something in a liquid means to soak it thoroughly.

steeply ADVERB

🔲 (sense 1) precipitous, sheer

steeped

ADJECTIVE If a person or place is steeped in a particular quality, they are deeply affected by it E.G. *an industry steeped in tradition*.

steeple steeples

NOUN a tall pointed structure on top of a church tower.

steeplechase steeplechases

NOUN a long horse race in which the horses jump over obstacles such as hedges and water jumps.

🔲 originally a race with a church steeple in sight as the goal

steer steers steering steered

VERB 1 To steer a vehicle or boat means to control it so that it goes in the right direction. 2 To steer someone towards a particular course of action means to influence and direct their behaviour or thoughts.

▶ NOUN 3 a castrated bull.

🔲 (sense 1) direct, guide, pilot

stem stems stemming stemmed

NOUN 1 The stem of a plant is the long thin central part above the ground that carries the leaves and flowers. 2 The stem of a glass is the long narrow part connecting the bowl to the base. ▶ VERB 3 If a problem stems from a particular situation, that situation is the original starting point or cause of the problem. 4 If you stem the flow of something, you restrict it or stop it from spreading E.G. *to stem the flow of refugees*.

stench stenches

NOUN a very strong, unpleasant smell.

stencil stencils stencilling stencilled

NOUN 1 a thin sheet with a cut-out pattern through which ink or paint passes to form the pattern on the surface below. ▶ VERB 2 To stencil a design on a surface means to create it using a stencil.

🔲 from Middle English *stanselen* meaning 'to decorate with bright colours'

step steps stepping stepped

NOUN 1 If you take a step, you lift your foot and put it down somewhere else. 2 one of a series of actions that you take in order to achieve something. 3 a raised flat surface, usually one that you can walk up or down. ▶ VERB 4 If you step in a particular direction, you move your foot in that direction. 5 If someone steps down or steps aside from an important position, they resign.

step-

PREFIX If a word like 'father' or 'sister'

has 'step-' in front of it, it shows that the family relationship has come about because a parent has married again E.G. *stepfather… stepsister.*

steppe steppes
Said "step" NOUN a large area of open grassland with no trees.
🔲 from Old Russian *step* meaning 'lowland'

stepping stone stepping stones
NOUN 1 Stepping stones are a line of large stones that you walk on to cross a shallow river. 2 a job or event that is regarded as a stage in your progress, especially in your career.

stereo stereos
ADJECTIVE 1 A stereo recording or music system is one in which the sound is directed through two speakers. ▶ NOUN 2 a piece of equipment that reproduces sound from records, tapes, or CDs directing the sound through two speakers.

stereotype stereotypes stereotyping stereotyped (PSHE)
NOUN 1 a fixed image or set of characteristics that people consider to represent a particular type of person or thing E.G. *the stereotype of the polite, industrious Japanese.* ▶ VERB 2 If you stereotype someone, you assume they are a particular type of person and will behave in a particular way.

sterile
ADJECTIVE 1 Sterile means completely clean and free from germs. 2 A sterile person or animal is unable to produce offspring.
sterility NOUN
🔲 (sense 1) germ-free, sterilized

sterilize sterilizes sterilizing sterilized; also spelt **sterilise**
VERB 1 To sterilize something means

to make it completely clean and free from germs, usually by boiling it or treating it with an antiseptic. 2 If a person or animal is sterilized, they have an operation that makes it impossible for them to produce offspring.

sterling
NOUN 1 Sterling is the money system of Great Britain. ▶ ADJECTIVE 2 excellent in quality E.G. *Volunteers are doing sterling work.*

stern sterner sternest; sterns
ADJECTIVE 1 very serious and strict E.G. *a stern father… a stern warning.* ▶ NOUN 2 The stern of a boat is the back part.

steroid steroids
NOUN Steroids are chemicals that occur naturally in your body. Sometimes sportsmen illegally take them as drugs to improve their performance.

stethoscope stethoscopes
NOUN a device used by doctors to listen to a patient's heart and breathing, consisting of earpieces connected to a hollow tube and a small disc.
🔲 from Greek *stēthos* meaning 'chest' and *skopein* meaning 'to look at'

stew stews stewing stewed
NOUN 1 a dish of small pieces of savoury food cooked together slowly in a liquid. ▶ VERB 2 To stew meat, vegetables, or fruit means to cook them slowly in a liquid.
🔲 from Middle English *stuen* meaning 'to take a very hot bath'

steward stewards
NOUN 1 a man who works on a ship or plane looking after passengers and serving meals. 2 a person who helps

a
b
c
d
e
f
g
h
i
j
k
l
m
n
o
p
q
r
s
t
u
v
w
x
y
z

to direct the public at a race, march, or other event.

📖 from Old English *stigweard* meaning 'hall protector'

stewardess stewardesses

NOUN a woman who works on a ship or plane looking after passengers and serving meals.

stick sticks sticking stuck

NOUN 1 a long, thin piece of wood. 2 A stick of something is a long, thin piece of it E.G. *a stick of celery*. ▶ VERB 3 If you stick a long or pointed object into something, you push it in. 4 If you stick one thing to another, you attach it with glue or sticky tape. 5 If one thing sticks to another, it becomes attached and is difficult to remove. 6 If a movable part of something sticks, it becomes fixed and will no longer move or work properly E.G. *My gears keep sticking*. 7 INFORMAL If you stick something somewhere, you put it there. 8 If you stick by someone, you continue to help and support them. 9 If you stick to something, you keep to it and do not change to something else E.G. *He should have stuck to the old ways of doing things.* 10 When people stick together, they stay together and support each other.

stick out VERB 1 If something sticks out, it projects from something else. 2 To stick out also means to be very noticeable.

stick up VERB 1 If something sticks up, it points upwards from a surface. 2 INFORMAL If you stick up for a person or principle, you support or defend them.

sticker stickers

NOUN a small piece of paper or plastic with writing or a picture on it, that you stick onto a surface.

sticking plaster sticking plasters

NOUN a small piece of fabric that you stick over a cut or sore to protect it.

stick insect stick insects

NOUN an insect with a long cylindrical body and long legs, which looks like a twig.

sticky stickier stickiest

ADJECTIVE 1 A sticky object is covered with a substance that can stick to other things E.G. *sticky hands*. 2 Sticky paper or tape has glue on one side so that you can stick it to a surface. 3 INFORMAL A sticky situation is difficult or embarrassing to deal with. 4 Sticky weather is unpleasantly hot and humid.

stiff stiffer stiffest

ADJECTIVE 1 Something that is stiff is firm and not easily bent. 2 If you feel stiff, your muscles or joints ache when you move. 3 Stiff behaviour is formal and not friendly or relaxed. 4 Stiff also means difficult or severe E.G. *stiff competition for places*. 5 A stiff drink contains a large amount of alcohol. 6 A stiff breeze is blowing strongly. ▶ ADVERB 7 INFORMAL If you are bored stiff or scared stiff, you are very bored or very scared.

stiffly ADVERB **stiffness** NOUN

stiffen stiffens stiffening stiffened

VERB 1 If you stiffen, you suddenly stop moving and your muscles become tense E.G. *I stiffened with tension.* 2 If your joints or muscles stiffen, they become sore and difficult to bend or move. 3 If fabric or material is stiffened, it is made firmer so that it does not bend easily.

stifle stifles stifling stifled
Said "sty-fl" VERB 1 If the atmosphere stifles you, you feel you cannot breathe properly. 2 To stifle something means to stop it from happening or continuing E.G. *Martin stifled a yawn.*
stifling ADJECTIVE

stigma stigmas
NOUN If something has a stigma attached to it, people consider it unacceptable or a disgrace E.G. *the stigma of mental illness.*

stile stiles
NOUN a step on either side of a wall or fence to enable you to climb over.

stiletto stilettos
NOUN Stilettos are women's shoes with very high, narrow heels.
🔳 from Italian *stilo* meaning 'dagger', because of the shape of the heels

still stiller stillest; stills
ADVERB 1 If a situation still exists, it has continued to exist and it exists now. 2 If something could still happen, it might happen although it has not happened yet. 3 'Still' emphasizes that something is the case in spite of other things E.G. *Whatever you think of him, he's still your father.* ▶ ADVERB OR ADJECTIVE 4 Still means staying in the same position without moving E.G. *Sit still… The air was still.* ▶ ADJECTIVE 5 A still place is quiet and peaceful with no signs of activity. ▶ NOUN 6 a photograph taken from a cinema film or video.
stillness NOUN

stillborn
ADJECTIVE A stillborn baby is dead when it is born.

stilt stilts
NOUN 1 Stilts are long upright poles on which a building is built, for example on wet land. 2 Stilts are also two long pieces of wood or metal on which people balance and walk.

stilted
ADJECTIVE formal, unnatural, and rather awkward E.G. *a stilted conversation.*

stimulant stimulants
NOUN a drug or other substance that makes your body work faster, increasing your heart rate and making it difficult to sleep.

stimulate stimulates stimulating stimulated
VERB 1 To stimulate something means to encourage it to begin or develop E.G. *to stimulate discussion.* 2 If something stimulates you, it gives you new ideas and enthusiasm.
stimulating ADJECTIVE **stimulation** NOUN
🔳 (sense 1) arouse, encourage, inspire

stimulus stimuli
NOUN something that causes a process or event to begin or develop.

sting stings stinging stung
VERB 1 If a creature or plant stings you, it pricks your skin and injects a substance which causes pain. 2 If a part of your body stings, you feel a sharp tingling pain there. 3 If someone's remarks sting you, they make you feel upset and hurt. ▶ NOUN 4 A creature's sting is the part it stings you with.
🔳 (sense 2) hurt, smart

stink stinks stinking stank stunk
VERB 1 Something that stinks smells very unpleasant. ▶ NOUN 2 a very unpleasant smell.
🔳 (sense 2) pong, stench

a
b
c
d
e
f
g
h
i
j
k
l
m
n
o
p
q
r
s
t
u
v
w
x
y
z

A
B
C
D
E
F
G
H
I
J
K
L
M
N
O
P
Q
R
S
T
U
V
W
X
Y
Z

stint stints

NOUN a period of time spent doing a particular job E.G. *a three-year stint in the army*.

stipulate stipulates stipulating stipulated

VERB; FORMAL If you stipulate that something must be done, you state clearly that it must be done. **stipulation** NOUN

stir stirs stirring stirred

VERB 1 When you stir a liquid, you move it around using a spoon or a stick. 2 To stir means to move slightly. 3 If something stirs you, it makes you feel strong emotions E.G. *The power of the singing stirred me.* ▶ NOUN 4 If an event causes a stir, it causes general excitement or shock E.G. *two books which have caused a stir*.

stirring stirrings

ADJECTIVE 1 causing excitement, emotion, and enthusiasm E.G. *a stirring account of the action.* ▶ NOUN 2 If there is a stirring of emotion, people begin to feel it.

stirrup stirrups

NOUN Stirrups are two metal loops hanging by leather straps from a horse's saddle, which you put your feet in when riding.

stitch stitches stitching stitched

VERB 1 When you stitch pieces of material together, you use a needle and thread to sew them together. 2 To stitch a wound means to use a special needle and thread to hold the edges of skin together. ▶ NOUN 3 one of the pieces of thread that can be seen where material has been sewn. 4 one of the pieces of thread that can be seen where a

wound has been stitched E.G. *He had eleven stitches in his lip.* 5 If you have a stitch, you feel a sharp pain at the side of your abdomen, usually because you have been running or laughing.

stoat stoats

NOUN a small wild animal with a long body and brown fur.

stock stocks stocking stocked

NOUN 1 Stocks are shares bought as an investment in a company; also the amount of money raised by the company through the issue of shares. 2 A shop's stock is the total amount of goods it has for sale. 3 If you have a stock of things, you have a supply ready for use. 4 The stock an animal or person comes from is the type of animal or person they are descended from E.G. *She was descended from Scots Highland stock.* 5 Stock is farm animals. 6 Stock is a liquid made from boiling meat, bones, or vegetables together in water. Stock is used as a base for soups, stews, and sauces. ▶ VERB 7 A shop that stocks particular goods keeps a supply of them to sell. 8 If you stock a shelf or cupboard, you fill it with food or other things.
▶ ADJECTIVE 9 A stock expression or way of doing something is one that is commonly used.

stock up VERB If you stock up with something, you buy a supply of it.

stockbroker stockbrokers

NOUN A stockbroker is a person whose job is to buy and sell shares for people who want to invest money.

stock exchange stock exchanges

NOUN a place where there is trading in

stocks and shares E.G. *the New York Stock Exchange.*

stocking stockings
NOUN Stockings are long pieces of thin clothing that cover a woman's leg.

stockman stockmen
NOUN a man who looks after sheep or cattle on a farm.

stock market stock markets
NOUN The stock market is the organization and activity involved in buying and selling stocks and shares.

stockpile stockpiles stockpiling stockpiled
VERB 1 If someone stockpiles something, they store large quantities of it for future use. ▶ NOUN 2 a large store of something.

stocktaking
NOUN Stocktaking is the counting and checking of all a shop's or business's goods.

stocky stockier stockiest
ADJECTIVE A stocky person is rather short, but broad and solid-looking.

stoke stokes stoking stoked
VERB To stoke a fire means to keep it burning by moving or adding fuel.

stomach stomachs stomaching stomached
NOUN 1 Your stomach is the organ inside your body where food is digested. 2 You can refer to the front part of your body below your waist as your stomach. ▶ VERB 3 If you cannot stomach something, you strongly dislike it and cannot accept it.

stone stones stoning stoned
NOUN 1 Stone is the hard solid substance found in the ground and used for building. 2 a small piece of rock. 3 The stone in a fruit such as a plum or cherry is the large seed in the centre. 4 a unit of weight equal to 14 pounds or about 6.35 kilograms. 5 You can refer to a jewel as a stone E.G. *a diamond ring with three stones.* ▶ VERB 6 To stone something or someone means to throw stones at them.

stoned
ADJECTIVE; INFORMAL affected by drugs.

stony stonier stoniest
ADJECTIVE 1 Stony ground is rough and contains a lot of stones or rocks. 2 If someone's expression is stony, it shows no friendliness or sympathy.

stool stools
NOUN 1 a seat with legs but no back or arms. 2 a lump of faeces.

stoop stoops stooping stooped
VERB 1 If you stoop, you stand or walk with your shoulders bent forwards. 2 If you would not stoop to something, you would not disgrace yourself by doing it.

stop stops stopping stopped
VERB 1 If you stop doing something, you no longer do it. 2 If an activity or process stops, it comes to an end or no longer happens. 3 If a machine stops, it no longer functions or it is switched off. 4 To stop something means to prevent it. 5 If people or things that are moving stop, they no longer move. 6 If you stop somewhere, you stay there for a short while. ▶ PHRASE 7 To **put a stop to** something means to prevent it from happening or continuing. ▶ NOUN 8 a place where a bus, train, or other vehicle stops during a journey. 9 If something that is moving comes to a stop, it no longer moves.
■ (sense 1) cease, desist, halt

a
b
c
d
e
f
g
h
i
j
k
l
m
n
o
p
q
r
s
t
u
v
w
x
y
z

stoppage stoppages
NOUN If there is a stoppage, people stop work because of a disagreement with their employer.

stopper stoppers
NOUN a piece of glass or cork that fits into the neck of a jar or bottle.

stopwatch stopwatches
NOUN a watch that can be started and stopped by pressing buttons, which is used to time events.

storage
NOUN The storage of something is the keeping of it somewhere until it is needed.

store stores storing stored
NOUN 1 a shop. 2 A store of something is a supply kept for future use. 3 a place where things are kept while they are not used. ▸ VERB 4 When you store something somewhere, you keep it there until it is needed.
▸ PHRASE 5 Something that is **in store for** you is going to happen to you in the future.
◼ (sense 1) hoard, stockpile, supply

storeroom storerooms
NOUN a room where things are kept until they are needed.

storey storeys
NOUN A storey of a building is one of its floors or levels.

stork storks
NOUN a very large white and black bird with long red legs and a long bill.

storm storms storming stormed
NOUN 1 When there is a storm, there is heavy rain, a strong wind, and often thunder and lightning. 2 If something causes a storm, it causes an angry or excited reaction E.G. *His words caused a storm of protest.* ▸ VERB 3 If someone storms out, they leave quickly, noisily, and angrily. 4 To storm means to say something in a loud, angry voice E.G. *'It's a fiasco!' he stormed.* 5 If people storm a place, they attack it.

stormy ADJECTIVE

story stories
NOUN 1 a description of imaginary people and events written or told to entertain people. 2 The story of something or someone is an account of the important events that have happened to them E.G. *his life story.*
◼ anecdote, tale, yarn

stout stouter stoutest
ADJECTIVE 1 rather fat. 2 thick, strong, and sturdy E.G. *stout walking shoes.* 3 determined, firm, and strong E.G. *He can outrun the stoutest opposition.*

stoutly ADVERB

stove stoves
NOUN a piece of equipment for heating a room or for cooking.

stow stows stowing stowed
VERB 1 If you stow something somewhere or stow it away, you store it until it is needed. 2 If someone stows away in a ship or plane, they hide in it to go somewhere secretly without paying.

straddle straddles straddling straddled
VERB 1 If you straddle something, you stand or sit with one leg on either side of it. 2 If something straddles a place, it crosses it, linking different parts together E.G. *The town straddles a river.*

straight straighter straightest
ADJECTIVE or ADVERB 1 continuing in the same direction without curving or

bending E.G. *the straight path… Amy stared straight ahead of her.* 2 upright or level rather than sloping or bent E.G. *Keep your arms straight.* ▶ ADVERB 3 immediately and directly E.G. *We will go straight to the hotel.* ▶ ADJECTIVE 4 neat and tidy E.G. *Get this room straight.* 5 honest, frank, and direct E.G. *They wouldn't give me a straight answer.* 6 A straight choice involves only two options.

straightaway
ADVERB If you do something straightaway, you do it immediately.

straighten straightens straightening straightened
VERB 1 To straighten something means to remove any bends or curves from it. 2 To straighten something also means to make it neat and tidy. 3 To straighten out a confused situation means to organize and deal with it.

straightforward
ADJECTIVE 1 easy and involving no problems. 2 honest, open, and frank.

strain strains straining strained
NOUN 1 Strain is worry and nervous tension. 2 If a strain is put on something, it is affected by a strong force which may damage it. 3 You can refer to an aspect of someone's character, remarks, or work as a strain E.G. *There was a strain of bitterness in his voice.* 4 You can refer to distant sounds of music as strains of music. 5 A particular strain of plant is a variety of it E.G. *strains of rose.* ▶ VERB 6 To strain something means to force it or use it more than is reasonable or normal. 7 If you strain a muscle, you injure it by moving awkwardly. 8 To strain food means to pour away the liquid from it.

▄ (sense 1) anxiety, stress
▄ (sense 6) overexert, tax

strained
ADJECTIVE 1 worried and anxious. 2 If a relationship is strained, people feel unfriendly and do not trust each other.

strait straits
NOUN 1 You can refer to a narrow strip of sea as a strait or the straits E.G. *the Straits of Hormuz.* ▶ PLURAL NOUN 2 If someone is in a bad situation, you can say they are in difficult straits.

straitjacket straitjackets
NOUN a special jacket used to tie the arms of a violent person tightly around their body.

strait-laced
ADJECTIVE having a very strict and serious attitude to moral behaviour.

strand strands
NOUN 1 A strand of thread or hair is a single long piece of it. 2 You can refer to a part of a situation or idea as a strand of it E.G. *the different strands of the problem.*

stranded
ADJECTIVE If someone or something is stranded somewhere, they are stuck and cannot leave.

strange stranger strangest
ADJECTIVE 1 unusual or unexpected. 2 not known, seen, or experienced before E.G. *alone in a strange country.*
strangely ADVERB **strangeness** NOUN
▄ (sense 1) curious, odd, peculiar
▄ (sense 2) alien, new, unfamiliar

stranger strangers
NOUN 1 someone you have never met before. 2 If you are a stranger to a place or situation, you have not been there or experienced it before.

a
b
c
d
e
f
g
h
i
j
k
l
m
n
o
p
q
r
s
t
u
v
w
x
y
z

strangle strangles strangling strangled

VERB To strangle someone means to kill them by squeezing their throat. **strangulation** NOUN

strangled

ADJECTIVE A strangled sound is unclear and muffled.

stranglehold strangleholds

NOUN To have a stranglehold on something means to have control over it and prevent it from developing.

strap straps strapping strapped

NOUN 1 a narrow piece of leather or cloth, used to fasten or hold things together. ▶ VERB 2 To strap something means to fasten it with a strap.

strapping

ADJECTIVE tall, strong, and healthy-looking.

strata

the plural of **stratum**.

strategic

Said "strat-**tee**-jik" ADJECTIVE planned or intended to achieve something or to gain an advantage E.G. *a strategic plan.*

strategically ADVERB

strategy strategies

NOUN 1 a plan for achieving something. 2 Strategy is the skill of planning the best way to achieve something, especially in war. **strategist** NOUN

stratum strata

NOUN The strata in the earth's surface are the different layers of rock.

straw straws

NOUN 1 Straw is the dry, yellowish stalks from cereal crops. 2 a hollow tube of paper or plastic which you use to suck a drink into your mouth.

▶ PHRASE 3 If something is **the last straw**, it is the latest in a series of bad events and makes you feel you cannot stand any more.

strawberry strawberries

NOUN a small red fruit with tiny seeds in its skin.

stray strays straying strayed

VERB 1 When people or animals stray, they wander away from where they should be. 2 If your thoughts stray, you stop concentrating. ▶ ADJECTIVE 3 A stray dog or cat is one that has wandered away from home. 4 Stray things are separated from the main group of things of their kind E.G. *a stray piece of lettuce.* ▶ NOUN 5 a stray dog or cat.

streak streaks streaking streaked

NOUN 1 a long mark or stain. 2 If someone has a particular streak, they have that quality in their character. 3 A lucky or unlucky streak is a series of successes or failures. ▶ VERB 4 If something is streaked with a colour, it has lines of the colour in it. 5 To streak somewhere means to move there very quickly.

streaky ADJECTIVE

stream streams streaming streamed

NOUN 1 a small river. 2 You can refer to a steady flow of something as a stream E.G. *a constant stream of people.* 3 In a school, a stream is a group of children of the same age and ability. ▶ VERB 4 To stream somewhere means to move in a continuous flow in large quantities E.G. *Rain streamed down the windscreen.*

streamer streamers
NOUN a long, narrow strip of coloured paper used for decoration.

streamline streamlines streamlining streamlined
VERB 1 To streamline a vehicle, aircraft, or boat means to improve its shape so that it moves more quickly and efficiently. 2 To streamline an organization means to make it more efficient by removing parts of it.

street streets
NOUN a road in a town or village, usually with buildings along it.

strength strengths
NOUN 1 Your strength is your physical energy and the power of your muscles. 2 Strength can refer to the degree of someone's confidence or courage. 3 You can refer to power or influence as strength E.G. *The campaign against factory closures gathered strength.* 4 Someone's strengths are their good qualities and abilities. 5 The strength of an object is the degree to which it can stand rough treatment. 6 The strength of a substance is the amount of other substances that it contains E.G. *coffee with sugar and milk in it at the correct strength.* 7 The strength of a feeling or opinion is the degree to which it is felt or supported. 8 The strength of a relationship is its degree of closeness or success. 9 The strength of a group is the total number of people in it.
▶ PHRASE 10 If people do something **in strength**, a lot of them do it together E.G. *The press were here in strength.*
▤ (sense 1) might, muscle
▤ (sense 3) force, intensity, power

strengthen strengthens strengthening strengthened
VERB 1 To strengthen something means to give it more power, influence, or support and make it more likely to succeed. 2 To strengthen an object means to improve it or add to its structure so that it can withstand rough treatment.
▤ fortify, reinforce

strenuous
Said "stren-yoo-uss" ADJECTIVE involving a lot of effort or energy.
strenuously ADVERB

stress stresses stressing stressed
NOUN 1 Stress is worry and nervous tension. 2 Stresses are strong physical forces applied to an object. 3 Stress is emphasis put on a word or part of a word when it is pronounced, making it slightly louder. ▶ VERB 4 If you stress a point, you emphasize it and draw attention to its importance.
stressful ADJECTIVE
▤ (sense 1) anxiety, pressure, strain
▤ (sense 3) accent, emphasis
▤ (sense 4) accentuate, emphasize

stretch stretches stretching stretched
VERB 1 Something that stretches over an area extends that far. 2 When you stretch, you hold out part of your body as far as you can. 3 To stretch something soft or elastic means to pull it to make it longer or bigger.
▶ NOUN 4 A stretch of land or water is an area of it. 5 A stretch of time is a period of time.

stretcher stretchers
NOUN a long piece of material with a

a
b
c
d
e
f
g
h
i
j
k
l
m
n
o
p
q
r
s
t
u
v
w
x
y
z

A B C D E F G H I J K L M N O P Q R S T U V W X Y Z

pole along each side, used to carry an injured person.

strewn

ADJECTIVE If things are strewn about, they are scattered about untidily E.G. *The costumes were strewn all over the floor.*

stricken

ADJECTIVE severely affected by something unpleasant.

strict stricter strictest

ADJECTIVE 1 Someone who is strict controls other people very firmly. 2 A strict rule must always be obeyed absolutely. 3 The strict meaning of something is its precise and accurate meaning. 4 You can use 'strict' to describe someone who never breaks the rules or principles of a particular belief E.G. *a strict Muslim.*

■ (sense 1) severe, stern
■ (sense 2) stringent

strictly

ADVERB 1 Strictly means only for a particular purpose E.G. *I was in it strictly for the money.* ► PHRASE 2 You say **strictly speaking** to correct a statement or add more precise information E.G. *Somebody pointed out that, strictly speaking, electricity was a discovery, not an invention.*

stride strides striding strode stridden

VERB 1 To stride along means to walk quickly with long steps. ► NOUN 2 a long step; also the length of a step.

strident

Said "stry-dent" ADJECTIVE loud, harsh, and unpleasant.

strife

NOUN; FORMAL Strife is trouble, conflict, and disagreement.

strike strikes striking struck

NOUN 1 If there is a strike, people stop working as a protest. 2 A hunger strike is a refusal to eat anything as a protest. A rent strike is a refusal to pay rent. 3 a military attack E.G. *the threat of American air strikes.* ► VERB 4 To strike someone or something means to hit them. 5 If an illness, disaster, or enemy strikes, it suddenly affects or attacks someone. 6 If a thought strikes you, it comes into your mind. 7 If you are struck by something, you are impressed by it. 8 When a clock strikes, it makes a sound to indicate the time. 9 To strike a deal with someone means to come to an agreement with them. 10 If someone strikes oil or gold, they discover it in the ground. 11 If you strike a match, you rub it against something to make it burst into flame.

strike off VERB If a professional person is struck off for bad behaviour, their name is removed from an official register and they are not allowed to practise their profession.

strike up VERB To strike up a conversation or friendship means to begin it.

striker strikers

NOUN 1 Strikers are people who are refusing to work as a protest. 2 In soccer, a player whose function is to attack and score goals.

striking

ADJECTIVE very noticeable because of being unusual or very attractive.
strikingly ADVERB

string strings stringing strung

NOUN 1 String is thin cord made of twisted threads. 2 You can refer to a row or series of similar things as a string of them E.G. *a string of islands… a string of injuries.* **3** The strings of a musical instrument are tightly stretched lengths of wire or nylon which vibrate to produce the notes. ▶ PLURAL NOUN **4** The section of an orchestra consisting of stringed instruments is called the strings.

string along VERB INFORMAL To string someone along means to deceive them.

string out VERB **1** If things are strung out, they are spread out in a long line. **2** To string something out means to make it last longer than necessary.

stringed
ADJECTIVE A stringed instrument is one with strings, such as a guitar or violin.

stringent
ADJECTIVE Stringent laws conditions are very severe or are strictly controlled E.G. *stringent financial checks.*

stringy-bark stringy-barks
NOUN any Australian eucalypt that has bark that peels off in long, tough strands.

strip strips stripping stripped
NOUN **1** A strip of something is a long, narrow piece of it. **2** A comic strip is a series of drawings which tell a story. **3** A sports team's strip is the clothes worn by the team when playing a match. ▶ VERB **4** If you strip, you take off all your clothes. **5** To strip something means to remove whatever is covering its surface. **6** To strip someone of their property or rights means to take their property or rights away from them officially.

stripe stripes
NOUN Stripes are long, thin lines,

usually of different colours.
striped ADJECTIVE

stripper strippers
NOUN an entertainer who does striptease.

striptease
NOUN Striptease is a form of entertainment in which someone takes off their clothes gradually to music.

strive strives striving strove striven
VERB If you strive to do something, you make a great effort to achieve it.

stroke strokes stroking stroked
VERB **1** If you stroke something, you move your hand smoothly and gently over it. ▶ NOUN **2** If someone has a stroke, they suddenly lose consciousness as a result of a blockage or rupture in a blood vessel in the brain. A stroke can result in damage to speech and paralysis. **3** The strokes of a brush or pen are the movements that you make with it. **4** The strokes of a clock are the sounds that indicate the hour. **5** A swimming stroke is a particular style of swimming. ▶ PHRASE **6** If you have a **stroke of luck**, then you are lucky and something good happens to you.

stroll strolls strolling strolled
VERB **1** To stroll along means to walk slowly in a relaxed way. ▶ NOUN **2** a slow, pleasurable walk.
▤ amble, saunter, walk

stroller strollers
NOUN In Australian English, a stroller is a pushchair.

strong stronger strongest
ADJECTIVE **1** Someone who is strong has powerful muscles. **2** You also say

a b c d e f g h i j k l m n o p q r s t u v w x y z

I want to see (C) your licen**C**e (licen**c**e) **SPELLING NOTE**

that someone is strong when they are confident and have courage. **3** Strong objects are able to withstand rough treatment. **4** Strong also means great in degree or intensity E.G. *a strong wind.* **5** A strong argument or theory is supported by a lot of evidence. **6** If a group or organization is strong, it has a lot of members or influence. **7** You can use 'strong' to say how many people there are in a group E.G. *The audience was about two dozen strong.* **8** Your strong points are the things you are good at. **9** A strong economy or currency is stable and successful. **10** A strong liquid or drug contains a lot of a particular substance. ▶ ADVERB **11** If someone or something is still going strong, they are still healthy or working well after a long time.

strongly ADVERB
▣ (sense 1) muscular, powerful
▣ (sense 4) acute, intense

stronghold strongholds
NOUN **1** a place that is held and defended by an army. **2** A stronghold of an attitude or belief is a place in which the attitude or belief is strongly held E.G. *Europe's last stronghold of male dominance.*

structure structures structuring structured
NOUN **1** The structure of something is the way it is made, built, or organized. **2** something that has been built or constructed. **3** If something has structure, it is properly organized E.G. *The days have no real structure.* ▶ VERB **4** To structure something means to arrange it into an organized pattern or system.

structural ADJECTIVE **structurally** ADVERB
▣ (sense 1) arrangement, construction, make-up

struggle struggles struggling struggled
VERB **1** If you struggle to do something, you try hard to do it in difficult circumstances. **2** When people struggle, they twist and move violently during a fight. ▶ NOUN **3** Something that is a struggle is difficult to achieve and takes a lot of effort. **4** a fight.

strum strums strumming strummed
VERB To strum a guitar means to play it by moving your fingers backwards and forwards across all the strings.

strut struts strutting strutted
VERB **1** To strut means to walk in a stiff, proud way with your chest out and your head high. ▶ NOUN **2** a piece of wood or metal which strengthens or supports part of a building or structure.

Stuart Stuarts
NOUN Stuart was the family name of the monarchs who ruled Scotland from 1371 to 1714 and England from 1603 to 1714.

stub stubs stubbing stubbed
NOUN **1** The stub of a pencil or cigarette is the short piece that remains when the rest has been used. **2** The stub of a cheque or ticket is the small part that you keep. ▶ VERB **3** If you stub your toe, you hurt it by accidentally kicking something.

stubble
NOUN **1** The short stalks remaining in the ground after a crop is harvested are called stubble. **2** If a man has

stubble on his face, he has very short hair growing there because he has not shaved recently.

stubborn

ADJECTIVE **1** Someone who is stubborn is determined not to change their opinion or course of action. **2** A stubborn stain is difficult to remove. **stubbornly** ADVERB **stubbornness** NOUN

≡ (sense 1) inflexible, obstinate, pig-headed

stuck

ADJECTIVE **1** If something is stuck in a particular position, it is fixed or jammed and cannot be moved E.G. His car's stuck in a snowdrift. **2** If you are stuck, you are unable to continue what you were doing because it is too difficult. **3** If you are stuck somewhere, you are unable to get away.

stuck-up

ADJECTIVE; INFORMAL proud and conceited.

stud studs

NOUN **1** a small piece of metal fixed into something. **2** A male horse or other animal that is kept for stud is kept for breeding purposes.

studded

ADJECTIVE decorated with small pieces of metal or precious stones.

student students

NOUN a person studying at university or college.

studied

ADJECTIVE A studied action or response has been carefully planned and is not natural E.G. She sipped her glass of white wine with studied boredom.

studio studios

NOUN **1** a room where a photographer or painter works. **2** a room

containing special equipment where records, films, or radio or television programmes are made.

studious

Said "styoo-dee-uss" ADJECTIVE spending a lot of time studying.

studiously

ADVERB carefully and deliberately E.G. She was studiously ignoring me.

study studies studying studied

VERB **1** If you study a particular subject, you spend time learning about it. **2** If you study something, you look at it carefully E.G. He studied the map in silence. ▶ NOUN **3** Study is the activity of studying a subject E.G. the serious study of medieval archaeology. **4** Studies are subjects which are studied E.G. media studies. **5** a piece of research on a particular subject E.G. a detailed study of the world's most violent people. **6** a room used for writing and studying.

stuff stuffs stuffing stuffed

NOUN **1** You can refer to a substance or group of things as stuff. ▶ VERB **2** If you stuff something somewhere, you push it there quickly and roughly. **3** If you stuff something with a substance or objects, you fill it with the substance or objects.

stuffing

NOUN Stuffing is a mixture of small pieces of food put inside poultry or a vegetable before it is cooked.

stuffy stuffier stuffiest

ADJECTIVE **1** very formal and old-fashioned. **2** If it is stuffy in a room, there is not enough fresh air.

≡ (sense 2) airless, close, fusty

stumble stumbles stumbling stumbled

VERB **1** If you stumble while you are

a
b
c
d
e
f
g
h
i
j
k
l
m
n
o
p
q
r
s
t
u
v
w
x
y
z

walking or running, you trip and almost fall. **2** If you stumble when speaking, you make mistakes when pronouncing the words. **3** If you stumble across something or stumble on it, you find it unexpectedly.

stump stumps stumping stumped

NOUN **1** a small part of something that is left when the rest has been removed E.G. *the stump of a dead tree*. **2** In cricket, the stumps are the three upright wooden sticks that support the bails, forming the wicket. ▶ VERB **3** If a question or problem stumps you, you cannot think of an answer or solution.

stun stuns stunning stunned

VERB **1** If you are stunned by something, you are very shocked by it. **2** To stun a person or animal means to knock them unconscious with a blow to the head.

stunning

ADJECTIVE very beautiful or impressive E.G. *a stunning first novel*.

stunt stunts stunting stunted

NOUN **1** an unusual or dangerous and exciting action that someone does to get publicity or as part of a film. ▶ VERB **2** To stunt the growth or development of something means to prevent it from developing as it should.

stupendous

ADJECTIVE very large or impressive E.G. *a stupendous amount of money*.

stupid stupider stupidest

ADJECTIVE showing lack of good judgment or intelligence and not at all sensible.

stupidity NOUN

■ foolish, obtuse, unintelligent

sturdy sturdier sturdiest

ADJECTIVE strong and firm and unlikely to be damaged or injured E.G. *a sturdy chest of drawers*.

sturgeon

Said "stur-jon" NOUN a large edible fish, the eggs of which are also eaten and are known as caviar.

stutter stutters stuttering stuttered

NOUN **1** Someone who has a stutter finds it difficult to speak smoothly and often repeats sounds through being unable to complete a word. ▶ VERB **2** When someone stutters, they hesitate or repeat sounds when speaking.

sty sties

NOUN a pigsty.

stye styes

NOUN an infection in the form of a small red swelling on a person's eyelid.

style styles styling styled

NOUN **1** The style of something is the general way in which it is done or presented, often showing the attitudes of the people involved. **2** A person or place that has style is smart, elegant, and fashionable. **3** The style of something is its design E.G. *new windows that fit in with the style of the house*. ▶ VERB **4** To style a piece of clothing or a person's hair means to design and create its shape.

■ (sense 2) elegance, flair, panache

stylish

ADJECTIVE smart, elegant, and fashionable.

stylishly ADVERB

■ chic, smart

A B C D E F G H I J K L M N O P Q R S T U V W X Y Z

suave

Said "swahv" ADJECTIVE charming, polite, and confident E.G. *a suave Italian.*

sub-

PREFIX 1 'Sub-' is used at the beginning of words that have 'under' as part of their meaning E.G. *submarine.*
2 'Sub-' is also used to form nouns that refer to the parts into which something is divided E.G. *Subsection 2 of section 49… a particular subgroup of citizens.*

📖 from Latin *sub* meaning 'under' or 'below'

subconscious

NOUN 1 Your subconscious is the part of your mind that can influence you without your being aware of it.
▶ ADJECTIVE 2 happening or existing in someone's subconscious and therefore not directly realized or understood by them E.G. *a subconscious fear of rejection.*
subconsciously ADVERB

subcontinent subcontinents

NOUN a large mass of land, often consisting of several countries, and forming part of a continent E.G. *the Indian subcontinent.*

subdue subdues subduing subdued

VERB 1 If soldiers subdue a group of people, they bring them under control by using force E.G. *It would be quite impossible to subdue the whole continent.* 2 To subdue a colour, light, or emotion means to make it less bright or strong.
■ (sense 1) control, overcome, quell

subdued

ADJECTIVE 1 rather quiet and sad. 2 not very noticeable or bright.

subject subjects subjecting subjected

NOUN 1 The subject of writing or a conversation is the thing or person being discussed. 2 In grammar, the subject is the word or words representing the person or thing doing the action expressed by the verb. For example, in the sentence 'My cat keeps catching birds', 'my cat' is the subject. 3 an area of study.
4 The subjects of a country are the people who live there. ▶ VERB 5 To subject someone to something means to make them experience it E.G. *He was subjected to constant interruption.* ▶ ADJECTIVE 6 Someone or something that is subject to something is affected by it E.G. *He was subject to attacks at various times.*

subjective

ADJECTIVE influenced by personal feelings and opinion rather than based on fact or rational thought.

subjunctive

NOUN In grammar, the subjunctive or subjunctive mood is one of the forms a verb can take. It is used to express attitudes such as wishing and doubting.

sublime

ADJECTIVE Something that is sublime is wonderful and affects people emotionally E.G. *sublime music.*

submarine submarines

NOUN a ship that can travel beneath the surface of the sea.

submerge submerges submerging submerged

VERB 1 To submerge means to go beneath the surface of a liquid. 2 If you submerge yourself in an activity, you become totally involved in it.

a
b
c
d
e
f
g
h
i
j
k
l
m
n
o
p
q
r
s
t
u
v
w
x
y
z

A
B
C
D
E
F
G
H
I
J
K
L
M
N
O
P
Q
R
S
T
U
V
W
X
Y
Z

submission submissions

NOUN **1** Submission is a state in which someone accepts the control of another person E.G. *Now he must beat us into submission.* **2** The submission of a proposal or application is the act of sending it for consideration.

submissive

ADJECTIVE behaving in a quiet, obedient way.

submit submits submitting submitted

VERB **1** If you submit to something, you accept it because you are not powerful enough to resist it. **2** If you submit an application or proposal, you send it to someone for consideration.

subordinate subordinates subordinating subordinated

NOUN **1** A person's subordinate is someone who is in a less important position than them. ▶ ADJECTIVE **2** If one thing is subordinate to another, it is less important E.G. *Non-elected officials are subordinate to elected leaders.* ▶ VERB **3** To subordinate one thing to another means to treat it as being less important.

subordinate clause subordinate clauses

NOUN (ENGLISH) In grammar, a subordinate clause is a clause which adds details to the main clause of a sentence.

subscribe subscribes subscribing subscribed

VERB **1** If you subscribe to a particular belief or opinion, you support it or agree with it. **2** If you subscribe to a magazine, you pay to receive regular copies.

subscriber NOUN

subscription subscriptions

NOUN a sum of money that you pay regularly to belong to an organization or to receive regular copies of a magazine.

subsequent

ADJECTIVE happening or coming into existence at a later time than something else E.G. *the December uprising and the subsequent political violence.*

subsequently ADVERB

subservient

ADJECTIVE Someone who is subservient does whatever other people want them to do.

subside subsides subsiding subsided

VERB **1** To subside means to become less intense or quieter E.G. *Her excitement suddenly subsided.* **2** If water or the ground subsides, it sinks to a lower level.

subsidence

NOUN If a place is suffering from subsidence, parts of the ground have sunk to a lower level.

subsidiary subsidiaries

Said "sub-**sid**-yer-ee" NOUN **1** a company which is part of a larger company. ▶ ADJECTIVE **2** treated as being of less importance and additional to another thing E.G. *Drama is offered as a subsidiary subject.*

subsidize subsidizes subsidizing subsidized; also spelt **subsidise**

VERB To subsidize something means to provide part of the cost of it E.G. *He feels the government should do much more to subsidize films.*

subsidized ADJECTIVE

subsidy subsidies
NOUN a sum of money paid to help support a company or provide a public service.

substance substances
NOUN 1 Anything which is a solid, a powder, a liquid, or a paste can be referred to as a substance. 2 If a speech or piece of writing has substance, it is meaningful or important E.G. *a good speech, but there was no substance.*
■ (sense 1) material, stuff

substantial
ADJECTIVE 1 very large in degree or amount E.G. *a substantial pay rise.* 2 large and strongly built E.G. *a substantial stone building.*

substantially
ADVERB Something that is substantially true is generally or mostly true.

substitute substitutes substituting substituted
VERB 1 To substitute one thing for another means to use it instead of the other thing or to put it in the other thing's place. ▶ NOUN 2 If one thing is a substitute for another, it is used instead of it or put in its place.
substitution NOUN
■ (sense 1) exchange, replace
■ (sense 2) alternative, replacement, surrogate

subterfuge subterfuges
Said "sub-ter-fyooj" NOUN Subterfuge is the use of deceitful or dishonest methods.
▥ from Latin *subterfugere* meaning 'to escape by stealth'

subtitle subtitles
NOUN A film with subtitles has a printed translation of the dialogue at the bottom of the screen.

subtle subtler subtlest
Said "sut-tl" ADJECTIVE 1 very fine, delicate, or small in degree E.G. *a subtle change.* 2 using indirect methods to achieve something.
subtly ADVERB **subtlety** NOUN

subtract subtracts subtracting subtracted
VERB If you subtract one number from another, you take away the first number from the second.

subtraction subtractions
NOUN (MATHS) Subtraction is subtracting one number from another, or a sum in which you do this.

suburb suburbs
NOUN an area of a town or city that is away from its centre.

suburban
ADJECTIVE 1 relating to a suburb or suburbs. 2 dull and conventional.

suburbia
NOUN You can refer to the suburbs of a city as suburbia.

subversive subversives
ADJECTIVE 1 intended to destroy or weaken a political system E.G. *subversive activities.* ▶ NOUN 2 Subversives are people who try to destroy or weaken a political system.
subversion NOUN

subvert subverts subverting subverted
VERB; FORMAL To subvert something means to cause it to weaken or fail E.G. *a cunning campaign to subvert the music industry.*

subway subways
NOUN 1 a footpath that goes underneath a road. 2 an underground railway.

a
b
c
d
e
f
g
h
i
j
k
l
m
n
o
p
q
r
s
t
u
v
w
x
y
z

A
B
C
D
E
F
G
H
I
J
K
L
M
N
O
P
Q
R
S
T
U
V
W
X
Y
Z

succeed succeeds succeeding succeeded

VERB **1** To succeed means to achieve the result you intend. **2** To succeed someone means to be the next person to have their job. **3** If one thing succeeds another, it comes after it in time E.G. *The explosion was succeeded by a crash.*

succeeding ADJECTIVE

■ (sense 1) be successful, do well, make it

success successes

NOUN **1** Success is the achievement of something you have been trying to do. **2** Someone who is a success has achieved an important position or made a lot of money.

successful ADJECTIVE **successfully** ADVERB

succession successions

NOUN **1** A succession of things is a number of them occurring one after the other. **2** When someone becomes the next person to have an important position, you can refer to this event as their succession to this position E.G. *his succession to the throne.* ► PHRASE **3** If something happens a number of weeks, months, or years **in succession**, it happens that number of times without a break E.G. *Borg won Wimbledon five years in succession.*

successive

ADJECTIVE occurring one after the other without a break E.G. *three successive victories.*

successor successors

NOUN Someone's successor is the person who takes their job when they leave.

succinct

Said "suk-**singkt**" ADJECTIVE expressing something clearly and in very few words.

succinctly ADVERB

succulent

ADJECTIVE Succulent food is juicy and delicious.

succumb succumbs succumbing succumbed

VERB If you succumb to something, you are unable to resist it any longer E.G. *She never succumbed to his charms.*

such

ADJECTIVE OR PRONOUN **1** You use 'such' to refer to the person or thing you have just mentioned, or to someone or something similar E.G. *Naples or Palermo or some such place.* ► PHRASE **2** You can use **such as** to introduce an example of something E.G. *herbal teas such as camomile.* **3** You can use **such as it is** to indicate that something is not great in quality or quantity E.G. *The action, such as it is, is set in Egypt.* **4** You can use **such and such** when you want to refer to something that is not specific E.G. *A good trick is to ask whether they have seen such and such a film.* ► ADJECTIVE **5** 'Such' can be used for emphasizing E.G. *I have such a terrible sense of guilt.*

suchlike

ADJECTIVE OR PRONOUN used to refer to things similar to those already mentioned E.G. *shampoos, talcs, toothbrushes, and suchlike.*

suck sucks sucking sucked

VERB **1** If you suck something, you hold it in your mouth and pull at it with your cheeks and tongue, usually to get liquid out of it. **2** To suck something in a particular direction means to draw it there with a powerful force. **3** INFORMAL To suck up to someone means to do things to please them in order to obtain praise or approval.

sucker suckers

NOUN **1** INFORMAL If you call someone a sucker, you mean that they are easily fooled or cheated. **2** Suckers are pads on the bodies of some animals and insects which they use to cling to a surface.

suckle suckles suckling suckled

VERB When a mother suckles a baby, she feeds it with milk from her breast.

sucrose

Said "**syoo**-kroze" NOUN; TECHNICAL Sucrose is sugar in crystalline form found in sugar cane and sugar beet.

suction

NOUN **1** Suction is the force involved when a substance is drawn or sucked from one place to another. **2** Suction is the process by which two surfaces stick together when the air between them is removed E.G. *They stay there by suction.*

Sudanese

Said "soo-dan-**neez**" ADJECTIVE
1 belonging or relating to the Sudan.
▶ NOUN **2** someone who comes from the Sudan.

sudden

ADJECTIVE happening quickly and unexpectedly E.G. *a sudden cry.*
suddenly ADVERB **suddenness** NOUN

sue sues suing sued

VERB To sue someone means to start a legal case against them, usually to claim money from them.

suede

Said "swayd" NOUN Suede is a thin, soft leather with a rough surface.
📖 from French *gants de Suède* meaning 'gloves from Sweden'

suffer suffers suffering suffered

VERB **1** If someone is suffering pain, or suffering as a result of an unpleasant situation, they are badly affected by it. **2** If something suffers as a result of neglect or a difficult situation, its condition or quality becomes worse E.G. *The bus service is suffering.*
sufferer NOUN **suffering** NOUN

suffice suffices sufficing sufficed

VERB; FORMAL If something suffices, it is enough or adequate for a purpose.

sufficient

ADJECTIVE If a supply or quantity is sufficient for a purpose, there is enough of it available.
sufficiently ADVERB

suffix suffixes

NOUN (ENGLISH) a group of letters which is added to the end of a word to form a new word, for example '-ology' or '-itis'.

suffocate suffocates suffocating suffocated

VERB To suffocate means to die as a result of having too little air or oxygen to breathe.
suffocation NOUN

suffrage

NOUN Suffrage is the right to vote in political elections.

suffragette suffragettes

NOUN a woman who, at the beginning of the 20th century, campaigned for women to be given the right to vote.

suffused

ADJECTIVE; LITERARY If something is

a
b
c
d
e
f
g
h
i
j
k
l
m
n
o
p
q
r
s
t
u
v
w
x
y
z

suffused with light or colour, light or colour has gradually spread over it.

sugar

NOUN Sugar is a sweet substance used to sweeten food and drinks.

suggest suggests suggesting suggested

VERB **1** If you suggest a plan or idea to someone, you mention it as a possibility for them to consider. **2** If something suggests a particular thought or impression, it makes you think in that way or gives you that impression E.G. *Nothing you say suggests he is mentally ill.*

▪ (sense 1) advocate, propose, recommend

▪ (sense 2) hint, imply

suggestion suggestions

NOUN **1** a plan or idea that is mentioned as a possibility for someone to consider. **2** A suggestion of something is a very slight indication or faint sign of it E.G. *a suggestion of dishonesty.*

▪ (sense 1) proposal, recommendation

suggestive

ADJECTIVE **1** Something that is suggestive of a particular thing gives a slight hint or sign of it.

2 Suggestive remarks or gestures make people think about sex.

▪ (sense 2) risqué, smutty

suicidal

ADJECTIVE **1** People who are suicidal want to kill themselves. **2** Suicidal behaviour is so dangerous that it is likely to result in death E.G. *a mad suicidal attack.*

suicide

NOUN People who commit suicide deliberately kill themselves.

🏛 from Latin *sui* meaning 'of oneself' and *caedere* meaning 'to kill'

suit suits suiting suited

NOUN **1** a matching jacket and trousers or skirt. **2** In a court of law, a suit is a legal action taken by one person against another. **3** one of four different types of card in a pack of playing cards. The four suits are hearts, clubs, diamonds, and spades.

▸ VERB **4** If a situation or course of action suits you, it is appropriate or acceptable for your purpose. **5** If a piece of clothing or a colour suits you, you look good when you are wearing it. **6** If you do something to suit yourself, you do it because you want to and without considering other people.

suitable

ADJECTIVE right or acceptable for a particular purpose or occasion.

suitability NOUN **suitably** ADVERB

▪ appropriate, apt, fitting

suitcase suitcases

NOUN a case in which you carry your clothes when you are travelling.

suite suites

Said "**sweet**" NOUN **1** In a hotel, a suite is a set of rooms. **2** a set of matching furniture or bathroom fittings.

suited

ADJECTIVE right or appropriate for a particular purpose or person E.G. *He is well suited to be minister for the arts.*

suitor suitors

NOUN; OLD-FASHIONED A woman's suitor is a man who wants to marry her.

sulk sulks sulking sulked

VERB Someone who is sulking is showing their annoyance by being silent and moody.

sulky ADJECTIVE

sullen
ADJECTIVE behaving in a bad-tempered and disagreeably silent way E.G. *a sullen and resentful workforce.*

sulphur
NOUN Sulphur is a pale yellow nonmetallic element which burns with a very unpleasant smell.

sultan sultans
NOUN In some Muslim countries, the ruler of the country is called the sultan.
🏛 from Arabic *sultan* meaning 'rule'

sultana sultanas
NOUN 1 a dried grape. 2 the wife of a sultan.

sum sums summing summed
NOUN 1 an amount of money. 2 In arithmetic, a sum is a calculation. 3 The sum of something is the total amount of it.
sum up VERB If you sum something up, you briefly describe its main points.

summarize summarizes summarizing summarized; also spelt **summarise**
VERB (EXAM TERM) To summarize something means to give a short account of its main points.

summary summaries
NOUN 1 A summary of something is a short account of its main points.
▶ ADJECTIVE 2 A summary action is done without delay or careful thought E.G. *Summary executions are common.*
summarily ADVERB
📇 (sense 1) précis, résumé, synopsis

summer summers
NOUN Summer is the season between spring and autumn.

summit summits
NOUN 1 The summit of a mountain is its top. 2 a meeting between leaders of different countries to discuss particular issues.

summon summons summoning summoned
VERB 1 If someone summons you, they order you to go to them. 2 If you summon up strength or energy, you make a great effort to be strong or energetic.

summons summonses
NOUN 1 an official order to appear in court. 2 an order to go to someone E.G. *The result was a summons to headquarters.*

sumptuous
ADJECTIVE Something that is sumptuous is magnificent and obviously very expensive.

sum total
NOUN The sum total of a number of things is all of them added or considered together.

sun suns sunning sunned
NOUN 1 The sun is the star providing heat and light for the planets revolving around it in our solar system. 2 You refer to heat and light from the sun as sun E.G. *We need a bit of sun.* ▶ VERB 3 If you sun yourself, you sit in the sunshine.

sunbathe sunbathes sunbathing sunbathed
VERB If you sunbathe, you sit in the sunshine to get a suntan.

sunburn
NOUN Sunburn is sore red skin on someone's body due to too much exposure to the rays of the sun.
sunburnt ADJECTIVE

sundae sundaes
Said "sun-day" NOUN a dish of ice cream with cream and fruit or nuts.

a
b
c
d
e
f
g
h
i
j
k
l
m
n
o
p
q
r
s
t
u
v
w
x
y
z

Sunday Sundays
NOUN Sunday is the day between Saturday and Monday.
📖 from Old English *sunnandæg* meaning 'day of the sun'

Sunday school Sunday schools
NOUN Sunday school is a special class held on Sundays to teach children about Christianity.

sundial sundials
NOUN an object used for telling the time, consisting of a pointer which casts a shadow on a flat base marked with the hours.

sundry
ADJECTIVE 1 'Sundry' is used to refer to several things or people of various sorts E.G. *sundry journalists and lawyers.* ▶ PHRASE 2 **All and sundry** means everyone.

sunflower sunflowers
NOUN a tall plant with very large yellow flowers.

sunglasses
PLURAL NOUN Sunglasses are spectacles with dark lenses that you wear to protect your eyes from the sun.

sunken
ADJECTIVE 1 having sunk to the bottom of the sea, a river, or lake E.G. *sunken ships.* 2 A sunken object or area has been constructed below the level of the surrounding area E.G. *a sunken garden.* 3 curving inwards E.G. *Her cheeks were sunken.*

sunlight
NOUN Sunlight is the bright light produced when the sun is shining.
sunlit ADJECTIVE

sunny sunnier sunniest
ADJECTIVE When it is sunny, the sun is shining.

sunrise sunrises
NOUN Sunrise is the time in the morning when the sun first appears, and the colours produced in the sky at that time.

sunset sunsets
NOUN Sunset is the time in the evening when the sun disappears below the horizon, and the colours produced in the sky at that time.

sunshine
NOUN Sunshine is the bright light produced when the sun is shining.

sunstroke
NOUN Sunstroke is an illness caused by spending too much time in hot sunshine.

suntan suntans
NOUN If you have a suntan, the sun has turned your skin brown.
suntanned ADJECTIVE

super
ADJECTIVE very nice or very good E.G. *a super party.*

super-
PREFIX 'Super-' is used to describe something that is larger or better than similar things E.G. *a European superstate.*
📖 from Latin *super* meaning 'above'

superb
ADJECTIVE very good indeed.
superbly ADVERB

supercilious
Said "soo-per-**sill**-ee-uss" ADJECTIVE If you are supercilious, you behave in a scornful way towards other people because you think they are inferior to you.

superego
NOUN; TECHNICAL Your superego is the part of your mind that controls your ideas of right and wrong and produces feelings of guilt.

A B C D E F G H I J K L M N O P Q R S T U V W X Y Z

superficial
ADJECTIVE **1** involving only the most obvious or most general aspects of something E.G. *a superficial knowledge of music*. **2** not having a deep, serious, or genuine interest in anything E.G. *a superficial and rather silly woman*. **3** Superficial wounds are not very deep or severe.
superficially ADVERB

superfluous
Said "soo-per-floo-uss" ADJECTIVE; FORMAL unnecessary or no longer needed.

superhuman
ADJECTIVE having much greater power or ability than is normally expected of humans E.G. *superhuman strength*.

superimpose superimposes superimposing superimposed
VERB To superimpose one image on another means to put the first image on top of the other so that they are seen as one image.

superintendent superintendents
NOUN **1** a police officer above the rank of inspector. **2** a person whose job is to be responsible for a particular thing E.G. *the superintendent of prisons*.

superior superiors
ADJECTIVE **1** better or of higher quality than other similar things. **2** in a position of higher authority than another person. **3** showing too much pride and self-importance E.G. *Jerry smiled in a superior way*. ► NOUN **4** Your superiors are people who are in a higher position than you in society or an organization.
superiority NOUN

superlative superlatives
Said "soo-per-lat-tiv" NOUN **1** In grammar, the superlative is the form of an adjective which indicates that the person or thing described has more of a particular quality than anyone or anything else. For example, 'quickest', 'best', and 'easiest' are all superlatives. ► ADJECTIVE **2** FORMAL very good indeed E.G. *a superlative performance*.

What is a Superlative?

Many adjectives have three different forms. These are known as the **positive**, the **comparative**, and the **superlative**. The comparative and superlative are used when you make comparisons.

The **positive** form of an adjective is given as the entry in the dictionary. It is used when there is no comparison between different objects:
  E.G. *Matthew is tall*.

The **superlative** form is usually made by adding the ending *-est* to the positive form of the adjective. It shows that something possesses a quality to a greater extent than all the others in its class or group:
  E.G. *Matthew is the **tallest** boy in his class*.

You can also express superlatives by using the words *most* or *least* with the positive (not the superlative) form of the adjective:
  E.G. *Matthew is the **most energetic** member of the family*.

Also look at the grammar box at **comparative**.

---

supermarket supermarkets
NOUN a shop selling food and household goods arranged so that

you can help yourself and pay for everything at a till by the exit.

supernatural

ADJECTIVE 1 Something that is supernatural, for example ghosts or witchcraft, cannot be explained by normal scientific laws. ► NOUN 2 You can refer to supernatural things as the supernatural.

superpower superpowers

NOUN a very powerful and influential country such as the USA.

supersede supersedes superseding superseded

Said "soo-per-seed" VERB If something supersedes another thing, it replaces it because it is more modern E.G. *New York superseded Paris as the centre for modern art.*

supersonic

ADJECTIVE A supersonic aircraft can travel faster than the speed of sound.

superstar superstars

NOUN You can refer to a very famous entertainer or sports player as a superstar.

superstition superstitions

NOUN Superstition is a belief in things like magic and powers that bring good or bad luck.

superstitious ADJECTIVE
🏛 from Latin *superstitio* meaning 'dread of the supernatural'

supervise supervises supervising supervised

VERB To supervise someone means to check and direct what they are doing to make sure that they do it correctly.

supervision NOUN **supervisor** NOUN
▄ oversee, superintend

supper suppers

NOUN Supper is a meal eaten in the evening or a snack eaten before you go to bed.

supplant supplants supplanting supplanted

VERB; FORMAL To supplant someone or something means to take their place E.G. *By the 1930s the wristwatch had supplanted the pocket watch.*

supple

ADJECTIVE able to bend and move easily.

supplement supplements supplementing supplemented

VERB 1 To supplement something means to add something to it to improve it E.G. *Many village men supplemented their wages by fishing for salmon.* ► NOUN 2 something that is added to something else to improve it.

supplementary

ADJECTIVE added to something else to improve it E.G. *supplementary doses of vitamin E.*

supplier suppliers

NOUN a firm which provides particular goods.

supply supplies supplying supplied

VERB 1 To supply someone with something means to provide it or send it to them. ► NOUN 2 A supply of something is an amount available for use E.G. *the world's supply of precious metals.* ► PLURAL NOUN 3 Supplies are food and equipment for a particular purpose.

support supports supporting supported

VERB 1 If you support someone, you agree with their aims and want them to succeed. **2** If you support someone who is in difficulties, you are kind, encouraging, and helpful to them. **3** If something supports an object, it is underneath it and holding it up. **4** To support someone or something means to prevent them from falling by holding them. **5** To support someone financially means to provide them with money. ► NOUN **6** an object that is holding something up. **7** Moral support is encouragement given to someone to help them do something difficult. **8** Financial support is money that is provided for someone or something. **supporter** NOUN **supportable** ADJECTIVE

supportive
ADJECTIVE A supportive person is encouraging and helpful to someone who is in difficulties.

suppose supposes supposing supposed
VERB **1** If you suppose that something is the case, you think that it is likely E.G. *I supposed that would be too obvious.* ► PHRASE **2** You can say **I suppose** when you are not entirely certain or enthusiastic about something E.G. *Yes, I suppose he could come.* **3** If something **is supposed** to be done, it should be done E.G. *You are supposed to report it to the police.* **4** If something **is supposed** to happen, it is planned or expected to happen E.G. *It was supposed to be this afternoon.* **5** Something that **is supposed** to be the case is generally believed or thought to be so E.G. *Wimbledon is supposed to be the best tournament of them all.* ► CONJUNCTION **6** You can use 'suppose' or 'supposing' when you are

considering or suggesting a possible situation or action E.G. *Supposing he were to break down under interrogation?*

supposed
ADJECTIVE 'Supposed' is used to express doubt about something that is generally believed E.G. *the supposed culprit.*
supposedly ADVERB

supposition suppositions
NOUN something that is believed and assumed to be true E.G. *the supposition that science requires an ordered universe.*

suppress suppresses suppressing suppressed
VERB **1** If an army or government suppresses an activity, it prevents people from doing it. **2** If someone suppresses a piece of information, they prevent it from becoming generally known. **3** If you suppress your feelings, you stop yourself expressing them.
suppression NOUN
☰ (sense 1) crush, quell, stop

supremacy
Said "soo-**prem**-mass-ee" NOUN If a group of people has supremacy over others, it is more powerful than the others.

supreme
ADJECTIVE **1** 'Supreme' is used as part of a title to indicate the highest level of an organization or system E.G. *the Supreme Court.* **2** 'Supreme' is used to emphasize the greatness of something E.G. *the supreme achievement of the human race.*
supremely ADVERB
☰ (sense 2) greatest, highest, paramount

a
b
c
d
e
f
g
h
i
j
k
l
m
n
o
p
q
r
s
t
u
v
w
x
y
z

Elaine and Emily shout EE when they mEEt to grEEt each other (-ee-)   **SPELLING NOTE**

A
B
C
D
E
F
G
H
I
J
K
L
M
N
O
P
Q
R
S
T
U
V
W
X
Y
Z

surcharge surcharges
NOUN an additional charge.

sure surer surest
ADJECTIVE **1** If you are sure about something, you have no doubts about it. **2** If you are sure of yourself, you are very confident. **3** If something is sure to happen, it will definitely happen. **4** Sure means reliable or accurate E.G. *a sure sign that something is wrong.* ► PHRASE **5** If you **make sure** about something, you check it or take action to see that it is done. ► INTERJECTION **6** Sure is an informal way of saying 'yes' E.G. *'Can I come too?' – 'Sure'.*

surely
ADVERB 'Surely' is used to emphasize the belief that something is the case E.G. *Surely these people here knew that?*

surf surfs surfing surfed
VERB **1** When you surf, you go surfing. **2** When you surf the Internet, you go from website to website reading the information. ► NOUN **3** Surf is the white foam that forms on the top of waves when they break near the shore.

surface surfaces surfacing surfaced
NOUN **1** The surface of something is the top or outside area of it. **2** The surface of a situation is what can be seen easily rather than what is hidden or not immediately obvious. ► VERB **3** If someone surfaces, they come up from under water to the surface.

surfboard surfboards
NOUN a long narrow lightweight board used for surfing.

surf club surf clubs
NOUN In Australia, a surf club is an organization of lifesavers in charge of safety on a particular beach, and which often provides leisure facilities.

surfeit
Said "sur-fit" NOUN If there is a surfeit of something, there is too much of it.

surfing
NOUN Surfing is a sport which involves riding towards the shore on the top of a large wave while standing on a surfboard.

surge surges surging surged
NOUN **1** a sudden great increase in the amount of something E.G. *a surge of panic.* ► VERB **2** If something surges, it moves suddenly and powerfully E.G. *The soldiers surged forwards.*

surgeon surgeons
NOUN a doctor who performs operations.

surgery surgeries
NOUN **1** Surgery is medical treatment involving cutting open part of the patient's body to treat the damaged part. **2** The room or building where a doctor or dentist works is called a surgery. **3** A period of time during which a doctor is available to see patients is called surgery E.G. *evening surgery.*

surgical
ADJECTIVE used in or involving a medical operation E.G. *surgical gloves.*

surgically ADVERB

surly surlier surliest
ADJECTIVE rude and bad-tempered.

surliness NOUN

surmise surmises surmising surmised
VERB; FORMAL To surmise something

means to guess it E.G. *I surmised it was of French manufacture.*

surmount surmounts surmounting surmounted
VERB 1 To surmount a difficulty means to manage to solve it. 2 FORMAL If something is surmounted by a particular thing, that thing is on top of it E.G. *The island is surmounted by a huge black castle.*

surname surnames
NOUN Your surname is your last name which you share with other members of your family.

surpass surpasses surpassing surpassed
VERB; FORMAL To surpass someone or something means to be better than them.

surplus surpluses
NOUN If there is a surplus of something there is more of it than is needed.
▤ excess, surfeit

surprise surprises surprising surprised
NOUN 1 an unexpected event. 2 Surprise is the feeling caused when something unexpected happens. ▶ VERB 3 If something surprises you, it gives you a feeling of surprise. 4 If you surprise someone, you do something they were not expecting.
surprising ADJECTIVE

surreal
ADJECTIVE very strange and dreamlike.

surrender surrenders surrendering surrendered
VERB 1 To surrender means to stop fighting and agree that the other side has won. 2 If you surrender to a temptation or feeling, you let it take control of you. 3 To surrender

something means to give it up to someone else E.G. *The gallery director surrendered his keys.* ▶ NOUN 4 Surrender is a situation in which one side in a fight agrees that the other side has won and gives in.
▤ (sense 1) give in, submit, yield
▤ (sense 4) capitulation, submission

surreptitious
Said "sur-rep-**tish**-uss" ADJECTIVE A surreptitious action is done secretly or so that no-one will notice E.G. *a surreptitious glance.*
surreptitiously ADVERB

surrogate surrogates
ADJECTIVE 1 acting as a substitute for someone or something. ▶ NOUN 2 a person or thing that acts as a substitute.

surround surrounds surrounding surrounded
VERB 1 To surround someone or something means to be situated all around them. ▶ NOUN 2 The surround of something is its outside edge or border.
▤ (sense 1) encircle, enclose

surrounding surroundings
ADJECTIVE 1 The surrounding area of a particular place is the area around it E.G. *the surrounding countryside.*
▶ PLURAL NOUN 2 You can refer to the area and environment around a place or person as their surroundings E.G. *very comfortable surroundings.*

surveillance
Said "sur-**vay**-lanss" NOUN Surveillance is the close watching of a person's activities by the police or army.
▥ from French *surveiller* meaning 'to watch over'

a
b
c
d
e
f
g
h
i
j
k
l
m
n
o
p
q
r
s
t
u
v
w
x
y
z

A
B
C
D
E
F
G
H
I
J
K
L
M
N
O
P
Q
R
S
T
U
V
W
X
Y
Z

survey surveys surveying surveyed

VERB 1 To survey something means to look carefully at the whole of it. 2 To survey a building or piece of land means to examine it carefully in order to make a report or plan of its structure and features. ▶ NOUN 3 A survey of something is a detailed examination of it, often in the form of a report.

■ (sense 1) look over, scan, view

surveyor surveyors

NOUN a person whose job is to survey buildings or land.

survival survivals

NOUN Survival is being able to continue living or existing in spite of great danger or difficulties E.G. *There was no hope of survival.*

survive survives surviving survived

VERB To survive means to continue to live or exist in spite of a great danger or difficulties E.G. *a German monk who survived the shipwreck.*

survivor NOUN

sus-

PREFIX 'Sus-' is another form of **sub-**.

susceptible

ADJECTIVE If you are susceptible to something, you are likely to be influenced or affected by it E.G. *Elderly people are more susceptible to infection.*

susceptibility NOUN

suspect suspects suspecting suspected

VERB 1 If you suspect something, you think that it is likely or is probably true E.G. *I suspected that the report would be sent.* 2 If you suspect something, you have doubts about

its reliability E.G. *He suspected her intent.* 3 If you suspect someone of doing something wrong, you think that they have done it. ▶ NOUN 4 someone who is thought to be guilty of a crime. ▶ ADJECTIVE 5 If something is suspect, it cannot be trusted or relied upon E.G. *a rather suspect holy man.*

suspend suspends suspending suspended

VERB 1 If something is suspended, it is hanging from somewhere E.G. *the television set suspended above the bar.* 2 To suspend an activity or event means to delay it or stop it for a while. 3 If someone is suspended from their job, they are told not to do it for a period of time, usually as a punishment.

suspender suspenders

NOUN Suspenders are fastenings which hold up a woman's stockings.

suspense

NOUN Suspense is a state of excitement or anxiety caused by having to wait for something.

suspension

NOUN 1 The suspension of something is the delaying or stopping of it. 2 A person's suspension is their removal from a job for a period of time, usually as a punishment. 3 The suspension of a vehicle consists of springs and shock absorbers which provide a smooth ride. 4 a liquid mixture in which very small bits of a solid material are contained and are not dissolved.

suspicion suspicions

NOUN 1 Suspicion is the feeling of not trusting someone or the feeling that something is wrong. 2 a feeling that

something is likely to happen or is probably true E.G. *the suspicion that more could have been achieved.*
■ (sense 1) distrust, misgiving, scepticism

suspicious
ADJECTIVE **1** If you are suspicious of someone, you do not trust them. **2** 'Suspicious' is used to describe things that make you think that there is something wrong with a situation E.G. *suspicious circumstances.*
suspiciously ADVERB
■ (sense 2) dubious, questionable, suspect

sustain sustains sustaining sustained
VERB **1** To sustain something means to continue it for a period of time E.G. *Their team-mates were unable to sustain the challenge.* **2** If something sustains you, it gives you energy and strength. **3** FORMAL To sustain an injury or harm means to suffer it.

sustainable
ADJECTIVE **1** capable of being sustained. **2** If economic development or energy resources are sustainable they are capable of being maintained at a steady level without exhausting natural resources or causing ecological damage E.G. *sustainable forestry.*

sustenance
NOUN; FORMAL Sustenance is food and drink.

swab swabs swabbing swabbed
NOUN **1** a small piece of cotton wool used for cleaning a wound. ► VERB **2** To swab something means to clean it using a large mop and a lot of water. **3** To swab a wound means to

clean it or take specimens from it using a swab.

swag swags
NOUN INFORMAL **1** goods or valuables, especially ones which have been gained dishonestly. **2** In Australian and New Zealand English, the bundle of possessions belonging to a tramp. **3** In Australian and New Zealand English, swags of something is lots of it.

swagger swaggers swaggering swaggered
VERB **1** To swagger means to walk in a proud, exaggerated way. ► NOUN **2** an exaggerated walk.

swagman swagmen
NOUN; INFORMAL In Australia and New Zealand in the past, a tramp who carried his possessions on his back.

swallow swallows swallowing swallowed
VERB **1** If you swallow something, you make it go down your throat and into your stomach. **2** When you swallow, you move your throat muscles as if you were swallowing something, especially when you are nervous. ► NOUN **3** a bird with pointed wings and a long forked tail.

swamp swamps swamping swamped
NOUN **1** an area of permanently wet land. ► VERB **2** If something is swamped, it is covered or filled with water. **3** If you are swamped by things, you have more than you are able to deal with E.G. *She was swamped with calls.*
swampy ADJECTIVE

swan swans
NOUN a large, usually white, bird with a long neck that lives on rivers or lakes.

a
b
c
d
e
f
g
h
i
j
k
l
m
n
o
p
q
r
s
t
u
v
w
x
y
z

A
B
C
D
E
F
G
H
I
J
K
L
M
N
O
P
Q
R
S
T
U
V
W
X
Y
Z

swap swaps swapping swapped
Rhymes with "stop" VERB To swap one
thing for another means to replace
the first thing with the second, often
by making an exchange with
another person E.G. *Webb swapped
shirts with a Leeds player.*
■ exchange, switch, trade

swarm swarms swarming
swarmed
NOUN 1 A swarm of insects is a large
group of them flying together. ▶ VERB
2 When bees or other insects swarm,
they fly together in a large group. 3 If
people swarm somewhere, a lot of
people go there quickly and at the
same time E.G. *the crowds of office
workers who swarm across the bridge.*
4 If a place is swarming with people,
there are a lot of people there.

swarthy swarthier swarthiest
ADJECTIVE A swarthy person has a dark
complexion.

swashbuckling
ADJECTIVE 'Swashbuckling' is used to
describe people who have the
exciting behaviour or appearance of
pirates.
🔲 from Middle English
swashbuckling meaning 'making a
noise by striking your sword against
a shield'

swastika swastikas
Said "swoss-tik-ka" NOUN a symbol in
the shape of a cross with each arm
bent over at right angles. It was the
official symbol of the Nazis in
Germany, but in India it is a good
luck sign.
🔲 from Sanskrit *svasti* meaning
'prosperity'

swat swats swatting swatted
VERB To swat an insect means to hit it

sharply in order to kill it.

swathe swathes
Rhymes with "bathe" NOUN 1 a long
strip of cloth that is wrapped around
something E.G. *swathes of white silk.*
2 A swathe of land is a long strip of
it.

swathed
ADJECTIVE If someone is swathed in
something, they are wrapped in it
E.G. *She was swathed in towels.*

sway sways swaying swayed
VERB 1 To sway means to lean or
swing slowly from side to side. 2 If
something sways you, it influences
your judgment. ▶ NOUN 3 LITERARY Sway
is the power to influence people E.G.
*under the sway of more powerful
neighbours.*

swear swears swearing swore
sworn
VERB 1 To swear means to say words
that are considered to be very rude
or blasphemous. 2 If you swear to
something, you state solemnly that
you will do it or that it is true. 3 If you
swear by something, you firmly
believe that it is a reliable cure or
solution E.G. *Some women swear by
extra vitamins.*

swearword swearwords
NOUN a word which is considered to
be rude or blasphemous, which
people use when they are angry.

sweat sweats sweating
sweated
NOUN 1 Sweat is the salty liquid
produced by your sweat glands
when you are hot or afraid. ▶ VERB
2 When you sweat, sweat comes
through the pores in your skin in
order to lower the temperature of
your body.

sweater sweaters
NOUN a knitted piece of clothing covering your upper body and arms.

sweatshirt sweatshirts
NOUN a piece of clothing made of thick cotton, covering your upper body and arms.

sweaty
ADJECTIVE covered or soaked with sweat.

swede swedes
NOUN a large round root vegetable with yellow flesh and a brownish-purple skin.
🔲 from Swedish turnip because it was introduced from Sweden in the 18th century

Swede Swedes
NOUN someone who comes from Sweden.

Swedish
ADJECTIVE 1 belonging or relating to Sweden. ▶ NOUN 2 Swedish is the main language spoken in Sweden.

sweep sweeps sweeping swept
VERB 1 If you sweep the floor, you use a brush to gather up dust or rubbish from it. 2 To sweep things off a surface means to push them all off with a quick, smooth movement. 3 If something sweeps from one place to another, it moves there very quickly E.G. A gust of wind swept over the terrace. 4 If an attitude or new fashion sweeps a place, it spreads rapidly through it E.G. a phenomenon that is sweeping America. ▶ NOUN 5 If you do something with a sweep of your arm, you do it with a wide curving movement of your arm.

sweeping
ADJECTIVE 1 A sweeping curve or

movement is long and wide. 2 A sweeping statement is based on a general assumption rather than on careful thought. 3 affecting a lot of people to a great extent E.G. sweeping changes.

sweet sweeter sweetest; sweets
ADJECTIVE 1 containing a lot of sugar E.G. a mug of sweet tea. 2 pleasant and satisfying E.G. sweet success. 3 A sweet smell is soft and fragrant. 4 A sweet sound is gentle and tuneful. 5 attractive and delightful E.G. a sweet little baby. ▶ NOUN 6 Things such as toffees, chocolates, and mints are sweets. 7 a dessert.
sweetly ADVERB **sweetness** NOUN
▤ (sense 5) charming, cute, delightful

sweet corn
NOUN Sweet corn is a long stalk covered with juicy yellow seeds that can be eaten as a vegetable.

sweeten sweetens sweetening sweetened
VERB To sweeten food means to add sugar or another sweet substance to it.

sweetener sweeteners
NOUN a very sweet, artificial substance that can be used instead of sugar.

sweetheart sweethearts
NOUN 1 You can call someone who you are very fond of 'sweetheart'. 2 A young person's sweetheart is their boyfriend or girlfriend.

sweet pea sweet peas
NOUN Sweet peas are delicate, very fragrant climbing flowers.

sweet tooth
NOUN If you have a sweet tooth, you like sweet food very much.

a b c d e f g h i j k l m n o p q r s t u v w x y z

swell swells swelling swelled swollen

VERB 1 If something swells, it becomes larger and rounder E.G. *It causes the abdomen to swell.* 2 If an amount swells, it increases in number. ▶ NOUN 3 The regular up and down movement of the waves at sea can be called a swell.

swelling swellings

NOUN 1 an enlarged area on your body as a result of injury or illness. 2 The swelling of something is an increase in its size.

sweltering

ADJECTIVE If the weather is sweltering, it is very hot.

swerve swerves swerving swerved

VERB To swerve means to suddenly change direction to avoid colliding with something.

swift swifter swiftest; swifts

ADJECTIVE 1 happening or moving very quickly E.G. *a swift glance.* ▶ NOUN 2 a bird with narrow crescent-shaped wings.

swiftly ADVERB

swig swigs swigging swigged

INFORMAL

VERB 1 To swig a drink means to drink it in large mouthfuls, usually from a bottle. ▶ NOUN 2 If you have a swig of a drink, you take a large mouthful of it.

swill swills swilling swilled

VERB 1 To swill something means to pour water over it to clean it E.G. *Swill the can out thoroughly.* ▶ NOUN 2 Swill is a liquid mixture containing waste food that is fed to pigs.

swim swims swimming swam swum

VERB 1 To swim means to move through water using various movements with parts of the body. 2 If things are swimming, it seems as if everything you see is moving and you feel dizzy. ▶ NOUN 3 If you go for a swim, you go into water to swim for pleasure.

swimmer NOUN

swimming

NOUN Swimming is the activity of moving through water using your arms and legs.

swimming bath swimming baths

NOUN a public swimming pool.

swimming costume swimming costumes

NOUN the clothing worn by a woman when she goes swimming.

swimming pool swimming pools

NOUN a large hole that has been tiled and filled with water for swimming.

swimming trunks

PLURAL NOUN Swimming trunks are shorts worn by a man when he goes swimming.

swimsuit swimsuits

NOUN a swimming costume.

swindle swindles swindling swindled

VERB 1 To swindle someone means to deceive them to obtain money or property. ▶ NOUN 2 a trick in which someone is cheated out of money or property.

swindler NOUN

📖 from German *Schwindler* meaning 'cheat'

swine swines

NOUN 1 OLD-FASHIONED Swine are pigs. 2 INFORMAL If you call someone a swine, you mean they are nasty and spiteful.

swing swings swinging swung
VERB 1 If something swings, it moves repeatedly from side to side from a fixed point. 2 If someone or something swings in a particular direction, they turn quickly or move in a sweeping curve in that direction. ▶ NOUN 3 a seat hanging from a frame or a branch, which moves backwards and forwards when you sit on it. 4 A swing in opinion is a significant change in people's opinion.

swipe swipes swiping swiped
VERB 1 To swipe at something means to try to hit it making a curving movement with the arm. 2 INFORMAL To swipe something means to steal it. 3 To swipe a credit card means to pass it through a machine that electronically reads the information stored in the card. ▶ NOUN 4 To take a swipe at something means to swipe at it.

swirl swirls swirling swirled
VERB To swirl means to move quickly in circles E.G. *The black water swirled around his legs.*

swish swishes swishing swished
VERB 1 To swish means to move quickly through the air making a soft sound E.G. *The curtains swished back.* ▶ NOUN 2 the sound made when something swishes.

Swiss
ADJECTIVE 1 belonging or relating to Switzerland. ▶ NOUN 2 someone who comes from Switzerland.

switch switches switching switched
NOUN 1 a small control for an electrical device or machine. 2 a change E.G. *a switch in routine.* ▶ VERB 3 To switch to a different task or topic means to change to it. 4 If you switch things, you exchange one for the other.

switch off VERB To switch off a light or machine means to stop it working by pressing a switch.

switch on VERB To switch on a light or machine means to start it working by pressing a switch.

switchboard switchboards
NOUN The switchboard in an organization is the part where all telephone calls are received.

swivel swivels swivelling swivelled
VERB 1 To swivel means to turn round on a central point. ▶ ADJECTIVE 2 A swivel chair or lamp is made so that you can move the main part of it while the base remains in a fixed position.

swollen
ADJECTIVE Something that is swollen has swelled up.
▣ distended, enlarged, puffed up

swoon swoons swooning swooned
VERB; LITERARY To swoon means to faint as a result of strong emotion.

swoop swoops swooping swooped
VERB To swoop means to move downwards through the air in a fast curving movement E.G. *A flock of pigeons swooped low over the square.*

swop
another spelling of **swap**.

sword swords
NOUN a weapon consisting of a very long blade with a short handle.

swordfish swordfishes or swordfish
NOUN a large sea fish with a long upper jaw.

a
b
c
d
e
f
g
h
i
j
k
l
m
n
o
p
q
r
s
t
u
v
w
x
y
z

there's a rAKE in the brAKEs (br<u>a</u>ke)   **SPELLING NOTE**

sworn

ADJECTIVE If you make a sworn statement, you swear that everything in it is true.

swot swots swotting swotted

INFORMAL

VERB 1 To swot means to study or revise very hard. 2 If you swot up on a subject you find out as much about it as possible in a short time.

▶ NOUN 3 someone who spends too much time studying.

sycamore sycamores

Said "sik-am-mor" NOUN a tree that has large leaves with five points.

syllable syllables

NOUN a part of a word that contains a single vowel sound and is pronounced as a unit. For example, 'book' has one syllable and 'reading' has two.

syllabus syllabuses or **syllabi**

NOUN The subjects that are studied for a particular course or examination are called the syllabus

✔ The plural *syllabuses* is much more common than *syllabi*.

symbol symbols

NOUN (RE) a shape, design, or idea that is used to represent something E.G. *The fish has long been a symbol of Christianity.*

▤ emblem, representation, sign

symbolic

ADJECTIVE Something that is symbolic has a special meaning that is considered to represent something else E.G. *Six tons of ivory were burned in a symbolic ceremony.*

symbolize symbolizes symbolizing symbolized; also spelt **symbolise**

VERB If a shape, design, or idea symbolizes something, it is regarded as being a symbol of it E.G. *In China and Japan the carp symbolizes courage.*

symbolism NOUN

symmetrical

ADJECTIVE (MATHS) If something is symmetrical, it has two halves which are exactly the same, except that one half is like a reflection of the other half.

symmetrically ADVERB

symmetry

NOUN (MATHS) Something that has symmetry is symmetrical.

sympathetic

ADJECTIVE 1 A sympathetic person shows kindness and understanding to other people. 2 If you are sympathetic to a proposal or an idea, you approve of it.

sympathize sympathizes sympathizing sympathized; also spelt **sympathise**

VERB To sympathize with someone who is in difficulties means to show them understanding and care.

sympathizer sympathizers; also spelt **sympathiser**

NOUN People who support a particular cause can be referred to as sympathizers.

sympathy sympathies

NOUN 1 Sympathy is kindness and understanding towards someone who is in difficulties. 2 If you have sympathy with someone's ideas or actions, you agree with them.

▶ PHRASE 3 If you do something in sympathy with someone, you do it to show your support for them.

▤ (sense 1) compassion, pity

symphony symphonies
NOUN a piece of music for an orchestra, usually in four movements.
📖 from Greek *sumphōnos* meaning 'harmonious'

symptom symptoms
NOUN 1 something wrong with your body that is a sign of an illness. 2 Something that is considered to be a sign of a bad situation can be referred to as a symptom of it E.G. *another symptom of the racism sweeping across the country.*
symptomatic ADJECTIVE

synagogue synagogues
Said "**sin**-a-*gog*" NOUN (RE) a building where Jewish people meet for worship and religious instruction.
📖 from Greek *sunagōgē* meaning 'meeting'

synchronize synchronizes synchronizing synchronized
Said "**sing**-kron-nize"; also spelt **synchronise**
VERB 1 (MUSIC) To synchronize two actions means to do them at the same time and speed. 2 To synchronize watches means to set them to show exactly the same time as each other.

syncopation
NOUN (MUSIC) Syncopation in rhythm is the stressing of weak beats instead of the usual strong ones.
📖 from Greek *suncopē* meaning 'cutting off'

syndicate syndicates
NOUN an association of business people formed to carry out a particular project.

syndrome syndromes
NOUN 1 a medical condition

characterized by a particular set of symptoms E.G. *Down's syndrome.* 2 You can refer to a typical set of characteristics as a syndrome E.G. *the syndrome of skipping from one wonder diet to the next.*

synod synods
NOUN a council of church leaders which meets regularly to discuss religious and moral issues.
📖 from Greek *sunodos* meaning 'meeting'

synonym synonyms
NOUN (ENGLISH) If two words have the same or a very similar meaning, they are synonyms.

synonymous
ADJECTIVE 1 Two words that are synonymous have the same or very similar meanings. 2 If two things are closely associated, you can say that one is synonymous with the other E.G. *New York is synonymous with the Statue of Liberty.*

synopsis synopses
NOUN a summary of a book, play, or film.

syntax
NOUN The syntax of a language is its grammatical rules and the way its words are arranged.

synthetic
ADJECTIVE made from artificial substances rather than natural ones.

syphon
another spelling of **siphon**.

Syrian Syrians
Said "**sirr**-ee-an" ADJECTIVE 1 belonging or relating to Syria. ▶ NOUN 2 someone who comes from Syria.

syringe syringes
Said "sir-**rinj**" NOUN a hollow tube with a part which is pushed down

a
b
c
d
e
f
g
h
i
j
k
l
m
n
o
p
q
r
s
t
u
v
w
x
y
z

I always visit my FRIend on a FRIday (<u>fri</u>end)   **SPELLING NOTE**

A
B
C
D
E
F
G
H
I
J
K
L
M
N
O
P
Q
R
S
T
U
V
W
X
Y
Z

inside and a fine hollow needle at one end, used for injecting or extracting liquids.

syrup syrups

NOUN a thick sweet liquid made by boiling sugar with water.

📖 from Arabic *sharab* meaning 'drink'

system systems

NOUN 1 (LIBRARY) an organized way of doing or arranging something according to a fixed plan or set of rules. 2 People sometimes refer to the government and administration

of the country as the system. 3 You can also refer to a set of equipment as a system E.G. *an old stereo system.* 4 In biology, a system of a particular kind is the set of organs that perform that function E.G. *the immune system.*

📑 (sense 1) method, procedure, routine

systematic

ADJECTIVE following a fixed plan and done in an efficient way E.G. *a systematic study.*

systematically ADVERB

I want to see (C) your licenCe (licen*c*e)

Tt

tab tabs
NOUN a small extra piece that is attached to something, for example on a curtain so it can be hung on a pole.

tabby tabbies
NOUN a cat whose fur has grey, brown, or black stripes.
📖 from Old French *tabis* meaning 'striped silk cloth'

tabernacle tabernacles
Said "**tab**-er-nak-kl" NOUN **1** a place of worship for certain Christian groups. **2** a sanctuary in which the ancient Hebrews carried the Ark of the Covenant as they wandered from place to place. **3** a Jewish temple.
📖 from Latin *tabernaculum* meaning 'tent'

table tables tabling tabled
NOUN **1** a piece of furniture with a flat horizontal top supported by one or more legs. **2** a set of facts or figures arranged in rows or columns. ► VERB **3** If you table something such as a proposal, you say formally that you want it to be discussed.

tablecloth tablecloths
NOUN a cloth used to cover a table and keep it clean.

tablespoon tablespoons
NOUN a large spoon used for serving food; also the amount that a tablespoon contains.

tablet tablets
NOUN **1** any small, round pill made of powdered medicine. **2** a slab of stone with words cut into it.

table tennis
NOUN Table tennis is a game for two or four people in which you use bats

to hit a small hollow ball over a low net across a table.

tabloid tabloids
NOUN (ENGLISH) a newspaper with small pages, short news stories, and lots of photographs.

taboo taboos
NOUN **1** a social custom that some words, subjects, or actions must be avoided because they are considered embarrassing or offensive E.G. *We have a powerful taboo against boasting.* **2** a religious custom that forbids people to do something. ► ADJECTIVE **3** forbidden or disapproved of E.G. *a taboo subject.*

tacit
Said "**tass**-it" ADJECTIVE understood or implied without actually being said or written.
tacitly ADVERB

taciturn
Said "**tass**-it-urn" ADJECTIVE Someone who is taciturn does not talk very much and so seems unfriendly.

tack tacks tacking tacked
NOUN **1** a short nail with a broad, flat head. **2** If you change tack, you start to use a different method for dealing with something. ► VERB **3** If you tack something to a surface, you nail it there with tacks. **4** If you tack a piece of fabric, you sew it with long loose stitches.

tackies or **takkies**
PLURAL NOUN; INFORMAL In South African English, tackies are tennis shoes or plimsolls.

tackle tackles tackling tackled
VERB **1** If you tackle a difficult task, you start dealing with it in a determined

The government licenSes Schnapps (licenₛes) **SPELLING NOTE**

way. **2** If you tackle someone in a game such as soccer, you try to get the ball away from them. **3** If you tackle someone about something, you talk to them about it in order to get something changed or dealt with. ▶ NOUN **4** A tackle in sport is an attempt to get the ball away from your opponent. **5** Tackle is the equipment used for fishing.

▤ (sense 1) deal with, undertake

tacky tackier tackiest
ADJECTIVE **1** slightly sticky to touch E.G. *The cream feels tacky to the touch.* **2** INFORMAL badly made and in poor taste E.G. *tacky furniture.*

tact
NOUN Tact is the ability to see when a situation is difficult or delicate and to handle it without upsetting people.
tactful ADJECTIVE **tactfully** ADVERB
tactless ADJECTIVE **tactlessly**
ADVERB

▤ delicacy, diplomacy, discretion

tactic tactics
NOUN **1** (PE) Tactics are the methods you use to achieve what you want, especially to win a game. **2** Tactics are also the ways in which troops and equipment are used in order to win a battle.
tactical ADJECTIVE **tactically** ADVERB

tactile
ADJECTIVE involving the sense of touch.

tadpole tadpoles
NOUN Tadpoles are the larvae of frogs and toads. They are black with round heads and long tails and live in water.
▥ from Middle English *tadde* meaning 'toad' and *pol* meaning 'head'

taffeta
Said "**taf**-fit-a" NOUN Taffeta is a stiff, shiny fabric that is used mainly for making women's clothes.

tag tags tagging tagged
NOUN **1** a small label made of cloth, paper, or plastic. **2** If you tag along with someone, you go with them or behind them.

tail tails tailing tailed
NOUN **1** The tail of an animal, bird, or fish is the part extending beyond the end of its body. **2** Tail can be used to mean the end part of something E.G. *the tail of the plane.* ▶ PLURAL NOUN **3** If a man is wearing tails, he is wearing a formal jacket which has two long pieces hanging down at the back. ▶ VERB **4** INFORMAL If you tail someone, you follow them in order to find out where they go and what they do. ▶ ADJECTIVE or ADVERB **5** The tails side of a coin is the side which does not have a person's head.

tail off VERB If something tails off, it becomes gradually less.

tailback tailbacks
NOUN a long queue of traffic stretching back from whatever is blocking the road.

tailor tailors tailoring tailored
NOUN **1** a person who makes, alters, and repairs clothes, especially for men. ▶ VERB **2** If something is tailored for a particular purpose, it is specially designed for it.

tailor-made
ADJECTIVE suitable for a particular person or purpose, or specifically designed for them.

taint taints tainting tainted
VERB **1** To taint something is to spoil it by adding something undesirable to

A B C D E F G H I J K L M N O P Q R S T U V W X Y Z

it. ▶ NOUN 2 an undesirable quality in something which spoils it.

taipan taipans
NOUN a large and very poisonous Australian snake.

take takes taking took taken
VERB 1 'Take' is used to show what action or activity is being done E.G. *Amy took a bath… She took her driving test.* 2 If something takes a certain amount of time, or a particular quality or ability, it requires it E.G. *He takes three hours to get ready.* 3 If you take something, you put your hand round it and hold it or carry it E.G. *Here, let me take your coat.* 4 If you take someone somewhere, you drive them there by car or lead them there. 5 If you take something that is offered to you, you accept it E.G. *He had to take the job.* 6 If you take the responsibility or blame for something, you accept responsibility or blame. 7 If you take something that does not belong to you, you steal it. 8 If you take pills or medicine, you swallow them. 9 If you can take something painful, you can bear it E.G. *We can't take much more of this.* 10 If you take someone's advice, you do what they say you should do. 11 If you take a person's temperature or pulse, you measure it. 12 If you take a car or train, or a road or route, you use it to go from one place to another.

take after VERB If you take after someone in your family, you look or behave like them.

take down VERB If you take down what someone is saying, you write it down.

take in VERB 1 If someone is taken in, they are deceived. 2 If you take

something in, you understand it.

take off VERB When an aeroplane takes off, it leaves the ground and begins to fly.

takeoff NOUN

take over VERB To take something over means to start controlling it.

takeover NOUN

take to VERB If you take to someone or something, you like them immediately.

takeaway takeaways
NOUN 1 a shop or restaurant that sells hot cooked food to be eaten elsewhere. 2 a hot cooked meal bought from a takeaway.

takings
PLURAL NOUN Takings are the money that a shop or cinema gets from selling its goods or tickets.

talc
NOUN Talc is the same as talcum powder.

talcum powder
NOUN Talcum powder is a soft perfumed powder used for absorbing moisture on the body.

tale tales
NOUN a story.

talent talents
NOUN Talent is the natural ability to do something well.

talented ADJECTIVE
☰ ability, flair, gift

talisman talismans
Said "**tal**-iz-man" NOUN an object which you believe has magic powers to protect you or bring luck.
📖 from Greek *telesma* meaning 'holy object'

talk talks talking talked
VERB 1 When you talk, you say things to someone. 2 If people talk,

a
b
c
d
e
f
g
h
i
j
k
l
m
n
o
p
q
r
s
t
u
v
w
x
y
z

especially about other people's private affairs, they gossip about them E.G. *the neighbours might talk.*
3 If you talk on or about something, you make an informal speech about it. ▶ NOUN **4** Talk is discussion or gossip. **5** an informal speech about something.

talk down VERB If you talk down to someone, you talk to them in a way that shows that you think you are more important or clever than them.

talkative
ADJECTIVE talking a lot.
☐ chatty, garrulous, loquacious

tall taller tallest
ADJECTIVE **1** of more than average or normal height. **2** having a particular height E.G. *a wall ten metres tall.*
▶ PHRASE **3** If you describe something as **a tall story**, you mean that it is difficult to believe because it is so unlikely.

tally tallies tallying tallied
NOUN **1** an informal record of amounts which you keep adding to as you go along E.G. *He ended with a reasonable goal tally last season.*
▶ VERB **2** If numbers or statements tally, they are exactly the same or they give the same results or conclusions.

Talmud
Said "**t**al-*mood*" NOUN The Talmud consists of the books containing the ancient Jewish ceremonies and civil laws.
📖 a Hebrew word meaning literally 'instruction'

talon talons
NOUN Talons are sharp, hooked claws, especially of a bird of prey.

tambourine tambourines
NOUN a percussion instrument made of a skin stretched tightly over a circular frame, with small round pieces of metal around the edge with the tambourine is beaten or shaken.

tame tamer tamest; tames taming tamed
ADJECTIVE **1** A tame animal or bird is not afraid of people and is not violent towards them. **2** Something that is tame is uninteresting and lacks excitement or risk E.G. *The report was pretty tame.* ▶ VERB **3** If you tame people or things, you bring them under control. **4** To tame a wild animal or bird is to train it to be obedient and live with humans.

tamper tampers tampering tampered
VERB If you tamper with something, you interfere or meddle with it.

tampon tampons
NOUN a firm, specially shaped piece of cotton wool that a woman places inside her vagina to absorb the blood during her period.

tan tans tanning tanned
NOUN **1** If you have a tan, your skin is darker than usual because you have been in the sun. ▶ VERB **2** To tan an animal's hide is to turn it into leather by treating it with chemicals.
▶ ADJECTIVE **3** Something that is tan is of a light yellowish-brown colour E.G. *a tan dress.*

tandem tandems
NOUN a bicycle designed for two riders sitting one behind the other.

tang tangs
NOUN a strong, sharp smell or flavour E.G. *the tang of lemon.*

tangy ADJECTIVE

tangata whenua
Said "**tang**-ah-tah **feh**-noo-ah" NOUN
Tangata whenua is a Maori term for
the original Polynesian settlers in
New Zealand, and their descendants.

tangent tangents
NOUN **1** A tangent of a curve is any
straight line that touches the curve
at one point only. ▶ PHRASE **2** If you **go
off on a tangent**, you start talking or
thinking about something that is not
completely relevant to what has
gone before.

tangerine tangerines
NOUN **1** a type of small sweet orange
with a loose rind. ▶ NOUN or ADJECTIVE
2 reddish-orange.

tangible
Said "**tan**-jib-bl" ADJECTIVE clear or
definite enough to be easily seen or
felt E.G. *tangible proof*.

tangle tangles tangling tangled
NOUN **1** a mass of things such as hairs
or fibres knotted or coiled together
and difficult to separate. ▶ VERB **2** If
you are tangled in wires or ropes,
you are caught or trapped in them
so that it is difficult to get free.

tango tangos
NOUN A tango is a Latin American
dance using long gliding steps and
sudden pauses; also a piece of music
composed for this dance.

taniwha taniwha or **taniwhas**
Said "**tun**-ee-fah" NOUN In New
Zealand, a monster of Maori legends
that lives in water.

tank tanks
NOUN **1** a large container for storing
liquid or gas. **2** an armoured military
vehicle which moves on tracks and is
equipped with guns or rockets.

tankard tankards

NOUN a large metal mug used for
drinking beer.

tanker tankers
NOUN a ship or lorry designed to carry
large quantities of gas or liquid E.G.
a petrol tanker.

tannin
NOUN a brown or yellow substance
found in plants and used in making
leather.

tantalizing or **tantalising**
ADJECTIVE Something that is tantalizing
makes you feel hopeful and excited,
although you know that you
probably will not be able to have
what you want E.G. *a tantalizing
glimpse of riches to come*.

tantamount
ADJECTIVE If you say that something is
tantamount to something else, you
mean that it is almost the same as it
E.G. *That would be tantamount to
treason*.

tantrum tantrums
NOUN a noisy and sometimes violent
outburst of temper, especially by a
child.

Tanzanian Tanzanians
Said "tan-**zan**-nee-an" ADJECTIVE
1 belonging or relating to Tanzania.
▶ NOUN **2** someone who comes from
Tanzania.

tap taps tapping tapped
NOUN **1** a device that you turn to
control the flow of liquid or gas from
a pipe or container. **2** the action of
hitting something lightly; also the
sound that this action makes. ▶ VERB
3 If you tap something or tap on it,
you hit it lightly. **4** If a telephone is
tapped, a device is fitted to it so that
someone can listen secretly to the
calls.

a
b
c
d
e
f
g
h
i
j
k
l
m
n
o
p
q
r
s
t
u
v
w
x
y
z

You must practiSe your Ss (practi**se**)　▶ **SPELLING NOTE**

tap-dancing

NOUN Tap-dancing is a type of dancing in which the dancers wear special shoes with pieces of metal on the toes and heels which click against the floor.

tape tapes taping taped

NOUN 1 Tape is plastic ribbon covered with a magnetic substance and used to record sounds, pictures, and computer information. 2 a cassette or spool with magnetic tape wound round it. 3 Tape is a long, thin strip of fabric that is used for binding or fastening. 4 Tape is also a strip of sticky plastic which you use for sticking things together. ▶ VERB 5 If you tape sounds or television pictures, you record them using a tape recorder or a video recorder. 6 If you tape one thing to another, you attach them using sticky tape.

tape measure tape measures

NOUN a strip of plastic or metal that is marked off in inches or centimetres and used for measuring things.

taper tapers tapering tapered

VERB 1 Something that tapers becomes thinner towards one end. ▶ NOUN 2 a thin candle.

tape recorder tape recorders

NOUN a machine used for recording sounds onto magnetic tape, and for playing these sounds back.

tapestry tapestries

NOUN a piece of heavy cloth with designs embroidered on it.

tar

NOUN Tar is a thick, black, sticky substance which is used in making roads.

tarantula tarantulas

Said "tar-rant-yoo-la" NOUN a large, hairy poisonous spider.

target targets

NOUN 1 something which you aim at when firing weapons. 2 The target of an action or remark is the person or thing at which it is directed. E.G. *You become a target for our hatred.* 3 Your target is the result that you are trying to achieve.

tariff tariffs

NOUN 1 a tax that a government collects on imported goods. 2 any list of prices or charges.

tarmac

NOUN Tarmac is a material used for making road surfaces. It consists of crushed stones mixed with tar. 🔲 short for *tarmacadam*, from the name of John McAdam, the Scottish engineer who invented it

tarnish tarnishes tarnishing tarnished

VERB 1 If metal tarnishes, it becomes stained and loses its shine. 2 If something tarnishes your reputation, it spoils it and causes people to lose their respect for you.

tarot

Said "tar-roh" NOUN A tarot card is one of a special pack of cards used for fortune-telling.

tarpaulin tarpaulins

NOUN a sheet of heavy waterproof material used as a protective covering.

tarragon

NOUN Tarragon is a herb with narrow green leaves used in cooking.

tarry tarries tarrying tarried

VERB; OLD-FASHIONED To tarry is to wait, or to stay somewhere for a little longer.

tarseal

NOUN In New Zealand English, tarseal

is the tarmac surface of a road.

tart tarts; tarter tartest

NOUN **1** a pastry case with a sweet filling. ▶ ADJECTIVE **2** Something that is tart is sour or sharp to taste. **3** A tart remark is unpleasant and cruel.

tartan tartans

NOUN Tartan is a woollen fabric from Scotland with checks of various colours and sizes, depending on which clan it belongs to.

tartar

NOUN Tartar is a hard, crusty substance that forms on teeth.

tarwhine tarwhines

NOUN an edible Australian marine fish, especially a sea bream.

task tasks

NOUN any piece of work which has to be done.

🔳 chore, duty, job

Tasmanian devil Tasmanian devils

NOUN a black-and-white marsupial of Tasmania, which eats flesh.

tassel tassels

NOUN a tuft of loose threads tied by a knot and used for decoration.

taste tastes tasting tasted

NOUN **1** Your sense of taste is your ability to recognize the flavour of things in your mouth. **2** The taste of something is its flavour. **3** If you have a taste of food or drink, you have a small amount of it to see what it is like. **4** If you have a taste for something, you enjoy it E.G. *a taste for publicity.* **5** If you have a taste of something, you experience it E.G. *my first taste of defeat.* **6** A person's taste is their choice in the things they like to buy or have around them E.G. *His taste in music is great.* ▶ VERB **7** When

you can taste something in your mouth, you are aware of its flavour. **8** If you taste food or drink, you have a small amount of it to see what it is like. **9** If food or drink tastes of something, it has that flavour.

taste bud taste buds

NOUN Your taste buds are the little points on the surface of your tongue which enable you to taste things.

tasteful

ADJECTIVE attractive and elegant.

tastefully ADVERB

tasteless

ADJECTIVE **1** vulgar and unattractive. **2** A tasteless remark or joke is offensive. **3** Tasteless food has very little flavour.

tasty tastier tastiest

ADJECTIVE having a pleasant flavour.

tatters

PLURAL NOUN Clothes that are in tatters are badly torn.

tattered ADJECTIVE

tattoo tattoos tattooing tattooed

VERB **1** If someone tattoos you or tattoos a design on you, they draw it on your skin by pricking tiny holes and filling them with coloured dye. ▶ NOUN **2** a picture or design tattooed on someone's body. **3** a public military display of exercises and music.

tatty tattier tattiest

ADJECTIVE worn out or untidy and rather dirty.

taught

the past tense and past participle of **teach**.

taunt taunts taunting taunted

VERB **1** To taunt someone is to speak to them about their weaknesses or

LEarn the principLEs (principle) ▸ SPELLING NOTE

failures in order to make them angry or upset. ▶ NOUN **2** an offensive remark intended to make a person angry or upset.

Taurus

NOUN Taurus is the second sign of the zodiac, represented by a bull. People born between April 20th and May 20th are born under this sign.

📖 from Latin *taurus* meaning 'bull'

taut

ADJECTIVE stretched very tight E.G. *taut wires*.

tavern taverns

NOUN; OLD-FASHIONED a pub.

tawdry tawdrier tawdriest

Said "taw-dree" ADJECTIVE cheap, gaudy, and of poor quality.

tawny

NOUN or ADJECTIVE brownish-yellow.

tax taxes taxing taxed

NOUN **1** Tax is an amount of money that the people in a country have to pay to the government so that it can provide public services such as health care and education. ▶ VERB **2** If a sum of money is taxed, a certain amount of it has to be paid to the government. **3** If goods are taxed, a certain amount of their price has to be paid to the government. **4** If a person or company is taxed, they have to pay a certain amount of their income to the government. **5** If something taxes you, it makes heavy demands on you E.G. *They must be told not to tax your patience*.

taxation NOUN

taxi taxis taxiing taxied

NOUN **1** a car with a driver which you hire to take you to where you want to go. ▶ VERB **2** When an aeroplane taxis, it moves slowly along the runway before taking off or after landing.

tea teas

NOUN **1** Tea is the dried leaves of an evergreen shrub found in Asia. **2** Tea is a drink made by brewing the leaves of the tea plant in hot water; also a cup of this. **3** Tea is also any drink made with hot water and leaves or flowers E.G. *peppermint tea*. **4** Tea is a meal taken in the late afternoon or early evening.

tea bag tea bags

NOUN a small paper bag with tea leaves in it which is placed in boiling water to make tea.

teach teaches teaching taught

VERB **1** If you teach someone something, you give them instructions so that they know about it or know how to do it. **2** If you teach a subject, you help students learn about a subject at school, college, or university.

teacher NOUN **teaching** NOUN

■ (sense 1) educate, instruct, train, tutor

teak

NOUN Teak is a hard wood which comes from a large Asian tree.

team teams teaming teamed

NOUN **1** a group of people who play together against another group in a sport or game. ▶ VERB **2** If you team up with someone, you join them and work together with them.

teamwork

NOUN Teamwork is the ability of a group of people to work well together.

teapot teapots

NOUN a round pot with a handle, a lid,

A B C D E F G H I J K L M N O P Q R S T U V W X Y Z

and a spout, used for brewing and pouring tea.

tear tears tearing tore torn
NOUN **1** Tears are the drops of salty liquid that come out of your eyes when you cry. **2** a hole that has been made in something. ▶ VERB **3** If you tear something, it is damaged by being pulled so that a hole appears in it. **4** If you tear somewhere, you rush there E.G. *He tore through busy streets in a high-speed chase.*
■ (sense 2) hole, rip, rupture
☑ When *tear* means 'a drop of salty water' (sense 1), it rhymes with *fear*. For all the other senses it rhymes with *hair*.

tearaway tearaways
NOUN someone who is wild and uncontrollable.

tearful
ADJECTIVE about to cry or crying gently.
tearfully ADVERB

tease teases teasing teased
VERB **1** If you tease someone, you deliberately make fun of them or embarrass them because it amuses you. ▶ NOUN **2** someone who enjoys teasing people.

teaspoon teaspoons
NOUN a small spoon used for stirring drinks; also the amount that a teaspoon holds.

teat teats
NOUN **1** a nipple on a female animal. **2** a piece of rubber or plastic that is shaped like a nipple and fitted to a baby's feeding bottle.

tea tree tea trees
NOUN a tree found in Australia and New Zealand with leaves that contain tannin, like tea leaves.

tech techs NOUN; INFORMAL a technical college.

technical
ADJECTIVE **1** involving machines, processes, and materials used in industry, transport, and communications. **2** skilled in practical and mechanical things rather than theories and ideas. **3** involving a specialized field of activity E.G. *I never understood the technical jargon.*

technical college technical colleges
NOUN a college where you can study subjects like technology and secretarial skills.

technicality technicalities
NOUN **1** The technicalities of a process or activity are the detailed methods used to do it. **2** an exact detail of a law or a set of rules, especially one some people might not notice E.G. *The verdict may have been based on a technicality.*

technically
ADVERB If something is technically true or correct, it is true or correct when you consider only the facts, rules, or laws, but may not be important or relevant in a particular situation E.G. *Technically, they were not supposed to drink on duty.*

technician technicians
NOUN someone whose job involves skilled practical work with scientific equipment.

technique techniques
NOUN **1** a particular method of doing something E.G. *these techniques of manufacture.* **2** Technique is skill and ability in an activity which is developed through training and

a
b
c
d
e
f
g
h
i
j
k
l
m
n
o
p
q
r
s
t
u
v
w
x
y
z

practice E.G. *Jim's unique vocal technique.*

techno-

PREFIX 'Techno-' means a craft or art E.G. *technology.*

🏛 from Greek *tekhnē* meaning 'a skill'

technology technologies

NOUN 1 (D&T) Technology is the study of the application of science and scientific knowledge for practical purposes in industry, farming, medicine, or business. 2 a particular area of activity that requires scientific methods and knowledge E.G. *computer technology.*

technological ADJECTIVE

technologically ADVERB

teddy teddies

NOUN A teddy or teddy bear is a stuffed toy that looks like a friendly bear.

🏛 named after the American President Theodore (Teddy) Roosevelt, who hunted bears

tedious

Said "**tee-dee-uss**" ADJECTIVE boring and lasting for a long time E.G. *the tedious task of clearing up.*

tedium

Said "**tee-dee-um**" NOUN the quality of being boring and lasting for a long time E.G. *the tedium of unemployment.*

tee tees teeing teed

NOUN 1 the small wooden or plastic peg on which a golf ball is placed before the golfer first hits it. ▶ VERB 2 To tee off is to hit the golf ball from the tee, or to start a round of golf.

teem teems teeming teemed

VERB 1 If a place is teeming with people or things, there are a lot of them moving about. 2 If it teems, it rains very heavily E.G. *The rain was teeming down.*

teenage

ADJECTIVE 1 aged between thirteen and nineteen. 2 typical of people aged between thirteen and nineteen E.G. *teenage fashion.*

teenager NOUN

teens

PLURAL NOUN Your teens are the period of your life when you are between thirteen and nineteen years old.

tee shirt

another spelling of **T-shirt.**

teeter teeters teetering teetered

VERB To teeter is to shake or sway slightly in an unsteady way and seem about to fall over.

teeth

the plural of **tooth.**

teethe teethes teething teethed

*Rhymes with "**breathe**"* VERB When babies are teething, their teeth are starting to come through, usually causing them pain.

teetotal

Said "**tee-toe-tl**" ADJECTIVE Someone who is teetotal never drinks alcohol.

teetotaller NOUN

tele-

PREFIX 'Tele-' means at or over a distance E.G. *telegraph.*

🏛 from Greek *tele* meaning 'far'

telecommunications

NOUN Telecommunications is the science and activity of sending signals and messages over long distances using electronic equipment.

telegram telegrams

NOUN a message sent by telegraph.

telegraph
NOUN The telegraph is a system of sending messages over long distances using electrical or radio signals.

telepathy
Said "til-**lep**-ath-ee" NOUN Telepathy is direct communication between people's minds.
telepathic ADJECTIVE

telephone telephones telephoning telephoned
NOUN 1 a piece of electrical equipment for talking directly to someone who is in a different place. ► VERB 2 If you telephone someone, you speak to them using a telephone.

telephone box telephone boxes
NOUN a small shelter in the street where there is a public telephone.

telescope telescopes
NOUN a long instrument shaped like a tube which has lenses which make distant objects appear larger and nearer.

teletext
NOUN Teletext is an electronic system that broadcasts pages of information onto a television set.

televise televises televising televised
VERB If an event is televised, it is filmed and shown on television.

television televisions
NOUN a piece of electronic equipment which receives pictures and sounds by electrical signals over a distance.

tell tells telling told
VERB 1 If you tell someone something, you let them know about it. 2 If you tell someone to do something, you order or advise them to do it. 3 If you can tell something, you are able to

judge correctly what is happening or what the situation is E.G. *I could tell he was scared.* 4 If an unpleasant or tiring experience begins to tell, it begins to have a serious effect E.G. *The pressure began to tell.*
■ (sense 1) inform, notify

teller tellers
NOUN a person who receives or gives out money in a bank.

telling
ADJECTIVE Something that is telling has an important effect, often because it shows the true nature of a situation E.G. *a telling account of the war.*

telltale
ADJECTIVE A telltale sign reveals information E.G. *the sad, telltale signs of a recent accident.*

telly tellies
NOUN; INFORMAL a television.

temerity
Said "tim-**mer**-it-ee" NOUN If someone has the temerity to do something, they do it even though it upsets or annoys other people E.G. *She had the temerity to call him Bob.*

temp temps
NOUN; INFORMAL a secretary who works for short periods of time in different places.

temper tempers tempering tempered
NOUN 1 Your temper is the frame of mind or mood you are in. 2 a sudden outburst of anger. ► PHRASE 3 If you **lose your temper**, you become very angry. ► VERB 4 To temper something is to make it more acceptable or suitable E.G. *curiosity tempered with some caution.*

temperament temperaments
Said "**tem**-pra-ment" NOUN Your

a
b
c
d
e
f
g
h
i
j
k
l
m
n
o
p
q
r
s
t
u
v
w
x
y
z

there's SAND in my SANDwich (sandwich)   SPELLING NOTE

temperament is your nature or personality, shown in the way you react towards people and situations E.G. *an artistic temperament*.

temperamental
ADJECTIVE Someone who is temperamental has moods that change often and suddenly.

temperate
ADJECTIVE A temperate place has weather that is neither extremely hot nor extremely cold.

temperature temperatures
NOUN 1 (SCIENCE) The temperature of something is how hot or cold it is. 2 Your temperature is the temperature of your body. ▶ PHRASE 3 If you **have a temperature**, the temperature of your body is higher than it should be, because you are ill.

tempest tempests
NOUN; LITERARY a violent storm.

tempestuous
Said "tem-**pest**-yoo-uss" ADJECTIVE violent or strongly emotional E.G. *a tempestuous relationship*.

template templates
NOUN a shape or pattern cut out in wood, metal, plastic, or card which you draw or cut around to reproduce that shape or pattern.

temple temples
NOUN 1 (RE) a building used for the worship of a god in various religions E.G. *a Buddhist temple*. 2 Your temples are the flat parts on each side of your forehead.

tempo tempos or tempi
NOUN 1 The tempo of something is the speed at which it happens E.G. *the slow tempo of change*. 2 (MUSIC); TECHNICAL The tempo of a piece of music is its speed.

temporary
ADJECTIVE lasting for only a short time.
temporarily ADVERB

tempt tempts tempting tempted
VERB 1 If you tempt someone, you try to persuade them to do something by offering them something they want. 2 If you are tempted to do something, you want to do it but you think it might be wrong or harmful E.G. *He was tempted to reply with sarcasm*.
☰ (sense 1) entice, lure

temptation temptations
NOUN 1 Temptation is the state you are in when you want to do or have something, even though you know it might be wrong or harmful. 2 something that you want to do or have, even though you know it might be wrong or harmful E.G. *There is a temptation to ignore the problem*.

ten
the number 10.
tenth

tenacious
Said "tin-**nay**-shuss" ADJECTIVE determined and not giving up easily.
tenaciously ADVERB **tenacity** NOUN

tenant tenants
NOUN someone who pays rent for the place they live in, or for land or buildings that they use.
tenancy NOUN

tend tends tending tended
VERB 1 If something tends to happen, it happens usually or often. 2 If you tend someone or something, you look after them E.G. *the way we tend our cattle*.
☰ (sense 1) be apt to, be inclined to, be liable to

tendency tendencies
NOUN a trend or type of behaviour that happens very often E.G. *a tendency to be critical.*

tender tenderest; tenders tendering tendered
ADJECTIVE 1 Someone who is tender has gentle and caring feelings. 2 If someone is at a tender age, they are young and do not know very much about life. 3 Tender meat is easy to cut or chew. 4 If a part of your body is tender, it is painful and sore. ▶ VERB 5 If someone tenders an apology or their resignation, they offer it. ▶ NOUN 6 a formal offer to supply goods or to do a job for a particular price.
☰ (sense 1) affectionate, gentle, loving

tendon tendons
NOUN a strong cord of tissue which joins a muscle to a bone.

tendril tendrils
NOUN Tendrils are short, thin stems which grow on climbing plants and attach them to walls.

tenement tenements
Said "ten-em-ent" NOUN a large house or building divided into many flats.

tenet tenets
NOUN The tenets of a theory or belief are the main ideas it is based upon.

tenner tenners
NOUN; INFORMAL a ten-pound or ten-dollar note.

tennis
NOUN Tennis is a game played by two or four players on a rectangular court in which a ball is hit by players over a central net.

tenor tenors
NOUN 1 a man who sings in a fairly high voice. 2 The tenor of something is the general meaning or mood that it expresses E.G. *the whole tenor of his poetry had changed.* ▶ ADJECTIVE 3 A tenor recorder, saxophone, or other musical instrument has a range of notes of a fairly low pitch.

tense tenser tensest; tenses tensing tensed
ADJECTIVE 1 If you are tense, you are nervous and cannot relax. 2 A tense situation or period of time is one that makes people nervous and worried. 3 If your body is tense, your muscles are tight. ▶ VERB 4 If you tense, or if your muscles tense, your muscles become tight and stiff. ▶ NOUN 5 The tense of a verb is the form which shows whether you are talking about the past, present, or future.
☰ (sense 1) anxious, nervous, uptight

What is a Tense?

The "tense" of the verb tells us whether the action is in the past, the present or the future.

Some forms of the verb indicate that the action has already happened. These forms are **past tenses**:

> E.G. *The captain **asked** Matthew for advice.*
> *The captain **has asked** Matthew for advice.*
> *The captain **was asking** Matthew for advice this morning.*
> *The captain **had asked** Matthew for advice that morning.*

Some forms of the verb indicate that the action is happening at the present time. These forms are **present tenses**:

CONTINUED ON NEXT PAGE →

Eddy Ant thinks mEAt is a grEAt trEAt to EAt (-ea-)   **SPELLING NOTE**

a
b
c
d
e
f
g
h
i
j
k
l
m
n
o
p
q
r
s
t
u
v
w
x
y
z

E.G. *I **see** some cause for optimism.*
*I **do see** some cause for optimism.*

Some forms of the verb indicate that the action will happen in the future. These forms are **future tenses**:

E.G. *They **will go** to Fiji in September.*
*They **will have gone** to Fiji by the end of September.*

Also look at the grammar boxes at **future**, **past tense**, and **present tense**.

tension tensions

NOUN **1** Tension is the feeling of nervousness or worry that you have when something dangerous or important is happening. **2** (D & T) The tension in a rope or wire is how tightly it is stretched.

tent tents

NOUN a shelter made of canvas or nylon held up by poles and pinned down with pegs and ropes.

tentacle tentacles

NOUN The tentacles of an animal such as an octopus are the long, thin parts that it uses to feel and hold things.

tentative

ADJECTIVE acting or speaking cautiously because of being uncertain or afraid.

tentatively ADVERB

tenterhooks

PLURAL NOUN If you are on tenterhooks, you are nervous and excited about something that is going to happen.
🔲 from the hooks called *tenterhooks* which were used to stretch cloth tight while it was drying

tenuous

Said "ten-yoo-uss" ADJECTIVE If an idea or connection is tenuous, it is so slight and weak that it may not really exist or may easily cease to exist E.G. *a very tenuous friendship.*

tenure tenures

Said "ten-yoor" NOUN **1** Tenure is the legal right to live in a place or to use land or buildings for a period of time. **2** Tenure is the period of time during which someone holds an important job E.G. *His tenure ended in 1998.*

tepee tepees

Said "tee-pee" NOUN a cone-shaped tent of animal skins used by North American Indians.

tepid

ADJECTIVE Tepid liquid is only slightly warm.

term terms terming termed

NOUN **1** a fixed period of time E.G. *her second term of office.* **2** one of the periods of time that each year is divided into at a school or college. **3** a name or word used for a particular thing. ▶ PLURAL NOUN **4** The terms of an agreement are the conditions that have been accepted by the people involved in it. **5** If you express something in particular terms, you express it using a particular type of language or in a way that clearly shows your attitude E.G. *The young priest spoke of her in glowing terms.* ▶ PHRASE **6** If you **come to terms with** something difficult or unpleasant, you learn to accept it. ▶ VERB **7** To term something is to give it a name or to describe it E.G. *He termed my performance memorable.*

terminal terminals
ADJECTIVE **1** A terminal illness or disease cannot be cured and causes death gradually. ► NOUN **2** a place where vehicles, passengers, or goods begin or end a journey. **3** A computer terminal is a keyboard and a visual display unit that is used to put information into or get information out of a computer. **4** one of the parts of an electrical device through which electricity enters or leaves.
terminally ADVERB

terminate terminates terminating terminated
VERB When you terminate something or when it terminates, it stops or ends.
termination NOUN

terminology terminologies
NOUN The terminology of a subject is the set of special words and expressions used in it.

terminus terminuses
Said "ter-min-uss" NOUN a place where a bus or train route ends.

termite termites
NOUN Termites are small white insects that feed on wood.

tern terns
NOUN a small black and white sea bird with long wings and a forked tail.

ternary
ADJECTIVE (MUSIC) Ternary form is a musical structure of three sections, the first and the second contrasting with each other and the third being a repetition of the first.

terrace terraces
NOUN **1** a row of houses joined together. **2** a flat area of stone next to a building where people can sit.

terracotta
NOUN a type of brown pottery with no glaze.
🏛 from Italian *terra cotta* meaning 'baked earth'

terrain
NOUN The terrain of an area is the type of land there E.G. *the region's hilly terrain.*

terrapin terrapins
NOUN a small North American freshwater turtle.

terrestrial
ADJECTIVE involving the earth or land.

terrible
ADJECTIVE **1** serious and unpleasant E.G. *a terrible illness.* **2** INFORMAL very bad or of poor quality E.G. *Paddy's terrible haircut.*

terribly
ADVERB very or very much E.G. *I was terribly upset.*

terrier terriers
NOUN a small, short-bodied dog.

terrific
ADJECTIVE **1** INFORMAL very pleasing or impressive E.G. *a terrific film.* **2** great in amount, degree, or intensity E.G. *a terrific blow on the head.*
terrifically ADVERB

terrify terrifies terrifying terrified
VERB If something terrifies you, it makes you feel extremely frightened.

territorial
ADJECTIVE involving or relating to the ownership of a particular area of land or water E.G. *a territorial dispute.*

territory territories
NOUN **1** The territory of a country is the land that it controls. **2** An animal's territory is an area which it

a
b
c
d
e
f
g
h
i
j
k
l
m
n
o
p
q
r
s
t
u
v
w
x
y
z

A B C D E F G H I J K L M N O P Q R S T U V W X Y Z

regards as its own and defends when other animals try to enter it.

terror terrors
NOUN **1** Terror is great fear or panic. **2** something that makes you feel very frightened.

terrorism
NOUN Terrorism is the use of violence for political reasons.
terrorist NOUN OR ADJECTIVE

terrorize terrorizes terrorizing terrorized; also spelt **terrorise**
VERB If someone terrorizes you, they frighten you by threatening you or being violent to you.

terse terser tersest
ADJECTIVE A terse statement is short and rather unfriendly.

tertiary
Said "ter-shar-ee" ADJECTIVE **1** third in order or importance. **2** Tertiary education is education at university or college level.

test tests testing tested
VERB **1** When you test something, you try to find out what it is, what condition it is in, or how well it works. **2** If you test someone, you ask them questions to find out how much they know. ▶ NOUN **3** a deliberate action or experiment to find out whether something works or how well it works. **4** a set of questions or tasks given to someone to find out what they know or can do.

testament testaments
NOUN **1** LEGAL a will. **2** a copy of either the Old or the New Testament of the Bible.

test case test cases
NOUN a legal case that becomes an example for deciding other similar cases.

testicle testicles
NOUN A man's testicles are the two sex glands that produce sperm.

testify testifies testifying testified
VERB **1** When someone testifies, they make a formal statement, especially in a court of law E.G. *Ismay later testified at the British inquiry.* **2** To testify to something is to show that it is likely to be true E.G. *a consultant's certificate testifying to her good health.*

testimonial testimonials
Said "tess-tim-**moh**-nee-al" NOUN a statement saying how good someone or something is.

testimony testimonies
NOUN A person's testimony is a formal statement they make, especially in a court of law.

testing
ADJECTIVE Testing situations or problems are very difficult to deal with E.G. *It is a testing time for his team.*

testis testes
NOUN A man's testes are his testicles.

test match test matches
NOUN one of a series of international cricket or rugby matches.

testosterone
Said "tess-**toss**-ter-rone" NOUN Testosterone is a male hormone that produces male characteristics.

test tube test tubes
NOUN a small cylindrical glass container that is used in chemical experiments.

tetanus
Said "**tet**-nuss" NOUN Tetanus is a painful infectious disease caused by germs getting into wounds.

tether tethers tethering tethered

VERB **1** If you tether an animal, you tie it to a post. ► PHRASE **2** If you are **at the end of your tether**, you are extremely tired and have no more patience or energy left to deal with your problems.

Teutonic

Said "tyoo-**tonn**-ik" ADJECTIVE; FORMAL involving or related to German people.

text texts

NOUN **1** The text of a book is the main written part of it, rather than the pictures or index. **2** Text is any written material. **3** a book or other piece of writing used for study or an exam at school or college.

textual ADJECTIVE

textbook textbooks

NOUN a book about a particular subject for students to use.

textile textiles

NOUN (U & T) a woven cloth or fabric.

texture textures

NOUN The texture of something is the way it feels when you touch it.

■ consistency, feel

Thai Thais

ADJECTIVE **1** belonging or relating to Thailand. ► NOUN **2** someone who comes from Thailand. **3** Thai is the main language spoken in Thailand.

than

PREPOSITION or CONJUNCTION **1** You use 'than' to link two parts of a comparison E.G. *She was older than me.* **2** You use 'than' to link two parts of a contrast E.G. *Players would rather play than train.*

thank thanks thanking thanked

VERB When you thank someone, you

show that you are grateful for something, usually by saying 'thank you'.

thankful

ADJECTIVE happy and relieved that something has happened.

thankfully ADVERB

thankless

ADJECTIVE A thankless job or task involves doing a lot of hard work that other people do not notice or are not grateful for E.G. *Referees have a thankless task.*

thanks

PLURAL NOUN **1** When you express your thanks to someone, you tell or show them how grateful you are for something. ► PHRASE **2** If something happened **thanks to** someone or something, it happened because of them E.G. *I'm as prepared as I can be, thanks to you.* ► INTERJECTION **3** You say 'thanks' to show that you are grateful for something.

thanksgiving

NOUN **1** Thanksgiving is an act of thanking God, especially in prayer or in a religious ceremony. **2** In the United States, Thanksgiving is a public holiday in the autumn.

thank you

You say 'thank you' to show that you are grateful to someone for something.

that those

ADJECTIVE or PRONOUN **1** 'That' or 'those' is used to refer to things or people already mentioned or known about E.G. *That man was waving.* ► CONJUNCTION **2** 'That' is used to introduce a clause E.G. *I said that I was coming home.* ► PRONOUN **3** 'That' is also used to introduce a relative clause E.G. *I followed Alex to a door that led inside.*

an ELegant angEL (angel)   **SPELLING NOTE**

a
b
c
d
e
f
g
h
i
j
k
l
m
n
o
p
q
r
s
t
u
v
w
x
y
z

A
B
C
D
E
F
G
H
I
J
K
L
M
N
O
P
Q
R
S
T
U
V
W
X
Y
Z

☑ You can use either *that* or *which* in clauses known as defining clauses. These are clauses that identify the object you are talking about. In the sentence *The book that is on the table is mine,* 'that' is on the table is a defining clause which distinguishes the book from other books that are not on the table. Some people think these types of clause should only be introduced by *that*, and *which* should be kept for nondefining clauses. These nondefining clauses add extra information about the object, but do not identify it. In the sentence *The book, which is on the table, is mine,* 'which is on the table' is a nondefining clause which gives the reader extra detail about the book.

thatch thatches thatching thatched

NOUN 1 Thatch is straw and reeds used to make roofs. ▶ VERB 2 To thatch a roof is to cover it with thatch.

thaw thaws thawing thawed

VERB 1 When snow or ice thaws, it melts. 2 When you thaw frozen food, or when it thaws, it returns to its normal state in a warmer atmosphere. 3 When people who are unfriendly thaw, they begin to be more friendly and relaxed. ▶ NOUN 4 a period of warmer weather in winter when snow or ice melts.

the

ADJECTIVE The definite article 'the' is used when you are talking about something that is known about, that has just been mentioned, or that you are going to give details about.

The Definite Article

The word *the* is known as the **definite article**. You use it before a noun to refer to a specific example of that noun:

E.G. *the kitchen table*
the school I attend

The definite article *the* may be used before singular and plural nouns. However, you cannot use the indefinite article *a* or *an* before a plural noun. You need to use the word *some* in this case:

E.G. *the tables* ➤ *some tables*
E.G. *the schools* ➤ *some schools*

Also look at the grammar box at **a**.

theatre theatres

Said "**theer**-ter" NOUN 1 (DRAMA) a building where plays and other entertainments are performed on a stage. 2 Theatre is work such as writing, producing, and acting in plays. 3 An operating theatre is a room in a hospital designed and equipped for surgical operations.
📖 from Greek *theatron* meaning 'viewing place'

theatrical

Said "thee-**at**-rik-kl" ADJECTIVE 1 (DRAMA) involving the theatre or performed in a theatre E.G. *his theatrical career.* 2 Theatrical behaviour is exaggerated, unnatural, and done for effect.

theatrically ADVERB

thee

PRONOUN; OLD-FASHIONED Thee means you.

theft thefts

NOUN Theft is the crime of stealing.
🔲 robbery, stealing

their

ADJECTIVE 'Their' refers to something belonging or relating to people or things, other than yourself or the person you are talking to, which have already been mentioned E.G. *It was their fault.*

☑ Be careful not to confuse *their* with *there*.

theirs

PRONOUN 'Theirs' refers to something belonging or relating to people or things, other than yourself or the person you are talking to, which have already been mentioned E.G. *Amy had been Helen's friend, not theirs.*

them

PRONOUN 'Them' refers to things or people, other than yourself or the people you are talking to, which have already been mentioned E.G. *He picked up the pillows and threw them to the floor.*

theme themes

NOUN 1 a main idea or topic in a piece of writing, painting, film, or music E.G. *the main theme of the book.* 2 a tune, especially one played at the beginning and end of a television or radio programme.

themselves

PRONOUN 1 'Themselves' is used when people, other than yourself or the person you are talking to, do an action and are affected by it E.G. *They think they've made a fool of themselves.* 2 'Themselves' is used to emphasize 'they' E.G. *He was as excited as they themselves were.*

then

ADVERB at a particular time in the past or future E.G. *I'd left home by then.*

theologian theologians

Said "thee-ol-**loe**-jee-an" NOUN someone who studies religion and the nature of God.

theology

NOUN Theology is the study of religion and God.

theological ADJECTIVE

theoretical

ADJECTIVE 1 based on or to do with ideas of a subject rather than the practical aspects. 2 not proved to exist or be true.

theoretically ADVERB

theory theories

NOUN 1 an idea or set of ideas that is meant to explain something E.G. *Darwin's theory of evolution.* 2 Theory is the set of rules and ideas that a particular subject or skill is based upon. ► PHRASE 3 You use **in theory** to say that although something is supposed to happen, it may not in fact happen E.G. *In theory, prices should rise by 2%.*

▤ (sense 1) conjecture, hypothesis

therapeutic

Said "ther-ap-**yoo**-tik" ADJECTIVE 1 If something is therapeutic, it helps you to feel happier and more relaxed E.G. *Laughing is therapeutic.* 2 In medicine, therapeutic treatment is designed to treat a disease or to improve a person's health.

therapy

NOUN Therapy is the treatment of mental or physical illness, often without the use of drugs or operations.

therapist NOUN

there

ADVERB 1 in, at, or to that place, point, or case E.G. *He's sitting over there.*

a b c d e f g h i j k l m n o p q r s t u v w x y z

▶ PRONOUN **2** 'There' is used to say that something exists or does not exist, or to draw attention to something E.G. *There are flowers on the table.*

☑ Be careful not to confuse *there* with *their*. A good way to remember that *there* is connected to the idea of place is by remembering the spelling of two other place words, *here* and *where*.

thereby
ADVERB; FORMAL as a result of the event or action mentioned E.G. *They had recruited 200 new members, thereby making the day worthwhile.*

therefore
ADVERB as a result.

thermal
ADJECTIVE **1** to do with or caused by heat E.G. *thermal energy.* **2** Thermal clothes are specially designed to keep you warm in cold weather.

thermometer thermometers
NOUN (SCIENCE) an instrument for measuring the temperature of a room or a person's body.

thermostat thermostats
NOUN a device used to control temperature, for example on a central heating system.

thesaurus thesauruses
Said "this-**saw**-russ" NOUN (LIBRARY) a reference book in which words with similar meanings are grouped together.
📖 from Greek *thēsauros* meaning 'treasure'

these
the plural of *this.*

thesis theses
Said "**thee**-siss" NOUN a long piece of writing, based on research, that is done as part of a university degree.

they
PRONOUN **1** 'They' refers to people or things, other than you or the people you are talking to, that have already been mentioned E.G. *They married two years later.* **2** 'They' is sometimes used instead of 'he' or 'she' where the sex of the person is unknown or unspecified. Some people consider this to be incorrect E.G. *Someone could have a nasty accident if they tripped over that.*

thick thicker thickest
ADJECTIVE **1** Something thick has a large distance between its two opposite surfaces. **2** If something is a particular amount thick, it measures that amount between its two sides. **3** Thick means growing or grouped closely together and in large quantities E.G. *thick dark hair.* **4** Thick liquids contain little water and do not flow easily E.G. *thick soup.* **5** INFORMAL A thick person is stupid or slow to understand things.

thicken thickens thickening thickened
VERB If something thickens, it becomes thicker E.G. *The clouds thickened.*

thicket thickets
NOUN a small group of trees growing closely together.

thief thieves
NOUN a person who steals.

thieving
NOUN Thieving is the act of stealing.

thigh thighs
NOUN Your thighs are the top parts of your legs, between your knees and your hips.

thimble thimbles
NOUN a small metal or plastic cap that you put on the end of your finger to protect it when you are sewing.

thin thinner thinnest; thins thinning thinned
ADJECTIVE **1** Something that is thin is much narrower than it is long. **2** A thin person or animal has very little fat on their body. **3** Thin liquids contain a lot of water E.G. *thin soup.*
▶ VERB **4** If you thin something such as paint or soup, you add water or other liquid to it.
■ (sense 2) lean, skinny, slim

thing things
NOUN **1** an object, rather than a plant, an animal, a human being. ▶ PLURAL NOUN **2** Your things are your clothes or possessions.
■ (sense 1) article, object

think thinks thinking thought
VERB **1** When you think about ideas or problems, you use your mind to consider them. **2** If you think something, you have the opinion that it is true or the case E.G. *I think she has a secret boyfriend.* **3** If you think of something, you remember it or it comes into your mind. **4** If you think a lot of someone or something, you admire them or think they are good.

third thirds
ADJECTIVE **1** The third item in a series is the one counted as number three. ▶ NOUN **2** one of three equal parts.

Third World
NOUN The poorer countries of Africa, Asia, and South America can be referred to as the Third World.

thirst thirsts
NOUN **1** If you have a thirst, you feel a need to drink something. **2** A thirst for something is a very strong desire for it E.G. *a thirst for money.*

thirsty ADJECTIVE   **thirstily** ADVERB

thirteen
the number 13.

thirteenth

thirty thirties
the number 30.

thirtieth

this these
ADJECTIVE OR PRONOUN **1** 'This' is used to refer to something or someone that is nearby or has just been mentioned E.G. *This is Robert.* **2** 'This' is used to refer to the present time or place E.G. *this week.*

thistle thistles
NOUN a wild plant with prickly-edged leaves and purple flowers.

thong thongs
NOUN a long narrow strip of leather.

thorn thorns
NOUN one of many sharp points growing on some plants and trees.

thorny thornier thorniest
ADJECTIVE **1** covered with thorns. **2** A thorny subject or question is difficult to discuss or answer.

thorough
Said "thur-ruh" ADJECTIVE **1** done very carefully and completely E.G. *a thorough examination.* **2** A thorough person is very careful in what they do and makes sure nothing has been missed out.

thoroughly ADVERB

thoroughbred thoroughbreds
NOUN an animal that has parents that are of the same high quality breed.

thoroughfare thoroughfares
NOUN a main road in a town.

those
the plural of **that.**

thou
PRONOUN; OLD-FASHIONED Thou means you.

a
b
c
d
e
f
g
h
i
j
k
l
m
n
o
p
q
r
s
t
u
v
w
x
y
z

A
B
C
D
E
F
G
H
I
J
K
L
M
N
O
P
Q
R
S
T
U
V
W
X
Y
Z

though
Rhymes with "show" CONJUNCTION
1 despite the fact that E.G. *Meg felt better, even though she knew it was the end.* 2 if E.G. *It looks as though you were right.*

thought thoughts
1 Thought is the past tense and past participle of **think**. ▶ NOUN 2 an idea that you have in your mind. 3 Thought is the activity of thinking E.G. *She was lost in thought.* 4 Thought is a particular way of thinking or a particular set of ideas E.G. *this school of thought.*
■ (sense 3) consideration, reflection, thinking

thoughtful
ADJECTIVE 1 When someone is thoughtful, they are quiet and serious because they are thinking about something. 2 A thoughtful person remembers what other people want or need, and tries to be kind to them.
thoughtfully ADVERB
■ (sense 1) meditative, pensive, reflective
■ (sense 2) caring, considerate, kind

thoughtless
ADJECTIVE A thoughtless person forgets or ignores what other people want, need, or feel.
thoughtlessly ADVERB

thousand thousands
the number 1000.
thousandth

thrash thrashes thrashing thrashed
VERB 1 To thrash someone is to beat them by hitting them with something. 2 To thrash someone in a contest or fight is to defeat them

completely. 3 To thrash out a problem or an idea is to discuss it in detail until a solution is reached.

thread threads threading threaded
NOUN 1 a long, fine piece of cotton, silk, nylon, or wool. 2 The thread on something such as a screw or the top of a container is the raised spiral line of metal or plastic round it. 3 The thread of an argument or story is an idea or theme that connects the different parts of it. ▶ VERB 4 When you thread something, you pass thread, tape, or cord through it. 5 If you thread your way through people or things, you carefully make your way through them.

threadbare
ADJECTIVE Threadbare cloth or clothing is old and thin.

threat threats
NOUN 1 a statement that someone will harm you, especially if you do not do what they want. 2 anything or anyone that seems likely to harm you. 3 If there is a threat of something unpleasant happening, it is very possible that it will happen.

threaten threatens threatening threatened
VERB 1 If you threaten to harm someone or threaten to do something that will upset them, you say that you will do it. 2 If someone or something threatens a person or thing, they are likely to harm them.
■ (sense 2) endanger, jeopardize

three
the number 3.

three-dimensional
ADJECTIVE A three-dimensional object or shape is not flat, but has height or

SPELLING NOTE   there's a rAKE in the brAKEs (br**ake**)

depth as well as length and width.

threesome threesomes
NOUN a group of three.

threshold thresholds
Said "thresh-hold" NOUN 1 the
doorway or the floor in the doorway
of a building or room. 2 The
threshold of something is the lowest
amount, level, or limit at which
something happens or changes E.G.
*the tax threshold… His boredom
threshold was exceptionally low.*

thrice
ADVERB; OLD-FASHIONED If you do
something thrice, you do it three
times.

thrift
NOUN Thrift is the practice of saving
money and not wasting things.

thrifty thriftier thriftiest
ADJECTIVE A thrifty person saves
money and does not waste things.

thrill thrills thrilling thrilled
NOUN 1 a sudden feeling of great
excitement, pleasure, or fear; also any
event or experience that gives you
such a feeling. ▶ VERB 2 If something
thrills you, or you thrill to it, it gives
you a feeling of great pleasure and
excitement.
thrilled ADJECTIVE   **thrilling** ADJECTIVE
■ (sense 1) buzz, kick

thriller thrillers
NOUN a book, film, or play that tells an
exciting story about dangerous or
mysterious events.

thrive thrives thriving thrived or
throve
VERB When people or things thrive,
they are healthy, happy, or successful.
thriving ADJECTIVE

throat throats
NOUN 1 the back of your mouth and

the top part of the passages inside
your neck. 2 the front part of your
neck.

throb throbs throbbing
throbbed
VERB 1 If a part of your body throbs,
you feel a series of strong beats or
dull pains. 2 If something throbs, it
vibrates and makes a loud, rhythmic
noise E.G. *The engines throbbed.*

throes
PLURAL NOUN 1 Throes are a series of
violent pangs or movements E.G.
death throes. ▶ PHRASE 2 If you are **in
the throes of** something, you are
deeply involved in it.

thrombosis thromboses
Said "throm-boe-siss" NOUN a blood
clot which blocks the flow of blood
in the body. Thromboses are
dangerous and often fatal.

throne thrones
NOUN 1 a ceremonial chair used by a
king or queen on important official
occasions. 2 The throne is a way of
referring to the position of being
king or queen.

throng throngs thronging
thronged
NOUN 1 a large crowd of people. ▶ VERB
2 If people throng somewhere or
throng a place, they go there in great
numbers E.G. *Hundreds of city
workers thronged the scene.*

throttle throttles throttling
throttled
VERB To throttle someone is to kill or
injure them by squeezing their
throat.

through
Said "threw" PREPOSITION 1 moving all
the way from one side of something
to the other E.G. *a path through the*

a
b
c
d
e
f
g
h
i
j
k
l
m
n
o
p
q
r
s
t
u
v
w
x
y
z

A B C D E F G H I J K L M N O P Q R S T U V W X Y Z

woods. **2** because of E.G. *He had been exhausted through lack of sleep.*
3 during E.G. *He has to work through the summer.* **4** If you go through an experience, it happens to you E.G. *I don't want to go through that again.*
▶ ADJECTIVE **5** If you are through with something, you have finished doing it or using it

☑ Do not confuse the spellings of *through* and *threw*, the past tense of *throw*.

throughout
PREPOSITION **1** during E.G. *I stayed awake throughout the night.* ▶ ADVERB **2** happening or existing through the whole of a place E.G. *The house was painted brown throughout.*

throve
the past tense of **thrive**.

throw throws throwing threw thrown
VERB **1** When you throw something you are holding, you move your hand quickly and let it go, so that it moves through the air. **2** If you throw yourself somewhere, you move there suddenly and with force E.G. *We threw ourselves on the ground.* **3** To throw someone into an unpleasant situation is to put them there E.G. *It threw them into a panic.* **4** If something throws light or shadow on something else, it makes that thing have light or shadow on it. **5** If you throw yourself into an activity, you become actively and enthusiastically involved in it. **6** If you throw a fit or tantrum, you suddenly begin behaving in an uncontrolled way.

🖹 (sense 1) chuck, fling, hurl
throwback throwbacks
NOUN something which has the

characteristics of something that existed a long time ago E.G. *Everything about her was a throwback to the fifties.*

thrush thrushes
NOUN **1** a small brown songbird.
2 Thrush is a disease of the mouth or of the vagina, caused by a fungus.

thrust thrusts thrusting thrust
VERB **1** If you thrust something somewhere, you push or move it there quickly with a lot of force. **2** If you thrust your way somewhere, you move along, pushing between people or things. ▶ NOUN **3** a sudden forceful movement. **4** The main thrust of an activity or idea is the most important part of it E.G. *the general thrust of his argument.*

thud thuds thudding thudded
NOUN **1** a dull sound, usually made by a solid, heavy object hitting something soft. ▶ VERB **2** If something thuds somewhere, it makes a dull sound, usually by hitting something else.

thug thugs
NOUN a very rough and violent person.
🏛 from Hindi *thag* meaning 'thief'

thumb thumbs thumbing thumbed
NOUN **1** the short, thick finger on the side of your hand. ▶ VERB **2** If someone thumbs a lift, they stand at the side of the road and stick out their thumb until a driver stops and gives them a lift.

thump thumps thumping thumped
VERB **1** If you thump someone or something, you hit them hard with your fist. **2** If something thumps

somewhere, it makes a fairly loud, dull sound, usually when it hits something else. **3** When your heart thumps, it beats strongly and quickly. ▶ NOUN **4** a hard hit E.G. *a great thump on the back.* **5** a fairly loud, dull sound.

thunder thunders thundering thundered
NOUN **1** Thunder is a loud cracking or rumbling noise caused by expanding air which is suddenly heated by lightning. **2** Thunder is any loud rumbling noise E.G. *the distant thunder of bombs.* ▶ VERB **3** When it thunders, a loud cracking or rumbling noise occurs in the sky after a flash of lightning. **4** If something thunders, it makes a loud continuous noise E.G. *The helicopter thundered low over the trees.*

thunderbolt thunderbolts
NOUN a flash of lightning, accompanied by thunder.

thunderous
ADJECTIVE A thunderous noise is very loud E.G. *thunderous applause.*

Thursday Thursdays
NOUN Thursday is the day between Wednesday and Friday.
📖 from Old English *Thursdæg* meaning 'Thor's day'; Thor was the Norse god of thunder

thus
ADVERB FORMAL **1** in this way E.G. *I sat thus for nearly half an hour.*
2 therefore E.G. *Critics were thus able to denounce him.*

thwart thwarts thwarting thwarted
VERB To thwart someone or their plans is to prevent them from doing or getting what they want.

thy
ADJECTIVE; OLD-FASHIONED Thy means your.

thyme
Said "time" NOUN Thyme is a bushy herb with very small leaves.

thyroid gland thyroid glands
NOUN Your thyroid gland is situated at the base of your neck. It releases hormones which control your growth and your metabolism.

tiara tiaras
Said "tee-ah-ra" NOUN a semicircular crown of jewels worn by a woman on formal occasions.

Tibetan Tibetans
ADJECTIVE **1** belonging or relating to Tibet. ▶ NOUN **2** someone who comes from Tibet.

tic tics
NOUN a twitching of a group of muscles, especially the muscles in the face.

tick ticks ticking ticked
NOUN **1** a written mark to show that something is correct or has been dealt with. **2** The tick of a clock is the series of short sounds it makes when it is working. **3** a tiny, blood-sucking, insect-like creature that usually lives on the bodies of people or animals.
▶ VERB **4** To tick something written on a piece of paper is to put a tick next to it. **5** When a clock ticks, it makes a regular series of short sounds as it works.

tick off VERB INFORMAL If you tick someone off, you speak angrily to them because they have done something wrong.

ticking NOUN

ticket tickets
NOUN a piece of paper or card which shows that you have paid for a

a
b
c
d
e
f
g
h
i
j
k
l
m
n
o
p
q
r
s
t
u
v
w
x
y
z

journey or have paid to enter a place of entertainment.

tickle tickles tickling tickled
VERB 1 When you tickle someone, you move your fingers lightly over their body in order to make them laugh. 2 If something tickles you, it amuses you or gives you pleasure E.G. *Simon is tickled by the idea.*

tidal
ADJECTIVE to do with or produced by tides E.G. *a tidal estuary.*

tidal wave tidal waves
NOUN a very large wave, often caused by an earthquake, that comes over land and destroys things.

tide tides tiding tided
NOUN 1 The tide is the regular change in the level of the sea on the shore, caused by the gravitational pull of the sun and the moon. 2 The tide of opinion or fashion is what the majority of people think or do at a particular time. 3 A tide of something is a large amount of it E.G. *the tide of anger and bitterness.*

tide over VERB If something will tide someone over, it will help them through a difficult period of time.

tidings
PLURAL NOUN; FORMAL Tidings are news.

tidy tidier tidiest; tidies tidying tidied
ADJECTIVE 1 Something that is tidy is neat and arranged in an orderly way. 2 Someone who is tidy always keeps their things neat and arranged in an orderly way. 3 INFORMAL A tidy amount of money is a fairly large amount of it. ▶ VERB 4 To tidy a place is to make it neat by putting things in their proper place.

tie ties tying tied
VERB 1 If you tie one thing to another or tie it in a particular position, you fasten it using cord of some kind. 2 If you tie a knot or a bow in a piece of cord or cloth, you fasten the ends together to make a knot or bow. 3 Something or someone that is tied to something else is closely linked with it E.G. *40,000 jobs are tied to the project.* 4 If you tie with someone in a competition or game, you have the same number of points. ▶ NOUN 5 a long, narrow piece of cloth worn around the neck under a shirt collar and tied in a knot at the front. 6 a connection or feeling that links you with a person, place, or organization E.G. *I had very close ties with the family.*
▤ (sense 1) bind, fasten

tied up
ADJECTIVE If you are tied up, you are busy.

tier tiers
NOUN one of a number of rows or layers of something E.G. *Take the stairs to the upper tier.*

tiff tiffs
NOUN a small unimportant quarrel.

tiger tigers
NOUN a large meat-eating animal of the cat family. It comes from Asia and has an orange coloured coat with black stripes.

tiger snake tiger snakes
NOUN a fierce, very poisonous Australian snake with dark stripes across its back.

tight tighter tightest
ADJECTIVE 1 fitting closely E.G. *The shoes are too tight.* 2 firmly fastened and difficult to move E.G. *a tight*

knot. **3** stretched or pulled so as not to be slack E.G. *a tight cord.* **4** A tight plan or arrangement allows only the minimum time or money needed to do something E.G. *Our schedule tonight is very tight.* ► ADVERB **5** held firmly and securely E.G. *He held me tight.*

tightly ADVERB **tightness** NOUN

■ (sense 3) stretched, taut

tighten tightens tightening tightened

VERB **1** If you tighten your hold on something, you hold it more firmly. **2** If you tighten a rope or chain, or if it tightens, it is stretched or pulled until it is straight. **3** If someone tightens a rule or system, they make it stricter or more efficient.

tightrope tightropes

NOUN a tightly-stretched rope on which an acrobat balances and performs tricks.

tights

PLURAL NOUN Tights are a piece of clothing made of thin stretchy material that fit closely round a person's hips, legs, and feet.

tiki tiki or **tikis**

NOUN In New Zealand, a small carving of an ancestor worn as a pendant in some Maori cultures.

tile tiles tiling tiled

NOUN **1** a small flat square piece of something, for example slate or carpet, that is used to cover surfaces. ► VERB **2** To tile a surface is to fix tiles to it.

tiled ADJECTIVE

till tills tilling tilled

PREPOSITION or CONJUNCTION **1** Till means the same as until. ► NOUN **2** a drawer or box in a shop where money is kept, usually in a cash register. ► VERB **3** To till the ground is to plough it for raising crops.

tiller tillers

NOUN the handle fixed to the top of the rudder for steering a boat.

tilt tilts tilting tilted

VERB **1** If you tilt an object or it tilts, it changes position so that one end or side is higher than the other. ► NOUN **2** a position in which one end or side of something is higher than the other.

■ (sense 1) incline, lean, tip

timber timbers

NOUN **1** Timber is wood that has been cut and prepared ready for building and making furniture. **2** The timbers of a ship or house are the large pieces of wood that have been used to build it.

time times timing timed

NOUN **1** Time is what is measured in hours, days, and years E.G. *What time is it?* **2** 'Time' is used to mean a particular period or point E.G. *I enjoyed my time in Durban.* **3** If you say it is time for something or it is time to do it, you mean that it ought to happen or be done now E.G. *It is time for a change.* **4** 'Times' is used after numbers to indicate how often something happens E.G. *I saw my father four times a year.* **5** 'Times' is used after numbers when you are saying how much bigger, smaller, better, or worse one thing is compared to another E.G. *The Belgians drink three times as much beer as the French.* **6** 'Times' is used in arithmetic to link numbers that are multiplied together E.G. *Two times three is six.* ► VERB **7** If you time something for a particular time, you

a
b
c
d
e
f
g
h
i
j
k
l
m
n
o
p
q
r
s
t
u
v
w
x
y
z

A
B
C
D
E
F
G
H
I
J
K
L
M
N
O
P
Q
R
S
T
U
V
W
X
Y
Z

plan that it should happen then E.G. *We could not have timed our arrival better.* **8** If you time an activity or action, you measure how long it lasts.

◼ (sense 2) interval, period, spell

timeless
ADJECTIVE Something timeless is so good or beautiful that it cannot be affected by the passing of time or by changes in fashion.

timely
ADJECTIVE happening at just the right time E.G. *a timely appearance.*
◼ opportune, well-timed

timer timers
NOUN a device that measures time, especially one that is part of a machine.

timescale timescales
NOUN The timescale of an event is the length of time during which it happens.

timetable timetables
NOUN **1** a plan of the times when particular activities or jobs should be done. **2** a list of the times when particular trains, boats, buses, or aeroplanes arrive and depart.

timid
ADJECTIVE shy and having no courage or self-confidence.

timidly ADVERB   **timidity** NOUN
◼ fearful, shy, timorous

timing
NOUN **1** Someone's timing is their skill in judging the right moment at which to do something. **2** The timing of an event is when it actually happens.

timpani
Said "tim-pan-ee" PLURAL NOUN Timpani are large drums with curved

bottoms that are played in an orchestra.

tin tins
NOUN **1** Tin is a soft silvery-white metal. **2** a metal container which is filled with food and then sealed in order to preserve the food. **3** a small metal container which may have a lid E.G. *a cake tin.*

tinder
NOUN Tinder is small pieces of dry wood or grass that burn easily and can be used for lighting a fire.

tinge tinges
NOUN a small amount of something E.G. *a tinge of envy.*
tinged ADJECTIVE

tingle tingles tingling tingled
VERB **1** When a part of your body tingles, you feel a slight prickling feeling in it. ▶ NOUN **2** a slight prickling feeling.
tingling NOUN or ADJECTIVE

tinker tinkers tinkering tinkered
NOUN **1** a person who travels from place to place mending metal pots and pans or doing other small repair jobs. ▶ VERB **2** If you tinker with something, you make a lot of small changes to it in order to repair or improve it E.G. *All he wanted was to tinker with engines.*

tinkle tinkles tinkling tinkled
VERB **1** If something tinkles, it makes a sound like a small bell ringing.
▶ NOUN **2** a sound like that of a small bell ringing.

tinned
ADJECTIVE Tinned food has been preserved by being sealed in a tin.

tinsel
NOUN Tinsel is long threads with strips of shiny paper attached, used as a

decoration at Christmas.

tint tints tinting tinted
NOUN 1 a small amount of a particular colour E.G. *a distinct tint of green*.
▶ VERB 2 If a person tints their hair, they change its colour by adding a weak dye to it.
tinted ADJECTIVE

tiny tinier tiniest
ADJECTIVE extremely small.
■ diminutive, minute

tip tips tipping tipped
NOUN 1 the end of something long and thin E.G. *a fingertip*. 2 a place where rubbish is dumped. 3 If you give someone such as a waiter a tip, you give them some money to thank them for their services. 4 a useful piece of advice or information. ▶ VERB 5 If you tip an object, you move it so that it is no longer horizontal or upright. 6 If you tip something somewhere, you pour it there quickly or carelessly.
tipped ADJECTIVE

tipple tipples
NOUN A person's tipple is the alcoholic drink that they normally drink.

tipsy tipsier tipsiest
ADJECTIVE slightly drunk.

tiptoe tiptoes tiptoeing tiptoed
VERB If you tiptoe somewhere, you walk there very quietly on your toes.

tirade tirades
Said "tie-**rade**" NOUN a long, angry speech in which you criticize someone or something.
🔲 from Italian *tirata* meaning 'volley of shots'

tire tires tiring tired
VERB 1 If something tires you, it makes you use a lot of energy so that you want to rest or sleep. 2 If you tire of

something, you become bored with it.

tired ADJECTIVE **tiredness** NOUN
■ (sense 1) exhaust, fatigue, weary

tireless
ADJECTIVE Someone who is tireless has a lot of energy and never seems to need a rest.

tiresome
ADJECTIVE A person or thing that is tiresome makes you feel irritated or bored.

tiring
ADJECTIVE Something that is tiring makes you tired.

tissue tissues
Said "**tiss**-yoo" NOUN 1 The tissue in plants and animals consists of cells that are similar in appearance and function E.G. *scar tissue… dead tissue*. 2 Tissue is thin paper that is used for wrapping breakable objects. 3 a small piece of soft paper that you use as a handkerchief.

tit tits
NOUN a small European bird E.G. *a blue tit*.

titanic
ADJECTIVE very big or important.
🔲 in Greek legend, the *Titans* were a family of giants

titillate titillates titillating titillated
VERB If something titillates someone, it pleases and excites them, especially in a sexual way.
titillation NOUN

title titles
NOUN 1 the name of a book, play, or piece of music. 2 a word that describes someone's rank or job E.G. *My official title is Design Manager*. 3 the position of champion in a

a
b
c
d
e
f
g
h
i
j
k
l
m
n
o
p
q
r
s
t
u
v
w
x
y
z

A
B
C
D
E
F
G
H
I
J
K
L
M
N
O
P
Q
R
S
T
U
V
W
X
Y
Z

sports competition E.G. *the European featherweight title.*

titled

ADJECTIVE Someone who is titled has a high social rank and has a title such as 'Princess', 'Lord', 'Lady', or 'Sir'.

titter titters tittering tittered

VERB If you titter, you laugh in a way that shows you are nervous or embarrassed.

TNT

NOUN TNT is a type of powerful explosive. It is an abbreviation for 'trinitrotoluene'.

to

PREPOSITION 1 'To' is used to indicate the place that someone or something is moving towards or pointing at E.G. *They are going to China.* 2 'To' is used to indicate the limit of something E.G. *Goods to the value of 500 pounds.* 3 'To' is used in ratios and rates when saying how many units of one type there are for each unit of another E.G. *I only get about 30 kilometres to the gallon from it.* ▶ ADVERB 4 If you push or shut a door to, you close it but do not shut it completely.

✓ The preposition *to* is spelt with one *o*, the adverb *too* has two *o*s, and the number *two* is spelt with *wo*.

toad toads

NOUN an amphibian that looks like a frog but has a drier skin and lives less in the water.

toadstool toadstools

NOUN a type of poisonous fungus.

toast toasts toasting toasted

NOUN 1 Toast is slices of bread made brown and crisp by cooking at a high temperature. 2 To drink a toast to someone is to drink an alcoholic drink in honour of them. ▶ VERB 3 If

you toast bread, you cook it at a high temperature so that it becomes brown and crisp. 4 If you toast yourself, you sit in front of a fire so that you feel pleasantly warm. 5 To toast someone is to drink an alcoholic drink in honour of them.
🔲 from Latin *tostus* meaning 'parched'

toaster toasters

NOUN a piece of electrical equipment used for toasting bread.

tobacco

NOUN Tobacco is the dried leaves of the tobacco plant which people smoke in pipes, cigarettes, and cigars.

tobacconist tobacconists

NOUN a shop where tobacco, cigarettes, and cigars are sold.

toboggan toboggans

NOUN a flat seat with two wooden or metal runners, used for sliding over the snow.
🔲 an American Indian word

today

ADVERB or NOUN 1 Today means the day on which you are speaking or writing. 2 Today also means the present period of history E.G. *the challenges of teaching in today's schools.*

toddle toddles toddling toddled

VERB To toddle is to walk in short, quick steps, as a very young child does.

toddler toddlers

NOUN a small child who has just learned to walk.

to-do to-dos

NOUN A to-do is a situation in which people are very agitated or confused E.G. *It's just like him to make such a to-do about a baby.*

toe toes

NOUN **1** Your toes are the five movable parts at the end of your foot. **2** The toe of a shoe or sock is the part that covers the end of your foot.

toff toffs

NOUN; AN INFORMAL, OLD-FASHIONED WORD a rich person or one from an aristocratic family.

toffee toffees

NOUN Toffee is a sticky, chewy sweet made by boiling sugar and butter together with water.

toga togas

NOUN a long loose robe worn in ancient Rome.

together

ADVERB **1** If people do something together, they do it with each other. **2** If two things happen together, they happen at the same time. **3** If things are joined or fixed together, they are joined or fixed to each other. **4** If things or people are together, they are very near to each other.

■ (sense 1) collectively, jointly

■ (sense 2) concurrently, simultaneously

✔ Two nouns joined by *together with* do not make a plural subject, so the following verb is not plural: *Jones, together with his partner, has had great success.*

togetherness

NOUN Togetherness is a feeling of closeness and friendship.

toil toils toiling toiled

VERB **1** When people toil, they work hard doing unpleasant, difficult, or tiring tasks or jobs. ▶ NOUN **2** Toil is unpleasant, difficult, or tiring work.

toilet toilets

NOUN **1** a large bowl, connected by a pipe to the drains, which you use when you want to get rid of urine or faeces. **2** a small room containing a toilet.

toiletries

PLURAL NOUN Toiletries are the things you use when cleaning and taking care of your body, such as soap and talc.

token tokens

NOUN **1** a piece of paper or card that is worth a particular amount of money and can be exchanged for goods E.G. *record tokens*. **2** a flat round piece of metal or plastic that can sometimes be used instead of money. **3** If you give something to someone as a token of your feelings for them, you give it to them as a way of showing those feelings. ▶ ADJECTIVE **4** If something is described as token, it shows that it is not being treated as important E.G. *a token contribution to your fees*.

told

Told is the past tense and past participle of **tell**.

tolerable

ADJECTIVE **1** able to be put up with. **2** fairly satisfactory or reasonable E.G. *a tolerable salary*.

tolerance

NOUN **1** A person's tolerance is their ability to accept or put up with something which may not be enjoyable or pleasant for them. **2** Tolerance is the quality of allowing other people to have their own attitudes or beliefs, or to behave in a particular way, even if you do not agree or approve E.G. *religious tolerance*.

tolerant ADJECTIVE

a
b
c
d
e
f
g
h
i
j
k
l
m
n
o
p
q
r
s
t
u
v
w
x
y
z

A
B
C
D
E
F
G
H
I
J
K
L
M
N
O
P
Q
R
S
T
U
V
W
X
Y
Z

tolerate tolerates tolerating tolerated

VERB 1 If you tolerate things that you do not approve of or agree with, you allow them. 2 If you can tolerate something, you accept it, even though it is unsatisfactory or unpleasant.

toleration NOUN

■ (sense 2) bear, endure, stand

toll tolls tolling tolled

NOUN 1 The death toll in an accident is the number of people who have died in it. 2 a sum of money that you have to pay in order to use a particular bridge or road. ▶ VERB 3 When someone tolls a bell, it is rung slowly, often as a sign that someone has died.

tom toms

NOUN a male cat.

tomahawk tomahawks

NOUN a small axe used by North American Indians.

tomato tomatoes

NOUN a small round red fruit, used as a vegetable and often eaten raw in salads.

tomb tombs

NOUN a large grave for one or more corpses.

tomboy tomboys

NOUN a girl who likes playing rough or noisy games.

tome tomes

NOUN; FORMAL a very large heavy book.

tomorrow

ADVERB OR NOUN 1 Tomorrow means the day after today. 2 You can refer to the future, especially the near future, as tomorrow.

ton tons

NOUN 1 a unit of weight equal to 2240 pounds or about 1016 kilograms. ▶ PLURAL NOUN 2 INFORMAL If you have tons of something, you have a lot of it.

tonal

ADJECTIVE involving the quality or pitch of a sound or of music.

tone tones toning toned

NOUN 1 Someone's tone is a quality in their voice which shows what they are thinking or feeling. 2 The tone of a musical instrument or a singer's voice is the kind of sound it has. 3 The tone of a piece of writing is its style and the ideas or opinions expressed in it E.G. *I was shocked at the tone of your leading article.* 4 a lighter, darker, or brighter shade of the same colour E.G. *The whole room is painted in two tones of orange.*

tone down VERB If you tone down something, you make it less forceful or severe.

tone-deaf

ADJECTIVE unable to sing in tune or to recognize different tunes.

tongs

PLURAL NOUN Tongs consist of two long narrow pieces of metal joined together at one end. You press the pieces together to pick an object up.

tongue tongues

NOUN 1 Your tongue is the soft part in your mouth that you can move and use for tasting, licking, and speaking. 2 a language. 3 Tongue is the cooked tongue of an ox. 4 The tongue of a shoe or boot is the piece of leather underneath the laces.

tonic tonics

NOUN 1 Tonic or tonic water is a colourless, fizzy drink that has a slightly bitter flavour and is often mixed with alcoholic drinks. **2** a medicine that makes you feel stronger, healthier, and less tired. **3** anything that makes you feel stronger or more cheerful E.G. *It was a tonic just being with her*.

tonight

ADVERB or NOUN Tonight is the evening or night that will come at the end of today.

tonne tonnes

Said "tun" NOUN (MATHS) a unit of weight equal to 1000 kilograms.

tonsil tonsils

NOUN Your tonsils are the two small, soft lumps in your throat at the back of your mouth.

tonsillitis

Said "ton-sil-lie-tiss" NOUN Tonsillitis is a painful swelling of your tonsils caused by an infection.

too

ADVERB **1** also or as well E.G. *You were there too*. **2** more than a desirable, necessary, or acceptable amount E.G. *a man who had taken too much to drink*.

☑ The adverb *too* has two *o*s, the preposition *to* is spelt with one *o*, and the number *two* is spelt with *wo*.

tool tools

NOUN **1** any hand-held instrument or piece of equipment that you use to help you do a particular kind of work. **2** an object, skill, or idea that is needed or used for a particular purpose E.G. *You can use the survey as a bargaining tool in the negotiations*.

▤ (sense 1) implement, instrument, utensil

toot toots tooting tooted

VERB If a car horn toots, it produces a short sound.

tooth teeth

NOUN **1** Your teeth are the hard enamel-covered objects in your mouth that you use for biting and chewing food. **2** The teeth of a comb, saw, or zip are the parts that stick out in a row on its edge.

toothpaste

NOUN Toothpaste is a substance which you use to clean your teeth.

top tops topping topped

NOUN **1** The top of something is its highest point, part, or surface. **2** The top of a bottle, jar, or tube is its cap or lid. **3** a piece of clothing worn on the upper half of your body. **4** a toy with a pointed end on which it spins. ▶ ADJECTIVE **5** The top thing of a series of things is the highest one E.G. *the top floor of the building*. ▶ VERB **6** If someone tops a poll or popularity chart, they do better than anyone else in it E.G. *It has topped the bestseller lists in almost every country*. **7** If something tops a particular amount, it is greater than that amount E.G. *The temperature topped 90°*.

▤ (sense 1) apex, height, peak

top hat top hats

NOUN a tall hat with a narrow brim that men wear on special occasions.

topic topics

NOUN a particular subject that you write about or discuss.

topical

ADJECTIVE involving or related to events that are happening at the time you are speaking or writing.

topping toppings

NOUN food that is put on top of other food in order to decorate it or add to its flavour.

a
b
c
d
e
f
g
h
i
j
k
l
m
n
o
p
q
r
s
t
u
v
w
x
y
z

A
B
C
D
E
F
G
H
I
J
K
L
M
N
O
P
Q
R
S
T
U
V
W
X
Y
Z

topple topples toppling toppled
VERB If something topples, it becomes unsteady and falls over.

top-secret
ADJECTIVE meant to be kept completely secret.

topsy-turvy
ADJECTIVE in a confused state E.G. *My life was truly topsy-turvy*.

Torah
NOUN The Torah is Jewish law and teaching.

torch torches
NOUN **1** a small electric light carried in the hand and powered by batteries. **2** a long stick with burning material wrapped around one end.

torment torments tormenting tormented
NOUN **1** Torment is extreme pain or unhappiness. **2** something that causes extreme pain and unhappiness E.G. *It's a torment to see them staring at me*. ▶ VERB **3** If something torments you, it causes you extreme unhappiness.

torn
1 Torn is the past participle of **tear**. ▶ ADJECTIVE **2** If you are torn between two or more things, you cannot decide which one to choose and this makes you unhappy E.G. *torn between duty and pleasure*.

tornado tornadoes or **tornados**
Said "tor-**nay**-doh" NOUN a violent storm with strong circular winds around a funnel-shaped cloud.

torpedo torpedoes torpedoing torpedoed
Said "tor-**pee**-doh" NOUN **1** a tube-shaped bomb that travels underwater and explodes when it hits a target. ▶ VERB **2** If a ship is

torpedoed, it is hit, and usually sunk, by a torpedo.

torrent torrents
NOUN **1** When a lot of water is falling very rapidly, it can be said to be falling in torrents. **2** A torrent of speech is a lot of it directed continuously at someone E.G. *torrents of abuse*.

torrential
ADJECTIVE Torrential rain pours down very rapidly and in great quantities.

torrid
ADJECTIVE **1** Torrid weather is very hot and dry. **2** A torrid love affair is one in which people show very strong emotions.

torso torsos
NOUN the main part of your body, excluding your head, arms, and legs.

tortoise tortoises
NOUN a slow-moving reptile with a large hard shell over its body into which it can pull its head and legs for protection.

tortuous
ADJECTIVE **1** A tortuous road is full of bends and twists. **2** A tortuous piece of writing is long and complicated.

torture tortures torturing tortured
NOUN **1** Torture is great pain that is deliberately caused to someone to punish them or get information from them. ▶ VERB **2** If someone tortures another person, they deliberately cause that person great pain to punish them or get information. **3** To torture someone is also to cause them to suffer mentally E.G. *Memory tortured her*.

torturer NOUN

Tory Tories
NOUN In Britain, a member or

supporter of the Conservative Party. 🏛 from Irish *toraidhe* meaning 'outlaw'

toss tosses tossing tossed
VERB **1** If you toss something somewhere, you throw it there lightly and carelessly. **2** If you toss a coin, you decide something by throwing a coin into the air and guessing which side will face upwards when it lands. **3** If you toss your head, you move it suddenly backwards, especially when you are angry, annoyed, or want your own way. **4** To toss is to move repeatedly from side to side E.G. *We tossed and turned and tried to sleep.*
▤ (sense 1) fling, sling, throw

tot tots totting totted
NOUN **1** a very young child. **2** a small amount of strong alcohol such as whisky. ► VERB **3** To tot up numbers is to add them together.

total totals totalling totalled
NOUN **1** the number you get when you add several numbers together. ► VERB **2** When you total a set of numbers or objects, you add them all together. **3** If several numbers total a certain figure, that is the figure you get when all the numbers are added together E.G. *Their debts totalled over 300,000 dollars.* ► ADJECTIVE **4** Total means complete E.G. *a total failure.*
totally ADVERB
▤ (sense 1) aggregate, sum, whole

totalitarian
Said "toe-tal-it-**tair**-ee-an" ADJECTIVE A totalitarian political system is one in which one political party controls everything and does not allow any other parties to exist.
totalitarianism NOUN

tote totes toting toted
VERB; INFORMAL To tote a gun is to carry it.

totem pole totem poles
NOUN a long wooden pole with symbols and pictures carved and painted on it. Totem poles are made by some North American Indians.

totter totters tottering tottered
VERB When someone totters, they walk in an unsteady way.

toucan toucans
Said "**too**-kan" NOUN a large tropical bird with a very large beak.

touch touches touching touched
VERB **1** If you touch something, you put your fingers or hand on it. **2** When two things touch, their surfaces come into contact E.G. *Their knees were touching.* **3** If you are touched by something, you are emotionally affected by it E.G. *I was touched by his thoughtfulness.* ► NOUN **4** Your sense of touch is your ability to tell what something is like by touching it. **5** a detail which is added to improve something E.G. *finishing touches.* **6** a small amount of something E.G. *a touch of mustard.* ► PHRASE **7** If you are **in touch** with someone, you are in contact with them.

touchdown touchdowns
NOUN Touchdown is the landing of an aircraft.

touching
ADJECTIVE causing feelings of sadness and sympathy.
▤ moving, poignant, sad

touchy touchier touchiest
ADJECTIVE **1** If someone is touchy, they are easily upset or irritated. **2** A touchy subject is one that needs to

A
B
C
D
E
F
G
H
I
J
K
L
M
N
O
P
Q
R
S
T
U
V
W
X
Y
Z

be dealt with carefully, because it might upset or offend people.

tough tougher toughest
Said "**tuff**" ADJECTIVE **1** A tough person is strong and independent and able to put up with hardship. **2** A tough substance is difficult to break. **3** A tough task, problem, or way of life is difficult or full of hardship. **4** Tough policies or actions are strict and firm E.G. *tough measures against organized crime.*

toughly ADVERB **toughness** NOUN **toughen** VERB

▪ (sense 2) durable, resilient, strong

toupee toupees
Said "**too-pay**" NOUN a small wig worn by a man to cover a bald patch on his head.

tour tours touring toured
NOUN **1** a long journey during which you visit several places. **2** a short trip round a place such as a city or famous building. ▶ VERB **3** If you tour a place, you go on a journey or a trip round it.

tourism
NOUN (GEOGRAPHY) Tourism is the business of providing services for people on holiday, for example hotels and sightseeing trips.

tourist tourists (GEOGRAPHY)
NOUN a person who visits places for pleasure or interest.

tournament tournaments
NOUN (PE) a sports competition in which players who win a match play further matches, until just one person or team is left.

tourniquet tourniquets
Said "**toor**-nik-kay" NOUN a strip of cloth tied tightly round a wound to stop it bleeding.

tousled
ADJECTIVE Tousled hair is untidy.

tout touts touting touted
VERB **1** If someone touts something, they try to sell it. **2** If someone touts for business or custom, they try to obtain it in a very direct way E.G. *volunteers who spend days touting for donations.* ▶ NOUN **3** someone who sells tickets outside a sports ground or theatre, charging more than the original price.

tow tows towing towed
VERB **1** If a vehicle tows another vehicle, it pulls it along behind it. ▶ NOUN **2** To give a vehicle a tow is to tow it. ▶ PHRASE **3** If you have someone **in tow**, they are with you because you are looking after them.

towards
PREPOSITION **1** in the direction of E.G. *He turned towards the door.* **2** about or involving E.G. *My feelings towards Susan have changed.* **3** as a contribution for E.G. *a huge donation towards the new opera house.* **4** near to E.G. *We sat towards the back.*

towel towels
NOUN a piece of thick, soft cloth that you use to dry yourself with.

towelling
NOUN Towelling is thick, soft cloth that is used for making towels.

tower towers towering towered
NOUN **1** a tall, narrow building, sometimes attached to a larger building such as a castle or church. ▶ VERB **2** Someone or something that towers over other people or things is much taller than them.

towering ADJECTIVE

town towns
NOUN **1** a place with many streets and

buildings where people live and work. **2** Town is the central shopping and business part of a town rather than the suburbs E.G. *She has gone into town.*

township townships
NOUN a small town in South Africa where only Black people or Coloured people were allowed to live.

towpath towpaths
NOUN a path along the side of a canal or river.

toxic
ADJECTIVE poisonous E.G. *toxic waste*.
🔲 from Greek *toxikon* meaning 'poison used on arrows' from *toxon* meaning 'arrow'

toxin toxins
NOUN a poison, especially one produced by bacteria and very harmful to living creatures.

toy toys toying toyed
NOUN **1** any object made to play with. ▶ VERB **2** If you toy with an idea, you consider it without being very serious about it E.G. *She toyed with the idea of telephoning him.* **3** If you toy with an object, you fiddle with it E.G. *Jessica was toying with her glass.*

toyi-toyi or **toy-toy**
NOUN In South Africa, a toyi-toyi is a dance performed to protest about something.

trace traces tracing traced
VERB **1** If you trace something, you find it after looking for it E.G. *Police are trying to trace the owner.*
2 (EXAM TERM) To trace the development of something is to find out or describe how it developed. **3** If you trace a drawing or a map, you copy it by covering it with a piece of

transparent paper and drawing over the lines underneath. ▶ NOUN **4** a sign which shows you that someone or something has been in a place E.G. *No trace of his father had been found.* **5** a very small amount of something.
tracing NOUN

track tracks tracking tracked
NOUN **1** a narrow road or path. **2** a strip of ground with rails on it that a train travels along. **3** a piece of ground, shaped like a ring, which horses, cars, or athletes race around. ▶ PLURAL NOUN **4** Tracks are marks left on the ground by a person or animal E.G. *the deer tracks by the side of the path.*
▶ ADJECTIVE **5** In an athletics competition, the track events are the races on a running track. ▶ VERB **6** If you track animals or people, you find them by following their footprints or other signs that they have left behind.

track down VERB If you track down someone or something, you find them by searching for them.

track record track records
NOUN The track record of a person or a company is their past achievements or failures E.G. *the track record of the film's star.*

tracksuit tracksuits
NOUN a loose, warm suit of trousers and a top, worn for outdoor sports.

tract tracts
NOUN **1** A tract of land or forest is a large area of it. **2** a pamphlet which expresses a strong opinion on a religious, moral, or political subject. **3** a system of organs and tubes in an animal's or person's body that has a particular function E.G. *the digestive tract.*

a
b
c
d
e
f
g
h
i
j
k
l
m
n
o
p
q
r
s
t
u
v
w
x
y
z

On WEDNESday Wayne WED NESta (<u>Wednes</u>day)   ▶ SPELLING NOTE

A
B
C
D
E
F
G
H
I
J
K
L
M
N
O
P
Q
R
S
T
U
V
W
X
Y
Z

traction

NOUN Traction is a form of medical treatment given to an injured limb which involves pulling it gently for long periods of time using a system of weights and pulleys.

tractor tractors

NOUN a vehicle with large rear wheels that is used on a farm for pulling machinery and other heavy loads.

trade trades trading traded

NOUN 1 (HISTORY) Trade is the activity of buying, selling, or exchanging goods or services between people, firms, or countries. 2 Someone's trade is the kind of work they do, especially when it requires special training in practical skills E.G. *a joiner by trade.* ▶ VERB 3 When people, firms, or countries trade, they buy, sell, or exchange goods or services. 4 If you trade things, you exchange them E.G. *Their mother had traded her rings for a few potatoes.*

■ (sense 1) business, commerce
■ (sense 3) deal, do business, traffic

trademark trademarks

NOUN a name or symbol that a manufacturer always uses on its products. Trademarks are usually protected by law so that no-one else can use them.

trader traders

NOUN a person whose job is to trade in goods E.G. *a timber trader.*

tradesman tradesmen

NOUN a person, for example a shopkeeper, whose job is to sell goods.

trade union trade unions

NOUN an organization of workers that tries to improve the pay and conditions in a particular industry.

tradition traditions

NOUN a custom or belief that has existed for a long time without changing.

■ convention, custom

traditional

ADJECTIVE 1 Traditional customs or beliefs have existed for a long time without changing E.G. *her traditional Indian dress.* 2 A traditional organization or institution is one in which older methods are used rather than modern ones E.G. *a traditional school.*

traditionally ADVERB

traditionalist traditionalists

NOUN someone who supports the established customs and beliefs of their society, and does not want to change them.

traffic traffics trafficking trafficked

NOUN 1 Traffic is the movement of vehicles or people along a route at a particular time. 2 Traffic in something such as drugs is an illegal trade in them. ▶ VERB 3 Someone who traffics in drugs or other goods buys and sells them illegally.

traffic light traffic lights

NOUN Traffic lights are the set of red, amber, and green lights at a road junction which control the flow of traffic.

traffic warden traffic wardens

NOUN a person whose job is to make sure that cars are not parked in the wrong place or for longer than is allowed.

tragedy tragedies

Said "**traj-id-ee**" NOUN 1 an event or situation that is disastrous or very sad. 2 a serious story or play, that usually ends with the death of the main character.

tragic

ADJECTIVE 1 Something tragic is very sad because it involves death, suffering, or disaster E.G. *a tragic accident*. 2 Tragic films, plays, and books are sad and serious E.G. *a tragic love story*.

tragically ADVERB

trail trails trailing trailed

NOUN 1 a rough path across open country or through forests. 2 a series of marks or other signs left by someone or something as they move along. ▶ VERB 3 If you trail something or it trails, it drags along behind you as you move, or it hangs down loosely E.G. *a small plane trailing a banner*. 4 If someone trails along, they move slowly, without any energy or enthusiasm. 5 If a voice trails away or trails off, it gradually becomes more hesitant until it stops completely.

trailer trailers

NOUN a small vehicle which can be loaded with things and pulled behind a car.

train trains training trained

NOUN 1 a number of carriages or trucks which are pulled by a railway engine. 2 A train of thought is a connected series of thoughts. 3 A train of vehicles or people is a line or group following behind something or someone E.G. *a train of wives and girlfriends*. ▶ VERB 4 If you train, you learn how to do a particular job E.G. *She trained as a serious actress*. 5 If you train for a sports match or a race, you prepare for it by doing exercises.

training NOUN

trainee trainees

NOUN someone who is being taught how to do a job.

trainers

PLURAL NOUN Trainers are special shoes worn for running or jogging.

trait traits

NOUN a particular characteristic or tendency E.G. *a very English trait*.

traitor traitors

NOUN (HISTORY) someone who betrays their country or the group which they belong to.

trajectory trajectories

Said "traj-**jek**-tor-ee" NOUN The trajectory of an object moving through the air is the curving path that it follows.

tram trams

NOUN a vehicle which runs on rails along the street and is powered by electricity from an overhead wire.

tramp tramps tramping tramped

NOUN 1 a person who has no home, no job, and very little money 2 a long country walk E.G. *I took a long, wet tramp through the fine woodlands*. ▶ VERB 3 If you tramp from one place to another, you walk with slow, heavy footsteps.

trample tramples trampling trampled

VERB 1 If you trample on something, you tread heavily on it so that it is damaged. 2 If you trample on someone or on their rights or feelings, you behave in a way that shows you don't care about them.

trampoline trampolines

NOUN a piece of gymnastic equipment consisting of a large piece of strong cloth held taut by

a
b
c
d
e
f
g
h
i
j
k
l
m
n
o
p
q
r
s
t
u
v
w
x
y
z

Elaine and Emily shout EE when they mEEt to grEEt each other (-ee-)   SPELLING NOTE

springs in a frame, on which a gymnast jumps to help them jump high.

trance trances
NOUN a mental state in which someone seems to be asleep but is conscious enough to be aware of their surroundings and to respond to questions and commands.

tranquil
Said "**trang**-kwil" ADJECTIVE calm and peaceful E.G. *tranquil lakes… I have a tranquil mind*.
tranquillity NOUN

tranquillizer tranquillizers; also spelt **tranquilliser**
NOUN a drug that makes people feel less anxious or nervous.

trans-
PREFIX Trans- means across, through, or beyond E.G. *transatlantic*.

transaction transactions
NOUN a business deal which involves buying and selling something.

transcend transcends transcending transcended
VERB If one thing transcends another, it goes beyond it or is superior to it E.G. *Her beauty transcends all barriers*.

transcribe transcribes transcribing transcribed
VERB If you transcribe something that is spoken or written, you write it down, copy it, or change it into a different form of writing E.G. *These letters were often transcribed by his wife Patti*.

transcript transcripts
NOUN a written copy of of something that is spoken.

transfer transfers transferring transferred
VERB 1 If you transfer something from one place to another, you move it

E.G. *They transferred the money to the Swiss account*. 2 If you transfer to a different place or job, or are transferred to it, you move to a different place or job within the same organization. ▶ NOUN 3 the movement of something from one place to another. 4 a piece of paper with a design on one side which can be ironed or pressed onto cloth, paper, or china.
transferable ADJECTIVE

transfixed
ADJECTIVE If a person is transfixed by something, they are so impressed or frightened by it that they cannot move E.G. *Price stood transfixed at the sight of that tiny figure*.

transform transforms transforming transformed
VERB If something is transformed, it is changed completely E.G. *The frown is transformed into a smile*.
transformation NOUN

transfusion transfusions
NOUN A transfusion or blood transfusion is a process in which blood from a healthy person is injected into the body of another person who is badly injured or ill.

transient
Said "**tran**-zee-ent" ADJECTIVE Something transient does not stay or exist for very long E.G. *transient emotions*.
transience NOUN

transistor transistors
NOUN 1 a small electrical device in something such as a television or radio which is used to control electric currents. 2 A transistor or a transistor radio is a small portable radio.

transit

NOUN 1 Transit is the carrying of goods or people by vehicle from one place to another. ▶ PHRASE 2 People or things that are **in transit** are travelling or being taken from one place to another E.G. *damage that had occurred in transit.*

transition transitions

NOUN a change from one form or state to another E.G. *the transition from war to peace.*

transitional

ADJECTIVE A transitional period or stage is one during which something changes from one form or state to another.

transitive

ADJECTIVE In grammar, a transitive verb is a verb which has an object.

transitory

ADJECTIVE lasting for only a short time.

translate translates translating translated

VERB To translate something that someone has said or written is to say it or write it in a different language.

translation NOUN **translator** NOUN

translucent

ADJECTIVE If something is translucent, light passes through it so that it seems to glow E.G. *translucent petals.*

transmission transmissions

NOUN 1 The transmission of something involves passing or sending it to a different place or person E.G. *the transmission of infectious diseases.* 2 The transmission of television or radio programmes is the broadcasting of them. 3 a broadcast.

transmit transmits transmitting transmitted

VERB 1 When a message or an electronic signal is transmitted, it is sent by radio waves. 2 To transmit something to a different place or person is to pass it or send it to the place or person E.G. *the clergy's role in transmitting knowledge.*

transmitter NOUN

transparency transparencies

NOUN 1 a small piece of photographic film which can be projected onto a screen. 2 Transparency is the quality that an object or substance has if you can see through it.

transparent

ADJECTIVE If an object or substance is transparent, you can see through it.

transparently ADVERB

☰ clear, limpid, see-through

transpire transpires transpiring transpired

VERB 1 FORMAL When it transpires that something is the case, people discover that it is the case E.G. *It transpired that he had flown off on holiday.* 2 When something transpires, it happens E.G. *You start to wonder what transpired between them.*

☑ Some people think that it is wrong to use *transpire* to mean 'happen'. However, it is very widely used in this sense, especially in spoken English.

transplant transplants transplanting transplanted

NOUN 1 a process of removing something from one place and putting it in another E.G. *a man who needs a heart transplant.* ▶ VERB 2 When something is transplanted, it is moved to a different place.

transport transports transporting transported

NOUN (GEOGRAPHY) 1 Vehicles that you

a b c d e f g h i j k l m n o p q r s **t** u v w x y z

A B C D E F G H I J K L M N O P Q R S T U V W X Y Z

travel in are referred to as transport E.G. *public transport.* **2** Transport is the moving of goods or people from one place to another E.G. *The prices quoted include transport costs.* ► VERB **3** When goods or people are transported from one place to another, they are moved there.
■ (sense 3) carry, convey, transfer

transportation
NOUN (GEOGRAPHY) Transportation is the transporting of people and things from one place to another.

transvestite transvestites
NOUN a person who enjoys wearing clothes normally worn by people of the opposite sex.
📖 from *trans-* and Latin *vestitus* meaning 'clothed'

trap traps trapping trapped
NOUN **1** a piece of equipment or a hole that is carefully positioned in order to catch animals or birds. **2** a trick that is intended to catch or deceive someone. ► VERB **3** Someone who traps animals catches them using traps. **4** If you trap someone, you trick them so that they do or say something which they did not want to. **5** If you are trapped somewhere, you cannot move or escape because something is blocking your way or holding you down. **6** If you are trapped, you are in an unpleasant situation that you cannot easily change E.G. *I'm trapped in an unhappy marriage.*
■ (sense 3) catch, snare
■ (sense 4) dupe, trick

trap door trap doors
NOUN a small horizontal door in a floor, ceiling, or stage.

trapeze trapezes

NOUN a bar of wood or metal hanging from two ropes on which acrobats and gymnasts swing and perform skilful movements.

trapezium trapeziums or **trapezia**
Said "trap-**pee**-zee-um" NOUN a four-sided shape with two sides parallel to each other.

trappings
PLURAL NOUN The trappings of a particular rank, position, or state are the clothes or equipment that go with it.

trash
NOUN **1** Trash is rubbish E.G. *He picks up your trash on Mondays.* **2** If you say that something such as a book, painting, or film is trash, you mean that it is not very good.

trauma traumas
Said "**traw**-ma" NOUN a very upsetting experience which causes great stress E.G. *the trauma of his mother's death.*
📖 from Greek *trauma* meaning 'wound'

traumatic
ADJECTIVE A traumatic experience is very upsetting.

travel travels travelling travelled
VERB **1** To travel is to go from one place to another. **2** When something reaches one place from another, you say that it travels there E.G. *Gossip travels fast.* ► NOUN **3** Travel is the act of travelling E.G. *air travel.* ► PLURAL NOUN **4** Someone's travels are the journeys that they make to places a long way from their home E.G. *my travels in the Himalayas.*
traveller NOUN **travelling** ADJECTIVE
■ (sense 1) go, journey

traveller's cheque traveller's cheques

NOUN Traveller's cheques are cheques for use abroad. You buy them at home and then exchange them when you are abroad for foreign currency.

traverse traverses traversing traversed

VERB; FORMAL If you traverse an area of land or water, you go across it or over it E.G. *They have traversed the island from the west coast.*

travesty travesties

NOUN a very bad or ridiculous representation or imitation of something E.G. *British salad is a travesty of freshness.*

trawl trawls trawling trawled

VERB When fishermen trawl, they drag a wide net behind a ship in order to catch fish.

trawler trawlers

NOUN a fishing boat that is used for trawling.

tray trays

NOUN a flat object with raised edges which is used for carrying food or drinks.

treacherous

ADJECTIVE 1 A treacherous person is likely to betray you and cannot be trusted. 2 The ground or the sea can be described as treacherous when it is dangerous or unreliable E.G. *treacherous mountain roads.*

treacherously ADVERB

■ (sense 1) disloyal, untrustworthy

treachery

NOUN Treachery is behaviour in which someone betrays their country or a person who trusts them.

treacle

NOUN Treacle is a thick, sweet syrup used to make cakes and toffee E.G. *treacle tart.*

tread treads treading trod trodden

VERB 1 If you tread on something, you walk on it or step on it. 2 If you tread something into the ground or into a carpet, you crush it in by stepping on it E.G. *bubblegum that has been trodden into the pavement.* ► NOUN 3 A person's tread is the sound they make with their feet as they walk E.G. *his heavy tread.* 4 The tread of a tyre or shoe is the pattern of ridges on it that stops it slipping.

treadmill treadmills

NOUN Any task or job that you must keep doing even though it is unpleasant or tiring can be referred to as a treadmill E.G. *My life is one constant treadmill of making music.*

treason

NOUN Treason is the crime of betraying your country, for example by helping its enemies.

treasure treasures treasuring treasured

NOUN 1 Treasure is a collection of gold, silver, jewels, or other precious objects, especially one that has been hidden E.G. *buried treasure.* 2 Treasures are valuable works of art E.G. *the finest art treasures in the world.* ► VERB 3 If you treasure something, you are very pleased that you have it and regard it as very precious E.G. *He treasures his friendship with her.*

treasured ADJECTIVE

treasurer treasurers

NOUN a person who is in charge of the finance and accounts of an organization.

a
b
c
d
e
f
g
h
i
j
k
l
m
n
o
p
q
r
s
t
u
v
w
x
y
z

LEt's measure the angLE (ang**l**e)   SPELLING NOTE

Treasury

NOUN The Treasury is the government department that deals with the country's finances.

treat treats treating treated

VERB 1 If you treat someone in a particular way, you behave that way towards them. 2 If you treat something in a particular way, you deal with it that way or see it that way E.G. *We are now treating this case as murder.* 3 When a doctor treats a patient or an illness, he or she gives them medical care and attention. 4 If something such as wood or cloth is treated, a special substance is put on it in order to protect it or give it special properties E.G. *The carpet's been treated with a stain protector.* 5 If you treat someone, you buy or arrange something special for them which they will enjoy. ▶ NOUN 6 If you give someone a treat, you buy or arrange something special for them which they will enjoy E.G. *my birthday treat.*

treatment NOUN

treatise treatises

Said "**tree**-tiz" NOUN a long formal piece of writing about a particular subject.

treaty treaties

NOUN a written agreement between countries in which they agree to do something or to help each other.

treble trebles trebling trebled

VERB 1 If something trebles or is trebled, it becomes three times greater in number or amount.

▶ ADJECTIVE 2 Treble means three times as large or three times as strong as previously E.G. *Next year we can raise treble that amount.*

tree trees

NOUN a large plant with a hard woody trunk, branches, and leaves.

trek treks trekking trekked

VERB 1 If you trek somewhere, you go on a long and difficult journey.

▶ NOUN 2 a long and difficult journey, especially one made by walking.

🔳 an Afrikaans word

trellis trellises

NOUN a frame made of horizontal and vertical strips of wood or metal and used to support plants.

tremble trembles trembling trembled

VERB 1 If you tremble, you shake slightly, usually because you are frightened or cold. 2 If something trembles, it shakes slightly. 3 If your voice trembles, it sounds unsteady, usually because you are frightened or upset.

trembling ADJECTIVE

tremendous

ADJECTIVE 1 large or impressive E.G. *It was a tremendous performance.*

2 INFORMAL very good or pleasing E.G. *tremendous fun.*

tremendously ADVERB

tremor tremors

NOUN 1 a shaking movement of your body which you cannot control. 2 an unsteady quality in your voice, for example when you are upset. 3 a small earthquake.

trench trenches

NOUN a long narrow channel dug into the ground.

trenchant

Said "**trent**-shent" ADJECTIVE Trenchant writing or comments are bold and firmly expressed.

trend trends
NOUN a change towards doing or being something different.

trendy trendier trendiest
ADJECTIVE; INFORMAL Trendy things or people are fashionable.

trepidation
NOUN; FORMAL Trepidation is fear or anxiety E.G. *He saw the look of trepidation on my face.*

trespass trespasses trespassing trespassed
VERB If you trespass on someone's land or property, you go onto it without their permission.
trespasser NOUN

tresses
PLURAL NOUN; OLD-FASHIONED A woman's tresses are her long flowing hair.

trestle trestles
NOUN a wooden or metal structure that is used as one of the supports for a table.

trevally trevallies
NOUN an Australian and New Zealand fish that is caught for both food and sport.

tri-
PREFIX three E.G. *tricycle.*

triad triads
Said "try-ad" NOUN 1 FORMAL a group of three similar things. 2 (MUSIC) TECHNICAL In music, a triad is a chord of three notes consisting of the tonic and the third and fifth above it.

trial trials
NOUN 1 the legal process in which a judge and jury decide whether a person is guilty of a particular crime after listening to all the evidence about it. 2 an experiment in which something is tested E.G. *Trials of the drug start next month.*

triangle triangles
NOUN 1 (MATHS) a shape with three straight sides. 2 a percussion instrument consisting of a thin steel bar bent in the shape of a triangle.
triangular ADJECTIVE

triathlon triathlons
Said "tri-**ath**-lon" NOUN a sports contest in which athletes compete in three different events.

tribe tribes
NOUN a group of people of the same race, who have the same customs, religion, language, or land, especially when they are thought to be primitive.
tribal ADJECTIVE

tribulation tribulations
NOUN; FORMAL Tribulation is trouble or suffering E.G. *the tribulations of a female football star.*

tribunal tribunals
Said "try-**byoo**-nl" NOUN a special court or committee appointed to deal with particular problems E.G. *an industrial tribunal.*

tributary tributaries
NOUN a stream or river that flows into a larger river.

tribute tributes
NOUN 1 A tribute is something said or done to show admiration and respect for someone E.G. *Police paid tribute to her courage.* 2 If one thing is a tribute to another, it is the result of the other thing and shows how good it is E.G. *His success has been a tribute to hard work.*

trice
NOUN If someone does something in a trice, they do it very quickly.

triceps
Said "try-seps" NOUN (PE) Your

a
b
c
d
e
f
g
h
i
j
k
l
m
n
o
p
q
r
s
t
u
v
w
x
y
z

triceps is the large muscle at the back of your upper arm that straightens your arm.

trick tricks tricking tricked
VERB 1 If someone tricks you, they deceive you. ▶ NOUN 2 an action done to deceive someone. 3 Tricks are clever or skilful actions done in order to entertain people E.G. *magic tricks*.

trickery
NOUN Trickery is deception E.G. *He accused the Serbs of trickery*.

trickle trickles trickling trickled
VERB 1 When a liquid trickles somewhere, it flows slowly in a thin stream. 2 When people or things trickle somewhere, they move there slowly in small groups or amounts. ▶ NOUN 3 a thin stream of liquid. 4 A trickle of people or things is a small number or quantity of them.

tricky trickier trickiest
ADJECTIVE difficult to do or deal with.

tricycle tricycles
NOUN a vehicle similar to a bicycle but with two wheels at the back and one at the front.

trifle trifles trifling trifled
NOUN 1 A trifle means a little E.G. *He seemed a trifle annoyed*. 2 Trifles are things that are not very important or valuable. 3 a cold pudding made of layers of sponge cake, fruit, jelly, and custard. ▶ VERB 4 If you trifle with someone or something, you treat them in a disrespectful way E.G. *He was not to be trifled with*.

trifling
ADJECTIVE small and unimportant.

trigger triggers triggering triggered
NOUN 1 the small lever on a gun which is pulled in order to fire it. ▶ VERB 2 If

something triggers an event or triggers it off, it causes it to happen. 🔟 from Dutch *trekken* meaning 'to pull'

trigonometry
Said "trig-gon-**nom**-it-ree" NOUN Trigonometry is the branch of mathematics that is concerned with calculating the angles of triangles or the lengths of their sides.

trill trills trilling trilled
VERB If a bird trills, it sings with short high-pitched repeated notes.

trillion trillions
NOUN; INFORMAL Trillions of things means an extremely large number of them. Formerly, a trillion meant a million million million.

trilogy trilogies
NOUN a series of three books or plays that have the same characters or are on the same subject.

trim trimmer trimmest; trims trimming trimmed
ADJECTIVE 1 neat, tidy, and attractive. ▶ VERB 2 To trim something is to clip small amounts off it. 3 If you trim off parts of something, you cut them off because they are not needed E.G. *Trim off the excess marzipan*. ▶ NOUN 4 If something is given a trim, it is cut a little E.G. *All styles need a trim every six to eight weeks*. 5 a decoration on something, especially along its edges E.G. *a fur trim*.
trimmed ADJECTIVE

trimming trimmings
NOUN Trimmings are extra parts added to something for decoration or as a luxury E.G. *bacon and eggs with all the trimmings*.

Trimurti
NOUN In the Hindu religion, the

Trimurti are the three deities
Brahma, Vishnu, and Siva.

Trinity

NOUN In the Christian religion, the
Trinity is the joining of God the
Father, God the Son, and God the
Holy Spirit.

trinket trinkets

NOUN a cheap ornament or piece of
jewellery.

trio trios

NOUN 1 a group of three musicians
who sing or play together; also a
piece of music written for three
instruments or singers. 2 any group
of three things or people together
E.G. *a trio of children's tales*.

trip trips tripping tripped

NOUN 1 a journey made to a place.
► VERB 2 If you trip, you catch your
foot on something and fall over. 3 If
you trip someone or trip them up,
you make them fall over by making
them catch their foot on something.
■ (sense 1) excursion, journey,
outing

tripe

NOUN Tripe is the stomach lining of a
pig, cow, or ox, which is cooked and
eaten.

triple triples tripling tripled

ADJECTIVE 1 consisting of three things
or three parts E.G. *the Triple Alliance*.
► VERB 2 If you triple something or if it
triples, it becomes three times
greater in number or size.

triplet triplets

NOUN Triplets are three children born
at the same time to the same
mother.

tripod tripods

Said "**try**-pod" NOUN a stand with
three legs used to support

something like a camera or telescope.

tripper trippers

NOUN a tourist or someone on an
excursion.

trite

ADJECTIVE dull and not original E.G. *his
trite novels*.

**triumph triumphs triumphing
triumphed**

NOUN 1 a great success or
achievement. 2 Triumph is a feeling
of great satisfaction when you win or
achieve something. ► VERB 3 If you
triumph, you win a victory or
succeed in overcoming something.

triumphal

ADJECTIVE done or made to celebrate a
victory or great success E.G. *a
triumphal return to Rome*.

triumphant

ADJECTIVE Someone who is triumphant
feels very happy because they have
won a victory or have achieved
something E.G. *a triumphant shout*.

trivia

PLURAL NOUN Trivia are unimportant
things.

trivial

ADJECTIVE Something trivial is
unimportant.
🔒 from Latin *trivialis* meaning 'found
everywhere'

troll trolls

NOUN an imaginary creature in
Scandinavian mythology that lives in
caves or mountains and is believed
to turn to stone at daylight.

trolley trolleys

NOUN 1 a small table on wheels. 2 a
small cart on wheels used for carrying
heavy objects E.G. *a supermarket trolley*.

trombone trombones

NOUN a brass wind instrument with a

a
b
c
d
e
f
g
h
i
j
k
l
m
n
o
p
q
r
s
t
u
v
w
x
y
z

A
B
C
D
E
F
G
H
I
J
K
L
M
N
O
P
Q
R
S
T
U
V
W
X
Y
Z

U-shaped slide which you move to produce different notes.

troop troops trooping trooped
NOUN 1 Troops are soldiers. 2 A troop of people or animals is a group of them. ▶ VERB 3 If people troop somewhere, they go there in a group.

trooper troopers
NOUN a low-ranking soldier in the cavalry.

trophy trophies
NOUN 1 a cup or shield given as a prize to the winner of a competition. 2 something you keep to remember a success or victory.
🏛 from Greek *tropē* meaning 'defeat of the enemy'

tropical
ADJECTIVE belonging to or typical of the tropics E.G. *a tropical island.*

tropics
PLURAL NOUN The tropics are the hottest parts of the world between two lines of latitude, the Tropic of Cancer, 23½° north of the equator, and the Tropic of Capricorn, 23½° south of the equator.

trot trots trotting trotted
VERB 1 When a horse trots, it moves at a speed between a walk and a canter, lifting its feet quite high off the ground. 2 If you trot, you run or jog using small quick steps. ▶ NOUN 3 When a horse breaks into a trot, it starts trotting.

trotter trotters
NOUN A pig's trotters are its feet.

trouble troubles troubling troubled
NOUN 1 Troubles are difficulties or problems. 2 If there is trouble, people are quarrelling or fighting E.G. *There*

was more trouble after the match.
▶ PHRASE 3 If you are **in trouble**, you are in a situation where you may be punished because you have done something wrong. ▶ VERB 4 If something troubles you, it makes you feel worried or anxious. 5 If you trouble someone for something, you disturb them in order to ask them for it E.G. *Can I trouble you for milk?*
troubling ADJECTIVE **troubled** ADJECTIVE
▣ (sense 1) difficulty, problem, worry
▣ (sense 5) bother, inconvenience

troublesome
ADJECTIVE causing problems or difficulties E.G. *a troublesome teenager.*

trough troughs
Said "**troff**" NOUN a long, narrow container from which animals drink or feed.

trounce trounces trouncing trounced
VERB If you trounce someone, you defeat them completely.

troupe troupes
Said "**troop**" NOUN a group of actors, singers, or dancers who work together and often travel around together.

trousers
PLURAL NOUN Trousers are a piece of clothing covering the body from the waist down, enclosing each leg separately.
🏛 from Gaelic *triubhas*

trout
NOUN a type of freshwater fish.

trowel trowels
NOUN 1 a small garden tool with a curved, pointed blade used for

planting or weeding. **2** a small tool with a flat blade used for spreading cement or plaster.

truant truants

NOUN **1** a child who stays away from school without permission. ▶ PHRASE **2** If children **play truant**, they stay away from school without permission.

truancy NOUN

truce truces

NOUN an agreement between two people or groups to stop fighting for a short time.

truck trucks

NOUN **1** a large motor vehicle used for carrying heavy loads. **2** an open vehicle used for carrying goods on a railway.

truculent

Said "truk-yoo-lent" ADJECTIVE bad-tempered and aggressive.

truculence NOUN

trudge trudges trudging trudged

VERB **1** If you trudge, you walk with slow, heavy steps. ▶ NOUN **2** a slow tiring walk E.G. *the long trudge home.*

true truer truest

ADJECTIVE **1** A true story or statement is based on facts and is not made up. **2** 'True' is used to describe things or people that are genuine E.G. *She was a true friend.* **3** True feelings are sincere and genuine. ▶ PHRASE **4** If something **comes true**, it actually happens.

truly ADVERB

▤ (sense 1) accurate, correct, factual

truffle truffles

NOUN **1** a soft, round sweet. **2** a round mushroom-like fungus which grows underground and is considered very good to eat.

trump trumps

NOUN In a game of cards, trumps is the suit with the highest value.

trumpet trumpets trumpeting trumpeted

NOUN **1** a brass wind instrument with a narrow tube ending in a bell-like shape. ▶ VERB **2** When an elephant trumpets, it makes a sound like a very loud trumpet.

truncated

ADJECTIVE Something that is truncated is made shorter.

truncheon truncheons

Said "trunt-shn" NOUN a short, thick stick that policemen carry as a weapon.

trundle trundles trundling trundled

VERB If you trundle something or it trundles somewhere, it moves or rolls along slowly.

trunk trunks

NOUN **1** the main stem of a tree from which the branches and roots grow. **2** the main part of your body, excluding your head, neck, arms, and legs. **3** the long flexible nose of an elephant. **4** a large, strong case or box with a hinged lid used for storing things. ▶ PLURAL NOUN **5** A man's trunks are his bathing pants or shorts.

truss trusses trussing trussed

VERB **1** To truss someone or truss them up is to tie them up so that they cannot move. ▶ NOUN **2** a supporting belt with a pad worn by a man with a hernia.

trust trusts trusting trusted

VERB **1** If you trust someone, you believe that they are honest and will

a b c d e f g h i j k l m n o p q r s t u v w x y z

not harm you. **2** If you trust someone to do something, you believe they will do it successfully or properly. **3** If you trust someone with something, you give it to them or tell it to them E.G. *One member of the group cannot be trusted with the secret.* **4** If you do not trust something, you feel that it is not safe or reliable E.G. *I didn't trust my arms and legs to work.* ▶ NOUN **5** Trust is the responsibility you are given to deal with or look after important or secret things E.G. *He had built up a position of trust.* **6** a financial arrangement in which an organization looks after and invests money for someone.

trusting ADJECTIVE

trustee trustees

NOUN someone who is allowed by law to control money or property they are keeping or investing for another person.

trustworthy

ADJECTIVE A trustworthy person is reliable and responsible and can be trusted.

trusty trustier trustiest

ADJECTIVE Trusty things and animals are considered to be reliable because they have always worked well in the past E.G. *a trusty black labrador.*

truth truths

NOUN **1** The truth is the facts about something, rather than things that are imagined or made up E.G. *I know she was telling the truth.* **2** an idea or principle that is generally accepted to be true E.G. *the basic truths in life.*
▤ (sense 1) fact, reality

truthful

ADJECTIVE A truthful person is honest and tells the truth.

truthfully ADVERB

try tries trying tried

VERB **1** To try to do something is to make an effort to do it. **2** If you try something, you use it or do it to test how useful or enjoyable it is E.G. *Howard wanted me to try the wine.* **3** When a person is tried, they appear in court and a judge and jury decide if they are guilty after hearing the evidence. ▶ NOUN **4** an attempt to do something. **5** a test of something E.G. *You gave it a try.* **6** In rugby, a try is scored when someone carries the ball over the goal line of the opposing team and touches the ground with it.
▤ (sense 1) attempt, endeavour, strive
▤ (sense 4) attempt, go, shot
☑ You can use *try to* in speech and writing: *try to get here on time for once.* *Try and* is very common in speech, but you should avoid it in written work: *just try and stop me!*.

trying

ADJECTIVE Something or someone trying is difficult to deal with and makes you feel impatient or annoyed.

tryst trysts

*Said "**trist**"* NOUN an appointment or meeting, especially between lovers in a quiet, secret place.

tsar tsars

*Said "**zar**"; also spelt* **czar**
NOUN a Russian emperor or king between 1547 and 1917.

tsarina tsarinas

*Said "**zah-ree-na**"; also spelt* **czarina**
NOUN a female tsar or the wife of a tsar.

tsetse fly tsetse flies
Said "tset-tsee" NOUN an African fly that feeds on blood and causes serious diseases in people and animals.

T-shirt T-shirts; also spelt **tee shirt**
NOUN a simple short-sleeved cotton shirt with no collar.

tuatara tuatara or **tuataras**
Said "too-ah-tah-rah" NOUN a large, lizard-like reptile found on certain islands off the coast of New Zealand.

tub tubs
NOUN a wide circular container.

tuba tubas
NOUN a large brass musical instrument that can produce very low notes.

tubby tubbier tubbiest
ADJECTIVE rather fat.

tube tubes
NOUN 1 a round, hollow pipe. 2 a soft metal or plastic cylindrical container with a screw cap at one end E.G. *a tube of toothpaste.*
tubing NOUN

tuberculosis
Said "tyoo-ber-kyoo-low-siss" NOUN Tuberculosis is a serious infectious disease affecting the lungs.

tubular
ADJECTIVE In the shape of a tube.

TUC
In Britain, an abbreviation for 'Trades Union Congress', which is an association of trade unions.

tuck tucks tucking tucked
VERB 1 If you tuck something somewhere, you put it there so that it is safe or comfortable E.G. *She tucked the letter into her handbag.* 2 If you tuck a piece of fabric into or under something, you push the loose ends inside or under it to make it tidy. 3 If something is tucked away, it is in a quiet place where few people go E.G. *a little house tucked away in a valley.*

tucker tuckers tuckering tuckered INFORMAL
NOUN 1 In Australian and New Zealand English, tucker is food. ▶ VERB 2 In Australian and New Zealand English, if you are tuckered out you are tired out.

Tudor Tudors
NOUN Tudor was the family name of the English monarchs who reigned from 1485 to 1603.

Tuesday Tuesdays
NOUN Tuesday is the day between Monday and Wednesday.
 from Old English *tíwesdæg* meaning 'Tiw's day'; Tiw was the Scandinavian god of war and the sky

tuft tufts
NOUN A tuft of something such as hair is a bunch of it growing closely together.

tug tugs tugging tugged
VERB 1 To tug something is to give it a quick, hard pull. ▶ NOUN 2 a quick, hard pull E.G. *He felt a tug at his arm.* 3 a small, powerful boat which tows large ships.

tug of war
NOUN A tug of war is a sport in which two teams test their strength by pulling against each other on opposite ends of a rope.

tuition
NOUN Tuition is the teaching of a subject, especially to one person or to a small group.

The government licenSes Schnapps (licenSes)   SPELLING NOTE

a b c d e f g h i j k l m n o p q r s **t** u v w x y z

A
B
C
D
E
F
G
H
I
J
K
L
M
N
O
P
Q
R
S
T
U
V
W
X
Y
Z

tulip tulips
NOUN a brightly coloured spring flower.
📖 from Turkish *tulbend* meaning 'turban', because of its shape

tumble tumbles tumbling tumbled
VERB **1** To tumble is to fall with a rolling or bouncing movement.
▶ NOUN **2** a fall.

tumbler tumblers
NOUN a drinking glass with straight sides.

tummy tummies
NOUN; INFORMAL Your tummy is your stomach.

tumour tumours
Said "tyoo-mur" NOUN a mass of diseased or abnormal cells that has grown in a person's or animal's body.

tumultuous
ADJECTIVE A tumultuous event or welcome is very noisy because people are happy or excited.

tuna
Said "tyoo-na" NOUN Tuna are large fish that live in warm seas and are caught for food.

tundra
NOUN The tundra is a vast treeless Arctic region.
📖 a Russian word

tune tunes tuning tuned
NOUN **1** a series of musical notes arranged in a particular way. ▶ VERB **2** To tune a musical instrument is to adjust it so that it produces the right notes. **3** To tune an engine or machine is to adjust it so that it works well. **4** If you tune to a particular radio or television station you turn or press the controls to select the station you want to listen

to or watch. ▶ PHRASE **5** If your voice or an instrument is **in tune**, it produces the right notes.

tuneful
ADJECTIVE having a pleasant and easily remembered tune.

tuner tuners
NOUN A piano tuner is a person whose job it is to tune pianos.

tunic tunics
NOUN a sleeveless garment covering the top part of the body and reaching to the hips, thighs, or knees.

Tunisian Tunisians
Said "tyoo-niz-ee-an" ADJECTIVE **1** belonging or relating to Tunisia.
▶ NOUN **2** someone who comes from Tunisia.

tunnel tunnels tunnelling tunnelled
NOUN **1** a long underground passage.
▶ VERB **2** To tunnel is to make a tunnel.

turban turbans
NOUN a head-covering worn by a Hindu, Muslim, or Sikh man, consisting of a long piece of cloth wound round his head.

turbine turbines
NOUN a machine or engine in which power is produced when a stream of air, gas, water, or steam pushes the blades of a wheel and makes it turn round.
📖 from Latin *turbo* meaning 'whirlwind'

turbot
Said "tur-bot" NOUN a large European flat fish that is caught for food.

turbulent
ADJECTIVE **1** A turbulent period of history is one where there is much uncertainty, and possibly violent change. **2** Turbulent air or water

currents make sudden changes of direction.

turbulence NOUN

tureen tureens
Said "tur-**reen**" NOUN a large dish with a lid for serving soup.

turf turves; turfs turfing turfed
NOUN Turf is short thick even grass and the layer of soil beneath it.

turf out VERB; INFORMAL To turf someone out is to force them to leave a place.

turgid
Said "tur-**jid**" ADJECTIVE LITERARY A turgid play, film, or piece of writing is difficult to understand and rather boring.

Turk Turks
NOUN someone who comes from Turkey.

turkey turkeys
NOUN a large bird kept for food; also the meat of this bird.

Turkish
ADJECTIVE 1 belonging or relating to Turkey. ▶ NOUN 2 Turkish is the main language spoken in Turkey.

turmoil
NOUN Turmoil is a state of confusion, disorder, or great anxiety E.G. *Europe is in a state of turmoil.*

turn turns turning turned
VERB 1 When you turn, you move so that you are facing or going in a different direction. 2 When you turn something or when it turns, it moves or rotates so that it faces in a different direction or is in a different position. 3 If you turn your attention or thoughts to someone or something, you start thinking about them or discussing them. 4 When something turns or is turned into

something else, it becomes something different E.G. *A hobby can be turned into a career.* ▶ NOUN 5 an act of turning something so that it faces in a different direction or is in a different position. 6 a change in the way something is happening or being done E.G. *Her career took a turn for the worse.* 7 If it is your turn to do something, you have the right, chance, or duty to do it. ▶ PHRASE 8 **In turn** is used to refer to people, things, or actions that are in sequence one after the other.
■ (sense 7) chance, go, opportunity

turn down VERB If you turn down someone's request or offer, you refuse or reject it.

turn up VERB 1 If someone or something turns up, they arrive or appear somewhere. 2 If something turns up, it is found or discovered.

turncoat turncoats
NOUN a person who leaves one political party or group for an opposing one.

turning turnings
NOUN a road which leads away from the side of another road.

turning point turning points
NOUN the moment when decisions are taken and events start to move in a different direction.

turnip turnips
NOUN a round root vegetable with a white or yellow skin.

turnout turnouts
NOUN The turnout at an event is the number of people who go to it.

turnover turnovers
NOUN 1 The turnover of people in a particular organization or group is the rate at which people leave it and

a
b
c
d
e
f
g
h
i
j
k
l
m
n
o
p
q
r
s
t
u
v
w
x
y
z

turnover are replaced by others. **2** The turnover of a company is the value of the goods or services sold during a particular period.

turnstile turnstiles
NOUN a revolving mechanical barrier at the entrance to places like football grounds or zoos.

turpentine
NOUN Turpentine is a strong-smelling colourless liquid used for cleaning and for thinning paint.

turps
NOUN Turps is turpentine.

turquoise
Said "tur-kwoyz" NOUN or ADJECTIVE **1** light bluish-green. ► NOUN **2** Turquoise is a bluish-green stone used in jewellery.

turret turrets
NOUN a small narrow tower on top of a larger tower or other buildings.

turtle turtles
NOUN a large reptile with a thick shell covering its body and flippers for swimming. It lays its eggs on land but lives the rest of its life in the sea.

tusk tusks
NOUN The tusks of an elephant, wild boar, or walrus are the pair of long curving pointed teeth it has.

tussle tussles
NOUN an energetic fight or argument between two people, especially about something they both want.

tutor tutors tutoring tutored
NOUN **1** a teacher at a college or university. **2** a private teacher. ► VERB **3** If someone tutors a person or subject, they teach that person or subject.

tutorial tutorials
NOUN a teaching session involving a tutor and a small group of students.

tutu tutus
Said "too-too" NOUN a short stiff skirt worn by female ballet dancers.

TV TVs
NOUN **1** TV is television. **2** a television set.

twang twangs twanging twanged
NOUN **1** a sound like the one made by pulling and then releasing a tight wire. **2** A twang is a nasal quality in a person's voice. ► VERB **3** If a tight wire or string twangs or you twang it, it makes a sound as it is pulled and then released.

tweak tweaks tweaking tweaked
VERB **1** If you tweak something, you twist it or pull it. ► NOUN **2** a short twist or pull of something.

twee
ADJECTIVE sweet and pretty but in bad taste or sentimental.

tweed tweeds
NOUN Tweed is a thick woollen cloth.

tweet tweets tweeting tweeted
VERB **1** When a small bird tweets, it makes a short, high-pitched sound. ► NOUN **2** a short high-pitched sound made by a small bird.

tweezers
PLURAL NOUN Tweezers are a small tool with two arms which can be closed together and are used for pulling out hairs or picking up small objects.

twelve
the number 12.
twelfth

twenty twenties
the number 20.
twentieth

twice
ADVERB Twice means two times.

twiddle twiddles twiddling twiddled
VERB To twiddle something is to twist it or turn it quickly.

twig twigs
NOUN A very small thin branch growing from a main branch of a tree or bush.

twilight
Said "twy-lite" NOUN **1** Twilight is the time after sunset when it is just getting dark. **2** The twilight of something is the final stages of it E.G. *the twilight of his career.*

twin twins
NOUN **1** If two people are twins, they have the same mother and were born on the same day. **2** 'Twin' is used to describe two similar things that are close together or happen together E.G. *the little twin islands.*

twine twines twining twined
NOUN **1** Twine is strong smooth string. ▶ VERB **2** If you twine one thing round another, you twist or wind it round.

twinge twinges
NOUN a sudden, unpleasant feeling E.G. *a twinge of jealousy.*

twinkle twinkles twinkling twinkled
VERB **1** If something twinkles, it sparkles or seems to sparkle with an unsteady light E.G. *Her green eyes twinkled.* ▶ NOUN **2** a sparkle or brightness that something has.

twirl twirls twirling twirled
VERB If something twirls, or if you twirl it, it spins or twists round and round.

twist twists twisting twisted
VERB **1** When you twist something you turn one end of it in one direction while holding the other end or turning it in the opposite direction.
2 When something twists or is twisted, it moves or bends into a strange shape. **3** If you twist a part of your body, you injure it by turning it too sharply or in an unusual direction E.G. *I've twisted my ankle.* **4** If you twist something that someone has said, you change the meaning slightly. ▶ NOUN **5** a twisting action or motion. **6** an unexpected development or event in a story or film, especially at the end E.G. *Each day now seemed to bring a new twist to the story.*
■ (sense 1) coil, wind
■ (sense 2) contort, distort

twisted
ADJECTIVE **1** Something twisted has been bent or moved into a strange shape E.G. *a tangle of twisted metal.* **2** If someone's mind or behaviour is twisted, it is unpleasantly abnormal E.G. *He's bitter and twisted.*

twit twits
NOUN; INFORMAL a silly person.

twitch twitches twitching twitched
VERB **1** If you twitch, you make little jerky movements which you cannot control. **2** If you twitch something, you give it a little jerk in order to move it. ▶ NOUN **3** a little jerky movement.

twitter twitters twittering twittered
VERB When birds twitter, they make short high-pitched sounds.

two
the number 2
☑ Do not confuse the spelling of the preposition *to*, the adverb *too*, and the number *two*.

two-faced
ADJECTIVE A two-faced person is not

a
b
c
d
e
f
g
h
i
j
k
l
m
n
o
p
q
r
s
t
u
v
w
x
y
z

honest in the way they behave
towards other people.

twofold

ADJECTIVE Something twofold has two
equally important parts or reasons
E.G. *Their concern was twofold:
personal and political.*

twosome twosomes

Said "too-sum" NOUN two people or
things that are usually seen together.

**two-time two-times two-timing
two-timed**

VERB; INFORMAL If you two-time your
boyfriend or girlfriend, you deceive
them, by having a romantic
relationship with someone else
without telling them.

two-up

NOUN In Australia and New Zealand,
two-up is a popular gambling game
in which two coins are tossed and
bets are placed on whether they
land heads or tails.

tycoon tycoons

NOUN a person who is successful in
business and has become rich and
powerful.

🏮 from Chinese *ta + chun* meaning
'great ruler'

type types typing typed

NOUN 1 A type of something is a class
of it that has common features and
belongs to a larger group of related
things E.G. *What type of dog should
we get?* 2 A particular type of person
has a particular appearance or
quality E.G. *Andrea is the type who
likes to play safe.* ▶ VERB 3 If you type
something, you use a typewriter or
word processor to write it.

typewriter typewriters

NOUN a machine with a keyboard with
individual keys which are pressed to
produce letters and numbers on a
page.

typhoid

Said "tie-foyd" NOUN Typhoid, or
typhoid fever, is an infectious disease
caused by dirty water or food. It
produces fever and can kill.

typhoon typhoons

NOUN a very violent tropical storm.
🏮 from Chinese *tai fung* meaning
'great wind'

typhus

NOUN Typhus is an infectious disease
transmitted by lice or mites. It results
in fever, severe headaches, and a skin
rash.

typical

ADJECTIVE showing the most usual
characteristics or behaviour.
typically ADVERB
▤ characteristic, standard, usual

typify typifies typifying typified

VERB If something typifies a situation
or thing, it is characteristic of it or a
typical example of it E.G. *This story is
one that typifies our times.*

typing

NOUN Typing is the work or activity of
producing something on a
typewriter.

typist typists

NOUN a person whose job is
typing.

**tyrannosaurus
tyrannosauruses**

Said "tir-ran-oh-saw-russ" NOUN a
very large meat-eating dinosaur
which walked upright on its hind
legs.
🏮 from Greek *turannos* meaning
'tyrant' and Latin *saurus* meaning
'lizard'

tyranny tyrannies
NOUN **1** A tyranny is cruel and unjust rule of people by a person or group E.G. *the evils of Nazi tyranny*. **2** You can refer to something which is not human but is harsh as tyranny E.G. *the tyranny of drugs*.
tyrannical ADJECTIVE

tyrant tyrants
NOUN a person who treats the people he or she has authority over cruelly and unjustly.
tyre tyres
NOUN a thick ring of rubber fitted round each wheel of a vehicle and filled with air.

a
b
c
d
e
f
g
h
i
j
k
l
m
n
o
p
q
r
s
t
u
v
w
x
y
z

LEarn the principLEs (principLe)   SPELLING NOTE

Uu

ubiquitous
Said "yoo-**bik**-wit-tuss" ADJECTIVE
Something that is ubiquitous seems
to be everywhere at the same time
E.G. *the ubiquitous jeans*.
▦ from Latin *ubique* meaning
'everywhere'

udder udders
NOUN the baglike organ that hangs
below a cow's body and produces
milk.

UFO UFOs
NOUN a strange object seen in the sky,
which some people believe to be a
spaceship from another planet. UFO
is an abbreviation for 'unidentified
flying object'.

Ugandan Ugandans
Said "yoo-**gan**-dan" ADJECTIVE
1 belonging or relating to Uganda.
▶ NOUN 2 someone who comes from
Uganda.

ugly uglier ugliest
ADJECTIVE very unattractive in
appearance.
▦ from Old Norse *uggligr* meaning
'terrifying'
▤ plain, unattractive, unsightly

UK
an abbreviation for **United
Kingdom**.

ulcer ulcers
NOUN a sore area on the skin or inside
the body, which takes a long time to
heal E.G. *stomach ulcers*.

ulterior
Said "ul-**teer**-ee-or" ADJECTIVE If you
have an ulterior motive for doing
something, you have a hidden
reason for it.

ultimate
ADJECTIVE 1 final or eventual E.G.
Olympic gold is the ultimate goal.
2 most important or powerful E.G.
the ultimate ambition of any player.
▶ NOUN 3 You can refer to the best or
most advanced example of
something as the ultimate E.G. *This
hotel is the ultimate in luxury.*
ultimately ADVERB

ultimatum ultimatums
Said "ul-tim-**may**-tum" NOUN a
warning stating that unless someone
meets your conditions, you will take
action against them.

ultra-
PREFIX 'Ultra-' is used to form
adjectives describing something as
having a quality to an extreme
degree E.G. *the ultra-competitive
world of sport today.*

ultramarine
NOUN or ADJECTIVE bright blue.
▦ from Latin *ultramarinus* meaning
'beyond the sea', because the
pigment was imported from abroad

ultrasonic
ADJECTIVE An ultrasonic sound has a
very high frequency that cannot be
heard by the human ear.

ultrasound
NOUN sound which cannot be heard
by the human ear because its
frequency is too high.

ultraviolet
ADJECTIVE Ultraviolet light is not visible
to the human eye. It is a form of
radiation that causes your skin to
darken after being exposed to the sun.

umbilical cord umbilical cords
Said "um-**bil**-lik-kl" NOUN the tube of

blood vessels which connects an unborn baby to its mother and through which the baby receives nutrients and oxygen.

umbrella umbrellas

NOUN a device that you use to protect yourself from the rain. It consists of a folding frame covered in cloth attached to a long stick.

umpire umpires umpiring umpired

NOUN **1** The umpire in cricket or tennis is the person who makes sure that the game is played according to the rules and who makes a decision if there is a dispute. ▶ VERB **2** If you umpire a game, you are the umpire.

umpteen

ADJECTIVE; INFORMAL very many E.G. *tomatoes and umpteen other plants.* **umpteenth** ADJECTIVE

un-

PREFIX Un- is added to the beginning of many words to form a word with the opposite meaning E.G. *an uncomfortable chair… He unlocked the door.*

unabashed

ADJECTIVE not embarrassed or discouraged by something E.G. *Samuel was continuing unabashed.*

unabated

ADJECTIVE or ADVERB continuing without any reduction in intensity or amount E.G. *The noise continued unabated.*

unable

ADJECTIVE If you are unable to do something, you cannot do it.

unacceptable

ADJECTIVE very bad or of a very low standard.

unaccompanied

ADJECTIVE alone.

unaccustomed

ADJECTIVE If you are unaccustomed to something, you are not used to it.

unaffected

ADJECTIVE **1** not changed in any way by a particular thing E.G. *unaffected by the recession.* **2** behaving in a natural and genuine way E.G. *the most down-to-earth unaffected person I've ever met.*

unaided

ADVERB or ADJECTIVE without help E.G. *He was incapable of walking unaided.*

unambiguous

ADJECTIVE An unambiguous statement has only one meaning.

unanimous

Said "yoon-**nan**-nim-mus" ADJECTIVE When people are unanimous, they all agree about something.

unanimously ADVERB **unanimity** NOUN

🔲 from Latin *unanimus* meaning 'of one mind'

unannounced

ADJECTIVE happening unexpectedly and without warning.

unarmed

ADJECTIVE not carrying any weapons.

unassuming

ADJECTIVE modest and quiet.

unattached

ADJECTIVE An unattached person is not married and is not having a steady relationship with someone.

unattended

ADJECTIVE not being watched or looked after E.G. *an unattended handbag.*

unauthorized or **unauthorised**

ADJECTIVE done without official permission E.G. *unauthorized parking.*

a
b
c
d
e
f
g
h
i
j
k
l
m
n
o
p
q
r
s
t
u
v
w
x
y
z

the QUeen stood on the QUay (quay) **SPELLING NOTE**

unavoidable

ADJECTIVE unable to be prevented or avoided.

unaware

ADJECTIVE If you are unaware of something, you do not know about it

✓ *Unaware* is usually followed by *of* or *that*. Do not confuse it with the adverb *unawares*.

unawares

ADVERB If something catches you unawares, it happens when you are not expecting it

✓ Do not confuse *unawares* with the adjective *unaware*.

unbalanced

ADJECTIVE 1 with more weight or emphasis on one side than the other E.G. *an unbalanced load… an unbalanced relationship.* 2 slightly mad. 3 made up of parts that do not work well together E.G. *an unbalanced lifestyle.* 4 An unbalanced account of something is an unfair one because it emphasizes some things and ignores others.

unbearable

ADJECTIVE Something unbearable is so unpleasant or upsetting that you feel you cannot stand it E.G. *The pain was unbearable.*

unbearably ADVERB

▤ insufferable, intolerable

unbeatable

ADJECTIVE Something that is unbeatable is the best thing of its kind.

unbelievable

ADJECTIVE 1 extremely great or surprising E.G. *unbelievable courage.* 2 so unlikely that you cannot believe it.

unbelievably ADVERB

▤ (sense 1) astonishing, incredible
▤ (sense 2) far-fetched, implausible

unborn

ADJECTIVE not yet born.

unbroken

ADJECTIVE continuous or complete E.G. *ten days of almost unbroken sunshine.*

uncanny

ADJECTIVE strange and difficult to explain E.G. *an uncanny resemblance.*

▥ from Scottish *uncanny* meaning 'unreliable' or 'not safe to deal with'

uncertain

ADJECTIVE 1 not knowing what to do E.G. *For a minute he looked uncertain.* 2 doubtful or not known E.G. *The outcome of the war was uncertain.*

uncertainty NOUN

unchallenged

ADJECTIVE accepted without any questions being asked E.G. *We can't let this enormous theft go unchallenged.*

uncharacteristic

ADJECTIVE not typical or usual E.G. *My father reacted with uncharacteristic speed.*

uncivilized or **uncivilised**

ADJECTIVE unacceptable, for example by being very cruel or rude E.G. *the uncivilized behaviour of football hooligans.*

uncle uncles

NOUN the brother of your mother or father or the husband of your aunt.

unclean

ADJECTIVE dirty E.G. *unclean water.*

unclear

ADJECTIVE confusing and not obvious.

uncomfortable

ADJECTIVE 1 If you are uncomfortable, you are not physically relaxed and feel slight pain or discomfort.

A B C D E F G H I J K L M N O P Q R S T U V W X Y Z

2 Uncomfortable also means slightly worried or embarrassed.
uncomfortably ADVERB

uncommon
ADJECTIVE **1** not happening often or not seen often. **2** unusually great E.G. *She had read Cecilia's last letter with uncommon interest.*
uncommonly ADVERB

uncompromising
ADJECTIVE determined not to change an opinion or aim in any way E.G. *an uncompromising approach to life.*
uncompromisingly ADVERB

unconcerned
ADJECTIVE not interested in something or not worried about it.

unconditional
ADJECTIVE with no conditions or limitations E.G. *a full three-year unconditional guarantee.*
unconditionally ADVERB

unconscious
ADJECTIVE **1** Someone who is unconscious is asleep or in a state similar to sleep as a result of a shock, accident, or injury. **2** If you are unconscious of something, you are not aware of it.
unconsciously ADVERB

uncontrollable
ADJECTIVE If someone or something is uncontrollable, they or it cannot be controlled or stopped E.G. *uncontrollable anger.*
uncontrollably ADVERB

unconventional
ADJECTIVE not behaving in the same way as most other people.

unconvinced
ADJECTIVE not at all certain that something is true or right E.G. *Some critics remain unconvinced by the*

plan.

uncouth
Said "un-**kooth**" ADJECTIVE bad-mannered and unpleasant.
▣ boorish, coarse, vulgar

uncover uncovers uncovering uncovered
VERB **1** If you uncover a secret, you find it out. **2** To uncover something is to remove the cover or lid from it.

undaunted
ADJECTIVE If you are undaunted by something disappointing, you are not discouraged by it.

undecided
ADJECTIVE If you are undecided, you have not yet made a decision about something.

undemanding
ADJECTIVE not difficult to do or deal with E.G. *undemanding work.*

undeniable
ADJECTIVE certainly true E.G. *undeniable evidence.*
undeniably ADVERB

under
PREPOSITION **1** below or beneath. **2** You can use 'under' to say that a person or thing is affected by a particular situation or condition E.G. *The country was under threat… Animals are kept under unnatural conditions.* **3** If someone studies or works under a particular person, that person is their teacher or their boss. **4** less than E.G. *under five kilometres… children under the age of 14.* ▶ PHRASE **5 Under way** means already started E.G. *A murder investigation is already under way.*

under-
PREFIX 'Under-' is used in words that describe something as not being

provided to a sufficient extent or not having happened to a sufficient extent.

underarm

ADJECTIVE **1** under your arm E.G. *underarm hair*. ▸ ADVERB **2** If you throw a ball underarm, you throw it without raising your arm over your shoulder.

undercarriage undercarriages

NOUN the part of an aircraft, including the wheels, that supports the aircraft when it is on the ground.

underclass

NOUN The underclass is the people in society who are the most poor and whose situation is unlikely to improve.

underclothes

PLURAL NOUN Your underclothes are the clothes that you wear under your other clothes and next to your skin.

undercover

ADJECTIVE involving secret work to obtain information E.G. *a police undercover operation*.

undercurrent undercurrents

NOUN a weak, partly hidden feeling that may become stronger later.

undercut undercuts undercutting undercut

VERB **1** To undercut someone's prices is to sell a product more cheaply than they do. **2** If something undercuts your attempts to achieve something, it prevents them from being effective.

underdeveloped

ADJECTIVE An underdeveloped country does not have modern industries, and usually has a low standard of living.

underdog underdogs

NOUN The underdog in a competition is the person who seems likely to lose.

underestimate underestimates underestimating underestimated

VERB If you underestimate something or someone, you do not realize how large, great, or capable they are.

underfoot

ADJECTIVE or ADVERB under your feet E.G. *the icy ground underfoot*.

undergo undergoes undergoing underwent undergone

VERB If you undergo something unpleasant, it happens to you.

underground

ADJECTIVE **1** below the surface of the ground. **2** secret, unofficial, and usually illegal. ▸ NOUN **3** The underground is a railway system in which trains travel in tunnels below ground.

undergrowth

NOUN Small bushes and plants growing under trees are called the undergrowth.

underhand

ADJECTIVE secret and dishonest E.G. *underhand behaviour*.

underlie underlies underlying underlay underlain

VERB The thing that underlies a situation is the cause or basis of it. **underlying** ADJECTIVE

underline underlines underlining underlined

VERB **1** If something underlines a feeling or a problem, it emphasizes it. **2** If you underline a word or sentence, you draw a line under it.

underling underlings

NOUN someone who is less important than someone else in rank or status.

undermine undermines
undermining undermined
VERB To undermine an idea, feeling, or
system is to make it less strong or
secure E.G. *You're trying to undermine
my confidence again.*
from the practice in warfare of
digging tunnels under enemy
fortifications in order to make them
collapse
subvert, weaken

underneath
PREPOSITION 1 below or beneath.
► ADVERB OR PREPOSITION 2 Underneath
describes feelings and qualities that
do not show in your behaviour E.G.
*Alex knew that underneath she was
shattered.* ► ADJECTIVE 3 The
underneath part of something is the
part that touches or faces the
ground.

underpants
PLURAL NOUN Underpants are a piece of
clothing worn by men and boys
under their trousers.

underpass underpasses
NOUN a road or footpath that goes
under a road or railway.

underpin underpins
underpinning underpinned
VERB If something underpins
something else, it helps it to
continue by supporting and
strengthening it E.G. *Australian skill is
usually underpinned by an immense
team spirit.*

underprivileged
ADJECTIVE Underprivileged people
have less money and fewer
opportunities than other people.

underrate underrates
underrating underrated
VERB If you underrate someone, you

do not realize how clever or valuable
they are.

understand understands
understanding understood
VERB 1 If you understand what
someone says, you know what they
mean. 2 If you understand a
situation, you know what is
happening and why. 3 If you say that
you understand that something is
the case, you mean that you have
heard that it is the case E.G. *I
understand that she's a lot better now.*
comprehend, follow, grasp, see

understandable
ADJECTIVE If something is
understandable, people can easily
understand it.
understandably ADVERB

understanding understandings
NOUN 1 If you have an understanding
of something, you have some
knowledge about it. 2 an informal
agreement between people.
► ADJECTIVE 3 kind and sympathetic.
(sense 1) comprehension, grasp,
perception

understatement
understatements
NOUN a statement that does not say
fully how true something is E.G. *To
say I was pleased was an
understatement.*

understudy understudies
NOUN someone who has learnt a part
in a play so that they can act it if the
main actor or actress is ill.

undertake undertakes
undertaking undertook
undertaken
VERB When you undertake a task or
job, you agree to do it.
undertaking NOUN

a
b
c
d
e
f
g
h
i
j
k
l
m
n
o
p
q
r
s
t
u
v
w
x
y
z

Eddy Ant thinks mEAt is a grEAt trEAt to EAt (-ea-)   SPELLING NOTE

A
B
C
D
E
F
G
H
I
J
K
L
M
N
O
P
Q
R
S
T
U
V
W
X
Y
Z

undertaker undertakers
NOUN someone whose job is to prepare bodies for burial and arrange funerals.

undertone undertones
NOUN 1 If you say something in an undertone, you say it very quietly. 2 If something has undertones of a particular kind, it indirectly suggests ideas of this kind E.G. *unsettling undertones of violence*.

undervalue undervalues undervaluing undervalued
VERB If you undervalue something, you think it is less important than it really is.

underwater
ADVERB OR ADJECTIVE 1 beneath the surface of the sea, a river, or a lake. ► ADJECTIVE 2 designed to work in water E.G. *an underwater camera*.

underwear
NOUN Your underwear is the clothing that you wear under your other clothes, next to your skin.

underwent
the past tense of **undergo**.

undesirable
ADJECTIVE unwelcome and likely to cause harm E.G. *undesirable behaviour*.

undid
the past tense of **undo**.

undisputed
ADJECTIVE definite and without any doubt E.G. *the undisputed champion*.

undivided
ADJECTIVE If you give something your undivided attention, you concentrate on it totally.

undo undoes undoing undid undone
VERB 1 If you undo something that is

tied up, you untie it. 2 If you undo something that has been done, you reverse the effect of it.

undoing
NOUN If something is someone's undoing, it is the cause of their failure.

undoubted
ADJECTIVE You use 'undoubted' to emphasize something E.G. *The event was an undoubted success*.
undoubtedly ADVERB

undress undresses undressing undressed
VERB When you undress, you take off your clothes.

undue
ADJECTIVE greater than is reasonable E.G. *undue violence*.
unduly ADVERB

undulating
ADJECTIVE; FORMAL moving gently up and down E.G. *undulating hills*.

undying
ADJECTIVE lasting forever E.G. *his undying love for his wife*.

unearth unearths unearthing unearthed
VERB If you unearth something that is hidden, you discover it.

unearthly
ADJECTIVE strange and unnatural.

uneasy
ADJECTIVE If you are uneasy, you feel worried that something may be wrong.
unease NOUN **uneasily** ADVERB
uneasiness NOUN

unemployed
ADJECTIVE 1 without a job E.G. *an unemployed mechanic*. ► NOUN 2 The unemployed are all the people who are without a job.

unemployment

NOUN Unemployment is the state of being without a job.

unending

ADJECTIVE Something unending has continued for a long time and seems as if it will never stop E.G. *unending joy*.

unenviable

ADJECTIVE An unenviable situation is one that you would not like to be in.

unequal

ADJECTIVE 1 An unequal society does not offer the same opportunities and privileges to all people. 2 Unequal things are different in size, strength, or ability.

uneven

ADJECTIVE 1 An uneven surface is not level or smooth. 2 not the same or consistent E.G. *six lines of uneven length*.

unevenly ADVERB

uneventful

ADJECTIVE An uneventful period of time is one when nothing interesting happens.

unexpected

ADJECTIVE Something unexpected is surprising because it was not thought likely to happen.

unexpectedly ADVERB

unfailing

ADJECTIVE continuous and not weakening as time passes E.G. *his unfailing cheerfulness*.

unfair

ADJECTIVE not right or just.

unfairly ADVERB

unfaithful

ADJECTIVE If someone is unfaithful to their lover or the person they are married to, they have a sexual relationship with someone else.

unfamiliar

ADJECTIVE If something is unfamiliar to you, or if you are unfamiliar with it, you have not seen or heard it before.

unfashionable

ADJECTIVE Something that is unfashionable is not popular or is no longer used by many people.

unfavourable

ADJECTIVE not encouraging or promising, or not providing any advantage.

unfit

ADJECTIVE 1 If you are unfit, your body is not in good condition because you have not been taking enough exercise. 2 Something that is unfit for a particular purpose is not suitable for that purpose.

unfold unfolds unfolding unfolded

VERB 1 When a situation unfolds, it develops and becomes known. 2 If you unfold something that has been folded, you open it out so that it is flat.

unforeseen

ADJECTIVE happening unexpectedly.

unforgettable

ADJECTIVE Something unforgettable is so good or so bad that you are unlikely to forget it.

unforgettably ADVERB

unforgivable

ADJECTIVE Something unforgivable is so bad or cruel that it can never be forgiven or justified.

unforgivably ADVERB

unfortunate

ADJECTIVE 1 Someone who is unfortunate is unlucky. 2 If you describe an event as unfortunate,

a
b
c
d
e
f
g
h
i
j
k
l
m
n
o
p
q
r
s
t
u
v
w
x
y
z

'i' before 'e' except after 'c'   SPELLING NOTE

you mean that it is a pity that it happened E.G. *an unfortunate accident*.

unfortunately ADVERB

unfounded
ADJECTIVE Something that is unfounded has no evidence to support it E.G. *unfounded allegations*.

unfriendly
ADJECTIVE 1 A person who is unfriendly is not pleasant to you. 2 A place that is unfriendly makes you feel uncomfortable or is not welcoming.

ungainly
ADJECTIVE moving in an awkward or clumsy way.
📖 from Old Norse *ungegn* meaning 'not straight'

unhappy unhappier unhappiest
ADJECTIVE 1 sad and depressed. 2 not pleased or satisfied E.G. *I am unhappy at being left out*. 3 If you describe a situation as an unhappy one, you are sorry that it exists E.G. *an unhappy state of affairs*.

unhappily ADVERB **unhappiness** NOUN

unhealthy
ADJECTIVE 1 likely to cause illness E.G. *an unhealthy lifestyle*. 2 An unhealthy person is often ill.

unheard-of
ADJECTIVE never having happened before and therefore surprising or shocking.

unhinged
ADJECTIVE Someone who is unhinged is mentally ill.

unhurried
ADJECTIVE Unhurried is used to describe actions or movements that are slow and relaxed.

unicorn unicorns
NOUN an imaginary animal that looks like a white horse with a straight horn growing from its forehead.
📖 from Latin *unicornis* meaning 'having one horn'

unidentified
ADJECTIVE You say that someone or something is unidentified when nobody knows who or what they are.

uniform uniforms
NOUN 1 a special set of clothes worn by people at work or school.
▶ ADJECTIVE 2 Something that is uniform does not vary but is even and regular throughout.

uniformity NOUN

unify unifies unifying unified
VERB If you unify a number of things, you bring them together.

unification NOUN

unilateral
ADJECTIVE A unilateral decision or action is one taken by only one of several groups involved in a particular situation.

unilaterally ADVERB

unimaginable
ADJECTIVE impossible to imagine or understand properly E.G. *a fairyland of unimaginable beauty*.

unimportant
ADJECTIVE having very little significance or importance.
■ insignificant, minor, trivial

uninhabited
ADJECTIVE An uninhabited place is a place where nobody lives.

uninhibited
ADJECTIVE If you are uninhibited, you behave freely and naturally and show your true feelings.

unintelligible
ADJECTIVE; FORMAL impossible to understand.

uninterested
ADJECTIVE If you are uninterested in something, you are not interested in it.

uninterrupted
ADJECTIVE continuing without breaks or interruptions E.G. *uninterrupted views*.

union unions
NOUN 1 an organization of workers that aims to improve the working conditions, pay, and benefits of its members. 2 When the union of two things takes place, they are joined together to become one thing.

unique
Said "yoo-**neek**" ADJECTIVE 1 being the only one of its kind. 2 If something is unique to one person or thing, it concerns or belongs to that person or thing only E.G. *trees and vegetation unique to the Canary islands*.

uniquely ADVERB **uniqueness** NOUN
☑ Something is either *unique* or *not unique*, so you should avoid saying things like *rather unique* or *very unique*.

unisex
ADJECTIVE designed to be used by both men and women E.G. *unisex clothing*.

unison
NOUN If a group of people do something in unison, they all do it together at the same time.
🏛 from Latin *unisonus* meaning 'making the same musical sound'

unit units
NOUN 1 If you consider something as a unit, you consider it as a single complete thing. 2 a group of people who work together at a particular job E.G. *the Police Support Unit*. 3 a machine or piece of equipment which has a particular function E.G. *a remote control unit*. 4 A unit of measurement is a fixed standard that is used for measuring things.

unite unites uniting united
VERB If a number of people unite, they join together and act as a group.

United Kingdom
NOUN The United Kingdom consists of Great Britain and Northern Ireland.

United Nations
NOUN The United Nations is an international organization which tries to encourage peace, cooperation, and friendship between countries.

unity
NOUN Where there is unity, people are in agreement and act together for a particular purpose.

universal
ADJECTIVE concerning or relating to everyone in the world or every part of the universe E.G. *Music and sports programmes have a universal appeal… universal destruction*.
universally ADVERB

universe universes
NOUN The universe is the whole of space, including all the stars and planets.

university universities
NOUN a place where students study for degrees.
🏛 from Latin *universitas* meaning 'group of scholars'

unjust
ADJECTIVE not fair or reasonable.
unjustly ADVERB

a
b
c
d
e
f
g
h
i
j
k
l
m
n
o
p
q
r
s
t
u
v
w
x
y
z

unjustified
ADJECTIVE If a belief or action is unjustified, there is no good reason for it.

unkempt
ADJECTIVE untidy and not looked after properly E.G. *unkempt hair*.

unkind
ADJECTIVE unpleasant and rather cruel. **unkindly** ADVERB **unkindness** NOUN
≡ cruel, nasty, uncharitable

unknown
ADJECTIVE 1 If someone or something is unknown, people do not know about them or have not heard of them. ▶ NOUN 2 You can refer to the things that people in general do not know about as the unknown.

unlawful
ADJECTIVE not legal E.G. *the unlawful use of drugs*.

unleaded
ADJECTIVE Unleaded petrol has a reduced amount of lead in it in order to reduce the pollution from cars.

unleash unleashes unleashing unleashed
VERB When a powerful or violent force is unleashed, it is released.

unless
CONJUNCTION You use 'unless' to introduce the only circumstances in which something will not take place or is not true E.G. *Unless it was raining, they played in the little garden*.

unlike
PREPOSITION If one thing is unlike another, the two things are different.

unlikely
ADJECTIVE 1 If something is unlikely, it is probably not true or probably will not happen. 2 strange and

unexpected E.G. *There are riches in unlikely places*.

unlimited
ADJECTIVE If a supply of something is unlimited, you can have as much as you want or need.

unload unloads unloading unloaded
VERB If you unload things from a container or vehicle, you remove them.

unlock unlocks unlocking unlocked
VERB If you unlock a door or container, you open it by turning a key in the lock.

unlucky
ADJECTIVE Someone who is unlucky has bad luck.
unluckily ADVERB
≡ hapless, unfortunate

unmarked
ADJECTIVE 1 with no marks of damage or injury. 2 with no signs or marks of identification E.G. *unmarked police cars*.

unmistakable or **unmistakeable**
ADJECTIVE Something unmistakable is so obvious that it cannot be mistaken for something else.
unmistakably ADVERB

unmitigated
ADJECTIVE; FORMAL You use 'unmitigated' to describe a situation or quality that is completely bad E.G. *an unmitigated disaster*.

unmoved
ADJECTIVE not emotionally affected E.G. *He is unmoved by criticism*.

unnatural
ADJECTIVE 1 strange and rather frightening because it is not usual

E.G. *There was an unnatural stillness.*
2 artificial and not typical E.G. *My voice sounded high-pitched and unnatural.*
unnaturally ADVERB

unnecessary
ADJECTIVE If something is unnecessary, there is no need for it to happen or be done.
unnecessarily ADVERB

unnerve unnerves unnerving unnerved
VERB If something unnerves you, it frightens or startles you.
unnerving ADJECTIVE

unobtrusive
ADJECTIVE Something that is unobtrusive does not draw attention to itself.

unoccupied
ADJECTIVE If a house is unoccupied, there is nobody living in it.

unofficial
ADJECTIVE without the approval or permission of a person in authority E.G. *unofficial strikes.*
unofficially ADVERB

unorthodox
ADJECTIVE unusual and not generally accepted E.G. *an unorthodox theory.*

unpack unpacks unpacking unpacked
VERB When you unpack, you take everything out of a suitcase or bag.

unpaid
ADJECTIVE **1** If you do unpaid work, you do not receive any money for doing it. **2** An unpaid bill has not yet been paid.

unpalatable
ADJECTIVE **1** Unpalatable food is so unpleasant that you can hardly eat it. **2** An unpalatable idea is so

unpleasant that it is difficult to accept.

unparalleled
ADJECTIVE greater than anything else of its kind E.G. *an unparalleled success.*

unpleasant
ADJECTIVE **1** Something unpleasant causes you to have bad feelings, for example by making you uncomfortable or upset. **2** An unpleasant person is unfriendly or rude.
unpleasantly ADVERB
unpleasantness NOUN

unpopular
ADJECTIVE disliked by most people E.G. *an unpopular idea.*

unprecedented
Said "un-press-id-en-tid" ADJECTIVE; FORMAL Something that is unprecedented has never happened before or is the best of its kind so far.

unpredictable
ADJECTIVE If someone or something is unpredictable, you never know how they will behave or react.

unprepared
ADJECTIVE If you are unprepared for something, you are not ready for it and are therefore surprised or at a disadvantage when it happens.

unproductive
ADJECTIVE not producing anything useful.
◼ fruitless, useless

unqualified
ADJECTIVE **1** having no qualifications or not having the right qualifications for a particular job E.G. *dangers posed by unqualified doctors.* **2** total E.G. *an unqualified success.*

unquestionable
ADJECTIVE so obviously true or real that

a
b
c
d
e
f
g
h
i
j
k
l
m
n
o
p
q
r
s
t
u
v
w
x
y
z

nobody can doubt it E.G. *His devotion is unquestionable.*

unquestionably ADVERB

unravel unravels unravelling unravelled

VERB 1 If you unravel something such as a twisted and knotted piece of string, you unwind it so that it is straight. 2 If you unravel a mystery, you work out the answer to it.

📖 from Dutch *ravelen* meaning 'to unpick'

unreal

ADJECTIVE so strange that you find it difficult to believe.

unrealistic

ADJECTIVE 1 An unrealistic person does not face the truth about something or deal with it in a practical way. 2 Something unrealistic is not true to life E.G. *an unrealistic picture.*

unreasonable

ADJECTIVE unfair and difficult to deal with or justify E.G. *an unreasonable request.*

unreasonably ADVERB

unrelated

ADJECTIVE Things that are unrelated have no connection with each other.

unrelenting

ADJECTIVE continuing in a determined way without caring about any hurt that is caused E.G. *unrelenting criticism.*

unreliable

ADJECTIVE If people, machines, or methods are unreliable, you cannot rely on them.

unremitting

ADJECTIVE continuing without stopping.

unrest

NOUN If there is unrest, people are angry and dissatisfied.

unrivalled

ADJECTIVE better than anything else of its kind E.G. *an unrivalled range of health and beauty treatments.*

unroll unrolls unrolling unrolled

VERB If you unroll a roll of cloth or paper, you open it up and make it flat.

unruly

ADJECTIVE difficult to control or organize E.G. *unruly children… unruly hair.*

unsatisfactory

ADJECTIVE not good enough.

unsaturated

ADJECTIVE Unsaturated oils and fats are made mainly from vegetable fats and are considered to be healthier than saturated oils.

unscathed

ADJECTIVE not injured or harmed as a result of a dangerous experience.

unscrew unscrews unscrewing unscrewed

VERB If you unscrew something, you remove it by turning it or by removing the screws that are holding it.

unscrupulous

ADJECTIVE willing to behave dishonestly in order to get what you want.

unseemly

ADJECTIVE Unseemly behaviour is not suitable for a particular situation and shows a lack of control and good manners E.G. *an unseemly squabble.*

unseen

ADJECTIVE You use 'unseen' to describe things that you cannot see or have not seen.

SPELLING NOTE Beautiful Elephants Are Usually Tiny (<u>beau</u>tiful)

unsettle unsettles unsettling unsettled

VERB If something unsettles you, it makes you restless or worried.

unshakable or **unshakeable**

ADJECTIVE An unshakable belief is so strong that it cannot be destroyed.

unsightly

ADJECTIVE very ugly E.G. *an unsightly scar.*

unskilled

ADJECTIVE Unskilled work does not require any special training.

unsolicited

ADJECTIVE given or happening without being asked for.

unsound

ADJECTIVE 1 If a conclusion or method is unsound, it is based on ideas that are likely to be wrong. 2 An unsound building is likely to collapse.

unspeakable

ADJECTIVE very unpleasant.

unspecified

ADJECTIVE You say that something is unspecified when you are not told exactly what it is E.G. *It was being stored in some unspecified place.*

unspoilt or **unspoiled**

ADJECTIVE If you describe a place as unspoilt or unspoiled, you mean it has not been changed and it is still in its natural or original state.

unspoken

ADJECTIVE An unspoken wish or feeling is one that is not mentioned to other people.

unstable

ADJECTIVE 1 likely to change suddenly and create difficulty or danger E.G. *The political situation in Moscow is unstable.* 2 not firm or fixed properly and likely to wobble or fall.

unsteady

ADJECTIVE 1 having difficulty in controlling the movement of your legs or hands E.G. *unsteady on her feet.* 2 not held or fixed securely and likely to fall over.

unsteadily ADVERB

unstuck

ADJECTIVE If something comes unstuck, it becomes separated from the thing that it was stuck to.

unsuccessful

ADJECTIVE If you are unsuccessful, you do not succeed in what you are trying to do.

unsuccessfully ADVERB

unsuitable

ADJECTIVE not right or appropriate for a particular purpose.

unsuitably ADVERB

unsuited

ADJECTIVE not appropriate for a particular task or situation E.G. *He's totally unsuited to the job.*

unsung

ADJECTIVE You use 'unsung' to describe someone who is not appreciated or praised for their good work E.G. *George is the unsung hero of the club.* from the custom of celebrating in song the exploits of heroes

unsure

ADJECTIVE uncertain or doubtful.

unsuspecting

ADJECTIVE having no idea of what is happening or going to happen E.G. *His horse escaped and collided with an unsuspecting cyclist.*

untangle untangles untangling untangled

VERB If you untangle something that is twisted together, you undo the twists.

a
b
c
d
e
f
g
h
i
j
k
l
m
n
o
p
q
r
s
t
u
v
w
x
y
z

Betty Eats Cakes And Uses Seven Eggs (<u>because</u>)   SPELLING NOTE

untenable
ADJECTIVE; FORMAL A theory, argument, or position that is untenable cannot be successfully defended.

unthinkable
ADJECTIVE so shocking or awful that you cannot imagine it to be true.

untidy untidier untidiest
ADJECTIVE not neat or well arranged.
untidily ADVERB

untie unties untying untied
VERB If you untie something, you undo the knots in the string or rope around it.

until
PREPOSITION or CONJUNCTION 1 If something happens until a particular time, it happens before that time and stops at that time E.G. *The shop stayed open until midnight… She waited until her husband was asleep.* 2 If something does not happen until a particular time, it does not happen before that time and only starts happening at that time E.G. *It didn't rain until the middle of the afternoon… It was not until they arrived that they found out who he was.*

untimely
ADJECTIVE happening too soon or sooner than expected E.G. *his untimely death.*

unto
PREPOSITION; OLD-FASHIONED Unto means the same as to E.G. *Nation shall speak peace unto nation.*

untold
ADJECTIVE You use 'untold' to emphasize how great or extreme something is E.G. *The island possessed untold wealth.*

untouched
ADJECTIVE 1 not changed, moved, or damaged E.G. *a small village untouched by tourism.* 2 If a meal is untouched, none of it has been eaten.

untoward
ADJECTIVE unexpected and causing difficulties E.G. *no untoward problems.*

untrue
ADJECTIVE not true.

unused
Said "un-**yoozd**" ADJECTIVE not yet used.
Said "un-**yoost**" ADJECTIVE If you are unused to something, you have not often done or experienced it.

unusual
ADJECTIVE Something that is unusual does not occur very often.
unusually ADVERB
■ exceptional, extraordinary, rare

unveil unveils unveiling unveiled
VERB When someone unveils a new statue or plaque, they draw back a curtain that is covering it.

unwanted
ADJECTIVE Unwanted things are not desired or wanted, either by a particular person or by people in general E.G. *He felt lonely and unwanted.*

unwarranted
ADJECTIVE; FORMAL not justified or not deserved E.G. *unwarranted fears.*

unwelcome
ADJECTIVE not wanted E.G. *an unwelcome visitor… unwelcome news.*

unwell
ADJECTIVE If you are unwell, you are ill.

unwieldy
ADJECTIVE difficult to move or carry because of being large or an awkward shape.

A B C D E F G H I J K L M N O P Q R S T U V W X Y Z

unwilling

ADJECTIVE If you are unwilling to do something, you do not want to do it.
unwillingly ADVERB

■ averse, loath, reluctant

unwind unwinds unwinding unwound

VERB 1 When you unwind after working hard, you relax. 2 If you unwind something that is wrapped round something else, you undo it.

unwise

ADJECTIVE foolish or not sensible.

unwitting

ADJECTIVE Unwitting describes someone who becomes involved in something without realizing what is really happening E.G. *her unwitting victims.*
unwittingly ADVERB

unworthy

ADJECTIVE; FORMAL Someone who is unworthy of something does not deserve it.

unwrap unwraps unwrapping unwrapped

VERB When you unwrap something, you take off the paper or covering around it.

unwritten

ADJECTIVE An unwritten law is one which is generally understood and accepted without being officially laid down.

up

ADVERB OR PREPOSITION 1 towards or in a higher place E.G. *He ran up the stairs, high up in the mountains.* 2 towards or in the north E.G. *I'm flying up to Darwin.* ▶ PREPOSITION 3 If you go up a road or river, you go along it. 4 You use 'up to' to say how large something can be or what level it

has reached E.G. *traffic jams up to 15 kilometres long.* 5 INFORMAL If someone is up to something, they are secretly doing something they should not be doing. 6 If it is up to someone to do something, it is their responsibility. ▶ ADJECTIVE 7 If you are up, you are not in bed. 8 If a period of time is up, it has come to an end. ▶ ADVERB 9 If an amount of something goes up, it increases.

up-and-coming

ADJECTIVE Up-and-coming people are likely to be successful.

upbringing

NOUN Your upbringing is the way that your parents have taught you to behave.

update updates updating updated

VERB If you update something, you make it more modern or add new information to it E.G. *He had failed to update his will.*

upgrade upgrades upgrading upgraded

VERB If a person or their job is upgraded, they are given more responsibility or status and usually more money.

upheaval upheavals

NOUN a big change which causes a lot of trouble.

uphill

ADVERB 1 If you go uphill, you go up a slope. ▶ ADJECTIVE 2 An uphill task requires a lot of effort and determination.

uphold upholds upholding upheld

VERB If someone upholds a law or a decision, they support and maintain it.

upholstery

NOUN Upholstery is the soft covering

a
b
c
d
e
f
g
h
i
j
k
l
m
n
o
p
q
r
s
t
u
v
w
x
y
z

on chairs and sofas that makes them comfortable.

upkeep
NOUN The upkeep of something is the continual process and cost of keeping it in good condition.

upland uplands
ADJECTIVE 1 An upland area is an area of high land. ▶ NOUN 2 Uplands are areas of high land.

uplifting
ADJECTIVE making you feel happy.

up-market
ADJECTIVE sophisticated and expensive.

upon
PREPOSITION 1 FORMAL Upon means on E.G. *I stood upon the stair.* 2 You use 'upon' when mentioning an event that is immediately followed by another E.G. *Upon entering the hall he took a quick glance round.* 3 If an event is upon you, it is about to happen E.G. *The football season is upon us once more.*

upper uppers
ADJECTIVE 1 referring to something that is above something else, or the higher part of something E.G. *the upper arm.* ▶ NOUN 2 the top part of a shoe.

upper class upper classes
NOUN The upper classes are people who belong to a very wealthy or aristocratic group in a society.

uppermost
ADJECTIVE or ADVERB 1 on top or in the highest position E.G. *the uppermost leaves… Lay your arms beside your body with the palms turned uppermost.* ▶ ADJECTIVE 2 most important E.G. *His family is now uppermost in his mind.*

upright
ADJECTIVE or ADVERB 1 standing or sitting up straight, rather than bending or lying down. 2 behaving in a very respectable and moral way.

uprising uprisings
NOUN If there is an uprising, a large group of people begin fighting against the existing government to bring about political changes.

uproar
NOUN If there is uproar or an uproar, there is a lot of shouting and noise, often because they are angry.
🏛 from Dutch *oproer* meaning 'revolt'
☰ commotion, furore, pandemonium

uproot uproots uprooting uprooted
VERB 1 If someone is uprooted, they have to leave the place where they have lived for a long time. 2 If a tree is uprooted, it is pulled out of the ground.

upset upsets upsetting upset
ADJECTIVE 1 unhappy and disappointed. ▶ VERB 2 If something upsets you, it makes you feel worried or unhappy. 3 If you upset something, you turn it over or spill it accidentally. ▶ NOUN 4 A stomach upset is a slight stomach illness caused by an infection or by something you have eaten.

upshot
NOUN The upshot of a series of events is the final result.

upside down
ADJECTIVE or ADVERB the wrong way up.

upstage upstages upstaging upstaged
VERB If someone upstages you, they

draw people's attention away from you by being more attractive or interesting.

upstairs

ADVERB 1 If you go upstairs in a building, you go up to a higher floor. ▶ NOUN 2 The upstairs of a building is its upper floor or floors.

upstart upstarts

NOUN someone who has risen too quickly to an important position and are too arrogant.

upstream

ADVERB towards the source of a river E.G. *They made their way upstream.*

upsurge

NOUN An upsurge of something is a sudden large increase in it.

uptake

NOUN You can say that someone is quick on the uptake if they understand things quickly.
🔲 from Scottish *uptake* meaning 'to understand'

uptight

ADJECTIVE; INFORMAL tense or annoyed.

up-to-date

ADJECTIVE 1 being the newest thing of its kind. 2 having the latest information.

up-to-the-minute

ADJECTIVE Up-to-the-minute information is the latest available information.

upturn upturns

NOUN an improvement in a situation.

upturned

ADJECTIVE 1 pointing upwards E.G. *rain splashing down on her upturned face.* 2 upside down E.G. *an upturned bowl.*

upwards

ADVERB 1 towards a higher place E.G. *People stared upwards and pointed.*

2 to a higher level or point on a scale E.G. *The world population is rocketing upwards.*

upward ADJECTIVE

uranium

Said "yoo-**ray**-nee-um" NOUN Uranium is a radioactive metal used to produce nuclear energy and weapons.

Uranus

NOUN Uranus is the planet in the solar system which is seventh from the sun.
🔲 named after the Greek god *Ouranos* who ruled the universe

urban

ADJECTIVE (GEOGRAPHY) relating to a town or city F.G. *urban development.*

urbane

ADJECTIVE well-mannered, and comfortable in social situations.

Urdu

Said "**oor**-doo" NOUN Urdu is the official language of Pakistan. It is also spoken by many people in India.

urge urges urging urged

NOUN 1 If you have an urge to do something, you have a strong wish to do it. ▶ VERB 2 If you urge someone to do something, you try hard to persuade them to do it.
▤ (sense 1) compulsion, desire, impulse
▤ (sense 2) beg, implore

urgent

ADJECTIVE needing to be dealt with as soon as possible.

urgently ADVERB **urgency** NOUN
▤ crucial, pressing

urinal urinals

Said "yoor-**rye**-nl" NOUN a bowl or trough fixed to the wall in a men's public toilet for men to urinate in.

a
b
c
d
e
f
g
h
i
j
k
l
m
n
o
p
q
r
s
t
u
v
w
x
y
z

I want to see (C) your licenCe (licence) SPELLING NOTE

A
B
C
D
E
F
G
H
I
J
K
L
M
N
O
P
Q
R
S
T
U
V
W
X
Y
Z

urinate urinates urinating urinated
Said "yoor-rin-ate" VERB When you urinate, you go to the toilet and get rid of urine from your body.

urine
Said "yoor-rin" NOUN the waste liquid that you get rid of from your body when you go to the toilet.

urn urns
NOUN a decorated container, especially one that is used to hold the ashes of a person who has been cremated.

us
PRONOUN A speaker or writer uses 'us' to refer to himself or herself and one or more other people E.G. *Why don't you tell us?*

US or **USA**
an abbreviation for 'United States of America'.

usage
NOUN 1 the degree to which something is used, or the way in which it is used. 2 the way in which words are actually used E.G. *The terms soon entered common usage.*

use uses using used
Said "yooz" VERB 1 If you use something, you do something with it in order to do a job or achieve something E.G. *May I use your phone?* 2 If you use someone, you take advantage of them by making them do things for you. *Said* "yoos" ▸ NOUN 3 The use of something is the act of using it E.G. *the use of force.* 4 If you have the use of something, you have the ability or permission to use it. 3 If you find a use for something, you find a purpose for it.
usable or **useable** ADJECTIVE
user NOUN

▤ (sense 1) apply, employ, utilize
▤ (sense 3) application, employment, usage

used
Said "yoost" VERB 1 Something that used to be done or used to be true was done or was true in the past.
▸ PHRASE 2 If you are **used to** something, you are familiar with it and have often experienced it. *Said* "yoozd" ▸ 3 ADJECTIVE A used object has had a previous owner.

useful
ADJECTIVE If something is useful, you can use it in order to do something or to help you in some way.
usefully ADVERB **usefulness** NOUN

useless
ADJECTIVE 1 If something is useless, you cannot use it because it is not suitable or helpful. 2 If a course of action is useless, it will not achieve what is wanted.

usher ushers ushering ushered
VERB 1 If you usher someone somewhere, you show them where to go by going with them. ▸ NOUN 2 a person who shows people where to sit at a wedding or a concert.

USSR
an abbreviation for 'Union of Soviet Socialist Republics', a country which was made up of a lot of smaller countries including Russia, but which is now broken up.

usual
ADJECTIVE 1 happening, done, or used most often E.G. *his usual seat.*
▸ PHRASE 2 If you do something **as usual**, you do it in the way that you normally do it.
usually ADVERB

The government licenSes Schnapps (licen<u>s</u>es)

■ (sense 1) customary, normal, regular

usurp usurps usurping usurped
Said "yoo-**zerp**" VERB; FORMAL If someone usurps another person's job or title they take it when they have no right to do so.

ute utes
Said "yoot" NOUN; INFORMAL In Australian and New Zealand English, a utility truck.

utensil utensils
Said "yoo-**ten**-sil" NOUN Utensils are tools E.G. *cooking utensils*.
🏛 from Latin *utensilis* meaning 'available for use'

uterus uteruses
Said "yoo-ter-russ" NOUN; FORMAL A woman's uterus is her womb.

utility utilities
NOUN **1** The utility of something is its usefulness. **2** a service, such as water or gas, that is provided for everyone.

utility truck utility trucks
NOUN In Australian and New Zealand English, a small motor vehicle with an open body and low sides.

utilize utilizes utilizing utilized; also spelt **utilise**
VERB; FORMAL To utilize something is to use it.
utilization NOUN

utmost
ADJECTIVE used to emphasize a particular quality E.G. *I have the utmost respect for Richard*.

utter utters uttering uttered
VERB **1** When you utter sounds or words, you make or say them.
▶ ADJECTIVE **2** Utter means complete or total E.G. *scenes of utter chaos*.
utterly ADVERB

utterance utterances
NOUN something that is said E.G. *his first utterance*.

a
b
c
d
e
f
g
h
i
j
k
l
m
n
o
p
q
r
s
t
u
v
w
x
y
z

Vv

v
an abbreviation for **versus**.

vacant
ADJECTIVE **1** If something is vacant, it is not occupied or being used. **2** If a job or position is vacant, no-one holds it at present. **3** A vacant look suggests that someone does not understand something or is not very intelligent.
vacancy NOUN **vacantly** ADVERB

vacate vacates vacating vacated
VERB; FORMAL If you vacate a room or job, you leave it and it becomes available for someone else.

vacation vacations
NOUN **1** the period between academic terms at a university or college E.G. *the summer vacation.* **2** a holiday.

vaccinate vaccinates vaccinating vaccinated
Said "vak-sin-ate" VERB To vaccinate someone means to give them a vaccine, usually by injection, to protect them against a disease.
vaccination NOUN

vaccine vaccines
Said "vak-seen" NOUN a substance made from the germs that cause a disease and is given to people to make them immune to that disease. 🏛 from Latin *vacca* meaning 'cow', because smallpox vaccine is based on cowpox, a disease of cows

vacuum vacuums vacuuming vacuumed
Said "vak-yoom" NOUN **1** a space containing no air, gases, or other matter. ► VERB **2** If you vacuum something, you clean it using a vacuum cleaner.

vacuum cleaner vacuum cleaners
NOUN an electric machine which cleans by sucking up dirt.

vagina vaginas
Said "vaj-jie-na" NOUN A woman's vagina is the passage that connects her outer sex organs to her womb. 🏛 from Latin *vagina* meaning 'sheath'

vagrant vagrants
NOUN a person who moves from place to place, and has no home or regular job.
vagrancy NOUN

vague vaguer vaguest
Said "vayg" ADJECTIVE **1** If something is vague, it is not expressed or explained clearly, or you cannot see or remember it clearly E.G. *vague statements.* **2** Someone looks or sounds vague if they are not concentrating or thinking clearly.
vaguely ADVERB **vagueness** NOUN
■ (sense 1) imprecise, indefinite, unclear

vain vainer vainest
ADJECTIVE **1** A vain action or attempt is one which is not successful E.G. *He made a vain effort to cheer her up.* **2** A vain person is very proud of their looks, intelligence, or other qualities. ► PHRASE **3** If you do something **in vain**, you do not succeed in achieving what you intend.
vainly ADVERB

vale vales
NOUN; LITERARY a valley.

valentine valentines
NOUN **1** Your valentine is someone you love and send a card to on Saint Valentine's Day, February 14th. **2** A

valentine or a valentine card is the card you send to the person you love on Saint Valentine's Day.

🏛 Saint Valentine was a 3rd century martyr

valet valets

Said "**val**-lit *or* **val**-lay" NOUN a male servant who is employed to look after another man, particularly caring for his clothes.

valiant

ADJECTIVE very brave.

valiantly ADVERB

valid

ADJECTIVE 1 Something that is valid is based on sound reasoning. 2 A valid ticket or document is one which is officially accepted.

validity NOUN

validate validates validating validated

VERB If something validates a statement or claim, it proves that it is true or correct.

valley valleys

NOUN a long stretch of land between hills, often with a river flowing through it.

valour

NOUN Valour is great bravery.

valuable valuables

ADJECTIVE 1 Something that is valuable has great value. ► PLURAL NOUN 2 Valuables are things that you own that cost a lot of money.

■ (sense 1) costly, expensive, precious

valuation valuations

NOUN a judgment about how much money something is worth or how good it is.

value values valuing valued

NOUN 1 The value of something is its

importance or usefulness E.G. *information of great value*. 2 The value of something you own is the amount of money that it is worth. 3 The values of a group or a person are the moral principles and beliefs that they think are important E.G. *the values of liberty and equality*.

► VERB 4 If you value something, you think it is important and you appreciate it. 5 When experts value something, they decide how much money it is worth.

valued ADJECTIVE   **valuer** NOUN

valve valves

NOUN 1 a part attached to a pipe or tube which controls the flow of gas or liquid. 2 a small flap in your heart or in a vein which controls the flow and direction of blood.

vampire vampires

NOUN In horror stories, vampires are corpses that come out of their graves at night and suck the blood of living people.

van vans

NOUN a covered vehicle larger than a car but smaller than a lorry, used for carrying goods.

vandal vandals

NOUN someone who deliberately damages or destroys things, particularly public property.

vandalize or **vandalise** VERB **vandalism** NOUN

vane vanes

NOUN a flat blade that is part of a mechanism for using the energy of the wind or water to drive a machine.

vanguard

Said "**van**-gard" NOUN If someone is in the vanguard of something, they are in the most advanced part of it.

a
b
c
d
e
f
g
h
i
j
k
l
m
n
o
p
q
r
s
t
u
v
w
x
y
z

I went to see (C) the doctor's new practiCe (practice)   **SPELLING NOTE**

A B C D E F G H I J K L M N O P Q R S T U V W X Y Z

vanilla

NOUN Vanilla is a flavouring for food such as ice cream, which comes from the pods of a tropical plant.

vanish vanishes vanishing vanished

VERB If something vanishes, it disappears or ceases to exist E.G. *The moon vanished behind a cloud.*

vanity

NOUN Vanity is a feeling of excessive pride about your looks or abilities.

vanquish vanquishes vanquishing vanquished

Said "**vang**-kwish" VERB; LITERARY To vanquish someone means to defeat them completely.

vapour

NOUN Vapour is a mass of tiny drops of water or other liquids in the air, which looks like mist.

variable variables

ADJECTIVE 1 Something that is variable is likely to change at any time. ▶ NOUN 2 In any situation, a variable is something in it that can change. 3 In maths, a variable is a symbol such as x which can represent any value or any one of a set of values.

variability NOUN

variance

NOUN If one thing is at variance with another, the two seem to contradict each other.

variant variants

NOUN 1 A variant of something has a different form from the usual one, for example *gaol* is a variant of *jail*.
▶ ADJECTIVE 2 alternative or different.

variation variations

NOUN 1 a change from the normal or usual pattern E.G. *a variation of the same route.* 2 a change in level,

amount, or quantity E.G. *a large variation in demand.*

varicose veins

PLURAL NOUN Varicose veins are swollen painful veins in the legs.

varied

ADJECTIVE of different types, quantities, or sizes.

variety varieties

NOUN 1 If something has variety, it consists of things which are not all the same. 2 A variety of things is a number of different kinds of them E.G. *a wide variety of readers.* 3 A variety of something is a particular type of it E.G. *a new variety of celery.* 4 Variety is a form of entertainment consisting of short unrelated acts, such as singing, dancing, and comedy.

■ (sense 2) assortment, mixture, range

various

ADJECTIVE Various means of several different types E.G. *trees of various sorts.*

variously ADVERB

■ different, miscellaneous, sundry
☑ You should avoid putting *different* after *various*: *the disease exists in various forms* not *various different forms.*

varnish varnishes varnishing varnished

NOUN 1 a liquid which when painted onto a surface gives it a hard clear shiny finish. ▶ VERB 2 If you varnish something, you paint it with varnish.

vary varies varying varied

VERB 1 If things vary, they change E.G. *Weather patterns vary greatly.* 2 If you vary something, you introduce

changes in it E.G. *Vary your routes as much as possible.*
varied ADJECTIVE

vascular
ADJECTIVE relating to tubes or ducts that carry fluids within animals or plants.

vase vases
NOUN a glass or china jar for flowers.

vasectomy vasectomies
Said "vas-**sek**-tom-ee" NOUN an operation to sterilize a man by cutting the tube that carries the sperm.

Vaseline
NOUN; TRADEMARK Vaseline is a soft clear jelly made from petroleum and used as an ointment or as grease.

vast
ADJECTIVE extremely large.
vastly ADVERB   **vastness** NOUN

vat vats
NOUN a large container for liquids.

VAT
NOUN In Britain, VAT is a tax which is added to the costs of making or providing goods and services. VAT is an abbreviation for 'value-added tax'.

vault vaults vaulting vaulted
Rhymes with "**salt**" NOUN 1 a strong secure room, often underneath a building, where valuables are stored, or underneath a church where people are buried. 2 an arched roof, often found in churches. ▶ VERB 3 If you vault over something, you jump over it using your hands or a pole to help.

VCR
an abbreviation for 'video cassette recorder'.

VDU VDUs
NOUN a monitor screen attached to a computer or word processor. VDU is an abbreviation for 'visual display unit'.

veal
NOUN Veal is the meat from a calf.

Veda Vedas
Said "**vay**-da" NOUN an ancient sacred text of the Hindu religion; also these texts as a collection.
Vedic ADJECTIVE

veer veers veering veered
VERB If something which is moving veers in a particular direction, it suddenly changes course E.G. *The aircraft veered sharply to one side.*

vegan vegans
Said "**vee**-gn" NOUN someone who does not eat any food made from animal products, such as meat, eggs, cheese, or milk.

vegetable vegetables
NOUN 1 Vegetables are edible roots or leaves such as carrots or cabbage.
▶ ADJECTIVE 2 'Vegetable' is used to refer to any plants in contrast to animals or minerals E.G. *vegetable life.*
📖 from Latin *vegetabilis* meaning 'enlivening'

vegetarian vegetarians
NOUN a person who does not eat meat, poultry, or fish.
vegetarianism NOUN

vegetation
NOUN Vegetation is the plants in a particular area.

vehement
Said "**vee**-im-ent" ADJECTIVE Someone who is vehement has strong feelings or opinions and expresses them forcefully E.G. *He wrote a letter of vehement protest.*
vehemence NOUN   **vehemently** ADVERB

a b c d e f g h i j k l m n o p q r s t u **v** w x y z

vehicle vehicles
Said "vee-ik-kl" NOUN **1** a machine, often with an engine, used for transporting people or goods. **2** something used to achieve a particular purpose or as a means of expression E.G. *The play seemed an ideal vehicle for his music.*
vehicular ADJECTIVE

veil veils
Rhymes with "male" NOUN a piece of thin, soft cloth that women sometimes wear over their heads.

vein veins
Rhymes with "rain" NOUN **1** Your veins are the tubes in your body through which your blood flows to your heart. **2** Veins are the thin lines on leaves or on insects' wings. **3** A vein of a metal or a mineral is a layer of it in rock. **4** Something that is in a particular vein is in that style or mood E.G. *in a more serious vein.*

veld
Said "felt" NOUN The veld is flat high grassland in Southern Africa.

veldskoen veldskoens
Said "felt-skoon" NOUN In South Africa, a veldskoen is a tough ankle-length boot.

velocity
NOUN; TECHNICAL Velocity is the speed at which something is moving in a particular direction.

velvet
NOUN Velvet is a very soft material which has a thick layer of fine short threads on one side.
velvety ADJECTIVE
📖 from Latin *villus* meaning 'shaggy hair'

vendetta vendettas
NOUN a long-lasting bitter quarrel

which results in people trying to harm each other.

vending machine vending machines
NOUN a machine which provides things such as drinks or sweets when you put money in it.

vendor vendors
NOUN a person who sells something.

veneer
NOUN **1** You can refer to a superficial quality that someone has as a veneer of that quality E.G. *a veneer of calm.* **2** Veneer is a thin layer of wood or plastic used to cover a surface.

venerable
ADJECTIVE **1** A venerable person is someone you treat with respect because they are old and wise. **2** Something that is venerable is impressive because it is old or important historically.

venerate venerates venerating venerated
VERB; FORMAL If you venerate someone, you feel great respect for them.
veneration NOUN

vengeance
NOUN **1** Vengeance is the act of harming someone because they have harmed you. ▶ PHRASE **2** If something happens **with a vengeance**, it happens to a much greater extent than was expected E.G. *It began to rain again with a vengeance.*

venison
NOUN Venison is the meat from a deer.
📖 from Latin *venatio* meaning 'hunting'

venom
NOUN **1** The venom of a snake, scorpion, or spider is its poison.

2 Venom is a feeling of great bitterness or spitefulness towards someone E.G. *He was glaring at me with venom.*

venomous ADJECTIVE

vent vents venting vented

NOUN **1** a hole in something through which gases and smoke can escape and fresh air can enter E.G. *air vents.* ► VERB **2** If you vent strong feelings, you express them E.G. *She wanted to vent her anger upon me.* ► PHRASE **3** If you **give vent** to strong feelings, you express them E.G. *Pamela gave vent to a lot of bitterness.*

ventilate ventilates ventilating ventilated

VERB To ventilate a room means to allow fresh air into it.

ventilated ADJECTIVE

ventilation

NOUN **1** Ventilation is the process of breathing air in and out of the lungs. **2** A ventilation system supplies fresh air into a building.

ventilator ventilators

NOUN a machine that helps people breathe when they cannot breathe naturally, for example if they are very ill.

ventriloquist ventriloquists

Said "ven-**trill**-o-kwist" NOUN an entertainer who can speak without moving their lips so that the words seem to come from a dummy.

ventriloquism NOUN

🏛 from Latin *venter* meaning 'belly' and *loqui* meaning 'to speak'

venture ventures venturing ventured

NOUN **1** something new which involves the risk of failure or of losing money E.G. *a successful venture in television films.* ► VERB **2** If

you venture something such as an opinion, you say it cautiously or hesitantly because you are afraid it might be foolish or wrong E.G. *I would not venture to agree.* **3** If you venture somewhere that might be dangerous, you go there.

■ (sense 1) enterprise, undertaking

venue venues

Said "**ven**-yoo" NOUN The venue for an event is the place where it will happen.

Venus

NOUN Venus is the planet in the solar system which is second from the sun.

🏛 named after the Roman goddess of love

veranda verandas

Said "ver-**ran**-da"; also spelt **verandah**

NOUN a platform with a roof that is attached to an outside wall of a house at ground level.

verb verbs

NOUN In grammar, a verb is a word that expresses actions and states, for example 'be', 'become', 'take', and 'run'.

→ *SEE BOX ON NEXT PAGE*

verbal

ADJECTIVE **1** You use 'verbal' to describe things connected with words and their use E.G. *verbal attacks on referees.* **2** 'Verbal' describes things which are spoken rather than written E.G. *a verbal agreement.*

verbally ADVERB

verdict verdicts

NOUN **1** In a law court, a verdict is the decision which states whether a prisoner is guilty or not guilty. **2** If you give a verdict on something, you give your opinion after thinking about it.

a
b
c
d
e
f
g
h
i
j
k
l
m
n
o
p
q
r
s
t
u
v
w
x
y
z

A
B
C
D
E
F
G
H
I
J
K
L
M
N
O
P
Q
R
S
T
U
V
W
X
Y
Z

What Is a Verb?

A verb is a word that describes an action or a state of being. Verbs are sometimes called "doing words".

Verbs of state indicate the way things are:

E.G. *Robert **is** a Taurus.*
*Anna **has** one sister.*

Verbs of action indicate specific events that happen, have happened or will happen:

E.G. *Anna **visits** the dentist.*
*The man **faxed** his order.*

Auxiliary verbs are used in combination with other verbs to allow the user to distinguish between different times, different degrees of completion, and different amounts of certainty:

E.G. *Anna **will** visit the dentist.*
*The man **is** faxing his order.*
*They **may** talk for up to three hours.*

A **phrasal verb** consists of a verb followed by either an adverb or a preposition. The two words taken together have a special meaning which could not be deduced from their literal meanings:

E.G. *The car **broke down** again.*
*When did you **take up** croquet?*

An **impersonal verb** is a verb that does not have a subject and is only used after *it* or *there*:

E.G. *It **rains** here every day.*

Modal Verbs

Can, could, may, might, must, should, would, and *ought* are called "modal verbs". They are usually used as auxiliary verbs to change the tone of the meaning of another verb:

E.G. *I wonder if you **can** come.*

Even when they are used on their own, they *suggest* another verb:

E.G. *I certainly **can**. (i.e. I certainly **can** come)*

There is no difference between the third person present and the other forms of the present tense. No form of the verb ends in *-s*:

E.G. *I **can** speak German.*
*She **can** speak German.*

These verbs do not have a present participle or a past participle.

The verb *could* may be used as the past tense of *can*:

E.G. *I **could** speak German when I was younger.*

You can talk about past time by using *could have, may have, might have, must have, should have, would have,* and *ought to have*:

E.G. *We **may have** taken a wrong turning.*
*She **must have** thought I was stupid.*

verge verges verging verged
NOUN 1 The verge of a road is the narrow strip of grassy ground at the side. ▶ PHRASE 2 If you are **on the verge** of something, you are going to do it soon or it is likely to happen soon E.G. *on the verge of crying.* ▶ VERB 3 Something that verges on

something else is almost the same as it E.G. *dark blue that verged on purple.*

verify verifies verifying verified
VERB If you verify something, you check that it is true E.G. *None of his statements could be verified.*
verifiable ADJECTIVE **verification** NOUN

veritable

ADJECTIVE You use 'veritable' to emphasize that something is really true, even if it seems as if you are exaggerating E.G. *a veritable jungle of shops*.

vermin

PLURAL NOUN Vermin are small animals or insects, such as rats and cockroaches, which carry disease and damage crops.

vernacular vernaculars

Said "ver-nak-yoo-lar" NOUN The vernacular of a particular country or district is the language widely spoken there.

verruca verrucas

Said "ver-roo-ka" NOUN a small hard infectious growth rather like a wart, occurring on the sole of the foot.

versatile

ADJECTIVE If someone is versatile, they have many different skills.

versatility NOUN

verse verses

NOUN 1 Verse is another word for poetry. 2 one part of a poem, song, or chapter of the Bible.

versed

ADJECTIVE If you are versed in something, you know a lot about it.

version versions

NOUN 1 A version of something is a form of it in which some details are different from earlier or later forms E.G. *a cheaper version of the aircraft.* 2 Someone's version of an event is their personal description of what happened.

versus

PREPOSITION 'Versus' is used to indicate that two people or teams are competing against each other.

vertebra vertebrae

Said "ver-tib-bra" NOUN Vertebrae are the small bones which form a person's or animal's backbone.

vertebrate vertebrates

NOUN (SCIENCE) Vertebrates are any creatures which have a backbone.

vertex vertexes or **vertices**

NOUN (MATHS) The vertex of something such as a triangle or pyramid is the point opposite the base.

vertical

ADJECTIVE (MATHS) Something that is vertical points straight up and forms a ninety-degree angle with the surface on which it stands.

vertically ADVERB

vertigo

NOUN Vertigo is a feeling of dizziness caused by looking down from a high place.

verve

NOUN Verve is lively and forceful enthusiasm.

very

ADJECTIVE or ADVERB 1 'Very' is used before words to emphasize them E.G. *very bad dreams… the very end of the book.* ▶ PHRASE 2 You use **not very** to mean that something is the case only to a small degree E.G. *You're not very like your sister.*

■ (sense 1) extremely, greatly, really

vessel vessels

NOUN 1 a ship or large boat. 2 LITERARY any bowl or container in which a liquid can be kept. 3 (SCIENCE) a thin tube along which liquids such as blood or sap move in animals and plants.

vest vests

NOUN a piece of underwear worn for warmth on the top half of the body.

a
b
c
d
e
f
g
h
i
j
k
l
m
n
o
p
q
r
s
t
u
v
w
x
y
z

A
B
C
D
E
F
G
H
I
J
K
L
M
N
O
P
Q
R
S
T
U
V
W
X
Y
Z

vestige vestiges
Said "**vest**-ij" NOUN; FORMAL If there is not a vestige of something, then there is not even a little of it left E.G. *They have a vestige of strength left.*

vestry vestries
NOUN The vestry is the part of the church building where a priest or minister changes into their official clothes.

vet vets vetting vetted
NOUN 1 a doctor for animals. ▶ VERB 2 If you vet someone or something, you check them carefully to see if they are acceptable E.G. *He refused to let them vet his speeches.*

veteran veterans
NOUN 1 someone who has served in the armed forces, particularly during a war. 2 someone who has been involved in a particular activity for a long time E.G. *a veteran of 25 political campaigns.*

veterinary
Said "**vet**-er-in-ar-ee" ADJECTIVE 'Veterinary' is used to describe the work of a vet and the medical treatment of animals.
🏛 from Latin *veterinae* meaning 'animals used for pulling carts and ploughs'

veterinary surgeon veterinary surgeons
NOUN the same as a **vet**.

veto vetoes vetoing vetoed
VERB 1 If someone in authority vetoes something, they say no to it. ▶ NOUN 2 Veto is the right that someone in authority has to say no to something E.G. *Dr Baker has the power of veto.*

vexed
ADJECTIVE If you are vexed, you are annoyed, worried, or puzzled.

VHF
NOUN VHF is a range of high radio frequencies. VHF is an abbreviation for 'very high frequency'.

via
PREPOSITION 1 If you go to one place via another, you travel through that place to get to your destination E.G. *He drove directly from Bonn via Paris.* 2 Via also means done or achieved by making use of a particular thing or person E.G. *to follow proceedings via newspapers or television.*

viable
Said "**vy**-a-bl" ADJECTIVE Something that is viable is capable of doing what it is intended to do without extra help or financial support E.G. *a viable business.*
viability NOUN

viaduct viaducts
NOUN a long high bridge that carries a road or railway across a valley.
🏛 from Latin *via* meaning 'road' and *ducere* meaning 'to bring'

vibrant
ADJECTIVE Something or someone that is vibrant is full of life, energy, and enthusiasm.
vibrantly ADVERB **vibrancy** NOUN

vibrate vibrates vibrating vibrated
VERB If something vibrates, it moves a tiny amount backwards and forwards very quickly.
vibration NOUN

vicar vicars
NOUN a priest in the Church of England.

vicarage vicarages
NOUN a house where a vicar lives.

vice vices
NOUN 1 a serious moral fault in someone's character, such as greed,

or a weakness, such as smoking.
2 Vice is criminal activities connected with prostitution and pornography.
3 a tool with a pair of jaws that hold an object tightly while it is being worked on.

vice-
PREFIX 'Vice-' is used before a title or position to show that the holder is the deputy of the person with that title or position E.G. *vice-president*.

viceregal
ADJECTIVE **1** of or concerning a viceroy.
2 In Australia and New Zealand, viceregal means of or concerning a governor or governor-general.

viceroy viceroys
NOUN A viceroy is someone who has been appointed to govern a place as a representative of a monarch.

vice versa
'Vice versa' is used to indicate that the reverse of what you have said is also true E.G. *Wives criticize their husbands, and vice versa.*

vicinity
Said "vis-**sin**-it-ee" NOUN If something is in the vicinity of a place, it is in the surrounding or nearby area.

vicious
ADJECTIVE cruel and violent.
viciously ADVERB **viciousness** NOUN

victim victims
NOUN someone who has been harmed or injured by someone or something.

victor victors
NOUN The victor in a fight or contest is the person who wins.

Victorian
ADJECTIVE **1** Victorian describes things that happened or were made during the reign of Queen Victoria.

2 Victorian also describes people or things connected with the state of Victoria in Australia.

victory victories
NOUN a success in a battle or competition.
victorious ADJECTIVE
▤ conquest, triumph, win

video videos videoing videoed
NOUN **1** Video is the recording and showing of films and events using a video recorder, video tape, and a television set. **2** a sound and picture recording which can be played back on a television set. **3** a video recorder. ▸ VERB **4** If you video something, you record it on magnetic tape for later viewing.

video recorder video recorders
NOUN A video recorder or video cassette recorder is a machine for recording and playing back programmes from television.

vie vies vying vied
VERB; FORMAL If you vie with someone, you compete to do something sooner than or better than they do.

Vietnamese
Said "vyet-nam-**meez**" ADJECTIVE
1 belonging or relating to Vietnam. ▸ NOUN **2** someone who comes from Vietnam. **3** Vietnamese is the main language spoken in Vietnam.

view views viewing viewed
NOUN **1** Your views are your personal opinions E.G. *his political views.*
2 everything you can see from a particular place. ▸ VERB **3** If you view something in a particular way, you think of it in that way E.G. *They viewed me with contempt.* ▸ PHRASE
4 You use **in view of** to specify the main fact or event influencing your actions or opinions E.G. *He wore a*

a
b
c
d
e
f
g
h
i
j
k
l
m
n
o
p
q
r
s
t
u
v
w
x
y
z

A
B
C
D
E
F
G
H
I
J
K
L
M
N
O
P
Q
R
S
T
U
V
W
X
Y
Z

lighter suit in view of the heat. **5** If something is **on view**, it is being shown or exhibited to the public.
◼ (sense 2) prospect, scene, vista

viewer viewers
NOUN Viewers are the people who watch television.

viewpoint viewpoints
NOUN **1** Your viewpoint is your attitude towards something. **2** a place from which you get a good view of an area or event.

vigil vigils
Said "vij-jil" NOUN a period of time, especially at night, when you stay quietly in one place, for example because you are making a political protest or praying.

vigilant
ADJECTIVE careful and alert to danger or trouble.

vigilante vigilantes
Said "vij-il-**ant**-ee" NOUN Vigilantes are unofficially organized groups of people who try to protect their community and catch and punish criminals.

vigorous
ADJECTIVE energetic or enthusiastic.
vigorously ADVERB **vigour** NOUN

Viking Vikings
NOUN The Vikings were seamen from Scandinavia who attacked villages in parts of north-western Europe from the 8th to the 11th centuries.

vile viler vilest
ADJECTIVE unpleasant or disgusting E.G. *a vile accusation… a vile smell.*

villa villas
NOUN a house, especially a pleasant holiday home in a country with a warm climate.

village villages

NOUN a collection of houses and other buildings in the countryside.
villager NOUN

villain villains
NOUN someone who harms others or breaks the law.
villainous ADJECTIVE **villainy** NOUN
◼ criminal, evildoer, rogue

vindicate vindicates vindicating vindicated
VERB; FORMAL If someone is vindicated, their views or ideas are proved to be right E.G. *My friend's instincts have been vindicated.*

vindictive
ADJECTIVE Someone who is vindictive is deliberately hurtful towards someone, often as an act of revenge.
vindictiveness NOUN

vine vines
NOUN a trailing or climbing plant which winds itself around and over a support, especially one which produces grapes.

vinegar
NOUN Vinegar is a sharp-tasting liquid made from sour wine, beer, or cider, which is used for salad dressing.
vinegary ADJECTIVE
▥ from French *vin* meaning 'wine' and *aigre* meaning 'sour'

vineyard vineyards
NOUN an area of land where grapes are grown.

vintage vintages
ADJECTIVE **1** A vintage wine is a good quality wine which has been stored for a number of years to improve its quality. **2** Vintage describes something which is the best or most typical of its kind E.G. *a vintage guitar.* **3** A vintage car is one made between 1918 and 1930. ▶ NOUN **4** a

grape harvest of one particular year
and the wine produced from it.

vinyl
NOUN Vinyl is a strong plastic used to
make things such as furniture and
floor coverings.

viola violas
Said "vee-**oh**-la" NOUN a musical
instrument like a violin, but larger
and with a lower pitch.

violate violates violating violated
VERB 1 If you violate an agreement,
law, or promise, you break it. 2 If you
violate someone's peace or privacy,
you disturb it. 3 If you violate a place,
especially a holy place, you treat it
with disrespect or violence.
violation NOUN

violence
NOUN 1 Violence is behaviour which is
intended to hurt or kill people. 2 If
you do or say something with
violence, you use a lot of energy in
doing or saying it, often because you
are angry.

violent
ADJECTIVE 1 If someone is violent, they
try to hurt or kill people. 2 A violent
event happens unexpectedly and
with great force. 3 Something that is
violent is said, felt, or done with
great force.
violently ADVERB

violet violets
NOUN 1 a plant with dark purple
flowers. ▶ NOUN OR ADJECTIVE 2 bluish
purple.

violin violins
NOUN a musical instrument with four
strings that is held under the chin
and played with a bow.
violinist NOUN

VIP VIPs

NOUN VIPs are famous or important
people. VIP is an abbreviation for
'very important person'.

viper vipers
NOUN Vipers are types of poisonous
snakes.

virgin virgins
NOUN 1 someone who has never had
sexual intercourse. ▶ PROPER NOUN
2 The Virgin, or the Blessed Virgin, is a
name given to Mary, the mother of
Jesus Christ. ▶ ADJECTIVE 3 Something
that is virgin is fresh and unused E.G.
virgin land.
virginity NOUN

virginal virginals
ADJECTIVE 1 Someone who is virginal
looks young and innocent.
2 Something that is virginal is fresh
and clean and looks as if it has never
been used. ▶ NOUN 3 a keyboard
instrument popular in the 16th and
17th centuries.

Virgo
NOUN Virgo is the sixth sign of the
zodiac, represented by a girl. People
born between August 23rd and
September 22nd are born under this
sign.

virile
ADJECTIVE A virile man has all the
qualities that a man is traditionally
expected to have, such as strength
and sexuality.
virility NOUN

virtual
Said "**vur**-tyool" ADJECTIVE Virtual
means that something has all the
characteristics of a particular thing,
but it is not formally recognized as
being that thing E.G. *The country is in
a virtual state of war*.
virtually ADVERB

a
b
c
d
e
f
g
h
i
j
k
l
m
n
o
p
q
r
s
t
u
v
w
x
y
z

virtual reality

NOUN Virtual reality is a situation or setting that has been created by a computer and that looks real to the person using it.

virtue virtues

NOUN **1** Virtue is thinking and doing what is morally right and avoiding what is wrong. **2** a good quality in someone's character. **3** A virtue of something is an advantage E.G. *the virtue of neatness.* ▶ A FORMAL PHRASE **4** **By virtue of** means because of E.G. *The article stuck in my mind by virtue of one detail.*

■ (sense 1) goodness, integrity, morality

virtuoso virtuosos or **virtuosi**

Said "vur-tyoo-**oh**-zoh" NOUN someone who is exceptionally good at something, particularly playing a musical instrument.

🔲 from Italian *virtuoso* meaning 'skilled'

virtuous

ADJECTIVE behaving with or showing moral virtue.

■ good, moral, upright

virus viruses

Said "**vie**-russ" NOUN **1** a kind of germ that can cause disease. **2** (ICT) a program that alters or damages the information stored in a computer system.

viral ADJECTIVE

visa visas

NOUN an official stamp, usually put in your passport, that allows you to visit a particular country.

viscount viscounts

Said "**vie**-kount" NOUN a British nobleman.

viscountess NOUN

Vishnu

PROPER NOUN Vishnu is a Hindu god and is one of the Trimurti.

visibility

NOUN You use 'visibility' to say how far or how clearly you can see in particular weather conditions.

visible

ADJECTIVE **1** able to be seen. **2** noticeable or evident E.G. *There was little visible excitement.*

visibly ADVERB

vision visions

NOUN **1** Vision is the ability to see clearly. **2** a mental picture, in which you imagine how things might be different E.G. *the vision of a possible future.* **3** Vision is also imaginative insight E.G. *a total lack of vision and imagination.* **4** an unusual experience that you have, in which you see things that other people cannot see, as a result of madness, divine inspiration, or taking drugs.

visionary NOUN or ADJECTIVE

visit visits visiting visited

VERB **1** If you visit someone, you go to see them and spend time with them. **2** If you visit a place, you go to see it. ▶ NOUN **3** a trip to see a person or place.

visitor NOUN

visor visors

Said "**vie**-zor" NOUN a transparent movable shield attached to a helmet, which can be pulled down to protect the eyes or face.

visual

ADJECTIVE relating to sight E.G. *visual problems.*

visualize visualizes visualizing visualized

Said "**viz**-yool-eyes"; also spelt **visualise**

VERB If you visualize something, you form a mental picture of it.

vital

ADJECTIVE **1** necessary or very important E.G. *vital evidence*. **2** energetic, exciting, and full of life E.G. *an active and vital life outside school*.

vitally ADVERB

■ (sense 1) essential, necessary

vitality

NOUN People who have vitality are energetic and lively.

vitamin vitamins

NOUN (D&T) Vitamins are organic compounds which you need in order to remain healthy. They occur naturally in food.

vitriolic

ADJECTIVE; FORMAL Vitriolic language or behaviour is full of bitterness and hate.

vivacious

Said "viv-**vay**-shuss" ADJECTIVE A vivacious person is attractively lively and high-spirited.

vivacity NOUN

vivid

ADJECTIVE very bright in colour or clear in detail E.G. *vivid red paint… vivid memories*.

vividly ADVERB   **vividness** NOUN

■ intense, powerful

vivisection

NOUN Vivisection is the act of cutting open living animals for medical research.

vixen vixens

NOUN a female fox.

vocabulary vocabularies

NOUN (ENGLISH) **1** Someone's vocabulary is the total number of words they know in a particular language. **2** The vocabulary of a language is all the words in it.

vocal

ADJECTIVE You say that someone is vocal if they express their opinions strongly and openly. (MUSIC)

vocation vocations

NOUN **1** a strong wish to do a particular job, especially one which involves serving other people. **2** a profession or career.

vocational

ADJECTIVE 'Vocational' is used to describe the skills needed for a particular job or profession E.G. *vocational training*.

vociferous

Said "voe-**sif**-fer-uss" ADJECTIVE; FORMAL Someone who is vociferous speaks a lot, or loudly, because they want to make a point strongly E.G. *vociferous critics*.

vociferously ADVERB

vodka vodkas

NOUN a strong clear alcoholic drink which originally came from Russia. 🔤 from Russian *vodka* meaning 'little water'

vogue

Said "vohg" PHRASE If something is **the vogue** or **in vogue**, it is fashionable and popular E.G. *Colour photographs became the vogue*.

voice voices voicing voiced

NOUN **1** Your voice is the sounds produced by your vocal cords, or the ability to make such sounds. ▶ VERB **2** If you voice an opinion or an emotion, you say what you think or feel E.G. *A range of opinions were voiced*.

void voids

NOUN **1** a situation which seems empty because it has no interest or

a
b
c
d
e
f
g
h
i
j
k
l
m
n
o
p
q
r
s
t
u
v
w
x
y
z

A B C D E F G H I J K L M N O P Q R S T U V W X Y Z

excitement E.G. *Cats fill a very large void in your life.* **2** a large empty hole or space E.G. *His feet dangled in the void.*

volatile
ADJECTIVE liable to change often and unexpectedly E.G. *The situation at work is volatile.*

volcanic
ADJECTIVE A volcanic region has many volcanoes or was created by volcanoes.

volcano volcanoes
NOUN a hill with an opening through which lava, gas, and ash burst out from inside the earth onto the surface.
📖 named after *Vulcan*, the Roman god of fire

vole voles
NOUN a small mammal like a mouse with a short tail, which lives in fields and near rivers.

volition
NOUN; FORMAL If you do something of your own volition, you do it because you have decided for yourself, without being persuaded by others E.G. *He attended of his own volition.*

volley volleys
NOUN **1** A volley of shots or gunfire is a lot of shots fired at the same time. **2** In tennis, a volley is a stroke in which the player hits the ball before it bounces.

volleyball
NOUN Volleyball is a game in which two teams hit a large ball back and forth over a high net with their hands. The ball is not allowed to bounce on the ground.

volt volts
NOUN a unit used to measure the force of an electric current.

voltage voltages
NOUN The voltage of an electric current is its force measured in volts.

volume volumes
NOUN **1** (MATHS) The volume of something is the amount of space it contains or occupies. **2** The volume of something is also the amount of it that there is E.G. *a large volume of letters.* **3** The volume of a radio, TV, or record player is the strength of the sound that it produces. **4** a book, or one of a series of books.

voluminous
Said "vol-**loo**-min-uss" ADJECTIVE very large or full in size or quantity E.G. *voluminous skirts.*

voluntary
ADJECTIVE **1** Voluntary actions are ones that you do because you choose to do them and not because you have been forced to do them. **2** Voluntary work is done by people who are not paid for what they do.
voluntarily ADVERB

volunteer volunteers volunteering volunteered
NOUN **1** someone who does work for which they are not paid E.G. *a volunteer for Greenpeace.* **2** someone who chooses to join the armed forces, especially during wartime.
▶ VERB **3** If you volunteer to do something, you offer to do it rather than being forced into it. **4** If you volunteer information, you give it without being asked.

voluptuous
Said "vol-**lupt**-yoo-uss" ADJECTIVE A voluptuous woman has a figure which is considered to be sexually exciting.
voluptuously ADVERB
voluptuousness NOUN

vomit vomits vomiting vomited
VERB 1 If you vomit, food and drink comes back up from your stomach and out through your mouth. ▶ NOUN 2 Vomit is partly digested food and drink that has come back up from someone's stomach and out through their mouth.

voodoo
NOUN Voodoo is a form of magic practised in the Caribbean, especially in Haiti.

vote votes voting voted
NOUN 1 Someone's vote is their choice in an election, or at a meeting where decisions are taken. 2 When a group of people have a vote, they make a decision by allowing each person in the group to say what they would prefer. 3 In an election, the vote is the total number of people who have made their choice E.G. *the average Liberal vote.* 4 If people have the vote, they have the legal right to vote in an election. ▶ VERB 5 When people vote, they indicate their choice or opinion, usually by writing on a piece of paper or by raising their hand. 6 If you vote that a particular thing should happen, you are suggesting it should happen E.G. *I vote that we all go to Holland.*
voter NOUN

vouch vouches vouching vouched
VERB 1 If you say that you can vouch for something, you mean that you have evidence from your own experience that it is true or correct. 2 If you say that you can vouch for someone, you mean that you are

sure that you can guarantee their good behaviour or support E.G. *Her employer will vouch for her.*

voucher vouchers
NOUN a piece of paper that can be used instead of money to pay for something.

vow vows vowing vowed
VERB 1 If you vow to do something, you make a solemn promise to do it E.G. *He vowed to do better in future.* ▶ NOUN 2 a solemn promise.

vowel vowels
NOUN (ENGLISH) a sound made without your tongue touching the roof of your mouth or your teeth, or one of the letters a, e, i, o, u, which represent such sounds.

voyage voyages
NOUN a long journey on a ship or in a spacecraft.
voyager NOUN

vulgar
ADJECTIVE 1 socially unacceptable or offensive E.G. *vulgar language.* 2 showing a lack of taste or quality E.G. *The most vulgar person who ever existed.*
vulgarity NOUN **vulgarly** ADVERB

vulnerable
ADJECTIVE weak and without protection.
vulnerably ADVERB **vulnerability** NOUN
■ defenceless, susceptible, weak

vulture vultures
NOUN a large bird which lives in hot countries and eats the flesh of dead animals.

vying
the present participle of **vie**.

a b c d e f g h i j k l m n o p q r s t u v w x y z

Ww

wacky wackier wackiest
ADJECTIVE; INFORMAL odd or crazy E.G.
wacky clothes.

wad wads
NOUN 1 A wad of papers or banknotes
is a thick bundle of them. 2 A wad of
something is a lump of it E.G. *a wad
of cotton wool*.

**waddle waddles waddling
waddled**
VERB When a duck or a fat person
waddles, they walk with short, quick
steps, swaying slightly from side to
side.

waddy waddies
NOUN a heavy, wooden club used by
Australian Aborigines as a weapon in
war.

wade wades wading waded
VERB 1 If you wade through water or
mud, you walk slowly through it. 2 If
you wade through a book or
document, you spend a lot of time
and effort reading it because you
find it dull or difficult.

wader waders
NOUN Waders are long waterproof
rubber boots worn by fishermen.

wafer wafers
NOUN 1 a thin, crisp, sweet biscuit
often eaten with ice cream. 2 a thin
disc of special bread used in the
Christian service of Holy
Communion.

waffle waffles waffling waffled
Said "wof-fl" VERB 1 When someone
waffles, they talk or write a lot
without being clear or without
saying anything of importance.
► NOUN 2 Waffle is vague and lengthy
speech or writing. 3 a thick, crisp

pancake with squares marked on it
often eaten with syrup poured over
it.

waft wafts wafting wafted
Said "wahft" VERB If a sound or scent
wafts or is wafted through the air, it
moves gently through it.

wag wags wagging wagged
VERB 1 When a dog wags its tail, it
shakes it repeatedly from side to
side. 2 If you wag your finger, you
move it repeatedly up and down.

wage wages waging waged
NOUN 1 A wage or wages is the
regular payment made to someone
each week for the work they do,
especially for manual or unskilled
work. ► VERB 2 If a person or country
wages a campaign or war, they start
it and carry it on over a period of time.

wager wagers
NOUN a bet.

wagon wagons; also spelt **waggon**
NOUN 1 a strong four-wheeled vehicle
for carrying heavy loads, usually
pulled by a horse or tractor.
2 Wagons are also the containers for
freight pulled by a railway engine.

waif waifs
Said "wayf" NOUN a young, thin person
who looks hungry and homeless.

wail wails wailing wailed
VERB 1 To wail is to cry loudly with
sorrow or pain. ► NOUN 2 a long,
unhappy cry.

waist waists
NOUN the middle part of your body
where it narrows slightly above your
hips.

waistcoat waistcoats
NOUN a sleeveless piece of clothing,

often worn under a suit or jacket, which buttons up the front.

wait waits waiting waited
VERB 1 If you wait, you spend time, usually doing little or nothing, before something happens. 2 If something can wait, it is not urgent and can be dealt with later. 3 If you wait on people in a restaurant, it is your job to serve them food. ▶ NOUN 4 a period of time before something happens. ▶ PHRASE 5 If you **can't wait** to do something, you are very excited and eager to do it.

waiter waiters
NOUN a man who works in a restaurant, serving people with food and drink.

waiting list waiting lists
NOUN a list of people who have asked for something which cannot be given to them immediately, for example medical treatment.

waitress waitresses
NOUN a woman who works in a restaurant, serving people with food and drink.

waive waives waiving waived
Said "wave" VERB If someone waives something such as a rule or a right, they decide not to insist on it being applied.

wake wakes waking woke woken
VERB 1 When you wake or when something wakes you, you become conscious again after being asleep. ▶ NOUN 2 The wake of a boat or other object moving in water is the track of waves it leaves behind it. 3 a gathering of people who have got together to mourn someone's death. ▶ PHRASE 4 If one thing follows **in the wake of** another, it follows it as a

result of it, or in imitation of it E.G. *a project set up in the wake of last year's riots.*
■ (sense 1) awaken, rouse

wake up VERB 1 When you wake up or something wakes you up, you become conscious again after being asleep. 2 If you wake up to a dangerous situation, you become aware of it.

waken wakens wakening wakened
VERB; LITERARY When you waken someone, you wake them up.

walk walks walking walked
VERB 1 When you walk, you move along by putting one foot in front of the other on the ground. 2 If you walk away with or walk off with something such as a prize, you win it or achieve it easily. ▶ NOUN 3 a journey made by walking E.G. *We'll have a quick walk.* 4 Your walk is the way you walk E.G. *his rolling walk.*

walk out VERB 1 If you walk out on someone, you leave them suddenly. 2 If workers walk out, they go on strike.

walkabout walkabouts
NOUN 1 an informal walk amongst crowds in a public place by royalty or by some other well-known person. 2 Walkabout is when an Australian Aborigine goes off to live and wander in the bush for a period of time.

walker walkers
NOUN a person who walks, especially for pleasure or to keep fit.

walking stick walking sticks
NOUN a wooden stick which people can lean on while walking.

Walkman
NOUN; TRADEMARK a small cassette

a
b
c
d
e
f
g
h
i
j
k
l
m
n
o
p
q
r
s
t
u
v
w
x
y
z

walk of life walks of life

NOUN The walk of life that you come from is the position you have in society and the kind of job you have.

walkover walkovers

NOUN; INFORMAL a very easy victory in a competition or contest.

walkway walkways

NOUN a passage between two buildings for people to walk along.

wall walls

NOUN 1 one of the vertical sides of a building or a room. 2 a long, narrow vertical structure made of stone or brick that surrounds or divides an area of land. 3 a lining or membrane enclosing a bodily cavity or structure E.G. *the wall of the womb.*

wallaby wallabies

NOUN an animal like a small kangaroo.
🔲 from *wolaba*, an Australian Aboriginal word

wallaroo wallaroos

NOUN a large, stocky kangaroo that lives in rocky or mountainous regions of Australia.

wallet wallets

NOUN a small, flat case made of leather or plastic, used for keeping paper money and sometimes credit cards.

wallop wallops walloping walloped

VERB; INFORMAL If you wallop someone, you hit them very hard.

wallow wallows wallowing wallowed

VERB 1 If you wallow in an unpleasant feeling or situation, you allow it to continue longer than is reasonable

or necessary because you are getting a kind of enjoyment from it E.G. *We're wallowing in misery.*
2 When an animal wallows in mud or water, it lies or rolls about in it slowly for pleasure.

wallpaper wallpapers

NOUN Wallpaper is thick coloured or patterned paper for pasting onto the walls of rooms in order to decorate them.

walnut walnuts

NOUN 1 an edible nut with a wrinkled shape and a hard, round, light-brown shell. 2 Walnut is wood from the walnut tree which is often used for making expensive furniture.
🔲 from Old English *walh-hnutu* meaning 'foreign nut'

walrus walruses

NOUN an animal which lives in the sea and which looks like a large seal with a tough skin, coarse whiskers, and two tusks.

waltz waltzes waltzing waltzed

NOUN 1 a dance which has a rhythm of three beats to the bar. ► VERB 2 If you waltz with someone, you dance a waltz with them. 3 INFORMAL If you waltz somewhere, you walk there in a relaxed and confident way.
🔲 from Old German *walzen* meaning 'to revolve'

wan

Rhymes with "on" ADJECTIVE pale and tired-looking.

wand wands

NOUN a long, thin rod that magicians wave when they are performing tricks and magic.

wander wanders wandering wandered

VERB 1 If you wander in a place, you

walk around in a casual way. **2** If your mind wanders or your thoughts wander, you lose concentration and start thinking about other things.

wanderer NOUN

■ (sense 1) ramble, roam, stroll

wane wanes waning waned
VERB If a condition, attitude, or emotion wanes, it becomes gradually weaker.

wangle wangles wangling wangled
VERB; INFORMAL If you wangle something that you want, you manage to get it by being crafty or persuasive.

want wants wanting wanted
VERB **1** If you want something, you feel a desire to have it or a need for it to happen. **2** INFORMAL If something wants doing, there is a need for it to be done E.G. *Her hair wants cutting.* **3** If someone is wanted, the police are searching for them E.G. *John was wanted for fraud.* ► NOUN **4** FORMAL A want of something is a lack of it.

wanting
ADJECTIVE If you find something wanting or if it proves wanting, it is not as good in some way as you think it should be.

wanton
ADJECTIVE A wanton action deliberately causes unnecessary harm or waste E.G. *wanton destruction.*

war wars warring warred
NOUN **1** a period of fighting between countries or states when weapons are used and many people may be killed. **2** a competition between groups of people, or a campaign against something E.G. *a trade war… the war against crime.* ► VERB **3** When two countries war with each other,

they are fighting a war against each other.

warring ADJECTIVE

■ (sense 1) battle, fighting, hostilities

■ (sense 3) battle, fight

waratah waratahs
Said "wor-ra-**tah**" NOUN an Australian shrub with dark green leaves and large clusters of crimson flowers.

warble warbles warbling warbled
VERB When a bird warbles, it sings pleasantly with high notes.

ward wards warding warded
NOUN **1** a room in a hospital which has beds for several people who need similar treatment. **2** an area or district which forms a separate part of a political constituency or local council. **3** A ward or a ward of court is a child who is officially put in the care of an adult or a court of law, because their parents are dead or because they need protection. ► VERB **4** If you ward off a danger or an illness, you do something to prevent it from affecting or harming you.

-ward or **-wards**
SUFFIX -ward and -wards form adverbs or adjectives that show the way something is moving or facing E.G. *homeward… westwards.*

warden wardens
NOUN **1** a person in charge of a building or institution such as a youth hostel or prison. **2** an official who makes sure that certain laws or rules are obeyed in a particular place or activity E.G. *a traffic warden.*

warder warders
NOUN a person who is in charge of prisoners in a jail.

a b c d e f g h i j k l m n o p q r s t u v **w** x y z

there's a rAKE in the brAKEs (br**a**ke)   **SPELLING NOTE**

A
B
C
D
E
F
G
H
I
J
K
L
M
N
O
P
Q
R
S
T
U
V
W
X
Y
Z

wardrobe wardrobes

NOUN **1** a tall cupboard in which you can hang your clothes. **2** Someone's wardrobe is their collection of clothes.

ware wares

NOUN **1** Ware is manufactured goods of a particular kind E.G. *kitchenware*. **2** Someone's wares are the things they sell, usually in the street or in a market.

warehouse warehouses

NOUN a large building where raw materials or manufactured goods are stored.

warfare

NOUN Warfare is the activity of fighting a war.

warhead warheads

NOUN the front end of a bomb or missile, where the explosives are carried.

warlock warlocks

NOUN a male witch.

warm warmer warmest; warms warming warmed

ADJECTIVE **1** Something that is warm has some heat, but not enough to be hot E.G. *a warm day*. **2** Warm clothes or blankets are made of a material which protects you from the cold. **3** Warm colours or sounds are pleasant and make you feel comfortable and relaxed. **4** A warm person is friendly and affectionate. ▸ VERB **5** If you warm something, you heat it up gently so that it stops being cold.

warmly ADVERB

warm up VERB If you warm up for an event or an activity, you practise or exercise gently to prepare for it.

warmth

NOUN **1** Warmth is a moderate amount of heat. **2** Someone who has warmth is friendly and affectionate.

warn warns warning warned

VERB **1** If you warn someone about a possible problem or danger, you tell them about it in advance so that they are aware of it E.G. *I warned him what it would be like*. **2** If you warn someone not to do something, you advise them not to do it, in order to avoid possible danger or punishment E.G. *I have warned her not to train for 10 days*.

■ (sense 1) alert, caution, notify

warn off VERB If you warn someone off, you tell them to go away or to stop doing something.

warning warnings

NOUN something said or written to tell people of a possible problem or danger.

warp warps warping warped

VERB **1** If something warps or is warped, it becomes bent, often because of the effect of heat or water. **2** If something warps someone's mind or character, it makes them abnormal or corrupt. **3** The warp in a piece of cloth is the stronger lengthwise threads.

warrant warrants warranting warranted

VERB **1** FORMAL If something warrants a particular action, it makes the action seem necessary E.G. *no evidence to warrant a murder investigation*. ▸ NOUN **2** an official document which gives permission to the police to do something E.G. *a warrant for his arrest*.

warranty warranties
NOUN a guarantee E.G. *a three-year warranty*.

warren warrens
NOUN a group of holes under the ground connected by tunnels, which rabbits live in.

warrigal warrigals
Said "wor-rih-gl" NOUN 1 In Australian English, a dingo. 2 In Australian English, a wild horse or other wild creature. ► ADJECTIVE 3 In Australian English, wild.

warrior warriors
NOUN a fighting man or soldier, especially in former times.

warship warships
NOUN a ship built with guns and used for fighting in wars.

wart warts
NOUN a small, hard piece of skin which can grow on someone's face or hands.

wartime
NOUN Wartime is a period of time during which a country is at war.

wary warier wariest
ADJECTIVE cautious and on one's guard E.G. *Michelle is wary of marriage*.
warily ADVERB

was
a past tense of **be**.

wash washes washing washed
VERB 1 If you wash something, you clean it with water and soap. 2 If you wash, you clean yourself using soap and water. 3 If something is washed somewhere, it is carried there gently by water E.G. *The infant Arthur was washed ashore*. ► NOUN 4 The wash is all the clothes and bedding that are washed together at one time E.G. *a typical family's weekly wash*. 5 The wash in water is the disturbance and waves produced at the back of a moving boat. ► PHRASE 6 If you **wash your hands of** something, you refuse to have anything more to do with it.

wash up VERB 1 If you wash up, you wash the dishes, pans, and cutlery used in preparing and eating a meal. 2 If something is washed up on land, it is carried by a river or sea and left there E.G. *A body had been washed up on the beach*.

washbasin washbasins
NOUN a deep bowl, usually fixed to a wall, with taps for hot and cold water.

washer washers
NOUN 1 a thin, flat ring of metal or plastic which is placed over a bolt before the nut is screwed on, so that it is fixed more tightly. 2 In Australian English, a small piece of towelling for washing yourself.

washing
NOUN Washing consists of clothes and bedding which need to be washed or are in the process of being washed and dried.

washing machine washing machines
NOUN a machine for washing clothes in.

washing-up
NOUN If you do the washing-up, you wash the dishes, pans, and cutlery which have been used in the cooking and eating of a meal.

wasp wasps
NOUN an insect with yellow and black stripes across its body, which can sting like a bee.

wastage
NOUN Wastage is loss and misuse of something E.G. *wastage of resources*.

a
b
c
d
e
f
g
h
i
j
k
l
m
n
o
p
q
r
s
t
u
v
w
x
y
z

I always visit my FRIend on a FRIday (friend)   **SPELLING NOTE**

A
B
C
D
E
F
G
H
I
J
K
L
M
N
O
P
Q
R
S
T
U
V
W
X
Y
Z

waste wastes wasting wasted

VERB 1 If you waste time, money, or energy, you use too much of it on something that is not important or necessary. 2 If you waste an opportunity, you do not take advantage of it when it is available. 3 If you say that something is wasted on someone, you mean that it is too good, too clever, or too sophisticated for them E.G. *This book is wasted on us.* ► NOUN 4 If an activity is a waste of time, money, or energy, it is not important or necessary. 5 Waste is the use of more money or some other resource than is necessary. 6 Waste is also material that is no longer wanted, or material left over from a useful process E.G. *nuclear waste.* ► ADJECTIVE 7 unwanted in its present form E.G. *waste paper.* 8 Waste land is land which is not used or looked after by anyone.

■ (sense 1) fritter away, misuse, squander

■ (sense 5) misuse, squandering

waste away VERB If someone is wasting away, they are becoming very thin and weak because they are ill or not eating properly.

wasted

ADJECTIVE unnecessary E.G. *a wasted journey.*

wasteful

ADJECTIVE extravagant or causing waste by using something in a careless and inefficient way.

■ extravagant, prodigal, spendthrift

wasteland wastelands

NOUN A wasteland is land which is of no use because it is infertile or has been misused.

wasting

ADJECTIVE A wasting disease is one that gradually reduces the strength and health of the body.

watch watches watching watched

NOUN 1 a small clock usually worn on a strap on the wrist. 2 a period of time during which a guard is kept over something. ► VERB 3 If you watch something, you look at it for some time and pay close attention to what is happening. 4 If you watch a situation, you pay attention to it or are aware of it E.G. *I had watched Jimmy's progress with interest.* 5 If you watch over someone or something, you care for them.

watch out VERB 1 If you watch out for something, you keep alert to see if it is near you E.G. *Watch out for more fog and ice.* 2 If you tell someone to watch out, you are warning them to be very careful.

watchdog watchdogs

NOUN 1 a dog used to guard property. 2 a person or group whose job is to make sure that companies do not act illegally or irresponsibly.

watchful

ADJECTIVE careful to notice everything that is happening E.G. *the watchful eye of her father.*

watchman watchmen

NOUN a person whose job is to guard property.

water waters watering watered

NOUN 1 Water is a clear, colourless, tasteless, and odourless liquid that is necessary for all plant and animal life. 2 You use water or waters to refer to a large area of water, such as a lake or sea E.G. *the black waters of* the lake. ► VERB **3** If you water a plant or an animal, you give it water to drink. **4** If your eyes water, you have tears in them because they are hurting. **5** If your mouth waters, it produces extra saliva, usually because you think of or can smell something appetizing.

water down VERB If you water something down, you make it weaker.

watercolour watercolours
NOUN **1** Watercolours are paints for painting pictures, which are diluted with water or put on the paper using a wet brush. **2** a picture which has been painted using watercolours.

watercress
NOUN Watercress is a small plant which grows in streams and pools. Its leaves taste hot and are eaten in salads.

waterfall waterfalls
NOUN A waterfall is water from a river or stream as it flows over the edge of a steep cliff in hills or mountains and falls to the ground below.

waterfront waterfronts
NOUN a street or piece of land next to an area of water such as a river or harbour.

watering can watering cans
NOUN a container with a handle and a long spout, which you use to water plants.

waterlogged
ADJECTIVE Land that is waterlogged is so wet that the soil cannot contain any more water, so that some water remains on the surface of the ground.

watermelon watermelons
NOUN a large, round fruit which has a

hard green skin and red juicy flesh.

waterproof waterproofs
ADJECTIVE **1** not letting water pass through E.G. *waterproof clothing*. ► NOUN **2** a coat which keeps water out.

watershed watersheds
NOUN an event or period which marks a turning point or the beginning of a new way of life E.G. *a watershed in European history*.

watersider watersiders
NOUN In Australian and New Zealand English, a person who loads and unloads the cargo from ships.

water-skiing
NOUN Water-skiing is the sport of skimming over the water on skis while being pulled by a boat.

water table water tables
NOUN The water table is the level below the surface of the ground at which water can be found.

watertight
ADJECTIVE **1** Something that is watertight does not allow water to pass through. **2** An agreement or an argument that is watertight has been so carefully put together that nobody should be able to find a fault in it.

waterway waterways
NOUN a canal, river, or narrow channel of sea which ships or boats can sail along.

waterworks
NOUN A waterworks is the system of pipes, filters, and tanks where the public supply of water is stored and cleaned, and from where it is distributed.

watery
ADJECTIVE **1** pale or weak E.G. *a watery*

a
b
c
d
e
f
g
h
i
j
k
l
m
n
o
p
q
r
s
t
u
v
w
x
y
z

smile. **2** Watery food or drink contains a lot of water or is thin like water.

watt watts
Said "wot" NOUN a unit of measurement of electrical power.

wattle wattles
Said "wot-tl" NOUN an Australian acacia tree with spikes of brightly coloured flowers.

wave waves waving waved
VERB **1** If you wave your hand, you move it from side to side, usually to say hello or goodbye. **2** If you wave someone somewhere or wave them on, you make a movement with your hand to tell them which way to go. **3** If you wave something, you hold it up and move it from side to side E.G. *The doctor waved a piece of paper at him.* ▶ NOUN **4** a ridge of water on the surface of the sea caused by wind or by tides. **5** A wave is the form in which some types of energy such as heat, light, or sound travel through a substance. **6** A wave of sympathy, alarm, or panic is a steady increase in it which spreads through you or through a group of people. **7** an increase in a type of activity or behaviour E.G. *the crime wave.*
■ (sense 3) brandish, flourish

wavelength wavelengths
NOUN **1** the distance between the same point on two adjacent waves of energy. **2** the size of radio wave which a particular radio station uses to broadcast its programmes.

waver wavers wavering wavered
VERB **1** If you waver or if your confidence or beliefs waver, you are no longer as firm, confident, or sure in your beliefs E.G. *Ben has never*

wavered from his belief. **2** If something wavers, it moves slightly E.G. *The gun did not waver in his hand.*

wavy wavier waviest
ADJECTIVE having waves or regular curves E.G. *wavy hair.*

wax waxes waxing waxed
NOUN **1** Wax is a solid, slightly shiny substance made of fat or oil and used to make candles and polish. **2** Wax is also the sticky yellow substance in your ears. ▶ VERB **3** If you wax a surface, you treat it or cover it with a thin layer of wax, especially to polish it. **4** FORMAL If you wax eloquent, you talk in an eloquent way.

way ways
NOUN **1** A way of doing something is the manner of doing it E.G. *an excellent way of cooking meat.* **2** The ways of a person or group are their customs or their normal behaviour E.G. *Their ways are certainly different.* **3** The way you feel about something is your attitude to it or your opinion about it. **4** If you have a way with people or things, you are very skilful at dealing with them. **5** The way to a particular place is the route that you take to get there. **6** If you go or look a particular way, you go or look in that direction E.G. *She glanced the other way.* **7** If you divide something a number of ways, you divide it into that number of parts. **8** 'Way' is used with words such as 'little' or 'long' to say how far off in distance or time something is E.G. *They lived a long way away.* ▶ PHRASE **9** If something or someone is **in the way**, they prevent you from moving freely or seeing clearly. **10** You say **by the way** when adding something to what you are

saying E.G. *By the way, I asked Brad to drop in.* **11** If you **go out of your way** to do something, you make a special effort to do it.

■ (sense 5) course, path, route

wayside

PHRASE If someone or something **falls by the wayside**, they fail in what they are trying to do, or become forgotten and ignored.

wayward

ADJECTIVE difficult to control and likely to change suddenly E.G. *your wayward husband.*

WC WCs

NOUN a toilet. WC is an abbreviation for 'water closet'.

we

PRONOUN A speaker or writer uses 'we' to refer to himself or herself and one or more other people E.G. *We are going to see Eddie.*

weak weaker weakest

ADJECTIVE **1** not having much strength E.G. *weak from lack of sleep.* **2** If something is weak, it is likely to break or fail E.G. *Russia's weak economy.* **3** If you describe someone as weak, you mean they are easily influenced by other people.

weakly ADVERB

■ (sense 1) feeble, frail, puny

weaken weakens weakening weakened

VERB **1** If someone weakens something, they make it less strong or certain. **2** If someone weakens, they become less certain about something.

weakling weaklings

NOUN a person who lacks physical strength or who is weak in character or health.

weakness weaknesses

NOUN **1** Weakness is lack of moral or physical strength. **2** If you have a weakness for something, you have a great liking for it E.G. *a weakness for whisky.*

wealth

NOUN **1** (GEOGRAPHY) Wealth is the large amount of money or property which someone owns. **2** A wealth of something is a lot of it E.G. *a wealth of information.*

■ (sense 1) fortune, prosperity, riches

wealthy wealthier wealthiest

ADJECTIVE having a large amount of money, property, or other valuable things.

■ affluent, rich, well-off

wean weans weaning weaned

VERB To wean a baby or animal is to start feeding it food other than its mother's milk.

weapon weapons

NOUN **1** an object used to kill or hurt people in a fight or war. **2** anything which can be used to get the better of an opponent E.G. *Surprise was his only weapon.*

weaponry NOUN

wear wears wearing wore worn

VERB **1** When you wear something such as clothes, make-up, or jewellery, you have them on your body or face. **2** If you wear a particular expression, it shows on your face. **3** If something wears, it becomes thinner or worse in condition. ▶ NOUN **4** You can refer to clothes that are suitable for a particular time or occasion as a kind of wear E.G. *beach wear.* **5** Wear is the amount or type of use that

a
b
c
d
e
f
g
h
i
j
k
l
m
n
o
p
q
r
s
t
u
v
w
x
y
z

Pla*i*ce the fish has a glittering 'EYE' (I) (pla*i*ce)　　**SPELLING NOTE**

A
B
C
D
E
F
G
H
I
J
K
L
M
N
O
P
Q
R
S
T
U
V
W
X
Y
Z

something has and which causes damage or change to it E.G. *signs of wear*.

wear down VERB If you wear people down, you weaken them by repeatedly doing something or asking them to do something.

wear off VERB If a feeling such as pain wears off, it gradually disappears.

wear out VERB When something wears out or when you wear it out, it is used so much that it becomes thin, weak, and no longer usable.

wear and tear

NOUN Wear and tear is the damage caused to something by normal use.

wearing

ADJECTIVE Someone or something that is wearing makes you feel extremely tired.

weary wearier weariest; wearies wearying wearied

ADJECTIVE 1 very tired. ▶ VERB 2 If you weary of something, you become tired of it.

wearily ADVERB   **weariness** NOUN

weasel weasels

NOUN a small wild animal with a long, thin body and short legs.

weather weathers weathering weathered

NOUN 1 (GEOGRAPHY) The weather is the condition of the atmosphere at any particular time and the amount of rain, wind, or sunshine occurring. ▶ VERB 2 If something such as rock or wood weathers, it changes colour or shape as a result of being exposed to the wind, rain, or sun. 3 If you weather a problem or difficulty, you come through it safely. ▶ PHRASE 4 If

you are **under the weather**, you feel slightly ill.

weather forecast weather forecasts

NOUN a statement saying what the weather will be like the next day or for the next few days.

weather vane weather vanes

NOUN a metal object on the roof of a building which turns round in the wind and shows which way the wind is blowing.

weave weaves weaving wove woven

VERB 1 To weave cloth is to make it by crossing threads over and under each other, especially by using a machine called a loom. 2 If you weave your way somewhere, you go there by moving from side to side through and round the obstacles. ▶ NOUN 3 The weave of cloth is the way in which the threads are arranged and the pattern that they form E.G. *a tight weave*.

weaver weavers

NOUN a person who weaves cloth.

web webs

NOUN 1 a fine net of threads that a spider makes from a sticky substance which it produces in its body. 2 something that has a complicated structure or pattern E.G. *a web of lies*. 3 The Web is the same as the **World Wide Web**.

webbed

ADJECTIVE Webbed feet have the toes connected by a piece of skin.

website websites

NOUN a publication on the World Wide Web which contains information about a particular subject.

SPELLING NOTE   I went to see (C) the doctor's new practiCe (practi<u>c</u>e)

wed weds wedding wedded or wed

VERB; OLD-FASHIONED If you wed someone or if you wed, you get married.

wedding weddings

NOUN ⟨RE⟩ a marriage ceremony.

wedge wedges wedging wedged

VERB 1 If you wedge something, you force it to remain there by holding it there tightly, or by fixing something next to it to prevent it from moving E.G. *I shut the shed door and wedged it with a log of wood.* ▸ NOUN 2 a piece of something such as wood, metal, or rubber with one pointed edge and one thick edge which is used to wedge something. 3 a piece of something that has a thick triangular shape E.G. *a wedge of cheese.*

wedlock

NOUN; OLD-FASHIONED Wedlock is the state of being married.

Wednesday Wednesdays

NOUN Wednesday is the day between Tuesday and Thursday.

📖 from Old English *Wodnes dæg* meaning 'Woden's day'

wee weer weest

ADJECTIVE; A SCOTTISH WORD very small.

weed weeds weeding weeded

NOUN 1 a wild plant that prevents cultivated plants from growing properly. ▸ VERB 2 If you weed a place, you remove the weeds from it.

weed out VERB If you weed out unwanted things, you get rid of them.

week weeks

NOUN 1 a period of seven days, especially one beginning on a Sunday and ending on a Saturday. 2 A week is also the number of hours you spend at work during a week

E.G. *a 35-hour week.* 3 The week can refer to the part of a week that does not include Saturday and Sunday E.G. *They are working during the week.*

weekday weekdays

NOUN any day except Saturday and Sunday.

weekend weekends

NOUN Saturday and Sunday.

weekly weeklies

ADJECTIVE or ADVERB 1 happening or appearing once a week. ▸ NOUN 2 a newspaper or magazine that is published once a week.

weep weeps weeping wept

VERB 1 If someone weeps, they cry. 2 If something such as a wound weeps, it oozes blood or other liquid.

weevil weevils

NOUN a type of beetle which eats grain, seeds, or plants.

weft

NOUN The weft of a piece of woven material is the threads which are passed sideways in and out of the threads held in a loom.

weigh weighs weighing weighed

VERB 1 If something weighs a particular amount, that is how heavy it is. 2 If you weigh something, you measure how heavy it is using scales. 3 If you weigh facts or words, you think about them carefully before coming to a decision or before speaking. 4 If a problem weighs on you or weighs upon you, it makes you very worried.

weigh down VERB 1 If a load weighs you down, it stops you moving easily. 2 If you are weighed down by a difficulty, it is making you very worried.

weigh up VERB If you weigh up a

a
b
c
d
e
f
g
h
i
j
k
l
m
n
o
p
q
r
s
t
u
v
w
x
y
z

weight weights weighting weighted

NOUN 1 (MATHS) The weight of something is its heaviness. 2 a metal object which has a certain known heaviness. Weights are used with sets of scales in order to weigh things. 3 any heavy object. 4 The weight of something is its large amount or importance which makes it hard to fight against or contradict E.G. *the weight of the law.* ► VERB 5 If you weight something or weight it down, you make it heavier, often so that it cannot move. ► PHRASE 6 If you **pull your weight**, you work just as hard as other people involved in the same activity.

weighted

ADJECTIVE A system that is weighted in favour of a particular person or group is organized in such a way that this person or group will have an advantage.

weightlifting

NOUN Weightlifting is the sport of lifting heavy weights in competition or for exercise.

weightlifter NOUN

weighty weightier weightiest

ADJECTIVE serious or important E.G. *a weighty problem.*

weir weirs

Rhymes with "near" NOUN a low dam which is built across a river to raise the water level, control the flow of water, or change its direction.

weird weirder weirdest

Said "weerd" ADJECTIVE strange or odd.

weirdly ADVERB

■ bizarre, odd, strange

weirdo weirdos

Said "weer-doe" NOUN; INFORMAL If you call someone a weirdo, you mean they behave in a strange way.

welcome welcomes welcoming welcomed

VERB 1 If you welcome a visitor, you greet them in a friendly way when they arrive. 2 'Welcome' can be said as a greeting to a visitor who has just arrived. 3 If you welcome something, you approve of it and support it E.G. *He welcomed the decision.* ► NOUN 4 a greeting to a visitor E.G. *a warm welcome.* ► ADJECTIVE 5 If someone is welcome at a place, they will be warmly received there. 6 If something is welcome, it brings pleasure or is accepted gratefully E.G. *a welcome rest.* 7 If you tell someone they are welcome to something or welcome to do something, you mean you are willing for them to have or to do it.

welcoming ADJECTIVE

weld welds welding welded

VERB To weld two pieces of metal together is to join them by heating their edges and fixing them together so that when they cool they harden into one piece.

welder NOUN

welfare

NOUN 1 The welfare of a person or group is their general state of health and comfort. 2 Welfare services are provided to help with people's living conditions and financial problems E.G. *welfare workers.*

welfare state

NOUN The welfare state is a system in which the government uses money from taxes to provide health care and education services, and to give benefits to people who are old, unemployed, or sick.

well better best; wells welling welled

ADVERB **1** If something goes well, it happens in a satisfactory way E.G. *The interview went well.* **2** in a good, skilful, or pleasing way E.G. *He draws well.* **3** thoroughly and completely E.G. *well established.* **4** kindly E.G. *We treat our employees well.* **5** If something may well or could well happen, it is likely to happen. **6** You use 'well' to emphasize an adjective, adverb, or phrase E.G. *He was well aware of that.* ▶ ADJECTIVE **7** If you are well, you are healthy. ▶ PHRASE **8** As well means also E.G. *He was a bus driver as well.* **9** As well as means in addition to E.G. *a meal which includes meat or fish, as well as rice.* **10** If you say you may as well or might as well do something, you mean you will do it although you are not keen to do it. ▶ NOUN **11** a hole drilled in the ground from which water, oil, or gas is obtained. ▶ VERB **12** If tears well or well up, they appear in someone's eyes.

well-advised

ADJECTIVE sensible or wise E.G. *Bill would be well-advised to retire.*

well-balanced

ADJECTIVE sensible and without serious emotional problems E.G. *a well-balanced happy teenager.*

wellbeing

NOUN Someone's wellbeing is their health and happiness.

well-earned

ADJECTIVE thoroughly deserved.

well-heeled

ADJECTIVE; INFORMAL wealthy.

well-informed

ADJECTIVE having a great deal of knowledge about a subject or subjects.

wellington wellingtons

NOUN Wellingtons or wellington boots are long waterproof rubber boots.

well-meaning

ADJECTIVE A well-meaning person tries to be helpful but is often unsuccessful.

well-off

ADJECTIVE; INFORMAL quite wealthy.

well-to-do

ADJECTIVE quite wealthy.

well-worn

ADJECTIVE **1** A well-worn expression or saying has been used too often and has become boring. **2** A well-worn object or piece of clothing has been used and worn so much that it looks old and shabby.

welly wellies

NOUN; INFORMAL Wellies are wellingtons.

Welsh

ADJECTIVE **1** belonging or relating to Wales. ▶ NOUN **2** Welsh is a language spoken in parts of Wales.

Welshman Welshmen

NOUN a man who comes from Wales. **Welshwoman** NOUN

welt welts

NOUN a raised mark on someone's skin made by a blow from something like a whip or a stick.

welter

NOUN; FORMAL A welter of things is a large number of them that happen or appear together in a state of confusion E.G. *a welter of rumours.*

a
b
c
d
e
f
g
h
i
j
k
l
m
n
o
p
q
r
s
t
u
v
w
x
y
z

LEarn the principLEs (principle)   SPELLING NOTE

wench wenches

NOUN; OLD-FASHIONED a woman or young girl.

wept

the past tense and past participle of weep.

were

a past tense of be.

werewolf werewolves

NOUN In horror stories, a werewolf is a person who changes into a wolf.
📖 from Old English *wer* + *wulf* meaning 'man wolf'

Wesak

Said "wess-suck" NOUN Wesak is the Buddhist festival celebrating the Buddha, held in May.

west

NOUN 1 The west is the direction in which you look to see the sun set. 2 The west of a place or country is the part which is towards the west when you are in the centre E.G. *the west of America.* 3 The West refers to the countries of North America and western and southern Europe.
▶ ADVERB OR ADJECTIVE 4 West means towards the west. ▶ ADJECTIVE 5 A west wind blows from the west.

westerly

ADJECTIVE Westerly means to or towards the west E.G. *France's most westerly region.*

western westerns

ADJECTIVE 1 in or from the west. 2 coming from or associated with the countries of North America and western and southern Europe E.G. *western dress.* ▶ NOUN 3 a book or film about life in the west of America in the nineteenth century.

West Indian West Indians

NOUN someone who comes from the West Indies.

westward or **westwards**

ADVERB Westward or westwards means towards the west E.G. *He stared westwards towards the clouds.*

wet wetter wettest; wets wetting wet or wetted

ADJECTIVE 1 If something is wet, it is covered in water or another liquid. 2 If the weather is wet, it is raining. 3 If something such as paint, ink, or cement is wet, it is not yet dry or solid. 4 INFORMAL If you say someone is wet, you mean they are weak and lacking confidence E.G. *Don't be so wet!* ▶ NOUN 5 In northern and central Australia, the wet is the rainy season.
▶ VERB 6 To wet something is to put water or some other liquid over it. 7 If people wet themselves or wet their beds, they urinate in their clothes or bed because they cannot control their bladder.

wetness NOUN

wet suit wet suits

NOUN a close-fitting rubber suit which a diver wears to keep his or her body warm.

whack whacks whacking whacked

VERB If you whack someone or something, you hit them hard.

whale whales

NOUN a very large sea mammal which breathes out water through a hole on the top of its head.

whaling

NOUN Whaling is the work of hunting and killing whales for oil or food.

wharf wharves

Said "worf" NOUN a platform beside a river or the sea, where ships load or unload.

what

PRONOUN **1** 'What' is used in questions E.G. *What time is it?* **2** 'What' is used in indirect questions and statements E.G. *I don't know what you mean.* **3** 'What' can be used at the beginning of a clause to refer to something with a particular quality E.G. *It is impossible to decide what is real and what is invented.* ▶ ADJECTIVE **4** 'What' can be used at the beginning of a clause to show that you are talking about the whole amount that is available to you E.G. *Their spouses try to earn what money they can.* **5** You say 'what' to emphasize an opinion or reaction E.G. *What nonsense!* ▶ PHRASE **6** You say **what about** at the beginning of a question when you are making a suggestion or offer E.G. *What about a drink?*

whatever

PRONOUN **1** You use 'whatever' to refer to anything or everything of a particular type E.G. *He said he would do whatever he could.* **2** You use 'whatever' when you do not know the precise nature of something E.G. *Whatever it is, I don't like it.* ▶ CONJUNCTION **3** You use 'whatever' to mean no matter what E.G. *Whatever happens, you have to behave decently.* ▶ ADVERB **4** You use 'whatever' to emphasize a negative statement or a question E.G. *You have no proof whatever… Whatever is wrong with you?*

whatsoever

ADVERB You use 'whatsoever' to emphasize a negative statement E.G. *I have no memory of it whatsoever.*

wheat

NOUN Wheat is a cereal plant grown for its grain which is used to make flour.

wheel wheels wheeling wheeled

NOUN **1** a circular object which turns on a rod attached to its centre. Wheels are fixed underneath vehicles so that they can move along. **2** The wheel of a car is its steering wheel. ▶ VERB **3** If you wheel something such as a bicycle, you push it. **4** If someone or something wheels, they move round in the shape of a circle E.G. *Cameron wheeled around and hit him.*

wheelbarrow wheelbarrows

NOUN a small cart with a single wheel at the front, used for carrying things in the garden.

wheelchair wheelchairs

NOUN a chair with wheels in which sick, injured, or disabled people can move around.

wheeze wheezes wheezing wheezed

VERB If someone wheezes, they breathe with difficulty, making a whistling sound, usually because they have a chest complaint such as asthma.

wheezy ADJECTIVE

whelk whelks

NOUN a snail-like shellfish with a strong shell and a soft edible body.

when

ADVERB **1** You use 'when' to ask what time something happened or will happen E.G. *When are you leaving?* ▶ CONJUNCTION **2** You use 'when' to refer to a time in the past E.G. *I met him when I was sixteen.* **3** You use 'when' to introduce the reason for an opinion, comment, or question E.G. *How did you pass the exam when you*

a
b
c
d
e
f
g
h
i
j
k
l
m
n
o
p
q
r
s
t
u
v
w
x
y
z

the QUeen stood on the QUay (<u>qu</u>ay) ▶ SPELLING NOTE

A
B *hadn't studied for it?* **4** 'When' is used
to mean although E.G. *He drives
when he could walk.*

C **whence**
ADVERB or CONJUNCTION; OLD-FASHIONED
D Whence means from where
☑ You should not write *from whence*
E because *whence* already means 'from
where'.

F **whenever**
G CONJUNCTION Whenever means at any
time, or every time that something
H happens E.G. *I still go on courses
whenever I can.*

I **where**
J ADVERB **1** You use 'where' to ask which
place something is in, is coming
K from, or is going to E.G. *Where is
Philip?* ▶ CONJUNCTION, PRONOUN, or ADVERB
L **2** You use 'where' when asking about
or referring to something E.G. *I
M hardly know where to begin.*
▶ CONJUNCTION **3** You use 'where' to
N refer to the place in which
O something is situated or happening
E.G. *I don't know where we are.*
P **4** 'Where' can introduce a clause that
contrasts with the other part of the
Q sentence E.G. *A teacher will be
listened to, where a parent might not.*
R
S **whereabouts**
NOUN **1** The whereabouts of a person
T or thing is the place where they are.
▶ ADVERB **2** You use 'whereabouts'
U when you are asking more precisely
where something is E.G.
V *Whereabouts in Canada are you from?*

W **whereas**
CONJUNCTION Whereas introduces a
X comment that contrasts with the
other part of the sentence E.G. *Her
Y eyes were blue, whereas mine were
brown.*
Z

whereby
PRONOUN; FORMAL Whereby means by
which E.G. *a new system whereby you
pay the bill quarterly.*

whereupon
CONJUNCTION; FORMAL Whereupon means
at which point E.G. *His enemies
rejected his message, whereupon he
tried again.*

wherever
CONJUNCTION **1** 'Wherever' means in
every place or situation E.G. *Alex
heard the same thing wherever he
went.* **2** You use 'wherever' to show
that you do not know where a place
or person is E.G. *the nearest police
station, wherever that is.*

wherewithal
NOUN If you have the wherewithal to
do something, you have enough
money to do it.

whet whets whetting whetted
PHRASE To **whet someone's appetite**
for something, means to increase
their desire for it.

whether
CONJUNCTION You use 'whether' when
you are talking about two or more
alternatives E.G. *I don't know whether
that's true or false.*

whey
Rhymes with "day" NOUN Whey is the
watery liquid that is separated from
the curds in sour milk when cheese
is made.

which
ADJECTIVE or PRONOUN **1** You use 'which'
to ask about alternatives or to refer
to a choice between alternatives E.G.
Which room are you in? ▶ PRONOUN
2 'Which' at the beginning of a clause
identifies the thing you are talking
about or gives more information

about it E.G. *certain wrongs which exist in our society.*

☑ See the usage note at *that*.

whichever

ADJECTIVE OR PRONOUN You use 'whichever' when you are talking about different alternatives or possibilities E.G. *Make your pizzas round or square, whichever you prefer.*

whiff whiffs

NOUN 1 a slight smell of something. 2 a slight sign or trace of something E.G. *a whiff of criticism.*

while whiles whiling whiled

CONJUNCTION 1 If something happens while something else is happening, the two things happen at the same time. 2 While also means but E.G. *Men tend to gaze more, while women dart quick glances.* ► NOUN 3 a period of time E.G. *a little while earlier.* ► PHRASE 4 If an action or activity is **worth your while**, it will be helpful or useful to you if you do it.

while away VERB If you while away the time in a particular way, you pass the time that way because you have nothing else to do.

whilst

CONJUNCTION Whilst means the same as while.

whim whims

NOUN a sudden desire or fancy.

☰ fancy, impulse

whimper whimpers whimpering whimpered

VERB 1 When children or animals whimper, they make soft, low, unhappy sounds. 2 If you whimper something, you say it in an unhappy or frightened way, as if you are about to cry.

whimsical

ADJECTIVE unusual and slightly playful E.G. *an endearing, whimsical charm.*

whine whines whining whined

VERB 1 To whine is to make a long, high-pitched noise, especially one which sounds sad or unpleasant. 2 If someone whines about something, they complain about it in an annoying way. ► NOUN 3 A whine is the noise made by something or someone whining.

whinge whinges whinging or whingeing whinged

VERB If someone whinges about something, they complain about it in an annoying way.

whinny whinnies whinnying whinnied

VERB When a horse whinnies, it neighs softly.

whip whips whipping whipped

NOUN 1 a thin piece of leather or rope attached to a handle, which is used for hitting people or animals. ► VERB 2 If you whip a person or animal, you hit them with a whip. 3 When the wind whips something, it strikes it. 4 If you whip something out or off, you take it out or off very quickly E.G. *She had whipped off her glasses.* 5 If you whip cream or eggs, you beat them until they are thick and frothy or stiff.

whip up VERB If you whip up a strong emotion, you make people feel it E.G. *The thought whipped up his temper.*

whip bird whip birds

NOUN an Australian bird whose cry ends with a sound like the crack of a whip.

a b c d e f g h i j k l m n o p q r s t u v w x y z

whiplash injury whiplash injuries

NOUN a neck injury caused by your head suddenly jerking forwards and then back again, for example in a car accident.

whippet whippets

NOUN a small, thin dog used for racing.

whirl whirls whirling whirled

VERB 1 When something whirls, or when you whirl it round, it turns round very fast. ▶ NOUN 2 You can refer to a lot of intense activity as a whirl of activity.

📖 from Old Norse *hvirfla* meaning 'to turn about'

whirlpool whirlpools

NOUN a small circular area in a river or the sea where the water is moving quickly round and round so that objects floating near it are pulled into its centre.

whirlwind whirlwinds

NOUN 1 a tall column of air which spins round and round very fast. ▶ ADJECTIVE 2 more rapid than usual E.G. *a whirlwind tour*.

whirr whirrs whirring whirred; also spelt **whir**

VERB 1 When something such as a machine whirrs, it makes a series of low sounds so fast that it sounds like one continuous sound. ▶ NOUN 2 the noise made by something whirring.

whisk whisks whisking whisked

VERB 1 If you whisk someone or something somewhere, you take them there quickly E.G. *We were whisked away into a private room.* 2 If you whisk eggs or cream, you stir air into them quickly. ▶ NOUN 3 a kitchen

tool used for quickly stirring air into eggs or cream.

whisker whiskers

NOUN The whiskers of an animal such as a cat or mouse are the long, stiff hairs near its mouth.

whisky whiskies

NOUN Whisky is a strong alcoholic drink made from grain such as barley.

📖 from Scottish Gaelic *uisge beatha* meaning 'water of life'

whisper whispers whispering whispered

VERB 1 When you whisper, you talk to someone very quietly, using your breath and not your throat. ▶ NOUN 2 If you talk in a whisper, you whisper.

whist

NOUN Whist is a card game for four players in which one pair of players tries to win more tricks than the other pair.

whistle whistles whistling whistled

VERB 1 When you whistle a tune or whistle, you produce a clear musical sound by forcing your breath out between your lips. 2 If something whistles, it makes a loud, high sound E.G. *The kettle whistled.* ▶ NOUN 3 A whistle is the sound something or someone makes when they whistle. 4 a small metal tube that you blow into to produce a whistling sound.

whit

NOUN FORMAL You say 'not a whit' or 'no whit' to emphasize that something is not the case at all E.G. *It does not matter one whit to the customer.*

white whiter whitest; whites

NOUN OR ADJECTIVE 1 White is the lightest

possible colour. **2** Someone who is white has a pale skin and is of European origin. ► ADJECTIVE **3** If someone goes white, their face becomes very pale because they are afraid, shocked, or ill. **4** White coffee contains milk or cream. ► NOUN **5** The white of an egg is the transparent liquid surrounding the yolk, which turns white when it is cooked.
whiteness NOUN

white-collar
ADJECTIVE White-collar workers work in offices rather than doing manual work E.G. *a white-collar union.*

white lie white lies
NOUN a harmless lie, especially one told to prevent someone's feelings from being hurt.

whitewash
NOUN **1** Whitewash is a mixture of lime and water used for painting walls white. **2** an attempt to hide unpleasant facts E.G. *the refusal to accept official whitewash in the enquiry.*

whither
ADVERB or CONJUNCTION; OLD-FASHIONED Whither means to what place E.G. *Whither shall I wander?*

whiting
NOUN a sea fish related to the cod.

whittle whittles whittling whittled
VERB If you whittle a piece of wood, you shape it by shaving or cutting small pieces off it.

whittle away or **whittle down**
VERB To whittle away at something or to whittle it down means to make it smaller or less effective E.G. *The 250 entrants had been whittled down to 34.*

whizz whizzes whizzing whizzed; also spelt **whiz**
VERB; INFORMAL If you whizz somewhere, you move there quickly.

who
PRONOUN **1** You use 'who' when you are asking about someone's identity E.G. *Who gave you that black eye?* **2** 'Who' at the beginning of a clause refers to the person or people you are talking about E.G. *a shipyard worker who wants to be a postman.*

whoa
Said "woh" INTERJECTION Whoa is a command used to slow down or stop a horse.

whoever
PRONOUN **1** 'Whoever' means the person who E.G. *Whoever bought it for you has to make the claim.* **2** 'Whoever' also means no matter who E.G. *I pity him, whoever he is.* **3** 'Whoever' is used in questions give emphasis to who E.G. *Whoever thought of such a thing?*

whole wholes
NOUN or ADJECTIVE **1** The whole of something is all of it E.G. *the whole of Africa… Have the whole cake.* ► ADVERB **2** in one piece E.G. *He swallowed it whole.* ► PHRASE **3** You use **as a whole** to emphasize that you are talking about all of something E.G. *The country as a whole is in a very odd mood.* **4** You say **on the whole** to mean that something is generally true E.G. *On the whole, we should be glad they are gone.*
wholeness NOUN

wholehearted
ADJECTIVE enthusiastic and totally sincere E.G. *wholehearted approval.*
wholeheartedly ADVERB

a b c d e f g h i j k l m n o p q r s t u v **w** x y z

A
B
C
D
E
F
G
H
I
J
K
L
M
N
O
P
Q
R
S
T
U
V
W
X
Y
Z

wholemeal

ADJECTIVE Wholemeal flour is made from the complete grain of the wheat plant, including the husk.

wholesale

ADJECTIVE OR ADVERB 1 Wholesale refers to the activity of buying goods cheaply in large quantities and selling them again, especially to shopkeepers E.G. *We buy fruit and vegetables wholesale.* ▶ ADJECTIVE 2 Wholesale also means done to an excessive extent E.G. *the wholesale destruction of wild plant species.* **wholesaler** NOUN

wholesome

ADJECTIVE good and likely to improve your life, behaviour, or health E.G. *good wholesome entertainment.*

wholly

Said "hoe-lee" ADVERB completely.

whom

PRONOUN Whom is the object form of 'who' E.G. *the girl whom Albert would marry.*

whoop whoops whooping whooped

VERB 1 If you whoop, you shout loudly in a happy or excited way. ▶ NOUN 2 a loud cry of happiness or excitement E.G. *whoops of delight.*

whooping cough

Said "hoop-ing" NOUN Whooping cough is an acute infectious disease which makes people cough violently and produce a loud sound when they breathe.

whore whores

Said "hore" NOUN; OFFENSIVE a prostitute, or a woman believed to act like a prostitute.

whose

PRONOUN 1 You use 'whose' to ask who something belongs to E.G. *Whose gun is this?* 2 You use 'whose' at the beginning of a clause which gives information about something relating or belonging to the thing or person you have just mentioned E.G. *a wealthy gentleman whose marriage is breaking up.*

☑ Many people are confused about the difference between *whose* and *who's. Whose* is used to show possession in a question or when something is being described: *whose bag is this?… The person whose car is blocking the exit. Who's,* with the apostrophe, is a short form of *who is* or *who has: who's that girl?… Who's got my ruler?*

why

ADVERB OR PRONOUN You use 'why' when you are asking about the reason for something, or talking about it E.G. *Why did you do it?… He wondered why she suddenly looked happier.*

wick wicks

NOUN the cord in the middle of a candle, which you set alight.

wicked

ADJECTIVE 1 very bad E.G. *a wicked thing to do.* 2 mischievous in an amusing or attractive way E.G. *a wicked sense of humour.*
wickedly ADVERB **wickedness** NOUN
🏛 from Old English *wicce* meaning 'witch'
▤ (sense 1) bad, evil, sinful

wicker

ADJECTIVE A wicker basket or chair is made from twigs, canes, or reeds that have been woven together.

wicket wickets

NOUN 1 In cricket, the wicket is one of the two sets of stumps and bails at which the bowler aims the ball. **2** The grass between the wickets on a cricket pitch is also called the wicket.

wide wider widest

ADJECTIVE **1** measuring a large distance from one side to the other. **2** If there is a wide variety, range, or selection of something, there are many different kinds of it E.G. *a wide range of colours.* ▸ ADVERB **3** If you open or spread something wide, you open it to its fullest extent.

widely ADVERB

■ (sense 2) broad, extensive, large

wide-awake

ADJECTIVE completely awake.

widen widens widening widened

VERB **1** If something widens or if you widen it, it becomes bigger from one side to the other. **2** You can say that something widens when it becomes greater in size or scope E.G. *the opportunity to widen your outlook.*

wide-ranging

ADJECTIVE extending over a variety of different things or over a large area E.G. *a wide-ranging survey.*

widespread

ADJECTIVE existing or happening over a large area or to a great extent E.G. *the widespread use of chemicals.*

■ common, general, universal

widow widows

NOUN a woman whose husband has died.

widowed

ADJECTIVE If someone is widowed, their husband or wife has died.

widower widowers

NOUN a man whose wife has died.

width widths

NOUN The width of something is the distance from one side or edge to the other.

wield wields wielding wielded

Said "weeld" VERB **1** If you wield a weapon or tool, you carry it and use it. **2** If someone wields power, they have it and are able to use it.

wife wives

NOUN A man's wife is the woman he is married to.

wig wigs

NOUN a false head of hair worn to cover someone's own hair or to hide their baldness.

🖾 short for *periwig* from Italian *perrucca* meaning 'wig'

wiggle wiggles wiggling wiggled

VERB **1** If you wiggle something, you move it up and down or from side to side with small jerky movements. ▸ NOUN **2** a small jerky movement or line.

wigwam wigwams

NOUN a kind of tent used by North American Indians.

🖾 from American Indian *wikwam* meaning 'their house'

wild wilder wildest; wilds

ADJECTIVE **1** Wild animals, birds, and plants live and grow in natural surroundings and are not looked after by people. **2** Wild land is natural and has not been cultivated E.G. *wild areas of countryside.* **3** Wild weather or sea is stormy and rough. **4** Wild behaviour is excited and uncontrolled E.G. *wild with excitement.* **5** A wild idea or scheme is original and crazy. ▸ NOUN **6** The wild is a free and natural state of living E.G. *There are about 200 left in the wild.* **7** The wilds are remote areas where few people live, far away from towns.

wildly ADVERB

a
b
c
d
e
f
g
h
i
j
k
l
m
n
o
p
q
r
s
t
u
v
w
x
y
z

'i' before 'e' except after 'c'   SPELLING NOTE

A
B
C
D
E
F
G
H
I
J
K
L
M
N
O
P
Q
R
S
T
U
V
W
X
Y
Z

wilderness wildernesses
NOUN an area of natural land which is not cultivated.

wildfire
NOUN If something spreads like wildfire, it spreads very quickly.

wild-goose chase wild-goose chases
NOUN a hopeless or useless search.

wildlife
NOUN Wildlife means wild animals and plants.

Wild West
NOUN The Wild West was the western part of the United States when it was first being settled by Europeans.

wiles
PLURAL NOUN Wiles are clever or crafty tricks used to persuade people to do something.

wilful
ADJECTIVE 1 Wilful actions or attitudes are deliberate and often intended to hurt someone E.G. *wilful damage*. 2 Someone who is wilful is obstinate and determined to get their own way E.G. *a wilful little boy*.

wilfully ADVERB
■ (sense 2) headstrong, stubborn

will
VERB 1 You use 'will' to form the future tense E.G. *Robin will be quite annoyed*. 2 You use 'will' to say that you intend to do something E.G. *I will not deceive you*. 3 You use 'will' when inviting someone to do or have something E.G. *Will you have another coffee?* 4 You use 'will' when asking or telling someone to do something E.G. *Will you do me a favour?… You will do as I say*. 5 You use 'will' to say that you are assuming something to be the case

E.G. *As you will have gathered, I was surprised*.

will wills willing willed
VERB 1 If you will something to happen, you try to make it happen by mental effort E.G. *I willed my eyes to open*. 2 If you will something to someone, you leave it to them when you die E.G. *Penbrook Farm is willed to her*. ▶ NOUN 3 Will is the determination to do something E.G. *the will to win*. 4 If something is the will of a person or group, they want it to happen E.G. *the will of the people*. 5 a legal document in which you say what you want to happen to your money and property when you die. ▶ PHRASE 6 If you can do something **at will**, you can do it whenever you want.

willing
ADJECTIVE 1 If you are willing to do something, you will do it if someone wants you to. 2 Someone who is willing is eager and enthusiastic E.G. *a willing helper*.

willingly ADVERB **willingness** NOUN
■ (sense 1) game, prepared, ready

willow willows
NOUN A willow or willow tree is a tree with long, thin branches and narrow leaves that often grows near water.

wilt wilts wilting wilted
VERB 1 If a plant wilts, it droops because it needs more water or is dying. 2 If someone wilts, they gradually lose strength or confidence E.G. *James visibly wilted under pressure*.

wily wilier wiliest
Said "wie-lee" ADJECTIVE clever and cunning.

wimp wimps

NOUN; INFORMAL someone who is feeble and timid.

win wins winning won

VERB **1** If you win a fight, game, or argument, you defeat your opponent. **2** If you win a prize, you get it as a reward for succeeding in something. **3** If you win something you want, such as approval or support, you succeed in getting it. ► NOUN **4** a victory in a game or contest.

win over VERB If you win someone over, you persuade them to support you.

wince winces wincing winced

VERB When you wince, the muscles of your face tighten suddenly because of pain, fear, or distress.

winch winches winching winched

NOUN **1** a machine used to lift heavy objects. It consists of a cylinder around which a rope or chain is wound. ► VERB **2** If you winch an object or person somewhere, you lift, lower, or pull them using a winch.

wind winds

Rhymes with "tinned" NOUN **1** a current of air moving across the earth's surface. **2** Your wind is the ability to breathe easily E.G. *Brown had recovered her wind.* **3** Wind is air swallowed with food or drink, or gas produced in your stomach, which causes discomfort. **4** The wind section of an orchestra is the group of musicians who play wind instruments.

wind winds winding wound

Rhymes with "mind" VERB **1** If a road or river winds in a particular direction, it twists and turns in that direction.

2 When you wind something round something else, you wrap it round it several times. **3** When you wind a clock or machine or wind it up, you turn a key or handle several times to make it work.

wind up VERB **1** When you wind up something such as an activity or a business, you finish it or close it. **2** If you wind up in a particular place, you end up there.

windfall windfalls

NOUN a sum of money that you receive unexpectedly.

wind instrument wind instruments

NOUN an instrument you play by using your breath, for example a flute, an oboe, or a trumpet.

windmill windmills

NOUN a machine for grinding grain or pumping water. It is driven by vanes or sails turned by the wind.

window windows

NOUN a space in a wall or roof or in the side of a vehicle, usually with glass in it so that light can pass through and people can see in or out.

window box window boxes

NOUN a long, narrow container on a windowsill in which plants are grown.

windowsill windowsills

NOUN a ledge along the bottom of a window, either on the inside or outside of a building.

windpipe windpipes

NOUN the tube which carries air into your lungs when you breathe.

windscreen windscreens

NOUN the glass at the front of a vehicle through which the driver looks.

a b c d e f g h i j k l m n o p q r s t u v **w** x y z

an ELegant angEL (ang<u>e</u>l)   SPELLING NOTE

A B C D E F G H I J K L M N O P Q R S T U V W X Y Z

windsurfing

NOUN Windsurfing is the sport of moving along the surface of the sea or a lake standing on a board with a sail on it.

windswept

ADJECTIVE A windswept place is exposed to strong winds E.G. *a windswept beach*.

windy windier windiest

ADJECTIVE If it is windy, there is a lot of wind.

wine wines

NOUN Wine is the red or white alcoholic drink which is normally made from grapes.

📖 from Latin *vinum* meaning 'wine'

wing wings

NOUN 1 A bird's or insect's wings are the parts of its body that it uses for flying. 2 An aeroplane's wings are the long, flat parts on each side that support it while it is in the air. 3 A wing of a building is a part which sticks out from the main part or which has been added later. 4 A wing of an organization, especially a political party, is a group within it with a particular role or particular beliefs E.G. *the left wing of the party*. ▸ PLURAL NOUN 5 The wings in a theatre are the sides of the stage which are hidden from the audience.

winged ADJECTIVE

wink winks winking winked

VERB 1 When you wink, you close one eye briefly, often as a signal that something is a joke or a secret. ▸ NOUN 2 the closing of your eye when you wink.

winkle winkles

NOUN a small sea-snail with a hard shell and a soft edible body.

winner winners

NOUN The winner of a prize, race, or competition is the person or thing that wins it.

▪ champion, victor

winning winnings

ADJECTIVE 1 The winning team or entry in a competition is the one that has won. 2 attractive and charming E.G. *a winning smile*. ▸ PLURAL NOUN 3 Your winnings are the money you have won in a competition or by gambling.

winter winters

NOUN Winter is the season between autumn and spring.

wintry

ADJECTIVE Something wintry has features that are typical of winter E.G. *the wintry dawn*.

wipe wipes wiping wiped

VERB 1 If you wipe something, you rub its surface lightly to remove dirt or liquid. 2 If you wipe dirt or liquid off something, you remove it using a cloth or your hands E.G. *Anne wiped the tears from her eyes*.

wipe out VERB To wipe out people or places is to destroy them completely.

wire wires wiring wired

NOUN 1 Wire is metal in the form of a long, thin, flexible thread which can be used to make or fasten things or to conduct an electric current. ▸ VERB 2 If you wire one thing to another, you fasten them together using wire. 3 If you wire something or wire it up, you connect it so that electricity can pass through it.

wired ADJECTIVE

wireless wirelesses

NOUN; OLD-FASHIONED a radio.

wiring

NOUN The wiring in a building is the system of wires that supply electricity to the rooms.

wiry wirier wiriest

ADJECTIVE **1** Wiry people are thin but with strong muscles. **2** Wiry things are stiff and rough to the touch E.G. *wiry hair*.

wisdom

NOUN **1** Wisdom is the ability to use experience and knowledge in order to make sensible decisions or judgments. **2** If you talk about the wisdom of an action or a decision, you are talking about how sensible it is.

wisdom tooth wisdom teeth

NOUN Your wisdom teeth are the four molar teeth at the back of your mouth which grow much later than other teeth.

wise wiser wisest

ADJECTIVE **1** Someone who is wise can use their experience and knowledge to make sensible decisions and judgments. ▶ PHRASE **2** If you say that someone is **none the wiser** or **no wiser**, you mean that they know no more about something than they did before E.G. *I left the conference none the wiser*.

■ (sense 1) judicious, prudent, sensible

wisecrack wisecracks

NOUN a clever remark, intended to be amusing but often unkind.

wish wishes wishing wished

NOUN **1** a longing or desire for something, often something difficult to achieve or obtain. **2** something desired or wanted E.G. *That wish came true two years later*. ▶ PLURAL

NOUN **3** Good wishes are expressions of hope that someone will be happy or successful E.G. *best wishes on your birthday*. ▶ VERB **4** If you wish to do something, you want to do it E.G. *We wished to return*. **5** If you wish something were the case, you would like it to be the case, but know it is not very likely E.G. *I wish I were tall*.

wishbone wishbones

NOUN a V-shaped bone in the breast of most birds.

wishful thinking

NOUN If someone's hope or wish is wishful thinking, it is unlikely to come true.

wishy-washy

ADJECTIVE; INFORMAL If a person or their ideas are wishy-washy, then their ideas are not firm or clear E.G. *wishy-washy reasons*.

wisp wisps

NOUN **1** A wisp of grass or hair is a small, thin, untidy bunch of it. **2** A wisp of smoke is a long, thin streak of it.

wispy ADJECTIVE

wistful

ADJECTIVE sadly thinking about something, especially something you want but cannot have E.G. *A wistful look came into her eyes*.

wistfully ADVERB

wit wits

NOUN **1** Wit is the ability to use words or ideas in an amusing and clever way. **2** Wit means sense E.G. *They haven't got the wit to realize what they're doing*. ▶ PLURAL NOUN **3** Your wits are the ability to think and act quickly in a difficult situation E.G. *the man who lived by his wits*. ▶ PHRASE **4** If someone is **at their wits' end**, they

a
b
c
d
e
f
g
h
i
j
k
l
m
n
o
p
q
r
s
t
u
v
w
x
y
z

are so worried and exhausted by problems or difficulties that they do not know what to do.

witch witches

NOUN a woman claimed to have magic powers and to be able to use them for good or evil.

witchcraft

NOUN Witchcraft is the skill or art of using magic powers, especially evil ones.

■ black magic, sorcery, wizardry

witch doctor witch doctors

NOUN a man in some societies, especially in Africa, who appears to have magic powers.

witchetty grub witchetty grubs

NOUN a large Australian caterpillar that is eaten by Aborigines as food.

with

PREPOSITION 1 'With' someone means in their company E.G. *He was at home with me.* 2 'With' is used to show who your opponent is in a fight or competition E.G. *next week's game with Brazil.* 3 'With' can mean using or having E.G. *Apply the colour with a brush… a bloke with a moustache.* 4 'With' is used to show how someone does something or how they feel E.G. *She looked at him with hatred.* 5 'With' can mean concerning E.G. *a problem with her telephone bill.* 6 'With' is used to show support E.G. *Are you with us or against us?*

withdraw withdraws withdrawing withdrew withdrawn

VERB 1 If you withdraw something, you remove it or take it out E.G. *He withdrew the money from his bank.* 2 If you withdraw to another place, you leave where you are and go

there E.G. *He withdrew to his study.* 3 If you withdraw from an activity, you back out of it E.G. *They withdrew from the conference.*

withdrawal withdrawals

NOUN 1 The withdrawal of something is the act of taking it away E.G. *the withdrawal of Russian troops.* 2 The withdrawal of a statement is the act of saying formally that you wish to change or deny it. 3 an amount of money you take from your bank or building society account.

withdrawal symptoms

PLURAL NOUN Withdrawal symptoms are the unpleasant effects suffered by someone who has suddenly stopped taking a drug to which they are addicted.

withdrawn 1 Withdrawn is the past participle of **withdraw.** ▶ ADJECTIVE 2 unusually shy or quiet.

wither withers withering withered

VERB 1 When something withers or withers away, it becomes weaker until it no longer exists. 2 If a plant withers, it wilts or shrivels up and dies.

withering

ADJECTIVE A withering look or remark makes you feel ashamed, stupid, or inferior.

withhold withholds withholding withheld

VERB; FORMAL If you withhold something that someone wants, you do not let them have it.

within

PREPOSITION or ADVERB 1 'Within' means in or inside. ▶ PREPOSITION 2 'Within' can mean not going beyond certain limits E.G. *Stay within the budget.*

3 'Within' can mean before a period of time has passed E.G. *You must write back within fourteen days.*

without
PREPOSITION **1** 'Without' means not having, feeling, or showing E.G. *Didier looked on without emotion.* **2** 'Without' can mean not using E.G. *You can't get in without a key.* **3** 'Without' can mean not in someone's company E.G. *He went without me.* **4** 'Without' can indicate that something does not happen when something else happens E.G. *Stone signalled the ship, again without response.*

withstand withstands withstanding withstood
VERB When something or someone withstands a force or action, they survive it or do not give in to it E.G. *ships designed to withstand the North Atlantic winter.*

witness witnesses witnessing witnessed
NOUN **1** someone who has seen an event such as an accident and can describe what happened. **2** someone who appears in a court of law to say what they know about a crime or other event. **3** someone who writes their name on a document that someone else has signed, to confirm that it is really that person's signature. ▶ VERB **4** FORMAL If you witness an event, you see it.
▣ (sense 1) bystander, observer, onlooker

witticism witticisms
Said "wit-tiss-izm" NOUN a clever and amusing remark or joke.

witty wittier wittiest
ADJECTIVE amusing in a clever way E.G.

this witty novel.
wittily ADVERB

wives
the plural of **wife**.

wizard wizards
NOUN a man in a fairy story who has magic powers.

wizened
Said "wiz-nd" ADJECTIVE having a wrinkled skin, especially with age E.G. *a wizened old man.*

wobbegong wobbegongs
Said "wob-bi-gong" NOUN an Australian shark with a richly patterned brown-and-white skin.

wobble wobbles wobbling wobbled
VERB If something wobbles, it shakes or moves from side to side because it is loose or unsteady E.G. *a cyclist who wobbled into my path.*
▣ from German *wabbeln* meaning 'waver'

wobbly
ADJECTIVE unsteady E.G. *a wobbly table.*

woe woes LITERARY
NOUN **1** Woe is great unhappiness or sorrow. ▶ PLURAL NOUN **2** Someone's woes are their problems or misfortunes.

wok woks
NOUN a large bowl-shaped metal pan used for Chinese-style cooking.

woke
the past tense of **wake**.

woken
the past participle of **wake**.

wolf wolves; wolfs wolfing wolfed
NOUN **1** a wild animal related to the dog. Wolves hunt in packs and kill other animals for food. ▶ VERB **2** INFORMAL If you wolf food or wolf it down, you eat it up quickly and greedily.

a
b
c
d
e
f
g
h
i
j
k
l
m
n
o
p
q
r
s
t
u
v
w
x
y
z

A
B
C
D
E
F
G
H
I
J
K
L
M
N
O
P
Q
R
S
T
U
V
W
X
Y
Z

woman women
NOUN 1 an adult female human being.
2 Woman can refer to women in general E.G. *man's inhumanity to woman*.

womanhood
NOUN Womanhood is the state of being a woman rather than a girl E.G. *on the verge of womanhood*.

womb wombs
Said "woom" NOUN A woman's womb is the part inside her body where her unborn baby grows.

wombat wombats
Said "wom-bat." NOUN a short-legged furry Australian animal which eats plants.

wonder wonders wondering wondered
VERB 1 If you wonder about something, you think about it with curiosity or doubt. 2 If you wonder at something, you are surprised and amazed at it E.G. *He wondered at her anger.* ► NOUN 3 Wonder is a feeling of surprise and amazement.
4 something or someone that surprises and amazes people E.G. *the wonders of science*.
■ (sense 4) marvel, miracle, phenomenon

wonderful
ADJECTIVE 1 making you feel very happy and pleased E.G. *It was wonderful to be together.* 2 very impressive E.G. *Nature is a wonderful thing*.

wonderfully ADVERB
■ (sense 2) amazing, magnificent, remarkable

wondrous
ADJECTIVE; LITERARY amazing and impressive.

wont
Rhymes with "don't" ADJECTIVE; OLD-FASHIONED If someone is wont to do something, they do it often E.G. *a gesture he was wont to use when preaching*.

woo woos wooing wooed
VERB 1 If you woo people, you try to get them to help or support you E.G. *attempts to woo the women's vote*.
2 OLD-FASHIONED When a man woos a woman, he tries to get her to marry him.

wood woods
NOUN 1 Wood is the substance which forms the trunks and branches of trees. 2 a large area of trees growing near each other.

wooded
ADJECTIVE covered in trees E.G. *a wooded area nearby*.

wooden
ADJECTIVE made of wood E.G. *a wooden box*.

woodland woodlands
NOUN Woodland is land that is mostly covered with trees.

woodpecker woodpeckers
NOUN a climbing bird with a long, sharp beak that it uses to drill holes into trees to find insects.

woodwind
ADJECTIVE Woodwind instruments are musical instruments such as flutes, oboes, clarinets, and bassoons, that are played by being blown into.

woodwork
NOUN 1 Woodwork refers to the parts of a house, such as stairs, doors or window-frames, that are made of wood. 2 Woodwork is the craft or skill of making things out of wood.

SPELLING NOTE there's a rAKE in the brAKEs (bra̲ke)

woodworm woodworm or woodworms
NOUN **1** Woodworm are the larvae of a kind of beetle. They make holes in wood by feeding on it. **2** Woodworm is damage caused to wood by woodworm making holes in it.

woody woodier woodiest
ADJECTIVE **1** Woody plants have hard tough stems. **2** A woody area has a lot of trees in it.

woof woofs
NOUN the sound that a dog makes when it barks.

wool wools
NOUN **1** Wool is the hair that grows on sheep and some other animals. **2** Wool is also yarn spun from the wool of animals which is used to knit, weave, and make such things as clothes, blankets, and carpets.

woollen woollens
ADJECTIVE **1** made from wool. ▶ NOUN **2** Woollens are clothes made of wool.

woolly woollier woolliest
ADJECTIVE **1** made of wool or looking like wool E.G. *a woolly hat.* **2** If you describe people or their thoughts as woolly, you mean that they seem confused and unclear.

woolshed woolsheds
NOUN In Australian and New Zealand English, a large building in which sheep are sheared.

woomera woomeras
NOUN a stick with a notch at one end used by Australian Aborigines to help fire a dart or spear.

word words wording worded
NOUN **1** a single unit of language in speech or writing which has a meaning. **2** A word can mean something brief said, such as a remark, statement, or conversation E.G. *a word of praise… Could I have a word?* **3** A word can also be a message E.G. *The word is that Sharon is exhausted.* **4** Your word is a promise E.G. *He gave me his word.* **5** The word can be a command E.G. *I gave the word to start.* ▶ PLURAL NOUN **6** The words of a play or song are the spoken or sung text. ▶ VERB **7** When you word something, you choose your words in order to express your ideas accurately or acceptably E.G. *the best way to word our invitations.*

wording
NOUN The wording of a piece of writing or a speech is the words used in it, especially when these words have been carefully chosen to have a certain effect.

word processor word processors
NOUN an electronic machine which has a keyboard and a visual display unit and which is used to produce, store, and organize printed material.

work works working worked
VERB **1** People who work have a job which they are paid to do E.G. *My husband works for a national newspaper.* **2** When you work, you do the tasks that your job involves. **3** To work the land is to cultivate it. **4** If someone works a machine, they control or operate it. **5** If a machine works, it operates properly and effectively E.G. *The radio doesn't work.* **6** If something such as an idea or a system works, it is successful E.G. *The housing benefit system is not working.* **7** If something works its way into a particular position, it gradually moves there E.G. *The cable had worked loose.* ▶ NOUN **8** People who

a
b
c
d
e
f
g
h
i
j
k
l
m
n
o
p
q
r
s
t
u
v
w
x
y
z

you'll brEAK that Electrical Aerial, Kitty (br**eak**)   **SPELLING NOTE**

A
B
C
D
E
F
G
H
I
J
K
L
M
N
O
P
Q
R
S
T
U
V
W
X
Y
Z

have work or who are in work have a job which they are paid to do E.G. *She's trying to find work.* 9 Work is the tasks that have to be done. 10 something done or made E.G. *a work of art.* 11 In physics, work is transfer of energy. It is calculated by multiplying a force by the distance moved by the point to which the force has been applied. Work is measured in joules. ▶ PLURAL NOUN 12 A works is a place where something is made by an industrial process E.G. *the old steel works.* 13 Works are large scale building, digging, or general construction activities E.G. *building works.*

■ (sense 4) control, handle, operate
■ (sense 5) function, go, run

work out VERB 1 If you work out a solution to a problem, you find the solution. 2 If a situation works out in a particular way, it happens in that way.

work up VERB 1 If you work up to something, you gradually progress towards it. 2 If you work yourself up or work someone else up, you make yourself or the other person very upset or angry about something.
worked up ADJECTIVE

workable
ADJECTIVE Something workable can operate successfully or can be used for a particular purpose E.G. *a workable solution… This plan simply isn't workable.*

workaholic workaholics
NOUN a person who finds it difficult to stop working and do other things.

worker workers
NOUN a person employed in a particular industry or business E.G. *a defence worker.*

workforce workforces
NOUN The workforce is all the people who work in a particular place.

workhouse workhouses
NOUN In the past a workhouse was a building to which very poor people were sent and made to work in return for food and shelter.

working workings
ADJECTIVE 1 Working people have jobs which they are paid to do. 2 Working can mean related to, used for, or suitable for work E.G. *the working week… working conditions.* 3 Working can mean sufficient to be useful or to achieve what is required E.G. *a working knowledge of Hebrew.* ▶ PLURAL NOUN 4 The workings of a piece of equipment, an organization, or a system are the ways in which it operates E.G. *the workings of the European Union.*

working class working classes
NOUN The working class or working classes are the group of people in society who do not own much property and who do jobs which involve physical rather than intellectual skills.

workload workloads
NOUN the amount of work that a person or a machine has to do.

workman workmen
NOUN a man whose job involves using physical rather than intellectual skills.

workmanship
NOUN Workmanship is the skill with which something is made or a job is completed.

workmate workmates
NOUN Someone's workmate is the

fellow worker with whom they do their job.

workout workouts
NOUN a session of physical exercise or training.

workplace
NOUN Your workplace is the building or company where you work.

workshop workshops
NOUN **1** a room or building that contains tools or machinery used for making or repairing things E.G. *an engineering workshop.* **2** a period of discussion or practical work in which a group of people learn about a particular subject E.G. *a theatre workshop.*

world worlds
NOUN **1** The world is the earth, the planet we live on. **2** You can use 'world' to refer to people generally E.G. *The eyes of the world are upon me.* **3** Someone's world is the life they lead and the things they experience E.G. *We come from different worlds.* **4** A world is a division or section of the earth, its history, or its people, such as the Arab World, or the Ancient World. **5** A particular world is a field of activity and the people involved in it E.G. *the world of football.* ▸ ADJECTIVE **6** 'World' is used to describe someone or something that is one of the best or most important of its kind E.G. *a world leader.* ▸ PHRASE **7** If you **think the world** of someone, you like or admire them very much.
🏛 from Old English *weorold* from *wer* meaning 'man' and *ald* meaning 'age'

worldly worldlier worldliest
ADJECTIVE **1** relating to the ordinary activities of life rather than spiritual things E.G. *opportunities for worldly pleasures.* **2** experienced and knowledgeable about life.

world war world wars
NOUN a war that involves countries all over the world.

worldwide
ADJECTIVE throughout the world E.G. *a worldwide increase in skin cancers.*

World Wide Web
NOUN The World Wide Web is another name for the Internet, the worldwide communication system which people use through computers.

worm worms worming wormed
NOUN **1** a small thin animal without bones or legs, which lives in the soil or off other creatures. **2** an insect such as a beetle or moth at a very early stage in its life. ▸ VERB **3** If you worm an animal, you give it medicine in order to kill the worms that are living as parasites in its intestines.

worm out VERB If you worm information out of someone, you gradually persuade them to give you it.

worn
1 Worn is the past participle of **wear**.
▸ ADJECTIVE **2** damaged or thin because of long use. **3** looking old or exhausted E.G. *Her husband looks frail and worn.*

worn-out
ADJECTIVE **1** used until it is too thin or too damaged to be of further use E.G. *a worn-out cardigan.* **2** extremely tired E.G. *You must be worn-out after the drive.*

worried
ADJECTIVE unhappy and anxious about a problem or about something

a
b
c
d
e
f
g
h
i
j
k
l
m
n
o
p
q
r
s
t
u
v
w
x
y
z

A
B
C
D
E
F
G
H
I
J
K
L
M
N
O
P
Q
R
S
T
U
V
W
X
Y
Z

unpleasant that might happen.

■ anxious, concerned, troubled

worry worries worrying worried

VERB 1 If you worry, you feel anxious and fearful about a problem or about something unpleasant that might happen. 2 If something worries you, it causes you to feel uneasy or fearful E.G. *a puzzle which had worried her all her life.* 3 If you worry someone with a problem, you disturb or bother them by telling them about it E.G. *I didn't want to worry the boys with this.* 4 If a dog worries sheep or other animals, it frightens or harms them by chasing them or biting them. ▶ NOUN 5 Worry is a feeling of unhappiness and unease caused by a problem or by thinking of something unpleasant that might happen E.G. *the major source of worry.* 6 a person or thing that causes you to feel anxious or uneasy E.G. *Inflation is the least of our worries.*

worrying ADJECTIVE

🏛 from Old English *wyrgan* meaning 'strangle'

■ (sense 1) be anxious, fret

■ (sense 2) bother, perturb, trouble

■ (sense 5) anxiety, concern

worse

ADJECTIVE or ADVERB 1 Worse is the comparative form of **bad** and **badly**. 2 If someone who is ill gets worse, they become more ill than before. ▶ PHRASE 3 If someone or something is **none the worse** for something, they have not been harmed by it E.G. *He appeared none the worse for the accident.*

worsen worsens worsening worsened

VERB If a situation worsens, it becomes more difficult or

unpleasant E.G. *My relationship with my mother worsened.*

■ decline, deteriorate, get worse

worse off

ADJECTIVE If you are worse off, you have less money or are in a more unpleasant situation than before E.G. *There are people much worse off than me.*

worship worships worshipping worshipped

VERB 1 (RE) If you worship a god, you show your love and respect by praying or singing hymns. 2 If you worship someone or something, you love them or admire them very much. ▶ NOUN 3 Worship is the feeling of respect, love, or admiration you feel for something or someone.

worshipper NOUN

■ (sense 2) adore, idolize, love

■ (sense 3) adoration, devotion

worst

ADJECTIVE or ADVERB Worst is the superlative of **bad** and **badly**.

worth

PREPOSITION 1 If something is worth a sum of money, it has that value E.G. *a house worth 85,000 dollars.* 2 If something is worth doing, it deserves to be done. ▶ NOUN 3 A particular amount of money's worth of something is the quantity of it that you can buy for that money E.G. *five pound's worth of petrol.* 4 Someone's worth is the value or usefulness they are considered to have.

worthless

ADJECTIVE having no real value or use E.G. *a worthless piece of junk.*

worthwhile

ADJECTIVE important enough to justify

the time, money, or effort spent on it
E.G. *a worthwhile career.*

worthy worthier worthiest
ADJECTIVE If someone or something is
worthy of something, they deserve it
E.G. *a worthy champion.*

would
VERB **1** You use 'would' to say what
someone thought was going to
happen E.G. *We were sure it would be
a success.* **2** You use 'would' when you
are referring to the result or effect of
a possible situation E.G. *If readers can
help I would be most grateful.* **3** You
use 'would' when referring to
someone's willingness to do
something E.G. *I wouldn't change
places with him if you paid me.* **4** You
use 'would' in polite questions E.G.
Would you like some lunch?

would-be
ADJECTIVE wanting to be or claiming to
be E.G. *a would-be pop singer.*

**wound wounds wounding
wounded**
NOUN **1** an injury to part of your body,
especially a cut in your skin and
flesh. ► VERB **2** If someone wounds
you, they damage your body using a
gun, knife, or other weapon. **3** If you
are wounded by what someone says
or does, your feelings are hurt.
wounded ADJECTIVE

wow
INTERJECTION Wow is an expression of
admiration or surprise.

WPC WPCs
NOUN In Britain, a female member of
the police force. WPC is an abbreviation
for 'woman police constable'.

**wrangle wrangles wrangling
wrangled**
VERB **1** If you wrangle with someone,

you argue noisily or angrily, often
about something unimportant. ► NOUN
2 an argument that is difficult to settle.
wrangling NOUN

wrap wraps wrapping wrapped
VERB **1** If you wrap something or wrap
something up, you fold a piece of
paper or cloth tightly around it to
cover or enclose it. **2** If you wrap
paper or cloth round something, you
put or fold the paper round it. **3** If
you wrap your arms, fingers, or legs
round something, you coil them
round it.

wrap up VERB If you wrap up, you
put warm clothes on.

wrapped up
ADJECTIVE; INFORMAL If you are wrapped
up in a person or thing, you give that
person or thing all your attention.

wrapper wrappers
NOUN a piece of paper, plastic, or foil
which covers and protects
something that you buy E.G. *sweet
wrappers.*

wrapping wrappings
NOUN Wrapping is the material used
to cover and protect something.

wrath
Said "roth" NOUN; LITERARY Wrath is
great anger E.G. *the wrath of his father.*

**wreak wreaks wreaking
wreaked**
Said "reek" VERB To wreak havoc or
damage is to cause it.

wreath wreaths
Said "reeth" NOUN an arrangement of
flowers and leaves, often in the
shape of a circle, which is put on a
grave as a sign of remembrance for
the dead person.

wreck wrecks wrecking wrecked
VERB **1** If someone wrecks something,

have a plEce of plE (pie**ce**)   **SPELLING NOTE**

a
b
c
d
e
f
g
h
i
j
k
l
m
n
o
p
q
r
s
t
u
v
w
x
y
z

A B C D E F G H I J K L M N O P Q R S T U V W X Y Z

they break it, destroy it, or spoil it completely. **2** If a ship is wrecked, it has been so badly damaged that it can no longer sail. ▶ NOUN **3** a vehicle which has been badly damaged in an accident. **4** If you say someone is a wreck, you mean that they are in a very poor physical or mental state of health and cannot cope with life.
wrecked ADJECTIVE

wreckage
NOUN Wreckage is what remains after something has been badly damaged or destroyed.

wren wrens
NOUN a very small brown songbird.

wrench wrenches wrenching wrenched
VERB **1** If you wrench something, you give it a sudden and violent twist or pull E.G. *Nick wrenched open the door.* **2** If you wrench a limb or a joint, you twist and injure it. ▶ NOUN **3** a metal tool with parts which can be adjusted to fit around nuts or bolts to loosen or tighten them. **4** a painful parting from someone or something.

wrest wrests wresting wrested
Said "rest" VERB; FORMAL If you wrest something from someone else you take it from them violently or with effort E.G. *to try and wrest control of the island from the Mafia.*

wrestle wrestles wrestling wrestled
VERB **1** If you wrestle someone or wrestle with them, you fight them by holding or throwing them, but not hitting them. **2** When you wrestle with a problem, you try to deal with it.
wrestler NOUN

wrestling
NOUN Wrestling is a sport in which

two people fight and try to win by throwing or holding their opponent on the ground.

wretch wretches
NOUN; OLD-FASHIONED someone who is thought to be wicked or very unfortunate. 🔠 from Old English *wrecca* meaning 'exile' or 'despised person'

wretched
Said "ret-shid" ADJECTIVE **1** very unhappy or unfortunate E.G. *a wretched childhood.* **2** INFORMAL You use wretched to describe something or someone you feel angry about or dislike E.G. *a wretched bully.*

wriggle wriggles wriggling wriggled
VERB **1** If someone wriggles, they twist and turn their body or a part of their body using quick movements E.G. *He wriggled his arms and legs.* **2** If you wriggle somewhere, you move there by twisting and turning E.G. *I wriggled out of the van.*
wriggly ADJECTIVE

wring wrings wringing wrung
VERB **1** When you wring a wet cloth or wring it out, you squeeze the water out of it by twisting it. **2** If you wring your hands, you hold them together and twist and turn them, usually because you are worried or upset. **3** If someone wrings a bird's neck, they kill the bird by twisting and breaking its neck.

wrinkle wrinkles wrinkling wrinkled
NOUN **1** Wrinkles are lines in someone's skin, especially on the face, which form as they grow old. ▶ VERB **2** If something wrinkles, folds or lines develop on it E.G. *silk so rich it doesn't wrinkle.* **3** When you wrinkle your nose, forehead, or eyes, you

tighten the muscles in your face so that the skin folds into lines.

wrinkled ADJECTIVE **wrinkly** ADJECTIVE
from Old English *wrinclian* meaning 'to wind around'
(sense 1) crease, fold

wrist wrists
NOUN the part of your body between your hand and your arm which bends when you move your hand.

writ writs
NOUN a legal document that orders a person to do or not to do a particular thing.

write writes writing wrote written
VERB 1 When you write something, you use a pen or pencil to form letters, words, or numbers on a surface. 2 If you write something such as a poem, a book, or a piece of music, you create it. 3 When you write to someone or write them a letter, you express your feelings in a letter. 4 When someone writes something such as a cheque, they put the necessary information on it and sign it.

write down VERB If you write something down, you record it on a piece of paper.

write up VERB If you write up something, you write a full account of it, often using notes that you have made.

writer writers
NOUN 1 a person who writes books, stories, or articles as a job. 2 The writer of something is the person who wrote it.

writhe writhes writhing writhed
Said "rieth" VERB If you writhe, you twist and turn your body, often because you are in pain.

writing writings
NOUN 1 Writing is something that has been written or printed E.G. *Apply in writing for the information.* 2 Your writing is the way you write with a pen or pencil. 3 Writing is also a piece of written work, especially the style of language used E.G. *witty writing.* 4 An author's writings are his or her written works.

written
1 Written is the past participle of **write.** ► ADJECTIVE 2 taken down in writing E.G. *a written agreement.*

wrong wrongs wronging wronged
ADJECTIVE 1 not working properly or unsatisfactory E.G. *There was something wrong with the car.* 2 not correct or truthful E.G. *the wrong answer.* 3 bad or immoral E.G. *It is wrong to kill people.* ► NOUN 4 an unjust action or situation E.G. *the wrongs of our society.* ► VERB 5 If someone wrongs you, they treat you in an unfair or unjust way.

wrongly ADVERB
(sense 2) erroneous, inaccurate, incorrect

wrongful
ADJECTIVE A wrongful act is regarded as illegal, unfair, or immoral E.G. *wrongful imprisonment.*

wrought iron
NOUN Wrought iron is a pure type of iron that is formed into decorative shapes.

wry
ADJECTIVE A wry expression shows that you find a situation slightly amusing because you know more about it than other people.

wryly ADVERB

a
b
c
d
e
f
g
h
i
j
k
l
m
n
o
p
q
r
s
t
u
v
w
x
y
z

I went to see (C) the doctor's new practiCe (practice)   SPELLING NOTE

X x

X or **x**
1 'X' is used to represent the name of an unknown or secret person or place E.G. *The victim was referred to as Mr X throughout Tuesday's court proceedings.* **2** People sometimes write 'X' on a map to mark a precise position. **3** 'X' is used to represent a kiss at the bottom of a letter, a vote on a ballot paper, or the signature of someone who cannot write.

xenophobia
Said "zen-nof-foe-bee-a" NOUN a fear or strong dislike of people from other countries.
xenophobic ADJECTIVE
📖 from Greek *xenos* meaning 'stranger' and *phobos* meaning 'fear'

Xerox Xeroxes
Said "zeer-roks" NOUN TRADEMARK **1** a machine that makes photographic copies of sheets of paper with writing or printing on them. **2** a copy made by a Xerox machine.

Xmas
NOUN; INFORMAL Xmas means the same as Christmas.

X-ray X-rays X-raying X-rayed
NOUN **1** a stream of radiation of very short wavelength that can pass through some solid materials. X-rays are used by doctors to examine the bones or organs inside a person's body. **2** a picture made by sending X-rays through someone's body in order to examine the inside of it.
▶ VERB **3** If you are X-rayed, a picture is made of the inside of your body by passing X-rays through it.

xylem
Said "zy-lem" NOUN; TECHNICAL Xylem is a plant tissue that conducts water and mineral salts from the roots and carries them through the plant. It forms the wood in trees and shrubs.

xylophone xylophones
Said "zy-lo-fone" NOUN a musical instrument made of a row of wooden bars of different lengths. It is played by hitting the bars with special hammers.

Yy

-y
SUFFIX '-y' forms nouns E.G. *anarchy*.
📖 from Old French *-ie*

yabby yabbies
NOUN a small edible Australian crayfish.

yacht yachts
Said "yot" NOUN a boat with sails or an engine, used for racing or for pleasure trips.

yachting
NOUN Yachting is the sport or activity of sailing a yacht.

yachtsman yachtsmen
NOUN a man who sails a yacht.

yachtswoman NOUN

yak yaks
NOUN a type of long-haired ox with long horns, found mainly in Tibet.

yakka or **yacker**
NOUN; INFORMAL In Australian and New Zealand English, yakka or yacker is work.

yam yams
NOUN a root vegetable which grows in tropical regions.

yank yanks yanking yanked
VERB 1 If you yank something, you pull or jerk it suddenly with a lot of force.
► NOUN 2 INFORMAL A Yank is an American
☑ When *Yank* means 'an American' it starts with a capital letter.

Yankee Yankees
NOUN the same as a Yank.

yap yaps yapping yapped
VERB If a dog yaps, it barks with a high-pitched sound.

yard yards
NOUN 1 a unit of length equal to 36 inches or about 91.4 centimetres.
2 an enclosed area that is usually next to a building and is often used for a particular purpose E.G. *a ship repair yard.*

yardstick yardsticks
NOUN someone or something you use as a standard against which to judge other people or things E.G. *He had no yardstick by which to judge university.*

yarn yarns
NOUN 1 Yarn is thread used for knitting or making cloth. 2 INFORMAL a yarn is a story that someone tells, often with invented details to make it more interesting or exciting E.G. *fishermen's yarns.*

yashmak yashmaks
NOUN a veil that some Muslim women wear over their faces when they are in public.

yawn yawns yawning yawned
VERB When you yawn, you open your mouth wide and take in more air than usual. You often yawn when you are tired or bored

yawning
ADJECTIVE A yawning gap or opening is very wide.

ye
AN OLD WORD; PRONOUN 1 Ye used to mean 'you'. ► ADJECTIVE 2 Ye also used to mean 'the'.

yeah
INTERJECTION; INFORMAL Yeah means 'yes'.

year years
NOUN 1 a period of twelve months or 365 days (366 days in a leap year), which is the time taken for the earth to travel once around the sun. 2 a

A
B
C
D
E
F
G
H
I
J
K
L
M
N
O
P
Q
R
S
T
U
V
W
X
Y
Z

period of twelve consecutive months, not always January to December, on which administration or organization is based E.G. *the current financial year.* ▶ PHRASE 3 If something happens **year in, year out**, it happens every year E.G. *a tradition kept up year in, year out.*

yearly ADJECTIVE OR ADVERB

yearling yearlings
NOUN an animal between one and two years old.

yearn yearns yearning yearned
Rhymes with "learn" VERB If you yearn for something, you want it very much indeed E.G. *He yearned to sleep.*

yearning NOUN

yeast yeasts
NOUN Yeast is a kind of fungus which is used to make bread rise, and to make liquids ferment in order to produce alcohol.

yell yells yelling yelled
VERB 1 If you yell, you shout loudly, usually because you are angry, excited, or in pain. ▶ NOUN 2 a loud shout.

yellow yellower yellowest; yellows yellowing yellowed
NOUN OR ADJECTIVE 1 Yellow is the colour of buttercups, egg yolks, or lemons. ▶ VERB 2 When something yellows or is yellowed, it becomes yellow, often because it is old. ▶ ADJECTIVE 3 INFORMAL If you say someone is yellow, you mean they are cowardly.

yellowish ADJECTIVE

yellow box yellow boxes
NOUN a large spreading Australian tree which is a source of honey.

yellow fever
NOUN Yellow fever is a serious

infectious disease that is found in tropical countries. It causes fever and jaundice.

yelp yelps yelping yelped
VERB 1 When people or animals yelp, they give a sudden, short cry. ▶ NOUN 2 a sudden, short cry.

yen
NOUN 1 The yen is the main unit of currency in Japan. 2 If you have a yen to do something, you have a strong desire to do it E.G. *Mike had a yen to try cycling.*

yes
INTERJECTION You use 'yes' to agree with someone, to say that something is true, or to accept something.

yesterday
NOUN OR ADVERB 1 Yesterday is the day before today. 2 You also use 'yesterday' to refer to the past E.G. *Leave yesterday's sadness behind you.*

yet
ADVERB 1 If something has not happened yet, it has not happened up to the present time E.G. *It isn't quite dark yet.* 2 If something should not be done yet, it should not be done now, but later E.G. *Don't switch off yet.* 3 'Yet' can mean there is still a possibility that something can happen E.G. *We'll make a soldier of you yet.* 4 You can use 'yet' when you want to say how much longer a situation will continue E.G. *The service doesn't start for an hour yet.* 5 'Yet' can be used for emphasis E.G. *She'd changed her mind yet again.* ▶ CONJUNCTION 6 You can use 'yet' to introduce a fact which is rather surprising E.G. *He isn't a smoker yet he always carries a lighter.*

yeti yetis
Said "yet-tee" NOUN A yeti, or
abominable snowman, is a large
hairy apelike animal which some
people believe exists in the
Himalayas.

yew yews
NOUN an evergreen tree with bright
red berries.

Yiddish
NOUN Yiddish is a language derived
mainly from German, which many
Jewish people of European origin
speak.
📖 from German *jüdisch* meaning
'Jewish'

yield yields yielding yielded
VERB 1 If you yield to someone or
something, you stop resisting and
give In to them E.G. *Russia recently
yielded to US pressure.* 2 If you yield
something that you have control of
or responsibility for, you surrender it
E.G. *They refused to yield control of
their weapons.* 3 If something yields,
it breaks or gives way E.G. *The handle
would yield to her grasp.* 4 To yield
something is to produce it E.G. *One
season's produce yields food for the
following year.* ▶ NOUN 5 A yield is an
amount of food, money, or profit
produced from a given area of land
or from an investment.

yippee
INTERJECTION 'Yippee!' is an exclamation
of happiness or excitement.

yob yobs
NOUN; INFORMAL a noisy, badly behaved
boy or young man.

yodel yodels yodelling yodelled
Said "yoe-dl" VERB When someone
yodels, they sing normal notes with
high quick notes in between. This
style of singing is associated with
the Swiss and Austrian Alps.

yoga
Said "yoe-ga" NOUN Yoga is a Hindu
method of mental and physical
exercise or discipline.
📖 from Sanskrit *yoga* meaning
'union'

yogurt yogurts; also spelt **yoghurt**
Said "yog-gurt or yoe-gurt" NOUN
Yogurt is a slightly sour thick liquid
made from milk that has had
bacteria added to it.

yoke yokes
NOUN 1 a wooden bar attached to two
collars which is laid across the necks
of animals such as oxen to hold
them together, and to which a
plough or other tool may be
attached. 2 LITERARY If people are
under a yoke of some kind, they are
being oppressed E.G. *two women
who escape the yoke of insensitive
men.*

yokel yokels
Said "yoe-kl" NOUN someone who lives
in the country and is regarded as
being rather stupid and old-
fashioned.

yolk yolks
Rhymes with "joke" NOUN the yellow
part in the middle of an egg.
📖 from Old English *geoloca*, from
geolu meaning 'yellow'

Yom Kippur
Said "yom kip-poor" NOUN Yom Kippur
is an annual Jewish religious holiday,
which is a day of fasting and
prayers. It is also called the Day of
Atonement.

yonder
ADVERB or ADJECTIVE; AN OLD WORD over
there E.G. *There's an island yonder.*

a b c d e f g h i j k l m n o p q r s t u v w x y z

yore

AN OLD-FASHIONED PHRASE **Of yore** means existing a long time ago E.G. *nostalgia for the days of yore.*

Yorkshire pudding Yorkshire puddings

NOUN In Britain, Yorkshire pudding is a kind of baked batter made of flour, milk, and eggs, and usually eaten with roast beef.

you

PRONOUN **1** 'You' refers to the person or group of people that a person is speaking or writing to. **2** 'You' also refers to people in general E.G. *You can get a two-bedroom villa quite cheaply.*

young younger youngest

ADJECTIVE **1** A young person, animal, or plant has not lived very long and is not yet mature. ▶ NOUN **2** The young are young people in general. **3** The young of an animal are its babies.
■ (sense 1) immature, undeveloped
■ (sense 3) babies, offspring, progeny

youngster youngsters

NOUN a child or young person.

your

ADJECTIVE **1** 'Your' means belonging or relating to the person or group of people that someone is speaking to E.G. *I do like your name.* **2** 'Your' is used to show that something belongs or relates to people in general E.G. *Your driving ability is affected by just one or two drinks.*

yours

PRONOUN 'Yours' refers to something belonging or relating to the person or group of people that someone is speaking to E.G. *His hair is longer than yours.*

yourself yourselves

PRONOUN **1** 'Yourself' is used when the person being spoken to does the action and is affected by it E.G. *Why can't you do it yourself?* **2** 'Yourself' is used to emphasize 'you' E.G. *Do you yourself want a divorce?*

youth youths

NOUN **1** Someone's youth is the period of their life before they are a fully mature adult. **2** Youth is the quality or condition of being young and often inexperienced. **3** a boy or young man. **4** The youth are young people thought of as a group E.G. *the youth of today.*

youthful ADJECTIVE

youth hostel youth hostels

NOUN a place where young people can stay cheaply when they are on holiday.

yo-yo yo-yos

NOUN a round wooden or plastic toy attached to a piece of string. You play by making the yo-yo rise and fall on the string.

Yugoslav Yugoslavs

Said "yoo-goe-slahv" ADJECTIVE **1** belonging or relating to the country that used to be known as Yugoslavia. ▶ NOUN **2** someone who came from the country that used be known as Yugoslavia.

Yule

NOUN; OLD WORD Yule means Christmas. 🔲 from Old English *geola* a pagan winter feast

yuppie yuppies

NOUN If you say people are yuppies, you think they are young, middle-class, and earn a lot of money which they spend on themselves

Zz

a
b
c
d
e
f
g
h
i
j
k
l
m
n
o
p
q
r
s
t
u
v
w
x
y
z

TIP Many words which sound as if they begin with letter *z* actually begin with letter *x*, for example *Xerox*, *xylem* and *xylophone*.

Zambian Zambians
Said "**zam**-bee-an" ADJECTIVE
1 belonging or relating to Zambia.
► NOUN 2 someone who comes from Zambia.

zany zanier zaniest
ADJECTIVE odd and ridiculous E.G. *zany humour*.
 from Italian *zanni* meaning 'clown'

zap zaps zapping zapped
VERB INFORMAL 1 To zap someone is to kill them, usually by shooting. 2 To zap also is to move somewhere quickly E.G. *I zapped over to Paris*.

zeal
NOUN Zeal is very great enthusiasm.
zealous ADJECTIVE

zealot zealots
Said "**zel**-lot" NOUN a person who acts with very great enthusiasm, especially in following a political or religious cause.

zebra zebras
NOUN a type of African wild horse with black and white stripes over its body.

zebra crossing zebra crossings
NOUN a place where people can cross the road safely. The road is marked with black and white stripes.

Zen or **Zen Buddhism**
NOUN Zen is a form of Buddhism that concentrates on learning through meditation and intuition.

zenith
NOUN LITERARY The zenith of something is the time when it is at its most successful or powerful E.G. *the zenith of his military career*.

zero zeros or **zeroes zeroing zeroed** 1 Zero is the number 0.
2 Zero is freezing point, 0° Centigrade. ADJECTIVE 3 Zero means there is none at all of a particular thing E.G. *His chances are zero*. ► VERB
4 To zero in on a target is to aim at or to move towards it E.G. *The headlines zeroed in on the major news stories*.
 from Arabic *sifr* meaning 'cipher' or 'empty'

zest
NOUN 1 Zest is a feeling of pleasure and enthusiasm E.G. *zest for life*.
2 Zest is a quality which adds extra flavour or interest to something E.G. *brilliant ideas to add zest to your wedding list*. 3 The zest of an orange or lemon is the outside of the peel which is used to flavour food or drinks.

zigzag zigzags zigzagging zigzagged
NOUN 1 a line which has a series of sharp, angular turns to the right and left in it, like a continuous series of 'W's. ► VERB 2 To zigzag is to move forward by going at an angle first right and then left E.G. *He zigzagged his way across the racecourse*.

Zimbabwean Zimbabweans
Said "zim-**bahb**-wee-an" ADJECTIVE
1 belonging or relating to Zimbabwe. ► NOUN 2 someone who comes from Zimbabwe.

A
B
C
D
E
F
G
H
I
J
K
L
M
N
O
P
Q
R
S
U
V
W
X
Y
Z

zinc

NOUN Zinc is a bluish-white metal used in alloys and to coat other metals to stop them rusting.

zing

NOUN; INFORMAL Zing is a quality in something that makes it lively or interesting E.G. *There's a real zing around the studio.*

zip zips zipping zipped

NOUN 1 a long narrow fastener with two rows of teeth that are closed or opened by a small clip pulled between them. ► VERB 2 When you zip something or zip it up, you fasten it using a zip.

zipper zippers

NOUN the same as a **zip**.

zodiac

Said "zoe-dee-ak" NOUN The zodiac is an imaginary strip in the sky which contains the planets and stars which astrologers think are important influences on people. It is divided into 12 sections, each with a special name and symbol.

📖 from Greek *zōdiakos kuklos* meaning 'circle of signs'

zombie zombies

NOUN 1 INFORMAL If you refer to someone as a zombie, you mean that they seem to be unaware of what is going on around them and to act without thinking about what

they are doing. 2 In voodoo, a zombie is a dead person who has been brought back to life by witchcraft.

📖 from an African word *zumbi* meaning 'good-luck charm'

zone zones

NOUN an area that has particular features or properties E.G. *a war zone.*

zoo zoos

NOUN a place where live animals are kept so that people can look at them.

zoology

Said "zoo-ol-loj-jee" NOUN Zoology is the scientific study of animals.

zoological ADJECTIVE **zoologist** NOUN

zoom zooms zooming zoomed

VERB 1 To zoom is to move very quickly E.G. *They zoomed to safety.* 2 If a camera zooms in on something, it gives a close-up picture of it.

zucchini

Said "zoo-**keen**-nee" PLURAL NOUN Zucchini are small vegetable marrows with dark green skin. They are also called **courgettes**.

Zulu Zulus

Said "zoo-loo" NOUN 1 The Zulus are a group of Black people who live in southern Africa. 2 Zulu is the language spoken by the Zulus.